THE COMPLETE FAMILY MEDICAL GUIDE

DR WARWICK CARTER MB. BS. FRACGP.

HB
HINKLER
BOOKS

This book is intended as a reference guide only, not a manual for self treatment. If you suspect that you have a medical problem, please seek competent medical care. The information presented here is designed to help you make informed choices about your health. It is not intended as a substitute for any treatment prescribed by your doctor.

Cover Design: Sam Grimmer
Illustrations: Jeff Lang
Editor: Dr Justin Coleman
Typesetting: Midland Typesetters, Maryborough, Victoria, Australia

The Complete Family Medical Guide
First published in this format in 2005 by Hinkler Books Pty Ltd
17–23 Redwood Drive
Dingley VIC 3172 Australia
www.hinklerbooks.com

ISBN: 1 7412 1897 7
Printed and bound in Australia

For Jane
my wife, supporter and best friend

"The most important thing you ever do in life,
is choose your parents"

"The most valuable thing you can ever own
is a boring medical history"

"The only thing worse than old age
is the alternative"

Introduction

This guide is designed to be just what its title states – a complete guide to everything about health and medicine that any reasonable family member would want to know, written in a way that is easy to understand, and extensively cross referenced to other topics that may be of interest.

In an easy to access A to Z format, the book comprehensively covers: –
- Abbreviations (doctors use all sorts of acronyms, abbreviations and notations to refer to complex ideas)
- Addictive substances (both legal and illegal – eg. alcohol, heroin, cocaine)
- Anatomy (the organs of the body – eg. liver, heart, kidneys)
- Bodily substances (eg. bile, blood, faeces)
- Cosmetic operations (improving our appearance – eg. breast augmentation, face lift)
- Curiosities (medicine is full of all sorts of strange abnormalities)
- Diseases (the illnesses diagnosed by doctors – eg. cancer, influenza, Tietze syndrome)
- Emergencies (what to do when disaster strikes – eg. choking, poisoning, bleeding)
- Investigations (how doctors investigate the body and its functions – eg. blood tests, x-rays)
- Lifestyle (the experiences we all go through – eg. bereavement, stress, masturbation)
- Medical history (famous people, symbols and events – eg. Hippocrates, Black Death, the caduceus)
- Medication groups (drugs and how they are classified – eg. benzodiazepines, narcotics, sedatives)
- Physiology (how the body works – eg. breast feeding, menopause, metabolism)
- Poisonous animals (what happens when they attack – eg. snake bite, bee sting, blue ringed octopus)
- Procedures (what doctors do to you – eg. biopsy, excision, colonoscopy)
- Signs (what doctors discover when they examine you – eg. enlarged liver, lumps, reflexes)
- Symptoms (abnormal feelings and their meanings – eg. backache, pain, wheeze)
- Treatments (the ways in which doctors treat illness – eg. chemotherapy, radiotherapy, surgery)

The cross referencing allows the book to be also used as a dictionary, so if a doctor uses an unknown term (eg. ecchymoses), looking up the term refers you to the common meaning and an explanation – in this case the reader will find that ecchymoses merely means a bruise.

Where appropriate, simple line drawings and diagrams are included to make the written explanation clearer.

Entries starting with a number are listed as though the number has been spelt (eg. 5HT RECEPTOR ANTAGONISTS are listed under 'F' for FIVE).

Over 4150 topics are covered in over 2100 entries in this encyclopaedic dictionary of health and medicine, to make it the most comprehensive guide of its size (and price) available anywhere for consumers of health care.

Dr. Warwick Carter
MB.BS., FRACGP, FAMA
Brisbane
July 2002

For more information on diseases and medications see the
companion volumes by Dr. Warwick Carter: –
"Complete Home Guide to Medical Illnesses"
"Complete Home Guide to Medication"
"1001 Medical Questions & Answers"

A

ABDOMEN

The abdomen (belly) is a cavity that contains the stomach, small and large intestines, liver, spleen, pancreas, bladder and kidneys. In women it also contains the ovaries and uterus. It is lined by a smooth membrane (the peritoneum) and extends from the pelvis to the diaphragm. The front and sides are formed by muscles, while the back is the vertebrae of the spine.

See also ASCITES; DIAPHRAGM; PELVIS; PERITONEUM; PERITONITIS; THORAX

ABDOMINAL DISTENSION
See BLOATING

ABDOMINAL FLUID
See ASCITES

ABDOMINAL LUMP

Abnormal lumps in the belly (abdomen) are more commonly found by doctors searching for the cause of abdominal pain, than by patients themselves. All masses found in the belly are significant and should be fully investigated to determine their exact cause.

The few causes that are not serious include pregnancy (a woman may not realise she is pregnant and become aware of a growth in her lower belly), scars in the muscle wall of the belly that form after a surgical operation or an injury may be felt as easily moved lumps, feeling the backbone of thin people (this bends forward just behind the umbilicus), constipation (causing a hard lump of faeces, usually in the lower left belly) and noticing the xiphisternum. The xiphisternum is a piece of firm cartilage attached to the lower end of the breast bone and if this becomes injured by a blow or by stress on the large abdominal muscles which partly attach to it, the xiphisternum may become slightly swollen and inflamed.

Cancer is, unfortunately, one of the most common causes of a lump in the belly. These are usually rock hard, tender and fixed (do not move when pushed). Cancer of any of the organs in the abdomen may be responsible, but the most common ones are those of the bowel, pancreas, ovary, bladder, liver and kidney. Often, other symptoms may be absent, but most cancers can be cured provided they are treated at the earliest possible time.

Crohn's disease is a thickening and inflammation of the small or large intestine. It is associated with variable bowel habits, belly pain and dark blood in the faeces. A firm, movable sausage-shaped lump is sometimes felt in thin people. It is a relatively uncommon condition, but early treatment by surgical removal of the affected sections of gut can sometimes prevent it spreading.

Hodgkin's disease is a cancer of lymph nodes that spreads at an early stage to involve the liver and spleen. Lymph nodes are scattered throughout the belly, and may enlarge to a size when they can be felt if affected by this disease.

An abscess is a collection of pus surrounded by a wall of fibrous tissue that forms at the site of an untreated infection. The most common site for an abscess is the appendix, low down on the right side of the belly, but other causes can be infection of the fallopian tubes (salpingitis, pelvic inflammatory disease), gall bladder and from any wound that penetrates into the belly cavity.

The aorta is the main large artery that takes blood from the heart to the abdomen and legs, and is between two and three cm. in diameter. If the thick wall of the aorta develops a weak spot, sometimes due to deposits of hard cholesterol, the artery may start to balloon out at one point to form a firm, pulsating lump known as an aneurysm. This aneurysm is at imminent danger of bursting, and if this occurs there is severe pain, and even in the best hospitals, half the patients die. Surgical correction of an aneurysm before it bursts, at the earliest opportunity, is therefore vital.

The uterus may be enlarged to form a lump in the lower abdomen not only by a pregnancy, but also by fibroids (hard masses of fibrous scar tissue in the muscular wall of the uterus). Heavy painful periods are the other common accompanying symptom.

Enlargement of the liver and spleen may be felt as a lump in the belly.

A hernia occurs when tissue pushes its way from one area, where it is normally present, into another area, where it is not. It may pass through a very narrow opening in this process. Hernias may move backwards and forwards freely, or become trapped. If tightly trapped, the blood and nerve supply to the herniated tissue may be restricted, and the tissue becomes painful and dies. If a piece of gut is in the hernia, the death of this tissue will cause gangrene, failure of the gut and death. A lump caused by a hernia may occur in the groin (inguinal or femoral hernia – may contain gut), around the umbilicus (umbilical hernia – usually contain fat, occasionally gut), at the site of a previous operation, or rarely may form a lump when weak areas between muscle are spread by increased pressure in the belly (ventral hernia above the umbilicus or lumbar hernia in the loin). Surgical correction is appropriate in most cases, but very large hernias in the elderly may be controlled by a truss.

Rarely, tumours and malformations of the vertebrae in the back may be felt in the abdomen of thin people.

See also ABDOMINAL PAIN; LIVER, ENLARGED; SPLEEN, ENLARGED and separate entries for diseases mentioned above.

ABDOMINAL PAIN

A pain in the belly (abdomen) is a very common symptom, and disorders of any of the organs (liver, spleen, intestine, bladder, uterus, ovaries, pancreas), glands, lymph nodes, arteries, veins or nerves may be responsible, as well as the structures around the area such as the muscles, ligaments, skin or the vertebrae in the back.

The doctor may make a diagnosis depending on the nature of the pain (sharp, ache, dull), whether it is constant or intermittent, if it is affected by eating or passing urine or faeces, if it starts in one area then moves to another, what tends to make the pain better or worse, and the presence of associated symptoms such as vomiting, diarrhoea, constipation, loss of appetite, fever, pain on passing urine and menstrual period problems.

Investigations to further aid a doctor may include blood tests, x-rays (but these show only bones, and unless a dye is injected, not soft tissue), CT scans (computerised cross sectional x-rays which show some soft tissues), ultrasound scans (using high frequency sound waves to examine organs), endoscopy (passing a flexible telescope tube in through the anus, mouth or urethra), and as a last resort, surgery.

A very large number of conditions may be responsible for pain in the belly. These include: –

• Constipation may cause discomfort anywhere in the belly, but most commonly in the lower left abdomen.

• Colic in children is an intermittent, painful spasm of the gut. It is common in babies at about six weeks of age, but may occur in older children and adults as a result of overeating, swallowing air (eg. with rapid eating or crying), anxiety and stress, or due to toxins in the food.

• Inflammation or infection of the gall bladder (cholecystitis) and gall stones (cholelithiasis) will cause an intermittent pain that is made worse by eating, particularly fatty foods. Gall stones moving down the duct from the liver or gall bladder to the intestine will cause severe pain whenever they are pushed along by the pressure of bile behind them.

• Infections of the gut by a virus (gastroenteritis) or bacteria (eg. typhoid, tuberculosis, shigellosis, brucellosis), or infestations by parasites (eg. giardiasis, bilharzia) may cause generalised abdominal pain, diarrhoea, vomiting and fever.

• A tear of a muscle in the belly wall, straining one of the ligaments in the groin, or inflammation of cartilages at the end of the ribs may result in pain and tenderness in the abdomen that may be difficult to differentiate from pain that is coming from inside the belly. Pain in these cases is usually aggravated by movement, and other bodily functions are unaffected.

• Inflammation (gastritis) or ulceration (peptic ulcer) of the stomach causes burning pain, that may be temporarily eased by eating food, but worsens after eating.

• Infections of the liver such as hepatitis, and cysts in the liver caused by parasites (eg. Hydatid cyst from eating poorly cooked pork).

• Cancer of the colon is a serious cause of discomfort and ache that gradually worsens to a severe pain. Alterations to the normal bowel habits, loss of appetite and blood in the faeces are other symptoms.

• Appendicitis may start as a dull ache in the central abdomen, but as the infection worsens, the pain will quickly increase and move to the right lower abdomen. It may be associated with nausea, loss of appetite, fever and diarrhoea.

• The irritable bowel syndrome causes painful spasms of the large intestine that are aggravated by stress and anxiety, and associated with diarrhoea and excess wind.

• Adhesions after surgery to the abdomen, particularly for the treatment of infections (eg. appendicitis, pelvic inflammatory disease), leave raw areas behind on the surface of organs that may adhere to each other and form bands that become twisted and inflamed.

• A stone in the kidney will cause a constant dull ache, but also excruciatingly severe pain that runs down into the groin (and testes, in men) every time it moves along with the pressure of urine behind it.

• Diverticulitis causes abdominal pain and diarrhoea.

• Infections of the bladder (cystitis) are far more common in women than men, and result in passing urine very frequently, pain when passing urine, blood in the urine and an ache in the lower abdomen.

• Nerves pinched in the back may cause pain along the course of that nerve as it runs around the belly.

• Cysts or tumours in the ovary, infections in the fallopian tubes (salpingitis), or an ectopic pregnancy (pregnancy developing in the fallopian tube or beside the ovary).

• Pelvic inflammatory disease is an infection of the fallopian tubes and other organs in the pelvis of a woman, often as a result of a sexually transmitted disease. A constant dull ache will be felt, that worsens with sex or menstrual periods.

• Muscular cramps of the uterus are responsible for the pain felt by women in this lower abdomen during menstrual periods. Fibroids (balls of fibrous scar tissue in the muscular wall of the uterus) may worsen these cramps.

• Shingles is an infection of a spinal nerve caused by the virus *Herpes zoster*.

• Tumours of the small intestine may cause pain anywhere in the belly, as the intestine wanders loosely throughout the belly cavity.

• Some medications (eg. anti-inflammatories) may have abdominal discomfort or pain as a side effect.

• Peritonitis is an infection of the membrane (peritoneum) that lines the belly cavity.

• Patients with coeliac disease (sprue) are unable to digest the protein gluten, which is found in cereal grains such as wheat, rye, barley and oats, but not in rice or corn. Eating any foods containing gluten will cause diarrhoea, belly discomfort, weight loss, excess wind and bloating.

There are many less common causes of abdominal pain including enlargement and inflammation of the spleen (eg. with glandular fever), intussusception, anaemia, psychiatric conditions, pneumonia, pleurisy (infection of the membrane around the lungs), pancreatitis, Crohn's disease, disorders of the heart, aortic aneurysm, Meckel's diverticulum, mesenteric adenitis, torsion of the testis, obstructions in the large bowel, endometriosis and ulcerative colitis.

See also ABDOMINAL LUMP; BACK PAIN; DYSPEPSIA; GROIN PAIN; LOIN PAIN and separate entries for diseases and organs mentioned above.

ABORTION

Provided the woman is less than twelve weeks pregnant, an abortion is a technically simple procedure, but more advanced pregnancies are more difficult to terminate.

On attending the clinic where the procedure is to be performed, the woman will be questioned about her overall health and the details of the pregnancy. She will be examined generally and internally, a pregnancy test may be performed, and an ultrasound scan of the lower belly should be done.

Once these details are completed, if she is determined to proceed, the woman will be taken to an operating theatre and usually a brief general anaesthetic will be given, although some clinics do use a form of local or spinal anaesthetic. While anaesthetised, a thin tube is introduced through the vagina and cervix and into the uterus (womb). Suction apparatus is attached to the other end of the tube, and the tube is moved around inside the uterus, sucking out the contents, which include the developing foetus and placenta.

There are several other techniques (eg. curette), but this is now the most common.

The operation lasts only ten to fifteen minutes, and the woman will wake up from the anaesthetic in a recovery room. After a couple of hours she will be allowed to go home, but should have an internal check by a doctor (often her own general practitioner) in the next day or two to ensure that there are no complications.

If the patient has any abnormal bleeding, discharge or develops a fever in the week or two after the abortion, she should see a doctor immediately.
See also CURETTE; PREGNANCY; UTERUS

ABORTION, SPONTANEOUS
See MISCARRIAGE

ABREACTION
Abreaction (or catharsis) is a technique used during psychoanalysis, in which the patient is desensitised to an unpleasant or disagreeable experience by thought, speech and action. An example of abreaction would be the following scenario: –
• If a person had an unpleasant encounter with a spider, and ever since has had an excessive fear of spiders, a psychiatrist would (over a period of weeks), gradually bring his patient closer and closer into contact with spiders in order to remove the fear. Initially, the patient would be told merely to think about spiders, and associate the thought of spiders with a pleasant thought (eg. a holiday, nice meal etc.). Once the patient was comfortable with thinking about spiders, he or she would be encouraged to talk about them. The next step may be seeing pictures of spiders, drawing spiders, and seeing dead spiders in a bottle. The final stages could be holding a dead spider in the hand, and then allowing a harmless live spider to run across the hand.

The same technique can be used for a wide range of fears including fear of flying, heights, enclosed rooms or other situations.
See also PHOBIA; PSYCHIATRY; PSYCHOANALYSIS

ABSENCE
See EPILEPSY

ABSCESS
An abscess is a collection of pus in a tissue cavity. There are two main types of abscesses – those under the skin, and those that occur in internal body organs (called an empyema on the surface of the lungs or brain). It is caused by the destruction of normal tissue by a bacterial, or rarely fungal, infection. If significant tissue destruction occurs, the destroyed cells accumulate as pus and an abscess forms.

An abscess may be a complication of a skin infection (cellulitis), follow surgery, appendicitis or a similar internal infection, or be due to a penetrating injury.

A skin abscess appears as a red, painful swelling that is initially hard to the touch, but as the pus formation increases, becomes soft and obviously fluid-filled. Eventually a head forms that bursts and allows the pus to escape. Particularly nasty abscesses may develop around the anus (pilonidal sinus) and require quite major surgery to drain the pus.

An internal abscess can occur in almost any organ, and may not be found until it is quite large. It causes a fever and a general feeling of being unwell. The organs most commonly affected include the brain, liver, breast, lung, tonsils (causing quinsy) and teeth. Internal abscesses may require an ultrasound scan or laparoscopy (operation) to confirm the diagnosis.

Skin abscesses are treated in the early stages by antibiotics given by mouth or injection, and hot compresses are applied to the area. Once pus is present, the abscess is drained by piercing it with a scalpel, scraping it out, and keeping the drain hole open with a small piece of cloth (a wick) to allow further pus to escape quickly.

With an internal abscess, antibiotics are used to stop the spread of the infection but will not cure the abscess, so the pus must eventually be removed by an open operation under a general or local anaesthetic.

Most abscesses will slowly reduce in size and heal. If left untreated, a patient may become severely ill, with new abscesses forming in surrounding tissues.
See also CELLULITIS; LIVER ABSCESS; LUNG ABSCESS; PILONIDAL SINUS; QUINSY

ABSORPTION OF FOOD, POOR
See MALABSORPTION

AC
The prescription notation 'ac' is derived from the Latin 'ante cibum' which means 'before food'.
See also PRESCRIPTION NOTATIONS

ACANTHOSIS NIGRICANS

Acanthosis nigricans is a skin condition of the neck, groin, palms and armpits that appears in four forms – true benign, benign, malignant and pseudo. All forms cause thick, ridged skin covered in multiple dark brown or black small polyps, giving the skin a velvety appearance. The diagnosis is confirmed by a skin biopsy.

True benign acanthosis nigricans is an inherited trait, that often runs in families, starts in childhood, is more common in girls and worsens with puberty. There is no specific treatment, but it often settles in early adult life.

Benign acanthosis nigricans is the mildest form and is often associated with hormonal abnormalities in Cushing syndrome, pituitary gland disorders or polycystic ovaries and develops in late childhood or early adult life. Treatment of the underlying hormonal imbalance is necessary.

Malignant acanthosis nigricans is a reaction to cancer in other parts of the body (eg. stomach, breast, lung) and starts in late life. It is the most severe form, and requires treatment of the underlying cancer.

Pseudo acanthosis nigricans occurs in obese women who have a dark complexion. Weight loss is the only treatment.
See also CUSHING SYNDROME and separate entries for other diseases mentioned above.

ACARBOSE
See HYPOGLYCAEMICS

ACCELERATED CONDUCTION SYNDROME
See WOLFF-PARKINSON-WHITE SYNDROME

ACETYLCHOLINE
See MIOTICS

ACHALASIA

Oesophageal achalasia is a loss of muscle contractions in the lower two thirds of the gullet (oesophagus), due to degeneration of the nerves supplying the muscles of the oesophagus, that usually starts between twenty-five and sixty years of age.

Patients experience gradually worsening difficulty in swallowing that initially affects solids more than liquids, fullness and discomfort behind the breast bone (sternum), regurgitation of unswallowed food (particularly at night), weight loss and cough. Inhalation of regurgitated food can cause a cough, lung damage and infections, and there is an increased risk of cancer in the oesophagus.

A barium swallow x-ray is diagnostic, while endoscopy (passing a flexible tube down the oesophagus) can further evaluate the severity of the disease and allow pressure measurements to be made in the oesophagus.

Dilation of the narrowed section of the oesophagus using a balloon can be performed, and medications (eg. nifedipine – a calcium channel blocker) that relax the lower oesophagus may be prescribed. Surgery is performed in intractable cases.
See also CALCIUM CHANNEL BLOCKERS; OESOPHAGUS

ACICLOVIR
See ANTIVIRALS

ACID TASTE

Waterbrash is a bitter acid taste in the back of the throat. It is invariably caused by hydrochloric acid coming up (refluxing) from the stomach into the throat, and may be associated with heartburn and burping. The reflux of acid may be caused by vomiting, overeating, rapid eating, excess alcohol, a hiatus hernia (part of the stomach slipping up from the belly into the chest) or a peptic ulcer. It is usually worse when lying down or bending over.
See also BURPING, EXCESSIVE; HEARTBURN; HIATUS HERNIA; REFLUX OESOPHAGITIS

ACCUPRIL
See ACE INHIBITORS

ACE INHIBITORS

Angiotensin converting enzyme (ACE) inhibitors are a class of drugs that prevent the contraction of the tiny muscles that circle around small arteries, by blocking the action of the chemical that is essential for the contraction of these tiny artery muscles. They are used for the treatment of high blood pressure and heart failure, and improve survival after heart attack.

Examples include captopril (Capoten), fosinopril (Monopril), quinapril (Accupril, Asig), perindopril (Coversyl), trandolapril (Odrik), lisinopril (Prinivil) and ramipril (Tritace).

Side effects may include a dry cough, swelling of ankles, rash, headache and dizziness. They should not be used in pregnancy, or with severe kidney or brain disease.

See also ANGIOTENSIN II RECEPTOR ANTAGONISTS; ANTIHYPERTENSIVES; DIGOXIN; HYPERTENSION

ACETABULUM
See HIP; PELVIS

ACETAMINOPHEN
See ANALGESICS

ACIDS
Acids are water soluble, sour tasting chemicals that turn litmus paper red, react with some metals to produce hydrogen, and combine with bases to produce salts. They are not commonly used internally in medicine today. Hydrochloric acid is naturally produced in the stomach to aid indigestion, and it may be given by mouth in an extremely dilute form to patients with indigestion and a natural lack of stomach acid. Glutamic acid can also be used in this way. Acids are available in capsule or liquid form and, unless taken in excess or by those who do not require the medication, cause virtually no side effects.

Acid ointments (eg. salicylic acid) and paints may be used on the skin to remove warts and small skin cancers. If the area being treated becomes painful, the acid should not be used for a few days until the pain subsides, then it may be applied again.

See also STOMACH; PEPTIC ULCER

ACNE
Acne, spots, pimples, zits. It doesn't matter what they are called, nobody likes to have them, or look at them. Acne can vary from the annual spot, to a severe disease that may cause both skin and psychological scarring. It is generally a curse of teenage years, but it may strike later in life too, particularly in women. Usually it is more severe in teenage males, but starts earlier in females. Acne affects Caucasians (whites) more than Negroes or Chinese races. The face, upper chest, upper back and neck are most commonly affected.

Acne vulgaris is a severe form that almost invariably results in scarring of the face, back and chest, while acne conglobata affects mainly the buttocks and chest and causes skin abscesses and severe inflammation.

Pimples are due to a blockage in the outflow of oil (known as sebum) from the thousands of tiny oil glands in the skin. This blockage can be caused by dirt (uncommon in our super-clean society), dead skin left behind during the normal regular regeneration of the skin surface, or a thickening and excess production of the oil itself.

Once the opening of the oil duct becomes blocked, the gland becomes dilated with the thick oil, then inflamed, and eventually infected. The result is a white head, with the surrounding red area of infection. Eventually this bursts, sometimes leaving a scar.

The most common cause of acne is the thickening of sebum caused by the hormonal changes of puberty. The severity of acne in a teenager will depend upon the degree of acne suffered by his/her parents, as this is a strongly inherited characteristic. Pregnancy, premenstrual syndrome (hormonal changes before a period), menopause and the oral contraceptive pill may all cause pimples.

Stress in the patient, either psychological or caused by disease, may make pimples worsen. A simple cold, or the onset of exams may see the number of spots increase dramatically.

Pressure from spectacles on the bridge of the nose or tight collars, increased skin humidity from a fringe of hair or nylon clothing, and excessive use of cosmetics that further block the oil duct openings, can all cause deterioration in a person's acne. Some chemicals or oils that a patient may encounter in the work place are also possible causes.

Treatment of asthma or other diseases with steroids (eg. prednisolone) may worsen acne. A tumour of the pituitary gland under the brain, or the adrenal glands on each kidney, may produce higher than normal levels of steroids and so mimic this problem.

The severity of acne also depends on hereditary factors. There is no evidence that diet, chocolate, vitamins or herbs have any effect on acne.

A number of conditions can cause a rash that looks like acne, but is not. The most common of these are rosacea and folliculitis barbae (ingrown facial hairs caused by blunt blade when shaving or other skin damage).

Rosacea is a skin disease of the face, found most commonly in middle-aged women, which causes excessive intermittent flushing of the face, then sores develop that are similar to a severe case of pimples.

Not much is to be gained by altering diet or taking vitamins or other herbs. A small number of sufferers may find that one particular food causes a fresh crop of spots, but these people usually quickly realise this and avoid the offending substance.

The first step in treatment involves keeping the skin clean with a mild soap and face cloth, and simple oil-drying, antiseptic and cleansing creams or lotions. Further treatment involves combinations of antibiotics (eg. tetracyclines) that may be taken in the short term for acute flare ups or in the long term to prevent acne, skin lotions or creams containing antibiotics and/or steroids, and changing a woman's hormonal balance by putting her on the oral contraceptive pill or using other hormones. In rare cases it is necessary to take the very potent medication isotretinoin (which can cause birth deformities if used during pregnancy), give steroid injections (eg. triamcinolone) into the skin around particularly bad eruptions, or to abrade away the skin around scars. The treatment of adults with maturity onset acne is more difficult than juvenile acne.

Picking acne spots can cause serious secondary bacterial infections that can spread deep into the skin (cellulitis).

Although acne cannot be cured, in the majority of cases reasonable control can be achieved. It eventually settles with age.
See also CHLORACNE; KERATOLYTICS; SEBACEOUS GLANDS; SKIN; TETRACYCLINES

ACNE ROSACEA
See ROSACEA

ACOUSTIC NEUROMA
An acoustic neuroma (acoustic neurinoma or Schwannoma) is usually a benign (noncancerous) tumour of the insulating sheath which covers the acoustic nerve (nerve which conducts the sense of hearing to the brain). It often develops at the point where the nerve passes through a small hole in the skull to enter the brain.

Patients develop a ringing noise (tinnitus), followed by deafness in the affected ear. As it increases in size other symptoms may include pain, dizziness and, because of pressure on other nearby nerves that supply the eye, a lack of tears in the eye and double vision. A headache does not occur until the tumour is very large. A CT scan can usually show the tumour accurately.

Surgical removal of the tumour in a very intricate operation is the only treatment option, but removing larger tumours may result in unavoidable permanent deafness and possibly other nerve damage.

The smaller the tumour at the time of surgery, the better the final result. Tumours less than two cm in diameter can normally be removed without any problem.
See also SCHWANNOMA; TINNITUS

ACQUIRED IMMUNE DEFICIENCY SYNDROME
See AIDS

ACROMEGALY
Acromegaly is excess growth in specific parts of the body due to over-production of growth hormone in the pituitary gland, which sits underneath the brain. Growth hormone is required for the normal growth of a child, but if it is produced inappropriately later in life, acromegaly results. The most common reason for this is a tumour in the pituitary gland, but occasionally tumours elsewhere can secrete the hormone.

Patients have excessive growth of the hands, feet, jaw, face, tongue and internal organs. They also suffer headaches, sweating, weakness, and loss of vision. A woman's menstrual periods will stop, and diabetes insipidus is a common complication of the disease and its treatment.

Blood tests can be used to prove the diagnosis, and x-rays and CT scans of the skull can detect the tumour.

Specialised microsurgery is performed through the nose and up into the base of the brain, to remove the tumour. Occasionally irradiation of the tumour may be performed. Usually hormone supplements must be taken long term to replace those normally produced by the destroyed pituitary gland. Treatment is very successful, particularly in younger adults.
See also DIABETES INSIPIDUS; HEAD LARGE

ACROMION
See SCAPULA

ACROPHOBIA
Acrophobia is an abnormal fear of heights.
See also PHOBIA

ACTH
See ADRENAL GLAND; PITUITARY
GLAND

ACTINIC KERATOSIS
See HYPERKERATOSIS

ACTINOMYCOSIS
Actinomycosis is an uncommon infection of
the skin, particularly the face, caused by the
bacteria *Actinomycoses,* which normally lives in
the mouth and assists with food digestion. If
the bacterium enters damaged tissue in other
parts of the body it may cause an infection.

The symptoms include hard, inflamed
lumps in the skin that develop into abscesses
and discharge pus. Other areas that may be
infected include tooth sockets after an extraction, and the gut. Other symptoms include a
fever, and constant severe pain in any infected
area.

Swabs are taken from the discharging
pus in an attempt to identify the responsible
bacteria, but the bacteria is often difficult to
identify

The infection is resistant to simple treatments, and a six-week or longer course of
penicillin and other antibiotics, initially by
injection, is necessary. Abscesses are surgically drained and affected tissue may need to
be excised (cut out). Cure is difficult, but
usually possible, although permanent scarring
may be left behind.
See also ABSCESS; BACTERIA

ACUPUNCTURE
Acupuncture is an ancient Chinese method of
healing used for at least four thousand years.
It is a system of healing in which the body's
inherent defence, repair and maintenance
systems are stimulated by means of the selective insertion of fine needles through the skin.
The points for insertion are located along the
meridians along which the energy (or chi),
according to the ancient Chinese tradition, is
perceived to flow through the body. The oldest
surviving description is the 'Yellow Emperor's
Classic of Internal Medicine' which was
written in China about 100 BC. By the sixth
century, the practice of acupuncture had been
codified and standardised throughout China,
and it remained one of the mainstays of
Chinese medical practice until outlawed in
1929 by the nationalist government of Chiang
Kai-shek. The practice of acupuncture continued in rural areas only, until the ban was lifted
by Mao Tse-tung in 1949.

The first information in Europe about
acupuncture was published by Dutch traders
to Japan in the late eighteenth century. In
1821, the Englishman J. M. Churchill published "A Treatise on Acpuncturation" under
the aegis of the Royal College of Surgeons and
brought knowledge of the practice into the
British area of influence.

In addition to the natural therapists who
practise traditional Chinese medicine, many
doctors and physiotherapists now also use
acupuncture and it has become an accepted
form of treatment, particularly for the relief of
pain, in orthodox medical practice. Scientifically, it is believed that acupuncture stimulates the release of endorphins. Endorphins
are a potent narcotic pain-killer that are naturally produced in small quantities in the body.
A full explanation for its actions in other diseases has not yet been found, and its use for
these is more controversial.

During acupuncture treatment, very fine
needles are inserted into various points on the
body. These points contain nerve endings,
and correspond to areas of reduced electrical
resistance on the skin. These areas can be
detected by a meter that measures electrical
resistance.

Acupuncture is believed to reduce pain by
at least two methods: –
• Firstly it stimulates the release in the brain
of chemical substances called endorphins,
which are the body's own painkillers.
• Secondly, stimulating nerves with acupuncture effectively overloads them so that they
are less able to carry pain messages to the
brain.

Other actions of acupuncture can include
raising the blood levels of white blood cells
and antibodies that fight infection, and producing a calming effect by the release of other
natural chemicals in the brain.

Acupuncture is a useful treatment for many
painful conditions, especially those caused by

muscle sprains or strains eg. strained neck, frozen shoulder, tennis elbow, low back pain, sciatica (provided it is not caused by a slipped disc), period pain, shingles and arthritis.

There are a number of other conditions for which acupuncture can be performed as an extra treatment in addition to orthodox Western medical methods. These include asthma, bronchitis, hay fever, anxiety, depression, dizziness, urinary frequency and the symptoms of menopause. It is absolutely essential that a patient receiving acupuncture treatment for any of these conditions is first assessed by a doctor. Under no circumstances should a patient stop or change any of their other treatments except in consultation with a doctor (it would be extremely dangerous for example, to stop using your asthma puffers or tablets).

Acupuncture can also be used to treat insomnia, morning sickness and to help stop smoking.

The needles used for acupuncture are even finer than those used for giving injections. Insertion is virtually painless, however sensations such as tingling, numbness or heaviness may be felt during treatment, and are part of the effect of acupuncture stimulating nerves.

The number of treatments necessary varies with the nature and severity of the complaint, and with the length of time it has been present. In some cases, for example an acute strained neck or morning sickness, relief may be obtained after two or three sessions. Other conditions such as low back pain which has been present for many years may require six to ten treatments before marked relief is evident. Usually the first signs of improvement are a return to normal sleep and improved range of movement.

For best results, the patient should be warm, relaxed and not overly hungry at the time of treatment. People who are physically exhausted, fasting or suffering from bleeding disorders should not undergo acupuncture treatment, and the practitioner should know if you are pregnant, taking warfarin tablets or have a pacemaker.
See also CHINESE MEDICINE; SHIATSU

ACUTE
An acute condition is one that is of recent or sudden onset. The opposite of chronic.
See also CHRONIC

ACUTE FEBRILE NEUTROPHILIC DERMATOSIS
See SWEET SYNDROME

ACUTE HEPATIC PORPHYRIA
Acute hepatic porphyria is one of a number of different uncommon types of porphyria, which is a liver disease.

It is an inherited disease that passes from one generation to the next but causes symptoms in only 10% of those affected.

Symptoms develop at the time of puberty with vague abdominal pains, nausea, vomiting and abnormal sensations. As the disease progresses, the abdominal pains may become severe, but nothing abnormal can be found in the abdomen. In advanced cases, nerve pain, paralysis, personality changes and fits may occur. The urine turns a dark purple colour, then brown, if left standing. Some patients may have the otherwise quiescent disease triggered by severe infections, starvation, some drugs or steroids. Complications include liver damage, which may progress to liver failure or liver cancer (hepatoma) and nerve damage which may cause varying forms of paralysis.

It is diagnosed by special blood tests. Treatment involves careful genetic counselling of families and avoiding factors (eg. crash diets, emotional stress, alcohol, certain drugs) that may precipitate an attack, and it is controlled by the use of a complex drug regime.

Acute hepatic porphyria may be controlled, but not cured, and death may occur due to the paralysis of the muscles of breathing.
See also LIVER; PORPHYRIA CUTANEA TARDA

ACUTE RENAL FAILURE
See KIDNEY FAILURE, ACUTE

ADAM'S APPLE
See LARYNX

ADAMS-STOKES SYNDROME
See STOKES-ADAMS ATTACK

ADD
See ATTENTION DEFICIT HYPERACTIVITY DISORDER

ADDICTION
See ALCOHOLISM; BENZODIAZEPINES; CANNABIS; COCAINE; ECSTASY;

GAMMA-HYDROXYBUTYRATE;
HEROIN; KETAMINE; LSD;
MARIJUANA; NARCOTICS;
STIMULANTS

ADDISON DISEASE

Addison disease is also known as adrenocorti-cal insufficiency and chronic hypoadrenocor-ticism. It is a rare underactivity of the outer layer (cortex) of the adrenal glands which sit on top of each kidney, and produce hormones (chemical messengers) such as cortisone that control the levels of vital elements in the body and regulate the breakdown of food. In most cases, the reason for adrenal gland failure is unknown, but tuberculosis is a possible cause.

The symptoms include weakness, lack of appetite, diarrhoea and vomiting, skin pig-mentation, mental instability, low blood pressure, loss of body hair and absence of sweating. Complications include diabetes, thyroid disease, anaemia, and eventual death. A sudden onset of disease is known as an Addisonian crisis, which may be rapidly fatal.

It is diagnosed by special blood tests that measure the body's response to stimulation of the adrenal gland.

Treatment involves a combination of medications (eg. steroids such as cortisone) to replace the missing hormones, and dosages vary greatly from one patient to another. Frequent small meals high in carbohydrate and protein are eaten, and infections must be treated rapidly. Patients must carry an emer-gency supply of injectable cortisone with them at all times. Treatment can give most patients a long and useful life, but they can-not react to stress (both physical and mental) adequately, and additional treatment must be given in these situations. The ultimate outcome depends greatly on the patient's ability to strictly follow all treatment regimes.
See also ADRENAL GLAND;
CONGENITAL ADRENAL
HYPERPLASIA; HORMONES;
WATERHOUSE-FRIDERICHSEN
SYNDROME

ADDISONIAN CRISIS
See ADDISON DISEASE

ADENITIS

Adenitis (or lymphadenitis) is an infection or inflammation of one or more lymph nodes, usually in the neck, armpit or groin. Lymph nodes are collections of white cells designed to remove and destroy invading bacteria and viruses. Sometimes the infection overwhelms the lymph node, or cancer spreads from another part of the body, causing it to become painful and enlarged.

Adenitis is characterised by red, sore and swollen lymph nodes, and the patient devel-ops a fever and feels ill. An untreated infec-tion may cause an abscess.

Blood tests may be performed to identify serious infections, or in cases where cancer is suspected.

If the infection is bacterial, the treatment is antibiotics. Viral infections, such as mumps and glandular fever, will need to run their course, with rest and painkillers the only treatment. Cancerous lymph nodes need to be surgically removed. Most bacterial infec-tions settle well with antibiotics. Cancer prog-nosis varies depending on the type.

All lymph nodes that cause discomfort must be examined by a doctor as the adenitis may be due to a cancer.
See also ABSCESS; CANCER; LYMPH
NODES ENLARGED AND/OR
PAINFUL; MESENTERIC ADENITIS

ADENOCARCINOMA OF THE LUNG
See LUNG CANCER

ADENOIDS

At the back of the nasal passages and top of the pharynx (throat) is a mass of lymph glands called the adenoids. Like all other lymph nodes, the adenoids help to combat infection but may themselves become infected, and if this infection persists, they may be surgically removed. Usually this is a relatively minor operation with no long-term adverse effects.

Enlarged adenoids may also block the opening to the Eustachian tube. This tube opens into the back of the nose beside the adenoids, and leads to the middle ear. If the Eustachian tube remains blocked, ear infections may occur.
See also EUSTACHIAN TUBE;
PHARYNX; TONSIL;
TONSILLECTOMY

ADENOSINE DIPHOSPHATE
See CREATINE; MUSCLE

ADENOSINE TRIPHOSPHATE
See CREATINE; MUSCLE

ADHD
See ATTENTION DEFICIT
HYPERACTIVITY DISORDER

ADHESIONS
Adhesions are a relatively uncommon but potentially serious and disabling complication of any surgery within the abdomen.

During an operation, minor damage to tissue in the abdominal cavity occurs. If two areas of damaged tissue come into contact they may heal together and form an adhesion, which is a tough fibrous band that can later stretch across the abdominal cavity between the two surgically damaged points. Adhesions are more common if there is an infection in the abdomen (eg. burst appendix), but sometimes occur after relatively minor surgery. They are also more common in short, overweight females, but the reason for this is unknown.

Many adhesions produce no symptoms, but if a loop of bowel is trapped it can become obstructed. Sometimes adhesions cause a persistent colic in the gut as the intestine winds tightly around the fibrous bands, or the adhesion may tear and bleed, leading to more pain. A bowel obstruction may rarely occur and lead to gangrene, perforation and peritonitis.

No totally diagnostic test is available, but sometimes abnormalities are seen on an ultrasound scan of the abdomen.

The only treatment is more surgery to cut away the adhesions, during which extreme care must be taken to prevent any bleeding into the abdomen and any unnecessary injury to the bowel. A few months or years after treatment the adhesions may re-form, and the symptoms start again. It is a very difficult problem to deal with, and often there is no permanent solution.
See also ASHERMAN SYNDROME

ADHESIVE CAPSULITIS
See FROZEN SHOULDER

ADIE'S PUPIL
See HOLMES-ADIE SYNDROME

ADOLESCENCE
Adolescence is the period between the start of puberty or sexual development and full matu-
rity. It generally begins in the early teens and ends around eighteen or twenty. Hence, the words 'adolescent' and 'teenager' are used interchangeably.
See also PUBERTY

ADP
See CREATINE; MUSCLE

ADRENAL GLAND
The adrenal glands are part of the system that produces the body's hormones (called the endocrine system). They sit on top of each kidney, a bit like a beanie. The glands are tiny – less than five cm long and weigh only a few grams – and yet produce more than three dozen hormones. The glands are divided into two quite distinct parts – an inner, reddish brown section called the medulla and an outer, yellow-coloured section called the cortex. Each part has its own distinct function.

Hormones are chemical messengers that help to determine the way the body functions. The hormones produced by the medulla in the adrenal gland include adrenaline which causes the well-known 'fight or flight' response to danger. The medulla is part of the autonomic (unconscious) nervous system, and when the body becomes aware of danger through one of its senses, these hormones literally spurt out making the heart beat faster, increasing the blood sugar level, altering the blood flow and generally increasing the body's capacity to deal with the emergency. Because many of the stresses of modern life do not require such a physical response, the release of adrenaline is

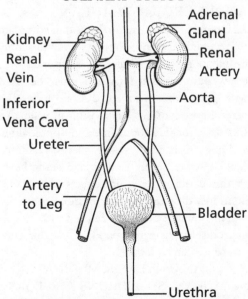
URINARY TRACT

sometimes inappropriate and the body has no way of using it up. If it happens too often it may eventually cause health problems.

The hormones produced by the cortex are steroids, of which there are three main groups. One group (aldosterone) controls the balance of minerals in the body. Another group regulates the use the body makes of carbohydrates, and also plays a part in our ability to handle stress (cortisone is the most important hormone of this group). The third group affects the operation of our sex glands and influences our sexual development. Steroids are made from cholesterol, so a certain amount of cholesterol is necessary in our diet, provided it isn't more than we need, which can cause heart problems.

Like other glands in the endocrine system, the adrenal cortex is controlled by the pituitary gland and its adrenocorticotrophic hormone (ACTH), amongst others.

If the adrenal glands are destroyed because of disease (eg. tuberculosis or cancer) or are overactive, the functioning of our entire body can be impaired. The most common disorders are Addison disease and Cushing syndrome.
See also ADDISON DISEASE; ALDOSTERONE; CUSHING SYNDROME; GLANDS; HORMONES; HYPOALDOSTERONISM; PHAEOCHROMOCYTOMA; PITUITARY GLAND

ADRENALINE
See ADRENAL GLAND; ADRENERGIC STIMULANTS; VASOCONSTRICTORS

ADRENERGIC STIMULANTS
Adrenergic stimulants are drugs that stimulate the nervous system. They are available only as injections or an inhaler. They interact with many other medications and must be used with great care in severe disease under the careful and constant supervision of a doctor. Examples include adrenaline and isoprenaline.

They are used in severe allergy reactions (anaphylaxis), severe asthma and some heart rhythm abnormalities. Side effects include palpitations, dizziness, pallor, tremor, headache and insomnia. They must be used with care in heart disease, neuroses, children and diabetes. Overdose can be fatal.
See also ANAPHYLAXIS; MEDICATION; STIMULANTS; VASOCONSTRICTORS

ADRENOCORTICAL HYPER-FUNCTION
See CUSHING SYNDROME

ADRENOCORTICOTROPHIC HORMONE
See ADRENAL GLAND; ALDOSTERONE; PITUITARY GLAND

ADRENOGENITAL SYNDROME
See CONGENITAL ADRENAL HYPERPLASIA

AESCULAPIUS
Aesculapius was the god of medical practice in the ancient Greek pantheon, so was included second only to Apollo (his father), the head of all the gods, in the list of those to whom the Hippocratic oath was directed. He was taught the art of healing by the centaur Chiron, and became a skilful physician, but Zeus (king of the gods) was afraid he would reveal his knowledge to mortals and so slew him with a lightening bolt. Ancient Greeks used to sleep in temples dedicated to Aesculapius in order to relieve their illnesses. Hygiae and Panacea were interpreted as the goddesses of health and healing.
See also CADUCEUS; HIPPOCRATES; HIPPOCRATIC OATH

AFFECTIVE DISORDER
See DEPRESSION

AFRICAN TICK BITE FEVER
See TYPHUS

AFRICAN TRYPANOSOMIASIS
See SLEEPING SICKNESS

AFTERBIRTH
See PLACENTA

AGAMMAGLOBULINAEMIA
Agammaglobulinaemia is an X-linked (only occurs in boys) inherited inability of the bone marrow and thymus gland to produce gammaglobulin, which is essential for establishing and maintaining the immune system. It is passed from one generation to the next by women.

Patients develop recurrent severe infections that start in infancy. There is an increased incidence of cancers.

Antibiotics are used to control infections,

immunoglobulin injections are given on a regular basis, and a bone marrow transplant may be tried. The prognosis is poor unless successful bone marrow transplant is possible.
See also GAMMAGLOBULIN; IMMUNODEFICIENCY; X-LINKED CONDITION

AGORAPHOBIA
Agoraphobia is an abnormal fear of open spaces.
See also PHOBIA

AGRANULOCYTOSIS
Agranulocytosis (malignant leucopenia) is a lack of white blood cells which are normally produced in the bone marrow, and a subsequent inability of the body to defend itself from infection.

There is often no apparent cause, but it may be due to a rare adverse reaction to some drugs (eg. sulphonamides, thiouracil), heavy metal poisoning or a complication of leukaemia and aplastic anaemia. It is diagnosed by examining blood and a bone marrow sample under a microscope.

Patients develop severe, uncontrollable bacterial and viral infections. Blood transfusion, and potent antibiotics by injection, are the only treatments, but the condition is often fatal.
See also APLASTIC ANAEMIA; LEUKAEMIA; WHITE BLOOD CELLS

AGRAPHIA
Agraphia is a medical term indicating difficulty with writing.
See also WRITING DIFFICULT

AID
See ARTIFICIAL CONCEPTION

AIDS
AIDS is an acronym for the acquired immune deficiency syndrome, which is an infection caused by a retrovirus known as the human immunodeficiency virus (HIV) which destroys the body's defence mechanisms and allows severe infections and cancers to develop.

The story begins in central Africa, where it is now believed a form of AIDS has existed in apes for thousands of years. These animals come into close contact with humans in this area, and are butchered and eaten by the local population. At some stage in the early part of the 1900s, the virus spread from apes to humans. In apes, due to natural selection over many generations, the virus causes few or no symptoms, and is harmless.

The AIDS virus has been isolated from old stored tissue samples dated in the 1950's, found in Kinshasa hospital, Zaire. From Africa, AIDS spread to Haiti in the Caribbean. Haiti was ruled by a vicious dictator (Papa Doc Duvalier), and many Haitian Negroes fled to Africa to avoid persecution. Once 'Papa Doc' and his son 'Baby Doc' were removed from power, these exiles returned, bringing AIDS with them. The virus mutated in humans and became more virulent, causing a faster and more severe onset of symptoms. Viruses mutate routinely (eg. different strains of influenza virus every year).

American homosexuals frequented Haiti because it was very poor, and sexual favours could be bought cheaply. They returned home from their holiday with the AIDS virus, and it has spread around the world from there. The first cases were diagnosed in California in 1981, although cases occurred in Sweden in 1978 in the family of a sailor who had visited Haiti, but the disease was not identified as AIDS until years later. There may also have been some movement of the disease directly through Africa to Algeria and France.

Fortunately for most of us, it is a relatively hard disease to catch. AIDS is spread by the transfer of blood and semen from one person to another. It was initially confined largely to homosexuals and drug addicts, but although these remain the most affected groups in developed countries, it is promiscuous heterosexual contact that is the most common method of transmission in poorer countries. In the early days of the disease, some unfortunate recipients of blood transfusions and other blood-derived medications were inadvertently given the AIDS virus. Tests are now available to allow blood banks to screen for AIDS.

AIDS can NOT be caught from any casual contact, or from spa baths, kissing, mosquitoes, tears, towels or clothing. The disease can be caught only by homosexual or heterosexual intercourse with a carrier of the disease, by using contaminated needles, or from blood from a carrier. If someone does come into sexual or blood contact with an AIDS carrier, it is possible for the virus to cross into their body. The body's defence mechanisms may then fight off the virus and leave the person with no illness whatsoever, or the AIDS virus may spread throughout the body to cause an HIV infection.

In 2001 there were 35 million people in the world with an HIV infection, 23 million of them in Africa and 95% in developing countries. There are seven million deaths worldwide every year from AIDS, and every day 20 000 people are infected with HIV. The incidence of HIV infection varies from two in every 100 000 people in China, to 115 in Australia, 2100 in Thailand, 20 000 in Uganda and over 50 000 in every 100 000 people in Botswana (the world's highest rate). Almost 1% of the entire adult population of the world is infected by HIV. The rate of infection is increasing in under-developed countries in Africa and Asia, but dropping in developed Western countries.

Those who are infected with the human immunodeficiency virus are said to be HIV positive. Once the HIV virus enters the body it may lie dormant for months or years. During this time there may be no or minimal symptoms, but it may be possible to pass the infection on to another sex partner, and babies may become infected in the uterus of an infected mother.

The disease has been classified into several categories. A patient can progress to a more severe category but cannot revert to less severe one. The categories are: –

• HIV category 1 – a glandular fever-like disease that lasts a few days to weeks with inflamed lymph nodes, fever, rash and tiredness.
• HIV category 2 – no symptoms.
• HIV category 3 – persistent generalised enlargement of lymph nodes.
• HIV category 4 (AIDS) – varied symptoms and signs depending on the areas of the body affected. May include fever, weight loss, diarrhoea, nerve and brain disorders, severe infections, lymph node cancer, sarcomas, and other cancers. Patients are very susceptible to any type of infection or cancer from the common cold to pneumonia, septicaemia and multiple rare cancers (eg. Kaposi sarcoma) because the body's immune system is destroyed by the virus.

Blood tests are positive at all stages of HIV infection, but there may be a lag period of up to three months or more from when the disease is caught until it can be detected.

There is no cure or vaccine available for AIDS or HIV infection at present. Prevention is the only practical way to deal with AIDS. Condoms give good, but not total, protection from sexually catching the virus, and drug addicts may be educated not to share needles.

Once diagnosed as HIV positive patients should not give up hope, because they may remain in the second stage for many years. Prolonging this stage can be achieved by the regular long-term use of potent antiviral and immunosupportive medications, stopping smoking, exercising regularly, eating a well-balanced diet, resting adequately and avoiding illegal drugs.

Patients may remain at the category 2 level for many years, possibly even decades. Up to half of those who are HIV positive do not develop category 4 disease for more than ten years. On the other hand, no one with category 4 HIV (AIDS) has lived more than a few months, and sufferers develop severe infections and cancers that eventually kill them.
See also ANTIVIRALS; KAPOSI SARCOMA; VIRUS

AIR SICKNESS
See MOTION SICKNESS

ALBINISM
Albinism is an uncommon condition in which there is a total lack of pigment in the skin and eyes. The skin is white, regardless of the race of the parents, and the iris (coloured part of the eyes) is pink. Both eyes and skin are very susceptible to damage by sunlight. Albinism is a defect of genes that occurs from the moment of conception, but it is not inherited, and an albino person will usually have normally pigmented children. There is no treatment for the condition other than carefully protecting skin and eyes from the sun.

Chediak-Higashi syndrome is an inherited condition that can pass to subsequent generations. It causes recurrent skin and lung infections, partial albinism and sometimes liver, spleen and lung damage.
See also CHEDIAK-HIGASHI SYNDROME; SKIN DEPIGMENTED; WHITE PATCHES ON SKIN

ALBINO
See ALBINISM

ALCOHOL

Ethyl alcohol (C^2H^5OH) or ethanol, is a colourless, liquid, organic compound produced by fermentation of carbohydrates (sugars) in fruit (eg. grapes) or grain (eg. wheat). Less commonly, it may be produced by fermenting vegetables or even milk and honey. It produces immediate effects on the human body as it is absorbed from the stomach rather than the intestine, reaching a maximum level ninety minutes after ingestion, then slowly dissipating. It is excreted through the kidneys over the subsequent twelve to fifteen hours.

Alcohol is normally consumed in the form of intoxicating liquids that have varying strengths of alcohol. The alcohol in beer varies from below 2% alcohol to over 8%. Wines vary from about 8% to over 14%, while fortified wines (eg. sherry, port) vary from 18% to 22% alcohol. Spirits (eg. gin, whisky, brandy, rum) and liqueurs usually contain 40% to 50% alcohol, but some overproof spirits go much higher.

In the body alcohol causes excitation of the brain, loss of inhibition and relief of tension and anxiety at low doses, but at higher doses it depresses the mood, sedates, impairs concentration, slows reflexes, impedes learning and memory, decreases coordination, slurs speech, changes sensation, weakens muscles and increases production of urine. Other effects may include abnormalities of the blood chemistry, nausea and vomiting. Self-injury as a result of falls and other accidents is very common amongst those affected by alcohol.

Long term abuse of alcohol (alcoholism) may have other serious effects on the brain, liver and other organs.

Levels of alcohol above 0.05% are considered sufficient to have significant adverse effects and to impair driving. Actual legal levels of alcohol in the blood vary from country to country. A level above 0.4% may be lethal.

Alcohol withdrawal (hangover) may cause tremor, headache, loss of appetite, nausea, sweating and insomnia. If the use of alcohol has been long term, withdrawal may cause delirium tremens.

See also ALCOHOLISM; BERIBERI; CIRRHOSIS; DELIRIUM TREMENS; WERNICKE-KORSAKOFF PSYCHOSIS

ALCOHOLISM

Alcohol abuse may be a temporary problem as a reaction to anxiety or stress, but it may lead to the chronic condition of alcoholism.

Alcoholism affects up to 3% of the adult population in developed countries. It is a disease in the same way that infections and cancer are diseases. It does no good to tell an alcoholic to 'pull yourself together' or 'stop drinking before it kills you'. They need professional counselling and treatment. The biggest problem faced by families and doctors is the denial by so many alcoholics that they have a problem.

When alcohol is swallowed, it is absorbed very rapidly from the stomach, and commences its actions on the brain and other organs. This of course is one of the attractions of alcohol – it can make you very happy very quickly, and this can lead to addiction in some people. The children of alcoholics are more likely themselves to become alcoholics, and should be very wary when using alcohol.

Blood tests on liver function and alcohol levels may confirm diagnosis, and an ultrasound scan of the liver may show damage (cirrhosis).

Alcoholism has two stages of development – problem drinking, and alcohol addiction. Problem drinking is the use of alcohol intermittently to ease tension and anxiety. It may be associated with the use of prescription drugs to control emotional problems. Alcohol addiction is more serious.

An alcoholic is someone who has three or more of the following symptoms or signs: –
• drinks alone
• tries to hide drinking habits from others
• continues to drink despite convincing evidence that it is damaging their health
• disrupts work or social life because of alcohol
• craves alcohol when none is available
• appears to tolerate the effects of alcohol well
• blacks out for no apparent reason
• binges on alcohol
• averages six standard alcoholic drinks a day
• has abnormal liver function blood tests

The social complications of alcohol are obvious and vary from the disruption of family life to poor performance at work and the risks of drink-driving.

The medical effects of alcoholism can be serious to the point where they can significantly alter the quality of life and shorten the life of the alcoholic. They include: –

• Cirrhosis. In this, the soft normal liver tissue is replaced by firm scar tissue that is unable to process the waste products of the body adequately. The other vital actions of the liver in converting and storing food products and producing chemicals essential to the body are also inhibited.

• Wernicke-Korsakoff psychosis. This syndrome causes brain damage with symptoms of depression, irrational behaviour and insanity. These conditions are related to vitamin deficiencies caused by an inadequate diet while on alcoholic binges.

• Degeneration of the cerebellum (the part of the brain that is at the back of the head) caused by alcoholism can cause permanent incoordination, difficulties in walking and performing simple tasks.

• Peripheral neuropathy is damage to the nerves supplying the body. It causes muscle cramps, pins and needles sensations and muscle pains.

Treatment involves counselling, professional treatment programs in hospital, supportive groups (eg. Alcoholics Anonymous) and medications to ease withdrawal and prevent relapses (eg. disulfiram, naltrexone). Withdrawal from alcohol may cause delirium tremens.

The medical effects of alcoholism can be serious to the point where they can significantly alter the quality of life and shorten the life of the alcoholic, and adversely impact on other members of the family.

See also ALCOHOL; BERIBERI; CIRRHOSIS; DELIRIUM TREMENS; FOETAL ALCOHOL SYNDROME; GAMMA-GLUTAMYL TRANSFERASE; PERIPHERAL NEUROPATHY; PSEUDOCUSHING SYNDROME; WERNICKE-KORSAKOFF PSYCHOSIS

ALDOSTERONE

Aldosterone is a hormone secreted by the outer part (cortex) of the adrenal glands, one of which sits on top of each kidney. It acts to control the amount of sodium, and therefore the amount of fluid, in the body. The secretion of aldosterone is itself controlled by fluid volume receptors in the adrenal cortex, and by other hormones produced in the adrenal gland and pituitary gland (ACTH).

The amount of aldosterone in the blood

can be measured by blood tests. The normal range is 100 to 400 pmol/L.

Low levels of the hormone may indicate adrenal gland disease or damage, or kidney failure, or it may be due to medications such as ACE inhibitors, beta-blockers, nonsteroidal anti-inflammatory drugs, cyclosporin and triamterene.

High levels occur in adrenal gland tumours, generalised body swelling (oedema), very severe hypertension, diuretic therapy, congestive cardiac failure and pregnancy.

See also ADRENAL GLAND; BLOOD TESTS; CONN SYNDROME; HYPOALDOSTERONISM; SODIUM and separate entries for medications and diseases mentioned above.

ALDOSTERONISM
See CONN SYNDROME

ALIMENTARY TRACT

The food we eat is the means by which our body is provided with nutrients and fuel to keep it functioning. Before it can be utilised, the food must be converted into a form that is able to be absorbed by the body. The process by which this occurs is called digestion, and the bodily organs involved in the process make up the alimentary tract or canal, which is also called the gastrointestinal tract or the digestive tract.

The alimentary tract starts at the mouth which takes in the food, breaking it up into small pieces with the teeth and tongue, and at the same time commencing the digestive process by the addition of saliva. With a swallow the food moves rapidly down the oesophagus (gullet) into the stomach, which is situated just below the bottom of the breastbone.

The stomach is shaped rather like a capital J, and the food enters at the top and leaves through the lower end. The sag of the J is a lake of food and hydrochloric acid. This acid is produced by cells lining the stomach, and it breaks down the basic structure of the food. The stomach itself is protected from being attacked by the acid by a thick layer of mucus on its walls. With contractions that sweep along the muscular walls of the stomach, the food is slowly moved towards the pylorus. This is a ring of muscle that surrounds the exit tube of the stomach. As a contraction

ALIMENTARY TRACT

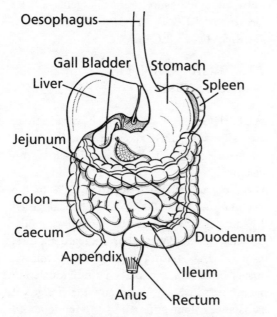

moves towards it, the muscle opens this valve to allow some but not all the food to pass into the next section of the digestive system.

The next tube is the small intestine, which starts with the duodenum, a section which is only 30–40cm. long. It is quite highly specialised, for its task is to add the final digestive juices and enzymes to the food that will break it down to its basic components. There is an opening in the side of the duodenum, and through this the bile from the liver and gall bladder is squirted onto the food, and the digestive enzymes from the pancreas are added. An enzyme is a protein that activates chemical reactions but is not itself changed or used up by the process. Each different enzyme has its own specific task and can only be used for that task. For example, one kind of enzyme deals with fats, another with carbohydrates, and yet another with proteins. Wave-like contractions from the gut steadily move the food along and churn it up so that the digestive juices are thoroughly mixed in.

The next section of the small intestine is the jejunum followed by the ileum. These sections are five to seven metres long, and are only loosely attached to the body so that they wind in slippery loops all over the abdominal cavity. At this stage, the food is in the form of a slurry from which the fine microscopic fingers that line the intestine absorb and engulf the proteins, carbohydrates and fats that are the basic components of all foodstuffs. By the time the food reaches the end of the small intestine and enters the next section of gut, only water, fibre and waste products are left.

The large intestine comes next. This is far larger in diameter and is about 1.5 to two metres long. The food moves very slowly through this section, as its task is to absorb as much water as necessary from the food. If the movement of food is too slow, the wastes dry out and you become constipated. If it is too fast, not enough water is removed and diarrhoea results.

The final thirty centimetres is the rectum. This fills the back of the pelvis and is basically a storage area for faeces. At the appropriate time, the muscle ring that forms the anus is relaxed, the muscles of the abdominal wall and rectum contract, and the unwanted wastes are eliminated after a journey that normally lasts two to three days.

See also ANUS; COLON; DUODENUM; ILEUM; JEJUNUM; LARGE INTESTINE; MOUTH; OESOPHAGUS; PHARYNX; SMALL INTESTINE; STOMACH

ALKALINISERS

Alkalinisers are designed to raise the pH (acidity) of the urine from a low value to a high value, making it more alkaline and less attractive to bacteria. They act to control the burning experienced with bladder infections (cystitis), and to control and prevent other minor urinary infections. They are also used to control excess acid in the stomach. They are available as a liquid, or as a powder that mixes with water to make a palatable drink. They should not be used regularly in the long term. Examples include citric acid and sodium citrotartrate. Side effects are rare, but diarrhoea may occur. They are safe in pregnancy, but should not be used in kidney or heart failure.

See also CYSTITIS; KIDNEY

ALLERGIC CONJUNCTIVITIS

Allergic (or atopic) conjunctivitis is an allergy reaction involving the surface of the eye.

If pollen, dust or other substance to which a person is allergic lands on the eye, an allergy reaction will occur. Allergic conjunctivitis is often associated with hay fever and often only occurs at certain times of the year.

The symptoms include redness, itching, blurred vision and watering of the eye. In severe cases the white of the eye may swell dramatically and balloon out between the eyelids. There may be a clear, stringy discharge from the eyes, as well as excessive tears, and if the lower eyelid is turned down it appears to be covered with a large number of tiny red bumps. Rarely, ulceration of the eye surface may occur.

Blood and skin tests can be undertaken to identify the responsible substance in some patients who are repeatedly affected.

It can be prevented by the regular use of sodium cromoglycate drops throughout the allergy time of year. Attacks can be treated by antihistamine tablets and eye drops such as levocabastine. Simple eye drops available over the counter from chemists and containing artery-constricting medications can be used in milder cases. Appropriate treatment usually settles the symptoms rapidly.
See also ALLERGY; CONJUNCTIVITIS; EYE; EYE PAIN; EYE RED; HAY FEVER

ALLERGIC ECZEMA
Allergic eczema is any red, scaling, itchy skin rash caused by an allergic reaction.

Many substances (allergens) have the ability to cause an allergic reaction in an individual. In most cases, the first exposure of a patient to a substance causes no reaction, but this sensitises the patient, and subsequent exposure can then cause an allergic reaction. Drugs, chemicals, metals, elements, plants, preservatives, rubber, cement, etc., may all be responsible. The reaction is worse if the patient is hot and sweaty, if the substance is caught in clothing, or is present at a point of skin flexion (eg. in the groin, under breasts, armpit). The condition is relatively uncommon in the young, and very common in the elderly. The sites of the rash correspond to the points where the allergen has touched the skin, and this may give a clue to its cause. Once a substance is suspected, it can be confirmed by patch testing, where a patch of the substance is applied to the skin, and the reaction noted.

If possible, the allergen should be avoided. Otherwise, the rash is controlled by steroid creams on weeping areas, and steroid ointments on dry and scaling areas. In severe cases, steroids may need to be given by tablet or injection. Unavoidable exposure to an allergen can cause a persistent rash that is difficult to treat.

Most patients respond well to treatment for a particular attack, but the rash may recur on subsequent exposure to the allergen.
See also ALLERGY; ATOPIC ECZEMA; DERMATITIS; ECZEMA

ALLERGIC RHINITIS
See HAY FEVER

ALLERGY
An allergy is an excessive reaction to a substance which in most people causes no reaction.

Significant allergies occur in 10% of the population. An allergy may be triggered by almost any substance including foods, pollens, dusts, plants, animals, feathers, furs, mould, drugs, natural or artificial chemicals, insect bites and gases. Some individuals are far more susceptible to a wide range of substances than others and the tendency to develop allergies may be inherited. Allergy reactions may be very localised (eg. at the site of an insect bite, or in just one eye), may occur suddenly or gradually, may last for a few minutes or a few months, may involve internal organs (eg. lungs), or be limited to the body surface (eg. skin or nose lining). When a person is exposed to a substance to which they are allergic, the body reacts by releasing excessive amounts of histamine from mast cells that are found in the lining of every body cavity and in the skin. Histamine is required at times to fight invading substances, but when released in excess, it causes tissue inflammation and an allergic reaction.

Screening blood tests can determine if a patient is suffering from an allergy. An allergy to specific substance can be detected by skin or blood tests. In the skin test, a minute amount of the suspected substance is scratched into a very small area of skin and the reaction of that skin area is then checked for a reaction a day or so later. In blood tests, specific antibodies to invading allergic substances are sought and identified.

The allergy reaction may cause a wide range of symptoms including itchy skin and eyes, diarrhoea, redness and swelling of tissues, a runny nose and skin lumps, depending on the area of the body affected.

Severe allergic reactions may kill a patient by causing the throat to swell shut, acting on the heart to cause irregular beats, or inducing a critical lung spasm. A small number of highly allergic patients must carry an emergency supply of injectable adrenaline (an adrenergic stimulant) with them at all times.

Treatment depends on where the allergy occurs, its severity, and its duration. Antihistamine drugs are the main treatment and may be given by tablet, mixture, injection, nose spray or cream, but some types may cause drowsiness. A severe attack may require steroid tablets or injections, adrenaline injections, or in very severe cases (anaphylaxis), emergency resuscitation. There are a number of medications (eg. sodium cromoglycate, steroid sprays, nedocromil sodium) that can be used on a regular basis to prevent allergic reactions.

If the substance that causes an allergy can be identified, further episodes may be prevented by desensitisation which involves giving extremely small doses of the allergy-causing substance to the patient by injection, and then slowly increasing the dose over many weeks or months until the patient can completely tolerate the substance.

Most allergies can be successfully treated and prevented, and some allergies can be cured by desensitisation.
See also ADRENERGIC STIMULANTS; ALLERGIC CONJUNCTIVITIS; ALLERGIC ECZEMA; ALLERGY TESTS; ANAPHYLAXIS; ANTIALLERGY EXTRACTS; ANTIHISTAMINES; ASTHMA; ATOPY; DERMOGRAPHISM; HAY FEVER; LATEX ALLERGY; URTICARIA

ALLERGY TESTS

The most common reason skin tests are carried out is to test for allergies (eg. a rash, hives, hay fever). The tests consist of the injection of various substances under the skin. These substances, called allergens, are found in cat fur, house dust, pollen from various plants, etc. Allergies to certain foods and drugs can also be tested. If the patient reacts to a particular injection, then the source of the allergy has been identified. The process is one of elimination, and consequently may be very slow.

Allergy testing can be especially important for people who react violently to things such as bee stings, since they may need desensitising treatment or to carry a supply of adrenaline in case of emergency.
See also ALLERGY; ANTIGEN; HIVES

ALLOPURINOL
See HYPOURICAEMICS

ALOPECIA AREATA

Alopecia areata is a common cause of patchy hair loss. There is a family history in about 20% of patients, or fungal infections and drugs used to treat cancer may be responsible, but in most cases no specific cause can be found. Stress and anxiety are not usually a cause. Alopecia areata is different to baldness in that it can occur at any age, in either sex, in any race, and is more common under twenty-five years of age.

Victims have a sudden loss of hair in a well-defined patch on the scalp or other areas of body hair (eg. pubic area, beard, eyebrows), and a bare patch two cm or more across may be present before it is noticed. The hairless area may slowly extend for several weeks before stabilising. Several spots may occur simultaneously, and may merge together as they enlarge. If the entire body is affected, the disease is called alopecia totalis, which is not a different disease, just a severe case of alopecia areata. Patients need to be careful to avoid sunburn to exposed scalp skin.

Treatment involves strong steroid creams, injections of steroids into the affected area, and irritant lotions.

In 90% of patients, regrowth of hair eventually recurs, although the new hair may be totally white and it may take many months or years. The further the bare patch is from the top of the scalp, the slower and less likely the regrowth of hair. It is rare to recover from total hair loss.
See also BALD; HAIR LOSS

ALOPECIA TOTALIS
See ALOPECIA AREATA

ALPHA-BLOCKERS

Alpha receptor blockers are drugs that block the reception of certain nerve signals to the arteries, and if these signals are not received, the artery relaxes, allowing more blood to flow through at a lower pressure. These drugs have undergone considerable refinement over the years, and most of the earlier ones that had significant side effects are no longer used. They are used to treat high blood pressure, heart failure, enlarged prostate gland and Raynaud's disease. They are available only as tablets and must be started in a very low dose, which is slowly increased over several weeks.

Examples of medications in this class (with brand names in brackets), include prazosin (Minipress) and doxazosin (Carduran). Side effects may include headache, drowsiness, nausea, palpitations and blurred vision. They must be used with care in pregnancy and liver disease.
See also ANTIHYPERTENSIVES; MEDICATION

ALPROSTADIL
Alprostadil is combined with prostaglandin e1 as an injection with the trade name Caverject. It is used for the treatment of impotence. An injection is given into the penis, about one third the way from the base, at the two o'clock or ten o'clock position. An erection usually occurs within ten minutes. Side effects may include pain and bruising at the injection site, and a prolonged erection. It should not be used in patients taking anticoagulants or with any infection in the blood or groin.
See also ERECTION; ERECTION PROLONGED AND PAINFUL; IMPOTENCE; SILDENAFIL

ALTERNATE THERAPIES
See ACUPUNCTURE; AYURVEDIC MEDICINE; CHELATION; CHINESE MEDICINE; CHIROPRACTIC; HOMEOPATHY; IRIDOLOGY; NATUROPATHY; ORTHOMOLECULAR MEDICINE; OSTEOPATHY; SHIATSU

ALTITUDE SICKNESS
Altitude (or mountain) sickness is caused by lack of oxygen from ascending rapidly to heights over 3000m. A slow ascent is less likely to cause problems than a rapid one. It is impossible to predict who will be affected, how rapidly or at what altitude.

Symptoms start with a headache, shortness of breath and excessive tiredness, followed by inability to sleep, nausea, vomiting, diarrhoea, abdominal pains and a fever. Fluid fills the lungs, patients start coughing up blood, the heart races, and they may eventually drown as blood fills the lungs. Permanent lung and other organ damage may result from a severe attack.

A rapid descent to a lower altitude is the only effective treatment for severe cases, although mild cases may recover with rest at high altitude. Fluid removing drugs (diuretics) may be used in an emergency to remove fluid from the lungs, and acetazolamide and dexamethasone may be given during the climb for prevention. Oxygen in cylinders is used by very high altitude climbers.

The condition may be life-threatening unless a lower altitude can be reached.
See also OXYGEN

ALUMINIUM HYDROXIDE
See ANTACIDS

ALZHEIMER DISEASE
Alzheimer disease (or senile dementia) used to be called second childhood, or the person was described as eccentric. Today it is recognised as the most common form of dementia in the elderly, but it may start as early as the mid-fifties.

It is named after the Wroclaw (Poland) neurologist Alois Alzheimer, who was born in 1864, and first described the disease in the medical literature.

The cause is a faster than normal loss of nerve cells in the brain, the exact cause of which is unknown, but studies suggest specific genes may predispose a person to the disease, and there is a familial tendency (runs in families from one generation to the next).

Initially it causes loss of recent memory, loss of initiative, reduced physical activity, confusion and loss of orientation (confused about place and time), then progresses to loss of speech, difficulty in swallowing which causes drooling, stiff muscles, incontinence of both faeces and urine, a bedridden state and eventually the patient is totally unaware of themselves or anything that is happening around them. Some patients may not deteriorate for some time, then drop to a lower level of activity quite suddenly. Admission to a nursing home or hospital is eventually necessary.

Reduced brain volume and wasting may show on a CT scan, but the diagnosis is primarily a clinical one made by a doctor after excluding all other forms of dementia by blood tests, x-rays, electroencephalogram (EEG) and sometimes taking a sample of the spinal fluid. The progress of the disease can be followed by tests of skill, general knowledge, simple maths, etc.

Medication is useful for restlessness and

insomnia, and a number of medications are now being used to slow the progression of the disease. In women, hormone replacement therapy after menopause reduces the incidence of Alzheimer disease, and slows its progress. Visits by the family general practitioner, physiotherapists, occupational therapists, home nursing care and health visitors are the main forms of management. Many claims have been made for various herbal remedies, but none have proved to be beneficial.

There is no cure, and treatments are aimed at keeping the patient content. From diagnosis to eventual death takes seven years on average.
See also BRAIN; DEMENTIA; MEMORY; MEMORY DISTURBED

AMAUROSIS FUGAX
Amaurosis fugax is a sudden, painless, temporary loss of vision due to a disruption to the blood supply to the optic nerve or brain. It may be associated with narrowing of the carotid artery in the neck, or a tiny blood clot in the arteries supplying the retina at the back of the eye.
See also BLINDNESS

AMBLYOPIA
Amblyopia is a decrease in vision in one or both eyes. There are numerous causes including squint, cataracts, severe short sight (myopia) or a lack of good nutrition, particularly vitamin B (often occurs in alcoholics and is aggravated by tobacco smoking). All causes result in degeneration of the light sensitive area (retina) at the back of the eye so patients experience dimness and blurring of vision and reduced colour differentiation. Permanent damage to optic nerve and blindness can occur with some causes.

Specific tests on visual function, and examination of the retina with an ophthalmoscope (magnifying light) will confirm the cause and diagnosis.

The cause must be treated by using spectacles, covering the better eye to stimulate the poorer one, eye muscle surgery or vitamin B supplements, good diet and not smoking. It will be steadily progressive to virtual blindness in affected eye(s) unless adequately treated.
See also EYE; VISION BLURRED

AMENORRHOEA
See MENSTRUAL PERIODS, FAILURE TO START; MENSTRUAL PERIODS, LACK OF

AMERICAN TRYPANOSOMIASIS
See CHAGAS' DISEASE

AMILORIDE
See DIURETICS

AMINO ACID
An organic substance that forms the building blocks for all proteins. About twenty different amino acids may come together in various combinations to form every protein in humans. On the other hand, all proteins eaten by humans are broken down into amino acids before being absorbed.

All amino acids contain NH2 connected to carbon, hydrogen and oxygen molecules in the following form of structure.
See also PROTEIN

AMINO ACID

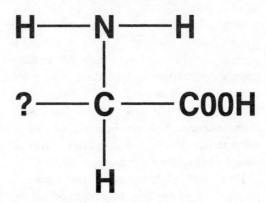

AMINOGLYCOSIDES
Aminoglycosides are a group of less commonly used antibiotics that can destroy certain types of bacteria causing infections in the urinary tract, skin, eye, ear, bone, lung and bloodstream. They are available as injections, tablets, powders and creams. They are most commonly used as creams and powders on the skin, or as injections for very severe infections. They can interact with cephalosporin antibiotics.

Examples include framycetin (Soframycin), gentamicin (Garamycin) and neomycin. Side effects may include a rash, nausea and headache.
See also ANTIBIOTICS; MEDICATION

AMINOPHYLLINE
See THEOPHYLLINES

AMIODARONE
See ANTIARRHYTHMICS

AMITRIPTYLINE
See ANTIDEPRESSANTS

AMLODIPINE
See CALCIUM CHANNEL BLOCKERS

AMMONIUM CHLORIDE
See EXPECTORANTS

AMNESIA
See MEMORY LOSS

AMNIOCENTESIS
In the uterus, a foetus is surrounded by amniotic fluid, which in turn is contained within the amniotic sac. Amniotic fluid is swallowed by the foetus, and urine and faeces produced by the foetus passes out into the amniotic fluid, so it contains cells of the baby's skin and other organs.

In amniocentesis a small amount of the amniotic fluid is drawn off, and the cells it contains are cultured and analysed under a microscope to give information about the health of the foetus. It will also disclose the baby's sex. The cells contain the baby's chromosomes which can be analysed to give information about many different genetic disorders (eg. Down syndrome).

There is a slightly increased risk of miscarriage (about one in 250) as a result of amniocentesis, and it will not usually be carried out unless there is some suspected problem with the foetus. Amniocentesis is not performed before fourteen weeks of pregnancy because until then there is not enough amniotic fluid present.

Amniocentesis may be performed when: –
• The mother is over forty years of age, especially if it is her first child, as there is an increased risk of the child having Down syndrome.
• One parent has a known chromosomal abnormality (eg. haemophilia).
• Diseases are known to run in either parent's family (eg. muscular dystrophy).
• The mother has had three or more miscarriages.

• There has been an earlier abnormal child.
• Initial pregnancy screening tests suggest a high risk of the foetus being abnormal.
• A close family member has an abnormal child.
• Rh incompatibility when the mother's blood differs from that of the baby.

Before the procedure, an ultrasound scan is performed so that the position of the foetus and placenta can be checked. The woman is then given a local anaesthetic in the abdomen, and a hollow needle is inserted through the belly wall into the uterus and about 15ml. of fluid is removed.

Before the test is undertaken the woman and her partner need to think about what they will do if the results prove that the foetus has an abnormality. If pregnancy termination is not an option under any circumstances, the test is pointless.
See also CHORIONIC VILLUS SAMPLING; PREGNANCY and separate entries for diseases mentioned above.

AMNIOTIC FLUID
Amniotic fluid is the liquid surrounding a foetus in the uterus of a pregnant woman. A sample may be obtained in a process called amniocentesis by putting a needle through the skin of the lower abdomen into the uterus and drawing off a small amount of amniotic fluid.

The amniotic fluid is created by the urine and faeces of the foetus, and by secretions from the placenta. The foetus is constantly swallowing and processing the fluid from about fifteen weeks onwards, and it aids the growth and nutrition of the foetus.

It is normally a pale yellow colour, but may be darker if the foetus is distressed. The dark colouration may only be noticed at the beginning of labour when the waters break with the rupture of the amniotic sac in which the fluid and foetus are contained.

The volume of amniotic fluid steadily increases throughout pregnancy until about thirty six weeks, after which it slowly decreases. At its peak, between 600 and 800 mls of fluid are present.

The amniotic fluid acts as a cushion for the foetus, protecting it from external bumps, jarring and shocks. It also allows the foetus to move relatively freely, and allows equal growth in all directions. It contains protein, sugars,

fats and electrolytes (sodium, potassium, salt etc.). Hormones and waste produced by the foetus are also present as these are excreted in the urine of the foetus.
See also AMNIOCENTESIS; OLIGOHYDRAMNIOS; PLACENTA; POLYHYDRAMNIOS

AMOEBA
A very primitive form of single-celled animal (protozoa) that has an undefined shape, and moves by changing its shape. It is controlled by a single nucleus and it ingests food particles into an inclusion vacuole by surrounding them with shape changes. It reproduces by effectively splitting in two. May cause diseases in man such as amoebic dysentery (amoebiasis).
See also AMOEBIASIS; PROTOZOA

AMOEBIASIS
Amoebiasis (amoebic dysentery) is an infestation of the gut with single-celled animals (amoebae) that is relatively common in many third-world countries. The swallowed amoebae usually infest the gut and liver, and very rarely the brain and lung. Amoebae are passed out with the faeces, and if this contaminates food or water, they can be picked up by others. Some people have very mild infections and act as carriers, steadily infecting more and more people.

The symptoms include abdominal pain, diarrhoea, mucus and blood in the faeces, fever, and in severe cases the bowel may rupture, leading to peritonitis and death. If the amoebae enter the liver from the gut, an abscess can form in the liver and cause severe pain.

It is diagnosed by finding the amoebae in the faeces when examined under a microscope, or by special blood tests that detect antibody changes caused by amoebae.

Spread of the infestation is controlled by strict attention to personal hygiene, cooking food and boiling water. It is treated with one or more of a number of drugs to kill the amoebae, but they all have significant side effects and may need to be used for several weeks. An abscess needs to be drained surgically. If left untreated, severely affected patients will die, but modern treatment methods lead to the total recovery of the majority.

See also ABSCESS; AMOEBA; DIARRHOEA

AMOEBIC DYSENTERY
See AMOEBIASIS

AMOROLFINE
See ANTIFUNGALS

AMOXYCILLIN
See PENICILLINS

AMPHETAMINE ABUSE
Amphetamines are synthetic stimulants that in some situations are used medically (eg. methylphenidate is used for the treatment of attention deficit disorder), but are also available illicitly as tablets ('speed'), or as a faster acting powder that is smoked ('ice'). Possibly one in every hundred people is dependent upon illicit drugs, and a far higher percentage have experimented with them at one time or another.

When used inappropriately, amphetamines cause increased activity, euphoria and a feeling of increased mental and physical ability. Tolerance develops quickly, and with time, higher and higher doses must be used to cause the same effect. Blood and urine tests can detect the presence of amphetamines.

The treatment options available are: –
• gradual withdrawal while receiving counselling and medical support
• immediate drug withdrawal ('cold turkey') while hospitalised
• half-way houses that remove the patient from the environment in which drug taking is encouraged.
• individual or group psychotherapy

Adverse effects include a rapid heart rate, sweating, dry eyes, increased blood pressure that may cause heart problems, confusion and disorientation. Long term use may cause delusions, paranoia, hallucinations, and serious psychiatric disturbances. Withdrawal results in severe depression and drowsiness.

Amphetamines are not as addictive as heroin, but more so than marijuana.
See also HEROIN; MARIJUANA; STIMULANTS

AMPHETAMINES
See AMPHETAMINE ABUSE; STIMULANTS

AMPHOTERICIN
See ANTIFUNGALS

AMPULLA OF VATER
See ENDOSCOPIC RETROGRADE
CHOLECYSTOPANCREATOGRAPHY;
PANCREAS

AMSTERDAM DWARF
See de LANGE SYNDROME

AMYLOIDOSIS
Amyloidosis is a rare disease in which millions of microscopic fibres made of a dense amyloid protein infiltrate and replace the normal tissue of different parts of the body. The kidneys, lungs, heart and intestine are commonly involved. The disease may be triggered by another disease, such as tuberculosis, rheumatoid arthritis, cancer or drug abuse, but in many cases no apparent cause can be found. The symptoms are extremely variable, depending on which organs are involved. Microscopic examination of a sample taken from an involved organ reveals a dense jelly formed by the protein fibres, rather than normal tissue.

No treatment is available, and on average, death occurs within three years of diagnosis from pneumonia, kidney infections or heart failure.

AMYOTROPHIC LATERAL SCLEROSIS
Amyotrophic lateral sclerosis is a rare form of motor neurone disease that affects the nerves that supply the muscles of the body. It is sometimes known as Lou Gehrig disease after a 1930s American baseballer who developed the condition.

The absolute cause unknown, but it may run in families, and results in a steadily progressive degeneration of the motor nerves in the body. Symptoms may include muscle weakness that usually starts in the hands or feet, muscle cramps and twitches, difficulty in swallowing and talking, drooling of saliva, inability to cough effectively, reduced tongue movement, and progressive weakness up the arms and legs. Eventually the muscles used for breathing are involved and lung infections such as pneumonia develop, and often lead to death within a few years of diagnosis.

Electrical tests of the motor nerves are used to determine how well they are functioning, and a nerve biopsy is diagnostic.

No cure is available, and treatment is aimed at relieving muscle spasm, assisting feeding, preventing infections, aiding breathing and making the patient as comfortable as possible. Physiotherapy on a very regular basis is essential.
See also MOTOR NEURONE DISEASE; MUSCLE WEAKNESS

ANABOLIC STEROIDS
Anabolic steroids are drugs that build up body tissue. They are used illegally by athletes and body builders to increase muscle mass, and are available as tablets and injections. There are many serious side effects and problems associated with their long-term use, including liver disease and damage, the development of male characteristics and cessation of periods in women, stunting of growth and early onset of puberty in children, swelling of tissue, water retention, infertility, personality disorders and voice changes. Other side effects may include excessive hairiness, and acne. In medicine they are used to treat short stature in boys, osteoporosis in women, aplastic anaemia, blood diseases and some types of cancer.

Examples of these medications include ethenolone (Primobolan) and nandrolone (Deca-Durabolin)
See also STEROIDS

ANAEMIA
Anaemia is a term indicating a low level of haemoglobin in the blood. Haemoglobin is a complex compound that is found in red blood cells, gives these cells their colour, and is used to transport oxygen in the blood from the lungs to the organs. A major component of the haemoglobin molecule is iron.

There are many different types of anaemia, which vary widely in their cause and severity. Symptoms include tiredness and weakness due to insufficient oxygen reaching the organs, pins and needles in the arms and legs, palpitations, abnormally curved fingernails, dizziness and shortness of breath. Skin and eye colour are poor guides to the severity of anaemia.

The level of haemoglobin in blood can be tested by a pathology laboratory. Further blood tests determine the type of anaemia present.

Treatment depends on the type of anaemia and its cause, but a blood transfusion may be necessary in severe cases.

See also APLASTIC ANAEMIA; BLOOD; FULL BLOOD COUNT; HAEMOGLOBIN; HAEMOLYTIC ANAEMIA; IRON; IRON DEFICIENCY ANAEMIA; PERNICIOUS ANAEMIA; RED BLOOD CELLS; SICKLE CELL ANAEMIA; SPHEROCYTOSIS; THALASSAEMIA BETA MAJOR

ANAEROBIC INFECTION

An infection anywhere in the body by bacteria that do not require oxygen (anaerobes). These bacteria include *Prevotella* in the lungs and throat, *Bacteroides* and *Clostridia* in the bowel and belly, and numerous types in the brain and female vagina and uterus.

The symptoms depend on the organ or tissue infected. Often multiple organs are involved, any pus produced is foul smelling, and numerous small abscesses form in infected organs. A culture of pus, fluid or tissue from an infected organ identifies responsible bacteria. Appropriate antibiotics can then be prescribed and surgical drainage of abscesses performed. There is usually a good response to appropriate antibiotics.

See also BACTERIA; INFECTION

ANAESTHESIA

Anaesthesia is a loss of pain sensation in one area of the body, or throughout the body.

See also ANAESTHETICS; EPIDURAL ANAESTHETIC; GENERAL ANAESTHETIC; LOCAL ANAESTHETIC; PAIN LOSS; SPINAL ANAESTHETIC

ANAESTHETIC

See ANAESTHETICS; EPIDURAL ANAESTHETIC; GENERAL ANAESTHETIC; LOCAL ANAESTHETIC; SPINAL ANAESTHETIC; SURGERY

ANAESTHETICS

Anaesthetics are drugs that cause the loss of sensation and pain. There are two main types, local and general.

Local anaesthetics are injections, creams, sprays, drops or gels that remove sensation at one point in the body. Examples include lignocaine (Xylocaine), prilocaine (Citanest), and bupivocaine (Marcaine). They may be combined with adrenaline to restrict blood flow to an area and prolong the anaesthetic effect, or included with drops and creams to ease pain in everything from ears to piles. Side effects are rare with local anaesthetics. Adrenaline-containing local anaesthetics should not be used in fingers, toes, ear lobes or penis.

More than twenty different general anaesthetics are used by doctors in hospital operating theatres. They may be inhaled (eg. halothane, nitrous oxide – laughing gas) or injected (eg. thiopentone).

See also KETAMINE and other forms of anaesthesia listed under ANAESTHETIC

ANAL BLEEDING

Bleeding from the anus at times when the patient is not passing a motion may be associated with piles or a fissure. Blood present on or in the faeces is covered under the "Faeces blood" entry.

With a pile (haemorrhoid), the bleeding tends to occur after passing a motion, and blood is present on the toilet paper, but it may occur at any time, particularly if straining with heavy lifting. Piles can be painless, or very painful, depending on the degree of inflammation and the presence of a blood clot within the pile.

A fissure in the anus, where the anus has overstretched and torn during an episode of constipation, can also cause intermittent bleeding similar to that of a pile. Keeping the motions soft and using a medicated ointment usually settles the problem.

See also ANAL FISSURE; ANUS; PILES; FAECES BLOOD

ANAL FISSURE

An anal fissure (fissure in ano) is a split in the anus. It develops when the anus has overstretched and torn during an episode of constipation.

Symptoms include intermittent pain and bleeding similar to that of a pile. Treatment involves keeping the motions soft and using a medicated ointment on the anus. Rarely, scarring and narrowing of the anus may occur. Generally the prognosis is good if constipation is controlled.

See also ANAL BLEEDING; ANUS; PILES

ANAL FISTULA

An anal fistula (fistula in ano) is a serious problem caused by a significant infection around the anus.

It starts when an abscess, bacterial infection or cancer damages the tissue between the rectum and skin, allowing a false tube (fistula) to form between the rectum inside the anus, and the skin beside the anus. Liquid faeces leaks through the fistula onto the skin which becomes inflamed and painful. A special dye may be injected into the drainage point of the fistula and then x-rayed to see where it runs. Rarely a fistula may develop between the last part of the rectum and the vagina or bladder.

Quite difficult surgery is necessary to close the fistula. The progress after surgery may be difficult, but most patients recover completely. *See also* ANUS; FISTULA; RECTUM

ANALGESIC NEPHROPATHY

Analgesic nephropathy is also known as papillary necrosis, and was a common kidney problem from the 1950s to 1970s due to regular and inappropriate use of the easily available analgesic (painkiller) phenacetin which was often combined with paracetamol and aspirin in excessive doses. It is uncommon now due to restrictions on this medication.

A microscopic part of the kidney structure (papilla) is damaged, dies (necrosis) and sloughs off to be passed in the urine.

Patients experience blood in the urine, kidney pain and stones, swelling of hands and feet, high blood pressure and eventually kidney failure, and the biochemical abnormalities in the blood may lead to a heart attack and stroke. Blood tests show kidney failure, and a microscopic examination of the urine shows damaged cells, while an ultrasound tests on the kidneys may also be abnormal.

Stopping phenacetin may prevent progression of the disease, but kidney damage is permanent and a kidney transplant or dialysis may be necessary. *See also* KIDNEY FAILURE, CHRONIC

ANALGESICS

Analgesics are drugs that reduce the sensation of pain. There are three main types – narcotics, salicylates (NSAIDs – nonsteroidal anti-inflammatory drugs) and paracetamol. Many analgesic preparations are combinations of two or more different medications.

Aspirin is classified as a salicylate. It may be used for the prevention of blood clots as well as pain and fever. Side effects may include heartburn, nausea and belly pain. It should be avoided in pregnancy, children (Reye syndrome may occur) and bleeding disorders.

Paracetamol (acetaminophen in North America) can be used to reduce fever as well as pain, and occurs in combination with many other types of drugs for the relief of cold symptoms and muscle spasm. Paracetamol is available in tablet or syrup forms, side effects are rare, and it can be used in the long term without problems, but overdosage has severe consequences, particularly in children. It is safe to use in pregnancy, but must be used with caution in liver and kidney disease. *See also* NARCOTICS; NSAID; REYE SYNDROME

ANAL INCONTINENCE
See INCONTINENCE OF FAECES

ANAL INFLAMMATION
See PROCTITIS

ANAL ITCH

An itchy anus is a relatively common problem, and most people will experience it at some time due to sweating, friction, uncomfortable underwear, irritating soaps or after episodes of diarrhoea.

Pruritus ani is a common condition that results in a persistently itchy anus caused by the patient themselves. For one of the reasons above or below, the anus becomes itchy. The patient then scratches the anus (sometimes while asleep) to irritate the delicate skin around the anus. The damaged skin then becomes itchier, leading to more scratching and then more itching – a vicious cycle. This can only be treated by never scratching the anus, not using soap on the area, never scratching, soothing creams, never scratching, loose underwear, never scratching, washing the area with plain water if sweaty, never scratching, dabbing rather than wiping with toilet paper after passing a motion, never scratching, using mild steroid creams in severe cases and never scratching (get the idea?).

Piles (haemorrhoids) and an anal fissure may also cause an anal itch.

Numerous infections of the bowel, anus and adjacent skin may cause an anal itch.

Examples include thrush (a fungal infection), worms (many different types, but thread worms most common in developed countries), molluscum contagiosum (virus that causes tiny blisters), gonorrhoea and syphilis (bacterial infection transmitted by anal sex) and condylomata accuminata (sexually transmitted warts).

Any condition of the bowel that causes diarrhoea may also cause anal itching. Examples include gastroenteritis (a viral infection), Crohn's disease (inflammation and thickening of a section of intestine) and diverticulitis (inflammation of small outpocketings in the large intestine).

Skin diseases that cause itching anywhere on the body may also occur around the anus. Various types of dermatitis, eczema and psoriasis (associated with red scaly plaques) are examples.

Other possible causes of an itchy anus include intertrigo, polyps or skin tags around the anus, poorly controlled or undiagnosed diabetes, and poor personal hygiene.
See also ANAL PAIN; ANUS; DIARRHOEA; SKIN ITCH and separate entries for diseases mentioned above.

ANAL PAIN

Pain in and around the anus may be embarrassing and cause problems with bowel movements, as well as being uncomfortable.

The most common cause is a pile that has a blood clot in it. Piles (haemorrhoids) are over-dilated veins around the anus, and are not harmful in themselves, but may cause discomfort and annoyance with repeated bleeding as well as pain.

A fissure occurs in the anus when the anus is overstretched and torn during an episode of constipation. This can cause both pain and intermittent bleeding similar to that of a pile.

If the tissue around or in the anus becomes infected through a sore or scratch, an abscess may form. A painful, tender lump will be felt, and passing a motion will be very uncomfortable. An anal fistula is a serious problem caused by an abscess or other infection forming a false tube from the rectum inside the anus, to the skin beside the anus. Liquid faeces may leak through this tube constantly, and it will be inflamed and painful.

Proctalgia fugax is a severe, brief, very sharp pain that is felt in the anus for a few seconds or minutes several times a day. Patients describe the sensation as having a thin knife pushed into the anal canal and twisted. It is caused by a spasm of the muscle that controls the opening and closing of the anus (the sphincter).

Lymphogranuloma venereum is a disease that may be transmitted by vaginal or anal sex to cause growths that become uncomfortable.

Some parasitic infestations of the bowel by worms and other organisms may result in anal pain, as well as diarrhoea, belly discomfort and poor food absorption.

Obviously, any injury to the anus may cause pain. Falling astride a bar or inserting objects into the anus are the most common causes of injury. Polyps beside the anus that become twisted or caught in clothing will also be painful.
See also ANAL FISSURE; ANAL ITCH; ANUS and separate entries for diseases mentioned above.

ANAL PROLAPSE
See RECTAL PROLAPSE

ANAPHYLACTOID PURPURA
See HENOCH-SCHOENLEIN SYNDROME

ANAPHYLAXIS

Anaphylactic shock is an immediate, severe, life-threatening reaction to an allergy-causing substance. Insect stings (eg. bees, hornets, wasps, ants) and injected drugs are the most likely causes. It is rare for inhaled, touched or eaten substances to cause this reaction.

The patient rapidly becomes sweaty, develops widespread pins and needles, may develop a generalised flush or red rash, or swelling in one or more parts of the body (possibly including the tongue, throat and eyelids), starts wheezing, becomes blue around the lips, may become incontinent of urine, loses consciousness, convulses and stops breathing. Swelling of the tongue and throat may cause death by suffocation if air is unable to pass into the lungs.

For first aid the patient is placed on their back with the neck extended to give the best possible airway and mouth-to-mouth resuscitation and external cardiac massage are performed if necessary. The patient must be taken to a hospital as quickly as possible.

Emergency medical assistance is necessary, as injection of a drug such as adrenaline (an adrenergic stimulant), hydrocortisone, aminophylline and an antihistamine (this is the preferred order) can reverse the reaction and save the patient's life. Patients who are aware that they may have an anaphylactic reaction often carry an adrenaline injection with them at all times to be used in an emergency.

Blood and skin tests to identify the responsible substance can be very carefully performed at a later time.

Patients usually respond well to appropriate treatment, but death may occur within minutes if medical help is not immediately available.
See ADRENERGIC STIMULANTS; ALLERGY; FIRST AID; RESUSCITATION; SHOCK

ANAPLASTIC CARCINOMA OF THE THYROID
See THYROID CANCER

ANCYCLOSTOMIASIS
See HOOKWORM

ANDERSEN SYNDROME
See GLYCOGEN STORAGE DISEASES

ANDROCUR
See SEX HORMONES

ANDROGENS
See SEX HORMONES

ANDROPAUSE
The male menopause (andropause) is a natural event that occurs in all men. After the andropause no male hormones are manufactured in the testes, the testes no longer produce sperm, and the man is infertile.

The male sex hormone (testosterone) is released from the testes into the blood in response to signals from the pituitary gland, which sits underneath the centre of the brain. These hormones affect every part of the body, but more particularly the penis, scrotum and body hair production. For an unknown reason, once a man reaches an age somewhere between the late sixties and late seventies, the pituitary gland stops sending messages to the testes, which results in the symptoms of the andropause.

The man experiences the gradual onset of a loss of interest in sex (low libido), difficulty in maintaining or achieving an erection of the penis, a lack of ejaculation during sex, thinning of body and pubic hair, and shrinking of the testicles. Osteoporosis may occur, particularly if there is a family history, or the andropause occurs at an early age. These symptoms are far subtler, and far less distressing than those that occur in the female menopause.

Blood tests can determine the levels of testosterone and the stimulating hormone released by the pituitary gland.

No treatment is normally necessary as it is a normal part of the ageing process, but if the andropause occurs earlier than normal, or following an injury or surgery to the testes or pituitary gland, testosterone supplements may be given by tablet, injection or implant.
See also MENOPAUSE; PITUITARY GLAND; SEX HORMONES; TESTICLE

ANENCEPHALY
Anencephaly is a congenital failure of the brain to develop. The infant has no forehead and minimal skull development behind the face. The condition is incompatible with life, and the infant usually dies within hours of birth.

ANEURYSM
An aneurysm is the ballooning out of one part of an artery (or the heart), at a point where the artery becomes weakened. There may be a slight bump on the side of an artery, a quite large bubble, or a long sausage-shaped extension along an artery. Any artery may be affected, but the most serious ones involve the aorta (the main artery down the back of the chest and abdomen – aortic aneurysm) and arteries in the brain (cerebral aneurysm). Different types are categorised by their shape. The most common are saccular or berry aneurysms, which are direct balloonings on the side of an artery. The most sinister are the dissecting aneurysms, where only part of the artery wall is damaged (often by cholesterol plaques – arteriosclerosis) and the blood penetrates in between the layers of the artery wall, slowly splitting them apart, and extending along the artery.

The weakness in arteries may be caused by plaques of cholesterol, high blood pressure, injury to the artery or a congenital (present

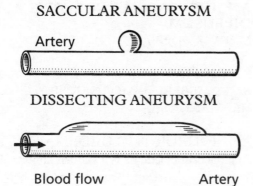

SACCULAR ANEURYSM

Artery

DISSECTING ANEURYSM

Blood flow   Artery

since birth) weakness in the wall of an artery. The heart wall may be damaged by a heart attack, and the weakened area can bulge out as an aneurysm. There is a slight hereditary tendency.

Usually there are no symptoms unless the aneurysm is very large or presses on a nerve, but the aneurysm may burst, leading to a massive loss of blood or damage to surrounding organs (eg. brain), or they may extend to the point where they put pressure on other arteries, and cut off the blood supply to vital organs (eg. kidney).

The condition is diagnosed by ultrasound, or on x-ray after special dye has been injected into the artery. Very large aneurysms may be seen on a plain x-ray. CT scans and magnetic resonance imaging (MRI) may also detect an aneurysm.

The rupture of an aneurysm on a major artery can lead to death within seconds, or a slow leak may allow surgeons enough time to undertake a major operation to repair or replace the leaking artery. If an aneurysm is found incidentally, it may be operated upon to prevent it bursting, or left alone and regularly checked for any increase in size. In the brain, a small aneurysm may be clipped with a tiny U-shaped piece of silver to prevent it from leaking.

It is vital for anyone with an aneurysm to control their blood pressure and avoid aggravating factors such as smoking and strenuous exercise.

The prognosis is extremely variable, depending on the site and severity of any rupture, but there is a significant overall mortality rate.
See also AORTA; AORTIC ANEURYSM; ARTERIOSCLEROSIS; ARTERY; NEUROSURGERY

ANGINA

Angina pectoris is pain caused by an inadequate blood supply (ischaemia) to part of the heart muscle due to a narrowing of one or more of the three small arteries that supply blood to the heart muscle. This narrowing may be due to hardening of the arteries, or a spasm of the artery caused by another disease, smoking, excitement, heavy meals or stress. Angina may lead to a heart attack, or a heart attack may cause angina, but they are two different problems. In a heart attack, part of the heart muscle dies.

The classical symptoms are a pressure-like, squeezing pain or tightness in the chest, usually central, that starts suddenly, often during exercise, and settles with rest, but may occur at almost any time and may extend into the left arm, neck, upper abdomen and back. It is uncommon during sleep. About 5% of all patients with angina will have a heart attack each year, and half of these will die from that heart attack. Heart failure can gradually affect those remaining, reducing their mobility and eventually leading to premature death. High blood pressure, diabetes and an irregular heart beat are unfavourable findings and will also lead to an early death.

Diagnosis may be difficult, as the pain has usually subsided when the patient sees a doctor, and all blood tests and electrocardiograms (ECG) may be normal. Sometimes a stress ECG must be performed under strict medical supervision to recreate the pain and observe the abnormal ECG pattern. Coronary angiography is a type of x-ray that can detect narrowed arteries around the heart. A more sophisticated test involves injecting radioisotopes into the bloodstream, and measuring their uptake by the heart muscle.

Prevention involves tablets or skin patches (eg. nitrates, beta-blockers or calcium channel blockers) that are used regularly to keep the arteries as widely dilated as possible. Smokers must stop smoking.

Treatment of an acute attack involves immediately resting, and spraying glyceryl trinitrate under the tongue, or placing a tablet containing nitroglycerine, nifedipine or a similar drug under the tongue to dilate the heart arteries and relieve the attack.

If a narrowed artery can be found it can be bypassed by a coronary artery bypass graft (CABG) operation. Balloon angioplasty is a technique that involves passing a tiny deflated balloon through the arteries in the leg or arm, into the heart, and then into the small narrowed arteries around the heart, then inflating it to enlarge the narrowed artery. Sometimes a stent (tube shaped metal grid) is left behind to ensure that the artery does not close down again.

Most people with angina can have their symptoms prevented and relieved by medication, and many patients with narrowed arteries can be successfully treated by surgery.
See also ANTIANGINALS; BALLOON ANGIOPLASTY; BETA-BLOCKERS; CALCIUM CHANNEL BLOCKERS; CHEST PAIN; CORONARY ARTERY BYPASS GRAFT; HEART; HEART ATTACK; INTERMEDIATE CORONARY SYNDROME

ANGININE
See ANTIANGINALS

ANGIOEDEMA
See URTICARIA

ANGIOGRAM
An angiogram is a contrast x-ray of a blood vessel. A dye that can be seen on an x-ray is injected into the vessel being investigated and a picture taken of the area where the problem is suspected. The patient is sedated but conscious during the procedure. An angiogram of an artery is called an arteriogram, and a venogram is an angiogram of a vein. Angiograms are usually used to detect blockages, such as a clot, or the narrowing of the wall of a blood vessel, such as occurs in arteriosclerosis.

If the patient has had a heart attack, if heart disease is suspected, or if they are to undergo a heart bypass operation, a coronary angiogram may be performed to see how much blood is getting through to the heart. This involves a catheter (thin tube) being inserted into an artery in the groin or arm and guided towards the heart where the dye is injected, and x-rays are then taken of the heart and coronary arteries which supply the heart. Sometimes a general anaesthetic is given, but normally it is performed under sedation.
See also ARTERIOSCLEROSIS; STRESS TEST; X-RAY

ANGIOKERATOMA CORPORIS DIFFUSUM
See FABRY DISEASE

ANGIOMA
See CAMPBELL de MORGAN SPOTS; HAEMANGIOMA

ANGIONEUROTIC OEDEMA
Angioneurotic oedema is a sudden abnormal swelling (oedema) of tissue around the body openings in the face (eye, nose or mouth). The face may be slightly itchy, but is not usually painful or tender. Rarely the swelling may be very severe and affect breathing. It is caused by an allergic reaction, usually to a pollen, dust, chemical or other substance that has blown into the eye or nose, food that has touched the lips, or from rubbing the face with a contaminated finger.

Antihistamine tablets or injections are given as treatment, but severe cases may need steroids.
See also ALLERGY; ANAPHYLAXIS; EYELID SWOLLEN

ANGIOPLASTY
See BALLOON ANGIOPLASTY

ANGIOSARCOMA
An angiosarcoma is a form of cancer involving arteries and veins, that often occurs in the liver or on the skin of the face and scalp, forming a red-purple tumour on the skin or in internal organs. The symptoms vary with the tumour location, and tumours may extend very deeply into the tissue of the face. Extensive surgical resection of tumour and surrounding tissue is the only treatment, and the prognosis is very variable depending on the stage of tumour development.
See also CANCER; SARCOMA; STEWART-TREVES SYNDROME

ANGIOSTRONGYLIASIS
Angiostrongyliasis (eosinophilic meningo-encephalitis) is an infestation of the brain and surrounding membranes (meninges) by the nematode worm *Angiostrongylus cantonensis*. It occurs on Pacific islands, in west Africa, south Asia and in the Caribbean.

The worms normally live in the gut of rats. Their eggs pass out with rat faeces, are eaten by snails, prawns or fish, and then pass to humans if these foods are eaten when poorly cooked. They may directly enter humans if foods contaminated by rat faeces (eg. salads) are eaten. The swallowed eggs hatch into larvae which migrate through the bloodstream to the brain and meninges. The incubation period is one to three weeks.

Patients develop a severe headache, fever, neck stiffness, nausea, vomiting and abnormal nerve sensations. The worms may spread into the eye and cause blindness. CT and MRI scans may show the presence of worms in the brain.

No specific treatment is available. Symptoms persist for several months until the worm dies, and then most patients recover completely. Rarely there may be permanent brain damage and death.
See also BRAIN; NEMATODE

ANGIOTENSIN CONVERTING ENZYME INHIBITORS
See ACE INHIBITORS

ANGIOTENSIN II RECEPTOR ANTAGONISTS
A new class of medications introduced in 1998 for the treatment of high blood pressure and other heart diseases was the angiotensin II receptor antagonists. Like ACE Inhibitors, they prevent the contraction of the tiny muscles that circle around small arteries by blocking the action of the chemical that is essential for the contraction of these tiny artery muscles, but with fewer side effects. They are available only as tablets but may be combined in the one tablet with a thiazide diuretic (hydrochlorothiazide).

Examples of medications in this class (with trade names in brackets) include candersartan (Atacand), irbesartan (Avapro, Karvea), and telmisartan (Micardis, Pritor).

Side effects may include sleep disturbances and depression. They should not be used in pregnancy, but low blood pressure is the only likely effect in overdose.
See also ACE INHIBITORS; DIURETICS; HYPERTENSION; MEDICATION

ANHIDROSIS
See SWEATING LACK

ANIMAL BITE
Bites by any animal, be they dog, cat, horse, human or even a lizard, are extremely likely to be followed by infection, and it is important to take steps to prevent this. First-aid measures consist of thoroughly washing the wound with soap, followed by antiseptic solution or cream, and then covering it with a clean dressing. Check for signs of infection for the first twenty-four to forty-eight hours. Most animal bites should be treated with antibiotics, and if there has been any significant breakage of the skin, a doctor should be consulted.

In areas of the world where rabies is endemic, it will be necessary to have a rabies vaccine if there is any suspicion that the animal may be rabid.
See also RABIES

ANKLE
The ankle joint is formed by the lower ends of the tibia (on the inside) and fibula, while the lower surface is the talus bone of the foot. Protrusions of the tibia and fibula form the lumps of bone on either side of the ankle (called the medial and lateral malleolus) and add stability to the joint. Thick strong ligaments run from the malleoli to the talus and calcaneus (the heel bone) to hold the joint together.
See also ANTERIOR IMPINGEMENT SYNDROME; CALCANEUS; FIBULA; FOOT; JOINT; TIBIA; TARSAL TUNNEL SYNDROME

ANKLE AND FOOT FROM FRONT

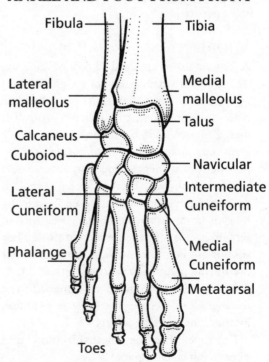

Fibula — Tibia

Lateral malleolus — Medial malleolus

Talus

Calcaneus

Cuboiod — Navicular

Lateral Cuneiform — Intermediate Cuneiform

Phalange — Medial Cuneiform

Metatarsal

Toes

ANKLE FRACTURE
See POTT'S FRACTURE

ANKYLOSING SPONDYLITIS
Ankylosing spondylitis (AS) is a long-term inflammation of the small joints between the vertebrae in the back. More common in men, it usually starts in the late twenties or early thirties, but progresses very slowly. The cause is unknown.

Symptoms start gradually with a constant backache that may radiate down the legs. Stiffness of the back becomes steadily worse, and eventually the patient may be bent almost double by a solidly fused backbone in old age (kyphosis). AS may be associated with a number of apparently unrelated conditions, including arthritis of other joints, heart valve disease, weakening of the aorta and inflammation of the eyes (uveitis). It is diagnosed by x-rays of the back, and specific blood tests.

Anti-inflammatory drugs such as indomethacin, naproxen, aspirin and (in resistant cases) phenylbutazone are prescribed. Regular physiotherapy can help relieve the pain and stiffness even in advanced cases.

AS may settle spontaneously for a few months or years, before progressing further. No cure is available, but treatment can give most patients a full life of normal length.
See also BACK; KYPHOSIS; SPINE; UVEITIS

ANOPHELES MOSQUITO
See MALARIA

ANORECTICS
Anorectic drugs are used to reduce appetite. These drugs do not reduce weight but act as an aid to controlling appetite while the patient complies with a strictly controlled diet. They are available in tablet and capsule form only. Anorectics should not be used for long periods, as dependence can occur. Some are stimulants, which may cause insomnia if used in the evening, and are used illegally by long-distance drivers and others who wish to remain awake for long periods of time. They should not be mixed with alcohol, and their use during pregnancy is controversial. Many drugs in this class have been removed from the market in recent years because of abuse, interactions and side effects.

Examples include diethylpropion and phentermine (Duromine).

See also FOOD; MEDICATION; OBESITY; ORLISTAT

ANOREXIA
Anorexia is a medical term that means a lack of appetite.
See also ANOREXIA NERVOSA; APPETITE, LACK OF; FAILURE TO THRIVE; GROWTH REDUCED; WEIGHT LOSS

ANOREXIA NERVOSA
Anorexia nervosa is an eating disorder that usually occurs in young white women in Western society. It is almost unknown in American Negroes and British Indians, and totally unknown in third-world countries. About one in every 200 women between thirteen and thirty in developed countries may be affected.

It may start with a psychological shock (eg. rejection by a boyfriend, fear of a new situation, stress at school, bad sexual experience) and is due to an inappropriate body image which makes the patient feel grossly overweight, or have an abnormal fear of becoming overweight, when they may in fact be normal or underweight.

Patients develop an extreme dislike of food accompanied by excessive exercising, a cessation of menstrual periods, diffuse hair loss, intolerance of cold, slow pulse, irregular heart beat and complex hormonal disorders. They may practice deceit to fool their family and doctors by appearing to eat normal meals but later vomit the food, use purgatives to clean out their bowel, or hide food during the meal. With time, they may become seriously undernourished and emaciated to the point of death, if adequate treatment is not available.

No specific blood or other test can confirm the diagnosis, but tests may be undertaken to ensure that there is no other cause for the weight loss or lack of appetite.

Treatment is very difficult, prolonged and requires the attention of expert psychiatrists and physicians. Initial hospital admission is almost mandatory, and any relapses should also be treated by hospitalisation. Punishment for not eating must be avoided, but friendly encouragement and persuasion by family and friends is beneficial in both improving the patient's self-esteem and food intake. Medications (eg. tricyclic antidepressants) are not successful without accompanying psychiatric help, which is required for many years.

Relapses are common, and suicide frequently attempted. The long term outcome can vary from complete recovery to death within a year or two. Statistically, 30% suffer some long term adverse health effects, and as many as 25% eventually die from the disease.
See also APPETITE, LACK OF; BULIMIA NERVOSA; FAILURE TO THRIVE; GROWTH REDUCED; WEIGHT LOSS

ANORGASMIA
See ORGASM, LACK OF

ANOSMIA
See SMELL LOSS

ANTACIDS
Drugs that neutralise acid in the stomach are antacids. A very large number of these medications are available without prescription as both mixtures and tablets. Sometimes they cause problems with the absorption of other medications if taken at the same time. They often contain multiple ingredients including aluminium hydroxide, magnesium hydroxide, and simethicone.
See also HEARTBURN; MEDICATION; PEPTIC ULCER

ANTAZOLINE
See VASOCONSTRICTORS

ANTERIOR CHEST WALL SYNDROME
See TIETZE SYNDROME

ANTERIOR COMPARTMENT SYNDROME
The anterior compartment syndrome is a common cause of leg pain in athletes. It is due to increased pressure in the rigid compartment between the bones in the lower leg (tibia and fibula) and the fibrous tissue surrounding the muscles from exercise stress (eg. long distance running).

Patients develop pain in the front and outside fleshy part of the lower leg that is worse with exercise. In severe cases there may be difficulty in pulling up the foot due to nerve compression.

Treatment involves rest, anti-inflammatory medications, physiotherapy, and rarely surgical relief of the pressure. Most cases settle slowly with treatment.
See also LEG PAIN; TIBIA

ANTERIOR IMPINGEMENT SYNDROME
The anterior impingement syndrome, or footballer's ankle, is a persistent painful inflammation of tissues around the ankle caused by repeated forced upward flexion of the ankle, as in kicking.

These athletes develop chronic ankle pain that is worse with running or descending stairs, ankle stiffness, and pain on upward flexion of the ankle.

An x-ray of the ankle shows bony growths on the upper surface of the talus bone at the top of the foot just in front of the ankle, and on the lower end of the tibia (shin bone).

Treatment involves rest, anti-inflammatory medications, and surgical removal of the bony overgrowths. Without rest, the pain steadily worsens until walking becomes impossible. The prognosis is good if a treatment plan is followed correctly.
See also ANKLE

ANTHELMINTICS
Helminths are different types of worms that infect the gut. The drugs that destroy these unwanted internal worms are called anthelmintics. There are many different types of helminths, including pinworms, hookworms, roundworms, and a number of rarer worms that are not normally found in Australia.

Most common anthelmintics can be purchased without prescription in mixture, tablet and granule formulations. It is important to treat all family members, and to carefully wash clothing and bedding at the time of treatment. A number of prescription drugs are available for the treatment of resistant cases or rarer types of infection.

Examples of these medications (with brand names in brackets) include mebendazole (Vermox) and pyrantel (Anthel, Combantrin). Diarrhoea may be a side effect.
See also MEDICATION; HOOKWORM; PINWORM

ANTHRAX
Anthrax is a bacterial skin, lung or intestinal infection that usually occurs in farmers, meat workers, veterinarians and others who come into close contact with animals. Infection of humans is uncommon.

The bacterium *Bacillus anthracis* which is found in cattle, horses, sheep, goats and pigs, is responsible. It may be caught by bacteria entering the body through scratches and grazes, or rarely by swallowing or inhalation into the lungs. Anthrax spores may remain inactive in the soil for decades, but it cannot be transmitted from one person to another. The natural incidence in Western countries is about one in 100 million people every year.

There are three different types of anthrax infection in humans: –
• Cutaneous anthrax – A sore appears at the site of entry (which may be in the mouth), then nearby lymph nodes become inflamed, a fever develops, followed by nausea, vomiting, headaches and collapse.
• Inhalation anthrax – After an incubation period of one to five days the patient develops flu-like symptoms with muscle aches and fever. This is followed two to five days later by difficulty in breathing, sweating, fever, rapid pulse and blue tinged skin. The patient collapses quickly with a severe form of pneumonia. It may also spread into the bloodstream.
• Gastrointestinal anthrax – Incubation period of one or two days, then nausea, vomiting, fever, loss of appetite, belly pain and bloody diarrhoea develop.

The diagnosis is confirmed by microscopic examination of smears from the skin sores, or from sputum samples. Specific blood tests may also be positive.

Treatment involves antibiotics such as ciprofloxacin or doxycycline by mouth or injection. A vaccine is available, but is only used by those who are at high risk because of their involvement with infected animals.

Treatment clears the skin and gastrointestinal forms of the disease effectively in most cases, but anthrax pneumonia is very serious, and a significant proportion of these patients die.
See also BACTERIA

ANTI-

A prefix derived from Greek and used in medicine to mean against, opposed to, or opposite.

For example, antibiotic means 'against life', in this case the life being that of bacteria.

ANTIALLERGY EXTRACTS

Antiallergy extracts are extracts of many different pollens, venoms and other substances that can be used in very slowly increasing dosages to desensitise a patient who is allergic to a particular substance. Each individual patient must be tested before treatment to determine the specific extracts required. They are available as injections or drops that are placed on the tongue. A large range of allergies can be treated by these means, but they must be used under strict medical supervision, as sudden severe allergic reactions may occur.
See also ALLERGY; ANTIHISTAMINES

ANTIANAEROBES

Metronidazole (Flagyl) and tinidazole (Fasigyn) are classed as both antianaerobic antibiotics and antitrichomonals. They destroy some microscopic animals that can infect the gut or vagina (eg. giardia, trichomonas), are used to treat the skin condition rosacea, and also kill bacteria that may be found deep inside the body where oxygen cannot reach (anaerobes). They can be given in tablet form as a single dose. Vancomycin is an antianaerobe normally used as a last resort antibiotic, when all others have failed.

Side effects may include a bad taste, nausea, diarrhoea and headache. They must be used with care in pregnancy, kidney and liver disease.
See also ANAEROBIC INFECTION; ANTIBIOTICS; MEDICATION; ROSACEA

ANTIANDROGENS
See SEX HORMONES

ANTIANGINALS

This large range of medications is used to treat angina (chest pain caused by a poor blood supply to the heart).

The tablets come in two types: –
• Those that are swallowed whole on a regular basis to prevent angina.
• Those that are dissolved under the tongue to rapidly relieve acute attacks of angina. A mouth spray (Nitrolingual) is also available to treat angina.

Examples of medications in this class (with brand names in brackets) include glyceryl trinitrate – colloquially known as nitroglycerine (Anginine, Nitro-Dur, Nitrolingual, Transiderm Nitro), isosorbide (Imdur, Isordil) and perhexilene (Pexid).

Side effects may include headache, flushing, rapid heart rate, dizziness, nausea and loss of appetite.

Because some antiangina medications (eg. isosorbide) can cause stomach upsets, a new method of putting the medication into the body by passing it directly through the skin has been developed. Patches of various strengths are now available to prevent angina. Dosage can also be adjusted by wearing a patch for only a certain period of the day. These treatments have remarkably few side effects but may cause skin rashes in some people, particularly if they are applied to the same place too often.

Great care must be taken when using antiangina drugs in patients with glaucoma, anaemia, low blood pressure and heart failure. Other groups of drugs, the beta-blockers and calcium channel blockers, are also used to treat and prevent angina.
See also ANGINA; BETA-BLOCKERS; CALCIUM CHANNEL BLOCKERS; MEDICATION

ANTIARRHYTHMICS

Antiarrhythmics are the drugs that keep the heart beating regularly. If the heart rhythm is uneven, beats are being missed, or extra beats are causing palpitations, doctors will prescribe an antiarrhythmic. There are a wide range of medications in this class that work in different ways depending on the type of heart rhythm irregularity, and they are available in both tablet and injection form.

Side effects do occur with antiarrhythmics, but they vary widely from drug to drug and patient to patient. It should be possible to vary the medication so that the effects of the drug adequately help the patient without causing significant side effects. These medications can also interact with other drugs, and some should not be used in certain diseases (eg. thyroid disorders). A doctor treating a patient with one of these drugs must be fully aware of the patient's medical history and all the other drugs the patient is taking.

Examples of drugs in this class include amiodarone, disopyramide, flecainide, mexiletine, procainamide, quinidine and sotalol.

Side effects may include a dry mouth, nausea, indigestion, ear noise, palpitations, fainting, slow heart rate and sun sensitivity.
See also BETA-BLOCKERS;

CALCIUM CHANNEL BLOCKERS; MEDICATION; PALPITATION

ANTIBIOTICS

Antibiotics are the most widely prescribed group of drugs, but most patients understand very little about them. Although there were chemical compounds used against infection before the Second World War, the isolation of penicillin from a mould grown in a laboratory by Alexander Fleming and Howard Florey in 1943 represented the first real exploitation of a purified natural substance that could kill bacteria. The very first supplies of penicillin came from the mould grown, due to wartime exigencies, in large numbers of bedpans. Most antibiotics today are produced as the result of chemical reactions (i.e. synthesised) as opposed to harvesting the drug from primitive life forms grown in bulk in areas that resembled mushroom farms.

Antibiotics are only effective against bacteria, and not against viral infections. Most of the infections seen by a general practitioner are caused by viruses, and there is no need for antibiotics in these cases. Antibiotics are used by doctors in several situations: –
• If the infection appears to be bacterial, the appropriate antibiotic will be selected to cure it. Samples or swabs may be taken so that the infecting bacteria and the correct antibiotic to kill it can be identified in a laboratory.
• If the problem is not clear-cut, or if there is some doubt as to the cause of a problem, an antibiotic may be prescribed to cover one of the possibilities. This may be the case with a severely sore throat.
• If a person has reduced immunity, is elderly, frail, liable to recurrent infections or due for an operation, an antibiotic may be used to prevent a bacterial infection. Women with recurrent bladder infections are one example.

Major problems can occur with the overuse of antibiotics. Cost is the first one, and as the government (i.e. you the taxpayer) pays part of the cost of everyone's antibiotics, this is a problem affecting you. Side effects are another problem, including altering the effectiveness of the oral contraceptive pill. The most important problem is the development of resistance which can enable bacteria to change in a way which makes them able to resist the actions of an antibiotic that was previously very effective. The need for new antibiotic agents is therefore always with us. Their development is a long and costly process involving huge investments by the drug companies. A good antibiotic deserves a long and effective life, and the needs of the public will be best served by the prescribing of antibiotics only when they are really needed, thus reducing the rate at which resistant strains develop.

The different types of antibiotics are dealt with separately in this text.
See also AMINOGLYCOSIDES; ANTIANAEROBES; CEPHALOSPORINS; FLEMING, ALEXANDER; FLOREY, HOWARD; MACROLIDES; MEDICATION; PENICILLINS; QUINOLONES; SULPHA ANTIBIOTICS; TETRACYCLINES

ANTIBODY

An antibody is a water soluble protein produced from globulins (eg. gammaglobulin) in the spleen, lymph nodes, thymus gland, liver or bone marrow in response to an antigen (foreign protein). Antibodies attack antigens to render them inactive and no longer infective.

In particular, antibodies are produced in response to an infection by a virus. The antibodies, once formed, are stored in the spleen and liver, so that when the person is exposed to the same infection a second time, the antibodies are already present and can react immediately to destroy the invading viruses and ward off any infection. This is why most viral infections (eg. chickenpox, measles) can be caught only once.

An antibody may be produced in response to a vaccine that contains selected protein particles from a virus (eg. measles), and thereby give immunity against that particular infection.

Bacteria produce too many different antigens for antibodies to be particularly effective in totally preventing an infection, but they still act to reduce the seriousness of subsequent infections, and eventually destroy the invader.
See also ANTIGEN; ANTIVENENE; GAMMAGLOBULIN; IMMUNE TESTS; PROTEIN; VACCINATION

ANTICOAGULANTS

Anticoagulants are drugs that stop blood from clotting at the normal speed. They are used in patients who have had strokes due to blood clots, clots in leg veins and clots in the heart and lung arteries. Aspirin is also a mild anticoagulant and can be used in small doses to prevent strokes. All anticoagulants should be stopped before any surgical procedure.

Patients on the stronger anticoagulants listed below, must be monitored carefully by their doctors and have blood tests regularly (an INR test) to ensure that the clotting factors in their blood are kept at the desirable level. Patients using anticoagulants will bruise and bleed more easily than normal, and care must be taken when using some antiarthritic medications, as they may cause bleeding into the gut while the patient is on anticoagulants. There are many precautions necessary with these drugs, which make compliance with a doctor's instructions vital.

Examples of these medications include heparin and warfarin (Coumadin, Marevan). Side effects may include abnormal bruising, nose bleeds, hair loss, itch, rash, fever and nausea.
See also BLOOD CLOTTING TEST; MEDICATION

ANTICONVULSANTS

This large class of drugs is used to control and prevent fits and convulsions caused by epilepsy and other diseases. Barbiturates and benzodiazepines are also used for this purpose. Patients must sometimes take quite large quantities of anticonvulsants, or combinations of several drugs to control their problem, and blood levels are usually checked, to arrive at the correct dosage. Anticonvulsants are nearly always used as tablets, but injections and mixtures of some drugs are available.

Side effects from anticonvulsants vary widely from one person to another and between drugs. They are usually worst when treatment is first started, and wear off as time passes. Common side effects may include drowsiness, incoordination, dizziness, double vision and nausea. Phenytoin may cause gum problems if used in the long term. All these drugs have a tendency to interact with other drugs, and the doctor must be made aware of all medications being taken and any other diseases (eg. diabetes) that may be present.

Examples (with common brand names in brackets) include carbamazepine (Tegretol), clonazepam (Rivotril), ethosuximide (Zarontin), gabapentin (Neurontin), lamotrigine (Lamictal), phenytoin (Dilantin), primidone

(Mysoline), sodium valproate (Epilim), sulthiame (Ospolot), tigabine (Gabitril), topiramate (Topamax) and vigabatrin (Sabril).
See also BARBITURATES; BENZODIAZEPINES; EPILEPSY; MEDICATION

ANTIDEPRESSANTS

Antidepressants are used to control depression. This is as much a disease as diabetes or high blood pressure but is often thought to be a mental disorder that patients can "pull themselves out of". Nothing could be further than the truth. Depression is caused by a biochemical imbalance in the brain, and requires appropriate medication to correct it before a tragedy occurs. There are many sub-classes of antidepressants including MAOI, RIMA, SNRI, SSRI, tetracyclics and tricyclics.

MAOI

Monoamine oxidase inhibitors (MAOI) are potent antidepressants that are only used in severe and chronic cases of depression. They are slow to become effective, and their effects may persist for a couple of weeks after they are stopped. They do not cause drowsiness, but they interact violently with many other drugs and some foods, including soy sauce, cheese, red wine and pickled foods. Any patient on MAOI should be given by their doctor a list of foods and drugs they must avoid. This list must be observed carefully, or serious side effects may occur. Other side effects may include dizziness, constipation, dry mouth, drowsiness and nausea. MAOI should not be taken in conjunction with tricyclic antidepressants, and only with extreme care by epileptic patients. If taken correctly, they can dramatically improve a depressed patient's life. Examples include phenelzine (Nardil) and tranylcypromine (Parnate).

RIMA

Reversible inhibitors of monoamine oxidase (RIMA) antidepressants are a very effective and safe antidepressant introduced in the early 1990s. The only one generally available is moclobemide (Aurorix). Side effects may include disturbed sleep and dizziness.

SNRI

Serotonin and noradrenaline reuptake inhibitors (SNRI) is a new class of antidepressants that was introduced in 1996 and is used in resistant cases of depression. Venlafaxine (Efexor) is the most common drug in this class. Side effects may include dizziness, drowsiness and a dry mouth.

SSRI

Selective serotonin reuptake inhibitors (SSRI) are a class of antidepressants which has received a great deal of publicity because of the extraordinary efficacy of one of its members – fluoxetine (Prozac). Introduced in 1992, this group has revolutionised the management of depression and anxiety because of its speed of action, safety and minimal side effects, and they are now the most widely used antidepressants. Other drugs in this class include paroxetine (Aropax), sertraline (Zoloft) and citalopram (Cipramil). Side effects may include nausea, drowsiness, sweating, tremor, a dry mouth and impotence.

TRICYCLICS

Tricyclic antidepressants were the most widely used drugs in this class until the introduction of SSRI, and are still very effective in treating most cases, but they are slow to act, taking two to four weeks to reach full effectiveness. They also cause some sedation, and so are normally taken at night. Other side effects may include a dry mouth, tremor, dizziness, constipation, rapid heart rate, blurred vision and excess sweating. Examples include amitriptyline (Tryptanol), clomipramine (Anafranil), dothiepin (Prothiaden), doxepin (Sinequan), imipramine (Tofranil), nortriptyline (Allegron) and trimipramine (Surmontil). Mianserin (Tolvon) is a variant on the tricyclic theme that tends to be safer in patients with heart problems.

HT RECEPTOR BLOCKERS

This is one of the newer classes of antidepressants. The only commonly used medication in this class is nefazodone (Serzone). It must be used with caution in pregnancy, breast feeding, children, brain, kidney, liver, heart and blood vessel disease, mania and epilepsy. It interacts with MAOI if used within two weeks, and medications that lower blood pressure. Common side effects include nausea, diarrhoea, low blood pressure, fainting and drowsiness. Unusual ones are vomiting and a painful prolonged erection of the penis (priapism). Another newer antidepressant is mirtazapine (Avanza, Remeron). Its use at present tends to be restricted to more severe depression that cannot be controlled by other classes of medication. It interacts with alcohol and

benzodiazepines (eg. Valium) and may cause increased appetite, weight gain, dizziness and headaches.
See also DEPRESSION; MEDICATION

ANTIDIARRHOEALS

Antidiarrhoeals are one of the most popular drug groups with patients. When you just have to go and go and go – and you want to stop – antidiarrhoeals are just the thing to help. There are some types of diarrhoea that they are not suitable for, including those associated with jaundice (yellow skin), bacterial gut infections, and diarrhoea during pregnancy. Diarrhoea has a vast number of causes, and the exact treatment chosen will depend on that cause. Many types of diarrhoea require no medication but a correct diet. The most commonly used antidiarrhoeals include diphenoxylate and atropine (Lomotil), kaolin (old fashioned and not particularly effective), codeine (also an analgesic – painkiller) and loperamide (Immodium).
See also DIARRHOEA; MEDICATION

ANTIDIURETIC HORMONE
See PITUITARY GLAND

ANTIEMETICS

Antiemetics are medicines that stop vomiting. They are often difficult to give in tablet or mixture form, so many of them are also available as an injection or suppository (for insertion into the back passage). There are many different drugs in this category, from the mild over-the-counter travel sickness pills such as dimenhydrinate (Andrumin, Travacalm), to the more effective and potent prescription drugs such as prochlorperazine (Stemetil), domperidone (Motilium) and metoclopramide (Maxolon). These are also available as injections. Prochlorperazine may also be used for Ménière's disease and for dizziness.

Side effects may include constipation, dry mouth, tremor, drowsiness and blurred vision.
See also ANTIHISTAMINES; ANTISPASMODICS; MEDICATION; NAUSEA AND VOMITING; OCULOGYRIC CRISIS

ANTIFUNGALS

Fungi are members of the plant kingdom and are one of the types of microscopic life that can infect human beings in many diverse ways. The most common site of infection is the skin, where they cause an infection that is commonly known as tinea. Fungi are also responsible for many gut infections, particularly in the mouth and around the anus. It is a rare infant who escapes without an attack of oral thrush. Around the anus, the fungus can cause an extremely itchy rash, but in women it may spread forward from the anus to the vagina to cause the white discharge and intense itch of vaginal thrush or candidiasis. The most serious diseases develop when fungal infections occur deep inside the body in organs such as the lungs, brain and sinuses. These diseases are very difficult to treat and it may take many months with potent antifungal drugs to bring them under control. Fortunately, this type of condition is relatively rare.

Antifungals include: –
• Imidazoles. Some of the most effective antifungals come from this class of antifungals, including clotrimazole (Canesten), econazole (Pevaryl) and miconazole (Daktarin). They can be used for fungal infections of skin, mouth, vagina and scalp and are safe in pregnancy and children.
• Amorolfine (Loceryl paint) which is used for severe fungal nail infections.
• Amphotericin (Fungilin, Fungizone) which is used for severe internal fungal infections, fungal mouth and gut infections.
• Fluconazole (Diflucan) which is a potent antifungal with many uses.
• Griseofulvin (Griseostatin, Grisovin) which is an oldie but a goodie that is used for fungal infections of skin, hair and nails, but may cause headache, nausea and sun sensitivity.
• Ketoconazole (Nizoral) which is used for significant fungal infections of skin and internal organs, and dandruff. Nausea may be a side effect.
• Nystatin (Mycostatin, Nilstat) is a long established and widely used antifungal that is safe in pregnancy and may be used for infections of skin, mouth, vagina and gut.
• Terbenafine (Lamisil) is a very effective medication for skin and nail fungal infections. It is available as a cream and tablet, but nausea, diarrhoea, rash and dizziness may be side effects of the tablets.
See also FUNGI; MEDICATION; PITYRIASIS VERSICOLOR; THRUSH; TINEA CRURIS

ANTIGEN

An antigen is any foreign matter containing a protein that enters the body to trigger an antibody response. It may be a virus, bacteria, fungus, snake venom, a splinter or a transplanted organ.

See also ANTIBODY; ANTIVENENE; BLOOD GROUPS; CANCER ASSOCIATED ANTIGEN; PROSTATE SPECIFIC ANTIGEN

ANTIHISTAMINES

Antihistamines are some of the most commonly used drugs. They are often found in cold and flu remedies that may be purchased without a prescription from chemists.

Histamine is a substance found in special cells (mast cells) in every part of the body, which is responsible for allergy reactions. If histamine is released from mast cells it causes swelling, itching, spasm of muscles, dilation of blood vessels and secretion of phlegm. Histamine release in the nose causes a runny nose and sneezing; in the lungs it may cause asthma; in the skin it causes hives (urticaria); in the gut it causes diarrhoea. Histamines may be released in response to an insect bite, to inhaling pollen or dusts, eating certain foods or drugs, or touching some plants.

Antihistamines counteract the histamine released into the tissues, and so control allergy reactions. They work well in the nose, sinuses and throat; reasonably well in the skin; but not at all well in the lungs and gut. Antihistamines are therefore used for hay fever, sneezing attacks, skin allergies and drug rashes. Some can be useful in treating dizziness, itches, nausea and migraine. Many of them produce some degree of lethargy and drowsiness, so care must be taken when driving and operating machinery. Alcohol should be avoided while taking sedating antihistamines. Children may be stimulated by sedating antihistamines, in direct contrast to adults. They are available as tablets, mixtures, nose sprays and some come as injections for severe allergy reactions. Promethazine is also available on prescription as a cream for certain allergic skin conditions.

Antihistamines are divided into two broad classes – those that have sedation as a common side effect and those that do not.

NON-SEDATING ANTIHISTAMINES

Non-sedating antihistamines include (with brand names in brackets) astemizole (Hismanal), fexofenadine (Telfast) and loratadine (Claratyne). These medications can be used only to treat allergies, and are of no use for the runny nose of a common cold.

SEDATING ANTIHISTAMINES

Sedating antihistamines include azatadine (Zadine), brompheniramine, cetrizine (Zyrtec – a newer and generally better medication), chlorpheniramine, dexchlorpheniramine (Polaramine), cyproheptadine (Periactin), pheniramine (Avil), promethazine (Phenergan) and trimeprazine (Vallergan). In addition to their anti-allergy properties, these can also be used for sedating children and drying nasal secretions during a common cold. Other side effects may include a dry mouth, constipation, incoordination, blurred vision and restlessness. They should be used with caution in glaucoma, liver disease, epilepsy, breast feeding, and severe heart and liver disease.

See also ALLERGY; MEDICATION

ANTIHYPERTENSIVES

Medications that control and reduce high blood pressure (hypertension) are called antihypertensives.

See also ACE INHIBITORS; ANGIOTENSIN II RECEPTOR ANTAGONISTS; ALPHA-BLOCKERS; BETA BLOCKERS; CALCIUM CHANNEL BLOCKERS; HEART; HYPERTENSION; METHYLDOPA

ANTI-INFLAMMATORY DRUGS

See NONSTEROIDAL ANTI-INFLAMMATORY DRUGS; STEROIDS

ANTIMALARIALS

Malaria is becoming an increasing problem in the world, as many forms of the disease are becoming resistant to the commonly used medications. Millions of people die of malaria in tropical countries every year, and the most resistant and virulent form in the world can be found in Papua New Guinea and the Solomon Islands. It is essential for travellers to any tropical country to discuss with their doctor, at least a month before their departure, the appropriate medications necessary to prevent malaria. Because it is spread by mosquitoes, important aspects of preventing malaria include insect repellents, protective clothing and mosquito nets. Generally speaking, the same drugs are used for both prevention and treatment of malaria, but they are given in much higher dosages for treatment.

Quinine, chloroquine and their derivatives (hydroxychloroquine, mefloquine) have been the mainstay of malaria treatment since quinine was first isolated from the South American cinchona tree bark by Spanish missionaries in the sixteenth century. Chloroquine-resistant forms of malaria are now present throughout south-east Asia and the south-west Pacific regions. The newer synthetic quinine derivatives (eg. mefloquine) overcome this problem. A number of other antimalarials (eg. pyrimethamine) are available to travellers to these countries and for those who do catch the disease.

Most of these medications have side effects, should not be used in pregnancy or infants, and are very dangerous in overdose. Chloroquine may cause nausea and diarrhoea, while hydroxychloroquine has a rash, itch, dry skin and nausea as side effects. Mefloquine's side effects include dizziness and vomiting. Pyrimethamine tends to have more side effects (eg. rash, nausea, colic, diarrhoea), and is better used for short periods of time if possible. It should not be used during pregnancy or breast feeding.

Prevention requires taking one or two tablets a week for two weeks before entering a malaria infected area, and continuing until a month after leaving it. Doxycycline, a tetracycline antibiotic, is also commonly used to prevent malaria.

Chloroquine can also be used to control rheumatoid arthritis.

Some antimalarials are used in strange ways to treat autoimmune diseases and muscle cramps amongst other conditions where they have been found to work serendipitously. Patients should not be surprised if their doctor prescribes these medications for conditions other than malaria.
See also ANTIRHEUMATICS; MALARIA; MEDICATION; TETRACYCLINES

ANTINEOPLASTICS
See CYTOTOXICS AND ANTINEOPLASTICS

ANTIPARASITICS
Antiparasitics are creams, shampoos or lotions that destroy microscopic animals (parasites) that can be found on the skin and in the hair.

Scabies, crabs, head lice and body lice are the common parasites. The medications are applied all over the body, or in just the affected area, depending on the parasite. The treatment is usually repeated after a few days, and other family members should be treated at the same time.

Examples include benzyl benzoate (Ascabiol), crotamiton (Eurax), maldison and permethrin (Lyclear, Quellada). Patients must avoid head, body openings and broken skin when applying these medications.
See also HEAD LICE; MEDICATION; SCABIES

ANTIPSYCHOTICS
A psychosis is a serious mental disorder, in which the patients normally have no idea that there is anything wrong with them. Many specific mental diseases fit into this category, and different antipsychotic drugs are known to be more useful in treating some types of psychoses. Psychoses are often characterised by agitation, anxiety, tension, personality changes and emotional disturbances. Common psychotic diseases include mania, some types of depression, and schizophrenia. Nearly all of the drugs that can correct these problems are available as tablets, and some as mixtures, wafers and injections.

Fluphenazine (Modecate) is a long-acting injectable antipsychotic that can be given on a monthly basis for long-term control of psychoses, particularly schizophrenia. This overcomes the problem of patients forgetting or refusing their medication.

The main class of antipsychotics is the phenothiazines. Examples include (with brand names in brackets) chlorpromazine (Largactil), fluphenazine (Modecate), pericyazine (Neulactil), promazine (Sparine), thioridazine (Melleril) and trifluoperazine (Stelazine). These may also be used for senile dementia, severe agitation, intractable vomiting, severe hiccups, severe anxiety, and to increase the effect of painkillers. Side effects may include drowsiness, dry mouth, rash, abnormal temperature, reduced alertness, constipation, blurred vision, a stuffy nose and tremor. They should only be used if essential in pregnancy and breast feeding, and not in depression or liver diseases, and alcohol must be avoided.

Two new and very effective antipsychotics are olanzapine (Zyprexa) and quetiapine

(Seroquel). They are rapidly acting, and have fewer side effects (eg. tiredness, weight gain) than the older medications and they are also very useful in the control of Alzheimer disease.

Haloperidol (Serenace) is one of the more potent antipsychotics. As well as being used for psychiatric disorders, it may also be used for alcoholism, severe vomiting, and the control of Tourette syndrome. Side effects are dose related and may include incoordination, drowsiness, spasms and tremor.

Lithium (Lithicarb) is a very effective medication used in manic-depressive psychoses and bipolar personalities, where patients swing wildly in their mood from very happy to excessively sad. Side effects may include weight gain, goitre and bloating. It should never be used in pregnancy.
See also DEMENTIA; MEDICATION; PSYCHOSES; SCHIZOPHRENIA

ANTIRHEUMATICS

An amazingly diverse range of drugs can be placed in the category of relieving rheumatoid arthritis. Most of them have found their place here serendipitously, when patients being treated for other diseases found that their rheumatoid arthritis was improved. There is no cure for rheumatoid arthritis, but by the use of painkillers, physiotherapy, NSAID (nonsteroidal anti-inflammatory drugs) and the antirheumatic drugs, control is normally possible. Penicillamine (not related to the antibiotic), gold, sulfasalazine and chloroquine (normally used for malaria) are antirheumatics. All these medications are slow to act, have significant side effects, and patients using them must be monitored very regularly by blood and urine tests. Because of these problems, they are only used in severe cases of rheumatoid arthritis where other treatment has failed. In the correct patients, remarkable relief from pain and swelling can be achieved.

Gold (Auranofin, Ridaura, Mycrosin) may be given by injection or tablets, but it can interfere with other medications, and because of its tendency to destroy white blood cells, blood tests must be ordered regularly. Penicillamine must not be used with gold. Side effects of both these medications may include a rash, fever, joint pains, itch and enlarged lymph nodes.
See also ANTIMALARIALS;

EXFOLIATIVE DERMATITIS; NSAID; RHEUMATOID ARTHRITIS

ANTISEPTICS

Antiseptics are medications that kill bacteria and other infecting organisms on the skin, in the mouth or other areas, without being absorbed into the body or blood. They may also be used to sterilise medical instruments and equipment. Something that is septic is infected, so antiseptics act against infection. They are available as lotions, creams, ointments, powders, pessaries (for vaginal use) and lozenges. A prescription is not normally required for their purchase (mupirocin is the exception). Allergy reactions (eg. to iodine preparations) can occur, and they should not be used near or in the eyes.

Examples include cetrimide, chlorhexidine, chloroxylenol (Dettol), triclosan (Phisohex, Sapoderm), mupirocin (Bactroban) and povidone-iodine (Betadine).
See also ANTIBIOTICS; MEDICATION

ANTISPASMODICS

Antispasmodics prevent or treat painful muscular spasm of hollow tubes within the body, such as the gut. If the gut goes into spasm, severe intermittent pains can develop in the abdomen. Irritable bowel syndrome, infantile colic, gastroenteritis and gut infections are just a few of the diseases that can cause this problem. There are a large number of antispasmodic drugs for the gut that vary from mild over-the-counter tablet and mixture preparations to potent prescription tablets such as dicyclomine (Merbentyl), mebeverine (Colofac), hyoscine (Buscopan) and propantheline. Some of these are also available as injections. Side effects may include a dry mouth and blurred vision. They should not be used in patients with glaucoma or prostate disease, and must be used with care in pregnancy.
See also GASTROENTERITIS; IRRITABLE BOWEL SYNDROME; MEDICATION

ANTITHYROID DRUGS

An overactive thyroid gland (hyperthyroidism) can cause a multiplicity of serious problems. The excess production of thyroxine hormone by the gland must be reduced before serious damage occurs to other organs

in the body. The drugs that act against the thyroid gland (antithyroid drugs) are carbimazole and propylthiouracil (PTU). They should not be used in the long term, unless regular blood tests are performed to assess any potential damage to blood cells or other organs. Because of their significant side effects, these tablets are often used only in the acute situation, until a cure by means of surgery or irradiation is undertaken.
See also HYPERTHYROIDISM; MEDICATION; THYROID GLAND

ANTITUSSIVES
See COUGH MEDICINES

ANTIVENENE
Antivenenes (antivenoms) are prepared by injecting slowly-increasing concentrations of a venom (antigen) into an animal such as a horse, and then purifying the antibodies (antivenom) produced from the animal's serum. The antivenene can then be used to counteract the effects of a venomous bite in a human, but repeated use of an antivenene may cause sensitisation to other proteins from the donor animal. An antivenene against a single venom or multiple venoms may be prepared.

Antivenenes are available for the bites and stings of many animals including several different snakes, funnel-web and red-back spiders and the box jellyfish.
See also ANTIBODY; ANTIGEN; SNAKE BITE; SPIDER BITE

ANTIVENOM
See ANTIVENENE

ANTIVIRALS
Until very recently, drugs that killed viruses and cured viral infections (antivirals) were limited to the idoxuridine eye drops and ointments used for cold sores and herpes simplex infections. Idoxuridine is far more effective if used early in the disease when the virus is multiplying.

Aciclovir (Zovirax) was the first antiviral tablet/injection that could attack viral infections from within the body, but it (and the newer famciclovir and valaciclovir) only acts against herpes zoster and herpes simplex viruses that cause cold sores, genital herpes and shingles.

A new inhaler that acts against the influenza virus, zanamvir (Relenza) was introduced in 1999, and a tablet, oseltamivir (Tamiflu) was introduced in 2001. Side effects are usually minimal to all these medications.

Numerous potent antivirals, such as zidovudine (Retrovir) and lamivudine are being used in combination to control AIDS.
See also AIDS; COLD SORE; GENITAL HERPES; INFLUENZA; MEDICATION; SHINGLES; VIRUS

ANURIA
See URINE REDUCED

ANUS
The anus has been described by some pundits as one of the smartest parts of the body, because what other structure could let gas out below while retaining solids and liquids above?

It consists of a narrow fleshy tube surrounded by a muscular ring that relaxes when faeces or wind is passed, but remains firmly closed at all other times. It connects the storage area for faeces (the rectum) with the outside of the body, is about three cm long, and can dilate to about two cm without discomfort.

The tissue between the anus and the base of the penis in a man or vulva in a woman is called the perineum.

A ring of veins around the anus may be damaged to form piles, and the anal canal can tear if overstretched.
See also ANAL FISSURE; ANAL FISTULA; ANAL TEAR; ANAL ITCH; ANAL PAIN; ANAL FISSURE; FAECES; PILES; PROCTITIS; RECTAL PROLAPSE; RECTUM

ANXIETY
Anxiety may be natural or unnatural. Natural anxiety is the type we all experience while expecting or experiencing a stressful event (eg. exam, job interview, dangerous journey), and may be eased by counselling, distraction (doing something else) or as a last resort using medication.

There are numerous causes of unnatural anxiety.

Depression is one common cause of anxiety. It may be a reaction to circumstances (eg. loss of job, death in the family), or may have no apparent cause (endogenous depression). Patients with endogenous depression have an imbalance of chemicals that normally occur in the brain to control mood. If too much of one chemical is produced, the patient becomes depressed. Postpartum depression occurs in some women after childbirth as a response to the effect on the brain of sudden changes in hormone levels. The symptoms may be the same as endogenous depression, but excessive anxiety about the infant, or neglect of the child, may also occur.

Hormonal effects may also come into play in the menopause and with premenstrual tension. Women may find that they become inappropriately anxious just before their periods, or for no reason during menopause as their sex hormone levels fluctuate dramatically.

A neurosis is an illness of the personality that may cause excessive anxiety, phobias (an inappropriate fear of something or some place), and physical distress (eg. shortness of breath, palpitations, nausea, abdominal pain, headache, faint). It is usually not possible to define the cause of the anxiety in patients with neuroses, and their phobias have no rational explanation.

As well as causing social and work disruption, long term alcoholism may result in neuroses, phobias, depression, irrational behaviour, poor coordination, difficulties in walking and performing simple tasks, and insanity.

Patients who have a serious disease, or who have had a near-death experience, may become excessively anxious. This is particularly common in patients who have had a heart attack, and who have some ongoing symptoms of heart disease.

See also ANXIETY NEUROSIS; ANXIOLYTICS; BARBITURATES; BENZODIAZEPINES; SOCIAL ANXIETY DISORDER and separate entries for diseases mentioned above.

ANXIETY NEUROSIS

An anxiety neurosis is also known as a nervous breakdown or panic attack.

A neurosis is an illness of the personality in which the patient is aware that a problem is present. In many psychiatric conditions, such as schizophrenia and psychosis, the patient is not aware that there is a problem. Both severe neuroses and depression may be politely referred to as a 'nervous breakdown'.

There is a tendency for anxiety neurosis to run in families from one generation to the next, and most are present before the age of twenty-five years. It is often not possible to define the cause of the anxiety, and patients may try to explain it as a result of some stress in their lives, but in most situations, when questioned closely, the anxiety is found to be 'free floating' and have no real basis. Panic attacks and neurotic episodes tend to be more common in the week immediately before a menstrual period. Caffeine (in coffee and cola drinks) has also been associated with the onset of attacks.

Patients with a neurosis are excessively anxious for no reason, may be unduly scared of something or some place (a phobia), and may become obviously distressed by their anxiety and/or fear. The distress may take the form of shortness of breath, palpitations, nausea, abdominal pain, headaches or a faint. Anxiety and fear can lead to panic attacks, during which the patient becomes breathless, tight in the chest, dizzy, nauseated, bloated, may vomit and collapse in a faint. These usually occur without warning, but once experienced, the patient will be extremely reluctant to place herself in similar circumstances again.

Many medications are available to assist patients through a crisis. Anxiolytics and sedatives are better used in the short term only, while antidepressants may be used for long periods without adverse effects. Additional treatment involves a mixture of behavioural therapy, psychotherapy and social counselling. Behavioural therapy involves gradually taking the patient through more and more stressful and fear-producing circumstances until the anxiety response wears off. Psychotherapy involves analysing the patient's reaction to their past and present situation. Group therapy may be employed to give additional encouragement. Social counselling requires a doctor, psychologist or social worker to advise the family and friends on how they should assist the patient. Activities that accentuate any phobias or anxieties will be discouraged, and the family will be taught how to encourage a more normal interaction with society by the patient.

The longer the neurosis has been present, the harder it will be to treat. Long-term treatment and encouragement by a sympathetic doctor is essential in all cases.

See also ANXIETY; ANXIOLYTICS; BENZODIAZEPINES; NEUROSES;

OBSESSIVE COMPULSIVE NEUROSES; PHOBIA; POST TRAUMATIC STRESS DISORDER; SOCIAL ANXIETY DISORDER; STRESS and separate entries for other diseases mentioned above.

ANXIOLYTICS

Anxiolytics are a group of medications that reduce anxiety. Most of the medications in this class are the benzodiazepines (eg. diazepam, oxazepam), which are dealt with separately. The other common anxiolytics designed for short-term use in anxiety states are buspirone (Buspar) and meprobomate (Equanil). They should be avoided during pregnancy and breast feeding, and they interact with alcohol. Buspirone does not cause dependence, but is slow to act. Side effects may include dizziness, insomnia, nausea and drowsiness. They should be used with caution in patients with liver disease, and when driving or operating machinery.
See also BARBITURATES; BENZODIAZEPINES; MEDICATION

AORTA

The aorta is the main artery leading from the heart. It passes up from the heart, then curves back and down beside the spine to end by dividing into the main arteries to the legs (common iliac arteries) at the back of the abdomen, just below the navel. It is about 2.5cm. in diameter, and has a thick muscular wall to withstand the varying pressure of blood within it.

Arteries branch from it to supply the head (carotid arteries), arms (brachial arteries), liver (hepatic artery), kidneys (renal arteries) and bowel (mesenteric arteries).

If weakened or damaged it may balloon out to form an aneurysm, which may burst without warning and cause massive internal bleeding.
See also AORTIC ANEURYSM; AORTIC VALVE; ARTERY; COARCTATION OF THE AORTA; HEART

AORTIC ANEURYSM

The aorta is the main large artery that takes blood from the heart to the abdomen and legs, and is between two and three cm. in diameter. If the thick wall of the aorta develops a weak spot, sometimes due to deposits of hard cholesterol in its wall, the artery may start to balloon out at one point to form a firm, pulsing lump known as an aneurysm. This aneurysm is at imminent danger of bursting, and if this occurs there is severe pain, and even in the best hospitals, half the patients die. Surgical correction of an aortic aneurysm at the earliest opportunity is therefore vital.
See also ANEURYSM; AORTA

AORTA AND MAIN ARTERIES
(AND THE ORGANS THEY SUPPLY)

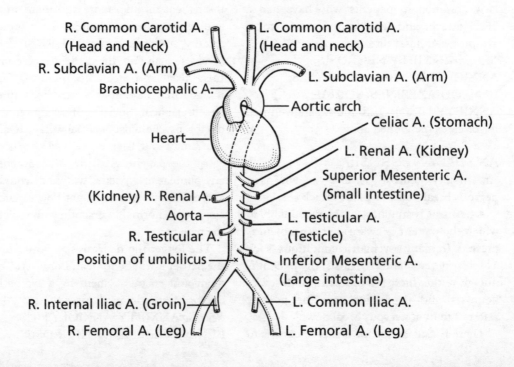

R. Common Carotid A. (Head and Neck)
L. Common Carotid A. (Head and neck)
R. Subclavian A. (Arm)
Brachiocephalic A.
L. Subclavian A. (Arm)
Aortic arch
Celiac A. (Stomach)
Heart
L. Renal A. (Kidney)
Superior Mesenteric A. (Small intestine)
(Kidney) R. Renal A.
Aorta
L. Testicular A. (Testicle)
R. Testicular A.
Position of umbilicus
Inferior Mesenteric A. (Large intestine)
R. Internal Iliac A. (Groin)
L. Common Iliac A.
R. Femoral A. (Leg)
L. Femoral A. (Leg)

AORTIC REGURGITATION
See AORTIC VALVE INCOMPETENCE

AORTIC STENOSIS
See AORTIC VALVE STENOSIS;
COARCTATION OF THE AORTA

AORTIC UNFOLDING
The aorta is the main artery of the body and is two to three cm. across. It starts from the top of the heart, bends (or folds) over, and then runs down the back of the chest and belly along the inside of the backbone. It looks like an upside down 'J'. With ageing, the bend in the aorta as it curls around from the top of the heart to run down the back of the chest becomes a less sharp bend. The aorta does not fold over on itself as much as it did before, and so in medical jargon, the aorta is said to be 'unfolded'. The unfolding may be revealed by an x-ray of the chest.

The aorta may be unfolded and dilated by an aneurysm, but in most cases it is merely a sign of advancing age, and nothing more.
See also AORTA; AORTIC ANEURYSM

AORTIC VALVE
The aortic valve is the tough cartilaginous valve in the heart that allows oxygenated blood to flow from the left ventricle when the heart contracts, into the aorta and thence throughout the body. When the heart relaxes, the valve closes to prevent blood flowing back from the aorta and into the heart. Failure or leakage of the valve makes the heart pumping action inefficient and has serious consequences.
See also AORTIC VALVE
INCOMPETENCE; AORTIC VALVE
STENOSIS; COARCTATION OF THE
AORTA; HEART; MITRAL VALVE

AORTIC VALVE INCOMPETENCE
Aortic valve incompetence (aortic regurgitation) is a leak of the aortic valve in the heart which sits between the left ventricle and the aorta, and normally stops blood that has been pumped out to the body from running back into the heart. The valve damage may be caused by rheumatic fever, endocarditis, high blood pressure, syphilis or a birth defect.

If only a slight leak is present, there will be no symptoms, but if the leak worsens, the patient will become short of breath, develop chest pain, and become very tired. There may be significant leakage before symptoms occur, and then the patient may deteriorate rapidly with heart failure. The defect is diagnosed by echocardiography (ultrasound) or passing a catheter through an artery and into the heart.

Medications to reduce blood pressure may give relief, but if possible, surgical correction should be undertaken once symptoms are present. The prognosis depends on the severity, but is good if regurgitation is mild or surgical replacement of the valve is possible.
See also AORTIC VALVE; HEART;
RHEUMATIC FEVER and separate entries for other diseases mentioned above.

AORTIC VALVE STENOSIS
Aortic valve stenosis is the narrowing of the aortic valve in the heart which sits between the left ventricle and the aorta, and normally stops blood that has been pumped out to the body from running back into the heart. An aortic valve stenosis prevents the blood from being easily pumped from the heart into the aorta and therefore to the rest of the body.

The problem may be congenital (present at birth), or may develop because of rheumatic fever or hardening of the valve from high blood pressure and/or high cholesterol levels.

Symptoms are often absent in mild cases, but when more serious, chest pain (that may progress to angina), fainting with exercise and an irregular heartbeat occur. Heart failure or a heart attack due to the excessive load placed on the heart muscle may occur in advanced cases.

The stenosis is diagnosed by hearing a typical murmur produced by the blood rushing through the narrowed valve, echocardiography (ultrasound) or passing a catheter through an artery and into the heart.

Once symptoms occur, surgery to correct the narrowing should be performed. There are good results if surgery is possible, but half those with symptoms will die within three years without surgery.
See also AORTIC VALVE; COARCTATION
OF THE AORTA; RHEUMATIC FEVER;
STENOSIS and separate entries for other diseases mentioned above.

APGAR SCORE
The Apgar score is a number that is given by doctors or midwives to a baby immediately after birth, and again five minutes later. The score gives a rough assessment of the

baby's general health. The name is taken from Dr Virginia Apgar, an American anaesthetist, who devised the system in 1953. The score is derived by giving a value of 0, 1 or 2 to each of five variables – heart rate, breathing, muscle tone, reflexes and colour. The maximum score is 10.

APGAR SCORE

SIGN	0	1	2
Heart rate	Absent	Below 100	Above 100
Breathing	Absent	Weak	Good
Muscle tone	Limp	Poor	Good
Reflexes	Nil	Poor	Good
Colour	Blue/ pale	Blue hands and feet	Pink

When estimated at birth, a baby is considered to be seriously distressed if the Apgar score is 5, and critical if the score is 3, when urgent resuscitation is necessary. The situation becomes critical if the score remains below 5 at five minutes after birth. A score of 7 or above is considered normal.
See also LABOUR; PREGNANCY

APHASIA
See SPEECH, DIFFICULT

APHTHOUS ULCER
See MOUTH ULCER

APLASTIC ANAEMIA
Aplastic anaemia is a very rare, but extremely serious form of anaemia caused by a failure of the bone marrow and spleen to produce new red blood cells. As old red blood cells die, they are not replaced, leading to a rapidly progressive and severe anaemia. Reasons for the failure of the blood cell production include poisons, toxins, insecticides, nuclear irradiation, severe viral infections and some drugs. In more than half the cases, no cause can be found.

In addition to the normal symptoms of anaemia of weakness, tiredness and pallor, these patients have a fever, bleeding into the skin, a rapid heart rate, and increased susceptibility to infection. Heart, lung and other organ failure may occur suddenly. It is diagnosed by examining a blood film under a microscope.

Repeated blood transfusion can keep the patient alive in the short term only, so any cause must be eliminated if it can be found. Steroid drugs may control the condition, but the only effective long term cure is a bone marrow transplant. The donor must be closely related to the patient, but cannot be one of the parents. Brothers and sisters are usually the best donors. The procedure involves taking a small amount of bone marrow from the pelvic bone or breast bone of the donor, and injecting it into the bone marrow of the patient. Unfortunately, rejection is a far greater problem with a bone marrow transplant than with other forms of transplant, and consequently, up to half the patients will eventually die from the condition.
See also ANAEMIA; BONE MARROW BIOPSY; TRANSPLANTS AND IMPLANTS

APOCRINE GLAND
See GLAND; SWEAT GLANDS

APOPHYSITIS OF THE TIBIAL TUBEROSITY
See OSGOOD-SCHLATTER'S DISEASE

APPENDECTOMY
The only effective treatment of appendicitis is surgery, and because of the serious consequences of a ruptured appendix, surgeons will remove the offending organ if there is a significant suspicion of appendicitis. Occasionally a normal appendix will be found in such cases, but it is far better to be safe than very sorry.

Removal of the appendix (appendectomy or appendicectomy) is a simple operation and takes about twenty minutes under a general anaesthetic. Unless there are complications, the patient should only have a small scar low down on the right side of the abdomen, often below the bikini line in women. Through this small incision, the appendix is found, the base is clamped, it is cut free of the surrounding structures and blood vessels, and then the base is cut through and the appendix removed. The stump of tissue from where the appendix was cut is carefully cleaned, and then oversewn to prevent any gut contents from leaking. The wound is then closed, with each layer of tissue being separately sutured.

If the surgeon is certain about the diagnosis, the appendix has not ruptured, and the patient is appropriate in other ways (eg. not overweight), the surgeon may consider removing the appendix by laparoscopy which is technically more difficult, but allows faster recovery. The operation is performed through three or four one centimetre incisions.

The removed appendix will be sent to a pathologist for further checking under a microscope so that the diagnosis can be confirmed and any other disease excluded. The patient will be in hospital between two and four days with an open operation, but only one or two days if performed through a laparoscope, and can return to work in seven to ten days. Removal of the appendix has no adverse effects on an individual.
See also APPENDICITIS; APPENDIX; LAPAROSCOPY

APPENDICECTOMY
See APPENDECTOMY

APPENDICITIS
Appendicitis is infection of the appendix, which is a narrow dead-end tube about twelve cm. long that attaches to the caecum (first part of the large intestine). It is an almost unknown condition in poorer countries for dietary reasons, and the lack of fibre in Western diets is often blamed for the infection, although its incidence is steadily falling due to better dietary education. In other mammals, particularly those that eat grass, the appendix is an important structure which aids in the digestion of cellulose, but in humans it serves no useful purpose.

If the narrow tube of the appendix becomes blocked by faeces, food, mucus or some foreign body, bacteria start breeding in the closed-off area behind the blockage. Pain develops around the navel, but soon moves to the lower right side of the abdomen just above the pelvic bone and steadily worsens. It is often associated with loss of appetite, slight diarrhoea and a mild fever. Depending on the position of the infected appendix, appendicitis can have variable symptoms, and sometimes, when it lies behind the caecum (retrocaecal appendicitis), its symptoms may be so misleading that the diagnosis is easily missed by a doctor. If untreated, the appendix becomes steadily more infected, full of pus, and eventually bursts to cause peritonitis.

There is no specific diagnostic test, but blood and urine tests and sometimes an ultra-

APPENDICITIS

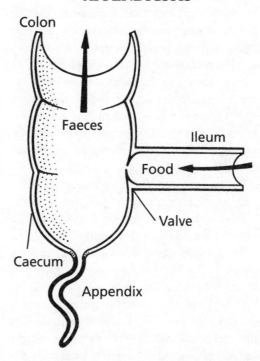

sound scan, are done to exclude other causes of pain.

The only effective treatment is surgical removal of the appendix in a simple operation (appendectomy).
See also APPENDECTOMY; APPENDIX; PERITONITIS

APPENDIX
The appendix is a dead-end hollow tube that can vary from five to twenty cm. in length and is about one cm. in diameter. It is attached at its open end to the caecum, which is part of the large intestine.

The appendix serves no useful purpose in humans, and a small number of people are born without one, but in more primitive animals it nurtures the bacteria that are necessary to digest the cellulose in grass. Rabbits have a huge appendix in proportion to the rest of their bowel.

The appendix floats relatively freely from its attachment, and may lie below, in front of, behind or beside the caecum. If the tube of the appendix becomes blocked by faeces or other material, it may become infected in appendicitis.
See also APPENDECTOMY; APPENDICITIS; CAECUM; LARGE INTESTINE.

APPETITE, EXCESS

An excessive appetite, continued hunger despite eating, and overeating are actually slightly different problems, but as they overlap considerably, all will be dealt with here.

Pregnancy is a very normal cause of excessive hunger. In the first three or four months of pregnancy, women often eat enormous amounts of food, with minimal increase in weight, due to their increased metabolic (body chemistry) activity.

Bulimia is a psychiatric condition in which anxious patients consume excessive amounts of food, often sweets or fatty foods, and then vomit to get rid of the food and so stay slim.

The thyroid gland in the front of the neck produces the hormone thyroxine, which acts as an accelerator for every cell in the body. If there is an excess of thyroxine (hyperthyroidism), all organs will function more rapidly, and symptoms will include sweating, weight loss, diarrhoea, malabsorption, hunger, nervousness, heat intolerance, rapid heart rate, warm skin, tremor and prominent eyes.

The early symptoms of diabetes are unusual tiredness, increased thirst and hunger, excess passing of urine, weight loss despite a large food intake, itchy rashes, recurrent vaginal thrush infections, pins and needles and blurred vision.

Damage to the pituitary gland under the brain, or the part of the brain (hypothalamus) that controls it, may result in inappropriate signals being sent to the thyroid, ovaries, testes, pancreas and other glands of the body to create an excessive appetite as well as other varied symptoms.

Patients with a peptic ulcer or stomach inflammation (gastritis) will find that food eases their pain, but unfortunately the pain returns an hour or so later. As a result they may eat excessively to control their discomfort.
See also OBESITY and separate entries for diseases mentioned above.

APPETITE, LACK OF

A vast range of problems may cause a loss of appetite (anorexia). Obviously, any condition that causes nausea or vomiting, or pain with eating (eg. dental disease, mouth ulcers) may be responsible, as may physical or emotional stress.

Psychological problems such as social isolation (particularly in the elderly), eating and behavioural fads, and prolonged anxiety will all have this effect.

Viral or bacterial infections as diverse as influenza, the common cold, urinary tract infections, pneumonia, gastroenteritis, hepatitis (liver infection) and glandular fever (infectious mononucleosis) will all reduce appetite. A fever, due to an infection or any other cause (eg. cancer) may also be responsible.

Serious illnesses of almost any major organ will reduce appetite. Examples include most types of cancer (loss of appetite is often a very early sign of bowel cancer and leukaemia), bowel inflammation or infection (eg. appendicitis, Crohn's disease), pancreatitis, heart failure (eg. after a heart attack), constant shortness of breath from lung damage (eg. emphysema), a stroke, or failure of the liver (eg. cirrhosis) or kidneys (eg. uraemia, glomerulonephritis).

A malfunction of any of the glands that control the body's hormone levels will also affect appetite. Under activity of the pituitary gland under the brain, the thyroid gland in the neck, and the adrenal glands on each kidney are examples.

Anorexia nervosa is a psychiatric condition that normally occurs in young women who have a distorted image of their own body. They believe that they are fat when they are not, and so starve themselves in order to lose excessive amounts of weight.

Patients with endogenous depression (for which there is no obvious cause) have an imbalance of chemicals that normally occur in the brain to control mood. They slowly become sadder and sadder, more irritable, anxious, unable to sleep, lose appetite and weight, and may feel there is no purpose in living.

Alcoholics may develop malnutrition due to loss of appetite and use the calories in alcohol for food.

Diabetes may cause both excess hunger if sugar levels are increased, or reduced appetite if the acidic toxins in the blood from the excess sugar build up to very high levels (ketosis).

Strangely, patients who are malnourished often have a poor appetite until they actually start eating, when they become ravenous, and food intake must be carefully regulated to prevent diarrhoea and vomiting.

Smoking will reduce appetite, and one of the reasons that many people gain weight after they stop smoking is that their appetite returns, and they can taste and enjoy food more.

Numerous medications may reduce appetite as a side effect. Examples include diuretics (remove fluid from body), digoxin (for heart disease), narcotics (for pain relief) and amphetamines (stimulants that are used occasionally by doctors, and often illegally). *See also* FEVER; NAUSEA AND VOMITING; WEIGHT LOSS and separate entries for diseases mentioned above.

APPETITE REDUCING MEDICATION
See ANORECTICS

ARACHNOPHOBIA
Arachnophobia is an abnormal fear of spiders.
See also PHOBIA

ARCUS SENILIS
Arcus senilis is a common eye pigmentation disorder in which there is deposition of fats around the edge of the iris (coloured part of the eye) in the elderly and those with abnormally high blood fat levels. A white ring can be seen around the iris of both eyes, but vision is unaffected. The blood fat levels of the patient should be checked, but no diagnostic tests are necessary. There is no cure, but it is a mild cosmetic problem only.
See also EYE

AREOLA
See BREAST; NIPPLE

ARGENTAFFINOMA
See CARCINOID SYNDROME

ARM
See ARM PAIN; ELBOW; HAND; HUMERUS; RADIUS; SHOULDER; WRIST

ARM FRACTURE
See COLLES' FRACTURE

ARM PAIN
Pain in the arm may come from the bones, muscles, ligaments, tendons, blood vessels, nerves and skin that make up the limb; or may start in the neck or chest (referred pain).

Any injury to the arm will cause pain at the point of injury. Bones may break, ligaments be strained, muscles tear, tendons rupture, joints dislocate or any number of other injuries to these structures. Over-use of these tissues may also cause pain as tendons stretch (tendinitis) and muscles become inflamed (repetitive strain injury).

Arthritis may affect the shoulder, elbow or wrist to cause arm pain. Osteoarthritis is the most common form, but rheumatoid arthritis, and even gout, may occur.

Fibromyositis occurs in large muscles that have been overused and damaged repeatedly by heavy work or exercise. Scattered muscle cells are replaced by fibrous scar tissue to disrupt the structure of the muscle and cause a deep ache that worsens with use.

Polymyalgia rheumatica is a generalised inflammation of muscles that particularly affects those in the hip, shoulder and arm, as well as causing a fever, tiredness and weight loss.

The painful arc syndrome causes pain during the mid-range movement of the shoulder joint as the arm is moved away from the body. It is caused by nipping of tissue between the top of the humerus (upper arm bone) and the shoulder blade.

The shoulder has a greater range of movement than any other joint in the body, and consequently has a very complex network of muscles, ligaments, bones and tendons to support it. These supporting structures are known as the rotator cuff. If there is a tear or rupture to any of the tissues that move and support the shoulder, due to injury, strain or ageing, pain will be felt with certain movements, depending upon which tissues are affected.

Referred pain is quite common, and is due to irritation of nerves in the neck or chest that then run down into the arm. If a nerve is pinched or damaged at any point along its long course, quite severe pain will be felt beyond that point.

The most significant cause of referred pain is that coming from the heart. This may be angina (a reduced blood supply to the heart muscle) or a heart attack (complete blockage of blood supply to one part of the heart muscle). The left arm is affected far more often than the right in these cases.

Nerve pinching may occur in the neck at the point where the nerve passes between the vertebrae as it leaves the spinal cord. Arthritis, a slipped disc or other injury may be responsible. Pain is felt along the course of the nerve down the arm. Some people are born with an extra rib in the neck above the normal first rib. This cervical rib can put pressure on the nerves running from the neck to the arm (Naffziger syndrome), affecting their function and causing pins and needles sensation, pain and weakness in the hand and arm.

Uncommon causes of arm pain include osteomyelitis (an infection of bone), septic arthritis (an infection of the fluid within a joint), tumours or cancer of bone (osteosarcoma), scapulo-costal syndrome, multiple myeloma (cancer of the cells in the bone marrow), and pronator syndrome.
See also BONE; BONE PAIN; ELBOW; HAND PAIN; MUSCLE; SHOULDER and separate entries for diseases mentioned above.

ARM WEAKNESS
See ERB-DUCHENNE PALSY; KLUMPKE PALSY

ARNOLD-CHIARI MALFORMATION
See SYRINGOMYELIA

ARRHYTHMIA
An arrhythmia is any irregular rhythm of the heart.
See also ATRIAL EXTRASYSTOLES; ATRIAL FIBRILLATION; LONG Q-T SYNDROME; LOWN-GANONG-LEVINE SYNDROME; PAROXYSMAL ATRIAL TACHYCARDIA; SICK SINUS SYNDROME; VENTRICULAR EXTRASYSTOLES; VENTRICULAR FIBRILLATION; WOLFF-PARKINSON-WHITE SYNDROME

ARSENIC
Arsenic (As) is an element used in industry and mining. It may be encountered in smelting (eg. gold, lead, zinc and nickel), wood preservatives, pesticides, herbicides and some folk remedies. It may be accumulated slowly by workers in such industries, or acute poisoning may occur if the mineral is swallowed.

Symptoms of acute poisoning include a difficulty in swallowing, vomiting, diarrhoea, thirst and poor urine output. Death may occur in two or three days. The lethal dose is about 150mg.

First aiders should induce vomiting if arsenic is recently swallowed, and the patient should go to hospital, where the stomach will be pumped out and activated charcoal given. Copious fluids are then given by a drip into a vein to flush out the poison, and medications are given to neutralise it.

Chronic poisoning is characterised by nerve damage affecting sensation and muscle control, kidney damage, skin changes and irritation of the nose and mouth lining.

The prognosis depends on age and weight of patient, and dose of arsenic.

Arsenic can be detected in hair samples indefinitely after death from the poison.
See also CYANIDE; STRYCHNINE

ARTERIAL GAS EMBOLISM
See BENDS

ARTERIAL PRESSURE POINTS
If direct pressure on a wound is not effective, or the area of damage is too widespread for direct pressure, bleeding from a wound can be stopped by applying pressure to the artery that supplies the area with blood. The best place to do this is to locate a pressure point between the wound and the heart where the artery can be pressed against a bone. The pressure point for the arm is halfway along the inside of the upper arm. For the leg, it is about halfway along the fold of skin in the groin that separates the thigh from the abdomen.
See also ARTERY; BLEEDING; FIRST AID

ARTERIOGRAM
See ANGIOGRAM

ARTERIOSCLEROSIS
Arteriosclerosis, or hardening of the arteries, is a degeneration of the arteries in the body, making them hard and inelastic. It is usually associated with atherosclerosis, which is the excessive deposition of hard fatty plaques and nodules within the artery and its wall.

It usually occurs in the elderly, and those who have a high blood level of cholesterol, but may also be caused and aggravated by high blood pressure. Hard fatty deposits form at points of turbulence within a major artery (eg. the junction of two arteries, or a bend in the artery) to narrow the artery and gradually restrict the flow of blood to the tissues beyond.

Symptoms depend on which arteries are affected. An affected artery is less able to cope with pressure changes and more likely to rupture, causing a leak of blood, sometimes into vital structures such as the brain. If a neck artery (carotid artery) is involved, patients cannot cope with sudden changes in position (eg. getting out of bed) without becoming dizzy or light-headed. If the leg arteries are involved, the leg muscles become painful, particularly when climbing slopes or stairs (claudication). If heart arteries are involved, angina occurs. If arteries to the brain are involved, the patient may develop a multitude of bizarre symptoms, become light headed, dizzy, confused, or black out as the brain does not receive sufficient blood to operate correctly.

An embolism occurs when a piece of the hard fat within the artery, breaks away and travels with the blood along the arteries to a point which is too narrow for it to pass. This causes no problem in most parts of the body, but if the blockage is in the heart or brain, a heart attack or stroke will occur.

Arteriosclerosis is diagnosed by doppler flow (ultrasound) studies on the movement of blood through arteries, and by angiograms (artery x-rays) in which an x-ray visible dye is injected to outline an artery. Cholesterol levels can be checked by a fasting blood test.

The condition is better prevented than treated, by keeping cholesterol levels and blood pressure within normal limits. Narrowed arteries can be opened slightly with medications that relax the muscles in the artery walls, or that ease the passage of blood cells through the narrowing, but in advanced cases, surgery is necessary.

There are three types of surgery possible: –
• Bypass grafts use tubes of synthetic material, or arteries or veins from elsewhere in the body, to bypass the blocked area.
• Endarterectomy involves opening the blocked artery and cleaning out the fatty deposits.
• Balloon angioplasty is used to dilate blocked arteries by passing a fine tube, with a deflated balloon at the end, along an artery and into the narrowed segment where the balloon is inflated, forcing open the blockage. Sometimes a stent (tube shaped metal grid) is left behind to keep the artery open.

Medication can help many cases, and surgery can be extremely successful in curing the condition.
See also ANGINA; ARTERY; CLAUDICATION; HEART ATTACK; HYPERCHOLESTEROLAEMIA; STENT; STROKE; TRANSIENT ISCHAEMIC ATTACK

ARTERIOVENOUS FISTULA

An arteriovenous fistula is an abnormal connection (fistula) between an artery and a vein. It may be congenital (developmental abnormality), or due to an injury or cancer. Sometimes a fistula is surgically created in the forearm for insertion of a shunt used for kidney dialysis.

The symptoms depend upon the site and severity. An abnormal pulsating lump may be seen or felt, or the fistula may reduce the blood supply to vital organs, and affect their function. Sometimes a blood clot can form in the turbulent blood flow in a fistula, and travel through the veins to the heart and lungs to cause a pulmonary embolus.

It is diagnosed by arteriography (x-ray of blood vessels) in which a dye is injected into an artery and its movement through the fistula into the vein recorded.

Surgical closure or destruction of the fistula is the only treatment, and results are usually very good.
See also ARTERY; FISTULA; PULMONARY EMBOLUS; VEIN

ARTERY

Arteries are part of the cardiovascular system by which blood circulates throughout the body. Arteries take blood away from the heart, whereas veins carry blood to the heart. Most arteries carry blood that has been enriched with oxygen by the lungs to other parts of the body, but the exception is the pulmonary artery which carries blood that has been depleted of oxygen on its journey throughout the body from the heart to the lungs, so that it can be replenished with oxygen.

At any given moment about 15% of our blood supply is in our arteries. So that blood can be carried throughout the entire body as efficiently as possible, blood in the arteries is carried at much higher pressure (the blood pressure) than blood in the veins. The two major arteries are the pulmonary artery and the aorta. The aorta is shaped rather like an upside down capital J and leads out of the left side of the heart, curves across the top of the chest, then passes down the back of the chest and abdomen to a point just below the umbilicus. Other arteries, extending through the body and becoming smaller as they go, branch out from the aorta and are fed by it.

Each time the heart contracts it pumps blood into the arteries. If an artery is healthy, it has strong muscular walls which are elastic enough to expand as the blood is pumped in and then contract before the next surge. If an artery is cut, it will bleed in rhythmic spurts, each spurt relating to the surge of blood caused by the regular pumping of the heart.

In general, arteries are situated along the inner surfaces of bones, which protect them from damage, and they are usually connected in such a way that, if one is damaged, the blood supply to an organ can still be maintained. An exception is the heart where there is no alternative method of blood supply, so that if an artery in the heart is blocked part of the heart muscle dies, causing a heart attack.
See also ANGIOGRAM; AORTA; ARTERIOSCLEROSIS; CLAUDICATION; HEART; VASODILATORS; VASOCONSTRICTORS; VEIN

ARTHRITIS

By strict definition, arthritis is inflammation in a joint – any joint from the jaw to the big toe – and a joint is a point at which two bones come together and normally can move in relation to each other. A joint itself is made up of the bones that form it, the ligaments, tendons and muscles that support it, the cartilages that stabilise it, the synovial fluid that fills it, and the synovial membrane that lines it.

There are hundreds of reasons for a joint to become inflamed and painful. A wide range of conditions that do not affect joints directly may have arthritis as an accompanying symptom.

Any injury to a joint that causes damage to the joint surfaces, bleeding into the joint, a tear to the cartilages or ligaments, or a break of the bones forming the joint, will lead to inflammation and pain in or around that joint.

Osteoarthritis is the most common form of arthritis. It is not strictly speaking a wear and tear injury to a joint, but can be considered as such without going into detailed physiology.

Rheumatoid arthritis is the other major cause of joint swelling and deformity associated with both pain and loss of function. The body develops antibodies that inappropriately reject the lining synovial membrane of the affected joint, in the same way that the body attempts to reject a donated transplanted kidney.

Many viral and bacterial infections that do not infect joints directly, may nevertheless cause joint pain by inflaming surrounding tissues. Examples include influenza, Ross River fever, mumps, glandular fever (infectious mononucleosis), brucellosis (caught from cattle), german measles (rubella), hepatitis, tuberculosis (TB), Lyme disease (transmitted by tics from mice and deer), syphilis and gonorrhoea (sexually transmitted diseases).

Gout is caused by the build up of excess levels of uric acid in the blood. Uric acid itself is a break-down product of proteins, particularly those found in red meat, offal and shellfish. If the uric acid reaches a critical level, particularly in joints that are put under considerable pressure (eg. ball of the foot), it may come out of solution and form crystals which under the microscope look like double ended needles which cause the severe pain, tenderness, redness and swelling of the joint.

Less common causes of arthritis include septic arthritis (bacterial infection of a joint), osteomyelitis (infection of bone), ankylosing spondylitis (long-term inflammation of the small joints between the vertebrae in the back), Osgood Schlatter's disease (inflammation of the knee in teenagers), synovitis (inflammation of the synovial membrane in every joint), psoriasis, systemic lupus erythematosus and other autoimmune diseases, and bursitis.

Almost any type of cancer, anywhere in the body, may cause arthritis if the cancer spreads to the joint or adjacent bones.

Damage to the nerves supplying a joint by severe diabetes, direct injury, spinal cord disease or nerve inflammation (neuralgia) may cause pain that appears to come from a joint.

There are many other rare causes of arthritis (eg. eosinophilia-myalgia syndrome).
See also BACK PAIN;

CHONDROCALCINOSIS;
CHONDROMALACIA PATELLAE;
JOINT; JOINT, RED; JOINT, SWOLLEN;
KNEE PAIN; NONSTEROIDAL ANTI-
INFLAMMATORY DRUGS; SHOULDER
PAIN and separate entries for diseases
mentioned above.

ARTHRITIS MEDICATIONS
See ANALGESICS; ANTIRHEUMATICS;
LINIMENTS; NONSTEROIDAL ANTI-
INFLAMMATORY DRUGS; STEROIDS

ARTHROSCOPY
Arthroscopy is a technique for the diagnosis
and treatment of joint problems. It has virtually revolutionised the treatment of knee
injuries, but joints as small as the jaw joint can
also be entered by an arthroscope. The patient
is usually given a general anaesthetic, but in
some cases a local anaesthetic can be used.

A knee arthroscopy is performed by an
orthopaedic surgeon who makes a small incision in the knee and inserts the thin tube that
is the arthroscope. This enables an examination of the inside of the knee to establish
what particular part is damaged (eg. cartilage, tendon, ligament) and then, if necessary, remedial surgery can be carried out
there and then, such as the removal of bits of
damaged cartilage. If required, separate incisions can be made to enable the surgeon
access to the damaged tissue, but these are
tiny and the whole operation is viewed by the
surgeon through the arthroscope. The advantages of having tiny cuts over a large incision
are obvious, not least from the point of view
of recuperation.
See also ENDOSCOPE; KNEE; KNEE
MENISCUS TEAR

ARTIFICIAL CONCEPTION
In recent times, techniques have been developed to enable conception to be carried out
artificially without the need for the act of
intercourse. At its simplest level, this is called
artificial insemination and involves male
sperm being deposited into the woman
usually by means of a syringe. This may be
undertaken when the woman's partner is
infertile and the couple decides to have a
child technically fathered by another man
with whom the woman does not wish to have
intercourse.

In vitro fertilisation (IVF) takes place
outside the human body and was first successfully carried out in England in 1978. 'In
vitro' means in glass, i.e. outside the body.

In IVF, an egg (ovum) is removed from the
ovary of a woman at a precise time that is
determined by hormones given to her in
order to stimulate ovulation (production of
an ovum or egg). The egg is removed under
general anaesthetic in a process known as
laparoscopy, in which two tubes, each about
1cm in diameter and 20-30cm long, are put
into the abdominal cavity through small cuts
on the surface of the abdomen. One cut may
be placed in the umbilicus to minimise scarring. The gynaecologist looks through one telescope tube, and through the other operates to
remove the egg.

The egg(s) obtained are placed in a special
nutrient solution in a test tube or flat glass
dish. To this is added sperm from the woman's
husband, or if the husband is infertile, another
donor's sperm may be used (AID – artificial
insemination by donor). The eggs are examined under a microscope, and any eggs that
are fertilised are then placed into the woman's
uterus (womb) using a fine tube that is passed
through the vagina and cervix into the uterus.
From this position, it is hoped that the fertilised egg(s) (embryos) will implant into the
wall of the uterus and grow into a baby (or
babies). The success rate with any one IVF
procedure is only about 20%, but in a series of
procedures, success rates in excess of 70%
have been achieved.

The newer technique is GIFT (gamete
intra-Fallopian transfer). A gamete is a technical name for an ovum (egg) or a sperm. In this
procedure, the egg is obtained in the same way
as for IVF, but it is then placed into the
woman's Fallopian tube along with a quantity
of the husband's or donor's sperm, and fertilisation occurs in the biologically normal place
– the Fallopian tube. The fertilised egg then
migrates down to the uterus in the normal
manner for implantation. The GIFT technique
is only useful in women who have a normal
Fallopian tube and a disease-free pelvis. Its
success rate is 35% for each procedure.

There are a number of other variations on
both these procedures that may be used.
See also GAMETE; INFERTILITY;
PREGNANCY; ZYGOTE

ARTIFICIAL INSEMINATION
See ARTIFICIAL CONCEPTION

As
See ARSENIC

AS
See ANKYLOSING SPONDYLITIS

ASBESTOSIS

Asbestosis is a lung disease caused by the inhalation of fine asbestos particles over a prolonged period of time. Asbestos particles are long, thin filaments, that easily become trapped in the small air tubes (bronchioles) of the lung. The lower part of the lungs is most commonly affected, and it occurs almost exclusively in asbestos factory workers, processors and miners who inhale free-floating particles of asbestos in their workplace. Swallowing small amounts of asbestos or touching asbestos in any form is harmless, but smoking will aggravate the condition.

Sufferers develop shortness of breath, cough, and in advanced cases, blue lips and swollen finger tips. As the disease progresses the patient may have no exercise tolerance and suffer symptoms similar to severe asthma or emphysema. It is easily diagnosed on chest x-ray.

No treatment is available other than removing the person from exposure to further asbestos dust and performing regular chest x-rays to detect mesothelioma as early as possible. Mesothelioma is a rapidly progressive form of lung cancer that occurs almost exclusively in asbestosis victims. Seven percent of those with asbestosis develop mesothelioma. Others suffer from varying degrees of lung impairment.
See also BREATH, SHORT OF;
EMPHYSEMA; LUNG; LUNG CANCER;
MESOTHELIOMA; SILICOSIS

ASCARIASIS

The roundworm *Ascaris lumbricoides* is one of a group of roundworms (known as nematodes) that may infest the human gut. Infestations are common in Indonesia, south-east Asia and other less developed countries.

Adult roundworms are between twenty and forty cm. long, and live in the small intestine. After fertilisation, the females release a large number of microscopic eggs that pass out in the faeces and can survive for many years in the soil. In areas where human faeces are used as a fertiliser, it is easy for them to be swallowed on food; or if sewerage contaminates the water supply, they may be swallowed in a drink. Once swallowed, the eggs hatch into larvae that burrow through the gut wall into the bloodstream and move through the heart into the lungs. There they penetrate into the small air tubes (bronchioles) of the lung, wiggle their way up through larger airways to the back of the throat from where they are swallowed again to enter the small intestine and grow into mature adults that may live for up to a year.

At all stages the larvae and worms can cause symptoms including a cough, shortness of breath, fever, wheezing, chest pain, abdominal pains and discomfort, nausea and gut obstruction. If severe infestations are left uncontrolled, the worms may move into the gall bladder and pancreas, rupture the bowel, and cause other severe complications that may result in death. The diagnosis is confirmed by finding eggs in the faeces.

A number of drugs are available to treat the disease, but they often have side effects. If patients are given the correct treatment at a relatively early stage of the disease, full recovery is normal.
See also NEMATODE; ROUNDWORM

ASCITES

Ascites is the accumulation of excessive amounts of fluid in the abdominal cavity. It is sometimes noticed by patients as a gain in weight or dull, heavy discomfort in the belly. If there is a lot of fluid, the abdomen will become swollen and distended. The fluid may come from inflammation of the belly lining (peritoneum), increased pressure in the veins draining blood from the belly or inflammation of the organs within the abdomen.

Common causes include cirrhosis, hepatitis, liver cancer, blockage of the vein draining the liver and other forms of liver damage. Cancer anywhere in the abdomen (eg. bowel, uterus, ovaries, pancreas), or spreading to the belly from other areas (eg. breast, lung) will inflame the peritoneum and allow fluid to escape through this membrane and into the belly cavity.

If the heart fails to pump effectively (congestive cardiac failure), it may be unable to adequately circulate blood around the body, and the pressure builds up in the veins of the belly, allowing serum (the clear fluid part of blood) to seep out of the veins and into the abdominal cavity. The feet and hands are also swollen, and the patient may cough because of a fluid buildup in the lungs.

Uncommon causes include hypothyroidism (underactive thyroid gland), lymphoma (cancer of the lymph nodes), nephrotic syndrome (kidney failure), pericarditis, malnutrition, Meig syndrome and bilharzia (schistosomiasis).

Fluid can be taken from the abdomen by a needle for analysis, while ultrasound and CT scans, and blood tests are used in an attempt to identify the cause.

The treatment depends on the cause of the ascites.
See also ABDOMEN and separate entries for diseases mentioned above.

ASHERMAN SYNDROME

Asherman syndrome is a complication of pregnancy. If part of the placenta (afterbirth) is retained after childbirth it must be removed, or the woman may continue to bleed, become infected or infertile. The operation is carried out using a small sharp edged spoon with a long handle (curette) to scoop out the remaining placental tissue. If it is carried out too vigorously, the lining of the uterus may be damaged and adhere to the opposite wall, obliterating the cavity inside the uterus where a baby would normally grow during pregnancy. This also prevents the lining of the uterus from developing in the future, menstrual periods stop, and the woman is infertile.

The diagnosis can be confirmed by hysteroscopy (looking into the uterus through a thin tube).

No effective treatment is available. The woman is unable to fall pregnant again, but is otherwise unaffected.
See also ADHESIONS; CURETTE; HYSTEROSCOPY; PLACENTA; UTERUS

ASCORBIC ACID
See VITAMIN C

ASPERGER SYNDROME

Asperger syndrome is a developmental disorder of unknown cause that may be a variant of autism, and is much more common in males.

Patients act inappropriately in social contacts, have a lack of empathy for others, have poor communication skills with poor speech patterns, lack facial expression, develop abnormal preoccupations, have variable intellectual disability and may be poorly coordinated. Other characteristics that sometimes occur include poor posture, poor imagination, inappropriate violence and the inability to memorise information. They may become involved in inappropriate activities.

No specific tests are available, and the diagnosis is made after extensive psychiatric and psychological assessment.

Drugs are not usually helpful, and treatment involves long term behaviour therapy by psychologists, psychiatrists and occupational therapists.
See also AUTISM; BEHAVIOUR THERAPY; VIOLENCE

ASPERGILLOSIS

Aspergillosis is a fungal infection of a wide range of tissues in the body including the ears, lungs, sinuses and skin (particularly burns) that is normally a minor irritation, but in patients who have poor immunity (eg. AIDS or taking chemotherapy for cancer), it may become critically serious if internal organs are infected. It is caused by the fungus *Aspergillus* which passes easily from one person to another.

It is often a very minor problem, and may cause no symptoms, but if the lungs are infected, it causes asthma-like symptoms with a wheeze and cough. The diagnosis is confirmed by examining sputum or other secretions that are infected, and by a specific antibody test on the blood.

Treatment depends on the severity. If internal organs are involved, high doses of potent antifungal drugs such as amphotericin B are used. Normally infection is not a problem, but half of the immunocompromised patients with lung aspergillosis will die, even in the best centres.
See also FUNGI

ASPIRIN
See ANALGESICS; NONSTEROIDAL ANTI-INFLAMMATORY DRUGS

ASTEATOTIC ECZEMA

Asteatotic dermatitis (eczema craquelé) is a common form of dermatitis, usually affecting older people who remain indoors in low humidity and with excess heating during cold weather. The drying of skin from excessive bathing and soap use is also a factor.

Patients develop dry, itchy, cracked, scaling, red skin, usually on the thighs and arms, but sometimes on the hands and trunk. If scratched excessively there may be permanent scarring and damage to the skin. The diagnosis can be confirmed by biopsy if necessary.

Patients should avoid soap, shower instead of bath, humidify the air in the home, and use moisturising creams and medium strength steroid creams. Resolution of the rash is slow initially, but cure is possible with good compliance with treatment.

See also ECZEMA; SKIN

ASTEMIZOLE
See ANTIHISTAMINES

ASTHENIA
See FATIGUE

ASTHMA
Asthma (known as wheezy bronchitis decades ago) is a temporary narrowing of, and excess production of phlegm in, the small airways (bronchioles) through which air flows into and out of the lungs. The narrowing is caused by a spasm in the tiny muscles which surround the bronchioles. One in ten people in Western countries suffers from some degree of asthma, but it is uncommon in developing countries.

The absolute cause is unknown, but certain triggers (eg. colds and other viral infections, temperature changes, allergies, exercise, smoke, dust and other irritants) may start an attack in susceptible individuals. Because it is more common in countries with good hygiene, there is a theory that exposure to bacteria, viruses and dirt in various forms at an early age gives some protection against asthma. The tendency to develop asthma runs in families, along with hay fever and some forms of eczema, to give a fifteen times greater chance of developing the condition.

Asthmatics have more trouble breathing out than breathing in. Attacks may build up slowly over many weeks and the individual may be barely aware of the deterioration in lung function, or a severe attack may start within a minute or two of exposure to a trigger. The narrowing of the airways causes shortness of breath and wheezing, coughing (particularly in children) and tightness and discomfort in the chest. Patients rarely can die rapidly from a sudden, severe asthma attack.

Asthma is diagnosed by respiratory function tests which involve blowing into a number of different machines which either draw a graph or give an electronic reading. The patient's response to medication is also checked on these machines. Once diagnosed it is important to identify any trigger substances if possible by trial and error, or with blood and skin tests.

The management of asthma is divided into two areas – prevention and treatment: –
• Prevention – all but the mildest asthmatics should be using steroid or anti-allergy inhalations to prevent attacks. Severe asthmatics may need to use prednisolone tablets to both prevent and treat their attacks. Those who react to specific substances may benefit from allergen desensitisation.
• Treatment – the best method is by aerosol inhalations which take the medication directly into the lungs where they act to dilate the airways and liquefy the thick mucus. Many of these can have their effectiveness and ease of use improved, particularly in children, if a spacing device or machine nebuliser is used. Mixtures and tablets are also available, but they work more slowly and have greater side effects. Very severe attacks may require oxygen by mask and injections of adrenaline, theophylline or steroids.

Asthma cannot be cured, but doctors can control the disease very effectively in the vast majority of patients.
See also ALLERGY; ASTHMA PREVENTION MEDICATION; ATOPY; BETA-2 AGONISTS; BRONCHODILATORS; HYPER-REACTIVE AIRWAYS DISEASE; LOEFFLER SYNDROME; LUNG; THEOPHYLLINES; WHEEZE

ASTHMA PREVENTION MEDICATION
The prevention of asthma is far more important than treatment, as most patients tend to under-treat or treat too late. Regular use of the appropriate preventer should mean that asthma treatment is rarely necessary. Prevention can be by means of steroid sprays which reduce inflammation in the airways, or the

almost inert allergy preventers.

Steroid sprays include beclomethasone (Aldecin, Becloforte, Becotide), budesonide (Pulmicort) and fluticasone (Flixotide). Side effects may include thrush infection of the mouth, sore mouth and throat, and a dry mouth. Rinsing the mouth after use prevents most of these problems. They should be used with caution in tuberculosis and pregnancy. Doctors should check the patient's lung function regularly to ensure an adequate dose. Many steroid sprays are now being combined in the one delivery device with beta-2 agonists (which treat asthma).

Airway allergy preventers are used less commonly and include sodium cromoglycate (Intal), and nedocromil sodium (Tilade). Side effects may include a hoarse voice and bad taste, but they are safe in pregnancy.
See also ASTHMA; BETA-2 AGONISTS; BRONCHODILATORS; MEDICATION; STEROIDS; THEOPHYLLINES

ASTIGMATISM
See VISION

ASTRAKHAN SPOTTED FEVER
See TYPHUS

ASTROCYTOMA
An astrocytoma is a slow growing, low grade malignant or benign tumour arising in the connective cells of the brain. The cause is unknown.

The symptoms are often very mild and confusing in the early stages, and as a result the tumour may be quite large before it is detected. Common symptoms include visual disturbances, abnormal pituitary gland function, paralysis of facial muscles, incoordination and difficulty in walking. Rarely it may become aggressively malignant and progress rapidly.

The tumour can be visualised by CT and MRI scans, but a biopsy is required for final diagnosis.

Treatment involves surgery to remove growth, and parts that cannot be removed are treated by drugs. Because of their size when diagnosed, they sometimes cannot be completely removed. They are often cured if complete surgical excision is possible, and the outcome is often better in children.
See also BRAIN; GLIOMA; NEUROSURGERY; PITUITARY GLAND

ATAXIA
See COORDINATION POOR; FRIEDREICH'S ATAXIA; WALK ABNORMAL

ATHEROSCLEROSIS
See ARTERIOSCLEROSIS

ATHETOSIS
See WRITHING

ATHLETE'S FOOT
Athlete's foot is a fungal infection of the toes technically known as tinea pedis. The responsible fungi can be found everywhere in the environment in the form of hardy microscopic spores that may survive for decades before being picked up and starting an infection. They multiply in the moist area between the toes, particularly in athletes who sweat and wear close fitting shoes that lead to the ideal warm, damp environment favoured by the fungi. A secondary bacterial infection of the damaged skin may occur.

The infection causes sore, red cracks in the skin under and between the toes. Swabs may be taken to identify the responsible fungus in resistant cases.

Treatment involves antifungal creams, lotions and powders, but in severe cases, antifungal tablets may be taken. Most patients respond well to treatment, but the infection often recurs, particularly if treatment is ceased too soon.
See also FUNGI; TINEA MANUM

ATOPIC CONJUNCTIVITIS
See ALLERGIC CONJUNCTIVITIS

ATOPIC ECZEMA
Atopic eczema or dermatitis, is an abnormal reaction of skin to an irritating substance. The rash may be triggered by changes in climate or diet, stress or fibres in clothing, and tends to occur in areas where the skin folds in upon itself (eg. groin, arm pits, inside elbows, eyelids). It is more common in winter and urban areas, has a peak incidence between six and twelve months of age, and there is a hereditary tendency. Up to a third of the population is atopic, but only 5% of children will develop this skin condition.

Patients develop an extremely itchy rash, but any blisters that form are rapidly destroyed by scratching which changes the normal appearance of the eczema, so that it appears as red, scaly, grazed skin that may be weeping because of a secondary bacterial infection. With repeated irritation, the skin may become hard, thickened, and pebbly.

In most cases, the responsible substance cannot be identified, but skin and blood tests can be performed to tell if a person has an atopic tendency.

Soothing moisturising creams and steroid creams are prescribed to reduce inflammation and itch, and soap substitutes are used to prevent drying the skin. In severe cases, steroid and antihistamine tablets are necessary. There is no cure, but effective control can be obtained in most cases. The majority of children grow out of the condition.
See also ALLERGIC ECZEMA; ATOPY; DERMATITIS; ECZEMA; SKIN

ATOPY
Atopy is the tendency to develop a sudden, excessive sensitivity to a substance. It is similar to allergy, but not the same, as no previous exposure to the substance is required. Hay fever, eczema and asthma may be atopic diseases.
See also ALLERGY; ASTHMA; ATOPIC ECZEMA; HAY FEVER

ATORVASTATIN
See HYPOLIPIDAEMICS

ATP
See CREATINE; MUSCLE

ATRIAL EXTRASYSTOLES
Atrial extrasystoles are abnormal heart beats caused by abnormal nerve impulses from a part of the left atrium (smaller chamber on the left side of the heart) that fires off before the normal heart pacemaker. Patients have a momentary irregularity in the heart beat that may occur very infrequently, or every three or four beats. Rarely it may progress to atrial flutter (multiple extrasystoles) or fibrillation. The diagnosis can be made by an electrocardiogram (ECG).

Often no treatment is necessary, but if the extrasystoles are frequent, medications can be given to regulate the heart rhythm. There is usually a good response to treatment.
See also ARRHYTHMIA; ATRIAL FIBRILLATION; HEART; HEART, EXTRA BEATS

ATRIAL FIBRILLATION
The heart has two small chambers (atria) which receive blood from the lungs and body through large veins, and two large chambers (ventricles) which pump blood out through arteries to the lungs and body. Atrial fibrillation occurs if the atria beat in a rapid uncoordinated manner, and as a result the ventricles (main pumping chambers of the heart) will receive only an intermittent blood supply from the atria, and will beat in a very irregular rhythm. If the atria beat rapidly, but not fast enough to cause irregular contractions by the ventricles, the condition is atrial flutter.

It may occur in normal people at times of stress, but more commonly as a reaction to heart damage such as a heart attack or infection. Other causes include an overactive thyroid gland, heart valve damage, severe high blood pressure, lung damage that restricts blood flow (eg. emphysema), or because of imbalances in body chemistry.

Patients have a very irregular pulse, tiredness due to low blood pressure, palpitations and sometimes chest pains, shortness of breath and fainting. An embolism (blood clot) that may cause a stroke or death if it travels through arteries to the brain may occur due to the formation of a clot in the heart with the irregular pressure patterns caused by the fibrillation. There is also an increased risk of heart failure and heart attack.

It is diagnosed by an electrocardiogram (ECG), but doctors can usually make the diagnosis by analysing the irregular heart beat rhythm.

Numerous medications or electric shock treatments to the heart (electrocardioversion) are available to control the heart rhythm. If the atrial fibrillation remains uncontrolled, an anticoagulant (eg. warfarin) should be used to prevent an embolism.

Most cases can be controlled by medication, but if persistent there is a small mortality rate due to complications.
See also ARRHYTHMIA; ATRIAL EXTRASYSTOLES; HEART; HEART, EXTRA BEATS

ATRIAL FLUTTER
See ATRIAL EXTRASYSTOLES; ATRIAL FIBRILLATION

ATRIAL SEPTAL DEFECT
An atrial septal defect is a congenital hole in the membrane (septum) between the two atria (smaller upper chambers) in the heart that creates an abnormal blood flow within the heart.

The symptoms are very variable depending on the size of the hole. Often there are no symptoms in an infant, but as the child grows symptoms may include blue tinged skin (cyanosis) from poor circulation of blood through lungs, thickened finger tips (clubbing) because of poor oxygen supply, slow growth rate, increased incidence of lung infections, tiredness and weakness. Complications include atrial fibrillation, cor pulmonale (high blood pressure in lungs), heart failure and the defect may be associated with mitral valve stenosis.

A characteristic murmur can be heard through a stethoscope. An electrocardiogram (ECG), echocardiogram (ultrasound of heart), and cardiac catheterisation (passing a pressure measuring tube through an artery or vein into the heart) all demonstrate heart abnormalities.

Very small holes may close spontaneously but if symptoms occur, open heart surgery to close the defect must be performed. This operation is very successful.
See also COR PULMONALE; HEART; VENTRICULAR SEPTAL DEFECT

ATRIAL TACHYCARDIA
See PAROXYSMAL ATRIAL TACHYCARDIA

ATRIUM
See HEART

ATROPHIC
See ATROPHY

ATROPHIC VAGINITIS
Atrophic, postmenopausal or senile vaginitis is a lack of vaginal moisture and lubrication. The vagina is kept moist by the production of mucus from glands in and around it, that become more active during sexual stimulation. After menopause, the female hormone oestrogen is no longer produced by the ovaries. This hormone stimulates the vaginal glands to produce mucus, but without oestrogen, they do not function. Blood tests can be used to measure oestrogen levels.

It is usually a condition of older women who complain of a dry, sore, itchy vagina. Ulceration and bacterial infection of the vagina may occur, and there is an increased risk of vaginal prolapse.

Simple moisturising creams can be applied when the vagina is irritated, but give only temporary relief. The best solution is to replace the missing oestrogen long term by using a vaginal cream once or twice a week, oestrogen tablets daily, skin patches once or twice a week, or implants every few months. Dosages must be slowly adjusted to suit each individual woman. The results of treatment are usually very good.
See also MENOPAUSE; VAGINA

ATROPHY
Atrophy is a medical term indicating the wasting or shrinking of tissue or an organ due to disease or lack of use. Often used as the adjective "atrophic".

ATROPINE
See ANTIDIARRHOEALS; BELLADONNA; CHOLINERGICS; MYDRIATICS

ATTENTION DEFICIT HYPERACTIVITY DISORDER
Attention deficit hyperactivity disorder (ADHD) is a very complex behaviour problem. A subtype is attention deficit disorder (ADD) in which there is no excess activity.

Patients are most commonly males who inherit the disorder from their father's side of the family, and it affects between 3% and 8% of primary school students. Boys show more aggressive and impulsive symptoms, while girls seem to have a lack of attention due to daydreaming.

These children are often fidgeting, unable to remain seated for long, unable to play quietly, easily distracted, unable to sustain attention, always impatient, have difficulty in following instructions, often move from one incomplete task to the next, talk excessively, often interrupt or intrude, do not seem to listen, have poor short term memory, often lose items and engage in physically dangerous activities. Most are average or above average in intelligence, but due to their genuine inability to pay attention and control their impulsiveness often do not take in all of the information in school. Thirty percent have a reading disorder and 10% to 15% have other academic disabilities. It may lead to criminal activity in the teens and early adult life.

Treatment involves behaviour modification with the assistance of a psychologist and the cooperation of the parents, social skills training, family counselling, psychostimulant medication (eg. methylphenidate) and occupational therapy. Many professionals have conflicting ideas about the best form of treatment, and it is a process of trial and error to find the best treatment for an individual. Diet modification is commonly thought to be useful, but there is no evidence to support this. Every individual will respond differently to treatment, but most grow out of the problem in their mid-teens.
See also BEHAVIOUR THERAPY;
EPISODIC DYSCONTROL SYNDROME;
HYPERKINETIC SYNDROME;
STIMULANTS; TOURETTE
SYNDROME; VIOLENCE

AUDIOMETER
See HEARING TESTS

AURICULOTEMPORAL SYNDROME
See FREY SYNDROME

AURISCOPE
The auriscope (otoscope) is an instrument very commonly used by doctors to examine the outer ear and ear drum. It consists of a cone shaped nozzle which is placed in the outer ear (usually with a clean protector over it), a light source and a magnifying glass. A power source (usually batteries) is contained in the handle.

Through the magnifier, the doctor can see all the structures in the outer ear and the ear drum, and any diseases (eg. infection, wax) that may be present.
See also EAR; OTITIS EXTERNA

AUTISM
Autism is a social developmental disorder that may be an abnormality in the development of the brain due to damage during growth as a foetus, at birth, or in the first years of life. The absolute cause is not known.

The child fails to develop normal social skills, language skills and communication skills. They are often excessively preoccupied with a particular type of behaviour and very resistant to change or education. Repetitive habits are common. Occasionally they have exceptional talents in a particular area (eg. maths or music – the idiot savant syndrome). Epilepsy occurs in up to 30% of cases.

There are no diagnostic tests, but CT brain scans sometimes show non-specific abnormalities. Electroencephalograms (EEG) are usually normal, except in those who develop epilepsy.

There is no effective treatment, and patients remain mentally below normal and most require care throughout their life, but life expectancy is close to normal.
See also ASPERGER SYNDROME; IDIOT SAVANT SYNDROME

AUTOIMMUNE DISEASES
Autoimmune diseases are a group of diverse conditions that cause the body to inappropriately reject some specific types of its own tissue, in the same way that transplanted organs or tissue may be rejected (eg. in rheumatoid arthritis, the synovial membrane lining a joint is rejected). Their absolute cause is unknown, but they often follow stress or viral infections.
See also HALO NAEVUS; HASHIMOTO THYROIDITIS; HYPERTHYROIDISM; IDIOPATHIC PULMONARY FIBROSIS; IMMUNE TESTS; KOEBNER PHENOMENON; MYASTHENIA GRAVIS; NEPHROTIC SYNDROME; PEMPHIGOID; PEMPHIGUS; POLYMYALGIA RHEUMATICA; PSORIASIS; RHEUMATOID ARTHRITIS; SCLERITIS; SCLERODERMA; SJÖGREN SYNDROME; SYNDROME X; SYSTEMIC LUPUS ERYTHEMATOSUS; TEMPORAL ARTERITIS; THROMBOCYTOPENIA; TRANSVERSE MYELITIS

AUTONOMIC NERVOUS SYSTEM
There are two networks of nerves in the body. One is under conscious control and, for

example, moves the legs to enable us to walk. The other network is unconscious and operates irrespective of any control on our part. This network is called the autonomic nervous system and is responsible for such bodily functions as the heart beating and digestion.

The autonomic system, in turn, is divided into two – the sympathetic and the parasympathetic system. These work in tandem and, in general, the sympathetic system stimulates activity, whereas the parasympathetic system stops or slows activity down.
See also NERVE; NERVOUS SYSTEM

AVAPRO
See ANGIOTENSIN II RECEPTOR ANTAGONISTS

AVASCULAR NECROSIS OF THE FEMORAL HEAD
This is death (necrosis) of the bone at the top end (head) of the femur (thigh bone) which forms the hip joint, caused by failure of the blood supply to the head of the femur. The absolute cause is unknown in most cases, but it may follow an injury or fracture to the femur, or inflammation (vasculitis) of an artery. It is a common problem in deep sea divers.

Patients develop severe hip pain that spreads down to the knee, and is made worse by movement or standing. Gradually the movement of the hip becomes more and more restricted, and the thigh muscles become thinner (wasted) on the affected side. It is diagnosed by characteristic changes on an x-ray.

Prolonged bed rest is the only treatment in early stages, but in advanced cases surgery to replace the head of the femur is necessary. There are reasonable results from surgery.
See also FEMUR

AVICENNA
Correctly known as Ibn Sina, Avicenna (980–1037) was an Islamic medical scholar whose book on medications was used for over 500 years throughout Medieval Europe.
See also GALEN

AYURVEDIC MEDICINE
Ayurvedic medicine is a system of healing which evolved amongst sages of the Brahmin cast in India 3000 years ago. There are several aspects which distinguish it from other forms of health care: –

• It focuses on establishing and maintaining the balance of life energies within a person, rather than treating individual symptoms.

• It recognizes the constitutional differences between individuals and therefore prescribes different treatments for different types of people. Although two people may appear to have the same symptoms, their constitutions may be very different and therefore call for very different remedies.

• It is a comprehensive system of health care which recognizes that ultimately all intelligence and wisdom flows from one absolute source. Health improves or deteriorates because of the absolute source acting through the laws of nature. Ayurveda assists nature by promoting harmony between the patient and nature by living a life of balance according to nature's laws.

• Ayurveda describes three fundamental universal energies which regulate all natural processes. That is, the same energies which produce effects in the various galaxies and star systems are operating at the level of human physiology. These three universal energies are known as the Tridosha.

• The ancient Ayurvedic physicians realised the need for preserving the harmonious connection between the mind and body and offered patients contemplative, dietary and herbal remedies for nurturing the subtler aspects of ones humanity. Ayurveda seeks to heal the mind-body complex and restore wholeness and harmony, and thereby restore health and well being.
See also ACUPUNCTURE; CHELATION; CHINESE MEDICINE; CHIROPRACTIC; HOMEOPATHY; IRIDOLOGY; NATUROPATHY; OSTEOPATHY; SHIATSU

AZATADINE
See ANTIHISTAMINES

AZATHIOPRINE
See IMMUNOSUPPRESSANTS

B

BABIES

A child grows faster during babyhood than at any other stage of its life, including adolescence. By the age of eighteen months a girl is usually half her adult height, and a boy is by the age of two years. There is little correlation between the rate of growth in childhood and eventual height. Many children grow quickly and then stop early so that they are short, whereas others seem to grow at a slower pace but continue until they outstrip everyone else. The most significant factor in determining height is heredity – the children of tall parents will usually also be tall. Nutrition is also significant, and a child who is poorly nourished is likely to be shorter than one who is well nourished. Advances in nutrition are the main reason for an overall increase in the height of populations of the developed world.

Body proportions of babies and children are markedly different from those in adults. A baby's head is disproportionately large compared with that of an adult, and its legs are disproportionately short. A baby's head is about a quarter of its length, but adults' heads are about one eighth of their height. Between birth and adulthood, a person's head almost doubles in size, the trunk trebles in length, the arms increase their length by four times, and the legs grow to about five times their original length.

At birth, babies have almost no ability to control their movements. At the age of about four weeks, a baby placed on its stomach can usually hold its head up. At about four months, the baby will usually be able to sit up with support, and at the age of seven months should be able to sit alone. At around eight months, most babies can stand with assistance, and will start to crawl at ten months. They can probably put one leg after the other if they are led at about eleven months, and pull themselves up on the furniture by one year. At about fourteen months a baby can usually stand alone, and the major milestone of walking will probably occur around fifteen months. These are average figures and many children will reach them much earlier and others much later. Physical development does not equate with mental development, and parents should not be concerned if their child takes its time about reaching the various stages – Einstein was so slow in learning to talk that his parents feared he was retarded.

Most newborn babies sleep most of the time – although there are wide variations and some babies seem to stay awake most of the day and night, to the distress of their parents. As they grow, a baby's need for sleep diminishes until a toddler requires about ten or twelve hours of sleep a night, with a nap in the daytime.

See also BABY FEEDING; BABY FLOPPY; CHILDREN; COMFORTERS; COT DEATH; DUMMIES; FAILURE TO THRIVE; PREMATURE BABY; TALKING; TEMPER TANTRUMS; THUMB SUCKING; TOILET TRAINING; VACCINATION OF CHILDREN

BABY COLIC
See INFANTILE COLIC

BABY FEEDING

A baby will normally be introduced to solids at about four months. These will consist of strained vegetables and fruits. At the beginning they are not a substitute for milk but are simply to get the baby used to them. Gradually solids become an integral part of the diet, and by six months the amount of milk can usually be reduced in proportion to solids in each meal.

Breast milk is the best possible food for a baby from birth, and no other milk is needed until one year of age, when cow's milk may be introduced. If the baby is not breast fed, infant formula is recommended for most of the first year, although many babies cope with ordinary cow's milk from six months. From the age of about six months it is safe to stop sterilising the bottles. Many babies are able to master the art of drinking out of a cup at about nine months. By the time a baby is a toddler, they should be eating much the same meals as the rest of the family, assuming these are nutritious and well-balanced. It is important that food is attractively prepared and presented so that it looks appetising.

Some parents become excessively anxious because their child seems to be a fussy eater, and they worry that the child will not receive adequate nutrition. This is usually because meals have become a battleground with a parent insisting on every last scrap being consumed. Once mealtimes become unpleasant, the child not unnaturally tries to avoid them. Children are like adults. Sometimes they are hungrier than other times, and they like some foods and dislike others. If you allow your child some individual choice in what and how much they eat, it is unlikely that problems will arise. If a child goes off a particular food for a period, respect their wish – it will usually be short-lived. It is unknown for a child voluntarily to starve him or herself to death.

There is growing evidence that children should not be overfed. A chubby child has long been regarded as desirably healthy and a tribute to its mother. No one would suggest that children ought to be thin and that a little extra fat does not provide the necessary fuel for a growing and energetic youngster, but increasingly it is being realised that fat children grow into overweight adults.
See also BABIES; CHILDHOOD

BABY, FLOPPY
A generalised lack of muscle tone in a newborn infant is an uncommon problem, but may be a sign of serious illness.

If the baby is floppy and not moving arms and legs spontaneously, a serious viral or bacterial infection caught before birth from the mother, or in the first few days of life, may be responsible.

Malnutrition in the mother causing poor nutrition of the baby, or poor nutrition of the baby after birth (often due to failure of breast feeding), is another cause.

Other less common causes of a floppy baby include cerebral palsy (spasticity), Down syndrome (mongolism), Ehlers-Danlos syndrome, Prader-Willi syndrome, myasthenia syndromes, muscular dystrophy (failure of muscle development), Werdig-Hoffmann disease (inherited progressive muscle wasting), Duchenne muscular dystrophy and other disorders that affect the nerve control of muscles.

Rarely, babies fed honey contaminated with dust containing *Clostridium botulinum* are affected by the toxin produced by this bacteria which results in muscle weakness.

Abnormalities of body chemical control may also cause weak muscles or poor muscle tone. Examples include rickets (lack of vitamin D), glycogen storage disease (inability to use sugar effectively for energy) and aminoaciduria (protein chemistry disorder).
See also FAILURE TO THRIVE; MUSCLE WEAKNESS

BABY MEASLES
See ROSEOLA INFANTUM

BABY NOT THRIVING
See FAILURE TO THRIVE

BACK
The back is made from twenty-four bones, called vertebrae, that sit one on top of the other. The bottom vertebra sits on top of the sacrum, which is really another five vertebrae that have fused together. The sacrum forms the back part of the pelvis. The top vertebra is specially modified to allow the skull to sit on it, and swivel in all directions.

When looked at from behind, the vertebrae form a straight line. From the side though, the bones of the back are aligned in several smooth curves. The back curves in at the waist, out over the back of the chest, and in again at the neck. This careful alignment of bones is maintained by ligaments (which are stout bands of fibrous tissue) and muscles that run along the length of the back. Between each vertebra is a cushion of cartilaginous material known as the disc. This has a semi-liquid centre (like a jelly filled balloon) and absorbs the shocks the body receives in walking, running and jumping.

The spinal cord runs through holes in the centre of each vertebra. This cord is an extension of the brain, and passes through every vertebra from the skull to waist level. Between each vertebra, the spinal cord sends out nerves that supply that section of the body. Nerves run out from the neck to supply the arms, and from the lower vertebrae to supply the legs.

The sacrum, that big bone at the bottom of the spine, is attached to the pelvis by a complex network of ligaments positioned just under the dimples that many people have on either side of their back, just above their buttocks.

See also BACK PAIN; SPINE; VERTEBRA

BACK PAIN

Back pain may occur when the intricate arrangement of bones, ligaments, discs, muscles and nerves that makes up the back becomes strained, torn, broken, stretched or otherwise disrupted.

The most common cause of back pain is ligamentous and muscular damage from incorrect lifting. Lifting and twisting simultaneously is particularly dangerous. A poor posture can also add to muscular and ligamentous strain.

In older people, arthritis may be the cause, when the smooth joints between the vertebrae become roughened and damaged by age and long years of use. This is osteoarthritis, but rheumatoid arthritis, which normally affects the hands and feet, may also affect the back.

A slight shift in the position of one vertebra on another, or inflammation of the surrounding tissues, may put pressure on a nerve, causing sciatica (leg pain) or localised back pain.

BACK PAIN

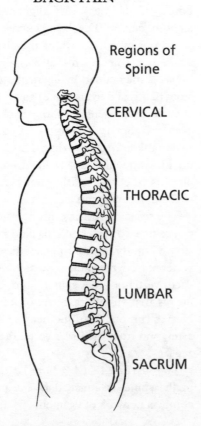

Regions of Spine

CERVICAL

THORACIC

LUMBAR

SACRUM

Direct injuries may fracture or dislocate the bones in the back, causing the spinal cord to be pinched, and paralysis of the body below that point.

There are discs of rubbery material between each vertebra that act as shock absorbers and allow movement between the vertebrae. These intervertebral discs may be damaged by a sudden injury, gradual deterioration with age or many years of heavy work. A damaged disc may bulge (slipped disc) and press on a nerve as it leaves the spinal cord, to cause pain in both the back and down the course of that nerve. Discitis is an inflammation of the disc that causes local pain without pressing directly on a nerve.

Fibromyositis occurs in large muscles that have been overused and damaged repeatedly by heavy work or exercise. Scattered muscle cells are replaced by fibrous scar tissue to disrupt the structure of the muscle and cause a deep ache that worsens with use.

Osteoporosis is a thinning of the bones that occurs mainly in women after the menopause, due to a lack of calcium in the bones. It may result in bones breaking easily anywhere in the body, but particularly in the back where the weak vertebrae may collapse and cause pain.

Any woman who has been pregnant will confirm the distressing pain that may be caused by that condition. Hormonal changes cause the ligaments throughout the body to slacken, and when this occurs in the back the vertebrae can shift slightly to cause considerable pain.

Menstrual period pain is a common cause of lower back pain, particularly in younger women who have not been pregnant.

Kidney stones may irritate the kidney to cause a dull ache on one side of the back, but if the stone starts moving down the ureter from the kidney to the bladder, excruciating pain will be felt running from the loin at the back to the groin at the front.

A peptic ulcer in the stomach is caused by the concentrated hydrochloric acid in the stomach penetrating the protective mucus that normally lines the organ, and eating into the stomach wall. A common symptom is severe pain in the belly or back that is eased by eating, but worse a few hours after eating.

Psychological and psychiatric conditions, including anxiety and depression, may cause

FEMALE PELVIS

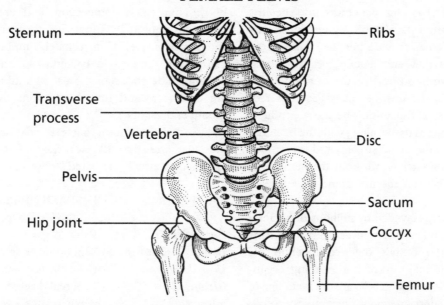

Sternum — Ribs

Transverse process —

Vertebra — Disc

Pelvis — Sacrum

Hip joint — Coccyx

— Femur

muscle spasms and inappropriate perception of minor aches and pains that are magnified into a significant problem.

Other causes of back pain include scoliosis (a sideways curvature of the spine), posterior facet syndrome (small joints at back of vertebra are inflamed), Paget's disease (in which the bones enlarge and soften in the back, legs and skull), Scheurmann's disease (an inflammation of the vertebrae in the centre of the back that is common in teenagers), hip disorders (eg. osteoarthritis, poor circulation) may be felt as a pain in the back, diffuse idiopathic spinal hyperostosis (spines on vertebrae) and ankylosing spondylitis (a long-term inflammation of the small joints between the vertebrae in the back).

Cancer from one part of the body to another is called metastatic carcinoma, and the back is one site where these spreading cancers may lodge.

Back pain does not necessarily arise from the back itself. Many diseases of the organs in the chest and belly may cause back pain. Conversely, quite severe damage to the back may cause pain anywhere from the belly to the big toe, without any pain being actually felt in the back.

A woman's organs of reproduction are a common source of back pain. Infections of the fallopian tubes (salpingitis) or uterus (pelvic inflammatory disease) may be felt in the back, as may endometriosis, a twisted ovarian cyst, and a prolapsed uterus (uterus slips down into the vagina).

There are many less common causes of back pain not covered in this list.
See also ARTHRITIS; SPINE; VERTEBRA and separate entries for diseases mentioned above.

BACLOFEN
See MUSCLE RELAXANTS

BACTERAEMIA

Bacteraemia is a common, low-grade bacterial infection of the blood, while a more severe infection is called septicaemia. It may be associated with other serious illnesses such as leukaemia, cancer and AIDS.

In most cases the infection spreads from the kidney, intestine, lung or gall bladder. Almost any type of bacteria may be responsible.

Symptoms include a fever, chills and rapid breathing. Some patients have a normal, or even low, temperature. Abnormal white blood cell levels can be used to make the diagnosis. Treatment involves taking the appropriate antibiotics, but sometimes the infection may spread to other organs, or worsen into septicaemia. Most patients recover well with treatment, but the condition is more serious in those with significant underlying disease.
See also SEPTICAEMIA and separate entries for diseases mentioned above.

BACTERIA

Tonsillitis, pneumonia, cystitis, school sores and conjunctivitis all have one thing in common – they are all caused by bacteria.

Bacteria are microscopic single-celled organisms that can penetrate into healthy tissues, and start multiplying into vast numbers. When they do this they damage the tissue that they are infecting, causing it to break down into pus. Because of the damage they cause, the involved area becomes red, swollen, hot and painful. The waste products of the damaged tissue, along with the bacteria, spread into the blood stream, and this stimulates the brain to raise the body temperature in order to fight off the infection. Thus a fever develops.

The body is invaded by millions of bacteria every day, but very few ever cause problems because the body's defence mechanisms destroy the majority of the invading organisms. The white blood cells are the main line of defence against infection. They rapidly recognise unwanted bacteria, and large numbers move to the area involved to engulf the bacteria and destroy them. It is only when these defences are overwhelmed that a noticeable infection develops.

Hundreds of bacteria are known to microbiologists (the doctors and scientists who study them), but only a few dozen cause significant infections in mankind. All these bacteria have specific names and can be identified under a microscope by experts who can tell them apart as easily as most of us can identify different breeds of dogs.

Every species of bacteria (and fungi, but not viruses) has two names – a family name (eg. Staphylococcus) which uses a capital initial letter and comes first, and a specific species name (eg: aureus) which uses a lower case initial letter and comes second. The golden staph bacteria which causes many serious throat infections is thus called *Staphylococcus aureus* but may be abbreviated to *S. aureus*.

When an infection occurs, the patient usually consults a doctor because of the symptoms. If the infection is bacterial, the appropriate antibiotics can be given to destroy the invading bacteria. Because different types of bacteria favour different parts of the body and lead to different symptoms, a doctor can make an educated guess about the antibiotic to use. When there is any doubt, a sample or swab is sent to a laboratory for expert analysis so that the precise organism can be identified, together with the appropriate antibiotic to kill it.

Many bacteria, particularly those in the gut, are beneficial to the normal functioning of the body. They can aid digestion, and prevent infections caused by fungi (eg. thrush) and sometimes viruses. Unfortunately, antibiotics can kill off these good bacteria too, and so common side effects of the use of antibiotics are diarrhoea, and fungal infections of the mouth and vagina.

The most common bacteria that attack humans, and the diseases they cause, or organs they attack, are listed below.

BACTERIA	DISEASE OR PLACE OF INFECTION
Bacteroides	Pelvic organs.
Bordetella pertussis	Whooping cough.
Brucella abortus	Brucellosis.
Chlamydia trachomatis	Venereal disease, pelvic organs, eye.
Clostridium perfringens	Gas gangrene, pseudomembranous colitis.
Clostridium tetani	Tetanus.
Corynebacterium diphtheriae	Diphtheria.
Escherichia coli	Urine, gut, Fallopian tubes, peritonitis.
Haemophilus influenzae	Ear, meningitis, sinusitis, epiglottitis.
Helicobacter pylori	Peptic ulcers.
Klebsiella pneumoniae	Lungs, urine.
Legionella pneumophilia	Lungs.
Mycobacterium leprae	Leprosy.
Mycobacterium tuberculosis	Tuberculosis.
Mycoplasma pneumoniae	Lungs.
Neisseria gonorrhoea	Gonorrhoea, pelvic organs.
Neisseria meningitidis	Meningitis.
Proteus	Urine, ear.
Pseudomonas aeruginosa	Urine, ear, lungs, heart.
Salmonella typhi	Typhoid fever.
Shigella dysenteriae	Gut infections.
Staphylococcus aureus	Lungs, throat, sinusitis, ear, skin, eye, gut, meningitis, heart, bone, joints.
Streptococcus pneumoniae	Throat, ear, sinusitis, lungs, eye, joints.
Streptococcus pyogenes	Sinuses, ear, throat, skin.

Streptococcus viridans	Heart.
Treponema pallidum	Syphilis.
Vibrio cholerae	Cholera.
Yersinia pestis	Plague.

See also ANAEROBIC INFECTION; *ESCHERICHIA COLI* INFECTION; FEVER; FUNGI; INFECTION; *MYCOPLASMA* INFECTION; *PSEUDOMONAS AERUGINOSA* INFECTION; RICKETTSIAL INFECTIONS; S*TAPHYLOCOCCUS AUREUS*; *STREPTOCOCCAL* INFECTION; VIRUS and separate entries for diseases mentioned above.

BAD BREATH
See BREATH, BAD

BAKER'S CYST
Joints contain a lubricating (synovial) fluid within a synovial membrane that totally encloses the joint. A Baker's cyst can form at the back of the knee when part of the synovial membrane pushes out between two muscles to form an outpocketing. These commonly occur in athletes who stress their legs (eg. long distance runners).

Patients notice a lump behind the knee that causes no discomfort, or it may become inflamed and tender, or most seriously, it may rupture to cause sudden severe pain. The cause can be proved by an ultrasound scan.

Treatment involves surgical excision before rupture. With a ruptured cyst the patient is rested, the leg is kept elevated, and steroids are injected into the knee to protect the joint lining from the loss of fluid and to seal the leak.
See also KNEE

BALANCE
See DIZZINESS; EAR

BALANITIS
Balanitis is an inflammation or infection of the head of the penis (the area normally covered by the foreskin in uncircumcised men) or the tip of the clitoris in women. It may be due to infection by bacteria (common), fungi (eg. thrush – also common), and micro-organisms such as amoebae and Trichomonas (uncommon). Irritants such as chemicals, urine (in incontinent men) and dermatitis may also be responsible.

The head of the penis or clitoris becomes tender, painful and there may be weeping sores present. A swab can be taken to identify the responsible organism. Treatment then involves using antibiotic or antifungal creams and/or tablets. Irritants must be removed, or the penis protected by a barrier cream or condom. Dermatitis may be difficult to treat and may require a variety of creams and ointments. In recurrent cases, circumcision may be necessary.
See also CHANCROID; PHIMOSIS

BALD
By far the most common form of baldness is that caused by hereditary tendencies in men. If your father or grandfather was bald, you have a good chance of developing the same problem. Baldness is a gender-linked genetic condition that is very rare in women, but passes through the female line to men in later generations. There are no cures available, and none are likely for some time to come.

There are many other causes for patchy or diffuse hair loss including ageing, skin diseases, stress, the menopause, lack of iron or zinc, an under active thyroid gland, drugs (particularly those used to treat cancer) and a dozen or more rare diseases.

Some people, particularly young women, develop patches of baldness that are scattered across their scalp. This condition is known as alopecia, and is very difficult to treat. Many cases settle by themselves after some months or years, but most require prolonged care by a dermatologist.

Almost always, male pattern baldness commences with gradual hair loss, starting at the front of the scalp on either side, or in a circular area on top. It is usually accompanied by excess hair on the body due to higher levels of testosterone. The connection between baldness and sexual potency is unproven.

Minoxidil tablets or scalp lotion may slow or stop hair loss, but the only real treatments are hair transplants, scalp flap rotation or a wig.
See also ALOPECIA AREATA; HAIR LOSS; TELOGEN EFFLUVIUM

BALLOON ANGIOPLASTY
When an artery becomes narrowed by fatty deposits, insufficient blood may reach the part of the body beyond the narrowing, particularly

during exercise, when more of the oxygen carried by the blood is required as fuel by the muscles. When this happens, pain occurs in the affected muscle. The area affected can be anywhere in the body, but most commonly involved are the heart, head and legs.

In past years, the only way to overcome this blockage was an operation to bypass the damaged area of artery, or to clean out the fatty deposits from inside the artery, but heart surgeons have now devised the technique of balloon angioplasty.

In this procedure, a fine tube is threaded into an artery, and moved along it until the blocked area is reached. The tube has a small balloon on the end of it. The hard tip of the tube is pushed through the obstructing fatty deposits, and then the balloon is gently blown up. This pushes aside the fat inside the artery, compresses it, and when the balloon is deflated, a clear channel is left for the blood to pass through. Sometimes a stent (tube shaped metal grid) is left behind to ensure that the artery does not close down again.

This delicate procedure saves the time, trauma and expense of a major operation, and is being used more and more where the blockage is not extensive. Large blockages will still need surgery, and sometimes the fat is too hard to be pushed away by the balloon.
See also ANGINA; STENT

BANTING, FREDERICK

Sir Frederick Grant Banting (1891–1941) was a Nobel–prize-winning Canadian physiologist who, in cooperation with then medical student Charles Best, first discovered in 1922 that a lack of insulin, produced in the pancreas, was responsible for diabetes. His discovery has saved the lives of millions of diabetics since then.
See also BEST, CHARLES; DIABETES MELLITUS TYPE ONE

BARBITURATES

Barbiturates are medications such as amylobarbitone and pentobarbitone that are now used primarily to control convulsions and to calm patients before operations, but they have been used in the past as sedatives and anti-anxiety drugs. They are addictive if given for long periods of time, and therefore have gone out of favour in recent years. They increase the effects of alcohol, are dangerous

in overdosage, and are available only on prescription. Examples include amylobarbitone, methylphenobarbitone (Prominal) and phenobarbitone.

Side effects include drowsiness, incoordination, slow breathing, nausea and drug dependence. They should never be used in pregnancy, be used with great care in the elderly and are very addictive.
See also ANXIETY; ANXIOLYTICS; MEDICATION

BARIUM ENEMA

This is an x-ray that shows the lower part of the gut from the anus up to the appendix, and sometimes the last part of the small intestine. This part of the gut is about one and a half to two metres long in an adult.

For a few days before the x-ray patients will have to use special medicines to clean out all the faeces from the gut. When they go to the radiologist's rooms, they will undress and lie on their side on a rather narrow table. A small tube is placed in the anus, and through this a mixture of barium will be run into the large intestine. An injection may be given in the arm to relax the gut during the procedure.

The patient is rolled around from side to side while x-rays are taken, and air will be introduced into the gut to display any abnormalities more readily. The procedure may be a little uncomfortable when the gut is inflated with air, but this settles rapidly.

After half to one hour, all the necessary pictures will have been taken and the patient is asked to go to the toilet to pass the barium mixture that was previously introduced. Bowel function will return to normal after a couple of days.

The procedure can diagnose most diseases of the lower gut, and will only be requested if a doctor considers there are good reasons for doing it.
See also BARIUM MEAL; COLONOSCOPY; X-RAY

BARIUM MEAL

Barium sulphate is a heavy, white radio-opaque powder used for contrast x-rays of the intestinal tract. If the upper intestines (eg. the duodenum or stomach) are being investigated, the powder will generally be flavoured and mixed with liquid which is then swallowed from a glass. This is called a barium

meal. The patient must fast for six hours before the x-ray. The mixture passes quickly into the stomach, enabling a picture to be taken and the presence of abnormalities noted. The doctor will prod the abdomen and ask the patient to move around to enable clear photographs to be obtained of the areas needing particular examination.
See also BARIUM ENEMA; GASTROSCOPY; X-RAY

BARMAH FOREST VIRUS
A viral blood infection that is more common in males than females and in the elderly, and is limited to the eastern states of mainland Australia. The virus passes from one person to another by mosquito bites. Carriers, who have no symptoms, can donate the virus to any mosquito that bites them.

Symptoms include arthritis that moves from joint to joint, muscle aches and pains, fevers that come and go, headaches and sometimes a rash. The diagnosis can be confirmed by a specific blood test.

Unfortunately there is no cure, but medication (eg. painkillers, nonsteroidal anti-inflammatories) can be given to relieve symptoms. The infection settles with time and rest over several months, but recurrences are possible.
See also ROSS RIVER FEVER

BARRETT SYNDROME
Also known as Barrett oesophagitis, this condition causes narrowing at the lower end of the oesophagus (gullet) from stomach acid reflux.

Reflux oesophagitis causes inflammation and ulceration of the lower part of the oesophagus, and if left untreated for years, repeated irritation causes scarring and narrowing. The patient suffers from difficult and painful swallowing as well as the symptoms of reflux oesophagitis. The diagnosis is confirmed by a barium meal x-ray or gastroscopy.

Medication can be used to control the acid reflux, or the stricture can be dilated by passing gradually larger dilators down the throat while the patient is anaesthetised. Occasionally more radical surgery is required.
See also HIATUS HERNIA; OESOPHAGUS; REFLUX OESOPHAGITIS

BARRIER CONTRACEPTION
See CONDOM; DIAPHRAGM CONTRACEPTIVE; SPERMICIDES

BARTHOLIN CYST
A swelling and infection of one of the mucus-secreting Bartholin's glands, which open through small ducts onto the inside lips of a woman's vulva, due to blockage of its duct. They produce mucus to keep the female genitals moist, and secrete extra fluid to act as a lubricant during sexual intercourse.

The woman experiences a tender, painful lump in the vulva that makes sex very painful, and even sitting uncomfortable. Occasionally, the duct may block intermittently, causing the cyst to swell and then subside. Antibiotics are given by mouth to settle the infection, and surgery is usually performed to drain away the pus and open up the cyst.
See also VAGINITIS; VULVA

BARTHOLIN GLAND
See BARTHOLIN CYST; VULVA

BARTONELLA HENSELAE
See CAT SCRATCH DISEASE

BARTTER SYNDROME
Bartter syndrome is a rare inherited kidney condition, far more common in females than males. It is caused by failure of the kidney to conserve adequate potassium in the blood, giving the body chemistry effects of Conn syndrome without the high blood pressure.

The condition presents as a child or young adult with short stature, who frequently passes large quantities of urine day and night (often causing bed wetting) and has muscle weakness. Some patients develop muscle spasms and cramps, a craving for salt, and in advanced stages vomiting and constipation occur. Numerous blood and urine tests are abnormal.

Indomethacin is used to reduce kidney inflammation, medication (eg. spironolactone) is given to reduce potassium loss, and potassium supplements are taken. There is no cure.
See also BED WETTING; CONN SYNDROME

BASAL CELL CARCINOMA
Also known as a rodent ulcer, these shiny, rounded lumps are a cancer of the deeper

(basal) layers of the skin. They are caused by prolonged exposure to sunlight, and occur most commonly on the face and back. They are not as serious as the more superficial squamous cell carcinomas (SCC), but occur at an earlier age than SCCs, although rarely before twenty-five years.

BCCs may be noticed as a spot that changes in size and colour, or they may present as an ulcer that fails to heal. The ulcer often has a pearly, rounded edge.

Whenever a BCC is suspected, it should be removed surgically. The specimen is then sent to a pathologist for examination to ensure that the diagnosis is correct, and that the entire tumour has been removed. Alternative treatments in more difficult areas include anticancer creams, irradiation, curetting and diathermy.

If correctly treated, they can be completely healed, but if left until large, significant plastic surgery may be necessary, as they will slowly invade deeper tissues, and after many years may cause death.
See also EXCISION; SKIN CANCER; SKIN ULCER

BASAL CELL PAPILLOMAS
See SEBORRHOEIC KERATOSES

BAT EARS
Prominent protruding ears are called bat ears. They are harmless, but may be cosmetically unacceptable. An operation can be performed to pin back the ears by taking a wedge of skin and tissue from behind the ear, and then the tissue is sewn down again. This is normally not performed until a child is a teenager and recovery takes only a couple of weeks.
See also PLASTIC SURGERY

BATTERED WIFE
See STOCKHOLM SYNDROME

BCC
See BASAL CELL CARCINOMA

BD
The prescription notation "bd" is derived from the Latin "bis die" which means "twice a day".
See also PRESCRIPTION NOTATIONS

BECKER MUSCULAR DYSTROPHY
Becker muscular dystrophy is an uncommon form of inherited muscle wasting that starts in late childhood or the early teens and results in a progressive and permanent weakening and wasting of muscles around the shoulders and hips. It can be diagnosed by electrical studies of muscle action and muscle biopsy. Unfortunately there is no effective treatment, but physiotherapy may be beneficial.
See also MUSCLE WEAKNESS; MUSCULAR DYSTROPHY

BECLOMETHASONE
See ASTHMA PREVENTION MEDICATION; STEROIDS

BED SORE
A bed sore (pressure ulcer) forms in skin on which the body rests and so most commonly affects areas such as the heels, buttocks, back of the head and the skin over the lower part of the backbone.

If the blood supply to the skin is significantly reduced, the affected skin dies. When pressure is applied to the skin for many hours without relief, the area will break down into an ulcer. Elderly, infirm, paralysed or unconscious patients who spend long periods in bed, or sitting, may not have the ability to move themselves or the sensation necessary to prompt movement, so that a particular area of skin may carry a great deal of the body's weight for a prolonged period of time.

Prevention involves moving the patient regularly so that no area bears pressure for too long. Sheep skins, ripple mattresses, water beds and other devices are placed under affected patients to spread their weight as much as possible.

Once present they are often difficult to heal, but may be cured by avoidance of any further pressure to the area, antibiotic dressings, special absorbent bandages or dressings and, in resistant cases, surgical treatment to cover the area with a skin graft. These sores may become infected very easily and require antibiotic treatment. Once affected, the same area is very susceptible to future damage, and extra precautions must be taken to avoid their recurrence.
See also SKIN ULCER

BED WETTING

Bed wetting (enuresis) is a medical problem that makes businessmen dread overnight trips to a conference, causes marriages to break up, stops teenagers from spending the night at a friend's, and drives the mothers of some children to desperation.

Normally, urine is retained in the bladder by the contraction of a ring shaped bundle of muscle that surrounds the bladder opening. When one wishes to pass urine, this ring of muscle relaxes, and the muscles in the wall of the bladder and around the abdominal cavity contract to squirt the urine out in a steady stream.

Those who are bed wetters tend to sleep very deeply, and during the deepest phases of this sleep, when all the main muscles of the body are totally relaxed, the sphincter ring muscle that retains the urine in the bladder, also relaxes. Because there is no associated contraction of the muscles in the bladder wall or elsewhere, the urine just dribbles out slowly in the night, not in a hard stream.

Many children are three or four years old before bladder control is obtained.

The first step is to investigate the patient to exclude any cause for bed wetting. Chronic urine infections, structural abnormalities of the bladder, and other rarer conditions may cause a weakness or excessive irritability of the bladder. These problems must be excluded by urine tests and x-rays.

In children lifestyle stresses (eg. family break up, moving home, hospital admission), social pressures (eg. poverty, overcrowding, lack of privacy) and excessively strict toilet training may cause psychological barriers to bladder control. Mental subnormality may make it impossible for a child to learn the reasons for bladder control.

Other uncommon possible causes include diabetes mellitus (lack of insulin production in the pancreas), diabetes insipidus, epilepsy, paraplegia, Bartter syndrome, spina bifida or a fracture of the pelvis.

A number of very rare brain disorders may also cause enuresis.

There are several steps in any treatment regime for this condition, but do not start before five years of age. They include: –
• Restrict fluids for three hours before bedtime, take child to the toilet during the night, and establish a reward system for dry nights.
• A bed-wetting alarm that consists of a moisture-sensitive pad that is placed under the patient, a battery and an alarm. When it becomes wet from the first small dribble of urine, it sounds the alarm, the patient is woken, and can empty the bladder before returning to sleep. After a few weeks use, most people learn to waken before the alarm.
• Amitriptyline (Tryptanol) is taken every night to alter the type of sleep. Over a few weeks, the dosage is slowly lowered and hopefully, the bad sleep habits and bed-wetting do not return.
• Desmopressin nasal spray at bedtime acts on the pituitary gland in the brain, and this instructs the kidney to reduce the amount of urine produced during the night.
• Psychotherapy in the most resistant cases.

Please remember that premature treatment can cause permanent sleep disturbances in a child. There are no serious long term medical consequences from bed wetting.
See also INCONTINENCE OF URINE

BEE AND WASP STING

A sting from a bee or wasp is often painful but recovery is usually swift and uneventful. However, a few people are allergic to such stings and their reaction may be far more severe. They are likely to experience considerable local pain, swelling and irritation, puffy eyelids and wheezy breathing. If the reaction is severe, it can affect the breathing apparatus and the heart, and if breathing becomes difficult and/or the tongue starts to swell, get medical help immediately as the person's life may be in danger.

Bee stings are barbed and are usually left behind in the skin with the venom sac attached.

If someone is stung by a bee or wasp: –
• remove the sting by scraping it sideways with your (clean) fingernail or the side of a knife. Make sure you do not pull or squeeze the sac of venom attached to the sting.
• Wipe the affected area clean and apply a block of ice wrapped in damp material, eg. a clean handkerchief.
• If the victim has an allergic reaction, apply pressure immobilisation and get them to a doctor.
• If their breathing or pulse stops, give mouth-to-mouth resuscitation or cardiopulmonary resuscitation.

In recent years, European wasps have become a particular problem. Unlike other wasps and bees, they do not release the sting into the skin of the victim but retain the ability to sting several times. This can be extremely painful and increase the possibility of an allergic reaction. The wasps are attracted to meat being cooked, and may be an unwelcome addition to barbecues. It is not unknown for them to crawl into an open can of drink, and then sting the victim in the mouth and throat. This can be extremely serious, since the airway may swell up and block. A wasp sting should be dealt with in the same way as a bee sting.
See also ANAPHYLAXIS; PRESSURE IMMOBILISATION; RESUSCITATION

BEHAVIOUR ABNORMAL
See ASPERGER SYNDROME; ATTENTION DEFICIT HYPERACTIVITY DISORDER; AUTISM; KLINEFELTER SYNDROME; SCHIZOPHRENIA; VIOLENCE

BEHAVIOUR THERAPY
Behaviour (behavioural) therapy is used by psychologists and psychiatrists to modify a patient's behaviour. In its basic principle, a patient is taught by rewards that acceptable behaviour is better than unacceptable behaviour, which may be punished by withholding a pleasure, or giving "time out" to the patient. It is a modification of the "carrot and stick" technique traditionally used with donkeys.

The technique can be applied in ways that vary in their sophistication to children, intelligent adults, mentally subnormal people, or to the confused elderly. It is vital that any reward be far more significant than the punishment.
See also ASPERGER SYNDROME; ATTENTION DEFICIT HYPERACTIVITY DISORDER; HYPERKINETIC SYNDROME; PSYCHIATRY; PSYCHOLOGIST

BEHÇET SYNDROME
Behçet syndrome is a serious condition of unknown cause that results in widespread, apparently unconnected symptoms such as recurrent severe mouth and genital ulcers, inflammation of the eye, arthritis and brain abnormalities such as convulsions, mental disturbances, partial paralysis and brain inflammation. Other symptoms may include rashes (eg. erythema nodosum), skin ulcers, inflamed veins and blindness.

Treatment is often unsatisfactory. Steroids and immune suppressant medications are used, but the condition usually follows a long course with spontaneous temporary remissions. It is often seriously disabling and sometimes fatal.
See also ERYTHEMA NODOSUM; STEROIDS

BELLADONNA
Belladonna is a white flower that is also known as deadly nightshade, and from it can be obtained the drug atropine. A high dose of atropine can cause death, but low doses are useful in medicine to stop diarrhoea, dry saliva and dilate the pupil.

Belladonna in Italian means 'beautiful lady'. It was named thus because the drug was used in a very dilute form to dilate the pupils of Italian women in the 17th and 18th century, in order to enhance their beauty. Large pupils are recognised by psychologists as a sign of sexual attraction.
See also CHOLINERGICS; MYDRIATICS; PUPIL LARGE

BELL'S PALSY
Facial muscles are controlled by a nerve which comes out of a hole in the skull just below and in front of the ear. From there, it spreads like a fan across the face to each of the tiny muscles that control facial expressions. Inflammation of the nerve at the point where it leaves the skull causes the facial muscles to stop working. The exact reason for this inflammation is unknown.

Patients with Bell's palsy experience a sudden paralysis of the facial muscles on one side only. They can no longer smile or close the eye properly. There may be some mild to moderate pain at the point where the nerve leaves the skull beside the ear, but this settles after a few days. There may also be a disturbance to taste sensation.

No treatment is necessary for most patients, but in the elderly, if the paralysis is total, or if there is severe pain, treatment with high doses of prednisone (a steroid) may be tried, provided it is started within five days of onset.

Two thirds of patients recover completely within a few weeks with no treatment. Most of the others obtain almost complete recovery, but 10% of patients are significantly affected long term by facial paralysis.

BELLY
See ABDOMEN

BELLY PAIN
See ABDOMINAL PAIN

BENDROTHIAZIDE
See DIURETICS

BENDS
The bends (also known as arterial gas embolism and caisson disease) is caused by the development of nitrogen gas bubbles in the blood due to sudden ascent from a deep dive.

In breathing, oxygen and nitrogen are taken into the lungs, and pass across a fine membrane to be dissolved into the blood. If the air pressure is high, more gases will be dissolved into the blood. Divers must breathe air at a pressure equivalent to the depth of water in which they are diving. When divers surface, they must do so slowly, or the lower pressure in shallow water or ashore will allow the dissolved gases to come out of solution and form tiny bubbles in the blood. The same phenomenon can be seen when the top is removed from a bottle of carbonated soft drink and it starts to fizz.

Symptoms may occur immediately or up to six hours later and depend on the fitness, age, and weight of the diver, and the amount of physical exertion undertaken. Joint pain, weakness, shortness of breath, dizziness, visual disturbances, pins and needles sensation, rashes, inability to speak, headache and confusion are common. Pain may be excruciating and if left untreated may progress to coma and death. The name 'bends' derives from the posture patients adopt in an attempt to relieve the pain.

The patient should be transported as quickly as possible to a decompression chamber where they are repressurised, and then over several hours or days the pressure is slowly reduced back to normal again. Even in the best centres, permanent joint damage from gas bubbles in joint fluid may occur, and a small percentage of patients die. Death is common without treatment.

BENIGN
A benign condition, growth or tumour is one that is not harmful, cancerous or malignant.
See also MALIGNANT

BENIGN PAROXYSMAL POSITIONAL VERTIGO
Benign paroxysmal positional vertigo (BPPV) is sometimes shortened to benign positional vertigo. It is an annoying but harmless cause of dizziness due to loose particles floating in the semicircular canals (vestibular apparatus) that control balance, situated in the inner ear. The cause is usually unknown, but it may follow a head injury.

Patients experience sudden, severe, brief episodes of dizziness that are worse lying down, and attacks are triggered by any movement of the head. Some patients find that a particular head movement (eg. looking up) starts an attack.

The Hall-Pike test is diagnostic. This involves lying the patient on their back with the head hanging down off the top of a bed. The head is then rotated and abnormal eye movements (nystagmus) are noted if the test is positive.

A series of head manoeuvres is carried out under the direction of a specialist doctor or physiotherapist to remove the loose particles from the vestibular apparatus. Surgery is a treatment of last resort, but drugs are not helpful.

Treatment is moderately successful, but the condition usually settles spontaneously after many months or years.
See also DIZZINESS; EAR;
LABYRINTHITIS; MÉNIÈRE's DISEASE;
VESTIBULITIS

BENZODIAZEPINES
Benzodiazepine anxiolytics are a group of medications that sedate and may cause dependency, and they also relieve anxiety, but the degree of sedation and dependency varies dramatically from one drug to another in the group and one patient to another. Dependency should not be a problem unless the drugs are used inappropriately. Some of these drugs (eg. diazepam) can also be used to relax muscle spasm and control convulsions. They should be stopped slowly, with a gradual reduction in dosage if they have been used for a long time. They will increase the effects of

alcohol, and care should be taken with driving and using machinery while taking them.

Examples include alprazolam (Xanax), bromazepam (Lexotan), clobazam (Frisium), clorazepate (Tranxene), diazepam (Ducene, Valium), lorazepam (Ativan), nitrazepam (Mogadon), oxazepam (Murelax, Serepax) and temazepam (Normison).

They are used for the short term relief of anxiety, muscle spasms, severe epilepsy, withdrawal from alcohol, before operations, and in cerebral palsy.

Side effects include reduced alertness, and they may cause dependence or addiction, tremor, incoordination and confusion.
See also ANXIETY; EPILEPSY; MEDICATION; SEDATIVES

BENZYDAMINE
See LINIMENT

BENZYL BENZOATE
See ANTIPARASITICS

BENZYL PEROXIDE
See KERATOLYTICS

BEREAVEMENT
The loss of a loved one is recognised as one of the most psychologically traumatic experiences we ever have, especially if the person is a spouse or a child. Everyone reacts to such a loss in their own way, but most people will experience a period of intense grief, which lessens as time passes so that gradually life returns to normal. The initial feeling is usually one of shock and numbness. Often the bereaved one acts as though the person is still alive. After a period varying from a few days to several weeks, realisation that the person really is dead will hit and usually be accompanied by feelings of deep sadness and loss. During this early period, thinking is usually muddled and concentration virtually non-existent. This is quite normal, and if possible it is usually wise to try to avoid making important decisions. Especially if the death has been unexpected, it is not uncommon for the bereaved person to experience feelings of anger at having been left. Financial difficulties resulting from the death may increase such feelings.

A person who has lost someone close to them may seem to lose motivation for life. They may be listless and lacking in energy, have difficulty in sleeping and lose weight. This is quite normal for a period of weeks, but if it continues for too long, medical help should be sought, as long-term depression needs treatment. It is not unusual for a bereaved person to become ill in the year following the death. There is some evidence that older people are more likely to die following the death of a partner.

Although grief is an individual matter, experience has shown that some courses of action may help. Many people find that seeing and touching the dead person helps them to come to terms with the fact that death has occurred and thus makes easier their acceptance of the loss. This seems to be particularly so with the death of a child. Someone who wants to spend time with the dead person should never be denied the opportunity of doing so.

Generally speaking the ability to experience and express grief is beneficial, and sedatives and antidepressants should be used only if necessary and only in consultation with a doctor. Grief is a perfectly natural emotion, and to deny it or try to suppress it artificially will do more harm than good. Nevertheless medications can sometimes usefully ease the pain if it becomes unbearable.

Relatives and friends need to be as supportive as they can, both immediately following the death, but also as time passes when the realisation of the loss may actually be more acute. Anniversaries, birthdays and Christmas are generally times when extra support is needed.
See also DEATH; DEATH, SUDDEN UNEXPECTED

BERIBERI
Beriberi is caused by a lack of thiamine (vitamin B1) in the diet of those who are malnourished, have food idiosyncrasies, overcook their food, in alcoholics (who obtain nutrition from alcohol and neglect normal food) and in those whose bodies use up abnormally large amounts of thiamine due to an overactive thyroid gland or prolonged fever.

In early stages patients experience a multitude of vague complaints including tiredness, loss of appetite, twitching, and muscle cramps and pains. In later stages swollen joints, shooting pains, paralysis of feet and hands, and heart abnormalities occur.

Thiamine supplements (initially by injection in severe cases) and a well-balanced diet rapidly control the condition, but permanent organ damage is possible in advanced cases.
See also ALCOHOL; ALCOHOLISM

BERNARD-SOULIER SYNDROME
The Bernard-Soulier syndrome is an inherited defect of platelets (blood cells essential for clotting) which fail to stick together to form a clot. Excessive bleeding occurs, particularly from mouth and nose. Bruises, red spots and red patches under skin appear, particularly on the feet. The condition is aggravated by aspirin.

Blood tests on platelet function and bleeding time are diagnostic.

Blood transfusions on a regular basis are the only treatment for this lifelong defect that may cause significant disability.
See also BLEEDING, EXCESSIVE;
PLATELETS

BEST, CHARLES
Charles Best (1899–1978) was a Canadian physiologist who, with Frederick Banting, first discovered in 1922 that a lack of insulin was responsible for the disease diabetes.
See also BANTING, FREDERICK;
DIABETES MELLITUS TYPE ONE

BETA-2 AGONISTS
Also known as sympathomimetics, beta-2 agonists are bronchodilators (dilators of the airways within the lungs) that are used in the treatment of asthma, bronchitis and airway spasm, and are available as pressure pack sprays, nebuliser additives, various inhalers (eg. Turbuhaler, Accuhaler), mixtures, tablets and injections. They act very rapidly if inhaled or injected but more slowly, and with more side effects, if taken as a mixture or tablet. Some forms have a very long action and can act effectively as both a preventer and a treatment.

Examples of short acting medications in this class include salbutamol (Respolin, Asmol, Ventolin), and terbutaline (Bricanyl), while long acting ones include eformoterol (Foradile, Oxis) and salmeterol (Serevent).

Side effects may include tremor, rapid heart rate, palpitations and headache.
See also ASTHMA; ASTHMA
PREVENTION MEDICATION;
MEDICATION

BETA-BLOCKERS
High blood pressure, migraine, irregular heartbeat, stage fright, prevention of heart attack, exam nerves, angina, overactive thyroid gland, tremors and glaucoma – all these diseases can be controlled, or treated, by the amazingly versatile group of drugs called beta-blockers. Some beta-blockers are very specific for particular diseases (eg. timolol is used only in eye drop form for glaucoma while atenolol acts mainly on the heart), but others (eg. propranolol) can act in virtually all areas. They are available on prescription in tablet and injection forms.

Beta receptors are present on certain nerves in the body, and blocking the action of these nerves with beta-blockers produces the desired effects. Because they can control a fine tremor and anxiety about performance, these drugs are banned in the Olympic and Commonwealth games, as they would give athletes such as archers and shooters an unfair advantage. Beta-blockers are generally very safe medications.

Examples include atenolol (Noten, Tenormin), metoprolol (Betaloc), oxprenolol (Corbeton), pindolol (Visken) and propranolol (Inderal).

Side effects may include low blood pressure, slow heart rate, cold hands and feet, nightmares, stuffy nose and impotence. They must not be used in asthmatics as they can trigger an asthma attack, and care must be used when giving them to diabetics.
See also ANGINA; BLOOD PRESSURE;
GLAUCOMA; HYPERTENSION;
MEDICATION; MIGRAINE

BETA CELL TUMOUR
See INSULINOMA

BETAHISTINE
See VASODILATORS

BETAMETHASONE
See STEROIDS

BEZOAR
See TRICHOBEZOAR

BICEPS BRACHII
When body builders show off the muscles in their upper arms, biceps brachii is the muscle that predominates. It is a Y shaped muscle,

with the two upper arms attached to the scapula (shoulder blade), while the lower arm inserts into the top end of the radius, just below the elbow joint. The muscle acts to bend the elbow, and is used in any lifting activity by the arm. The belly of the muscle bulges on the front of the upper arm when the elbow is bent.
See also MUSCLE; RADIUS; SCAPULA

BIGUANIDES
See HYPOGLYCAEMICS

BILE
Bile is a thick yellow-green liquid containing salts that break down fat into small droplets so that it can more easily be digested. Bile is manufactured constantly in the liver, but because it may be required only a few times a day, it is carried from the liver through ducts to the gall bladder, a small pear-shaped bag lying just under the liver, where it is stored until it is needed. If the gall bladder has to be removed for some reason, the duodenum simply receives the necessary bile directly from the liver. Bile is required to help in the digestion of food, but as we do not eat constantly, it is not needed in the gut all the time.
See BILIRUBIN; DUODENUM; GALL BLADDER; LIVER

BILHARZIA
See SCHISTOSOMIASIS

BILIARY COLIC
See GALLSTONES

BILIRUBIN
Bilirubin is a yellowish brown pigment found in bile, which is produced in the liver and stored in the gall bladder. It is produced by the break down of red blood cells and haemoglobin. Excessive amounts in the blood stream indicate excessive destruction of red blood cells, or liver damage. It may form stones in the gall bladder if the concentration becomes excessive. Bile is responsible for the brown colour of faeces. A bilirubin level under 20 µmol/L is considered normal in an adult.
See also BILE; BLOOD TESTS; GALL BLADDER; GILBERT SYNDROME; LIVER; LIVER FUNCTION TESTS

BILLING'S METHOD
See NATURAL FAMILY PLANNING

BINGE PURGE SYNDROME
See BULIMIA NERVOSA

BIOPSY
A biopsy is the removal of a small piece of tissue from an organ or part of the body so that it can be examined under a microscope to detect the presence of abnormal or diseased cells. Biopsies are particularly important in the diagnosis of cancer.

In a skin biopsy a piece of skin is cut away, after giving a local anaesthetic. If the required tissue is from an internal organ (eg. the liver, kidney or lung) a hollow needle is inserted which will suck the tissue out. A local anaesthetic may be applied to the skin. In an endoscopic biopsy, a fine tube with both a lens and a light is passed into the body so that the inside can be seen. A tiny knife in the head of the tube then removes a small specimen of tissue.

Once the tissue has been extracted, it is placed in preservative and sent to the laboratory, where it is set in wax and finely sliced. The slices are then mounted on a glass slide and stained with various dyes which highlight different characteristics. Abnormal cells can be identified and treatment can be decided upon according to the results. During an operation, a biopsy can be performed on abnormal tissue, and the tissue can be snap-frozen, sliced and examined under a microscope immediately.
See also BONE MARROW BIOPSY; BREAST BIOPSY; LYMPH NODE BIOPSY

BIOTIN
See VITAMIN H

BIPOLAR AFFECTIVE DISORDER
See DEPRESSION; MANIA; MANIC-DEPRESSIVE

BIRD FANCIER'S LUNG
See PSITTACOSIS

BIRTH
See LABOUR; PREGNANCY

BISACODYL
See LAXATIVES

BITE
See ANIMAL BITE; BEE STING; BLUE RINGED OCTOPUS AND CONE SHELL; BOX JELLYFISH; FIRST AID; IRUKANDJI SYNDROME; RESUSCITATION; SNAKE BITE; TICKS

BITTER TASTE
See WATERBRASH

BLACK DEATH
The Black Death purportedly arrived in Europe at Messina on the northeast tip of Sicily, at the end of 1346 on a Genoan merchant ship from the Crimea on the Black Sea.

The disease had already spread across Asia from its endemic home in northwest India, where as recently as the 1990s, epidemics have been reported, but on a dramatically smaller scale than that which struck Europe in the fourteenth century. Other contemporary sources give China as the site of the original outbreak. Whichever it was, the impact on Europe altered the history of that continent, and resulted in the emancipation of the serfs due to the acute labour shortages.

From Italy the plague spread slowly and steadily across Europe, reaching Paris and Madrid by the middle of 1348, London by the end of that year, Scotland a year later, and finally Stockholm by the end of 1350. There were amazing escapes, with cities such as Milan and Nuremberg (Germany), and most of modern day Belgium and Poland escaping the devastation, while the populations of other areas such as Florence and Vienna were almost completely wiped out.

Overall one third of the entire population of the continent died in three years, causing enormous social, religious and economic upheaval. For the next 500 years there were sporadic outbreaks of plague, but nothing to equal the Black Death.

Patients developed large, pus-filled glands (buboes) in the neck, groin and armpit. This was followed by a high fever, severe muscle pain, headache, rapid heart rate, profound tiredness and a coma. The infection then spread to the blood and caused black spots (bruises – thus the "Black Death") under the skin. A pneumonia or meningitis also developed, and almost invariably, these complications were fatal.

The true cause of the Black Death was unknown then, but today it is known that a bacterium called *Yersinia pestis* is responsible for a disease known as bubonic plague that has all these symptoms. It normally infects rats, and passes from one rat to another in fleas. If a flea carrying the bacteria bites a human, that person will develop the disease.
See also BUBONIC PLAGUE

BLACK EYE
A bruised or black eye can be relieved by an ice pack (not the traditional piece of steak). Be careful not to bring the eye into direct contact with the ice but wrap the ice in a damp cloth and alternately leave it on and remove it from the eye for about ten minutes at a time.

If the eyeball seems to be injured or the victim is unable to see properly, seek medical attention. The eye should be padded and bandaged shut while travelling to the doctor or hospital.
See also EYE INJURY

BLACK FAECES
See FAECES, BLACK

BLACK MOLE
See BLUE NAEVUS; MELANOMA

BLACK NAIL
See NAIL DISCOLOURED; SUBUNGAL HAEMATOMA

BLACKOUT
See FAINT

BLACK SPOTS IN VISION
See VISUAL BLACK SPOTS

BLACKWATER FEVER
See MALARIA

BLADDER
The urinary bladder is situated deep in the pelvis behind the pubic bone and is linked to the kidneys by two long tubes called the ureters, and to the outside of the body by another tube called the urethra. The kidneys constantly manufacture urine from the body's waste products. The bladder is a hollow bag in which urine is stored before being excreted at a convenient time. It has a capacity of about 500mL, and as it fills up, the elastic walls are stretched, giving rise to the urge to urinate.

LONGITUDINAL SECTION OF FEMALE PELVIS

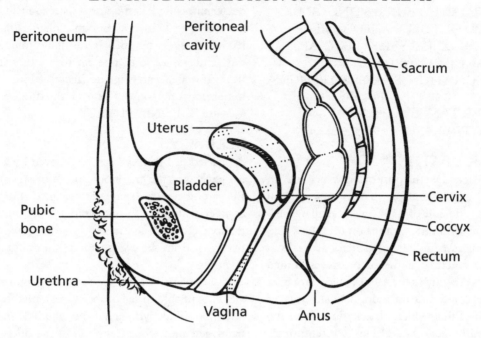

On an appropriate signal from the brain, the muscles around the bladder contract at the same time as a ring of muscle at the bottom of the bladder is relaxed, allowing the collected urine to pass into the urethra and from there to the outside.
See also CYSTITIS; CYSTOSCOPY; KIDNEYS; URETER; URETHRA; URINATION PAIN

BLADDER INFECTION
See CYSTITIS

BLAND DIET
A bland diet consists of vegetables (cooked without any sauces or spices), fish, chicken breast (no skin), most forms of cereal (eg. bread, corn flakes), and fruit taken in moderation. Fatty, fried and dairy foods should be avoided. This type of diet is used to settle the bowel in many conditions, but particularly in chronic diarrhoea.

BLANKET COMFORTER
See COMFORTER

BLASTOCYST
The ball of stem cells that forms from a zygote immediately after conception is called a blastocyst. The blastocyst travels down the Fallopian tube to the uterus where it implants in the wall, seven days after fertilisation. Once implanted it becomes an embryo.

See also CONCEPTION; EMBRYO; STEM CELL; ZYGOTE

BLASTOCYSTIS
Blastocystis is an organism (protozoan) that is widespread in every part of the world, and normally lives in the human intestine without causing any symptoms. Symptoms occur only in cases where there is a very heavy infestation, the patient is particularly sensitive to the organism, or the patient has a deficient immune system (eg. AIDS). It spreads from person to person by a wide range of intermediates that include everything from the house fly to the earth worm, as well as other animals and humans.

Often there are no symptoms, but when they occur patients develop diarrhoea, belly pains, nausea and loss of appetite. Rarely, an infestation of the lungs may occur. The diagnosis can be made by examining a sample of faeces under a microscope.

Usually no treatment is necessary, as the infestation is self-limiting and settles in a few days, but if required, the antibiotic metronidazole is used to clear the organism from the gut.
See also ANTIANAEROBES; DIARRHOEA; PROTOZOA

BLASTOMYCOSIS
Blastomycosis is a serious fungal infection of the lungs and skin caused by the fungus

Blastomycoses dermatitidis which is found in the soil in tropical areas, and may be inhaled in dust. Person to person infection does not occur, and infection is far more common in men than women.

Symptoms include a severe pneumonia-like illness with fever, mucus-producing cough, muscle pains, tiredness, weight loss and skin sores. It may spread to brain, bone, joints, lymph nodes, prostate gland and cause skin ulcers that are slow to heal. Sputum samples and swabs from skin sores can be taken in an attempt to identify the responsible fungus, and a chest x-ray is abnormal.

Treatment involves regular injections into a vein with potent antifungal drugs (eg. amphotericin B, ketaconazole) for several months, but it is difficult to cure, and the mortality rate is 15%.
See also FUNGI

BLEEDING

A person who is bleeding severely may die from blood loss if it is not stopped. Blood can be lost rapidly from a severed or torn artery, and it is vital to act quickly to avoid shock and unconsciousness. Severe blood loss is when an adult loses one litre of blood or a child as little as 300mL.

There are three ways bleeding can be controlled: –
• Press directly on the wound, which will stop the blood flow and encourage clotting.
• Raise the wounded part so the pressure is reduced.
• Press on the artery supplying the wounded area so the blood supply is cut off. Do not use a tourniquet.

Severe bleeding is often very alarming but it can be controlled relatively simply. The steps involved are: –
• Lie patient flat and if possible raise the injured part (although not if a fracture is suspected since moving it may make it worse).
• Apply direct pressure to the wound. Ideally, a dressing should be used, but if none is available use a piece of clothing, or even the hand. If the wound is gaping, hold its edges firmly together. If there is anything in the wound, try to press around it rather than directly on it. Unless the foreign body is lying loose on top of the wound, do not remove it – it may be plugging the wound and therefore reducing blood loss.

• Bind the wound up so that pressure is maintained – use clothing torn into strips if no dressing is available.
• If blood oozes through the binding, do not remove the binding – add more (eg. a towel). If a dressing is removed once it has been applied, it will dislodge the blood clot that will have formed and bleeding will start again.
• Get medical help or take the victim to hospital as soon as possible.
• Keep checking the victim for signs of shock or a cessation of bleeding or circulation. If necessary give mouth to mouth resuscitation or cardiopulmonary resuscitation.
See also ARTERIAL PRESSURE POINTS; ANAL BLEEDING; BLEEDING, EXCESSIVE; BRUISING, EXCESSIVE; COUGHING BLOOD; FAECAL BLOOD; FIRST AID; NOSEBLEED; RESUSCITATION; URINE BLOOD; VAGINAL BLEEDING ABNORMAL; VOMITING BLOOD.

BLEEDING, EXCESSIVE

The medical term haemorrhage is used to describe an excessive loss of blood.

There are some people who are born with defects in the chemical pathways that cause blood to clot, or who develop a lack of one of the essential elements for clotting, and become bleeders. Instead of stopping within a few minutes of an injury, bleeding may persist for hours, and the slightest injury may cause massive bruises, or bleeding into joints that leads to arthritis. Haemophilia (lack of factor VIII) and Christmas disease (lack of factor IX) are inherited diseases of excessive bleeding. These diseases only occur in males, but females act as the carriers from one generation to the next.

Some people develop diseases which destroy the platelets in the blood stream. Platelets are cell-like structures in the blood which stick together to form a clot. Without adequate numbers, excess bleeding occurs, and multiple small bruises may develop under the skin. Diseases as diverse as virus infections, german measles, drug reactions and rare cancer-like conditions may lead to a lack of platelets (thrombocytopenia). Often there is no apparent cause for the problem.

Other uncommon causes for excessive bleeding include aplastic anaemia (a very serious, and potentially fatal condition in which bone marrow fails to produce blood cells), disseminated intravascular coagulation (a rare condition in which clotting occurs within normal arteries and veins in one area of the body), a lack of vitamin K or vitamin C (scurvy), von Willebrand disease and the Bernard-Soulier syndrome (inherited platelet defect).

Drugs designed to reduce clotting (eg. warfarin, heparin, aspirin) may be taken to prevent strokes and heart attacks, but in excess will cause bleeding.
See also BLEEDING; BLOOD; PREGNANCY BLEEDING; SKIN RED SPOTS and separate entries for diseases mentioned above.

BLEOMYCIN
See CYTOTOXICS AND ANTINEOPLASTICS

BLEPHARITIS
Blepharitis is a common inflammatory condition of the eyelid edges caused by a bacterial infection, allergy or a reaction to an environmental factor.

Both eyelids become red, covered with scales, sore and itchy. In advanced cases the eyelashes may fall out, and ulcers form on the lid margins. Treatment involves cleaning away the scales several times a day with moist cotton wool, which may be dipped in baby shampoo, and applying antibiotic ointment to the affected areas of the eyelids. It is often difficult to cure and often recurrent.
See also EYELID DISEASE

BLIGHTED OVUM
See MISCARRIAGE

BLINDNESS
Loss of the sense of vision is one of the most devastating things that a person can experience. Fortunately, sudden total blindness is rare, but a partial loss of sight is quite common.

Causes include a serious injury to the eye, or damage to the part of the brain that is responsible for perceiving vision (eg. by a stroke,

tumour, cancer, abscess or direct injury), or an ulcer on the surface of the eye (cornea) caused by infection, injury or an object in the eye.

Other common causes include trachoma (a type of conjunctivitis), a cataract (clouding of the lens in the eye that causes gradual loss of sight over many years, usually in the elderly), glaucoma (an increase in the pressure of the jelly like fluid inside the eye) and macular degeneration (due to a poor blood supply to the retina at the back of the eye in the elderly).

Uncommon causes include retinal detachment (the light sensitive retina at the back of the eye becomes detached from the globe of the eye), inflammation of the optic nerve (optic neuritis), extremely high blood pressure (malignant hypertension), diabetes, bleeding into the fluid in the eye, Behçet syndrome, craniopharyngioma (form of brain tumour), retinitis pigmentosa, Lowe syndrome and Vogt-Koyanagi-Harada syndrome.

Certain poisons (eg. methanol) and medication overdoses (eg. quinine) will damage or destroy the retina.
See also AMAUROSIS FUGAX; CATARACT; EYE; GLAUCOMA; VISION, BLURRED; VISION, HALF LOST and separate entries for most diseases mentioned above.

BLIND SPOT
When we see something, light reaching the retina at the back of the eye stimulates nerve cells which convert it into electrical impulses and send these along the optic nerve to the brain. The point where the optic nerve leaves the retina has no light sensitive cells and so forms a blind spot. You can find your blind spot by the following simple test.

Hold this page at arms length and close your left eye. Look at the cross with the right eye, and move the page slowly towards you. When the dot disappears, its image has fallen on the blind spot of the right eye.
See also EYE

BLISTERS
Blisters on the skin can vary in size from pin heads to several centimetres across. They may

BLIND SPOT TEST

be full of clear fluid, or creamy pus, and there may be one or hundreds of them.

A single blister full of clear fluid may be due to an insect or spider bite, which can often appear as a clear blister in the centre of a small red patch of skin. A significant burn will cause a clear blister to arise at the site of the burn.

Multiple blisters full of clear fluid may be due to contact dermatitis (a red rash that then develops multiple tiny blisters), shingles (painful blistering rash on one specific area of the body – this is a medical emergency, as the viral infection can be completely cured if treated within seventy-two hours of the rash starting), erythema multiforme, and herpes simplex ('type one' causes cold sores on the face, while 'type two' causes genital herpes).

Drug eruptions occur when a patient is sensitive or allergic to a medication, and they may cause multiple large clear fluid-filled blisters on many areas of the body.

Chickenpox is the most common infection to cause small, scattered fluid-filled blisters. The rash usually starts on the head or chest as red pimples, then spreads onto the legs and arms, and develops into blisters before drying up and scabbing over.

Shingles is an infection of a spinal nerve caused by the same virus that causes chickenpox. At times of stress or reduced immunity, the virus may start to multiply again in one particular nerve, causing sharp pain that gradually moves along the nerve on one side only. It may occur from the back to the front of the abdomen, or on the face or a limb. Shortly after the pain starts, a patchy blistering rash will appear in a line along the course of the nerve.

Genital herpes and cold sores are caused by different forms of the *Herpes simplex* virus. Genital herpes causes a blister which bursts to form a very painful, tender, shallow ulcer that persists for ten to twenty days.

Multiple blisters filled with a creamy substance may be due to molluscum contagiosum (a common viral infection of the skin in children), impetigo (school sores – a bacterial infection), cellulitis (a skin infection, that in severe cases may break down the overlying skin to form large slack pus-filled blisters) and erysipelas (a superficial infection of skin that causes blisters similar to cellulitis).

Virtually every child will eventually develop hand, foot and mouth disease, which is caused by a *Coxsackie* virus. In severe cases a child will develop blisters on the soles and palms, and mouth ulcers that persist for three to five days before settling.

Less common causes of skin blisters include cellulitis (skin infection), pemphigoid (a skin disease usually of elderly women), pemphigus (an autoimmune skin disease), erythema multiforme, porphyria, lichen planus, epidermolysis-bullosa (inherited) and toxic epidermal necrolysis (a severe but rare skin condition caused by exposure to a toxin or poison which causes large clear fluid filled blisters to form on extensive areas of the body).

A number of other unusual skin diseases may cause large blistering, often associated with peeling of large amounts of skin, as though the patient had been sunburned.
See also PUSTULES; SKIN and separate entries for diseases mentioned above.

BLOATING

When a patient feels bloated, their intestine is full of excess gas, and they may burp excessively and pass excess wind (flatulence). Consuming too much gassy fluid, be it lemonade, beer or champagne, can add an uncomfortable amount of gas to the intestine. Foods such as beans and cereals may ferment in the gut to create gas. Severe constipation will give the sensation of bloating due to the retention of faeces and fluid as well as gas.

Other possible causes include infection with bacteria such as *Giardia*, the irritable bowel syndrome (characterised by intermittent belly pain, irregular bowels, bloating and indigestion), the gas bloat syndrome (a complication of surgery to the stomach), and a partial or complete obstruction of the gut by a tumour, cancer, twisting (eg. volvulus), polyp, intussusception (infolding of gut) or Crohn's disease (thickened gut wall).
See also BURPING, EXCESSIVE; FLATULENCE and separate entries for diseases mentioned above.

BLOCKED TEAR DUCT
See CONJUNCTIVITIS

BLOOD

One of the many miracles of human life is blood. It is a liquid that transports the necessary elements of existence to every cell in the body, but if allowed to leak out of a vein, artery or capillary, will rapidly solidify to prevent further loss. Clotting is accepted as normal, but more than a score of different chemicals, cells and enzymes are involved in an extremely complex interaction to convert this liquid into a solid.

Blood also delivers oxygen collected from the air and nutrients extracted from food to every cell, and it also gathers up waste products such as carbon dioxide and uric acid and transports them to appropriate organs for eventual disposal. Blood also protects against infection and regulates temperature and fluid levels.

The channels through which blood flows are the arteries and veins. The main pumping mechanism forcing the blood along is the heart. Veins carry the blood to the heart, and arteries carry it away from the heart.

About 55% of blood is a straw-coloured fluid called plasma. The rest is made up of three different types of cells with totally different functions. Red blood cells transport oxygen and carbon dioxide, white blood cells help to fight infection, and platelets assist in blood clotting.

Plasma itself is over 90% water. The remaining 10% contains just about everything the body needs to function – glucose, protein, salts, vitamins, chemicals, hormones and infection-fighting antibodies – as well as the waste products to be discarded. The proportions vary according to the particular needs of the body.

Serum is the clear yellowish watery fluid that remains if the chemicals responsible for clotting are removed from plasma.
See also BLEEDING; PLATELETS; RED BLOOD CELLS; SPLEEN; WHITE BLOOD CELLS

BLOOD CLOTTING TEST
A clotting or coagulation test measures how long it takes the blood to clot. This test may be ordered for someone who bruises or bleeds excessively to find out if they suffer from a hereditary disease such as haemophilia, or one of the many other diseases that can reduce clotting.

Patients with a high risk of blood clots forming in the heart, an artery or vein, which may result in a heart attack, lung damage or stroke, may be placed on anticoagulant drugs (eg. warfarin). Clotting tests are carried out regularly to monitor the effect of these drugs and to ensure that a balance is maintained between preventing a clot forming and stopping the blood clotting at all.

These tests are often reported as a ratio (international normalised ratio – INR) which measures how much longer the patient takes to stop bleeding than normal. A person with an INR of 3 takes three times as long to stop bleeding as a normal person. The doctor will determine the INR which is desirable for the patient (usually between 2 and 3.5), depending upon their diagnosis.
See also ANTICOAGULANTS; BLOOD TESTS

BLOOD GAS ANALYSIS
Oxygen is extracted from the air by the lungs and transferred to the blood to be pumped throughout the body. The oxygen is exchanged with the waste product, carbon dioxide, which is contained in blood that has been used. If the lungs are diseased, this exchange process will not take place efficiently, and the blood will retain carbon dioxide and will not receive adequate oxygen.

Blood gas analysis measures the concentration of oxygen and carbon dioxide in the blood and can tell if lung diseases such as asthma, pneumonia, emphysema or pneumoconiosis may be present. The blood sample is taken by a needle directly puncturing an artery in the groin or wrist. The blood must not come into contact with air before being analysed, so the test is normally performed in a hospital or laboratory.
See also BLOOD TESTS; LUNG; PEAK EXPIRATORY FLOW RATE; VITAL CAPACITY

BLOOD GLUCOSE
See BLOOD SUGAR

BLOOD GROUPS
Antigens are proteins that stimulate the production of antibodies to fight infection, and different antigens are found in different types of blood. If a person with antigens of one kind receives blood with antigens of a different kind, antibodies will be produced to cause a transfusion reaction. The main antigens to cause problems are named A and B. The blood group you have depends on the presence of these antigens in your blood. The four

blood types are A, B, AB, and O. People in the A group have A antigens in their blood, people in the B group have B antigens, and people in AB have both. O denotes people who have neither A nor B antigens. There is no specific logic to the naming of the blood groups as A and B, merely convenience. Patients who need a blood transfusion must be given blood from the same group to avoid a reaction. The blood group is inherited from the parents, and so can be used as a basic test of paternity.

About 45% of Europeans have group O blood. Group O blood can also be given in an emergency because it does not have either the A or B antigens. Type B blood is the most common type in Asian races.

Another antigen contained in blood is called the Rhesus (Rh) factor, but not everyone has it. People who do have it (about 85% of the population) are said to be Rh positive. People who do not have it are Rh negative. If Rh positive blood is given to an Rh negative person, they may produce antibodies to fight off the foreign invader and so destroy the transfused blood. Once the antibodies have been produced and are in the system, a further transfusion of Rh positive blood can be fatal.

There are many other types of antigens in blood (eg. M, N, S, U) that can have varying adverse effects when a blood transfusion is given.
See also ANTIGEN; ARTERIES;
CIRCULATORY SYSTEM; HEART;
SERUM SICKNESS; TRANSFUSION
REACTION; VEINS

BLOOD POISONING
See SEPTICAEMIA

BLOOD PRESSURE
Blood pressure is just that – the pressure of the blood against the walls of the main arteries.

The pumping action of the heart causes waves of pressure. As the muscle contracts, a spurt of blood is forced out into the arteries, and as the muscle relaxes so that the heart can refill, the pressure eases. The period of contraction is called systole and the period of relaxation is known as diastole.

The pressure can be measured by a sphygmomanometer which measures pressure by using a column of mercury, a spring gauge, or electronically. The pressure is usually expressed as two numbers representing each extreme of pressure. The systolic pressure in a young healthy adult usually varies from about 90 to 120mm of mercury and the diastolic pressure between 60 and 80mm. Hence a reading might be, say, 90/60 or 120/80. A blood pressure of up to 145/85 is considered normal in a middle-aged person.

Blood pressure varies between individuals and according to age (older people tend to have slightly increased blood pressure), physical activity, and physical and emotional well being.

In general, low blood pressure is preferable to high blood pressure. Higher than normal pressure over an extended period can be a sign of underlying disease or itself lead to major health problems. Very low blood pressure can also be a problem, for example severe shock can cause the blood pressure to fall so that not enough blood is transported through the body to keep it functioning properly.
See also ACE INHIBITORS; ALPHA
BLOCKERS; BETA-BLOCKERS;
CALCIUM CHANNEL BLOCKERS;
DIURETICS; HYPERTENSION;
HYPOTENSION;
SPHYGMOMANOMETER

BLOOD SUGAR
See GLUCOSE, BLOOD

BLOOD TAKING
Blood is extracted by inserting a hollow needle into a vein and allowing an amount of blood to flow into an attached tube. The blood will usually be taken from a vein at the bend in the elbow, but if that is not sufficiently prominent, it may be taken the forearm or the back of the hand. Once sufficient blood has been obtained, the needle is withdrawn and a pad of dressing or cotton wool pressed on to the point of entry to stop the blood flow. For very minor blood tests where not much blood is needed, such as for a simple sugar test, enough blood may be obtained from a prick in the finger.

If the blood test is to measure the proportions of oxygen and carbon dioxide in the blood (a blood gas analysis), it will be taken from an artery, because arterial blood contains oxygen absorbed from the air in the lungs. In this case, blood will be taken with a needle and syringe from the arm, wrist or groin. This is more uncomfortable than taking blood from a vein and the patient may be given a local anaesthetic.

Usually the blood can be taken at any time of the day, unless the test is for glucose, cholesterol, triglycerides or other measures of metabolism (how the body converts food into energy), in which case the test is ordered in the morning after a twelve hour fast, or at particular times after eating a certain measured amount of food. Blood tests to measure the amount of some drugs in the body are also taken at specific times after the medication is swallowed.
See also BLOOD

BLOOD TESTING

Blood is made up of cells suspended in straw coloured fluid called plasma. Blood serum is the fluid that separates from clotted blood or blood plasma when it is allowed to stand. Most tests are carried out on serum. When blood is collected, it is placed in a plain glass or plastic tube in which it clots. If the blood cells or plasma are to be examined, some of the sample is put into a different tube containing a chemical that stops it clotting (a whole blood sample). The cells and clot are then separated from the plasma or serum by spinning the tube in a centrifuge.

Most blood tests are carried out by machines called auto-analysers and are available within twelve hours of the sample reaching the laboratory. Unusual or specialised tests may take a few days, since they are performed in batches once or twice a week.
See also BLOOD TAKING; PATHOLOGY

BLOOD TESTS

Blood tests are the most useful and commonly ordered of all diagnostic tests. A blood test can not only give information about your blood (eg. whether it contains infection-causing bacteria, drugs or alcohol), but also shows many changes involving quite separate organs. For example, if the liver is malfunctioning, the problem will almost certainly show up in blood tests. Consequently, blood tests are used not only for information on the blood itself but to diagnose disorders of many of the organs and systems of the body.

The blood tests described further in this text are listed below.

See also ALDOSTERONE; BILIRUBIN; BLOOD; BLOOD CLOTTING TESTS; BLOOD GAS ANALYSIS; BLOOD GROUPS; BLOOD TAKING; CANCER ASSOCIATED ANTIGEN; CREATININE; ELECTROLYTES; ESR; FULL BLOOD COUNT; GAMMA-GLUTAMYL TRANSFERASE; GLUCOSE, BLOOD; HAEMOGLOBIN; IMMUNE TESTS; IRON; LIPIDS; MBA; PATHOLOGY; PHOSPHORUS; POTASSIUM; PROSTATE SPECIFIC ANTIGEN; THYROID FUNCTION TESTS; URIC ACID; ZINC

BLOOD TRANSFUSION REACTION
See TRANSFUSION REACTION

BLOOD UNDER NAIL
See SUBUNGUAL HAEMATOMA

BLOODY FAECES
See FAECES BLOOD

BLOOM SYNDROME

Bloom syndrome is an extremely rare familial genetic abnormality that occurs in Jews. These children are small at birth, have light sensitive skin, underdeveloped cheeks, leukaemia and other malignant diseases. Some have spider naevi (blood vessels) on the facial skin. People who are carriers of the gene, but do not suffer from the syndrome, are more likely to develop cancers. No treatment is available and death in adolescence is common.
See also RILEY-DAY SYNDROME

BLUE BABY
See VENTRICULAR SEPTAL DEFECT

BLUE BOTTLE JELLYFISH
See JELLYFISH STING

BLUE NAEVUS

A blue naevus is a benign (non-cancerous) blue coloured mole that may be found anywhere on the body, and usually appears on older children and teenagers, but may develop at any age. It is caused by overproduction of pigment in the deeper layers of the skin by melanocytes (skin cells that are responsible for pigment production). No treatment is necessary unless the mole is cosmetically

unacceptable, when it can be surgically excised.
See also NAEVUS

BLUE NAIL
See NAIL DISCOLOURED

BLUE-RINGED OCTOPUS AND CONE SHELL
Blue-ringed octopus and cone shells are often found in rock pools along the Australian coastline. They are extremely poisonous with venom that acts very quickly. A cone shell sting is usually painful, but that of the blue-ringed octopus is not necessarily painful at all. The blue-ringed octopus is an attractive creature that invites handling – but never touch one! It is yellowish in colour, with blue bands that become iridescent when the octopus is disturbed.

Indications that a person has been stung include numbness of the lips and tongue (usually within minutes), muscular weakness and inability to breathe. First aiders should : –
• reassure and calm the victim
• send for medical help
• make sure the victim is not left unattended
• start mouth-to-mouth resuscitation as soon as breathing starts to weaken. Keep it up until medical help arrives as the victim will not be able to breathe for themselves.
• apply cardiopulmonary resuscitation if the victim's pulse stops
See also FIRST AID; RESUSCITATION

BLUE SKIN
See SKIN BLUE

BLURRED VISION
See VISION, BLURRED

BODY DYSMORPHIC DISORDER
See OBSESSIVE COMPULSIVE NEUROSIS

BOERHAAVE SYNDROME
Boerhaave syndrome is the spontaneous rupture of the oesophagus (gullet), often following gluttonous overeating. Patients have sudden severe chest pain and then collapse, and sometimes die. Gastroscopy reveals the rupture. Surgical repair of oesophagus is essential, but there may be a permanent stricture (narrowing) at the site of repair.
See also OESOPHAGUS

BOIL
A boil (or furuncle) is a small superficial abscess that develops when a hair follicle becomes infected by bacteria. As a result, people who are very hairy will develop more boils. Commonly affected areas are the armpits, buttocks and groin.

Patients develop an acutely painful, red and tender lump, which gradually enlarges, causing more and more pain until it ruptures, discharging pus.

Treatment involves antibiotic tablets, applying antiseptic or antibiotic ointment to the boil, and when pus is obviously present, lancing the boil with a scalpel or needle. Repeated attacks may require long-term antibiotic treatment, antiseptic soaps and antiseptic lotions applied regularly.

In some cases infection can spread to cause boils in other areas, or in severe cases, the infection may enter the blood stream to cause septicaemia. Boils should never be squeezed, as the pus they contain may rupture internally, and spread through the blood stream to the brain and other vital organs.

A carbuncle is several boils in a limited area that join together to form an interconnecting infected mass that will degenerate into an abscess.
See also ABSCESS; BACTERIA; FURUNCULOSIS, EAR

BONE
The bones of the skeleton safeguard the internal organs and support the body. The rib cage shields the heart and lungs and the skull protects the brain. Bone is active living tissue, able to repair itself when damaged, and a major contributor to the ongoing functioning of the body.

The skeleton can be seen as early as eight weeks in a developing foetus, but at that stage it is not bone but cartilage (gristle). Gradually the cartilage is transformed into bone by the laying down of calcium, phosphorus and other hard minerals in the cartilage. In most bones, the process of change is well under way by the time of birth, but it is not completed until the age of about sixteen years in girls and eighteen or more years in boys. Children's bones are therefore flexible and able to withstand the rough and tumble games they are subjected to.

In an adult body, bone makes up about

sixteen percent of its total weight. A person's height is determined by the length of their bones, particularly those in the thighs (the femurs). Bone is also extraordinarily strong – about four times stronger under stretching than its equivalent weight in steel or aluminium.

Adults have fewer bones than children. A baby is born with 350 bones. Many of these then fuse as the child grows, and by the time a person has reached twenty to twenty-five years of age, they will typically have 206 permanent bones.

Bone is classified into four types according to shape – long, short, flat and irregular. The long bones are those in the arms and legs, and are thin, hollow and light, enabling ease of movement. The short bones include those in the wrists and ankles and are geared to provide strength as well as limited movement. Flat bones include most of those in the skull, the breast bone, ribs and the shoulder blades. Irregular bones are those that don't fit into the other categories and include some of the skull bones and the bones of the spine (the vertebrae).

All bones consist of two different types of bone – hard (compact) bone on the outside encasing spongy (cancellous) bone on the inside. The combination gives both elasticity and strength, and the proportions of hard and spongy tissue in individual bones (or even within the same bone) vary depending on which quality is the more important in the function of that particular bone.

The spongy interior of most bones is filled with marrow, a soft gelatinous substance that produces white blood cells (to fight infection), red blood cells (to carry oxygen) and platelets (which help stop bleeding). Bone marrow is crucial to the maintenance of life. Blood vessels and nerves pass into the spongy interior of a bone through small channels in the hard outer layer. Surrounding and protecting each bone is a thin tough membrane called the periosteum.

Generally speaking, bones grow from a point near each end. Bone growth is stimulated by hormones produced by the pituitary and thyroid glands. The long bones, where most growth takes place during childhood, grow at only one end. These growing ends are separated from the main part of the bone by cartilage, and it is by the constant formation of new cartilage which is then replaced by bone that growth takes place. Growth stops when cartilage is no longer formed and the growing end and the parent bone become one.

All bones are constantly renewed. Old bone is absorbed into the bloodstream to be eventually eliminated from the body and new bone is laid down. If a bone is broken, it will eventually heal perfectly because of this ongoing regeneration.

The high calcium content of bone means that it acts as a reserve store of calcium. If the calcium levels in the blood get too low, calcium is drawn from the bones.

The largest bone in the body is the femur (thigh bone) while the smallest is the stapes in the middle ear.
See also CALCIUM; FEMUR; FIBULA; FRACTURE; HUMERUS; PELVIS; RADIUS; RED BLOOD CELLS; RIB; SESAMOID BONE; SKELETON; SKULL; STERNUM; TIBIA; ULNAR; VERTEBRA; WHITE BLOOD CELLS

BONE BREAK
See FRACTURE

BONE CANCER
There are many different forms of bone cancer depending on which bone cell types are involved, including osteomas, fibrosarcoma, enchondroma (start in cartilage), chondrosarcoma, osteoclastoma (giant cell tumours), osteosarcoma and Ewing tumours. The most common type is that which spreads from cancer in another tissue (metastatic cancer) such as the breast and prostate.

Osteosarcoma (osteogenic sarcoma) is a form of bone cancer that occurs in teenagers and young adults, and is more common in males than females. The knee and elbow are the most commonly affected areas.

Common symptoms are bone pain and swelling, although many types of bone cancer may show no symptoms until the disease is quite advanced. Painful or swollen joints and limitation of joint movement are also possible. Diagnosis involves x-rays, CT scans, bone scans, bone biopsy and blood tests.

These cancers are treated using a combination of amputation, surgical removal, irradiation and drugs, depending on the exact type of cancer present. The outcome is extremely variable, depending on the type of cancer, the

stage at which it is diagnosed, the position in the body, the age of the patient and the response to treatment, but the outcome is better the further out along the limb the cancer develops. The overall cure rate is only fifty percent. For cancer in the forearm or lower leg, seventy percent are cured, but for cancers in the pelvis or breast bone, there are virtually no survivors. Metastatic cancers usually have a far poorer outcome than cancers that actually start in the bone.
See also BONE; CANCER; EWING TUMOUR

BONE FRACTURE
See FRACTURE

BONE INFECTION
See OSTEOMYELITIS

BONE LUMP
Most lumps felt on a bone are not serious, but because some may be, all should be checked by a doctor, and probably x-rayed. Many lumps felt by the patient as being in the bone, are actually in the tissue around the bone. Examples include ganglions (firm cysts) on the wrist and ankle, swellings associated with arthritis in a joint, and scars or cysts in fibrous tissue around a joint.

Lumps are often found on bones at the site of a recent fracture. The bone may no longer be painful or tender, but a lump may persist at the site of the break for months, or even years, afterwards.

The bone is covered by a very fine membrane (periosteum). If a bone close to the skin (eg. shin) is knocked hard, bleeding may occur under the periosteum to cause a firm, tender lump, that may be slowly transformed into bone before eventually subsiding.

Cysts can occur in bone from birth, or may slowly develop at a later age, but usually in childhood. They are quite harmless unless they are uncomfortable or disfiguring.

Lumps may appear in the growing plates (the point in long bones where growth occurs) of rapidly growing children, particularly just below the knee.

The most serious cause of a bone lump is a cancer (osteoma or sarcoma). Cancer may start in bone itself, in the surrounding tissues, or may spread from a primary cancer in a distant organ (eg. breast, bowel) to start a new growth in bone. Most, but not all, bone cancers are tender and painful.
See also ARTHRITIS; BONE CANCER

BONE MARROW BIOPSY
A bone marrow biopsy is most commonly carried out in cases of suspected leukaemia and certain anaemias. The bone marrow is responsible for the production of new blood cells, and an analysis of bone marrow can give vital information if this production seems to have been disrupted and has caused disease.

Marrow is obtained through a needle inserted into the cavity of either the breastbone or the pelvic bone. A local anaesthetic is given, but there will usually be some pain as the needle reaches the interior. A smear of the bone marrow extracted is examined to assess such things as the number of cells, the internal chemistry and the maturity of the cells, and the presence of abnormal cells.
See also APLASTIC ANAEMIA; LEUKAEMIA

BONE PAIN
See ARM PAIN; FRACTURE; FOOT PAIN; LEG PAIN

BONE SCAN
See DUAL PHOTON DENSITOMETRY; NUCLEAR SCAN

BONE, WEAK
See FRACTURE; OSTEOGENESIS IMPERFECTA; OSTEOPOROSIS; PAGET'S DISEASE OF BONE; RICKETS

BORBORYGMI
See BOWEL NOISY

BORNHOLM DISEASE
Also known as pleurodynia, Bornholm disease is a *Coxsackie* virus infection that attacks the pleura at the point where the diaphragm attaches to the ribs at the back of the chest. The pleura is the smooth membrane that surrounds the lungs within the chest. The disease is named after a Danish island.

Patients experience sudden, severe, lower chest pain that is aggravated by chest movements such as a deep breath or cough. Other symptoms include a fever, headache, nausea, and sore throat. There is marked tenderness of the lower ribs.

Unfortunately no cure is available. The patient is given rest and aspirin until the disease settles, usually after two or three weeks.
See also COXSACKIE VIRUS INFECTION

BORRELIA
See RELAPSING FEVER

BOTTLE FEEDING
Although cow's milk is part of the normal diet of most Western nations, it is not suitable for young babies. The naturally intended food for babies is breast milk, and a baby who is not being breastfed must be fed with special formulas developed to approximate breast milk, which has more sugar and less protein than cow's milk.

Provided the manufacturer's instructions are followed exactly, most babies will thrive on formula. It is quite wrong to think that a slightly stronger formula might give the baby more nourishment. If the mixture is made stronger than the manufacturer recommends, the baby will get too much fat, protein, minerals and salt, and not enough water.

Milk, especially when at room temperature, is an ideal breeding ground for bacteria, and it is therefore essential that formula is prepared in a sterile environment. Bottles, utensils, measuring implements, teats and anything used in the preparation of a baby's food must be boiled and stored in one of the commercially available sterilising solutions. Carers should also wash their hands before embarking on preparation. Made-up formula must be stored in the refrigerator. If these precautions are not followed, the baby may develop gastroenteritis and require hospitalisation.

The baby should be allowed some say in how much food s/he needs. Carers will generally be advised by the hospital or baby health clinic how much to offer the baby (calculated according to weight), but just as breastfed babies have different needs that can vary from feed to feed, so too do bottle-fed babies. Mothers often feel that the baby should finish the last drop in the bottle. But within reason, babies can generally be relied upon to assess their own needs quite satisfactorily.

Just as with breastfed babies, it is generally considered best to feed a baby as and when they are hungry. In the first few weeks this may be at irregular and frequent intervals. It takes about three or four hours for a feed to be digested, and as the baby's digestive system matures, signs of hunger will normally settle down into a regular pattern.

The rate at which babies feed also varies. Some like to gulp down their formula, while others like to take things easy. The rate of feed can upset a baby if it is too fast or slow for its liking. Teats with different hole sizes can be purchased, and a small hole can be enlarged with a hot needle. Frequent breaks from the bottle during a feed in order to let a burp come up and the milk go down can also smooth the progress of the feed and avoid stomach discomfort afterwards.
See also BABIES; BABY FEEDING; BREAST FEEDING

BOTULISM
Botulism is an extremely severe form of food poisoning. Home-preserved fruits and vegetables, and very rarely commercially canned foods, may be responsible for harbouring the bacterium *Clostridium botulinum* which is capable of producing an extremely potent poison (toxin) that attacks the nervous system.

Twelve to thirty-six hours after eating inadequately preserved food, the patient develops double vision, difficulty in swallowing and talking, a dry mouth, nausea and vomiting. The muscles become weak, and breathing becomes steadily more difficult. The patient must be hospitalised immediately and put upon an artificial breathing machine (ventilator) to maintain lung function once the paralysis occurs. An antitoxin is also available for injection.

Death occurs in about 70% of patients unless adequate medical treatment in a major hospital is readily available. In the best circumstances, up to 25% of patients will still die.
See also FOOD POISONING

BOWEL
See LARGE INTESTINE;
SMALL INTESTINE

BOWEL CANCER
See COLORECTAL CANCER

BOWEL MOVEMENTS IRREGULAR
Irregular bowel habits need to be investigated thoroughly by a doctor, as they may be an

early sign of many different bowel diseases. It may be that something simple like stress and anxiety, hormonal changes during the month, or different foods may be responsible for the problem. Unfortunately, diverticulitis, ulcerative colitis and bowel cancer can also first show up as alternating diarrhoea and constipation.
See also CONSTIPATION; DIARRHOEA

BOWEL NOISY

Onomatopoeia is the term used to describe words that sound like what they mean. The grunts, groans and baarrrooms of the stomach are alliteratively described as borborygmi by doctors and they are due to an overactive intestine as it moves food from one end of the gut to the other.

Some people have more active intestines than others, but everyone suffers this complaint with infections and some other disorders. The problem can be aggravated by nervous swallowing of air, hunger, eating rapidly or drinking large amounts of aerated drinks.

A viral infection of the intestine (gastroenteritis) will cause vomiting and/or diarrhoea, and overactivity of the gut. A partial gut obstruction caused by twisting of the bowel, a polyp, tumour, abscess or cancer, can make it difficult for food to pass the obstruction. The bowel muscles contract more vigourously to move the food along, and create a gurgling noise.
See also COLON; SMALL INTESTINE

BOWELS, LOOSE
See DIARRHOEA

BOWEN'S DISEASE

Bowen's disease is a precancerous skin condition that may be found anywhere on the body. It is caused by exposure to sunlight or arsenic compounds and appears as a sharply edged red patch covered with a fine scale. Biopsy or excision is required to make the diagnosis.

Spots should be surgically removed or chemically destroyed, as they can progress to become a squamous cell carcinoma (SCC).
See also INTRAEPITHELIAL CARCINOMA; SKIN CANCER; SQUAMOUS CELL CARCINOMA OF SKIN

BOW LEGS

Technically called genu varum, bow legs are normal in toddlers and a common condition of young children, diagnosed when a significant outward bending of the legs is observed when the child stands straight and the ankles are together. If severe cases are left untreated, the child develops an awkward way of walking and possible knee and ankle discomfort.

In virtually all cases the problem corrects itself without any treatment. In rare cases a wedge may be inserted into the outside edge of the shoes to turn the foot slightly inwards. Very rarely, if the problem continues into the early teenage years and causes difficulty in walking or abnormal appearance and posture, an operation may be necessary.
See also KNEE; KNOCK KNEES

BOXING

The aim of boxing is to render your opponent unconscious, or to injure him sufficiently that he is unable to continue, or to injure him so that he cannot injure you. It is therefore not surprising that a significant number of the participants in this activity suffer from permanent brain, eye and other bodily injuries that destroy the quality of their life, and shorten their lifespan.

During the 1990s, seven percent of amateur boxing matches in the United Kingdom were won by a knock out, and that amounts to a lot of brain damaged people. Every episode of unconsciousness associated with a head injury leaves some permanent damage, but it is not necessary to be knocked out to become 'punch drunk'. Mohammed Ali was knocked out only once in his career, but he now suffers from advanced cerebral degeneration, and is barely able to care for himself.

In the professional arena, with longer bouts and no protection, the head injuries are more severe, and eye damage may cause permanent blindness, as the light-sensitive retina separates from the back of the eye in response to successive blows. Retinal detachment is normally an uncommon disease of the elderly, but is far more common amongst boxers, at a far younger age.

The outstanding feature in the brains of dead boxers is the massive number of altered nerve cells spread throughout the brain, which must have significantly altered the thought patterns and activity of the boxer in life. Injuries occur in most sports, from fractures in rugby to injuries from a hard ball in cricket, and even golfers strain backs and joints, but no other sport comes close to the trail of wrecked bodies and premature death created by boxing. No other sport has the stated aim of damaging the opponent, and in the other marshal arts such as judo and karate, deliberately injuring your opponent can count against the competitor.

That we allow the barbarity of boxing to continue in this modern age is a poor comment on the standards of our times. Psychiatrists also question the sadistic motives of those who attend boxing matches, and pay a premium for ringside seats so that they can see the blood, sweat and agony at close quarters.
See also HEAD INJURY

BOX JELLYFISH

The box jellyfish (sea wasp) is the most dangerous creature found in Australian tropical waters. A severe sting will lead to failure of the respiratory and circulatory systems in minutes. The box jellyfish has a small body with long tentacles. It is colourless and so can be difficult to see. It occurs in northern waters, especially between October and March, and bathers are generally warned to stay out of the sea during these months. However, beaches are increasingly being meshed to keep the jellyfish out, and then swimming is safe. An antivenene is available.

The most effective first aid treatment for all jellyfish stings, including the box jellyfish, is ordinary household vinegar as this renders the tentacles harmless within thirty seconds. Anyone who lives in or is travelling in areas where dangerous jellyfish stings are a possibility should check that supplies of vinegar are available.

A box jellyfish sting will cause immediate and intense pain. The so-called 'frosted ladder' pattern from the tentacles can be seen along the line of the sting. The victim will quickly become irrational and find it difficult, then impossible, to breathe.

You SHOULD NOT: –
• try to remove the tentacles with your fingers, as undischarged venom cells may sting you
• rub the sting, as this will spread the venom

You SHOULD: –
• liberally cover the affected area with vinegar

• apply a firm compression bandage to the area
• observe the victim closely and apply mouth-to-mouth resuscitation if breathing stops and cardiopulmonary resuscitation if the pulse stops
• get medical help quickly

If there is no vinegar available, apply a firm compression bandage
See also IRUKANDJI SYNDROME; JELLYFISH STING; RESUSCITATION

BRACHIORADIALIS PRURITUS
See ITCHY UPPER ARM SYNDROME

BRACHMANN-de LANGE SYNDROME
See de LANGE SYNDROME

BRADYCARDIA
See PULSE SLOW; SICK SINUS SYNDROME

BRAIN

The brain is the central organ of the nervous system. It coordinates the operation of all the organs and tissues making up the body. The brain is often likened to a computer, but no computer yet developed has anything like the same complexity as the human brain. There are several billion cells in the brain, each of which is connected to about one thousand other cells. These connections keep changing all the time in order to allow us to function, coordinate and remember.

The brain weighs about 1300 grams and, proportional to body weight, is larger than that of any other animal.

It is surrounded by three layers of fibrous membrane, the meninges, which acts as both a support and protection.

The brain interprets signals from the senses and controls body functions, both conscious and automatic. It is also the site of memory, learning, thinking and reasoning.

The brain consists of three main divisions: the cerebrum, the cerebellum, and the brain stem.

Some of the substances carried by the blood to other parts of the body could damage the brain. The blood vessels servicing the brain are therefore less porous than other blood vessels. Oxygen, which is made up of small molecules, is allowed into the brain but

BRAIN

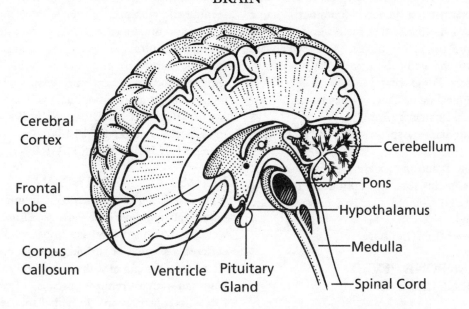

Cerebral Cortex

Frontal Lobe

Corpus Callosum

Ventricle

Pituitary Gland

Cerebellum

Pons

Hypothalamus

Medulla

Spinal Cord

harmful chemicals composed of large molecules are blocked. However, alcohol and most anaesthetics also have small molecules and can pass through easily.

The hard bony skull with its underlying cushion of cerebrospinal fluid protects the brain from external harm.

We still don't fully understand the functioning of the brain and how information is learned and transferred to memory, but it involves the making of additional connections between the billions of nerve cells in the brain, each of which may have thousands of connections to other brain nerve cells. It is generally acknowledged that factors such as heredity, previous experiences, the external environment, personality, character and intelligence all play a part in our brain's operation.

The brain creates four different types of electrical waves. Slow alpha waves occur when we are relaxed. Very fast beta waves are produced with concentration. Very slow delta waves occur during sleep. Theta waves are very regular waves of medium frequency that develop during meditation and creative thought. The brain usually produces a mixture of these waves.

See also BRAIN STEM; CEREBRUM; CEREBELLUM; CEREBROSPINAL FLUID; CRANIAL NERVES; ELECTROENCEPHALOGRAM; INTELLIGENCE QUOTIENT; MEMORY; MENINGES; NERVOUS SYSTEM; STROKE

BRAIN CANCER OR TUMOUR
See ASTROCYTOMA; CRANIOPHARYNGIOMA; GLIOMA; MENINGIOMA; PINEALOMA; RETINOBLASTOMA

BRAIN HAEMORRHAGE
See STROKE; SUBARACHNOID HAEMORRHAGE; SUBDURAL HAEMATOMA

BRAIN STEM
The brain stem is at the bottom of the brain and extends down through an opening in the skull to merge with the spinal cord. As a continuation of the spinal cord, the brain stem is the passage for all the nerve fibres from the body to the rest of the brain. In also controls most of the automatic body functions, for example breathing, digestion and the beating of the heart. By means of the hypothalamus in its upper section, the brain stem also controls our temperature, appetite and aspects of our metabolism.
See also BRAIN; NERVOUS SYSTEM

BRAIN SURGERY
See NEUROSURGERY

BRAIN WAVES
See ELECTROENCEPHALOGRAM

BRAND NAMES
The terminology of medications can be confusing. Every medication has at least three

names – a chemical name which is used only by scientists, a generic (common) name which is specific to that medication, and one or more brand (or trade) names which are given to the medication by the various manufacturers. For example: –

• Chemical name: Acetyl salicylic acid.
• Generic name: aspirin.
• Brand names: Aspro, Astrix, Cartia, Disprin etc.

Some brand names are listed after generic names in this text, but only those that have become household names (eg. Viagra) are indexed.
See also MEDICATION

BREAKBONE FEVER
See DENGUE FEVER

BREAST
Also known as the mammary glands, the breasts are glands that develop on the chest wall of women at puberty. Some women have breasts that are higher or lower on the chest, but when kneeling on all fours so the breast is hanging down, the nipple is usually over the fourth to sixth rib on each side. Some women have round breasts, while others have a more tubular shape. The size, shape and position of the breast is determined genetically, so women are likely to have similar shaped and sized breasts to that of their mother and both maternal and paternal grandmothers.

The primary function of breasts is to produce milk to feed babies, but they also have a very important role to play as secondary sexual characteristics and thereby to attract a suitable male partner.

The milk glands are arranged into fifteen to twenty groups (lobes), each of which drains separately through ducts in the nipple. The amount of milk-producing glandular tissue is similar in all breasts, regardless of their size. Larger breasts merely have more fat in them.

During pregnancy the glandular tissue increases to enlarge the breasts, and makes them tender at times. The same phenomenon occurs to a minor extent just before a menstrual period in many women due to the increased level of oestrogen (sex hormone produced by the ovaries) in the bloodstream.

The breast also contains fibrous tissue to give it some support. The stretching of these fibres causes the breast to sag after breast feeding and with age.

When stimulated by suckling, muscles in the nipple contract to harden and enlarge it so that the baby can grip and suck on it. A similar response occurs with sexual activity, cold temperature or emotional excitement.
See also BEAST CANCER; BREAST ENLARGED; BREAST FEEDING; BREAST LUMP; BREAST PAIN; NIPPLE

BREAST AUGMENTATION
Women desiring breast enlargement (augmentation) fall into three broad groups. Those who were born with small breasts, those who have suffered a sagging or shrinkage of the breasts after breast feeding or with age, and those who have had a breast removed because of cancer (breast reconstruction). Provided the patient is healthy, will benefit from the procedure, and is willing to have the operation there are no other criteria to be met.

The operation involves a two- or three-day stay in hospital. Techniques vary from one surgeon to another, but normally a small cut is made under each breast, and through this a plastic bag of silicone or saline gel (a prosthesis) is inserted to increase the size and improve the shape of the breast.

Often a small tube is left behind in the wound to drain off excess fluids that may accumulate. Bandages are tightly bound around the chest and breasts for a few days.

The patient should rest for a week to ten days after the operation before returning to normal duties. The stitches are taken out in two stages about one and two weeks after the operation. After six weeks the breasts feel and look completely natural, and the tiny scar is hidden under the breast fold when standing so that the briefest bikini can be worn.

Complications are unusual, but include excess bleeding and infection. The most common postoperative problem is breast capsule contraction. This occurs months after the procedure and is caused by the body laying down too much fibrous tissue around the implant, which results in the breast feeling firmer than normal.

There has never been any link demonstrated between this operation and the development of breast cancer. The woman can still breast feed after the operation, and can still check herself routinely for breast lumps.

An attractive bust may improve a woman's self image and esteem, but the operation should not be done for the wrong reasons. It will probably not save a dicey marriage, men will not start rushing to the door and sex life is not suddenly going to improve.
See also BREAST; PLASTIC SURGERY

BREAST BIOPSY

If preliminary examinations of a lump in the breast indicate that there is a suspicion of cancer, the doctor may order a breast biopsy. This may be performed by inserting a hollow needle into a cyst or lump in the breast to extract fluid that contains cells, or some of the tissue may be removed with a knife. A needle biopsy may or may not require a local anaesthetic and takes only a few minutes; it is usually done in the outpatients department of a hospital, or in the doctor's surgery. An open surgical biopsy may also be done in the outpatients department with a local anaesthetic, but more frequently it involves admission to hospital and a general anaesthetic.
See also BREAST CANCER; BREAST LUMP

BREAST BONE
See STERNUM

BREAST CANCER

Mammary carcinoma is the technical name for this all too common cancer that affects one in every eleven women at some time in her life.

The absolute cause is unknown but it is more common in women who have a close relative (mother, sister, daughter) with the disease, in women who have not had a pregnancy, have not breast fed, have had a first pregnancy after thirty-five years, in white women, those who have had uterine cancer, and in higher socioeconomic groups. On the other hand, women who start their periods late, breast feed their babies and those who have an early menopause have a lower incidence of breast cancer. About 2% of all breast cancers occur in men as they have a tiny amount of breast tissue present just under the nipple.

The symptoms are a hard, fixed, tender lump in the breast. The nipple skin itself can become cancerous (Paget's disease of the nipple) causing a thick, firm, rubbery feeling to the nipple. There are many other causes of lumps in the breast and less than one in ten breast lumps examined by a doctor is cancerous.

One method of detecting breast cancer is monthly self examination. The diagnosis is confirmed by an x-ray mammogram, ultrasound scan of the breast and needle biopsy.

The most common form of treatment is a lumpectomy in which only the cancer itself is removed, but if it is too large for this procedure a simple mastectomy, in which only the breast is removed, may be performed, leaving a cosmetically acceptable scar and scope for later plastic reconstruction of the breast. Often the lymph nodes under the arm will be removed at the same time. A course of radiotherapy and/or chemotherapy (drugs) may also be given.

A radical mastectomy in which the breast, underlying muscle and all the lymph nodes in the armpit and other nearby areas are all removed is done rarely, and only for very advanced cancer.

Up to two thirds of all patients with breast cancer can be cured. In early cases the cure rate rises to over 90%. In advanced cases the cancer may spread to nearby lymph nodes, the lungs and bones.
See also BREAST LUMP;
FIBROADENOMA OF THE BREAST;
MAMMOGRAM; NIPPLE DISCHARGE;
PAGET'S DISEASE OF THE NIPPLE

BREAST DISCHARGE
See NIPPLE DISCHARGE

BREAST ENLARGED

Breasts are normally a female characteristic, developing at puberty in the early teenage years, but any human of any age or either sex, is able to develop breasts if given the sex hormone oestrogen. Those men who have decided to change their apparent sex, and those who wish to be transvestites, may take oestrogen in order to develop breasts, but there are a number of medical conditions that can also cause gynaecomastia (abnormal breast enlargement).

Some boys going through puberty find that they are developing small lumps of tissue behind their nipples. This is caused by an imbalance in the sex hormones during this delicate stage of development. Most settle in a few months or a year, but a small number continue to develop excessive amounts of breast tissue and require an operation to remove it.

In men the menopause (andropause) occurs in the seventies, while in women it occurs in the late forties and early fifties. As testosterone levels drop in elderly men, the small amount of oestrogen that is present in the system of all men, may no longer be suppressed by the testosterone, and start stimulating breast tissue development.

Women taking oestrogen as a hormone replacement therapy after the menopause, or in the oral contraceptive pill, may notice an increase in their breast size.

Obesity is an often overlooked cause for breast enlargement in both sexes, as fat may deposit in the breast area more easily than in the surrounding chest tissue.

Other causes of breast enlargement include liver failure (oestrogen normally produced by a man or woman may not be broken down and removed from the body at the normal rate), cancer or tumours of the testicle that may prevent the normal production of testosterone, or in some cases (eg. teratoma) may start to produce oestrogen instead, Klinefelter syndrome (only affects males who have additional X chromosomes matched with a single Y chromosome), Addison's disease (adrenal glands do not produce sufficient quantities of vital hormones), and a rare form of lung cancer (oat cell carcinoma) will affect sex hormone balance and cause breast enlargement in both sexes.
See also BREAST; BREAST REDUCTION and separate entries for diseases mentioned above.

BREAST ENLARGEMENT
See BREAST AUGMENTATION

BREAST EXAMINATION
It is commonly advised that women are taught how to check their breasts for lumps by a doctor, and perform this easy procedure every month. Women who are still menstruating should do this after their period has just finished.

The first step is inspecting the breasts in a mirror, with the arms at the sides and then raised above the head. Women should get to know the shape and size of their breasts, and note any changes that occur.

The next step is to lie down, and with one hand behind the head, examine the opposite breast with the free hand. This should be done by resting the hand flat on the chest below the breast, and then creeping the fingers up over the breast by one finger breadth at a time. Do this twice, once over the inside half of the breast, and then over the outside half. Check under the nipple with the finger tips and finally check the arm pit for lumps. Repeat the procedure on the other breast.
See also BREAST; MAMMOGRAM

BREAST FEEDING
Breast feeding is technically known as lactation.

After birth, a woman's breasts automatically start to produce milk to feed the baby. The admonition "breast is best" features prominently on cans of infant formula and on advertising for breast milk substitutes in many third-world countries, and there is little doubt that it is true. Because of poverty, poor hygiene and poorly prepared formula, bottle-feeding should be actively discouraged in disadvantaged areas.

Unfortunately, for a variety of reasons, not all mothers are capable of breast feeding. Those who can't should not feel guilty, but should accept that this is a problem that can occur through no fault of theirs, and be grateful that there are excellent feeding formulas available for their child.

Breast feeding protects the baby from some childhood infections and also helps the mother by stimulating the uterus to contract to its pre-pregnant size more rapidly.

Babies don't consume much food for the first three or four days of life. Nevertheless, they are usually put to the breast shortly after birth. For the first few days the breasts produce colostrum, a very watery, sweet milk, which is specifically designed to nourish the newborn. It contains antibodies from the mother which help prevent infections.

Breast feeding may be started immediately after birth in the labour ward. All babies are born with a sucking reflex, and will turn towards the side on which their cheek is stroked. Moving the baby's cheek gently against the nipple will cause most babies to turn towards the nipple and start sucking. Suckling at this early stage gives comfort to both mother and child. In the next few days, relatively frequent feeds should be the rule to give stimulation to the breast and build up the milk supply. The breast milk slowly becomes thicker and heavier over the next week, naturally compensating for the infant's increasing demands.

After the first week, the frequency of feeding should be determined by the mother and child's needs, not laid down by any arbitrary authority. Each will work out what is best for them, with the number of feeds varying between five and ten a day.

Like other beings, babies feed better if they are in a relaxed comfortable environment, with a relaxed comfortable mother. A baby who is upset will not be able to concentrate on feeding, and if the mother is tense and anxious, the baby will sense this and react, and she will not be able to produce the "let-down reflex" which allows the milk to flow. The milk supply is a natural supply and demand system. If the baby drinks a lot, the breasts will manufacture more milk in response to the vigorous stimulation. Mothers of twins can produce enough milk to feed both babies because of this mechanism.

While milk is being produced, a woman's reproductive hormones are suppressed and she may not have any periods. This varies greatly from woman to woman: some have regular periods while feeding, some have irregular bleeds, and most have none. Breast feeding is sometimes relied upon as a form of contraception, but this is not safe. The chances of pregnancy are only reduced, not eliminated. The mini contraceptive pill, condoms, and the intrauterine device can all be used during breast feeding to prevent pregnancy.

It is important for the mother to have a nourishing diet throughout pregnancy and lactation. The mother's daily protein intake should be increased and extra fresh fruit and vegetables should be eaten. Extra iron can be obtained from egg yolk, dark green vegetables (eg. spinach), as well as from red meat and liver. Extra fluid is also needed.
See also BOTTLE FEEDING; BREAST FEEDING FAILURE; BREAST MILK INADEQUATE; BREASTS ENGORGED; NIPPLE CRACKED; NIPPLE DISCHARGE; NIPPLE INVERTED; WEANING

BREAST FEEDING CESSATION
See WEANING

BREAST FEEDING FAILURE
Most women hope to feed their newborn child for the first few months of life, but unfortunately not all women succeed. The most common reason for failure is emotional or physical stress. The harder the woman tries to succeed, the more she fails. Being relaxed with the baby, the concept of breast feeding, and the physical and emotional surroundings is vital.

There are other reasons for being unable to breast feed. A mother who has a significant illness, be it an infection, dietary problems, cancer or any other form of debilitation, is not going to be as successful at breast feeding as a woman who is in perfect health. In primitive areas of the world, malnutrition may be a factor, but even in developed countries, a fad diet may lack vital nutrients and have an adverse effect. Rarely, damage to the pituitary gland under the brain may be responsible.
See also BREAST FEEDING; BREAST MILK INADEQUATE; WEANING

BREAST FIBROADENOMA
See FIBROADENOMA OF THE BREAST

BREAST INFECTION
See MASTITIS

BREAST LUMP
Breast lumps probably arouse more concern among women than any other condition. This is because of the fear of cancer in an organ that is so significantly associated with femininity and sexuality.

It is important to understand that there are many other causes of lumps in the breast, so if a lump develops, particularly in a young woman, the chances are that it is NOT a cancer. Less than one breast lump in ten seen by a doctor proves to be malignant. The most important method of detecting breast cancer and lumps is self examination by the woman. All women should be taught how to check their breasts for lumps by a doctor, and should perform this easy procedure every month.

After examining the breast, a general practitioner may arrange for an x-ray mammogram, ultrasound scan of the breast or a needle biopsy. These tests show the inside structure of the breast and can sometimes differentiate between cysts, cancers and fibrous lumps. If all the features of the examination and investigations in a young woman indicate that the lump is benign, it is safe to watch the lump, with regular checks by a doctor, because many disappear after a few months.

In an older woman, or if the lump persists, it should be removed by a small operation. In the majority of cases this is the only treatment necessary, and the scar should be almost invisible on even the most liberated beaches. If the lump is found to be cancerous, a more extensive operation may be necessary.

The earlier a cancer is diagnosed, the better the chance of cure, so surgeons have good reason for advising removal of a lump which appears to be benign, rather than waiting until an obvious cancer appears.

Infections in the breast (mastitis), particularly during breast feeding, will cause hard, tender, painful, red lumps. Blocked milk ducts during breast feeding might also be felt as a lump. If not cleared rapidly, mastitis may eventuate.

Other causes of breast lumps include cysts, over stimulation of the breast by hormones (eg. hormone replacement therapy, contraceptive pill, pregnancy), collections of fibrous tissue (fibroadenoma), mammary dysplasia and lumps of scar tissue in damaged fat caused by an injury to the breast.
See also BREAST CANCER;
BREAST EXAMINATION and separate entries for diseases mentioned above.

BREAST MILK
See BREAST FEEDING; BREAST MILK INADEQUATE; NIPPLE DISCHARGE

BREAST MILK INADEQUATE
If the milk supply appears to be inadequate, increasing the frequency of feeds will increase the breast stimulation, and the reflex between the breast and the pituitary gland under the brain is also stimulated. This gland then increases the supply of hormones that cause the production of milk. Sometimes, medications that stimulate the pituitary gland can be used to increase milk production, or even induce milk production in mothers who adopt a baby.

A mother who is tense and anxious about her new baby may have trouble breast feeding. The mother should be allowed plenty of time for feeding and relaxation so that she becomes more relaxed and never feels rushed. A lack of privacy can sometimes be a hindrance to successful breast feeding. Lots of reassurance, support from family, and advice from doctors, health centre nurses or associations that support nursing mothers can help her through this difficult time.

The best way to determine if the baby is receiving adequate milk is regular weighing at a child welfare clinic or doctor's surgery. Provided the weight is steadily increasing, there is no need for concern. If the weight gain is very slight, or static, and increasing the frequency of feeds fails to improve the breast milk supply, then as a last resort supplementation of the breast feeds may be required. It is best to offer the breast first, and once they appear to be empty of milk, a bottle of suitable formula can be given to finish the feed.
See also BOTTLE FEEDING; BREAST FEEDING; BREAST FEEDING FAILURE

BREAST MOUSE
See FIBROADENOMA OF THE BREAST

BREAST PAIN
Any direct injury or blow to the breast may cause bruising and pain.

Many women experience painful tender breasts for a few days before each menstrual period. If this becomes a significant problem, medications are available to ease the discomfort.

In early pregnancy, one of the first signs of the pregnancy, other than missing a menstrual period, may be unusually sore and enlarged breasts.

The hormonal disturbances of the menopause may over stimulate breast tissue to cause varying soreness. In the same way, excess oestrogen in hormone replacement therapy or the contraceptive pill will have the same effect.

Infections in the breast (mastitis), particularly during breast feeding, will cause hard, tender, painful, red lumps. If left untreated, an abscess may develop in the breast tissue.

Breast cancer may present as a painful lump in the breast, but sometimes there may be a firm painful area behind the nipple, with virtually no lump that can be felt. Large

breasted women may not be able to feel a cancerous lump, but may experience pain on pressing on the affected area.
See also BREAST; BREAST LUMP

BREAST REDUCTION

Women with very large breasts can find them to be both uncomfortable and embarrassing. They develop fungal and heat rashes under the breast, and tired shoulder and back muscles from supporting them. They get in the way when performing some tasks, and make the woman look fatter than she is. Many women gain enormous benefit by having a breast reduction operation performed, and the sooner such a procedure is undertaken, the better.

There are a number of different ways of reducing the breast size, but in the most common operation, a slice of tissue and fat is removed from the underside of the breast, so that the resulting scar is in the fold under the breast, and barely noticeable. If nothing further was done, the nipple would be left pointing at the floor instead of straight ahead, so a further vertical cut must be made, to allow the nipple to be moved further up the smaller breast. The resultant vertical scar is below the nipple on an area of the breast that is rarely exposed to public view.

After the operation, the woman will feel much more comfortable, she will still be able to breast feed, and no one except her most intimate friends will ever know.
See also BREASTS UNEVEN

BREASTS ENGORGED

One of the most common breast problems is engorgement, which is not only uncomfortable but may lead to difficulty in feeding and to infection. If the breasts are swollen and overfilled with milk, expressing the excess milk usually relieves the discomfort. This can be done by hand under a shower or into a container, or with the assistance of a breast pump. At other times, expressed milk may be kept and given to the baby by a carer while the mother is out or at work. Breast feeding need not tie the mother to the home.

The infant may find it difficult to suckle on an overfilled breast, so expressing a little milk before the feed may be helpful. A well fitted, supportive bra is essential for the mother's comfort. Mild analgesics such as aspirin may be necessary, particularly before feeds, so that the feeding itself is less painful. Heat, in the form of a warm cloth or hot shower, will help with the expression of milk and with releasing milk from blocked areas of the breast.

Engorgement usually settles down after a few days or a week, but if the problem persists, fluid tablets can be used to reduce the amount of total fluid in the body and make it more difficult for the body to produce milk. In severe cases, partial suppression of the milk supply may be necessary.
See also BREAST FEEDING

BREASTS UNEVEN

Most women have slight differences in the sizes of their breasts, in the same way that most of us have one foot or hand a fraction larger than the other. All humans (male and female) have a tiny nodule of breast tissue present behind the nipple from birth. At puberty, the oestrogens in women stimulate this tissue to grow into a breast. The degree of stimulation, the size of the original nodule, and (most importantly) hereditary tendencies will determine your breast size. In some women the breast tissue on one side does not react as much to the stimulating hormones as the other side.

Some women are born with no nodule of breast tissue behind one nipple, and therefore there is nothing there for the hormones to stimulate at puberty.

There is no magical medication, cream or diet that will correct uneven breasts, but plastic surgery will improve a woman's self image and appearance dramatically.
See also BREAST AUGMENTATION; BREAST REDUCTION

BREATH BAD

Bad breath (halitosis), and its social implications, may be a major problem to a patient. The addictive habit of smoking is often to blame. Smoking causes the tongue to become deprived of its normal lubrication, and it becomes hairy and coated. This in turn traps microscopic food particles that decay in the crevasses of the tongue causing the offensive odours.

Dental health is the other major factor involved. The gums may become very slightly detached from the teeth, forming tiny pockets in which food may become trapped. This is periodontal disease, and the breakdown of saliva, food, bacteria and other foreign bodies in these pockets causes the production of rotten egg gas (hydrogen sulphide).

Sinusitis and other infections of the nose (eg. rhinitis), throat (eg. tonsillitis) and lungs (eg. bronchitis, pneumonia) can cause bad breath because of the infected saliva and pus present in the airways. Damaged and scarred lungs will become infected more readily, or may have a constant low level of infection present in them (eg. bronchiectasis, emphysema).

Fad diets that have excess protein and not enough carbohydrates are another cause, because the breakdown products of proteins are highly volatile acids that are expelled in the breath.

Alcoholics have halitosis because the alcohol alters the balance of micro-organisms that normally live in the gut, causing an increase in the number of odour producing bacteria.

Other causes of bad breath include liver failure, hepatitis, diabetes, some types of cancer, dehydration and some drugs, such as those used to treat angina, certain tranquillisers, lithium (used in psychiatry), griseofulvin (for fungal infections), penicillamine (for rheumatoid arthritis) and fluid tablets (diuretics).
See also MOUTH; SMOKING and separate entries for diseases and medications mentioned above.

BREATHING DIFFICULT
Stridor is the term used to describe difficulty in breathing in. Patients may actually whistle as they try to draw breath, and it is far more common in children than adults.

Many different bacterial and viral infections of the throat may cause stridor, including laryngitis (infection of vocal cords), diphtheria (now mainly prevented by vaccination), glandular fever (infectious mononucleosis), tracheitis (infection of windpipe) and most significantly, croup.

Croup is a viral infection of the throat in children which causes swelling of the tissues in the throat that results in a seal-like barking cough, difficulty on breathing in, and excessive chest movement with breathing, in a child under five years of age.

A particularly sinister cause in small children is the inhalation of a foreign body (eg. peanut, plastic block) into the windpipe (trachea) or larynx where it causes a partial obstruction of the airway.

A growth, polyp, cyst, tumour, haemorrhage (bleed) or abscess in the throat may also be responsible.
See also BREATH, SHORT OF; COUGH; LUNG; WHEEZE and separate entries for diseases mentioned above.

BREATHING RAPID
Hyperventilation is the term used by doctors for rapid breathing, usually at a rate above thirty-five breaths per minute in an adult. Rapid shallow breathing may alter the balance of carbon dioxide and oxygen in the lungs, and thus the blood. The blood becomes more alkali, and irritates small muscles, particularly in the hands, which go into spasm. This is known as tetany (totally different to a tetanus infection) and patients have fingers and sometimes wrist, forearms and feet, which are pointed in a firm spasm. Hormonal and calcium imbalances in the blood may also cause tetany. Breathing into a paper bag for a few minutes increases the level of carbon dioxide in the lungs, slows the breathing and eases the spasm.

Obviously, exercise will cause rapid breathing, but so will pain, anxiety, fright, hysteria and a high fever of any cause.

Most bacterial and viral infections cause a fever, and therefore might be responsible for hyperventilation, but infections of the lungs and throat are more likely to be responsible.

Common causes of hyperventilation include a blood clot in one of the major arteries within the lungs (pulmonary embolus), pneumothorax (occurs if air escapes from the lung into the chest cavity), and a stroke (cerebrovascular accident).

An uncommon cause is Rett syndrome, an inherited condition of girls that causes episodes of hyperventilation, seizures, subnormal mentality, constipation and repetitive hand movements.

Some medications (eg. adrenaline, pseudoephedrine – used for runny noses) may cause rapid breathing as a side effect.

See also BREATH, SHORT OF; FEVER; LUNG and separate entries for diseases mentioned above.

BREATH, SHORT OF

If a person runs up stairs, become emotionally excited or upset, or exercises in any way, they will become short of breath, but the better their state of fitness, the longer it takes.

Most medically significant causes of dyspnoea (shortness of breath) are related to the lungs, the throat (mouth, pharynx, larynx) and the heart.

Common lung causes include asthma (a temporary narrowing of the tubes through which air flows into and out of the lungs), any significant infection of the lungs (eg. bronchitis, pneumonia, bronchiolitis), chronic obstructive airways diseases (eg. chronic bronchitis, emphysema, bronchiectasis), cystic fibrosis (a birth defect of lung function) and a pneumothorax (air escapes from the lung into the chest cavity).

Less common lung causes of dyspnoea include lung collapse because of a chest injury, a blood clot in one of the major arteries within the lungs (pulmonary embolism), fluid accumulation within the pleura that surrounds the lung (pleural effusion), the rupture of an artery in the lung, asbestosis or silicosis, carbon monoxide poisoning, infantile respiratory distress syndrome (hyaline membrane disease) and sarcoidosis.

Throat causes for shortness of breath include croup (a viral infection of the throat in children), severe postnasal drip (which may clog the throat and make breathing difficult), and an abscess, polyp or tumour in the throat or on the vocal cords may affect breathing.

The heart may also be responsible with conditions such as congestive cardiac failure (a damaged heart is unable to beat effectively enough to clear blood out of the lungs and pump it out to the rest of the body), a heart attack (myocardial infarct) or damaged valves in the heart (particularly a narrowed mitral valve).

Other less common possible causes for this symptom include gross obesity (may restrict the muscles available to move the chest and lungs), a stroke (cerebrovascular accident), reflux oesophagitis, severe scoliosis, an overactive thyroid gland, various nerve and muscle disorders that affect muscle contraction, and imbalances in the vital electrolytes (sodium, potassium, chloride) in blood due to kidney disease, abnormal diet, medications or injury, which may affect the function of both lungs and heart.

There are many other rarer causes.
See also BREATHING DIFFICULT; BREATHING RAPID; BLUE SKIN; COUGH; LUNG; WHEEZE and separate entries for diseases mentioned above.

BREATH TEST

Strange as it may seem, the cause of a peptic ulcer in the stomach can be determined by a test on the breath. A small amount of radioactive urea is swallowed on an empty stomach. After fifteen minutes, samples of breath are collected and the amount of radioactive carbon present is measured. The test can confirm the presence of the bacteria *Helicobacter pylori* as the cause of a peptic ulcer. The amount of radioactivity is extremely small and completely safe, and the test is quick and easy for the patient.
See also PEPTIC ULCER

BREECH BIRTH

Babies normally come into the world head first, but occasionally the wrong end fits into the mother's pelvis and cannot be dislodged. About 3% of babies are in the breech position at birth. They are normally delivered by a caesarean section, but may be delivered normally with the assistance of forceps to protect the head.

Breech labours tend to take longer than head first ones, and there can be more problems for the baby, as the cord will be compressed during the delivery before the head is free to start breathing. Even so, the vast majority of breech births result in no long-term complications to the mother or child.
See also CAESAREAN SECTION; LABOUR

BRIQUET SYNDROME

The Briquet syndrome (somatisation disorder) is a psychiatric disorder of perceived illness that is a form of hysteria. A family history is common.

Patients have multiple, unexplained, recurrent symptoms with no physical basis, and all investigations are normal.

Psychiatric counselling is the only treatment, but the condition is usually intractable.
See also CONVERSION DISORDER; HYPOCHONDRIA

BRITTLE BONE DISEASE
See OSTEOGENESIS IMPERFECTA

BROKEN BONE
See FRACTURE; PLASTER

BROMHEXINE
See EXPECTORANTS; MUCOLYTICS

BROMPHENIRAMINE
See ANTIHISTAMINES

BRONCHI
See LUNG

BRONCHIAL CARCINOMA
See LUNG CANCER

BRONCHIECTASIS
Bronchiectasis is a disease involving scarring and permanent over-dilation of damaged air carrying tubes (bronchi) within the lungs. The bronchi may be damaged from birth by cystic fibrosis or childhood immune deficiencies, or may develop in adult life due to recurrent attacks of bronchitis, pneumonia or the inhalation of toxic gases, but smoking is by far the most common cause.

A constant cough that brings up large amounts of foul phlegm is the main symptom. Patients may cough up blood, become anaemic and lose weight. An x-ray of the chest reveals characteristic changes and can confirm the diagnosis.

Treatment involves regular physiotherapy to clear the chest of sputum and antibiotics when necessary to control infection. Other medications to open up the clogged airways (bronchodilators), to liquefy sputum (mucolytics) and to assist the coughing (expectorants) may be necessary. It is essential for smokers to quit. In severe cases where a limited part of the lung is badly affected, that section may be surgically removed.

The disease is usually very slowly progressive, but aggressive treatment slows this process.
See also BRONCHITIS, CHRONIC; EMPHYSEMA; LUNG; PNEUMONIA; SMOKING

BRONCHIOLITIS
The respiratory syncitial virus (RSV) is usually responsible for bronchiolitis, a lung infection of children under two years of age. The infant develops a cough and wheeze, shortness of breath and a runny nose. In severe cases, the child may be very weak, blue around the mouth and dehydrated.

Antibiotics cannot cure this viral condition but are sometimes given to prevent pneumonia. Bronchodilator medications may be used but often are of little help. Placing the child in a warm room with a humidifier, or in a steam tent may give relief. More severe cases will require hospitalisation, where steroids are given and oxygen may be administered into a steam tent to assist with breathing.

The vast majority of cases settle without complications in a few days to a week.
See also BRONCHITIS, ACUTE; LUNG

BRONCHITIS, ACUTE
Bronchitis is a very common infection of the major tubes (bronchi) that carry air within the lungs, but it occurs in two very different forms, acute and chronic.

The acute form is commonly caused by viruses, occasionally by bacteria, and rarely by fungi. It spreads easily from one person to another on the breath. The symptoms include a fever, chest aches and pains, headache, tiredness, and a productive cough with dark yellow or green mucus. The diagnosis is confirmed by listening to the chest through a stethoscope. In early stages, x-rays may be normal, but later show characteristic changes. Sputum may be cultured to identify any bacteria present, and the correct antibiotic to treat it.

Viral infections settle with time, rest, inhalations, bronchodilators (to open up the bronchi) and physiotherapy. If a bacterium is responsible, antibiotics can be prescribed. Bacterial infections settle rapidly with antibiotics, but viral bronchitis takes about ten days to fade in most patients, but may persist for several weeks in the elderly or debilitated.
See also ANTIBIOTICS; BRONCHITIS, CHRONIC; LUNG; PNEUMONIA

BRONCHITIS, CHRONIC
This form of bronchitis is a long term inflammation of the larger airways (bronchi) in the lungs. The cause may be repeated attacks of acute bronchitis, long-standing allergies, or constant irritation of the bronchi by noxious gases, particularly those found in tobacco smoke (most common cause).

Patients have a persistent moist cough, shortness of breath (particularly with exertion), constant tiredness, blue lips and swollen ("clubbed") finger tips. The thickened and scarred bronchi and poor air entry to the lungs, show up quite markedly on a chest x-ray.

Physiotherapy, bronchodilators (medications to improve air flow), and antibiotics if a bacterial infection is present, are the main treatments. It is a semi-permanent condition for which there is no effective cure, but treatment can keep the condition under control for many years. Sometimes it may progress to emphysema.
See also ANTIBIOTICS; BRONCHITIS, ACUTE; EMPHYSEMA; PNEUMONIA

BRONCHITIS, WHEEZY
See ASTHMA

BRONCHODILATORS
Bronchodilators are medications used to treat asthma and bronchitis. The bronchi are the tubes in the lung that contain air. Bronchodilators open these tubes to their maximum extent to allow more air to enter and leave the lungs. Bronchodilators are classified as either beta-2 agonists or theophyllines.
See also BETA-2 AGONISTS; MEDICATION; THEOPHYLLINES

BRONCHOGENIC CARCINOMA
See LUNG CANCER

BRONCHOPNEUMONIA
See PNEUMONIA

BRONCHOSCOPY
Bronchoscopy is the examination of the bronchial tubes and the inside of the lungs through an endoscope (thin flexible tube). It is usually used if a tumour is suspected or to investigate a serious disease such as chronic bronchitis. The patient must fast for six hours before the test is performed. The procedure is performed in a hospital day surgery centre, or as an inpatient. The throat and airways will be anaesthetised, so the procedure is not very uncomfortable and takes about half an hour.
See also ENDOSCOPE; LUNG

BROWN NAIL
See NAIL DISCOLOURED

BROWN PATCHES ON SKIN
Naevi and birth marks may appear as flat brown patches scattered across the skin. More naevi develop with age and sun exposure. Most naevi, and almost invariably all birth marks, are not cancerous, but rarely a skin cancer may develop in them, so any brown patch that changes in colour, shape or size should be checked by a doctor.

Café-au-lait (white coffee) spots are an inherited condition in which hundreds of small brown patches appear on the skin from birth.

An area of skin that has been severely inflamed for any reason may become permanently brown due to persistent damage after the inflammation has settled.
See also NAEVUS; SKIN PIGMENTATION EXCESS

BROWN-SÉQUARD SYNDROME
The Brown-Séquard syndrome is an uncommon spinal cord condition caused by injury, transverse myelitis, overgrowth of arteries (haemangioma), tumours or compression of the spinal cord. The symptoms include muscle spasm and loss of position sense on one side of the body, loss of pain and temperature sense on the opposite side, with light touch sensation preserved and muscle strength lost on both sides. The cause is treated if possible, but often there is no cure.
See also HAEMANGIOMA; SPINAL CORD; TRANSVERSE MYELITIS

BRUCELLOSIS
Undulant fever or brucellosis is a bacterial infection of cattle, goats and pigs, which can spread to humans, and most commonly infects meat workers, veterinarians and farmers. The bacteria *Brucella abortus*, *Brucella melitensis* or other species of *Brucella*, enter a human through a cut or graze in the skin, or are swallowed. It is found in raw meat and unprocessed milk.

Patients initially experience a fever, tiredness and intermittent sweats. After several weeks, further symptoms of headache, swollen painful joints, loss of appetite and abdominal pains (from a large spleen and/or liver) develop. The fever may come and go for many months in a low-grade chronic form of the disease (thus undulant fever).

Specific blood tests are used to make the diagnosis.

Treatment involves taking antibiotics (eg. tetracycline) and rest until all symptoms have settled. Animals may be vaccinated to prevent them from catching the disease, but not humans. Occasionally the infection may spread to involve the lung, brain and heart, causing specific problems in those areas. Long-term complications include arthritis, and bone weakness.

There is good response to treatment, but symptoms may recur over several years and require further courses of treatment.
See also Q FEVER; TETRACYCLINES

BRUISE

A bruise (ecchymosis or haematoma in medical jargon) occurs when part of the body is struck by a blunt object to cause rupture of blood vessels under the skin, when internal structures rupture blood vessels by their movement (eg. a fracture of a bone), blood vessels are ruptured by over-stretching when a joint is overextended (eg. a severe sprain), or blood fails to clot rapidly when a blood vessel receives minor damage.

If an artery ruptures, a bruise will form very rapidly, with swelling and a blue/black tinge to the overlying skin. A bruise develops more slowly and with less swelling if a vein ruptures. It is far harder to rupture a muscular, thick walled artery than a thin walled vein. Blood under pressure can track its way between layers of tissue so that bruising may occur not only at the site of the injury, but some distance away (eg. a kick to the calf may cause a spot bruise on the calf, but a day or two later bruising may appear around the ankle).

Patients on a medication which is prescribed to reduce the speed at which blood clots form (eg. warfarin, to prevent strokes or heart attacks), will bruise far more easily than normal people. Aspirin, anti-inflammatory medications (for arthritis) and other less commonly used drugs may also increase bleeding, and therefore bruising.

Women bruise more than men, particularly around the menopause, because hormonal changes may make blood vessel walls weaker, and allow them to rupture easily. Many women complain of multiple small bruises on their arms and legs, in places where they cannot recall any significant injury.

Other common causes of abnormal bruising include thrombocytopenia (a lack of platelets in the blood), Cushing syndrome (over production of steroids in the body, or taking large doses of cortisone), and leukaemia (cancer of the white blood cells).

Less common causes include AIDS, failure of the liver or kidney, haemophilia, scurvy and aplastic anaemia.

Some snakes and spiders kill their victims by injecting a substance that prevents blood from clotting when they bite. Bruising at the bite site is common.

When a bruise is likely, or first develops after an injury, the affected area should be cooled with ice, elevated and rested. The ice should not be applied directly to the skin, but wrapped inside a cloth. Elevation of the area reduces the pressure in the veins, and slows blood loss from the ruptured blood vessel. Any exercise or movement involving an area with a ruptured blood vessel will force more blood out into the tissues.

With time and rest the swelling will reduce, the bruise will go from blue/black to purple, brown and finally yellow before disappearing. There may be some residual swelling and firmness at the bruise site due to the formation of fibrous scar tissue and the skin over the area may dry out and flake off.

If there is no apparent cause for a bruise, medical advice should be sought.
See also BLEEDING, EXCESSIVE and separate entries for diseases mentioned above.

BRUXISM

Bruxism is the abnormal and excessive grinding of teeth. It is commonly a sign of stress or tension, may be a nervous habit, or during sleep can occur with nightmares. It is very common in patients with mental retardation.

If the underlying cause cannot be corrected, a mild muscle relaxing and anxiety reducing medication (eg. diazepam) is the appropriate treatment. A dentist should check the teeth regularly. A special dental plate can be worn at night to stop the teeth wearing down. Prolonged bruxism may cause permanent damage to the teeth.
See also TEMPOROMANDIBULAR JOINT DYSFUNCTION

BS
'BS' is an abbreviation used to indicate that the doctor has a Bachelor of Surgery qualification, which is part of basic medical degree.
See also GENERAL PRACTITIONER; MEDICAL TRAINING

BUBONIC PLAGUE
Also known as the "Black Death" when it devastated Europe in the fourteenth century, bubonic plague is a severe generalised bacterial infection that is very rare in developed nations, but still present in many poorer Asian and African countries.

The cause is the bacterium *Yersinia pestis* which normally infects rats, and passes from one rat to another, or from rat to humans, by the bite of a flea. The symptoms include large, pus-filled glands (buboes) in the neck, groin and armpit, accompanied by a high fever, severe muscle pain, headache, rapid heart rate, profound tiredness and eventually coma. The infection may spread to the blood and cause black spots (bruises – thus the "Black Death") under the skin.

The diagnosis can be confirmed by special blood tests and cultures from the discharging glands.

Treatment involves isolation in hospital, antibiotics and intravenous drip feeding. It may be prevented by a plague vaccine or taking tetracycline tablets every day. In good hospitals virtually all patients will recover, but untreated the death rate exceeds 50%, and death may occur more commonly and within a few hours in patients who are malnourished or in poor health. Complications such as meningitis and pneumonia are fatal without excellent medical care.
See also BACTERIA; BLACK DEATH

BUDD-CHIARI SYNDROME
The Budd-Chiari syndrome is a rare syndrome affecting liver function, caused by a blood clot blocking the main vein leading from the liver, because of a liver tumour or blood clotting disease.

The liver and spleen become dramatically enlarged, causing abdominal pain and fluid accumulation in the belly. There may be significant bleeding into the upper intestine. The syndrome is diagnosed by CT and ultrasound scans, liver biopsy and radionucleotide scans. Liver transplant is the only treatment option, and the syndrome is usually fatal within two years of diagnosis unless a liver transplant can be performed.
See also LIVER

BUDESONIDE
See ASTHMA PREVENTION MEDICATION; STEROIDS

BUERGER'S DISEASE
Also known as smoker's foot, and technically known as thromboangiitis obliterans, Buerger's disease occurs only in smokers, and nearly always in men. Abnormal blood clot formation associated with inflammation and obliteration of arteries results in the progressive loss of fingers, toes, then arms and legs.

Toxins in tobacco smoke cause inflammation in sections of the small arteries in the hands and feet which causes a clot to form in the artery, and the tissue beyond the blockage becomes painful, white and eventually gangrenous. It starts in the fingers and toes, and slowly moves further up the arteries in the arms and legs.

The initial symptoms include pain in the foot when walking, which settles with rest. Red tender cords caused by clot-filled (thrombosed) arteries may be felt under the skin, and a finger or toe may be white and have reduced sensation. The next stage is characterised by pain at rest, loss of pulses in the hands and feet and ulcers around the nails. Cold weather aggravates symptoms. Further progression results in gangrene.

Doctors try to stop patients from smoking, but they are far more addicted than the average smoker, and success is rare. Surgery to the nerves supplying the arteries to make them totally relax may be tried, but amputation of affected tissue is usually necessary. A limb may eventually be totally amputated, but often over several operations as each successive area becomes deprived of blood.
See also SMOKING

BUFFALO HUMP
See CUSHING SYNDROME

BULIMIA NERVOSA
Also known as the binge-purge syndrome, this is a psychiatric disturbance of body perception almost invariably occurring in middle to upper class young females, that may be

associated with anorexia nervosa. The main difference between these diseases is the way in which the patients see themselves – the bulimic has a fear of being fat, the anorexic has a desire to be thin.

There is no known specific cause, but patients tend to be high achievers, perfectionists, desperately eager to please others and have an anxious personality.

Symptoms are characteristically a voracious and continuous consumption of huge quantities of food followed by purging, vomiting and the use of fluid tablets or laxatives in order to maintain a normal weight. Patients are secretive, and appear to eat normally in public, but binge eat and vomit in private. Other symptoms may be menstrual irregularities, sore throat, bowel problems, dehydration, lethargy, and dental problems due to the repeated exposure of the teeth to stomach acid. Suicide can be a risk in severe cases.

Close family support, psychotherapy and careful medical monitoring over a period of several years are the main forms of treatment.

Most patients recover, and go on to lead normal lives
See also ANOREXIA NERVOSA

BULLOUS IMPETIGO
See SCALDED SKIN SYNDROME

BULLOUS PEMPHIGOID
See PEMPHIGOID

BUNDLE OF HIS
See HEART

BUNION
Hallux valgus is the technical term for a common bunion.

If the big toe is constantly pushed across towards the smaller toes by tight shoes, it may become semi-permanently deformed in this direction. The end of the long bone in the foot behind the toe bones then pushes against the skin. A protective, fluid-filled sac (a bursa) forms between the bone end and the skin and slowly enlarges to form a tender and painful bunion. They usually start in childhood but may not cause significant discomfort until adult life.

A number of surgical procedures are available to correct the deformity, but in elderly people it may be preferable for a protective pad to be worn inside soft or especially made shoes.
See also FOOT

BUPIVOCAINE
See ANAESTHETICS

BURN
A burn is damage to body tissues by excess heat. A burn can be caused by fire, contact with something hot, boiling water or steam (scald), electricity, the sun, or excess friction. They are classified according to three degrees of severity. First degree refers to burns where the skin has reddened, such as in sunburn. Second degree burns are where the superficial layers of skin are damaged, such as in a blister from hot coffee. Third degree burns are when the full thickness of the skin has been burnt away.

Burns are painful and distressing, and all but minor burns are serious and need medical attention. Third degree burns are sometimes less painful as the nerve endings will have been destroyed. Extensive burns may lead to fluid loss and shock, and the victim will need urgent help.

The first aid treatment of burns involves the following steps: –
• If necessary put out the flames. Hold a rug or blanket in front of you as you approach so that you will not get burnt yourself, and envelop the victim in it. Wrap it tightly around the victim to smother the flames and lower them to the ground. You can also use water to douse the flames but make sure you do not create scalding steam.
• Remove hot clothing if it will come off easily, but do NOT remove any fragments sticking to the skin because you may remove the skin with it.
• Cool the burnt area with cold water. If the victim is comfortably able to move and the burn is easily accessible, eg. on an arm, hold the burn under cold water for at least twenty minutes. If not, gently apply cold compresses.
• Do NOT prick or break any blisters and do not apply any lotions, ointments, or oily dressings as they will have to be removed later, which will be painful and damaging.
• Cover the burnt area with a clean (sterile if possible) non-stick dressing. If not available, use a wet cloth.

• Bandage the burnt area lightly – a torn up sheet is ideal. If the burns are on the face, cut holes for the eyes, mouth and nose.

• Allow the victim to rest in a comfortable position, if possible using pillows for support. Raise injured limbs to reduce swelling and fluid loss. If the face is burnt, try to keep the victim sitting up.

• Give frequent sips of water to replace lost fluids – but NOT alcohol.

• Watch for signs of shock and treat if necessary.

• Give mouth-to-mouth resuscitation or cardio-pulmonary resuscitation if required.

Once under medical care, second degree burns are treated with antibiotic creams or other dressings. Third degree burns usually require skin grafts unless very small.

Extensive second and third degree may be life threatening because of the loss of body fluids through the burn area and the absorption of large amounts of toxic waste products into the blood that can cause kidney and liver failure.

Once in a hospital burns unit a patient can be kept alive on a ventilator, and fluids can be replaced through drips into a vein. Antiseptic paints, creams, amniotic sac membrane (recovered from the placenta of mothers who have just delivered a baby) or pig skin may be used to protect wounds after the burnt tissue has been cleaned or cut away (surgical debridement). Pressure may be applied in various ways to reduce scarring. Skin taken from unburned areas of the body is grafted to areas that have been totally destroyed in a late stage of treatment. Tissue cultures of the patient's own skin cells, or those of a donor, are used in severe cases to replace missing skin.

Rehabilitation from a severe burn takes months or years, and may involve plastic surgery to correct contractures (tight scars) or improve appearance. Physiotherapists, occupational therapists, and even speech pathologists (for inhaled hot gas burns) will all play a part.
See also FIRST AID; KIDNEY FAILURE, ACUTE; RESUSCITATION; SHOCK; SUNBURN

BURNING VULVA SYNDROME
See VULVODYNIA

BURPING, EXCESSIVE
Burping is bringing up air or gas from the stomach into the mouth. That air has to get in to the stomach in the first place to be burped, and in the vast majority of cases, it gets in by being swallowed.

People who eat quickly tend to swallow air with their food. If a person is nervous, before an exam or interview etc., they may swallow more often as a sign of anxiety and take in extra air. Drinking fizzy liquids such as lemonade or beer will also take gas in to the stomach. If small amounts of gas are swallowed, it will move on into the gut to be absorbed or passed through the anus as flatus. Otherwise excess gas tries to escape by going up and out through the mouth.

This is not as easy as it seems because there is a muscular valve at the top of the stomach that stops the food and acid in the stomach from running back up the gullet into the mouth while bending or lying down. Only when sufficient pressure builds up, or the person can relax the muscular valve themselves, can the air escape, causing the often unexpected and embarrassing explosion. When the gas escapes, it may take small amounts of acid and food with it, causing heartburn or nausea at the same time.

A hiatus hernia occurs when part of the stomach pushes up through the diaphragm (the sheet of muscle that separates the chest and abdominal cavities) into the chest. The muscle ring that prevents stomach acid from coming back up into the oesophagus then fails to work effectively, allowing reflux oesophagitis to occur very easily.

The excess amounts of acid present in the stomach of patients with a peptic ulcer may also damage the muscle ring at the lower end of the oesophagus, and increase the amount of burping.
See also ACID TASTE; DYSPEPSIA; FLATULENCE and separate entries for diseases mentioned above.

BURR HOLE
See NEUROSURGERY

BURSA
See BURSITIS; SYNOVIAL FLUID

BURST EAR DRUM
See TYMPANIC RUPTURE

BURSITIS

Every moving joint in the body contains synovial fluid to lubricate it. This fluid is produced in small sacs (bursae) that surround the joint. The fluid passes from the bursae through tiny tubes into the joint space, from where it is slowly absorbed into the bone ends. Bursitis is inflammation or infection of a bursa due to an injury to the area, an infection entering the joint or bursa, or by arthritis. The most common sites for bursitis are the point of the elbow, over the kneecap (housemaid's knee), and the buttocks.

Patients present to a doctor with a swelling of a joint, or joint surrounds, which may or may not be painful. The skin over the bursa may become red.

In cases of simple inflammation, local heat, rest, splinting and painkillers are the only treatments required. Recurrent or persistent cases may have the synovial fluid in the bursa removed by a needle, and steroids injected back into the sac to prevent further accumulation of fluid. If the bursa becomes infected, antibiotic therapy and surgical drainage of pus are necessary.

See also HOUSEMAID'S KNEE; JOINT; SYNOVIAL FLUID

BUSPIRONE
See ANXIOLYTICS

BUTOXYL ETHYL NICOTINATE
See LINIMENT

BUZZING EARS
See TINNITUS

C

C²H⁵OH
See ALCOHOL

CABG
See CORONARY ARTERY BYPASS GRAFT

CACHEXIA
Cachexia is the weakness and wasting of a body due to a serious illness.
See also CANCER; WEIGHT LOSS

CADUCEUS
Aesculapius was the Greek god of medicine, and son of Apollo (god of truth, light and prophecy), and the nymph Coronis. The symbol of Aesculapius is a coarse rod or staff entwined by a single serpent. The serpent embodies renewal of youth and health as it periodically sheds its skin, enlarges and emerges as a transformed creature.

The caduceus, a winged rod entwined by two serpents, was the symbol of the swift messenger Mercury, the messenger of the gods (also the god of science and trade) in Greek mythology. In classical Greece, a herald's wand or staff showed that the bearer was a sacred person and not to be molested. Originally a straight branch from which two twigs grew, the twigs were then pulled back and twined around the branch. Later the twigs were interpreted as snakes.

Mercury was also identified with Hermes and the Egyptian god Thoth, whose characteristics included wisdom and eloquence.

In the 16th and 17th centuries, the caduceus was associated with wise and eloquent individuals, including some physicians. However, in the early 19th century it was adopted by a medical publisher as a sign, not that he published medical books, but that he was a commercial deliverer of information.

By a misconception, the caduceus became the insignia of the US Army Medical Corps in 1902. Before then, it had no medical relevance. The sign became widely recognised after the exposure it had during World War I. It thereafter became frequently used and popular.

At various times, the cross of the Knights of Malta (the Maltese Cross), who were hospitaliers in the Crusades to the Middle East in medieval times has been combined in various forms with both the staff of Aesculapius and the Caduceus.

The staff of Aesculapius is the true symbol of the physician.
See also AESCULAPIUS; EYE OF HORUS; HIPPOCRATES

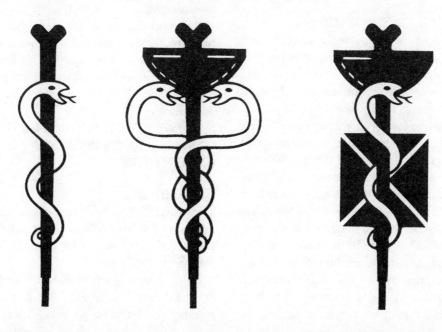

CAECUM

The large intestine begins in the lower part of the abdomen on the right side and is divided into three parts. The first part, consisting of a small pouch into which the ileum of the small intestine opens, is known as the caecum (pronounced 'seekum'). The second part is the colon, and the third part is the rectum.

Opening off the caecum is the small dead-end tube of the appendix.

See also APPENDIX; COLON; ILEUM

CAECUM AND APPENDIX

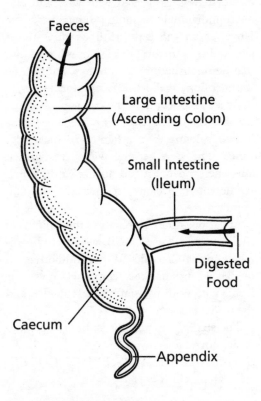

Faeces

Large Intestine
(Ascending Colon)

Small Intestine
(Ileum)

Digested
Food

Caecum

Appendix

CAESAREAN SECTION

Julius Caesar was purportedly delivered from his dead mother, alive and well, after her belly was cut open immediately upon her demise, giving rise to the common name for the operative delivery of a baby. In the last 2000 years the operation has been considerably refined to the point where about a quarter of all babies are now delivered in this manner.

There are obvious situations where a caesarean section is the only choice for the obstetrician. These include a baby that is presenting side on instead of head first, a placenta (after-birth) that is over the birth canal, a severely ill mother, a distressed infant that may not survive the rigours of the passage through the birth canal, and the woman who has been labouring for many hours with no success.

Caesarean sections may also be performed if the mother has had a previous operative birth, if she is very small, if previous children have had birth injuries or required forceps delivery, for a baby presenting bottom first, if the baby is very premature or delicate, in multiple pregnancies where the two or more babies may become entangled, and in a host of other combinations and permutations of circumstances that cannot be imagined in advance. The decision to undertake the operation is often difficult, but it will always have to be up to the judgement and clinical acumen of the obstetrician, in consultation with the mother if possible, to make the final decision.

The operation is extremely safe for both mother and child. A spinal or epidural anaesthetic is given to the mother, and the baby is usually delivered within five minutes. A general anaesthetic is these days only given in some specific circumstances. After delivery the longer and more complex task of repairing the womb and abdominal muscles is undertaken. In most cases, the scar of a caesarean is low and horizontal, below the bikini line, to avoid any disfigurement.

With epidural or spinal anaesthesia, a needle is placed in the middle of the mother's back, and through this an anaesthetic is introduced. The woman feels nothing below the waist, and although sedated is quite awake and able to participate in the birth of her baby, seeing it only seconds after it is delivered by the surgeon. Some doctors and hospitals allow the woman's partner to be present during these deliveries.

Recovery from a caesarean is slower than for normal childbirth, but most women leave hospital within seven days. It does not affect breast feeding or the chances of future pregnancies, and does not increase the risk of miscarriage.

See also EPIDURAL ANAESTHETIC;
LABOUR; PREGNANCY; SPINAL
ANAESTHETIC

CAFFEINE

The caffeine in coffee, tea, cocoa and cola drinks acts as a stimulant, but depending on the strength, there may be more caffeine in tea than in coffee.

Caffeine acts on the body to increase alertness, increase the rate at which the body metabolises (burns) food, and increase urine production. In large doses, it may produce headache, irritability, insomnia, psychiatric conditions and stomach upsets, and it can aggravate diabetes, heart disease, depression and anxiety disorders. If taken before going to bed, a short, less restful sleep can be expected. People who have any of the foregoing conditions should limit their caffeine intake.

There are some connections between moderate to large doses of caffeine and problems such as miscarriage, premature birth and still-birth in pregnancy. Pregnant women should therefore limit themselves to two to four cups of tea, coffee or cola a day.
See also STIMULANTS

CAISSON DISEASE
See BENDS

CALCANEUS
The calcaneus is the heel bone. The Achilles tendon attaches to the back of the bone, and the talus (ankle bone) sits on top of it. In front are the bones of the foot, the navicular on the big toe side, and the cuboid on the other.
See also ANKLE; FOOT

CALCITONIN
See CALCIUM;
HYPERPARATHYROIDISM;
HYPOPARATHYROIDISM;
PARATHYROID GLAND

CALCITRIOL
See VITAMIN D

CALCIUM
Calcium (Ca) is a mineral that makes up the main part of the structure of bones. Two percent of the weight of the body is due to calcium, with half in the bones and half in solution in the blood and other bodily fluids. The level of calcium in the bones and blood is controlled by two hormones, parathormone (which raises blood calcium) and calcitonin (which lowers blood calcium) which are produced in the parathyroid glands in the neck. Calcium is essential for the production of many enzymes, for muscle contraction, and for electrical conduction in nerves, as well as bone structure.

The absorption of calcium from the gut is dependent on vitamin D, which is obtained by sun irradiation of cholesterol in the skin.

The amount of calcium in the blood and urine can be measured. The normal range in the blood after fasting for eight hours is 2.2–2.7 mmol/L (9-10.8 mg/100 mL). High levels in the blood may indicate parathyroid gland over-activity, bone tumours, excess vitamin A or D, excess calcium absorption from the diet, lymphomas, sarcoidosis and other cancers, dehydration, hyperalbuminaemia, kidney failure, multiple myeloma, Paget's disease of bone, or an over active thyroid gland. Prolonged application of the tourniquet during blood collection may falsely raise the levels. Medications such as diuretics, lithium and tamoxifen may also be responsible.

Low levels of blood calcium may be due to a lack of vitamin D, chronic illness, an underactive parathyroid gland, kidney failure, pregnancy and hyperventilation (rapid breathing).

The amount of calcium found in urine is strongly affected by the diet. High levels may be found in osteoporosis.
See also BLOOD TESTS; BONE; MINERALS; HYPERCALCAEMIA; OSTEOMALACIA; PARATHYROID GLAND; RICKETS; VITAMIN D

CALCIUM CHANNEL BLOCKERS
Calcium is essential for the contraction of the tiny muscles around the arteries. When these muscles contract, the artery becomes smaller and narrower. Calcium channel blockers prevent the calcium from entering the muscle cells through tiny channels in the membrane surrounding the cell. These muscle cells cannot then contract easily, remain relaxed, and do not narrow the artery. The wider an artery, the less resistance is placed on the blood flowing through it, and the lower the blood pressure. Because they prevent the contraction of all arteries, they reduce the strain on the heart, and some of these drugs can therefore be used to treat angina (a lack of blood to the heart muscle) as well as high blood pressure and a rapid heart rate.

Calcium channel blockers are quite safe and are normally used in tablet form, although some can be given as injections. They can interact with a number of drugs, so doctors must be aware of all the patient's medications.

Examples of drugs in this class include amlodipine (Norvasc), diltiazem (Cardizem), felodipine (Agon, Plendil), nifedipine (Adalat) and verapamil (Cordilox, Isoptin).

Side effects may include constipation, tiredness, headache, swelling of feet, dizziness, indigestion and hot flushes. They should be used only if essential in pregnancy, and not in heart failure or low blood pressure. Care should be taken when used in patients with diabetes.

See also ANGINA; ANTIANGINALS; HYPERTENSION; MEDICATION

CALCIUM PYROPHOSPHATE DEPOSITION DISEASE
See CHONDROCALCINOSIS; PSEUDOGOUT

CALF CRAMP
See MUSCLE CRAMP

CALLOSITY
See CALLUS

CALLUS
A callus (callosity) is an abnormal thickening of skin keratin caused by recurrent injury to, or rubbing of, the skin. The patient should remove any pressure to the area if possible (eg. correct footwear, protective pads), and can then carefully peel away the layers of keratin with a scalpel or apply salicylic acid ointment. A callus may become painful, and rarely infected, if trimmed excessively.
See also SKIN

CALORIES
See KILOJOULES AND CALORIES

CALYMMATOBACTERIUM GRANULOMATIS
See GRANULOMA INGUINALE

CAMPBELL de MORGAN SPOTS
Campbell de Morgan spots are also known as cherry angiomas and senile haemangiomas. They are a common skin disorder affecting the trunk of older people caused by overgrowth of blood vessels in the skin. There is a genetic tendency to develop them.

Patients develop red to maroon, raised, dome shaped growths on the skin a few millimetres across, that steadily increase in number with age. Normally no treatment is necessary, but cautery, laser treatment or surgical excision can be used if cosmetically unacceptable.
See also HAEMANGIOMA; VENOUS LAKE

CAMPHOR
See COUGH MEDICINES; LINIMENT

CAMPYLOBACTER JEJUNI
Campylobacter jejuni is a bacterium that may infect the intestine (enteritis) to cause fever, cramping belly pains and watery diarrhoea. Infection occurs worldwide in both developed and developing countries. It spreads from one person to another or from animals by water or food (particularly dairy products) that are contaminated by faeces. Its incubation period is two to six days.

Treatment involves a diet with minimal fat and plenty of fluids. If the infection is prolonged, antibiotics such as erythromycin may be used. Usually it settles without treatment in a few days, but rarely may persist for weeks.
See also GASTROENTERITIS; SHIGELLOSIS

CANCER
Cancer, the crab of astrology, is so named because the ancients could see the abnormal cancer cells clawing their way into the normal tissue, destroying everything in their path. Doctors now understand a great deal about cancer, but do not fully understand what starts the process. Although the specific cause of cancer is unknown in many cases, sun exposure, a low-fibre diet and smoking are well-known precipitating factors.

Cancer (malignancy or neoplasm) occurs when otherwise normal cells start multiplying at an excessive rate, and the cells made by the rapid process of reproduction are abnormal in shape, size and function. Although they may have some slight resemblance to the cells around them, cancer cells cannot perform the correct work of that type of cell, and they prevent the normal cells around them from working properly, thus enabling the cancerous cells to spread.

Cancer is not just one disease process – dozens of different types of cancer occur in different parts of the body, and each type causes different problems and responds differently to treatment. Several different types of cancer can be found in the lungs for example. There are, however, two main groups of cancers according to the type of tissue affected: –

• Sarcomas are tumours originating in connective tissue (bone, cartilage, muscle and fibre).

• Carcinomas are tumours originating in the epithelial cells (tissue comprising the external and internal linings of the body).

The early signs of cancer are: –
• a lump or thickening anywhere in the body
• sores that will not heal
• unusual bleeding or discharge
• change in bowel or bladder habits
• persistent cough or hoarseness,
• change in a wart or mole
• indigestion or difficulty in swallowing
• loss of weight for no apparent reason

Investigation of a cancer depends upon the organ involved and may include blood tests, urine tests, sputum tests, faeces tests, x-rays, endoscopy, radioactive scans, ultrasound scans, microscopic examinations and magnetic resonance imaging. Treatment may involve surgery to remove the growth, drugs that are attracted to and destroy abnormal cells, irradiation of the tumour with high-powered x-rays, specifically developed vaccines or combinations of these methods.

Over half of all cancers can be cured, and that excludes the skin cancers that rarely cause death. The cure rate is far higher in those who present early to a doctor, because the less the cancer has spread, the easier it is to treat.
See also CANCER ASSOCIATED ANTIGEN; CYTOTOXICS AND ANTINEOPLASTICS; IMMUNOTHERAPY and names of individual types of cancer (eg. BREAST CANCER; LUNG CANCER).

CANCER ASSOCIATED ANTIGEN
Blood tests are available for specific antigens that are produced against some types of cancer (eg. breast, pancreas, liver, colon, ovary, uterus and prostate cancer). The most commonly ordered of these tests is the prostate specific antigen (PSA).

These tests are unreliable as a way of detecting cancer as there is no absolute value in any one person above which a cancer can be said to be present, but a series of tests over a period of months or years may show increasing levels of the antigen which may indicate the presence of a particular cancer. The tests are particularly useful in following the progress of treatment in a patient (if successful, antigen levels should decrease steadily), or in watching a patient who has a bad family history of a particular type of cancer. Raised levels may also occur with infection, inflammation or enlargement of the organ.
See also ANTIGEN; BLOOD TESTS; CANCER; PROSTATE SPECIFIC ANTIGEN

CANCER MEDICATIONS
See CYTOTOXICS AND ANTINEOPLASTICS

CANCER OF THE CERVIX
See CERVICAL CANCER

CANDESARTAN
See ANGIOTENSIN II RECEPTOR ANTAGONISTS

CANDIDA ALBICANS
See THRUSH

CANNABIS
See MARIJUANA

CAPGRAS SYNDROME
Also known as L'Illusion de sosies, Capgras syndrome is a rare cause of psychosis.

The cause is unknown, but it may be a form of, and associated with, schizophrenia.

Patients have a psychotic delusion that a near relative has been replaced by a double or impersonator. It is a phenomenon that may be temporary in the elderly. There are no specific diagnostic tests, but an EEG (electroencephalogram) is often abnormal.

No specific treatment or cure is available, but medications used for schizophrenia may be tried, although control is often unsatisfactory.
See also PSYCHOSES; SCHIZOPHRENIA

CAPITATE BONE
See WRIST

CAPOTEN
See ACE INHIBITORS

CAPSAICIN
See LINIMENT

CAPSULITIS
See FROZEN SHOULDER

CAPTOPRIL
See ACE INHIBITORS

CARBACHOL
See MIOTICS

CARBAMAZEPINE
See ANTICONVULSANTS

CARBIMAZOLE
See ANTITHYROID DRUGS

CARBOHYDRATE
Carbohydrates are molecules that contain carbon, hydrogen and oxygen. They are the body's preferred source of energy as the process of digestion converts them into forms of sugar that the body can use easily. Sugar, bread, pasta, potatoes and cereals are all rich in carbohydrates. Sugar, however, is not the best means of getting adequate carbohydrate as it has no minerals, vitamins or fibre, and is not always metabolised properly because it enters the bloodstream too quickly.
See also FAT; FIBRE; PROTEIN

CARBON DIOXIDE
Carbon dioxide (CO_2) is a colourless gas that makes up a mere 0.3% of the atmosphere. It is a waste product of humans produced by the fermentation or metabolism (use for energy) of carbohydrates and other carbon containing foods. It is expelled from the body through the lungs as we breathe out.

It is sometimes used in medicine in its solid form ('dry ice') to freeze skin spots. Its most common use is to add the bubbles to all fizzy soft drinks.

It has the unusual ability to sublime, which is passing from the solid to the gas (or gas to solid) forms directly without becoming a liquid in between these two states.
See also BLOOD GAS ANALYSIS; CRYOTHERAPY; OXYGEN

CARBON MONOXIDE POISONING
Poisoning can occur by inhalation of carbon monoxide (CO), which is a colourless and odourless gas produced by the burning of carbon containing material. Carbon monoxide binds to haemoglobin in the blood to form carboxyhaemoglobin, which prevents the haemoglobin from carrying oxygen to all tissues in the body.

CO may be inhaled by accidental or deliberate (suicide) inhalation of automobile exhaust gas, smoke in a fire, or unvented combustion heater fumes.

Initially symptoms include headache, dizziness, belly pain, nausea and shortness of breath. Later symptoms include red skin, confusion, fainting, coma, convulsions and death. Permanent brain damage is possible in survivors of severe poisoning. The level of carbon monoxide in the blood can be measured to determine the severity of poisoning.

The patient should be immediately removed from the gas source, and artificial respiration should be applied if necessary. In hospital or an ambulance, oxygen 100% is given using a close fitting mask to flush the carbon monoxide out of the blood.

The prognosis depends on the level of exposure, but is usually good if the patient is resuscitated without coma or convulsions occurring.
See also RESUSCITATION

CARBOXYHAEMOGLOBIN
See CARBON MONOXIDE POISONING

CARBUNCLE
See BOIL

CARCINOID SYNDROME
Carcinoid syndrome (argentaffinoma) is a rare cancer that starts in argentaffin cells inside the small intestine, stomach or lung. Argentaffin cells are responsible for producing a number of essential hormones (eg. serotonin) for the functioning of the gut and body in general. When these cells become cancerous, they produce excessive amounts of these hormones, which causes unusual symptoms.

The syndrome may develop very rapidly, and patients can become severely ill in a few days. Symptoms include hot flushes of the face, swelling of the head and neck, diarrhoea and stomach cramps, asthma and bleeding into the skin. Blood or urine tests can be carried out to find the high levels of serotonin and other hormones. The site of the cancer is often very difficult to find, as it is usually very small and slow growing. It also tends to spread at an early stage to other areas, so even if the original is removed, the syndrome may continue due to the production of hormones in high levels by newly formed and very small cancers in multiple sites.

Prednisone (a steroid) is used in the emergency treatment of the disease, and other medications are given to control the other symptoms. Drugs such as interferon can sometimes be used to destroy the cancer cells.

Because of its slow growth rate, it may take ten or fifteen years for the disease to progress from the stage of being a nuisance that requires constant medication, to being life-threatening. *See also* CANCER

CARCINOMA
See CANCER

CARDIA
See HEART

CARDIAC ANGIOGRAM
See ANGIOGRAM

CARDIAC GLYCOSIDES
See DIGOXIN

CARDIAC SPHINCTER
See STOMACH

CARDIOMYOPATHY
Hypertrophic cardiomyopathy means enlarged heart muscle disease ('hypertrophic' means over developed, 'cardio' refers to the heart, 'myo' to muscle, and 'pathy' to disease). Diseases and weakness of the heart muscle such as this are very common in older people due to the ageing process.

Almost any disease, from an infection to a heart attack, can cause cardiomyopathy and so the term may be used when the exact nature of the heart disease present is unknown. Drugs, tumours and high blood pressure may also be responsible.

Cardiomyopathy may be a trivial illness that is barely noticed by the patient, or may cause tiredness, weakness, shortness of breath and chest pains (angina). It can be a progressive disease that leads inevitably to death or the need for a heart transplant. The condition is diagnosed by chest x-ray demonstrating an enlarged heart, ECG (electrocardiogram) and echocardiogram.

Medications such as digoxin, captopril, disopyramide, sotalol and a number of others may be prescribed to strengthen the heart muscle and make it contract more efficiently.

The prognosis depends on the cause, but in most cases can be controlled reasonably. *See also* ANGINA; CONGESTIVE CARDIAC FAILURE; HEART

CARDIOPULMONARY RESUSCITATION
See DROWNING; HEART ATTACK; RESUSCITATION

CARDIOVASCULAR SYSTEM
See ARTERIES; CIRCULATORY SYSTEM; HEART; VEINS

CARDURAN
See ALPHA BLOCKERS

CARMUSTINE
See CYTOTOXICS AND ANTINEOPLASTICS

CAROTENAEMIA
Vitamin A is found in leafy green vegetables, dairy products, liver and yellow coloured foods such as carrots, pumpkin, mangoes, paw paws, oranges and apricots that contain large quantities of a yellow substance known as carotene. Excess levels of carotene and vitamin A (hypervitaminosis A) therefore occur simultaneously in most cases.

Carotenaemia is caused by taking excessive amounts of vitamin A tablets or eating large quantities of yellow fruit and vegetables. Huge quantities must be consumed, but patients who develop a craving for one particular type of food can consume sufficient for the symptoms to appear in a few weeks.

The symptoms may include loss of appetite and weight, yellow colouring of the skin (particularly the palms and soles, but unlike liver diseases, not the whites of the eyes), brittle nails, dry and cracked skin, sore gums, headaches and other more bizarre symptoms. It can cause deformities to the foetus of a pregnant woman, and therefore large doses of vitamin A should be avoided during pregnancy.

All blood tests remain normal, but yellow palms and soles are diagnostic features.

The only treatment is not eating the offending foods and vitamin supplements. Almost invariably the condition resolves

slowly over a few weeks without long-term damage.
See also VITAMIN A

CAROTID ARTERY

The main arteries leading up through the neck from the aorta to the head are the carotid arteries. There is one artery on each side of the neck which divides into internal and external branches to supply respectively the brain and other organs inside the skull, and the muscles and tissues outside the skull.

Narrowing of the carotid artery from fatty deposits (arteriosclerosis) may lead to a restricted blood supply to the brain and strokes or transient ischaemic attacks.
See also ARTERIOSCLEROSIS; AORTA; STROKE; TRANSIENT ISCHAEMIC ATTACK

CAROTID BODY TUMOUR

A carotid body tumour (chemodectoma) is a very rare tumour of a small body in the neck at the point where the carotid artery (main artery to head) branches into external and internal arteries. The external carotid artery supplies the face and the internal carotid artery goes to the brain. The carotid body is used to detect the chemistry of the blood, and particularly the amount of oxygen in the blood, so that a drop in blood oxygen stimulates the brain to increase blood pressure, heart rate and breathing rate. The tumour is often benign, or rarely an extremely slowly progressive form of cancer.

Patients develop a pulsing tender lump in the neck to one side or the other of the trachea (windpipe). Ultrasound scans are used in making the diagnosis while treatment involves surgical removal in younger and middle-aged patients, or observation only in the elderly. There are very significant risks of surgery due to possible damage to the carotid artery and the blood supply to the brain. Elderly patients usually die with the tumour rather than from the tumour.
See also CAROTID ARTERY; CAROTID SINUS SYNDROME

CAROTID SINUS SYNDROME

Carotid sinus syndrome is a disease affecting the carotid body, a tiny pressure sensitive structure at both sides of the front of the neck at the point where the main artery to the head (carotid artery) divides into internal and external branches. Excessive sensitivity of the carotid body results in inappropriate nerve signals being sent to the heart and blood vessels. It is more common in the elderly.

Symptoms include low blood pressure, slow heart rate, dizziness and fainting. Massaging the carotid body can trigger the symptoms.

A pacemaker is inserted to regulate heart rate, and most, but not all, patients are controlled by this treatment. Many are not diagnosed until serious falls from fainting have occurred.
See also CAROTID BODY TUMOUR

CARPAL TUNNEL SYNDROME

The carpal tunnel syndrome is a form of repetitive strain injury to the wrist caused by excessive compression of the arteries, veins and nerves that supply the hand as they pass through the carpal tunnel in the wrist. This tunnel is shaped like a letter 'D' lying on its side and consists of an arch of small bones which is held in place by a band of fibrous tissue. If the ligaments become slack, the arch will flatten, and the nerves, arteries and tendons within the tunnel will become compressed. It is far more common in women and in those undertaking repetitive tasks or using vibrating tools and in pregnancy.

SCHEMATIC CROSS SECTION OF WRIST SHOWING CARPAL TUNNEL

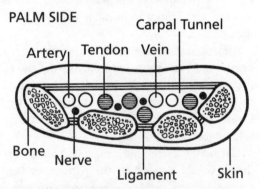

PALM SIDE

BACK OF WRIST

Patients experience numbness, tingling, pain and weakness in the hand. X-rays of the wrist, and studies to measure the rate of nerve conduction in the area confirm the diagnosis.

Splinting the wrist, fluid tablets to reduce swelling, nonsteroidal anti-inflammatory medications, and occasionally injections of

steroids into the wrist are the main treatments. Most patients will eventually require minor surgery to release the pressure. Permanent damage to the structures in the wrist and hand can occur if not treated, but the operation normally gives a lifelong cure.
See also de QUERVAIN
TENOSYNOVITIS; GUYTON CANAL
SYNDROME; TARSAL TUNNEL
SYNDROME; WRIST PAIN

CAR SICKNESS
See MOTION SICKNESS

CARTILAGE
Cartilage (gristle) is a tough, elastic, flexible, white or cream connective tissue that is found in many parts of the body. Within joints it acts as a shock absorber, forms the structure of the outer ears and tip of the nose, strips of cartilage join the ends of the ribs to the side of the sternum (breast bone), and between the vertebrae of the back forms the discs.

In a foetus there are no bones, but bone forms in cartilage as the foetus matures, and after birth most of the remaining cartilage that forms the structure of the body is gradually replaced by bone.

Cartilage has a very poor blood supply, and so is very slow to heal if damaged.
See also BONE; JOINTS;
OSTEOCHONDRITIS DESSICANS; RIB

CAST
See PLASTER

CASTRATION
Castration is the removal of the testicles. In horses the operation is called gelding.

It is used in medicine to treat some serious forms of prostate cancer by removing all possible sources of testosterone which may stimulate the cancer.

This mutilating operation was performed on choir boys until a century ago to prevent their voice breaking and thus ruining their career. The "castrati" were admired as the best singers in the world for centuries.

Castration was also used in many societies, but particularly those of the Middle East, to create eunuchs who would protect their masters and particularly their women in the harem, but without being able to get them pregnant.

Slaves were sometimes castrated to make them more docile.

Some members of the British aristocracy believed until late last century that hemi-castration (removal of one testicle) would give them male heirs, as sperm from the right testicle was meant to produce sons, sperm from the left daughters.
See also TESTICLES

CATARACT
A cataract is a clouding of the lens in the eye, that usually occurs slowly over a number of years, and gradually reduces vision until it is the equivalent of looking through frosted glass. A lens affected by a cataract can usually be surgically replaced with an artificial lens.

By far the most common cause of a cataract is a slow clouding of the lens with advancing age. There is no specific cause for this, but people who live and work outdoors in very sunny climates seem to get the problem more. A small number of children have a genetic or inherited predisposition to develop a cataract early in life. Some babies are born with the problem. Patients with diabetes suffer the premature development of cataracts.

Uncommon causes of cataracts include ultraviolet, x-ray or gamma ray irradiation to the eye, exposure of a foetus to german measles (rubella) caught by the mother, damage to the eyes at birth due to lack of oxygen and a number of rare syndromes.

The condition can be diagnosed by examining the eye with an ophthalmoscope (magnifying light).

Cataracts are initially treated with powerful spectacles, but eye surgery to replace the damaged lens is the best solution. Only one eye (usually the worst one) will be operated upon initially. Once this has recovered, the second eye may be repaired. The procedure can be done under a general or local anaesthetic, and involves cutting open the top of the eye at the edge of the iris (the coloured part of the eye), removing the damaged lens by gentle suction, and inserting an artificial lens in its place. This new lens is not mobile, and cannot change shape, thus spectacles are normally still required for close work, and sometimes distant vision as well.

The most noticeable effect after the operation is the brightness of the world. Colours in particular appear far brighter than the washed out appearance they have through a cloudy lens.

Complications may include dislocation of the new lens, or infection of the eye, but they are uncommon.

More than 95% of patients achieve excellent results with surgery.
See also EYE; OPHTHALMOSCOPY and separate entries for diseases mentioned above.

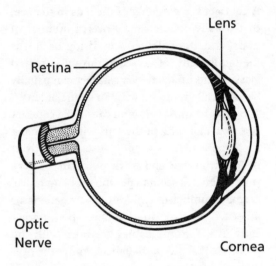

CATARRH
The excessive flow of phlegm down the back of the pharynx (throat) is called catarrh.
See also POST-NASAL DRIP

CATATONIC SYNDROME
Catatonia (catatonic syndrome) is a psychiatric or neurological (brain damage) disorder that affects muscle control. It is usually associated with schizophrenia, but may be due to brain tumours or inflammation, strokes, drugs, poisons and body chemistry disorders.

Patients develop increased muscle tone at rest that disappears during movement, sudden impulsive movements and excitement. Multiple investigations (eg. blood tests, CT scan) must be carried out to determine the cause. Treatment involves hospitalisation, medications (eg. haloperidol, fluphenazine, thiothixene), psychotherapy, behavioural and social therapy.
See also SCHIZOPHRENIA

CAT CRY
See CRI DU CHAT SYNDROME

CATHARSIS
See ABREACTION

CATHETER
A catheter is a tube used in medicine to drain fluid from one area to another, and usually from the inside of the body (eg. bladder) to the outside.
See also FOLEY CATHETER

CAT SCAN
See CT SCAN

CAT SCRATCH DISEASE
Cat scratch disease is a curious condition caused by a scratch from a cat claw, often to the face. The bacterium *Bartonella henselae*, that may be present on cat paws, is responsible. When a person is scratched by a cat, the bacteria enter the damaged tissue.

A few days after being scratched, about one third of patients develop a scab-covered sore at the site of the scratch. Between one and three weeks later, a fever and headache occur and are accompanied by enlarged lymph nodes in the groin and the side of the neck or armpit nearest the scratch. Occasionally the infected nodes develop into an abscess. No specific tests are available to confirm the diagnosis, and blood tests merely show that an infection is present, but not what has caused the infection.

No treatment is available or necessary, but sometimes it is necessary to surgically drain an abscess. It usually settles spontaneously within a week or two, but very rarely a form of encephalitis (brain inflammation) and skin rashes may occur.
See also ENCEPHALITIS

CAUCASIANS
See RACE

CAULIFLOWER EAR
A cauliflower ear (haematoma auris) is scarring and disfigurement of the ear from repeated bruising and swelling that usually occurs in boxers and rugby players. Draining of any blood collections in the ear as soon as they occur will reduce long term deformity. Plastic surgery to the ear will reduce disfigurement. The problem stabilises within a month or two of injury, then remains long term unless surgically treated.
See also EAR; HAEMATOMA

CAUSALGIA

Causalgia (also known as complex regional pain syndrome type two) is a complex abnormal reaction to a nerve injury resulting in excessive inappropriate stimulation of the nerve.

Three phases of the condition occur: –
• Phase one – swelling and intermittent severe burning pain of the forearm and hand, or lower leg and foot, starting within three months of a nerve injury.
• Phase two – thin, shiny, cool skin that sweats excessively, replaces normal skin on the affected limb three to six months after the injury, and pain continues.
• Phase three – after a further three to six months, the skin becomes very thin, scar tissue develops in the limb, and affected joints become contracted, painful and immobile.

There are no specific diagnostic tests, but electromyography (EMG – measurement of electrical impulses in muscles) may be abnormal.

Treatment is often unsatisfactory. Physiotherapy, anti-inflammatory drugs and steroids have been tried, but permanent disability involving the affected limb is common.
See also REFLEX SYMPATHETIC DYSTROPHY SYNDROME

CAVERJECT
See ALPROSTADIL

CCF
See CONGESTIVE CARDIAC FAILURE

CEFACLOR
See CEPHALOSPORINS

CEFUROXIME
See CEPHALOSPORINS

CELECOXIB
See NONSTEROIDAL ANTI-INFLAMMATORY DRUGS

CELIAC DISEASE
See COELIAC DISEASE

CELL

Cells are the basic building blocks of virtually every form of life. The human body is made of over two hundred different types of cells, each type performing a different function, but usually arranged in groups (tissue) of identical cells that perform the same function. The average cell is only 0.02mm. across, and can only be seen using a microscope.

Every cell has a semipermeable membrane that surrounds the cytoplasm that makes up the body of the cell. There are numerous structures inside the cell including a nucleus which is the control centre of the cell, ribosomes which are filamentous structures that manufacture proteins, mitochondria which act as the power houses of the cell by converting carbohydrates into energy, and lysosomes (Golgi bodies) which are the storage areas within the cells. The red blood cells are the exception to this rule, and contain no nucleus and few other structures. The chromosomes are found in the nucleus.

Growth and repair occur because cells have the ability to divide and duplicate themselves. Millions of cells die and are replaced in the body every second. Some cells may live as long as the person (eg. brain cells), while some cells lining the intestine last only two or three days before being shed. Red blood cells live for three or four months.

Stem cells are the basic cells in an embryo from which all other cells may be formed, and some of these persist in the adult.

Cells can have extremely diverse tasks. They may convey messages as nerve cells, create mucus in the gut, secrete hormones in the glands, lay down dense calcium containing structures to form bone, grow hairs, or be elastic and stretch and rebound in the skin and joints.
See also RED BLOOD CELLS; SPERM; STEM CELL; WHITE BLOOD CELLS

CELLULITIS

Cellulitis is a bacterial infection of the tissue immediately under the skin that may start from a bite or wound, but sometimes occurs for no apparent reason.

The area affected is hot, red, tender, swollen and painful. The infected area slowly spreads, and once the lymphatic system becomes involved, red streaks may run towards the nearest lymph nodes (adenitis), and the patient will develop a fever and become quite ill.

A swab may be taken from any sore to determine the type of bacteria responsible, and the appropriate antibiotic to treat it is

then prescribed. An abscess may develop in the tissue if treatment is delayed, and rarely, the infection may spread to the blood to cause septicaemia. Most cases respond rapidly to antibiotics.
See also ABSCESS; ADENITIS; ERYSIPELAS; SEPTICAEMIA

CENTRAL NERVOUS SYSTEM
The term central nervous system is used to describe the main thought processing, sensation and control areas of the nervous system including the brain (and all its parts) and the spinal cord.
See also BRAIN; CEREBRUM; CEREBELLUM; NERVOUS SYSTEM; SPINAL CORD

CEPHALEXIN
See CEPHALOSPORINS

CEPHALOSPORINS
Cephalosporins are a group of relatively strong antibiotics. They are divided by doctors into first, second and third generation cephalosporins. In general terms, as you go from first to third generation drugs, they increase in strength but decrease in the number of types of bacteria they are active against.

First generation cephalosporins (eg. cefaclor, cephalexin, cefuroxime) are commonly used by general practitioners. They are active against a very wide range of bacteria, and are particularly useful in chest, urinary, skin and joint infections. They can interact with aminoglycoside antibiotics, and must be used with care in patients with kidney failure. Side effects (eg. diarrhoea) are uncommon with the first generation capsules and mixtures, but more likely with the third generation cephalosporins which are given by injection.
See also ANTIBIOTICS; MEDICATION

CEREBELLUM
The cerebellum is a small part of the brain that lies at the back of the skull and top of the brain stem that leads to the spinal cord. Its function is to maintain balance, muscle coordination and posture.
See also BRAIN; CEREBRUM; DANDY-WALKER SYNDROME; FRIEDREICH'S ATAXIA; SPINAL CORD

CEREBRAL INFARCT
See STROKE

CEREBRAL PALSY
Cerebral palsy (spasticity) is a brain condition causing abnormal uncontrolled muscle spasms. It is usually due to abnormal development of the brain before birth, or rarely to brain damage around the time of birth because the baby is deprived of oxygen for several minutes.

Symptoms vary dramatically from one patient to another depending on the area of brain damaged. Some have slight difficulty in controlling one limb; others may be unable to talk clearly, yet others may be totally unable to care for themselves in any way. Mental functioning may be completely normal, or there may be significant mental retardation.

Electroencephalograms (EEG) which measure brain waves, electromyelograms (EMG) which measure the electrical conduction in muscles, and CT scans of the brain and spine may be abnormal, but blood tests are usually normal.

Most help comes from teams of nurses, physiotherapists, occupational therapists, social workers and volunteers. Medications may be used to treat skin, intestinal and arthritic complications. Operations to correct deformities and release spasm in limbs can complement medications which reduce the uncontrollable twitching that may occur. Paramedical staff can teach the patient how to control an unwilling body, and emotional and psychiatric support is often necessary.

Cerebral palsy is often associated with epilepsy due to brain damage, and there is a high incidence of arthritis, pressure ulcers, chest infections, peptic ulcers, and emotional and social problems.

Although there is no cure, some symptoms can be eased, but life expectancy is slightly less than average.
See also BRAIN; EPILEPSY

CEREBROSPINAL FLUID
Cerebrospinal fluid (CSF) surrounds the brain and spinal cord, and fills the spaces (ventricles) within the brain. In the brain are a number of ventricles, one of which contains a network of veins (the choroid plexus) that secretes the CSF, which passes through small ducts to the outside of the brain. From there it

flows down and around the spinal cord in the back, from where it is absorbed into the blood. The CSF protects and nurtures the brain, and acts as a shock absorber. It may become infected or altered by diseases in the brain and spinal cord, and a sample can be taken for analysis by putting a needle between the vertebrae in the lower back (a spinal tap or lumbar puncture).
See also BRAIN; HYDROCEPHALUS; LUMBAR PUNCTURE; SPINAL CORD

CEREBROVASCULAR ACCIDENT
See STROKE

CEREBRUM
The cerebrum is the largest part of the brain, mushrooming out from the brain stem. It fills almost all of the top part of the skull and is the centre of most of the brain's activity. Nerves throughout the body travel via the spinal cord, up through the brain stem and into the cerebrum.

The cerebrum is divided into two halves or hemispheres. Because the nerve fibres cross over as they travel from the spinal cord up the brain stem, each of the two halves controls the opposite side of the body, i.e. the left side of the brain controls the right side of the body, and vice versa. For activities such as speech, one side of the brain will be dominant. Generally the left side is dominant in a right-handed person. This means that if a right-handed person has a stroke affecting the left side of the brain, they may lose the capacity to speak as well as the use of their right hand.

The outer layer of the cerebrum consists of grey-coloured matter called the cortex. This is the part of the brain that thinks, and is thought to be concerned with memory, intelligence and imagination. It also deals with information fed in from the senses, for example whether something is hot or cold or bitter, and what the response should be, for example whether the arm should be snatched away from burning heat or the person should spit out the bitter substance in case it is poisonous. The cortex selects those sensations that are important and ignores those that are irrelevant. A common analogy is to imagine a room full of people at a party. You will be conscious of the buzz of conversation but will not be aware of the specific words unless someone mentions your name, in which case, because it is important to you, you will probably pick it up. This illustrates the brain's operation perfectly. Hundreds of sensations are impinging on it at any given time, but it selects only the important ones and reacts to them.

The surface of the cortex is arranged in folds so that the area of the brain is as large as possible. It is these folds that give the brain its easily recognised ruffled appearance.

The inner part of the cerebrum is white in colour and is where emotions such as anger, pleasure, pain, fear, sexual desire and affection are thought to originate.
See also BRAIN; CEREBELLUM; SPINAL CORD

CERIVASTATIN
See HYPOLIPIDAEMICS

CERUMEN
See EAR WAX

CERVICAL CANCER
Cancer of the cervix involves the part of the uterus (womb) which opens into the top of the vagina. It is one of the more common forms of female cancer, and more common in women who have multiple sexual partners, smokers, and much more common in women who have been infected with the human papilloma virus which causes genital warts.

There may be no symptoms for several years after the cancer is present, then abnormal vaginal bleeding, foul discharge, pain and/or bleeding on intercourse, and discomfort in the lower abdomen may occur.

The cancer may be detected at an early stage by a Pap smear test. If a Pap smear result is suspicious, the cervix will be more closely examined through a microscope that looks into the vagina (a colposcope). Biopsy of a suspicious area can then confirm the diagnosis.

It is easily treated in early stages by burning away the cancerous area with diathermy or laser, or a cone-shaped area of tissue may be excised. These forms of treatment do not interfere with the woman's ability to fall pregnant, or function normally in her sexual responses. Only if the cancer is advanced is a hysterectomy required or radiation therapy used. If left untreated the cancer may spread to the lymph nodes in the pelvis, the uterus, ureters and other organs.

99% of early stage cancer is cured, 65% of cases with medium stage survive, but only 5% of those with spread outside the pelvis are alive after five years. Regular Pap smears can therefore save lives.

See also GENITAL WART; PAP SMEAR

CERVICAL CAP

Like the diaphragm, the cervical cap is a barrier method of contraception, but it is much smaller because it fits tightly over the cervix, rather than filling the vagina. There are several types of cervical caps, but the one most commonly used attaches to the cervix by suction. The cap must be fitted carefully. It should be used in the same way as the diaphragm, with spermicides and following the same precautions. It has about the same reliability as the diaphragm. The cervical cap is most commonly used in Europe.

See also CONTRACEPTION

CERVICAL RIB SYNDROME

See NAFFZIGER SYNDROME

CERVIX

The cervix is the narrow passage at the lower end of the uterus, which connects with the vagina. It allows blood to flow out of the uterus during the menstrual period, and sperm to enter after intercourse for possible fertilisation of an egg. The cervix is normally filled with mucus, the composition of which changes at different stages of the menstrual cycle. It is usually thick to stop bacteria and other infections from entering the uterus, but when an egg is released (ovulation) it becomes thinner so as to make it easier for sperm to enter and fertilise the egg. Some forms of birth control are based on a woman analysing the consistency of the cervical mucus she produces, since it is an obvious indicator of when an egg is about to be released.

When a baby is due to be born and the mother goes into labour, the canal through the centre of the cervix expands in a few hours to many times its normal diameter of about three millimetres up to about ten centimetres to allow the baby out. The first stage of labour is when the muscles of the wall of the uterus start contracting while at the same time the muscle fibres of the cervix relax to allow expansion.

If the cervix opens abnormally during

FEMALE REPRODUCTIVE SYSTEM

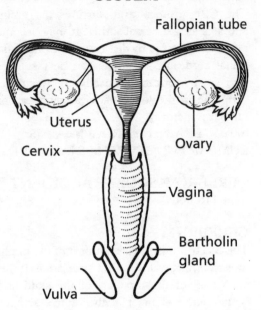

pregnancy, the foetus may escape and the woman will have a miscarriage. Some women have a cervix that is prone to weakness (an incompetent cervix), and if detected early enough, the cervix can be held closed by stitches, a procedure generally carried out under general anaesthetic. The stitches are removed when labour begins or at about the thirty-eighth week of pregnancy.

Sometimes the delicate cells forming the inner lining of the cervix spread to cover the tip and replace the stronger tissue normally occurring there. This is called cervical erosion and makes the cervix more vulnerable to infection. It may cause a heavy discharge and bleeding after intercourse. Generally the treatment for cervical erosion is to destroy the unwanted cells by heat (cauterisation) or laser. This is painless and usually only requires attendance at a clinic or hospital as an outpatient.

The most serious condition affecting the cervix is cervical cancer. Like most cancers, this can be effectively treated if it is detected early. The method of detection is a Pap smear, and all women should have one every two years. Deaths from cervical cancer are second only to deaths from breast cancer, but the death rate could be dramatically reduced if all women had regular Pap smears.

See also CERVICAL CANCER; COLPOSCOPY; PAP SMEAR; UTERUS; VAGINA

CESTODES
See TAPEWORMS

CETRIMIDE
See ANTISEPTICS

CETRIZINE
See ANTIHISTAMINES

CFS
See CHRONIC FATIGUE SYNDROME

CHAGAS' DISEASE
Chagas' disease (American trypanosomiasis) is an infestation by the protozoan (single celled) parasite *Trypanosoma cruzi* that is widespread in tropical America from Texas to Bolivia. It is transmitted from wild animals to humans by bug bites to the skin or bug faeces in the eye.

The disease goes through three stages – acute, latent and chronic. Initially a sore develops on skin at the site of a bite or in the eye, and in many patients, no other symptoms ever occur until after a latent stage, lasting ten to thirty years, when a chronic stage with heart disease occurs causing irregular heart rhythm, congestive heart failure, and pulmonary thromboses (blood clots in lung). A minority of patients go through an acute illness which causes enlarged lymph nodes near the bite, fever, tiredness, headache, and enlarged liver and spleen. Acute heart or brain infection may be rapidly fatal. Long term infection may cause severe heart disease. The disease is diagnosed by specific blood tests, but may be undetectable in the latent stage.

Treatment is generally unsatisfactory. Medications may be tried in the acute stage, but are of no use in the chronic stage.

Chagas' disease is fatal in 10% of acute illnesses, and death from heart disease may occur in the chronic stage.
See also SLEEPING SICKNESS and separate entries for diseases mentioned above.

CHALAZION
A chalazion is a bacterial infection of an oil gland (Meibomian gland) deep within an eyelid due to blockage of the duct draining the gland. Patients develop a painful, red, tender swelling in an eyelid.

Treatment involves antibiotic eye ointment, and sometimes either cutting open or cutting out the infected gland. The condition may be recurrent, and rarely infection can spread further into the eyelid, but there is a good response to treatment.
See also EYELID; MEIBOMIAN CYST

CHANCROID
Chancroid is a sexually transmitted infection caused by the bacteria *Haemophilus ducreyi*, that is rare in developed countries, and more common in the tropics and Asia.

Three to five days after sexual contact with a carrier, a sore develops on the penis or vulva which rapidly breaks down to form a painful ulcer. Several sores and ulcers may be present at the same time. Lymph nodes in the groin then swell up into hard, painful lumps, that may degenerate into an abscess and discharge pus. The patient is feverish and feels ill. Some patients develop a mild form with minimal symptoms, but they can transmit the disease. This is particularly common in women, where the sores may be hidden internally in the vagina. The condition is diagnosed by taking swabs from the sores and identifying the bacteria present in the pus, or skin tests that often remain positive for life.

Antibiotics (eg. azithromycin, ciprofloxacin) cure the infection, but balanitis (infection of penis head) and phimosis (contracture of foreskin) are possible complications.
See also BALANITIS; PHIMOSIS; VENEREAL DISEASES

CHANGE OF LIFE
See MENOPAUSE

CHARCOT-MARIE-TOOTH DISEASE
Charcot-Marie-Tooth disease is a gradually progressive degeneration of nerves that supply the arms and legs, caused by a familial (runs in families) genetic abnormality. Patients initially have an abnormal gait (way of walking) and foot deformities in late childhood or early adult life. The gait gradually worsens over several years with weakness and loss of sensation in the legs, and later the arms. Paralysis of both arms and legs is the eventual result. The diagnosis is confirmed by a nerve biopsy. There is no treatment and no cure.
See also MUSCLE WEAKNESS

CHARNLEY, JOHN

John Charnley (1911–1982) was a Lancashire (England) orthopaedic surgeon who produced the first practical artificial hip joint replacement with a plastic cup and stainless steel ball.
See also HIP FRACTURE; HIP REPLACEMENT

CHÉDIAK-HIGASHI SYNDROME

The Chédiak-Higashi syndrome is a familial (runs through families) failure of white blood cells to function or develop. Patients have recurrent skin infections, partial albinism (loss of skin pigment) and a lack of white blood cells. Some patients have a large liver and spleen, and severe respiratory infections. Blood tests show abnormal and low number of white cells. Antibiotics can be used for bacterial infections, and steroids, bone marrow transplants and vitamin C supplements may also be helpful. The prognosis is poor.
See also ALBINISM

CHELATION

Proponents of chelation therapy claim that a series of twenty or more, three-hour long intravenous injections of a chemical called EDTA, will totally change a patient's life and that it will cure, or dramatically improve, everything from hardening of the arteries and strokes, to senility and cancer. Diabetes and rheumatoid arthritis are also sometimes mentioned. The injections are usually undertaken only after a long and expensive series of high technology investigations.

As well as the course of injections, treatment may include large doses of mineral supplements, vitamins, thyroid extract and hormones, all of which may have serious side effects. The mineral supplements are actually necessary, to counteract some of the complications of the EDTA that is run into the patient's veins, as this chemical drains all metals out of the body, and can cause kidney damage, low calcium levels, diarrhoea, tetany and death.

EDTA and chelation therapy are actually used by doctors to treat heavy metal poisoning by substances such as lead and mercury.

There is no scientific evidence that chelation therapy will achieve the numerous claims made for it. The claims are made by a skilful combination of accepted facts and reasonably accurate statements about theories concerning many diseases, interleaved with a subtle mixture of statements which are not supported by any scientific evidence.
See also LEAD POISONING; MERCURY POISONING

CHEMODECTOMA

See CAROTID BODY TUMOUR

CHERRY ANGIOMA

See CAMPBELL de MORGAN SPOTS

CHEST

See CHEST PAIN; HEART; LUNG; RIB; STERNUM

CHEST PAIN

A pain in the chest is a very distressing symptom as patients are often concerned that it may be serious, and rightly so. Because chest pains might be caused by a life threatening condition involving the heart or lungs, medical help should be sought rapidly unless there is an obvious cause. Other organs that may cause chest pain include the oesophagus, breast bone, ribs, aorta (main artery of the body), thymus gland, lymph nodes, smaller arteries, veins or nerves, as well as the structures around the area such as the muscles, ligaments, skin, breasts or the vertebrae in the back.

The doctor may be guided as to the diagnosis by the nature of the pain (sharp, ache, dull, pressure), whether it is constant or intermittent, if it is affected by eating, exercising, coughing or taking a deep breath, if it starts in one area then moves to another, what tends to make the pain better or worse, and the presence of associated symptoms such as vomiting, cough, shortness of breath, loss of appetite, fever and pain on swallowing.

Investigations to further aid a doctor may include blood tests, x-rays (but these show only bones, and not soft tissue), CT scans (computerised cross sectional x-rays which show some soft tissues), electrocardiograms (ECG – read the electrical activity of the heart), lung function tests (blowing into various machines), endoscopy (passing a flexible telescope tube in through the mouth and down the oesophagus or into the lungs), and as a last resort, surgery.

Common causes of chest pain include: –
• An injury to the chest that causes bruising, fractured ribs, muscle or ligamentous tears, may cause pain in varying parts of the chest

that is usually worsened by any movement.

• Viral infections frequently cause generalised muscle inflammation, resulting in aches and pains in varying muscle bundles, including those in the chest and back.

• Arthritis of the vertebrae in the back may cause pinching of nerves and pain not only in the back, but running around the sides of the chest to the front as well. Changes in position often vary this pain.

• A heart attack (myocardial infarct) occurs when one of the small arteries supplying the heart muscle becomes blocked by a piece of clot or debris from a cholesterol plaque. Pain may occur in any part of the chest, neck, jaw or arms (left more than right), but the usual sites for pain are the left chest, lower front of neck, central chest and front of left shoulder. It is usually described as a crushing pressure or severe ache rather than a sharp pain. It is not affected by movement, eating or coughing, and does not usually vary in intensity. If in doubt, see a doctor now!

• Angina is a pressure-like, squeezing pain or tightness in the chest, usually central, that starts suddenly, often during exercise, and settles with rest.

• Pneumonia is a bacterial infection of the tiny air bubbles (alveoli) that form the major part of the lung and enable oxygen to cross into the bloodstream. The symptoms include fever, cough and chest pains.

• Pleurisy causes severe localised pain that is worse with breathing, coughing or any movement of the chest.

• The stomach contains concentrated hydrochloric acid, and is protected from this by a thick lining of mucus. If the acid comes back up into the unprotected oesophagus (reflux oesophagitis), intense burning may be felt behind the breast bone, as well as a bitter taste, shortness of breath and burping.

• A hiatus hernia may cause burning pain behind the breast bone, burping and an acid taste at the back of the tongue.

• Tietze syndrome, which is a painful, tender swelling of one or more of the cartilages that join the end of each rib to the side of the breast bone.

• A blood clot (pulmonary embolus) in one of the major arteries within the lungs (pulmonary thrombosis) will cause severe damage to that section of lung beyond the clot, leading to its collapse, pain and shortness of breath.

• If an aneurysm on the aorta starts to enlarge, leak or bursts, pain may be felt in this area that varies from an ache to severe pain, depending on the degree of damage.

Less common causes include pneumothorax, a foreign body (eg. food, small toy) caught in the oesophagus or a bronchus, shingles, bronchiectasis (lung damage), myocarditis (infection of the heart muscle), various abnormalities of the heart structure that may be present at birth (eg. Fallot's tetralogy), severe anaemia, failure of the major valves in the heart (particularly the mitral valve between the left ventricle and atrium), cancer in the lymph nodes within the chest, cardiac neuroses (excessive concern about heart disease), slipping rib syndrome and Bornholm disease (pleurodynia).

Problems in the abdomen such as cholecystitis (inflammation or infection of the gall bladder) or a peptic ulcer, and the back (pinched nerve from arthritis between the vertebrae) may also cause chest pain.
See also BACK PAIN; HEARTBURN; THORAX and separate entries for diseases mentioned above.

CHEYNE-STOKES RESPIRATION

Cheyne-Stokes respiration is characterised by breaths that gradually decrease in frequency until a temporary stop occurs. Breathing then restarts slowly and the frequency of breaths builds to a maximum before the cycle repeats itself.

It is a serious abnormality of breathing, due to damage to the respiratory (breathing) centre in the brain from a stroke or tumour, meningitis, uraemia (kidney failure), drug (eg. narcotic, barbiturate) overdose or advanced heart disease (eg. congestive cardiac failure). It is the final stage of many long term fatal diseases.

In most cases, it is a sign of imminent death, but if the cause can be treated, the condition may be reversed.
See also DEATH; ICHABOD SYNDROME

CHICKENPOX

Chickenpox (varicella) is a generalised infection caused by the virus *Herpes zoster*. Infection occurs when the virus passes to another person from the fluid-filled blisters that cover the body of patients, or in their breath and saliva. Patients are infectious for a day or two before the spots appear, and remain infectious for about eight days. The incubation period is ten to twenty-one days.

Early symptoms are similar to those of a cold, with a vague feeling of being unwell, headache, fever and sore throat. The rash usually starts on the head or chest as red pimples, then spreads onto the legs and arms, and develops into blisters before drying up and scabbing over. New spots may develop for three to five days, and it may be two weeks or more before the last spot disappears. The diagnosis can be confirmed by blood tests, but none are usually necessary.

Treatment involves bed and home rest until the patient feels well, and medications to relieve the itch (eg. calamine lotion, antihistamines), fever and headache. There is a vaccine available to prevent the disease.

Complications are more common in adults, and include chest infections and a type of meningitis. It is unusual for the pockmarks to scar unless a secondary bacterial infection occurs.

Complete recovery within ten days is normal. Once a person has had chickenpox, it is unlikely (but not impossible) that they will ever catch it again.

After recovery, the chickenpox virus never leaves the body but migrates to the nerves along the spinal cord where it remains forever. The virus may be reactivated years later at times of stress to give the patient the painful rash of shingles.
See also SHINGLES; VIRUS

CHICLERO ULCER
See CUTANEOUS LEISCHMANIASIS

CHILBLAINS
Chilblains are a mild form of frostbite caused by exposure to extreme cold.

Itchy, red skin spots develop on the fingers, toes and other exposed areas such as the nose. The spot may form a blister, and the itching is aggravated by warmth.

Treatment involves gradual warming in a warm room. The fingers or toes should NOT be immersed in hot water or placed near a heater or fire, nor should the area be rubbed or massaged as this may cause further damage. Sometimes damaged skin may become infected and require antibiotics. Recurrent chilblains can lead to a permanent scar

forming at the site, but if not exposed to further cold, the skin will heal in a day or two.
See also FROSTBITE

CHILD ABUSE
The physical abuse of a child is not so much a symptom, but a cry for help in many cases, from a parent who is not coping with the stress of child care. At some stage in the first few months of their baby's life, most parents feel like throwing their bundle of joy out of the window. Fortunately, the vast majority of parents resist this desire, but there is no doubt that children can become irritating, frustrating and maddening to the most loving of parents. Inexperienced parents and a new baby who cries day and night can lead to irrational thinking and spontaneous actions which are quite out of character and later will be profoundly regretted. Child abuse in this situation is understandable but still inexcusable. Parents must seek help from their doctor or child welfare officer before this stage is reached.

In other situations, child abuse may be more callous or sadistic. An unwanted child may be abused in order to extract unwarranted revenge. A father may hurt a child to indirectly hurt his wife or girlfriend. Some parents are simply nasty people who are violent in all their human relationships. Many child abusers were themselves abused as children.

Child abuse can be physical, psychological or sexual. Whichever form it takes, it can be difficult to detect and may continue for a long time before the child comes to the notice of a responsible person and is given protection. A person who abuses a child rarely does it when anyone else is around. If a person becomes suspicious that a child is being abused, they should talk to a doctor or children's hospital. Child abuse may be suspected if a child has repeated bruising or burn marks and the parents delay or fail to obtain medical help, offer implausible or inconsistent explanations for the injuries, or if their reactions to the injuries seem strange. The most reliable indication of continued cruelty or neglect is often failure of the child to grow at the normal rate. Children made unhappy by repeated abuse do not thrive, and their weight drops well below the average for their age.

Neglect is as much a form of child abuse as deliberate injury. Poor hygiene and under- or over-clothing an infant may be due to lack of knowledge, but lack of food and failure to obtain attention for illnesses, skin diseases, infected eyes and injuries is unacceptable abuse.

There is sometimes a fine line between discipline by the parents, temper tantrums by the child, and criminal abuse of the child. Casual observation by an outsider may give a false impression, but if the child shows signs of injury or the problem continues consistently, then the family requires help. This help is readily available from the family general practitioner, paediatricians, community nurses and welfare workers, and special teams attached to most children's hospitals.

Some parents realise that assistance in dealing with a difficult child is required, but are afraid to seek it because of the consequences. If help is sought voluntarily, it would be exceptional for any charges to be laid against the parents. Putting a parent in jail is rarely seen as a solution for either the child or the family as a whole. Rather, every effort is made to solve the problem by counselling, medications and care. Sometimes the child can be removed from the family for a short period, if it is thought this will help to relieve stress, modify abnormal behaviour patterns in the child, and lead to normal future family life. Only those who consistently refuse to accept their responsibilities as parents and reject offers of professional assistance are likely to find the law invoked against them.

Child abuse is not new; it has occurred throughout history, and is probably occurring less now than in Victorian times when child labour was the norm. However, society today is far more aware of the problem and less inclined either to accept it or sweep it under the carpet.

Many areas have a child abuse hot line that can be called in an emergency, and any information supplied will be treated confidentially. *See also* CHILDHOOD; FAILURE TO THRIVE; PAEDOPHILIA; POLLE SYNDROME

CHILDHOOD

The years from two to adolescence are mostly taken up with growing, being educated, and learning to interact with the family and society at large. By the time children are five and ready to start school, most of their behaviour problems will have settled down.

A growing child needs a well-balanced diet to provide all the kilojoules, vitamins and minerals that are essential to maintain physical and mental development. The child's diet should include meat and fish with plenty of fresh vegetables and fruit, as well as adequate calcium, usually from milk, to ensure strong and healthy bones.

Some children start to dislike sleep and to rebel against going to bed. Generally a child will be more amenable to an early bedtime if a regular routine is adhered to and there is no question that bedtime has arrived. A child who persistently appears for a chat after being put to bed, or constantly asks for a drink of water or to go to the toilet, should have his or her request met once and then be put to bed firmly with no further excuses for delay allowed. Of course, many children develop a fear of the dark at this time, and if this is the reason for a toddler's reluctance to stay in bed, a night light may solve the problem.

Children should have their teeth checked every six months to ensure that the teeth are growing as they should and that they are free from decay. Checks on hearing and vision are normally carried out through the school system. A child who is suspected of having difficulties with hearing or seeing should be tested without delay, as these handicaps can affect all areas of learning and general ability to function. It is vitally important to make sure that a child has strong, healthy feet, and this depends almost entirely on their shoes. All children should have shoes that support their feet, protect them and allow them freedom to grow.

The childhood years are affected by repeated infectious viral diseases. Serious diseases such as measles, mumps, rubella and whooping cough are now rare since the introduction of immunisation programs. Scarlet fever and other bacterial infections can be cured readily by antibiotics. Coughs and colds are part and parcel of school life, and most children will get such infections every few months. An otherwise healthy child will usually have a few days of feeling off-colour and then fight off the infection and return to health.

Accidents are a hazard of the childhood years. Obviously this is because a normal healthy child leads an active outdoor life, riding bicycles, swimming, climbing trees and

taking part in various other activities. Falls, fractures, knee injuries, sprained ankles and dislocated shoulders are commonplace in the five to twelve age group. Fortunately, most of these heal quickly and completely if given appropriate care. Nevertheless some accidents should not happen. Parents need to give their child a basic understanding of safety, and to steer a balance between allowing the child freedom to explore and develop its independence, and sufficient supervision and protection to ensure that serious injury does not occur. The odd sprained wrist or ankle from falling off a bike is probably inevitable in an active youngster's life, but being knocked off the bike by a car with possible serious and lifelong repercussions is a quite different matter.
See also BABIES; BABY FEEDING; CHILD ABUSE; FAILURE TO THRIVE; TALKING; TOILET TRAINING; VACCINATION OF CHILDREN

CHILD NOT THRIVING
See FAILURE TO THRIVE

CHINESE MEDICINE
Traditional Chinese medicine has its own internal diagnostic system which arises out of the ancient philosophy and custom governing the discipline.

In addition to acupuncture, traditional Chinese medicine also uses herbalism and a combination of acupuncture and herbs in moxibustion or moxa treatment, in which acupuncture points on the body are stimulated by the heat from burning a stick of special herbs. The remedial therapies in this discipline include various massage techniques, acupressure, exercise and relaxation techniques such as tai chi.
See also ACUPUNCTURE; AYURVEDIC MEDICINE; SHIATSU

CHIROPODY
See PODIATRY

CHIROPRACTIC
Chiropractic is a healing art designed to relieve ailments by manipulation and adjustment of the spine. The technique and the fundamental theory that most human ailments result from a slight misalignment of the vertebrae, causing nerve interference, were developed by the American M. Palmer

in 1895. He adjusted the spine of a man who had been deaf for many years, and the man regained his hearing.

Chiropractors believe that, because the nervous system (brain, spinal cord and nerves) controls all the other systems of the body, adjusting the spine can affect other more distant parts of the body. The adjustment of the spine is perceived as removing misalignments between the vertebrae called subluxations, or abnormal movements between vertebrae called fixations. When subluxations or fixations are removed, normal movement returns to the spinal joints, nerve and muscle irritations are eased and tension is relieved. It is claimed that subluxation in particular parts of the spine may induce disorders of other organs, such as the kidney, stomach, lungs and liver, and increase the body's likelihood of contracting disease.

Orthodox medicine does not accept that spinal adjustment can cure diseases within distant organs.
See also MANIPULATION; NATUROPATHY; OSTEOPATHY

CHLAMYDIAL INFECTION
Infection of tissue such as the lung, eye, genitals and urinary tract by the intracellular bacterium *Chlamydiae* can be cured by antibiotics such as tetracyclines and erythromycin (a macrolide).
See also LYMPHOGRANULOMA VENEREUM; MACROLIDES; NON-SPECIFIC URETHRITIS; PSITTACOSIS; TETRACYCLINES; TRACHOMA

CHLOASMA
Chloasma (melasma) is a pigmentation disorder of the skin that occurs almost invariably in women, and more commonly in those with a dark complexion. The deposits of pigment on the forehead, cheeks, upper lip, nose and nipples are often triggered by pregnancy or starting the oral contraceptive pill.

Treatment is unsatisfactory. Numerous blanching agents have been tried with minimal success, but the pigmentation usually fades slowly over several years.
See also FACE PIGMENTED; NIPPLE; PREGNANCY; SKIN PIGMENTATION, EXCESS

CHLORACNE
This rare skin condition chloracne, occurs as a

reaction to toxic chemicals (eg. dioxin, chlorbenzene, polychlorbiphenyls, chlorophenol, pyrazole) found in insecticides, herbicides and wood preservatives. The chemicals may be touched, inhaled or swallowed.

Whiteheads and blackheads similar to acne (pimples) that are not inflamed (red), develop on the skin of the cheeks, neck, armpits and groins. Because the chemicals are stored in body fat, more pimples may develop for some time after exposure to the chemicals has ceased.

The source of exposure must be identified and further exposure prevented. Antibiotics and isotretinoin are used to slowly clear pimples.

After an attack the palms and soles may be excessively sweaty, the liver may be damaged, excess fat is found in the blood, impotence may occur, patients may become tired and nervous, and porphyria cutanea tarda may develop. Provided there is no more exposure to the responsible chemicals, the pimples usually clear within two years.
See also ACNE; PORPHYRIA CUTANEA TARDA

CHLORHEXIDINE
See ANTISEPTICS

CHLOROQUINE
See ANTIMALARIALS; ANTIRHEUMATICS

CHLOROXYLENOL
See ANTISEPTICS

CHLORPHENIRAMINE
See ANTIHISTAMINES

CHLORPROMAZINE
See ANTIPSYCHOTICS

CHLORPROPAMIDE
See HYPOGLYCAEMICS

CHLORTHIAZIDE
See DIURETICS

CHOKING
Choking occurs when a foreign body gets stuck in the airway so that breathing is obstructed. When choking occurs, the victim may have a violent fit of coughing and the face

and neck will become deep red, turning to purple. They will make a superhuman effort to breathe, and if unsuccessful will claw the air and clutch at the throat before turning blue in the face and collapsing.

Often the object will be dislodged by the coughing. If not, try to remove it with your finger – but be extremely careful not to push it down further. If that is unsuccessful, two or three sharp blows between the shoulder blades may clear it. Make sure the person is in a position in which the object can fall out easily – eg. an adult should sit and lean forward. If the victim is lying down, turn them gently to one side.

If this fails, there are several ways in which you may proceed: –
• Place your arms around the victim's chest from behind, with your clenched fists over the breast bone. As suddenly and as hard as you can, push on the breast bone and squeeze the chest (Heimlich manoeuvre).
• Lie the patient in the coma position on their side on the floor, give several sharp blows between the shoulder blades and then, if necessary, give several firm quick pushes on the side of the chest wall below the arm pit.
• Place the victim on a table so that they are hanging over the edge from the waist up, with the top of their head on the floor. Try the chest compression (Heimlich manoeuvre) again so that it is aided by gravity.

If all these measures fail and the victim is unconscious, lie them on their back and tilt the head backwards to maximise the airway. Sit astride the victim and place the heel of your hand on the upper abdomen just above the navel. Cover it with the heel of your other hand. Give a sharp downward and forward thrust towards the victim's head. Give up to four thrusts if necessary. If the victim does not splutter and start breathing, start mouth-to-mouth resuscitation.

As the victim starts breathing normally, place them in the lateral or coma position and get medical help. It is especially important to tell the doctor if chest compression has been used, so that the internal organs can be checked.

If all efforts to dislodge the object fail, you will have to blow air past it by using mouth-to-mouth resuscitation until medical help is obtained.

If you have a child who is choking, sit down

and lie the child face down across your lap, with the head low. Give two or three blows between the shoulder blades with the heel of your hand. If this is unsuccessful, administer chest compression. A baby can be held upside down in your arms while you slap it between the shoulder blades or administer chest compression.

See also HEIMLICH MANOEUVRE; RESUSCITATION; UNCONSCIOUS

CHOLECYSTECTOMY

A cholecystectomy (gall bladder removal) is normally performed because there are stones in the gall bladder that are causing pain or discomfort. Ideally, the operation is performed at a time when there is no infection present in the gall bladder, and after the patient has lost any excess weight. This is not always possible, and some of these operations must be performed while the patient is quite ill with cholecystitis (gall bladder infection).

If the surgeon is certain about the diagnosis, the gall bladder is not infected, and the patient is appropriate in other ways (eg. not overweight), the surgeon may consider removing the gall bladder by laparoscopy which is technically more difficult, but allows faster recovery. Only three or four small incisions are made in the belly, and the patient may only remain in hospital two or three days.

If a traditional open operation is performed due to risk factors or complications, the incision is usually diagonal just below the edge of the ribs on the right side, but in some cases it may be vertical between the bottom of the breast bone and the umbilicus. Through this incision, the surgeon sees the liver, which must be pushed aside so that access to the gall bladder can be obtained. Patients are in hospital for about five days and off work for three to four weeks. Those involved in heavy manual labour may require six weeks to recover.

In both operations the gall bladder is carefully dissected away from the liver and removed, and then the duct that drains away the bile is cut. Through this opening into the common bile duct that connects the liver to the gut a fine tube is placed, and dye that can be seen on x-ray is injected into this duct to ensure that no other stones are present and that the bile will be able to flow freely after the operation. If no other stones are found, a drain will sometimes be left in the common bile duct to drain excess bile in the period after the operation when the damaged tissues may swell and cause blockages. The incision is closed with the other end of the drain left coming through the skin. The drain is removed after a few days when the common bile duct and surrounding structures have recovered from the operation.

See also CHOLECYSTITIS; GALL BLADDER; GALLSTONES; LAPAROSCOPY

CHOLECYSTITIS

Cholecystitis is an infection or inflammation of the gall bladder that almost always occurs in the presence of gallstones. Many different bacteria can be responsible for the infection.

Patients develop pain in the upper right abdomen and behind the lower right ribs that often goes through to the back. They also have a fever, indigestion, nausea and sometimes irregular bowel habits.

Ultrasound scans can detect gallstones, and sometimes thickening of the wall of the gall bladder which is characteristic of infection. Rarely there may be spread of the infection to the liver and other surrounding tissues, and sometimes an abscess forms in or around the gall bladder. Blood tests are often normal, but sometimes show non-specific signs of infection or liver stress.

Antibiotics are used to settle the gall bladder infection, then surgery is necessary to remove the stones (cholecystectomy).

See also CHOLECYSTECTOMY; GALL BLADDER; GALLSTONES

CHOLELITHIASIS

See GALLSTONES

CHOLERA

Cholera is a severe infection of the bowel that occurs in areas with poor hygiene. The responsible bacterium, *Vibrio cholerae*, may be swallowed with contaminated water or food. The bacteria multiply rapidly in the body to irritate the gut, cause diarrhoea, and then pass out in faeces, contaminate water supplies, and infect others.

Patients develop very severe diarrhoea with blood in the faeces and rapid dehydration that may lead to death. A huge amount of fluid is lost from the body in a short time. The patient also shivers, has a below normal temperature, shallow breathing, muscle cramps and becomes comatose. Samples of faeces cultured in a laboratory can identify the responsible bacteria.

Replacing fluid loss by a drip into a vein (preferable) or an electrolyte mixture by mouth, is imperative to prevent death. An emergency mixture to rehydrate a patient can be made by mixing a level teaspoon of salt and eight level teaspoons of sugar or glucose into a litre of boiled water. This should be given freely to more than replace the fluid lost in the diarrhoea. A course of tetracycline antibiotic will kill the infecting bacteria in the gut, but will not relieve symptoms. A vaccination against cholera is available.

Untreated, the death rate varies from 35% to 80%, but with proper care, 98% should survive. From the time of onset to death from dehydration can be a matter of a day or two in adults and only a few hours in children.
See also DIARRHOEA;
GASTROENTERITIS; SHIGELLOSIS;
TYPHOID FEVER

CHOLESTASIS
See CHOLESTATIC JAUNDICE

CHOLESTATIC JAUNDICE
Cholestasis (cholestatic jaundice) is a failure of bile to move out of the liver, allowing it to build up in the liver and overflow into the bloodstream as bilirubin to cause jaundice (yellow skin). It may be due to an inherited characteristic (benign familial recurrent cholestasis), a complication of pregnancy, a serious side effect of some medications and drugs, after surgery to the liver and due to mechanical ventilation in critically ill patients.

As well as jaundice, the patient has a loss of appetite, nausea, itchy skin, tiredness, abdominal discomfort and diarrhoea. Ultrasound scans and needle biopsy of the liver are sometimes necessary to determine the cause and seriousness of the condition, and to differentiate it from other types of jaundice.

The cause must be treated if possible (eg. stop any medication that may be responsible, deliver baby early in pregnancy). Most cases recover without further treatment being necessary, but the inherited form recurs many times during the patient's life. Sophisticated medications can be used if necessary to reduce the level of bilirubin in the blood.

The prognosis depends on the cause, but most cases recover satisfactorily, although this may take many months.
See also JAUNDICE; LIVER

CHOLESTEATOMA
A cholesteatoma is a serious complication of middle ear infections or blockage of the Eustachian tube (which runs through the centre of the head from the middle ear to the back of the nose to equalise ear pressure).

A sac on the ear drum develops which is

BILE AND PANCREAS DRAINAGE

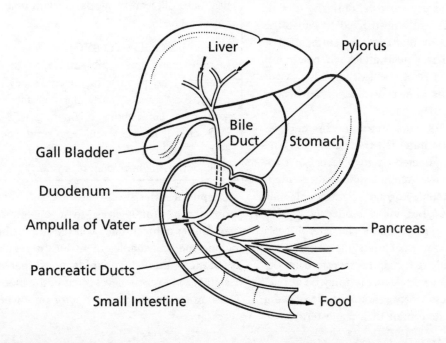

filled with chronically infected material that antibiotics cannot reach. The infected sac slowly enlarges and eats away surrounding bone, including the fine bones which transmit sound vibrations from the ear drum to the hearing mechanism in the inner ear. The symptoms are minimal until the condition is well advanced when ear discomfort and deafness occur. It is diagnosed by examining the ear with an otoscope (magnifying light).

Surgical removal of the sac of infected material usually gives a good result. If left too long before treatment, permanent deafness may occur.

See also EAR; EUSTACHIAN TUBE; OTITIS MEDIA

CHOLESTEROL

A yellow/white fatty substance called cholesterol is responsible for a large proportion of the heart attacks, strokes, circulatory problems and kidney disease in the Western world. Yet cholesterol is essential for the normal functioning of the human body. It is responsible for cementing cells together, is a major constituent of bile, and is the basic building block for sex hormones. Only in excess (when the patient is said to have hypercholesterolaemia) is it harmful.

About 70% of the body's cholesterol is actually manufactured in the liver, and only 30% is obtained through the diet. If too much cholesterol is carried around in the blood stream, it may be deposited in gradually increasing amounts inside the arteries. Slowly, the affected artery narrows, until the flow of blood is sufficiently obstructed to cause the area supplied by that artery to suffer. If that area is the heart, a heart attack will result; if it is the brain, a stroke will occur. This deposition of fat is known as arteriosclerosis, or hardening of the arteries.

The level of cholesterol in the body is determined by inherited traits and diet. The people most affected by high levels of cholesterol are overweight middle-aged men. Women, and some normal weight people may be affected too, but not as frequently.

It has been proved that if cholesterol levels that are within normal limits, the risk of heart attack is greatly reduced. It is therefore important for anyone who feels they may be at risk, and everyone at forty years of age, to have a blood test to determine their cholesterol level.

For this test to be accurate, it is necessary to starve for twelve hours (usually overnight), and avoid alcohol for seventy-two hours before the blood sample is taken.

If the cholesterol level is below 5.5 mmol/L, there is no need for concern. If it is above 5.5 mmol/L, the doctor will probably order tests to find out what types of cholesterol are present. Lower levels of cholesterol are of concern in patients who have diabetes, a history of heart attack or stroke, smokers and with some other diseases. Levels should also be lower in young people than old, and males than females.

There are two main subgroups of cholesterol – high density (which protect you from heart attacks and strokes) and low density (which are bad for you). The ratio between these two types of cholesterol will determine the treatment (if any) that is required.

If the patient is found to be in the high risk group, there are several measures they can take to bring the levels back to normal. The first step is to stop smoking, limit alcohol intake, take more exercise and lose weight if obese. If these measures are insufficient, doctors will recommend a diet that is low in fat and cholesterol. On this, many people return to within normal cholesterol levels after a month or two.

A low cholesterol diet has the following rules: –

FOODS ALLOWED
vegetables, chicken breast, cereals, margarine, fruit and nuts, dark chocolate, fish, olive oil, lean meat, pasta, skim milk, wine and beer

FOODS TO AVOID
sausages, hamburgers, pies, mince, chicken skin and legs, pizza, offal (liver, kidneys, tripe), roast meats (particularly surface), game meat, lamb chops, calamari, prawns, milk chocolate, eggs and egg products, oysters, and all dairy products (cream, milk, butter, yoghurt, cheese, custard)

Despite a strict diet, there are still some people who cannot keep their cholesterol levels under control. They will require further lifelong medical management by the regular use of medications (hypolipidaemics) that are designed to lower the level of fat in the blood. These are prescribed by a doctor only when necessary.

Once the fatty deposits of cholesterol are deposited inside the arteries, they remain there permanently. There are new drugs that may partially remove these deposits over many years, and surgical techniques are available to clean out clogged arteries, but diet has little effect at this late stage. As in all diseases, prevention is much better than cure.
See also ARTERIOSCLEROSIS; FAT; HYPOLIPIDAEMICS; LIPIDS; TRIGLYCERIDE; XANTHOMATOSIS

CHOLESTEROL LOWERING MEDICATIONS
See HYPOLIPIDAEMICS

CHOLESTYRAMINE
See HYPOLIPIDAEMICS

CHOLINERGICS
Cholinergics are a class of medication normally used in injection form to reduce the amount of saliva before an operation, to correct a very slow heart beat, to reduce the severity of diarrhoea, and to relieve the spasm pain associated with kidney stones and gall stones. They are also used by doctors as eye drops to enlarge the pupil. They are an old-fashioned treatment for asthma. Atropine is the only commonly used drug in this class.
See also BELLADONNA; MEDICATION

CHONDROCALCINOSIS
Chondrocalcinosis (calcium pyrophosphate deposition disease) is a form of arthritis due to damage from deposition of calcium pyrophosphate crystals in the cartilages lining major joints. It may be a familial condition (passed from one generation to the next), or due to abnormalities in the body's metabolic processes (eg. diabetes mellitus, hypothyroidism, haemochromatosis).

Affected joints become painful and swollen and x-rays show abnormal calcium deposits. Anti-inflammatory medications are used in treatment, and although recurrent attacks usually occur, each attack can be reasonably controlled.
See also PSEUDOGOUT

CHONDROMALACIA PATELLAE
Chondromalacia patellae is a disease of the knee cap (patella) that occurs only in

KNEE JOINT

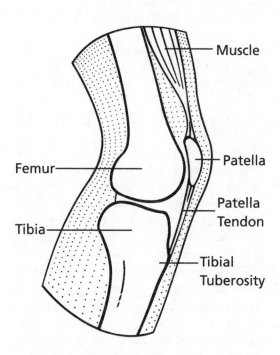

teenagers and young adults. The patella is designed to glide smoothly over the end of the femur (the thigh bone) as the knee is bent and straightened. The under-surface of the patella is covered with a very smooth layer of cartilage, but in chondromalacia, the cartilage becomes softened, pitted, uneven and damaged, and the knee cap grates across the femur instead of gliding. The cause is often difficult to determine, but it may be caused by recurrent dislocation of the knee cap, or by falling repeatedly on the knee.

Patients experience pain deep in the knee which is worse on bending the knee or kneeling. When the knee is moved, a fine grating sensation may be felt. Arthroscopy (looking into the knee joint through a thin tube) may be necessary. Treatment involves firm bandaging and rest, but sometimes splinting or a plaster cast may be required for a few weeks. If pain persists for months, surgery to modify or remove the knee cap may be necessary. Rarely, permanent knee pain may occur and resist all treatment, but the majority of cases settle with simple treatments.
See also ARTHRITIS; ARTHROSCOPY; PATELLA; PATELLO-FEMORAL PAIN SYNDROME

CHONDROSARCOMA
See BONE CANCER

CHOREA
See JERKING; HUNTINGTON'S
CHOREA; SYDENHAM'S CHOREA

CHORIOCARCINOMA
See CHORIOCARCINOMA OF THE
UTERUS; TESTICULAR CANCER

CHORIOCARCINOMA OF THE UTERUS
A choriocarcinoma of the uterus (invasive uterine mole) is a rare form of cancer involving the placenta during pregnancy. Four percent of women with uterine moles (abnormal excessive placental development) develop cancer in the abnormal tissue. This may occur some time after apparently successful treatment of the mole. It can also very rarely occur with an apparently normal pregnancy and a live baby. It may sometimes be successfully treated with surgical removal of the uterus (hysterectomy) and cytotoxic drugs, but the prognosis is poor for the mother, and the foetus invariably dies.
See also UTERINE MOLE; UTERUS

CHORIONIC VILLUS SAMPLING
Chorionic villus sampling (CVS) is a relatively new technique that can be used in the same situations and for the same reasons as amniocentesis (sampling the fluid around a foetus). Primarily it checks for chromosomal abnormalities in a developing foetus. CVS has the advantage over amniocentesis in that it can be performed as early as eight weeks after conception. The results are therefore known earlier, and if a termination of pregnancy is desired because of a serious abnormality in the foetus, this can be undertaken at a far earlier stage of pregnancy when it is physically safer and less stressful to the mother.

The chorionic villi are the microscopic fingers of the placenta that penetrate into the wall of the mother's uterus to enable the blood supplies of the foetus and mother to interact and exchange nutrition, wastes and oxygen. The placenta has the same chromosomal make-up as the foetus, so analysing a sample of cells from the chorionic villi of the placenta gives the same result as analysing cells from the foetus itself.

CVS involves collecting a small amount of placental tissue by passing a very fine tube into the vagina and through the cervix into the uterus, and sucking up a small amount of the placenta into a syringe. Only a tiny number of cells is required, as after removal they are cultured to increase their number before being examined for abnormal chromosomes.

There is a risk of miscarriage with this procedure, as with amniocentesis, but it is only one or two in every 100 tests. For this reason the test is only undertaken if there is some initial suspicion that an abnormal result may be obtained (eg. if a previous child or a close family member has some chromosomal abnormality).
See also AMNIOCENTESIS; PLACENTA;
PREGNANCY; UTERUS

CHRISTMAS DISEASE
Christmas disease (factor IX deficit, haemophilia B) is named after a patient with Christmas as his surname, who had the disease. It is an inherited lack of factor IX, one of the essential factors responsible for the clotting of blood. The gene for the disease is carried by women on the X chromosome, but can only affect men (sex linked inheritance). Statistically, half the children of a woman who carries the responsible gene will have the disease. The incidence is one in 40,000 people.

Symptoms include excessive bleeding from a cut, severe bruising from a minor injury, bleeding into joints to cause arthritis, internal bleeding into the gut and other organs. Specific blood tests can confirm the diagnosis.

Injections of the missing coagulation factor are given to prevent excessive bleeding when it occurs. Insufficient supplies are available for it to be given regularly to prevent bleeding, as the factor can only be obtained from blood donations.

Arthritis, infertility, damage to other organs from bleeding, chronic weakness, and a shorter than normal life span may occur.
See also BLEEDING, EXCESSIVE;
HAEMOPHILIA A; von WILLEBRAND
DISEASE

CHROMOSOME
Chromosome means 'coloured body' in Greek, because the chromosome was originally seen through a microscope as an unidentified coloured body in the nucleus of a cell after using stains to see the structures of the cell more clearly.

There are forty-six chromosomes in every

cell in a human body with the exception of the ova (egg cells) in women and the sperm in men which have only twenty-three chromosomes each. Half of the chromosomes are obtained from each parent, and unite into twenty-three pairs. Each chromosome in the pair looks identical except in men where the sex chromosomes are a very small Y chromosome matched with a much larger X chromosome.

The sex of an individual is determined by the X and Y chromosomes. Males have one X and one Y chromosome (XY), while females have two X chromosomes (XX). Sperm come from the father and so may contain either an X or a Y chromosome, while the ova come from the mother and can only contain an X chromosome. The sex of a child is therefore determined by whether a sperm with an X or Y chromosome fertilises an ovum.

On each chromosome there are thousands of genes which carry the genetic information of each individual.

Each chromosome is made up of DNA (deoxyribonucleic acid) in the form of a double helix. This is like a rubber ladder twisted into a spiral. Each rung of the ladder is formed by a set combination of amino acids that form a code. Segments of that code form a gene.

A chromosome is capable of exactly duplicating itself with every cell reproduction.

The human genome project, which was completed in 2000, mapped the position of every rung of the ladder of DNA on every chromosome and identified many of the over 30 000 genes.

See also AMINO ACID; CELL; DNA; GENE; X-LINKED CONDITION

CHRONIC
A chronic medical condition is one that is persistent or long standing. The opposite of acute.
See also ACUTE

CHRONIC BRONCHITIS
See BRONCHITIS, CHRONIC

CHRONIC CYSTIC MASTITIS
See MAMMARY DYSPLASIA

CHRONIC FATIGUE SYNDROME
Chronic fatigue syndrome (CFS) has been given many different names in various places, including myalgic encephalomyelitis (ME), post-viral syndrome, Royal Free disease (named after a London hospital), and Tapanui flu (in New Zealand). It is characterised by a persistent tiredness and easy fatigue that persists for many months for no obvious reason.

The condition is may be caused by a virus, but some patients find that certain foods aggravate the condition. It is possible that it is actually several diseases that overlap with their symptoms, and may be due to a combination of infection, immune deficiencies, autoimmune type condition (where the body rejects its own tissue), chronic inflammation, stress and psychiatric disturbances. It is a matter of debate whether the distressing symptoms cause the psychological problems, or vice versa.

The diagnosis can only be confirmed if in the following list, both major criteria are met, plus six symptoms and two signs from the minor criteria.

MAJOR CRITERIA
• New, persistent or intermittent, debilitating fatigue severe enough to reduce or impair average daily activity below 50% of normal activity for a period of more than six months.
• Exclusion of all other causes by thorough clinical evaluation, and blood tests

MINOR CRITERIA – SYMPTOMS
• Generalised fatigue lasting more than twenty-four hours following levels of exertion that would have been easily tolerated previously.
• Vague headache.
• Unexplained general muscle weakness.
• Muscle pains.
• Arthritis that moves from joint to joint without any apparent damage to the joint.
• One or more of the following problems: –
    • avoidance of bright lights
    • forgetfulness
    • irritability
    • confusion
    • poor concentration
    • depression
    • intermittent visual disturbances
    • difficulty thinking
• Inability to sleep, or excessive sleepiness.
• Rapid onset over hours or days of major criteria.

MINOR CRITERIA – SIGNS
Documented by a physician on at least two occasions at least a month apart.
• Mild fever greater than 38.6°C.

• Sore throat with no pus present.
• Tender enlarged lymph nodes in neck or arm pit

There are no specific diagnostic tests, but numerous blood tests may show minor abnormalities. Tests are always performed to exclude any other possible cause.

There is no specific treatment available, but patients can benefit by having an understanding doctor who may use antidepressants, anti-inflammatory medication, steroids and other drugs that may be helpful. Although there is no cure, with time, most cases slowly improve, but some patients are left with long term tiredness so severe that they are unable to return to work or undertake normal daily activities.
See also AUTOIMMUNE DISEASES; FATIGUE

CHRONIC OBSTRUCTIVE AIRWAYS (PULMONARY) DISEASE
Chronic obstructive airways (pulmonary) disease is a term that covers a group of irreversible conditions (chronic bronchitis, emphysema, pneumoconiosis) that permanently affect the lung and its function.
See also BRONCHITIS, CHRONIC; EMPHYSEMA; PNEUMOCONIOSIS

CHRONIC RENAL FAILURE
See KIDNEY FAILURE, CHRONIC

CHYME
See STOMACH

CIGUATERA POISONING
This is a form of seafood poisoning caused by eating reef fish that contain the ciguatera toxin. The fish itself is not affected, and there are no tests for differentiating safe from toxic fish. Generally the larger the fish, the more likely it is to be toxic. The poison is produced at certain seasons by a microscopic animal (Dinoflagellida) that proliferates on tropical reefs. This is eaten by very small fish, which are then eaten by bigger fish, which are then eaten by still bigger fish. There may be a dozen steps along this chain, with the poison being steadily concentrated in the fish tissue at every step. Ciguatera is present in a low concentration in most reef fish, but only when it exceeds a certain concentration does it cause problems in humans. There are far

higher concentrations in the gut, liver, head and roe of reef fish, which should never be eaten or used to make fish soup, and it cannot be destroyed by cooking.

Symptoms vary dramatically from one patient to another, depending on the amount of toxin eaten, the size of the victim, and the individual reaction. They may include unusual skin sensations and tingling, diarrhoea, nausea, abnormal sensation, headaches and irregular heartbeats. Unusual tingling sensations may persist for years, and subsequent serious attacks may be triggered by eating tiny amounts of ciguatera that may be present in fish that others can eat without adverse effects.

There are no diagnostic tests, and no specific treatment or antidote, but medication may be used to control symptoms.

Patients with a mild reaction usually recover in a few days as the toxin is naturally eliminated from the body, but severe attacks may cause symptoms for a couple of months. Death is rare, but possible, usually occurs within thirty-six hours of the onset of the attack, and is caused by the effects of the toxin on the heart and blood vessels.
See also FOOD POISONING

CIMETIDINE
See H2 RECEPTOR ANTAGONISTS

CINCHONA
See ANTIMALARIALS

CIPROFLOXACIN
See QUINOLONES

CIRCULATORY SYSTEM
The circulatory system is the means by which blood circulates throughout the body. The blood travels along a complex network of narrow channels, all interlinked so that they flow into or out of the heart. These channels, or blood vessels, together with the four chambers of the heart, form a completely enclosed system. The only time any blood escapes from it is if it is damaged as a result of injury.

The vessels carrying blood from the heart out to the body organs and tissues are arteries. They get gradually smaller the further out they extend. The smallest arteries are called arterioles. The vessels by which the used blood is returned to the heart to be pumped through the system again are veins. The smallest veins are called venules. Linking the arterioles and venules are even tinier blood vessels called capillaries. The capillaries have tissue-thin transparent walls that allow the exchange of fluids between the blood and body cells, and blood and air in the lungs.

All cells require energy and oxygen, and produce waste products that must be discarded. Oxygen is carried along the arteries leading from the lungs into the smaller arterioles and thence into the capillaries where it seeps through the walls into the cells. At the same time, the waste product carbon dioxide goes through the process in reverse, passing from the cells back into the capillaries to be carried away in the bloodstream for eventual elimination.

There are two main circuits of blood vessels. Those carrying blood between the heart and the lungs for oxygenation are called the pulmonary vessels. The arteries and veins supplying the rest of the body with food and oxygen are called the systemic vessels.
See also ARTERIES; HEART; LYMPHATIC SYSTEM; VEINS.

CIRCUMCISION

Circumcision as a religious ritual is known in many different cultures, but the idea that circumcision is normal in countries of the British Commonwealth is relatively recent. It started only at the end of last century, and appears to stem from the hygiene problems, penile infections and subsequent adult circumcisions suffered by soldiers in the Crimean wars, and to some extent in the First World War. Fathers at that time swore that they would not put their sons through such agony in adult life, and started the ritual of infant circumcision.

Today there is no medical reason to support the continuation of this ritual. Hygiene is not a problem in modern society, and it is possible for parents and children to adequately clean their penis as much as their ears or any other part of the anatomy. The vast majority of the medical profession can now see no advantages to the procedure.

Some men will need to be circumcised later in life, but fewer than 1% of men will need this operation for infections, tight bands, cancer or other reasons. Some of us will also need to have our appendix removed later in life, but this is not a valid reason for removing

it at birth.

Cancer of the penis has been used as a good reason for circumcision. It is true that the incidence of penile cancer is higher in uncircumcised men, but it is a rare cancer that is detected at an early stage in most cases. On the other hand, the wives of circumcised men are more likely to develop cancer of the cervix.

The procedure can be done under local anaesthetic using clamps and a scalpel, or using a device (Plastibel) which makes it technically easier for the doctor to cut off the foreskin and minimise the risk of bleeding. The procedure can be done in a doctor's surgery, and hospitalisation is not necessary.

There are risks associated with the procedure. Although any bleeding from the penis may appear to be adequately controlled when the child leaves the surgery, catastrophic bleeding may occur unnoticed into a nappy that night. Scarring of the penis due to infection may also occur.

Removing the foreskin may adversely affect the man in later life. The foreskin is the most sexually sensitive part of the penis, and if excess is removed, it may decrease sexual pleasure. Plastic surgeons are now able to refashion the foreskin by an operation that moves some of the skin on the penis further down the shaft.
See also PARAPHIMOSIS; PENIS; PHIMOSIS

CIRCUMSCRIBED DERMATITIS
See LICHEN SIMPLEX

CIRRHOSIS

Cirrhosis is a slowly developing form of damage to the liver, which results in it becoming hard and enlarged, as normal tissue is replaced by fibrous scar tissue. There are many possible causes including recurrent attacks of hepatitis A, one attack of hepatitis B or C, other liver infections, excess alcohol intake, gall stones, a number of rare diseases that affect the liver (eg. haemochromatosis, Wilson's disease, Gaucher's disease), toxins, poisons (eg. arsenic) and drugs (eg. methotrexate, isoniazid). The diagnosis is confirmed by blood tests, and ultrasound and/or CT scans of the liver.

The symptoms may include itchy skin without a rash, jaundice (yellow skin), diarrhoea and abdominal discomfort.

Other than a liver transplant, there is no cure for cirrhosis. Patients must stop all further alcohol intake to reduce further damage. Vitamin supplements and nutritious diets are recommended, and medication can be prescribed to ease some symptoms. The liver tends to become steadily more damaged until it ceases to function completely.
See also ALCOHOLISM; HEPATITIS A; HEPATITIS B; LIVER; PERIPHERAL NEUROPATHY; PORTAL HYPERTENSION

CISAPRIDE
See PROKINETIC AGENTS

CISPLATIN
See CYTOTOXICS AND ANTINEOPLASTICS

CITALOPRAM
See ANTIDEPRESSANTS

CITANEST
See ANAESTHETICS

CITRIC ACID
See OTHER

CJD
See CREUTZFELDT-JAKOB DISEASE

"CLAP"
See GONORRHOEA

CLARITHROMYCIN
See MACROLIDES

CLAUDICATION
Claudication is a term used to describe an aching pain in muscles, usually in the calf of the leg, but it may occur in any muscle group, and is caused by a poor blood supply to the muscle. The pain is usually worse with exercise (particularly climbing slopes or stairs with leg pain), and eases with rest.

The arteries to one or both legs may be narrowed by cholesterol deposits (arteriosclerosis) and an adequate amount of blood may not get through. Any activity will require extra supplies of oxygen and nutrition, which the narrowed arteries cannot supply.

A doppler ultrasound scan can show reduced blood flow in affected arteries.

Medications are given to strengthen the heart and open arteries, but surgery may be necessary to bypass the blockage.
See also ARTERY; ARTERIOSCLEROSIS; CHOLESTEROL; LEG PAIN

CLAUSTROPHOBIA
Claustrophobia is an abnormal fear of enclosed spaces.
See also PHOBIA

CLAVICLE
The collar bone (clavicle) braces the shoulder and prevents it from coming too far forwards when pulling or lifting. The outer end of the bone joins with a side arm of the scapula (shoulder blade) that curves out across the top of the shoulder joint (the acromion). The inner end moves against the upper end of the scapula (breast bone).

If fractured, it usually heals itself in six to eight weeks provided the shoulder is kept as still as possible.
See also JOINT; SHOULDER; STERNUM

CLEFT LIP AND PALATE
During development as a foetus, the face forms in three pieces – a central one (nose) and two sides (eyes and cheeks). These normally fuse together very early in foetal development, but sometimes the fusion is incomplete, resulting in a gap between the pieces which is seen as a cleft in one or both sides of the upper lip that may extend into the palate which forms the roof of the mouth. The deformity may vary from a barely noticeable notch just off centre in the upper lip, to a complete wide split of the upper lip and full length of the palate on both sides.

Sometimes a cleft lip or palate can be detected late in pregnancy by an ultrasound scan of the foetus. After birth, sophisticated x-rays and CT scans of the face and skull will be undertaken before any surgical repair, to accurately determine the extent of the problem.

In the vast majority of cases, a cleft lip is not associated with any other physical or mental abnormality.

The aims of treatment are to ensure that the child has good speech, to enhance facial appearance, and to produce the best possible jaw function and dental bite. Surgical repair of the lip is normally performed between two and six months after birth. Infants with a double cleft lip must have special dental treatment to reshape their upper jaw prior to surgical repair of the lip. The palate repair is normally done at about one year of age. The upper jaw does not grow as well as the lower jaw, so special dental and orthodontic care is necessary until the child has finished growing. Patients also need careful monitoring to ensure their hearing is adequate. Modern surgery now makes it possible to correct the problem in older people who have a poorly repaired or unrepaired cleft palate, and very good results are usually obtained.

There are a small number of rare syndromes which have other features as well as a cleft lip and palate. These include: –
• Meckel syndrome, with extra fingers and toes, under-developed kidneys, incomplete formation of the skull and sometimes eye defects.
• Patau syndrome, which is caused by the presence of an extra chromosome 13 and/ or 15, and features extra fingers and toes, heart malformations, small eyes and brain malformations.
• Wolf-Hirschhorn syndrome, with mental retardation, growth retardation, and abnormal nose.
See also FACE ABNORMAL; LIP-PIT SYNDROME; PALATE and separate entries for diseases mentioned above.

CLERAMBAULT SYNDROME
See de CLERAMBAULT SYNDROME

CLIMACTERIC
See MENOPAUSE

CLITORIS
See VULVA

CLOFIBRATE
See HYPOLIPIDAEMICS

CLONAZEPAM
See ANTICONVULSANTS

CLONING
Cloning is the use of genetic technology to exactly replicate a living organism. The genetic material (chromosomes) in a single cell of one organism can be taken and have specific methods applied to it so that it reproduces itself repeatedly and grows into a new organism that has the identical genetic characteristics of the donor.

Virtually every form of life can be, and has been cloned, including human embryos. The widest use of cloning is in agriculture, but the ethics of such scientific endeavours when applied to humans are still a matter of significant debate.
See also GENE; PARTHENOGENESIS

CLOSTRIDIAL MYOSITIS
See GANGRENE, GAS

CLOSTRIDIUM TETANI
See TETANUS

CLOTRIMAZOLE
See ANTIFUNGALS

CLOTTING
See BLEEDING, EXCESSIVE; BLOOD; BLOOD CLOTTING TEST; COAGULATION; DISSEMINATED INTRAVASCULAR COAGULATION; HAEMOPHILIA; PLATELETS; THROMBOSIS

CLOMIPHENE
Clomiphene (Clomid) is a medication used to stimulate ovulation in infertile women. It must be taken cyclically as directed by a doctor and often for many months before success occurs. Side effects may include hot flushes, bloating, belly pain and multiple pregnancies. It should not be used in women with liver disease.
See also INFERTILITY; MEDICATION

CLOMIPRAMINE
See ANTIDEPRESSANTS

CLOSTRIDIUM DIFFICILE INFECTION
See BACTERIA; GAS GANGRENE; PSEUDOMEMBRANOUS COLITIS

CLUBBING OF FINGERS
See FINGER TIPS SWOLLEN

CLUB FOOT
A club foot (technically called talipes equinovarus), is a congenital defect in the development of the foot that is more common in boys than girls, and one or both

feet may be affected.

The foot is turned in so that the sole of the foot faces the other foot, and if the infant was to walk, it would walk on the outside edge of the foot. It is often associated with under development of the muscles that move the ankle joint.

Treatment should begin soon after birth by splinting the foot into the correct position for many months in mild cases, and surgery to correct the deformity in more severe cases and those that do not respond to splinting. If treatment is delayed, there may be permanent deformity of the foot, due to a distorted growth of the bones around the ankle. There are usually good results from treatment.
See also FOOT

CLUMSINESS

People who are clumsy move awkwardly and cannot manipulate objects skillfully. The most common causes of clumsiness are due to the effects of alcohol, illegal drugs (eg. marijuana, heroin) and prescribed drugs that cause sedation (eg. sleeping tablets, antihistamines). There are numerous medical causes of clumsiness.

In a stroke (cerebrovascular accident) various parts of the brain may be affected by having the blood supply cut off by a blockage in an artery, or a blood vessel in the brain may burst causing bleeding and damage to part of the brain. The onset is almost instantaneous, may be associated with a wide variety of symptoms from paralysis and headache to muscle weakness, loss of sensation, anaesthesia, confusion and coma. A transient ischaemic attack (TIA) is a temporary spasm or blockage of an artery in the brain. It can cause effects similar to that of a stroke, but only for a short period of time.

Migraines are often associated with visual symptoms including flashing lights, shimmering, seeing zigzag lines and loss of part of the area of vision. Nausea, vomiting and poor coordination are also common.

Parkinson disease is caused by degeneration of part of the brain that co-ordinates muscle movement. The usual symptoms are tremor, shuffling walk and increased muscle tone, but in advanced cases muscle weakness of the face may occur.

Alzheimer disease (senile dementia or second childhood), is one of the most common forms of dementia in the elderly. It is characterised by loss of recent memory, loss of initiative, reduced physical activity, confusion, and then it gradually progresses to loss of speech, difficulty in swallowing, stiff muscles, incontinence of both faeces and urine, and a bedridden state in which the patients are totally unaware of themselves or anything that is happening around them.

Uncommon causes of clumsiness include hypothyroidism (underactive thyroid gland); damage to the spinal cord in the back from an injury, tumour, slipped disc or arthritis; alcoholism; a tumour, cyst, cancer or abscess in the brain; multiple sclerosis, hydrocephalus, motor neurone disease and muscular dystrophies.
See also BRAIN; COORDINATION, LACK OF and separate entries for diseases mentioned above.

CLUSTER HEADACHE

A cluster headache is a severe, intermittent one-sided headache that occurs in clusters lasting from days to weeks. Attacks may be triggered by alcohol, stress, exercise, certain foods and glare. They are more common in middle-aged men.

Patients experience severe, one-sided pain around the eye that occurs daily for weeks and then subsides, only to flare again months later. The pain may be quite disabling, and is often accompanied by a congested nostril on the same side as the headache, a watery red eye and weakness on the affected side of the face. Unfortunately, there are no specific diagnostic tests available, and the diagnosis rests on the clinical acumen of the doctor.

Once present, these headaches are very difficult to control. Normally it is a matter of trial and error to determine the most effective treatment regime in any individual. The inhalation of pure oxygen may settle an otherwise intractable attack in a few minutes. Prevention is far better than cure, and medications such as propranolol, ergotamine, lithium and amitriptyline can be used on a regular basis to prevent further attacks. In severe cases prednisone is prescribed.
See also HEADACHE; MIGRAINE

CMV
See CYTOMEGALOVIRUS INFECTION

COAGULATION

The process by which liquid blood turns into a solid clot is called coagulation. This complex process involves the interaction of platelets and numerous factors within blood.
See also BLEEDING, EXCESSIVE; BLOOD; BLOOD CLOTTING TEST; CHRISTMAS DISEASE; DISSEMINATED INTRAVASCULAR COAGULATION; HAEMOPHILIA; PLATELETS

COAGULATION TEST
See BLOOD CLOTTING TEST

COAD (COPD)

Chronic obstructive airways (pulmonary) disease (COAD or COPD) is a term that covers a group of irreversible conditions (chronic bronchitis, emphysema, pneumoconiosis) that permanently affect the lung and its function.
See also BRONCHITIS, CHRONIC; EMPHYSEMA; PNEUMOCONIOSIS

COARCTATION OF THE AORTA

Coarctation of the aorta (aortic stenosis) is a congenital (present since birth) narrowing of the aorta, which is the main artery running from the heart through the chest and down the back of the abdomen. Only a short segment is normally affected and the severity of symptoms depends on the degree of narrowing. The condition is usually diagnosed at birth or shortly afterwards, although milder cases may not be detected until the child undergoes rapid growth in the early teenage years. It is more common in boys than girls, and often associated with abnormalities of the aortic heart valve.

Children with aortic stenosis develop headaches, leg pain with exercise and frequent nosebleeds. The blood pressure is high in the arms, but low in the legs. Severe coarctation can restrict blood flow to the lower half of the body and cause heart failure as it strives to pump the blood past the obstruction. It is usually discovered by hearing a characteristic murmur when listening to the chest, caused by the blood rushing through the narrowed section of the aorta. The diagnosis can be confirmed by an ultrasound scan.

Surgical correction of the narrowing with a synthetic patch to open up the aorta to its correct diameter is the only treatment. The results of surgery are very good, but without surgery, 75% of babies die in the first year of life.
See also AORTA; AORTIC VALVE STENOSIS

COCAINE

Cocaine (crack, coke) is a naturally derived addictive stimulant substance that is manufactured from the leaves of the coca plant which is native to South America. It is available as a white crystalline powder, and can be administered by sniffing it into the nostrils (most common), injection into a vein, or smoking. It is usually diluted with sugars such as lactose and glucose to less than 50% purity. Users tend to be depressed and have a poor self-image and ego. Possibly one in every 100 people is dependent upon illicit drugs in Western society, and a far higher percentage have experimented with them at one time or another.

Cocaine has no recognised medical uses (although local anaesthetics and blood vessel constrictors are derived from it), but is used illegally as a psychoactive drug to cause euphoria (artificial happiness).

The more refined version of cocaine known as 'crack' is the only form that can be smoked. It is ten times more potent than cocaine base, and is therefore more dangerous. All forms are highly addictive, and whether they are smoked, sniffed or injected, cocaine works within seconds to cause euphoria (artificial happiness), mood enhancement, increased energy and stimulates the brain to increase all sensations. After use, many people feel worse than before, hence they want to repeat the artificial high. With continued use, the duration of the pleasant effects becomes shorter and shorter, requiring further doses every fifteen to thirty minutes to maintain the desired effect.

Side effects include severe damage to nostrils (if inhaled), fever, headache, irregular heart rate, dilation of pupils, loss of libido, infertility, impotence, breast enlargement and tenderness in both sexes, menstrual period irregularities, abnormal breast milk production, and may lead to a desire for more frequent use or stronger drugs of addiction. It will also aggravate psychiatric disturbances. Cocaine should never be used in pregnancy as it increases the risk of malformation and heart disease in the baby.

Less commonly it may cause high blood pressure, perforation of the nasal septum, difficulty in breathing, convulsions, stroke, dementia and a heart attack.

Cocaine interacts with may legal medications and illegal drugs including stimulants, antidepressants, sedatives, alcohol, heroin, marijuana and other medications acting on the brain.

Blood and urine tests can detect the presence of cocaine.

An overdose can cause convulsions, difficulty in breathing, irregular heart rate, coma and death may occur.

The treatment options available for addiction are: –
• gradual withdrawal while receiving counselling and medical support
• immediate drug withdrawal ('cold turkey') while hospitalised
• halfway houses that remove the patient from the environment in which drug taking is encouraged
• individual or group psychotherapy

The long term outcome for addicts is reasonably good, as cocaine is not as addictive as heroin, but more addictive than marijuana.
See also ECSTASY; GAMMA-HYDROXYBUTYRATE; HEROIN; KETAMINE; LSD; MARIJUANA; MEDICATION; MESCALINE; STIMULANTS

COCHLEA
See EAR

CODEINE
See ANTIDIARRHOEALS; COUGH MEDICINES; NARCOTICS

COELIAC DISEASE
Coeliac disease (spelt celiac in the USA) is also known as coeliac sprue and non-tropical sprue. It is a congenital disease of the small intestine that usually starts in childhood, and persists into early adult life, often settling in middle age. It is caused by a genetic error that prevents the small intestine from absorbing fats and, to a lesser extent, carbohydrates and protein, because the intestine becomes sensitised to gluten. Gluten is a protein found in wheat, oats, barley and rye cereals, and may be used as a bulking agent in prepared foods such as sausages.

Patients are unable to tolerate any form of gluten in their intestine. If it is eaten they develop large, foul-smelling, frothy, fatty motions. This causes weight loss, anaemia and generalised weakness due to lack of nutrition and a failure to absorb vitamins A, D, E and K (the fat soluble vitamins). Rashes and weak bones, as well as a failure to grow and foul diarrhoea may occur if untreated.

It is initially diagnosed by a series of blood and faeces tests, but the final diagnosis can only be confirmed by taking a biopsy (sample) of the lining of the small intestine.

Patients respond to a diet free of gluten, high in calories and protein, and low in fat.

In most patients coeliac disease is completely controlled by diet. Once they reach adult life, many patients find they can slowly introduce gluten-containing products to their diet without ill effect.
See also GLUTEN; TROPICAL SPRUE

COELIAC SPRUE
See COELIAC DISEASE

COFFIN-LOWRY SYNDROME
The Coffin-Lowry syndrome is a developmental abnormality affecting multiple organs that has sex linked inheritance, and affects only boys, but females act as carriers.

Patients have prominent lips, coarse facial features, tapering fingers, reverse eye slant, mental retardation and excess curvature of the spine (kyphosis and scoliosis).

There are no specific diagnostic tests, no treatment is available, and there is no cure.
See also SCOLIOSIS

COFFIN-SIRIS SYNDROME
The Coffin-Siris syndrome is a familial (runs in families) developmental abnormality in which both parents must be carriers. Patients have poorly developed toenails, are very hairy at birth but have sparse hair in later life, suffer mental retardation and coarse facial features.

There are no specific diagnostic tests, and no treatment is available, but life expectancy is reasonable.
See also NAIL UNDERDEVELOPED

COGAN SYNDROME
Cogan syndrome is a rare ear, eye and other

organ inflammatory condition with rapid onset in young adults. The cause is unknown.

Patients develop eye surface inflammation, ringing in the ears (tinnitus), dizziness and deafness. Some patients develop a fever, enlarged tender lymph nodes, joint aches and pains, belly pain, enlarged spleen, black faeces from blood leaking into the bowel and heart abnormalities (eg. aortic valve disease).

Non-specific blood tests showing inflammation are positive, but there is no specific diagnostic test.

Medications such as corticosteroids and cyclophosphamide are used in treatment, although the disease course is variable and self-limiting.

COITUS INTERRUPTUS

Coitus interruptus is a method of contraception in which no artificial aids are used. It requires the man to withdraw his penis from the woman's vagina before orgasm so that his sperm is not ejaculated into her. This has the disadvantage of being very unreliable since sperm sometimes leak out before ejaculation, and in any event the man's timing has to be accurate – frequently difficult to achieve. It can also take the edge off full sexual enjoyment for both partners, especially the man.
See also CONTRACEPTION

COKE
See COCAINE

COLCHICINE
See HYPOURICAEMICS

COLD, COMMON

A common cold (coryza is the technical term) is a very common viral infection of the upper respiratory tract. One or more of several hundred different rhinoviruses may be responsible. A cold is a distinct entity from influenza, which is caused by a different group of viruses.

Colds spread from one person to another in droplets of moisture in the breath, in a cough or in a sneeze. Once inhaled, the virus settles in the nose or throat and starts multiplying rapidly. Crowds, confined spaces (eg. buses, aircraft) and air conditioners that recycle air are renown for spreading the virus. Most adults have a cold every year or two, usually in winter. Children, because they have not been exposed to these viruses before and so have no immunity to them, may have ten or more infections a year.

A sore throat and nose, runny and/or blocked nose, sneezing, cough, phlegm in the back of the throat, headache, intermittent fever and tiredness are the main symptoms. A secondary bacterial infection may cause pharyngitis or sinusitis.

No cure or prevention is possible. The symptoms can be eased by aspirin or paracetamol for headache and fever, and medications for the cough, sore throat, runny nose and blocked sinuses. The more the patient rests, the faster the infection will go away. Many vitamin and herbal remedies are touted as cures or preventatives, but when subjected to detailed trials, none can be proved to be successful.

Colds usually last about a week, but some people have a briefer course, while in others the first cold may lower their defences so that they can catch another one, and then another, causing cold symptoms to last for many weeks. *See also* DECONGESTANTS; INFLUENZA; LARYNGITIS; MUCOLYTICS; NOSE DISCHARGE; PHARYNGITIS; SINUSITIS; VIRUS

COLD INTOLERANCE

Some people seem to be able to tolerate hot or cold conditions better than others. Acclimatisation plays a major part in this phenomenon. If you normally live in a tropical climate, and visit a cold climate, you will wear more clothes than the locals in order to remain warm, but there are also a couple of medical conditions which have intolerance of cold conditions as a feature.

The thyroid gland in the front of the neck produces the hormone thyroxine, which acts as an accelerator for every cell in the body. If there is a lack of thyroxine (hypothyroidism), all organs will function slowly, and symptoms will include intolerance of cold, constipation, weakness, hoarse voice, heavy periods, dry skin, hair loss, slow heart rate and anaemia.

A blood clot in one of the major arteries within the lungs (pulmonary thrombosis) will cause severe damage to that section of lung beyond the clot, leading to its collapse, pain, shortness of breath and cold intolerance. The severity of symptoms will depend on the size of the artery blocked and the amount of lung tissue damaged.

Malnutrition will prevent the body from generating sufficient internal heat because of a lack of fuel.

See also HYPOTHYROIDISM

COLD SORE

Cold sores are a common skin infection, usually around the nose or mouth, caused by the virus *Herpes simplex* type 1.

Initially, the infection is caught as a child, when it is a simple mouth infection. The virus then migrates to the nerve endings around the lips and nose, and remains inactive there for many years. It may later reactivate at times of stress or illness to cause cold sores. It is passed from one person to another by direct contact (eg. kissing). Sixty percent of the population are infected and remain carriers throughout their lives. Sores are uncommon before five years of age, and the incidence decreases in old age. Recurrences tend to develop at the same spot.

Active infection is characterised by redness and soreness of the affected area, followed a day or two later by an eruption of small blisters, which rapidly burst to leave a shallow, weeping, painful ulcer. In severe cases, there may be a mild fever, and the lymph nodes in the neck may become tender and enlarged. An additional bacterial infection, is the only common complication. If necessary, the diagnosis can be confirmed by taking special swabs from the sore.

If treated by appropriate antiviral creams and lotions (eg. aciclovir, idoxuridine) immediately the redness and discomfort is felt and before the blisters form, it may be possible to stop further progress. Once the cold sore is established, a cure is not normally possible, but drying, antiseptic and anaesthetic creams or lotions may be used. Patients who are severely affected on a regular basis may use expensive aciclovir or famciclovir tablets continuously to prevent infections.

The sore heals and the pain eases in about a week. Some patients have only one attack of cold sores in their lives, while others develop one every month. Over many years, most patients find that their attacks become less frequent.

See also ANTIVIRALS; GENITAL HERPES; WHITLOW; VIRUS

COLESTIPOL
See HYPOLIPIDAEMICS

COLIC

Colic describes a pain that comes and goes in cycles, and usually refers to pain in the abdomen. The length and frequency of the cycle (eg. colicky pain from the small intestine lasts a shorter time but recurs more frequently than colic in the large intestine) may help doctors to determine the cause and site of the pain.

See also ABDOMINAL PAIN; GALL STONES; INFANTILE COLIC; INTESTINAL COLIC; IRRITABLE BOWEL SYNDROME; KIDNEY STONE

COLITIS

Colitis is any form of inflammation or infection affecting the colon, which is part of the large intestine.

See also COLON; DIVERTICULITIS; PSEUDOMEMBRANOUS COLITIS; ULCERATIVE COLITIS

COLLAR BONE
See CLAVICLE

COLLES' FRACTURE

A Colles' fracture is a common fracture of the forearm bones (ulna and radius) which are bent back and broken just above the wrist. It is usually caused by landing on the outstretched hand during a fall. The fracture is diagnosed by an x-ray.

Symptoms include pain, swelling, tenderness and a backwards deformity of the forearm bones just above the wrist.

The bones must be put back into place under an anaesthetic if the deformity is significant, and held in position by plaster. Persistent deformity will occur if the bones are incorrectly aligned.

COLLES' FRACTURE OF FOREARM BONES

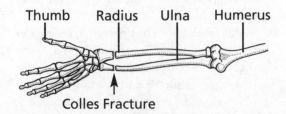

Thumb   Radius   Ulna   Humerus

Colles Fracture

The fracture normally heals well after six weeks in plaster in an adult, or three to four weeks in a child.

See also FRACTURE; SCAPHOID
FRACTURE; SMITH'S FRACTURE

COLON

The colon is the major part of the large intestine and consists of a large loop that circuits the belly. Dividing the ileum of the small intestine from the colon is a muscular valve that opens to let food into the colon but otherwise remains closed to prevent the food passing back into the small intestine.

The colon starts at the caecum and passes up through the abdomen as the ascending colon. When it reaches just below the liver, it makes a sharp turn and travels across the abdomen to the left side near the spleen as the transverse colon. It then makes a sharp downwards turn and becomes the descending colon. This extends down the left side of the abdomen to the pelvis. At the bottom of the descending colon is an S-bend, called the sigmoid colon, which empties into the rectum.

Food that is not digested in the small intestine passes into the colon. Here most of the water content is extracted to be reabsorbed into the bloodstream, and the remaining semisolid waste passes into the rectum to be stored until it is eliminated from the body through the anus.

At 65mm, the large intestine is nearly twice the diameter of the small intestine, and is 1.5 to 2 metres in length from caecum to anus.

See also CAECUM; COLONOSCOPY; COLORECTAL CANCER; COLOSTOMY; CONSTIPATION; DIVERTICULITIS; GASTRO-COLIC REFLEX; LARGE INTESTINE; RECTUM

COLONIC CANCER
See COLORECTAL CANCER

COLONOSCOPY

A colonoscopy is an examination of the large bowel or colon using a colonoscope, which is a flexible tube which combines the features of magnification and illumination. It is two metres long and enables the doctor to view the entire colon.

For the lower third of the colon, an instrument called a sigmoidoscope may be used, which is rigid but shorter than the colonoscope and enables an examination of the bowel for polyps, tumours and other diseases. The instrument used for seeing inside the rectum and anus is called a proctoscope.

Before having a colonoscopy, the patient will be given a laxative or an enema and then be instructed to drink only clear fluids for the day before the test is performed. A solution must also be drunk in the day before the test

LARGE INTESTINE

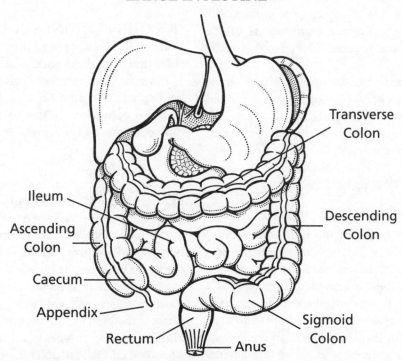

Transverse Colon

Ileum

Ascending Colon

Caecum

Appendix

Rectum

Anus

Descending Colon

Sigmoid Colon

to thoroughly cleanse the bowel. It is unusual to feel any discomfort during the procedure as an effective sedative is given. The examination takes about an hour.
See also COLON; COLORECTAL CANCER; ENDOSCOPE

COLORECTAL CANCER

Colorectal cancer is cancer of the large bowel, which forms the last two metres of the intestine.

The absolute cause is unknown, but a low fibre diet may be a factor and there is a family tendency. It is more common in men, and most develop in the last ten centimetres of the gut.

Symptoms include alteration in normal bowel habits, passing blood with the faeces, weight loss, colicky pains in the abdomen and constant tiredness. A large cancer can be felt as a hard lump in the abdomen. If left untreated, a gut obstruction, or perforation which allows faeces to leak into the abdomen and causes peritonitis, will occur.

A colonoscopy and/or barium enema x-ray will confirm the diagnosis. Blood tests may show anaemia due to the constant slow leaking of blood from the cancer. People with a bad family history can have a faeces sample tested for blood. Treatment involves major surgery to remove the cancer, the bowel for some distance above and below the cancer, and the surrounding lymph nodes. Up to 3% of patients may die during or immediately after surgery. Regular examinations of the colon are then required lifelong to detect any recurrence.

If the cancer has not spread away from the large intestine, two out of three patients will survive for five years. If the cancer has spread, the survival rate drops steadily, depending on the degree of spread.
See also CANCER; COLON; COLOSTOMY; RECTUM

COLOSTOMY

If the lower part of the bowel (the colon) is involved in a cancer, it may be impossible to reconnect the gut to the anus after the cancer has been removed. A stoma called a colostomy is created when surgeons bring part of the colon through the front wall of the abdomen so that the patient can pass faeces through this opening and not through the anus. If the cancer is higher in the large intestine, the colostomy may be temporary, as the gut can be reconnected after the cancer affected area has recovered from the initial operation.
See also COLON; ILEOSTOMY; STOMA

COLOUR

See COLOUR BLIND; COLOUR BLINDNESS TEST; NAIL DISCOLOURED; SKIN COLOUR; SKIN BLUE; SKIN PIGMENTATION EXCESS; SKIN RED

COLOUR BLIND

Colour blindness is an inherited condition that nearly always occurs in men, and is an inability to differentiate between colours, usually red and green. Rarely all colour vision is lost with the patient seeing only black and white.

Ishihara test-cards covered in coloured dots, with numbers hidden amongst the dots, are used to diagnose the form of colour blindness.

No treatment or cure is available. Usually it is merely a nuisance, and most patients live happily with the problem, adapting so completely that they are not aware of its existence. Those planning to work as an electrician or commercial pilot, or in some other areas where colour differentiation is vital, may not be allowed to undertake these careers.
See also COLOUR BLINDNESS TEST

COLOUR BLINDNESS TEST

Colour blindness is tested by means of specially designed plates with patterns made up of different coloured dots. This is known as the Ishihara test, after Shinobu Ishihara, the Japanese ophthalmologist who first devised this sophisticated system of coloured dots in 1917.

To test whether a patient can distinguish between red and green, they will be shown a page covered with dots in various shades of green with a numeral in the middle composed of red dots. People who are able to distinguish between red and green will be able to pick out the figure, whereas the plate will appear to be all the one colour to those who can't tell the difference between red and green. Other plates with different patterns and colour combinations test other types of colour blindness.
See also COLOUR BLIND; EYE

COLPOSCOPY

A colposcope is a microscope that illuminates and magnifies the cells covering the cervix and vaginal walls. It is especially useful in the early diagnosis of cancer of the cervix, and as a follow-up to an abnormal result from a Pap smear.

A metal speculum is used to open the vagina in the same way as for a Pap smear test. The colposcope is then moved into position just outside the vagina (it never actually enters the vagina and therefore is not, strictly speaking, an endoscope) and focuses on the cervix which is magnified about ten to fifteen times. The cervix may be painted with solutions of water and vinegar and water and iodine, which shows up abnormal cells. A tissue sample will be taken of anything suspicious.

Colposcopy is painless and takes only about fifteen minutes.

If the colposcopy fails to pinpoint the diseased cells (most likely in women over thirty-five since cervical tissue retracts with age and cannot be seen as easily) or the full extent of the suspicious cells cannot be determined, a cone biopsy (in which a cone shaped section of tissue is excised from around the opening of the cervix) may be taken. Because of the larger amount of tissue removed in a cone biopsy, it also serves as a form of treatment. More recently, laser techniques have been developed as a form of treatment to burn off abnormal cells after a normal biopsy has been taken. This is a much less invasive procedure than a cone biopsy and has a considerably reduced risk of bleeding and other complications.
See also CERVIX; ENDOSCOPE

COLOUR OF URINE ABNORMAL
See URINE COLOUR ABNORMAL

COMA

A coma is an unrousable loss of consciousness.

The severity and depth of a coma is measured by the Glasgow Coma Scale.

Many causes of a coma relate to the brain but other diseases and conditions may be responsible. A wide range of blood, urine, x-ray, CT and ultrasound scan, and cerebrospinal fluid (CSF, the fluid around the brain) tests will be performed in order to determine the cause.

The brain is suspended in cerebrospinal fluid inside the bony skull. Any blow to the head will make the brain rattle around inside the skull, and it may be bruised or damaged. A fractured skull may cause a laceration of the brain. This damage can cause unconsciousness that may persist for seconds, minutes, occasionally hours and rarely for months.

In a stroke (cerebrovascular accident) various parts of the brain may be affected by having its blood supply cut off by a blockage in an artery, or a blood vessel in the brain may burst causing bleeding and damage to part of the brain. The onset is almost instantaneous, may be associated with a wide variety of symptoms from paralysis and headache to weakness, loss of sensation, anaesthesia, confusion and coma. Tumours, cancers, an abscess or cyst in the brain can have a similar effect to a stroke.

The brain is supported and completely surrounded by a three-layered membrane (the meninges) which contain the cerebrospinal fluid. If these meninges are infected by a virus or bacteria (meningitis) the patient may experience headache, fever, fits, neck stiffness and in severe cases may become comatose. Encephalitis is an infection of the brain which may be confused with meningitis. The symptoms include headache, intolerance of bright lights, fever, stiff neck, lethargy, nausea, vomiting, sore throat, tremors, confusion, convulsions, stiffness and paralysis. This can progress to coma, and sometimes to death.

If too much cerebrospinal fluid is produced, or insufficient is absorbed, the pressure of this fluid in and around the brain will gradually increase (hydrocephalus). The resultant pressure on the brain will affect its function and result in headaches, personality changes, memory loss, reduced intelligence, convulsions and coma.

Epilepsy is a condition that causes recurrent seizures (fits). Fits can vary from very mild absences in which people just seem to lose concentration for a few seconds, to uncontrolled bizarre movements of an arm or leg, to the grand mal convulsion in which an epileptic can thrash around quite violently and lose control of bladder and bowel. A prolonged period of confusion or coma may follow a fit.

Degeneration of the brain may occur steadily in various forms of dementia, including Alzheimer disease. Confusion, forgetfulness, poor coordination, incontinence and irritability will gradually worsen. The final stage of these degenerative conditions is coma.

Patients with an intense form of hysteria as a reaction to severe fright, fear, shock or some psychiatric conditions, may appear to be in a coma, and act completely as though they are unconscious, although there is no physical cause.

Overdoses of alcohol, illegal drugs (eg. heroin) and many different medications may cause a life threatening coma. Numerous poisons, attempted suicide with a car exhaust (carbon monoxide poisoning), snake and venomous spider bites may also cause a loss of consciousness.

Dehydration from lack of water or excessive sweating in a hot climate, or due to severe diarrhoea with cholera or other bowel infections, may have coma as an end result.

Very low blood pressure (hypotension) caused by loss of blood (eg. into the body or from a deep wound), heart attack or other serious disease, will lead to collapse and coma that may lead to death.

An irregular heart beat (palpitation) may prevent sufficient blood from reaching the brain.

Diabetes is caused by a lack of insulin production in the pancreas (type 1 or juvenile diabetes), or is due to the cells of the body becoming resistant to insulin and preventing it from transporting sugar from the blood and into the cell (type 2 or maturity onset diabetes). The early symptoms are unusual tiredness, increased thirst and hunger, excess passing of urine, weight loss despite a large food intake, itchy rashes, recurrent vaginal thrush infections, pins and needles and blurred vision. An excess of insulin or diabetic tablets can lower blood sugar levels excessively (hypoglycaemia) to cause a coma. Conversely, uncontrolled diabetes may cause a coma due to excessive blood sugar levels (hyperglycaemia).

Severe bacterial infections, particularly septicaemia when the blood itself is infected, can cause a persistent high fever that affects the brain and other organs, leading to confusion, convulsions and coma.

Less common causes of coma include suffocation, lack of oxygen at high altitude, a near drowning experience, severe asthma, pneumothorax, pneumonia, heart failure, heart attack, failure of the liver or kidney, severe hypothyroidism (underactive thyroid gland), severe allergy reaction (anaphylaxis), very high blood pressure (malignant hypertension), serious tropical diseases that have associated high fevers (eg. typhoid fever, yellow fever) and Addison disease.

A coma is always serious and needs immediate medical treatment, but correct treatment will depend on identifying the cause. The prognosis depends on the cause and is very unpredictable. Some comas last for years while others may be quite brief.
See also CONCUSSION; FAINT; GLASGOW COMA SCALE; UNCONSCIOUS and separate entries for diseases mentioned above.

COMA POSITION
See UNCONSCIOUS

COMA SCALE
See GLASGOW COMA SCALE

COMFORTERS
Some children develop an attachment for a particular toy or article. This may be a teddy bear or soft toy, or simply a piece of blanket which gives the child a feeling of comfort and security. Some children only require their comforter before settling down to go to sleep, others carry it around all day. Provided the object can be kept reasonably clean, clearly its presence is harmless, and the child should not be deprived of it. On the other hand, some parents seem to feel that their child should have a favourite teddy or some such toy, and insist on the child taking it to bed when the child seems completely disinterested. Even young children are capable of making up their own minds about what they need in the way of comforters, and parents might sometimes ask themselves whether the behaviour they are insisting on is for the child's benefit or the parents'.

When a parent desires to reduce the child's dependence on a comforter, repeated washing will remove all familiar smells, and reduce its desirability.
See also BABIES

COMMON COLD
See COLD, COMMON

COMMON ILIAC ARTERY
See AORTA

COMPLEX REGIONAL PAIN SYNDROME TYPE ONE
See REFLEX SYMPATHETIC DYSTROPHY SYNDROME

COMPLEX REGIONAL PAIN SYNDROME TYPE TWO
See CAUSALGIA

COMPUTERISED AXIAL TOMOGRAPHY
See CT SCAN

CONCEPTION
Conception occurs when as a result of sexual intercourse (or by an some medical procedure), a female egg is fertilised by a male sperm. Once a month, fourteen days before the beginning of the next menstrual period, a microscopically small egg (ova) is released from one of a woman's ovaries, and travels down a Fallopian tube towards the womb (uterus). During this journey, the egg may encounter sperm released by the woman's male partner during intercourse.

If one sperm penetrates the egg, the egg is fertilised, in a process called conception, and if the fertilised egg successfully implants into the wall of the uterus, the woman becomes pregnant. Once an egg has been fertilised by one sperm, it immediately becomes impenetrable to other sperm, even though millions of sperm are deposited as a result of any single ejaculation.

If, perchance, two eggs are released and fertilised, there will be two babies or twins.
See also ARTIFICIAL CONCEPTION; FALLOPIAN TUBE; SEX CHOICE; ZYGOTE

CONCUSSION
Concussion is due to bruising of part of the brain, from a moderate to severe blow on the head (generally at the back) or a severe shake of the body. Symptoms can vary in severity from mere giddiness and a headache for an hour or two, to a complete loss of consciousness, sometimes lasting for weeks. The range of symptoms includes temporary, partial or complete loss of consciousness, 'seeing stars', shallow breathing, nausea and vomiting, paleness, coldness and clamminess of the skin, blurred or double vision, and possibly loss of memory.

A skull x-ray and CT scan may be performed to exclude fracture or other complications, but do not specifically diagnose concussion.

The first-aider should lie the patient down, keep them warm and comfortable, apply cold compresses to the brow or the site of injury, and not give anything to eat or drink for the first few hours after the injury. Medical attention should be sought. Paracetamol may be used for pain, but aspirin should be avoided. Keep the victim under observation for at least twenty-four hours for signs of more serious injury.

There may be slow bleeding into the brain, which can cause problems hours or days later. The symptoms are a worsening headache, continued vomiting, drowsiness, stupor, deliriousness or other mental changes, collapse, fits, blackouts, giddiness, clear or bloodstained fluid draining from the nose or ears. If any of these symptoms occur, get medical advice immediately.

In most cases, complete recovery within a few hours or days is normal.
See also COMA; HEAD INJURY; SUBDURAL HAEMATOMA; UNCONSCIOUS

CONDOM
The condom is the simplest barrier method of artificial contraception and the only reversible contraceptive so far developed which is used by men. A condom is a thin rubber sheath which is placed on the penis before penetration. When the man ejaculates, the sperm are held in a reservoir at the tip.

Condoms have the advantage that they are cheap and readily available. They are not completely foolproof because the rubber can tear or they can come off, but if they are used in accordance with instructions they are very effective. Used with a spermicide, the failure rate has been estimated as only 3%. Condoms have the further advantage that they not only protect the woman against becoming pregnant, but they may also protect both partners against some sexually transmitted diseases, and since the advent of the AIDS virus, anyone engaging in sex with a partner who is not long-term and well known to them should use a condom.

Some men complain that the rubber lessens the sensation ("like showering with a raincoat" is a common analogy), but modern ultra-thin rubbers reduce this disadvantage considerably, and the risks of engaging in unprotected sex in this day and age make such objections foolish in the extreme. On the other hand, men who suffer from premature ejaculation may be helped by a thicker condom as it does reduce sensation slightly.

Condoms are not new. In eighteenth century France, the renowned philanderer Casanova used a thin pig's bladder as an early condom or "French letter". Prior to this there were similar devices made from leather or gut which were far less comfortable.

As a historical curiosity, in the 1920s, condoms were considered a danger to the well-being of a woman as it was considered necessary for a woman to absorb semen from her vagina on a regular basis to maintain good health.

See also CONTRACEPTION; FEMALE CONDOM

CONDYLOMATA ACCUMINATA
See GENITAL WARTS

CONE BIOPSY
See COLPOSCOPY; PAP SMEAR

CONE SHELL
See BLUE RINGED OCTOPUS AND CONE SHELL

CONFUSION
People may become confused over time, place, happenings, other people and even who they are. There are many obvious causes for varying degrees of confusion, including alcohol intoxication, recovery from a general anaesthetic, the time shift of jet lag, the use of illegal drugs (eg. marijuana, cocaine), and the side effects or overdosage of prescribed drugs (eg. sedatives, narcotics, steroids, antidepressants, digoxin). There are also numerous medical conditions which may be responsible.

The brain is suspended in a fluid (cerebrospinal fluid – CSF) inside the bony skull. Any blow to the head will make the brain rattle around inside the skull, and it may be bruised or damaged. A fractured skull may cause a laceration of the brain. This damage can cause merely a headache, or confusion, fits and unconsciousness.

Alzheimer disease (senile dementia or second childhood) is one of the most common forms of dementia in the elderly, but unfortunately it may strike as early as the mid-fifties and cause extreme distress to spouses, family and friends. It is characterised by loss of recent memory, loss of initiative, reduced physical activity, confusion, loss of orientation (patients become confused about where they are and dates), and then it gradually progresses.

In a stroke (cerebrovascular accident) part of the brain is affected by having its blood supply cut off by a blockage in an artery, or a blood vessel in the brain may burst causing bleeding and damage to part of the brain. The onset may be associated with paralysis in various parts of the body, headache, shortness of breath and other abnormalities that can vary from minor discomfort and confusion to widespread paralysis and coma.

A tumour, cancer, cyst or abscess in the brain may have an effect similar to that of a stroke.

A transient ischaemic attack (TIA) is a temporary spasm or blockage of an artery in the brain. It can also cause effects similar to that of a stroke, but only for a short period of time.

Encephalitis is a bacterial or viral infection of the brain. The symptoms include headache, intolerance of bright lights, fever, stiff neck, lethargy, nausea, vomiting, sore throat, tremors, confusion, convulsions, stiffness and paralysis.

After many types of epileptic fit, patients often experience a period of confusion and headache which is known as a postictal state. This may last for a few minutes or a few hours.

Uncommon causes of confusion include a high fever, heart attack, pulmonary thrombosis (a clot of blood affecting one of the arteries in the lungs), psychiatric conditions (eg. depression and schizophrenia), severe stress, fear, a bad accident or assault.

See also DEMENTIA and separate entries for diseases mentioned above.

CONGENITAL
A congenital condition is one that has been present since birth.

See also FAMILIAL; GENETIC

CONGENITAL ADRENAL HYPERPLASIA

Congenital adrenal hyperplasia (or the adrenogenital syndrome) is a condition affecting the adrenal glands which sit on top of each kidney, in which they are over stimulated to produce abnormal steroids in the body which affect sexual development. The condition is familial (runs in families), but both parents must be carriers for the condition to be present.

In girls the clitoris becomes enlarged, high blood pressure occurs, and at puberty the breasts are very small, pubic hair pattern is masculine, hair may develop excessively on the body, and female characteristics are reduced. A rare form causes excessive development of male characteristics in boys. The diagnosis is confirmed by specific blood and genetic tests.

Surgical correction of abnormal genitalia can be performed, and medication is given to correct hormonal imbalances. Infertility and confused gender assignment can occur if treated late, but there are good results if treated very early. Patients have a relatively normal life expectancy.
See also ADDISON DISEASE; CONN SYNDROME

CONGENITAL DISLOCATION OF HIP
See HIP DISLOCATION

CONGENITAL SYPHILIS
See SYPHILIS

CONGESTIVE CARDIAC FAILURE

Congestive cardiac failure (CCF) is also known as heart failure or ventricular failure. It is a failure of the heart to pump blood effectively.

Many conditions may be responsible for CCF, including heart attacks, heart infection (endocarditis, myocarditis, pericarditis), narrowing or leaking of heart valves, high blood pressure, narrowing of the aorta (aortic stenosis), irregular heart rhythm, alcoholic heart damage, severe anaemia and an overactive thyroid gland (hyperthyroidism). In many elderly patients, there can be a multitude of causes, or no specific cause at all for heart failure. In these cases, the condition is treated as a disease in itself.

Patients complain of being short of breath when exercising or climbing stairs, or in more advanced cases they may be short of breath constantly or only when lying down at night. Other symptoms include a hard dry cough, passing excess urine at night, general tiredness and weakness, a rapid heart rate, weight loss, chest and abdominal discomfort and swelling of the feet, ankles and hands. Severely affected patients may be unable to speak a full sentence without taking a breath and a blue tinge develops on and around the lips. Angina and a heart attack may occur.

The diagnosis can often be made without resorting to any tests. The exact cause of the CCF may be found by blood tests, chest x-rays and electrocardiograms (ECG). Echocardiograms and cardiac catheterisation (passing a tube through a vein into the heart) are sometimes undertaken if surgical treatment is being contemplated.

Treatment involves correction of any specific cause for the heart failure if possible, lowering high blood pressure and controlling any irregular heart rhythm. Sometimes surgical correction of a heart valve deformity is possible. A diet low in salt, and avoiding strenuous exercise can often be beneficial. Medications to remove excess fluid from the body (diuretics) and to strengthen the action of the heart (eg. digoxin, ACE inhibitors) are in common use. More sophisticated drugs are available for use in difficult cases. Oxygen may be supplied to seriously ill patients.

Unless an underlying correctable cause can be found, heart failure cannot be cured, only controlled. The condition usually slowly worsens with time, but it may take many years before serious incapacitation or death occurs.
See also ANAEMIA; AORTIC VALVE STENOSIS; COR PULMONALE; ENDOCARDITIS; HYPERTENSION; HYPERTHYROIDISM; MYOCARDITIS; PERICARDITIS and separate entries for medications mentioned above.

CONJUNCTIVITIS

Conjunctivitis is an inflammation of the outer surface (conjunctiva) of the eye, due to an allergy, or a viral or bacterial infection.

A bacterial conjunctivitis is the most common form, and is due to bacteria infecting the thin film of tears that covers the eye. It is very easily passed from one person to another (eg. a patient rubs their eyes with a hand, then shakes hands, and the second person then rubs their eyes). Babies suffering from a blocked tear duct may have recurrent infections. Tears are produced in the lacrimal gland beyond the outer edge of the eye, move across the eye surface and then through a tiny tube at the inner edge of the eye that leads to the nose. If the duct is too small in an infant, or is blocked by pus or phlegm, the circulation of tears is prevented and infection results.

Any one or more of a number of viruses may infect the cornea to cause conjunctivitis. This form is not quite as easily transmitted as bacterial conjunctivitis.

Bacterial conjunctivitis causes the formation of yellow or green pus in the eyes which may stick the eyelids together. The eyes are bloodshot and sore, and almost invariably the infection involves both eyes. If allowed to persist, it may cause scarring of the eye surface and a deterioration in sight.

Viral conjunctivitis causes slight pain or an itch, redness of the eye and often a clear sticky exudate.

Rarely, resistant infections make it necessary to take a swab from the eye to determine the exact bacteria or virus responsible, but in most cases, no investigations are necessary.

Bacterial conjunctivitis is easily treated with antibiotic drops or ointment on a regular basis until the infection clears. A blocked tear duct may be probed and cleared if conjunctivitis persists in a baby for several months, but most grow out of the problem.

Viral conjunctivitis is the more difficult form to treat as there is no cure for most viral infections, but *Herpes* virus infections can be cured by antiviral drops. Soothing drops and ointment may be used, but time is the main treatment, and the infection may persist for several weeks until the body's own defences overcome it.
See also ALLERGIC CONJUNCTIVITIS; EYE; EYE PAIN; EYE RED; TRACHOMA

CONN SYNDROME

Conn syndrome is also known as aldosteronism and hyperaldosteronism. It is a rare disease due to overactivity of the adrenal glands which sit on top of each kidney.

A tumour in one of the adrenal glands, or other even rarer diseases, cause excessive amounts of the hormone aldosterone to be produced by the gland. Aldosterone controls the amount of salt in the body. If the level of salt in the blood drops, more aldosterone is secreted by the adrenal gland, and it acts on the kidney to reduce the amount being lost in the urine. The tumour is not a cancer, but the increased aldosterone production causes excess salt to be retained in the body.

Excess salt causes high blood pressure, increased urine production, muscle weakness, pins and needles sensations, headache and thirst. The syndrome may be the cause of high blood pressure that does not respond to normal treatments.

The diagnosis is confirmed by blood tests, and a CT or MRI scan. Radioactive substances that concentrate in the abnormal adrenal gland may also be given to a patient in whom the disease is suspected, and the degree of concentration of the substance in each adrenal gland can then be measured.

The tumour of the adrenal gland can be removed surgically, but medications may be required to control the symptoms and high blood pressure before the operation. Most cases can be cured by surgery, while the others can be controlled by medication.
See also ALDOSTERONE; BARTTER SYNDROME; CONGENITAL ADRENAL HYPERPLASIA; HYPERTENSION

CONSTIPATION

We have all experienced the strain and discomfort of constipation at some stage of our lives as a result of changes in diet, dehydration or reduced activity, but if it persists a specific cause should be sought so that long term complications do not occur.

Normal bowel activity can vary from two or three times a day to two or three times a week, or even once a week in some individuals. Constipation increases with age and is far more common in the elderly than the young.

To be medically significant, constipation must cause discomfort in the abdomen, pain around the anus, bleeding, tears (both pronunciations of the word are appropriate), piles or another problem.

Hard dry motions are usually due to inadequate fluid intake, eating too much junk food with too little fibre, or lack of exercise. May also be due to repeatedly ignoring signals to pass a motion and allowing the bowel to become distended, which reduces the urge to eliminate and the problem becomes self-perpetuating.

The major complications of persistent constipation are piles (bleeding under the skin caused by over stretching of the anus and straining), anal tears (fissures) and megacolon (an overdilated lower end of gut that cannot contract properly). All these problems can worsen constipation as well as being a result of the problem, as patients with piles and tears are reluctant to pass motions because of pain, while megacolon prevents normal lower bowel contraction to move faeces along.

Bedridden patients often find they become constipated due to the lack of activity and body movement. Even a healthy person who becomes less active because of a broken leg or bad dose of the flu will suffer the same effects.

Changes in diet, particularly if more protein and less fibre is suddenly eaten, and lack of fluid (dehydration) will both cause the faeces to harden and dry.

In the last three months of pregnancy, many women find that constipation becomes a problem as the growing baby puts pressure on the bowel.

A prolapse of the bowel occurs when it bulges forward into a woman's vagina, or slides out through the anus due to weakening of the support structures with pregnancy or age. Straining to pass a motion only worsens the prolapse without moving the faeces.

Many different medications can have constipation as a side effect. Examples include codeine, narcotics (eg. morphine), antacids, anticonvulsants (for epilepsy and fits), antidepressants, diuretics (fluid tablets) and iron.

Less common causes of constipation include hypothyroidism (underactive thyroid gland), tumours or cancers of the last part of the large intestine, irritable bowel syndrome, depression, neuroses and psychiatric disturbances, Hirschsprung disease, diabetes mellitus, persistent high levels of calcium in the blood stream (hypercalcaemia) from kidney or parathyroid gland disease, and abnormal balances of sodium, potassium or chloride in the blood.

Extensive investigations (eg. colonoscopy, barium enema x-ray) may be necessary to determine the cause in persistent cases.

Treatment of constipation should be aimed at treating the underlying cause if possible. Dietary methods are the next choice, and only if neither is possible should laxatives or other medications be used. Patients should change their diet by avoiding white bread, pastries, biscuits, sweets and chocolates, and adding plenty of fluids and fibre containing foods such as cereals, vegetables and fruit. If necessary, fibre supplements may be used. Laxatives are the next step, but dependence can develop rapidly. They vary in effectiveness and strength, but the weakest ones (eg. paraffin, other oils, senna and cascara) should be tried first. As a last resort, enemas may be used to clear out the lower gut.

Long term unrelieved constipation may result in megacolon.

The prognosis depends on the cause, but the condition can usually be well managed by appropriate treatment.
See also ANUS; COLON; CONSTIPATION IN PREGNANCY; FAECES; LAXATIVES; MEGACOLON; RECTUM and separate entries for diseases mentioned above.

CONSTIPATION IN PREGNANCY

Constipation is common in pregnancy and is thought to be due to a loosening of the muscles of the digestive tract caused by hormonal changes. In late pregnancy the enlarging womb presses on the intestines and aggravates the condition. It is not dangerous, but if worrying, a faecal softener can be used. No medications, including laxatives, should be used during pregnancy without discussing them with a doctor.
See also CONSTIPATION

CONSTRICTIVE PERICARDITIS
See PERICARDITIS

CONTACT DERMATITIS

Contact dermatitis (housewife's dermatitis or irritant eczema) is one of the most common forms of dermatitis.

Soaps, medicated creams, detergents, chemicals, solvents, cosmetics, perfume, jewellery, metals, rubber, animals and plants are the most common substances causing contact dermatitis. Substances that a person has used or touched regularly for many years without any adverse effect may suddenly cause a reaction. This is particularly common with solvents, dyes, rubber, inks and cosmetics. The rash is more common on exposed parts of the body, but may occur on other areas if, for example, underclothes are washed in a detergent to which the patient reacts.

The affected area of skin is red, itchy, swollen, burns and may blister. After a few days, it may become crusted and weep. The dermatitis may become secondarily infected by bacteria, when antibiotics are required.

A person's reaction to suspect agents may be investigated, but these tests, in which a patch of skin is exposed to a substance to test its response, are often inconclusive.

If the substance causing the dermatitis can be identified and avoided, the problem is solved. Gloves can be used to avoid detergents, soap substitutes used for washing, and changes in occupation to avoid solvents. If the irritating substance can be tracked down, it may be possible to desensitise the patient. The main treatment is a steroid cream, lotion or ointment. Placing a plastic dressing over the dermatitis and cream increases the effectiveness of the treatment. In severe cases, steroids may need to be given in tablet form, or even by injection.

Provided the causative agent is not touched again, the dermatitis should settle with treatment, and not recur.

See also DERMATITIS

CONTINUOUS POSITIVE AIRWAY PRESSURE MACHINE

Patients who snore excessively or develop sleep apnoea may be assisted by a continuous positive airway pressure (CPAP) machine that increases the air pressure in the mouth, throat and major airways of the lungs. The machine is about the size of a shoebox, and from it runs a flexible hose that is attached to a mask. The mask is firmly applied to the face by means of elastic straps over the head, and the machine turned on. An electric motor pumps air into the mask at an adjustable pressure, and this higher pressure keeps the airway open while the patient sleeps to prevent the partial collapse of the airways, which is the cause of snoring and sleep apnoea. Despite this description, many patients find that their sleep is less disturbed and more refreshing using this device, and their partners are certainly relieved by their quieter and more restful bedmate.

These machines can sometimes be used in severely ill patients who would otherwise require a tracheotomy (hole cut through the front of the neck into the trachea – windpipe) in order for them to be able to breathe.

See also SLEEP APNOEA; SNORING

CONTRACEPTION

Attempts to find some way of having sex without producing babies have a long history. Documents from Mesopotamia, 4000 years ago, record that a plug of dung was placed in the woman's vagina to stop conception. In Cleopatra's Egypt, small gold trinkets were inserted into the uterus of the courtesans as a form of early intrauterine contraceptive device. At the same time, camel herders pushed pebbles into the wombs of the female camels so that they would not get pregnant on long caravan treks. More recently, in the eighteenth century in France, the renowned philanderer Casanova used a thin pig's bladder as an early condom or 'French letter'. Before this there were similar devices made from leather or gut. Finding a safe, effective and reliable contraceptive has proved a difficult task.

Today, a very wide range of safe and effective contraceptives are available. They include: –
CONTRACEPTIVE PILL
Available since 1962, the contraceptive pill has revolutionised modern life. It is probably the safest and most effective form of reversible contraception. There are many different dosage forms and strengths, so that most women can find one that meets their needs. The main types are the monophasic (constant dose) two-hormone pill, the biphasic (two phase) and triphasic (three phase) hormone pills in which the hormone doses vary during the month, and the mini-pill which contains only one hormone.
MORNING-AFTER PILL
The morning-after pill is a short course of a high dose of sex hormones (often an oral contraceptive) which must be taken within seventy two hours of sexual intercourse. Two doses are taken twelve hours apart and they are often given with a second medication to prevent vomiting, which is the most common side effect.
MEDROXYPROGESTERONE
INJECTIONS
Medroxyprogesterone injections are a means of contraception in which a synthetic form

of the female sex hormone progesterone is injected, causing the ovaries to stop producing eggs. One injection lasts for twelve weeks or more depending on the dose given.

IMPLANTS

It is possible to have a small rod-shaped, hormone-containing implant inserted into the flesh on the inside of the upper arm. This gives almost 100% protection against pregnancy for three years. In most women, their periods cease for this time, but in some, irregular bleeding leads to the implant being removed. It is essential for the implant to be removed after the three year period.

SPERMICIDES

Spermicides are creams, foams, gels and tablets which act to kill sperm on contact. A spermicide must be inserted no more than twenty minutes before intercourse and a new application must be used before each ejaculation. Generally the use of spermicides is advised with a diaphragm or condom.

CONDOM

The condom is the simplest barrier method of artificial contraception. A condom is a thin rubber sheath which is placed on the penis before penetration. When the man ejaculates, the sperm are held in the rubber tip. There is also a female version of the condom, which is a thin rubber or plastic pouch that is inserted into the vagina.

DIAPHRAGM

The diaphragm for women works on a similar principle as the condom in that it provides a physical barrier to the sperm meeting the egg. A diaphragm is a rubber dome with a flexible spring rim. It is inserted into the vagina before intercourse, so that it covers the cervix. It is best used with a spermicidal cream or jelly to kill any sperm that manage to wriggle around the edges.

CERVICAL CAP

Like the diaphragm, the cervical cap is a barrier method of contraception, but it is much smaller because it fits tightly over the cervix, rather than filling the vagina. The cap must be fitted very carefully and should be used with spermicides.

CONTRACEPTIVE SPONGE

A contraceptive sponge is impregnated with spermicide and is inserted into the vagina so that it expands to cover the cervix. Like a diaphragm it is inserted before intercourse but is disposable and thrown away after use.

INTRAUTERINE DEVICE

The IUD is a piece of plastic shaped like a T, that may be covered by a thin coil of copper wire or may be impregnated with a hormone. It is inserted by a doctor through the vagina and cervix to sit inside the uterus (womb). The device can remain in place for two or three years before its needs to be changed.

NATURAL FAMILY PLANNING

Natural family planning is a form of periodic abstinence from sex (not having sex at those times of the month when a woman is fertile). The trick is knowing just what are the safe and not so safe times. Obviously, it is essential for both sexual partners in this situation to co-operate fully in the contraceptive process. The man must be as aware of the woman's cycle as she is herself. For this reason alone, this method of contraception does not suit all couples.

TUBAL LIGATION

A tubal ligation (having the tubes tied, clipped or blocked) is an operation that usually renders a woman permanently unable to have children. As a contraceptive it is almost 100% effective, but as with all surgical procedures, failures may occur, and women should be aware of this when they have the procedure.

VASECTOMY

A vasectomy is procedure in which the vas deferens (sperm tubes) of a man are cut and tied or clipped in order to prevent him from fathering children. It is a simpler operation than the sterilisation (tubal ligation) of a woman. It should be considered a permanent procedure at the time it is performed, but there is always a small risk that the cut sperm tubes may spontaneously reconnect at a later time making the man fertile again.

See also SEX HORMONES and separate entries for these methods of contraception for more detail.

CONTRACEPTIVE PILL

The development of the oral contraceptive pill in 1959, and its widespread release in 1962, revolutionised the lives of modern women, and changed society as a whole forever. For the first time there was an effective, safe, reliable, easy to use, reversible contraceptive that did not interfere with lovemaking and had no aesthetic drawbacks.

The oral contraceptive pill is the safest and

most effective form of reversible contraception. There are many different dosage forms and strengths, so that most women can find one that meets their needs. The main types are the monophasic (constant dose) two-hormone pill, the biphasic (two phase) and triphasic (three phase) hormone pills in which the hormone doses vary during the month, and the one hormone mini-pill.

The pill has several positive benefits besides almost perfect prevention of pregnancy. It regulates irregular periods, reduces menstrual pain and premenstrual tension, may increase the size of the breasts, reduces the severity of acne in some women, and libido (the desire for sex) is often increased. It even reduces the incidence of some types of cancer.

Two different hormones control the menstrual cycle. At the time of ovulation, the levels of one hormone drops, and the other rises, triggering the egg's release from the ovary. When the hormones revert to their previous level two weeks later, the lining of the uterus (womb) is no longer able to survive and breaks away, giving the woman a period.

The pill maintains a more constant hormone level, and thus prevents the release of the egg. In fact, it mimics the hormonal balance that is present during pregnancy, so the side effects of the pill are also those of pregnancy. The body, being fooled into thinking it is pregnant by the different hormone levels, does not allow further eggs to be released from the ovaries. With the triphasic pills, the level of both hormones rises at the normal time of ovulation, and then drops slightly thereafter to give a more natural hormonal cycle to the woman, while still preventing the release of an egg.

The hormones commonly used in contraceptive pills include ethinyloestradiol, levonorgestrel, norethisterone, gestodene, and mestranol. There are some specialised types of contraceptive pills which have added benefits such as the improvement of acne when the hormones cytoperone and ethinyloestradiol (Diane) are combined.

When the pill is stopped (or the sugar pills started) at the end of the month, the sudden drop in hormone levels cause a hormone withdrawal bleed (period) to start. If the woman stops taking the pill, her normal cycle should resume very quickly (sometimes immediately) and she is able to become pregnant.

If taken correctly, the pill is very effective as a contraceptive. But missing a pill, or suffering from diarrhoea or vomiting can have a very pregnant result. Some antibiotics can also interfere with the pill. If any of these things occur, continue to take the pill but use another method of contraception until at least seven active pills (not the sugar ones taken when you have your period) have been taken.

In its early days there were some questions raised about the wisdom of long-term reliance on the pill, but a woman on today's pill is taking a hormone dose that is only 4% the strength of the original. It is much safer to take the contraceptive pill for many years than it is to have one pregnancy, and that is the realistic basis on which to judge the safety of any contraceptive.

A few women do have unwanted side effects from the contraceptive pill. These can include headaches, break-through bleeding, nausea, breast tenderness, increased appetite and mood changes. If these problems occur, they can be assessed by a doctor, and a pill containing a different balance of hormones can be prescribed. Rarely, a serious complication such as a blood clot in a vein may occur.

Although the contraceptive pill is very safe, there are some women who should not use it. Those who have had blood clots, severe liver disease, strokes or bad migraines must not take the pill. Heavy smokers, obese women and those with diabetes must be observed closely, and probably should not use the pill after thirty-five years of age.

There is no need these days to take a break from the pill every year or so. This may have been the case in earlier years, but is no longer necessary. It is possible (and safe) to take the active pills of a monophasic (constant dose) contraceptive pill without a break for three months or more, then have a one week break when a period will occur. This way the woman will only have four periods a year, but some women have break through bleeds when attempting this.

In its most commonly used forms, the pill is a combination of the hormones oestrogen and progesterone. There is also a "mini pill" which contains only a progestogen hormone and is suitable for some women, including breast feeding mothers, who cannot take the combined pill. The mini pill is less reliable than the combined pill and is more likely to give rise to irregular bleeding, but serious side effects are much less common. It is vital to take it at the same time each day.

The effects of the pill are readily reversible. If a woman decides to become pregnant, she could find herself in that state in as little as two weeks after ceasing the pill, with no adverse effects on the mother or child.
See also CONTRACEPTION; MORNING AFTER PILL; SEX HORMONES

CONTRACEPTIVE SPONGE
This device is a sponge impregnated with spermicide which is inserted into the vagina so that it expands to cover the cervix. Like a diaphragm it is inserted before intercourse but is disposable and thrown away after use. It does not need to be fitted by a doctor and can be bought over the counter from pharmacies.
See also CONTRACEPTION; DIAPHRAGM

CONVERSION DISORDER
A conversion disorder is more commonly called hysteria, and is a psychiatric disorder related to stress resulting in the conversion of inner psychological conflicts into physical symptoms. There may be a serious preceding emotional upset, and it tends to occur more among the poorly educated and in some cultures (eg. southern European, Middle East).

Patients experience varying abnormalities of bodily function for no apparent or discoverable reason. Fitting and paralysis are common effects. All tests are normal, including electromyography (electrical testing of muscles) and EEG (electroencephalogram). 'Doctor shopping' may result in dependence on sedatives and pain-killers.

Treatment involves psychiatric counselling, behaviour modification, and family involvement in socialisation. The long term management is difficult, and success depends on combination of psychiatrist, patient and family.
See also BRIQUET SYNDROME; HYPOCHONDRIA; STRESS

CONVULSION
A fit or a convulsion is a result of a disturbance in the functioning of the brain. The main task of anyone present at a seizure is to protect the sufferer from harm. Do not restrict their movements, since the spasms and jerking are automatic and trying to stop them may cause injury. Simply move any objects that may be a danger and, if necessary, remove false teeth (but do not prise the mouth open or force objects into it). Protect the head from banging against the floor by putting something flat and soft (such as folded jacket) under it. If necessary loosen the person's collar so they can breathe more easily. Artificial respiration will probably be impossible, and the sufferer will breathe normally again at the end of the seizure, generally after a minute or so. The sufferer may fall asleep once the seizure has ended, in which case place them in the coma position (on side with legs bent) and allow them to wake naturally. There may be a card or tag on the person saying what to do in case of a seizure – look for this and follow the instructions.

Although relatively uncommon, and very distressing when they do occur, there are scores of causes for a convulsion that vary from the obvious to the extremely obscure.

Everyone thinks of epilepsy and other serious diseases when fitting occurs, but a simple faint, severe bacterial and viral infections, high fever and a sudden shock or intense fear can trigger a convulsion. Overdoses of numerous prescribed and illegal drugs, as well as alcohol, strychnine and cyanide poisoning may also be responsible.

Children sometimes have convulsions because of a sudden rise in temperature. These febrile convulsions consist of body rigidity, twitching, arched head and back, rolling eyes, a congested face and neck, and bluish face and lips. Generally the seizure will end quite quickly, but the carer should ensure that the airway is clear, turn the child on to the side if necessary, remove clothing, bathe or sponge the child with lukewarm water, and when the convulsion has eased obtain medical attention.

Epilepsy is a condition that causes recurrent seizures (fits). Some people are born with epilepsy, while others acquire the disease later in life after a brain infection, tumour or injury. Brain degeneration in the elderly, removing alcohol from an alcoholic or heroin from an addict, or an excess or lack of certain chemicals in the body can also cause epilepsy. Fits can vary from very mild absences in which people just seem to lose concentration for a few seconds, to uncontrolled bizarre movements of an arm or leg, to the grand mal convulsion in which an epileptic can thrash around quite violently and lose control of bladder and bowel.

A head injury from any cause may cause immediate or delayed fitting because of injury to the brain, or bleeding into or around the brain. Bleeding may also be caused by the spontaneous rupture of a weakened artery or vein in the skull, and the resultant pressure on the brain can have many varied effects.

The brain is supported and completely surrounded by a three layered membrane (the meninges) which contain the cerebrospinal fluid. If these meninges are infected by a virus or bacteria (meningitis) the patient may experience headache, fever, fits, neck stiffness and in severe cases may become comatose.

Encephalitis is an infection of the brain itself, which may be confused with meningitis. The symptoms include headache, intolerance of bright lights, fever, stiff neck, lethargy, nausea, vomiting, sore throat, tremors, confusion, convulsions, stiffness and paralysis.

Severe dehydration caused by excess sweating and/or lack of fluid in a hot environment, particularly if exercising, may cause collapse and fitting. This may be combined with excessive body temperature (hyperthermia), which aggravates the problem. Marathon runners who collapse and start twitching are often suffering from these problems.

Low blood sugar levels caused by excessive doses of insulin or other sugar lowering medications in diabetics may starve the brain of essential nutrients and affect its function.

Children who have behaviour problems may have severe temper tantrums which can appear to be similar to a convulsion. If the child is a very determined breath holder, the end stage may be collapse and fitting due to lack of oxygen reaching the brain, which usually settles quite quickly.

A lack of oxygen from near drowning, suffocation or smoke inhalation may also have adverse effects on the brain that trigger fitting.

Hysteria may occur because of fear, anxiety or some other type of stress, and the hysterical reaction may result in collapse, convulsions and coma.

Uncommon causes of convulsions include a stroke (cerebrovascular accident), a tumour or cancer affecting the brain or surrounding structures within the skull, significant liver or kidney disease, abnormal migraines, hydrocephalus, malignant hypertension (extremely high blood pressure), eclampsia (a rare complication of pregnancy) and a lack of thyroxine (hypothyroidism).

Rapid shallow breathing may alter the balance of carbon dioxide and oxygen in the lungs, and thus the blood. The blood becomes more alkali, and irritates small muscles, particularly in the hands, which go into spasm and may appear to be a convulsion. This is known as tetany (totally different to tetanus infection) and patients have fingers and sometimes wrist, forearms and feet, which are pointed in a firm spasm. Hormonal and calcium imbalances in the blood may also cause tetany.

Numerous rare syndromes, inherited conditions and congenital abnormalities (eg. tuberous sclerosis, Landau-Kleffner syndrome, Sturge-Weber syndrome, Creutzfeldt-Jakob syndrome, Lennox-Gestaut syndrome, Tourette syndrome) may also be responsible. *See also* FEBRILE CONVULSION; EPILEPSY; UNCONSCIOUS and separate entries for diseases mentioned above.

COORDINATION, POOR
Ataxia (a lack of coordination) is closely associated with clumsiness, but ataxic patients also have an unsteady and almost uncontrolled way of walking. When one muscle contracts to bend a joint, the opposite muscle, which normally straightens the joint, must be coordinated to relax simultaneously, and vice versa. Numerous diseases that affect the brain and spinal cord (an extension of the brain down through the vertebrae in the back) may be responsible for problems in this delicate system.

Alcoholism may affect many of the vital centres in the brain, and may actually damage the nerves in the spinal cord that are responsible for coordinating muscle action.

Pressure on the spinal cord caused by a growth, tumour or cancer of the cord itself, or the surrounding bone and other tissues, may also affect its function. Other conditions in the back including a disc protrusion (slipped disc) and severe arthritis, have similar effects.

Direct injury, tumours, cysts, a ruptured artery or vein, an abscess or cancer that affects the parts of the brain responsible for muscle movement and coordination will have obvious effects. The cerebellum at the back bottom part of the brain is the most vital area for coordination activities.

In a stroke (cerebrovascular accident) part of the brain is affected by having its blood supply cut off by a blockage in an artery, or a blood vessel in the brain may burst causing bleeding and damage to part of the brain. The symptoms can vary from minor discomfort and confusion to widespread paralysis and coma. Transient ischaemic attacks (TIA) are sometimes called mini-strokes and can have similar but temporary effects.

Other causes of poor coordination may include abnormalities of body chemistry caused by diseases of the liver, kidney or other organs, Friedreich's ataxia (an inherited condition), Wernicke-Korsakoff psychosis, Creutzfeldt-Jakob syndrome, Angleman syndrome (also known as the happy puppet syndrome), Bassen-Kornzweig syndrome (abetalipoproteinaemia) and many rarer conditions.
See also BRAIN; CLUMSINESS and separate entries for diseases mentioned above.

CO POISONING
See CARBON MONOXIDE POISONING

COPPER
Copper (Cu) is found in minute amounts in most body tissue, and to excess in Wilson disease. It is essential for red blood cell formation. There are no recognised diseases in humans due to a lack of copper as it is so widespread in the diet.
See also WILSON DISEASE

CORI SYNDROME
See GLYCOGEN STORAGE DISEASES

CORNEA
See EYE

CORNEAL ULCER
See EYE ULCER

CORONARY ARTERY BYPASS GRAFT
Three main coronary arteries supply the necessary blood to the thick heart muscle. If one of these arteries becomes narrowed or partially blocked, angina will occur. If it becomes totally blocked, the patient will suffer a heart attack. If a narrowed segment of coronary artery is discovered by special x-rays (angiogram), this partial blockage can be bypassed by a graft using an artery from the front wall of the chest or a vein from the leg.

A coronary artery bypass graft (CABG) operation is a major but routine procedure in many hospitals, and is successful in relieving angina and preventing heart attacks.

Under a general anaesthetic, the skin over the breast bone (sternum) is incised, and the breast bone itself is split open. Sometimes part of a rib is removed to give access to the heart. When the heart is seen, the blocked artery (or arteries in most cases) are identified, and the graft is sewn onto the side of the artery above and below the blockage. This allows the blood to bypass the blockage and to supply the heart muscle normally. The breast bone is stapled together and the skin is closed with sutures. The patients remain in hospital for seven to ten days, and will take up to six weeks to recover, but after that time they will find they have far more energy, no angina, and less shortness of breath than before. Most people claim it makes them feel ten years younger.

Close follow-up by the surgeon and/or general practitioner is necessary for some months after the procedure, and special tablets may be needed for the first few weeks or months.
See also ANGINA; ANGIOGRAM; HEART; HEART ATTACK

COR PULMONALE
Cor pulmonale is also known as pulmonary hypertension or right heart failure. It results in enlargement of the right side of the heart (which pumps blood through the lungs), and increased blood pressure in the lungs.

Lungs damaged by emphysema, smoking, inhaled coal dust or asbestos, recurrent lung infections or a number of rarer lung diseases may be so abnormal that the blood has difficulty in passing through them. The right side of the heart must work harder to force the blood through the damaged lungs, which causes a significant rise in the blood pressure in the right heart and lungs. This causes further damage to arteries and worsens the disease. The heart muscle thickens and enlarges, and because of the lung damage, inadequate oxygen enters the blood, which further compounds the problem.

Patients have a cough that produces clear or bloodstained phlegm, a wheeze, shortness of breath with any exertion and general weakness. In advanced cases the ankles may be swollen, nausea and indigestion may occur, and the liver enlarges. Patients are more susceptible to lung infections such as bronchitis and pneumonia.

The diagnosis can be made by a chest x-ray and an electrocardiogram (ECG). Other investigations include cardiac catheterisation (passing a tube through a vein into the heart to measure the blood pressure), echocardiography and angiography.

Medication can be prescribed to strengthen the heart, open the lungs and cure any lung infection. Physiotherapy can help drain phlegm from the lungs, and oxygen may be used to relieve the shortness of breath.

Unfortunately, no cure is possible and patients steadily deteriorate over many years to eventually die from heart attacks, pneumonia or other complications of the disease.
See also CONGESTIVE CARDIAC FAILURE; EMPHYSEMA; HEART; LUNG

CORTICOSTEROIDS
See STEROIDS

CORYNEBACTERIUM DIPHTHERIAE
See DIPHTHERIA

CORYNEBACTERIUM MINUTISSIUM
See ERYTHRASMA

CORYZA
See COLD, COMMON

COSTAL CARTILAGE
See RIB; TIETZE SYNDROME

COSTEN SYNDROME
Costen syndrome is a jaw joint abnormality caused by abnormal stress on the jaw (temporomandibular) joint and muscles used in chewing.

The symptoms include ear pain and discomfort, a headache in the temples, ringing in the ears (tinnitus), impaired hearing, and the top and bottom teeth do not meet properly (malocclusion). X-rays of the temporomandibular joint with the mouth open and closed show the abnormality.

Dental or surgical correction of malocclusion gives reasonable results.
See also MANDIBLE

COSTOCHONDRAL SYNDROME
See TIETZE SYNDROME

COSTOCHONDRITIS
See TIETZE SYNDROME

COT DEATH
The sudden infant death syndrome (SIDS) or cot death is the sudden unexpected death of an apparently normal healthy child in whom a subsequent detailed post-mortem examination reveals no cause for the death. A baby is put to bed and some hours later is found dead. There is no evidence of disturbed sleep and no cry is heard.

It affects two out of every 1000 children between the ages of one month and one year.

The cause is unknown, but there are many theories. It is not infectious or contagious, nor are the deaths due to suffocation, choking or allergies. It occurs in both bottle and breast fed babies and there is no relationship between immunisation and cot death. There is no evidence that vitamins, dietary supplements or any medication can prevent the syndrome. If one baby in a family dies from cot death, there is some evidence that subsequent babies are at a higher risk. Another theory implicates high body temperatures due to over wrapping or dressing a baby, so that the baby cannot sweat effectively.

Babies who sleep face down are more susceptible to cot death, and it is strongly recommended that babies should never be placed on their stomach to sleep.

It is imperative that the parents receive adequate and immediate counselling by trained professionals as they develop an acute sense of guilt, thinking that they are in some way responsible, and fear that someone will blame them for the death of their child due to neglect or mistreatment, but this is not so. Other children in the family will also be affected because they are often unable to understand or accept the tragedy.

Some parents have found their child on the

verge of death, lying blue in the cot and not breathing, and rousing them has started breathing again. After such an event, these babies can be monitored by a sensing device that sounds an alarm if breathing stops for more than a few seconds. Only a very select group of infants require this type of care.

Interestingly, the incidence of cot death halved in the decade between 1990 and 2000, but it is not known why.
See also DEATH, SUDDEN UNEXPECTED

CO-TRIMOXAZOLE
See SULPHA ANTIBIOTICS

COUGH
A cough is one of the most common conditions presenting to doctors, and the causes can vary from the totally innocuous to the deadly serious. A cough may be dry or moist, hard, productive, painful, associated with a wheeze, persistent or intermittent, and the phlegm produced may be clear, yellow, brown, green or blood stained, and all these characteristics and more assist the doctor in making a diagnosis.

Many causes come from the throat and lungs (respiratory tract), but anything from heart failure to thyroid gland disease may cause a cough.

Any bacterial or viral infection (eg. common cold, influenza) of the respiratory tract, from the nose to the lungs, may cause a cough. In the nose, excess phlegm production with a common cold may not only cause the nose to run, but phlegm may run back into the throat (a postnasal drip) to irritate this and stimulate a cough. An infection in the sinuses will cause a similar effect. The throat itself may be inflamed with minimal phlegm, but irritated to produce a hard dry cough. In the lungs, infections can cause inflammation of the major air tubes (bronchi) to cause bronchitis, or pus may accumulate in the tiny bubbles (alveoli) from which oxygen is absorbed into the blood to cause pneumonia.

Smoking is the most common cause of a persistent cough. 'Smoker's cough' typically occurs on waking, eases after half an hour or so, then flares after each cigarette during the day, and worsens again as temperatures drop at night.

Allergy reactions in the nose (hay fever) and throat can create copious amounts of clear phlegm that pour down the back of the throat, as well as out the front on the nose.

Asthma is a temporary narrowing of the tubes through which air flows into and out of the lungs (the bronchi). Symptoms may include shortness of breath, wheezing, difficulty in breathing out easily, coughing (particularly in children) and a tightness and discomfort in the chest.

Other lung diseases that may cause a cough include emphysema, bronchiectasis, pleurisy, an inhaled foreign body such as a peanut, lung cancer (bronchial carcinoma), pulmonary embolism (blood clot in an artery supplying the lung), smoke inhalation, near drowning, toxic gases (eg. exhaust fumes), hyper-reactive airways disease (a condition similar to asthma in which there is wheezing, cough and shortness of breath), whooping cough (pertussis), tuberculosis (TB), cystic fibrosis, Q fever, brucellosis, psittacosis, Legionnaire's disease, sarcoidosis, anthrax and an abscess in the lung.

Conditions outside the lungs which may cause a cough include congestive cardiac failure, reflux oesophagitis, a foreign body in an ear (eg. hard wax, peanut) in a child may cause a cough even though the lung itself is not infected, psychogenic (the patient coughs repeatedly to attract attention, then subconsciously develops a habit of coughing constantly), aortic aneurysm that puts pressure on the trachea, damage to the valves (eg. mitral valve) between the chambers of the heart, pericarditis and a goitre.

Many medications, but particularly those used for heart failure and high blood pressure (ACE inhibitors) may have a cough as a side effect.

There are many other rare and unusual causes of coughing.
See also ACE INHIBITORS; BREATH, SHORT OF; COUGHING BLOOD; COUGH MEDICINES; CROUP; LUNG; SMOKING; WHEEZE and separate entries for diseases mentioned above.

COUGHING BLOOD
Any prolonged bout of coughing can result in the coughing up of blood, or blood stained phlegm (haemoptysis), caused by damage to the pharynx (throat), larynx (voice box), trachea (main airway) or bronchi (smaller

airways) in the lungs. As a result, bronchitis, pneumonia and many other infections that cause a cough may cause the problem. The occasional coughing up of blood under these circumstances is usually of no significance, but when the coughing of blood, particularly when not mixed with much phlegm, becomes a regular occurrence, assessment by a doctor is essential.

A bleeding nose will not only lose blood out through the nostrils, but some will run down the back of the nose into the throat, from where it may be coughed up. If the bleeding comes from a polyp, tumour or cancer at the back of the nose, nearly all the bleeding will be back into the throat.

An injury to the chest, such as a fractured rib that pierces the lung, or a crush injury that damages the lung (eg. car accident), will cause bleeding into the airways and haemoptysis.

Bronchiectasis occurs if the tubes within the lung that carry air (the bronchi) are damaged, scarred and permanently overdilated. The damage can be present from birth in diseases such as cystic fibrosis, or be caused in childhood by immune deficiencies. Bronchiectasis may develop in adult life due to recurrent attacks of pneumonia or to the inhalation of toxic gases (eg. smoking). Patients have a constant cough that brings up large amounts of foul phlegm, and they may cough up blood, become anaemic, lose weight, have chest pains and develop frequent attacks of pneumonia and other lung infections that are triggered by minor stress, a cold or flu.

Lung cancer (bronchial carcinoma) is usually a result of smoking. The early warning signs are weight loss, a persistent cough, a change in the normal type of cough, coughing blood and worsening breathlessness.

A blood clot in one of the major arteries within the lungs (pulmonary thrombosis) will cause severe damage to that section of lung beyond the clot, leading to its collapse, cough, pain and shortness of breath.

Tuberculosis (TB) causes a productive cough, haemoptysis, night sweats, loss of appetite, fever, weight loss and generalised tiredness.

Tumours, polyps, cancer or ulceration of the pharynx, larynx, trachea or other airways can cause bleeding that irritates the airway or lung to trigger coughing.

Less common causes of coughing up blood include: –
• an inhaled foreign body (eg. peanut)
• damage to the valves (eg. mitral valve) between the chambers of the heart which may lead to back pressure into the lungs leading to a build up of blood in the lungs which can leak into the airways to irritate them and cause a cough which brings up blood tinged phlegm
• an abnormality in the blood clotting mechanism (eg. a lack of platelets in the blood, haemophilia)
• cystic fibrosis
• an abscess in the lungs
• rare tropical diseases (eg. hookworm, ascariasis)
• inflammation from smoke inhalation, near drowning, toxic gases (eg. exhaust fumes) or other irritants
See also COUGH; LUNG; WHEEZE and separate entries for diseases mentioned above.

COUGH MEDICINES
Antitussives are the mixtures, lozenges or tablets that stop coughing. They act by directly soothing the inflamed throat, decreasing the sensitivity of the part of the brain that triggers the spasm of coughing, decreasing the amount of phlegm in the throat, anaesthetising the throat, reducing inflammation, reducing pain, and by almost any combination of these methods. There are dozens of different cough mixtures (antitussives). They differ from expectorants which are designed to increase coughing but make the coughing more effective so that phlegm can be cleared from the lungs and throat.

Codeine is one of the most common ingredients of cough mixtures and acts as a suppressor of the brain's cough centre and as a painkiller. It is a mild narcotic, and its main side effect is constipation. There are a number of related drugs (eg. pholcodine, dihydrocodeine, dextromethorphan) which act in a similar way.

Most antitussives are available without prescription and have minimal side effects. Many have an alcohol base and also contain mild narcotics or antihistamines, so care must be taken with driving and operating machinery.

Other cough suppressants may include

guaiphenesin, senega, camphor and thymol. Antihistamines, decongestants, mucolytics and analgesics are often combined with these ingredients.

The only potent antitussive that requires a prescription is hydrocodone, which may have drowsiness and blurred vision as side effects, and is addictive.
See also COUGH; EXPECTORANTS; LUNG; MEDICATION

COX-2 INHIBITORS
See NONSTEROIDAL ANTI-INFLAMMATORY DRUGS

COXIELLA BURNETTI
See Q FEVER

COXSACKIE VIRUS INFECTION
There are two main types of *Coxsackie* virus (A and B), but these are further broken down into more than fifty subtypes.

The symptoms depend on where the infection occurs. It may cause viral meningitis, cold-like symptoms, fevers, ulceration of the mouth and throat (herpangina), inflammation of the pleura around the lungs (Bornholm disease), hand foot mouth disease, myositis (inflammation of muscles), and inflammation of the heart or the pericardium that surrounds the heart. Rarely, if the heart is infected, it may be permanently damaged.

There is no cure other than time and rest, but symptoms may be eased by appropriate medication when necessary. Most patients recover uneventfully unless the heart is involved.
See also BORNHOLM DISEASE; HAND FOOT MOUTH DISEASE; MENINGITIS; STOMATITIS

CPAP
See CONTINUOUS POSITIVE AIRWAY PRESSURE MACHINE

CPR
See RESUSCITATION

CRABS
Crabs (pubic pediculosis) is an infestation of the pubic hair with the lice (parasitic insect) *Phthirus pubis*, that lives by sucking blood from the soft pubic skin. It is caught by being in close bodily contact with someone who already has an infestation (eg. during sex), but as the lice can survive away from humans for a time, it can also be caught from borrowed clothing, towels or bedding.

Often there are no symptoms and many people are unaware of the presence of lice. In others the lice cause an itchy rash in the pubic area, which may be raw and bleeding from constant scratching. Secondary skin infections may develop in these sores, and this infection can cause further symptoms including a fever and enlarged glands in the groin. Lice may be seen by examining the pubic hair through a magnifying glass.

A number of lotions are available to kill the crabs. The affected individual, and all sex partners, must be treated simultaneously to prevent reinfestations occurring. All clothing and bedding must be thoroughly washed in hot water. A repeat treatment after twenty four hours and again after seven days is advisable in order to kill any lice that have hatched in the interim. Antibiotics may be required to treat secondary infections.

Correct treatment should result in a complete cure.
See also ANTIPARASITICS; HEAD LICE

CRACK
See COCAINE

CRACKED NIPPLES
See NIPPLES, CRACKED

CRADLE CAP
See SEBORRHOEIC ECZEMA

CRAMP, MUSCULAR
See MUSCLE CRAMP

CRANIAL NERVES
Twelve nerves on each side run out from the brain through holes in the skull to supply the body directly rather than via the spinal cord. These cranial nerves are all known by both their name and number, as listed in the table below.

No.	NAME	FUNCTION
1	Olfactory	Smell.
2	Optic	Sight.
3	Oculomotor	Eye movement.
4	Trochlear	Pupil size, downwards eye movement.
5	Trigeminal	Head sensation, jaw movement.

No.	NAME	FUNCTION
6	Abducent	Outwards eye movement.
7	Facial	Face movement, taste, tear and saliva secretion.
8	Vestibu- locochlear	Hearing, balance.
9	Glosso- pharyngeal	Taste; tongue, ear and pharynx sensation; pharynx movement.
10	Vagus	Gut movement and sensation, taste, external ear sensation.
11	Accessory	Movement of pharynx, larynx, head, shoulder and gut.
12	Hypoglossal	Tongue movement.

See also BRAIN; NERVE; SKULL

CRANIOPHARYNGIOMA

Craniopharyngiomas are uncommon slowly growing brain tumours that occur in the centre of the brain, and put pressure on the optic (vision) nerve. They are more common in children and young adults, but their cause is unknown.

Patients develop partial or total blindness in one or both eyes, headache, vomiting, personality and mental changes. Short stature, failure of puberty in children and other hormonal abnormalities may occur due to pressure on the pituitary gland. It can be diagnosed by a CT or MRI scan.

Treatment involves irradiation and sometimes surgery, but is generally unsatisfactory. *See also* BLINDNESS; BRAIN; VISION HALF LOST

CRANIOSTENOSIS

Craniostenosis is a congenital deformity of the head in which the skull fails to grow and expand due to premature fusion of the joints (sutures) between the bones that make up the skull. This results in brain damage, mental retardation, convulsions and a small deformed skull. The closed sutures can be seen on x-ray.

Sometimes surgical splitting of sutures is attempted, but generally no treatment is available and life expectancy is significantly shortened.
See also HEAD SMALL; SKULL

CRANIOTOMY
See NEUROSURGERY

CRANIUM
See SKULL

CRAWLING SENSATION ON SKIN

Formication is the name given to the sensation of thousands of ants crawling over the skin, even though there are no ants actually present.

It may be caused by damage to the brain (eg. by a stroke), or nerves of sensation (eg. by compression of the nerve around arthritic joints or in the spine) that gives inappropriate signals to the brain.

Numerous psychiatric conditions (eg. schizophrenia, other psychoses) may cause the brain to incorrectly perceive that the skin is being irritated.

Some medications, particularly in overdose, may have formication as a side effect. *See also* SKIN and separate entries for diseases mentioned above.

CREATINE

Creatine is a naturally occurring amino acid, it is not a hormone or a stimulant. Amino acids are the building blocks from which proteins are made, and they are found in a variety of foods, with the richest source being lean red meat. A one kilogram steak contains about five grams of creatine. Nearly all the creatine in the body is stored in muscle cells, but it is made in the liver, kidney, and pancreas.

Creatine increases the amount of water held in muscles, thus increasing their bulk, and making creatine attractive to muscle builders.

Muscles require energy to move, which comes from a molecule called adenosine triphosphate, (ATP). During exercise, muscles break down ATP into ADP (adenosine diphosphate). When ATP is broken down, creatine phosphate comes in and releases phosphate to change ADP back to ATP. As creatine phosphate levels drop during exercise, performance deteriorates as skeletal muscle only stores enough creatine and ATP for about ten seconds of high intensity activity.

Those who use creatine phosphate supplements may increase the level of creatine in muscles, which increases the amount of phosphate available to convert ADP back to ATP, therefore increasing muscle performance and decreasing recovery time.

Creatine supplements should be used in conjunction with vigourous training to obtain any athletic or muscle building benefit. It may briefly increase peak power, delay fatigue, and increase energy during high intensity exercise.

Creatine is absorbed better into the body from the intestine if taken with a fruit drink or sugar.

Dosages are usually high for the first five days with 10 to 20 grams of creatine phosphate taken every day, after that 2 to 5 grams a day is all that is necessary. After a week of additional creatine supplementation, there may be a 10% to 20% increase in creatine stored in the body. There is considerable variability in creatine absorption between individuals, and those with a low initial creatine concentration will show a greater benefit. Trained athletes often have higher natural stores of creatine than non-athletes, so they will not benefit as much from supplements.

Creatine supplementation does improve performance with intermittent short exercises lasting no longer than twenty seconds (eg. body building, sprinting, throwing, jumping). It does not improve long term aerobic exercise (medium or long distance running, swimming, cycling).

The most common side effects from creatine in normal doses are a rash, shortness of breath, vomiting, diarrhoea, nervousness, anxiety, fatigue and migraines. Uncommon serious side effects include muscle inflammation, seizures and irregular heart beat. Excessive doses can cause kidney damage. There are no adverse effects from long term use at low dosages; in fact there is some evidence that it may improve cholesterol levels.

There are some experiments being undertaken to see if creatine helps patients with muscle wasting diseases such as muscular dystrophy. Early results are encouraging.
See also AMINO ACID; MUSCLE; PROTEIN

CREATININE
The level of creatinine in the blood is probably the most sensitive test for kidney function. If the levels of this substance are raised, the kidney is not functioning adequately due to diseases as diverse as kidney stones, glomerulonephritis, cancer, cysts, diabetes and old age. A creatinine level under 11 mmol/L is considered normal.
See also BLOOD TESTS; KIDNEY; UREA

CREEPING ERUPTION
See CUTANEOUS LARVA MIGRANS

CREST SYNDROME
The name of this syndrome is an acronym for its symptoms: –
• Calcinosis (the formation of hard calcium containing nodules under the skin)
• Raynaud's phenomenon (fingers and toes to become cold and blue)
• Oesophageal (Esophageal – American spelling) inflammation causing difficulty in swallowing
• Sclerodactyly (thickening and hardening of the skin on the fingers and toes)
• Telangiectasia (multiple dilated blood vessels in the skin)

It is known as CRST syndrome if the oesophagus is not involved.

The cause is unknown, but it can be diagnosed by a biopsy of affected tissue.

There is no cure, and the condition is usually slowly progressive, but medications can be given to ease symptoms. Scleroderma may be a complication.
See also RAYNAUD'S PHENOMENON; SCLERODERMA

CRETINISM
Cretinism is hypothyroidism (under active thyroid gland) in a child, a condition which occurs in one in every 4000 births.

The thyroid gland in the front of the neck is responsible for producing a substance called thyroxine which acts on every cell in the body to control the rate at which it works. In cretinism, the thyroid gland fails to function correctly from birth to cause impaired brain development and mental retardation (which may be severe). It is diagnosed by specific blood tests that are routinely performed on all babies at birth.

Thyroxine tablets or mixture control the problem, but there may be some degree of brain damage due to lack of thyroxine in the foetus before birth. Most cretins can function normally in society with their intelligence and functional capacity only slightly below average. No further deterioration occurs once treatment is started.
See also HYPOTHYROIDISM; THYROID GLAND

CREUTZFELDT-JAKOB DISEASE

Creutzfeldt-Jakob disease (CJD) or spongieform encephalitis is a prion (virus-like) infection of the brain.

Rare spontaneous cases have occurred where the source of infection is unknown, but in more recent times it has been spread by the use of growth hormone extracted from the pituitary gland of corpses, and given to children who have inadequate growth. Rarely, transmission has also occurred through some corneal and meninges organ transplants. In the United Kingdom during the late 1980s and early 1990s, cattle were fed a protein supplement that included the ground up carcasses of sheep. Some of these sheep suffered from a disease called scrapie, which was caused by the same prion as CJD. These cattle developed mad cow disease, and when slaughtered for consumption by humans, passed on the prion to cause CJD.

There may be no symptoms for years after the prion enters the body, before it activates and attacks the brain. Progressive dementia, tremors, incoordination, drowsiness, emotional instability and speech difficulties then occur.

The diagnosis is difficult and no treatment is available. The infection leads inevitably to death, often within a year of diagnosis.
See also KURU; PRION

CRI DU CHAT SYNDROME

Cri du chat syndrome is a rare congenital brain development abnormality that causes mental retardation, wide apart eyes, a small head, round face, low set ears, and a cat-like cry ("cri du chat") as a newborn. The cat cry disappears with age. Diagnostic chromosome studies show deletion of the short arm of the 5th chromosome. There is no treatment or cure.
See also MENTAL RETARDATION

CRIGLER-NAJJAR SYNDROME

Crigler-Najjar syndrome is the congenital lack of an enzyme from the liver that results in liver failure and severe jaundice (yellow skin) in newborn infants. It may result in permanent brain damage and premature death. Blood tests will show the abnormal liver function and lack of enzyme.

Phenobarbitone can sometimes be used to slow the progress of the disease, but the prognosis is poor.
See also JAUNDICE; LIVER; TOURETTE SYNDROME

CRIME

See CHILD ABUSE; INCEST; RAPE; VIOLENCE

CROHN'S DISEASE

Crohn's disease (regional enteritis) is a chronic inflammation and thickening of the wall of the intestine that usually occurs in the lower part of the small intestine (ileum), but may occur anywhere between the stomach and the anus. It usually affects young adults, and despite treatment, often continues for the rest of the patient's life. When the intestine of these patients is examined at operation, segments of bowel from a few centimetres to a metre or more in length are found to have a wall that is several times thicker and much firmer than normal. It may vary from a minor irritation to being a very serious disease as patients have episodes of relatively good health for months or years, then become acutely ill again. The cause is unknown.

The symptoms include moderate to severe intermittent lower abdominal pain (colic), alternating diarrhoea and constipation (with the diarrhoea being more common), intermittent fever, loss of appetite, passing excess wind and weight loss. In severe cases the bowel may rupture into the bladder, vagina or through the skin around the anus, bowel obstruction may occur, as may bowel perforation and, in rare cases, death.

The diagnosis is confirmed by a barium meal x-ray and follow through, or if the lower intestine (colon) is involved, a barium enema or colonoscopy. Treatment involves surgically removing the worst affected segments of intestine, and controlling diarrhoea and pain with medication, followed by a high-calorie, high-vitamin, low-residue diet with calcium supplements. Vitamin injections are sometimes necessary if food absorption is very poor. Anaemia, dehydration and diarrhoea are signs of a poorly maintained diet. Antibiotics are given to treat bowel infections, and steroids to control flare-ups of the disease.

There is no permanent cure. Even after extensive surgery, 60% of patients develop new affected segments of intestine. Although the mortality rate of patients is slightly increased, most live relatively normal and long lives.

See also ABDOMINAL PAIN; BARIUM MEAL; COLIC; COLONOSCOPY; CONSTIPATION; DIARRHOEA; ILEUM

CROMOGLYCATE
See ASTHMA PREVENTION MEDICATION

CROTAMITON
See ANTIPARASITICS

"CROTCH ROT"
See TINEA CRURIS

CROUP
Croup (or stridor) causes a harsh whistling when breathing in, and is usually followed by a cough.

By far the most common cause is a minor viral respiratory infection of children under five years of age, affecting the pharynx (lower throat). If a constant high fever occurs, and the child becomes particularly lethargic, a bacteria may be responsible. The condition may be very distressing to both child and parents, but is rarely serious.

Affected children have a seal-like barking cough, difficulty with taking a breath in, and excessive chest movement with breathing. There is usually only a slight fever, and minimal throat pain. Very rarely, the child may develop severe swelling in the throat that totally obstructs breathing, which is a critical emergency.

Medications and steam will ease the symptoms. Nurse the child in a warm, moist, steamy environment (eg. use a vaporiser). Paracetamol is given for fever or discomfort, and lots of fluid to prevent dehydration. In more serious cases, prednisone is prescribed and a steam and oxygen tent may be used in hospital to assist breathing. The vast majority of children recover spontaneously within a day or two.

There are many other causes of croup including: –
• Epiglottitis. The epiglottis is a piece of cartilage that sticks up at the back of the tongue to stop food from entering the windpipe (trachea) when swallowing. If this becomes infected by bacteria (eg. *Haemophilus influen-*

zae B – Hib), it can swell up rapidly and cause a very sore throat, fever and obvious illness.
• Glandular fever (infectious mononucleosis), caused by the Epstein-Barr virus. Patients usually have a sore throat, raised temperature, croupy cough, large glands in the neck and other parts of the body, extreme lethargy, and generally feel absolutely lousy for about a month.
• The incidence of diphtheria in children is now low due to vaccination. It causes a sore throat, thick grey sticky membrane across the throat, fever, nasal discharge, croup, hoarse voice and obvious illness, with overwhelming tiredness and muscle aches.
• Foreign bodies (eg. peanut, small toy), polyps, cysts, tumours, bruising, an abscess and other growths in the larynx or throat may irritate the area to cause a croupy cough.
• Laryngomalacia is a rare condition of children in which the cartilage of the larynx (voice box) is softened, and collapses when the patient breathes in heavily with exercise, to cause croup.
See also COUGH; PHARYNX; VIRUS; WHEEZE and separate entries for diseases mentioned above.

CRST SYNDROME
See CREST SYNDROME

CRYING, ABNORMAL
See BABIES; TEARS, ABNORMAL

CRYOTHERAPY
Cryotherapy (freezing) to remove skin tumours or sunspots is usually carried out using a liquid nitrogen spray or probe cooled to –196°C, although carbon dioxide snow (dry ice) is sometimes used. Stinging is felt at the time of freezing, and often a slight ache later as the area thaws. Pain-killers are not normally needed, but some patients may wish to use paracetamol tablets after the procedure.

The frozen sites may go through any or all of the following stages during recovery: –
• Dry, swollen, mildly inflamed areas. These should be left uncovered except when a dressing is necessary to prevent the area becoming dirty (eg. if gardening with a freeze site on the hand). Avoid using make-up on the site until inflammation settles.
• Blistering. If the blister is intact and contains

clear fluid, leave it alone. Bursting a blister makes it more likely to become infected. If the blister is very uncomfortable, it may be drained by pricking with a needle that has been soaked in disinfectant or methylated spirits.

• Blistering with weeping. Clean lesions as often as practical with saline (salty water). Continue until sore is dry, which usually takes several days, but occasionally two to three weeks.

• Dry crusts. Apply Vaseline or petroleum jelly three times a day.

• Infection. This is uncommon, but if the freeze site has a red border more than 2mm. wide surrounding it, is painful, or a pus filled blister is present, it is infected. Avoid prolonged wetting and dry well after a shower. Burst infected blisters with a disinfected needle, and apply an antiseptic ointment three times a day. If these measures don't lead to rapid improvement, return to see your doctor.

Almost every spot treated by cryotherapy will develop some scar. All scars are bright pink for one to four months, then usually fade. White scars may persist for many months after this, especially where a particularly thick or malignant lesion has required a longer freeze spraying time.

Keloid scarring is a less common form of healing which appears as a pink smooth nodule (proud flesh) in the centre of the freeze site, or as a thin straight ridge of thickened scar tissue. Keloid scars may last for several years, but eventually most fade and flatten. Scarring can be reduced by treatment with steroid creams that can be prescribed by a doctor.

Tumour recurrence is most commonly seen as a faint pink or slightly scaling area two to three millimetres wide arising adjacent to a freeze site. A recurrence is often larger than it looks, but is usually treated by excision rather than refreezing.
See also CARBON DIOXIDE;
DIATHERMY; EXCISION

CRYPTOCOCCOSIS
Cryptococcosis is an infection of the lungs caused by the fungus *Cryptococcosis neoformans* which is caught by inhalation of the fungal spores into the lungs. The fungus is often carried by pigeons, and found in their droppings, which when dry can be inhaled as a dust.

Often there are no symptoms. Those with severe infections may have chest pain and a cough. Those with reduced immunity (eg. AIDS) develop pneumonia-like symptoms. Uncommonly, it may spread from lungs to brain to cause a serious form of encephalitis. Rarely it may spread to skin and bones.

Diagnosis is difficult. Chest x-ray shows abnormalities, but are not diagnostic. Sputum tests may be positive for the fungus, but are usually negative. A biopsy of the lung is often necessary to make the diagnosis.

Often no treatment is necessary, but in severe cases antifungal medications (eg. amphotericin B, flucytosine) are given. The infection usually settles spontaneously in lungs, but it may be fatal if the brain is infected.
See also ENCEPHALITIS; FUNGI

CRYPTOGENIC FIBROSING ALVEOLITIS
See IDIOPATHIC PULMONARY FIBROSIS

CRYPTORCHIDISM
See TESTICLE UNDESCENDED

CRYPTOSPORIDIOSIS
Cryptosporidiosis is a common parasitic infestation of the gut of humans and animals, which spreads from animals to humans in water contaminated by faeces.

Usually there are minimal symptoms, but when they occur may include watery diarrhoea, belly discomfort and pains, and less commonly weight loss, nausea and a mild fever. It normally only causes symptoms in patients with a damaged immune system (eg. AIDS) or other illnesses.

The diagnosis can be made by examining a sample of faeces under a microscope.

Treatment involves a low fat diet, medications to ease diarrhoea and plenty of fluid. No medication is effective against the parasite itself, but there are no long term complications and the prognosis is very good.
See also CAMPLYLOBACTER
ENTERITIS; SHIGELLOSIS

CSF
See CEREBROSPINAL FLUID

CT SCAN
CT stands for computerised tomography. The term CAT scan (computerised axial tomography scan) is less used by the medical profession nowadays. CT scans are a combination of x-rays and computers.

When x-ray machines were first developed, they were a marvelous way of enabling doctors to see breaks and abnormalities in bones. They were not so successful at showing up soft tissues. Furthermore they took pictures from only one direction at one point in the body, thus limiting how much of the body could be seen at any one time and at what angle. Modern day CT scanners take pictures of soft tissue such as tumours, and send x-rays from all sides – around the entire circumference of 360 degrees – with no greater amount of radiation than regular x-rays. The computer then builds these cross-sectional images up into a two dimensional slice. CT scanners can also take pictures at every point through the body, fractions of millimetres apart. This means not only that the picture is extraordinarily accurate, but also that very precise measurements are possible (eg. in the case of a tumour).

CT scanners can also guide a doctor during a biopsy and may help in surgery. By far the greatest application of the scanners is in the area of malignancies to assess whether there is a tumour, how big it is and how far it has spread. A CT scan can also be used after a stroke to tell what part of the brain has been affected. Scanning is invaluable for suspected cancers deep within the abdomen, such as in the liver.

Until a few years ago CT scanners were enormously expensive both to buy and to run, and only the main hospitals could afford to acquire them and to employ the skilled technicians needed to operate them. By the mid 1990's, CT scanners were available in many suburban and regional x-ray centres, and CT scans are now routinely ordered by general practitioners to diagnose back pain, head injuries and abdominal lumps.

Having a CT scan is quick, painless and safe. Sometimes a dye is introduced into the body before the scan is started, either by injection or swallowing, so that the particular organ under investigation will show up more clearly. For the scan itself, the patient lies on a narrow bench to which they are firmly strapped to prevent movement that would blur the picture, and the scanner moves over the body. The machine rotates around as it takes the x-rays and may be slightly noisy.
See also MRI SCAN; X-RAYS

Cu
See COPPER

CULDOSCOPY
Culdoscopy is a type of endoscopy for observing a woman's internal reproductive organs. The culdoscope is inserted through a tiny incision in the top of the vagina. It is used in the diagnosis of disorders of the uterus and the endometrium (the lining of the uterus). The woman will normally be given a general anaesthetic. Culdoscopy is now less commonly used than laparoscopy.
See also ENDOSCOPE; HYSTEROSCOPY

CUNEIFORM BONE
See WRIST

CURETTE
A curette is actually a sharp-edged spoon used by surgeons to clean out the inside of any small cavity within the body (eg. an abscess). The name of this surgical instrument is now often applied by gynaecologists to the actual operation of cleaning out the contents of the womb (uterus), which is one of the most common surgical procedures.

The uterus is a thick muscular sack, lined with special cells that rapidly multiply during the month to accept any pregnancy that may occur. If no pregnancy develops, the lining of cells breaks away, and causes bleeding that a woman recognises as her monthly menstrual period. If this delicate process is affected by one or more of several diseases and fails to operate correctly, many different complications can occur. A curette can be used to both diagnose and cure many of these problems.

The procedure only takes ten minutes, but will involve a visit to hospital, and a brief general anaesthetic. Once the patient is asleep, the doctor will use an instrument to look into the vagina. Through this, the opening into the uterus (the cervix) can be seen. This is normally closed, and a series of successively larger smooth rods are slid through the cervix to gradually dilate it. For this reason the operation is sometimes called a dilation and curettage (D & C). Once the cervix is wide enough, a small curette is passed into the uterus, and is scraped along the inside of the uterus in sweeping motions to remove all the cells and tissue inside the womb. These are collected for later examination under a microscope by a pathologist.

It is often difficult for doctors to exactly determine why a woman is having heavy, painful or irregular periods. The pathologist can report the type of cells that are present in the scrapings removed from the uterus, thus enabling an accurate diagnosis to be made. One common reason for problem periods is the failure of the uterus to clear all the cells and tissue during a period. The curette will give the uterus a very thorough cleaning, and as a result, the procedure often cures the period problems at the same time as the diagnosis is made.

It is normal to perform a curette after a miscarriage. When a miscarriage occurs, some unwanted tissue may be left behind, and it is necessary for this to be removed to prevent any infection in the uterus and allow another pregnancy to start. More than one in every ten pregnancies end prematurely as a miscarriage.

When termination of pregnancy (abortion) is indicated, it may be performed by a dilation and curettage of the uterus. Suction is often used to empty the uterus before final curettage.

Infertility may be due to the incorrect development of the womb lining. A curette to remove and analyse this lining can help gynaecologists determine the cause of the infertility, and hopefully overcome the problem.

Cancer of the uterus (endometrial carcinoma) is not particularly common but very difficult to diagnose. It usually has the symptoms of abnormal vaginal bleeding and discharges. A curette would pick up the abnormal cancer cells, and these would enable a diagnosis to be made at an early stage when successful treatment is more likely.

Other than a slight ache low down in the abdomen, similar to a period cramp, there are no after-effects from a curette. Complications are rare, and the menstrual periods usually start again three to six weeks after the operation.
See also ABORTION; ASHERMAN SYNDROME; ENDOMETRIAL CARCINOMA; MENSTRUAL PERIODS HEAVY; MISCARRIAGE; UTERUS

CURVATURE OF THE SPINE
See ANKYLOSING SPONDYLITIS; KYPHOSCOLIOSIS; KYPHOSIS; SCOLIOSIS; SPINE; VERTEBRA

CUSHING SYNDROME
Cushing syndrome is also known as adrenocortical hyperfunction and hyperadrenocorticism. It is a syndrome resulting from excessive amounts of steroids in the blood.

The hypothalamus is the part of the brain that decides how much natural steroid is required. It sends nerve messages to the pituitary gland, which sits under the centre of the brain and it in turn sends a chemical message to the adrenal glands that sit on top of each kidney. The adrenals produce the steroids required by the body. Tumours or overactivity (may be triggered by pregnancy or stress) in the hypothalamus, pituitary gland or adrenal gland can result in the overproduction of steroids.

Cushing syndrome may also be due to taking excessive amounts of steroids (eg. prednisone) for medical reasons.

Patients develop a fat face, fatty deposits on the upper back (called a buffalo hump), obesity of the abdomen and chest with thin arms and legs, high blood pressure, impotence, cessation of menstrual periods, skin infections and pimples, headaches, backache, excess hair growth on the face and body, mood changes, excessive bruising, thinning of the bones (osteoporosis – which can cause bones to fracture easily), stretch marks on the breasts and abdomen, kidney stones, and generalised weakness. Strokes, heart attacks, broken bones, diabetes, increased susceptibility to infections (particularly of the skin and urine), and psychiatric diseases may be complications.

Complex blood tests can confirm the diagnosis, but finding the cause of the syndrome can be very difficult, and CT scans and magnetic resonance imaging (MRI) may be used to find very small tumours.

If a tumour can be found in the adrenal or pituitary gland, it is surgically removed. Other treatments include irradiation of the pituitary gland, or removal of both adrenal glands. Drug treatment is generally unsuccessful, but if both adrenal glands are removed it is necessary to supply steroids and other hormones by taking tablets or having injections regularly. If the Cushing syndrome is due to taking steroid medication, the dosage of this should be reduced if possible. Nelson syndrome (skin and tongue pigmentation, and enlargement of the pituitary gland under the brain) is a complication of treatment.

The prognosis depends on the cause. Some tumours of the adrenal or pituitary glands are very aggressive and spread to other areas to continue the syndrome, and these patients have a poor life expectancy. In others, a life-long cure may be obtained by removing a localised tumour. If caused by excessive steroid medication, the syndrome is cured by stopping the medication, but the patient may require the steroids for control of asthma, rheumatoid arthritis or other diseases, and they must tread a very narrow path between the side effects of the medication and the necessary treatment of a disease.
See also ADRENAL GLAND; BRAIN; HYPOPITUITARISM; PITUITARY GLAND; PSEUDOCUSHING SYNDROME

CUT
There are three essentials in dealing with any cut (laceration). The first is to stop bleeding, the second to prevent infection, and the third to repair the wound.

No matter how large the wound, the best way to stop bleeding is to apply pressure directly over the injury. Tourniquets should not be used. A piece of clean cloth several layers thick (eg. a clean folded handkerchief) is the best and usually most convenient dressing. Paper tissues tend to disintegrate and contaminate the wound.

The cloth should be applied over the bleeding area and held there firmly by the person giving first aid or the victim. If it is likely to be some time before further treatment can be given, the dressing can be held in place by a firm bandage, provided it is not so tight as to cause pain or restrict the supply of blood to the parts of the body beyond the bandage.

If an arm or a leg is involved, that part of the body should be elevated above the level of the heart. Unless the wound is minor, the patient should lie down to avoid fainting or shock.

Provided medical attention is readily available, no other first aid is necessary, as the doctor will ensure the cleanliness of the wound and its repair. If there is likely to be a significant delay before a doctor can be seen, it is prudent to clean any dirt out of the wound with a diluted antiseptic, or clean water if no antiseptic is available. Ensure that bleeding has stopped first, and do not disturb any clots that may have formed.

Minor cuts will heal without suturing, provided the edges of the wound are not gaping. If the edges do not lie comfortably together, if a joint surface is involved, if the wound continues to bleed, or if the scar may be cosmetically disfiguring, then it is essential to have the cut correctly repaired by taping or sutures.
See also BLEEDING; FIRST AID; SUTURING

CUTANEOUS LARVA MIGRANS
Cutaneous larva migrans, or creeping eruption, is a skin infestation by a larval nematode worm. The rash is caused by the burrowing of hookworm larvae through the skin. The larvae hatch from dog or cat faeces, mature in the soil and then penetrate human skin.

Patients develop red, very itchy, twisting tracks several centimetres long, in and under the skin. Large blisters may form later. Secondary bacterial infection of skin may occur due to damage by both the larvae and scratching.

A skin biopsy is sometimes used to make the diagnosis. Treatment involves medication by mouth and ointment to kill the larvae, and other creams to ease the skin irritation.

The larvae cannot mature in humans, and die after several weeks, and then the skin tracks slowly heal.
See also VISCERAL LARVA MIGRANS

CUTANEOUS LEISCHMANIASIS
Cutaneous leischmaniasis has numerous local names in different parts of the world including Chiclero's ulcers, Oriental sore and uta. It is an ulcerating skin infection caused by the protozoan (single celled animal) *Leischmania tropica, Leischmania aethiopica, Leischmania mexicana,* or *Leischmania peruviana* depending upon the geographic location. It is transmitted from one person to another by sand flies. Occurs throughout the tropics in Asia, Africa and particularly America.

The symptoms depend upon which protozoan is causing the disease, and vary from a self-healing ulcer (Oriental sore), to persistent multiple mutilating sores and ulcers (Chiclero's ulcers), or widespread non-ulcerating plaques on the skin. Secondary bacterial infection of sores can allow rapid spread of the protozoa and gross disfigurement.

Smears taken from the ulcer edge show the protozoan under a microscope, and specific blood tests may be positive.

Single ulcers are treated with heat packs, cryotherapy (freezing), radiotherapy or specific ointments. Widespread disease is difficult to treat but numerous medications may be tried. Antibiotics are given for secondary infections.

The prognosis depends on the infecting organism and form of disease. Single ulcers often heal after a few months, but widespread disease may be steadily progressive without treatment.
See also KALA-AZAR; PROTOZOA

CUTIS HYPERELASTICA
See EHLERS-DANLOS SYNDROME

CVA
See STROKE

CVS
See CHORIONIC VILLUS SAMPLING

CYANIDE
Correctly called hydrocyanic acid, cyanide is a potent poison that can be inhaled or swallowed. It has rapid toxic effects on many tissues in the body, causing them to fail due to an inability to process essential oxygen.

Cyanide is used in fumigation, photography, electroplating, rubber processing, metal cleaning and some other industries. It is found naturally in numerous seeds including cherry, plum, peach, pear and apricot. Lethal dose depends on form, but is about 250mg. of sodium cyanide.

The symptoms of poisoning include headache, fainting, dizziness, anxiety, rapid heart rate, burning in the mouth and throat, shortness of breath, high blood pressure, nausea, vomiting, bitter almond breath, coma, convulsions and finally death.

Some medications may be effective as an antidote. The emergency treatment is pure oxygen given by a close fitting mask. The prognosis depends on age, weight and fitness of patient, and dose of cyanide.
See also STRYCHNINE

CYANOCOBALAMIN
See VITAMIN B

CYANOSIS
See SKIN BLUE

CYCLOPENTOLATE
See MYDRIATICS

CYCLOSPORIN
See OTHER

CYCLOTHYMIA
See DEPRESSION

CYPROHEPTADINE
See ANTIHISTAMINES

CYST
A cyst is a fluid, semi-fluid or gas filled cavity within the body or on the skin.
See also BAKER'S CYST; BARTHOLIN CYST; HYDATID CYST; LIPOMA; MEIBOMIAN CYST; MYXOID CYST; NABOTHIAN CYST; OVARIAN CYST; POLYCYSTIC KIDNEY; POLYCYSTIC OVARIAN SYNDROME; SEBACEOUS CYST

CYSTIC FIBROSIS
Cystic fibrosis (fibrocystic disease) is a congenital disease of all mucus glands in the body due to genetic damage that occurs in one in every 2000 children. There is no known cause, and there is nothing parents can do to prevent the occurrence of the disease.

The symptoms are extremely varied because it is a disease of mucus glands throughout the body, but particularly those in the lungs and gut. In the lungs, the mucus becomes thick and sticky, the lungs clog up, become infected, and the lung tissue is destroyed. In the gut, excess mucus is produced, food cannot be absorbed correctly, and diarrhoea occurs. Because the glands in the reproductive organs are involved, these patients are usually sterile, and so cannot pass the disease on to their children. Glands in the skin produce sweat that is far saltier than that of normal people. Severe lung infections, lung damage and heart failure may eventually occur.

The diagnosis is confirmed by measuring the amount of salt in sweat, chest x-rays, abnormal lung function tests, and faeces tests. The condition cannot be detected before birth, but screening of parents to see if they are potential carriers is sometimes successful.

Treatment with physiotherapy several times every day to clear the lungs is critical. Antibiotics are used to treat lung infection, and medications to open up the airways (bronchodilators) and loosen the thick mucus (mucolytics) are prescribed. Regular vaccination against lung infections are essential. As a final solution, a heart and lung transplant may be performed.

There is no cure, and the outcome depends on the patient's dedication to following a comprehensive treatment program. Many survive into their thirties with continued intensive therapy, and with lung and heart transplants, a long life is possible.
See also LUNG

CYSTITIS
Cystitis is an infection of the urinary bladder that usually occurs in women, with less than 10% occurring in men because of the longer length of their urethra (the tube leading from the bladder to the outside).

A bacterial infection can enter the bladder by coming up the urethra from outside the body, or through the bloodstream to the kidneys and then the bladder. Entry from the outside is far more common, and often due to irritation of the urethra with sex. Slackness of the muscle ring that controls the release of urine from the bladder can also allow bacteria to enter the bladder. This damage may be caused by childbirth or prolapse of the womb, and may eventually cause incontinence during a cough or laugh.

The symptoms include burning pain on passing urine, pain in the pelvis, the desire to pass urine very frequently and blood may be seen in the urine. The infection may spread up the ureters to the kidneys to cause acute pyelonephritis.

The urine can be cultured to identify the responsible bacteria and correct antibiotic. Further investigations such as x-rays and ultrasound scans of the bladder and kidneys may be performed, to exclude more serious causes of recurrent cystitis.

Appropriate antibiotic tablets for a week or two, and urinary alkalinisers (in the form of a powder that makes a fizzy drink) result in a rapid cure in most patients. Drinking extra fluid will help wash the infection out of the bladder, while passing urine immediately after sex sometimes prevents infections.
See also ALKALINISERS; BLADDER; INTERSTITIAL CYSTITIS; PYELONEPHRITIS, ACUTE

CYSTOCOELE
See VAGINAL PROLAPSE

CYTOMEGALOVIRUS INFECTION
A cytomegalovirus (CMV) infection is an extremely common viral infection affecting between 10% and 25% of the entire population at any one time. The infection rate may be in excess of 80% in homosexual men. It may be a serious illness in patients who have reduced immunity due to treatment with cytotoxic drugs for cancer, have suffered other serious illnesses, are anaemic, suffering from AIDS or other immune affecting diseases, or who are extremely run-down from stress or overwork.

The virus passes from one person to another in saliva or as droplets in the breath, but may also spread through blood transfusions or sexual contact. In all but a tiny percentage of infected people, there are absolutely no symptoms, and they appear and feel totally well. Adults with reduced immunity develop a fever, headaches, overwhelming tiredness, muscle and joint pains, enlarged lymph nodes and a tender liver. In patients with severely reduced immunity, pneumonia and hepatitis may develop.

If a pregnant woman with reduced immunity acquires a significant CMV infection, her baby may be affected in the womb and be born with liver damage (jaundice), enlarged liver and spleen, poor ability to clot blood, bruises, mental retardation, and one in six are deaf.

The infection can be detected by specific blood tests, and the virus may be found in sputum, saliva, urine and other body fluids.

There is no specific treatment. Aspirin and/or paracetamol are used to control fever and pain, and prolonged rest is required for recovery.

An uneventful recovery is expected in normal patients. In immune compromised patients, pneumonia and hepatitis may be fatal.

See also VIRUS

CYSTOSCOPY

A cystoscopy is an examination of the inside of the bladder and urethra. The end of a thin tube called a cystoscope is inserted through the urethra (the tube linking the bladder with the outside) into the bladder, where the combination of light and magnification enables the doctor to observe any abnormalities, such as stones, tumours or disorders of the bladder lining.

In men, a cystoscope may be used in the investigation of cancer of the prostate. The man will be given an anaesthetic, general or local, depending on the circumstances, and the tiny tube will be gently guided up through the penis until it reaches the prostate, which is situated at the base of the bladder.

Small tumours or stones can often be removed by means of a special instrument inserted through the cystoscope and if so, there will be no need for surgery.

Fine tubes called catheters can be passed along a cystoscope and guided into each ureter (the tubes leading from the bladder up to the kidneys). This enables a specimen of urine to be obtained from each kidney so that the doctor can find out which one is diseased.

See also BLADDER; ENDOSCOPE; PROSTATE GLAND; URETHRA

CYTARABINE
See CYTOTOXICS AND ANTINEOPLASTICS

CYTOPERONE
See CONTRACEPTIVE PILL

CYTOTOXICS AND ANTINEOPLASTICS

The cytotoxics and antineoplastics form a large, diverse group of drugs (very few will be listed here) that are used to destroy cancer cells within the body in a process known as chemotherapy. 'Cyto' means cell, so 'cytotoxic' means toxic (harmful) to cells, while antineoplastic means 'against cancer'. These drugs can be given by tablet or injection, and different drugs are used to attack different types of cancer. Unfortunately they are not all as specific in attacking cancer cells as we would wish, and normal cells may also be attacked and destroyed. The balance between giving enough of the drug to kill the cancer cells and not enough to kill too many normal cells is a very fine one.

The effectiveness of cytotoxic drugs varies dramatically from one patient to another and one disease to another. Some forms of cancer are very susceptible to cytotoxic drugs (eg. acute leukaemias), while others are resistant. Side effects are very common, and again variable. Nausea, vomiting, diarrhoea, belly pain, mouth ulcers, rash, infertility, muscle pain, loss of hair, weight loss, fatigue and headaches are just a few of the many complications possible. Patients taking this type of medication will be closely monitored by their doctors through regular blood tests and clinic visits. Long-term treatment for many months is usually required, and other medications may be added to control the side effects.

Examples include bleomycin, carmustine, chlorambucil, cisplatin, cytarabine, daunorubicin, etoposide, fosfestrol, goserelin, mercaptopurine, methotrexate and tamoxifen.

See also CANCER; MEDICATION

D

D & C
See CURETTE

da COSTA SYNDROME
The da Costa syndrome is a heart function abnormality that is also known as the effort syndrome. It is characterised by persistent palpitations that are triggered by anxiety, exercise or stress, but have no other sinister underlying cause.

An ECG (electrocardiogram) shows a rapid heart rate but no other abnormality, and the blood pressure shows a high systolic and low diastolic reading (wide pulse pressure).

The syndrome is resistant to psychiatric care and beta-blocker medications are used to successfully control the symptoms, but cure is difficult.
See also HEART; PALPITATIONS

DANAZOL
See SEX HORMONES

DANDRUFF
Dandruff is a very common form of scalp irritation. It is actually a disease in itself, but most people describe a scalp that is shedding copious quantities of skin scale as dandruff.

Over a period of a few weeks, the skin totally replaces itself. New cells are produced deep in the skin, slowly move out as new cells are produced beneath them, thin out to form a hard scaly layer, and eventually slough off. Dandruff is an acceleration of this natural process in which the rate at which cells are produced on the scalp is increased, so that the excess cells produced form a scale on the skin. The underlying skin may become inflamed and itchy. It is thought that a mild fungal infection of the scalp causes this increased rate of cell loss. Emotional stress, overworking, hot climates and a poor diet all aggravate dandruff.

Dandruff must be differentiated from other skin diseases such as psoriasis, dermatitis, eczema, neurodermatitis and other fungal infections. A biopsy is sometimes necessary to make the diagnosis.

Seborrhoeic dermatitis is an inflammation of the scalp that is more common in babies, when it is known as cradle cap.

Good scalp hygiene, and an antidandruff lotion or shampoo are the main treatments, but excessive use of shampoos or soap may aggravate the problem by further drying and irritating the scalp. Resistant cases may be helped by steroid scalp lotions and antifungal lotions or gels.

Most patients have recurrences, with bad and good periods, often for no apparent reason, but reasonable control is normally possible.
See also PSORIASIS; SEBORRHOEIC ECZEMA; SKIN; TINEA CAPITIS

DANDY-WALKER SYNDROME
The Dandy-Walker syndrome is a rare brain developmental abnormality, in which there is failure of the central portion of the cerebellum (lower back part of brain) to develop.

Children with the condition have a very large head, vomiting, irritability, poor head control, cleft palate, and abnormal side to side eye movements (nystagmus). Some patients have an abnormal way of walking (gait), headaches, multiple cysts in the kidneys, abnormal lumbar vertebrae, subnormal mentality and delayed muscle control.

MRI and CT scans of the skull are abnormal and can be used to confirm the diagnosis.

Brain surgery may prevent further deterioration of symptoms, but there is no cure.
See also BRAIN; CEREBELLUM

DANTROLENE
See MUSCLE RELAXANTS

DARIER DISEASE
A rare skin condition that usually starts between eight and fifteen years of age, Darier disease affects the face, back, scalp, groin and armpits. It is an inherited disorder causing the production of abnormal keratin (hardening substance in skin) that may worsen with heat and sweating.

Patients develop small, brown, firm lumps

on the skin that slowly enlarge and become covered in greasy scales. They may appear as small pits on the soles and palms. The diagnosis can be confirmed by a skin biopsy.

Salicylic acid and retinoic acid ointments are used in treatment.

In serious cases the lumps in the skin may merge together to form a hard crusted plaque, and the nails become brittle, ridged and discoloured in persistent cases. Secondary bacterial infections may also occur. The syndrome may be associated with subnormal mentality and reduced height in some patients.

In the early stages, the disease may settle spontaneously, but if it becomes prolonged the disease is difficult to control.
See also SKIN

DARIER'S SIGN
See URTICARIA PIGMENTOSA

DATE OF DELIVERY
See PREGNANCY DATES

DAUNORUBICIN
See CYTOTOXICS AND ANTINEOPLASTICS

DAY SURGERY
Day surgery is becoming increasingly common for procedures as varied as in-vitro fertilisation, cataracts, gastroscopy and hernia repairs. The patient attends the day surgery centre early on the day of operation, a light general anaesthetic or other form of anaesthetic is administered, the operation is performed, and after a few hours of recovery, the patient can go home again.
See also GENERAL ANAESTHETIC; SURGERY and separate entries for procedures mentioned above.

DE-
A prefix derived from the Latin and used in medicine to indicate down or away (eg. depressed, dementia, defaecation).

DEAF
It is hard for most of us to imagine a totally silent world, and there are actually very few people classified as deaf who can hear absolutely nothing. Most deaf people hear a blur of noise that is not quite comprehensible, and this can be more annoying than total silence. The worst affected are those who cannot hear any intelligible sound, and are sufferers from tinnitus (a constant buzzing in the ears).

If excessive quantities of wax, or a foreign body (eg. tiny toy or foam packing ball in children) blocks the outer ear canal, hearing will be reduced in that ear.

The gradual decrease in hearing associated with advancing age is the most common form of deafness. This is basically due to thickening of the ear drum, wear and tear on the tiny bones that conduct the vibrations of the ear drum to the hearing apparatus in the inner ear, and a loss of sensitivity in the spiral tube that senses the vibrations, and turns them into nerve impulses in the brain. The higher frequencies of sound disappear first, and this cuts out a lot of hearing discrimination, so that conversation in a noisy room melts into a constant blur of sound.

Middle ear infections (otitis media) are a very common cause of temporary deafness in children that, if left untreated, may progress to glue ear and a permanent partial loss of hearing.

Any infection of the nose, sinuses or throat may cause partial deafness due to pressure on the Eustachian tube, which connects the middle ear to the back of the nose, and normally opens to allow equalisation of air pressure with changes in altitude.

The ear drum may be damaged and rupture with changes in air pressure (barotrauma) that cannot be equalised because of a blocked Eustachian tube. Diving and flying are the common causes for this problem, particularly if there is a rapid change in pressure.

Direct injury to the ear drum may occur from trying to clean the ear with a bobby pin or cotton bud, or a sharp object accidentally entering the ear. Rarely, the delicate bony mechanism inside the ear may also be injured, leading to permanent deafness.

Ménière's disease may occur after a head injury or ear infection, but in most patients it has no apparent cause. It is more common in men, and with advancing age. The cause is a build-up in the pressure of the fluid inside the hearing and balance mechanisms of the inner ear. The increase in pressure causes a constant high-pitched ringing noise (tinnitus) in the ear. Other symptoms include dizziness,

EAR

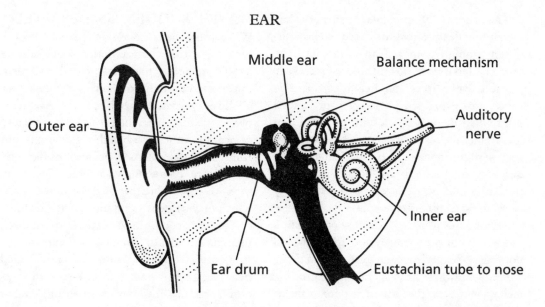

Outer ear

Middle ear

Balance mechanism

Auditory nerve

Inner ear

Ear drum

Eustachian tube to nose

nausea and slowly progressive permanent deafness.

Uncommon causes of deafness include otosclerosis, a cholesteatoma (foul smelling growth in the ear), bony growths in the outer ear canal (exostoses), a fracture of the skull around the ear and a lack of thyroxine (hypothyroidism).

A number of medications may have temporary (or very rarely, permanent) deafness as a side effect. These include aspirin, beta-blockers (used for high blood pressure and heart disease), quinine, aminoglycosides (an antibiotic) and cancer treating drugs (cytotoxics).

Numerous generalised infections, such as measles, mumps and meningitis, may cause temporary or permanent deafness.

Infection of a woman in the early months of pregnancy with german measles (rubella), cytomegalovirus or toxoplasmosis may affect her unborn child to cause permanent and total deafness.

Total deafness in an ear is usually associated with congenital (developmental) defects, surgery to the ear, severe head injuries or tumours in or around the ear.
See also EAR; EUSTACHIAN TUBE; TINNITUS; TYMPANIC RUPTURE and separate entries for diseases mentioned above.

DEATH

Until recently, death was defined as occurring when breathing ceased and the heart stopped beating. Modern advances in methods of resuscitation and artificial respiration, however, have led to the need to rethink the definition. It is now possible for the heart to be kept beating and breathing to be maintained by machines, and unless the brain has ceased to function the person may recover and start breathing independently again. Consequently death is now defined as the cessation of electrical activity in the brain. Once this has occurred, there is no possibility of the person ever regaining consciousness, and life has ceased.

The process of death is essentially due to a lack of blood, and thus oxygen, first in the brain and spinal cord and then in the rest of the body. If the brain is deprived of oxygen for only about five minutes, it will be irreversibly damaged.

From the patient's perspective, death is usually similar to slipping into a deep sleep – calm and painless.

In death, the body is still, movement and respiration are absent, no pulse can be felt or heart sounds heard over the chest. The eyes are glazed. The pupils are dilated, and when light is shone into them there is no response. Within minutes, the body starts to feel cold, the skin turns pale and blood drains down to the lower part of the body (causing the flanks and buttocks to discolour). Within a period of about four hours, the body becomes stiff as the stored energy is released, causing the muscles to contract – rigor mortis. This may last for 48 hours, but it may be considerably less than this. After death many of the cell membranes break down and decomposition sets in.

The advent of transplant surgery has meant that death sometimes needs to be diagnosed promptly, since if an organ is to be transplanted it must be removed as quickly as possible while it is still healthy. A fear is sometimes expressed of being pronounced dead when there is still a faint possibility of life. In fact the tests carried out by doctors in such circumstances are quite clear-cut and definite, and there is no possibility that a person would be declared dead when they were, in fact, still alive.

About two thirds of deaths occur in a hospital or nursing home, and the staff will normally be experienced in dealing with dying patients and their needs. There is a growing feeling, however, that unless a person needs specialised hospital care, dying at home amid familiar surroundings is preferable to the inevitably impersonal surroundings of a hospital. In recent times there has been a growth in the number of hospices – small hospitals devoted entirely to the care of the terminally ill. These provide expert nursing care, control of pain and other symptoms, and emotional support for both the dying patient and the family.

After death, certain legal formalities must be followed. A doctor must issue a certificate stating the cause of death. If the person has died after a long illness, the attending doctor will normally complete the certificate as a matter of course, but in other cases or if there are any suspicious circumstances the coroner will be informed. The coroner may order a post-mortem examination to determine the cause of death, and if this raises further questions, an inquest (inquiry into the death by the court) may be ordered.

When a medical certificate is issued, it must be taken to the registrar of births, deaths and marriages, generally within about a week, and a death certificate will be issued. A death certificate is required before a funeral can be held and before the deceased's will can be dealt with. A further certificate will be necessary if a cremation is to be performed.
See also BEREAVEMENT; CHEYNE-STOKES RESPIRATION; DEATH, SUDDEN UNEXPECTED; ELECTROENCEPHALOGRAM; EUTHANASIA; ICHABOD SYNDROME; MORTALITY; PALLIATIVE CARE

DEATH, SUDDEN UNEXPECTED

When someone is elderly, or has been very ill for some time, some emotional preparation can be made for the death, but the sudden, unexpected death of someone is distressing for all those associated with the patient. Accidents of various forms are the most common cause of death in otherwise healthy individuals, but sometimes disease may be responsible, and even more distressingly, suicide. There are many diseases, particularly those of the heart, which may cause sudden unexpected death.

The most common causes of sudden unexpected death include a heart attack (myocardial infarct), failure of an enlarged heart (cardiomyopathy) from long term high blood pressure, myocarditis (a serious viral or bacterial heart muscle infection), pericarditis (inflammation or infection of the pericardial sac that surrounds and supports the heart), damage to the valves within the heart (eg. aortic valve), aortic aneurysm rupture, and a stroke (cerebrovascular accident).

In children, cot death (sudden infant death syndrome – SIDS) is the sudden unexpected death of an apparently normal healthy child in whom a subsequent detailed post-mortem examination reveals no cause for the death. Two or three out of every 1000 children between the ages of one month and one year will die from this distressing condition. Abnormalities of the heart valves, structure or arteries may have minimal symptoms in a child, and be undetectable until the heart suddenly fails to cope with the child's growing body.
See also BEREAVEMENT; DEATH; HEART and separate entries for diseases mentioned above.

DECA-DURABOLIN
See ANABOLIC STEROIDS

de CLERAMBAULT SYNDROME

Also known as erotomania, de Clerambault syndrome takes the form of a fixed single-minded psychiatric delusion (monomania).

Patients usually have an inadequate, dependent personality, often after a period of real dependency on a person (eg. doctor during pregnancy and labour). They have a fixed delusional conviction that another is in love with them despite minimal contact. The majority of patients are female and may persecute or stalk the victim, who is often a doctor, film star, sportsman or other famous person.

There is no diagnostic test, and the condition is diagnosed by psychiatric assessment.

Psychoanalysis, and drugs such as phenothiazines and clomipramine are used in treatment.

Legal action may need to be taken to stop stalking, and the person who is the object of affection is sometimes attacked and harmed if advances are rejected.

Treatment is extremely difficult and often unsuccessful, and certification is occasionally necessary.
See also NEUROSES

DECONGESTANTS

Decongestants relieve stuffy noses, ease tight coughs and loosen mucus plugs. They are contained in a large number of proprietary cough and cold mixtures, tablets and nose drops, and work with varying degrees of efficacy.

Examples include oxymetazoline, phenylephrine and pseudoephedrine.

Side effects may include nose burn, sneezing, dry nose, insomnia, rapid heart and over excitement. They should be used with care in patients with hypertension, and are not designed for long term use.
See also COLD, COMMON; MEDICATION; VASOCONSTRICTORS

DEEP VEIN THROMBOSIS

A deep vein thrombosis (DVT) is a blood clot (thrombosis) in one of the veins deep inside the calf or thigh muscles. Since 2000 this has also been given the nickname 'economy class syndrome' due to the risks of developing a blood clot on long distance flights in cramped conditions.

The clot may occur more commonly after surgery, with heart failure, poor circulation, cancer, varicose veins, or as an uncommon side effect of oral contraceptives, but often there is no apparent cause.

The patient experiences pain and tightness in the calf which is worse when walking. It may be diagnosed by ultrasound scan or special x-ray (venogram) of the leg. Blood tests can show that there is a blood clot somewhere in the body, but not its location.

Anticoagulant drugs, elevation of the legs,

firm elastic stockings and strict bed rest are the main treatments. In complex or persistent cases surgery may be undertaken to remove the clot or prevent its spread to the lungs. As a form of prevention, patients having major operations may be given special stockings to wear during and after the operation, the foot of the bed may be elevated, and leg exercises encouraged. After a thrombosis, further clots may be prevented by low dose aspirin or medications such as warfarin.

If the clot in the veins becomes fragile, small pieces may break off and travel to the heart and then into the lungs where one of the small lung (pulmonary) arteries becomes blocked (pulmonary embolism). The lung beyond this blockage then dies which may have serious effects for the patient. Women who have had blood clots anywhere in the body should not use the contraceptive pill.

With appropriate treatment, most patients recover in four to six weeks without complications.
See also ANTICOAGULANTS; BLOOD CLOTTING TEST; POSTPHLEBITIC SYNDROME; PULMONARY EMBOLISM; SUPERFICIAL VENOUS THROMBOSIS; THROMBOSIS; ULTRASOUND

DEFAECATION

Defaecation is the act of passing faeces through the anus. A literal Latin translation would be 'faeces away'.
See also ANUS; FAECES; GASTRO-COLIC REFLEX

DEFIBRINATION SYNDROME

The defibrination syndrome is an uncommon life threatening abnormality of blood clotting.

It may be caused by a very severe infection, or shock after an accident may cause inappropriate blood clotting within arteries and veins. This causes the level of fibrinogen in the blood to drop to a low level. Fibrinogen is essential for the clotting of blood, so patients with this critical problem, then start to bleed profusely. Rarely it may follow childbirth.

After suffering excessive internal clotting which may affect their brain, heart, lungs, limbs and other organs, patients start to bleed excessively internally (eg. into the gut and kidney), externally (eg. intractable nose bleeds) and into the skin (eg. massive bruises).

The condition can be diagnosed by specific blood tests.

Treatment involves the rapid transfusion of freshly donated compatible blood and other blood concentrates to stop bleeding, heparin given intravenously to stop abnormal clotting, and treating the underlying cause of the syndrome if possible. Unfortunately, permanent organ damage is common in the few survivors. *See also* BLOOD; SHOCK

DEHYDRATION
Dehydration is a lack of water in the body. As the human body is almost 70% (7/10ths) water, even a small drop in the total amount of water in the body can have significant effects.

Patients who lose less than 5% (1/20th) of their body water will feel thirsty, have a dry mouth, but few other symptoms.

More severe dehydration resulting in a loss of 5% to 10% (1/10th) of the body water will cause sunken eyes, loose skin, rapid heart rate, minimal passing of urine, and depression of the soft spot at the front of a baby's skull.

Dehydration in excess of 10% may be life threatening, particularly in children. Symptoms include altered mood, poor concentration, drowsiness, irritability, weak pulse, cold white hands and feet, loose folds of skin and eventually loss of consciousness.

Dehydration may be caused by loss of fluid in diarrhoea, copious vomiting, excessive sweating (eg. exercise, heat) which also causes a loss of sodium in salt, passing excess urine (eg. taking too many fluid tablets, diabetes insipidus and other diseases); or by lack of fluid intake, usually when fluids are not readily available.

Blood tests can accurately determine the degree of dehydration.

Treatment involves giving a solution of water and electrolytes (vital elements) by mouth if possible, or intravenously. In an emergency, a mixture containing a level teaspoon of salt and eight level teaspoons of sugar or glucose in a litre of boiled water may be given by mouth. Plain water should not be given, as it will pass straight through the body. Because of their lower body weight, children will dehydrate far more rapidly than adults.

A decrease of 5% in water volume can cause significant disease, and a 10% loss may be fatal in children. Fortunately there is a very good response to correct treatment.

See also DIARRHOEA; HEAT STROKE; SWEATING, EXCESS; SODIUM; VOMITING AND NAUSEA

DEJA VU
Deja vu is a feeling of intense familiarity when encountering an unfamiliar situation, person or place. It is a normal phenomenon that occurs occasionally in all people, but when it occurs regularly, it may be a sign of significant disease.

Some forms of epilepsy, particularly petit-mal epilepsy, in which there are momentary absences of concentration rather than any form of convulsion, may have deja vu as a common characteristic.

A stroke (cerebrovascular accident) may also have temporary deja vu as an accompanying phenomenon.

Patients who have experienced severe stress, fear, a bad accident or assault may suffer from the post traumatic stress syndrome. Symptoms may include sleeplessness, nightmares, intrusive thoughts, anxiety, loss of concentration, depression, withdrawal from friends and activities, confusion, recurrent minor illnesses, poor general health and abnormal perceptions which may be described as deja vu.

Numerous psychiatric conditions may have deja vu as a symptom. Schizophrenia is the most common mental disease to do this as it causes the sufferer to have a distorted view of the world because of delusions and hallucinations.

If the problem is persistent, epilepsy medications in very low doses are usually very effective.
See also EPILEPSY; POST-TRAUMATIC STRESS DISORDER and separate entries for other diseases mentioned above.

de LANGE SYNDROME
The de Lange syndrome is an uncommon congenital cause of dwarfism that is also known as Amsterdam dwarfism, and Brachmann-de Lange syndrome.

These children have a small head, severe mental retardation, bushy eyebrows that meet in centre, low birth weight and failure to thrive, low hair line, and excess hair on the skin. There are no specific diagnostic tests and no treatment is available. Patients rarely survive beyond ten years.
See also GROWTH REDUCED

DELIRIUM TREMENS

Delirium tremens (DTs) is a complication of alcoholism that occurs when an alcoholic is deprived of alcohol. Symptoms may start within twenty-four to seventy-two hours and include mental confusion, tremor, hallucinations, excessive sensitivity to all sensations, body chemistry disturbances, sweating, occasionally seizures and rarely death. Body chemistry disorders may be detected by blood tests.

Medications to reverse adverse effects of alcohol withdrawal are given, along with intravenous fluids and observation in hospital.

The DTs can be successfully managed in hospital, but may be dangerous in other situations.
See also ALCOHOL; ALCOHOLISM

DEMENTIA

Dementia is a mental disorder in which the patient develops confusion, irrational behaviour, inappropriate reactions, poor or jumbled speech patterns, hallucinations (both visual and auditory) and loss of short term memory. Some patients become uninhibited in their language and habits, and may act in a socially unacceptable manner. Symptoms are often worse at night. It is a permanent condition, as opposed to confusion, which may be temporary.

By far the most common cause of dementia in the elderly is Alzheimer disease (senile dementia or second childhood), but unfortunately it may strike as early as the mid-fifties and cause extreme distress to spouses, family and friends. It is characterised by loss of recent memory, loss of initiative, reduced physical activity, confusion, loss of orientation (patients become confused about where they are and dates), and then it gradually progresses to loss of speech, difficulty in swallowing (drooling results), stiff muscles, incontinence of both faeces and urine, and a bedridden state in which the patient is totally unaware of themselves or anything that is happening around them. It is caused by a faster than normal loss of nerve cells in the brain.

Damage to the brain from an injury (eg. fractured skull), lack of oxygen (eg. near drowning), essential surgery, abscess, tumour or cancer may affect brain function to cause dementia at any age.

In a stroke (cerebrovascular accident) part of the brain is affected by having its blood supply cut off by a blockage in an artery, or a blood vessel in the brain may burst causing bleeding and damage to part of the brain including dementia of sudden onset.

The brain is supported and completely surrounded by a three-layered membrane (the meninges) which contain the cerebrospinal fluid. If these meninges are infected by a virus or bacteria (meningitis) the patient may experience headache, fever, fits, neck stiffness and in severe cases may suffer permanent brain damage. Encephalitis is an infection of the brain tissue itself that may be confused with meningitis as it has similar symptoms and consequences.

Less common causes of dementia include hydrocephalus (increased pressure of the fluid within the brain), pernicious anaemia, failure of the kidneys (uraemia), liver failure, AIDS, Wernicke-Korsakoff syndrome (often secondary to alcoholism), punch drunk syndrome (from boxing), and a number of poisons such as organophosphates (in insecticides), glue sniffing, and drugs (eg. amphetamines, barbiturates) which may cause permanent damage to the brain.

There are many other rare causes of dementia.

There are no diagnostic blood or other tests, but in advanced stages, a CT scan of the brain will show abnormalities.

The patient should be kept in a pleasant, safe, non-threatening environment with adequate medical, nursing, physiotherapy, occupational therapy and general support services. Medications may be given for irrational behaviour, hallucinations and violent tempers, but do not affect the disease process.

Unfortunately there is no cure for most causes, and patients progressively deteriorate.
See also ALZHEIMER DISEASE; ANTIPSYCHOTICS; BRAIN; CONFUSION; DIOGENES SYNDROME and separate entries for diseases mentioned above.

DEMONS-MEIGS SYNDROME
See MEIGS SYNDROME

DENGUE FEVER

Dengue (or breakbone) fever is a generalised viral infection that is very common in many tropical countries of the world. The virus spreads from person to person by the bite of the Aedes mosquito, and the incubation period is usually three to seven days, but may stretch out to two weeks.

Symptoms include the sudden onset of a high fever, chills, and a severe aching of the back, head and legs (thus breakbone fever). Over the next few days a sore throat, blotchy skin and depression develop. These symptoms then totally cease for a day or two, before the second phase of the disease commences. This is similar to the first phase, but generally milder, and is usually accompanied by a rash that starts on the hands and feet and spreads to cover the entire body with the exception of the face. In severe cases, skin bleeding, and bleeding into the gut with accompanying diarrhoea can occur.

The diagnosis can be confirmed by specific blood tests, but there is no cure and no vaccine. Aspirin and anti-inflammatories (eg. ibuprofen) are given for fevers and pains, and prolonged rest is required. Patients may become dehydrated because of diarrhoea, and require fluid replacement.

Eventually complete recovery occurs, but may take several months.
See also MUSCLE PAIN; VIRUS

DENTAL PLAQUE
Dental plaque, like dental decay, is preventable in most people. Plaque is a soft deposit around the teeth caused by bacteria in the mouth which can and should be constantly removed as it forms. Some of it is removed naturally. At one time when diets were more natural, a good deal was removed by the action of tough and fibrous foods. Wild animals and native tribes use this method, but modern man and domesticated animals need some further assistance. A professional mechanical removal with a scaler can be maintained by constant polishing with a very soft toothbrush, dental floss and soft wooden stimulators.

If plaque is left to accumulate, it causes irritation to the gums and bone. In many cases it is converted by other bacteria into a hard deposit called tartar or calculus, which no amount of brushing will remove. It must be scaled off with a sharp instrument by a dental hygienist, dentist, or periodontist (a dental specialist in this field). If left, tartar or calculus traps more plaque which is harder to remove and in turn becomes more calculus. Some

people can build up enormous deposits in a very short time. Hard calculus deposits can trap not only plaque but food debris which can putrefy and cause bad breath or halitosis. Regular professional removal of calculus enables most people to keep their teeth clean, polished and healthy. Gums that are irritated by plaque or calculus become inflamed and suffer from gingivostomatitis.
See also DENTISTRY; GINGIVOSTOMATITIS; GUM PAIN; PERIODONTICS; MOUTH; STOMATITIS; TEETH

DENTISTRY
Dentistry is the art and science of caring for the teeth and jaws and their related structures by university-trained dentists supported by various auxiliaries, such as dental hygienists and dental technicians. The dental specialities include paedodontics (children's dentistry), endodontics (root fillings), periodontics (gum diseases), orthodontics (tooth straightening), prosthodontics (dentures and bridges), and oral and maxillofacial surgery (surgery of the mouth and jaws).
See also DENTAL PLAQUE; FLUORIDATION; ORTHODONTICS; PAEDODONTICS; PERIODONTICS; TEETH; TOOTH DISCOLOURED; TOOTH LOOSE

DEOXYRIBONUCLEIC ACID
See DNA

DEPIGMENTED SKIN
See ALBINISM; SKIN DEPIGMENTED

DEPRESSION
Depression is also known as an affective disorder, melancholia or a nervous breakdown. It is a medical condition, not just a state of mind, which affects 30% of people at some time in their life. Patients are not able to pull themselves together and overcome the depression without medical aid, although a determination to improve the situation certainly helps the outcome.

Depression may be a symptom (having a bad day and feeling sad), personality type (inherited with the genes), reaction (depressed because of loss of job, death in family etc.) or a disease (depression due to chemical imbalances in the brain). It is usually a mixture of several of these.

There are two main types of depression, endogenous and reactive, with very different causes.

Endogenous depression has no obvious reason for the constant unhappiness, and patients slowly become sadder and sadder, more irritable, unable to sleep, lose appetite and weight, and feel there is no purpose in living. They may feel unnecessarily guilty, have a very poor opinion of themselves, feel life is hopeless and find it difficult to think or concentrate. After several months they usually improve, but sometimes it can take years. It is due to an imbalance of chemicals that normally occur in the brain to control mood. If too much of one chemical is produced, the patient becomes depressed – if too much of another, the patient becomes manic. They are not able to pull themselves together and overcome the depression without medical aid, but doctors can alter the abnormal chemical balance by giving antidepressant medications. When they do start to improve, some patients with depression go too far the other way and become over-happy or manic. These patients are said to be manic depressive, have bipolar personality (generally severe swings of mood) or cyclothymic disorder (milder mood changes).

Reactive depression is the sadness that occurs after a death in the family, loss of a job, a marriage break-up or other disaster. Patients are depressed for a definite reason, and with time, will be often be able to cope with the situation, although some patients do require medical help.

There are no diagnostic blood tests or brain scans to prove these diagnoses, and the final diagnosis depends on the clinical acumen of the doctor.

There are many other causes of depression that overlap between the two types above or have totally independent causes.

The elderly often become depressed because they are confused, ill, unable to sleep as well as they would like, in discomfort, have no pleasure in life and can see no future. A change in attitude, environment and a bit of medication may often change their outlook dramatically.

The hormonal changes associated with pregnancy and menopause are often triggers for significant clinical depression. Postnatal depression usually occurs just after the birth of a child, with the sudden drop in the level of hormones. The mother feels inadequate, helpless and unable to cope. Urgent medical assistance is vital. In the menopause, the varying hormone levels may cause wide variations in mood that can be corrected by hormone replacement therapy.

Many women find that the normal sex hormone variations during the month will also cause mood changes, with depression and irritability being particularly common just before a menstrual period (premenstrual tension – PMT).

Many other diseases may have depression as a component, but doctors must be careful to differentiate between depression caused by the disease process itself, and depression in the patient because they are upset at having the disease.

Possible medical causes for depression include a tumour, cyst, abscess, cancer or infection of the brain; a stroke (cerebrovascular accident); hypothyroidism (a lack of thyroxine); Parkinson disease (a degeneration of part of the brain that co-ordinates muscle movement); serious viral infections (eg. AIDS, hepatitis, influenza, glandular fever); pernicious anaemia; systemic lupus erythematosus (an autoimmune disease); multiple sclerosis (a nerve disease that can affect any nerve in the body in a random and intermittent way); and abnormalities in the levels of potassium, sodium, bicarbonate and chloride (electrolytes) in the blood due to kidney or other diseases.

A number of medications may have depression as a side effect, including cortisone, methyldopa (used for high blood pressure), beta blockers (used for heart disease) and various hormones (including the contraceptive pill).

There are many rarer medical causes of depression.

Numerous medications (antidepressants) that control the production or activity of the depressing chemicals in the brain are available to treat depression, but most antidepressant drugs work slowly over several weeks. Hospitalisation in order to use high doses of drugs or other treatments, and to protect the patient from the possibility of suicide, is sometimes necessary when the disease is first diagnosed.

The other form of treatment used is shock therapy (electroconvulsive therapy – ECT), which is a safe and often very effective method of giving relief to patients with severe chronic depression.

Untreated depression may lead to attempted or actual suicide, which can be seen as a desperate plea for help.

Depression is not a diagnosis that patients should fear, as medication and counselling by a general practitioner, psychologist or psychiatrist will cure or control the vast majority of cases.
See also ANTIDEPRESSANTS; BIPOLAR AFFECTIVE DISORDER; ELECTROCONVULSIVE THERAPY; MANIA; NEUROSES; POSTNATAL DEPRESSION; PREMENSTRUAL TENSION; SEASONAL AFFECTIVE DISORDER and separate entries for other diseases mentioned above.

DEPRESSION MEDICATIONS
See ANTIDEPRESSANTS

de QUERVAIN TENOSYNOVITIS
De Quervain tenosynovitis (or tenovaginitis) is an inflammatory condition of the wrist caused by repetitive wrist action. The prominent bone (radial styloid) at the side of the wrist above the thumb becomes painful, tender and swollen, and there is pain with wrist movement.

Anti-inflammatory medications, rest (in a splint if necessary), and steroid injections around the radial styloid are the main forms of treatment. There is a good response to treatment.
See also CARPAL TUNNEL SYNDROME; WRIST PAIN

de QUERVAIN THYROIDITIS
De Quervain thyroiditis (or sub-acute thyroiditis) is a relatively common form of thyroid gland inflammation that occurs most commonly in women between twenty-five and forty-five, and is thought to be the result of a viral infection.

Patients experience painful swelling of the thyroid gland at the front of the neck, pain around the neck to the ears, difficulty in swallowing and symptoms of hyperthyroidism such as rapid heart rate and excess sweating.

The condition is diagnosed by blood tests and biopsy of the thyroid gland, but there is no specific cure available. Aspirin usually relieves the pain and swelling, and propranolol controls the thyrotoxicosis. Complications may include heart damage from the excess production of thyroid hormone.

Satisfactory control of the thyroid inflammation is usually possible, and it settles spontaneously with time.
See also HYPERTHYROIDISM; THYROID GLAND; THYROIDITIS

DERMATITIS
Any inflammation of the skin can be called dermatitis, so there are many different types of dermatitis.

It is often very difficult to determine any cause, for although the skin is the most visible of our organs, its diseases are very diverse and often difficult to diagnose.

In most cases simple steroid anti-inflammatory creams will control dermatitis, but it may become persistent and widespread.

For further information see the specific types of dermatitis.
See also ATOPIC ECZEMA; DERMATITIS ARTEFACTA; CONTACT DERMATITIS; DERMATITIS HERPETIFORMIS; ECZEMA; EXFOLIATIVE DERMATITIS; NEURODERMATITIS; PERIORAL DERMATITIS; PHOTODERMATITIS; POMPHOLYX; PSORIASIS; RASH; SKIN; SKIN RED

DERMATITIS ARTEFACTA
Dermatitis artefacta is a rash that is deliberately self-inflicted to attract attention or obtain special treatment. Patients may be disturbed psychiatrically, prisoners, deprived of affection or attention, senile or confused. They may use heat, sharp instruments, sandpaper, chemicals or their fingernails to create the rash. Women are five times more likely to have the condition than men.

The rash can be extraordinarily varied in its form, and quite bizarre in its presentation. It usually does not respond to treatment, and occurs on unusual parts of the body. Treatment involves psychiatric counselling and medication, and dressings that cannot be easily removed by the patient. Plaster casts may occasionally be necessary to stop a patient constantly picking at an ulcer that will not

heal. Sometimes the rash may become infected or gangrenous, but if effective psychiatric care given, treatment is usually successful.
See also DERMATITIS

DERMATITIS HERPETIFORMIS
This is an uncommon blistering itch that occurs on the elbows, knees and backside. There are several different causes, including gluten, which is found in many cereals.

Patients develop small, intensely itchy, fluid-filled blisters on red, inflamed skin. Often appears scratched and bleeding because of the almost irresistible itching. The diagnosis can be confirmed by a biopsy of a skin blister.

Treatment requires avoiding gluten containing cereals, and using very potent steroid creams or tablets.

The rash can be cured by avoiding any cause that can be discovered, otherwise control may be difficult.
See also DERMATITIS; GLUTEN

DERMATOFIBROMA
Dermatofibromas (histiocytomas) are common non-cancerous fibrous skin lumps that usually occur on the legs and arms. Their cause is unknown, but they may arise at the site of a minor injury such as an insect bite or thorn prick.

Patients develop firm yellow-brown nodule in the skin, which if squeezed forms a dimple because the skin is tethered to the nodule. No treatment is necessary unless the lumps are cosmetically unacceptable, when they can be removed surgically, frozen (cryotherapy) with liquid nitrogen or injected with a steroid. They usually persist for years unless surgically removed.
See also SKIN LUMPS

DERMATOMYOSITIS
Dermatomyositis is a rare disease that combines a persistent rash with muscle weakness. When it occurs without the rash (which is present in only 40% of cases) it is called polymyositis. The cause is unknown, but it commonly attacks those in late middle-age.

Patients experience a gradually progressive weakness and pain of the muscles in the neck, upper arms, shoulder, buttocks and thighs. Patients may also develop a dusky red rash on the cheeks and nose, shoulders and upper chest and back. The eyelids are often swollen and appear bruised. Unusual symptoms include redness and bleeding under the nails, cold hands, and a scaly rash over the knuckles.

The condition is diagnosed by blood tests, muscle biopsy and by measuring the muscle's electrical activity.

Drugs such as steroids, methotrexate and azathioprine are commonly used in treatment.

One in ten patients risk developing cancer, and there is no cure. Most patients can lead a relatively normal life, although a minority are disabled by muscle weakness.
See also MUSCLE WEAKNESS

DERMIS
See SKIN

DERMOGRAPHISM
Dermographism is an exaggerated skin response that usually occurs in young adults when the skin is rubbed. It is caused by the excessive release of histamine into the skin. In severe cases, pressure from clothing (eg. belts, bra straps), chairs, clapping hands, tools or even kissing may start the reaction.

In normal skin, firmly rubbing a blunt rounded object over the skin produces a white line for a few seconds. In about one third of people, the white line is followed by a red line and slight swelling of the underlying skin which subsides quickly. In the approximately 4% of the population who suffer from dermographism this response is exaggerated, so that the red line and swelling of the skin persists for many minutes, and sometimes hours. The response is often worse when the patient is anxious, after a hot bath or in warm weather.

Antihistamine tablets will both prevent and treat the reaction.

Dermographism may be a temporary phenomenon that lasts for a few months, or may persist life long.
See also ALLERGY

de TONI-FANCONI-DEBRÉ SYNDROME
See FANCONI SYNDROME

DEXAMPHETAMINE
See STIMULANTS

DEXCHLORPHENIRAMINE
See ANTIHISTAMINES

DEXTROCARDIA

Dextrocardia is a congenital condition in which the heart is located on the right side of the chest instead of the left.
See KARTAGENER SYNDROME

DEXTROMETHORPHAN
See COUGH MEDICINES

DEXTROPROPOXYPHENE
See NARCOTICS

DIABETES

The term diabetes is derived from the Greek word for syphon and indicates that water goes through the person with the disease. There are three totally distinct medical conditions called diabetes, and all have the symptoms of excessive thirst and the frequent passing of urine. It was not possible for doctors to differentiate between the three forms of diabetes until the end of the eighteenth century, so the name of diabetes has stuck with all of them because of their similar symptoms.

Diabetes insipidus is a rare disease caused by a disorder of the pituitary gland.

Diabetes mellitus type one (juvenile diabetes or insulin dependent diabetes) develops in children and young adults due to a lack of insulin production by the pancreas.

Diabetes mellitus type two (maturity onset diabetes or non-insulin dependent diabetes) is the most common form and develops in middle aged and elderly people as the cells in their body develop resistance to insulin.
See also DIABETES IN PREGNANCY; DIABETES INSIPIDUS; DIABETES MELLITUS TYPE ONE; DIABETES MELLITUS TYPE TWO; HYPOGLYCAEMICS; INSULIN; INSULINOMA

DIABETES IN PREGNANCY

Pregnancy may trigger diabetes in a woman who was previously well but predisposed towards this disease. One of the reasons for regular antenatal visits to doctors and the urine tests taken at each visit is to detect diabetes at an early stage. If diabetes develops, the woman can be treated and controlled by regular injections of insulin. In some cases, the diabetes will disappear after the pregnancy, but it often recurs in later years.

If the diabetes is not adequately controlled, serious consequences can result. In mild cases, the child may be born grossly overweight but otherwise be healthy. In more severe cases, the diabetes can cause a miscarriage, eclampsia, malformations of the foetus, urinary and kidney infections, fungal infections (thrush) of the vagina, premature labour, difficult labour, breathing problems in the baby after birth, or death of the baby within the womb.

Diabetic women tend to have difficulty in becoming pregnant, unless their diabetes is very well controlled.
See also DIABETES MELLITUS TYPE ONE; PREGNANCY and separate entries for diseases mentioned above.

DIABETES INSIPIDUS

Diabetes insipidus is an uncommon type of pituitary gland failure. This gland lies under the centre of the brain and controls all other glands in the body. The condition may be triggered by a head injury, or develop slowly over many months because of a brain infection, tumour or stroke. It occurs when the pituitary gland fails to produce the hormone vasopressin that controls the rate at which the kidney produces urine. Without this hormone, the kidney constantly produces large amounts of dilute urine.

Patients have a huge urine output, are constantly thirsty, lose weight, develop headaches and muscle pains, become easily dehydrated, and may have an irregular heart beat. The diagnosis can be confirmed by a series of ingenious blood and urine tests after exposing the patient to varying degrees of water intake.

It can be controlled by regular injections of vasopressin which last from one to three days. Milder cases can be treated with a nasal spray containing a synthetic form of vasopressin, but this only lasts for a few hours.

Although diabetes insipidus cannot be cured, it is usually well controlled. Some cases do settle spontaneously, but most patients require life long treatment.
See also DIABETES; PITUITARY GLAND

DIABETES MEDICATIONS
See HYPOGLYCAEMICS; INSULIN

DIABETES MELLITUS TYPE ONE

Diabetes mellitus type one is also known as insulin dependent diabetes mellitus (IDDM) or juvenile diabetes, and causes excessive levels of glucose in the blood.

Glucose is used as fuel by every cell in the body. When glucose is eaten, it is absorbed into the blood from the small intestine. Once it reaches a cell, it must cross the fine membrane that forms its outer skin. This is normally impermeable to all substances, but insulin has the ability to combine with glucose and transport it across the membrane from the blood into the interior of the cell. Insulin is made by cells in the Islets of Langerhans in the pancreas, which sits in the centre of the abdomen.

Only 10% of diabetics suffer from this form of diabetes mellitus which is caused by a lack of insulin production by the pancreas. Most people develop this type as a child or in early adult life.

Symptoms include excessive tiredness, thirst, excess passing of urine, weight loss despite a large food intake, itchy rashes, recurrent vaginal thrush infections, pins and needles and blurred vision. Patients become steadily weaker because their muscles and other organs cannot work properly.

The diagnosis can be confirmed by blood and urine glucose levels and a glucose tolerance test (GTT).

By measuring the amount of glucose in certain blood cells, the average blood glucose level over the past three months can also be determined. The level of insulin can also be measured in blood.

Daily self-testing is advisable to ensure that disease control is adequate. Both blood and urine tests for glucose are available, but the blood tests are far superior.

Diet is an essential part of treatment because the amount of glucose eaten is not normally constant, and diabetics lack the means of adjusting the amount of glucose in their blood with insulin. The diet must restrict the number of kilojoules (calories) being eaten, and sugar in all its forms should be eaten only with great caution. Fat should not account for more than a third of the total calories, and cholesterol intake should be restricted. Protein should be obtained more from poultry and fish than red meats. Carbohydrates other than sugar can be consumed freely. Grains and cereals with a high fibre content should be the main part of the diet. Artificial sweeteners such as aspartame (NutraSweet) can be used to flavour food and

drinks. Fat cells can react abnormally to insulin very easily, and so overweight diabetics must lose weight. Exercise is encouraged on a regular daily basis. Patients should carry glucose sweets with them at all times to use if their blood sugar levels drop too low.

When first diagnosed, patients are often quite ill, and most are hospitalised for a few days to stabilise their condition. Insulin injections must be given regularly several times a day for the rest of their life. Initially derived from pigs and cattle, human insulin has now been produced by genetic engineering techniques. Insulin cannot be taken by mouth as it is destroyed by acid in the stomach, but can be injected into any part of the body covered by loose skin, although the same site should not be used repeatedly. The newer pen-style delivery systems enable diabetics to easily dial the required dose and inject as necessary with minimal inconvenience. There are many different types of insulin that vary in their speed of onset and duration of action.

The complications of type one diabetes mellitus include an increased risk of both bacterial and fungal skin and vaginal infections, the premature development of cataracts in the eye, microscopic haemorrhages and exudates that destroy the retina at the back of the eye, damage to the kidneys that prevents them from filtering blood effectively, poor circulation to the extremities (hands and feet) that may cause chronic ulcers and even gangrene to the feet, the development of brown skin spots on the shins, and sensory nerve damage (diabetic neuropathy) that alters the patient's perception of vibration, pain and temperature.

There are also complications associated with treatment such as a 'hypo' in which too much insulin is given, excess exercise undertaken or not enough food is eaten, and blood glucose levels drop (hypoglycaemia) to an unacceptably low level. The patient becomes light-headed, sweats, develops a rapid heart beat and tremor, becomes hungry, then nauseated before finally collapsing unconscious. Glucose drinks or sweets given before collapse can reverse the process, but after collapse, an injection of glucose is essential. In an emergency, a sugary syrup or honey introduced through the anus into the rectum may allow a diabetic to recover sufficiently to take further sugar by mouth. Rarer complications of treatment are adverse reactions to pork or beef insulin, and damage to the fat under the skin if the same injection site is used too frequently. Diabetic ketoacidosis is the most severe complication.

On the other hand, with the correct treatment and careful control, patients should live a near-normal life, with a near-normal life span.

See also BANTING, FREDERICK; BEST, CHARLES; DIABETES; DIABETES IN PREGNANCY; DIABETES MELLITUS TYPE TWO; DIABETIC KETOACIDOSIS; GLUCOSE, BLOOD; GLUCOSE TOLERANCE TEST; INSULIN; INSULINOMA; PANCREAS

DIABETES MELLITUS TYPE TWO

Diabetes mellitus type two is also known as maturity onset diabetes or non-insulin dependent diabetes mellitus (NIDDM).

Glucose is used as fuel by every cell in the body. When glucose is eaten, it is absorbed into the blood from the small intestine. Once it reaches a cell, it must cross the fine membrane that forms its outer skin. This is normally impermeable to all substances, but insulin has the ability to combine with glucose and transport it across the membrane from the blood into the interior of the cell. Insulin is made in the pancreas, which sits in the centre of the abdomen.

Nine out of ten diabetics suffer from the maturity onset form of diabetes mellitus, which is far more common in obese patients. There is adequate insulin production, but cells throughout the body fail to respond to the insulin, so glucose cannot enter the cell.

The symptoms include excessive tiredness, thirst, excess passing of urine, visual problems, skin infections and sensory nerve problems. Many patients are totally without symptoms when the diagnosis is discovered on a routine blood or urine test.

Blood and urine glucose levels are high in untreated or inadequately treated patients. A blood glucose tolerance test (GTT) is performed to confirm the diagnosis and determine its severity.

By measuring the amount of glucose in certain blood cells, the average blood glucose level over the past three months can also be determined.

Regular blood testing of glucose levels is also necessary, but normally on a weekly rather than daily basis. Urine tests are often inaccurate in the elderly, as their kidney function may be reduced to the point where glucose cannot enter the urine.

Watching the diet is essential because the amount of glucose eaten is not normally constant, but the medication levels do not normally vary from day to day. The diet must restrict the number of kilojoules (calories) being eaten, and sugar in all its forms should be eaten only with great caution. Fat should not account for more than a third of the total calories, and cholesterol intake should be restricted. Protein should be obtained more from poultry and fish than red meats. Carbohydrates other than sugar can be consumed freely. Grains and cereals with a high fibre content should be the main part of the diet. Artificial sweeteners such as aspartame (NutraSweet) can be used to flavour food and drinks. Fat cells can react abnormally to insulin very easily, and so overweight diabetics must lose weight. Exercise is encouraged on a regular daily basis.

Education of patients with diabetes is very important, so that they understand what they can and cannot eat and drink. Older people who develop diabetes can often have the disease controlled by diet alone or a combination of tablets and diet. Tablets (eg. metformin, glimepride, tolbutamide, chlorpropamide, glibenclamide, glipizide) make the cell membrane respond to insulin again. Weight loss is a vital part of treatment because if normal weight levels can be maintained, the disease may disappear.

Diabetics have an increased risk of both bacterial and fungal skin and vaginal infections, the premature development of cataracts in the eye, microscopic haemorrhages and exudates that destroy the retina at the back of the eye, damage to the kidneys that prevents them from filtering blood effectively, poor circulation to the extremities (hands and feet) that may cause chronic ulcers and even gangrene to the feet, the development of brown skin spots on the shins, and sensory nerve damage (diabetic neuropathy) that alters the patient's perception of vibration, pain and temperature. High blood pressure is more common than in the average person of their age.

There are also complications associated with treatment such as a "hypo" which is usually due to excessive medication. As a result blood glucose levels drop (hypoglycaemia) to an unacceptably low level. The patient becomes light-headed, sweats, develops a rapid heart beat and tremor, becomes hungry, then nauseated before finally collapsing unconscious. Glucose drinks or sweets given before collapse can reverse the process, but after collapse, an injection of glucose is essential. Diabetic ketoacidosis is the most severe complication.

With the correct treatment and careful control, patients should live a near-normal life, with a near-normal life span.
See also DIABETES; DIABETES MELLITUS TYPE ONE; DIABETIC KETOACIDOSIS; GLUCOSE, BLOOD; GLUCOSE TOLERANCE TEST; HYPOGLYCAEMICS

DIABETIC KETOACIDOSIS

Ketoacidosis is a severe complication or initial presentation of diabetes mellitus. It is due to a build-up of waste products and glucose in the bloodstream because of untreated or under-treated diabetes. Patients who are careless about their treatment, diet and self-testing may be affected. Almost invariably, it is the juvenile insulin dependent diabetics who develop this complication.

The symptoms include mental stupor, nausea, vomiting, shortness of breath and eventually coma. Blood sugar levels are very high and other blood and urine tests are abnormal.

Treatment involves the emergency injections of insulin, but urgent hospital treatment is necessary to control the situation adequately. If left untreated, death will occur due to kidney, heart or brain damage.

The prognosis is good with prompt medical care, but permanent organ damage may occur if treatment is delayed.
See also DIABETES MELLITUS TYPE ONE; DIABETES MELLITUS TYPE TWO

DIABETIC NEUROPATHY
See DIABETES MELLITUS TYPE ONE; DIABETES MELLITUS TYPE TWO

DIALYSIS
First developed in 1945 by Dutchman Willem Kolff, haemodialysis is a means of removing wastes and toxins from the blood of a patient whose kidneys have failed or been removed.

The patient is connected through a permanent shunt in the arm to a dialysis machine which uses the principle of diffusion across a membrane to clean the blood that constantly passes from the artery in the arm through a pump to the machine and then back to a vein in the arm. Patients with kidney failure attend a hospital or clinic a couple of times a week for a few hours to undertake the procedure, or use a portable unit at home. Between nine and fifteen hours of dialysis are normally required every week for good health.

Peritoneal dialysis is a more primitive procedure in which a large amount of fluid is run through a catheter (soft tube) into the peritoneal cavity within the abdomen, left for a few hours, then drained out again, along with many of the wastes and toxins that have diffused from the blood into the fluid across the peritoneal lining (membrane).

Both forms of dialysis can be abandoned if the patient receives a kidney transplant.
See also CATHETER; KIDNEY FAILURE, ACUTE; SHUNT; TRANSPLANTS AND IMPLANTS

DIANE
See CONTRACEPTIVE PILL

DIAPHORESIS
See SWEATING EXCESS

DIAPHRAGM
The diaphragm is a sheet of muscle that runs across the body to separate the chest from the abdomen (belly). It is shaped like a dome, curved upwards towards the chest. It is attached to the ribs and vertebrae.

It contracts down to aid breathing in, and relaxes back when breathing out.

There are holes in the diaphragm to allow the oesophagus (gullet), aorta and inferior vena cava (main vein from the lower body) to pass from the chest into the abdomen. If the hole for the oesophagus becomes stretched, part of the stomach may slip up into the chest to form a hiatus hernia.
See also HIATUS HERNIA; OESOPHAGUS

DIAPHRAGM CONTRACEPTIVE
The diaphragm is a contraceptive device used

by women that provides a physical barrier to the sperm meeting the egg. A diaphragm is a rubber dome with a flexible spring rim. It is inserted into the vagina before intercourse, so that it covers the cervix, or entry to the uterus. It should be used with a spermicidal cream or jelly to kill any sperm that manage to wriggle around the edges. A woman must be measured by a doctor for a diaphragm of the correct size and she will also need to be instructed how to insert it properly.

Most women find a diaphragm easy enough to use, and it has a high reliability. Some women find the fact that it has to be inserted before intercourse aesthetically displeasing, but generally it presents no problems. It can be put in place some time before if necessary, but must be left in place for at least six hours after intercourse to ensure that all the sperm are dead before removal. Its failure rate of between 10% and 15% makes it less reliable than condoms.
See also CONTRACEPTIVES

DIARRHOEA

Diarrhoea is the frequent and excessive discharge of watery fluid from the bowel. Diarrhoea is really a symptom of disease rather than a disease itself.

Absolutely everyone experiences diarrhoea at some time. The ten metres of an adult human gut is very sensitive to irritants, and any irritation of the lower half, particularly the last two metres (the large intestine), will result in diarrhoea.

Diarrhoea may be considered by a patient to be the more frequent passing of motions that are softer than usual, but to be medically significant, the motions must be at least part liquid and be passed more than four times a day.

Diarrhoea can be caused by conditions of the intestine, or diseases outside the gut that alter the body's chemistry or other functions.

By far the most common cause of diarrhoea is a viral infection of the intestine (viral gastroenteritis). This infection is passed from one person to another by close contact or on the breath, and usually occurs in epidemics, often in springtime. The usual symptoms are six to twelve hours of vomiting followed by one to three days of diarrhoea, and painful gut spasms usually occur.

Food poisoning is due to bacteria, or a toxin produced by bacteria, being present in food. The diagnosis is most strongly suspected when a whole family or group of people is affected simultaneously. The symptoms and the severity of the attack will depend upon the bacteria causing the poisoning, the amount eaten, and the age and general health of the victim. Most attacks of food poisoning occur abruptly, within eight hours (and often one or two hours) of eating the contaminated food, but some types may take up to twenty-four hours to give symptoms. The patient suddenly starts vomiting, and has explosive diarrhoea associated with intermittent belly pain.

Bacterial gastroenteritis is usually more severe than the viral form, and includes infections by bacteria such as *Shigella*, *Salmonella typhi* (causes typhoid) and *Yersinia*. These are usually responsible for the 'Delhi belly' and 'Montezuma's revenge' suffered by travellers to less developed countries. *Vibrio cholerae* is the bacteria responsible for cholera, the most severe of the bacterial gut infections.

Giardia lamblia is a microscopic animal that can easily enter the body and cause an infection (giardiasis) in the small intestine. It passes from one person to another by poor personal hygiene. The condition is far more common in children than adults, who may have no symptoms.

Other common intestinal causes of diarrhoea include the irritable bowel syndrome, diverticulitis (infected outpocketings of the large bowel), lactose intolerance (a reaction to the sugar in milk), appendicitis, cancer of the rectum or colon (large intestine), food allergies (eg. eggs, milk, chocolate, peanuts), ulcerative colitis (lining of the large intestine becomes ulcerated and bleeds), Crohn's disease (a thickening and inflammation of the small or large intestine), intussusception (an infolding of the gut on itself), surgery to shorten the intestine (prevents adequate absorption of fluids) and, strangely, severe constipation may actually present as diarrhoea because liquid faeces from further up the bowel can seep around the outside of a large faecal mass in the rectum that is impossible to pass through the anus.

Uncommon intestinal causes of diarrhoea include regular anal sex (causes inflammation of the rectum), pseudomembranous colitis, amoebiasis (an infestation of the gut with microscopic animals), blastocystis, bilharzia, a blood clot in an artery supplying the bowel, tropical sprue and Whipple's disease.

Conditions outside the intestine may also cause diarrhoea. These include psychological, physical or emotional stress, fear and anxiety (may cause involuntary spasms of the gut), psychiatric conditions (eg. depression), excess thyroxine (hyperthyroidism), pernicious anaemia, deficiencies of other essential vitamins (eg. vitamin B3 in the disease pellagra) and minerals, diabetes mellitus, inflammation or infection of the organs in the pelvis around the rectum (eg. bladder, vagina), an abscess in the pelvis, Addison's disease, cirrhosis (damage to the liver), septicaemia (bacterial infection of the blood), alcoholism, AIDS, the toxic shock syndrome and uraemia (kidney failure).

There are many medications that may have diarrhoea as a side effect. Examples include antibiotics (particularly penicillin), antacids, methyldopa (for high blood pressure), beta blockers (for heart disease), theophylline (for asthma and bronchitis), colchicine (for gout), digoxin (for heart disease) and quinine (for malaria). Over-use of laxatives will naturally result in diarrhoea.

There are dozens of other rare causes of diarrhoea.

Faeces may be examined to determine the cause, along with blood tests and sometimes colonoscopy and x-rays.

Treatment involves determining and treating the cause if possible. Mild attacks are dealt with by diet and fluids, more serious ones require medication to slow the flow, and severe attacks may need fluids to be replaced by an intravenous drip.

Dehydration is the main complication, and the risk is much greater in children under five years of age.

See also ANTIDIARRHOEALS;
DYSENTERY; FAECES;
GASTROENTERITIS; TRAVELLER'S
DIARRHOEA and separate entries for diseases mentioned above.

DIASTOLIC PRESSURE

The heart contracts regularly to pump blood through the arteries under high (systolic) pressure. When the heart relaxes between beats, the blood continues to flow due to the lower (diastolic) pressure exerted by the elasticity of the artery walls.

See also HYPERTENSION

DIATHERMY

Diathermy is the destruction of tissue by heat produced by a high frequency electric current.

There are two types of diathermy – unipolar and bipolar.

Unipolar electrocautery or diathermy is used to remove skin warts, plantar warts, genital warts, skin tags, polyps, keratoses, some types of skin cancer and other growths on the skin (all these are known as lesions). The skin is cleaned with a water based antiseptic solution, then an anaesthetic injection is given under, into and around the lesion to numb it and prevent any pain during the procedure. This will sting for fifteen to thirty seconds.

After the anaesthetic has taken effect (only a few seconds) the area is cleaned and carefully dried. Then an electric probe is placed within a millimetre or two of the lesion. Using a foot control, the doctor will activate an electric current through the probe, and a spark will jump from the tip of the probe to the lesion being treated. This spark will gradually destroy the lesion.

The patient may feel a fluttering sensation on the skin, and smell burning during the procedure, but should feel no pain. If pain is felt, more anaesthetic can be given.

At the end of the procedure, the patient is effectively left with a graze at the site of the diathermy procedure. This will heal in the same way as all grazes, with a scab, that will come off after ten to fourteen days. There should be only mild discomfort after the anaesthetic wears off, unless the procedure has been performed on a particularly sensitive area such as the sole, when paracetamol may be needed for a day or two.

When the graze caused by the diathermy heals, a red mark will remain, but this will usually fade to a white patch over a month or two. A scar is always left after the procedure, but the colour (red or white), size and severity of the scarring will depend on the size of the lesion treated, the position on the body, and the depth of the diathermy necessary to remove the lesion. The face will usually heal well, while the back and legs often heal poorly. A very small number of patients will develop a keloid (raised red) scar that can be gradually reduced with further treatment.

Diathermy cannot guarantee that there will be no recurrence of any wart or skin cancer after the treatment, and about one in ten warts and skin cancers may come back after months or years. Any recurrence should be bought to the attention of a doctor.

Bipolar diathermy is only used on patients who are fully anaesthetised in an operating theatre as an electric current must pass through the body. A pointed probe is touched to the desired place on the body, and the electric current passes in a concentrated form through this place to destroy it, then disperses through the body without causing further damage to exit through a large plate that is often strapped to the back of the thigh, thus completing the electrical circuit. This form of diathermy is used to stop bleeding during an operation, and the diathermy probe may be used to cut through soft tissues while simultaneously sealing all blood vessels. Large arteries will still need to be tied off if cut.
See also SHORT-WAVE DIATHERMY

DIC
See DISSEMINATED INTRAVASCULAR COAGULATION

DICHOTOMY
Dichotomy is the splitting of medical fees between two doctors, and it is considered to be one of the worst possible breaches of medical ethics. An example of dichotomy would be the specialist who paid a GP to refer patients to him/her.
See also MEDICAL ETHICS

DICLOFENAC
See NONSTEROIDAL ANTI-INFLAMMATORY DRUGS

DICYCLOMINE
See ANTISPASMODICS

DIEFFENBACHIA POISONING
See POISONOUS PLANTS

DIENOESTROL
See SEX HORMONES

DIET
See ANORECTICS; DIETICIANS; FOOD; GASTROENTERITIS; VEGETARIAN DIET; WEIGHT LOSS DIET

DIETICIANS
Dieticians (or nutritionists) are professionals who have undertaken a course of training at a university or technical college, from where they have received a Bachelor of Science degree and/or a diploma in dietetics (or nutrition). They assist the normal medical treatment of many diseases (eg. diabetes, high cholesterol levels, liver disease, gout, heart disease, constipation and diarrhoea). They can also offer advice on diets associated with food allergies, the correct diet for pregnant or breast feeding mothers, the nutrition of babies, and correcting problems of obesity or underweight.
See also FOOD; WEIGHT LOSS DIET

DIETHYLPROPION
See ANORECTICS

DIFFICULT SWALLOWING
See SWALLOWING PAINFUL

DIFFICULT URINATION
See URINATION DIFFICULT

DIFFUSE IDIOPATHIC SPINAL HYPEROSTOSIS
Diffuse idiopathic spinal hyperostosis (DISH, skeletal hyperostosis or Forestier disease) is an abnormal calcification of the vertebrae in the back. It may also affect elbows, hands and feet, and affects 5% of men over the age of sixty-five. The cause is unknown, but it is more common in diabetics and gout sufferers.

Stiffness and pain in the central back, and sometimes in hands, elbows and feet, are the main symptoms. Sudden severe pain due to nerve entrapment is a complication.

X-rays of the back show abnormal bony spurs and areas of calcification. Disc spaces may also be narrowed.

Treatment involves anti-inflammatory medication, and sometimes steroid tablets or injections. Rarely, surgery may be performed to remove spurs that are painful.

The condition is very slowly progressive, but control with medication is usually very good.
See also BACK PAIN; SPINE; VERTEBRA

DIFLUNISAL
See NONSTEROIDAL ANTI-INFLAMMATORY DRUGS

di GEORGE SYNDROME
Di George syndrome (thymic hypoplasia) is a congenital failure of the thymus gland (which

lies behind the upper end of the breast bone), and parathyroid glands (which lie in the front of the neck) to develop properly.

Newborn babies with the condition develop muscle spasms, recurrent severe infections, and have wide spread eyes. Abnormal blood tests and lymph node biopsy confirm the diagnosis.

Thymic tissue transplantation is the only treatment possible.

Unusual cancers are possible, and death inevitable unless successful thymus transplant performed.
See also IMMUNODEFICIENCY; NEZELOF SYNDROME; THYMUS

DIGESTION
See GALL BLADDER; PANCREAS; SMALL INTESTINE

DIGESTIVE ENZYMES
Digestive enzymes are normally produced in the stomach, gall bladder and pancreas (whose enzyme is pancrease) to break down food into a form suitable for digestion. If these organs are unable to produce adequate enzymes, pancrease and hydrochloric acid can be given in a tablet or capsule form during or after a meal. Because they are natural products (often obtained from pigs), side effects are rare unless they are taken in excess or away from meals.
See also PANCREAS; STOMACH

DIGESTIVE TRACT
See ALIMENTARY TRACT

DIGOXIN
The foxglove flower has been known for centuries to control and assist patients with 'dropsy', which we now call congestive heart failure. Many mediaeval doctors made their reputation by curing the shortness of breath and swollen legs suffered by these patients by prescribing the regular use of foxglove tea. The active ingredient in the foxglove is digitalis, which has now been further refined to digoxin (Lanoxin). This is the only commonly used medication in a class called cardiac glycosides. It is available in injection, tablet and mixture forms, and must only be used in the appropriate patients, as there are some heart diseases that it can aggravate. It can also interact with many other medications. Side effects are uncommon (eg. nausea, rash, slow heart rate)

and are usually associated with excess dosage.

It is used in the treatment of heart failure and irregular heart beats, but is now being replaced with more sophisticated drugs including the ACE inhibitors. Digoxin should be used with care in patients with kidney and thyroid disease, and a lower dose is necessary in the elderly.
See also ACE INHIBITORS; MEDICATION

DIHYDROCODEINE
See COUGH MEDICINES

DILANTIN
See ANTICONVULSANTS

DILATION AND CURETTAGE
See CURETTE

DILTIAZEM
See CALCIUM CHANNEL BLOCKERS

DIMENHYDRINATE
See ANTIEMETICS

DIOGENES SYNDROME
Diogenes syndrome is a social disorder that is more a symptom of an underlying problem than a disease in itself. Numerous psychiatric disturbances (eg. schizophrenia) may be responsible.

Victims are usually recluses who live alone in filth and squalor, and are usually male. They may be involved in drug abuse and mentally subnormal.

Numerous blood and other tests should be performed to determine the cause of any mental disorder.

Doctors can treat any underlying cause, then specifically treat psychoses and dementia.

The syndrome is named after a Greek eccentric who founded a group of stoics in about 300 BC who rejected all comforts.
See also DEMENTIA; PSYCHOSIS; SCHIZOPHRENIA

DIPHENOXYLATE
See ANTIDIARRHOEALS

DIPHTHERIA
Diphtheria is a childhood respiratory infection that is now rare in developed countries.

It is caused by infection of the throat and

trachea (the tube leading to the lungs) by the bacterium *Corynebacterium diphtheriae* which releases a toxin that is responsible for most of the symptoms and complications. It spreads from one person to another in the breath, and the incubation period is two to seven days.

Symptoms include a sore swollen throat, fever, nasal discharge, hoarse voice, overwhelming tiredness, weakness and muscle aches. A thick, grey, sticky discharge forms a membrane across the throat that the patient constantly fights to clear. The diagnosis is confirmed by throat swabs, and heart involvement by an electrocardiogram (ECG).

Rapid, early treatment is critical and involves diphtheria antitoxin injection, antibiotics (kill the bacteria but do not remove the toxin), and medications to control or prevent complications. In severe cases a tracheotomy (cut into the front of the throat) is performed to allow air into the lungs. It can be totally prevented by vaccination in infancy.

Severe cases may affect the heart, nose, skin and nerves. Survivors may be affected for life by damage to the heart or lungs.

The death rate varies from 10% to 30%, and most deaths occur within the first day or two. Survivors improve in a few days, but must be kept at rest for at least three weeks to prevent complications, as it will take this time to for all the toxin to be removed from the body.
See also SCHICK TEST; WHOOPING COUGH

DIPLOPIA
See DOUBLE VISION

DISC
See SPINE; VERTEBRA

DISCHARGE
See EAR DISCHARGE; EYE DISCHARGE; NIPPLE DISCHARGE; PENIS DISCHARGE; VAGINAL DISCHARGE

DISCITIS
Discitis is an inflammation and/or infection of one of the intervertebral discs that separate the vertebra in the back from one another. The infection may spread through the bloodstream, often from the kidneys or bladder, or may come from an injury to the disc. The inflamed disc enlarges and pushes forward to pinch the spinal cord.

Patients experience pain at the site of the disc inflammation in the back, and limited movement of that section of the back. Pain is often eased by bending the neck or back forward. A CT scan will show the damaged disc and surrounding inflammation.

Urgent surgery to remove the pressure on the spinal cord caused by the bulging disc is necessary. Antibiotics are also used.

In some cases, pressure on the spinal cord may cause permanent damage to the cord and limited sensation and movement below that level of the back.

The prognosis is good if treated early, but discitis may result in paraplegia or quadriplegia (depending on level in the back involved) if left untreated.
See also BACK PAIN; SPINE; VERTEBRAE

DISCOID ECZEMA
Discoid or nummular eczema is a persistent rash that is often confused with a fungal infection. The cause is unknown, but it usually occurs in young adults.

The rash appears as discs of scaling, red, thickened skin on the back of the forearms and elbows, back of the hands, front of the legs and the tops of the feet. The affected areas can vary in size from a few millimetres to three centimetres or more. The diagnosis can be confirmed by biopsy.

Steroid creams and tablets are effective, but antihistamine tablets are sometimes needed for the itch.

The rash heals rapidly with correct treatment, but unfortunately, there is a tendency for recurrences. Attacks usually cease after six to twelve months.
See also ECZEMA

DISCOID LUPUS ERYTHEMATOSUS
Discoid lupus erythematosus is an uncommon disfiguring inflammatory skin disease. Its cause is an autoimmune condition in which the body inappropriately rejects patches of skin for no known reason.

Patients develop distinct red plaques on the face (particularly the cheeks), scalp and ears that worsen with sun exposure. Permanent facial hair loss and loss of pigmentation in dark skinned races may also occur. The diagnosis is confirmed by a skin biopsy and some specific blood tests may be abnormal. Treatment involves protecting the affected skin from the sun, strong steroid creams, injections of steroids into the spots and medications such as chloroquine, dapsone and retinoic acid. All these must be used with great care as they have significant side effects.

The condition is often persistent, and only 60% of patients adequately controlled.
See also SYSTEMIC LUPUS ERYTHEMATOSUS

DISH
See DIFFUSE IDIOPATHIC SPINAL HYPEROSTOSIS

DISLOCATION
A dislocation occurs when the surfaces of a joint that normally slide across each other are totally displaced, one from the other. If there is partial separation of the joint surfaces, the condition is called subluxation.

DISLOCATION TYPES

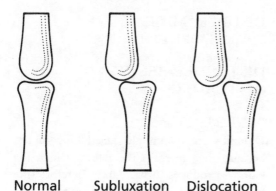

Normal   Subluxation   Dislocation

Diagram demonstrating the difference between subluxation and dislocation of a joint.

A dislocation can be a birth defect (eg. congenital dislocation of the hips), due to a severe injury (almost any joint in the body), spontaneous for no apparent reason but caused by disease in a joint (eg. the dislocation of a toe joint severely affected by arthritis), abnormal twisting of a joint (eg. dislocation of the patella – knee cap), or recurrent, when after previous dislocation the joint dislocates very easily in the future (eg. shoulder). A dislocation caused by injury may also be associated with a fracture, and anyone treating a dislocation must be aware of this possibility.

Inevitably, cartilages and ligaments, and possibly muscles and tendons around a dislo-

cated joint will also be stretched, strained or torn by the dislocation. A dislocated joint will be painful, swollen and difficult or impossible to move. The skin over the dislocated joint will have different contours to the same joint on the other side of the body. An x-ray is the only definitive way to make the diagnosis.

A dislocation can be associated with complications, such as pinching a nerve or blood vessel, which may cause severe pain beyond the dislocation, and a poor blood supply that can result in tissue death and gangrene. Other complications involve the joint itself, and repeated dislocations can damage the smooth surfaces of the joint and lead to persistent pain after the dislocation has been reduced and to the premature development of arthritis.

A dislocation is treated by replacing the bones of the joint back into their correct position. Immediately after the injury, this can sometimes be done quite easily, even with major joints, as the damaged muscles around the joint will not yet have gone into a spasm. This spasm can later make the reduction of dislocations very difficult without an anaesthetic to relax the muscles.

Those giving first aid may attempt the reduction of a dislocation, but if not readily successful should not persist, as there may be a fracture or other complication present. In severe cases, a joint may need to be replaced in its correct position by an open operation. The hip is a common example of this. Severely damaged ligaments and cartilages around a joint may also need to be surgically repaired.

After the joint has been correctly replaced, little or no rest is required. A major joint may require one or two days of limited use, but prolonged rest of the joint can lead to the formation of scar tissue and a permanent limitation of movement. Movement of the joint through its maximum possible range, without putting it under any stress (eg. avoid weights), is the best way of bringing a joint back to full recovery as quickly as possible. The exception to this rule is the situation when a fracture is also present. The fracture will require immobilisation to allow healing. Physiotherapy will then be required at a later date to fully mobilise the joint once the fracture has healed.

Joints that dislocate repeatedly (eg. the shoulder) may require an operation to tighten the ligaments and muscles around the joint to prevent further dislocations.

See also FIRST AID; FRACTURE; HIP DISLOCATION; SHOULDER DISLOCATION

DISSEMINATED INTRAVASCULAR COAGULATION

Disseminated intravascular coagulation (DIC) is a rare and horrendous blood reaction to many different types of severe disease (eg. septicaemia, cancer). Excessive blood clotting occurs within normal arteries and veins in one area, which uses up all the available blood clotting factors in the body, so that excessive bleeding occurs elsewhere.

The blood supply to an organ (eg. kidney, liver, brain), finger or limb may be cut off partially or completely to cause loss of function, gangrene or scarring. This is followed by severe and damaging bleeding internally to other organs, externally into the skin and from most body openings.

The diagnosis can be confirmed by specific blood tests.

Transfusion of fresh blood to replace lost clotting factors is the only treatment. Amputation of affected fingers, toes, or limbs may be necessary, and permanent organ (eg. stroke if brain affected) or limb damage is probable.

Sudden death occurs in severe cases, and most survivors are damaged in some way.
See also BLEEDING, EXCESSIVE; BLOOD CLOTTING TEST

DISSEMINATED LUPUS ERYTHEMATOSUS
See SYSTEMIC LUPUS ERYTHEMATOSUS

DISSEMINATED SCLEROSIS
See MULTIPLE SCLEROSIS

DISSEMINATED SUPERFICIAL ACTINIC POROKERATOSIS

Disseminated superficial actinic porokeratosis (DSAP) is an unusual inherited condition that increases the risk of sun damage to the skin in people of European descent.

Half the children of an affected parent will have the condition, but only if they have excessive sun exposure will it be a problem. New spots may also be caused by ultraviolet light in sun lamps. The average age of onset is about forty, and severity increases steadily with age. It does not occur in childhood.

Spots begin as a 1–3 mm cone-shaped lump, brownish red or brown in colour and usually around a hair follicle. The spot expands and a slightly raised dark brown ring develops and spreads out to a diameter of ten millimetres or more. The skin within the ring is thin and mildly reddened or slightly brown, and sometimes may ulcerate and crust. Sweating is absent in affected areas and sun exposure may cause itching. The condition becomes more prominent in the summer and may improve in winter. Affects sun exposed areas, appearing mainly on the cheeks, forearms and lower legs and occurs more frequently in women than men. The diagnosis can be confirmed by a skin biopsy.

There is no satisfactory treatment, but cryotherapy (freezing) and creams containing 5 fluoro-uracil, tretinoin or alpha hydroxy acid may be tried. It is important to reduce sun exposure by wearing long sleeved shirts and slacks and using sunscreens.
See also DERMATITIS; SKIN

DISOPYRAMIDE
See ANTIARRHYTHMICS

DISTENDED BELLY
See BLOATING

DIURETICS

Diuretics are commonly called fluid tablets because they increase the rate at which the kidney produces urine, and therefore the frequency with which the patient has to visit the toilet to pass urine. Common diuretics all come as tablets, and some are available as injections.

The most common side effect of diuretics is washing out of the body (with the increased urine production) essential elements that should remain in the body. Potassium is the element most commonly lost, and as a result, many patients are given potassium (K) supplements to take while using diuretics, but sodium may also be lost. Some types of diuretics are not as likely as others to cause this problem and others (eg. Hydrene, Dyazide) are combined with a second drug to prevent the loss of potassium. This side effect may also be overcome by taking the tablets only five days a week, or in some other intermittent pattern. Blood tests are often ordered to assess the levels of potassium (and other elements) in patients on diuretics.

The most common group of diuretics are the thiazides. These include bendrothiazide (Aprinox), chlorthiazide (Chlotride), hydrochlorothiazide and methyclothiazide. They are used to increases urine output in patients with high blood pressure, heart failure and fluid retention. Side effects may include nausea, stomach cramps, headache and biochemical disturbances. They should be used only if essential in pregnancy and breast feeding, and must be avoided in patients with gout.

Other diuretics include amiloride, frusemide (Lasix – in the class of loop diuretics), indapamide (Natrilix), spironolactone (Aldactone), and triamterene. They increases urine output in patients with high blood pressure, kidney failure, fluid retention and heart failure. Spironolactone also has the interesting effect of removing excess body and facial hair in women if used regularly for six months or more. Side effects may include weakness, thirst, dizziness, cramps, flushing and blood chemistry imbalances. They should be used only if essential in pregnancy and breast feeding, and must be avoided in a jaundiced patient.

See also HYPERTENSION; KIDNEY; MEDICATION

DIVERTICULAR DISEASE
See DIVERTICULITIS

DIVERTICULITIS
Diverticulitis is infection or inflammation occurring in diverticulae (outpocketings) that develop on the colon (large intestine). When no infection or inflammation is present, the condition is called diverticular disease of the colon. It is very common in older people, but the incidence is slowly decreasing in developed countries as the amount of fibre in the diet is increasing.

If fibre is lacking in the diet, almost everything eaten is absorbed, and there is little to pass on in the faeces. If there is no bulk in the motions, there is a tendency towards constipation, and pressure builds up in the colon as the hard, dry food remnants are moved along towards the anus. The pressure increases in the last metre or so of the bowel to cause ballooning out of the bowel wall between the muscle bands that run along and around the gut. With time, these outpocketings become permanent and form small diverticulae in which faecal particles can be trapped to cause infection and inflammation.

Patients experience intermittent cramping pains in the lower abdomen, alternating constipation and diarrhoea, excess flatus (wind), and noisy bowels. A barium enema x-ray or colonoscopy of the large bowel can confirm the diagnosis.

Acute attacks are treated with antibiotics and medications that reduce gut spasm. Sometimes treatment must be continued long term to prevent recurrences. Fibre supplements are added to the diet, and faecal softeners prevent constipation. In severe cases, surgery may be necessary to remove the affected sections of bowel, particularly if the bowel starts to bleed from chronic irritation or if an abscess forms. If fibre is added to the diet once the disease is present, it will not lead to a cure, but will prevent the formation of more diverticulae and therefore limit the severity of the disease.

Uncommonly, an abscess may form in one of the diverticulae, and this may rupture causing peritonitis.

Acute attacks normally settle quickly with treatment, but once diverticulae are present, they are permanent, and periodic infections usually occur.

See also BARIUM ENEMA; COLITIS; COLON; COLONOSCOPY; DIARRHOEA

DIVERTICULAR DISEASE OF THE COLON

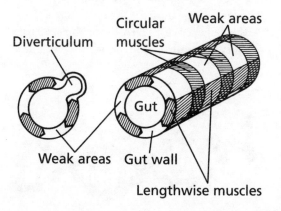

DIZZINESS
Dizziness (vertigo) can be one of the most annoying and distressing of symptoms. The patient may feel otherwise well, but is unable to function because the world constantly revolves around them. It may also be

associated with other symptoms, particularly vomiting and nausea.

The ear is made of three main sections – the outer ear canal (where wax can accumulate) which ends at the ear drum; the middle ear between the ear drum and the start of the hearing mechanism which connects through the eustachian tube with the back of the nose and contains three small bones that magnify the vibrations caused by sound; and the inner ear which contains both the hearing mechanism and three semicircular canals which are responsible for balance. It is often diseases or disorders of these semicircular canals (the vestibular apparatus), or its connections in the brain, which cause dizziness, but other diseases which indirectly affect the balance mechanism and brain may also cause the problem.

A middle ear infection (otitis media) is a very common cause of temporary deafness, pain, fever and dizziness, particularly in children. They are often associated with a common cold, and if left untreated, may progress to a permanent partial loss of hearing.

Ménière's disease may occur after a head injury or ear infection, but in most patients it has no apparent cause. It causes a constant high-pitched ringing noise (tinnitus) in the ear, dizziness, nausea and slowly progressive permanent deafness.

Motion sickness is due to an effect on the brain that is unable to reconcile the motion being seen by the eyes and that felt by the balance mechanism. Dizziness, nausea and vomiting may result.

The semicircular canals that control balance are known as the labyrinth. If this structure becomes inflamed or infected (labyrinthitis) the patient will become dizzy, abnormal eye movements will occur and noises may be heard in the ear.

The Eustachian tube connects the middle ear to the back of the nose and enables the air pressure in the ear to equalise with that outside when there is a change in altitude. If the tube becomes blocked, pressure in the ear will increase, causing pain, deafness and dizziness.

Uncommon ear causes of dizziness include mastoiditis (infection of the mastoid bone behind the ear), benign paroxysmal positional vertigo, eighth (auditory) nerve inflammation or tumour, shingles (herpes zoster infection)

involving the ear, vestibular neuronitis (inflammation of the nerve endings in the inner ear), endolymphatic hydrops (increased pressure in the inner ear) and a fractured skull involving the inner ear.

Other causes of vertigo that occur outside the ear include migraines (headaches that are often associated with visual symptoms, nausea and vomiting), a stroke (cerebrovascular accident), transient ischaemic attacks, temporal epilepsy, a serious head injury, rapid shallow breathing (hyperventilation), altitude sickness, hypotension (low blood pressure), hardening of the arteries (arteriosclerosis), and a tumour, cyst, cancer, abscess, bleed (after a head injury) or infection (eg. meningitis, encephalitis) affecting the parts of the brain responsible for balance (particularly the cerebellum at the bottom back of the brain).

Many different heart diseases (eg. infection, irregular rhythm) and anaemia may affect blood pressure, and cause dizziness as well as chest pain and other symptoms.

Some medications may have dizziness as an unwanted side effect. Examples include phenytoin (for epilepsy), benzodiazepines, barbiturates (strong sedatives), gentamicin and streptomycin (antibiotics), nonsteroidal anti-inflammatory drugs (for arthritis), and high doses of aspirin.

There are many other uncommon and rare conditions that may cause vertigo.
See also EAR; HALL-PIKE TEST; LIGHTHEADED; NAUSEA AND VOMITING and separate entries for diseases mentioned above.

DNA

DNA (deoxyribonucleic acid) is the key to life and genetics.

Discovered in 1953 by biologists James Watson (USA – born 1928) and Francis Crick (UK – born 1916), DNA forms the structure of every chromosome in the form of a double

DNA

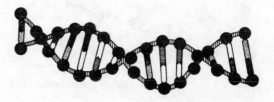

helix. This is like a twisted rubber ladder. Each rung of the ladder is formed by a set combination of amino acids that form a code. Segments of that code form a gene.

Only four amino acids make up the code – adenine (A), thymine (T), guanine (G) and cytosine (C). A always pairs with T, and G with C, allowing exact reproduction of the chromosome.
See also AMINO ACID; CHROMOSOME; GENE

DOCTOR TRAINING
See MEDICAL TRAINING

DOG BITE
See ANIMAL BITE

DOMPERIDONE
See ANTIEMETICS

DONOVANOSIS
See GRANULOMA INGUINALE

DOPPLER STUDIES
When listening to a fast moving vehicle approaching you, its engine noise changes pitch as the vehicle passes you and moves away. This change in the pitch of a sound due to movement is known as the doppler effect. This same effect can be used to measure the movement of fluids (usually blood) within the body.

Using a blunt probe that is placed against the skin, a high pitched sound wave (ultrasound) is passed into the body, and the reflection of the sound wave from stationary tissue and moving blood is measured and compared. In this way, the rate at which the blood is flowing can be determined.

The carotid artery in the neck is the most common one to be examined, but other arteries near the surface of the body (eg. in the groin) may also be checked to see if there is any blockage of the blood flow caused by a clot or build up of a cholesterol plaque.

There is absolutely no discomfort to the patient during the procedure, and they only have to lie still for a few minutes.
See also ECHOCARDIOGRAPHY; ULTRASOUND

DORSAL
The term dorsal is used by doctors to describe the back of the body. The dorsal part of the hand is the back, and in the same way the dorsal part of the lower leg is the calf. Fish commonly have a dorsal fin (eg. the back fin of a shark).
See also LATERAL; VENTRAL

DOTHIEPIN
See ANTIDEPRESSANTS

DOUBLE PNEUMONIA
Pneumonia occurs when bacteria enter the tiny air bubbles that make up the lung, and starts multiplying to cause an infection. Usually only one part of the lungs, often at the bottom of the lung, is affected at first, but the problem soon spreads to other parts of the lung. Normally only one lung is affected but if the patient is particularly unlucky and both lungs are affected, the patient is said to be suffering from double pneumonia.
See also LUNG; PNEUMONIA

DOUBLE VISION
Everyone normally sees double, because we have two eyes, but the brain learns from infancy to merge the two images into one seamless image. Double vision (diplopia) is seeing two images instead of one, rather like a badly ghosting television set. It is a disorienting and confusing symptom that can be caused by eye or brain diseases, or conditions elsewhere in the body that have an effect on these organs.

A squint occurs if the eyes do not align properly, and look in slightly different directions. If a squint occurs from infancy, the image from one eye is suppressed by the brain, and the child effectively sees with only one eye. A squint developing later in life is usually due to damage to the nerves supplying the muscles that control eye movement, or damage to the muscles themselves. The damage is usually a result of a tumour, cancer, direct injury (eg. fractured skull) or inflammation of the nerves or muscles.

An injury to an eye or surrounding bone or other tissue, that prevents it from moving normally, will also cause double vision.

Migraines are often associated with visual symptoms including flashing lights, double vision, shimmering, seeing zigzag lines and loss of part of the area of vision.

In a stroke (cerebrovascular accident)

various parts of the brain may be affected by having its blood supply cut off by a blockage in an artery, or a blood vessel in the brain may burst causing bleeding and damage to part of the brain. The onset is almost instantaneous, may be associated with a variety of symptoms from paralysis and headache to weakness, loss of sensation, double vision, anaesthesia, confusion and coma.

A head injury, causing concussion, may affect the part of the brain responsible for receiving and interpreting sight, as may a tumour, cyst, cancer, abscess or infection affecting the relevant parts of the brain.

Less common causes of double vision include myasthenia gravis (a disease affecting muscle control), multiple sclerosis (a nerve disease), Wernicke-Korsakoff psychosis, and hyperthyroidism (excess thyroxine production).
See also SQUINT; VISION and separate entries for diseases mentioned above.

DOWN SYNDROME
Down syndrome is also known as mongolism and trisomy 21. It is a genetic defect due to the presence of three copies of chromosome 21 instead of two (normally one from each parent), causing various body and organ malformations. It occurs in one in every 600 births overall, but rises to a rate of one in every 100 for mothers over forty years of age.

The symptoms vary considerably between individuals. Common characteristics include poor muscle tone, joints that move further than normal, slanted eyes, a flattened facial appearance (accounting for the former name of "mongolism"), small stature, some degree of intellectual disability, small nose, a short broad hand and finger prints that have a whorl with the loop on the thumb side of the finger tip and other abnormal features. Other characteristics may include a fissured protruding tongue, short neck, widely spaced first and second toes, dry skin, sparse hair, small genitals, small ears, poorly formed teeth, keratoconus (protruding eye surface) and a squint.

It is usually easily recognised and diagnosed at birth. Diagnosis before birth is possible from the fifteenth week of pregnancy by amniocentesis (taking a sample of fluid from around the foetus) or chorionic villus (placenta) biopsy.

There is no specific treatment, but plastic surgery may help some deformities. Patients require more than average medical attention for ear, nose and throat infections. More severe health problems include abnormal heart formation, abnormal formation of the intestines (especially the duodenum), a clouded lens in the eye, infertility and a higher than normal incidence of leukaemia may occur.

There is no cure, but provided there are no serious heart abnormalities, the life expectancy is close to normal. Good education and physiotherapy are effective in helping patients achieve a relatively normal life.
See also AMNIOCENTESIS; CHORIONIC VILLUS SAMPLING; CHROMOSOME; KERATOCONUS

DOXAZOSIN
See ALPHA BLOCKERS

DOXEPIN
See ANTIDEPRESSANTS

DOXYCYCLINE
See ANTIMALARIALS; TETRACYCLINES

DRACUNCULIASIS
See GUINEA WORM

DRESSLER SYNDROME
Dressler syndrome is a complication of a heart attack causing inflammation of the pericardium (fibrous sac that contains the heart). The symptoms include chest pain and fever. Some patients develop lung inflammation (pneumonitis) and shortness of breath.

Blood tests and an ECG (electrocardiogram) can be used to differentiate the syndrome from new heart attack. Treatment involves indomethacin and corticosteroids, but the syndrome settles with or without treatment.
See also HEART ATTACK; PERICARDITIS

DROWNING
Drowning is due to immersion in a swimming pool, dam, river, the ocean or any other water. Fresh water drowning is more serious than salt water due to greater lung damage.

Drowning occurs because the lungs partially fill with water and the larynx (windpipe) goes into spasm and blocks air from entering the lungs. Breathing stops, often after vomiting swallowed water, and the heart will stop beating soon afterwards.

In hospital, blood tests and chest x-rays may be done after the patient is stabilised to check for lung damage and the level of oxygen in blood.

Cardiopulmonary resuscitation should be started as soon as possible (in the water if necessary) and continued for at least an hour. Transfer the patient to a hospital as quickly as possible. Resuscitation is continued in hospital until doctors determine it is no longer appropriate. Follow-up nursing is usually in an intensive care unit.

Permanent lung or brain damage is possible if resuscitation is started too late, but competent cardiopulmonary resuscitation can save an amazing number of lives.
See also RESUSCITATION

DRUG RASH
See FIXED DRUG ERUPTION

DRUGS
See ALCOHOL; CANNABIS; COCAINE; ECSTASY; GAMMA-HYDROXYBUTYRATE; HEROIN; KETAMINE; LSD; MARIJUANA; MEDICATION; MESCALINE; STIMULANTS

DRUSEN
Drusen is a degenerative condition of the retinal macular (central area of light sensitive cells at the back of the eye) in late middle age and the elderly. Patients experience steadily worsening central vision, while edge (peripheral) vision is often normal.

The condition is diagnosed by examining the eye through a magnifying light (ophthalmoscope) and injecting a bright dye (fluorescein) into the artery supplying the eye.

No treatment is available, and the condition is slowly progressive.
See also MACULAR DEGENERATION

DRY EYE
See DRY EYE SYNDROME; EYE DRY

DRY EYE SYNDROME
The dry eye syndrome (xerophthalmia) is a very common problem, with the incidence increasing with age, and is due to reduced tear production. Patients experience dry scratchy irritated eyes.

A small piece of blotting paper placed under lower eye lid remains dry (Schirmer tear test) in patients with the syndrome.

Treatment involves artificial tear drops or ointment, lubricating inserts under lower lids, and surgical blockage of tear duct at inner corner of eye to prevent tear drainage. Complications include eye ulcers and infections. There is no cure, but it can be reasonably controlled with treatment. Severe forms of the syndrome are known as keratoconjunctivitis sicca.
See also EYE DRY; KERATOCONJUNCTIVITIS SICCA

DRY ICE
See CARBON DIOXIDE

DRY MOUTH
See MOUTH DRY

DRY SKIN
See SKIN DRY AND SCALY

DSAP
See DISSEMINATED SUPERFICIAL ACTINIC POROKERATOSIS

DTs
See DELIRIUM TREMENS

DUAL PHOTON DENSITOMETRY
The density of bone can be ascertained from the amount of mineral contained in it. Dual photon densitometry is a type of bone scan that is able to measure the mineral content of bone and is a way of diagnosing the onset of osteoporosis, or thinning of the bones.

The patient lies on a bed with a very mild source of radiation under it, and a long-armed scanner then moves slowly down the body emitting photon beams, which can determine the density of the tissue they are passing through. The procedure takes about half an hour and is completely painless. A screening test may involve only checking the density of the bone in the forearm.

A bone scan cannot necessarily predict osteoporosis in normal people but is very useful for high-risk subjects or people who already have signs of osteoporosis, so that remedial treatment such as bisphosphonate

drugs, hormone replacement therapy and calcium supplements can be administered.
See also NUCLEAR SCAN; OSTEOPOROSIS

DUANE SYNDROME

Duane syndrome is a rare congenital abnormality of nerve supply to eye muscles due to absence of the 6th nerve, which supplies some eye movement muscles. Vision remains normal. Patients are unable to move the eye horizontally resulting in a variable squint. There is no cure, but the severity of squint may be reduced by surgery.
See also EYE; SQUINT

DUBIN-JOHNSON SYNDROME

The Dubin-Johnson syndrome is a congenital developmental abnormality of the liver that causes jaundice (yellow skin) in a newborn infant. Blood tests show high levels of bilirubin, a liver biopsy is abnormal and the gall bladder cannot be seen on special x-rays (cholecystogram) as it does not contain any bile. No treatment is necessary as the condition settles slowly.
See also LIVER; ROTOR SYNDROME

DUBOWITZ SYNDROME

This is a a rare developmental abnormality that is familial, but both parents must be carriers.

The Dubowitz syndrome is characterised by a low birth weight baby with drooping eyelids (ptosis), small jaw, sparse hair, short stature, mild mental retardation and eczema. No treatment is available, and there is no cure.
See also EYELID DROOP; MENTAL RETARDATION

DUCHENNE MUSCULAR DYSTROPHY

Duchenne muscular dystrophy is a progressive and permanent gender-linked inherited condition affecting only males. Females can be carriers, and statistically half the sons of a carrier are affected.

The symptoms start in infancy or early childhood, and progress rapidly with worsening weakness of the pelvic, shoulder, arm and leg muscles resulting in inability to walk by twelve years of age. Eventually the muscles essential for breathing are affected. The condition can be diagnosed by specific blood tests, electrical studies of muscle action, and muscle biopsy.

There is no effective treatment and no cure is available, but physiotherapy is beneficial. Curvature of the spine (kyphoscoliosis) is the main complication. It eventually leads to death in the twenties or thirties.
See also KYPHOSCOLIOSIS; MUSCLE WEAKNESS

DUCTUS ARTERIOSUS

The ductus arteriosus is a short artery that connects the pulmonary artery and the aorta to enable blood to bypass the lungs (which are not in use) before birth. The ductus normally closes shortly after birth.
See also FALLOT'S TETRALOGY; PATENT DUCTUS ARTERIOSUS

DUE DATE
See PREGNANCY DATES

DUMMIES

The use of a dummy always causes arguments. If a parent prefers a child to suck a dummy to a thumb, or uses a dummy as a pacifier, there is no good reason why not, provided the dummy can be kept clean. To coat a dummy with honey or some other sweet substance is forbidden, as it will cause dental problems and almost inevitably will lead to the child developing a propensity for sweet foods, which can cause lifelong problems.
See also THUMB SUCKING

DUMPING SYNDROME

The dumping (or postgastrectomy) syndrome is a complication of gastrectomy, an operation in which part of the stomach is surgically removed for diseases such as cancer and incurable peptic ulcers. It occurs in 10% of postgastrectomy patients because of sudden overstretching of the now small stomach by food, and stimulation of the vagus nerve, which supplies the stomach, intestine and heart.

Patients experience sweating, rapid heart rate, pallor, belly discomfort and cramps, nausea and weakness. Some develop fainting, vomiting and diarrhoea. All symptoms occur within twenty minutes of eating.

Frequent small meals with low carbohydrate content and no fluids with meals, is the

main treatment. Sedatives and anticholinergics (stomach muscle relaxing medication) are sometimes used. There is no cure.
See also STOMACH

DUODENAL ULCER
See PEPTIC ULCER

DUODENUM
The duodenum is the first section of the small intestine, and at one end connects to the valve at the bottom of the stomach (the pylorus) and at the other end merges into the jejunum. It is attached to the back wall of the abdomen with a fine sheet of tissue that contains the blood and lymphatic vessels which carry the digested food to be processed for absorption by the liver.

The alkaline nature of the mucus in the duodenum protects it from being damaged by the acidity of the partly digested food entering from the stomach. The mucus also contains numerous enzymes, each designed to work on particular types of food. There is a special enzyme to break down proteins, one to break down carbohydrates and a different one again to break down fats.

Additional digestive juices from the liver and the pancreas also enter the small intestine through the duodenum. The pancreas produces the enzyme pancrease and the liver produces bile – a thick greenish-yellow liquid containing bile salts which act to break down fat globules, not unlike detergent. These juices are conveyed to the duodenum through two ducts, respectively called the pancreatic

duct and the bile duct, which normally join together just before entering the duodenum. Bile does not come directly from the liver but is stored in the gall bladder and released as needed when food enters the small intestine.

The partly digested food continues from the duodenum through the jejunum and into the ileum where digestion is completed.
See also GALL BLADDER; ILEUM; JEJUNUM; LIVER; PANCREAS

DUPUYTREN CONTRACTURE OF HAND
A fibrous sheet (the palmar aponeurosis) stretches under the skin of the palm to give it a smooth appearance, strength and firmness, and to protect and control the movement of the muscle tendons that cross under it to the fingers. If damaged, the palmar aponeurosis may become scarred, contract and thicken into hard lumps that can be felt under the skin. As the damage progresses, the contraction of the fibrous sheet pulls on the tendons that run underneath it to prevent their free movement. This is a Dupuytren contracture of the hand.

The cause is unknown, but may be due to a poor blood supply to the hand (eg. diabetes), the use of vibrating tools (eg. jack hammers), or injury to the hand from repeated blows (eg. catching cricket balls). Men are affected more than twice as often as women and there is a tendency for the condition to occur in successive generations.

Patients develop one or more hard, fixed nodules under the skin of the palm that gradually extend length wise along the palm to cause discomfort and loss of finger mobility. Eventually the fingers cannot be fully extended, and contract into a claw-like appearance. The ring and little fingers are usually more severely affected than the others.

A relatively minor and successful operation can be performed to carefully cut away the thickened part of the palmar aponeurosis and free the tendons. Without treatment there is complete loss of hand function as it contracts into a fist. Unfortunately, a slow recurrence after operation, which may require further surgery, is quite common.

Rarely a similar condition can occur in the sole of the foot (Ledderhose disease).
See also HAND; LEDDERHOSE DISEASE

DUODENUM

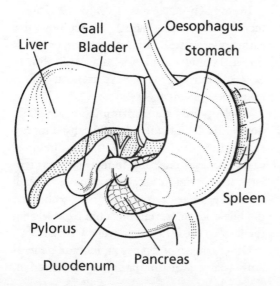

Liver · Gall Bladder · Oesophagus · Stomach · Spleen · Pylorus · Pancreas · Duodenum

DUROMINE
See ANORECTICS

DVT
See DEEP VEIN THROMBOSIS

DWARF
See de LANGE SYNDROME; GROWTH REDUCED

DYDROGESTERONE
See SEX HORMONES

DYS-
"Dys-" is a prefix derived from the Greek that is used in medicine to indicate something that is abnormal, difficult or impaired (eg. dyslexia means difficulty in reading and writing).

DYSARTHRIA
See SPEECH DIFFICULT

DYSENTERY
Dysentery is severe diarrhoea with blood and/or mucus in the motions, and associated with abdominal pains (colic). Due to infection of the bowel by a bacteria or amoeba.
See also AMOEBIASIS; DIARRHOEA; SHIGELLOSIS

DYSHIDROSIS
See POMPHOLYX

DYSHIDROTIC DERMATITIS
See POMPHOLYX

DYSKINESIA
See MOVEMENT ABNORMAL

DYSLEXIA
Dyslexia is a developmental abnormality in which reading and writing are a problem. Word learning and language ability are affected. The cause is unknown, but rarely, it may be due to brain injury.

It is a disorder that affects the ability of children (and in brain injury, adults) to read, write and understand words despite normal intelligence and educational opportunity. Other symptoms may include delayed development of speech, difficulty in remembering the names of objects, inability to rhyme words, confusing the position of sounds in long multisyllabic words, inability to choose the correct word, poor time organisation and poor memory.

Intensive teaching and training is the main treatment. Drug treatments are available, but their use is very controversial.

Although it is a lifelong problem, many develop the ability to function in society with basic reading and writing skills.
See also ATTENTION DEFICIT DISORDER

DYSMENORRHOEA
See MENSTRUAL PERIODS PAINFUL

DYSPAREUNIA
See SEXUAL INTERCOURSE PAIN

DYSPEPSIA
Belly pains that are made worse by eating are referred to as dyspepsia.

The stomach contains concentrated hydrochloric acid that is used to digest food. Extra amounts are secreted when food is eaten, or even the smell of food may trigger acid secretion. The stomach is lined with thick mucus that protects it from being digested by the acid it contains. Gastritis is an inflammation of the stomach caused by the mucus lining becoming too thin, or excessive acid secretion. Upper belly pain, often made worse after eating, and burping, are the most common symptoms. If the acid succeeds in damaging the stomach or small intestine, a peptic ulcer will develop, and pain may become more constant.

Severe anxiety, and physical or emotional stress, may increase acid production and cause gastritis or inflammation of the first part of the small intestine (the duodenum).

If stomach acid runs up into the unprotected gullet (oesophagus), particularly after eating a large meal, intense burning pain will be felt behind the breast bone, and a bitter taste and burping may be experienced. This is reflux oesophagitis.

Cholecystitis is an inflammation or infection of the gall bladder, usually caused by gall stones that have formed within it. In most cases it causes pain and indigestion, particularly after eating a fatty meal, but if the gall bladder becomes very swollen it may obstruct the bile duct to prevent bilirubin from leaving the liver to cause jaundice (yellow skin).

Other causes of dyspepsia include pancreatitis (damage to the pancreas by infection, gall stone, alcoholism or a cancer), irritable bowel syndrome, cancer of the stomach and food allergies.

Some medications (eg. nonsteroidal anti-inflammatory drugs used for arthritis) may also irritate the stomach.

See also ABDOMINAL PAIN; BURPING, EXCESSIVE; CHEST PAIN; HEARTBURN; STOMACH; SWALLOWING, PAINFUL OR DIFFICULT

DYSPHAGIA
See SWALLOWING PAINFUL

DYSPNOEA
See BREATH, SHORT OF

DYSTROPHIA ADIPOSGENITALIS
See FRÖHLICH SYNDROME

DYSURIA
See URINATION PAIN

E

EAR

The ears are the organs of hearing and of balance. The ear consists of three parts – the outer, middle and inner ear. The outer and middle parts are concerned with hearing, and parts of the inner ear are concerned with balance as well as hearing.

The outer ear consists of the part we can see, i.e. the ear flap (pinna) guarding the ear canal, which links the outer ear with the middle ear. The ear canal is also protected by tiny hairs, sweat glands and oil glands which produce wax to stop particles of dust and dirt from getting in. The ear canal is about 2.5cm long.

At the end of the ear canal is a six-sided box which is the middle ear. Four sides of the box are made of bone but the fifth side opens into the Eustachian tube and the sixth side, which is the one facing into the ear canal, is covered by the thin, transparent membrane that forms the eardrum. Inside the box are the three tiniest bones in the human body, commonly called after their respective shapes the hammer, the anvil and the stirrup, but more correctly known as the malleus, incus and stapes. The stapes is the smallest bone in the body. Sound waves are collected by the outer ear, passed down the ear canal to vibrate the eardrum and then into the middle ear where the sounds are amplified by the tiny bones.

The Eustachian tube connects the middle ear to the back of the nose. In essence, sound consists of small fluctuations in air pressure and this tube enables the same pressure to be maintained in the middle ear as in the outside atmosphere, so that the middle ear can pick up the sound waves. If the outside pressure alters more quickly than the middle ear can adjust to, such as when we are flying or diving, the ear will hurt. The familiar pop of the ears in these circumstances is the pressure adjusting by air suddenly moving through the eustachian tube. The connection of the tube to the throat means that phlegm and mucus sometimes travel along it and cause middle-ear infections.

The inner ear is filled with fluid and contains the cochlea (named because it is shaped like a cockle or snail shell) which is the part where hearing occurs. Sound passes from the middle ear through a fluid-filled chamber and into the cochlea where, in a tiny hair-lined section called the organ of Corti, it is converted into nerve impulses. These nerve impulses are then transmitted to the brain by the auditory nerve which registers them as sounds.

The inner ear is also the organ of balance. Above the cochlea are three semicircular

EAR

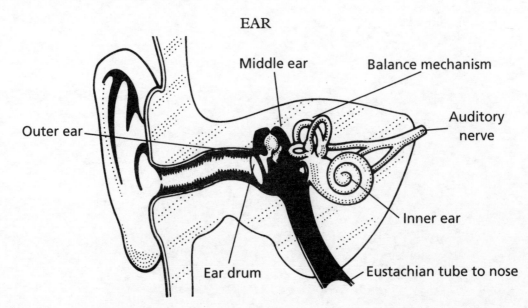

Outer ear

Middle ear

Balance mechanism

Auditory nerve

Inner ear

Ear drum

Eustachian tube to nose

canals set at different angles (the vestibular apparatus). These are filled with fluid which moves as the head moves. Highly sensitive hairs pick up the movement and send impulses to the brain indicating the position of the head and body.

See also AURISCOPE; CAULIFLOWER EAR; DEAF; DIZZINESS; EARACHE; EAR DISCHARGE; EAR SMELL; EAR WAX; EUSTACHIAN TUBE; GROMMET; HEARING TESTS; MYRINGOTOMY; OTITIS EXTERNA; OTITIS MEDIA; PINNA; TINNITUS; TRAGUS; TYMPANIC RUPTURE; VALSALVA MANOEUVRE and other entries for ear symptoms and diseases.

EARACHE

Ear pain is a very common problem, particularly in children, and because the pain is often caused by a buildup of pressure inside the middle ear, normal (and even prescribed) pain killers are often not effective. Only reducing the pressure will ease the pain.

It is often difficult to tell if a child has an ear infection, but this trick may help. If moving the outer ear causes pain, a middle ear infection is a possibility. If pressure on the tragus (the firm lump of cartilage immediately in front of the ear canal) causes pain, an outer ear infection is possible. If neither causes pain, an ear infection is unlikely.

A direct injury to the ear from a blow or fall may cause bleeding, bruising, swelling and pain to the ear and surrounding tissues.

Wax is normally produced in the ear canal by specialised glands, and slowly moves out of the canal to keep it clean. If excess amounts of wax are produced, dirt or dust gets into the canal, water swells the wax in the canal, or attempts are made to clean the canal with a cotton bud or other implement, the wax may become swollen, hard and tightly packed in the canal to cause pain and deafness.

Otitis externa (swimmer's ear) is a bacterial or fungal (tropical ear) infection of the ear canal. The ear becomes very painful, and as the infection progresses, a smelly discharge usually develops.

Middle ear infections (otitis media) are a very common cause of temporary deafness in children, that if left untreated, may progress to a permanent partial loss of hearing. The ear is painful, the child is feverish, and when a doctor examines the ear, a red bulging ear drum can be seen.

If phlegm from the nose enters the middle ear cavity through the Eustachian tube, or other secretions accumulate in the cavity, it is difficult for them to escape back through the Eustachian tube to the back of the nose, particularly if the adenoids which surround the opening of the tube into the nose are swollen. This is glue ear, and may be responsible for recurrent infections in the ear, deafness and low grade ear discomfort.

Blockage of the Eustachian tube with phlegm will prevent pressure equalisation between the middle ear and the outside if there is an altitude change (eg. taking off in an aircraft) or pressure change (eg. scuba diving). Intense pain will be felt in the ear because of distortion of the sensitive ear drum with the pressure difference. In the worst cases, the ear drum will burst, the pain will ease, but the ear will be deaf until the ear drum heals.

If bacteria or viruses enter the sinuses, an infection (sinusitis) may result and thick pus is produced. The sinuses becomes very painful and tender, then waste products from the infection enter the blood stream, and cause a fever, headaches and the other unpleasant sensations of any major infection. It is quite easy for the infection to spread through the Eustachian tube from the back of the nose to the middle ear.

The common cold (coryza) may be caused by one or more of several hundred different viruses. It may cause a sore throat, runny nose, cough, fever, headache, earache and general tiredness.

The sensory nerves that supply the teeth run along the top and bottom jaws to a point just in front of the ear where they enter the skull. Any infection or disease of a tooth can inflame the nerve running from that tooth, but the pain may be felt in the ear because of the course the nerve follows to the brain. Babies who are teething often pull at their ears because of this phenomenon.

Less common causes of earache include a foreign body in the ear canal (eg. a small toy, nut, insect), mastoiditis (infection in the bone behind the ear), a furuncle (boil in the ear), a cholesteatoma (foul smelling growth in the ear canal), parotitis (infection of the parotid salivary gland), and arthritis, diseases or other inflammations of the jaw joint.

There are many uncommon and rare causes of ear pain. Some of these include shingles (*Herpes zoster* virus infection) involving the ear (Ramsay Hunt syndrome), nerve inflammation or tumour (neuroma), temporal arteritis (inflammation of the artery in the temple) and Hand-Schueller-Christian syndrome.
See also EAR; EAR WAX; EUSTACHIAN TUBE and separate entries for most diseases mentioned above.

EAR BUZZING
See TINNITUS

EAR DISCHARGE
An ear may discharge wax, blood, pus, serum (the pale yellow liquid part of blood without the cells) or cerebrospinal fluid (CSF – the fluid that surrounds and supports the brain).

The most common substance to be discharged is wax, and if a patient has a fever, the higher temperature may melt the wax in the ear canal, allowing it to flow out more easily than normal.

If there is a foreign body in the ear canal (eg. a small toy, nut, insect), the irritation may cause pain, bleeding, dermatitis (and a watery discharge of serum) and infection with pus formation.

Otitis externa (swimmer's ear) is a bacterial or fungal (tropical ear) infection of the ear canal. The ear becomes very painful, and as the infection progresses, a smelly discharge usually develops.

Middle ear infections (otitis media) are a very common cause of temporary deafness in children that, if left untreated, may progress to a permanent partial loss of hearing. The ear is painful, the child is feverish, and when a doctor examines the ear, a red bulging ear drum can be seen. If the drum bursts, pus will discharge from the ear, but the pain will diminish.

Other causes include a furuncle (a boil in the ear), weeping dermatitis or eczema in the ear canal, a severe head injury in which the skull around the ear is fractured (some of the cerebrospinal fluid that surrounds and supports the brain may leak into the ear canal) and rarely, tumours or cancers in the ear canal will discharge and bleed.
See also EAR; EARACHE; FURUNCULOSIS, EAR

EAR DRUM RUPTURE
See TYMPANIC RUPTURE

EAR INFECTION
See FURUNCULOSIS, EAR; MASTOIDITIS; OTITIS EXTERNA; OTITIS MEDIA

EAR NOISE
See TINNITUS

EAR, NOSE AND THROAT
See EAR; NOSE; LARYNX; PHARYNX; OTORHINOLARYNGOLOGY

EAR PAIN
See EARACHE

EAR PROTRUDING
See BAT EARS

EAR SMELL
The most common cause of a smelly ear is otitis externa (swimmer's ear). This is a bacterial or fungal (tropical ear) infection of the ear canal. The ear becomes very painful and as the infection progresses, a smelly discharge develops.

Other causes include a middle ear infection (otitis media) and a cholesteatoma (foul smelling growth in the ear from a sac on the ear drum which is filled with chronically infected material).
See also EAR; EAR DISCHARGE and separate entries for diseases mentioned above.

EAR VENTILATION TUBE
See GROMMET

EAR WAX
Technically, ear wax is known as cerumen. It is secreted naturally in the outer ear canal by special glands, and slowly moves out to clear away dust and debris that enters the ear. It also acts to keep the skin lining the canal lubricated and to protect it from water and other irritants. The ear is designed to be self-cleaning, and over-zealous attempts to clean it may pack the wax down hard on the eardrum or damage the ear canal.

Ear wax may cause problems if excess is produced, the wax is too thick, the ear canal is narrow, or the person works in a dusty and dirty environment. When wax builds up on the eardrum, it cannot transmit vibrations on to the inner ear, and so causes varying degrees of deafness, itching, and sometimes pain. Water entering the ear during bathing or swimming may cause the wax to swell.

Cerumen may be removed by syringing, suction or fine forceps. In syringing, warm water is gently squirted into the ear to dislodge the wax, with large lumps being removed by forceps. The use of wax-softening drops may be necessary to facilitate the removal of particularly large or hard accumulations of wax. Those with recurrent problems should use wax-softening drops on a regular basis.

Ear wax normally causes no problems, and merely fulfils its cleaning role, but sometimes an infection may start in the skin of the outer ear canal under the wax causing significant pain.

Strangely, it has been discovered that women who have soft ear wax have a much higher risk of breast cancer than those with hard ear wax.
See also EAR

EATING, EXCESSIVE
See APPETITE, EXCESS

EATING, PAINFUL
See DYSPEPSIA

EBOLA VIRUS
The Ebola virus is an extremely contagious form of viral haemorrhagic fever (viral infection of the blood) that occurs in central and west Africa, and the Philippines. The virus is spread by monkeys and from person to person in conditions of poor hygiene. Outbreaks have occurred in the Congo, Sudan, Ivory Coast and the Philippines. Epidemics are often hospital based, but good personal hygiene and using masks and gowns prevents the spread of infection.

Victims develop muscle pains, headache, sore throat, joint pains, diarrhoea, vomiting, red eyes and abnormal bleeding, and blood tests show significant abnormalities. There is no cure or vaccine for prevention, and treatment is restricted to managing the symptoms and nursing care in strict isolation. Internal bleeding causes death in about 80% of patients.
See also LASSA FEVER; MARBURG VIRUS

EBSTEIN ANOMALY
The Ebstein anomaly is the congenital abnormal development of the tricuspid valve and some nerve pathways in heart. The tricuspid valve between the atrium and ventricle on the right side of the heart is under developed, slips down into the right ventricle, and leaks (is incompetent or regurgitates). This results in right heart failure (cor pulmonale), and some patients develop blue skin (cyanosis), paroxysmal atrial tachycardia or Wolff-Parkinson-White syndrome. Echocardiography (ultrasound scan of heart) is used to confirm the diagnosis.

Medication is used to control heart contraction (eg. propranolol), followed by surgery to replace tricuspid valve and cut abnormal nerve pathways in the heart, but some patients have irreparable heart defects. Treatment gives reasonable results from treatment.
See also COR PULMONALE;
ECHOCARDIOGRAM; HEART;
TRICUSPID VALVE INCOMPETENCE

EBV
See GLANDULAR FEVER

ECCHYMOSIS
See BRUISING, ABNORMAL

ECG
See ELECTROCARDIOGRAM

ECHINOCOCCOSIS
See HYDATID DISEASE

ECHOCARDIOGRAPHY
Echocardiography is a highly sophisticated form of ultrasound used to investigate the inner workings of the heart and in particular the heart valves.

While lying down, the patient's chest is smeared with gel, and an instrument is placed on the chest and moved slowly from one point to another over the heart. The instrument sends out high frequency sound waves and receives back an echo of these waves as they are reflected by the heart. The reflected waves are recorded on a moving sheet of paper to give a complex tracing. Specialist doctors (usually cardiologists) interpret this tracing to see if the heart valves are working properly (eg. if they are leaking or narrowed) and to check the contraction of each chamber of the heart.

Because performing echocardiography involves no risk, no pain and no discomfort for the patient, the procedure is often carried out before progressing to more sophisticated and invasive tests on the heart. If no abnormalities show on the echocardiogram, the other tests may be unnecessary.
See also HEART; ULTRASOUND

ECLAMPSIA
See PRE-ECLAMPSIA AND ECLAMPSIA

E. COLI INFECTION
See ESCHERICHIA COLI INFECTION

ECONAZOLE
See ANTIFUNGALS

ECONOMY CLASS SYNDROME
See DEEP VEIN THROMBOSIS

ECSTASY
Ecstasy is a synthetic stimulant that comes as a tablet and has found favour in dance clubs since the mid 1990s. There is no easy or definite way in which to determine if someone is using Ecstasy unless a specific blood test is performed. From a parent's point of view, it is almost impossible, as the symptoms of its use could also be explained by the variable moodiness of the average teenager.

The symptoms of Ecstasy are rapid in onset and brief in duration. The rapid onset explains its popularity as the user gets a high quickly after taking the tablet. The effects are increased if used with alcohol, as this increases its rate of absorption, and this also explains the fatalities that can occur.

Serious adverse effects result in an irregular heart beat that may become so serious that a heart attack and death occurs. Most users experience a period of increased perception of sounds, sights and smells that makes the world seem a more exciting place. It can also result in sexual disinhibition, hallucinations and general euphoria.

After the high has worn off the user may be moody, drowsy, have red and sore eyes, be nauseated and vomit, and have poor coordination.
See also COCAINE; GAMMA-HYDROXY BUTYRATE; HEROIN; KETAMINE; LSD; MARIJUANA; MESCALINE; STIMULANTS

ECT
See ELECTROCONVULSIVE THERAPY

ECTOPIC PREGNANCY
A foetus normally grows within the womb (uterus). An ectopic pregnancy is one that starts and continues to develop outside the uterus. About one in every 200 pregnancies is ectopic. Conditions such as pelvic inflammatory disease and salpingitis increase the risk of ectopic pregnancies, as they cause damage to the Fallopian tubes. Other infections in the pelvis (eg. severe appendicitis) may also be responsible for tube damage.

ECTOPIC PREGNANCY

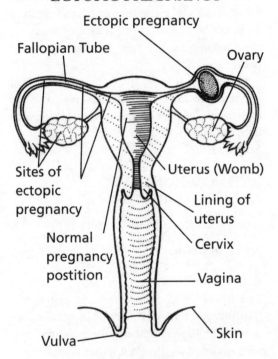

Female reproductive organs showing possible sites of ectopic pregnancy

Symptoms of an ectopic pregnancy may be minimal until a sudden crisis from rupture of blood vessels occurs, but most women have abnormal vaginal bleeding or pains low in the abdomen in the early part of the pregnancy. Many ectopic pregnancies fail to develop past an early stage, and appear to be a normal miscarriage. Serious problems can occur if the ectopic pregnancy does continue to grow.

The most common site for an ectopic pregnancy is the Fallopian tube, which leads from the ovary to the top corner of the womb. A pregnancy in the tube will slowly dilate the tube until it eventually bursts. This will cause severe bleeding into the abdomen and is an urgent, life-threatening situation for the mother. Other possible sites for an ectopic pregnancy include on or around the ovary, in the abdomen or pelvis, or in the narrow angle where the Fallopian tube enters the uterus.

If an ectopic pregnancy is suspected, an ultrasound scan can be performed to confirm the exact position of any pregnancy. If the pregnancy is found to be ectopic, the woman must be treated in a major hospital. Surgery to save the mother's life is essential, as a ruptured ectopic pregnancy can cause the woman very rapidly to bleed to death internally. If the ectopic site is the Fallopian tube, the tube on that side is usually removed during the operation. With early diagnosis and improved surgical techniques, the tube may not have to be removed. Even if it is lost, the woman can fall pregnant again from the tube and ovary on the other side.

It is rare for a foetus to survive any ectopic pregnancy.
See also FALLOPIAN TUBE; PREGNANCY

ECTROPION

Ectropion is the out-turning of the lower eyelid, due to slackness of tissue in the eyelid with ageing or injury. Tears cannot be retained in the eye and trickle down the cheek, and there is an increased risk of eye surface infection or ulceration. Surgery can be performed to tighten up the lower lid.
See also EYE DRY; EYELID DISEASE

ECZEMA

The term eczema describes a large number of skin diseases that cause itching and burning of the skin. The many different forms of eczema also have innumerable causes, both from within the body (eg. stress) and outside (eg. allergies, chemicals).

The appearance of eczema depends more on its position on the body, duration, severity and degree of scratching than the actual cause. Typically it appears as red, swollen, itchy skin that is initially covered with small fluid-filled blisters that quickly break down to a scale or crust.

No investigations are usually necessary, but a biopsy can be diagnostic.

Treatment depends upon the cause of eczema, but steroid creams and tablets are commonly used.

The main complication is a secondary bacterial infection of the skin.
See also ALLERGIC ECZEMA; ASTEATOTIC ECZEMA; ATOPIC ECZEMA; CONTACT DERMATITIS; DISCOID ECZEMA; GRAVITATIONAL ECZEMA; LICHEN SIMPLEX; PHOTOSENSITIVE ECZEMA; SEBORRHOEIC ECZEMA; SKIN; SKIN RED; SKIN ITCH; VARICOSE ECZEMA

ECZEMA CRAQUELÉ
See ASTEATOTIC ECZEMA

EDWARDS SYNDROME

Edwards syndrome (trisomy 18) is a rare congenital developmental disorder caused by the presence of three copies of chromosome 18 instead of two. Patients have a small jaw, heart malformations and rounded soles (rocker-bottom feet). There is no cure or treatment available.

EEG
See ELECTROENCEPHALOGRAM

EFFORT SYNDROME
See da COSTA SYNDROME

EFFUSION

Effusion is a medical term that indicates the presence of a fluid, such as blood or serum, in a place where it should not be present.
See also PLEURAL EFFUSION

EHLERS-DANLOS SYNDROME

Ehlers-Danlos syndrome (cutis hyperelastica or the elastic skin syndrome) is a congenital abnormality of skin development with eight clinically and genetically different variants. Patients have over extendable joints, excessively elastic and fragile skin, scarring of skin and growths on their knees and elbows, and premature arthritis may occur. It is diagnosed by a skin biopsy. There is no treatment or cure available, but life expectancy is normal.
See also SKIN THIN

EISENMENGER SYNDROME

Eisenmenger syndrome is the failure of an artery near the heart (the ductus arteriosus, that bypasses the lungs before birth) to close immediately after birth. This causes an abnormal blood flow through the lungs and heart, and high blood pressure in the lungs (cor pulmonale). A machinery-like murmur can be heard through a stethoscope, and an ECG (electrocardiogram), echocardiogram (ultrasound of heart), and cardiac catheterisation (passing a pressure-measuring tube through an artery or vein into the heart) are all abnormal.

Medication (indomethacin) is sometimes successful to close the artery, but surgery is often needed to close the ductus arteriosus and prevent permanent lung or heart damage. Patients get good results from treatment, but it is fatal if untreated.
See also COR PULMONALE; PATENT DUCTUS ARTERIOSUS

EJACULATION
The ejaculation of semen from the penis is the culmination of sexual intercourse in men, and makes it possible for his female partner to fall pregnant. Ejaculation may also be stimulated by masturbation.

The man feels a buildup of pressure in the base of the penis and testicles, and then with a release of pressure and pleasure, the semen is forced down the urethra by contraction of the seminal vesicles in the groin and the muscles at the base of the penis. Ejaculation may last in an intense phase for ten to thirty seconds, but semen may leak from the penis for some minutes afterwards. The penis usually becomes flaccid and soft shortly after ejaculation.
See also EJACULATION FAILURE; EJACULATION, LACK OF; EJACULATION PREMATURE; EJACULATION RETROGRADE; IMPOTENCE; MASTURBATION; ORGASM; PENIS; SEXUAL INTERCOURSE; TESTICLE

EJACULATION FAILURE
An inability to ejaculate (ejaculatory failure or retarded ejaculation) during sexual intercourse is the male equivalent of a failed orgasm in the female. Some men can ejaculate when masturbating, or with oral sex, but not with vaginal sex. This problem may be a drug side effect or due to psychological problems, an inhibited personality, subconscious or conscious anxiety, or fear of losing self-control. Any significant underlying disease should be excluded.

Treatment involves progressive desensitisation with the assistance of a co-operative sex partner, who initially masturbates the patient to ejaculation, and over a series of weeks, learns to bring him almost to the point of ejaculation by hand stimulation before allowing vaginal sex. Another technique involves additional stimulation of the penis during intercourse by the woman massaging the penis with her fingers while the man thrusts in and out of the vagina. Distracting the man from consciously holding back the ejaculation by passionate kissing or other stimulation of the face or back during intercourse may also help. Reasonable results can be achieved with commitment to the treatment program.
See also EJACULATION; EJACULATION, LACK OF

EJACULATION, LACK OF
The male ejaculation or discharge of semen at the time of sexual intercourse sometimes goes awry, and instead of travelling from the sperm storage sac (seminal vesicle) in the groin, into the penis and out through the urethra, the ejaculate goes backwards into the urinary bladder.

Causes include prostate surgery or disease, injury to the pelvis or the spinal cord, diabetes, or a tumour of the spinal cord. It may also be due to psychological stress, a stroke, tumour or cancer in the brain, compression to, or damage of, the nerves in the pelvis, Parkinson's disease, or to an abnormality the individual was born with (when it will usually become evident soon after puberty).

Sometimes it may be a side effect of medications such as those used to treat high blood pressure, psychiatric conditions or fluid excess (diuretics). Often no cause can be found.
See also EJACULATION; EJACULATION FAILURE; EJACULATION RETROGRADE; PENIS; SEXUAL INTERCOURSE

EJACULATION PREMATURE
Premature ejaculation can be very embarrassing for a man. He is just about to have sex, or has just started, when he finds he is no longer able to control himself and he ejacu-

lates his sperm. The penis then becomes soft and flaccid. This leaves his partner sexually frustrated, makes pregnancy impossible and may damage the relationship.

The most common cause is psychological stress, including emotional upsets and performance anxiety. The more the man tries to please his partner, the more trouble he may have with the problem. The man may also be over-stimulated, excited and foreplay may have been too intense.

There are virtually no diseases or physical conditions, which cause this problem.

Therapists can teach appropriate techniques that involve the co-operation of the partner, to overcome premature ejaculation.

One simple technique is the penis squeeze. If a man feels that ejaculation is imminent, he indicates this to his partner, and all sexual activity ceases. The man, or his partner, uses the thumb and forefinger to squeeze the penis firmly from above and below, about one third the way down the shaft from the head of the penis. This will cause the sensation of imminent ejaculation to cease and the penis may start to become less rigid. Sexual activity can then recommence.
See also EJACULATION, LACK OF; PENIS; SEXUAL INTERCOURSE

EJACULATION RETROGRADE
Retrograde ejaculation occurs if semen is ejaculated from the sac at the base of the penis (seminal vesicle), but instead of passing along the urethra in the penis to the outside, it travels in the other direction and enters the bladder. It is usually a complication of surgery in the area (eg. to the prostate), due to advanced diabetes or a side effect of some uncommon drugs. The man has the sensation of orgasm during sex, but no ejaculation occurs.

Unfortunately, no treatment is available, but the resultant infertility may be overcome by microsurgical techniques to remove sperm from the man and artificially inseminate a woman.
See also EJACULATION; EJACULATION, LACK OF; SEMINAL VESICLE

EKBOM SYNDROME
See RESTLESS LEGS SYNDROME

ELASTIC SKIN SYNDROME
See EHLERS-DANLOS SYNDROME

ELBOW
The joint formed by the humerus above and the radius and ulnar below. It can move in only one plane, forward and back, as it is a hinge joint. The joint is enclosed in a synovial membrane filled with lubricating synovial fluid.
See also HUMERUS; JOINT; MONTEGGIA FRACTURE; SYNOVIAL FLUID

ELBOW JOINT

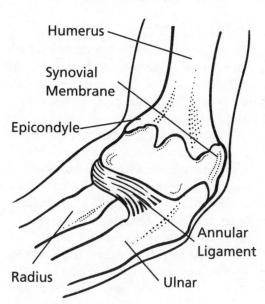

Humerus

Synovial Membrane

Epicondyle

Annular Ligament

Radius   Ulnar

ELDERLY FALLING
See FALL, UNEXPECTED

ELECTRICAL TESTS
See ELECTROCARDIOGRAM; ELECTROENCEPHALOGRAM; ELECTROMYOGRAM

ELECTRIC SHOCK
See ELECTROCUTION

ELECTROCARDIOGRAM
The heart is a muscular bag that pumps blood by contracting and relaxing. Messages for the muscle to contract are carried electrically from one part of the heart to another. An electrocardiogram or electrocardiogram (ECG) is a machine that measures the electrical activity of the heart to produce a tracing that can sometimes be used to diagnose heart disease.

Early ECG recordings were made by putting both the patient's arms and a leg in a bucket of salty water (which conducts electricity), and putting a wire from an instrument for measuring changes in electrical current (a galvanometer) into each bucket. Modern electrocardiographs are more sophisticated but work on the same principle, using electrodes (metal plates or plastic patches covered in a gel) and leads instead of wires and buckets of water. A present day ECG machine is relatively small – about the size of a shoe box – but still quite expensive. An electrocardiogram is the single most important test for coronary heart disease due to narrowing of the arteries.

To have an ECG the patient is asked to strip to the waist (including removal of the bra in women) so ten electrodes can be attached to the chest, arms and legs. They are held in place by elastic straps, suction caps or sticky pads. There is no discomfort or pain of any kind. While lying quietly, the doctor will twist dials and move levers on the machine to measure the electrical activity being picked up from the body by the ten different leads. If the patient moves to any significant degree, the electrical activity generated in the muscles may interfere with the reading.

The machine will produce a graph consisting of a continuous wiggly line that looks like a landscape of steep mountains and deep valleys and represents the activity of the heart. The graph may appear on either a screen or on a long strip of paper. A normal healthy heart has a characteristic pattern. Any irregularity in the heart rhythm or damage to the heart muscle will show up as being different from the normal pattern.

NORMAL ECG TRACING

The different bumps in the printout are identified by letters of the alphabet. The small bump marked P shows the activity of the atrium (the upper chamber of the heart). The QRS zigzag is the contraction of the ventricles (lower heart chamber) and the T wave is the recharging of the heart ready for the next beat.

The ECG may show enlargement of the heart, irregular beats, damage to the heart

(eg. by a heart attack), poor blood supply to the heart, abnormal position of the heart, high blood pressure, abnormal nerve pathways, and even an imbalance in the blood chemicals that control heart activity.

The interpretation of an ECG reading is a very complex task, and may take considerable time. Doctors receive special training in this art during their course. Twelve different lines are recorded in an ECG one after another (or simultaneously on very sophisticated machines) and each line has its own normal and abnormal characteristics. As an example, the figure above is characteristic of lead IV, but if the Q wave was much larger and there was a smoothing of the angle between the S and T waves, the ECG would be indicating that a heart attack may have recently occurred. Others of the twelve leads would also have to show abnormal characteristics to confirm the diagnosis.

The letters P, Q, R, S and T used to identify the main waves of an ECG tracing were chosen arbitrarily by William Einthoven, the Dutch physician who invented the ECG in 1903.

Unfortunately the cardiograph only shows what is happening to the heart at the moment the reading is taken. It cannot always predict what will happen to the heart in the future. It is not unknown for a patient to have a heart attack only minutes after a normal ECG. For this reason, if there is significant suspicion (not just for routine investigations), an exercise ECG (heart stress test) will be performed.

Electrocardiograms are sometimes performed as a routine part of a medical examination, but more commonly if a doctor is suspicious about a patient's health.
See also HEART; HOLTER MONITOR; STRESS TEST

ELECTROCAUTERY
See DIATHERMY

ELECTROCONVULSIVE THERAPY
Electroconvulsive therapy (ECT, shock treatment) has been used successfully by psychiatrists since the 1930s to treat severe depression and other mental disease, but it has been subjected to much media criticism and vilification by consumer groups in the past few decades. The adverse reactions to shock treatment come mainly from a misunderstanding

of the procedure and what it can and cannot achieve.

A patient about to undergo ECT is thoroughly examined and an electroencephalogram (EEG) and x-rays of the back and neck may be performed. The patient will be stopped from eating or drinking for eight hours before the treatment.

For the procedure, patients are usually taken to a specially equipped room or operating theatre. They are asked to empty their bladder. Electrodes are attached to the temples and then a brief general anaesthetic is administered. During this anaesthetic, which lasts only a couple of minutes, an electric current is passed through the brain. This electric current causes an epileptic-like seizure that lasts five to fifteen seconds, but because the patients are anaesthetised, the actual body and muscle movement is only slight or non-existent, and no pain or discomfort is felt. Patients recover rapidly from the anaesthetic, but are confused for about an hour. They may lose any memory of events in the few hours before the shock treatment was given, and may suffer a dull headache for a day or two. There are no other side effects, and normal activity can be resumed an hour or so after the procedure.

The ECT is repeated up to three or four times a week for eight to twelve or more treatments. Occasionally, more intensive programs of shock treatment are carried out under strictly monitored conditions. Up to 70% of patients with severe depression are significantly improved by ECT, and overall it is more effective than medication in these patients.

See also DEPRESSION; ELECTROENCEPHALOGRAM; PSYCHIATRY

ELECTROCUTION

It is most important to remember that a person who has been electrocuted is a source of electrical energy until they are removed from the source of the current. If touched, the person may pass on a deadly electric current. The first thing a rescuer should try to do is switch off the power or break the connection between the victim and the appliance. If the accident involves low voltage current, such as that used in homes and for lights and heating in shops and offices, find the switch and turn

it off, if possible by pulling out the plug. If the power can't be turned off, DO NOT TOUCH THE VICTIM DIRECTLY, but stand on a rubber mat or wear rubber-soled shoes and try to separate the victim from the source of the current with something made from dry wood (eg. a chair or a broom handle). Avoid anything damp or wet, since water is a very efficient conductor of electricity.

If the accident involves high voltage current, stay well away from the victim until an expert turns off the power – high voltage current can travel through the ground and give you a shock from up to six metres.

The seriousness of an electric shock depends on how strong the charge is, how long the victim was exposed to it, and how well they were insulated. Death by electrocution is most likely to occur if the victim was in contact with water.

The burns from electrocution are usually more serious than they appear, as there may be a burn track through the inside of the body from the point of contact to the point of earthing.

A patient who survives an electrocution may develop cataracts several months later. *See also* FIRST AID

ELECTROENCEPHALOGRAM

An electroencephalogram (EEG) is a recording of the electrical activity of the brain in the same way as an ECG measures the electrical activity of the heart.

For an EEG, electrodes are attached to the scalp, often using a close fitting rubber cap (like a bathing cap) to which the electrodes are attached. There will normally be about eight electrodes attached to the electroencephalograph (the machine that does the recording). The procedure is completely painless. The minute electrical waves produced by the nerve cells of the brain as it sends messages throughout the body are transmitted to the machine and reproduced as wavy lines on a strip of paper. The patient will usually lie quietly while the recording is taking place, but may be asked to open and close their eyes and to breathe heavily and lights may be flashed before their eyes. If there is no abnormality, the pattern will be fairly regular. The recording takes about half an hour to an hour.

Normal brain waves occur at a rate of about fifty per second. A departure from this can indicate abnormalities such as epilepsy, a tumour, degeneration of the tissues of the brain, or other serious disorders of the central nervous system. In someone with epilepsy, brain activity can suddenly jump to as many as 500 messages a second.

The most common reason for an EEG is suspected epilepsy, but only the brain activity at the time the test is being carried out is measured. There are EEG test patterns typical of epileptic seizures, but it is possible to have epilepsy and to have a normal EEG, simply because there is no unusual brain activity at the time of the test. If a person is having seizures and produces a normal EEG, there will be a need for further testing.

An EEG can be used to establish death. Nowadays, it is possible for the heart to be kept beating artificially, virtually indefinitely. Consequently it may be necessary to establish that the person's brain has ceased to function and therefore that there is no possibility of a return to consciousness. A completely flat EEG, with no peaks and valleys, which persists for an extended period of time, can provide irrefutable evidence of brain death and that life no longer exists.
See also BRAIN; EPILEPSY

ELECTROLYTES
The levels of the ions (electrically charged particles) of sodium, potassium, chloride and bicarbonate in the blood must be in perfect balance in the body in order to maintain the acidity of the blood within very narrow boundaries. They are collectively known as electrolytes, and all can be very accurately measured. If the level of these ions varies significantly from the normal range, the electrical activity of the brain and nerves and the function of the heart and other organs may be adversely affected.

Conditions such as severe diarrhoea, prolonged vomiting, dehydration, kidney failure, massive infection, diabetes and starvation can affect electrolyte levels.
See also BLOOD TESTS; MBA

ELECTROMYOGRAM
An electromyogram (EMG) shows the electrical activity of the muscles. Every time they move, muscles create an electric current, and if a person is paralysed, an EMG can determine whether the paralysis is due to a muscle disorder or to a disorder of the nerves.

For an EMG, an electrode is passed through the skin and attached to a muscle. The electricity produced in the muscle is then picked up and transferred to the electromyograph (the machine doing the recording). A graph of the activity is then viewed on a screen or printed onto a continuous strip of paper. There may be some brief discomfort as the electrode needle is inserted. Sometimes an electric current is passed into the muscle to test its activity, and a tingling sensation from the current may persist for about a day. The test lasts for about thirty to sixty minutes. Periodic EMGs are often used to measure the progress of someone who is recovering from some form of paralysis.

A similar test can be carried out on the nerves. In this case, an electrode is taped to the skin over the nerve.
See also MUSCLE

ELECTROPHYSICAL TREATMENT
See SHORT-WAVE DIATHERMY; ULTRASOUND

ELEPHANTIASIS
See FILARIASIS

ELEPHANT MAN DEFORMITY
See PROTEUS SYNDROME

ELLIS-van CREVELD SYNDROME
The Ellis-van Creveld syndrome is a familial developmental abnormality of heart and limbs, but both parents must be carriers of the defective gene. These babies are born with extra fingers and toes, their tongue is tied to the floor of the mouth, and they have small nails, short arms and legs, small chest and holes in the heart (atrial septal defect, ventricular septal defect). There are no specific diagnostic tests, but an echocardiogram (ultrasound of heart), and cardiac catheterisation (passing a pressure measuring tube through an artery or vein into the heart) can demonstrate the heart abnormalities, and surgical repair of heart and cosmetic defects are undertaken when possible.
See also ATRIAL SEPTAL DEFECT; ECHOCARDIOGRAM; VENTRICULAR SEPTAL DEFECT

EMBOLISM
See BENDS; PULMONARY EMBOLISM

EMBRYO
Each month, a microscopically small egg (ovum, plural ova) is released from one of a woman's ovaries and travels down the Fallopian tube towards the uterus. If during this journey the egg encounters sperm released by the woman's partner, the egg may be fertilised, and the woman becomes pregnant. Once penetrated by the sperm, the egg starts multiplying, from one cell to two, then four, eight, sixteen and so on, doubling in size with each division.

After ten days, the growing embryo consists of a fluid-filled ball, only a couple of millimetres across. At this point it attaches to the wall of the uterus and continues to grow, drawing all its needs from the mother through the placenta.

For the first twelve weeks, the developing baby is called an embryo. The growth of the embryo is rapid to start with, but slows down as maturity approaches. The embryo soon becomes the size of a grain of rice, and then a tadpole (both in size and appearance). By the end of the first month, it is about eight millimetres long, with four small swellings at the sides, called limb buds, which will develop into arms and legs.

FIVE WEEK OLD EMBRYO

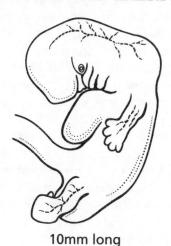

10mm long

At eight weeks of pregnancy, the embryo is two cm. long, and the nose, ears, fingers and toes are identifiable. Most of the internal organs form in the next four weeks, and by twelve weeks when the baby is 5.5 centimetres long, a pumping heart can be detected, and the baby is moving, although too weakly yet to be detected by the mother. It is during the first three months that the embryo is most prone to the development of abnormalities caused by drugs (eg. thalidomide, isotretinoin) or infections (eg. German measles).

Once it is three months old, the baby is called a foetus.
See also BLASTOCYST; FOETUS; PREGNANCY

EMBRYOMA
See TESTICULAR CANCER

EMERGENCY
See ANAPHYLAXIS; ANIMAL BITE; ARTERIAL PRESSURE POINTS; BEE STING; BLEEDING; BOX JELLYFISH; BURN; CARBON MONOXIDE POISONING; CHOKING; CONVULSION; CUT; DISLOCATION; ELECTROCUTION; EYE FOREIGN BODY; EYE INJURY; FAINT; FEBRILE CONVULSION; FIRST AID; FRACTURE; HEART ATTACK; INSECTICIDE POISONING; JELLYFISH STING; NOSEBLEED; OVERDOSE; POISONING; POISONOUS PLANTS; RESUSCITATION; SCORPION STING; SHOCK; SNAKE BITE; SPLINTER; STONEFISH; SUFFOCATION; UNCONSCIOUS; VOMITING BLOOD.

EMG
See ELECTROMYOGRAM

EMPHYSEMA
Emphysema is a form of chronic obstructive airways disease caused by permanent destruction of the small air-absorbing sacs (alveoli) in the lungs. It is caused by smoking, exposure to other noxious gases, or recurrent attacks of bronchitis or pneumonia. With these irritants the alveoli break down into larger cavities which are surrounded by scar tissue and have less surface area to absorb oxygen. About 3% of the population develop emphysema, and most are smokers.

The symptoms are constant shortness of breath, repetitive coughing, a barrel shaped chest and excessive sputum. Because of their constant exertion to breathe, patients become wasted and emaciated and may develop recurrent attacks of bronchitis and pneumonia, right heart failure (cor pulmonale) and pneumothorax.

It is diagnosed by a chest x-ray and by blowing into machines (eg. spirometer, peak flow meter) that analyse lung function. There may also be changes in blood tests and electrocardiograms (ECG).

Treatment involves physiotherapy to make the damaged lung work as effectively as possible, drugs by tablet or spray to open up the lungs to their maximum capacity, and antibiotics to treat infection. In severe cases, steroids by inhalation or tablet are given, and as a last resort oxygen is used, while vaccination against influenza and pneumonia may prevent a fatal illness. Smokers must stop their habit.

No cure is possible and the condition is slowly progressive with the complications eventually causing death.
See also BREATH, SHORT OF; BRONCHITIS, CHRONIC; COR PULMONALE; LUNG; LUNG CANCER; PNEUMONIA; PNEUMOTHORAX

EMPYEMA
See ABSCESS

ENCEPHALITIS
Encephalitis is any infection or inflammation of the brain tissue.
See also ANGIOSTRONGYLIASIS; BRAIN; CREUTZFELDT-JAKOB DISEASE; HENDRA VIRUS; JAPANESE ENCEPHALITIS; MENINGITIS; MURRAY VALLEY ENCEPHALITIS; RABIES; REYE SYNDROME

ENCEPHALOPATHY
See WERNICKE-KORSAKOFF PSYCHOSIS

ENCHONDROMA
See BONE CANCER

ENDEMIC
An endemic disease is one that has been present for a long time in a specific place or group of people.
See also EPIDEMIC

ENDOCARDITIS
Endocarditis is a bacterial or fungal infection inside the heart, usually on the heart valves. It normally develops slowly over many weeks or months in an already damaged heart, or may rarely cause sudden illness in a previously healthy person. The heart valves may be malformed from birth, damaged by disease (eg. rheumatic fever), distorted by cholesterol deposits, scarred by heart attacks or an artificial heart valve may have been inserted to replace a damaged valve.

Symptoms are many and varied, and some patients, particularly the elderly, may have almost no early symptoms. Most patients have a fever, and other complaints include night sweats, fatigue, tiredness, palpitations, rapid heart rate, loss of appetite, chills, joint pains, muscle pains, weight loss, swollen joints, paralysis, headache, chest pain, nose bleeds and other minor problems. Small, transient, red, raised, tender patches on the finger tips (Osler's nodes) may be diagnostic. The infection causes clumps of bacteria to grow inside the heart, and pieces can break off and travel through the arteries to cause severe problems elsewhere in the body. In the brain they can block an artery and cause a stroke, while in other organs they may cause blindness, kidney failure, joint damage and bowel problems. Almost any part of the body may be affected. Further complications such as heart attack and stroke can occur years after the disease appears to have been cured.

It is diagnosed by taking blood and culturing it in the laboratory in order to detect any bacteria, while other blood tests and an ECG (electrocardiogram) may also be diagnostic.

Urgent hospital treatment is essential, where large doses of antibiotics, often penicillin, are given by injection for several weeks. Other treatments include correction of anaemia and controlling the damage done to other organs. Major heart surgery is sometimes required, particularly if the infection is fungal. Prevention is better than cure, and patients who have had rheumatic fever or any other heart disease should have a preventative course of penicillin before and during an operation or dental procedure.

Sixty percent of patients with endocarditis recover completely, while another 30% survive but with significant restrictions on their lifestyle caused by damage to the heart or other organs. Death occurs in about 10%. If untreated, death is inevitable. When a fungus is responsible (most commonly in

intravenous drug abusers), the outcome is far worse.
See also HEART; OSLER, WILLIAM; RHEUMATIC FEVER

ENDOGENOUS DEPRESSION
See DEPRESSION

ENDOLYMPHATIC HYDROPS
Endolymphatic hydrops is caused by an increase in the pressure in the endolymphatic fluid, which fills the balance-sensing semicircular canals (vestibular apparatus) in the inner ear. It is due to a viral infection (eg. mumps, German measles), syphilis, head injury, or it may start for no apparent reason.

Patients experience intermittent dizziness, varying deafness, ringing in the ears (tinnitus) and a feeling of pressure or fullness in the ears. Symptoms usually occur as attacks that build up slowly, then fade, lasting for hours or days. Sometimes permanent deafness and poor balance may occur.

Hearing tests (audiometry), caloric tests (irrigating the ear with alternating warm and cold water), electrical tests of ear function and CT scans may be used to exclude other diseases and aid in the diagnosis, but there is no definitive diagnostic test.

Numerous medications (eg. prochlorperazine, betahistine, sedatives, diuretics, droperidol, urea) are used to ease dizziness, but their success rate is not high, although combinations work better than one drug alone. Surgery to the balance mechanism or its nerves is a last resort option. Usually symptoms gradually settle after many attacks over several years.
See also EAR; DIZZINESS; LABYRINTHITIS; MÉNIÈRE'S DISEASE; TINNITUS; VESTIBULITIS

ENDOMETRIAL ABLATION
See MICROWAVE ENDOMETRIAL ABLATION

ENDOMETRIAL CARCINOMA
Endometrial carcinoma is cancer of the lining of the uterus (the endometrium). The endometrium increases steadily in thickness during the month to become receptive to any fertilised egg that may be present, so that it can implant and grow into a foetus. If no egg is implanted, the endometrium is shed each month as a menstrual period.

The absolute cause of this cancer is unknown, but the incidence is increased in women who use oestrogen hormone replacement therapy without a balancing dose of progestogen. Obesity and being childless are other risk factors.

Abnormal vaginal bleeding in a postmenopausal woman is the only symptom. There are no early symptoms and the cancer may be well advanced by the time bleeding occurs. In advanced stages, tender lymph nodes may occur in the groin and an enlarged uterus may be felt, and the cancer spreads early to surrounding organs (eg. bladder, ovary).

Taking a sample of the cells within the uterus and examining them can confirm the diagnosis. An ultrasound scan can sometimes show an abnormality, but doesn't demonstrate the underlying cause.

A total hysterectomy (removing the uterus and ovaries) is the primary treatment, followed by appropriate chemotherapy with oestrogen opposing drugs (eg. tamoxifen). The prognosis varies widely depending on the degree of spread at the time of treatment. Overall five year survival is about 70%.
See also CANCER; CHORIOCARCINOMA OF THE UTERUS; CURETTE; UTERUS; VAGINAL BLEEDING ABNORMAL

ENDOMETRIOSIS
Endometriosis is the presence of cells that normally line the uterus (womb) in abnormal positions in the pelvis and abdomen. Two percent of all women are affected at some time.

The uterus is lined with endometrial cells that during the second half of a woman's monthly cycle may accept a fertilised egg and allow it to grow into a baby. If no pregnancy occurs, these cells degenerate, break away from the inside of the uterus, and are carried out of the body in a woman's period. From the top of the uterus, a Fallopian tube leads out to each of the two ovaries. In a small number of women, the endometrial cells go into and through these tubes to settle in abnormal positions around the ovary, on the outside of the uterus, or in the pelvic cavity, where they can start growing and spread further. These cells still respond to the woman's hormonal cycle every month, and will bleed with every period, releasing blood in places where it can cause symptoms. The abnormally positioned endometrial cells can also irritate the bladder, settle on the outside of the intestine, or they may block the Fallopian tubes to cause infertility.

Symptoms depend on the site of the endometrial deposits, but pelvic pain, often worse at the time of a period, is usual. They may also cause uterus and bowel cramps, diarrhoea and frequent passage of urine due to bladder irritation. The condition can only be diagnosed by examining a woman's pelvis by means of an open operation or laparoscopy.

Various medications (eg. hormones, danocrine) taken as tablets, implants or nasal sprays for many months settle mild to moderate cases. Removal of endometrial deposits is normally possible by laparoscopy (passing a number of small tubes into the abdomen), but open operation may be necessary to remove large amounts of abnormal tissue. As a last resort, a hysterectomy may be performed.

Most patients are cured with medication and/or surgery, but some will be left permanently infertile. Artificial means of fertilisation can help these women conceive, as their ovaries still function normally.
See also INFERTILITY; SEX HORMONES; UTERUS

ENDOMETRIUM
See ENDOMETRIOSIS; MENSTRUAL PERIOD; UTERUS

ENDOSCOPE
An endoscope is a long, usually flexible tube, with a lens at one end and a light source and an eyepiece at the other. The end with the lens is inserted into the patient, light passes down the tube so that the relevant area is illuminated, and the eyepiece enables the area to be magnified so the doctor can see what is there.

Early endoscopes, which are still used and are very effective for some diagnoses, consisted of a hollow tube made of metal, often with a light bulb. More sophisticated fibreoptic endoscopes are the most common form now. They consist of hundreds of fibreglass or plastic fibres down which a light is directed and which reflects back the image by means of what are effectively tubular mirrors. The plastic rods are so thin that they bend easily,

making the endoscope flexible enough to bend around up to 180°. This kind of endoscope can literally see around corners.

An endoscope is usually inserted into the body through one of its normal openings, such as the mouth, the urethra or the anus. Sometimes, however, there is a need for a small incision in the skin.

Individual endoscopes have been developed for many parts of the body, including the abdominal cavity, oesophagus, rectum, bladder, lungs, stomach, intestines, uterus, nasal sinuses and several joints. Each has its own name, depending on what part of the body it is intended to investigate. Hence, a gastroscope looks the stomach, a bronchoscope looks at the bronchial passages and the lungs, and an arthroscope examines the inside of joints.

Most endoscopes have special equipment so that a sample of tissue can be removed for further analysis (a biopsy). It is possible to use an endoscope to perform surgery, such as a hernia repair or a tubal ligation (tying a woman's Fallopian tubes). Endoscopes are also used to locate and remove foreign objects that have found their way into organs such as the stomach and lungs.

Some endoscopies can be carried out in the doctor's surgery, others need a trip to hospital, and a few need a general anaesthetic. Usually the patient will be sedated and given painkilling medication, and the procedure is rarely uncomfortable.
See also ARTHROSCOPY; BIOPSY; BRONCHOSCOPY; COLONOSCOPY; COLPOSCOPY; CULDOSCOPY; CYSTOSCOPY; ENDOSCOPIC RETROGRADE CHOLECYSTOPANCREATOGRAPHY; GASTROSCOPY; HYSTERECTOMY; HYSTEROSCOPY; LAPAROSCOPY; TUBAL LIGATION

ENDOSCOPIC RETROGRADE CHOLECYSTOPAN CREATOGRAPHY
Endoscopic retrograde cholecystopancreatography (ERCP) is a method of investigating, and sometimes treating, diseases of the bile duct, gall bladder and pancreas.

While the patient is sedated, an endoscope (thin flexible tube) is passed through the mouth, down the oesophagus (gullet), through

BILE AND PANCREAS DRAINAGE

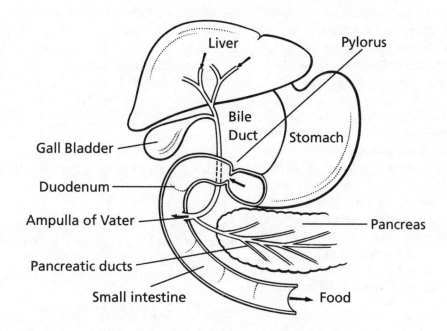

the stomach and into the duodenum (first part of the small intestine).

The bile duct connects the gall bladder with the pancreatic duct, which carries digestive juices (enzymes) from the pancreas. Just after they join, the combined ducts open into the side of the duodenum (the opening is called the ampulla of Vater).

The opening of this duct can be seen through the endoscope, and a tiny tube can be passed through the endoscope and threaded into this opening. A dye that is visible on x-rays can then be injected up the duct to outline its course and any abnormalities (eg. stone, cancer) that may be present in the bile duct or pancreatic ducts.

If a stone is found just inside the ampulla, a wire is passed through the opening, pulled tight onto one side of the opening, and then an electric current is passed to heat the wire. This burns the side of the ampulla, and effectively opens it up to a greater diameter to allow the stone to pass. Any blood vessels cut are cauterised by the hot wire.

The process is quite routine, and has few complications. Recovery only takes a few hours. Uncommonly there may be unwanted damage to the duodenum, ampulla or ducts.
See also ENDOSCOPE; GALLSTONES

ENERGY
See KILOJOULES AND CALORIES

ENERGY, LACK OF
See LETHARGY

ENGORGED BREASTS
See BREASTS ENGORGED

ENOPHTHALMOS
See EYE SUNKEN

ENOXACIN
See QUINOLONES

ENT
'ENT' is an abbreviation for ear, nose and throat, and often used when referring to doctors who specialise in diseases of these organs (otorhinolaryngologists).
See also OTORHINOLARYNGOLOGY

ENTERIC FEVER
See TYPHOID FEVER

ENTERITIS
See CAMPYLOBACTER JEJUNI;
CROHN'S DISEASE;
GASTROENTERITIS; SHIGELLOSIS

ENTEROBIUS VERMICULARIS
See PINWORM

ENTHESITIS
Enthesitis is inflammation of the point where a muscle, ligament or tendon attaches to a

bone, caused by recurrent excessive stress on, or overloading of, the muscle, ligament or tendon. Pain occurs at the insertion point when the muscle is used, and there is tenderness to pressure over the insertion point even when the muscle is relaxed. In severe cases the muscle is unable to be used due to pain and permanent damage or complete rupture of the insertion is possible.

Initial treatment is rest, ice, compression and elevation of the affected part, with anti-inflammatory medication to ease the swelling and discomfort. After the acute phase, options include an exercise program directed by a physiotherapist, continued use of anti-inflammatory medication, ultrasound stimulation of the affected area, and injection of a steroid and local anaesthetic around the area. Most cases respond well, if rather slowly, to treatment.
See also TENNIS ELBOW

ENTROPION
Entropion is an inturning of the eyelashes due to eyelid injury or infection, resulting in the eyelashes rubbing irritatingly on the eye surface, and ulceration or infection of the eye surface may occur. Plucking the eyelashes gives temporary relief, but the problem often recurs when they regrow. It is cured by surgery to permanently destroy a small number of damaged eyelashes, or change the shape of the eyelid. There are good results from treatment, but blindness from corneal scarring is possible if left untreated long term.
See also EYE; EYELID DISEASE

ENURESIS
See BED WETTING

ENZYMES
See DIGESTIVE ENZYMES

EOSINOPHILIA-MYALGIA SYNDROME
The eosinophilia-myalgia syndrome is a food intolerance triggered by ingestion of a large amount of the protein L-tryptophan in a sensitised person. Severe muscle and joint pain, cough, shortness of breath, swelling of feet and ankles, thick skin, rashes and nerve pain occur, and a large number of reactive white blood cells (eosinophils) are seen in a blood sample. There is no specific treatment, but sufferers must avoid eating L-tryptophan. Most patients

recover quickly, but one in a hundred die within a few hours.
See also ARTHRITIS; MUSCLE PAIN

EPI-
'Epi-' is a prefix derived from the Greek word for 'above', and used in medicine to indicate on, above or near to (eg. epigastrium means above the stomach).

EPICONDYLITIS
See GOLFER'S ELBOW; TENNIS ELBOW

EPIDEMIC
An epidemic is the increased incidence of a particular disease in an area or group of people for a specific period of time.
See also ENDEMIC

EPIDEMIC POLYARTHRITIS
See ROSS RIVER FEVER

EPIDERMIS
See SKIN

EPIDERMOLYSIS BULLOSA
Epidermolysis bullosa is a rare familial (runs in families) skin disease of which there are several subtypes. The slightest injury to the skin causes large, firm blisters. In infants blisters develop on knees and hands as the child starts to crawl, but later may occur anywhere. In severe forms the disease continues throughout life, the fingers may become bound together by scar tissue, the mouth and throat may be involved, and nails and teeth may be damaged. On healing, blisters leave behind a scar that causes significant disfigurement and cancer may develop in the affected tissue. The diagnosis is confirmed by a skin biopsy.

Steroids are the only treatment available, but are not particularly effective, so avoiding injury to the skin is imperative. There is no cure, and the subtypes vary in severity from an inconvenience to life-threatening.
See also BLISTERS

EPIDERMOPHYTON
See FUNGI; TINEA CAPITIS; TINEA CORPORIS; TINEA CRURIS

EPIDIDYMIS
See TESTICLE

EPIDIDYMO-ORCHITIS

Epididymo-orchitis is a bacterial or viral infection of the testicle and epididymis. The sperm produced in a testicle passes into a dense network of fine tubes that forms a lump on the back of the testicle called the epididymis. These join up to form the sperm tube (vas deferens) that takes the sperm to the penis. Epididymo-orchitis is an infection of both the epididymis and testicle. Orchitis is an infection of the testicle alone, but the infection is almost invariably present in both places.

TESTICLE AND EPIDIDYMIS

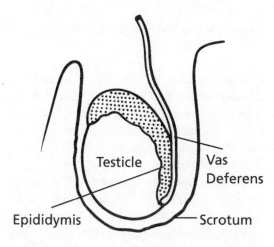

Men with a bacterial epididymo-orchitis are acutely uncomfortable, have a painful swollen testicle, and a fever. Occasionally an abscess will form, which must be surgically drained. A painful testicle can also be caused by torsion of the testis, which is a surgical emergency requiring immediate treatment. Any boy or man, particularly in the teenage years or early twenties, who develops a painful testicle, must see a doctor immediately – day or night.

Blood tests may show the presence of infection in the body, and treatment involves appropriate antibiotics, aspirin or paracetamol for pain relief. Ice may be applied to the scrotum and a supportive bandage or jockstrap worn. If the infection is caused by a virus such as mumps, there is no effective treatment available. With the correct treatment, bacterial epididymo-orchitis resolves in a couple of days, and usually does not cause any problems with fertility or masculinity. In cases of viral infection, there may be problems with fertility in later life.
See also TESTICLE; TORSION OF THE TESTIS

EPIDURAL ANAESTHETIC

An epidural anaesthetic is very similar to a spinal anaesthetic, but the injection into the back does not penetrate as deeply and does not enter the cerebrospinal fluid. The spinal cord is wrapped in three layers of fibrous material (the meninges), and this anaesthetic is given into the very small space between the outer two layers (dura mater and arachnoid mater). It is outside the dura – thus 'epidural'. The procedure is technically more difficult than a spinal anaesthetic, but the side effects are less severe. Epidural anaesthetics are used most commonly to relieve the pain of childbirth.
See also ANAESTHETICS; EPIDURAL ANAESTHETIC; GENERAL ANAESTHETIC; LOCAL ANAESTHETIC; MENINGES; SPINAL ANAESTHETIC

EPIGLOTTIS

The epiglottis is a leaf shaped piece of cartilage that projects upwards, towards the back of the tongue from the base of the pharynx. The epiglottis moves back and forward to direct food into the top of the oesophagus (gullet) and prevent food from entering the larynx and trachea.

If the epiglottis fails to function properly, and food or fluid goes into the larynx, a coughing reflex is stimulated to force it back up and then down into the correct path.
See also EPIGLOTTITIS; LARYNX; OESOPHAGUS; PHARYNX

EPIGLOTTITIS

The epiglottis is a piece of cartilage that sticks up at the back of the tongue to stop food from entering the wind pipe (trachea) when swallowing. Epiglottitis is an uncommon bacterial infection (most commonly by *Haemophilus influenzae* B – HiB) of the epiglottis that is an acute medical emergency requiring urgent hospitalisation, as it can swell up rapidly and block the throat. Infection is most common in children under five years of age who develop a very sore throat, fever and obvious illness. In young children, if the epiglottis swells excessively, or is disturbed by trying to eat solids or by the 'tongue depressor' stick of a doctor examining the mouth, it can cover the wind pipe completely and rapidly cause death through suffocation. For this reason a doctor will give the throat only a cursory examination

LOCATION OF EPIGLOTTIS AT BACK OF TONGUE

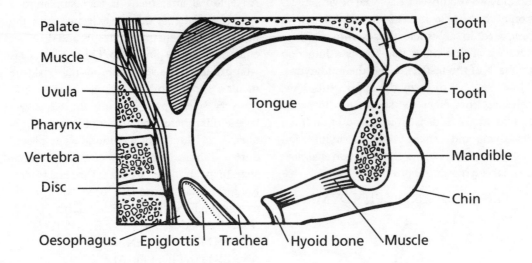

Palate — Muscle — Uvula — Pharynx — Vertebra — Disc — Tongue — Tooth — Lip — Tooth — Mandible — Chin — Oesophagus — Epiglottis — Trachea — Hyoid bone — Muscle

before arranging the immediate transfer of the child to hospital. If the airway is obstructed in hospital, an emergency tracheotomy (an operation to make a hole into the wind pipe through the front of the neck) is performed to allow the child to breathe.

The diagnosis is confirmed by a side-on x-ray of the neck that shows the swollen epiglottis. Throat swabs are taken to identify the infecting bacteria, and sometimes blood tests are also performed.

Antibiotics are given to cure the infection and paracetamol to reduce fever and pain. Some hospitals routinely anaesthetise children and put a tube through the mouth or nose and down the throat to prevent the airway from blocking. The infection usually settles in a few days, and provided there has been no airway obstruction, the outcome is excellent. Epiglottitis is far less common now that a series of vaccinations against Haemophilus influenzae B (HiB) is routinely given to all children, starting at two months of age.

See also EPIGLOTTIS; *HAEMOPHILUS INFLUENZAE* B INFECTION; PHARYNX

EPILEPSY

Epilepsy is a brain condition causing recurrent seizures (fits). It may be congenital or acquired later in life after a brain infection, tumour, injury or with brain degeneration in the elderly. Chemical imbalances in the body, kidney failure and removing alcohol from an alcoholic or heroin from an addict may also trigger the condition. Fits are caused by a short-circuit in the brain after very minor and localised damage. This then stimulates another part of the brain, and then another, causing a seizure. Triggers such as flickering lights, shimmering televisions, certain foods, emotional upsets, infections or stress can start fits in some patients.

The symptoms vary from very mild absences in which people just seem to lose concentration for a few seconds or stumble (petit mal epilepsy), to uncontrolled bizarre movements of an arm or leg and abnormal sensations (temporal lobe epilepsy or partial seizures), to a grand mal convulsion which last for a minute or two and during which the patient becomes rigid, falls to the ground, stops breathing, muscles go into spasm, abnormal movements occur and the patient may urinate, pass faeces and become blue. Petit mal epilepsy is far more common in children and teenagers than adults. Patients normally remain conscious during partial seizures. After recovering from a grand mal fit, the patient has no memory of the event, is confused, drowsy, disoriented and may have a severe headache, nausea and muscle aches. Many patients with epilepsy develop warning auras before an attack which can be a particular type of headache, change in mood, tingling, light-headedness or twitching. Status epilepticus is a condition where one grand mal attack follows another without the patient regaining consciousness between attacks.

Epilepsy can be investigated by an EEG (electroencephalogram) to measure the brain waves, blood tests to exclude other diseases and a CT scan of the brain to find any structural abnormality.

Many different anti-epileptic drug combinations in tablet or mixture form are used to control epilepsy, and regular blood tests ensure that the dosage is adequate. Medication must be continued long term, but after several years without fits, a trial without medication may be undertaken. Epileptics must not put themselves in a position where they can injure themselves or others.
See also ANTICONVULSANTS; BARBITURATES; BENZODIAZEPINES; CEREBRAL PALSY; CONVULSION; ELECTROENCEPHALOGRAM; LANDAU-KLEFFNER SYNDROME; STURGE-WEBER SYNDROME

EPILIM
See ANTICONVULSANTS

EPILOIA
See TUBEROUS SCLEROSIS

EPISCLERITIS
Episcleritis is a common inflammation of the outer surface of the eye in young adults that causes discomfort, tenderness and redness of one section of the white of the eye. No treatment is usually necessary, as most cases settle without treatment in one or two weeks, but persistent cases may become lumpy and thickened and require steroid eye drops.
See also EYE; EYE RED; SCLERITIS

EPISODIC DYSCONTROL SYNDROME
The episodic dyscontrol syndrome is a psychiatric disturbance of no known cause that is not related to recognised mental disorders (eg. schizophrenia). Its characteristics are physical abuse of family, severe episodes of alcohol intoxication, impulsive sexual misconduct, and irresponsible social behaviour. Patients almost invariably end up in prison for violent crimes. Patients must avoid alcohol, and take medication (eg. phenytoin, thioridazine), but most do not respond to treatment and require legal restraints.
See also ATTENTION DEFICIT HYPERACTIVITY DISORDER; VIOLENCE

EPISPADIAS
See HYPOSPADIAS

EPISTAXIS
See NOSE BLEED

EPSTEIN-BARR VIRUS
See GLANDULAR FEVER

EQUINE MORBILLIVIRUS
See HENDRA VIRUS

ERB-DUCHENNE PALSY
Erb-Duchenne palsy is a rare complication of pulling too hard on the head during a difficult delivery of a baby, which stretches and damages the nerves running from the neck across the top of the shoulder to the muscles in the upper arm. The muscles are not damaged, but without a nerve supply, they cannot function.

Patients are unable to move the upper arm away from the body, to fully bend the elbow, or to turn the hand so that the palm faces backwards when the arm is beside the body. The arm hangs limply by the side, and if treatment is unsuccessful, it appears withered and wasted as the child grows older.

Splinting the shoulder in a position that allows the nerves to grow back and recover is necessary immediately after birth. More than nine out of ten cases recover with adequate treatment, usually within a month, but sometimes it takes six months.
See also KLUMPKE PALSY; MUSCLE WEAKNESS

ERB MUSCULAR DYSTROPHY
Erb muscular dystrophy (limb-girdle dystrophy) is a rare gradually progressive muscle-wasting disease that may occur in the one family in successive generations, or appear for no apparent reason. It affects the muscles around the shoulder and pelvis, and progresses at a variable rate from its onset between ten and thirty years of age to cause severe disability in mid-life. A muscle biopsy is diagnostic, but no treatment is available other than physiotherapy and occupational therapy. The severity varies significantly between patients, some being only moderately inconvenienced while others are severely disabled and unable to care for themselves.
See also MUSCLE WEAKNESS

ERB PALSY
See ERB-DUCHENNE PALSY

ERCP
See ENDOSCOPIC RETROGRADE
CHOLECYSTOPANCREATOGRAPHY

ERECTION
Normally the male penis is soft and flaccid, but if sexually stimulated it becomes firm and erect. This is a reflex that cannot be consciously controlled by the man, and in fact if the man does try to consciously control an erection it is more likely to fail.

Stimulation of the penis, other sensitive areas of the body (eg. nipple, small of back) and mental sexual imagery will result in a reflex in the nerves at the lower end of the spinal cord that sends a signal to muscle rings (valves) around the veins in the base of the penis that drain blood from the organ. These valves close, preventing blood from escaping from the penis while blood continues to be pumped into the organ through the arteries as normal. As a result it blows up in the same way as a sausage shaped balloon, the pressure of blood within the penis being the same as the maximum blood pressure elsewhere in the vascular system.

The penis has a long sponge filled sac (corpus cavernosum) along each side that fills with the blood under pressure to support the organ when erect.

When ejaculation occurs or sexual stimulation ceases the valves around the veins open and allow the blood to drain out of the penis, and it becomes soft again.

An inability to obtain an erection is called impotence.
See also ALPROSTADIL; ERECTION
PROLONGED AND PAINFUL;
IMPOTENCE; PENIS; SILDENAFIL

ERECTION FAILURE
See IMPOTENCE

ERECTION PROLONGED AND PAINFUL
The penis normally becomes erect and hard with sexual stimulation, and subsides after ejaculation or cessation of stimulation. Rarely the penis may remain hard and erect when not stimulated, and this can cause considerable pain in the penis and the man cannot usually pass urine while the erection persists. This condition is called priapism.

If the penis remains erect and hard for several hours, there may be an inadequate blood supply to the tissues of the penis, and these may become scarred and permanently damaged. Priapism should be dealt with if the erection has not subsided within two hours.

Treatment involves hot packs around the penis, taking the medication pseudoephedrine (Sudafed) found in many cold remedies, and as a last resort, doctors can put a needle into the penis to drain out the excess blood.

Causes of priapism include an injury to the penis during sex or at an earlier time that has caused the formation of scar tissue, a calculus in the bladder, psychiatric conditions, damage to the spinal cord from an injury or tumour, drug abuse (eg. alcohol, marijuana, cocaine), medications (eg. prazosin, psychotropics, heparin, vasodilators) and an excessive dose of the drug alprostadil (Caverject) which is used to stimulate an erection.

There are many rare causes, including leukaemia, sickle cell anaemia, multiple myeloma and a stroke, which may need to be excluded by doctors after an episode of priapism.
See also ALPROSTADIL; EJACULATION;
ERECTION; MASTURBATION; PENIS
and separate entries for diseases mentioned above.

ERGOCALCIFEROL
See VITAMIN D

ERGOTAMINES
Acute migraine attacks can be treated by the use of painkillers and sedatives, or the use of specific drugs that deal with the over-dilated arteries that cause migraine. The ergotamine class of drugs work in this way. Some are combined with other medications and painkillers to improve their effect. All must be used as soon as a migraine attack starts, and they may cause significant side effects in some people. They may also interact with other drugs, and are available as tablets (for both swallowing and dissolving under the tongue), suppositories (anal use), and injections.

This class of drugs was the mainstay of migraine treatment for many years, but has now been superseded in many cases by the newer 5HT receptor agonists.

Examples include dihydroergotamine (Dihydergot) and ergotamine (Ergodryl). Side effects may include nausea, diarrhoea,

pins and needles and chest pain. They should not be used in pregnancy, heart or liver disease.
See also 5HT RECEPTOR AGONISTS; MIGRAINE

EROTOMANIA
See de CLERAMBAULT SYNDROME

ERYSIPELAS
Erysipelas is an infection of the skin, caused by any one of a large number of bacteria, but usually *Streptococci*. It most commonly involves the cheek, but any area of the body may be affected. It may start at the site of a scratch, crack or bite, but often there is no apparent cause.

The skin is red, swollen, painful and hot, and the patient may be feverish, shiver and feel very ill. Fluid-filled blisters sometimes develop on the infected area. Swabs may be taken to identify the responsible bacteria, then an antibiotic (eg. penicillin, erythromycin) capsule or tablet is prescribed. It was a very serious disease and often killed children before effective antibiotics were available, but now recovery is rapid once antibiotics are started, and it usually heals without scarring.
See also CELLULITIS; ERYTHRASMA; *STREPTOCOCCAL* INFECTION

ERYTHEMA
See FACE RED; SKIN RED

ERYTHEMA INFECTIOSUM
See FIFTH DISEASE

ERYTHEMA MULTIFORME
Erythema multiforme (which can be loosely translated as 'red spots of many shapes') is an acute inflammation (redness) of the skin and moist (mucus) membranes lining body cavities. It may be triggered by drugs, bacterial or viral infections, cold sores and other *Herpes* infections, or may appear for no apparent reason. Seventy-five percent occur after a *Herpes* or cold sore infection, and half of the remainder is caused by drugs – particularly sulpha antibiotics. Attacks caused by cold sores and other infections tend to be mild, but those that occur as a result of drug sensitivity can be very severe.

Patients experience the sudden development of several types of rash simultaneously.

The easiest rash to identify appears as multiple red, sore rings on the skin with a pale centre that vary in diameter from a few millimetres to two or three centimetres. Other forms include red patches, swollen lumps, fluid-filled blisters, itchy red stripes and painful hard dome-shaped bumps. The insides of the mouth and the vagina, and the eye surface, may be involved with ulcers developing in some cases. The rash may occur anywhere, but is more common on the front of the leg, over the shoulders, above and below the elbow on the outside of the arm, and on the soles and palms. Most patients have only a mild fever, but those severely affected may be acutely ill with a very high fever and generalised weakness, and rarely it may progress to the Stevens-Johnson syndrome. No blood or other tests can confirm the diagnosis.

If a drug is suspected as the cause, it is immediately ceased, while if an infection is thought responsible, this is treated appropriately. The discomfort can be minimised with painkillers such as paracetamol and aspirin, and with creams, lotions and dressings to ease the skin irritation. Steroid tablets are taken in severe cases.

There is no cure, but the vast majority of cases are mild and settle in two to four weeks, but severe cases may persist for up to six weeks, and in rare cases, with lung involvement (Stevens-Johnson syndrome) in the elderly or chronically ill, death may occur. Recurrent attacks are quite common.
See also COLD SORE; SKIN RED; STEVENS-JOHNSON SYNDROME

ERYTHEMA NODOSUM
Erythema nodosum is an unusual skin inflammation for which the cause is often unknown, but it may be a reaction to certain bacterial infections, medications (eg. penicillin) or more serious underlying diseases (eg. leukaemia, tuberculosis, syphilis, hepatitis B or ulcerative colitis).

Very tender, painful red lumps develop on the front of the leg, usually below the knees, while less commonly affected areas include the arms, face and chest. Patients also have a fever, joint pains and general tiredness, and skin ulcers may be a complication. The diagnosis is confirmed by a skin lump biopsy, and other tests are done to find any underlying cause.

If a cause can be found, this is treated (eg. infection) or removed (eg. ceasing medication), but there is no specific treatment. Steroids and painkillers may ease the symptoms. The condition lasts about six weeks before slowly disappearing with no serious after-effects, but recurrences are common.
See also LEUKAEMIA; LOEFFLER SYNDROME; SKIN NODULES; SKIN RED

ERYTHRASMA
Erythrasma is a common superficial infection of the outermost layer of the skin caused by the bacteria *Corynebacterium minutissium* that usually affects the groin, armpit and under the breasts. It causes well defined, red-brown, scaling, slightly itchy patches that slowly enlarge and become wrinkled. A culture of skin scrapings can identify the responsible bacteria and antibiotic tablets (eg. tetracycline, erythromycin) and ointments (eg. fusidic acid) are used to cure the infection.
See also ERYSIPELAS

ERYTHROCYTES
See ESR; RED BLOOD CELLS

ERYTHROCYTE SEDIMENTATION RATE
See ESR

ERYTHRODERMA
See EXFOLIATIVE DERMATITIS

ERYTHROMYCIN
See MACROLIDES

ERYTHROPOIETIC PROTOPORPHYRIA
Erythropoietic protoporphyria is sometimes called 'sunlight allergy'. It is a distressing inherited excessive skin reaction to sun exposure that normally starts in childhood, has an incidence of one in 100 000 people and affects both sexes equally. Red, swollen, crusted, irritated, painful, raised patches develop on sun exposed areas of the body, particularly the face. The rash starts minutes to hours after sun exposure, and slowly settles after hours or days. Milder attacks may involve skin pain with minimal rash, but areas of skin frequently affected by attacks may develop scars, skin thickening and wrinkling, and there is a higher than normal incidence of gall stones and liver damage (cirrhosis).

Specific blood tests can detect abnormalities that aid in diagnosis, and a skin biopsy is also abnormal.

Sun avoidance is essential, and beta-carotene used regularly reduces the severity of the reaction. Although it is a life long condition, its severity slowly decreases with age.
See also LIGHT SENSITIVE SKIN; PORPHYRIA CUTANEA TARDA

ESCHERICHIA COLI INFECTION
Escherichia coli (*E. coli*) is a bacteria normally found in the gut where it usually causes no harm, but if it finds its way into other organs, or overgrows to excessive numbers in the gut, it may cause a serious infection. The symptoms depend on the site of infection (eg. cystitis, pyelonephritis, pneumonia, diarrhoea, septicaemia, cholecystitis). A swab or sample can be taken from the infected area to determine the bacteria responsible for infection and appropriate antibiotic to treat it. Some forms are resistant to common antibiotics, making control more difficult, but most respond rapidly to correct treatment.
See also BACTERIA and separate entries for diseases mentioned above.

ESOPHAGUS
See OESOPHAGUS

ESOTROPIA
See SQUINT

ESR
The erythrocyte sedimentation rate (ESR) or haematocrit, is a frequently performed blood test that gives an indication of inflammation, infection or cancer in the body, but gives no indication of where the disease is located, or the nature of the disease. It is a measure of the rate at which erythrocytes (red blood cells) settle in a thin tube. The higher the rate, the more significant the result. It is a warning sign to doctors to watch out for some significant disease, but may be raised in anything from a simple viral infection or pregnancy to a heart attack or most types of cancer.

An ESR under 20 mm/Hr. is considered normal in an adult, but higher levels are common in the elderly.

See also BLOOD TESTS;
RED BLOOD CELLS

ESSENTIAL HYPERTENSION
See HYPERTENSION

ESSENTIAL TREMOR
An essential or familial tremor, is an inherited muscle tremor that usually commences in the twenties. It causes a tremor of the hands at rest that worsens with emotional upsets and slowly deteriorates with advancing age. Attempts may be made to find a cause using investigations such as a CT scan of the brain, but all are negative. Numerous medications to reduce tremor are available, and although there is no cure, reasonable control is usually possible.
See also PARKINSON DISEASE;
TREMOR

ETHAMBUTOL
See TUBERCULOSIS MEDICATIONS

ETHANOL
See ALCOHOL

ETHENOLONE
See ANABOLIC STEROIDS

ETHICS
See MEDICAL ETHICS

ETHINYLOESTRADIOL
See CONTRACEPTIVE PILL; SEX HORMONES

ETHOSUXIMIDE
See ANTICONVULSANTS

ETOPOSIDE
See CYTOTOXICS AND ANTINEOPLASTICS

EUNUCH
See CASTRATION

EUSTACHIAN TUBE
The Eustachian tube is a thin tube that passes through the centre of the head from the back of the nose to the bottom of the middle ear. Its opening into the nose is surrounded by lymph tissue called the adenoids. Its purpose is to equalise pressure between the middle ear cavity and the outside air when a person changes altitude. The pop you feel when changing rapidly (eg. taking off in an aircraft) is caused by air passing through this tube.

It may become blocked with phlegm and mucus, or allow these to pass into the middle ear to cause a glue ear or middle ear infection (otitis media).

It is named after the Italian anatomist and student of Versalius, Bartolommeo Eustachio (1524-74).
See also DIZZINESS; EAR; EUSTACHIAN TUBE BLOCKAGE; OTITIS MEDIA

EUSTACHIAN TUBE BLOCKAGE
Any condition which causes the excess production of phlegm (eg. common cold, sinusitis, hay fever), particularly if there is a sudden

DIAGRAMMATIC REPRESENTATION OF THE CONNECTION BETWEEN THE EAR AND NOSE

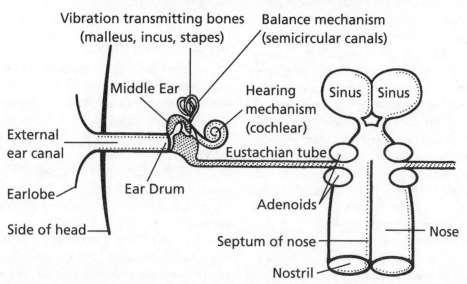

change in altitude (eg. flying), can cause a blockage of the Eustachian tube. This tube runs from the middle ear to the back of the nose, and is used to equalise air pressure between the middle ear and the outside air with changes in altitude.

Pressure discomfort occurs in the ear and may become painful, with accompanying deafness and a constant feeling that swallowing will ease the discomfort. It is worsened by changes in altitude which may cause the ear drum to burst. Persistent blockage may lead to a middle ear infection (otitis media). The bulging ear drum can be seen using an otoscope (magnifying light), and sometimes specific pressure tests are carried out on the ear drum.

Treatments may include steam inhalations, medications (eg. pseudoephedrine, bromhexine), decongestant nasal sprays and the valsalva manoeuvre (holding the nose, closing mouth and trying to breathe out to force air into the ears). In persistent cases a small slit may be put in the ear drum (myringotomy) to ease the pressure. It usually settles slowly without treatment, and slightly faster with treatment, but sometimes may persist for weeks.
See also CHOLESTEATOMA; DEAF; EAR; EUSTACHIAN TUBE; GLUE EAR; OTITIS MEDIA; TYMPANIC RUPTURE; VALSALVA MANOEUVRE

EUTHANASIA
Euthanasia is taking deliberate action to end the life of a person who is suffering from an incurable disease and is highly likely to die in the near future, but is suffering excessively during the process of dying.

Passive euthanasia is the withholding of medication or medical procedures (eg. surgery), or stopping medical support (eg. a respirator) that would briefly prolong the patient's life. This is frequently undertaken by doctors in the appropriate circumstances, usually after discussions with the patient (if possible) or his/her relatives. Increasing the level of narcotic pain relief, muscle relaxants for spasm, and other medications, to the point where a patient is comfortable, may result in the slowing or suppression of breathing to the point where inadequate oxygen to sustain life can be obtained, or a fatal lung infection (eg. pneumonia) develops.

A 'living will' in the form of an advance health directive (a type of statutory declaration) is now available in some countries. This can direct doctors (and advise relatives) about the patient's wishes on passive euthanasia and medical intervention should they become critically ill.

Active euthanasia is intervening to give drugs that will deliberately and rapidly end life. Normally an intravenous injection of a general anaesthetic is given to render the patient unconscious, followed by drugs to paralyse breathing and stop the heart. Death usually occurs within a minute or two. This form of euthanasia was briefly legal in Australia's Northern Territory in 1997, and continues to be legal in some countries (eg. Netherlands).
See also DEATH; PALLIATIVE CARE

EWING TUMOUR
A Ewing tumour is a form of bone cancer that usually occurs in young adults, but may develop in children. Almost any bone in the body may be affected, including the vertebrae of the back. There is pain, swelling and tenderness at the site of the tumour, and the patient develops a fever and becomes anaemic. Pathological fractures may occur in the weakened bone. The diagnosis is made by x-ray and bone biopsy, and treatment involves surgical removal if possible, plus irradiation and potent anticancer (cytotoxic) drugs. With intensive treatment a 50% cure rate can be achieved.
See also BONE CANCER; FRACTURE

EXANTHEMA
See VIRAL EXANTHEMA

EXANTHEM SUBITUM
See ROSEOLA INFANTUM

EXCISION
An area of skin is excised (cut out) to remove a skin cancer, a mole that is annoying or cosmetically unacceptable, to improve the appearance of a scar, or part of a growth may be removed to see if it is malignant.

After lying down in a position that makes the area to be excised easily accessible, the area will be cleaned with a solution that destroys most of the germs on the skin. The doctor will then inject an anaesthetic around the area to be excised, or sometimes into the base of a finger or toe, to anaesthetise the area. The injection stings for about fifteen seconds, and two or more injections may be necessary in larger areas. The area injected will become numb within a few seconds, and no further pain or discomfort should be experienced. If any discomfort is felt, tell the doctor immediately, and further anaesthetic can be injected.

A tray with instruments, solutions, drapes, swabs, sutures etc. will have been placed near you and the doctor will wear sterile gloves. The doctor will thoroughly clean the skin again, then take a drape from the tray, and arrange it near or around the area to be excised.

Using a scalpel, which has an edge sharper than a razor, the doctor will cut around the lesion being excised. The patient may feel pressure, but no pain. It is not possible to cut out closely around the lesion, as a round hole cannot be closed without using plastic surgery techniques to extend the size of the wound, so in most cases, a diamond shaped excision is made, and the scar is usually about three times longer than the lesion is wide. Over the next few minutes, the doctor will cut out the area of concern, and in most cases put the tissue removed into a bottle of preservative for further analysis by a pathologist.

The repair of the wound then commences with stitches (or sometimes tape or staples) being inserted to close the wound. This often takes longer than the excision of the lesion and, once again, the patient should feel no pain.

Once the wound is closed, a dressing will be applied (unless the wound is on a sensitive area where it is inappropriate) and the patient can go home. The anaesthetic will last for one to three hours (depending on which type has been used), but after it has worn off there should be nothing more than a slight ache and paracetamol is normally the only medication necessary.

There may be some slight ooze of blood onto the dressing in the first hour or two, but not for longer, and the dressing may need to be changed at this time. The wound should be kept clean, dry, and if possible, covered until the stitches are removed. The patient can normally have a shower, but not a bath or a swim.

If the wound becomes red, painful, discharges pus or a fever develops, return to see the doctor immediately. Otherwise, the stitches will be removed in a few days or weeks, depending on the area affected and the size of the wound. Sometimes only some of the stitches are removed, and a further visit is necessary for removal of the remainder.

The scar will continue to heal after the stitches are removed. It will form a red line initially, but this usually fades to a white line after a few months. The scar will not reach its final form until a year after the excision.

Some parts of the body heal better than others. The face and hands heal very well, while the back, chest and lower leg heal poorly and will scar more. Scars on areas of tension often spread, and will not appear as neat as scars that are not under tension.
See also CRYOTHERAPY; DIATHERMY; LOCAL ANAESTHETIC

EXERCISE ELECTROCARDIOGRAM
See STRESS TEST

EXFOLIATIVE DERMATITIS
Exfoliative dermatitis (generalised erythroderma) is a form of dermatitis in which there is extensive peeling of skin. It is often associated with foods or drugs, such as gold injections (used for rheumatoid arthritis), sulphonamide antibiotics, some diabetes tablets and some anti-inflammatory medications. Exposure to heavy metals (eg. lead in battery factories) may also be responsible.

There is widespread scaling, peeling and redness of the skin, and patch testing of the skin may be undertaken to determine the cause. Removal of the substance that causes the rash is the obvious treatment, and steroid creams can be used to ease the inflammation. Rarely the condition may become very severe and debilitating, but in most cases the outcome is good, particularly if the trigger substance can be found, but may still take many months to settle.

MOLE

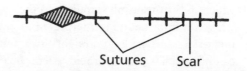

Mole   Excision lines   Wound   Sutures   Scar

See also ANTIRHEUMATICS;
DERMATITIS

EXOPHTHALMOS
See EYE PROTRUDING

EXPECTORANTS
Expectorants aid the removal of phlegm and mucus from the respiratory passages of the lung and throat by coughing. They act by liquefying tenacious, sticky mucus so that it does not adhere firmly to the walls of the air passages, and can therefore be shifted up and out by the microscopic hairs that line these passages and by the forced expiration of air in coughing. They are usually combined in a mixture with other medications such as mucolytics, decongestants, antihistamines, bronchodilators or antitussives.

The traditional expectorants include senega, ammonium chloride, and potassium iodide, all of which taste absolutely foul. Bromhexine (a mucolytic) and methoxyphenamine are more recently developed expectorants with a slightly better taste.

The side effects of expectorants are minimal. Many different brands are available from chemists without a prescription.
See also ANTIHISTAMINES, SEDATING;
BRONCHODILATORS; COUGH
MEDICINES; DECONGESTANTS;
MEDICATION; MUCOLYTICS

EXPOSURE
See HYPOTHERMIA

EXTERNAL CARDIAC COMPRESSION
See RESUSCITATION

EXTERNAL HORDEOLUM
See STYE

EXTRASYSTOLE
See ATRIAL EXTRASYSTOLES; HEART, EXTRA BEATS; VENTRICULAR EXTRASYSTOLES

EYE
Light enters the eyes and stimulates nerves which in turn transmit impulses to the brain where the information is interpreted as visual images. Light travels in straight lines, but it can be bent if it passes through a lens, be that

THE EYE

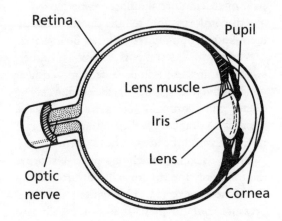

in a camera or the human eye. The degree of bending can be precisely controlled by the shape of the lens and the shape of the lens in the human eye can be changed by tiny muscles attached to it.

Each eye is a slightly flattened sphere consisting of three layers. The outer layer is called the sclera and forms the white of the eye, except for the very front section which is transparent to allow light in and is called the cornea. The second layer is the choroid and contains the blood vessels that service the eye. The front of the choroid forms the iris, which is the part that gives the eyes their colour depending on the inherited genes. In the centre of the iris is a small gap called the pupil. Muscles in the iris enlarge or reduce the size of the pupil according to the amount of light – the more light the smaller the pupil. Just behind the iris is the lens.

The innermost layer of the eye, curving around the back of the eyeball sphere, is the retina. This is a light-sensitive structure containing nerve cells, commonly called rods and cones because of their shapes. The rods are sensitive to dim light and will function in near-darkness but do not produce a very sharp image. The cones are sensitive to colour. When you go into a darkened room such as a theatre, it is difficult to see for the first few moments. This is the time it takes the rods to adjust to the change in light. The nerves in the retina all meet together to form the optic nerve, which connects to the brain.

Between the lens and the cornea is a chamber filled with a watery fluid, called the aqueous humour. The ball of the eye behind the lens and in front of the retina is filled with a jelly-like substance called vitreous humour. It is this that gives the eyeball its firmness and maintains its spherical shape.

Light passes through all the transparent layers starting with the cornea, then through the pupil and aqueous humour, the lens, followed by the vitreous humour to finally impinge on the retina. All these layers refract (bend) the light so that light from the large area outside is focused in the small area of the retina. The most important refractive body is the cornea, which is responsible for about 70% of the process. The lens focuses the light according to whether it is for near or distance vision. When the light reaches the retina, the nerve cells convert it into electrical impulses and send these along the optic nerve to the brain, which records visually the objects we are looking at. Just like the lens of a camera, the lens of the eye produces an upside down image. The brain is responsible for the right-side-up, three-dimensional view that we eventually get. If the optic nerve is damaged, it can cause blindness even though the eyes themselves are still functioning. The point where the optic nerve leaves the retina has no rods and cones and so forms a blind spot.

The eye is one of the most mobile organs in the body. Each eye has a set of six external muscles so that it can move in all directions.

Because the eyes are so sensitive, the body provides a great deal of protection for them. They are set in two bony sockets in the skull. Externally they are guarded by the eyebrows and the eyelids. The eyebrows help to ward off blows, shield the eyes from sunlight and deflect sweat so that it does not run into the eyes. The eyelids form a protective covering, while the fringe of eyelashes stops dust and dirt getting in. When an eyelid blinks, it wipes a film of antiseptic tears over the eye. The inner surface of both upper and lower eyelids, as well as the eyes themselves, are covered by a transparent membrane called the conjunctiva. This helps to keep the eyes moist so that they can move freely.
See also ASTIGMATISM; BLIND; BLIND SPOT; CATARACT; COLOUR BLINDNESS TEST; CATARACT; CONJUNCTIVITIS; ECTROPION; EYE DRY; EYE PAIN; EYE PARALYSED; EYE PROTRUDING; EYE RED; EYE ULCER; FLASH BURN TO EYE; FLOATER IN EYE; GLAUCOMA; MYDRIATICS; NYSTAGMUS; OPHTHALMOSCOPY; PINGUECULUM; PTERYGIUM; PUPIL LARGE; PUPIL SMALL; REFRACTIVE SURGERY; SQUINT; TEARS; TONOMETRY; UVEITIS; VISION; VISUAL ACUITY and other diseases and symptoms associated with the eye.

EYE CANCER
See RETINOBLASTOMA

EYE DISCHARGE
The eye may discharge tears when the person is emotionally upset or the eye is inflamed, or may discharge pus with an eye infection.

The causes of a watery discharge include allergic conjunctivitis (the eye reacts to pollen, dust, a chemical or other substance with itching, redness and watering), a foreign body (eg. speck of dirt, inturned eyelash), flash burn (from watching a welding arc), ultraviolet lights, iritis (inflammation of the coloured part of the eye), scleritis (inflammation of the whites of the eyes), glaucoma (increase in the pressure of the jelly-like fluid inside the eye), and an infection of the eye with the virus *Herpes simplex*.

A creamy or green thick discharge may be caused by bacterial conjunctivitis, viral conjunctivitis, and trachoma (a type of conjunctivitis caused by *Chlamydia*).
See also EYE; TEARS, EXCESS and separate entries for diseases mentioned above.

EYE DRY
Tears are produced in glands (lacrimal glands) beyond the outer corner of the eye, and are released onto the eye surface through a small tube (duct) to keep the eye surface moist. Excess tears drain through the tear duct at the inner corner of the eye into the back of the nose. If too many tears are produced, they will overflow the eye and the person will be seen to be crying. If too few tears are produced, the eye will dry out and become itchy and irritated. Technically, dry eyes are called xerophthalmia.

Dry eyes are a very common problem with old age, as the lacrimal glands wear out. The lower lid may also become slack, and separate from the eye surface with age (a condition called ectropion), allowing tears

EYE FROM FRONT

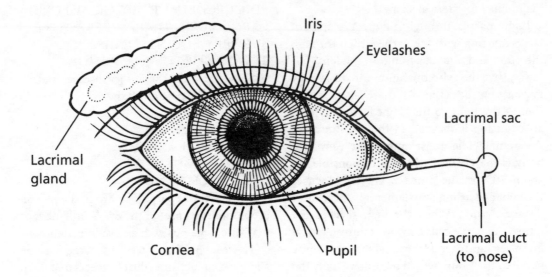

Iris

Eyelashes

Lacrimal sac

Lacrimal gland

Cornea

Pupil

Lacrimal duct (to nose)

to escape from the eye. Lubricating drops and ointments are used to overcome the problem.

A deficiency of vitamin A in the diet will cause dry skin, dry eyes, shallow ulcers on the eye surface and poor night vision.

Keratoconjunctivitis sicca is an inflammation of the eye surface similar to eczema on the skin, with which it is often associated.

A viral infection of the eye (viral conjunctivitis) may affect tear production and cause eye drying, as well as redness and soreness.

Trachoma is a type of conjunctivitis (superficial eye infection) caused by an organism known as *Chlamydia*. It is very common in areas of low hygiene where flies can transmit the infection from one person to another. A mild trachoma infection may not be very noticeable and may cause no symptoms at all. In more severe cases, eye pain, intolerance to bright lights, and a weeping swollen eye may develop. The lacrimal gland can also be damaged so that the eye dries out.

Damage to the lacrimal gland from an injury, infection or irradiation (eg. treatment of a skin cancer) may prevent tear production.

Some medications may have dry eyes as a side effect. Examples include antihistamines, blood pressure medications, pseudoephedrine (used for a runny nose) and some psychiatric drugs.

Uncommon causes of a dry eye include cirrhosis (liver failure), rheumatoid arthritis, diabetes, erythema multiforme (an acute inflammation of the skin), Sjögren's syndrome (an autoimmune disease) and Riley-Day syndrome.

See also DRY EYE SYNDROME; EYE; TEARS and separate entries for diseases mentioned above.

EYE FLOATER
See FLOATER IN EYE

EYE FOREIGN BODY
See EYE INJURY

EYE INFECTION
See CONJUNCTIVITIS; TRACHOMA

EYE INJURY
Any injury to the eye is potentially serious and should receive expert assessment and treatment. An injured eye should not be rubbed, nor should it be opened and examined since it is very easy to do further damage. If the victim is wearing contact lenses, they may be able to remove the lenses themselves, but otherwise it is best left to a doctor. It is especially important to act quickly if any chemical has entered the eye.

Foreign bodies in the eye are relatively common and can usually be dealt with at home. Simply washing the face with cool water, ensuring some gets into the eyes, will often remove loose bits of grit. If a single bit is embedded in the under-surface of the upper lid and the lid is pulled back over a match, it may be possible to remove it with the moistened cotton bud. Do not touch the eye surface. If bits of grit adhere to the eye itself, unless they can be washed away easily, a doctor's attention is needed.

A bruised or black eye can be relieved by an ice pack (not the traditional piece of steak). Be careful not to bring the eye into direct contact with the ice. Wrap the ice in a damp cloth and alternatively leave it on and remove it from the eye for about twenty minutes at a time. If the eyeball seems to be injured or the victim is unable to see properly, get a doctor. The eye can be padded and bandaged shut while travelling to the doctor or hospital.

It is essential that chemicals in the eye are washed out immediately. Tilt the victim's head to the affected side, hold the eyelids gently apart and rinse the eye for at least ten minutes (preferably twenty). Make sure that the water does not splash or flow into the other eye.

See also EYE; EYE FOREIGN BODY

EYELID

There are two eyelids on each eye, an upper and lower. The upper one is much larger and more active than the lower. The eyelid consists of skin, a moist membrane on the inside of the lid (which folds back to form the conjunctiva over the front of the eye), a fibrous plate (tarsal plate) which gives rigidity to the eyelid, eyelashes (which shade the eye), sweat glands, Meibomian glands (oil glands that lubricate the eyelashes) and the tiny tarsal muscles.

The medical term for the eyelid is the palpebrae.

The epicanthus is the fold of skin that covers the inner corner of the eye (the canthus). This is more prominent in oriental people.

See also EYE; EYELID DISEASE; EYELID DROOP; EYELID SWOLLEN; MEIBOMIAN CYST; TEARS; TIC

EYELID DISEASE

Any of the structures that make up the eyelid may become affected by injury, infection, inflammation or disease.

The eyelid muscles may become fatigued by excessive hours without sleep, and start twitching uncontrollably.

A stye (or sty) is a bacterial infection of one of the superficial tiny sweat or oil glands on the margin of the eyelid. There is often no apparent reason for a stye developing, but

rubbing the eye, or an injury to the eye, is a possible cause. The infected gland becomes painful, red and swollen, and fills with pus. A stye is really a miniature abscess.

A chalazion is a bacterial infection of a deeper gland (Meibomian gland) within the eyelid to cause a painful, red, tender swelling.

Blepharitis is a superficial bacterial infection of the eyelid margin around the base of the eyelashes. It is often associated with dandruff.

Entropion is the inturning of the eyelid that results in eyelashes rubbing irritatingly on the eye surface. It may be caused by eyelid injury or infection.

Ectropion is the out-turning of the lower eyelid which allows tears to trickle down the cheek, and is a common problem in the elderly.

Other causes of eyelid disease include allergic dermatitis, xanthelasma (yellow fatty deposits on the eyelid), skin cancer, ptosis and hyperthyroidism (excess thyroxine production).

See also EYELID DROOP and separate entries for diseases mentioned above.

EYELID DROOP

Drooping of the eyelid(s) is known as ptosis, and may be caused by damage to the nerve controlling the eyelid muscle or a number of rarer syndromes.

Bell's palsy is a peculiar condition in which the nerve that controls the movement of muscles on one side of the face stops working. The cause is unknown. The onset is quite sudden and one side of the face becomes totally paralysed in a matter of hours. The patient feels well, and has no other medical problems or areas that are affected.

Myasthenia gravis causes a varying weakness of the muscles that control the eyelids, the movement of the eyes (double vision results) and swallowing. The weakness varies in severity during the day and may disappear entirely for days or weeks before recurring but, over a period of months or years, the attacks become more severe. It is most common in young women and the symptoms are caused by a blocking of the nerves that supply the affected muscles.

Uncommon causes of ptosis include the Guillain-Barré syndrome (progressive symmetrical weakness of the limbs and face), Horner syndrome (nerves are compressed in the brain, neck or upper chest), Wernicke-Korsakoff psychosis (due to vitamin deficiencies caused by an inadequate diet while on alcoholic binges) and Dubowitz syndrome (mental retardation). Ptosis may also be caused by damage to the nerve which controls eyelid movement (third nerve) by a tumour, bleeding, abscess or other disease in the nerve, brain or skull.

There are numerous other rare causes.
See also EYELID and separate entries for diseases mentioned above.

EYELID SWOLLEN

Swelling (oedema) of an eyelid can be due to an injury, bruise or bite, but sometimes more significant conditions may be responsible.

The most common cause is angioneurotic oedema, which is a sudden, severe swelling of the eyelid and other tissues around the eye caused by an allergy reaction. The trigger is usually a pollen, dust, chemical or other substance that has blown into the eye, or from rubbing the eye with a contaminated finger. The affected tissue may be slightly itchy, but is not usually painful or tender.

Another cause is hypothyroidism (an underactive thyroid gland). Obstruction of the major veins draining the head because of a tumour, clot, cancer, abscess or other disease will cause blood to be retained in the head, resulting in headache and swelling of many facial tissues, including the eyelids.
See also ANGIONEUROTIC OEDEMA; EYELID; HYPOTHYROIDISM

EYELID TWITCH
See TIC

EYE MOVEMENT ABNORMAL
See NYSTAGMUS

EYE OF HORUS

Horus was the Ancient Egyptian sky god who was depicted in the form of a falcon, and whose eyes were the sun and the moon. During a battle between Horus and the earth god Seth, the left eye of Horus (the moon eye) was blinded. The eye was then cured by the healing god, Thoth. This battle continued every month, explaining in myth the waxing and waning of the moon. Because of this recurring miracle, the eye of Horus became a powerful symbol of healing in the ancient world.

The eye of a falcon is oval in shape, with a trailing taper leading to the lacrimal gland, and the eye covets (markings) are a vertical triangular slash, and a lazy trailing marking below the eye, as shown in the diagram below.

The left eye of Horus was used throughout Ancient Egypt, and later in modified form in Ancient Greece, to signify the healing power of a potion or medication.

With time and abbreviation, the full symbol became modified to the Rx symbol we know today, which is often interpreted to mean 'recipe'. It is often written in a flowing old English style script to differentiate it from the main part of the prescription, and is still used to mark the start of a prescription for 21st. century treatments.
See also CADUCEUS; HIPPOCRATIC OATH

EYE PAIN

Eye pain may come from the eye itself, structures around the eye, or from nerve irritation associated with other conditions.

A foreign body (eg. speck of dirt, loose eyelash) in the eye will irritate it to cause pain (particularly on eye movement), redness and watering from the affected eye. After the irritant is removed, an ulcer may be left behind, which will cause eye irritation for some days until it heals.

Bacterial conjunctivitis is very common in children but may occur at any age. The eyes (and both are usually involved) are red, sore and a yellow/green discharge forms that may stick the eyelids together overnight. Viral conjunctivitis is a viral infection of the eye surface. It is far less common than a bacterial infection, but much harder to treat. A watery, pale yellow, slightly creamy discharge occurs, the eyes are itchy, slightly sore and sometimes red.

Glaucoma is due to an increase in the pressure of the jelly-like fluid inside the eye. This may come on gradually, or may be quite sudden. Early symptoms include an eye ache or pain, blurred vision, seeing halos around objects, red eye, a gradual loss of peripheral vision and watering of the eye.

Iritis is an inflammation of the iris (the coloured part of the eye). The inflammation can be due to an infection such as toxoplasmosis, tuberculosis or syphilis, or it may be associated with inflammatory diseases in other parts of the body, including psoriasis, ankylosing spondylitis, and some bowel conditions. Almost invariably, only one eye is involved. It will suddenly become red and painful, a watery discharge will develop, and the vision is blurred.

Other eye causes of pain include scleritis (inflammation of the whites of the eyes), looking at a welding arc (flash burn) or ultraviolet lights, trachoma (a type of conjunctivitis caused by *Chlamydia* , and an infection of the eye with the virus *Herpes simplex* .

Eye pain originating outside the eye may be due to sinusitis, migraine, cluster headache (usually associated with excess sweating of one or both sides of head), Ramsay Hunt syndrome (form of shingles affecting the face), excess thyroxine (hyperthyroidism), Reiter syndrome, Sjögren syndrome and ankylosing spondylitis (long-term inflammation of the small joints between the vertebrae that may sometimes involve the eyes).
See also EYE; EYE RED; FACE PAIN; PHOTOPHOBIA and separate entries for diseases mentioned above.

EYE PARALYSED
The inability to move the eye in one or more directions is a rare, but serious symptom.

Reasons for this problem may include a stroke affecting the part of the brain that controls eye movement, Steele-Richardson-Olszewski syndrome (a variation of Parkinson's disease), Parinaud syndrome (tumour or inflammation of the pineal gland at the front of the brain), Wernicke-Korsakoff psychosis

(vitamin deficiency usually from alcoholism), Cogan syndrome and Tolosa-Hunt syndrome (painful paralysis of one eye, a drooping eyelid and enlargement of the pupil because of pressure on nerves to the eye caused by an aneurysm on the carotid artery).
See also EYE; NYSTAGMUS and separate entries for diseases mentioned above.

EYE PINK
See ALBINISM; EYE RED

EYE PROTRUDING
A patient with slightly protruding eyes in comparison to the face is said to have proptosis or exophthalmos.

The thyroid gland in the front of the neck produces the hormone thyroxine, which acts as an accelerator for every cell in the body. Excess thyroxine (hyperthyroidism) will cause sweating, weight loss, diarrhoea, malabsorption of food, nervousness, heat intolerance, rapid heart rate, warm skin, tremor and prominent eyes.

A tumour, cancer or infection of the eye, the eye socket, surrounding tissues, skull or the brain behind the eye will cause one eye only to become more prominent.

Other possible causes of exophthalmos include Cushing syndrome (over production of steroids in the body, or taking large doses of cortisone), very severe high blood pressure (malignant hypertension), clots in the veins behind an eye, Hand-Schueller-Christian syndrome, Apert syndrome and Sturge-Weber syndrome.
See also EYE and separate entries for diseases mentioned above.

EYE RED
Red eyes are a very common problem, and may be due to overuse, inadequate rest and too much alcohol, as well as any one of a number of diseases.

A foreign body (eg. speck of dirt, loose eyelash) in the eye will irritate it to cause pain (particularly on eye movement), redness and watering from the affected eye. After the irritant is removed, an ulcer may be left behind, that will cause eye irritation for some days until it heals. Chemical irritation from a substance splashed in an eye, or pool chlorine that is too strong, will cause a similar effect.

Bleeding into the white of the eye after an injury will cause a dramatic red patch.

Bacterial conjunctivitis is very common in children but may occur at any age. The eyes (and both are usually involved) are red, sore and a yellow/green discharge forms that may stick the eyelids together overnight. Viral conjunctivitis is a viral infection of the eye surface. It is far less common than a bacterial infection, but much harder to treat. A watery, pale yellow, slightly creamy discharge occurs, the eyes are itchy, slightly sore and sometimes red.

Allergic conjunctivitis, in which the eye is reacting to a pollen, dust, chemical or other substance that has entered the eye, will cause itching, redness and watering. Often only one eye is affected.

Iritis is an inflammation of the iris (the coloured part of the eye). The eye will suddenly become red and painful, a watery discharge will develop, and the vision is blurred. Bright lights will aggravate the eye pain and the pupil is small.

A pingueculum or pterygium (growth on the eye surface) may become irritated and red.

Uncommon causes of a red eye include trachoma (eye infection caused by *Chlamydia*), glaucoma, cluster headaches, episcleritis, Reiter syndrome, Behçet syndrome and Stevens-Johnson syndrome.

The use of the illegal drug cocaine is also associated with eye redness.
See also EYE; EYE PAIN and separate entries for diseases mentioned above.

EYE SUNKEN

The eyes may appear sunken in (enophthalmos) because of tiredness or prolonged illness of any sort, but there are some significant medical conditions that may be responsible.

Dehydration because of lack of fluid intake, or excess fluid output (eg. diarrhoea, sweating) will result in a loss of tissue tone, and cause the eyes to sink into the head.

Malnutrition from the unavailability of food, or diseases such as anorexia nervosa, will decrease body fat, including the fat pad which normally sits behind each eye.

A significant weight loss due to serious disease (eg. cancer, heart failure), or deliberate dieting, will also shrink the eye fat pad.

The thyroid gland in the front of the neck produces the hormone thyroxine, which acts as an accelerator for every cell in the body. If there is a lack of thyroxine, all organs will function slowly, and symptoms will include intolerance of cold, constipation, weakness, hoarse voice, heavy periods, sunken eyes, dry skin, hair loss, slow heart rate and anaemia.

A tumour of the tear producing lacrimal gland at the outside corner of the eye may put pressure on the front of the eye, and cause swelling of the tissue around the eye, to make it appear sunken into the head.
See also EYE and separate entries for diseases mentioned above.

EYE ULCER

Ulceration of the cornea, the transparent outside covering on the front of the eye, may be caused by injuries to the surface of the eye (eg. scratch), or infections. *Herpes simplex*, the virus that causes cold sores and genital herpes, is the most common cause of all eye ulcers. Fungal infections causing ulcers are commonly seen in farm workers, but may develop in others when steroid eye drops are being used. Bacterial conjunctivitis seldom causes ulcers unless treatment is neglected. Two rare causes are a deficiency of vitamin A (eg. in people on fad diets, or with inability to absorb vitamin A because of diseases of the bile duct) which results in a very dry eye, and prolonged exposure of the eye in unconscious patients who do not blink.

Pain and watering occurs in the eye, there is redness of the whites of the eye, and a discharge of sticky pus occurs if an infection is responsible. Permanent scarring of the cornea and reduced vision may occur if the ulcer is left untreated. A swab may be taken from the eye to identify the organism responsible for an infection.

Appropriate eye drops are prescribed for bacterial and fungal eye infections. Serious *Herpes* virus infections can be treated with special antiviral eye drops and ointment, and through a microscope, minor surgery to remove the active viral areas at the edge of the ulcer may be undertaken. If necessary, a scarred cornea can be surgically replaced by a corneal transplant.

The prognosis depends on the cause and response to treatment. Ulcers caused by an injury usually heal within a few days without treatment. Most viral infections settle without treatment after a few weeks of discomfort, but in some patients, particularly those who are otherwise in poor health or on potent drugs for other serious diseases, the infection can steadily worsen to cause severe eye ulceration. Bacterial and fungal infections respond rapidly to treatment, and there is usually a good result from corneal transplantation. *See also* COLD SORE; CONJUNCTIVITIS; EYE; VITAMIN A

EYE WATERY
See EYE DISCHARGE; TEARS EXCESS

F

FABRY DISEASE

Fabry disease (angiokeratoma corporis diffusum) is a rare, inherited inborn error in body chemistry that affects the skin and internal organs of males. Tiny dark red raised spots appear on the lower abdomen, buttocks, penis and scrotum. The heart and brain are also affected to cause transient ischaemic attacks, strokes, angina, heart attacks (myocardial infarction) and excruciating attacks of body pain. Women who carry the gene but who do not actually develop the disease may develop cataracts in their eyes. It is diagnosed by a biopsy of skin spots and family history. No specific treatment is available, but the symptoms may be eased.

See also ANGINA; HAEMANGIOMA; TRANSIENT ISCHAEMIC ATTACK

FACE

See EYE; FACE ABNORMAL; FACE PAIN; FACE PIGMENTED; FACE RED; FACE SWOLLEN; FACE, WEAK MUSCLES; MANDIBLE; MAXILLA; MOUTH; NOSE; SINUS; ZYGOMA

FACE ABNORMAL

Abnormalities in the appearance of the face are usually due to injury, or are congenital (present since birth). Injuries can cause any conceivable deformity, and some congenital conditions cause horrendous abnormalities. Plastic surgeons are now very skilled in reconstructing the bones, covering muscles and skin to create dramatic improvements in appearance.

Cushing syndrome is caused by an over-production of steroids such as cortisone in the body, or taking large doses of cortisone to control a wide range of diseases, including asthma and rheumatoid arthritis. Headache, obesity, thirst, easy bruising, impotence, menstrual period irregularities, a swollen red face, acne, high blood pressure, bone pain and muscle weakness are common symptoms of this syndrome.

Some of the birth defects that can cause abnormal facial appearance include: –

• Apert syndrome, which may be associated with fingers and toes fusing together and protruding eyes.

• Coffin-Lowry syndrome, which may be associated with prominent lips.

• Down syndrome, which may be associated with mental retardation, and a broad face with slanted eyes.

• Fragile X syndrome, which may be associated with overactivity, small testes and mental retardation.

• Moebius syndrome, which may be associated with drooping eyelids, paralysed eyes and poor facial expression.

• Rubenstein-Taybi syndrome, which may be associated with an underdeveloped lower jaw and heart abnormalities.

• Sturge-Weber syndrome, which may be associated with convulsions and large red stains across the face and other parts of the body.

• William syndrome, which may be associated with prominent lips and drooping cheeks.

See also CLEFT LIP AND PALATE; FACE PAIN; FACE RED and separate entries for most diseases mentioned above.

FACE LIFT

A plastic surgeon can make the changes of ageing less apparent by means of a face lift. Face lifts are not confined to Hollywood actresses and vain millionaire's wives: many ordinary people, men and women, have this very common operation, and most find that it changes their outlook on life as dramatically as their appearance.

From the outset it is important to realise that a face lift will not make a person look like their son or daughter, let alone their favourite television star, but it will significantly soften the wrinkles on the face, particularly those under the eyes, and will remove double chins and other sagging tissue.

The first step in considering a face lift is to discuss the matter with a general practitioner who will assess the situation sympathetically, and unless there is a medical reason not to proceed, will refer the patient on to a plastic surgeon. Plastic surgeons have undertaken six years postgraduate training in this speciality, and many have practised in specialised clinics overseas.

The plastic surgeon will carefully assess the face and probably take photos before explaining what can and cannot be done. He or she may show before and after photos of other patients who have had a similar procedure. Costs will also be discussed, as these are often expensive procedures for which there may be no medical insurance coverage. If a decision is made to proceed, a hospital booking will be made. The patient is usually admitted the day before for assessment by the anaesthetist.

Under the general anaesthetic, the surgeon will make incisions in front of the ears, then behind the hairline above the ear, across the top of the forehead and down the other side. Through this he or she will gently lift the skin off the face and forehead, remove excess amounts of fat under the skin, tighten up the skin itself, then sew up the long incision very finely so that it cannot be seen. Separate incisions may be made under the eyes and under the chin to tighten up the tissue in those areas.

The face is then firmly bandaged, and when the patient awakes they may be blind-folded for a day or two. The skin on the face will feel tight and sore, and when the bandages first come off it will look bruised, but after a few weeks the new person will emerge.
See also PLASTIC SURGERY

FACE PAIN

The most common causes of pain in the face are sinusitis and problems with the teeth.

The sinuses in the front of the skull are lined with a moist membrane, similar to that inside the nose. If the membrane becomes infected, it starts secreting thick mucus or pus, which rapidly blocks the small holes which drain fluid from the sinuses. The sinus then fills with mucus or pus, and pressure builds up to cause the severe pain of sinusitis. There is usually also tenderness below or above the eyes.

The teeth may become infected, a nerve can become exposed, the gums around a tooth may be inflamed or infected, or a tooth root may become abscessed. All these dental problems can cause facial pain, sometimes running from the affected tooth up to the ear on that side. The tooth or gum is usually also tender.

Other causes of face pain include trigeminal neuralgia (inflammation of the main sensory nerve of the face), infection of the face tissue by bacteria (cellulitis), migraines, cluster headaches, infected salivary glands (sialitis), Ramsay Hunt syndrome (form of shingles affecting the face), muscle spasms (from excessive talking, shouting, chewing etc.), and disorders of the jaw joint including injury, arthritis and dislocation.

Rare causes of facial pain may include tumours of the sinuses, nose and nerves in the face; infections in the mouth; temporal arteritis (inflammation of the artery in the temple) and carotodynia.
See also EYE PAIN; FACE ABNORMAL; HEADACHE; SINUSITIS and separate entries for most diseases mentioned above.

FACE PIGMENTED

Chloasma is a mark of motherhood, as it results in pigment being deposited in the skin of the forehead, cheeks and nipples. Unfortunately, it is also an uncommon side effect of using the contraceptive pill. The pigmentation affects some women far more than others, and some races more than others. If a woman's mother, sister or grandmother has the problem, they are more likely to have it too.

Nothing can be done to prevent or treat the pigmentation of chloasma, but it will fade slowly with time after the pregnancy, or once the contraceptive pill is ceased. Cosmetics can be used to hide the pigmentation if necessary.

Other forms of facial pigmentation may be caused by most of the conditions that cause skin pigmentation elsewhere on the body. In older people, the face may appear pigmented from many years of sun exposure, while the rest of the body may be quite unaffected.
See also SKIN COLOUR; SKIN PIGMENTATION EXCESS

FACE PRESENTATION

During birth, normally the baby presents the crown (top) of its head in the opening of the uterus, with the neck bent and the chin on the chest. This lets the smallest diameter of the head pass through the birth canal. In a very small number of cases, the neck becomes extended (bent back) instead of flexed (bent forward), and the face presents itself to the outside. This is a significant problem, as the largest diameter of the head is trying to force its way through the birth canal. The result is a very long labour and possible damage to both mother and baby.

Obstetricians can sometimes disengage (push up) the head from the pelvis and bring it back down again with the crown of the head presenting, but in most cases a caesarean section is the treatment of choice.
See also LABOUR; PREGNANCY

FACE RED

An excessively red face (facial erythema) is most commonly caused by sunburn and flushing from embarrassment.

Other possible causes include rosacea (a skin rash that causes bright red cheeks with raised bumps), seborrhoeic dermatitis (very common in babies causing a blistering red rash), many forms of dermatitis (eg. contact dermatitis) and sometimes the overuse of steroid creams for treating dermatitis can result in skin redness that is very difficult to treat.

Less common causes of facial erythema may include perioral dermatitis (around mouth), psoriasis, excess sensitive to sunlight, systemic lupus erythematosus (red rash across the cheeks and bridge of the nose in a butterfly pattern), erysipelas (serious infection of the skin on the face) and birthmarks.
See also FLUSH, ABNORMAL; SKIN RED and separate entries for diseases mentioned above.

FACE SWOLLEN

Injury, infection and inflammation are the main causes of swelling (oedema) of any tissue. Because the face has very delicate tissues, and many openings to the outside world, it is particularly susceptible to all these problems.

Obvious causes of swelling are blows to the face, insect bites and infection of the skin and tissue under the skin (cellulitis). In the face, infections can spread rapidly to vital organs (eyes, ears, throat) so rapid treatment with appropriate antibiotics is essential.

The facial swelling that brings people to the doctor most rapidly is the sudden onset of massive swelling, usually around the eyes, caused by angioneurotic oedema. This is an acute allergy reaction to some substance (pollen, dust, chemical etc.) that has landed on the surface of the eye, and been absorbed into the underside of the upper and/or lower eyelids to make them swell dramatically and rapidly to the point where it may be impossible to open the eye. The same effect can occur around the mouth and nose.

Other causes of facial swelling include Cushing syndrome (due to over production of steroids, or taking large doses of cortisone), an overactive thyroid gland (hyperthyroidism), a parotid gland tumour and severe dermatitis on the face.

Obstruction to the veins draining blood from the face is a rare, but serious, cause of facial swelling.
See also FACE PAIN; OEDEMA

FACE, WEAK MUSCLES

The most common causes for weakness of the muscles of the face are Bell's palsy and a stroke.

Bell's palsy is a peculiar condition in which the nerve that controls the movement of muscles on one side of the face stops working. The cause is unknown. The onset is quite sudden, and a patient may find that one side of his or her face becomes totally paralysed in a matter of hours. The usual course is that the weakness completely recovers without treatment or discomfort in two to ten weeks.

In a stroke (cerebrovascular accident) the part of the brain that controls movement on one side of the face is affected by having its blood supply cut off by a blockage in an artery, or by a blood vessel in the brain bursting, causing bleeding and damage to part of the brain. The onset is almost instantaneous, may be associated with paralysis in other parts of the body, headache and other abnormalities that can vary from minor discomfort and confusion to widespread paralysis and coma.

Less common causes of facial muscle weakness include Parkinson's disease (degeneration of part of the brain that coordinates muscle movement), multiple sclerosis (nerve disease) and motor neurone disease (progressive and permanent degeneration of the nerves that control muscle movement). Tumours, abscesses and bleeding outside the brain put pressure on the part of the brain that controls the muscles of the face and thus can cause them to become weak or paralysed.

The Guillain-Barré syndrome is a rare condition that usually occurs in young people and causes progressive symmetrical weakness of the limbs and face, numbness in hands and feet, nerve pain, difficulty in speaking and swallowing. It often follows a viral infection, and although treatment is unsatisfactory, 80% of patients recover.

See also PARALYSIS and separate entries for diseases mentioned above.

FACTOR VII DEFICIT
See HAEMOPHILIA A

FACTOR IX DEFICIT
See CHRISTMAS DISEASE

FAECES
The body disposes of solid waste as faeces through the anus. It consists mainly of fibre (cellulose), fats, protein and small amounts of inorganic substances such as iron and phosphorus. At least two thirds of the total weight of faeces is made up of water but if the person has diarrhoea, water may make up over 95% of the faeces. Bacterial debris also makes up a very large part of faeces.

Faeces is usually passed once or twice a day, but some people are comfortable passing faeces only two or three times a week. The amount passed varies markedly from one person to another, and depends greatly upon the diet. The more fibre in the diet, the greater the volume of faeces.

See also ANUS; COLON; CONSTIPATION; DIARRHOEA; FAECES, ABNORMAL DESIRE TO PASS; FAECES COLOUR ABNORMAL; FAECES BLOOD; STEATORRHOEA

FAECES, ABNORMAL DESIRE TO PASS
Tenesmus is the technical term for the desire to pass faeces despite there being no faeces present in the rectum (last part of the large intestine). Diarrhoea causes a similar sensation, but in this case, there is good reason to go to the toilet so that the watery faeces can escape.

The most common cause is a mass in the anal canal. This may be a swollen internal pile (haemorrhoid), a tumour or cancer, polyps, or inflammation of the anal canal or rectum from infection or ulceration (eg. ulcerative colitis).

Inflammation and infection of organs in the pelvis such as the bladder and uterus, which rest on the rectum, can cause irritation in the rectum and this inflammation results in tenesmus.

A foreign body inserted into the rectum will also give this sensation.

Because the range of conditions that can be responsible for tenesmus include some very serious ones, a doctor's checkup is essential to determine the exact cause of the sensation. *See also* CONSTIPATION; DIARRHOEA and separate entries for diseases mentioned above.

FAECES BLACK
See FAECES BLOOD; FAECES COLOUR ABNORMAL

FAECES BLOOD
Faecal blood may be fresh (bright red), old (dark red or black), on the outside of the stool, or mixed in with the faeces. It must always be checked by a doctor to ensure that there is no serious cause for the bleeding.

Persistent bleeding of small amounts of blood into the gut may first be detected because the patient is anaemic, and only on special tests can the blood be detected in the faeces.

Bright red blood on the outside of the faeces may be due to bleeding piles (haemorrhoids) when the bleeding tends to occur for a minute or two after passing a motion, a fissure in the anus (the anus has overstretched and torn during an episode of constipation), and disorders of coagulation (faulty blood clotting mechanism).

Bright red blood mixed in with the faeces may be due to dilated blood vessels and polyps in the rectum, a cancer in the rectum, ulcerative colitis (lining of the large intestine becomes inflamed and ulcerated), polyps in the large intestine, and diverticulitis (formation of numerous small outpocketings of the large gut due to increased pressure in the intestine from inadequate fibre in the diet).

Dark blood in the faeces (melaena) is due to blood that has been altered by the digestive process to appear very dark or black. Bleeding anywhere from the mouth down may appear in the faeces in this form. Common causes include a peptic ulcer in the stomach, oesophageal ulceration, cancer of any part of the intestine, Crohn's disease (thickening and inflammation of the small or large intestine), increased pressure of the blood in the veins draining the intestine (portal hypertension) and excessive doses of

drugs such as warfarin and aspirin. The colour of the blood in the faeces depends upon the part of the gut affected.
See also FAECES COLOUR ABNORMAL; FAECES TESTS and separate entries for diseases mentioned above.

FAECES COLOUR ABNORMAL

Most changes in the colour of the faeces are due to changes in diet, but occasionally may be due to serious disease. Any persistent change in the colour of the faeces needs to be checked by a doctor. Take along a sample in a clean, clear glass bottle so it can be inspected and analysed.

Dark faeces may be due to iron and bismuth medications, red wine and certain fruits, but blood is another possibility which can herald serious disease.

Green/yellow faeces is caused by excess bile in the faeces. Bile is produced in the liver, stored in the gall bladder and released onto food in the first part of the small intestine to aid in digestion. Excess can be caused by diarrhoea (the bile moves through the gut too quickly to be digested), bowel infections and starvation (inadequate food for the bile to work on).

Bright yellow faeces occurs in bottle fed babies, and rarely older children and adults, who have dairy products as the main source of their diet.

Faeces takes its usual mid-brown colour from digested bile. If this is lacking, due to obstruction of the bile duct from the gall bladder to the intestine, or because liver disease is preventing bile production, the stools will be an off-white clay colour. Determining the cause of the lack of bile is essential.

Excess fat in the faeces (steatorrhoea) causes the faeces to be pale yellow.

Only blood can cause red faeces.

Iron tablets may cause black faeces but even if the patient is taking iron supplements, black faeces must be checked by a doctor to ensure the discolouration is not due to blood from a cancer or other disease in the intestine.
See also FAECES BLOOD; STEATORRHOEA and separate entries for diseases mentioned above.

FAECES INCONTINENCE
See INCONTINENCE OF FAECES

FAECES TESTS

Faeces is the solid waste eliminated from our body. Like urine, because faeces have passed through much of the body, an analysis of its composition can be an indication of abnormalities and disorders existing in the body. A faeces sample is collected by using a disposable plastic spoon to place a small amount of faeces into a sterile plastic container.

One of the most straightforward reasons for testing the faeces is the suspected presence of parasites or worms in the intestines. In such a case, the eggs, body parts or entire creatures can often be seen quite easily in the faeces.

The colour of the faeces can indicate something abnormal. For example, black or red faeces may indicate bleeding in the stomach or intestines, while tan or white faeces may be a sign of liver or gall bladder problems.

Even if nothing untoward can be seen in the faeces, chemical tests may show, for example, that blood is in fact present. An analysis of the fat and salt content of the faeces provides a means of assessing if food is being properly digested and absorbed, or if there is some digestive disorder present. A culture test performed on the faeces may be carried out to determine a possible infectious cause of diarrhoea.
See also BILIRUBIN; CONSTIPATION; DIARRHOEA

FAILURE TO THRIVE

Failure to thrive is a term use to describe babies and young children under two years of age who are lighter than 97% of children their age, and who do not put on weight or develop at the expected rate.

The most common cause is neglect and starvation, and sometimes this can be difficult for doctors to detect, and it is only when the child is hospitalised, or information is given by friends or relatives, that this problem becomes apparent.

Persistent infection, particularly of the urine, is another common cause. Infections may be low grade and not apparent, and urine infections may have no symptoms in young children, and collection of urine samples is difficult, making them hard to detect.

Infestations of the gut with various worms and parasites must be excluded by examination of a sample of faeces in a laboratory.

Genetic factors must also be considered. If

both parents are very small, then the child may be also be small, but completely healthy.

A wide range of uncommon diseases can cause failure to thrive. If one of the common causes above cannot be found, it may be necessary to undertake extensive investigations to find a long term disease that is affecting the child's growth. Examples include diabetes (rare under two years), pyloric stenosis (narrowing of the outlet of the stomach), Down syndrome (mongolism), Turner syndrome (girls born with only one X chromosome instead of two), Fanconi syndrome (failure of the kidneys), major heart valve and artery abnormalities (eg. Fallot's tetralogy, patent ductus arteriosus), cystic fibrosis (failure of the glands throughout the body), coeliac disease (intolerance to gluten in flour), failure of any of the body's major hormone producing glands (eg. thyroid gland, pituitary gland, adrenal glands and parathyroid glands) and a diet deficient in iron or other essential nutrients.

Numerous other rare congenital and acquired conditions may also cause failure to thrive.
See also BABIES; CHILDHOOD; FLOPPY BABY; GROWTH REDUCED; WEIGHT LOSS and separate entries for diseases mentioned above.

FAINT

A faint (syncope) is a sudden, unexpected loss of consciousness, that may be preceded for a few seconds by a feeling of light headedness. If a person has fainted, they should be made to lie flat with their legs raised to increase the flow of blood to the brain. Tilt the head backwards and make sure the airways are clear. Loosen any tight clothing. The person should regain consciousness within a few minutes. If the victim does not recover spontaneously within a short period, turn them on their side in the coma position and get medical help. Recovery usually occurs within a minute or two, and it is not associated with any convulsion or passing of urine or faeces.

Low blood pressure (hypotension) and poor blood supply to the brain are the absolute causes of a faint, and these in turn may be due to a number of conditions including stress, anxiety, fright, over exertion, lack of sleep, lack of food, heat, dehydration, lack of ventilation, prolonged standing and hormonal fluctuations.

A significant infection of any sort, such as a bad dose of influenza, pneumonia or gastroenteritis, may lead to a faint, particularly if the patient is trying to push on and not rest.

Stokes-Adams attacks are caused by a sudden change in the heart rate, with the heart slowing down markedly for a few seconds or minutes, and then recovering. It is due to a problem with the conduction of electrical impulses through the heart muscle.

Other causes of a faint include the vasovagal syndrome (response to stress), a heart attack (myocardial infarct), a pulmonary thrombosis (blood clot in the lung), a stroke (cerebrovascular accident), sudden changes in emotional state, transient ischaemic attacks (temporary blocking of a small artery in the brain by a blood clot), low blood sugar (hypoglycaemia from starvation, or overuse of insulin or sugar lowering tablets in a diabetic), micturition syncope (faint that occurs when urine passed), pregnancy, hardening of the arteries (arteriosclerosis), severe anaemia, dehydration, alcohol intoxication, and the effects of many drugs (eg. those that lower blood pressure, narcotics, sleeping tablets, anxiety relieving medications).

There are many less common causes of fainting including narrowing (stenosis) of the main artery from the heart to the body (the aorta), sudden episodes of irregular heart beat, high blood pressure (may sometimes cause a faint as the increased pressure on the brain prevents it from working properly), migraines, epilepsy (may be mistaken for a faint), a severe allergy reaction (anaphylaxis), the Shy-Drager syndrome and the Wolff-Parkinson-White syndrome (peculiar abnormality of the electrical conduction system in the heart).

Some psychiatric patients may fake a faint as an attention seeking device.

No investigations are usually necessary, but if repeat attacks occur, the more serious diseases above that may cause this condition (eg. low blood sugar, low blood pressure, irregular heart beat, infections, anaemia) must be excluded by blood tests and electrocardiographs.

The patient usually recovers quickly once lying down, but should only rise slowly and when completely well.
See also COMA; LIGHTHEADED; POSTURAL HYPOTENSION;

UNCONSCIOUS and separate entries for diseases mentioned above.

FALLOPIAN TUBE

The two Fallopian tubes that make up part of a woman's reproductive system are named after Gabriello Fallopio, a 16th century Italian doctor and anatomist who lectured at the University of Padua.

One Fallopian tube leads from each ovary to the uterus. They are about 10-12.5cm long and the end near the ovaries is rather like a bent hand with its extended fingers encircling the ovary, although not actually touching it. At the other end the tube blends with the upper corner of the uterus.

Once a month, about halfway between menstrual periods, one ovary releases an egg (ova). The egg is swept into the Fallopian tube by the waving fingers and transported down to the uterus. If, on its passage through the tube, the egg is fertilised by a male sperm introduced during sexual intercourse, pregnancy will result when the fertilised egg implants in the wall of the uterus.

Occasionally, the fertilised egg becomes implanted in the wall of the Fallopian tube, a situation called an ectopic pregnancy. This is a dangerous and usually very painful occurrence, as the fertilised egg rapidly becomes too large for the tube and can cause it to rupture. If an ectopic pregnancy occurs, the tube will usually have to be removed by surgery, but the woman can still become pregnant via the other tube.

If the egg passes down the tube without being fertilised, it will simply pass out of the body when the woman has her period.

A woman who is certain she does not want any more children may elect to have her Fallopian tubes tied (tubal ligation). This involves an operation to close the Fallopian tubes so that the egg and the sperm cannot meet.
See also CONCEPTION; ECTOPIC PREGNANCY; OVARY; SALPINGITIS; TUBAL LIGATION; UTERUS

FALLOT'S TETRALOGY

Fallot's tetralogy is a developmental abnormality of the heart of no known cause that is present at birth and results in four defects: –
• a hole between the lower chambers (ventricles) of the heart
• narrowing of the artery leading to the lungs (pulmonary artery)
• the opening of the heart into the aorta is shifted from the left side of the heart to the right
• enlargement of the right side of the heart

If the aorta abnormality is missing, it is known as Fallot's trilogy.

The baby is blue, very short of breath, very weak, and fails to thrive. The diagnosis is confirmed by special x-rays of the heart and chest, echocardiograms (ultrasound pictures of heart function), electrocardiograms (ECG), measurement of oxygen concentration in blood, and catheters inserted into heart through veins. Open heart surgery, often on several occasions, is necessary, but most patients respond well to the surgery and can lead a normal life.
See also AORTA; DUCTUS ARTERIOSUS;

FALLOT'S TETRALOGY

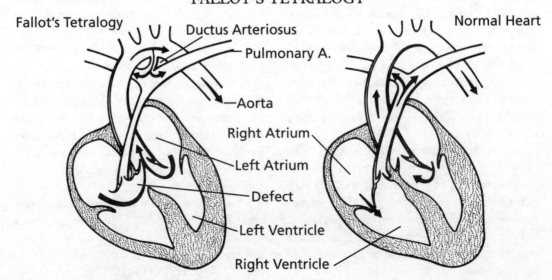

Fallot's Tetralogy — Ductus Arteriosus — Pulmonary A. — Aorta — Right Atrium — Left Atrium — Defect — Left Ventricle — Right Ventricle — Normal Heart

ECHOCARDIOGRAM; HEART; PATENT
DUCTUS ARTERIOSUS;
VENTRICULAR SEPTAL DEFECT

FALL, UNEXPECTED

Sudden falls, particularly in the elderly, may
be due to a multiplicity of conditions, often a
combination of different medical and environmental factors.

Poor vision and balance are common in
older people, and may combine to cause falls,
particularly when in unfamiliar surroundings.

Anaemia, and narrowing and hardening of
the arteries (arteriosclerosis from cholesterol
deposits in arteries) may cause dizziness and
instability.

A transient ischaemic attack is a temporary
blocking of a small artery in the brain by a
blood clot, piece of plaque from a cholesterol
deposit in an artery, or spasm of an artery,
which results in that part of the brain failing
to function for a short time.

Parkinson's disease causes poor muscle
coordination and tremor. The limbs may not
do what they are told to do as quickly as the
person may wish, leading to an abnormal and
unsteady style of walking.

Dementia caused by brain degeneration
(eg. Alzheimer disease) may lead to inappropriate expectations of the individual, and
trying to do too much too quickly.

Arthritis may affect major joints in the
limbs and back, and sudden stabs of pain or
poor function may result in a fall.

Muscle weakness from general deterioration
with age obviously makes it more difficult to
remain upright. Various diseases (eg. multiple
sclerosis) may cause muscle weakness in far
younger people.

Poor nutrition may lead to inadequate
energy to walk and move properly, and thus
predisposes to falls.

Medications can have increased side effects
in the elderly, and may lead to confusion,
weakness and falling. Sedatives, blood pressure lowering medications and drugs to treat
anxiety and depression are particularly likely
to cause these problems.

Excess alcohol intake can cause anyone of
any age to fall unexpectedly.
See also DIZZINESS; FAINT; KNEE
UNSTABLE; MUSCLE WEAKNESS and
separate entries for diseases mentioned above.

FAMCICLOVIR
See ANTIVIRALS

FAMILIAL

A familial condition is an inherited one that
tends to run in a family from one generation to
the next, but may skip a generation or become
apparent in cousins or other relatives.
See also CHROMOSOME;
CONGENITAL; GENETIC

FAMILIAL MEDITERRANEAN
FEVER

Familial Mediterranean fever is an inherited
condition that occurs only in people from the
Middle East and eastern Mediterranean area.
The cause is unknown, but it is slightly more
common in males than females.

Starting in the teens or twenties, the patient
develops recurrent, severe attacks of a high
fever, arthritis, belly pains and pleurisy (inflammation of the membrane over the lungs). Skin
rashes sometimes occur. All symptoms settle
after twenty-four to forty-eight hours, but will
recur after a period that can vary from days
to months or even years. Amyloidosis may
develop as an uncommon complication. There
is no specific blood or other test that can
diagnose the condition, and so many patients
are not diagnosed until they have had several
attacks.

Medication is given to relieve the pain and
inflammation during attacks, and the prognosis is good unless amyloidosis develops.
See also AMYLOIDOSIS

FAMILIAL POLYPOSIS
See POLYPOSIS COLI

FAMILIAL TREMOR
See ESSENTIAL TREMOR

FAMILIARITY, ABNORMAL
See DEJA VU

FAMILY PHYSICIAN
See GENERAL PRACTITIONER

FAMOTIDINE
See H2 RECEPTOR ANTAGONISTS

FANCONI SYNDROME

The Fanconi syndrome (de Toni-Fanconi-
Debré syndrome) is a rare defect of kidney

function that may be congenital (present from birth) or follow diseases such as cystinosis, glycogen storage diseases, Wilson disease and others. The kidney fails to adequately deal with numerous chemicals and elements, resulting in abnormalities in the blood levels of calcium, phosphate, potassium and sugar. The bone disease osteomalacia and kidney failure may develop, while eye and brain abnormalities may accompany the congenital form.

It is diagnosed by specific blood and urine tests, then supplements of missing calcium and potassium are given, and the patient must increase water intake and observe specific dietary restrictions. The prognosis is good if carefully managed.
See also GLYCOGEN STORAGE DISEASES; OSTEOMALACIA; WILSON DISEASE

FART
See FLATULENCE

FASCIA
See FOOT

FASCIITIS
See PLANTAR FASCIITIS

FAT
The main function of fats is to provide energy, although minute amounts are used in growth and repair. Fats enable energy to be stored and play a role in insulation. Most fats come from animal products, although some are found in plant foods such as olives, peanuts and avocados. Excess fat is laid down in the body as fatty tissue and is the main cause of obesity.

Depending on chemical composition, fats in food are either saturated or unsaturated. Saturated fats are more likely to increase the amount of cholesterol in the body and therefore increase the risk of heart disease. Broadly speaking, animal fats, especially those in milk, butter, cheese and meat are highly saturated, whereas the fat in fish, chicken, turkey and vegetable products is unsaturated. Most of the fat in chicken and turkey is in the skin, which can be removed.

Cholesterol and triglycerides are types of fat that are found only in animal products such as meat, eggs and dairy products. These fats can also be manufactured by the body from other types of fat, and they are essential in the body for the formation of many chemicals including sex hormones. The rate at which cholesterol and triglyceride are manufactured by the body is determined to a considerable extent by inheritance. Excess levels of these fats in the blood stream can cause hardening of the arteries, heart attacks and strokes.
See also CARBOHYDRATE; CHOLESTEROL; FIBRE; LIPIDS; LIPOMA; OBESITY; PROTEIN; STEATORRHOEA; TRIGLYCERIDE

FAT CYST
See LIPOMA

FATIGUE
Fatigue is different to lethargy in that fatigue occurs with exercise, while lethargy is a tiredness that prevents any exercise in the first place. There is a great overlap in the causes of the two problems, so they will be dealt with together under this heading.

Fatigue is a very common problem, and trying to determine its cause can be extremely difficult, as often there are no other symptoms to give the examining doctor any clues.

There may be lifestyle factors causing fatigue, such as excessive working hours, shift work, stress, long term anxiety, grief, poor quality or inadequate diet, a sedentary lifestyle, obesity, and both a lack of sleep and over-sleeping. These may be overlooked by the patient as they feel their way of life is relatively normal, but when a doctor analyses these factors, the problem may become obvious.

Any internal infection – bacterial (eg. urinary infection, bronchitis, tuberculosis), viral (eg. hepatitis, glandular fever, influenza) or fungal – will cause a person to tire excessively. In fact any long term illness, persistent pain or even a recurrent allergy reaction can cause this effect.

Snoring may be a sign of sleep apnoea (stopping breathing for half a minute or so while asleep) which results in a disturbed and unrefreshing sleep.

Other causes of fatigue may include cancer anywhere in the body, anaemia (due to an excessive loss of blood, or a failure of the body to produce sufficient red blood cells), heart diseases of any sort (eg. heart failure, angina, heart attack, damage to valves in the heart, myocarditis, endocarditis, subacute endocarditis), lung diseases (eg. asthma, pneumonia, emphysema, pulmonary thrombosis), poorly controlled diabetes, imbalances in any of the substances in the blood (eg. sodium, potassium, calcium, magnesium, sugar and iron), failure or overactivity of the endocrine glands (eg. thyroid, pituitary, adrenal), and depression (causes mood disorders, difficulty in sleeping, a loss of interest in life, early morning waking and both lethargy and fatigue).

The chronic fatigue syndrome is a controversial diagnosis but may explain a persistent tiredness with numerous other symptoms that can vary from depression and irritability, to arthritis and fevers.

Less common causes of fatigue may include a stroke (cerebrovascular accident), autoimmune diseases (eg. rheumatoid arthritis, systemic lupus erythematosus, scleroderma, multiple sclerosis), leukaemia, agranulocytosis (a lack of white cells that leads to recurrent infections), thalassaemia (an inherited lack of vital blood ingredients), polycythaemia vera (an excessive number of red blood cells), kidney and liver disease, and AIDS.

Many medications can cause fatigue, and all medications being taken must be considered a potential cause of fatigue until specifically excluded. Antihistamines, sedatives, pain relievers, narcotics, beta-blockers (for heart disease, high blood pressure and migraines), and drugs used to control epilepsy and psychiatric conditions are particular suspects.

Recreational drugs (eg. marijuana, ecstasy, heroin, cocaine, LSD) may initially cause a high, but this is often followed by a low and persistent fatigue, that is only relieved by another dose of the drug, rapidly leading to a vicious cycle of addiction.

There are many other rare causes of fatigue.
See also SLEEP EXCESS and separate entries for diseases mentioned above.

FATIGUE FRACTURE
See STRESS FRACTURE

FAVUS
Favus (witkop in southern Africa) is an infection of the scalp by the fungus *Trichophyton schoenleinii*, which causes redness of the scalp followed by matting of the hair and gradual formation of a thick off-white crust on the skin. Permanent skin damage and hair loss

occurs with severe infections. Examination of the skin under a microscope shows characteristic changes. Griseofulvin or other antifungal tablets are taken for several weeks to cure the infection.
See also FUNGI

FBC
See FULL BLOOD COUNT

Fe
See IRON

FEAR
See PHOBIA

FEBRILE CONVULSION
Small children under the age of about four sometimes have convulsions because of a rapid rise in temperature. The actual temperature is not as important as the rate at which the temperature rises. These febrile convulsions generally consist of body rigidity, twitching, arched head and back, rolling eyes, a congested face and neck, and bluish face and lips. This can be extremely alarming for parents, but generally the seizure will end quite quickly.

The carer should: –
• ensure the airway is clear, turning the child onto the side if necessary
• remove the child's clothing
• bathe or sponge the child with lukewarm water
• when the convulsion has eased, cover them lightly and obtain medical attention.

Prevention involves keeping the child cool with cool sponging and regular paracetamol.
See also CONVULSION

FEET
See FOOT

FELODIPINE
See CALCIUM CHANNEL BLOCKERS

FELTY SYNDROME
Felty syndrome results in the premature destruction of red and white blood cells by the spleen and is often associated with advanced rheumatoid arthritis. Patients have a very large spleen and a low level of both red and white blood cells in the bloodstream.

Significant discomfort is felt in the abdomen because of the enlarged spleen, which may put pressure on veins that pass through it. This pressure can cause dilation of the veins that surround the upper part of the stomach, and these dilated veins may ulcerate and bleed especially if attacked by the acid in the stomach, put under stress by vomiting or damaged by food entering the stomach. Other symptoms include a fever, leg ulcers, darkly pigmented skin patches, and tiny blood blisters under the skin. Patients may become quite ill, very anaemic and vomit blood, and if the bleeding continues, patients may die from loss of blood into the stomach.

The diagnosis is confirmed by blood tests that estimate the type and age of cells in the blood stream. Surgical removal of the spleen is the only treatment. After removal of the spleen patients react more slowly to infections and must ensure they are treated early in the course of any bacterial or viral infection. Regular influenza and pneumococcal vaccinations are recommended.
See also RHEUMATOID ARTHRITIS; SPLEEN

FEMALE CONDOM
A female condom is now available. This is rather like a small sausage shaped plastic bag with a firm broad rim at its opening. The rim is placed against the vulva, and the woman or her partner pushes the bag up into the vagina where it feels to be too large, but this allows for movement of the penis and enlargement of the vagina during sex. They are easy to use, comfortable and, provided they do not break, give good protection against both pregnancy and venereal disease.
See also CONDOM

FEMORAL HERNIA
A femoral hernia is a hernia due to a small piece of intestine being forced through a point of weakness in the groin, just underneath the skin, where the femoral artery passes through a small hole as it leaves the abdomen and travels to the front of the thigh. They are much more common in women than men and are caused by pressure in the abdomen from heavy work, lifting or childbirth.

A small lump is felt under the skin of the groin, and may be intermittently painful. It is common for the trapped intestine to become pinched, twisted, and gangrenous. The diagnosis is made by examination, and no tests are normally required, but an ultrasound scan may be necessary in fat patients.

Routine surgical repair of the hernia is necessary, but if constant pain occurs in the hernia, surgery is urgent. The recurrence rate after surgery is about 5%.
See also HERNIA

FEMUR
The femur (thigh bone) runs from the pelvis to the knee. It is the largest bone in the body at forty-four to fifty cm. in length. Most of a person's height is determined by the length of the femur.

The top end is modified into a large ball which sits on a neck of bone which is at an angle to the main body of the bone. The ball fits into a socket in the pelvis to form the hip joint. The angle of the neck of the femur enables humans to walk erect with parallel legs. The neck of the femur is the part of the bone most commonly broken, particularly in the elderly.

At the lower end the bone has two drumlike protuberances which rest on the top of the tibia to form the knee joint.
See also BONE; HIP FRACTURE; KNEE; PATELLA; PELVIS; TIBIA

FESTINATION
See WALK ABNORMAL

FETUS
See FOETUS

FEVER
The normal active human has a temperature of about 37°C. The word 'about' is used advisedly, because the temperature is not an absolute value. A woman's temperature rises by up to half a degree after she ovulates in the middle of her cycle. Many people have temperatures a degree below the average with no adverse effects. The body temperature will also vary slightly depending on the time of day, food intake and the climate. All these factors must be taken into account when the notion of a normal temperature is considered.

A fever (pyrexia) is a sign that the body is fighting an infection, inflammation, or invasion by cancer or foreign tissue. A fever may be beneficial to the patient, because many germs (viruses particularly) are temperature sensitive, and are destroyed by the fever. However, a fever over 40°C should be reduced by using paracetamol or aspirin and cool baths.

An infection by a bacteria (eg. pneumonia, tuberculosis, tonsillitis, ear infection, urinary infection), virus (eg. common cold, influenza, hepatitis, chickenpox, AIDS) or fungus (eg. serious fungal infections of lungs) is by far the most common cause of a fever. A viral infection usually causes a fever that comes and goes during the day, often with a sudden onset in the morning and evening, followed by a slow decline to normal over the next couple of hours. Bacterial infections tend to cause a constant fever, usually over 38.5°C. This is because bacteria reproduce like all animals, at random times, while viruses tend to reproduce all at once, so the body is subjected to a sudden doubling of the number of viruses, which stimulates the brain to increase the body temperature.

Infections can occur in any tissue or organ of the body, and other symptoms will depend upon where the infection is sited. An untreated bacterial infection will result in pus formation, and an abscess full of pus may form at any site of infection (eg. under the skin, in the lung, at the root of a tooth, in the bowel) and continue to cause a fever.

Other causes of a fever include appendicitis, malaria (caused by a mosquito borne parasite), many different cancers (usually when well advanced), leukaemia, inflammation of tissue, a severe allergy reaction, rejection of a transplanted organ, autoimmune diseases (eg. rheumatoid arthritis, scleroderma, systemic lupus erythematosus), rheumatic fever, haemolytic anaemia (the body destroys its own blood cells), a blood clot in the lung (pulmonary embolus) and liver failure from cirrhosis (hardening of the liver).

Medications can sometimes cause a fever as a side effect (eg. methyldopa used for blood pressure).

Illegal drugs such as amphetamines, cocaine and LSD are well known to cause a fever as well as tremors and sometimes convulsions.

Rare causes of a fever include agranulocytosis, sarcoidosis, toxic shock syndrome, brain tumour, stroke, head injury, Felty syndrome, Stevens-Johnson syndrome, very high blood pressure, neuroleptic malignant syndrome and the Riley-Day syndrome.
See also TEMPERATURE;

TEMPERATURE MEASUREMENT and separate entries for most diseases mentioned above.

FEXOFENADINE
See ANTIHISTAMINES

FIBRE
Thread-like strands of cellulose or cell products that are not normally digested by humans. Fibre is that part of vegetables, cereal or fruits which is left over in the intestine, cannot be digested, and is passed out in the faeces.

Fibre in food does not cause indigestion because it cannot be digested, and does not always look stringy. For example, peas and beans are high in fibre, cucumber is very low, and celery is in between. The average person should eat forty grams of fibre a day.

A high-fibre diet is one way of overcoming obesity, since it makes the stomach feel full and so makes one feel less hungry, but there are fewer kilojoules to be absorbed from the food into the body. Furthermore, the fibre residue in the bowel increases the size and wetness of the stools, and so eases defecation and prevents constipation. The down side may be an increase in flatulence (wind).

Diseases that benefit from a high-fibre diet include diverticulitis (small outpocketings of the large bowel), diabetes, gallstones, arteriosclerosis (hardening of the arteries), cancer of the bowel, varicose veins, piles and hernias. The incidence of these diseases is significantly less in populations who eat high-fibre diets. Moderation, however, is important. A diet made up entirely of fibre-based foods would lack essential nutrients, fats, carbohydrates and vitamins.
See also CARBOHYDRATE; FAT; FOOD; PROTEIN

FIBRILLATION
Fibrillation is the very rapid, uncoordinated, spontaneous contraction of a muscle, including the heart muscle.
See also ATRIAL FIBRILLATION; VENTRICULAR FIBRILLATION

FIBROADENOMA OF THE BREAST
A fibroadenoma of the breast is a common benign growth of the breast, often affecting young women. The cause is usually unknown, but it may be the result of an injury to the

breast. The lump in the breast feels round and firm (but not hard) and is hard to catch hold of, tending to slide out from between the fingers when squeezed (thus sometimes known as a breast mouse), because it is not attached to surrounding tissue. It is not usually tender or painful.

Mammography (breast x-ray) and ultrasound may be used initially, but in most cases a needle biopsy is necessary to confirm the diagnosis. If it is confirmed to be a benign fibroadenoma, it may be left untreated, but if in any doubt, it should be surgically removed. Fibroadenomas persist long term if not removed.
See also BIOPSY; BREAST CANCER; BREAST LUMP; MAMMARY DYSPLASIA

FIBROCYSTIC DISEASE
See CYSTIC FIBROSIS

FIBROCYSTIC DISEASE OF THE BREAST
See MAMMARY DYSPLASIA

FIBROIDS OF THE UTERUS
The uterus (womb) is made up of muscular, fibrous and glandular tissue. After childbirth, the uterus shrinks back to its usual size, but the stress on the uterus during pregnancy may result in some minor injury to the fibrous tissue in its wall, and after the uterus shrinks, it may repair itself in an abnormal way by the formation of one or more hard fibrous balls in the wall of the uterus, which are called fibroids.

When the uterus contracts to force out the blood and wastes during a period, the fibroids distort the uterus causing painful cramps and sometimes heavy menstrual bleeding. Fibroids can usually be detected on pelvic examination, but the diagnosis may be confirmed by an ultrasound scan of the abdomen, laparoscopy or special x-rays of the uterus.

The treatments available include a hysterectomy to completely remove the uterus, or if the woman wishes to have more children, the individual fibroids can be removed from the uterus.
See also UTERUS

FIBROMYALGIA SYNDROME
See FIBROSITIS

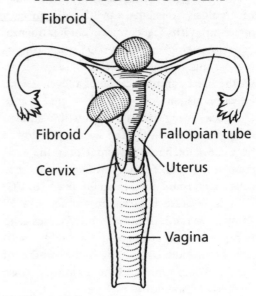

FIBROIDS DISTORTING THE FEMALE REPRODUCTIVE SYSTEM

Fibroid
Fibroid
Cervix
Fallopian tube
Uterus
Vagina

FIBROMYOSITIS
See FIBROSITIS

FIBROSARCOMA
See BONE CANCER

FIBROSITIS
Fibrositis (fibromyalgia syndrome or fibromyositis) is the replacement of some muscle fibres with scar tissue after injury to the muscle from over use or repetitive use, resulting in widespread inflammation of muscles that is more common in women, particularly in middle age. The syndrome may be temporary, recur regularly, or in rare cases last for years.

The main symptoms are aching, tender and stiff muscles in varying parts of the body that may be aggravated by poor sleep. Other symptoms include tiredness, insomnia, bladder irritability and passing urine frequently. Touching certain areas of muscle may cause sudden, severe pain, while nearby areas are quite unaffected. The discomfort is eased by heat and worsened by cold.

Heat, massage, exercise, anti-inflammatory drugs, and medication to relax the patient and assist in sleeping are the main treatments. Some patients are helped by physiotherapy. The syndrome persists intermittently for some months then usually subsides, regardless of what treatment is given. The treatments usually give relief while disease process continues its course.
See also MUSCLE PAIN

FIBULA

The fibula is the smaller of the two bones in the lower leg (the tibia is the other one). It does not form part of the knee joint, because its upper end attaches to the tibia, but at its lower end it forms part of the ankle joint. The lump of bone on the outside of the ankle is the lower end of the fibula. It acts as a strut in the leg, but carries virtually no weight, and if badly broken the top half may be removed rather than repaired.

See also JOINT; TIBIA

LOWER LEG

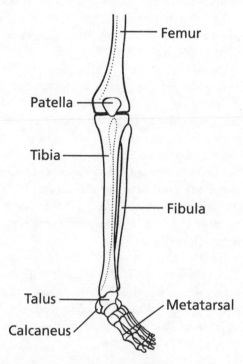

FIEVRE BOUTONNEUSE
See TYPHUS

FIFTH DISEASE

Fifth disease (erythema infectiosum) is a common childhood viral disease caused by the *Parvovirus* that last from two to five days, but occasionally may persist for weeks. It occurs in epidemics every few years and virtually every child will eventually develop the infection before their teenage years.

The infection is characterised by red flushed cheeks (slapped cheeks appearance), paleness around the mouth and a red patchy rash on the arms and legs. Many children will have very mild symptoms that may be overlooked, or confused with German measles. Rarely, joints may become sore and inflamed.

Complete recovery is normal and no treatment is necessary.

See also GERMAN MEASLES; VIRUS

FILARIASIS

Filariasis (elephantiasis) is a disease of the lymphatic system (waste drainage ducts) that occurs in tropical Asia, Africa and America, caused by a microscopic worm (filarial nematode) that is transmitted from one person or animal to another by mosquito bites.

Inflammation of the lymph nodes occurs and a fever develops. After repeated attacks, the lymph channels of the lymphatic system that carry waste products become blocked by the worm. Wastes cannot escape from the legs, arms and scrotum, which slowly enlarge to a huge size to give the characteristic appearance of elephantiasis.

It is diagnosed by seeing the infecting worm in a drop of blood under a microscope.

Treatment involves elevation of the affected limb, medication to kill the worm, and surgery to remove the swollen tissue. Amputation of a limb is sometimes necessary. Filariasis is difficult to treat, the effective use of damaged limbs may never return, and long term medication may be necessary. Residents of affected areas should avoid mosquito bites and take medication constantly to prevent the disease.

See also LYMPHATIC SYSTEM

FINGER

See FINGER TIPS SWOLLEN; HAND; HAND PAIN; NAIL; NAIL PAIN; TRIGGER FINGER

FINGER NAIL

See NAIL; NAIL ABNORMAL; NAIL PAIN

FINGER TIPS SWOLLEN

Clubbing of the fingers is a term used in medicine to describe swelling of the tissue immediately behind the finger nails so that the groove between the nail and flesh disappears, and becomes raised and rounded. The nail is also markedly rounded and raised. It is a phenomenon that is often looked for by doctors as a sign of serious disease, but rarely noted by patients.

Clubbing is caused by overgrowth of the soft tissue and underlying bone at the tip of the fingers due to a lack of oxygen in the blood, while the actual amount of blood reaching the area is increased.

Long standing diseases of the lungs, heart, or less commonly the bowel, are the cause of clubbing. It is not specific as to the type of disease in these organs, but common examples include emphysema (usually caused by smoking), tuberculosis, bronchiectasis (damage to the tubes in the lung leading to repeated infection), asbestosis and cancer in the lungs, abnormal heart valves, holes in the heart and abnormal blood vessels in the heart, regional enteritis (inflammation of part of the intestine) and Crohn's disease (thickening and ulceration of part of the wall of the small and/or large intestine).

Less common causes include cystic fibrosis (which causes thick secretions in the lungs and bowel) and sarcoidosis (infiltration of abnormal tissue into the lungs and other organs).

Some people are born with clubbing of the fingers, and in others it is a family trait, passing from one generation to the next. In both these situations, it is not significant medically.

See also NAIL and separate entries for diseases mentioned above.

FIRST AID

First aid is the initial care of someone who has been injured or become unexpectedly ill. Some injuries and illnesses are minor and require no more than first aid. Other emergencies are life-threatening, and prompt and appropriate first aid can mean the difference between life and death, or at the very least permanent disablement.

Everyone should undertake a basic first aid course taking only four hours to complete, or a full course of only fifteen hours of study over three or four days or nights. It is difficult to learn many of the necessary skills by reading about them, and nothing substitutes for hands-on experience.

First aid is proven to work and is based on sound modern principles. Some people killed in road accidents would have survived if adequate first aid had been available. Similarly, with near-drowning it has been estimated 60% of children resuscitated by a person trained in first aid survive, compared with only 30% if the rescuer is untrained.

The goals of first aid are to sustain life, to prevent the illness or injury from becoming worse, and to promote recovery. It is important to recognise that reassurance and making the person as comfortable as possible is an important part of administering first aid.

At the scene of an emergency, keep calm and allocate priorities. Speed may be crucial, but panic and confusion will not help and may deny the injured person the attention they need.

The main task in any emergency is to keep the victim alive. Whatever the injury, the victim will die or suffer irreparable damage to vital organs, in particular the brain, within three or four minutes unless oxygenated blood is kept circulating throughout the body.

The first step is to carry out the DRABC (danger, response, airway, breathing, circulation) of first aid: –

DANGER
You are of no use to the victim if you suffer the same fate. Look around the scene before you do anything. If the emergency is a road traffic accident, turn off the damaged car engine and position your own car prominently, with hazard lights flashing, ensuring oncoming traffic can see the danger. If electrocution is involved, turn off the power if possible (DO NOT enter the area if electric wires are live).

RESPONSE
Talk to the victim. If s/he doesn't respond to your voice, pinch the skin or squeeze a finger hard. Within fifteen seconds you should be able to determine whether the victim is conscious or unconscious.

AIRWAY
Make sure the airway is not being blocked by any foreign matter (eg. false teeth, particles of food or vomit, seaweed, etc.). Provided the neck has not been injured, turn the victim's head to one side and sweep the index finger around the inside of the mouth and under the tongue to remove anything there. Loosen any clothing around the neck, such as a tie or scarf. Make sure the tongue is not blocking the airway. To do this, tilt the head back by placing one hand on the forehead and the other hand under the angle of the lower jaw. Gently tilt the head back at the same time lifting the jaw upward and forward. It can be quite difficult to keep a child's airway clear. Generally the head of a small child should be kept horizontal without tilting the head. Support the lower jaw but be careful not to press on the tissues of the

neck. If it is safe to do so, place the victim on their side in the coma or lateral position (see Unconscious entry). This stops the tongue from falling backwards into the throat and ensures that any vomit or saliva cannot flow into the lungs. The coma position should not be used if the victim might have a fractured neck or spine, unless their breathing becomes noisy, laboured or irregular.

BREATHING

Make sure the victim is breathing – watch or feel the chest for movement. If none can be detected, place an ear close to the nose and mouth to hear whether there is any air passing in or out. If there is no sign of breathing start resuscitation (see separate entry).

CIRCULATION

If the heart stops beating, the blood will stop circulating. The external indication of a beating heart is the pulse. The two most easily accessible pulses are in the wrist and the neck. The neck (carotid) pulse is usually the most appropriate, because if the person is seriously ill or shocked, the wrist pulse may be too weak to feel even though it is present. One can find the neck pulse by locating the thick cord of muscle running along the side of the neck; then find the larynx, which has the Adam's apple in front; place the first and second fingers lightly on the front of the muscle at the level of the Adam's apple. If there is no sign of a pulse, start cardiopulmonary resuscitation (see Resuscitation entry).

The next step is to control serious bleeding and take measures against shock. If the victim is unconscious, put them in the recovery position. Do not give anything to eat or drink (it may be vomited and cause the victim to choke if they lapse into unconsciousness or if they later have to be given an anaesthetic). Keep the victim warm and as comfortable as possible.
See also ANAPHYLAXIS; ANIMAL BITE; ARTERIAL PRESSURE POINTS; BEE STING; BLEEDING; BOX JELLYFISH; BURN; CHOKING; CONVULSION; CUT; DISLOCATION; ELECTROCUTION; EYE FOREIGN BODY; EYE INJURY; FAINT; FEBRILE CONVULSION; FRACTURE; INSECTICIDE POISONING; JELLYFISH STING; NOSEBLEED; OVERDOSE; POISONING; RESUSCITATION; PULSE; SCORPION STING; SHOCK; SLING; SNAKE BITE; SPLINTER; SPRAIN; STONEFISH; STRAPPING; SUFFOCATION; UNCONSCIOUS

FISTULA

A fistula is an abnormal opening or the formation of a false passage (connection) between two hollow organs, or the inside and outside of the body. Most commonly, fistulae may form between an artery and a vein (arteriovenous fistula), the bowel and bladder (rectovesical fistula), bowel and vagina (rectovaginal fistula), bowel and skin (anal fistula) or gall bladder and bowel (choledocoduodenal fistula). The contents of one organ (eg. intestine) can leak into the other (eg. bladder), and may cause serious damage or infection to one or both of the organs involved. The symptoms will vary depending on the organs.

Fistulae may be caused by an injury, abscess, infection, stone, inflammation or cancer. The tissue between the two organs is damaged, allowing a fistula to form between them. Sometimes fistulas are surgically produced to drain an otherwise blocked organ (eg. gall bladder to bowel).

During an investigation of a fistula a special dye may be injected into the fistula and then x-rayed to see where it runs.

Quite difficult surgery is often necessary to close a fistula, but most patients recover completely.
See also ANAL FISTULA; ARTERIOVENOUS FISTULA

FISTULA IN ANO
See ANAL FISTULA

FIT
See CONVULSION; EPILEPSY

5HT RECEPTOR AGONISTS

Acute migraine attacks can be treated by the use of painkillers and sedatives, or the use of specific drugs that deal with the over-dilated arteries that cause migraine. The 5-hydroxy tryptamine receptor agonists are a class of drugs introduced in the early 1990s that acts to rapidly treat migraines and cluster headaches by acting on specific receptors in brain arteries, causing the arteries to constrict. Overdilation of arteries in the brain is the cause of migraine pain and other symptoms. They are available as tablets, injections and nose sprays.

Examples of medications in this class

include naratriptan (Naramig), sumatriptan (Imigran) and zolmitriptan (Zomig).

Side effects may include chest pain, tingling, flushing, dizziness, weakness and fatigue. They should be used with caution in pregnancy, and avoided in heart disease or after a stroke.
See also ERGOTAMINES; MIGRAINE; MIGRAINE PREVENTERS

FIVE-HYDROXYTRYPTAMINE RECEPTOR AGONISTS
See 5HT RECEPTOR AGONISTS

FIXED DRUG ERUPTION
A fixed drug eruption is a persistent skin rash caused by a reaction to a drug (eg. blood pressure medications, antibiotic, arthritis drugs, oral contraceptives, thiazide diuretics (fluid tablets), food colouring), that may have been taken for years without previous reaction.

Patients develop a widespread, itchy, red, patchy, raised rash, and a biopsy is sometimes necessary to confirm the diagnosis. It is necessary to stop taking the suspected drug, then use steroid creams and antihistamine tablets. In severe cases steroid tablets may be necessary. The rash may persist for months or years after causative drug ceased, but most eventually subside.
See also SKIN ITCH

FLANK PAIN
See LOIN PAIN

FLASH BURN TO EYE
A flash burn is a superficial burn to the surface of the eye (cornea) caused by looking at a welding arc or ultraviolet light for a prolonged time. The eye is very painful, red and sometimes swollen, but the pain may not develop until six to twelve hours after exposure. Severe or recurrent eye burns can cause scarring and blindness that can only be corrected by a corneal transplant.

Patients are prescribed eye drops and painkilling tablets, and it is necessary to cover the eye until it has recovered. Most settle completely within twenty-four hours. The only effective first-aid measure is a cold, wet compress.
See also EYE PAIN; KERATITIS

FLASHES IN VISION
See VISUAL FLASHES

FLAT FEET
A flat foot (pes planus) occurs when the arch on the inside of the foot is in continuous contact with the ground when the person is standing barefoot on a smooth hard surface, and the foot may also be slightly twisted outwards. All infants are flat-footed, as the arch only develops after the age of two years. In children a flat foot is an inherited or congenital disorder, while in adults the causes include obesity (because the foot must carry excess weight), severe foot arthritis and occupations requiring prolonged standing.

Most patients have no symptoms or discomfort, but some have an awkward gait, knock-knees and distorted shoes. No treatment other than well fitting shoes is normally required, but wedging of the shoes to tilt the foot outwards, weight reduction, arch supports, foot exercises and physiotherapy are occasionally used. In later life, patients are more likely to develop arthritis in the foot and strain their feet more easily.
See also FOOT; PES CAVUS

FLATULENCE
Gas can get into the bowel by being swallowed (when eating too quickly, or by nervous swallowing when anxious), drinking fizzy fluids (eg. beer, champagne, lemonade), fermentation of food in the gut, and by the process of diffusion. The last of these occurs when oxygen dissolved in the blood passes (diffuses) across the bowel wall into the gut. Once in the gut, gas must escape through either the mouth (burping) or anus (flatulence or fart).

Diet affects the fermentation of food. Fibre containing foods such as beans, peas, dried fruit, corn and bran are well known to be responsible.

Almost any bacterial infection of the gut will cause flatulence due to excessive fermentation. Other conditions that may cause this include Crohn's disease (a thickening and ulceration of part of the gut) and diverticulitis (outpocketings of the last part of the large intestine which harbour fermenting bacteria). If the gas is smelly, it is more likely to be due to fermentation, and the problem may be settled by using antibiotics to reduce the number of fermenting bacteria in the gut.

Diffusion of gas into the gut varies from person to person, and some people naturally produce more gas this way than others.

Charcoal tablets may absorb excess gas in the gut, and reduce both flatulence and burping.
See also BURPING and separate entries for diseases mentioned above.

FLAT WARTS
See PLANE WARTS

FLECAINIDE
See ANTIARRHYTHMICS

FLEMING, ALEXANDER
Alexander Fleming was a Scottish scientist who discovered penicillin in 1929 and, with the assistance of Howard Florey, manufactured the first effective broad-spectrum antibiotic in 1941.
See also ANTIBIOTICS; FLOREY, HOWARD

FLESH EATING DISEASE
See NECROTISING FASCIITIS

FLINDERS ISLAND SPOTTED FEVER
See TYPHUS

FLOATER IN EYE
A floater is a collection of cells or protein in the thick fluid that fills the eyeball, which casts a shadow on the light-sensitive retina at the back of the eye. The floater forms because of bleeding into the eye, a detached retina or infection, or no cause may be found. Diabetes, leukaemia, high blood pressure and rarer conditions may cause bleeding into the eye.

Patients notice a spot in the field of vision that may continue to move across the visual field after the moving eye comes to rest – thus the name floater. Because a serious condition may be responsible, all patients with floaters must be investigated to exclude any disease. A detached retina can be repaired by a laser in the early stages, but if left, may cause permanent blindness.

They are only treated if causing significant trouble, but if necessary, a laser can destroy the floater while a doctor uses a microscope to look into the eye. Most floaters dissipate with time.
See also EYE; VISUAL BLACK SPOTS

FLOPPY BABY
See BABY FLOPPY

FLOREY, HOWARD
Howard Florey was an Australian who discovered the use of penicillin and won the Nobel Prize in collaboration with Alexander Fleming and Ernst Chain in 1941.
See also ANTIBIOTICS; FLEMING, ALEXANDER

FLU
See INFLUENZA

FLUCLOXACILLIN
See PENICILLINS

FLUCONAZOLE
See ANTIFUNGALS

FLUID EXCESS IN TISSUES
See OEDEMA

FLUID IN ABDOMEN
See ASCITES

FLUID LACK
See DEHYDRATION

FLUID TABLETS
See DIURETICS

FLUNITRAZEPAM
See SEDATIVES

FLUORIDATION
Fluoridation of public water supplies is the adjustment of the natural fluoride level of the water upwards or downwards to the optimum level needed to minimise tooth decay in a population and maximise bone strength.

In the early part of the 20th century, it was discovered in the USA that minute traces of the element fluorine (in the form of the fluoride ion) drastically reduced dental decay in a population. This turned out to be probably one of the most significant discoveries in the field of public preventive medicine ever made. Until that time, dental decay was all but universal in its incidence, and devastating in its destruction of an important part of the body. When a simple adjustment of the fluoride level matched the level in naturally occurring waters which produced decay-resistant teeth, it brought under control one of the most widespread of the incurable diseases.

In Australia, the first community to apply the new-found method was Beaconsfield in

Tasmania, which fluoridated its water supply in 1953. From that time, most of the nation (except Queensland) has followed suit. All capital cities (except Brisbane) have fluoridated water supplies, as have most provincial centres. The consequent reduction in tooth decay has been dramatic. It has not been eliminated, but so reduced that control of the disease appears possible.

In latter years, further assistance has been available by the almost universal incorporation of fluoride into toothpaste, conferring further benefit. Further supplementation by the ingestion of fluoride tablets or drops in non-fluoridated areas is beneficial, and should be undertaken under professional guidance.
See also DENTISTRY; TEETH

FLUORIDE
See FLUORIDATION; MINERALS

FLUOXETINE
See ANTIDEPRESSANTS

FLUOXYMESTRONE
See SEX HORMONES

FLUPHENAZINE
See ANTIPSYCHOTICS

FLUSH, ABNORMAL
Many people have a facial flush (redness and hot feeling) when they are embarrassed, and this is a completely normal characteristic, particularly in women with fine skin. Abnormal flushes may occur occasionally, or may be almost constant.

The menopause is a very common cause of sudden, unexpected flushing when sex hormone levels surge instead of being released in a very slowly varying pattern. The woman usually feels the flush far more than others can see it, as the skin in women of this age has usually thickened somewhat over the years, particularly if they live in a sunny climate.

Sex hormone treatment can also cause abnormal flushing, particularly if the dosage is incorrect.

Excessive indulgence in alcohol can cause obvious flushing that may persist for several hours after over imbibing. Repeated excessive use of alcohol can result in liver and blood vessel damage that causes a persistent red face, although technically, this is not flushing.

A fever of almost any cause can cause flushing that lasts for hours or days.

Other causes of flushing may include an overactive thyroid gland (hyperthyroidism), a severe allergy reaction (anaphylaxis), Cushing syndrome (caused by over production in the body, or over use, of cortisone), phaeochromocytoma (tumour of the adrenal glands that causes very high blood pressure), diseases of the hormone-controlling pituitary gland in the centre of the brain, impaired drainage of blood from the head caused by narrowing of the major veins in the neck or upper chest, and the carcinoid syndrome (characterised by diarrhoea, palpitations and wheezing).
See also FACE RED; FEVER; SKIN RED and separate entries for diseases mentioned above.

FLUTICASONE
See ASTHMA PREVENTION MEDICATION; STEROIDS

FLUVASTATIN
See HYPOLIPIDAEMICS

FOETAL ALCOHOL SYNDROME
Excessive alcohol consumption by the mother for a prolonged period during pregnancy causes damage to the foetus before birth and numerous deformities collectively known as the foetal alcohol syndrome. The baby is small at delivery, and has excessive body hair, small finger nails, underdevelopment of the central part of the face and mild mental retardation. Less common symptoms include a small head and small jaw, poor coordination, poor concentration and reduced muscle tone.

It is a clinical diagnosis made on a history from the mother, and observation. No treatment is available for the baby, and if recovery to normal developmental levels does not occur by one year of age, further improvement is unlikely.

Mothers should be advised as strongly as possible not to drink alcohol to excess during pregnancy.
See also ALCOHOLISM

FOETUS
A baby in a mother's womb is called a foetus after three months of age, and appears like a perfectly formed but tiny baby. Before this it is referred to as an embryo.

The foetus floats in a fluid filled sack, like a balloon full of water. The foetus drinks the fluid, and also excretes into it through its kidneys and bowels.

One side of the balloon is a special outgrowth of the baby which forms the placenta, while the rest is a fine, but tough, transparent membrane. The baby is connected to the placenta by the umbilical cord, which at birth is between fifteen and 120 cm long, and runs from the navel to the centre of the placenta. The arteries and veins in the placenta fan out and penetrate into the wall of the uterus to interact with the mother's circulatory system. This enables the baby to draw oxygen and food from the mother's system, and send waste products to the mother for removal.

At sixteen weeks, the foetus is twelve cm. long and its sex can be determined. The skin is bright red because it is transparent, and the blood can be seen through it. The kidneys are functioning and producing urine, which is passed into the amniotic fluid.

The 'quickening' is the time when the mother becomes aware of the baby's movements. It occurs between sixteen and eighteen weeks (the latter in first pregnancies). The mother usually becomes quite elated at this time, as she realises that there really is a baby inside her. The movements become gradually stronger throughout pregnancy, until it is possible to trace the movement of a limb across the belly. Babies vary dramatically in how much they move – some are very active indeed, while others are relatively quiet. During the last couple of weeks of pregnancy the baby does not move as much, as the amount of space available becomes more restricted.

By twenty-four weeks, the skin is the normal colour. This is the earliest that a baby has a reasonable chance of surviving outside the mother, although infants are still at high risk if born before thirty-two weeks. By that stage, development is complete, and the last eight weeks are merely a growth stage.

By thirty-eight weeks, the baby has settled upside down in the uterus. During this period, the head sinks down into the mother's pelvis and is said to 'engage' ready for birth.

The miracle is completed when labour starts. The trigger for this is not accurately known, but a series of nervous and hormonal stimuli dilates the cervix that guards the opening into the womb, and starts the rhythmic contractions of the womb which will bring another human being out into the world.

See also EMBRYO; LABOUR; PLACENTA; PREGNANCY

FOLEY CATHETER

A Foley catheter is a long, thin rubber or synthetic tube that has a double lumen (tube opening), and a smooth rounded tip. It is used to drain urine from the bladder. There is an opening at the side of the tip to collect urine.

The larger diameter tube carries the urine from the bladder to the outside, while the smaller diameter tube (which is inside the larger one) is used to blow up a balloon at the tip of the catheter once it has been inserted into the bladder, to prevent it from slipping out again.

At the outside end of the catheter, the two tubes separate, with the larger one leading to a urine collection bag, while the smaller one leads to a one-way valve which prevents the escape of the water inserted to blow up the balloon.

The catheter must be inserted under strictly aseptic conditions to prevent infection from entering the bladder.

Sometimes the acronym IDC (in dwelling catheter) is used to indicate the presence of a Foley catheter in a patient.

FOLEY CATHETER

In an emergency, a Foley catheter can be inserted into the nose and then inflated to stop an intractable nose bleed.
See also BLADDER; INCONTINENCE OF URINE

FOLIC ACID
Folic acid is sometimes classed as vitamin M. It is essential for the basic functioning of cells, and extra amounts may be needed during pregnancy, breast feeding, and in the treatment of anaemia and alcoholism. It assists in the uptake and utilisation of iron. During pregnancy, supplements may prevent spinal cord defects in the baby.
See also VITAMINS

FOLLICLE STIMULATING HORMONE
See PITUITARY GLAND

FOLLICULAR CYST
See OVARIAN CYST

FOLLICULITIS
Folliculitis is a bacterial (most common) or fungal (yeast) infection of hair follicles which occurs mainly on the neck, armpits, upper lip and groins, and is more common in men than women. Numerous different bacteria and fungi may be responsible. *Staphylococcus aureus* is the most common bacteria, while *Pityrosporum* is the most common fungus. Infection is more likely in diabetics, the obese, those with poor hygiene or with oily skin, and at times of stress.

A sore, tender, and sometimes itchy pus-filled blister appears on the skin surrounded by red skin. A boil or abscess may form, and the latter will need to be cut open and drained.

Antibiotic or antifungal ointments are applied to the sores, and in severe cases antibiotic tablets are taken. A swab may be taken from a blister in resistant cases to identify the bacteria or fungus responsible for the infection and thus the correct antibiotic or antifungal to treat it. Personal hygiene must be scrupulous, and the long-term use of antibiotics and antiseptic soaps may be required. The infection is often difficult to cure, and attacks may recur for several months or years, and any underlying cause (eg. diabetes) must be cured or controlled.
See also ABSCESS; BOIL; HAIR; SKIN LUMPS; *STAPHYLOCOCCUS AUREUS*

FONG SYNDROME
The Fong, or nail-patella, syndrome is a congenital abnormality of finger and toe nails, and the knee cap. These children have gross nail defects, small or absent knee caps, bony outgrowths of the pelvic bone, elbow joint abnormalities and sometimes kidney failure. Excess protein is found in the urine, and x-rays show bony abnormalities. Plastic and orthopaedic surgery is performed, but patients have persistent knee problems and premature arthritis.
See also NAIL UNDERDEVELOPED

FOOD
All animals require food appropriate to their needs. The food requirements of humans can best be demonstrated by the food pyramid, which shows which foods are required and in what proportions.

A healthy diet contains adequate quantities of six groups of substances – proteins, carbohydrates, fats, fibre, vitamins, and minerals. The first three contain kilojoules (ie. produce energy) and the second three do not. It is also essential to have a supply of safe drinking water, as a person can live for weeks without food, but only a few days without water.

A good, well balanced diet should include: –
• protein from foods such as fish or other seafood, poultry, very lean meat, or eggs, dried peas, beans or lentils
• some salad and three or four vegetables, including at least one serve of a green leafy variety and one yellow/orange variety such as carrots
• two or three pieces of fruit
• cereal or grains, such as rice
• bread (some dieticians recommend that this should be wholemeal or wholegrain but others are content with white bread)
• some dairy products, preferably low-fat for most adults (women in particular should ensure that they get an adequate supply of milk, yogurt or cheese to prevent the loss of calcium in their bones after menopause which causes osteoporosis).
See also CAFFEINE; CARBOHYDRATE; DIETICIANS; FAT; FIBRE; KILOJOULES AND CALORIES; OBESITY; PROTEIN; VEGETARIAN DIET; VITAMINS; WEIGHT LOSS DIET

HEALTHY FOOD PYRAMID

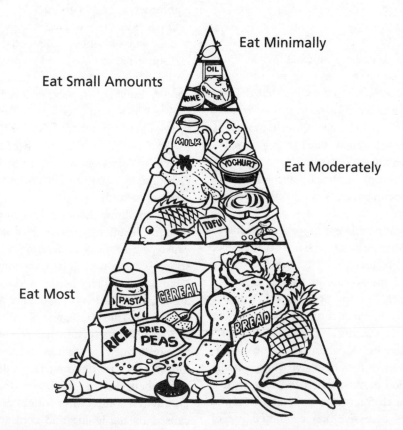

FOOD ABSORPTION POOR
See MALABSORPTION

FOOD POISONING

Food poisoning is an illness involving the intestine caused by eating food contaminated by bacteria, or a toxin produced by bacteria. Many different types of bacteria may be responsible. Foods that are particularly likely to be responsible are dairy products, fish, chicken or other meat that has been inadequately refrigerated, fried foods, meat dishes that have been reheated, and stale bread.

Patients develop nausea, vomiting, diarrhoea, a fever and stomach cramps, and small amounts of blood may be vomited or passed in the motions. Most attacks develop suddenly, within one to eight hours of eating the contaminated food, but may take up to twenty-four hours.

No specific investigation can diagnose the cause in an individual, but a suspect food can be tested to see if it is contaminated. Food poisoning is strongly suspected when a number of people are affected simultaneously, but it may be confused with gastroenteritis.

Usually no treatment is necessary other than a clear fluid diet. In the very young and elderly, dehydration may be a problem, and intravenous drips in hospital may be required. Antibiotics are rarely necessary, and most attacks settle within six to twelve hours.
See also BOTULISM; CIGUATERA POISONING; DIARRHOEA; GASTROENTERITIS; NAUSEA AND VOMITING; TYPHOID

FOOT

The foot contains twenty-one bones, often extra sesamoid bones, and a large number of small muscles, long tendons and tough ligaments that hold bones together. The arch of the foot acts as a spring and shock absorber when walking and running. The sole of the foot has a strong sheet of fibrous tissue, the plantar fascia, underneath it, to keep the sole smooth and tough and maintain the curvature of the arch. Many of the muscles that move the foot are actually in the calf, and connected to the bones of the foot by tendons.
See also ANKLE; CALCANEUS; CLUB FOOT; FLAT FEET; FOOT PAIN; PES CAVUS; PLANTAR FASCIITIS; PODIATRY; SESAMOID BONE

FOOTBALLER'S ANKLE
See ANTERIOR IMPINGEMENT SYNDROME

FOOT PAIN

The feet are constantly exposed to shock and injury with every step, and when jumping or running are added, it is amazing that the feet do not suffer more injuries, as it is often only a small area on the ball of the foot that is taking the entire weight. The foot is a complex structure with twenty-one bones, nearly thirty joints, and dozens of muscles and tendons in a small structure that is remarkably flexible and strong.

Overweight people are more susceptible to foot injury because the pressure on their feet is so much greater.

A strain from overuse or sudden injury to the ligaments, tendons, bones or other tissues in the foot is the most common cause of pain in the foot. Ligaments and tendons may tear, or bones may break, when the tissue is suddenly stressed, or they may give way gradually over a period of time when the foot is over used. A march fracture is an example of the latter, when excessive unaccustomed use of the feet on a long march may cause some small bones in the forefoot to crack.

Osteoarthritis is not, strictly speaking, a wear and tear injury to a joint, but can be considered as such without going into detailed physiology. The lining of a joint, often in the ball of the foot degenerates with time, and becomes inflamed, resulting in pain with any movement or pressure on the joint.

Gout is a classic cause of foot pain. It is caused by a buildup of uric acid, a protein waste product, in the blood and in the lubricating synovial fluid inside joints. Joints put under greater pressure will usually affected by gout when the excess uric acid forms microscopic double pointed needle shaped crystals in the synovial fluid. These crystals cause agonisingly sharp pain in the affected joint.

The arch of the foot is maintained by a strong band of fibrous tissue that runs from the heel to the base of the toes along the outside edge of the foot under the sole. This is known as the plantar fascia, and it can be stretched or torn by injury, resulting in the disabling foot pain of plantar fasciitis, which is difficult to treat.

There are many other obvious causes of foot pain such as ingrown toe nails, fungal or bacterial infections of nails, corns, bunions, plantar warts and bruising.

Other causes of foot pain include an infection of the tissue or bones in the foot, developmental abnormalities (eg. pes cavus), synovitis (inflammation of the synovial membrane lining a joint), bursitis (excessive synovial fluid accumulated in a joint), tendinitis (from over use or stretching of a tendon), a poor blood supply to the foot (eg. in diabetes, hardening of the arteries), ulceration of the skin and Raynaud's phenomenon (spasm of arteries when tissue is exposed to cold).

Any condition that can affect muscles, bone, tendons, ligaments, skin or even fat tissue can cause pain in the foot. Examples include heel spurs, bone cancer (often accompanied by a painful lump), erythema nodosum (generalised inflammation of tissues accompanied by a rash), vasculitis (inflamed blood vessels), pernicious anaemia (insufficient red blood cells to supply oxygen to tissues distant from the lungs), Morton's neuroma (a swollen damaged nerve between the bones in the forefoot), Dupuytren contractures (ridges under the sole caused by hardening and contracture of the tissues around tendons), Marfan syndrome (very tall people with heart abnormalities), blood clots in veins, and impingement syndromes (where ligaments, tendons and bones pinch each other).

See also FOOT; GOUT and separate entries for most diseases mentioned above.

FOREIGN BODY IN EYE
See EYE FOREIGN BODY

FORMICATION
See CRAWLING SENSATION ON SKIN

FORCEPS DELIVERY

Babies are sometimes reluctant to enter into the world and must be assisted out by a doctor. Forceps have been used for 150 years to help the baby's head through the pelvis. They can be used not just to help pull out the child, but to turn the head into a more appropriate position if the head is coming out at the wrong angle. In a breech birth (bottom first), the forceps actually protect the head as it follows, and they prevent the cervix from clamping around the neck.

Forceps consist of two spoon-shaped

stainless steel blades. They slide around the side of the baby's head and fit snugly between the wall of the vagina and the head. Once placed carefully in position, the doctor, in time with the contractions, will apply traction (and sometimes rotation) to deliver the head. The baby may be born with some red marks on its face and head from the forceps, but they disappear after a few weeks.

Another method of assisted delivery is vacuum extraction, in which a suction cap (ventouse) is attached to the baby's head, and traction is applied to the cap to help pull out the baby.
See also LABOUR

FOREARM
See RADIUS; ULNAR; WRIST

FOREARM FRACTURE
See COLLES' FRACTURE

FORESKIN
See CIRCUMCISION; PENIS

FORESTIER DISEASE
See DIFFUSE IDIOPATHIC SPINAL HYPEROSTOSIS

FOSFESTROL
See CYTOTOXICS AND ANTINEOPLASTICS

FOSINOPRIL
See ACE INHIBITORS

FOXGLOVE
See DIGOXIN

FRACGP
'FRACGP' is the abbreviation for a Fellow of the Royal Australian College of General Practitioners – a postgraduate qualification by training and examination indicating that a doctor is a skilled and qualified general practitioner.
See also GENERAL PRACTITIONER; MEDICAL TRAINING

FRACOG
'FRACOG' is the abbreviation for a Fellow of the Royal Australian College of Obstetricians and Gynaecologists – a postgraduate qualification by training and examination indicating

that a doctor is a skilled and qualified specialist in childbirth and women's diseases.
See also MEDICAL TRAINING

FRACP
'FRACP' is the abbreviation for a Fellow of the Royal Australian College of Physicians – a postgraduate qualification by training and examination indicating that a doctor is a skilled and qualified specialist physician.
See also MEDICAL TRAINING

FRACR
'FRACR' is the abbreviation for a Fellow of the Royal Australian College of Radiologists – a postgraduate qualification by training and examination indicating that a doctor is a skilled and qualified specialist in x-rays, CT scans, ultrasound etc.
See also MEDICAL TRAINING

FRACS
'FRACS' is the abbreviation for a Fellow of the Royal Australian College of Surgeons – a postgraduate qualification by training and examination indicating that a doctor is a skilled and qualified specialist surgeon.
See also MEDICAL TRAINING

FRACTURE
A broken bone, or fracture (break and a fracture mean the same thing), is usually caused by abnormal violence, pressure, force or twisting being applied to a bone.

There are several different types of fracture: –
• Hair line fracture – tiny crack part way through a bone.
• Greenstick fracture – abnormal flexion in a child's soft bone, wrinkling one surface only.
• Simple fracture – a single break across the whole width of a bone.
• Avulsion fracture – a small fragment of bone is pulled off at the point where a muscle, tendon or ligament attaches.
• Impacted fracture – the forcible shortening of a bone as one fragment of bone is pushed into another.
• Comminuted fracture – two, three or more breaks in the one bone.
• Depressed fracture – a piece of bone (often in the skull) is pushed in below the level of the surrounding bone.
• Compound fracture – the skin over the fracture is broken by a bone end.

TYPES OF BONE FRACTURE

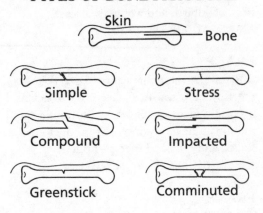

• Pathological fracture – a break in a bone weakened by osteoporosis, cancer or other disease.

Fractures cause pain that worsens with use of the bone, swelling and tenderness at the site of the fracture, bruising over or below the fracture, and a loss of function of the limb or area. Pathological fractures may be relatively pain free in some cases.

To apply first aid for a fracture: –
• keep the victim as warm and comfortable as possible
• gently remove clothing from any open wound and cover it with a clean (preferably sterile) dressing
• do not try to manipulate the bone or joint, as further (potentially very serious) damage may be caused
• move the affected area as little as possible and immobilise the fracture
• if the injury is in the arm, use a sling, or strap the arm to the body. If the leg is injured, strap the injured leg to the uninjured leg. Alternatively, make a splint from a broom handle, branch or a rolled-up newspaper (remembering to protect any open wound).
• do not give the victim anything to eat or drink, as the setting of the fracture may require an anaesthetic

For healing, the bone fragments must be aligned as perfectly as possible after manipulation (under an anaesthetic if necessary), and fixed in position with plaster, pins, plates, or screws. It is normally necessary to prevent movement in the joints at either end of the broken bone. The exact treatment will vary considerably from one bone to another, with some fractures requiring minimal fixation (eg. fracture of humerus – upper arm bone), while others require major surgery (eg. fracture of hip). Movement at the fracture site may cause failure to heal, and chronic pain may occur. Fractures requiring surgery and compound fractures are susceptible to infection. Death of bone tissue can occur if small fragments of bone are present.

The majority of fractures can be successfully treated with an eventual return to full function of the bone.
See also BONE; COLLES' FRACTURE; MARCH FRACTURE; OSTEOGENESIS IMPERFECTA; OSTEOPOROSIS; PATHOLOGICAL FRACTURE; PLASTER; POTT'S FRACTURE; SCAPHOID FRACTURE; SLING; SMITH'S FRACTURE; STRESS FRACTURE

FRACTURE, ABNORMAL
See PATHOLOGICAL FRACTURE

FRAGILE X SYNDROME
The fragile X syndrome is an inherited cause of mental retardation in males caused by an abnormal gene carried on the X chromosome. Men have only one X sex chromosome matched to a small Y sex chromosome, while women have two X sex chromosomes and thus the faulty gene's activity can be replaced by the one on the good X chromosome. Women carry the abnormal gene from one generation to the next.

Fragile X symptoms may include mental retardation, excess activity, epilepsy and autism. They are often large babies, with large ears, forehead and jaw. Short sightedness, enlarged testes, cleft palate and slack joints are other possible complications.

It is diagnosed by examination of the genes in a cell sample taken from the blood after birth, or by a sample from the placenta taken before birth.

There is no cure for this life-long disability, and treatment involves the use of appropriate support services and medication to reduce the excitement and excess activity, while genetic counselling of families is essential.
See also AUTISM; EPILEPSY; MENTAL RETARDATION

FRAMYCETIN
See AMINOGLYCOSIDES

FRANCE'S TRIAD

France's triad is the simultaneous occurrence of asthma, aspirin sensitivity and allergic rhinitis (hay fever) in a patient for no known reason. These diseases must be treated individually.
See also ALLERGY; ASTHMA; HAY FEVER

FRANZCP

'FRANZCP' is the abbreviation for a Fellow of the Royal Australian and New Zealand College of Psychiatrists – a postgraduate qualification by training and examination indicating that a doctor is a skilled and qualified specialist psychiatrist.
See also MEDICAL TRAINING

FRCGP

'FRCGP' is the abbreviation for a Fellow of the Royal College of General Practitioner – an English postgraduate qualification by training and examination indicating that a doctor is a skilled and qualified general practitioner.
See also MEDICAL TRAINING

FRCP

'FRCP' is the abbreviation for a Fellow of the Royal College of Physicians – an English postgraduate qualification by training and examination indicating that a doctor is a skilled and qualified specialist physician.
See also MEDICAL TRAINING

FRCS

'FRCS' is the abbreviation for a Fellow of the Royal College of Surgeons – an English postgraduate qualification by training and examination indicating that a doctor is a skilled and qualified specialist surgeon.
See also MEDICAL TRAINING

FRECKLES

See SKIN PIGMENTED

FREEZING

See CRYOTHERAPY

'FRENCH LETTER'

See CONDOM

FREQUENT URINATION

See URINATION FREQUENT

FREY SYNDROME

The Frey, or auriculotemporal, syndrome is the abnormal functioning of a nerve on the side of the head after injury, infection or surgery. Flushing and sweating of the ear and temple on one side of the head occurs with eating. Some success can be obtained from surgery to the nerve, but the problem may persist long term.
See also SWEATING EXCESS

FRIEDREICH'S ATAXIA

Friedreich's ataxia (spinocerebellar degeneration) is an inherited condition causing degeneration of nerves in the cerebellum (lower back part of the brain) and spinal cord which usually starts in childhood or early adult life. Patients develop an abnormal way of walking, incoordination, clumsiness, weakness and have abnormal sensations. Heart inflammation and degeneration is a complication. Nerve conduction studies, CT and MRI scans are used to confirm the diagnosis. No treatment is available and death in early adult life is normal.
See also CEREBELLUM; COORDINATION POOR; SPINAL CORD

FRIGIDITY

Frigid is a term, now outdated, usually intended to describe a woman who is unable to experience any pleasure or arousal from sexual stimulation. Anorgasmia is a term used to indicate an inability to have an orgasm. Frigidity is usually a psychological problem and not a physical one, and may be the result of a woman's strict upbringing, a loathing for sex that has been conditioned by an oppressive mother or violent father, an unfortunate early sexual experience, an unwanted pregnancy, a rape or other assault. Other causes include pain with intercourse, postnatal depression after birth, life stress (eg. moving house or changing jobs), and the hormone drop associated with menopause. Certain prescribed drugs and hormones may also be responsible.

With sexual stimulation there is no lubrication of the vagina, enlargement of the nipples or clitoral tenseness. In extreme cases it may be responsible for infertility.

Treatment requires a very understanding partner and a very slow teaching process, usually with the help of a psychiatrist or psychologist. Stimulation of non-erotic parts of the body to relax the woman over a period

of weeks, followed by stimulation of more erotically sensitive areas, slowly breaks down the barriers. Most women respond to appropriate treatment after many sessions over several months.
See also LIBIDO LACKING, ORGASM, LACK OF

FRÖHLICH SYNDROME

Fröhlich syndrome (dystrophia adiposgenitalis) is a rare condition that has its onset after puberty when there is a loss of sexual function and libido due to a lack of sex hormones, which in turn may be due to a tumour of the pituitary gland in the centre of the brain.

The symptoms are a lack of sexual development and activity, the skin becomes thin and wrinkles prematurely, body hair is scanty, scalp hair becomes very fine, and fat may deposit around the buttocks and genitals. All hormones must be checked by blood tests, and a CT or MRI scan of the pituitary gland is performed. There is no cure, but long term control possible by sex hormone supplements and surgery to remove any pituitary tumour.
See also LIBIDO LACKING; PITUITARY GLAND

FRONTAL BONE

The bones forming the forehead at the front of the skull. The two frontal bones fuse together at about six years of age.
See also SKULL

FROSTBITE

Frostbite is the freezing of living tissue due to exposure of flesh to very cold conditions that occurs most commonly in the toes, but also in the fingers, ears and nose. The severity of the frostbite depends on the depth to which the freezing has penetrated. Early symptoms are numbness, itching and a pricking sensation. As the freezing penetrates deeper, stiffness and shooting pains will occur, the skin becomes white or yellow, and the toe or finger becomes immobile. Freezing of the skin itself is not particularly serious, but if the freezing penetrates to the bone, the tissue will die, and the finger or toe requires amputation. Late stages of frostbite are characterised by blistering, swelling, black colouration and gangrene.

Treatment involves slow and gradual thawing of frozen tissue in warm water. Rapid rewarming or overheating further damages the tissue. Never warm an area affected by frostbite by rubbing or massage. If two people are present, thawing each other's toes by placing them in the other person's armpit is an ideal method. After thawing, the tissue should be kept protected and warm. No dressings should be applied, but the affected areas should be left exposed in a warm room. Antiseptics may be applied to blisters and antibiotics given for infection. Only after several days or weeks is amputation of affected fingers or toes considered, as recovery may occur from an apparently hopeless situation. Moist gangrene is an indication for immediate amputation. Any area that has been frostbitten will be more susceptible to frostbite in future.
See also CHILBLAINS; HYPOTHERMIA

FROZEN SHOULDER

A frozen shoulder (adhesive capsulitis) is a shoulder that becomes stiff and limited in its range of movement for no apparent reason, although overuse of the joint may be an aggravating factor. The joint stiffness usually starts slowly and worsens gradually over a period of days or weeks, and there may also be a constant ache in the joint. X-rays are taken to exclude other causes, but in a frozen shoulder the X-rays are normal.

Treatment involves constant gentle movement with more structured exercises under the supervision of a physiotherapist. Anti-inflammatory drugs and mild to moderate strength painkillers are prescribed, and in severe cases, steroid tablets are taken or injections given into the joint. If recovery is delayed, the shoulder may be moved around while the patient is anaesthetised to break down any adhesions that have formed. Most cases last six to twelve months, then slowly recover regardless of any treatment.
See also SHOULDER

FRUSEMIDE
See DIURETICS

FULL BLOOD COUNT

A full blood count (FBC) is the most frequently performed of all blood tests. It gives an enormous amount of information about the blood and the state of overall health. A drop of blood is smeared across a glass slide and examined under a microscope, and the number of different types of cells present is counted. Computers now automatically do these counts very rapidly.

Blood cells consist of three different types – red cells (erythrocytes), white cells (leucocytes) and platelets (thrombocytes). Red cells carry the red pigment haemoglobin, which is used to transport oxygen. There are several different types of white cells that fight infection, and platelets are one of the main factors that enable blood to clot.

A blood count determines the number of all these cells, their size, and the proportions in which they exist, as well as the amount of haemoglobin present. Diseases as diverse as anaemia, infection and some types of cancer may be diagnosed by this test.

If you are anaemic, you will have insufficient haemoglobin or too few red blood cells. If you have a bacterial infection it is likely that your white blood cells will increase in number (leucocytosis) to fight it, while a viral infection often decreases white blood cell levels (leucopenia) as the virus destroys them. A lack of platelets (thrombocytopenia) will cause excessive bruising and bleeding as the blood is unable to clot normally.
See also BLOOD TESTS;
HAEMOGLOBIN; LEUCOCYTOSIS;
LEUCOPENIA; PLATELETS; RED
BLOOD CELLS; WHITE BLOOD CELLS

FULMINANT MENINGOCOCCAEMIA
See WATERHOUSE-FRIDERICHSEN SYNDROME

FUNCTIONAL INDIGESTION
See IRRITABLE BOWEL SYNDROME

FUNGI
Mushrooms, the green slime that forms on stagnant pools, and tinea are all related. They are fungi. Fungi are members of the plant kingdom, and are one of the types of microscopic life that can infect human beings in many diverse ways.

The most common site of infection is the skin, where they cause an infection commonly known as tinea, or ringworm. The fungus that causes tinea can be found everywhere in the environment in the form of hardy spores. These are microscopic in size and may survive for decades before being picked up and starting an infection. Between the toes the fungus causes a type of tinea commonly known as athlete's foot. This is because athletes sweat and wear close fitting shoes that lead to the ideal warm, damp environment favoured by fungi. Similar infections in the groin cause a red, itchy, rapidly spreading rash. In both situations, creams or lotions are used to kill off the fungus before it spreads too widely. The rash is often slow to clear, because the treatments destroy the fungus, and do not necessarily heal the rash. The body heals the rash itself once the infection is controlled.

Unfortunately, fungal skin infections tend to recur because the fungus in its cyst form is resistant to many types of treatment. The active forms of the fungus are killed, but the spores may remain in the skin pores to reactivate once the treatment is ceased. To prevent this condition, keep the affected areas cool by wearing the correct clothing and foot wear, and dry carefully when wet.

Fungi are also responsible for many gut infections, particularly in the mouth and around the anus. It is a rare infant that escapes without an attack of oral thrush. The white plaques that form on the tongue and insides of the cheeks are familiar to most mothers, and this is due to one of a number of fungi. Paints or gels used in the mouth usually bring it rapidly under control.

Around the anus, the fungus can cause an extremely itchy rash, but in women it may spread forward from the anus to the vagina to cause the white discharge and intense itch of vaginal thrush or candidiasis. The movement from the anus to vagina is aided by nylon underwear, tight clothing (particularly jeans), wet bathers and most importantly, sex.

Fungi live normally in the gut, and are in balance with the bacteria that are meant to be there to help with the digestion of our food. Antibiotics may kill off the good bacteria, allowing the fungal numbers to increase dramatically, or they may migrate to unwanted areas. In these circumstances, they can cause trouble.

The most serious diseases develop when fungal infections occur deep inside the body in organs such as the lungs, brain and sinuses. These diseases are very difficult to treat and it may take many months with potent antifungal drugs to bring them under control. Fortunately, this type of condition is relatively rare.

The most obvious form of fungal infection is ringworm. This is not really a worm, but a fungal infection growing outward from a central spore, in exactly the same way that mushroom rings form in the garden in damp weather.

Every species of fungus (and bacteria, but not viruses) has two names – a family name (eg. Candida) which uses a capital initial letter and comes first, and a specific species name (eg: albicans) which uses a lower case initial letter and comes second. The fungus which causes thrush is thus called 'Candida albicans' but may be abbreviated to 'C. albicans'.

Common fungi, and the diseases they cause or the tissues they attack, include: –

FUNGUS	TYPE OR PLACE OF INFECTION
Aspergillus	Lungs, brain.
Blastocystis hominis	Lungs.
Blastomycoses dermatitidis	Lungs, skin.
Candida albicans	Mouth, vagina, penis (thrush).
Coccidioides immitis	Lungs.
Histoplasma capsulatum	Lungs.
Microsporum audouinii	Scalp (cradle cap), nails.
Pityrosporum orbiculare	Skin (tinea versicolor).
Pneumocystis carinii	Lungs (usually in AIDS patients).
Trichophyton mentagrophytes	Feet (athlete's foot), nails.
Trichophyton rubrum	Skin, nails.
Trichophyton tonsurans	Scalp.

See also ANTIFUNGALS; ASPERGILLOSIS; ATHLETE'S FOOT; BLASTOMYCOSIS; CRYPTOCOCCOSIS; FAVUS; INFECTION; ONYCHOGRYPHOSIS; OTITIS EXTERNA; PITYRIASIS VERSICOLOR; THRUSH; TINEA

FUNGAL NAIL INFECTION
See ONYCHOGRYPHOSIS

FUNGAL SKIN INFECTION
See ATHLETE'S FOOT; PITYRIASIS VERSICOLOR; TINEA

FUNNEL WEB SPIDER BITE
See SPIDER BITE

FURUNCLE
See BOIL; FURUNCULOSIS, EAR

FURUNCULOSIS, EAR
Otic furunculosis is a boil that involves a hair follicle in the outer canal of the ear caused by bacteria such as *Staphylococcus aureus* (the golden staph) which invade the roots of the fine hairs in the ear canal, often after an injury to the ear canal from a cotton bud, hair pin or other foreign object.

An excruciatingly painful swelling develops that may completely close the ear canal. If the infection is deeper, there may be less swelling and only a patch of redness on one side of the ear canal. The pain is aggravated by chewing and may spread to the lymph nodes on that side of the neck, and eventually it may burst and discharge pus. Most furuncles burst spontaneously, but some deep-seated infections may form an abscess that must be lanced to drain the pus. Rarely, the infection can penetrate to bone and from there to the sinuses or brain.

A swab is taken to culture the particular bacteria that is causing the infection, and to select the correct antibiotic. Furuncles are more common in diabetics and, in cases of recurrent infection, tests should be done to exclude any other disease. X-rays are occasionally necessary to ensure that surrounding bone has not been damaged.

A wick (thin ribbon of cloth or tiny material tube) soaked in an antibiotic and soothing ointment is gently placed in the ear canal and changed every day or two, and a course of antibiotics by tablet or injection is also given. Heat can help relieve the pain, but scratching the ear canal with any object is forbidden. Most respond well to appropriate treatment.
See also ABSCESS; BOIL; EARACHE; OTITIS EXTERNA; *STAPHYLOCOCCUS AUREUS*

G

GABAPENTIN
See ANTICONVULSANTS

GAIT
Gait is a term that describes the way in which a person walks, particularly the rhythm of the walk.
See also WALK ABNORMAL

GAIT ABNORMAL
See WALK ABNORMAL

GALACTOKINASE
See GALACTOSAEMIA

GALACTORRHOEA
See NIPPLE DISCHARGE

GALACTOSAEMIA
Galactosaemia is a congenital lack of the liver enzyme galactokinase that is responsible for the metabolism (break down) of galactose, which is one of the sugars in milk. These infants vomit, fail to thrive, and develop liver disease, mental retardation, frequent infections and eye cataracts. A specific diagnostic test can be performed on red blood cells. A strict dietary avoidance of all milk products will prevent all the symptoms except mental retardation.
See also MENTAL RETARDATION

GALACTOSE
Galactose is a form of sugar that is formed by the breakdown of lactose, the main sugar in milk.
See also GALACTOSAEMIA

GALEN
Claudius Galen was born in Pergamon (in present-day Turkey) in about 130 and died about 200AD. He was a Greek physician in Rome, chief physician to the gladiators, and very well respected. He was an anatomist who dissected apes and extrapolated their anatomy to that of humans. His mistaken ideas about the circulation of blood and numerous anatomical structures (eg. he thought there was an opening between the left and right sides of the heart) persisted unchallenged until the 15th century. He was a believer in the humoral theory of disease, in that imbalances between the four humours of the body (phlegm, blood, yellow bile, black bile) were responsible for all illness.
See also HIPPOCRATES

GALL BLADDER
The liver, which sits behind the lower ribs on the right side of the body, produces bile at a more or less constant rate. This bile moves through a series of collecting ducts, which join up to form the common bile duct. This duct leads to the small intestine. There is a side duct to the common bile duct that leads to the gall bladder.

Bile is required to help in the digestion of food, but as we do not eat constantly, it is not needed in the gut all the time. There is a valve at the lower end of the common bile duct where it opens into the intestine. This valve opens when food passes to allow bile to be added to the food in the gut. When the valve is closed, the bile must be stored, and this is done in the gall bladder.

The gall bladder is a storage area for bile not immediately required, so the bile from the liver is directed into it when the valve is

THE LIVER AND GALL BLADDER

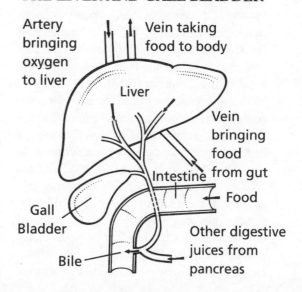

Artery bringing oxygen to liver

Vein taking food to body

Liver

Vein bringing food from gut

Intestine

Food

Gall Bladder

Bile

Other digestive juices from pancreas

closed. When extra bile is required in the gut to digest food, the gall bladder contracts to squeeze the bile out through the open valve onto the food.

If the gall bladder is removed, the bile trickles into the gut constantly and, although not an ideal situation, the bile and food will eventually mix together, and digestion will occur, with minimal consequences to you or your gut.
See also CHOLECYSTECTOMY; CHOLECYSTITIS; DUODENUM; GALLSTONES; LIVER; PANCREAS

GALL BLADDER REMOVAL
See CHOLECYSTECTOMY

GALLSTONES
The development of one or more stones in the gall bladder is called cholelithiasis.

The liver produces bile which is stored in the gall bladder. Bile is required to help in the digestion of food, and when this is required in the gut, the gall bladder contracts to squeeze out the bile. If the bile becomes too concentrated it may precipitate out as a stone. Up to 10% of men over sixty years of age, and 20% of women over sixty have some gallstones.

Larger stones may block the bile duct, and when the gall bladder contracts with eating, the movement of the stone in the duct causes severe intermittent pain (biliary colic) in the upper right side of the abdomen. The pain can also be felt in the back at the lower end of the shoulder blade. Indigestion, burping and passing wind rectally (farting), are common. If the stone becomes stuck, constant severe pain results, and an emergency operation is required to clear it. Infection of the gall bladder (cholecystitis) may occur when its drainage is blocked by a stone. The patient is feverish, nauseated and in constant pain. In extreme cases, an infected gall bladder will rupture and cause peritonitis.

The presence of gallstones may be confirmed by an ultrasound scan, or special x-rays (cholecystograms) taken after swallowing (or having injected) a dye which concentrates in the bile. In difficult cases, x-rays of the gall bladder can be performed by passing a gastroscope into the small intestine and then injecting dye through the opening into the bile duct (endoscopic retrograde cholecystopancreatography – ERCP). Blood tests to check liver function are usually normal unless a gallstone is blocking the bile duct and preventing waste products leaving the liver.

A low fat diet will reduce demands on the gall bladder for bile and reduce painful spasms. The most effective treatment is surgery to remove the gall bladder (cholecystectomy). The operation can be performed by open exposure of the gall bladder or by laparoscopic surgery. If stones are very low in the common bile duct they may be removed by an instrument that is passed through the mouth and stomach into the intestine (an endoscope). Patients who are too ill for an operation may use a drug that slowly dissolves some gallstones over many months. Lithotripsy is a treatment in which the stones are shattered by a high-frequency sound wave, but it is only suitable for a small number of cases.
See also CHOLECYSTECTOMY; CHOLECYSTITIS; ENDOSCOPE; ENDOSCOPIC RETROGRADE CHOLECYSTOPANCREATOGRAPHY; GALL BLADDER; LIVER

GAMBLING
Gambling becomes a medical problem (pathological) when the person has a preoccupation with gambling for its own sake, that becomes more intense when under stress. Pathological gambling is a psychiatric illness, a form of obsessive compulsive neurosis, which normally starts in the teenage years, but intensifies in early adult life and may be triggered by stress. The children of pathological gamblers are more likely to develop the problem.

Most victims are men who gamble alone, then try to conceal their gambling and losses, gamble more when they lose, are unable to confine losses to a budget, borrow money to gamble, and may steal money to gamble. They experience an intolerable buildup of tension when there is an opportunity to gamble, which can only be relieved by partaking in the bet. Serious family, social and financial losses may occur.

Group therapy run by psychiatrists, psychologists and groups such as Gamblers Anonymous are the most successful treatments. Only rarely are drugs prescribed to quieten a particularly manic phase. Often, not until a crisis such as bankruptcy, gaol or separation from a wife results will the sufferer seek, or be forced to undertake, any form of treatment.

See also OBSESSIVE COMPULSIVE
NEUROSIS

GAMETE
Any reproductive cell, either a sperm or an
ovum (egg), is called a gamete.
See also ARTIFICIAL CONCEPTION;
ZYGOTE

GAMETE INTRA-FALLOPIAN TRANSFER
See ARTIFICIAL CONCEPTION

GAMMAGLOBULIN
Gammaglobulin is a protein found in blood
and used by the body to fight infection as it is
the basic building block for creating antibodies. Additional gammaglobulin can be injected
to prevent or treat specific infections, particularly those caused by a virus.
See also AGAMMAGLOBULINAEMIA;
ANTIBODY; IMMUNODEFICIENCY

GAMMA-GLUTAMYL TRANSFERASE
Gamma glutamyl transferase (Gamma GT or
GGT) is an enzyme released mainly from the
liver, and in some situations from the kidneys,
when these organs are under stress or damaged. It can be measured in the blood to determine how well the liver is functioning. The
normal range is under forty-five units/litre.

Very high levels are an indication of alcoholism, liver cancer, liver abscess, or obstruction to the drainage of bile from the liver.
Levels that are only slightly raised may be
caused by recent intake of alcohol, pancreatitis, heart attack, hepatitis, fatty liver, cirrhosis,
obesity, anorexia nervosa, porphyria, some
kidney diseases, kidney cancer and medications such as tricyclic antidepressants, phenytoin, barbiturates and a paracetamol overdose.
See also LIVER FUNCTION TESTS

GAMMA-HYDROXYBUTYRATE
Gamma-hydroxybutyrate (GHB) is an illegal
drug that is used to give effects similar to those
of alcohol. As with many such substances, it
has many alternative names including GBH,
grievous bodily harm, Georgia home boy,
liquid ecstasy and goop.

It was developed in the 1960s as an anaesthetic, but abandoned because of adverse side
effects such as nausea, dizziness, vomiting, low
blood pressure, poor coordination, collapse,
disorientation, fits and loss of consciousness.
It is now illegal to manufacture, posses or sell
the substance in many countries.

It is available as a powder that is often
mixed with water, and is colourless and taste-
less. As a result it can be used to spike drinks,
and make the user comatose. It has been used
as a rape drug.

If used regularly, it will increase the desire
of the user for the effects that are considered
beneficial such as an increase in mood, relaxation, disinhibition, and enhanced perception
(particularly of music). As a result it is often
used at rave dance parties.

The drug takes effect in about twenty
minutes, and lasts one or two hours.

Overdoses may be fatal, particularly when
combined with alcohol or other illegal drugs
that affect the brain.
See also COCAINE; ECSTASY; HEROIN;
KETAMINE; LSD; MARIJUANA;
MESCALINE; STIMULANTS

GANGLION
Ganglion is a medical term indicating a nerve
junction or a bundle of nerves. Ganglia are
found throughout the body, but most importantly just outside the spinal cord where the
nerves from the spine join with those running
out to the body and limbs.

The solar plexus (stellate ganglion) is a
junction of sympathetic nerves that lies in
front of the vertebrae behind the upper part
of the abdomen.

Other important ganglia include the celiac
ganglia in the abdomen beside the aorta that
supply many of the organs in the belly, and
the geniculate ganglia that supply the facial
nerves.
See also GANGLION CYST; NERVE;
SPINAL CORD

GANGLION CYST
A ganglion of a tendon is a benign thin-walled
cyst filled with a thick, clear fluid that develops on a tendon of the wrist, hand or foot. It
has nothing to do with a nerve ganglion.

Tendons slide within fibrous sheaths which
prevent the tendon from slipping out of position around a joint. The tendon is surrounded
by a thin film of lubricating fluid within the
sheath. A tiny puncture in the sheath allows
some of the lubricating fluid around the

tendon to escape and form a disfiguring hard lump on the back of the hand, wrist or less commonly on the top of the foot. Painful bleeding may occur into the ganglion, or pressure on a nerve may cause also cause pain. Rarely the ganglion may become infected.

FORMATION OF A GANGLION CYST

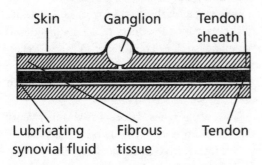

Treatments available are either a minor operation in which the ganglion is cut away from the tendon, or a needle is inserted into the ganglion to withdraw the thick fluid within, and a small amount of a steroid solution is then injected. Many settle spontaneously, but they may recur after injection, while most are permanently cured by surgery.
See also TENDON

GANGRENE, GAS
Gas gangrene (clostridial myositis) is caused by the *Clostridium welchii* bacterium, which can infect a deep wound into which air cannot penetrate, and cause death of that tissue. These anaerobic (without air) bacteria are widespread in the environment, but cannot survive if exposed to oxygen. In tissue without oxygen they produce a chemical (toxin) that destroys damaged muscle and produces a foul-smelling gas.

The wound becomes painful and swollen, and surrounding skin discolours. Pressure over the area produces a crackling sound as tiny gas bubbles in the damaged tissue burst and a smelly discharge issues from the wound. The patient becomes feverish, delirious and comatose. Destruction of red blood cells, and damage to the liver and kidney are possible complications.

A swab taken from the wound shows the bacteria under a microscope and gas bubbles in infected tissue can be seen on an x-ray.

Massive doses of penicillin and gas gangrene antitoxin are given by injection, but this is only beneficial if given very early in the infection. Surgery to cut away affected tissue is essential. High-pressure oxygen chambers that are normally used to treat divers with the bends may force oxygen into the tissues to destroy the bacteria. The prognosis depends on the site of the wound and the severity of the infection, but there is a significant death rate.
See also SUBCUTANEOUS EMPHYSEMA

GARDNER SYNDROME
Gardner syndrome is an inherited inflammatory condition of the large bowel. Patients have multiple polyps in the large bowel that may bleed and progress to bowel cancer, multiple skin cysts, bony growths on the jaw, and other tumours of soft tissue throughout the body. A colonoscopy or barium enema x-ray is used to make the diagnosis.

Regular colonoscopy is necessary to remove bleeding and cancerous growths, and it is sometimes necessary for part or all of the large gut to be removed. The prognosis is good, provided regular colonoscopies prevent cancer or detect it early.
See also COLORECTAL CANCER; POLYPOSIS COLI

GARBLED VERBIAGE
See VERBAL GARBAGE

GAS EMBOLISM
See BENDS

GAS FROM BOWEL
See BURPING; FLATULENCE

GAS GANGRENE
See GANGRENE, GAS

GAS IN URINE
See URINE GASSY

GASTR-
'Gastr-' is a prefix derived from the Greek word for stomach, and used in medicine to refer to the stomach, its diseases and procedures (eg. gastritis, gastroscopy).
See STOMACH

GASTRIC CARCINOMA
See STOMACH CANCER

GASTRIC ULCER
See PEPTIC ULCER

GASTRINOMA
See ZOLLINGER-ELLISON SYNDROME

GASTRITIS
Gastritis is an inflammation of the stomach that may be caused by many factors including stress, gut infections, drugs (particularly aspirin and anti-arthritis drugs), alcohol excess, overindulgence in food, stomach cancer and allergies.

Patients develop intermittent symptoms of nausea, vomiting, loss of appetite, a feeling of fullness, upper abdominal discomfort or pain, and possibly indigestion for a few hours or days, or constant discomfort for weeks or months. Sometimes it can progress to a peptic ulcer and rarely stomach cancer. Gastroscopy reveals an inflamed, red stomach lining.

The treatment depends upon the cause. Antacids or anti-ulcer drugs (eg. H2 receptor antagonists, proton pump inhibitors) will ease the inflammation, and anti-anxiety drugs may be used when appropriate. Drug-induced gastritis will require the removal of the drug responsible, substituting other drugs or, if the medication is essential, adding anti-ulcer or antacid medications to control the continuing symptoms.

See also ANTACID; GASTROSCOPY; H2 RECEPTOR ANTAGONISTS; PEPTIC ULCER; PROTON PUMP INHIBITORS; STOMACH

GASTROENTERITIS
Gastroenteritis is a viral infection of the gut. The Rotavirus is one of the most common viruses responsible, particularly in children, and it often appears in epidemics, usually in spring or early summer. It passes from one person to another through contamination of the hands and food.

Patients develop an uncomfortable feeling in the stomach, gurgling, cramping pains and then vomiting. A few hours later the vomiting starts to ease, and diarrhoea develops. The infection lasts from one to three days and young children may become rapidly dehydrated and require urgent hospitalisation.

Usually no investigations are necessary, but faeces tests may be performed if another cause is suspected and blood tests are sometimes necessary to assess dehydration.

The treatment involves a specific diet to replace the fluid and vital salts that are lost from the body due to vomiting and diarrhoea, and then careful reintroduction of foods. In adults, medications can be used to slow diarrhoea, and paracetamol can be used for belly pain at all ages. Some children develop an intolerance to milk sugar (lactose) after the infection, and this may prevent them from returning to a normal diet for weeks or months.

GASTROENTERITIS DIET
Take small amounts of food and fluids very frequently (every hour), rather than large amounts three times a day.

DAY 1 – CLEAR FLUIDS ONLY
• Repalyte, Hydralyte and Gastrolyte (available from chemists and taste better if cold) are best. In milder cases for a short time you may use white grape juice, clear soups, Bonox, very dilute flat lemonade, very dilute cordial and frozen cordial. Average 50 mLs. an hour for a child, 100 mLs. an hour for an adult.
• Do not drink plain water.
• Isomil, Prosobee, Infasoy etc. can be used as a milk substitute in infants.
• Lactose free milk ('Lactaid') may be used.
• Breast milk is perfect for infants even with gastroenteritis.

DAY 2 – LIGHT DIET
• Continue clear fluids and add bread, toast, boiled rice, dry biscuits (eg. quarter slice of bread, half a dry biscuit every half hour) .

DAY 3 – ADD NUTRITION
• Boiled vegetables, fruits, white meats (chicken breast, fish), cereals.

DAY 4 – GRADUALLY INCREASE FOOD INTAKE
• Until return to normal.

AVOID
• All dairy products (eg: milk, cream, cheese, butter, ice cream, custard, yoghurt), eggs, red meat, fatty and fried foods until completely better.

See also CAMPYLOBACTER JEJUNI; DEHYDRATION; DIARRHOEA; NAUSEA AND VOMITING; SHIGELLOSIS

GASTROINTESTINAL TRACT
See ALIMENTARY TRACT; ANUS; APPENDIX; CAECUM; COLON;

DUODENUM; ILEUM; JEJUNUM; MOUTH; OESOPHAGUS; PHARYNX; RECTUM; STOMACH

GASTRO-COLIC REFLEX

The gastro-colic reflex is more evident in animals (eg. dogs) than humans in which dilation of the stomach from eating stimulates a desire to pass faeces (defaecate).

See also COLON; FAECES; REFLEX; STOMACH

GASTRO-OESOPHAGEAL REFLUX

see REFLUX OESOPHAGITIS

GASTROSCOPY

Gastroscopy is a technique by which a doctor can look inside the oesophagus, stomach and small intestine to detect a peptic ulcer, reflux or tumour.

A gastroscope is an instrument about one metre long, consisting of a highly flexible thin tube. There is a light at the end that is inserted, and a box at the end remaining outside with various controls so that the doctor can manipulate the tube on its way down and see everything that is present. Long flexible forceps can pass down the tube and take a sample of tissue from inside the intestine.

The patient will have to fast overnight and then go to hospital or day surgery centre for a few hours.

The patient is sedated to prevent gagging and the gastroscope is passed through the mouth and throat and into the stomach. The procedure is not painful or uncomfortable. The doctor will turn on the light in the endoscope and darken the room to maximise the degree of illumination. The patient will be asked to lie in different positions to bring areas into view, and will comply normally, but because of the sedation they will usually have no memory of these instructions or the procedure itself. When the investigation is complete, the doctor will slowly withdraw the instrument. The whole procedure takes about ten minutes.

The patient is allowed to go home when the sedation wears off, but should arrange for someone to escort them.

See also ENDOSCOPE; STOMACH

GASTROSTOMY

If the oesophagus (gullet) is damaged or missing it is impossible to swallow food. An opening (stoma) can be made through the upper part of the abdomen into the stomach (a gastrostomy), and food is then placed directly into the stomach and can continue on its normal way through the rest of the intestine. The gastrostomy is often created by an endoscope (laparoscope) being inserted through the skin into the stomach, and the procedure is called percutaneous endoscopic gastrostomy (PEG).

See also ENDOSCOPE; LAPAROSCOPY; STOMA; STOMACH

GAUCHER DISEASE

Gaucher disease is an inherited condition that is more common in eastern Europeans and Jews, that causes the excess accumulation of fat in cells throughout the body due to the lack of a liver enzyme. The symptoms include enlargement of the spleen, anaemia, damage to bones in the back and thigh, and bone pain. Fractures of softened bones and poor liver function may occur, and sometimes there is lung involvement. It is diagnosed by specific blood tests and tissue biopsy, but no treatment is available. Patients can expect a reasonable life expectancy unless the lungs become damaged.

GAY

See HOMOSEXUALITY

GBH

See GAMMA-HYDROXYBUTYRATE

GEMFIBRIZOL

See HYPOLIPIDAEMICS

GENDER CHOICE

See SEX CHOICE

GENE

The gene is the basic unit by which inherited characteristics are passed from one generation to the next. Thousands of genes are found on each chromosome, and a total of between 30 000 and 40 000 genes exist in every cell of the body. A gene is one segment of DNA on a chromosome.

Genes direct the formation of enzymes, hormones, proteins and every other chemical responsible for the functioning and shaping of the body.

See also AMINO ACID; CHROMOSOME; CLONING; DNA; PARTHENOGENESIS; RACE

GENERAL ANAESTHETIC

It is normal to admit a patient who is having an operation under general anaesthetic to hospital six to twenty-four hours before the operation is scheduled. During this time, routine tests and checks are performed, and the anaesthetist will check the heart, lungs and other vital systems. If the operation is an emergency one, these checks will be performed in the theatre to save time. If the surgeon is concerned about the patient, s/he may arrange for the patient to be seen in the anaesthetist's rooms several days before the operation so that any complications can be sorted out well in advance.

About an hour before an operation, the patient is changed into an easily removable gown and given an injection to dry up the saliva and induce relaxation. Shortly before the operation, s/he is put onto a trolley and wheeled into the theatre suite. In many hospitals, the normal bed is wheeled all the way.

In the theatre the patient is transferred to the operating table under a battery of powerful lights. While breathing oxygen through a mask, a needle is placed in a vein and a medication is injected to induce sleep and relax the muscles. This is not at all frightening, and is just like going to sleep naturally.

The drugs used last only a short time, and the anaesthesia is maintained by gases that are given through a mask or by a tube down the throat. The anaesthetist regularly checks the pulse, blood pressure, breathing and heart during the operation to ensure there is no variation from the normal. When the operation is finished, the anaesthetist turns off the gases and gives another injection to wake up the patient.

The first memory after the operation is of the recovery room where the patient stays under the care of specially trained nurses and the anaesthetist until fully awake.

Side effects of a general anaesthetic can include a sore throat (from the tube that was placed down the throat), headache, nausea, vomiting and excessive drowsiness (all side effects of the medications).
See also ANAESTHETICS; EPIDURAL ANAESTHETIC; SPINAL ANAESTHETIC

GENERALISED ERYTHRODERMA
See EXFOLIATIVE DERMATITIS

GENERAL PRACTITIONER

General practitioners (GPs) or family physicians are the front-line doctors of medical practice. They must be capable of dealing with absolutely any patient presenting with any symptoms, signs or problem. The breadth of knowledge required is enormous, and the responsibility taken for a patient's welfare is equally significant.

General practitioners are now effectively specialists, as they must undertake postgraduate training, must be selected for a training post by a Royal College, must complete a difficult multi-part exam, must undertake continuing medical education, and are specifically registered by a government board as a GP after obtaining their FRACGP (Fellow of the Royal Australian College of General Practitioners).

GPs deal with the unfiltered public. Specialists have all their patients checked by a general practitioner before they are seen. The general practitioner has the far more difficult problem of dealing with the undifferentiated patient who may present with anything from an infected fingernail to a heart attack, or worse still, vague symptoms that are distressing but non specific, and which may be the result of almost any disease known to medical science. One of the great joys of general practice is the lack of routine, and the impossibility of boredom – the GP never knows what is going to come through his/her door next.

Having a regular GP whom they trust can be invaluable to the health and welfare of a family.
See also MEDICAL TRAINING

GENERIC MEDICATION
See BRAND NAMES; MEDICATION

GENETIC

A genetic condition is one that is determined by the genes on the individual's chromosomes. They are usually familial (run in families).
See also CHROMOSOME; CONGENITAL; FAMILIAL; GENE

GENITAL HERPES

Genital herpes is a contagious viral infection of the genitals caused by the *Herpes simplex* type 2 virus, which is caught by sexual contact with someone who already has the disease. It is possible, but unlikely, for the virus to be caught in hot spa baths and from a shared wet towel. If sores are present, there is a good chance of passing the disease on, but a patient is also infectious for several days before a new crop of sores develops. Condoms can give limited protection against spreading the disease.

Once a person is infected with the virus, it settles in the nerve endings around the vulva or penis and remains there, usually for the rest of that person's life. With stress, illness or reduced resistance, the virus starts reproducing and causes painful blisters and ulcers on the penis or scrotum (sac) in the male; and on the vulva (vaginal lips), and in the vagina and cervix (opening into the womb) of the female. The first attack may occur only a week, or up to some years, after the initial infection. An attack will last for two to four weeks and then subside, but after weeks, months or years, a further attack may occur. Women are affected more severely and frequently than men. The incidence of gynaecological cancer is increased in women with the infection and in rare cases it can cause encephalitis (brain infection).

If a baby catches the infection from the mother during delivery, it can cause severe brain damage in the child. For this reason, if a woman has a history of repeated herpes infections, the baby may be delivered by caesarean section.

The infection is diagnosed by taking a swab from the ulcer or a blood test.

Antiviral tablets and ointments will control an attack, but must be started within seventy two hours of its onset, or they can be taken continually for months or years to prevent further attacks. Good control is possible with modern medications.
See also ANTIVIRALS; COLD SORE; ENCEPHALITIS; GENITAL ULCER; VENEREAL DISEASES; VIRUS

GENITAL ITCH
The genitals (penis and scrotum in the male, vulva and vagina in the female) may become itchy for similar, or totally different reasons in males and females.

Any skin condition that causes itching can also affect the genital skin. Common examples are eczema, reactive dermatitis and psoriasis.

If you have an itch of any cause, and scratch it, the scratching will further irritate the skin, leading to yet more itching and scratching, The condition becomes self perpetuating, although the cause of the original itch has long gone. If it itches, do NOT scratch it!

Excessive sweating in an area that is usually well covered and constricted by clothing is a common cause of skin irritation and itching. The damaged skin can then become infected by fungi and/or bacteria to cause a painful, oozing rash. Prevention is better than cure, and regular washing of the area when sweaty, loose clothing and cotton underwear (nylon may look sexy, but is not good for skin) can all help.

Over washing of the area on the other hand, particularly with strong soaps, can remove all natural protective oil, and lead to dry itchy skin. Minimal use of soap and thorough rinsing is a better approach.

Other causes common to both sexes include an allergy reaction (eg. to soaps, clothing, antiperspirants, toiletries, perfumes, contraceptive creams, lubricants etc.), infestation of the pubic hair (eg. with scabies, lice or crabs), genital herpes, genital warts (caused by the human papilloma virus) and poorly controlled diabetes (due to excessive sweating and superficial infections of the affected skin by fungi and bacteria).

Psychiatric conditions, including depression, may often include itching of the more private parts of the body as one of their symptoms. This may be because the mind becomes focussed inwards, magnifying minor irritations and excluding the outside world.

Conditions that may cause genital itching in women include thrush (fungal infection of the vagina), vaginal infections by bacteria or parasites (eg. Trichomonas), excessive natural vaginal secretions (leucorrhoea often due to excess oestrogen), infection of the bladder (cystitis), urinary incontinence (urine can irritate the genital skin), and a lack of oestrogen in older women after the menopause. Cancer of the vulva may first be noted as a hard area of itchy skin. The burning vulva syndrome is a rare condition that causes exquisite tenderness and itching of the vulva, but its cause is unknown.

In men a genital itch may be due to fungal and bacterial infections under the foreskin of the penis, venereal diseases that cause a penile discharge (eg. gonorrhoea, chlamydia) and, rarely, cancer of the penis.

See also ANAL ITCH; SKIN ITCH and separate entries for diseases mentioned above.

GENITALS
The external organs of sexual intercourse and reproduction in both sexes are referred to as the genitals.
See also PENIS; SEXUAL INTERCOURSE; TESTICLE; VAGINA; VULVA

GENITAL ULCER
Almost any condition that can cause an ulcer on the skin elsewhere on the body can also cause an ulcer on the genital skin. A common example is the bacterial infection of a minor skin irritation to cause impetigo (school sores).

An injury to the area is an obvious cause, but sometimes injury may be forgotten if it happens in the heat of a sexual encounter, especially if artificial aids are used to increase sexual stimulation.

Skin cancers are a possibility that should not be overlooked.

The most common reason for an ulcer to develop on the penis and scrotum of the male, and on the vulva and in the vagina of a woman is a venereal (sexually transmitted) disease. These include genital herpes (causes a blister which bursts to form a painful, tender, shallow ulcer), syphilis (causes a painless ulcer at the original site of infection), and rarer venereal diseases such as chancroid, donovanosis and lymphogranuloma venereum.

Behçet syndrome is a rare condition that causes eye inflammation, arthritis, genital ulceration and sometimes convulsions.
See also SKIN ULCER and separate entries for diseases mentioned above.

GENITAL WARTS
Genital or venereal warts (condylomata accuminata) are a sexually transmitted viral infection caused by the human papilloma virus (HPV), which is transmitted from one person to another only by sexual intercourse or other intimate contact, but condoms can give some protection against the infection. It is not possible to catch it from toilet seats or spa baths. The incubation period varies from one to six months.

Warts, sometimes of a large size, grow on the penis in men and in the genital area of women. They initially appear as flat, pale areas on the skin, or as dark-coloured, irregularly shaped lumps. Both men and women can be carriers without being aware they are infected, and in women genital warts may develop internally where they are difficult to detect. A significant proportion of women with this infection will develop cancer of the cervix which can only be detected at an early stage by regular Pap smears. Anyone with genital warts should also have tests performed to check for the presence of other venereal diseases.

Small warts can be more easily seen if a special stain is applied to the skin, then treatment can be given with antiviral cream applied three times a week for up to four months, acid paints or ointments, freezing with liquid nitrogen, or burning with electric diathermy or laser. The treatment is often prolonged and warts tend to recur, but with careful watching and rapid treatment of any recurrence the infection will eventually settle.
See also CERVICAL CANCER; PAP SMEAR; VENEREAL DISEASES; WART

GENITOURINARY SYSTEM
See BLADDER; KIDNEY; OVARY; PENIS; TESTICLE; URETER; URETHRA; VAGINA; VULVA

GENTAMICIN
See AMINOGLYCOSIDES

GENU VALGUM
See KNOCK KNEES

GENU VARUM
See BOW LEGS

GEOGRAPHIC TONGUE
Smooth, red patches with greyish margin are scattered over the tongue in a map-like pattern in patients with geographic tongue. There are no symptoms other than the strange appearance of tongue. It is caused by the excessive shedding of the cells on the surface of the tongue, and may be due to an allergy or severe infection, but usually has no apparent cause. No treatment is necessary and it usually settles after a few weeks.
See also TONGUE DISCOLOURED

GERMAN MEASLES
German measles (rubella) is a contagious viral infection caused by a Togavirus, which is

widespread in the community, and causes epidemics every few years. It spreads from one person to another with coughs and sneezes, but can be caught only once in a lifetime. An infection in a child may be so mild that it is completely overlooked. The incubation period is two to three weeks.

Infection occurs most commonly in children, and produces a fine rash over the body that lasts only two or three days, is not itchy, and is not accompanied by the sore eyes and cold symptoms associated with common measles. There are often some enlarged lymph nodes at the back of the neck, and in severe cases there may be a fever, runny nose and joint pains.

If a pregnant woman catches the disease between the sixth and twelfth weeks of pregnancy, infection may cause blindness, deafness, heart damage and other serious defects to her child. Because of this, a blood test is sometimes done to confirm the disease or determine the immune status of a pregnant woman.

Paracetamol for fever and discomfort is all the treatment that is necessary.

An effective vaccine is available, and all children are now given mumps, measles and rubella as a combined vaccine at one and five years of age.
See also FIFTH DISEASE; MEASLES; ROSEOLA INFANTUM; SKIN RED; VIRUS

GERMS
See BACTERIA; FUNGI; PRIONS; PROTOZOA; VIRUS

GESTODENE
See CONTRACEPTIVE PILL

GGT
See GAMMA-GLUTAMYL TRANSFERASE

GHB
See GAMMA-HYDROXYBUTYRATE

GIANT CELL ARTERITIS
See TEMPORAL ARTERITIS

GIANT CELL TUMOURS
See BONE CANCER

GIARDIASIS
Giardia lamblia is the parasite responsible for a very common protozoan (microscopic single celled animal) infection of the intestine, that is far more common in children than adults. The parasite can enter the small intestine via the mouth and pass from one person to another by poor personal hygiene. Eggs are found in the faeces, and faecal contamination of water supplies is a common method of infection. From the time Giardia eggs are swallowed, it may be one to three weeks before symptoms develop or the adult parasite (trophozite) which is only 0.00014 centimetres (14 micrometres) long, can be found in the faeces.

Most patients have no symptoms, but more severe cases may cause mild diarrhoea, foul-smelling stools, smelly flatus (farts), general tiredness, an uncomfortable feeling in the abdomen, nausea, vomiting, burping and cramping pains in the abdomen. In persistent cases, particularly amongst indigenous people (eg. Aborigines) and children in third-world countries, malnutrition occurs from the constant diarrhoea which prevents proper food absorption. People with the parasite but without symptoms can easily pass on the infection.

It is diagnosed by examining a sample of faeces under a microscope and identifying the eggs or the live giardia.

Most cases clear spontaneously after many weeks or months, but a number of different single-dose treatments are available as tablets or mixtures to cure the infestation. It is essential to treat all members of the patient's family, and any other close contacts at the same time, and the vast majority of cases settle rapidly with treatment. The only form of prevention is scrupulous personal hygiene.
See also DIARRHOEA; PROTOZOA

GIDDY
See DIZZINESS

GIFT
See ARTIFICIAL CONCEPTION

GIGANTISM
See HEIGHT EXCESSIVE

GILBERT SYNDROME

Gilbert syndrome is an uncommon inherited cause of poor liver function due to the lack of a specific enzyme (glucuronyl transferase) that breaks down proteins in the liver. There are usually no symptoms, but it may cause a dark complexion (mild jaundice) from a persistent excess level of bilirubin in the blood. Liver function blood tests are consistently abnormal and patients are more susceptible to other forms of liver damage (eg. from excess alcohol).

No treatment is normally necessary, but in selected cases medication can be given to trigger the activity of the missing enzymes. No cure is available, but usually there are no adverse effects suffered by the patient.
See also BILIRUBIN; LIVER

GILLES de la TOURETTE SYNDROME
See TOURETTE SYNDROME

GINGIVA
See GUM PAIN; TEETH

GINGIVITIS
See DENTAL PLAQUE; GINGIVOSTOMATITIS; GUM PAIN

GINGIVOSTOMATITIS

Gingivostomatitis (Vincent's angina) is an inflammation of the gums (gingivitis) and mouth lining (stomatitis) due to bacterial infection, poor hygiene, malnutrition, or it may be associated with malignancy (eg. leukaemia). Patients suffer ulceration and pain of the gums, and the inside of the mouth and lips. A swab taken from an ulcer shows the responsible bacteria, and blood tests show the presence of infection. Appropriate antibiotic and anti-inflammatory mouth washes and gels are effective in curing the condition.
See also DENTAL PLAQUE; GUM PAIN; STOMATITIS

GLAND

A gland is an organ or group of cells that secretes (produces) various substances used in keeping the body functioning. Lymph nodes are often referred to as glands, particularly in the neck, but this is incorrect terminology.

EXOCRINE GLANDS
Some glands have ducts to carry their secretions to various parts of the body, and these are called exocrine glands. There are dozens of different exocrine glands, which include the: –
• liver which produces bile
• mammary glands (breasts) which produce milk
• sweat glands
• sebaceous (oil) glands in the skin
• lacrimal glands (above the outer corner of the eyes) which produce tears
• salivary glands (produce saliva) in the mouth
• Meibomian glands in the eyelids (lubricate eyelashes)
• Bartholin glands in the vulva (lubricate the vagina)
• prostate gland (produces part of the semen)
• apocrine glands in the armpit and groin (produce thick sweat and pheromones – sexual stimulants)
• areolar glands in the nipple (lubricate the nipple in breast feeding)
There are numerous other glands within the intestine and other organs of the body.

ENDOCRINE GLANDS
Glands without ducts are called endocrine glands and secrete hormones (chemical messengers) which are released directly into the bloodstream. Some glands are large organs such as the liver, pancreas and kidneys, but more commonly they are very tiny. The endocrine glands are enormously important in the functioning of the body. Endocrine glands generally work in conjunction with one another, so that the release of a hormone in one gland will influence the operation of a different gland. Among other things they influence growth, metabolism (rate at which body functions) and sexual development. The other endocrine glands include the: –
• pituitary gland at the base of the brain.
• thyroid gland in the front of the neck.
• parathyroid glands, four of which lie behind the thyroid gland.
• adrenal glands on top of the kidneys.
• islets of Langerhan in the pancreas, under the stomach.
• thymus in the lower neck.
• ovaries in women and the testes in men
See also ADRENAL GLAND; BARTHOLIN CYST; BREAST; HORMONES; LIVER; LYMPHATIC SYSTEM; MEIBOMIAN CYST; OVARY;

PANCREAS; PARATHYROID GLAND;
PITUITARY GLAND; PROSTATE;
SALIVARY GLAND; SEBACEOUS
GLANDS; SWEAT GLANDS; TESTICLE;
THYMUS; THYROID GLAND.

GLANDS ENLARGED AND/OR PAINFUL
See ADENITIS; GLANDULAR FEVER;
LYMPH NODES ENLARGED AND/OR
PAINFUL

GLANDS OF ZEISS
See STYE

GLANDULAR FEVER
Glandular fever (infectious mononucleosis or
the kissing disease) is a very common viral
infection of the lymph nodes (incorrectly
called glands) in the neck, armpit, groin and
belly, that almost invariably occurs in
teenagers or in the early twenties. It is caused
by the Epstein-Barr virus (EBV) which is
passed from one person to another through
the breath. The patient is infectious during
the stage of tender lymph nodes, and good
personal hygiene is important to prevent
further spread.

Patients have a sore throat, raised temperature, large lymph nodes in the neck and other
parts of the body, extreme tiredness, and they
generally feel miserable. It usually lasts about
four weeks, but in some patients it may
persist for several months. Some antibiotics
(eg. penicillin) can cause a widespread rash
if taken while glandular fever is present.
Other complications are very uncommon,
but include secondary bacterial infections,
infected spleen, or in even rarer cases the
liver, heart and brain may be involved.

A blood test can prove the diagnosis, but
may not turn positive until ten days after the
onset of the symptoms. This test is unreliable
in children before puberty.

There is no specific cure, and patients must
rest as much as possible, take aspirin or
paracetamol for the fever and aches, and use
gargles for the sore throat. Recurrences are
possible in the following year or two at times
of stress or lowered resistance.
See also ADENITIS; LYMPHATIC
SYSTEM; LYMPH NODES ENLARGED
AND/OR PAINFUL

GLANS
See PENIS

GLASGOW COMA SCALE
The depth of a patient's coma may be
assessed by the Glasgow coma scale. The
score is derived from the following observa-
tions and points: –

	POINT SCORE
EYE OPENING (E)	
• Spontaneous opening	4
• Open to verbal command	3
• Open to pain	2
• No response	1
MOTOR RESPONSES (M)	
• Obeys verbal command	6
• Responds to painful stimuli by: –	
• localises pain	5
• withdraws from painful stimulus	4
• abnormal flexion	3
• extensor response	2
• no response	1
VERBAL RESPONSES (V)	
• Oriented and converses	5
• Disoriented and converses	4
• Inappropriate words	3
• Incomprehensible sounds	2
• No response	1

COMA SCORE = E + M + V
3 = very deeply comatose.
15 = completely conscious and alert

See also COMA; UNCONSCIOUS

GLAUCOMA
Glaucoma is an increase in the pressure of the
half-set jelly-like fluid inside the eyeball that
damages the eye and affects the vision. The
eye is filled with a thick clear fluid (aqueous
humour) that is slowly secreted by special
cells within the eye, while in another part of
the eye the fluid is removed, allowing a slow
but steady renewal. If there is a blockage to
the drainage of the fluid from the eye while
new fluid continues to be secreted, the pressure inside the eye increases, and damage
occurs to the light-sensitive retina at the back
of the eye. Other conditions may also cause
glaucoma, including eye tumours, infections,
injury and, in rare cases, drugs (eg. steroids)
may be responsible.

Three types of glaucoma occur – chronic, acute and congenital: –

• Chronic glaucoma (open-angle glaucoma) is the most common type with a slow onset over years. It usually occurs in both eyes simultaneously and runs in families. Initially it affects the peripheral vision, which is how far can be seen to the sides and up and down while looking straight ahead. One in every seventy-five people over the age of forty have this type of glaucoma.

• Acute glaucoma (angle-closure glaucoma) is the worst type, as it develops in a few hours or days, but usually involves only one eye. There is a rapid deterioration in vision, severe pain, rainbow-coloured halos around lights, nausea and vomiting. It may start after a blow to the eye, or for no discernible reason. Immediate treatment of acute glaucoma is essential if the sight of the eye is to be saved, but even with good treatment, permanent blindness can occur.

• Congenital glaucoma occurs in babies who are born with the condition. The earliest sign is the continual overflow of tears from the eye, and the baby turns away from lights rather than towards them as a normal.

Glaucoma is diagnosed in most cases by measuring the pressure of the fluid within the eye. This can be done by anaesthetising the eye surface with eye drops and then resting a pressure measuring instrument (tonometer) on the surface of the eye while the patient is lying down, or by using a machine that directs a puff of air onto the eye to measure the pressure. Glaucoma may also be detected by measuring deterioration in peripheral vision using a computerised device, charts or by following a white dot on a large black screen. More complex tests include examining the eye through a microscope to determine the nature and seriousness of the glaucoma.

The excessive pressure in the eye caused by glaucoma can be reduced by eye drops, which are usually beta-blockers, and/or tablets that remove some fluid from the eye.

Beta-blocker eye drops include betaxolol (Betoptic), latanoprost (Xalantan), levobunolol (Betagan) and timolol. Their side effects may include blurred vision, headache and a small pupil. They should be used with caution in asthma and heart disease. The other commonly used eye drop for glaucoma is carbachol pilocarpine (Pilopt). It may cause blurred vision

but otherwise has minimal side effects.

The tablet used to treat glaucoma is acetazolamide (Diamox). Side effects may include pins and needles, excess urination and a poor appetite. It must be used with caution in pregnancy, and not in patients with liver disease.

In serious cases, laser microsurgery to the tiny drainage canals in the front of the eye is necessary. Congenital glaucoma always requires surgical treatment.

Without treatment, glaucoma progresses inexorably to total blindness, but if the disease is detected early, glaucoma in most patients can be successfully controlled but not cured.
See also BETA-BLOCKERS; EYE; TONOMETRY; VISION BLURRED; VISUAL HALO

GLENOID
See SCAPULA; SHOULDER

GLIBENCLAMIDE
See HYPOGLYCAEMICS

GLIMEPRIDE
See HYPOGLYCAEMICS

GLIOBLASTOMA
See GLIOMA

GLIOMA
A glioma (glioblastoma or malignant astrocytoma) is a form of brain cancer arising from the cells that support and surround the nerve cells in the brain. The cause is unknown, but there is a higher incidence in some families and occupations (eg. petroleum processing). The very variable symptoms may include personality changes, seizures, weakness in some areas and abnormal sensations. Bleeding into the tumour may suddenly worsen the symptoms.

CT and MRI scans can usually identify the location of the tumour, but a biopsy is necessary to make a definitive diagnosis. Brain surgery is then performed to remove the tumour, followed by radiation therapy. Unfortunately the prognosis for these aggressive tumours is very poor.
See also ASTROCYTOMA; BRAIN; CRANIOPHARYNGIOMA; GLIOMA; MEDULLOBLASTOMA; MENINGIOMA; NEUROSURGERY; PINEALOMA; RETINOBLASTOMA

GLIPIZIDE
See HYPOGLYCAEMICS

GLOBUS
Globus hystericus is an intermittent spasm of the muscles in the oesophagus (gullet) that occurs in emotionally stressed people, particularly women. Patients have the sensation of a constant lump in the throat that they feel will interfere with swallowing, but usually does not. All investigations of the oesophagus and throat are normal.

The condition usually settles after some months in most patients with time and reassurance, but sometimes anti-anxiety medication is necessary.
See also OESOPHAGUS; SWALLOWING PAINFUL

GLOMERULONEPHRITIS
Glomerulonephritis is a degenerative disease of the glomeruli and nephrons in the kidneys that occurs in two forms – acute and chronic. Glomeruli are microscopic cups in the kidney where the waste products are filtered out of the blood to form urine, while the nephron is the tiny tube that carries the urine away from the glomerular cup. Thus the term glomerulonephritis (inflammation of the glomeruli and nephrons).

Acute glomerulonephritis is often triggered by a bacterial infection but may start as a result of other diseases in the body or for no identifiable reason. It is more common in children than adults, in third-world countries and amongst Aborigines, but quite rare in affluent societies.

Some patients do not recover from acute glomerulonephritis, and they develop worsening kidney function which results in chronic glomerulonephritis.

Patients with the acute form feel tired, have no appetite, develop headaches, have a low-grade fever and the tissues may become swollen. About 5% of patients develop the nephrotic syndrome and permanent kidney damage.

Chronic glomerulonephritis usually has no symptoms until the kidneys start to fail and excessive levels of waste products build up in the bloodstream. Symptoms may then include a low urine output, loin (kidney) pain, swelling of the ankles and around the eyes, cloudy urine and there may be an increase in blood pressure. Infection, injury or strenuous exercise may cause a sudden deterioration in kidney function.

The diagnosis is confirmed by examining the urine under a microscope, when blood cells and cell fragments are seen, and blood tests can determine how effectively the kidneys are functioning.

The treatment of acute glomerulonephritis involves antibiotics for any infection that is present, and keeping the patient at rest until the kidneys recover. In severe cases, a special low-protein, high-carbohydrate diet is required, and medication may be required to lower the blood pressure. In the rare cases that deteriorate further, an artificial kidney machine may be needed for a short time. Most patients recover completely in a month or so, but in severe cases it may take a year or more. Very rarely, death may occur.

There is no specific treatment for chronic glomerulonephritis other than continuation of the low-protein, high-carbohydrate diet, and a large intake of fluids is also desirable. Most patients live relatively normal lives for twenty or thirty years before kidney failure occurs, at which point dialysis or a kidney transplant is necessary.
See also KIDNEY; NEPHROTIC SYNDROME

GLOSSITIS
See TONGUE PAIN

GLUCOSE, BLOOD
Blood sugar (glucose) tests are used to diagnose hyperglycaemia and hypoglycaemia (too much or too little sugar in the bloodstream) which may be associated with diabetes. Diabetics must regularly measure their blood glucose levels, and should aim to keep them at a fasting level below 8 mmol/L and above 3.5 mmol/L. A level over 10 is considered to be dangerous, and below 3.5 there is a risk of having a "hypo" due to excessive medication lowering the level too much.

A very sneaky test that measures the amount of a type of glucose present in red blood cells (glycated haemoglobin or HbA1c) can be used to give an average blood glucose level over a period of three months. This should give an average reading of between 5 and 7 to be perfect. A level over 9 is quite dangerous.

See also BLOOD TESTS;
DIABETES MELLITUS TYPE ONE;
DIABETES MELLITUS TYPE TWO;
GLUCOSE TOLERANCE TEST

GLUCOSE TOLERANCE TEST

Blood and urine glucose levels are high in untreated or inadequately treated patients with diabetes mellitus. A blood glucose tolerance test (GTT) may be performed to confirm the diagnosis. After fasting for twelve hours, a blood sample is taken, then a sweet drink is swallowed, and further blood samples are taken at regular intervals for two or three hours. The pattern of absorption and elimination of blood glucose is measured to confirm the diagnosis of diabetes mellitus.
See also DIABETES MELLITUS TYPE ONE; DIABETES MELLITUS TYPE TWO; GLUCOSE, BLOOD;

GLUCURONYL TRANSFERASE
See GILBERT SYNDROME

GLUE EAR

A glue ear develops when phlegm and mucus from the nose pass up the thin Eustachian tube into the middle ear. It is difficult for these thick, sticky secretions to escape through the Eustachian tube to the back of the nose, particularly if the adenoids which surround the opening of the tube into the nose are swollen.

There is a feeling of blockage in the affected ear similar to that felt when descending (more common) or ascending a mountain and being unable to pop the ears clear. The glue may also be responsible for a middle ear infections (otitis media) and deafness.

Examination of the ear by an otoscope (magnifier and light) shows an opaque and bulging ear drum, and special instruments can measure the pressure in the middle ear. The surgical insertion of a small tube (grommet) through the ear drum to relieve the pressure is often necessary. Recurrent cases may require the surgical removal of the adenoids, which are lymph nodes surrounding the nasal opening into the Eustachian tubes. There are very good results after appropriate treatment, but the problem may recur after the grommets fall out.
See also ADENOIDS; EAR; EUSTACHIAN TUBE BLOCKAGE; GROMMET; MYRINGOTOMY; OTITIS MEDIA

GLUTAMIC ACID
See ACIDS

GLUTEN

Gluten is a protein found in many cereals including wheat, oats and rye. There is no gluten in rice or potatoes.

Some patients are intolerant of gluten, and if it is eaten they develop significant symptoms, depending on their form of intolerance. Diseases that may be associated with gluten intolerance include coeliac disease and dermatitis herpetiformis.
See also COELIAC DISEASE; DERMATITIS HERPETIFORMIS

GLUTEUS MAXIMUS

The largest muscle in the body is the gluteus maximus, which forms the buttocks on which we sit, and acts to extend the hip and straighten the leg in walking. In cattle, rump steak comes from this muscle.
See also MUSCLE

GLYCATED HAEMOGLOBIN
See BLOOD SUGAR

GLYCERYL TRINITRATE
See ANTIANGINALS

GLYCOGEN STORAGE DISEASES

The glycogen storage diseases are a number of rare inherited or congenital conditions including McArdle syndrome, von Gierke syndrome, Cori syndrome, Hers syndrome, Pompe syndrome and Andersen syndrome. All these conditions involve missing or inactive enzymes and other natural chemicals in the liver, which are necessary to process carbohydrates in food into glycogen and make it available to the body as a form of energy fuel.

The different diseases vary in their symptoms and effects depending upon which enzymes and chemicals are affected. Most patients have low blood sugar, large livers, short stature, subnormal mentality, and may bleed excessively and fail in their development to progress through puberty. Other forms cause muscle pain and weakness.

The diagnosis can be confirmed by appropriate blood tests and a liver biopsy. Special diets and a liver transplant sometimes assist in relieving the symptoms. The prognosis varies from minimal effects throughout life to death

in infancy, depending on which type of glycogen storage disease is present.
See also LIVER

GOITRE

A goitre is any enlargement of the thyroid gland which lies in the front of the neck just below the Adam's apple. This gland releases a hormone (thyroxine) into the blood stream which acts as an accelerator for every cell in the body. If there is too much thyroxine in the blood stream, the cells (and the tissue they form) will work too fast (resulting in diarrhoea, palpitations, sweating, weight loss etc.), while a lack of thyroxine causes cell function to become too slow (resulting in constipation, slow heart rate, dry skin, weight gain etc.).

An enlarged thyroid gland indicates that it is malfunctioning either by producing too much (hyperthyroidism) or too little (hypothyroidism) of the hormone thyroxine. A goitre can also be an inherited characteristic, due to the development of cysts or tumours in the gland, or a lack of iodine in the diet (iodine is essential for the production of thyroxine).

Thyrotoxicosis (hyperthyroidism) is a goitre associated with excessive production of thyroxine. Surgery is usually necessary to cure the problem, but medication may slow down the effects in the short term.

Myxoedema (hypothyroidism) is the opposite, as there is a lack of thyroxine being released into the blood, and feedback mechanisms make the gland swells in an attempt to make more of the hormone. Thyroid hormone can be given in tablet form on a regular basis to overcome this defect.

Cysts may form in the thyroid gland, and are usually of no consequence unless they enlarge sufficiently to cause an obvious deformity.

Other causes of a goitre include thyroid cancer (a hard lump in the gland), Hashimoto's thyroiditis (inflammation of the thyroid gland) and de Quervain thyroiditis (rare condition that results in a painful goitre).

Sometimes, swelling of tissue behind the thyroid gland may push it forward to make it appear that a goitre is present. Examples include enlarged lymph nodes in the neck, and tumours and cysts of the larynx (wind pipe).

Blood tests can determine the activity of the thyroid gland and the amount of thyroxine being produced and an ultrasound or radionucleotide scan will show any tumours or cysts.

The treatment of a goitre depends on the cause – surgery for an overactive gland or thyroid supplements for an underactive one. In most developed countries a goitre due to a lack of iodine has been eliminated since the introduction of iodised table salt, bread and milk. The enlargement usually settles with appropriate treatment.
See also HYPERTHYROIDISM;
HYPOTHYROIDISM; THROAT LUMP;
THYROID GLAND and separate entries for diseases mentioned above.

GOLD
See ANTIRHEUMATICS

GOLDEN STAPH
See STAPHYLOCOCCUS AUREUS

GOLFER'S ELBOW

Golfer's elbow (medial epicondylitis) is an inflammation of the tendon that runs around the bony lump (epicondyle) on the inside of the elbow. It is caused by overstraining of the extensor tendon at the inner back of the elbow due to excessive bending and twisting movements of the arm. In golfers it is not normally one stroke that strains the tendon, but repeated episodes of over stretching caused by hitting the ground with the club during a stroke. This leads to tears of the minute fibres in the tendon, forming scar tissue which is then broken down again by further strains. It may also occur in tradesmen who undertake repetitive tasks, and cleaners, musicians and many others who may put excessive strain on their elbows.

Painful inflammation occurs, which can be constant or may only occur when the elbow is moved or stressed. The whole forearm can ache in some patients, especially when trying to grip or twist with the hand.

Prolonged rest is the most important treatment, while exercises to strengthen the elbow and anti-inflammatory drugs may also be used. Cortisone injections may be given in resistant cases. The strengthening exercises are done under the supervision of a physiotherapist and involve using your wrist to raise and lower a weight with the palm facing up.

Some patients find pressure pads over the tendon, or elbow guards (elastic tubes around the elbow) help relieve the symptoms and prevent recurrences by adding extra support. The condition is not easy to treat and can easily become chronic, but no matter what form of treatment is used, most cases seem to last for about eighteen months and then settle spontaneously.
See also ELBOW; TENDON; TENNIS ELBOW

GONADOTROPHINS
See TROPHIC HORMONES

GONORRHOEA
Gonorrhoea ('clap') is a common sexually transmitted bacterial infection caused by the bacterium *Neisseria gonorrhoeae* which can only be caught by having sex with a person who already has the disease. It has an incubation period of three to seven days after contact. Some degree of protection can be obtained by using a condom.

The symptoms vary significantly between men and women.

In women there may be minimal symptoms with a mild attack, but when symptoms do occur they include a foul discharge from the vagina, pain on passing urine, pain in the lower abdomen, passing urine frequently, tender lymph nodes in the groin, and fever. If left untreated the infection can involve the uterus and Fallopian tubes to cause salpingitis and pelvic inflammatory disease which can result in infertility and persistent pelvic pain. Babies born to mothers with the infection can develop gonococcal conjunctivitis (eye infection).

In men symptoms are usually obvious with a yellow milky discharge from the penis, pain on passing urine and, in advanced cases, inflamed lymph nodes in the groin. If left untreated the prostate can become infected, which can cause scarring of the urine tube (urethra), permanent difficulty in passing urine and reduced fertility.

With anal intercourse, a rectal infection with gonorrhoea can develop and cause an anal discharge, mild diarrhoea, rectal discomfort and pain on passing faeces.

Oral sex can lead to the development of a gonococcal throat infection.

Gonorrhoea may also enter the bloodstream and cause septicaemia. An unusual complication is gonococcal arthritis, which causes pain in the knees, ankles and wrists. Other rarer complications include infections of the heart, brain and tendons.

The diagnosis is confirmed by examining a swab from the urethra, vagina or anus under a microscope and culturing the bacteria on a nutrient substance. There are no blood tests available to diagnose gonorrhoea. Other sexually transmitted diseases should also be tested for when gonorrhoea is diagnosed, as they may be contracted at the same time. For this reason, blood tests are often ordered when treating anyone with any form of venereal disease.

Gonorrhoea has been readily treated with a course of penicillin until recently, but many strains are now resistant to penicillin and more potent antibiotics are required. All sexual contacts of the infected person need to be notified as they may be carriers of the disease and unaware of the presence of the infection. After treatment, a follow-up swab is important to ensure that the infection has been adequately treated. More than 95% of cases of gonorrhoea can be cured by the appropriate antibiotics.
See also PELVIC INFLAMMATORY DISEASE; SALPINGITIS; SEPTICAEMIA; VENEREAL DISEASES

GOODPASTURE SYNDROME
Goodpasture syndrome is a rare failure of the body's immune system that results in shortness of breath, coughing, recurrent nose bleeds, significant anaemia, kidney damage and iron deposition in vital organs throughout the body. The cause is unknown, but it can be diagnosed by blood tests and a lung biopsy. Treatment is often unsatisfactory, and involves potent medications, artificial cleaning of the blood by dialysis, and kidney transplantation.
See also IMMUNODEFICIENCY

GOSERELIN
See CYTOTOXICS AND ANTINEOPLASTICS

GOUT
Gout is caused by excess blood levels of uric acid (hyperuricaemia), which is produced as a normal breakdown product of protein in the diet. Normally uric acid is removed by the

kidneys, but if excess is produced or the kidneys fail to work efficiently, high levels build up in the body and precipitate as crystals in the lubricating fluid of a joint. Under a microscope the crystals look like double ended needles. An alcoholic binge or eating a lot of meat can start an attack in someone who is susceptible, and there is a tendency for the disease to run in families. Most victims are men and it usually starts between thirty and fifty years of age.

The main symptom is an exquisitely tender, red, swollen and painful joint. The most common joint to be involved is the ball of the foot, but almost any joint in the body may be involved. In severe attacks, a fever may develop, along with a rapid heart rate, loss of appetite and flaking of skin over the affected joint. Attacks usually start very suddenly, often at night, and may occur every week or so, or only once in a lifetime. In chronic cases, uric acid crystals can form lumps (tophi) under the skin around joints and in the ear lobes. More seriously, the crystals may damage the kidneys and form kidney stones.

High levels of uric acid found on blood tests confirm the diagnosis, and a needle may be used to take a sample of fluid from within the joint for analysis in difficult cases.

The management of gout takes two forms – treatment of the acute attack, and prevention of any further attacks.

Acute attacks are cured by the combination of nonsteroidal anti-inflammatory drugs (eg. indomethacin) and colchicine (a hypouricaemic). Aspirin is contraindicated in acute gout as it may elevate serum uric acid levels and aggravate the symptoms. Rest of the affected joint to control the pain and prevent further damage is important.

Prevention involves taking tablets (eg. allopurinol, probenecid) daily for the rest of the patient's life to prevent further attacks, not consuming excess alcohol, keeping weight under control, drinking plenty of liquids to prevent dehydration, avoiding overexposure to cold, not exercising to extremes and avoiding foods that contain high levels of purine-producing proteins which metabolise to uric acid (eg. prawns, shellfish, liver, sardines, meat concentrates and game birds). If the prevention tablets are missed an attack of gout can follow very quickly.

Gout can be controlled and prevented easily in most cases, provided the patient understands the problem and co-operates with treatment.
See also ARTHRITIS; HYPOURICAEMICS; JOINT RED; NONSTEROIDAL ANTI-INFLAMMATORY DRUGS; PSEUDOGOUT; URIC ACID

GP
See GENERAL PRACTITIONER

GRAFT
A graft is a piece of tissue that is taken from one part of the body and placed in a different part in order to repair or replace damaged tissue. Bone grafts to help heal a fracture or fuse a joint (eg. in the back) are one example.

Grafts may be placed in the same body from which they are taken, or placed in a different person, when there may be immune reactions to the transplanted tissue.
See also GRAFT VERSUS HOST DISEASE; TRANSPLANTS

GRAFT VERSUS HOST DISEASE
Graft versus host disease (GvHD) is an uncommon but severe immune reaction affecting the whole body due to a reaction between tissue donated by one person and the body of the recipient of the tissue. It is most common after bone marrow transplantation for diseases such as leukaemia and aplastic anaemia, where it occurs mildly in 8% of transplants, and seriously in about 1%. There are two forms of the disease, acute and chronic. Symptoms start two to twelve weeks after the transplant in acute cases, and more than three months later in chronic cases.

The symptoms of acute GvHD are very variable depending on organs affected. Mild symptoms include itchy skin, skin pain and soreness, and tender soles and palms. With more severe cases, symptoms may include nausea, vomiting, red patches or lumps in and on the skin, fever, jaundice (yellow skin) from liver damage, mouth and nostril sores, belly pain, diarrhoea, eye ulceration, blistering and shedding of inflamed skin, ulcers in the oesophagus, bleeding into the lung and coughing of blood, and massive loss of skin similar to severe burn. The acute form may be a life threatening condition, as patient has little or no immunity to any form of infection, and severe bacterial, viral or fungal infections may start in skin or lungs, and spread to blood to cause septicaemia.

Chronic GvHD causes weight loss, flat-topped red raised small skin lumps and, in more severe cases, hair loss, skin pigment loss (white patches) or gain (dark patches or areas), liver damage and jaundice.

Numerous blood tests may be abnormal, but there is no specific diagnostic test.

Prednisone by mouth is the main treatment, while skin creams containing steroids are used in milder cases. Ultraviolet light with associated medication may also be useful but severe cases require a drip with steroids and other potent medications.

Most acute forms respond well to treatment but if secondary infections occur, the outlook is poor. Chronic GvHD settles slowly with time and treatment.
See also ANTIBODY; APLASTIC ANAEMIA; LEUKAEMIA; TRANSPLANTS AND IMPLANTS

GRAND MAL
See EPILEPSY

GRANULOMA ANNULARE
Granuloma annulare causes one or more ring shaped lumps of 1-3cm. diameter to develop on the back of the hands, elbows or top of the feet. The lumps are covered with normal skin but vary in colour from red to white. They are harmless, but slightly disfiguring. The cause is unknown although the may be associated with diabetes, and they are more common in teenagers and young adults. The diagnosis is confirmed by a skin biopsy.

No ideal treatment exists. Application of potent steroid creams, or injections of steroids into the skin lesion are sometimes successful, while cryotherapy (freezing), ultraviolet light and medications used to treat cancer are other options. Spontaneous regression is possible over years.
See also SKIN LUMPS

GRANULOMA INGUINALE
Granuloma inguinale (donovanosis or granuloma venereum) is caused by the bacteria *Donovania* or *Calymmatobacterium granulomatis* which passes from one person to another during sexual intercourse. The incubation period is one to twelve weeks and it causes painless nodules on or around the genitals that break down to shallow ulcers, and may join together into progressively larger ulcers that spread up onto the lower abdomen. Infection of the ulcers with other bacteria will cause them to fill with pus and become foul smelling. Microscopic examination of a biopsy or swab smear from the edge of an ulcer reveals the responsible bacteria and confirms the diagnosis.

Treatment is difficult, and it may be necessary to take antibiotics such as tetracycline for several months. Relapses are common unless the full antibiotic course is completed.
See also GENITAL ULCER; TETRACYCLINES; VENEREAL DISEASES

GRANULOMA VENEREUM
See GRANULOMA INGUINALE

GRAVE'S DISEASE
See HYPERTHYROIDISM

GRAVITATIONAL ECZEMA
Gravitational eczema occurs mainly in older women due to poor drainage of veins in the legs from varicose veins, thromboses or other circulatory problems. Excessive pressure of blood in the veins increases the fluid pressure in the tissue to create the rash.

The symptoms are an itchy, red, blotchy rash affecting the lower legs and a firm, swollen leg that is worse after standing and eased by raising the leg (eg. after resting overnight in bed). Hot weather aggravates the problem. The rash may ooze and become infected by bacteria, and scratching may break down the skin, resulting in thickening and permanent pigmentation due to scar formation. In severe cases, ulcers may form. An ultrasound scan may be used to check circulation.

Patients should avoid prolonged standing and, when seated, should place their leg on a footstool and elevate the foot of the bed slightly at night. Steroid creams will ease the itch and irritation, and moisturising creams should be used regularly to keep the skin soft and supple. Condy's solution compresses may be used to dry up oozing, and antibiotics are prescribed for any infection that may develop. Patients must never scratch the

affected skin. In severe cases, elastic pressure stockings may be used to reduce the collection of blood in the leg, or surgery to remove varicose veins may be considered.
See also ECZEMA; SKIN ITCH

GREENSTICK FRACTURE
See FRACTURE

'GRIEVOUS BODILY HARM'
See GAMMA-HYDROXYBUTYRATE

GRISEOFULVIN
See ANTIFUNGALS

GRISTLE
See CARTILAGE

GROIN PAIN
The groin is the dip in the flesh where the thigh joins the belly.

By far the most common reason for pain in this area is a strain (stretch or tear) to the large ligaments and muscles that support the pelvis and belly. A strain can occur because of a sudden injury, but may also be the result of repetitive use over a period of time (eg. constantly twisting and squatting while cleaning or gardening). These injuries can only be healed by rest and time, but medications and physiotherapy may ease the discomfort.

A nerve may be injured or trapped as it passes through the groin into the leg or genitals. This may result in constant aching, or sudden severe stabs of pain.

A hernia is another common cause of groin pain, and again can occur suddenly or gradually. An inguinal hernia occurs when gut forces its way down the canal through which the blood vessels, nerves and sperm tube (vas deferens) run from the belly to the testicle. A femoral hernia occurs when the gut comes out under the pubic bone through the gap created for the passage of the femoral artery and vein that run to and from the leg.

Torsion of the testis is a medical emergency in which the testicle twists around and cuts off the blood vessels that supply it. Pain occurs in both the testicle and the groin. Surgery must be performed within twelve hours or the testicle will die.

Other causes of groin pain include arthritis in the hip, infection or inflammation of the pelvic bone (very serious but rare), and organs within the pelvis and lower belly can cause pain in the groin if they are infected or inflamed (eg. tumours or cysts of the ovary, endometriosis, appendicitis, infections of the prostate gland and an abscess in the pelvic cavity).
See also ABDOMINAL PAIN; PELVIC PAIN

GROMMET
A grommet is a short tube (ear ventilation tube), ridged at both ends and often made of teflon, which is inserted through the eardrum to ventilate the middle ear.

The ear is one of the most complex organs, and is made from a diversity of materials found nowhere else in the body. Tiny, finely balanced bones interact with super sensory nerve hairs and amazingly tough sheets of cartilage, but all on a microscopic scale. The ear is composed of three main parts. Interference with any of these three areas can cause deafness. The outer ear is the ear canal which leads into the eardrum. Beyond the solid sheet of tissue which forms the eardrum is the middle ear. This contains three tiny bones which magnify and transmit the vibrations of the eardrum, that are caused by a noise, across the cavity of the middle ear to a similar but much smaller membrane. This smaller membrane separates the middle ear from the inner ear. The inner ear is the third part of the ear structure, and contains a fine spiral shaped canal that gives us our ability to hear.

Except for the three tiny bones it contains, the middle ear is normally empty. To keep this space ventilated, a fine tube runs through the skull from the middle ear to the back of the nose. This is the Eustachian tube. When you drive up a steep hill, you swallow and your ears 'pop'. This is caused by air rushing through the Eustachian tubes to equalise the pressure inside and outside the ear. When a person has a cold, hay fever or other causes of excess phlegm and mucus production in the nose, the Eustachian tube may become blocked, and unable to function.

In some people, particularly children who have narrower Eustachian tubes, the middle ear may become full of a mixture of phlegm and mucus known as 'glue'. The glue material is too thick to pass easily back down the Eustachian tube to the nose and if it remains

GROMMET TUBE

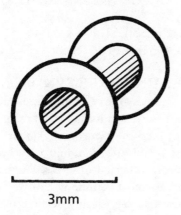

3mm

in the middle ear it may cause serious long-term problems.

A glue ear can be effectively treated by inserting a grommet. Under a general anaesthetic, the surgeon puts a small hole in the eardrum (a myringotomy), sucks out most of the glue, and inserts a grommet into the hole in the eardrum. This grommet does not drain any further secretions from the middle ear but allows air to enter the ear so that there is no air pressure difference to push further rubbish up from the nose and into the ear.

After three to six months, the grommet falls out, and the eardrum usually heals up perfectly afterwards. It is then hoped that no further attacks of glue ear occur. These can be prevented by careful treatment of all colds and nasal infections.

The use of the simple grommet, which is only 3mm. or so long, has prevented a great deal of deafness in children, and may prevent more serious complications, such as an abscess in the ear or brain.
See also EAR; EUSTACHIAN TUBE BLOCKAGE; GLUE EAR; MYRINGOTOMY

GROVER DISEASE

Grover disease (transient acantholytic dermatosis) is an itchy skin condition of the chest and back that usually affects men over fifty, and much less commonly women or younger people. It frequently follows sweating or some unexpected heat stress to cause the sudden onset of very itchy spots on the central back, mid chest and occasionally elsewhere. A skin biopsy can be used to confirm diagnosis.

Treatment is unsatisfactory, as it is necessary for patients to remain cool and avoid sweating. A mild steroid lotion can be applied frequently to give temporary relief. Most cases settle in six to twelve months, but occasionally it may last longer.
See also SKIN ITCH

GROWING PAINS

Growing pains or, technically, the limb-pain syndrome, occur in children who have significant intermittent pain in their legs and (less commonly) their arms for no obvious reason. It may be due to softening of bones at times of rapid growth, and there is a tendency for the condition to recur within the one family in successive generations. It affects up to one third of all children of both sexes between the ages of six and fourteen years.

Growing children experience a deep ache in the limbs that occurs between joints (not at the joint), often worse at night and equal on both sides. No specific tests are necessary, but it is important for other causes of limb pain to be excluded. Reassurance, paracetamol and heat packs are the only necessary treatments as the condition always settles spontaneously.
See also LEG PAIN

GROWTH HORMONE
See PITUITARY GLAND

GROWTH INCREASED
See HEIGHT EXCESSIVE

GROWTH REDUCED

Before a parent becomes concerned about the failure of a child to grow in height or weight, they should look at themselves. If both parents are small, it is unlikely that the child is going to reach average height. Genetics play a vital part in development and growth, and many of the causes of abnormally reduced growth are due to a defect in the individual's genes.

A child deprived of adequate nutrition will obviously not reach his or her expected height or weight, and anyone who suffers from a long term illness will have their growth affected. Examples include conditions as varied as severe asthma, underactive thyroid gland, heart disease (eg. hole in the heart), kidney infections or failure, coeliac disease (inability to digest gluten in wheat), other conditions in which food is poorly absorbed, deficiencies of vitamins or minerals (particularly zinc),

Crohn's disease (thickening and ulceration of a segment of gut) and cystic fibrosis (thick mucus in lungs and gut).

Steroid drugs, used to control some long term diseases, can reduce growth as a side-effect.

Psychiatric conditions such as anorexia nervosa may severely affect the nutrition of teenagers (particularly girls) and prevent them from ever reaching their expected height or weight.

The pituitary gland in the centre of the brain controls every other gland (eg. thyroid, ovary, testes) in the body. If this becomes diseased or damaged by a tumour, it will have generalised adverse effects including altered growth rates.

Precocious puberty is the term for a very early development of adult sexual characteristics. Growth may cease early when this occurs, resulting in the individual being shorter than expected.

Foetal alcohol syndrome is caused by the mother drinking excessive amounts of alcohol during pregnancy, and results in a small baby that grows very slowly in the first few years of life. Small amounts of social drinking and even the occasional episode of drunkenness during pregnancy do NOT cause this problem (although they are not advisable).

A large number of rare syndromes that affect the individual's genetic make-up, bodily functions and general health can affect growth and result in dwarfism. A few of these include: –
• Bassen-Kornzweig syndrome (poor food absorption, poor coordination)
• de Lange syndrome (mental retardation, small head, hairy skin)
• Down syndrome (broad face, mental retardation, slanted eyes)
• Hurler syndrome (abnormal facial development, inflamed joints)
• Noonan syndrome (wide neck, prominent chest)
• Turner syndrome (female who fails to develop sexually due to a genetic defect)
• von Gierke syndrome (low blood sugar, persistent diarrhoea)
• Russell-Silver syndrome (uneven size of body sides)
See also FAILURE TO THRIVE; PITUITARY GLAND and separate entries for most diseases mentioned above.

GTT
See GLUCOSE TOLERANCE TEST

GUAIPHENESIN
See COUGH MEDICINES

GUILLAIN-BARRÉ SYNDROME
The Guillain-Barré syndrome (Landry-Guillain-Barré syndrome) is a rare inflammation of nerves (neuropathy) that usually follows a viral infection, injury, surgery, vaccination or a period of stress. The nerves in the legs are most commonly involved and the muscles that they supply become paralysed, and sensation to the affected areas may also be lost. No specific diagnostic investigations are available.

Steroids are used in treatment, but their use is controversial, and up to 20% of patients are left with a permanent disability. Most patients slowly recover, but in rare cases the muscles of breathing may be paralysed, which can result in death.
See also MUSCLE PAIN; MUSCLE WEAKNESS; NEUROPATHY

GUINEA WORM
Dracunculiasis (Guinea worm disease) is a worm infestation that occurs only in west and central Africa, and uncommonly in south Asia and Arabia.

The worm *Dracunculus medinensis* is caught by swallowing water contaminated by microscopic crustaceans (copepods – water fleas) that contain the worm larva. In the stomach these are released, burrow through the stomach wall into the bloodstream, and migrate to the fat under the skin where they mature. After mating the male worm dies, but the mature female worm, which may be sixty to eighty cm. long, moves to the skin surface where it forms a sore, and through this discharges eggs every time the skin comes into contact with water. The eggs are then swallowed by the copepods where the cycle starts again. The worms eventually die and emerge through the skin sore, or occasionally remain under the skin. The full cycle takes nine to fourteen months.

Patients experience generalised itching, fever, shortness of breath and nausea when larvae are in the blood. Redness, burning and itching occurs at the site of skin sores, usually on the foot or leg. After the worm dies a red, tender ulcer forms.

When examined under a microscope, smears from skin sores show eggs to confirm the diagnosis.

The patient should rest with affected leg elevated. Worms can be individually removed by exposing one end and then slowly drawing them out a centimetre at a time over several days. Medications cannot kill worms, but may encourage them to be expelled through a sore. Secondary bacterial infection of an ulcer can spread to the surrounding skin (cellulitis). Abscesses can form under the skin (particularly if a worm is broken during removal), in joints or rarely in other organs that are reached by worms.

The ulcers heal after a month or two and most patients recover eventually.

GULLET
See OESOPHAGUS

GUM PAIN
Gingivitis is inflammation or infection of the gums. This may be caused by injury to the gums (eg. biting on a bone, poorly fitting dentures or plate), or by a bacteria, virus or fungus infecting the gum tissue.

Mouth ulcers may occur on the gums to create a tender eroded area.

A number of dental diseases may cause gum pain, including an abscess of a tooth root, decay of a tooth and exposure of the base of the tooth to make it sensitive. A gap may develop between the gum and tooth, and debris may accumulate there, become infected and cause gum pain.

Other causes of gum pain include scurvy (caused by a lack of vitamin C in the diet), iron and vitamin B deficiencies, Behçet syndrome (causes recurrent mouth and gum ulcers, genital ulcers, eye inflammation, arthritis and brain damage), Reiter syndrome (causes conjunctivitis, inflammation of the urethra, arthritis and painful ulceration of the gums), and Hand-Schueller-Christian syndrome (rare condition that causes skull bone defects, diabetes insipidus, protruding eyes and ear inflammation as well as sore gums).

Rarely, cancer of the gums can occur, which results in a hard painful lump.

In most cases a dentist, rather than a doctor, is the first person to contact in cases of gum pain, unless there are also symptoms elsewhere in the body.

See also MOUTH PAIN and separate entries for diseases mentioned above.

GUMS
See GUM PAIN; MOUTH; TEETH

GUMS, BLUE LINE ON
Rarely, a fuzzy dark blue line may be noticed running around the gums just beyond the edge of the teeth. This may be caused by the deposition of lead sulphide in the gums, and is a sign of significant lead poisoning.

In developed countries, anyone who works with lead (eg. in a battery factory) is now tested regularly for lead levels in the blood, which prevents the problem reaching this stage.
See also LEAD POISONING

GUT
See CAECUM; COLON; DUODENUM; ILEUM; JEJUNUM; LARGE INTESTINE; RECTUM; SMALL INTESTINE

GUT PAIN
See ABDOMINAL PAIN

GUTTAE
The prescription notation 'guttae' is from the Latin word for 'drops' and usually referring to 'eye drops'.
See also PRESCRIPTION NOTATIONS

GUTTAE PARAPSORIASIS
See PITYRIASIS LICHENOIDES

GUTTAE PSORIASIS
Guttae psoriasis is a very active form of the skin disease psoriasis that is more common in teenagers and young adults and may follow a Streptococcal bacterial infection. Patients experience the sudden appearance of multiple small, red, scale covered patches on the arms, leg and trunk that may gradually enlarge and merge, and it may progress to normal psoriasis. Usually no investigations are necessary, but if the diagnosis is in doubt it may be confirmed by a skin biopsy.

One or more of numerous skin preparations including coal tar, dithranol, calcipotriol and steroid creams are used in treatment. It may disappear spontaneously after a few weeks, or persist for many years, and is controlled, but not cured, by medication.
See also PITYRIASIS LICHENOIDES;

PSORIASIS; RED PATCHES ON SKIN;
SKIN DRY AND SCALY

GUYTON CANAL SYNDROME

The Guyton canal syndrome is a loss of sensation in the fifth finger and half the fourth finger, and wasting and weakness of some muscles in the hand, due to the ulnar nerve becoming trapped as it passes the wrist. An electromyogram (EMG) can detect the affected muscles. Anti-inflammatory medications are prescribed and an operation to release the ulnar nerve at the wrist is performed. Permanent muscle weakness and loss of sensation can occur if not treated adequately, but there are good results with correct treatment.

See also CARPAL TUNNEL SYNDROME; ELECTROMYOGRAM; HAND WEAK

GvHD

See GRAFT VERSUS HOST DISEASE

GYNAECOLOGICAL PAIN

See GENITAL ULCER; PELVIC PAIN; SEXUAL INTERCOURSE PAIN; VAGINA

GYNAECOLOGY

Gynaecology is the science of dealing with medical problems that are specific to women. Doctors specialising in this field are known as gynaecologists, and often also deal with obstetrics (the science of pregnancy and birth).

See also BREAST; OVARY; SEXUAL INTERCOURSE; UTERUS; VAGINA

GYNAECOMASTIA

See BREAST ENLARGED

H

H2 RECEPTOR ANTAGONISTS

Peptic ulcers have caused belly pains for millennia, and were poorly treated until a significant advance in medication occurred in the late 1970s with the introduction of cimetidine, the first of the H2 receptor antagonists. These drugs are distantly related to antihistamines and act to cure ulcers of the stomach, duodenum and oesophagus by reducing the amount of acid secreted into the stomach. This also enables them to control reflux oesophagitis (heartburn), which may accompany a hiatus hernia, and inflammation of the stomach (gastritis) caused by excess acid. Treatment is usually rapidly effective, but must be continued for weeks or months to prevent relapses. This class of medication is now being replaced by the more potent proton pump inhibitors.

Examples of drugs in this class include cimetidine (Tagamet), famotidine (Pepcidine), nizatadine (Tazac) and ranitidine (Zantac). Side effects are usually minimal, but may include occasional headache, diarrhoea, rash, breast enlargement in men, dizziness and tiredness. Cimetidine can sometimes interact with other drugs that control epilepsy and blood clotting.

Cimetidine has sometimes been used to treat cases of multiple skin warts with some success, but the mode of action is unknown.
See also PEPTIC ULCER;
PROTON PUMP INHIBITORS;
ULCER MEDICATIONS

HAEMANGIOMA

A haemangioma (angioma) is a localised overgrowth of arteries and veins in the skin, intestine, spinal cord, brain or inside other organs. It appears as a red lump that blanches (turns white) with pressure. Haemangiomas may bleed dramatically if injured, and in the gut may cause steady blood loss and anaemia. They may also put pressure on nerves (eg. in spine) to cause pain or loss of nerve function.

No investigations are necessary for haemangiomas in the skin. Internal haemangiomas may be detected by angiography (injecting dye into a blood vessel and taking an x-ray), CT or MRI scans, gastroscopy or colonoscopy. Surgical removal is performed if the spot is cosmetically unacceptable or causing symptoms.
See also CAMPBELL de MORGAN
SPOTS; FABRY DISEASE; STRAWBERRY
NAEVUS; VENOUS LAKE

HAEMATEMESIS
See VOMITING BLOOD

HAEMATOCRIT
See ESR

HAEMATOMA

A haematoma is a collection of blood in tissue under the skin or in an internal organ due to injury to the tissue or organ, or to an abnormal bleeding tendency.

The symptoms depend on the site of the haematoma. If a person is kicked in the leg, there may be a haematoma in the underlying muscle, with a firm, tender swelling at that site, usually with overlying bruising, and pain if the affected muscle is used. If deeper organs in the body (eg. liver, kidney, brain) are involved, there may be discomfort around that organ, vague bruising at the site of injury and signs of damage to the organ (eg. blood in the urine with kidney injury, unconscious from brain injury). Pressure on the affected organ may affect its function, and serious consequences can result from subdural haematomas within the skull putting pressure on the brain. Persistent soreness and a lump of scar tissue may occur with muscular haematomas.

An ultrasound scan of muscles in the arms or legs, or organs within the abdomen, can show a haematoma. Within the skull, a CT scan is necessary. Blood tests for a bleeding disorder may be performed if there is no obvious injury to cause the haematoma.

Smaller haematomas are slowly removed as the body gradually destroys the blood collection over weeks or months. Larger haematomas may need to be surgically removed or drained, particularly if they occur within the skull.

See also BRUISE; CAULIFLOWER EAR;
SUBDURAL HAEMATOMA

HAEMATURIA
See URINE BLOOD

HAEMOCHROMATOSIS

Haemochromatosis is a congenital condition of iron metabolism that is far more common in males than females. The body stores excessive amounts of iron in the liver, pancreas, kidneys, heart, testes and other tissues.

It is a very slowly progressive condition that usually causes no problems until over the age of fifty. Common symptoms include liver enlargement and reduced liver function, joint pains, heart enlargement, impaired heart function, diabetes, dark skin discolouration and impotence. It is diagnosed by specific blood tests and a liver biopsy.

Bloodletting on a regular basis to remove iron from the body is the main method of dealing with the disease. This may need to be continued weekly for some years to adequately drain iron out of the system. Drugs are also available to increase the rate at which iron is excreted through the kidneys and urine. Damage already caused to the body's vital organs by the excess levels of iron (eg. diabetes, liver and heart failure) cannot be reversed.

Good control, but not a permanent cure, is possible once diagnosed.
See also IRON

HAEMODIALYSIS
See DIALYSIS

HAEMOGLOBIN

Haemoglobin (Hb) is a red coloured protein found in red blood cells (erythrocytes). It transports oxygen from the lungs to every cell in the body. When combined with oxygen, haemoglobin becomes a brighter red colour than when the oxygen is removed, thus making arterial blood a redder colour than blood from veins.

Haemoglobin is formed in bone marrow. A main ingredient of the protein is iron, so a lack of iron can cause a drop in haemoglobin production – the disease of anaemia. Excess haemoglobin may occur in haemochromatosis. When red blood cells die, the iron is salvaged and reused, while the rest of the cell is destroyed by the liver and passes out of the body through the bile.

There is a different form of haemoglobin found in the foetus (HbF), which combines more effectively with oxygen, but this form disappears during the first few months of life.

Haemoglobin can combine with other substances that act as poisons, including lead and carbon monoxide from exhaust fumes.

A haemoglobin level of 135 to 180 g/L is considered normal in an adult male, while a range of 115 to 165 g/L is normal for an adult woman.
See also ANAEMIA; BLOOD TESTS;
FULL BLOOD COUNT;
HAEMOCHROMATOSIS; IRON;
JAUNDICE; RED BLOOD CELLS

HAEMOGLOBIN S
See SICKLE CELL ANAEMIA

HAEMOLYTIC ANAEMIA

Haemolytic anaemia is a form of anaemia caused by the excessive destruction of red blood cells because of an uncommon complication of many diseases including kidney failure, liver failure, transfusion with incompatible blood, cancer, both viral and bacterial infections, and exposure to some drugs and poisons.

Tiredness and weakness are the usual symptoms, but fever and jaundice (yellow skin) may also be present. In severe cases, the patient may become semiconscious, have severe abdominal pain, and bruise easily. It is diagnosed by blood tests and examining the red blood cells under a microscope.

Emergency treatment involves transfusing the patient with concentrated red blood cells. Prednisone (a steroid) is the usual drug used, but some patients do not respond, and more exotic and toxic drugs are then required. The spleen is responsible for destroying red blood cells, and if this becomes overactive, surgical removal may control the disease. Some patients require years of treatment, and in a small number the condition is resistant to treatment and fatal. Most cases respond well to treatment and recover in a few months.
See also ANAEMIA

HAEMOLYTIC-URAEMIC SYNDROME

The haemolytic-uraemic syndrome (uraemic

syndrome) is a serious condition of red blood cell destruction resulting in kidney failure. Microscopic damage to, and clogging of, the tiny blood vessels in the kidneys occurs due to excessive destruction of red blood cells, resulting in poor filtration of the blood and failure to remove waste products that then build up in the body. It may be a side effect of severe gut infections or an inappropriate response to pregnancy or drugs.

The symptoms are the passing of bloody urine, tiredness and weakness due to anaemia, and excessive bruising and bleeding due to a drop in the number of platelets (cells in the blood essential for clotting) which in turn may cause extensive internal bleeding.

The condition is diagnosed by blood tests and kidney biopsy, but treatment is difficult and usually involves blood transfusions. In about 30% of patients the kidneys fail, and dialysis (artificial kidney machine) is required. Although most patients recover, even in the best hospitals some patients do not survive.
See also ANAEMIA; DIALYSIS; HAEMOLYTIC ANAEMIA; KIDNEY FAILURE, CHRONIC

HAEMOPHILIA A

Haemophilia A is an inherited lack of factor VIII, one of the essential factors responsible for the clotting of blood. The gene for the disease is carried by women on the X chromosome, but can only affect men.

These people have excessive bleeding from a cut, severe bruising from a minor injury, bleeding into joints to cause arthritis and internal bleeding into the gut and other organs. The excessive bleeding may result in arthritis, infertility, damage to other organs from bleeding, chronic weakness, and a shorter than normal life span. Specific blood tests can confirm the diagnosis.

Injections of the missing coagulation factor must be given to prevent excessive bleeding when it occurs. Insufficient is available to be given regularly to prevent bleeding at present, but genetic technologies are likely to change this in the near future. The factor is obtained from blood donations at present, but in the future may be obtained from genetically modified pig milk.

The severity may vary from one patient to another and no permanent cure is available. Statistically, half the children of a woman who carries the responsible gene will have the disease, but the overall incidence is only one in 10,000.
See also CHRISTMAS DISEASE; von WILLEBRAND DISEASE; X-LINKED CONDITION

HAEMOPHILIA B
See CHRISTMAS DISEASE

HAEMOPHILUS DUCREYI
See CHANCROID

HAEMOPHILUS INFLUENZAE B INFECTION

Haemophilus influenzae B (HiB) is a bacterial infection that in children causes meningitis or epiglottitis, and in adults may affect numerous organs. It is spread by close contact and can cause infections in any age group, but is far more serious in children.

In children it may cause: –
• Meningitis, which is an infection of the meninges (covering of the brain) that results in a fever, irritability, lethargy, seizures and coma. The onset of meningitis may be so rapid that the child may be permanently affected (eg. by deafness, learning difficulties and other forms of brain damage) before any treatment can work.
• Epiglottitis, which is a life threatening infection of a piece of cartilage at the back of the throat that may swell and block the airways.

In adults it may cause a serious form of pneumonia and less serious types of throat infection, sinusitis, middle ear infection, bronchitis, joint infection, skin infection, heart infection and meningitis. Adults with reduced immunity (eg: in AIDS) may have the same serious infections as children.

Blood and fluid from the spinal cord can be tested to confirm the diagnosis.

Infections in adults can be readily treated with appropriate antibiotics (usually as tablets), with minimal long term complications. In children far more potent antibiotics are needed, and they must be given by injection. The swollen epiglottis (piece of cartilage at the back of the throat) may choke the child before the antibiotics can work, so urgent hospitalisation and intubation (placing a tube into the throat to permit breathing) is essential. A vaccine for infants is now available to prevent HiB infections.

Good recovery occurs if the infection is diagnosed and treated early, but permanent damage or death are possible in children if treatment is delayed.
See also EPIGLOTTITIS; MENINGITIS; PNEUMONIA

HAEMOPTYSIS
See COUGHING BLOOD

HAEMORRHAGE
See BLEEDING, EXCESSIVE

HAEMORRHOIDS
See ANAL BLEEDING; PILES

HAIR
With the exception of the lips, the palms of the hands and the soles of the feet, the body is entirely covered with hair but, depending on the part of the body, it grows in different densities, patterns and colour. There are two types of hair – vellus hairs which are fine and downy and which account for most of the body hair, and terminal hairs which are longer and darker and which occur in the scalp, eyebrows, eye lashes, the pubic region, the armpits and on the lower part of the male face.

The main function of hair is to act as antennae for touch sensors located at the base of each hair, but it also serves other useful purposes. The hair on the head cushions blows to the head and stops the head being burnt by the sun. Hairs in the nose filter out particles of grit and dust. Eyelashes prevent foreign bodies getting into the eyes. Eyebrows serve as sweat bands absorbing and diverting perspiration so that it does not drip into the eyes.

Each threadlike hair is made up of a structure of dead cells filled with a protein called keratin. A hair develops in a tiny tube called a follicle, situated below the surface of the skin. All hair follicles are present at birth – generally about five million, of which 100 000 to 200 000 are on the head. The hair develops from cells within the follicle and pushes its way up through the top layer of the skin to the outside. By the time it reaches the outside, the cells will gradually have died and hardened to form hair. The fact that visible hair is dead is evidenced by the fact that if a hair is pulled out, pain is felt at the root, whereas cutting hair, even close to the skin, is completely painless.

The hairs on the head are continuously shed and replaced by new hairs growing from the follicle. Over 100 hairs are normally lost a day, the only obvious sign of which may be a clogged drain after washing. One hair takes about three years from the time it starts to grow to the time it drops off. Hair grows at the rate of twelve to sixteen centimetres a year.

The type of hair on the scalp depends largely on the size and shape of the hair follicle. A hair follicle that is small in diameter will produce fine hair. Conversely, coarse hair grows from a large follicle. If the follicle is circular it will produce straight hair, and if it is oval it will produce curly hair. Whether hair is coarse or fine also depends on its structure. A single strand of hair consists of an outer scaly casing called the cuticle, and a soft fibrous inner cortex. In coarse hair the cuticle is up to four times as thick in proportion to the cortex as it is in fine hair.

Hair colour depends on the amount of pigment called melanin in the hair. The hair colour is inherited from parents, although exactly how is not fully understood. It is known that dark colours are dominant over light colours, so if a child has one fair and one dark parent, the child is more likely to be dark than fair. Grey or white hair has no pigment. For no known reason, the body stops producing melanin with ageing, making grey or white hair one of the most familiar signs of old age.

Although all the hair follicles are present at birth, not all are functioning. Some, such as those in the pubic area and under the arms, are inactive until puberty, when they are stimulated into production by the sex hormones. The production of hair in puberty increases far more in boys than it does in girls.

If a hair follicle is damaged, hair growth may continue, but once a follicle is destroyed, hair will not grow again in that spot.

Each hair follicle has tiny oil glands (sebaceous glands) and an erector muscle that contracts under certain circumstances (eg. fright) so that the hair stands on end. Similarly if the body is cold, the muscle will contract and cause goose pimples.
See also BALD; FOLLICULITIS; HAIR LOSS; HIRSUTISM; SEBACEOUS GLANDS; TOUCH

HAIR BALL
See TRICHOBEZOAR

HAIR EXCESS ON BODY
See HIRSUTISM

HAIR LOSS
A healthy adult loses at least 100 hairs a day from their head, so only excessive hair loss above this level is abnormal. Hair may be lost in small patches (alopecia areata), large areas (alopecia totalis, baldness), or there may be diffuse loss of hair from all over the head (telogen effluvium).

The most common type of hair loss is male pattern baldness, which may start in the late teens and progress to total loss of all scalp hair. There is a strong hereditary tendency in this condition which cannot be reversed.

Diffuse hair loss (telogen effluvium), when the person notices large quantities of hair coming out in their brush or comb, is a common and distressing problem, but must be very severe before anyone else notices the problem. It occurs more in women than men, and may be related to the menstrual cycle, with more hair loss occurring at certain times of the month. Prolonged stress and anxiety, or a sudden severe shock (eg. death in the family) may trigger significant hair loss. The menopause is another time when dramatic hair loss may occur, but this stabilises once the menopause is passed. There is not usually a permanent loss of hair in these cases, but the hair becomes more fragile at its root, and breaks away from the scalp. The number of hair follicles remains the same though, and the site where a hair breaks off immediately starts producing more hair.

The hair density tends to decrease with age, and an older people will have fewer hair growing follicles on their scalp than when they were young. This occurs far more after the menopause, which in women occurs about twenty years earlier than in men. Unfortunately there is nothing that can be done to reverse this process, but there are products available which will thicken the remaining hair to make it appear that more is present.

A sudden loss of weight, either by diet or disease, is often associated with diffuse hair loss.

After pregnancy, the combination of a sudden change in hormone levels with the delivery of the baby and breast development for milk production, and the physical and mental stress of looking after and breast feeding an infant, may result in diffuse hair loss.

Alopecia areata causes a small area of the scalp to be completely hairless. The area starts as just a tiny patch, but may slowly spread to result in hairless patches a few centimetres across. In the worst case, the entire scalp may be affected (alopecia totalis). There is often no apparent cause, but sometimes extreme stress, psychiatric disturbances and drugs may be found responsible.

Less common causes of hair loss include fad diets lacking in essential nutrients (eg. proteins, iron, zinc), diseases of the hormone secreting glands of the body (eg. pituitary gland in the brain, thyroid gland in the neck, testes and ovaries), autoimmune diseases in which the body inappropriately rejects some of its own tissue (eg. systemic lupus erythematosus), excessive intake of vitamin A either as vitamin supplements or eating large quantities of orange coloured foods (eg. carrots, paw paw) and diabetes mellitus.

Drugs used to combat cancer are well known to cause serious hair loss, often involving the entire scalp, but other drugs may also cause the problem, although usually not as significantly. Examples include anticoagulants that prevent blood clots (eg. warfarin), lithium (for psychiatric conditions), beta-blockers (for heart disease and high blood pressure) and the oral contraceptive pill.

There are many rarer causes of scalp hair loss, some of which include liver failure, uraemia (kidney failure), tumours or cancers anywhere in the body (particularly those involving the testes or ovaries), trichotillomania (psychiatric condition in which the patient pulls out handfuls of their own hair) and Fröhlich syndrome.
See also BALD; HAIR and separate entries for diseases mentioned above.

HAIRY CELL LEUKAEMIA
See LEUKAEMIA, HAIRY CELL

HAJDU-CHENEY SYNDROME
The Hajdu-Cheney syndrome is an inherited developmental abnormality of joints, teeth and facial structure. The child presents with

slack joints, premature tooth loss, small unusually shaped face, small jaw, unusual eye and eyebrow shape, slow growth, excess body hair, generalised weakness and pain, and sometimes finger abnormalities. No treatment or cure is available.

HALCION
See SEDATIVES

HALITOSIS
See BREATH BAD

HALL-PIKE TEST
The Hall-Pike test is a diagnostic test for the cause of dizziness. It involves lying the patient down with the head hanging down off the top of a bed. The head is then rotated and abnormal eye movement (nystagmus) is noted if the test is positive.

HALL PIKE TEST

Start position   Finish position

See BENIGN PAROXYSMAL POSITIONAL VERTIGO

HALLUCINATION
Hallucinating is experiencing something that is not really there. Hallucinations may be visual (sight), auditory (sound), olfactory (smell), tactile (touch) or taste.

Unfortunately, in our society the most common cause of hallucinations is the use of illegal psychoactive drugs such as marijuana, heroin, LSD and amphetamines. These effects can last for some time after the use of the substance (up to a month with marijuana which is absorbed into, and later released from, body fat) which can make driving a vehicle rather scary and dangerous.

Alcohol can be another cause of hallucinating (pink elephants?) when consumed to excess, but it may also cause long term brain damage (Wernicke encephalopathy) which may cause hallucinations. Withdrawal from alcohol after a long period of excessive intake (delirium tremens) may also trigger the problem.

Numerous psychiatric disorders may cause a wide range of hallucinations (eg. schizophrenia, affective disorders, mania), as well as inflammation of the brain due to infection (encephalitis), epileptic fits (the attack of epilepsy may be characterised by an hallucination and no other problem such as convulsions or loss of consciousness) and post-hypnotic suggestions may make a person experience effects that are not real.

Medications may sometimes cause hallucinations, particularly if given in an excessive dose (eg. phenothiazines).
See also ALCOHOL; HEROIN; LSD; MARIJUANA; SCHIZOPHRENIA and separate entries for diseases mentioned above.

HALO
See VISUAL HALO

HALO NAEVUS
A halo naevus is an area of depigmentation around a benign pigmented spot (naevus) that is common in Caucasian children and young adults. It is an autoimmune response to the presence of the naevus that appears as a dark brown spot surrounded by an area of abnormally white skin. The naevus often disappear over a few years.
See also AUTOIMMUNE DISEASES; BROWN PATCHES ON SKIN; NAEVUS

HALOPERIDOL
See ANTIPSYCHOTICS

HALOTHANE
See ANAESTHETICS

HAMATE BONE
See WRIST

HAMSTRING MUSCLES
The group of three muscles responsible for bending the knee (biceps femoris, semitendinosus and semimembranosus) at the back of the thigh are collectively known as the hamstrings. The top ends of these muscles are attached to the back and bottom of the pelvis. The strings are the tendons that run from the muscles to the back and top of the tibia (shin bone) and can be felt as cords at either side of the back of the knee.

See also MUSCLE; QUADRICEPS MUSCLE

HAND

The hand is an extraordinarily flexible, delicate and intricate structure with thirty-one joints in the wrist and beyond, connecting twenty-seven bones which are manipulated by thirty-six muscles and numerous tendons coming from muscles in the forearm. This is all covered by some of the most delicate and sensitive skin on the body, yet it must withstand extreme forces when undertaking many of the activities of daily living. Three major nerves (median, ulnar and radial nerves) run between the hand and brain, as well as two large arteries (radial and ulnar arteries) and several veins.

The palm of the hand has a strong sheet of fibrous tissue, the palmar aponeurosis, underneath it, to keep the palm smooth and tough. Many of the muscles that move the hand are actually in the forearm, and are connected to the bones of the hand by tendons.
See also DUPUYTREN CONTRACTURE OF HAND; HAND PAIN; HAND SPASM; HAND WEAK; NAIL; WRIST

HAND FOOT MOUTH DISEASE

Hand foot mouth disease is an infection that virtually every child will eventually catch caused by a *Coxsackie* virus. The infection is usually so mild that it causes no symptoms, but in severe cases a child will develop blisters on the soles and palms, and mouth ulcers. It may be accompanied by a mild intermittent fever, headache and irritability. Paracetamol is the only treatment necessary. The rash persists for three to five days before settling without any problems.
See also *COXSACKIE* VIRUS INFECTION

HAND PAIN

Damage to any of the bones, joints, muscles, tendons, ligaments, cartilages, nerves, blood vessels in the hand, or the skin covering it, may cause pain. Bruises, fractures and strains are the most common reasons for hand pain.

Diseases of the skin, joints and bone that can occur elsewhere in the body may also cause hand pain.

Rheumatoid arthritis (an inflammation of the joint lining) tends to affect small joints in the hands and feet more than larger joints. The affected joints become stiff, painful and swollen, but may have periods of remission when symptoms ease. Osteoarthritis (a wearing out of the joint lining) may also affect joints in the hands.

Inflammation of the tendons and the sheath covering them (tenosynovitis) can result from injury, strain or overuse (repetitive strain injury, occupational overuse syndrome). The affected tendons will not only become painful, but swollen and weak and the effect on the adjacent nerves causes a burning pain in the hand.

The carpal tunnel syndrome is caused by inflammation in the narrow tunnel on the palm side of the wrist through which all the hand-flexing tendons, nerves and blood vessels that supply the hand must run. If any

BONES OF THE HAND

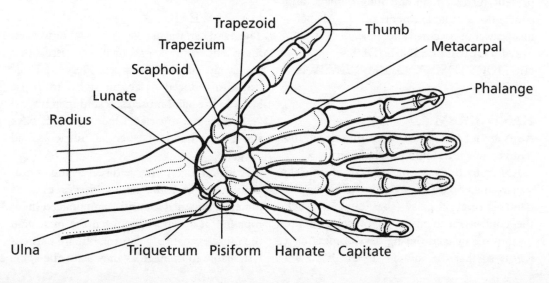

Trapezoid
Trapezium
Scaphoid
Lunate
Radius
Thumb
Metacarpal
Phalange
Ulna   Triquetrum   Pisiform   Hamate   Capitate

of these tissues are damaged or strained, they will swell to place pressure on the adjacent nerves, and therefore pain. Common causes of the carpal tunnel syndrome are pregnancy, weight gain, an underactive thyroid gland, diabetes, rheumatoid arthritis and systemic lupus erythematosus (SLE).

Other less common causes of hand pain include Raynaud's disease and phenomenon (the hands become blue, then red and white before swelling up), neuralgia (inflammation or injury to nerves), cellulitis (infection of soft tissue), infections of joints, de Quervain tenovaginitis (the radius bone at the side of the wrist above the thumb becomes painful, tender and swollen) and polycythaemia rubra vera (excessive number of red blood cells). *See also* ARM PAIN; ARTHRITIS; BONE PAIN; SKIN PAIN; WRIST PAIN and separate entries for diseases mentioned above.

HAND-SCHUELLER-CHRISTIAN DISEASE

Hand-Schueller-Christian disease is one of a group of congenital diseases known as histiocytosis X or Langerhans cell histiocytosis, that occurs in children. The disease causes diabetes insipidus, patchy bony absorption in the skull, protruding eyes, lung damage and outer ear inflammation. Other symptoms may include skin rashes and gum inflammation and in advanced cases numerous organs may fail.

The diagnosis can be made by skull x-rays, biopsy of skin rashes, bone marrow biopsy and chest x-rays. Treatment involves irradiation of the bone lesions, very potent medications to prevent further bone and lung damage and conventional management of the diabetes insipidus, but no cure is possible. *See also* DIABETES INSIPIDUS; HISTIOCYTOSIS X; LETTERER-SIWE DISEASE

HAND SPASM

A spasm of one or more of the muscles in the hand can be intermittent or long term.

A common cause of long term muscle spasm in any part of the body, including the hand, is cerebral palsy (spasticity) in which the control mechanisms of muscles in the brain are damaged during development as a foetus so that the muscles in the hand are constantly and inappropriately told to contract. The result is a useless hand that is hooked into a claw shape.

Other causes of a claw hand caused by muscle spasm are damage to the nerves in the spinal cord that control the muscles of the hand, stretching or pinching of the ulnar and median nerves in the arm, and the carpal tunnel syndrome (inflammation in the narrow tunnel on the palm side of the wrist through which all the hand-flexing tendons, nerves and blood vessels that supply the hand must run).

Rapid shallow breathing (hyperventilation) can cause the amount of carbon dioxide in the lungs to increase. This dissolves in the blood to make it more alkali (high pH) than normal, and small muscles in the hand are sensitive to this change in the blood to the point that they go into spasm with the wrist bent and fingers and thumb bunched together and pointed towards the wrist. This is known as tetany (totally different to the disease tetanus) and can be cured by getting the patient to breathe into a paper bag for a few minutes while they slow down their breathing with repeated reassurance. Hyperventilation may start after a shock, surprise, injury or vigourous exercise.

Erb-Duchenne palsy results in a permanent hand spasm and is caused by damage to the delicate network of nerves (brachial plexus) in the armpit. This is most common if the arm of a baby is pulled too hard during a difficult birth, but may occur later in life with other injuries to the armpit. *See also* MUSCLE CRAMP; MUSCLE TONE EXCESSIVE; TIC; TREMOR and separate entries for diseases mentioned above.

HAND WEAK

The hand can waste (shrink in size) or weaken if any one of the nerves or blood vessels that supply the hand is damaged. Nerve damage causes a reduced or absent signal from the brain to the hand muscles, resulting in wasted and weakened muscles. Blood vessel damage starves the hand of essential nutrients and oxygen.

A wide range of nerve diseases and conditions can affect the hand. Nerves may be pinched, inflamed (neuritis) or damaged (neuropathy) at any point between the brain and the muscles that they control, but are particularly liable to damage as they leave the spine in the neck, and at the major joints (shoulder, elbow, wrist) where they are subjected to stretching or pinching by the movement of the joint. Arthritis in, or injury to, these joints makes the nerves more likely to be damaged. Tumours in the brain, spinal cord or on the nerves (neurofibromas) can have the same effect.

Some people are born with an extra rib (cervical rib) above the normal first rib. Nerves to the arm and hand must stretch to pass over this cervical rib and, as the child grows and develops, they may be over-stretched and function poorly.

The brachial plexus is an intricate network of nerves in the armpit that interconnect to act as a switchboard for impulses going between the hand and arm, and the brain. It can be affected by injury to the armpit from a direct blow, use of crutches that are too long, a tumour, infection, abscess or irradiation in the treatment of cancer in the area (particularly breast cancer).

Generalised diseases of nerves such as motor neurone disease, multiple sclerosis and polio can affect the nerves to the hand as well as nerves in other parts of the body.

The arteries supplying the hand can be damaged or pinched where they must negotiate sharp turns at the joints. If arteries are hardened or narrowed by deposits of cholesterol within them (atherosclerosis) they are more easily damaged or blocked. Aneurysms (swellings on the side of arteries) may also put pressure on arteries supplying the hand.

The carpal tunnel syndrome is caused by inflammation in the narrow tunnel on the palm side of the wrist through which all the hand-flexing tendons, nerves and blood vessels that supply the hand must run. If any of these tissues are damaged or strained, they will swell to place pressure on the adjacent nerves and arteries, and therefore cause loss of function and wasting of the muscles in the hand. Common causes of the carpal tunnel syndrome are pregnancy, weight gain, an underactive thyroid gland, diabetes, rheumatoid arthritis and systemic lupus erythematosus (SLE).

Muscle diseases which cause general wasting in the body (myopathy) may also affect the hand. A specific muscle wasting disease, the myopathy of Gower, affects the hands only.

Inclusion body myositis is a rare condition that results in the progressive destruction of muscle cells in the hands, forearms, feet and lower legs. It only affects elderly people.

An underactive thyroid gland in the neck produces reduced amounts of the hormone thyroxine, which is essential for the function of every cell in the body. Generalised muscle wasting and weakness occurs.
See also HAND; MUSCLE WEAKNESS and separate entries for diseases mentioned above.

HANSEN'S DISEASE
See LEPROSY

HARDENING OF THE ARTERIES
See ARTERIOSCLEROSIS

HARE LIP
See CLEFT LIP AND PALATE

HARLEQUIN SYNDROME
The harlequin syndrome is a rare, congenital, disfiguring disease due to abnormal skin formation. The child is born with very thick, hard plates of skin separated by deep cracks, and there may also be absence of the ears, and out-turning of the lips and eyelids to give a grotesque appearance. There is an inability to move joints freely due to skin hardening.

The diagnosis is confirmed by skin biopsy and treated with moisturising cream in large quantities, but death within days or weeks of birth is usual, and many die before birth.

HARVEY, WILLIAM
William Harvey (1578-1657) was an English physician and anatomist who also worked in Padua, Italy, and became a professor of medicine in London. He made one of the greatest discoveries in medicine – the circulation of blood – in 1628. Prior to his work it was thought that arteries contained air and blood was stored in the liver. He realised that the heart was a pump, and recognised the relationship between arteries and veins in the circulation. He was originally lampooned in the popular press for his ideas and castigated by his colleagues, but in 1672 his ideas were accepted by a decree of Louis XIV of France.
See also HEART

HASHIMOTO THYROIDITIS
Hashimoto thyroiditis is an inflammation of

the thyroid gland in the front of the neck that occurs for no known reasons, but is possibly an autoimmune disease. It may occur at any age, but tends to run in families and is far more common in women.

Patients have a gradual enlargement of the thyroid gland (goitre) over many months or years, and the gland becomes firm, but not tender or painful. Many patients have no other symptoms, and the gland enlargement may be barely noticeable, but in others the gland may gradually cease to function and the patient becomes tired, listless and has other symptoms of hypothyroidism. A rapidly progressive form of the disease is also known.

It is diagnosed by blood tests and treated by taking thyroid hormone tablets (thyroxine) on a daily basis indefinitely. The long term outcome is usually very good with normal life expectancy.
See also AUTOIMMUNE DISEASES; de QUERVAIN THYROIDITIS; GOITRE; HYPOTHYROIDISM; RIEDEL THYROIDITIS; THYROID GLAND; THYROIDITIS

HASHISH
See MARIJUANA

HAY FEVER
Hay fever (allergic rhinitis) is an allergy reaction affecting the lining of the nose that may be due to any one of several million different pollens, microscopic animals such as the house dust mite, skin scale or hair particles from animals. When the sensitive moist membranes that line the nose first come into contact with the sensitising particle (an allergen), there is no reaction, but the body's immune system is primed to react to the next invasion. On the second exposure the large immunoglobulin proteins, which act to defend the body against invasion by any foreign matter, react violently. They cluster around mast cells that rupture and release histamine into the nasal tissues. This causes the tissue to become inflamed. After a few hours or days, the body destroys the histamine released, and the tissues return to normal.

Ten percent of the population is affected. The nose drips constantly and is clogged, the patient sneezes repeatedly, has red eyes, bad breath and a constant drip of phlegm down the throat, but it usually occurs for only a few weeks or months of the year. A secondary bacterial infection may develop to cause sinusitis. Blood tests may show an increase in certain types of cells and immunoglobulins.

Antihistamines and pseudoephedrine tablets or nose sprays are used to counteract the histamine released into the tissue and ease the symptoms, but some types of antihistamine may cause drowsiness. Steroid nasal sprays and/or anti-allergy sprays used regularly prevent the nose from reacting to allergens. Patients who suffer repeatedly can have blood or skin tests performed to determine exactly which dusts and pollens cause the hay fever and if a cause can be found, a course of twenty or more weekly injections may be given to permanently desensitise the patient. The last resort is surgery in which part of the lining of the nasal cavity is removed by burning (diathermy) and some of the curly bones within the nose (turbinates) are cut out so there is less membrane to secrete phlegm.
See also ALLERGY; ATOPY; NOSE; NOSE DISCHARGE; VASOMOTOR RHINITIS

Hb
See HAEMOGLOBIN

HbF
See HAEMOGLOBIN

HbA1C
See GLUCOSE, BLOOD

HEAD
See ACROMEGALY; CRANIAL NERVES; FACE PAIN; HEADACHE; HEAD LARGE; HEAD SMALL; SKULL

HEADACHE
A headache is probably the most common symptom to be experienced by mankind, and may be associated with problems of any of the multiple complex structures in the head, or disorders of many of the body's other organs. Fatigue, stress and anxiety may in themselves cause a headache, or may trigger muscle spasms in the temples and scalp that are responsible for the pain.

Any infection by a bacteria (eg. tonsillitis, sinusitis, ear infection, bronchitis, urinary infection), virus (eg. influenza, common cold, glandular fever, hepatitis), fungus or parasite (eg. malaria), may cause a headache, as may a fever of any cause.

Injury to any part of the head may cause a headache, but sometimes, and very seriously, the headache may occur some days after the injury due to slow bleeding from an leaking vein within the skull.

A headache is more significant when not associated with any other symptoms elsewhere in the body. The most common headaches to fit into this category are tension headaches, migraine and cluster headache.

A tension (muscle spasm) headache causes a dull, persistent pain with varying intensity that is often described as a pressure or tightening around the scalp. It occurs as a localised band around and across head and is not aggravated by exercise or alcohol. The muscles at the top of the neck, in the forehead and over both temples go into prolonged contraction which tightens the scalp, causing pressure on the skull, and further increases the strain on the muscles. Tension headaches are episodic, often in association with stress. Depression and anxiety are common accompanying symptoms. The pain may last for thirty minutes or a week. Muscle spasm headaches usually have a cause (eg. stress, infection, psychiatric disturbance, eye strain), which should be rectified if possible. Simple medications such as aspirin or paracetamol, sometimes in combination with muscle relaxants, are readily available to ease both the muscle spasm and pain. Commercially available combinations (eg. Fiorinal, Mersyndol, Panalgesic) are useful in the short term, but often cause drowsiness. Mild heat and massaging the tense muscles will give temporary relief. Relief of chronic anxiety by talking through the problems with a doctor or counsellor, accepting help to deal with a stressful situation, and using an anti-anxiety medication may also be useful.

Migraines are often associated with visual symptoms including flashing lights, shimmering, seeing zigzag lines and loss of part of the area of vision. They usually occur on only one side of the head, are described as throbbing, and cause intolerance of exercise, light and noise. Nausea and vomiting are common. Migraines occur periodically, and may last for a few hours to several days. The patient often looks pale and drawn.

Cluster headaches are not common, but cause a very characteristic pattern of headache, usually associated with excess sweating of one or both sides of head. They occur in episodes once or twice a year to cause severe pain around or behind one eye which spreads to a temple, the jaw, teeth or chin. They often begin during sleep, and other effects may include a red, watery eye, drooping eyelid, altered pupil in the eye, stuffy nose and flushed face. Cluster headaches may be triggered by alcohol, temperature changes, wind blowing on the face or excitement. They usually last for fifteen minutes to three hours, and are named because of their tendency to occur in clusters for several weeks.

Many people fear that their headache may be due to a brain tumour, but this is actually very rare. Most brain tumours cause other symptoms that lead to their diagnosis well before a headache develops. Cancerous and benign tumours may develop not only in the brain tissue itself, but in the other structures within the skull such as the pituitary gland, membranes around the brain (meninges), sinuses and eyes. Most brain tumours are benign and can be cured by surgery.

Anything that puts abnormal pressure on the brain may cause headaches. An abscess caused by an untreated infection in the brain or an injury that penetrates the skull, is one possibility. Bleeding inside the skull caused by an injury or rupture to a blood vessel is another. An aneurysm is the ballooning out of one side of an artery. The aneurysm may put pressure on the brain to cause a headache, or rupture to cause very severe effects on the brain function.

Viral or bacterial infections of the brain (encephalitis) or surrounding membranes (meningitis) will almost invariably cause a headache.

Inflammation of nerves in the scalp and face may appear to be a headache, when really it is the tissue outside the skull that is affected. Trigeminal neuralgia is one relatively common example, as is the pain of neuralgias associated with pinched nerves in the neck that spread from the base of the skull up the back of the head and as far forward as the hairline.

Psychiatric disorders as varied as phobias (abnormal fears), depression, post-traumatic stress disorder and excessive anxiety may cause headaches.

Other common causes of headache include

eye disorders that vary from increased pressure within the eye (glaucoma) to poor vision (resulting in eye muscle strain) and inflammation of the eye (iritis); menopause, menstrual periods (premenstrual tension), contraceptive pills, pregnancy and other fluctuations in the level of the sex hormone oestrogen; inflammation or infection of the teeth (eg. abscess or dental decay), jaw joint (eg. arthritis), neck (eg. arthritis or ligamentous strain), nose (eg. large polyp) or sinuses (eg. polyp or infection); cancer of any tissue in the body (cause headaches due to the release of toxins into the blood); an under active and over active thyroid gland (hypothyroidism and hyperthyroidism); diseases of other glands (eg. adrenal glands, testes, parathyroids); extreme high blood pressure (eg. phaeochromocytoma) and anaemia (a lack of haemoglobin and/or red blood cells).

A wide range of medications (eg. for control of high blood pressure, epilepsy and cancer) may cause headache as a side effect.

Uncommon causes of headache include SUNCT syndrome (variant of cluster headache), poorly controlled diabetes (either high sugar levels from lack of treatment, or low blood sugar from excess medication), severe allergy reactions (anaphylaxis), acromegaly (thickening and enlargement of the bones in the skull and legs), Cushing syndrome (over production or over dosage of steroids), low blood pressure (eg. from excessive medication, sudden change in position, shock or fright), failure or inflammation of any of the body's major organs (eg. kidneys, spleen or liver), pre-eclampsia (severe complication of pregnancy that is associated with a rise in blood pressure), autoimmune diseases (eg. systemic lupus erythematosus, rheumatoid arthritis, scleroderma), inflammation of arteries in the neck (carotodynia) or temples (giant cell or temporal arteritis), Paget's disease (softening of bone throughout the body), toxic shock syndrome and many other causes that have not been included. Almost any abnormality in the body may result in some kind of headache when our brain, or its surrounding structures, perceives the disorder in body function.

See also CLUSTER HEADACHE;
MIGRAINE and separate entries for diseases mentioned above.

HEAD INJURY

Any patient who sustains a head injury, even if it appears to be mild, should be checked by a doctor. If after being checked the person shows no serious signs of damage, he or she can go home and expect that recovery will follow within twenty-four hours. However, rarely, complications may follow at any time over the next few days.

The brain is housed, very compactly, in the rigid skull, and cannot tolerate any increase in pressure. If pressure increases due to bleeding or swelling from fluid then pressure is exerted on the base of the brain which contains the vital centres controlling such functions as breathing and heart action.

Someone should keep the patient under close observation over the next twenty-four hours at least, and take them to a doctor immediately if any of the features below are noticed. The problems may occur gradually and certain warning signs will develop that indicate the pressure will have to be relieved by surgery.

Watch for: –
• Unconsciousness or undue drowsiness.
• Confused, irrational or delirious behaviour.
• Headache which continues.
• Bleeding from an ear.
• Repeated vomiting.
• Fits or spasms.
• Blurred or double vision.

Other points to consider: –
• Diet – food and drink should be consumed in moderation for twenty-four hours.
• Alcohol – nil for twenty-four hours.
• Drugs – no medication unless instructed by doctor. Paracetamol is allowed.
• Rest – no physical exercise for twenty-four hours. Use a flat pillow. Do not drive a vehicle.
See also COMA; CONCUSSION;
GLASGOW COMA SCALE;
SUBARACHNOID HAEMORRHAGE;
SUBDURAL HAEMATOMA

HEAD, LARGE

A child may be born with a large head or develop one during infancy, or it may be a problem that starts in adult life. In infancy the usual cause is hydrocephalus, and if this occurs before birth, the large head may obstruct labour necessitating delivery by caesarean section.

The brain is surrounded by a supportive fluid (cerebrospinal fluid – CSF) and interconnected cavities within the brain also contain CSF. If there is too much CSF produced, or insufficient absorbed, the pressure of this fluid in and around the brain will gradually increase to cause the steadily enlarging head of babies who have hydrocephalus.

Acromegaly is caused by excess production of growth hormone in the pituitary gland, which sits underneath the brain. This hormone is required during the normal growth of a child, but if it is produced inappropriately later in life, abnormal bone growth occurs in the hands, feet, jaw, face, tongue and internal organs. Patients also suffer from headaches, sweating, weakness and loss of vision. The most common reason for the excess production of growth hormone is the development of a tumour in the pituitary gland, but occasionally tumours elsewhere can secrete abnormal amounts of the hormone.

Proteus syndrome is a very rare condition that causes unequal bone growth in the head, arms and legs to greatly increase the head size, and wrinkled bumps form on the face, feet and hands. This is believed to be the cause of John Merrick's 'Elephant Man' deformity.
See also ACROMEGALY;
HYDROCEPHALUS and separate entries for diseases mentioned above.

HEAD LICE
This is an infestation of the hairs on the scalp by the 2-3 mm long human head louse, *Pediculus capitis*, which is an insect that lives on human hairs and survives by sucking blood from the skin. They are very common and spread from one person to another very quickly by close contact, by sharing a brush or comb, or by wearing another person's hat. The female louse lays eggs and glues them to the hairs. They hatch after six days, grow into adults capable of further reproduction in about ten days and live for four to six weeks. The nits that can be seen firmly attached to hairs are the egg cases. Often there are no symptoms, but in severe cases there may be a mild itching on the scalp. The most common areas for them to congregate are the forehead and behind the ears.

It is advisable to treat all the members of a family with lotions or shampoos that contain malathion or gamma benzene hexachloride. Treatment should be repeated weekly for two or three weeks to kill insects as they hatch.

The hair does not need to be cut short unless there are repeated infestations. Eggs that remain after treatment should be removed by a fine comb. Another very effective method of treatment is to wash the hair and apply conditioner, but do not rinse out the conditioner, and the lice will be unable to grasp the hair and can be combed out.

Lice cannot survive for long away from humans, so clothing and pillows need only normal washing and no special treatment. If there is any doubt about the diagnosis, or the problem becomes recurrent, medical advice should be sought. Exclusion of children with head lice from school is only necessary until proper treatment has been given. A cure is possible with correct treatment.
See also ANTIPARASITICS; CRABS

HEAD PAIN
See FACE PAIN; HEADACHE

HEAD, SMALL
An obviously small head (microcephaly) may be an inherited characteristic because one or both parents have a small head, or it may be a sign of a serious underlying defect. Several rare congenital (present since conception) conditions may cause significant microcephaly.

Angleman syndrome (also known as the happy puppet syndrome) is due to a genetic defect and causes damage to lungs and liver, deep set eyes, mental retardation and a prominent forehead on a small head.

De Lange syndrome (also known as Amsterdam dwarfism) is a rare genetic defect that results in microcephaly, severe mental retardation, bushy eyebrows that meet in the centre, low birth weight, below normal growth, excessive body and head hair and death in late childhood.

Langer-Giedion syndrome is another rare genetic defect. It is characterised by sparse hair, bulbous nose, bony protrusions and a small head, but intelligence is often reasonable, and defects can be corrected by plastic surgery.

Craniostenosis is caused by a premature fusing of the sutures between the bones of the skull, thereby preventing normal growth of the skull.
See also CRANIOSTENOSIS; de LANGE
SYNDROME; MENTAL RETARDATION

HEARING
See DEAF; EAR; HEARING TESTS;
TINNITUS

HEARING TESTS
The most basic test for hearing simply involves the doctor talking and making sounds to see if the patient can hear them. Generally the doctor will sit about six metres away, whisper numbers and then repeat them in a normal voice. You will listen first with one ear and then with the other. An experienced doctor can assess hearing loss quite accurately using this method.

A similar test uses a tuning fork to test the ability to hear tones conducted by air and by the bones of your head.

A more scientific way of evaluating hearing is using an audiometer. This is a device that produces pure tones of a certain pitch and loudness. The first part of the test measures the ability to hear air-conducted sounds and involves listening through earphones to tones of different pitch and volume, or to spoken words. The patient is asked to signal when they can hear something, or to repeat the words. The second part of the test measures the ability to hear bone-conducted sounds. For this, an oscillating device is placed on the bone behind each ear, and the patient is asked to signal when a tone is heard.
See also DEAF; EAR

HEART
Despite the emotional mystique often attributed to it, the heart is simply a very efficient pump. It is crucial to the maintenance of life, but no more so than many other organs such as the liver or kidneys.

The heart (cardia) is the centre of the circulatory system. It lies high up behind the breastbone (sternum) and between the lungs, and is not unlike a mango both in shape and size. One corner extends outwards towards the left nipple.

Basically the heart is a muscular pump with four separate chambers into which enter the major blood vessels carrying blood to and from the rest of the body. The two upper chambers (the atria) which receive blood are much smaller than the two lower chambers (the ventricles) which pump it out.

The right side of the heart deals with blood that has been used throughout the body and so is depleted of oxygen. This blood comes into the heart via the upper right chamber, passes immediately through a valve into the lower right chamber and a split second later is pumped out into the lungs where the poisonous carbon dioxide it has collected in the body is removed and the blood is replenished with oxygen. The oxygen-enriched blood is then dealt with by the left side of the heart. It travels from the lungs into the upper left chamber and is pumped out through the lower left chamber to the rest of the body for another circuit.

The left and right sides of the heart are roughly similar in shape but the left side, which has to be strong enough to pump blood to the furthest parts of the body – even the fingers and toes – is larger and more muscular. Hence the heart has a somewhat asymmetrical appearance. The two sides of the heart are completely sealed from one another. To get from one side of the heart to another, blood has to go through the lungs or the entire circulatory system.

When it leaves the left side of the heart, the blood passes into the major artery, the aorta, and from there travels along the network of arteries into the smaller arterioles and finally into capillaries from where it is absorbed into the cells. From there it moves back through the veins to the heart again, completing the cycle. It takes about twenty seconds for one blood cell to complete the full cycle. In the major arteries, blood travels at about two kilometres an hour.

At rest, the heart beats at about seventy times a minute. With exercise or increased activity the rate increases until it may reach as much as 200 beats a minute. The number of beats a minute is called the heart or pulse rate. Each contraction moves about 80mLs of blood, but that adds up to over 8000 litres a day.

The heart rate is regulated by electrical impulses generated by the pacemaker within the heart. Without any assistance, the heart would beat about forty times a minute. However, this would not be enough for all the activities the body is required to perform so there is a sort of spark plug to push the rate up higher. This consists of a group of special nerves, forming what is commonly known as a pacemaker, which produces an electrical charge and raises the heart rate as demand

HEART

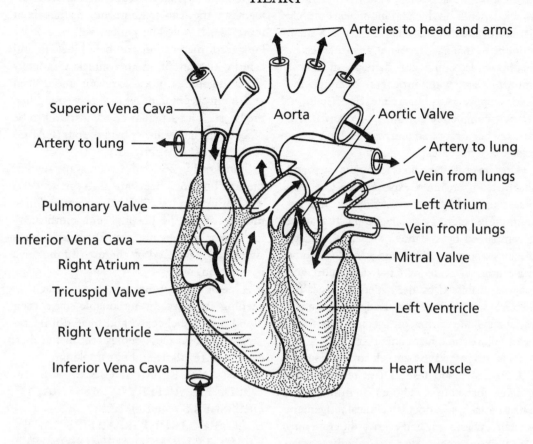

Arteries to head and arms

Superior Vena Cava

Aorta

Aortic Valve

Artery to lung

Artery to lung

Vein from lungs

Pulmonary Valve

Left Atrium

Inferior Vena Cava

Vein from lungs

Right Atrium

Mitral Valve

Tricuspid Valve

Left Ventricle

Right Ventricle

Inferior Vena Cava

Heart Muscle

requires. The pacemaker is located on the right atrium, and a large nerve (the bundle of His) connects it to the two ventricles.

The heart is made up of three main layers. The outer fibrous layer is called the pericardium and is generally surrounded by a thin protective layer of fat. The innermost layer is called the endocardium and is a thin smooth lining for the inner surfaces of the heart chambers and valves. The middle layer or myocardium is the thickest and most important. It consists mostly of muscle and it is the contraction and relaxation of this muscle that results in the heart's pumping action. In normal circumstances, this pump continues to operate without stopping for our entire life, probably seventy or eighty years. If the pumping system fails in any way (eg. due to the heart not receiving enough oxygen, the lungs becoming damaged by disease, clots blocking an artery, extreme blood loss or any other cause) the victim will become severely ill or die.

See also ANGINA; AORTA; AORTIC VALVE; ARTERIES; BLOOD PRESSURE; CARDIOMYOPATHY; CHEST PAIN; CONGESTIVE CARDIAC FAILURE; ECHOCARDIOGRAPHY; ELECTROCARDIOGRAM; ENDOCARDITIS; FALLOT'S TETRALOGY; HARVEY, WILLIAM; HEART ATTACK; HEART MURMUR; HYPERTENSION; INTERMEDIATE CORONARY SYNDROME; MITRAL VALVE; MYOCARDITIS; PACEMAKER; PALPITATIONS; PULMONARY VALVE; PULSE; SPHYGMOMANOMETER; TRICUSPID VALVE; VEIN etc.

HEART ATTACK

A heart attack (myocardial infarct, MI) is caused by a blockage of the arterial blood supply to heart muscle for sufficient time to cause the affected muscle to die and be replaced by fibrous scar tissue. All the blood to the heart muscle passes through three small coronary arteries. If one of these is blocked, one part of the heart muscle cannot obtain sufficient blood and it dies. The arteries may be blocked by fatty deposits because the patient is overweight or has high cholesterol levels, by clots or fat globules breaking off from damaged blood vessels elsewhere in the body, or by damage to the artery from high blood pressure. The severity of a heart attack depends on the amount of heart muscle damaged, and its position in the heart. A small amount of damage in a vital area may cause death, while significant damage in a less important area will not be fatal. In angina the blood supply to the heart muscle is reduced but not completely cut off, so no permanent damage occurs, but angina may lead to a heart attack in some cases.

A severe crushing pain is felt in the chest and shortness of breath is experienced. The pain builds up rapidly in waves, then persists for some time before gradually fading. It may be accompanied by sweating, weakness, anxiety, dizziness, cough, nausea and vomiting. Some heart attacks create minimal discomfort and may be dismissed by the patient as a passing attack of severe indigestion. Long-term complications include angina, an irregular heartbeat, heart failure and a heart aneurysm.

It is diagnosed by an electrocardiogram (ECG) and blood tests. These tests may be negative for a couple of hours after the start of a heart attack, so a doctor's clinical judgement is vital. A chest x-ray and echocardiogram may also be performed. After the initial recovery period, echocardiography, coronary angiography and nuclear scans may be performed to find the cause of the heart attack and to determine further surgical or medical treatment.

If someone is having a heart attack, call an ambulance and if necessary carry out mouth-to-mouth or cardiopulmonary resuscitation. If the victim is conscious, help them into a position in which they are comfortable, and loosen clothing around the neck, chest and waist. Give them a soluble aspirin to suck in the mouth, as aspirin reduces the rate at which blood clots and so can protect against the worsening of a heart attack. If the victim is breathing but unconscious, place them on their side in the coma position.

Once the patient is under the care of a doctor, their chance of survival is good, because medication can be given to stop an abnormal heartbeat, relieve pain and ease the intense anxiety of the patient. Once in hospital, treatment in a coronary care unit will include drugs to break up the blood clot blocking the coronary artery and a complex cocktail of other medications given through a drip into a vein to regulate the functioning of the heart. After a few days, the patient is moved to a normal ward and after ten to fourteen days they can go home for a further six or more weeks rest. The patient will be put on long term medication (eg. beta-blockers and aspirin) to prevent another attack. Gradually increasing levels of exercise are undertaken over many weeks in order to slowly strengthen the heart. If a particular artery is found to be blocked, coronary artery bypass graft (CABG) surgery may be performed.

Statistically, 20% of patients die within the first hour of a heart attack, a further 10% will die in hospital, 5% will die within three months of leaving hospital and another 3% in every year thereafter, but the death rate is significantly lowered by the use of long term medication.

A person can prevent a heart attack by keeping their weight reasonable, have their blood pressure checked and treated if necessary, avoiding excess cholesterol in the diet, exercising regularly and not smoking.
See also ANEURYSM; ANGINA; CORONARY ARTERY BYPASS GRAFT; DRESSLER SYNDROME; ELECTROCARDIOGRAM; FIRST AID; HEART; INTERMEDIATE CORONARY SYNDROME; RESUSCITATION; STOKES-ADAMS SYNDROME; UNCONSCIOUS

HEARTBEAT RAPID
See TACHYCARDIA

HEARTBURN
Heartburn is a form of indigestion which causes a burning pain behind the breast bone in the centre of the chest. It is often associated with burping and a bitter taste at the back of the throat. The cause is a leakage of concentrated hydrochloric acid from the stomach up into the gullet (oesophagus) which runs from the back of the throat, down through the chest to the stomach. The stomach is lined with a thick layer of acid resistant mucus, but the oesophagus lacks this protection, and any stomach acid entering it causes burning pain.

Common simple causes include over eating, rapid eating, excess alcohol consumption and advanced pregnancy (pressure of the enlarged womb causes acid to be forced up into the oesophagus from the stomach). Smoking can be an aggravating factor in all causes of heartburn.

More serious causes include inflammation of the oesophagus from acid repeatedly coming up from the stomach (reflux oesophagitis) and a hiatus hernia (part of the stomach slips up into the chest cavity).

Sometimes a peptic ulcer (ulceration of the stomach from excess acid production) or, rarely, a cancer of the stomach or oesophagus, may cause heartburn.

A number of serious conditions may cause pain in the chest that can be mistaken for heartburn. A heart attack is the most common of these, but a blood clot in the lungs, angina, (reduced blood supply to the heart) and inflammation of the membrane around the heart (pericarditis) may also be responsible. As a result, any heartburn not responding rapidly to simple medications (eg. antacids) must be checked by a doctor.
See also ANTACIDS; CHEST PAIN; H2 RECEPTOR ANTAGONISTS; HEARTBURN IN PREGNANCY; OESOPHAGUS and separate entries for diseases mentioned above.

HEARTBURN

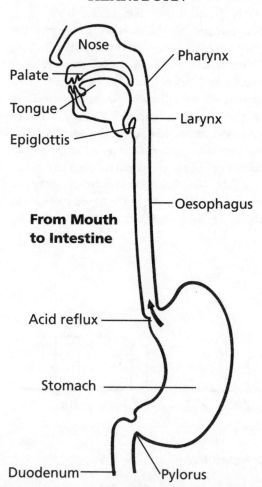

From Mouth to Intestine

Nose
Pharynx
Palate
Tongue
Larynx
Epiglottis
Oesophagus
Acid reflux
Stomach
Duodenum
Pylorus

HEARTBURN IN PREGNANCY
Indigestion or heartburn affects about half of all pregnant women because during pregnancy the muscle that closes off the upper part of the stomach from the oesophagus (gullet) loosens and allows digestive juices from the stomach to flow back up the oesophagus and irritate it. In late pregnancy the enlarging uterus presses on the stomach and aggravates the condition.

Heartburn can be very uncomfortable but is not harmful. Symptoms may be reduced by eating small, frequent meals so that there is never too much food present but always enough to absorb the stomach acid. Antacids can usually be taken safely at most stages of pregnancy, and may be used to relieve more severe symptoms. The problem disappears when the baby is born.
See also HEARTBURN; PREGNANCY

HEART, EXTRA BEATS
Occasional extra irregular beats (extrasystoles) of the heart are relatively common, and are of no concern provided they do not occur more than once a minute. If they occur more frequently than this for several hours, and for no apparent reason, consult a doctor.

Common causes include unusually vigorous exercise, smoking, overindulgence in alcohol or coffee (caffeine), illegal drugs and medications such as pseudoephedrine (Sudafed), salbutamol (Ventolin) or digoxin (Lanoxin).

Some people are born with electrical short circuits in the heart which cause multiple extrasystoles, and the necessity for treatment will depend upon the effects these extra beats have on the function of the heart and body.

Extrasystoles may also be caused by significant diseases such as a heart attack, heart muscle disease, abnormalities of the heart pacemaker and its connecting nerves, very high blood pressure, severe allergy reaction (anaphylaxis), an over active thyroid gland in the neck (hyperthyroidism) and imbalances in the essential blood chemistry (eg. too little or too much salt or potassium).
See also ARRHYTHMIA; HEART; PALPITATIONS and separate entries for diseases mentioned above.

HEART FAILURE
See CARDIOMYOPATHY; CONGESTIVE CARDIAC FAILURE; COR PULMONALE

HEART FAST
See PALPITATIONS

HEART INFECTION
See ENDOCARDITIS; MYOCARDITIS; PERICARDITIS

HEART MEDICATIONS
See ACE INHIBITORS; ALPHA BLOCKERS; ANTIANGINALS; ANTIARRHYTHMICS; BETA-BLOCKERS; CALCIUM CHANNEL BLOCKERS; DIGOXIN; DIURETICS

HEART MURMUR
A heart murmur is any abnormal sound heard by a doctor when listening to the heart through a stethoscope or with another amplifying device. Only in very rare situations is a patient aware of a heart murmur themselves. An abnormality in the rhythm of the heart, when it beats irregularly, slowly, rapidly, has extra beats or misses beats, is not a murmur.

Heart murmurs are caused by a disturbance to the smooth flow of blood through the heart, due to an abnormality in one of the four valves in the heart, a structural abnormality of the heart (eg. abnormal hole between two chambers) or an increased rate of flow through the heart. Doctors will describe murmurs in several different ways, which enables them to communicate what they are hearing to other doctors, but will mean little to a layperson.

Many murmurs are of no consequence and, particularly in infants, may disappear as the child grows older.

At birth, an artery beside the heart which enables blood to bypass the lungs while they are not in use in the mother's womb, must close to enable blood to circulate effectively through the lungs so that the blood can receive sufficient oxygen to supply the body. If this artery (the ductus arteriosus) fails to close, a constant 'machinery' murmur may be heard. Surgery or medication may be used to close this abnormal artery.

Doctors describe the heart as having two main sounds, a softer first sound and a louder second sound, caused by the closing of different valves. Between the two sounds which are closer together, the heart is contracting. In the slightly longer gap between the end of the second sound and the start of the next first sound, the heart is relaxed.

Murmurs heard between the first and second heart sounds are called 'systolic' murmurs, and may be caused by vigourous exercise, leakage of the mitral or tricuspid valves (between the upper and lower chambers of the heart on each side), narrowing of the pulmonary and aortic valves (that open into the arteries supplying the lung and body), a hole between the two sides of the heart (septal defect), severe anaemia, a high fever, heart muscle disease, and a number of rare conditions. The way in which the murmur fluctuates between the two heart sounds will give the doctor further clues as to the cause.

Murmurs heard after the second heart sound, and before the start of the next first sound, are called 'diastolic' murmurs. They may be caused by narrowing of the mitral or tricuspid valves, leakage of the aortic or pulmonary valves, anaemia, a hole in the heart or the failure of the ductus arteriosus to close.

Other less common murmurs may be caused by an increase in the blood pressure in the lungs, electrical conduction disturbances

HEART SOUNDS

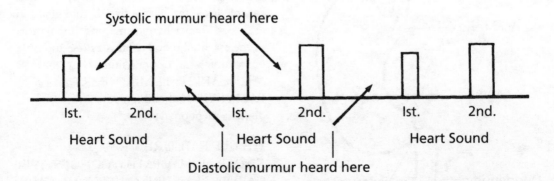

Systolic murmur heard here

1st. 2nd. 1st. 2nd. 1st. 2nd.

Heart Sound | Heart Sound | Heart Sound

Diastolic murmur heard here

in the heart, failure of a damaged heart to contract properly or an aneurysm (dilation) of one part of the heart wall.
See also ECHOCARDIOGRAPHY; HEART and separate entries for diseases mentioned above.

HEART SLOW
See PULSE SLOW

HEART SURGERY
See CORONARY ARTERY BYPASS GRAFT

HEART TUMOUR
See MYXOMA

HEART VALVE
See AORTIC VALVE; FALLOT'S TETRALOGY; MITRAL VALVE; PULMONARY VALVE; TRICUSPID VALVE

HEAT STROKE
Heat stroke is a failure of temperature regulation by the brain due to overloading the body's cooling mechanisms due to a combination of a hot environment, exertion and dehydration. It is a common problem in endurance athletes, soldiers and the elderly.

Victims develop a fever over 41°C, sweating stops, they becomes dizzy, weak, nauseated, confused, start vomiting and eventually become comatose and may convulse. Extreme cases may cause kidney failure, muscle breakdown, irregular heart beat, heart attack, liver failure and blood clots (thromboses), with blood tests showing abnormal biochemistry and high levels of white blood cells.

First aid is cool (not cold) water immersion or water spray and fan, followed by intravenous fluids and medication to control shivering and prevent fitting. Regular blood tests are performed to monitor progress. It may be fatal if untreated, but responds well to appropriate management, although permanent organ damage is possible.
See also DEHYDRATION; SWEATING LACK

HEAVY METAL POISONING
See LEAD POISONING; MERCURY POISONING; PEWTER

HEEL BONE
See CALCANEUS

HEEL SPUR
Beneath and behind the heel, large ligaments and tendons attach to the calcaneus (heel bone). The attachment can be stressed and inflamed by prolonged over use or by a sudden injury. After injuring a tendon or ligament attachment, the healing process will involve both the tendon or ligament and the bone to which it attaches. During the healing process, part of the ligament or tendon may be replaced by bone, leading to a spur of bone jutting out from the calcaneus. Spurs are subject to further injury and may have tiny microscopic stress fractures in them, involving the equally tiny nerves in the area, causing chronic pain.

Pain and tenderness occur at the site of the spur formation behind or under the heel and are worsened by exercise. Spurs can be seen on an x-ray.

Prolonged rest and thick padded insoles in shoes will ease the pain, but further use often results in a recurrence. Active treatment involves the use of painkillers, heat, anti-inflammatory medications, physiotherapy, steroid injections or, as a last resort, an operation to remove the spur. Steroid injections are often very effective, but if used too frequently, can actually damage the surrounding tissue. Satisfactory treatment is sometimes difficult but usually eventually succeeds.
See also CALCANEUS; FOOT PAIN

HEIGHT
See GROWTH REDUCED; HEIGHT EXCESSIVE

HEIGHT EXCESSIVE
Very tall people are usually that way because their parents (or grandparents) were also tall. Most of a tall person's height comes from the increased length of the femur, tibia and fibula bones in the legs. The better nutrition and health of people in the last few decades has also meant people are becoming steadily taller every generation. The average height of men has risen by more than three centimetres in the last fifty years.

Some children grow faster and earlier than others, so a child at twelve may be far taller than others of the same age, but may stop growing sooner and have an average final height. Children who start puberty earlier than normal will often be tall early in life, but normal in adulthood. Special x-rays of the wrist can be done between about eight and fifteen years of age to give a reasonably accurate estimate of final height. Only if this gives an estimate of a severely abnormal height will any medical steps be taken to prevent the growth.

A wide range of medical conditions and rare syndromes may cause excessive growth. The classic one is a disease or a tumour of the pituitary gland in the brain, or a tumour in the brain itself, which results in the excessive production of growth hormone from the gland. This hormone determines the rate at which the body grows in childhood and the teens. If control of its release from the pituitary gland is lost, or too much is produced, the person will grow inappropriately. Surgery to the pituitary gland is essential to control this serious problem, as major organs of the body may be adversely affected by being too large.

A failure of puberty to occur may result in growth continuing into the twenties. Diseases which affect the function of the testes (eg. Klinefelter syndrome) or ovaries (eg. multiple large cysts) may cause this problem.

In children, overactivity of the thyroid gland in the neck or the adrenal glands on top of each kidney may also cause gigantism.

Marfan syndrome is a genetic defect that causes long limbs and fingers, a thin body and heart defects.

XYY syndrome occurs when two Y carrying sperm fuse with one X carrying egg at the moment of conception. These men are very tall, strong, of large build and inclined to violence.
See also PITUITARY GLAND and separate entries for diseases mentioned above.

HEIGHT FEAR
See ACROPHOBIA

HEIGHT REDUCED
See GROWTH REDUCED

HEIMLICH MANOEUVRE
The Heimlich manoeuvre is a method of relieving a person who is choking on inhaled food or other object.

The helper should wrap their arms around the victim's chest from behind, and place the clenched fists over the breast bone. Then as suddenly and as hard as possible, they should pull back on the breast bone and squeeze the victim's chest between their fists and arms, and their own chest. The procedure may need to be repeated several times, but there is a risk of breaking ribs, particularly if the victim is smaller than the helper.
See also CHOKING

HEINER SYNDROME
The Heiner syndrome is a cow's milk allergy reaction in the lungs with the symptoms of anaemia, persistent lung inflammation (eg. asthma) and infection (eg. bronchitis). Blood tests show an inflammatory reaction and presence of large numbers of inflammatory cells, and a chest x-ray may be abnormal. Patients must avoid dairy products and lung symptoms are treated. Serious lung infections and permanent scarring of lungs may occur. In most patients reasonable control is possible, but no cure exists.
See also ASTHMA; BRONCHITIS; LUNG

HELICOBACTER PYLORI
See PEPTIC ULCER

HELMINTHS
Helminths is a collective term for worms derived from the Greek word *helminis* which means worm. It includes most types of worm that may invade humans.
See also GUINEA WORM; HOOKWORM; HYDATID DISEASE; PINWORM; STRONGYLOIDIASIS; TAPEWORM; TRICHURIASIS; WORMS

HEMIANOPIA
See VISION HALF LOST

HEMIPLEGIA
See MUSCLE WEAKNESS; PARAPLEGIA AND QUADRIPLEGIA

HENDRA VIRUS
The Hendra virus (equine morbillivirus) is a very rare paramyxovirus infection of the brain that spreads from bats to horses and then humans causing a form of encephalitis. Only two cases have ever occurred, both in Queensland in 1994, and the disease is named after the Brisbane suburb in which the racecourse

was located at which the first case was diagnosed. Headache, fever, rash, drowsiness, disorientation and convulsions are the observed symptoms. No treatment is available other than general supportive measures in hospital, and both patients affected died.

See also VIRUS

HENOCH-SCHOENLEIN SYNDROME

The Henoch-Schoenlein syndrome (anaphylactoid purpura) is a generalised inflammation of small blood vessels resulting in the formation of small red spots in the skin. It may be a complication of a number of different diseases, but its cause is often unknown. It is more common in children.

Small, slightly raised dilated blood vessels (purpura) appear on the skin as red or purple patches about five to ten millimetres across. There may also be bleeding into the intestine, lungs, kidneys and joints to cause belly pain, coughing of blood, blood in the urine and arthritis.

It is diagnosed by biopsy of one of the purpura in the skin, but no treatment is normally necessary as the condition is self-limiting and usually settles without serious long term problems in one to six weeks. If the kidneys become involved medical treatment is necessary, as long term kidney damage may occur.

See also SKIN RED SPOTS

HEPARIN
See ANTICOAGULANTS

HEPARINOID
See LINIMENT

HEPAT-

'Hepat-' is a prefix used in medicine to indicate conditions affecting the liver (eg. hepatitis, hepatomegaly). It is derived from both the Greek and Latin word for the liver (*hepar*).

HEPATOLENTICULAR DEGENERATION
See WILSON DISEASE

HEPATIC ABSCESS
See LIVER ABSCESS

HEPATIC CARCINOMA
See LIVER CANCER

HEPATIC METASTASES
See METASTATIC CANCER

HEPATITIS

Hepatitis is a term that indicates any inflammation or infection of the liver. There are many different types and causes of hepatitis.
See also GALLSTONES; HEPATITIS A; HEPATITIS B; HEPATITIS C; HEPATITIS D; HEPATITIS E; JAUNDICE; LIVER

HEPATITIS A

Hepatitis A (infective hepatitis) is a viral infection of the liver caught by eating food that has been contaminated by someone who has the disease. The virus lives in the liver, but large numbers pass down the bile duct into the gut and into the faeces. If sufferers are not careful with their personal hygiene, the virus may be passed on to someone else. When hepatitis A virus particles are swallowed, they are absorbed with the food into the bloodstream and migrate to the liver where, after an incubation period lasting two to six weeks, they start multiplying and cause damage to liver cells. Patients may pass on the virus for a week or two before they develop any symptoms. The vital preventative factor is the standard of hygiene in the community.

The liver is used by the body to process food and eliminate waste products through bile which passes into the gut. If the liver is damaged, it cannot work efficiently, and the main constituent of bile (bilirubin) builds up in the blood stream. Because of the yellow colour of bilirubin, the skin slowly turns a dark yellow (jaundice). The whites of the eyes are affected first, and this may be the only sign of the disease in a dark-skinned person. Other symptoms are nausea, vomiting, marked tiredness, loss of appetite, generalised aches and pains, fever and a large tender liver.

Blood tests are available to diagnose the type of hepatitis and monitor its progress.

The main treatment is bed rest and a diet low in protein and high in carbohydrate, and alcohol is forbidden. Sometimes it is necessary to give medication for nausea and vomiting and to feed severely affected patients by a drip into a vein for a short time. If it continues to worsen, drugs may be used to reduce the liver damage. In rare cases (two in 1000), the disease may progress despite all efforts of doctors and result in death, but this is more common in the elderly. Hepatitis A can be prevented by a vaccine that may be combined with the vaccine against hepatitis B.

There is usually an initial worsening of the symptoms, followed by a slow recovery period that may take from one to four months. In children, it may occur entirely without symptoms. Permanent liver damage is uncommon. *See also* HEPATITIS B; HEPATITIS C; HEPATITIS D; HEPATITIS E; JAUNDICE; LIVER; VIRUS

HEPATITIS B

Hepatitis B (serum hepatitis) is a viral infection of the liver that can only be caught by intimate contact with the blood or semen of a person who has the disease or is a carrier of the disease. Examples include receiving blood from a carrier, using a contaminated needle, rubbing a graze or cut on an infected person's graze or cut, being bitten by an infected person, or most commonly by having sex (homosexual or heterosexual) with him or her. Ninety percent of babies born to mothers who are carriers catch the disease. The highest incidences are amongst homosexual men, drug addicts who share needles, Australian Aborigines, and the disease is widespread in southeast Asia. Blood banks screen all donations for hepatitis B. Splashes of blood into an eye or onto a cut or graze can spread the disease, and doctors, dentists, nurses and other health workers are therefore at risk.

There is a long incubation period of six weeks to six months, and the infection cannot be detected during this period. Once active it causes the patient to become very ill with a liver infection, fever, jaundice (yellow skin), nausea and loss of appetite. Some patients develop only a very mild form of the disease but they are still contagious and may suffer the long term effects.

Blood tests are available to diagnose the type of hepatitis and monitor its progress.

Treatment involves bed rest and a diet low in protein and high in carbohydrate, and alcohol is forbidden. Sometimes it is necessary to give medication for nausea and vomiting and to feed severely affected patients by a drip into a vein for a short time. If it continues to worsen, drugs may be used to reduce the liver damage. It is possible to vaccinate against hepatitis B.

Patients must ensure they are no longer infectious before having sex with anyone and should have regular blood tests throughout their life to detect any liver damage. Nine out of ten patients recover completely after a few weeks, but one in ten becomes a chronic carrier. Ten percent of patients develop cirrhosis, failure of the liver or liver cancer, and about one percent of patients develop a rapidly progressive liver disease that causes death. *See also* HEPATITIS A; HEPATITIS C; HEPATITIS D; HEPATITIS E; JAUNDICE; LIVER CANCER; VIRUS

HEPATITIS C

Hepatitis C is a viral infection of the liver transmitted from one person to another through blood contamination – most often the sharing of needles by drug users. All blood donations are screened for this virus. Sexual transmission is possible but uncommon, and the incubation period is six to seven weeks.

The symptoms are usually mild, and the patient may only be vaguely unwell for a few days, but a minority progress to develop jaundice, liver enlargement and nausea. About a quarter of patients develop permanent liver damage, often after many years.

Blood tests are available to diagnose the type of hepatitis and monitor its progress.

Treatment involves bed rest and a diet low in protein and high in carbohydrate, and alcohol is forbidden. Sometimes it is necessary to give medication for nausea and vomiting and to feed severely affected patients by a drip into a vein for a short time. If it continues to worsen, drugs may be used to reduce the liver damage. Unfortunately it is not yet possible to vaccinate against hepatitis C.

No cure is available, but many patients lead normal long lives, although about a quarter eventually develop cirrhosis and liver failure. *See also* CIRRHOSIS; HEPATITIS A; HEPATITIS B; HEPATITIS D; HEPATITIS E; JAUNDICE; LIVER; VIRUS

HEPATITIS D

Hepatitis D is a viral infection of the liver that can only be caught by patients who already have hepatitis B. The two diseases may be caught at the same time or separately. Hepatitis D is much more common in intravenous drug users with hepatitis B than in patients who have caught hepatitis B in other ways, and it is also more prevalent in countries around the Mediterranean.

If hepatitis D is caught at a later time than hepatitis B, there are usually no symptoms, but the second infection increases the risk of developing serious liver disease. Blood tests are available to diagnose the type of hepatitis and monitor its progress.

Usually no treatment is necessary, but in severe cases, drugs may be used to reduce the liver damage. There is no specific vaccine against hepatitis D, but vaccination against hepatitis B effectively prevents both diseases.

No cure is available, and most patients lead normal lives, but many eventually develop cirrhosis, liver failure or liver cancer. *See also* CIRRHOSIS; HEPATITIS A; HEPATITIS B; HEPATITIS C; HEPATITIS E; JAUNDICE; LIVER CANCER; VIRUS

HEPATITIS E
Hepatitis E is a viral infection of the liver caught from contaminated food and water in the same way as hepatitis A. It is rare in western countries with the highest incidence being in central Asia, Algeria and Mexico. Patients become jaundiced, are nauseated and tired, vomit, have no appetite, and develop aches, pains, a fever and a large tender liver. Blood tests are available to diagnose the type of hepatitis and monitor its progress.

The immediate death rate from hepatitis E is far higher than in other types of hepatitis, and may occur within a day or two of symptoms appearing. The death rate is far higher in pregnant women. Even so, most patients recover completely and there are no long term liver problems. There is no vaccine available, but a gammaglobulin injection will give short term protection. Scrupulous personal hygiene is vital.
See also HEPATITIS A; HEPATITIS B; HEPATITIS C; HEPATITIS D; JAUNDICE; LIVER

HEPATITIS F
There is no form of hepatitis known as hepatitis F.

HEPATITIS G
The GB virus was at one time thought to be a cause of hepatitis G, but recent research has found that although present in some patients with hepatitis, it was not actually responsible for the symptoms. The GB virus is transmitted from one person to another through blood contamination such as the sharing of needles by drug users, and probably by sex. The GB virus is found in about 2% of all people, and interestingly, it seems to confer some resistance to the progression of the AIDS virus from the early stages of the disease to the more serious later stages. Hepatitis G is a disease that was once thought to exist, but has now been removed from the list of liver infections.
See also HEPATITIS A; HEPATITIS B; HEPATITIS C; HEPATITIS D; HEPATITIS E

HEPATOLENTICULAR DEGENERATION
See WILSON DISEASE

HEPATOMA
See LIVER CANCER

HEPATOMEGALY
See LIVER ENLARGED

HERALD PATCH
See PITYRIASIS ROSEA

HERBALISM
See NATUROPATHY

HERNIA
A hernia occurs when tissue pushes its way from one area, where it is normally present, into another area, where it is not. It may pass through a very narrow opening in this process. Some hernias move back and forwards freely: others become trapped. If tightly trapped, the blood and nerve supply to the herniated tissue may be restricted and the tissue becomes painful and dies. If a piece of gut is in the hernia, the death of this tissue will cause gangrene, failure of the gut and death. A lump caused by a hernia may occur in the groin (inguinal or femoral hernia – may contain gut), around the umbilicus (umbilical hernia – usually contain fat, occasionally gut), at the site of a previous operation, or rarely may form a lump when weak areas between muscle are spread by increased pressure in the belly (ventral hernia above the umbilicus or lumbar

hernia in the loin). Surgical correction is appropriate in most cases, but very large hernias in the elderly may be controlled by a truss.

See also ABDOMINAL LUMP; FEMORAL HERNIA; HIATUS HERNIA; INCISIONAL HERNIA; INGUINAL HERNIA; SPIGELIAN HERNIA; UMBILICAL HERNIA

HEROIN

Narcotics, including codeine, pethidine, morphine and oxycodone, are derived from heroin and can be abused if taken regularly or excessively. Heroin is normally injected by addicts directly into a vein, but it may also be inhaled or eaten, when it has a much slower effect.

Heroin is refined from the milky juice of the opium poppy. Most abusers have personality disorders, antisocial behaviour or are placed in situations of extreme stress. Possibly one in every 100 people in developed countries is dependent upon illicit drugs, and a far higher percentage has experimented with them at one time or another.

It causes exaggerated happiness, relief of pain, a feeling of unreality, and a sensation of bodily detachment. Contracted pupils that do not respond to light are one sign of use. Tolerance develops quickly and, with time, higher and higher doses must be used to cause the same effect.

Heroin is often combined with abuse of alcohol, smoking and synthetic drugs. Physiological problems include vomiting, constipation, brain damage (personality changes, paranoia), nerve damage (persistent pins and needles or numbness), infertility, impotence, stunting of growth in children, difficulty in breathing (to the point of stopping breathing if given in high doses) and low blood pressure.

Withdrawal causes vomiting, diarrhoea, coughing, twitching, fever, crying, excessive sweating, generalised muscle pain, rapid breathing and an intense desire for the drug. These symptoms can commence within eight to twelve hours of the last dose, and peak at one to three days after withdrawal. Mild symptoms may persist for up to six months. As sterile techniques are often not followed when self-injecting, the veins and skin at the injection site become infected and scarred.

Blood and urine tests can detect the presence of narcotics.

The treatment options available for heroin or other narcotic addiction are: –
• Gradual withdrawal while receiving counselling and medical support.
• Immediate drug withdrawal ('cold turkey') while hospitalised in a specialised unit, sometimes combined with other drugs that are used temporarily to reduce the symptoms associated with the drug withdrawal.
• Substitution of heroin with a prescribed medication (eg. methadone) on a medium to long-term basis before it is slowly withdrawn.
• Naltrexone may be used to flush heroin from the body, and relieve the addiction within a few days, a process that must be undertaken under strict supervision in a specialised clinic. Naltrexone may also be used long term to reduce the desire for heroin.
• Halfway houses that remove the patient from the environment in which drug taking is encouraged.
• Individual or group psychotherapy.
• Education of intravenous drug users of the dangers associated with their habit (eg. the development of AIDS or hepatitis B).

One quarter of heroin addicts will die within ten years of commencing the habit as a direct result of the heroin use, and a rising proportion will die from complications of the intravenous injections such as AIDS, septicaemia and hepatitis B, C and D.

See also AIDS; COCAINE; ECSTASY; GAMMA-HYDROXYBUTYRATE; HEPATITIS B; KETAMINE; LSD; MARIJUANA; MESCALINE; NARCOTICS; STIMULANTS

HERPANGINA
See COXSACKIE VIRUS INFECTION; STOMATITIS

HERPES SIMPLEX TYPE ONE
See COLD SORE; ERYTHEMA MULTIFORME; WHITLOW

HERPES SIMPLEX TYPE TWO
See GENITAL HERPES

HERPES ZOSTER
See CHICKENPOX; RAMSAY-HUNT SYNDROME; SHINGLES

HERS SYNDROME
See GLYCOGEN STORAGE DISEASES

HIATUS HERNIA
In a hiatus hernia, part of the stomach slips up through the hole in the diaphragm where the oesophagus passes from the chest to the abdomen. They may be caused by increased pressure in the abdominal cavity from heavy lifting, obesity, tension (muscle spasm occurs), or slack ligaments in the diaphragm in the elderly.

There are two types of hiatus hernia: –
• Paraoesophageal hiatus hernias occur when a pocket of stomach slips up through the hole in the diaphragm beside the oesophagus. Most are small, but sometimes a large proportion of the stomach may push up into the chest.
• Sliding hiatus hernias (90% of hiatus hernias) result from the stomach sliding up into the chest, pushing the oesophagus further up into the chest.

Patients usually describe heartburn (usually worse at night when lying down, or after a meal), excessive burping, a bitter taste on the back of the tongue (waterbrash), difficulty in swallowing and sometimes pain from ulceration inside the hernia or pinching of the hernia. Further symptoms may include a feeling of fullness, and palpitations if a large hernia pushes onto the heart. Bleeding may occur from ulcers that form in the damaged part of the stomach.

A barium meal x-ray or gastroscopy is used to confirm the diagnosis.

Paraoesophageal hiatus hernias should be surgically repaired, unless the patient is elderly or in poor health, while sliding hiatus hernia can usually be treated with diet and medications that reduce the amount of acid secreted by the stomach or increase the emptying rate of the stomach and strengthen the valve at the lower end of the oesophagus. Frequent small meals, rather than three large meals a day, and a diet low in fat and high in protein is beneficial. Obese patients must lose weight.

Medications are usually very successful in controlling symptoms, and the results of surgery are generally good.
See also BARIUM MEAL; DIAPHRAGM; GASTROSCOPY; HERNIA; OESOPHAGUS; REFLUX OESOPHAGITIS; STOMACH

HiB INFECTION
See HAEMOPHILUS INFLUENZAE B INFECTION

HICCOUGH
See HICCUP

HICCUP
Hiccups (hiccoughs) are caused by repeated spasms of the diaphragm, which is a sheet of muscle across the body between the chest and the abdomen. When the diaphragm muscle contracts we breathe in, and the muscles relax as we breathe out. When the diaphragm contracts spasmodically, a small amount of air is suddenly forced into the lungs, causing the characteristic sound. Simple causes of hiccups include emotional stress, smoking, drinking excess alcohol, over eating, rapid eating, sudden changes in temperature, swallowing air when nervous and indigestion.

More seriously, hiccups may be due to inflammation of organs that touch the diaphragm. In the abdomen, the stomach may be inflamed by a peptic ulcer or hiatus hernia (part of the stomach slips up into the chest), or a diseased liver may irritate the diaphragm. In the chest, pleurisy (inflammation of the membrane around the lungs), pneumonia or heart disease may be the cause.

Irritation of the phrenic nerve, which runs from the brain to the diaphragm and controls its action, may cause hiccups. Tumours of the nerve or brain, or pinching of the nerve on its long route through the neck and chest, may be responsible.

Rarely, psychiatric disturbances may have intermittent hiccups as an attention-seeking feature.

The hiccups may be cured by a counter irritation or relieving the stomach pressure. Drinking water, holding a deep breath, a fright, swallowing a teaspoon full of table sugar, and burping are well-known remedies. Medications can be given to relax the diaphragm muscle in persistent cases. Rarely they may persist for days, weeks, months or years, and the causes need to be investigated and treated in these cases.
See also DIAPHRAGM and separate entries for diseases mentioned above.

HIGH BLOOD PRESSURE
See HYPERTENSION

HIP

The hip joint is the strongest in the body. The socket (acetabulum) is formed at the point where the three fused bones that make up the pelvis meet. The femur (thigh bone) has a ball at its upper end that forms the other half of the joint. The joint can move in every direction as well as rotate.

When a hip is broken, it is actually the neck of bone which joins the ball to the main part of the femur at an angle that breaks.
See also FEMUR; HIP DISLOCATION; HIP FRACTURE; HIP REPLACEMENT; JOINT; PELVIS; PERTHES' DISEASE

HIP JOINT

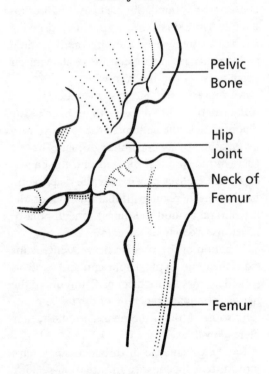

Pelvic Bone

Hip Joint

Neck of Femur

Femur

HIP DISLOCATION

The hip may be dislocated at birth (congenital dislocation), dislocated in a major injury (traumatic dislocation), or dislocated because of severe arthritis or joint infection (pathological dislocation). All types of dislocation are diagnosed by an x-ray.

CONGENITAL DISLOCATION

Some babies are born with one or both hips dislocated, or able to be easily dislocated. This is five times more common in girls than boys. There is a delay in walking, uneven skin folds on the buttocks and back of the legs, limping and a doctor can detect abnormal movement in the hips soon after birth. If detected early, most patients can be effectively cured by putting the baby's legs in a 'frog position' (widely spread) in a special splint or double nappies for three months. If this is not successful, or if the condition is not diagnosed until after the child is six months old, an operation to correct the dislocation is required. Good long term results are obtained with early treatment but in severe cases, an artificial hip may need to be inserted once the patient is fully grown.

TRAUMATIC DISLOCATION

Traumatic dislocation is a very serious injury that occurs in severe accidents. The hip joint is forcibly torn from its socket, and the surrounding ligaments and muscles are badly damaged. The dislocation may be associated with a fracture. Severe pain is felt in the hip and the patient is unable to move the leg. An operation is usually necessary to repair the damage, many months convalescence are required and permanent arthritis is often a consequence.

PATHOLOGICAL DISLOCATION

Pathological dislocation occurs because the joint is worn away, and weak elderly patients with very severe arthritis of the hip may dislocate the joint quite easily. In younger patients, a severe infection of the hip may partially destroy the joint and allow it to dislocate. There is often minimal pain, but patients are unable to walk or bear weight on the affected leg. Treatment depends on the degree of disability and the patient's general health, but an operation to replace the hip joint may be undertaken. Permanent disability is common, depending on the patient's general health.
See also DISLOCATION; FEMUR; HIP; HIP FRACTURE

HIP FRACTURE

A hip fracture is actually a fracture of the top of the thigh bone (the femur) that normally does not directly involve the hip joint itself. It usually occurs in elderly people, particularly women when falling on the side, often when the bone is thinned by osteoporosis. There is pain and loss of function of the hip, but some patients manage to disguise the injury remarkably well. An x-ray is used to confirm the diagnosis.

Orthopaedic surgeons usually totally replace the hip joint and the ball at the top of the femur, and patients are mobile again in only a few days. Other cases require surgery to fix the fracture in position with steel pins or screws, or many weeks in traction in bed. Failure to heal is common when the fracture is pinned and screwed and death of a fragment of bone due to an inadequate blood supply may occur. Infection is a rare possible complication with a hip replacement, and most hip replacements are very successful, but results are affected by the general health of the patient.

See also CHARNLEY, JOHN; FEMUR; FRACTURE; HIP REPLACEMENT; OSTEOPOROSIS

HIP NECROSIS
See AVASCULAR NECROSIS OF THE FEMORAL HEAD

HIPPOCRATES
Hippocrates is known as the founder of medicine and a significant ancient philosopher. His oath has traditionally been taken by all new medical graduates, but in recent decades, this tradition has fallen by the wayside, and copies of legislation and ethical guidelines from medical organisations have taken its place. Although the oath has anachronisms such as not performing castrations, and not seducing slaves, its basic tenets still hold true.

Almost nothing is actually known about the man, Hippocrates, and some scholars have even cast doubt upon his very existence, considering him to have been an ideal physician set up as an example, rather than a person. The name Hippocrates was actually quite a common one, and was adopted by many physicians of the era.

No true drawing or bust of Hippocrates exists, so all representations that appear in print are the imagination of the artist as to how the ideal ancient Greek physician should appear. If he did live, it was in the fifth century BC, and for most of his life on the small Aegean island of Cos, and he purportedly survived to the very ripe old age of 104. He may have died in the northern Greek city of Thessaly (Thessalonika).

Nine different treatises have been credited to him by those scholars who believe in his existence, while another seven may be his work. They cover a wide range of topics from gynaecology to psychiatry, as well as ethics and philosophy. One is devoted to nutrition,

and recommends that two meals be eaten each day. Other suggestions are that wine, figs and ass's milk are beneficial. While the first two are still regarded as beneficial (in moderation of course), the last is rather difficult to obtain.

Hippocrates believed that the brain, and not the heart (or liver as was believed by the Egyptians), was the site of the soul, personality and intelligence. It was the brain that brought humans joy and happiness, sadness and grief, fear and terror. It was the site of mental diseases and sexual desire.

When it came to explaining the function of the brain, a lack of science let him down. He was a great philosopher, but his belief in imbalances of heat and cold, and moisture and dryness in the brain leading to its disorders does not match with modern scientific knowledge. However, bearing in mind that others at the time believed psychiatric conditions were due to possession by evil spirits, and the possessed should be tortured to remove the spirit, Hippocrates treatments were rather kinder.

Although the science of Hippocrates has dated, much of his philosophy has not, and although doctors are now constrained by laws and lawyers, regulations and bureaucrats, guidelines and academics, parliamentary acts and politicians, his ethical attitudes still ring true down the centuries. Long may they continue to be heard.

See also AESCULAPIUS; GALEN; HIPPOCRATIC OATH; MEDICAL ETHICS

HIPPOCRATIC OATH
"I swear to Apollo the physician, and to Aesculapius, and to Hygeia (goddess of health), and to all the gods and goddesses whom I name my witnesses, that I shall fulfil to the best of my ability and judgement, this oath and covenant.

"My teacher who instructed me in this art to hold equal to my parents, and his male descendants to hold as my brothers, to teach them this art and all the medical knowledge, should they ask me to, without any reward or covenant, and to do so to all those that have taken the medical oath and to none other.

"According to my power and judgement to use the medical knowledge for the benefit of those that suffer, as judged by myself to be fair, and to avoid from doing any harm or injustice.

"Not to give to anyone any lethal drug, even if

he asks of me, and neither to suggest such. Also not supply any woman with the means for abortion.

"To preserve pure and immaculate my life and art, not to castrate even that may ask me to, but to leave this to manual labourers.

"In any homes I enter, to do so for the good and benefit of those that suffer, and to abstain from any premeditated injustice or harm of any kind or sexual actions upon the bodies of women or men, be they free citizens or slaves.

"Anything that I may see or hear during the course of treatment, even outside the space where such treatment is being conducted, even during the course of the daily life of men, I cannot invoke, but on the contrary, to conceal and keep forever secret.

"This oath of mine, keeping it and without ever violating, may I have as assistant throughout all my life and in the conduct of my art as well, so that I may have the respect of all men. But should I ever transgress it and commit perjury, that I may be punished with the opposites."
See also EYE OF HORUS; HIPPOCRATES; MEDICAL ETHICS; PRAYER OF MAIMONEDES

HIP REPLACEMENT
Artificial hips were first implanted in the 1950s by the Lancashire surgeon John Charnley. In a hip replacement operation for severe arthritis of the joint, a long cut is made by the orthopaedic surgeon along the outside of the thigh and over the hip joint. Through this, the top end of the thigh bone (femur) is exposed, and just below the start of the hip joint, the bone is sawn through to remove the top one centimetre of the femur and the part of the bone that forms the head of the femur and the hip joint itself. The inside of the femur (where the marrow is situated) is then reamed out for a distance of about 10cm, and the hip joint socket on the side of the pelvis is partly drilled away. Special glue is then poured into the top of the femur from where the marrow has been removed, and the long spindle of the new steel hip joint is inserted down into the bone. The glue hardens rapidly and fixes it in position. A plastic socket is glued onto the side of the pelvis in a similar way, and the new hip joint is put into position. The tissues are closed with sutures.

Within a day or two, physiotherapists will start the patient walking on the new, strong, pain-free hip, and most patients leave hospital within seven to ten days.

See also CHARNLEY, JOHN; HIP; HIP FRACTURE; TRANSPLANTS AND IMPLANTS

HIRSCHSPRUNG DISEASE
Hirschsprung disease is a congenital disease of the large intestine, far more common in boys than girls, caused by a failure of development of the nerves supplying the large intestine (colon). Without these nerves, the intestine cannot contract to move along the faeces. The collection of faeces dilates the colon to an enormous size (megacolon). The disease tends to occur in successive generations.

It is usually diagnosed soon after birth as the baby is severely constipated, has a distended belly, refuses to feed, is lethargic, small in size, and is very irritable. Foul smelling diarrhoea may develop as a late symptom. The diagnosis is confirmed by an x-ray of the gut (barium enema), and taking a biopsy of the colon.

Initially, excess faeces is removed by a tube placed up through the anus, but in due course an operation to remove the affected section of gut is necessary. Without treatment most affected babies will die, but after the operation, these children progress very well and have only minor long-term problems.
See also BARIUM ENEMA; COLON; MEGACOLON

HIRSUTISM
Hirsutism is the medical term for the presence of excess body hair in both sexes, and facial hair in women.

There are obvious racial and family reasons for a hairy body, with some races and families carrying genes that predispose to the growth of hair on the chest, belly, back, buttocks, arms and legs. Facial hair in men also varies between races, with southern Asians having a scanty beard, while northern Europeans can grow a thick bushy beard.

Hair is normally present on all areas of skin except the palms and soles. Hirsutism is often the presence of coarse dark coloured hair rather than fine body coloured hair.

At puberty, both sexes develop hair on the lower abdomen above the genitals and in the arm pits, but sometimes excessive hair growth may occur in other areas, including the face of girls. This problem usually settles down over a few years as the hormone levels stabilise.

The menopause, and associated hormonal changes, may see the growth of hair on the face and chest of women.

Women whose periods cease for no apparent reason may be suffering from a hormonal imbalance that results in hirsutism. Other women naturally have a hormonal makeup that allows normal menstrual periods and fertility, but still inappropriately stimulates body and facial hair growth.

Other causes of hirsutism include tumours and diseases of the pituitary gland in the brain, tumours or injury of the testes or ovaries, failure of the thyroid gland in the neck to produce sufficient thyroxine (hypothyroidism), starvation, severe psychological stress (may affect hormone production), the Stein-Leventhal syndrome (causes multiple cysts in the ovaries to affect their function), Cushing syndrome (over production, or excessive use of cortisone) and foetal alcohol syndrome (babies born to alcoholic mothers).

Numerous medications may have hirsutism as a side effect, including cortisone, oral contraceptive pills, minoxidil, diazoxide, streptomycin, muscle building anabolic steroids, phenytoin and metoclopramide.

Anyone with hirsutism for no obvious cause should have the condition investigated. Most forms can be successfully treated by dealing with the cause, or using medications that reduce the growth of body hair (eg. spironolactone, antiandrogens). Individual hair electrolysis permanently removes that particular hair.
See also HAIR and separate entries for diseases and drugs mentioned above.

HISTAMINE
See ALLERGY; ANTIHISTAMINE; URTICARIA PIGMENTOSA

HISTIOCYTOMA
See DERMATOFIBROMA

HISTIOCYTOSIS X
Histiocytosis X or Langerhans cell granulomatosis, are a group of diseases of no known cause that result in replacement of lung, bone and intestinal tissue by fibrous scar tissue. Hand-Schueller-Christian disease and Leterrer-Siwe disease are the main types of histiocytosis X. They tend to occur in young smokers to cause worsening shortness of breath,

chronic cough, and gradual destruction of the lungs, with a spontaneous pneumothorax being a possible complication. The diagnosis can be confirmed by chest x-ray, CT scan and lung biopsy.

Patients must stop smoking. Numerous treatments have been tried with varying success including medications normally used for asthma, the drug penicillamine (not the antibiotic penicillin), irradiation and lung transplant. The condition is usually slowly progressive despite treatment.
See also HAND-SCHUELLER-CHRISTIAN DISEASE; LETERRER-SIWE DISEASE; SMOKING

HISTOPLASMOSIS
Histoplasmosis is an uncommon infection of the lungs caused by the fungus *Histoplasma capsulatum* which is present in soil and can be inhaled to cause a form of pneumonia. Most cases are very mild and may pass unnoticed or cause mild flu-like symptoms, but sometimes a moderately severe lung infection may develop, and in rare cases a severe and fatal pneumonia occurs. It is most common in southeast Asia, South America and Africa, and is very rare in developed countries.

The symptoms depend on the severity of the infection but in severe cases resemble those of a normal pneumonia with a cough, wheeze, shortness of breath, marked tiredness and a fever. The lung damage from a severe pneumonia may be permanent.

It is diagnosed after examining a sample of sputum and culturing it to determine the infecting organism. There is also a specific blood test, and x-rays of the chest show a characteristic pattern. Minor cases require no treatment, but more severe ones are treated with specific antifungal medications. With correct treatment, only the elderly or invalids are likely to die or develop long-term complications.
See also PNEUMONIA

HISTORY OF MEDICINE
See AESCULAPIUS; AVICENNA; BANTING, FREDERICK; BEST, CHARLES; BLACK DEATH; CADUCEUS; CHARNLEY, JOHN; EYE OF HORUS; FLEMING, ALEXANDER; FLOREY, HOWARD; GALEN; HARVEY, WILLIAM; HIPPOCRATES;

HIPPOCRATIC OATH; JENNER, EDWARD; LAËNNEC, RENÉ; MEDICAL ETHICS; OSLER, WILLIAM; PANACEA; PRAYER OF MAIMONEDES; ROENTGEN, WILHELM; STETHOSCOPE

HIV
See AIDS

HIVES
See URTICARIA

HOARSE VOICE
A hoarse voice can vary from an occasional croak to being unable to speak above a whisper. The cause is inflammation of the vocal cords in the voice box (larynx) at the top of the windpipe (trachea). The tension and vibrations of these cartilaginous cords determines the tone, pitch and other characteristics of the voice.

Viral, bacterial and rarely fungal infections of the throat are the most common cause of hoarseness, and are usually accompanied by a sore throat, fever and other aches and pains. Many different organisms may be responsible, but viruses cannot be cured by antibiotics. Anti-inflammatory medications such as aspirin and ibuprofen (eg. Nurofen, Brufen) are most useful in easing the inflammation.

Straining the vocal cords by speaking for a prolonged time, or shouting (eg. cheering at a sporting match) will cause swelling and inflammation of the cords, which results in hoarseness.

Puberty, and the hormonal changes associated with it, may cause croaky changes in the voice of boys that may be thought to be hoarseness, but is really just deepening of the voice with the onset of manhood.

Less common causes of hoarseness include an inhaled foreign body (particularly in a child), inhaling hot gases (eg. if caught in a fire), allergy reactions (from inhaled pollens), reflux of stomach acid up into the throat that is then inhaled (reflux oesophagitis), hypothyroidism (lack of thyroxine from an underactive thyroid gland), and a tumour, cyst, polyp or nodule on the vocal cords.

Unusual causes include a stroke (cerebrovascular accident), diphtheria, a laryngeal web (a fine membrane of tissue that may form across part of the vocal cords in an infant), damage to the nerve supplying the vocal cords from an injury or tumour, tuberculosis (TB), laryngomalacia and a number of rarer conditions.

See also LARYNX; SPEECH DIFFICULT and separate entries for diseases mentioned above.

HODGKIN'S LYMPHOMA
Hodgkin's lymphoma or disease is a form of cancer of the lymph nodes. The cause is unknown, but it tends to occur more in males, young adults and the elderly, and there may be a genetic tendency. The group of lymphomas that do not fulfil all the criteria to be called Hodgkin's disease are called 'non-Hodgkin's lymphomas'.

Patients develop painless swellings of the lymph nodes, often in the neck, armpit and groin. Other symptoms include tiredness, fever, weight loss, night sweats and a generalised itch, and it may spread to other lymph nodes and organs in other parts of the body. The diagnosis is confirmed by removing an involved lymph node and examining it under a microscope.

Most patients can be classified into different stages (one to four) depending upon the degree of spread of the disease. The treatment varies depending on the stage of the disease and involves various combinations of irradiation, cytotoxic (anticancer) drugs, and surgery. Survival depends upon the staging, and the higher the staging the worse the outcome.

See also CYTOTOXICS AND ANTINEOPLASTICS; LYMPH NODES ENLARGED AND/OR PAINFUL; NON-HODGKIN'S LYMPHOMA

HOLE IN THE HEART
See VENTRICULAR SEPTAL DEFECT

HOLMES-ADIE SYNDROME
The Holmes-Adie syndrome (Adie's pupil) is a congenital abnormality of the pupils that is more common in women. The pupils in the eyes are different sizes, respond poorly to light stimulation and tendon reflexes in the arms and legs may be slower than normal. Patients may be adversely affected by bright light, or find it difficult to see in dim light. It is a harmless condition and no treatment is necessary.

See also EYE

HOLTER MONITOR

A Holter monitor is a relatively simple device that measures every heart beat for twenty four hours onto a cassette tape. Leads from the patient go to the recorder, and an ECG (electrocardiogram) reading is taken of the electrical activity of the heart. The patient can push a button to indicate that they are feeling an abnormality, and this will also be recorded on the tape.

Once disconnected from the patient, the tape can be played back through a machine that prints out, or displays on a screen, the day long ECG, and any abnormality of heart rhythm can be seen. Often the cause of the abnormality can be determined.
See also ARRHYTHMIA; ELECTROCARDIOGRAM; FAINT; HEART; STOKES-ADAMS ATTACK

HOMEOPATHY

Homeopathy is a method of treating disease by the use of very small amounts of herbal, mineral or animal substances which in healthy individuals produce symptoms similar to those of the disease being treated. For example, someone who presented to a homeopath with vomiting would be prescribed a very dilute mixture of a substance that was known to cause vomiting. This approach of treating 'like with like' was introduced by a German doctor, Samuel Hahnemann (1755-1843) at the end of the 18th century. Some of the homeopathic substances can be toxic when undiluted but, at the very high dilution of the therapeutically used dose, the toxic properties are lost. The effectiveness of such preparations has not been supported by modern pharmacology. As a form of therapy used by medical practitioners, homeopathy has been most widespread in Britain.
See also AYURVEDIC MEDICINE; CHINESE MEDICINE; CHIROPRACTIC; IRIDOLOGY; NATUROPATHY; OSTEOPATHY

HOMO SAPIENS SAPIENS
See RACE

HOMOSEXUALITY

Homosexuality (having intimate sexual contact with a person of the same sex) in men or women is not considered to be a medical abnormality, but a variation of normal behaviour. There are many theories as to why some people are homosexual, but no absolute reason is known. 6% of adult men and 3% of adult women have partaken in some form of homosexual activity, but only about 3% of men and half that number of women are exclusively homosexual. Homosexual women may be referred to as lesbians.

There is a higher incidence of sexually transmitted diseases than for heterosexuals, mainly because of promiscuity. AIDS is the most common of these, although in undeveloped countries this is a condition that is spread by heterosexual sex (between men and women) more than anal intercourse. Gay bowel syndrome is an inflammation of the lower bowel caused by anal intercourse that results in a constant urge to pass faeces (tenesmus), rectal discomfort and diarrhoea.

Individuals who have trouble accepting their sexual orientation because of peer or society pressures may require psychiatric assistance.
See also AIDS

HOOKWORM

One quarter of the entire population of the world is affected by hookworm (Ancylostomiasis), which is an infestation of the gut by the nematode worm *Ancylostoma duodenale*. The eggs of the adult hookworm, which is one cm long, pass out in the faeces, and if the faeces fall onto moist ground, the larvae will hatch from the eggs. The larvae remain active in moist soil for up to a week and during that time a larva may penetrate the skin of the foot of any person who treads on it. The larva then migrates through the bloodstream to the lung, where it breaks into the air-carrying passageways of the lung. From there it is carried with sputum up into the throat, where it is swallowed, enters the gut, develops into an adult worm and starts the process all over again. It may be caught in all the tropical countries of the world.

Patients develop an itch at the site of skin penetration, a cough, wheeze and fever while the larvae are in the lung, and mild abdominal discomfort and diarrhoea when there are a large number of worms in the gut, but only in patients who are otherwise ill or malnourished does a hookworm infestation cause significant problems.

Examination of a sample of faeces under a

microscope reveals the worm or its eggs, and drugs are available to successfully destroy the worms.

See also ANTHELMINTICS; ROUNDWORM

HORDEOLUM, EXTERNAL
See STYE

HORMONE REPLACEMENT THERAPY

Sex hormones are produced by the ovary in women and the testes in men to give to each gender its characteristic appearance.

In women, the sex hormones produced for the first time at puberty cause breast enlargement, hair growth in the armpit and groin, ovulation, the start of menstrual periods and later act to maintain a pregnancy.

If the sex hormones are reduced or lacking, these characteristics disappear. This happens naturally during the female menopause. After the menopause, the breasts sag, pubic and armpit hair becomes scanty, and the periods cease due to the lack of sex hormones.

Hormone tablets are the main method of menopause control. While passing through the menopause, it is usual to take one hormone (oestrogen – eg. Premarin) for three weeks, and a different hormone (progestogen – eg. Provera) is added in for the last seven to fourteen days, and then no hormones are taken for a week. After the menopause has been completed and all periods have stopped, it is usual to take both the oestrogen and progestogen constantly. Other dosage regimes may be recommended.

If oestrogen is taken without progestogen, there is over-stimulation of the endometrial tissue in the uterus (womb) which can increase the risk of cancer of the uterus. When the two are taken together, either cyclically (progestogen for only part of the month) or constantly (both hormones all the time) there is no increased risk of uterine cancer. In a hysterectomy the uterus is removed, and so women who have had a hysterectomy cannot have an increased risk of cancer of the uterus, so these women only need to take the oestrogen, the progestogens being unnecessary.

These hormones maintain the body in a near normal balance, while underneath the artificial hormones, the natural menopause is occurring, so that when the tablets are stopped after a year or two, the menopausal symptoms will have gone.

HRT can be given as tablets, patches, skin or vaginal creams, implants or injection.

Every woman must assess her own needs in consultation with her doctor regarding her lifestyle expectations and the risks of using HRT. Many women are now continuing hormone replacement therapy (HRT) for many years after the menopause to prevent osteoporosis (and the resultant fractured bones), and to slow ageing. Generally speaking, HRT has been a major advance in the health of women, who now outlive men by an average of more than seven years.

The points for and against hormone replacement therapy are outlined as simply as possible as follows:

ADVANTAGES: –
• Prevents osteoporosis (thinning of bones) and fractures.
• Slows the development of wrinkles and keeps the skin moist and more elastic.
• Increases libido (sexual desire).
• Lubricates the vagina and enhances sexual pleasure.
• Slows the sagging of breasts by maintaining breast tissue.
• Relieves the hot flushes, depression, bloating and other symptoms of menopause.
• Regulates irregular periods to make them milder and less painful.
• Significantly reduces the risk of colon cancer.

DISADVANTAGES: –
• Slightly increases risk of breast cancer if taken for more than four years.
• Increases risk of blood clots in the veins (deep venous thrombosis) and brain (stroke).
• Slightly increases risk of heart disease if taken for more than four years.
• Menstrual periods may restart, or continue, for a year or so after HRT commences.
• May cause breast tenderness if dosage too high.
• Nausea and belly cramps may occur.
• Migraines may be aggravated.

Except under special circumstances, women who have had cancer of the breast, uterus or cervix, or have had hormonal mastitis (breast pain), endometriosis, blood clots (thromboses) or strokes, should not use HRT.

See also MENOPAUSE; SEX HORMONES; UTERUS

HORMONES

Hormones are produced naturally in the body by many different glands, including the thyroid and parathyroid glands (in the neck), the pancreas (in the abdomen), the pituitary gland (in the brain), the adrenal glands (on top of the kidneys), the ovary and testes (produce sex hormones). Most of these are listed under their individual type of hormone (eg. sex hormones). Hormones are chemicals that travel from the producing gland, directly into the bloodstream, and then around the body. They reach and act upon every cell in the body through the bloodstream.

The thyroid gland in the neck produces the hormone thyroxine, which acts to control the rate at which every cell in the body works. It is the accelerator of the body. If thyroxine is lacking, the patient becomes tired and slow. This is a common condition in middle-aged and elderly women. The thyroid hormone not being produced by the thyroid gland can be given as a tablet (thyroxine) by mouth. If used at the correct dosage, as determined by regular blood tests, there should be minimal side effects.

The pituitary gland produces a range of hormones, most of which control other glands. The pituitary gland is therefore the 'conductor' of the glandular and hormonal 'orchestra' of the body.
See also ADRENAL GLAND; GLAND; INSULIN; OVARY; PANCREAS; PITUITARY GLAND; SEX HORMONES; TESTES; THYROID GLAND; TROPHIC HORMONES

HORNER SYNDROME

Horner syndrome is a bizarre combination of symptoms involving the eye and sweat glands caused by compression of a special network of nerves (autonomic nervous system) in the chest due to lung cancer or pneumothorax, or in the brain due to a tumour. It may be the first sign of a quite advanced lung cancer. The syndrome is characterised by a drooping eyelid, contracted pupil and a sunken eye, and reduced sweating.

Numerous investigations must be undertaken to find the cause, including x-rays, CT and MRI scans. It is necessary to correct the underlying cause of the nerve compression, usually by surgery.
See also AUTONOMIC NERVOUS SYSTEM; LUNG CANCER; PANCOAST SYNDROME; PNEUMOTHORAX

HORUS
See EYE OF HORUS

HOSTAGE SYNDROME
See STOCKHOLM SYNDROME

HOT FLUSH
See FLUSH, ABNORMAL

HOUSEMAID'S KNEE

Housemaid's knee is the rather old-fashioned name for a condition that is technically known as pre-patellar bursitis, and also commonly known as water on the knee. It is a swelling and inflammation of the bursa on the front of the kneecap. Bursae are small sacs that are connected by a fine tube to a joint cavity. Several are present near every joint, and secrete the synovial fluid which acts as a lubricant for the joint. One of the bursae supplying the knee is in front of the kneecap, and it may be damaged by prolonged kneeling or a blow to cause a painful swelling. Uncommonly, a serious bacterial infection may occur in the knee.

Treatment involves rest, strapping, avoiding kneeling and occasionally draining the excess fluid from the knee. The results of treatment are good, but a recurrence is possible.
See also BURSITIS; KNEE; SYNOVIAL FLUID

HOUSEWIFE'S DERMATITIS
See CONTACT DERMATITIS

HPV INFECTION
See GENITAL WARTS; PLANE WARTS; PLANTAR WARTS; WART

HRT
See HORMONE REPLACEMENT THERAPY

HUMAN BITE
See ANIMAL BITE

HUMAN IMMUNODEFICIENCY VIRUS
See AIDS

HUMAN PAPILLOMAVIRUS
See GENITAL WARTS; PLANE WARTS;
PLANTAR WARTS; WART

HUMERUS
The humerus is the only bone in the upper part of the arm between the shoulder and elbow. At its upper end it has a ball that fits into the socket of the scapula (shoulder blade). The shoulder has more movement than any other joint in the body.
See also ELBOW; HUMERUS FRACTURE; SCAPULA; SHOULDER

UPPER ARM

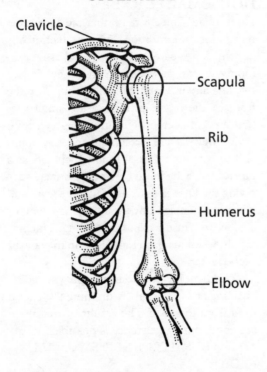

Clavicle
Scapula
Rib
Humerus
Elbow

HUMERUS FRACTURE
A fracture of the upper arm bone (humerus) usually occurs near the shoulder joint after a severe injury, but in the elderly it may occur after a relatively minor fall or twisting force. Severe pain and swelling occurs at the site of the fracture, with an inability to move the arm. It is diagnosed by an x-ray.

It is not practical to immobilise the humerus because it would require a plaster that encased the chest and shoulder, and extended down the arm to the elbow. Most heal very well if the arm is left hanging by the side while the wrist is supported by a sling. Sometimes the elbow is strapped to the body. No attempt should be made to use the arm. A false joint may form at the site of the fracture

in the elderly with poor healing, or with excessive use of the arm during healing.

The prognosis is good in most cases, with healing in six to eight weeks, but in the elderly healing may be slow and painful.
See also FRACTURE; HUMERUS

HUNGER
Physical sensation associated with the desire for food and contractions of the stomach, and stimulated by a feedback mechanism between sensors in the brain and the stomach.
See also APPETITE, EXCESS; APPETITE, LACK OF; THIRST

HUNNER ULCER
See INTERSTITIAL CYSTITIS

HUNTER SYNDROME
The Hunter syndrome (mucopolysaccharoidosis type II) is a rare inherited abnormality of the metabolic system in which patients are unable to eliminate certain substances (mucopolysaccharides) from the body. Stiff joints, grotesque facial appearance, enlarged spleen and liver, heart abnormalities and mild mental retardation are the usual characteristics, while deafness may also be a problem. It is diagnosed by specific blood and bone marrow tests and x-rays. Surgery may be performed for heart and facial abnormalities, but no cure is possible, although patients have a reasonable life expectancy.
See also HURLER SYNDROME

HUNTINGTON'S CHOREA
Huntington's chorea is a distressing, congenital condition that affects muscle function and coordination and is passed to half the children of a patient. Because the symptoms do not become apparent until between thirty and fifty years of age, it has often already been passed to the next generation before diagnosis. It is likely that all cases in existence can be traced back to previous sufferers.

In mid-life, patients develop irregular, random movements of the arms, legs and face; irritability, mood changes, antisocial behaviour, restlessness, fidgeting, mental deterioration, premature senility and rigid muscles. The symptoms develop very slowly over many years and serious psychiatric disturbances may also occur.

The chromosomal location of the gene that

carries the condition from one generation to the next has been identified and the children of a patient can now decide if they wish to know if they are carrying the abnormal gene. This decision will obviously have dramatic effects upon their future lifestyle.

No effective treatment is available, but some psychiatric drugs can control mood changes, and muscle relaxants may ease the abnormal movements. The inevitable progression cannot be halted and usually death occurs within ten to twenty years of symptoms developing.
See also JERKING; SYDENHAM'S CHOREA

HURLER SYNDROME

Hurler syndrome (mucopolysaccharoidosis type 1) is a rare inherited abnormality of the metabolic system in which patients are unable to eliminate certain substances (mucopolysaccharides) from the body. These children have a grotesque facial appearance, short stature, stiff joints, spinal deformities, mental retardation, heart abnormalities, blindness and enlarged liver and spleen. Heart failure often occurs early in life. It is diagnosed by specific blood and bone marrow tests and x-rays. Surgery is possible for heart and facial abnormalities, but no cure is possible. It is similar to, but more serious than, Hunter syndrome, and patients usually die in childhood.
See also HUNTER SYNDROME; SPLEEN ENLARGED

HUTCHISON MELANOTIC FRECKLE

A Hutchison melanotic freckle (lentigo maligna) is an irregular flat black-blue pigmented spot, usually on the face of the middle aged or elderly, that slowly enlarges. It is diagnosed by biopsy, and small spots may be frozen (cryotherapy), but larger spots are surgically excised. Rarely they develop into a malignant melanoma. Without treatment, they slowly enlarge and thicken.
See also MELANOMA; SKIN PIGMENTATION EXCESS

HUTCHISON PRURIGO
See PHOTODERMATITIS

HYALINE MEMBRANE DISEASE
See RESPIRATORY DISTRESS SYNDROME, INFANT

HYDATID DISEASE

Hydatid disease or echinococcosis, is an infestation of human tissue by the larva of the tapeworm *Echinococcus*. The normal life cycle of *Echinococcus* requires infested meat to be eaten by a dog or other carnivore. The larva enters the gut and grows into a tapeworm which then passes eggs out in the faeces to contaminate grass and soil. The normal hosts are cattle, sheep and other grazing animals which eat the contaminated grass and are eventually killed by the *Echinococcus* infestation in their body. This allows the carcass to be eaten by meat-eating animals, and the life cycle of the parasite starts again. If a human eats food that has been contaminated by the faeces of an infected animal (usually dogs or other meat-eating animals), the larva migrates to the liver, lung, spleen or brain, where it forms a cyst that remains life-long. The disease is rare in developed countries, but widespread in South America, around the Mediterranean, in east Africa and central Asia.

After the cyst forms in the body, it usually remains dormant for many years, often causing no symptoms. Over a decade or more the cyst slowly enlarges, until the pressure it exerts on its surroundings causes problems. With liver cysts, there may be pain in the upper part of the abdomen, nausea, vomiting and jaundice. In the lung, the cysts may cause part of the lung to collapse, pain and shortness of breath. In the brain symptoms occur earlier, and even a small cyst may cause convulsions or severe headaches. If a cyst ruptures, the reaction in the body to the sudden release of a large number of larvae may cause sudden death or severe illness and the formation of multiple cysts in other parts of the body. If multiple cysts are present, the long-term outlook is grave.

The condition is diagnosed by seeing the cyst on a CT or ultrasound scan. Specific blood tests can be performed to determine whether or not a person has a cyst somewhere in their body, but discovering the actual site of the cyst may then prove very difficult.

If possible, a cyst should be removed surgically. It is vital for the surgeon not to rupture the cyst during its removal, because the spilled larvae can then spread through the body. In other cases, or as an additional form of treatment, potent medications may be prescribed to kill the larvae, but the cyst will

remain. Provided the disease is not widespread, the results of treatment are good. Dogs in affected areas can be treated regularly to prevent them carrying the disease.
See also TAPEWORMS; WORMS

HYDATIDIFORM MOLE
See UTERINE MOLE

HYDATID OF MORGAGNI
The hydatid of Morgagni is a small, unnecessary tissue sac that hangs loosely from the top of the testis in the male and the Fallopian tube in the female. In men, it is possible for the sac to become twisted, gangrenous and painful. Sudden onset of severe testicular pain and tenderness occurs. It may be confused with torsion of the testis, which is a surgical emergency that requires treatment within a few hours and also has the same symptoms. The diagnosis is only made during surgery, after ensuring that the testis itself has not become twisted and gangrenous. During the operation the offending piece of tissue is removed, with no subsequent adverse effects upon the potency or masculinity of the patient. Recovery is usually complete within three or four days.
See also TESTICLE; TORSION OF THE TESTIS

HYDRAMNIOS
See OLIGOHYDRAMNIOS; POLYHYDRAMNIOS

HYDROCELE
A hydrocele is a common problem due to a collection of excess fluid around a testicle. The testes are surrounded by a fine layer of tissue called the tunica vaginalis. At almost any age, fluid may accumulate between the testicle and the tunica to cause swelling. This may follow an injury or infection in the scrotum, or occur for no apparent reason.

The swelling is painless and there is no discomfort, but the testicle may slowly enlarge to the size of a tennis ball or more. Other cysts and growths that can occur in the scrotum, including cancer (which may not be painful) must be excluded by an ultrasound scan.

In infants the problem sometimes settles without treatment, but in adults a needle is used to drain off the fluid. Unfortunately the fluid often re-accumulates, and a minor surgical procedure may be necessary to give a permanent cure. There is no permanent damage to the testicle or its function.
See also SPERMATOCELE; TESTICLE

HYDROCEPHALUS
The brain and spinal cord are surrounded by cerebrospinal fluid (CSF). In the brain are a number of cavities, one of which contains a network of veins (the choroid plexus) that secretes the CSF, which passes through small ducts to the outside of the brain. From there the CSF flows down and around the spinal cord in the back, from where it is absorbed into the blood. Hydrocephalus occurs when excess CSF accumulates in or around the brain.

There are two types of hydrocephalus: –
• Obstructive hydrocephalus occurs if CSF cannot escape from the cavities within the brain due to a blockage in the draining tubes.
• Communicating hydrocephalus occurs when there is a blockage of the circulation down the spinal cord and the fluid cannot be absorbed back into the bloodstream.

Both types are usually caused by a developmental abnormality of the foetus, or may develop in later life because of brain infections, tumours in the brain or skull, cysts in the brain, blood clots and other rarer conditions.

In babies with hydrocephalus, the soft skull is grossly dilated by the excess fluid. In older children or adults, the harder skull is unable to expand, so symptoms include a severe headache, personality changes, partial paralysis or loss of consciousness. Other symptoms will depend upon the effect of the increased fluid pressure on the brain. It is diagnosed by a CT or MRI scan.

Treatment involves inserting a tube (shunt) into the skull to drain away the excess CSF. The tube has a one way valve allowing the CSF to escape, but preventing other fluids or infection from entering the brain. The far end of the tube is inserted into a vein in the neck or chest, or is run all the way through the chest, and allowed to drain into the abdominal cavity. Shunts can become blocked and require replacement or clearing occasionally. Any brain damage that occurs before the condition is treated may be permanent.

Treatment is usually very successful in controlling the condition and allows the patient

to lead a normal life with minimal impairment of body function or intelligence.
See also BRAIN; CEREBROSPINAL FLUID; HEAD LARGE

HYDROCHLORIC ACID
Hydrochloric acid (HCl) is produced in a very concentrated form in the stomach by parietal cells in the stomach wall, to aid digestion.
See also ACIDS; STOMACH

HYDROCHLOROTHIAZIDE
See DIURETICS

HYDROCODONE
See COUGH MEDICINES

HYDROCORTISONE
See STEROIDS

HYDROCYANIC ACID
See CYANIDE

HYDROPHOBIA
An abnormal fear of water or drinking is called hydrophobia.
See also RABIES

HYDROXYCHLOROQUINE
See ANTIMALARIALS

HYGIAE
Hygiae was the goddess of health in ancient Greek mythology, from whose name the word hygiene is derived.
See also AESCULAPIUS

HYMEN
The hymen (maidenhead) is a thin membrane across the opening of the vagina. It has a large hole in it to allow menstrual blood to escape, and normally covers only a third of the vaginal opening. It is often gradually torn open by the insertion of tampons and vigorous exercise, with the first experience of sexual intercourse completing its destruction.

There may be slight bleeding with initial intercourse if the hymen has not previously been torn.

Rarely, the hymen may be complete and has no hole, so that menstrual blood accumulates in the vagina with no way to escape.
See also VAGINA

HYOSCINE
See ANTISPASMODICS

HYPER-
'Hyper-' is a prefix used in medicine to mean high, excess, over or above.

HYPERACTIVE
See OVERACTIVE

HYPERADRENOCORTICISM
See CUSHING SYNDROME

HYPERAESTHESIA
See TOUCH

HYPERALDOSTERONISM
See CONN SYNDROME

HYPERCALCAEMIA
Hypercalcaemia is excess calcium in the body and blood. Causes include hyperparathyroidism, sarcoidosis, excess vitamin D and cancer. Cancer can affect bone directly or indirectly (eg. metastatic breast or prostate cancer) causing the release of calcium.

The symptoms include a loss of appetite, nausea, vomiting, constipation, passing excess urine, muscle weakness, confusion, tremor, psychiatric disturbances and tiredness. Abnormal nerve conduction in the heart may lead to significant abnormalities of rhythm. Blood tests can demonstrate high calcium levels.

It is necessary to treat any cause if possible. Fluids given by a drip into a vein can dilute high calcium levels, followed by diuretics (fluid tablets) to wash it out of the body. Other medications (eg. diphosphonates) can then be used to bind calcium and reduce inflammation (eg. prednisone).
See also CALCIUM; CANCER;
HYPERPARATHYROIDISM;
SARCOIDOSIS; VITAMIN D

HYPERCHOLESTEROLAEMIA
See CHOLESTEROL

HYPEREMESIS GRAVIDARUM
See MORNING SICKNESS

HYPERHIDROSIS
See SWEATING EXCESS

HYPERKERATOSIS

A hyperkeratosis (actinic or solar keratosis) is a common form of damage to skin exposed to the sun, particularly as a youth and on fair skinned people, that may develop into a squamous cell carcinoma (SCC). It appears as a patch of rough, raised and scaling skin, but it is not red or itchy. It may be treated by acid ointments, anticancer cream (5-Fluorouracil), freezing (cryosurgery), burning (diathermy) or surgical excision. In some elderly patients with very large affected areas it may not be practical to remove all the spots, but they should be checked regularly so that any changing in appearance can be treated.
See also CRYOTHERAPY; DIATHERMY; SEBORRHOEIC KERATOSES; SQUAMOUS CELL CARCINOMA OF THE SKIN

HYPERKINETIC SYNDROME

The hyperkinetic syndrome is a developmental form of minimal brain dysfunction that starts before birth. These children have an early onset of personality problems, overactivity, poor coordination of limbs, learning disorders, and antisocial behaviour. It may be associated with epilepsy, and criminal activity is common in early adult life. An EEG (electroencephalogram) may be abnormal.

Treatments available include behaviour modification techniques, drugs such as methylphenidate and dexamphetamine, special education programs, and environmental modification. Although the condition persists, satisfactory control is usually possible.
See also ATTENTION DEFICIT HYPERACTIVITY DISORDER; BEHAVIOUR THERAPY; ELECTROENCEPHALOGRAM; OVERACTIVE

HYPERLIPIDAEMIA
See CHOLESTEROL; LIPIDS; TRIGLYCERIDE

HYPERMETROPIA
See VISION

HYPERMOBILITY SYNDROME

Hypermobility syndrome is a congenital slackness of ligaments resulting in a dramatically increased ability to move joints beyond their normal limits, which is associated with intermittent joint pain, tenderness and swelling, and ease of joint dislocation. Fingers may bend back at a right angle, the thumb may be able to bend back to touch the forearm, the knees and elbows bend back beyond 10°, and patients can rest palms easily on floor when bending from waist with knees straight. X-rays may show joint damage.

Joint protection, physiotherapy, joint supports and splints, exercise program, counselling, anti-inflammatory drugs, pain killers, local anaesthetic and steroid injections are used in treatment, but osteoarthritis may develop early and there may be disability from recurrent sprains or dislocations.
See also JOINT

HYPERNATRAEMIA
See SODIUM

HYPEROPIA
See LONG SIGHTED

HYPERPARATHYROIDISM

Four small parathyroid glands sit behind the thyroid gland in the neck and secrete the hormone calcitonin, which controls the amount of calcium in the bones and blood. If these glands become overactive (hyperparathyroidism), excess calcitonin is secreted, resulting in calcium being taken out of the bones and into the blood. It is a rare disease that may be caused by a tumour or cancer in one of the parathyroid glands, but often no cause can be found.

The bones become brittle and painful and break easily, and the high level of calcium in the blood causes kidney stones and damage (which can result in thirst and the passing of large quantities of urine), high blood pressure, constipation and peptic ulcers in the stomach. Damage to the kidneys may occur, and they may eventually fail.

The diagnosis is confirmed by finding high levels of calcium in the blood and urine, and CT scans are used to determine the site of the affected gland.

Delicate surgery is necessary to remove the overactive gland and patients must take copious amounts of fluid to flush out the kidneys. There are no drugs that can be used. The surgery is successful in most cases, but without treatment the disease will steadily progress until serious complications result.

See also CALCIUM;
HYPOPARATHYROIDISM; KIDNEY
STONE; PARATHYROID GLAND

HYPERPROLACTINAEMIA

Hyperprolactinaemia is the excessive production of the hormone prolactin by the pituitary gland in the centre of the brain. Prolactin is the hormone which is responsible for breast milk production. The disease may be due to underactive ovaries or testes, or more commonly a tumour in the pituitary gland. Uncommonly, it may be due to side effects of some drugs or an underactive thyroid gland.

Abnormal milk production by the breasts occurs in both women (much more commonly) and men, and women usually stop their menstrual periods. The blood level of prolactin is increased, and a pituitary gland tumour can be detected by a CT scan. The disease is controlled by the drug bromocriptine, while surgery or radiotherapy to the pituitary gland can be used to treat a tumour.
See also PITUITARY GLAND

HYPER-REACTIVE AIRWAYS DISEASE

Hyper-reactive airways disease is an inflammatory lung condition similar to asthma that often follows a viral infection of the upper airways or lungs, or may be due to inhalation of irritant gases or an allergy. The symptoms are persistent wheezing, cough and shortness of breath. There are more allergy type symptoms and less phlegm production than in asthma, and lung function tests and chest x-ray are usually normal. Inhaled steroids (eg. beclomethasone, budesonide, fluticasone) or anti-inflammatories (eg. ipratropium) are used in treatment. Rarely, in persistent cases, prednisone tablets are prescribed. The condition settles spontaneously eventually, but responds well to treatment.
See also ASTHMA; LUNG

HYPERTENSION

Hypertension is high blood pressure, an excessive pressure of blood within the arteries, that occurs in 20% of adults over forty years of age.

The heart contracts regularly to pump blood through the arteries under high (systolic) pressure. When the heart relaxes between beats, the blood continues to flow due to the lower (diastolic) pressure exerted by the elasticity of the artery walls. Hypertension occurs when one, or both, of these pressures exceeds a safe level. Blood pressure readings are written as systolic pressure/diastolic pressure (eg. 125/70) and are measured with a sphygmomanometer.

Blood pressure varies with exercise, anxiety, age, fitness, smoking and drinking habits, weight and medications. In a very elderly person 160/90 may be acceptable, but in a young woman, 110/60 would be more appropriate. Life insurance companies generally require the blood pressure to be under 136/86 for the person to be acceptable at normal rates. The numbers are a measure of pressure in millimetres of mercury.

The arteries of a person with high blood pressure will become hardened, brittle and may eventually rupture, causing a stroke, heart attack or other serious injury to vital organs.

The majority of patients have 'essential' hypertension, for which there is no single identifiable cause. The identifiable causes include smoking, obesity, kidney disease, oestrogen-containing medications (eg. the contraceptive pill), hyperparathyroidism, phaeochromocytoma and a number of other rare diseases. High blood pressure may also be a complication of pregnancy (pre-eclampsia), when it can lead to quite serious consequences.

The majority of patients have no symptoms for many years, but those who do have symptoms complain of headaches and tiredness, although only when the blood pressure is very high do the further symptoms of nausea, confusion, and disturbances in vision occur.

Once diagnosed, blood and urine tests are performed to see if there is any specific cause, and x-rays of the kidneys and an electrocardiogram (ECG) may also be performed.

Hypertension is prevented by keeping weight within reasonable limits, not eating excessive amounts of salt, not smoking, and by exercising regularly. There is no cure, but hypertension can be successfully controlled by taking tablets regularly, lifelong. A wide range of medications is available (eg, diuretics, alpha blockers, beta-blockers, calcium channel blockers, ACE inhibitors etc.), but it takes days or weeks for the tablets to work. Regular checks are essential until the correct dosage is determined, then blood pressure checks every three to six months are necessary.

Untreated high blood pressure causes strokes and heart attacks at an earlier age than would be expected with normal blood pressure. Other complications include kidney damage and bleeding into an eye. A rapidly progressive condition known as malignant hypertension can sometimes develop and cause remarkably high levels of blood pressure.

Once controlled, there is no reason why the patient should not lead a full and active working, sporting and sexual life. Untreated, most patients with only moderate hypertension die within twenty years.

See also ACE INHIBITORS; ALPHA-BLOCKERS; BETA-BLOCKERS; BLOOD PRESSURE; CALCIUM CHANNEL BLOCKERS; DIURETICS; ELECTROCARDIOGRAM; HEART ATTACK; PHAEOCHROMOCYTOMA; PORTAL HYPERTENSION; SMOKING; SYNDROME X

HYPERTENSION, PULMONARY
See COR PULMONALE

HYPERTHYROIDISM
Hyperthyroidism (thyrotoxicosis or Grave's disease) is overactivity of the thyroid gland, which sits in the front of the neck and is responsible for secreting a hormone called thyroxine. This acts as the accelerator for every cell in the body. If the level of thyroxine is high, the cells function at an increased rate and if the level of thyroxine is low, the cells function at a less than normal rate. The most common cause is an autoimmune disease, in which antibodies attack the thyroid gland and over stimulate it, but there are numerous other rarer causes.

Patients sweat excessively, lose weight, are nervous, tired, cannot tolerate hot weather and have a mild diarrhoea. Other effects include a rapid heart rate, slightly protruding eyes, warm skin and a slight tremor. Patients also tend to fidget, dart quickly in their activity, and speak rapidly. The thyroid gland may be grossly enlarged (a goitre) or normal size.

The complications are serious. The weight loss and muscle wasting may become permanent, liver damage and heart failure may be fatal, psychiatric disturbances may lead to hospitalisation, eye scarring may lead to blindness, and infertility may occur.

The level of thyroxine and gland activity can be measured by blood tests and abnormalities may also be seen on an electrocardiogram (ECG).

The overactivity can only temporarily be controlled by medication, but a cure can be obtained by surgically removing most of the thyroid gland or destroying it by giving the patient radioactive iodine (iodine 131) which concentrates in the gland as it is an essential component of thyroxine. Because there is usually insufficient thyroid gland left behind after these procedures to produce adequate amounts of thyroxine, it is necessary for most patients to take thyroxine tablets on a daily basis.

If treated early, the prognosis is excellent, but if treatment is delayed until complications occur the outcome is far less favourable.

See also ANTITHYROID DRUGS; AUTOIMMUNE DISEASES; GOITRE; HASHIMOTO THYROIDITIS; IODINE; THYROID FUNCTION TESTS; THYROID GLAND; THYROIDITIS

HYPERTONIC
See MUSCLE TONE INCREASED

HYPERTRIGLYCERIDAEMIA
See TRIGLYCERIDE

HYPERTROPHIC CARDIOMYOPATHY
See CARDIOMYOPATHY

HYPERURICAEMIA
See GOUT; URIC ACID

HYPERVENTILATION
See BREATHING, RAPID

HYPERVITAMINOSIS A
See CAROTENAEMIA; VITAMIN A

HYPNIC JERKS
Hypnic jerks are experienced by everyone as brief, sudden muscle jerks while falling asleep. Unlike dreams, this phenomenon can be clearly remembered. They are harmless and no treatment is necessary.
See also JERKING

HYPNOTICS
See SEDATIVES

HYPO-
'Hypo-' is a prefix used in medicine to mean low, under or below.

See also DIABETES MELLITUS TYPE ONE

HYPOALDOSTERONISM

Hypoaldosteronism is an uncommon kidney disorder in which blood levels of potassium and sodium are abnormal due to a lack of the hormone aldosterone, which is produced in the adrenal glands. Numerous diseases may be responsible (eg. diabetes mellitus), or it may be inherited, a side effect of drugs (eg. heparin), occur after severe blood loss in an injury, as a result of brain diseases affecting the pituitary gland, after surgery for a tumour of the adrenal glands (which sit on top of each kidney), or may occur spontaneously for no obvious reason. Kidney and heart failure are possible. There is abnormal urine production and fluid retention, and blood tests show high potassium levels, and other abnormalities of body chemistry.

Specific types of steroids are given long term to treat the condition, and a low salt diet is essential. There is no cure, but control is reasonable in most patients.
See also ADRENAL GLAND; ALDOSTERONE; DIABETES MELLITUS TYPE ONE; HEPARIN; PITUITARY GLAND

HYPOCHONDRIA

Hypochondria is the false belief by a person that they are ill. In most cases they are not deliberately faking an illness, but really believe that the symptoms they are experiencing are a sign of significant disease.

At any time, all of us have some discomfort in our body. Normally we accept this for what it is, an excess pressure on some part, abnormal position, overeating, constipation, full bladder, hunger, or symptoms of a minor infection (eg. common cold). Hypochondriacs increase these minor discomforts out of all proportion to reality. Because of anxiety, the symptom may actually worsen, which makes them even more anxious, which further aggravates the symptom. This vicious cycle can be very difficult to break.

True hypochondria is a psychiatric condition that requires regular medication to control. Unfortunately, many patients do not accept the diagnosis, and keep seeking further investigation and treatment from a variety of doctors.

Munchausen syndrome is one of the more famous extremes of hypochondria, and is named after a famous 18th century German baron who suffered from the condition. Patients falsify symptoms by elaborate means in order to obtain medical attention, medications, investigations and surgery.

Briquet syndrome is a form of hysteria which results in the patient presenting with multiple, unexplained (and unexplainable) symptoms which have no physical basis. It tends to run in families, and treatment is difficult.

SHAFT syndrome has a name which is an acronym for its main symptoms. They are sad, hostile, anxious, frustrated, tenacious patients who praise a doctor excessively to obtain unnecessary surgery, then have worsening or imagined symptoms after surgery, for which the doctor is blamed.

Hypochondria is a neurosis that may be helped by psychotherapy, but care must be taken by doctors not to miss a true medical condition that may be present, or arise during treatment. The prognosis is generally poor, and the delusion persists life long.
See also BRIQUET SYNDROME; CONVERSION DISORDER; PSYCHOSES and separate entries for most diseases mentioned above.

HYPOGASTRIC PAIN
See PELVIC PAIN

HYPOGASTRIUM

The hypogastrium is the area of the lower abdomen just above the pubic bone and in front of the bladder.
See also PELVIC PAIN

HYPOGLYCAEMIA

Hypoglycaemia is a medical term for low blood sugar. The patient becomes light-headed, sweats, develops a rapid heart beat and tremor, becomes hungry, then nauseated before finally collapsing unconscious. It is usually a complication of excessive medication (eg. insulin, hypoglycaemics) for diabetes mellitus.
See also DIABETES MELLITUS TYPE ONE; DIABETES MELLITUS TYPE TWO; HYPOGLYCAEMICS

HYPOGLYCAEMICS

Hypoglycaemics are drugs that lower the level

of sugar (glucose) in the bloodstream by allowing the sugar to cross the membrane surrounding a cell and to enter the interior of the cell. They are used mainly in the maturity onset (type two) form of diabetes mellitus.

Alteration to the dosage of all types of hypoglycaemics may be required with changes in exercise, or diet, surgery or the occurrence of other illnesses, particularly if a fever is present. A doctor should be consulted immediately in these situations. As well as treatment with hypoglycaemics, all diabetics must remain on an appropriate diet for the rest of their lives. Regular blood tests and urine tests are essential for the adequate control of all forms of diabetes. Some patients now use small machines the size of a thick credit card, to test their own blood sugar.

Hypoglycaemics fall into two main groups – tablets and injections. Insulin, normally produced by the pancreas to transport sugar across the cell membrane, can only be given by injection, and is invariably required in type one diabetes which has its onset in children and young adults. Maturity onset (type two) diabetes has its onset in the middle aged and elderly, and is normally treated by hypoglycaemic tablets and diet, but sometimes insulin is also required. The hypoglycaemic tablets fall into several sub-classes.

Biguanide hypoglycaemics tend to be used more in obese patients. Metformin (Diabex, Diaformin) is the only commonly used medication in this subclass. Side effects may include nausea and belly discomfort. It should not be used in pregnancy or alcoholics.

The sulfonylureas is a class of tablets used only in maturity onset (type two) diabetes. Excessive use, or overdosage, can cause a 'hypo' attack as in insulin overuse. Examples include chlorpropamide (Diabinese), glimepride (Amaryl), glibenclamide (Daonil, Euglucon), glipizide (Minidiab) and tolbutamide (Rastinon). Side effects include nausea, weakness and belly discomfort. They should not be used in pregnancy, thyroid disease, and severe liver or kidney diseases, and should not be combined with insulin.

Acarbose (Glucobay) is used in difficult-to-control mature onset diabetes. Side effects include nausea and diarrhoea. It must be used with caution in pregnancy, and blood tests to check liver function must be performed regularly.

See also DIABETES MELLITUS TYPE TWO; INSULIN; MEDICATION

HYPOLIPIDAEMICS

The term 'hypo' means low (as opposed to 'hyper', meaning high), lipids are fats, and the term 'aemia' refers to the blood (compare 'anaemia' – lack of blood), so a hypolipidaemic is a drug that lowers fat in the blood. The fats include both cholesterol and triglycerides. An excess of either, or both, of these in the bloodstream can cause narrowing, hardening and blockage of arteries, which result in serious diseases such as strokes and heart attacks. A combination of diet and drugs is used to control excess levels of fat in the bloodstream. Diet alone may be sufficient in many patients.

Fat-lowering hypolipidaemics include tablets in the newer statins subclass which are generally more convenient, effective and have fewer side effects than the older medications such as clofibrate and probucol (tablets), colestipol and cholestyramine (powders to mix with water) which are taken after meals to remove fats from the blood. These older medications can be useful additive treatment to the statins, and in some diabetics and obese patients, but they interact with a number of other medications that may be essential for the patient's well-being. The powders must always be mixed with water, and not swallowed dry.

The drugs in the statins class include atorvastatin (Lipitor), cerivastatin (Lipobay), fluvastatin (Lescol, Vastin), pravastatin (Pravachol) and simvastatin (Lipex, Zocor). Side effects may include constipation, diarrhoea, excess wind, nausea and headache. They should not be used in pregnancy or severe liver disease. Regular blood tests are necessary to check liver function and fat levels.

Cholestyramine (Questran) is an old-fashioned medication used to reduce blood cholesterol, the itch of liver failure, and in some other intestinal diseases. Side effects include constipation, belly discomfort, excess wind, heartburn and a rash. It must be used with care in pregnancy, and not in gall bladder disease. The powder must always be mixed with water, and not swallowed dry.

Clofibrate (Atromid S) is another older style medication that reduces both blood cholesterol and triglyceride levels. Side effects may include nausea, vomiting and diarrhoea. Must be used with care in pregnancy, and not in patients with liver failure.

Colestipol (Colestid) is a hypolipidaemic used in difficult cases. Its most common side effect is constipation. It must not be used in patients with diabetes or thyroid disease. The powder must always be mixed with water, and not swallowed dry.

Gemfibrizol (Jezil, Lopid) also reduces both blood cholesterol and triglyceride levels. Side effects may include heartburn, belly pains, nausea and diarrhoea. It must be used with caution in pregnancy, and may reduce fertility.

Nicotinic acid is one of the oldest medications used to reduce blood cholesterol and triglycerides, and it also aids poor circulation. Side effects may include a rash, itch, nervousness, heart changes and stomach upsets. It must be used with care in pregnancy, and not in patients with peptic ulcer or a recent heart attack.

Probucol (Lurselle) is reserved for patients with severe high blood cholesterol level. Side effects include diarrhoea, nausea, excess wind and belly pains. It must be used with care in pregnancy, and not in patients with a recent heart attack or heart disease.
See also CHOLESTEROL; FAT;
MEDICATION; TRIGLYCERIDE

HYPONATRAEMIA
Hyponatraemia is a medical term indicating a low level of sodium (Na), and therefore usually salt, in the blood.
See also SODIUM

HYPOPARATHYROIDISM
The four parathyroid glands behind the thyroid gland in the neck regulate the amount of calcium in the blood and bones. In hypoparathyroidism, the glands secrete inadequate amounts of the hormone calcitonin, which results in excessive amounts of calcium being taken from the blood and into the bones. It is a rare condition that may occur after thyroid gland surgery, or may be spontaneous for no apparent reason.

Symptoms may include spasms of the small muscles in the hands and feet, tingling lips, tiredness, wheezing, muscle cramps, fungal infections, abdominal pains, anxiety attacks, and behavioural alterations. If present for some time, the nails will become thin and brittle, the teeth will be deformed, cataracts may develop in the eyes, and the skin becomes dry and scaly. Untreated, it may cause irregular heartbeat, reduced growth in children, anaemia and mental retardation.

The diagnosis is confirmed by measuring the amount of calcium in the blood, and x-rays show very dense bones and calcium deposits in abnormal areas (eg. brain).

Treatment may be an emergency in serious cases. Calcium injections and tablets, and vitamin D tablets are used, and once stabilised on treatment, the long-term outlook is good, but damage already done to eyes, teeth and other tissues may be irreversible. Very regular blood tests, follow-up visits, and lifelong medication are essential.
See also HYPERPARATHYROIDISM;
PARATHYROID GLAND

HYPOPITUITARISM
The pituitary gland sits in the centre of the brain and secretes hormones into the blood stream that control every other hormone-producing gland in the body (eg. thyroid gland, adrenal gland, ovary, testes). Hypopituitarism (Simmonds disease) occurs if the pituitary fails to produce the appropriate regulating hormones. If the gland fails to produce all the possible hormones it is called panhypopituitarism. The causes include a tumour or abscess of the pituitary gland, head injury, stroke, swollen blood vessels, malnutrition or other rare and complex reasons.

When the pituitary gland is underactive, every other gland it controls will also become underactive and the patient will have reduced sexual desire and activity, lose pubic hair, men will stop growing a beard and women will stop having monthly periods. Infertility may be a problem in both sexes. Other problems include weakness, tiredness, poor resistance to infections, low blood pressure, vision defects, and becoming stressed easily. Sometimes only part of the pituitary gland is underactive, so only some glands will malfunction. The diagnosis can be confirmed by blood tests, CT and MRI scans.

Treatment involves correcting the cause, if possible, by surgery or irradiation, and giving hormone supplements by tablet or injection. The prognosis depends on the cause, but in most cases the condition can be well controlled.

See also CUSHING SYNDROME;
PITUITARY GLAND

HYPOSPADIAS

Hypospadias is a congenital developmental abnormality in which the tube carrying the urine through the penis (the urethra) fails to close properly in the foetus, and the opening is on the lower side of the penis rather than the end. Very rarely the opening may be on top of the penis (epispadias). The urethral opening can occur anywhere from the base of the penis to very near the end, depending on the severity of the abnormality. These men are more likely to develop urinary infections, must pass urine sitting down, and later in life when having sex, will ejaculate through the abnormal opening in a place that makes it difficult for their partner to fall pregnant.

An operation can be performed to correct the abnormality and place the urethral opening in the usual position at the end of the penis. The operation is completely successful in the vast majority of patients, and the man's future sex life should be completely normal.
See also PENIS ABNORMAL

HYPOSTATIC ECZEMA
See VARICOSE ECZEMA

HYPOTENSION

Hypotension is excessively low blood pressure. The heart contracts regularly to pump blood through the arteries under high (systolic) pressure. When the heart relaxes between beats, the blood continues to flow due to the lower (diastolic) pressure exerted by the elasticity of the artery walls. Hypotension occurs when one, or both, of these pressures drops to a low level. Blood pressure readings are written as systolic pressure/diastolic pressure (eg. 125/70) and are measured with a sphygmomanometer. Blood pressure varies with exercise, anxiety, age, fitness, smoking and drinking habits, weight and medications. The numbers are a measure of pressure in millimetres of mercury.

Low blood pressure only causes concern when it causes symptoms or is detected in the course of investigation of other diseases (eg. someone with a suspected heart attack). Hypotension is a relative condition – the blood pressure is low compared to what it should be – and not an absolute one. A young woman may have a blood pressure of 90/50 and be

perfectly well, but the same pressure in an elderly person may have serious consequences.

Hypotension may be due to a sudden change in position (postural hypotension), a serious injury resulting in blood loss (shock), heart attack, heart failure, dehydration, alcoholism, serious infections, heat stroke, pregnancy, a large number of less common diseases, and some drugs. It causes dizziness, light headedness, fainting and headaches.

The cause of the low blood pressure needs to be treated, rather than the blood pressure itself. In a very small number of people no specific cause can be found, and a medication may be given to raise the blood pressure slightly.
See also HYPERTENSION; POSTURAL HYPOTENSION; SHOCK; SPHYGMOMANOMETER

HYPOTHERMIA

Hypothermia, or exposure, is an abnormally low body temperature below 35°C due to being in cold conditions without adequate protection. Cold air alone can cause hypothermia, but if combined with wind, hypothermia occurs more rapidly. Cold water is the most serious cause, and death may occur in as little as a few minutes in icy water. An inadequately clad person may suffer hypothermia after only half a day in a climate where the temperature does not drop below 20°C. Even in tropical waters shipwreck victims may die from hypothermia. Alcoholics may neglect themselves and even in relatively mild conditions suffer from hypothermia due to inadequate clothing, shelter and nutrition.

The blood vessels to the skin contract so that victims feel far colder to the touch than expected. Other symptoms are weakness, drowsiness, irritability, irrational behaviour and poor coordination. As the temperature drops further, delirium, coma and death from an irregular heartbeat occur. The temperature of the patient must be measured using a rectal (through the anus) thermometer as the skin temperature and mouth temperature are often inaccurate.

The treatment depends on the severity of the hypothermia. Mild cases respond well to good warm clothing, warm bed and rest. Shared body heat may be appropriate.

Moderate to severe cases will require hospitalisation for warmed air or oxygen, warm drinks, and warm fluids through a drip into a vein to heat the core of the body. This may be followed by immersion in a lukewarm bath that may have its temperature increased slowly over several hours. Heated blankets may also be used.

Patients who appear to have died because of hypothermia must be given mouth-to-mouth resuscitation and external heart massage for several hours while continuing to warm the body. Recovery may not occur until the body temperature rises to 32°C or more. Patients (particularly children) have been known to recover fully after prolonged periods of immersion or apparent death, with appropriate resuscitation, as the low temperature protects the brain and body from damage. Rapid warming, and warming the surface of the body only (which may cause premature dilation of the arteries in the skin), can cause heart irregularities and death.

The prognosis depends upon the severity, prior health and age, but children recover far better than the elderly.
See also FROSTBITE

HYPOTHYROIDISM

Hypothyroidism is underactivity of the thyroid gland, which sits in the front of the neck and is responsible for secreting a hormone called thyroxine. This acts as the accelerator for every cell in the body. If the level of thyroxine is high, the cells function at an increased rate. If the level of thyroxine is low, the cells function at a less than normal rate. In children, hypothyroidism causes cretinism. The thyroid gland tends to fail with advancing age, particularly in women. It may be associated with an enlarged thyroid gland (goitre), and less commonly cysts or tumours may destroy the gland tissue.

Tiredness, weakness, muscle cramps, constipation, dry skin, headaches, nervousness, intolerance to cold weather and a hoarse voice are the most common symptoms. In more severe cases additional symptoms may include thinning of the hair, skin thickening, brittle nails, weight gain, shortness of breath, a thick tongue and a slow heart rate. The symptoms are referred to as myxoedema. The drop in thyroxine levels is usually gradual over many years and the symptoms may be overlooked until the disease is quite advanced. It is diagnosed by blood tests that measure the amount of thyroxine, and other thyroid-related substances.

Thyroxine tablets are taken long term to replace that not being produced by the gland. Patients usually notice a remarkable improvement in their quality of life as the thyroxine replacement tablets start to work. With adequate treatment the patient should lead a normal active life, but untreated, there is an increased risk of developing severe infections and heart failure, and premature death will occur.
See also CRETINISM; GOITRE; THYROID GLAND; THYROIDITIS

HYPOTONIA
See MUSCLE TONE REDUCED

HYPOURICAEMICS

Uric acid is the substance that, in excess, causes gout. Hypouricaemics are those drugs that reduce the level of uric acid in the blood, and treat or prevent gout. Colchicine can be used to both treat and prevent gout, but allopurinol (Zyloprim) and probenecid (Benemid) are used only for the long-term prevention of the disease. They are only available as tablets. Side effects of allopurinol and probenecid are minimal, but a rash is possible, and they must not be used during an acute attack as this may make the attack worse.

Colchicine is a very effective gout treatment, but diarrhoea is a very common side effect, and nausea may occur.

Once a patient has gout, regular medication should be taken for many years to prevent a recurrence of the joint pain and the kidney damage that may also occur. It must be used with caution in the elderly, pregnant, and those with diseased kidneys, heart or gut.

Probenecid is also used to prolong the effectiveness of penicillin, as it prevents its excretion through the kidneys.
See also GOUT; MEDICATION; URIC ACID

HYSTERECTOMY

Hysterectomy is a term which many women misunderstand and fear, yet it is one of the most common surgical procedures performed. Before a hysterectomy, a woman should be thoroughly investigated by blood tests, ultrasound examinations, and possibly x-rays and laparoscopy, to determine if there is any method of relieving her symptoms other than removal of the uterus.

The operation derives its name from a period over 150 years ago when it was thought that the uterus was a source of mental disturbance and caused hysteria in women. A hysterectomy was a very radical cure.

The female sexual organs consist of four main parts – the vagina which is used in intercourse, the womb (uterus) and its opening into the vagina called the cervix, the Fallopian tubes that carry the egg from the ovaries to the womb, and the two ovaries. It is only the uterus, tubes and one ovary that are removed from most women in a hysterectomy. Both ovaries and/or the vagina may be removed if the operation is for cancer.

Because the vagina and one ovary are normally left behind, the woman is able to have a normal sex life after the operation. The vagina remains the same size, and the female hormones that stimulate sexual responses and maintain the normal breast shape and body hair continue to be released in adequate amounts from the remaining ovary. Once she has recovered fully from the operation, the woman and her partner should notice no significant difference in their normal sexual relationships, and the woman will still be able to experience an orgasm.

Women who have the operation before their menopause will still experience the problems commonly associated with the change later in their life, and the resultant hot flushes, depression, bloating, headaches and other symptoms may need further medical treatment.

Because the uterus is responsible for producing the blood loss that occurs with monthly periods, a hysterectomy stops any further bleeding, but a woman may still experience the symptoms of premenstrual tension, and sometimes detect the bodily changes associated with ovulation. This is because the remaining ovary continues to produce hormones in the normal cyclical manner, as though the uterus was still there to respond. If both ovaries are removed, the woman undergoes an instant menopause, and must take hormone replacement therapy long term.

Hysterectomies are performed for many different reasons, the most serious being cancer (which may result in more major surgery to remove the surrounding lymph nodes as well). Most operations are for milder diseases and complaints, which may still be very distressing to the individual woman.

These problems include uterine growths (eg. fibroids), endometriosis (a type of pelvic bleeding disorder), ovarian diseases and, most commonly, for intractable heavy and painful periods.

There are three main methods of performing a hysterectomy – an open operation, vaginal hysterectomy and laparoscopic hysterectomy.

In the open operation, a horizontal incision is made into the lower part of the belly, the abdominal cavity is opened, and the uterus and other attached organs are removed. The wound, which is about twelve to fifteen cm. long, is then sutured closed. A hospital stay of five or six days is necessary, and it may be six to eight weeks before a return to normal activities.

In a vaginal hysterectomy, there is no scar on the abdomen as the entire operation is performed through the vagina. The recovery time is not quite as long as for the open operation, but the operation is more technically difficult, and in most centres has been replaced by laparoscopic hysterectomy.

Laparoscopic hysterectomies were first performed in the late 1980s, and are now the most common form of the operation, but not all women are suitable candidates. It involves four incisions in the abdomen, each about one centimetre long, and through these thin tubes are introduced. These laparoscopic tubes are used to see what is happening inside the abdomen using a camera or direct vision, and to introduce instruments to perform the operation. When the uterus and tubes have been cut free from the supporting structures, they are removed through the vagina. There is much less pain after this operation, the hospital stay is only one or two nights, and patients recover completely in two to three weeks. There are fewer complications than with open surgery as less tissue damage occurs.

An alternative to hysterectomy in some circumstances (eg. heavy bleeding) is microwave endometrial ablation.

Most women who have the operation for good reasons are very grateful because they no longer need to spend a week or more each month cloistered away from society because of menstrual flooding and cramps.

Any woman contemplating a hysterectomy, or who has been advised to have one, should take along a list to ensure that her gynaecologist or general practitioner adequately answers all her questions and concerns. Obtaining a second opinion from another gynaecologist may further reassure the woman that the operation is her best option. In this way, many problems can be avoided.

See also ENDOMETRIOSIS; FALLOPIAN TUBE; FIBROID; MICROWAVE ENDOMETRIAL ABLATION; OVARY; UTERUS

HYSTERIA
See BRIQUET SYNDROME; CONVERSION DISORDER; HYPOCHONDRIASIS

HYSTEROSCOPY
A hysteroscopy is an endoscopic examination of the inside of the uterus using a hysteroscope, which is a thin flexible tube that is passed through the vagina and cervix into the uterus (womb). The doctor can look through the instrument to examine the inside of the uterus and the openings into the Fallopian tubes. Hysteroscopy is used to help diagnose disorders of the uterus and the endometrium (lining of the uterus). The patient will be sedated or given a general anaesthetic.

See also CULDOSCOPY; ENDOSCOPE; LAPAROSCOPY; MICROWAVE ENDOMETRIAL ABLATION; UTERUS

I

IATROGENIC

An iatrogenic condition or disease is one that has been caused by the treatment, investigation or management of the patient by doctors or other medical staff. Side effects of medications and complications of surgery or investigations are the most common causes.

IBN SINA
See AVICENNA

IBS
See IRRITABLE BOWEL SYNDROME

IBUPROFEN
See NONSTEROIDAL ANTI-INFLAMMATORY DRUGS

ICHABOD SYNDROME

The ICHABOD syndrome is a sign of imminent death from any chronic cause. The disease name is an acronym for a number of clinical signs used by doctors to predict death in a patient with a longstanding incurable disease. As well as being an acronym, the syndrome name may also be derived from the Old Testament daughter-in-law of Eli who, before dying in childbirth, named her son Ichabod, which translates as 'the glory has departed'.

The components of the acronym are: –
• Immobility – fewer than 20% of patients can stand within two days before death
• Confusion and coma – 40% become comatose and 30% confused in the two days before death
• Homeostatic (body function regulation) failure – failure of temperature regulation, blood pressure control and circulation to hands and feet are common in the two days before death
• Anorexia (loss of appetite) – very common in final week before death
• Blood – blood test changes indicative of imminent death
• Observation – occasional (rather than regular) observation of facial appearance shows marked deterioration in personality features

• Dyspnoea (shortness of breath) – 30% of patients become short of breath in last two days. Cheyne-Stokes respiration is very common in last few hours.
See also CHEYNE-STOKES RESPIRATION; DEATH

ICHTHYOSIS

Ichthyosis is an uncommon congenital (present since birth) skin condition due to a lack of oil glands in the skin. Numerous subtypes are known (eg. ichthyosis vulgaris – most common type; X-linked ichthyosis – affects males only; ichthyosis linearis circumflexa – affects babies). Widespread scaling, dryness and thickening of the skin occur, and the diagnosis is confirmed by a skin biopsy.

Massive quantities of moisturising creams and oils must be applied to the skin, but the skin is more susceptible to other skin diseases, sun damage and poor healing. No cure is possible.
See also SKIN DRY AND SCALY

ICTERUS
See JAUNDICE

IDC

'IDC' is the acronym for an 'in dwelling catheter' which is a tube used to drain urine from the bladder.
See FOLEY CATHETER

IDDM
See DIABETES MELLITUS TYPE ONE

IDIOPATHIC

Idiopathic is a medical term meaning that a condition or disease has no known cause.

IDIOPATHIC PULMONARY FIBROSIS

Idiopathic pulmonary fibrosis (cryptogenic fibrosing alveolitis) is an uncommon (one in 10 000 people) condition of middle aged and elderly people in which normal lung tissue is replaced by fibrous tissue. The cause is unknown, but it may be a form of autoimmune disease in which the body rejects its own tissue.

Patients develop progressively worsening shortness of breath, crackling breath sounds, coughing and attacks of bronchitis. Pneumonia and heart failure may also develop. It is diagnosed by chest x-ray, nuclear scans, lung function tests, lung biopsy and blood tests.

Lung transplantation may help some patients, steroids may slow the progress of the disease, and a number of innovative medications are being used experimentally, but the condition is usually slowly progressive until the lungs and/or heart fail. Patients without treatment survive two to four years after diagnosis.
See also AUTOIMMUNE DISEASES; LUNG

IDIOPATHIC THROMBO-CYTOPENIC PURPURA
See THROMBOCYTOPENIA

IDIOT SAVANT SYNDROME
The cause of the idiot savant syndrome is unknown, but it may be due to one area of the brain over-developing before birth at the expense of other areas. The patient is usually subnormal in all areas of mental activity except one narrow field (eg. maths, music) in which they are extraordinarily talented. Mental tests are used to differentiate areas of skill from areas of below normal function. Intensive education is necessary to develop life skills and areas of subnormal ability.
See also AUTISM

IDOXURIDINE
See ANTIVIRALS

IEC
See INTRAEPITHELIAL CARCINOMA

ILEAL CONDUIT
Surgeons have devised some ingenious ways of helping patients with very difficult problems. One of these is for the patient who has no bladder function due to injury or disease. The ureter (the tube that carries urine from the kidney to the bladder) is implanted into the side of an isolated piece of ileum (small intestine) to form an artificial bladder known as an ileal conduit. One end of this 30cm segment of intestine is closed off, while the other is formed into a stoma, allowing the patient to urinate through this into a plastic bag.
See also BLADDER; ILEOSTOMY; ILEUM; STOMA

ILEOLUMBAR SYNDROME
The ileolumbar syndrome is a strain to the ligaments in the lower back from lifting and twisting movements. Patients have sciatica (pain running down the back of the leg), and pain and tenderness in the buttocks. Bending sideways away from painful side worsens the pain. There are no specific tests, and x-rays and CT scans of the back are usually normal.

Anti-inflammatory medications, physiotherapy and injection of local anaesthetic and long lasting steroid into the tender area are the main treatments. The condition often recurs, although treatment is usually successful.
See also BACK PAIN; STRAIN

ILEOSTOMY
Some diseases of the bowel may necessitate the small intestine being made into a stoma (opening onto the skin). The lower part of the small intestine is technically known as the ileum, and so a stoma in this part of the gut is called an ileostomy, and food will leave the body in a semi-digested state through this opening and into a collecting bag. The small intestine is responsible for the absorption of food into the body and contains acids and digestive juices which may attack the skin. As a result these people have more problems dealing with their stoma than those with a colostomy.
See also ILEAL CONDUIT; ILEUM; STOMA

ILEUM
The ileum is the third and final part of the small intestine, leading from the jejunum at its top end and connecting into the side of the caecum at its lower end. It is lined with millions of tiny finger-like projections (villi) that are finer and smaller than those found in the jejunum. These act to absorb food into the bloodstream and lymphatic system. It is about 2cm. in diameter and five or six metres long.

Those parts of the food that cannot be used are passed into the large intestine eventually to be eliminated.

The ileum's name is very aptly derived

INTESTINAL TRACT

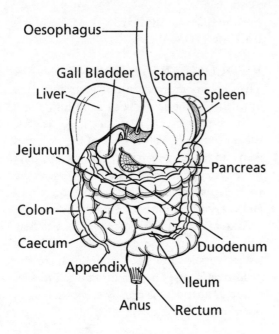

from the Latin word for twist, as it twists and turns in multiple loose loops in the belly.

See also CAECUM; GALL BLADDER; ILEAL CONDUIT; ILEOSTOMY; JEJUNUM; LARGE INTESTINE; PORTAL SYSTEM

ILIAC ARTERY
See AORTA

ILIAC BONE
See PELVIS

ILIOTIBIAL BAND FRICTION SYNDROME

The iliotibial band friction syndrome is a leg injury that usually occurs in long distance runners who run on side-sloped surface (eg. beach, road shoulder). Pain occurs on the outside of the knee with walking, there is tenderness when pressure is applied to outside lower end of femur (thigh bone), and a grating sensation may be felt in the knee joint with walking. Rest, anti-inflammatory medications and physiotherapy are the only treatments, but most cases settle eventually.

See also KNEE PAIN

ILLEGAL DRUGS

See CANNABIS; COCAINE; ECSTASY; GAMMA-HYDROXYBUTYRATE; HEROIN; KETAMINE; LSD; MARIJUANA; MESCALINE

IMDUR
See ANTIANGINALS

IMIDAZOLES
See ANTIFUNGALS

IMIGRAN
See 5HT RECEPTOR AGONISTS

IMIPRAMINE
See ANTIDEPRESSANTS

IMMERSION
See DROWNING

IMMUNE TESTS

During a viral infection, antibodies are produced to fight the virus. These antibodies remain even after the infection has cleared, and prevent most viral infections from developing again. This is immunity. Rubella (German measles) and chickenpox are examples of infections which, once suffered, will not usually recur. A blood test may be performed to find out if a patient is immune to a particular disease. For example, a doctor may want to know if a woman has had rubella (which can harm the foetus if the mother develops it during early pregnancy) or whether she should be immunised against it.

For some reason not yet fully understood, the body can start producing antibodies to its own tissues. In effect, the body fights against itself and is the cause of its own destruction. This is called autoimmune disease, examples of which include rheumatoid arthritis (the body develops antibodies against the synovial tissue lining some joints) and the more widespread systemic lupus erythematosus (SLE). The presence of these specific disease antibodies can also be detected by a blood test.

Sometimes tests are carried out to detect the presence of antigens themselves (antigens are substances the body regards as foreign and to which it will develop antibodies). The presence of particular antigens in the blood indicates that the organism is still active and that, even though the symptoms have subsided, the person may be a carrier of the disease (eg. hepatitis B).

The progress of certain diseases can be assessed by testing the blood for specific immunoglobulins (antibodies) which differ according to whether the disease is current or past. Many infectious diseases such as glandular fever, AIDS, various forms of hepatitis, Ross River fever and measles can be diagnosed and followed by these tests.

A 'T cell' count tests the number and proportion in the blood of a type of white cell (T lymphocyte) which is an indication of the progress of immune deficiency diseases such as AIDS.

See also ANTIBODY; ANTIGEN; AUTOIMMUNE DISEASES; BLOOD TESTS; IMMUNODEFICIENCY

IMMUNISATION
See TRAVEL IMMUNISATION; VACCINATION

IMMUNITY
See ANTIBODY; ANTIGEN; IMMUNE TESTS; LYMPH NODES; VACCINATION; WHITE BLOOD CELLS

IMMUNODEFICIENCY
The immune system is centred on the thymus gland (which sits behind the top of the breast bone), the bone marrow and lymph nodes (mainly in the armpit, groin and neck). These produce white blood cells and antibodies (molecules that attack specific viruses or bacteria) which circulate in the bloodstream to detect and destroy invading germs. Immunodeficiency (a lack of immunity to infection) is a rare condition that is caused by a lack of or abnormal white blood cells, or a lack of immunoglobulin, which is the building block of antibodies. Most cases occur in children, and usually within a year of birth.

A number of very rare diseases are responsible for immunodeficiency, including di George syndrome (a failure of the thymus to develop), Goodpasture syndrome, Wiskott-Aldrich syndrome (an inherited failure to produce white cells), and agammaglobulinaemia (a lack of gamma immunoglobulin). Acquired immune deficiency syndrome (AIDS) is also a form of immunodeficiency in which the white cells are destroyed by the virus causing AIDS.

Immunodeficiency causes frequent severe infections, sometimes patients bleed and bruise easily, and there is an increased incidence of cancer. It is diagnosed by blood tests and biopsy of bone marrow and other organs.

Medications may slow the progress of the condition and resultant infections can be treated, but patients with most forms of immunodeficiency cannot be cured, and children often die early in life.

See also AGAMMAGLOBULINAEMIA; AIDS; di GEORGE SYNDROME; GOODPASTURE SYNDROME; IMMUNE TESTS; WISKOTT-ALDRICH SYNDROME

IMMUNOGLOBULIN
See IMMUNE TESTS

IMMUNOSUPPRESSANTS
Immunosuppressants are used to suppress (control or reduce) the immune reaction that occurs after the transplantation of foreign tissue into a body. They may also be used in the treatment of some types of cancer and defects in immunity that allow a few rare diseases to arise within the body. They are the drugs that have made possible the transplanting of the kidney, liver, heart and other organs, as the body normally uses its immune system to reject these donated organs. There are many different drugs in this class (eg. azathioprine, cyclosporin, interferon), all with significant complications and precautions attached to their use, and are used only by doctors who specialise in this type of work. They are available both in tablet and injection form.

See also TRANSPLANTS AND IMPLANTS

IMMUNOTHERAPY
Immunotherapy is the enhancement of the body's natural immunity as a method of preventing, or (more recently) of treating disease. Immunisation against a wide range of diseases such as polio, influenza, measles, typhoid, mumps, etc., is a well known role of this area of medicine. Immunisation against smallpox has resulted in the total elimination of this disease.

The new role of immunotherapy is in treating cancer, and specifically engineered antibodies are now being used to destroy some types of cancer cells. Antibodies are normally produced by the body as a reaction to an invading organism. Antibodies against the measles virus are produced by an attack of measles. The antibodies destroy the invading virus, and they remain for the rest of the patient's life to prevent a further measles attacks.

With genetic engineering techniques that have been developed within the last decade, specific antibodies have already been designed to detect certain types of cancer, and their use experimentally to treat these cancers is under way.

Cancer cells from the patient are cultured artificially, and a vaccine to destroy these cells is developed. This vaccine is then given to the patient, quite often with very good results. Unfortunately this process is very time consuming, technically difficult and expensive, and a vaccine must be developed specifically for each patient. Leukaemias, melanomas and lymphomas (lymph gland cancers) are the main areas of success to date.

Immunotherapy is a new science, and medical practitioners are only just beginning to grasp its complexity and potential. Almost certainly immunotherapy will be as significant in the future as the first antibiotics were in 1940.
See also ANTIBODY; IMMUNODEFICIENCY; VACCINATION

IMOVANE
See SEDATIVES

IMPETIGO
Impetigo or school sores, is a very common skin infection that virtually every child will catch, but it may also occur in adults. Several different bacteria may be responsible, but the most common is *Staphylococcus aureus* ('golden staph'). This is a serious infection inside the body, but relatively mild on the skin. Impetigo spreads from one person to another by close contact, and sometimes an infected animal may act as a source. Once one sore develops on the skin, scratching with fingers can rapidly spread the infection to other parts of the body. It is more common in warm climates and in summer.

An itchy, red, raised, weeping or crusting sore appears. If there are a many sores, the patient may feel generally unwell, but normally there are no other symptoms. In newborn babies, impetigo may spread rapidly and become serious, so for this reason, infected children should be kept away from infants.

If necessary, swabs can be taken from the sores to confirm the diagnosis, determine the infecting bacteria, and select the correct antibiotic.

Treatment involves antibiotic mixtures or tablets, and an antibiotic cream. Antiseptic soaps, not sharing towels and bedding, and careful personal hygiene can be used to prevent the spread of infection, and a child must be excluded from school until the sores start to heal. With correct treatment, the sores will heal without scarring in a few days.
See also BACTERIA; SCALDED SKIN SYNDROME; *STAPHYLOCOCCUS AUREUS*

IMPINGEMENT SYNDROMES
See ANTERIOR IMPINGEMENT SYNDROME; SHOULDER IMPINGEMENT SYNDROME

IMPLANTS
See TRANSPLANTS AND IMPLANTS

IMPOTENCE
Impotence is the inability of a man to obtain a firm erection of the penis when sexually stimulated. It is a very common problem, and something that every man experiences at some time, particularly in middle age and older.

Women are sometimes mystified by the process of erection, but it is one over which the man has no direct control as it is a local reflex in the pelvis triggered by sexual excitement. The penis contains two sausage shaped sponge-filled tubes (corpora cavernosa) that fill with blood under pressure when a muscular ring closes off the drainage veins behind the base of the penis.

A wide range of diseases may cause impotence, and these must be excluded by appropriate investigations before a psychological cause is diagnosed, or impotence treatment is given. If a cause is found, it should be specifically treated to resolve the problem. Only if no particular cause can be diagnosed should the various impotence treatments available be used.

A lot of impotence is caused by a psychological feedback mechanism. For one of the reasons listed below, a man may fail to develop an erection when attempting sex. He feels embarrassed and ashamed about this, particularly if it is with a new partner. The next time he tries to have sex he will be anxious as to whether he will be able to perform. This anxiety makes him concentrate on trying to get an erection, which is an almost certain way in which to prevent an erection. After two failures, the anxiety increases, which further decreases the chance of success at subsequent attempts. It requires patient understanding by the man's partner and the continuing advice of a doctor, to overcome this erection failure cycle.

Common causes of impotence include the overuse of alcohol (which increases the desire, while reducing the ability), stress and anxiety in any aspect of life, difficult circumstances (eg. lack of privacy), heavy smoking, illegal drugs (eg. marijuana, heroin) and medications (eg. those used to lower blood pressure and improve depression, sedatives, cimetidine, clofibrate, digoxin).

Other possible causes of impotence include depression, pituitary gland disease (gland in the brain which controls all other glands including the testes), testicular diseases or injury, and poorly controlled diabetes mellitus (sugar diabetes). High levels of cholesterol may cause hardening of the arteries (atherosclerosis), making it difficult for the blood to get into the penis, and cancer of the prostate gland may interfere with the normal nerve and blood vessel reflexes that allow an erection.

Rare causes of impotence include Peyronie's disease (a replacement of the blood filled sacs by fibrous scar tissue), a 'fracture' of the erect penis, multiple sclerosis, paraplegia and quadriplegia, lead poisoning, Klinefelter syndrome and Fröhlich syndrome.

Psychological factors may be overcome by avoiding planning sex, but relaxing and waiting until the right circumstances occur spontaneously. Mutual heavy petting and erotic stimulation (but without the expectation of sex), sexual toys, pornography and vacuum pumps to create an erection may be used. Once spontaneous erections develop, sex may start again. Numerous medications are also available including: –
• alprostadil (Caverject) injections into the penis
• alprostadil (Muse) pellets may be inserted into the urethra (urine tube in the penis)
• sildenafil (Viagra) tablets

Several other medications are under development (eg. apomorphine).
See also ALPROSTADIL; EJACULATION, LACK OF; EJACULATION PREMATURE; LIBIDO LACKING; PENIS; SEXUAL INTERCOURSE; SILDENAFIL

INCEST
Incest is sexual contact between members of a family, usually between father and daughter or brother and sister, but between mother and son or with grandparents is also possible. A child is the usual victim, although once established as a practice, it may persist into adult life.

It is a form of deviant sexual behaviour, and is not tolerated in any society. It may be used as a form of domination over a weaker person, to satisfy aberrant sexual desires or because of psychological and sexual immaturity.

It is unusual for the victim to report the crime as they are normally frightened of the perpetrator. As a result, the abuse may continue for many years. It is therefore essential for anyone who is aware of incest to bring the matter to the attention of a doctor or the police so that both parties can receive help in recovering from the emotional and psychological trauma that incest causes.

Long term counselling is often needed for the victim, and continued psychiatric management for the perpetrator.
See also CHILD ABUSE; RAPE

INCISIONAL HERNIA
In older, obese or debilitated people, the deeper tissue may break down after an operation on the belly, allowing part of the bowel to escape through the deeper layers of the wound to the area just under the skin, to cause an incisional hernia. A wound infection may be responsible, but often the deeper tissue gives way after a fit of coughing or under the strain of supporting the belly after an operation.

A lump is seen and felt under the skin of the belly, and other symptoms are usually minimal, but sometimes intermittent discomfort, and occasionally pain, at the site of the hernia may occur. Rarely, intestine may become caught and twisted in the hernia, causing severe pain, and eventually gangrene of the intestine.

A corset is usually all that is required to control the hernia, but in some circumstances, further surgery, often with insertion of some surgical mesh to strengthen the area, will be required. There is a significant risk of recurrence after further surgical repair. Most cause no serious problem, but may be annoying.

See also HERNIA

INCLUSION BODY MYOSITIS

Inclusion body myositis is a rare form of progressive muscle wasting and weakness in the elderly with a very slow insidious onset and no known cause. Patients experience gradually worsening muscle weakness, which starts in the hands and feet and moves towards the trunk. It is diagnosed by muscle biopsy and tests on the electrical activity within muscles (electromyography – EMG). No specific treatment is available, but progression of the disease may be slowed by medication in some patients.

See also MUSCULAR WEAKNESS

INCONTINENCE OF FAECES

Severe diarrhoea from any cause can be an obvious and embarrassing cause of incontinence of faeces (soiling), due to the massive amounts of hard-to-control fluid present in the lower bowel.

The inability to control the passing of faeces may be due to psychological or psychiatric conditions, particularly in the elderly. A loss of inhibitions associated with dementia (eg. Alzheimer disease) is a common cause, while psychiatric patients may use it as an attention-seeking device.

In children, behavioural disorders or emotional stress may be responsible.

Soiling may be due to damage to the brain (eg. a stroke, cerebral palsy) or the nerves supplying the muscle ring around the anus (eg. paraplegia, fractured pelvis).

In advanced pregnancy the pressure on the lower bowel from the growing baby may make control of faeces difficult. Damage to the anus from a difficult birth may be a temporary, or very rarely a permanent, cause of faecal incontinence. Surgery can be performed to control the problem in these cases.

Any surgery to the anus, for problems as diverse as piles and cancer, may be responsible for loss of control.

A greatly dilated lower bowel (megacolon) may cause large amounts of hard faeces to collect just inside the anus, and remain for a long time, while watery faeces flow around the outside of this faecal mass in the bowel, to leak out through the anus.

See also COLON; DIARRHOEA; FAECES and separate entries for diseases mentioned above.

INCONTINENCE OF URINE

This is the inability to control the outflow of urine so that wetting of clothing or bedding occurs. It is a problem that affects women far more than men. Repeated urinary infections may be a complication.

In women, there is normally an acute angle between the bladder and the opening into the urethra (tube leading to the outside). If this angle is reduced for any reason, the woman will become more prone to urinary incontinence.

Alcohol and caffeine are both known to increase the production of urine, and if too much of the former is consumed, the person may lose his or her inhibitions and urinate inappropriately.

A sudden severe fright, shock or extreme fear may cause loss of bladder control.

An infection of the bladder or kidney will result in the frequent, painful passage of small amounts of urine. Women may find their control of urination to be compromised with these infections.

Childbirth can cause damage to the muscles that control the release of urine, and may result in long term problems, so that every time the woman laughs, coughs or exercises, she passes a small amount of urine. The loss of muscle tone in the floor of the pelvis can result in the same problem. The muscle tone in this area is maintained by the female hormone, oestrogen, so the lack of oestrogen at menopause predisposes to incontinence. Obesity will further aggravate the problem. Pelvic floor exercises supervised by a physiotherapist, hormone replacement therapy, weight loss and surgery can all help control these causes of incontinence.

A number of medications may aggravate incontinence. Examples include blood pressure medications (particularly prazosin), fluid producing medications (diuretics), tranquillisers, lithium and some depression treating drugs (tricyclics).

Other causes of urinary incontinence include surgery to the pelvis and genitals (eg. hysterectomy), a stroke, loss of consciousness, epileptic fit, damage to the brain (eg. cerebral palsy, tumour, Parkinson's disease), senility or dementia (eg. Alzheimer disease), tumours or stones in the bladder, pelvic injury, multiple sclerosis, injury to the spinal cord (eg. paraplegia or quadriplegia), poorly controlled diabetes mellitus and diabetes insipidus.

A fistula (abnormal opening) between the bladder and vagina may be caused by a very difficult childbirth, particularly in poorer countries. These poor women constantly dribble urine through their vagina.

Rarer causes include severe allergy reactions affecting the genitals, psychiatric disorders (eg. severe depression) and birth abnormalities of the bladder structure.

X-rays of the bladder and kidneys, and cystoscopy (looking into the bladder through a thin tube) can be used to investigate the cause of the incontinence. Incontinence is not a disease but a symptom, and the responsible disease needs to be diagnosed before any treatment can start.
See also BED WETTING; BLADDER;
FOLEY CATHETER and separate entries for diseases mentioned above.

INCOORDINATION
See CLUMSINESS; COORDINATION, LACK OF

INCUS
See EAR

INDAPAMIDE
See DIURETICS

INDIAN TICK TYPHUS
See TYPHUS

INDIGESTION
See ABDOMINAL PAIN; BURPING, EXCESSIVE; CHEST PAIN; DYSPEPSIA; HEARTBURN

INDOMETHACIN
See NONSTEROIDAL ANTI-INFLAMMATORY DRUGS

INDUCTION OF LABOUR
A pregnancy that goes beyond about forty-two weeks can put the baby at risk because the placenta starts to degenerate. It is therefore sometimes necessary to start (induce) labour artificially. Labour may also be induced for a number of other reasons, including diseases of the mother (eg. pre-eclampsia, diabetes), and problems with the baby (eg. foetal distress from a twisted cord or separating placenta).

Labour can be induced in a number of ways, including rupturing the membranes through the vagina, stimulating the cervix, by tablets or (most commonly) medication given through a drip into a vein in the arm. Using these methods, doctors can control the rate of labour quite accurately to ensure that there are no problems for either mother or baby.
See also FOETUS; LABOUR; PRE-ECLAMPSIA AND ECLAMPSIA; PREGNANCY

INDWELLING CATHETER
See FOLEY CATHETER; IDC

INFANTILE COLIC
Infantile or six-week colic is probably caused by spontaneous spasms of the small intestine, but no reason for these spasms has ever been proven. Some experts suggest anxiety in the mother, particularly in a family without extended family support, may cause anxiety in the infant, and subsequent gut spasms.

The baby starts screaming for no apparent reason, draws the legs up and looks pale. After a few minutes, the attack subsides, and the infant appears normal, then after a short interval, the screaming starts again. This pattern repeats itself several times a day. No tests can be performed to confirm the diagnosis.

Changes in diet and formula, different foods for the mother of breastfed infants, alterations to feeding times and positions, increases or decreases in the degree of attention paid to the child, and antispasmodic drugs and paracetamol can all be tried, with varying degrees of success. The problem always goes away in due course, usually at twelve to sixteen weeks of age.
See also ABDOMINAL PAIN; COLIC; INTESTINAL COLIC

INFARCT
An infarct is the death of tissue due to a lack of blood supply. The artery supplying a tissue or organ may be blocked by a clot, fatty plaque or may be squeezed by the growth of a tumour.
See also HEART ATTACK; STROKE

INFECTION

An infection is the invasion of tissue by a bacteria, virus, prion or fungus, which multiply and spread to cause cell damage and/or destruction and unwanted symptoms. About eighty different bacteria, hundreds of different viruses and a score of different fungi cause infection in humans. Many of these organisms exist in the body without causing an infection.

Symptoms vary depending on the tissue involved, and the type and severity of infection, but most cause a fever, pain, swelling and redness of the infected tissue. Swabs, biopsies and blood tests may be performed to determine the infecting organism and the appropriate treatment.

Most bacteria and fungi are susceptible to antibiotics and antifungal agents, but most viral infections cannot be treated, although many can be prevented by vaccination (eg. measles, hepatitis B, influenza), some may have their reproduction slowed by medication (eg. AIDS) and a very small number may have their reproduction completely blocked by antiviral agents (eg. genital herpes, influenza). Untreated infections may form abscesses or spread through the bloodstream to other organs or to the whole body.
See also ANAEROBIC INFECTION; BACTERIA; FUNGI; INFESTATION; PRION; PUS; VIRUS and specific types of infection (eg. ABSCESS; CELLULITIS; ERYSIPELAS; PERITONITIS; SEPTICAEMIA; TONSILLITIS)

INFECTIOUS MONONUCLEOSIS
See GLANDULAR FEVER

INFERTILITY

It takes two to tango, and to make a baby. Fertility is the joint property of a man and a woman, and infertility may be due to factors in either or both.

For a pregnancy to occur, an egg must be released from one of a woman's ovaries, move into the Fallopian tube, then down towards the uterus. At the same time, sperm released during ejaculation by a man must move from the vagina through the cervix and uterus and into a fallopian tube which contains a recently released egg. One sperm and an egg must then fuse together, start dividing into a multi celled structure, and implant into the lining of the woman's uterus, where it can obtain nutrition from the mother and continue to grow.

If sex is infrequent, then it may occur at times when the woman is not ovulating (releasing an egg). Conception can occur in a woman on only five or six days a month, so if sex occurs only once a month, those vital days may be missed. This is actually a quite common cause of apparent infertility in this busy modern society where both potential parents may work, are stressed and over tired. Occasionally, poor sexual technique, with ejaculation near the outside of the vagina, may be a problem.

Rarely, a woman may be allergic to, and develop antibodies against, her partner's sperm, which are rejected and destroyed by her body. Sperm from another man are not normally affected.

Extremely fit athletes of both sexes who exercise very vigourously may have their fertility affected as sperm counts drop and ovulation fails to occur.

Diseases of the pituitary gland in the brain, hypothyroidism (an underactive thyroid gland in the neck), poorly controlled diabetes mellitus and a deficiency of vital minerals (eg. zinc) may also be responsible for infertility in both sexes.

MALE INFERTILITY

Male infertility is far easier to investigate than female, so the male is often checked first by being asked to provide a fresh sample of ejaculated semen for analysis in a laboratory. If this shows that the sperm are alive and healthy, and the joint factors above are absent, then investigation of the woman can commence. An abnormal sample of semen will result in extensive detailed investigations to determine the cause of the abnormality.

If a man is impotent (unable to sustain an erect penis) then obviously successful intercourse is not possible.

Other causes of male infertility include the regular wearing of tight clothing while exercising (eg. bike pants, keeping the testes against the warm flesh in the groin and overheating them), premature ejaculation (resulting in the man ejaculating semen before penetration of the vagina), surgery to the prostate gland (may cause impotence or retrograde ejaculation), damage or infection to the testes (resulting in reduced sperm production. The testes may be compromised by failure to develop normallym, torsion of both testes, undescended testes, bacterial or viral infections (including infection of the testes during mumps), tumours or cancer, and irradiation or direct injury.

Genetic diseases such as Klinefelter syndrome will result in poorly functioning testes.

When he enters a new relationship, it is not unknown for a man to deliberately forget, or subconsciously repress the memory, that he has previously had a vasectomy, and the discovery of this during a physical examination may prove embarrassing to both parties.

FEMALE INFERTILITY
Investigation of female infertility can involve relatively old-fashioned but simple methods such as keeping accurate temperature charts, or more complex regular blood tests of hormone levels, specialised x-rays, and surgical examination of the ovaries using a laparoscope (telescope-like tube into the belly).

Vaginismus is the term used for a strong spasm of the muscles in the vagina that prevents the penis from entering. It usually results from anxiety or stress related to sex, lack of privacy, inadequate foreplay, sexual inhibitions due to a puritanical background, pain or discomfort associated with sex, or other psychological problems.

The cervix may be damaged by surgery for cancer or severe infection, or injured by an object placed in the vagina. The resultant scarring may prevent the passage of sperm.

Endometriosis is a sinister disease which is due to cells that normally line the inside of the uterus becoming displaced, and moving through the fallopian tubes to settle around the ovary, in the tubes themselves, or on other organs in the belly. In these abnormal positions they proliferate, and when a menstrual period occurs, they bleed as though they were still in the uterus. This results in pain, adhesions, damage to the organs they are attached to, and infertility.

Other causes of female infertility include abnormalities of the uterus due to poor development, fibroids (hard lumps in the wall of the uterus) or polyps in the uterus, infections of the fallopian tubes (salpingitis), cancer or tumours in the ovaries, ovarian cysts, the polycystic ovarian syndrome, hydrosalpinx (blockage of the fallopian tubes with fluid from persistent inflammation), Turner syndrome and Asherman syndrome (complication of surgically clearing out the uterus after a miscarriage or for heavy bleeding after childbirth).
See also ARTIFICIAL CONCEPTION; CLOMIPHENE; CONCEPTION; SEMEN TEST and separate entries for diseases mentioned above.

INFESTATION
An infestation is the invasion of the body by an insect (eg. lice, scabies, maggots), worm (eg. ascariasis) or other parasite.
See also ASCARIASIS; CRABS; INFECTION; SCABIES; TRICHURIASIS; WORMS

INFLAMED EYE
See EYE RED

INFLAMMATION
Inflammation is a reaction of tissues in the body to injury or infection, characterised by redness, swelling, pain and heat developing in the affected tissue, due to leakage of fluid (serum) from blood vessels.

INFLUENZA
Influenza (the flu) is a debilitating generalised viral infection caused by one of the more than eighty known strains of the influenza virus. Influenza was originally a disease of pigs and ducks, passing to humans only after these animals were domesticated seven thousand years ago. It was once thought to be due to 'influences in the atmosphere', thus giving its name. The various flu virus strains are named after the places where they were first isolated. It spreads by microscopic droplets in a cough or sneeze from one person to another.

Muscular aches and pains, overwhelming tiredness, fever, headache, cough, runny nose, stuffed sinuses, painful throat and nausea are the main symptoms. It can be a very serious disease, but deaths are now rare except in the elderly and debilitated.

Influenza can now be cured, but only if the antiviral medication (zanamivir or oseltamivir) is given within the first thirty-six hours of symptoms developing. Otherwise rest and time, aspirin, anti-inflammatory drugs and medications to help the phlegm and cough are given. A light, nutritious diet that contains minimal fat, and a higher than normal fluid intake are sensible.

Flu can be prevented by an annual vaccination, which gives more than 80% protection from contracting the infection, but only for one year. Unfortunately the vaccine does not prevent the common cold, and many people who complain that their flu shot has not worked are suffering from a cold caused by a different group of viruses. Amantadine tablets will prevent some forms of flu while they are being taken. Secondary bacterial infections of the throat, sinuses, lungs and ears may occur, which can be treated with antibiotics.

Influenza normally lasts for seven to ten days, and the vast majority of patients recover without complications.
See also ANTIVIRALS; COLD, COMMON; VIRUS

INGROWN NAIL
An ingrown toenail occurs with penetration of the tip of the nail edge into the flesh at the side of the nail, most commonly on the big toe. The nail has usually been torn, or cut too short, or shoes are too tight. This allows the skin at the end of the toe to override the end of the nail, so that when the nail grows, the corner of the nail cuts into the flesh and causes damage, pain and infection in the affected flesh beside the nail.

The infection is treated with antibiotic ointments and tablets, while the ingrown corner of the nail must be allowed to break free of the skin by avoiding shoes, and pulling the flesh away from the ingrowing nail corner with tape or regular massage. If this is unsuccessful, one of a number of minor operations may be necessary. The most common operations involve cutting away the excess flesh that is growing over the nail, or cutting away a wedge of the nail, nail bed and tissue beside the nail (a wedge resection) to permanently narrow the nail. Surgery usually cures an ingrown toenail, but there is still a 20% recurrence rate.
See also NAIL; PARONYCHIA; ZADEK PROCEDURE

INGUINAL
Inguinal is a medical term that refers to the groin.
See also GROIN PAIN

INGUINAL HERNIA
Inguinal hernias occur only in men.

The testicles develop inside the abdomen, and before birth they migrate down into the scrotum. As they move down, they leave behind them a tube called the inguinal canal. Through this canal run the arteries, veins and nerves that supply the testicles, and the vas deferens (a duct that carries the sperm from the testicle to the base of the penis). Shortly before birth, the inguinal canal closes, leaving just enough room for the vital supplies to pass to and from the testes. The inguinal canal remains a source of weakness in the strong muscle wall of the abdomen, and it may tear open again, allowing some of the gut to protrude under the skin of the groin as a hernia.

These hernias may be caused by excess pressure on the lower part of the belly by heavy lifting, prolonged coughing or some other form of strain. Men who are overweight and have their muscles weakened by fat deposits are more likely to develop them, and the slackening of muscle tone with advancing age can also lead to a rupture. There is also a hereditary tendency, so that if your father had a hernia, your chances of developing one are increased. In some little boys the tube does not close properly, and this allows a small amount of fat or intestine to move down the tube from the inside of the abdomen, to form a hernia just under the skin beside the penis.

Usually the only symptom is a small lump in the groin that may be only mildly annoying after exercise, or may become intermittently painful. Occasionally the gut inside the hernia may become strangled in the inguinal canal, causing severe pain and the trapped section of gut becomes gangrenous. This requires urgent surgery.

In fat men, an ultrasound scan may be needed to confirm the diagnosis.

Surgical repair of the hernia as is usually performed as an elective procedure, but up to 20% of repaired inguinal hernias will recur. A tight sensation in the groin, that may be occasionally painful, may follow the surgery.
See also HERNIA; TESTICLE

INR
See BLOOD CLOTTING TEST

INSECTICIDE POISONING

Stronger insecticides that contain organophosphate chemicals (eg. parathion, fenthion and malathion) may cause poisoning in humans by swallowing, inhaling or touching. Wheezing, contracted pupils, excessive sweating, nausea, vomiting, watery eyes, and diarrhoea are the common symptoms, and blood tests show serious abnormalities. In severe cases, symptoms can progress to muscle weakness, convulsions, coma and death.

First aid is vital. If the poison has been swallowed, the patient must be made to vomit, and then given milk. The patient must be thoroughly washed to remove any poison from the skin, and contaminated clothing must be removed. Mouth-to-mouth resuscitation and external cardiac massage may be necessary. Those giving first aid must be careful not to contaminate themselves. In hospital, emergency treatment and medication to neutralise the poison can be given.

The prognosis depends upon the type of poison, its dosage, and the age and fitness of the patient.
See also POISONING

INSECTS
See BEE STING; SCORPION STING; SPIDER BITE; TICKS

INSOMNIA

Insomnia is an inability to sleep – either a difficulty in getting to sleep, or waking repeatedly or for prolonged periods, after initially falling asleep. Sleep is as essential for the normal functioning of the human body as food and drink. Doctors do not completely understand why we need sleep, but they do understand what happens when we are asleep.

There are two main types of sleep – deep sleep and REM sleep. REM stands for rapid eye movements, and several times a night, the level of sleep lightens, and while the eyelids remain closed, the eyes themselves move around rapidly. It is during this stage of sleep that dreams occur, and it is the more valuable form of sleep. If a volunteer is observed, and woken every time s/he starts REM sleep, s/he will remain tired and irritable, and obtain little benefit from the sleep. REM sleep does not start until an hour or so after first falling asleep, and long periods of deep sleep occur between each episode.

Unfortunately, many sleeping tablets induce deep sleep, but tend to prevent REM sleep, so that people using them do not benefit from their sleep as much as those who sleep naturally. This is one of the reasons that doctors are reluctant to use them until all other avenues have been explored.

The amount of sleep needed varies dramatically from one person to another. Some require only three or four hours a day; most require seven or eight hours; others may need ten hours. As we age, our sleep needs change too. An infant requires sixteen or more hours of sleep a day; in middle age, eight hours is normal; but the elderly need only five or six hours sleep.

The problem here is that older people may have less to occupy their days, and so look forward to the escape of eight hours sleep every night, but find they cannot obtain it because their bodies do not require that much. This is further exacerbated by the low activity levels of many elderly people, and any midday naps they take. As a result, some elderly people seek help in obtaining extra sleep from their doctors by means of sleeping pills. This is not true insomnia, merely a desire for extra sleep, above what is biologically necessary.

There are, of course, those who genuinely cannot get to sleep for a variety of reasons, and 15% of the population fall into this category.

Specific causes of insomnia include stress and anxiety (including post-traumatic stress disorder), pain, depression, menopause and its associated hormonal fluctuations, snoring, the restless legs syndrome and Cushing syndrome (over production in the body of, or excessive medication with, cortisone).

Numerous drugs, both illegal and prescribed, may cause sleeplessness. Examples include alcohol, caffeine, marijuana, cocaine, slimming pills and pseudoephedrine (Sudafed) for runny noses.

There are many things other than medication that can be done to ease the problem.

There are simple steps that anyone can use to aid sleep: –
• Bed is for sleep and sex only, not for watching television or reading.
• Go to bed when you feel tired, not when the clock tells you to.
• Do not lie down or nap during the day.
• Do not have a clock in the bedroom.

• Avoid exercise immediately before bed. Take time to wind down before going to bed.

• Avoid drinks containing caffeine such as tea, coffee or cola. Caffeine is a stimulant.

• Do not smoke before going to bed.

• Relax by having a long warm bath and/or a warm milk drink before going to bed.

• Lose weight if you are obese. A slight weight loss can significantly improve sleep.

• Avoid eating a full meal immediately before bedtime. Give your food a couple of hours to settle.

• If you cannot sleep once in bed, get up and read a book or watch television for half an hour before returning to bed. Never lie in bed tossing and turning.

• Learn to relax by attending specific relaxation classes, which your doctor may recommend. Follow up by listening to relaxation tapes.

• Instead of counting sheep or worrying about your problems, focus your mind on a pleasant incident in your past (such as a holiday, journey or party) and remember the whole event slowly in intricate detail from beginning to end.

• Remember that the harder you try to fall asleep, the less likely you are to succeed, so relax!

If all else fails, and sleep is still impossible, a doctor can prescribe medications that can be taken, ideally for a short time only, to relieve the problem.
See also BENZODIAZEPINES; SEDATIVES; SLEEP STUDIES

INSULIN

Insulin is a natural hormone produced by cells in the islets of Langerhans, which are in the pancreas (an organ in the centre of the abdomen). It is essential for insulin to be present in the blood, because without it cells cannot absorb glucose. Unfortunately, insulin is destroyed by the acid and digestive juices in the stomach and gut, and therefore cannot be given in tablet form. It is currently only available as an injection, but experiments with an inhaled form are under way.

Insulin was derived from the pancreas of cattle or pigs for sixty years up to the early 1990s, since it was originally identified and isolated by the Canadian doctors, Banting and Best. Because it was derived from animals, there were occasional reactions to the foreign animal protein present in the insulin. Since 1990, genetically engineered human insulin has almost totally replaced the animal insulin. The new form causes virtually no adverse reaction after injection.

There are many different types of insulin available. They vary in their speed of action (how quickly they work after injection) and their duration of action (how long they last after injection). Some can be given by doctors as an injection directly into the bloodstream in acutely ill patients; others are combinations of long and short-acting insulins that enable diabetics to have only one or two injections a day, rather than four or more of the short-acting types. Each diabetic will have trials of a number of these combinations to find the one best suited to them.

There are a number of ways of administering insulin injections, including the traditional syringe and needle, injecting guns, and a new type of calibrated tube that looks like a ball point pen and is easy to carry in a pocket or purse but injects very precise doses of insulin.

Insulin is almost always required in the juvenile (type one) form of diabetes, and occasionally in the maturity onset (type two) form.

Overuse of insulin or a reduction in normal food intake or exercise, can lead to a sudden drop in blood glucose and collapse of the patient. Most diabetics are aware of the onset of a hypoglycaemia ('hypo') attack, and are prepared to deal with it by sucking a glucose sweet or swallowing a sweetened drink.
See also DIABETES MELLITUS TYPE ONE; DIABETES MELLITUS TYPE TWO; HYPOGLYCAEMICS; PANCREAS

INSULIN DEPENDENT DIABETES
See DIABETES MELLITUS TYPE ONE

INSULINOMA

An insulinoma is an uncommon tumour of the insulin-producing beta cells in the pancreas gland. Insulin is a hormone that lowers the level of sugar (glucose) in the blood to cause hypoglycaemia. 90% of tumours are benign, while the remaining 10% are cancerous. They usually occur between fifty and seventy years of age, but may occur at any age. The cause is unknown.

Symptoms may include tiredness, headaches, slurred speech, visual disturbances and confusion. Eating relieves symptoms, which may result in weight gain. If food is not eaten, tremor, palpitations, irregular heart rhythm, coma and death may follow. A cancerous tumour can spread to other organs (metastasise).

Blood tests show low glucose and high insulin levels, and the tumour may be found by a CT or MRI scan.

Treatment involves surgical removal of the tumour, and chemotherapy for the spread of any cancer. Good results are obtained from surgery, but cancerous tumours eventually kill about half those affected. If left untreated, both forms are eventually fatal.

See also DIABETES MELLITUS TYPE ONE; INSULIN; PANCREAS

INSULIN RESISTANCE SYNDROME
See SYNDROME X

INTELLECTUAL DISABILITY
See MENTAL RETARDATION

INTELLIGENCE QUOTIENT

Intelligence is more than just the ability to learn – it includes the ability to apply knowledge and use common sense. There are many different types of intelligence including mathematical, verbal, spatial, reasoning and musical intelligence.

Attempts have been made to measure intelligence for hundreds of years, but because intelligence itself is poorly defined, its measurement is almost impossible, and many older intelligence tests have now been discredited. The first widely used IQ (intelligence quotient) test was the Stanford-Binet test, which was developed in the early twentieth century. Standard IQ tests cannot measure manual dexterity, musical talent, or emotional factors which influence performance.

There is very little benefit in having a very high IQ on a test if the person is unable to apply that intelligence in any useful way. As a result, a pure IQ test is a very poor measure of how successful an individual will be in society.

There are many factors that can influence an individual's score on an IQ test including tiredness, illness, distractions and even if the person has done similar tests before.

The IQ score is a statistically calculated number, and an individual's results may vary from one IQ test to another. The test targets a specific range of more easily measured human abilities.

Statistically the following statements are true about IQ scores obtained by taking a typical IQ test: –
• An IQ of below 50 is incompatible with functioning normally in society.
• An IQ of 80 is higher than 7% of all persons taking the test.
• An IQ of 90 is higher than 25% of all persons taking the test
• An IQ of 100 is higher than 50% of all persons taking the test.
• An IQ of 110 is higher than 75% of all persons taking the test.
• An IQ of 120 is higher than 93% of all persons taking the test.
• An IQ of 130 is higher than 98% of all persons taking the test.

It can be seen that half of all people have an IQ between 90 and 110.

IQ tests may be useful in predicting an individual's academic potential, but application to study and interest in the topics are also vital in academic achievement.

A high IQ is certainly no guarantee that a person will achieve happiness or be psychiatrically stable and, conversely, a low IQ does not mean that an individual is worthless or unable to achieve significant goals and contribute to society. A menial labourer may have a high IQ but be unable to apply that IQ usefully, while a high achiever may have an average IQ but has assiduously applied him/her self to achieving a particular aim. History is filled with stories of humans of limited intellectual ability who have nevertheless been among humankind's most important contributors.

A person with a low IQ may have children with high IQ and vice versa, but there is certainly a genetic tendency for people to have children with a similar IQ.

Environment can also play a major part in IQ. Children raised in an inquiring and mentally stimulating environment are more likely to achieve well in society, do well academically and have higher IQ scores.

It is very important to remember that all IQ tests are culturally sensitive. If Aborigines drafted an IQ test, most of Western civilisation would probably fail it.

See also BRAIN; MEMORY; MENTAL RETARDATION

INTERCOURSE
See SEXUAL INTERCOURSE

INTERCOURSE PAIN
See SEXUAL INTERCOURSE PAIN

INTERFERON
See OTHER

INTERMEDIATE CORONARY SYNDROME
The intermediate coronary syndrome (unstable angina) is an intermediate stage between angina and myocardial infarct (heart attack). It is caused by damage to the arteries supplying the heart muscle from high blood pressure, excess cholesterol in the blood and other causes.

Patients experience chest pain (angina) that varies in nature, severity, duration, spread, timing and cause from one attack to another or even during attacks. Sometimes these attacks may develop into a heart attack.

Rest, nitrates given under the tongue or inhaled, and medications to prevent attacks are used in treatment. If possible, coronary artery bypass graft surgery is performed. The mortality is 15% per annum.
See also ANGINA; ANTIANGINALS; CORONARY ARTERY BYPASS GRAFT; HEART ATTACK

INTERNATIONAL NORMALISED RATIO
See BLOOD CLOTTING TEST

INTERSTITIAL CYSTITIS
Interstitial cystitis (Hunner ulcer) is a persistent inflammation and ulceration of the bladder. The cause is not exactly known but may be an autoimmune disease (inappropriate rejection by the body of its own tissue), allergy, or unidentified bacteria or virus. Some cases may be associated with cancer of the bladder. Middle aged women are most commonly affected.

The inflammation, scarring and reduced capacity of the bladder results in the frequent painful passing of bloodstained urine. A biopsy of the bladder wall through a cystoscope (instrument passed through the urethra into the bladder) is essential for diagnosis.

Possible treatments include forced dilation of the bladder under anaesthesia, laser or other heat applied to ulcers, drugs to reduce bladder muscle spasm, and surgery to enlarge the bladder or divert urine into an isolated loop of small intestine that opens onto the belly wall. Unfortunately, the treatments are generally unsuccessful, and symptoms to some extent persist long term.
See also BLADDER; CYSTOSCOPY

INTERTRIGO
Intertrigo is an inflammatory skin condition caused by heat, sweat and friction in those who are overweight, have poor personal hygiene, live in the tropics, or suffer from diabetes.

Red, damaged, moist, itchy and burning skin occurs in places where the skin folds back upon itself, such as under the breasts, in the groin and armpit, and in skin folds of the abdomen and neck in obese people. In advanced cases, the skin may crack, bleed, become painful and fungal and/or bacterial infections may develop on the damaged skin.

Treatment involves scrupulous hygiene, controlling diabetes, using antibiotics and antifungals to remove infection, losing weight, and applying drying powders to the affected areas. A piece of soft cloth placed under bulky breasts, and a well-fitted bra may help. Plastic surgery to reduce large breasts or excessive skin on the belly may be appropriate. Unfortunately most patients remain overweight, are not consistent in their hygiene, and the problem persists or recurs.
See also SKIN RED; SKIN ITCH

INTERVERTEBRAL DISC PROLAPSE
Vertebral discs are cushions between the bony vertebrae that form the backbone. They are like a small, thick walled balloon, with walls made of rubbery ligaments and cartilage. The hollow centre is filled with a dense fluid, which acts as a shock absorber when walking or running. Prolapses usually affect the discs between the last three or four vertebrae, but any disc from the skull down may be involved. If an excessive amount of pressure is put on a disc from heavy lifting, long term wear and tear or other injury, it may collapse and bulge out between the vertebrae (prolapse or slip) to put pressure on nerves or the spinal cord.

Patients experience severe back pain and/or pain in the buttock or leg (sciatica), numbness and other altered sensation, and in extreme cases muscle weakness and paralysis. The space between vertebrae is seen to be narrower than normal on an x-ray, and a CT or MRI scan shows the bulging disc.

Treatment involves physiotherapy and exercises, anti-inflammatory medications, painkillers, back supports, steroids, back injections or surgery. Permanent damage to nerves is possible if treatment is delayed. The condition is usually slowly progressive, but good results are obtained from surgery in severe cases.

See also BACK PAIN; SCIATICA; SPINE; VERTEBRA

INTESTINAL COLIC
Intestinal colic is a recurrent intermittent abdominal pain due to spasm of the intestine that may be caused by a number of conditions, including an obstruction to the gut (eg. by a cancer, tumour, twisting of the gut, adhesions, swallowed foreign body), infections of the intestine, gastroenteritis, food poisoning, overindulgence in food, parasites in the gut, dehydration and even extreme stress and anxiety.

Serious causes of prolonged colic must be excluded by blood tests, x-rays, colonoscopy and gastroscopy, but any treatment depends on the cause, as colic is a symptom rather than a disease.

See also ABDOMINAL PAIN; COLIC; INFANTILE COLIC

INTESTINE
See ABDOMINAL PAIN; BOWEL NOISY; CAECUM; COLON; DUODENUM; DYSPEPSIA; FAECES BLOOD; ILEUM; INTESTINAL COLIC; JEJUNUM; LARGE INTESTINE; MALABSORPTION; NAUSEA AND VOMITING; RECTUM; SMALL INTESTINE; STOMACH; SWALLOWING DIFFICULT

INTRACEREBRAL HAEMORRHAGE
See SUBARACHNOID HAEMORRHAGE

INTRAEPITHELIAL CARCINOMA
An intraepithelial carcinoma (IEC) is a common cancer in the outer layers of skin, similar to, but deeper in the skin than, a squamous cell carcinoma. They usually occur in patients who are over fifty years of age and they are caused by prolonged exposure to sunlight. The rims of the ears, the face, scalp, arms and hands are commonly affected.

The cancer appears as an unsightly red spot covered in fine white scales that may be itchy or sore. Small IECs are easily removed by burning with a diathermy machine or freezing with liquid nitrogen. If larger, or if the diagnosis is not certain, it is necessary to excise the spot and surrounding tissue. Any IEC that recurs after freezing or burning must be surgically excised. Rarely they may spread by blood or lymphatics to other parts of the body.

Treatment is very effective in early stages of the disease.

See also BOWEN'S DISEASE; HYPERKERATOSIS; KERATOACANTHOMA; SQUAMOUS CELL CARCINOMA OF SKIN

INTRAUTERINE DEVICE
The intrauterine device (IUD) is a piece of plastic shaped like a '7', 'T' or 'S', that may be covered by a thin coil of copper wire or contain a hormone such as progestogen. It is inserted by a doctor through the vagina and cervix to sit inside the uterus (womb). The IUD acts by irritating the lining of the uterus and preventing the egg from implanting so no pregnancy can develop. The IUD can also be used as an after sex contraceptive device if inserted within five days of unprotected intercourse

The insertion of the device is done very simply by a general practitioner or gynaecologist, takes only a few minutes, and is usually pain free. Through a speculum (a collapsible metal tube) the doctor will examine the entrance to the womb (the cervix) and check the shape and size of the uterus. Then, while

IUD IN UTERUS

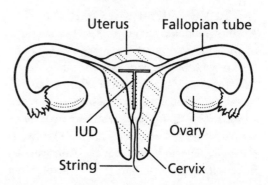

holding the cervix carefully with a special pair of forceps, the IUD is slowly pushed through the cervix canal into the uterus. It is only 3mm in diameter when inserted, but once inside the uterus it springs open to its '7', 'T' or 'S' shape and is held in position by the arms of the device pushing on the uterine walls. It is normal to insert the IUD immediately after a menstrual period, but may be inserted at other times if the woman wants immediate protection.

Once in place, the woman is not aware of its presence. After each period she should feel for the fine thread which will normally hang into the vagina. This is used to remove the IUD at a later time. The device can remain in place for two or three years before it needs to be changed, but a doctor should check it every year, and you should also have a routine Pap smear test every two years.

The IUD has one great advantage – you cannot forget to take it or use it. Once in place it can be relied upon to give 97% protection against pregnancy. When you want to become pregnant, or no longer require contraception, the device is easily removed. Your doctor will merely pull on the short thread left outside the uterus (but inside the vagina), and the IUD will fold up on itself, enabling it to be gently withdrawn.

Not all women are suited to the use of IUDs. Only about 40% of women still have them in place a year after insertion. Sometimes they can fall out, they may cause heavy and painful periods, or rarely they can cause infections of the uterus resulting in permanent infertility. During insertion, it very rarely may penetrate the uterus to cause serious peritonitis. The devices are normally used, and have fewer side effects, in women who have had a pregnancy, but there are smaller devices available for women who have had no children.
See also CONTRACEPTIVES

INTRAVENOUS PYELOGRAM

An intravenous pyelogram (IVP) is an x-ray of the kidneys and the urinary system. The soft tissues of the kidneys and the ureters (the tubes leading from the kidneys to the bladder) do not show up well on a plain x-ray, so an iodine compound which is opaque to x-rays is injected into the patient. The dye is normally injected into a vein (intravenous injection) in the arm and travels through the

bloodstream until it reaches the kidneys a few seconds later, when the x-ray is taken. The harmless dye is then removed from the blood by the normal filtering process of the kidneys so that it becomes part of the urine and is eliminated from the body.

The pyelogram shows the sizes of the kidneys and ureters, whether their shape and function are normal, and the position of any stone. If there is a stone blocking one of the ureters, only the kidney and that part of the ureter above the blockage shows.

A tight belt around the belly compresses the ureters for the first few minutes of the procedure and concentrates the dye in the kidneys. When the belt is released, the x-rays show the dye flowing down the ureters to the bladder.

In a retrograde pyelogram, dye is introduced through a tube passed into the bladder and up a ureter into the kidney's drainage system.
See also KIDNEY; X-RAY

INTUSSUSCEPTION

An intussusception is an uncommon type of obstruction of the small or large gut that usually occurs in children.

A polyp growing in the gut is picked up by the waves of muscular contraction that normally move food along. As the polyp moves down the gut it pulls the piece of gut it is attached to along with it, to cause an infolding of the gut into itself. This is an intussusception.

The child has obstruction of the gut, severe intermittent waves of pain, red jelly motions and paralysis of the intestine. The intussusception can be relieved by a barium enema (special x-ray) or colonoscopy (passing a flexible telescope in through the anus) if the large bowel is involved, but in the small intestine surgery is necessary.

It is usually completely cured by appropriate

INTUSSUSCEPTION

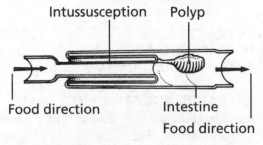

THE INFOLDING OF GUT IN AN
INTUSSUSCEPTION CAUSED BY A POLYP

treatment, but bowel perforation may rarely occur.

See also BARIUM ENEMA; COLON; COLONOSCOPY; LARGE INTESTINE

INVASIVE UTERINE MOLE
See CHORIOCARCINOMA OF THE UTERUS

INVERTED NIPPLE
See NIPPLE INVERTED

IN VITRO FERTILISATION
See ARTIFICIAL CONCEPTION

IODINE
Iodine (I) is essential for the formation of the hormone thyroxine in the thyroid gland in the neck. A lack of iodine will lead to a goitre and hypothyroidism. A lack in children may cause the permanent brain damage of cretinism, and as a result iodine is added to salt and bread to ensure that everyone has sufficient in their diet. Seafood is another excellent source. Adults require 150 micrograms a day in their diet, but an excess is not harmful. The amount of iodine in the body is not normally measured directly by doctors.

Iodine is used in many different medications, particularly antiseptics.

Taking extra iodine after a nuclear attack will help to protect the body from radiation injury.

See also ANTISEPTICS; HYPERTHYROIDISM; HYPOTHYROIDISM; MINERALS; THYROID GLAND

IQ
See INTELLIGENCE QUOTIENT

IRBESARTAN
See ANGIOTENSIN II RECEPTOR ANTAGONISTS

IRIDOLOGY
Iridology is not a form of treatment but a diagnostic tool used by many naturopaths. It involves examining the condition of the iris (the coloured part) of both eyes of the patient. Photographs are often taken of the iris for later detailed examination.

Charts of the iris, divided into segments like a complicated clock face, are available,

and were initially prepared by the American, Bernard Jensen. An abnormality, fleck or colour, or swirl of lines in an area of the iris can be interpreted from the chart to represent a problem in a particular part of the body.

Iridology is meant to be used in conjunction with other methods of diagnosis, but there is no scientific evidence for the rationale behind iridology.

See also CHINESE MEDICINE; CHIROPRACTIC; HOMEOPATHY; NATUROPATHY; OSTEOPATHY

IRIS
See EYE

IRITIS
See UVEITIS

IRON
Iron (Fe) is essential in the diet and body in order for the blood's red oxygen carrying pigment haemoglobin to be manufactured. Iron can be lost from the body during bleeding from an injury or with heavy menstrual periods, or inadequate amounts of iron may be taken into the body due to a poor diet or it may be inadequately absorbed. High iron levels may be a sign of haemochromatosis.

During pregnancy, additional iron is required in the diet for the needs of the developing foetus. Iron levels are routinely measured during pregnancy, and to investigate the cause of anaemia.

An iron level of 15 to 30 µmol/L is considered normal.

See also ANAEMIA; FULL BLOOD COUNT; HAEMOCHROMATOSIS; HAEMOGLOBIN; IRON DEFICIENCY ANAEMIA; IRON POISONING; PERNICIOUS ANAEMIA

IRON DEFICIENCY ANAEMIA
Iron deficiency anaemia is the most common form of anaemia. Iron is essential for the manufacture of haemoglobin which transports oxygen in the blood. If iron levels are low, haemoglobin levels drop and the body becomes starved of oxygen. It is usually found in women who have very heavy periods or are pregnant, and in those with an iron deficient diet. Serious causes include slow bleeding into the gut from a peptic ulcer or cancer.

Tiredness, weakness and pallor are the

main symptoms. Anaemia is diagnosed by appropriate blood tests, then the cause of the anaemia must be determined by more extensive investigations.

Iron supplements by mouth are the main treatment. Iron is found in many foods including meat, poultry, fish, eggs, cereals and vegetables. Vitamin C and folic acid assist in the absorption of iron from the gut into the blood, and because of this, iron tablets often contain folic acid, and sometimes vitamin C as well. Some patients with severe degrees of anaemia due to lack of iron, or to intestinal diseases that reduce the absorption of iron, may require iron injections, but usually they can return to tablets, and then a good diet, after only a few shots.
See also ANAEMIA; HAEMOGLOBIN; IRON

IRON POISONING
Taking excessive amounts of iron into the body, either deliberately or accidentally, can result in vomiting, diarrhoea, black coloured faeces, a rapid and irregular heart rate, low blood pressure, convulsions, and eventually coma and death. Early symptoms may commence within an hour of taking excess iron.

Iron is found in tablets used to treat iron deficiency states and anaemia, many tonics and anti-vomiting drugs. 2000 mg of iron taken at once is sufficient to cause iron poisoning in an adult, but lesser amounts can be very serious in a child. The amount of iron in the body can be measured by blood tests.

First-aiders should induce vomiting to remove any recently swallowed iron, then urgent hospitalisation is necessary. Medications are given to bind the iron and remove it from the body, then a drip is inserted into a vein to correct the dehydration caused by vomiting and diarrhoea. Even after apparent recovery, liver, pancreas and kidney failure may occur at a later date. The prognosis depends upon the amount of iron taken, and the weight, age and health of the patient.
See also IRON

IRREGULAR HEART BEAT
See HEART, EXTRA BEATS

IRRITABLE BOWEL SYNDROME
The irritable bowel syndrome (IBS) has many other names, including functional indigestion, mucus colitis, nervous dyspepsia and spastic colon. It causes abnormal spasms of the muscles in the wall of the large intestine.

The gut is a long tube with bands of muscle running along and around it. The movement of the food from one end to the other is the result of rhythmic contractions of these muscles, which send waves and ripples along the gut to push food along. Nutrients are removed from the gut, and only non-absorbable fibre and roughage remains to be passed out through the anus. Up to 20% of adults have symptoms of the irritable bowel syndrome at some time, but only a fraction of these people require medical treatment.

If the diet consists of large amounts of refined foods with little fibre content, the bulk of the faeces is reduced. When the muscles in the large intestine contract, they may have very little to push along, and this may lead to spasms of the gut. People with tense personalities or continuing stress will find that their intestine acts more rapidly than normal due to over stimulation. Over a number of years, the combination of a low-fibre diet, anxiety, stress and hereditary factors may lead to the development of this syndrome, which is more common in women.

Abdominal pain occurs due to intense spasms of the bowel muscle, and patients experience alternating constipation and diarrhoea, excess passage of wind by mouth and anus, nausea, loss of appetite and mucus on the stools. Once established, the pattern may be very difficult to break, as the symptoms cause further anxiety in the victim, which in turn exacerbates the original symptoms.

No definite tests can prove the diagnosis, but all other causes must be excluded by exhaustive investigations such as an x-ray of the large intestine (barium enema) or colonoscopy.

Treatment requires a diet high in fibre and low in dairy products and processed foods, plus high-fibre dietary supplements in some cases. Regular meal and toilet habits should be established, and tobacco and alcohol intake should be restricted. Reassurance is very important, and anti-anxiety drugs, anti-depressants and psychotherapy may all prove useful. In severe cases, drugs are used to alter the activity of gut muscles, and occasionally painkillers are also necessary. IBS usually persists intermittently for many years.

See also ABDOMINAL PAIN; BARIUM ENEMA; COLIC; COLON; COLONOSCOPY

IRRITANT ECZEMA
See CONTACT DERMATITIS

IRUKANDJI SYNDROME
The Irukandji syndrome is named after an Aboriginal tribe that lived north of Cairns, Australia, and is an excessive and abnormal response to the sting of the tiny transparent jellyfish *Caukia barnesi* (named after the Cairns doctor, Jack Barnes, who discovered it) which is found in the waters of tropical Australia.

The lungs fill with fluid causing severe shortness of breath, and patients experience excruciating widespread pain, a rapid heart rate, profuse sweating, generalised shaking and very high blood pressure. Narcotic painkillers and other painkillers in high doses are given through a drip, diuretics (fluid removing drugs) are prescribed and machine ventilation through a tube into the throat may be necessary. Permanent brain damage and death are rarely possible, but most patients recover, although some may have long term nerve damage and pain.
See also BOX JELLYFISH

ISHIHARA TEST
See COLOUR BLINDNESS TEST

ISCHAEMIA
Ischaemia is a medical term indicating an inadequate blood supply to an organ or tissue due to damaged or diseased arteries. Myocardial ischaemia is a lack of blood to the muscles of the heart.
See also NECROSIS

ISCHAEMIC HEART DISEASE
See ANGINA; HEART ATTACK; INTERMEDIATE CORONARY SYNDROME

ISCHIUM
See PELVIS

ISLETS OF LANGERHANS
See DIABETES MELLITUS TYPE ONE; INSULIN; PANCREAS

ISONIAZID
See TUBERCULOSIS MEDICATIONS

ISOPRENALINE
See ADRENERGIC STIMULANTS

ISORDIL
See ANTIANGINALS

ISOSORBIDE
See ANTIANGINALS

ISOTOPE SCAN
See NUCLEAR SCAN

ISOTRETINOIN
See KERATOLYTICS

ISRAELI SPOTTED FEVER
See TYPHUS

ITCH
See ANAL ITCH; GENITAL ITCH; NIPPLE ITCH; SKIN ITCH

ITCHY UPPER ARM SYNDROME
The itchy upper arm syndrome (brachioradialis pruritus) is a real disease despite its descriptive name, and is an abnormal response of the skin to long term sun damage and the constant release of the irritating substance histamine from allergy (mast) cells in the affected skin.

Patients with chronic sun damage to their skin may develop intense itching and burning on outer surface of arm that is worse in summer, but they have no apparent rash. A skin biopsy shows the presence of excessive numbers of mast cells.

Very strong steroid creams or ointments can be tried, but the condition is generally resistant to treatment.
See also ALLERGY; SKIN ITCH

-ITIS
'-itis' is a suffix that indicates the presence of infection and/or inflammation (eg. tonsillitis, appendicitis).

IVF
See ARTIFICIAL CONCEPTION

IVP
See INTRAVENOUS PYELOGRAM

J

JAPANESE ENCEPHALITIS

Japanese encephalitis is a viral infection of the brain that is transmitted from animals such as pigs and horses to humans by a mosquito bite. It is found in areas where rice paddies occur throughout east and south Asia and on some Pacific islands. Symptoms include a fever, belly pains, dizziness, sore throat, cough, headache, neck stiffness, nausea, vomiting, tiredness, disturbed mental functions, disorientation, coma and sometimes death. It may cause permanent brain damage in up to half of survivors, with personality changes, fatigue and inability to concentrate.

Tests on blood and the fluid around the brain are abnormal and can confirm the diagnosis, but no specific treatment is available, although it can be prevented by a vaccine.

Acute attacks last for one to three weeks, but complete recovery may take months. The overall mortality rate is up to 50%, but worsens in children.
See also BRAIN; ENCEPHALITIS

JAUNDICE

Jaundice (icterus) is a yellow colour in the skin caused by high levels of bilirubin in the blood. Bilirubin is a waste product of the body, caused by the break down of the oxygen-carrying haemoglobin in red blood cells. It is removed from the blood by the liver, before passing into the gall bladder, and then onto the food in the small intestine to assist in digestion. Bilirubin also gives faeces its dark yellow/brown appearance.

In dark skinned people, jaundice may only be seen as a yellowing of the whites of the eyes.

Jaundice may be confused with carotenaemia which is a yellowing of the soles and palms caused by excessive levels of vitamin A (carotene) in the blood, and is due to eating excessive quantities of yellow food (eg. carrots, pumpkins, paw paw) or supplements with large amounts of vitamin A.

There are numerous medical conditions that may cause jaundice.

An obstruction to the bile duct drainage from the liver to the small intestine will prevent bilirubin from escaping into the gut. It continues to build up in the liver, and overflows back into the blood from where it is deposited in the skin. The obstruction may be caused by a gall stone in the bile duct, cancer in the liver (hepatoma), secondary cancer in the liver that has spread from elsewhere (eg. breast, bowel), or a tumour in the pancreas which presses on and constricts the bile duct.

Cholecystitis is an inflammation or infection of the gall bladder, usually caused by gallstones that have formed within it. In most cases it causes pain and indigestion, but if the gall bladder becomes very swollen it may obstruct the bile duct to prevent bilirubin from leaving the liver.

Many newborn infants are jaundiced for a short time after birth. This is caused by immaturity of the liver, and the change from a primitive form of haemoglobin (foetal haemoglobin – HbF) which breaks down to form bilirubin, while a more mature form of haemoglobin is made in the spleen and bone marrow to replace it. In severe untreated cases, the high levels of bilirubin may damage the brain, so careful monitoring and treatment if bilirubin levels rise too high, is essential. The jaundice can be eased by ultraviolet light, which penetrates the child's delicate skin to destroy bilirubin. Sun will destroy bilirubin, as can be demonstrated by dog faeces, which turns white after being out in the sun for a week or so.

Cirrhosis is damage to the liver that results in its normal tissue being replaced by scar tissue. As the disease progresses the liver is unable to function successfully, and it cannot clear bilirubin out of the blood, resulting in jaundice. Cirrhosis may be caused by serious long lasting infections (eg. hepatitis B), poisons or excessive alcohol intake over a long period.

Hepatitis is an infection of the liver by a virus. There are many different types of hepatitis, but the most common are hepatitis A (caught from contaminated food) and hepatitis B (caught by intimate contact with an infected person's blood or semen). In the acute stages, all types of hepatitis will cause jaundice, but the long term consequences will depend upon the type of hepatitis and the individual's response to it.

Other causes of jaundice include malaria (transmitted by a mosquito in tropical areas), severe viral infections (eg. cytomegalovirus of babies, glandular fever), severe bacterial infections (eg. syphilis, leptospirosis, *Clostridia*), Gilbert syndrome (an inherited condition in which the liver fails to adequately clear bilirubin from the blood), yellow fever (severe infection of the liver transmitted by mosquitoes in central Africa and tropical America), pancreatitis (excruciatingly painful inflammation of the pancreas), and severe anaemia caused by the rapid break down of red blood cells (eg. sickle cell anaemia, haemolytic anaemia) .

Some medications may have jaundice as a side effect. Examples include chlorine, sulpha antibiotics and the general anaesthetic halothane.

There are many rarer causes of jaundice including Hodgkin's disease (cancer of the lymph tissue), a thrombus (clot) in the vein leading from the liver, sclerosing cholangitis (progressive blockage of the drainage tubes of the liver with inflamed scar tissue), parasites that invade the liver (eg. Hydatid cysts, Echinococcus), thalassaemia major (an inherited condition that causes the red blood cells to be fragile and break down very rapidly) and the Dubin-Johnson syndrome (children who are born without a gall bladder).
See also BILE; GALL BLADDER; HAEMOGLOBIN; HEPATITIS A; HEPATITIS B; LIVER and separate entries for diseases mentioned above.

JAW JOINT
See MANDIBLE; TEMPOROMANDIBULAR JOINT DYSFUNCTION

JEJUNUM
The jejunum is the second part of the small intestine, leading from the duodenum at the top end and merging into the ileum at its lower end. By the time the small intestine becomes the jejunum, it has tapered from about 5cm to about 3cm in diameter. It winds in loose loops around the abdominal cavity, and is connected to the back wall of the belly by the mesentery that carries blood vessels, lymph ducts and nerves. It is about 4 metres long.

The primary task of the jejunum is to absorb food from the gut. The absorbable nutrients from digested food pass through the millions of tiny finger like projections (villi) lining the jejunum and into blood or lymph vessels. Some (mostly fats) will go through the lymphatic system, and others will journey through a special series of veins (portal system) to the liver for further processing so that they can be utilised by the body's cells to keep them alive and functioning.

The end products of the digestive processes consist of amino acids which come from the protein we eat, sugar in its simplest form, and fats.

The name jejunum comes from the Latin word for empty, as this part of the bowel was usually found to be empty after death.
See also DUODENUM; GALL BLADDER; ILEUM; LYMPHATIC SYSTEM; PANCREAS; PORTAL SYSTEM

JELLYFISH STING
Many jellyfish have stinging tentacles and, rarely, extensive stings can lead to respiratory failure and cardiac arrest, but most stings, although painful, are not life-threatening. One of the most common stingers in this category is the bluebottle or Portuguese man-of-war. Not surprisingly, the bluebottle is bright blue in colour, and consists of an air-filled sac with long threadlike tentacles. Often washed up on the beach by the tide, bluebottles are tempting targets for 'popping' by the unwary – a hazardous undertaking unless wearing shoes.

A person who has been stung by a jellyfish will usually have some surface indication of what has happened. The area subjected to the sting may display whip marks, goose pimples, or wheals. The burning pain may be mild or severe. Minor stings may give rise to backache, pain in the chest, vomiting, aching limbs and sometimes loss of coordination, with some difficulty in breathing coming on ten to forty minutes after the sting.

The best treatment is to pour household vinegar over the area of the sting. This destroys still-active sting cells. Do not rub the area with sand, as this causes more venom to be absorbed. If no vinegar is available, pick off the tentacles with tweezers or scrape them off with a blunt edge (eg. cardboard, swim flipper) but not the fingers.

If the stings are severe: –
• keep the victim at rest and calm
• treat for shock
• if breathing or pulse stops, carry out mouth-to-mouth resuscitation or cardiopulmonary resuscitation
• get medical help
See also BOX JELLYFISH; IRUKANDJI SYNDROME; RESUSCITATION; SHOCK

JENNER, EDWARD

Edward Jenner was a Gloustershire (England) physician who was born in 1749 and died in 1823. He was the discoverer of vaccination as a method of protecting people from disease. He noticed that milkmaids who had the blisters of cowpox on their hands, a cattle disease, did not catch smallpox. He scratched the material from cowpox blisters into the skin of a boy, then exposed him some time later to smallpox (an experiment that would be considered grossly unethical today). The boy did not catch smallpox, so Jenner then started using his technique widely and encouraged other physicians to follow his example. The scourge of smallpox has now been totally eradicated from the planet due to Jenner's pioneering work.
See also SMALLPOX; VACCINATION

JERKING

Numerous medical conditions may be responsible for unwanted muscle jerks.

Hypnic jerks are experienced by everyone as brief, sudden muscle jerks while falling asleep. Unlike dreams, this phenomenon can be clearly remembered. They are harmless and no treatment is necessary.

Chorea is the technical term given to continual, purposeless jerking of the arms and legs. It is a rare symptom, but always a sign of serious disease.

The most common cause is an uncommon side effect of medications such as phenytoin (Dilantin), phenothiazines (eg. Largactil, Melleril) and a very rare side effect of the oral contraceptive pill. Amphetamines used illegally (eg. speed) may also be a cause. In these cases, the problem usually subsides soon after the drug is ceased.

Other possible causes of chorea include Huntington's chorea (a devastating inherited condition that does not make its presence felt until the patient is middle aged), dementia (eg. Alzheimer disease), Sydenham's chorea (a complication of rheumatic fever) and chorea gravidarum (caused by hormonal imbalances during pregnancy).

Other very rare causes include systemic lupus erythematosus (with arthritis and generalised organ inflammation), an overactive thyroid gland, carbon monoxide poisoning, polycythaemia rubra vera (excess red blood cells) and the Lesch-Nyhan syndrome (associated with retarded mentality, gout and self mutilation).
See also CONVULSIONS; MUSCLE CRAMP; TIC; TREMOR; WRITHING and separate entries for diseases mentioned above.

JET LAG

Jet lag is encountered on long intercontinental flights, and it is worse when flying east (against time) than flying west. It does not occur flying north-south (eg. on flights from Australia to Japan). Children are particularly upset by time changes and may take several days to adjust, becoming irritable and restless in the meantime.

The best way to deal with very long flights is to have a stopover. If only one stopover is possible, it should be taken when flying east (eg. from Europe to Australia or Australia to America).

The main symptoms of jet lag are tiredness, headaches, nausea, aching muscles, dizziness and disorientation. The best way to deal with the problem is to adjust to the local time zone as soon as possible. Start having the meals at the same time as the locals, even though you may feel like breakfast at 9 p.m., and go to bed near your normal time by the local clocks.

The air in aircraft is very dry and at a lower pressure than that on the ground. The dry air dehydrates passengers rapidly, and they should ensure that they have plenty to drink on the flight, but avoid alcohol. The low air pressure may cause severe pain and occasionally significant damage if the ears are blocked or the person has a cold.

Unless lucky enough to be in a first class seat, there may not be a great deal of leg room. As a result, most passengers tend to remain in the one position for long periods

JET LAG RECOVERY TIME

$$\text{REST TIME in hours} = \left(\frac{\text{Travel Time in hours}}{2} + \text{Time zones in excess of 4} + \text{Departure time coefficient} + \text{Arrival time coefficient} \right) \times 2$$

1 Time Zone = 1 Hour Difference in Time

TIME PERIOD	0800–1200	1200–1800	1800–2200	2200–0100	0100–0800
Departure Time Coefficient	0	1	3	4	3
Arrival Time Coefficient	4	2	0	1	3

$$\text{REST TIME in hours} \left(\frac{16}{2} + 3 + 1 + 2 \right) \times 2 = 28 \text{ hours}$$

of time. This will cause blood to pool in the feet and legs, which will swell up to the point that it may be difficult to replace shoes removed for comfort. This problem can be minimised by moving around the aircraft as much as possible, without inconveniencing the other passengers and staff, and leaving the aircraft for a long walk at every stop en route.

Adjust to the local time zone as soon as possible after the start of the flight. Small, frequent carbohydrate rich meals and extra fluids during the flight will aid recovery, but alcohol will slow it. Analgesic preparations (eg. paracetamol and aspirin) and a mild sleeping tablet (eg. temazepam) may be useful. The hormone melatonin, normally produced by the time regulating pineal gland at the front of the brain, is being used by some doctors to reset the body clocks and prevent jet lag, but the use of this drug is still controversial.

If someone really needs to find out how long it will take to recover from jet lag after a long trip, the equation shown here can be used. The example above allows for a 16-hour trip crossing seven time zones (seven hours time difference), leaving at 5 p.m. and arriving at 1 p.m. local time.
See also TRAVEL IMMUNISATION; TRAVEL MEDICINE

JEWISH DISEASES
See BLOOM SYNDROME; GAUCHER DISEASE; RILEY-DAY SYNDROME

JOHANSON-BLIZZARD SYNDROME
The rare Johanson-Blizzard syndrome is an inherited abnormality of connective tissue development, but both parents must carry the gene for an infant to be affected. The baby has abnormal nose structure, failure of the anus to form, underdeveloped and poorly functioning skin, deafness, mild mental retardation, and failure to gain weight and height. Plastic surgery may be used to correct some deformities, but no cure is available.

JOHANSSON-SINDING-LARSEN SYNDROME
The Johansson-Sinding-Larsen syndrome is a form of damage to the knee cap in athletic adolescents caused by overuse and stress on the knee joint with recurrent knee extension in sports that require running and/or kicking. It results in damage to the lower end of the patella (kneecap) at the point where ligaments attach to the tibia (shin bone). Abnormal bone growth may occur down this ligament from the patella.

Patients experience knee pain and tenderness at the lower edge of the patella in a teenager. An x-ray of the knee may show abnormal bone deposits in some cases. Rest, and a splint if severe, is the appropriate treatment.
See also KNEE PAIN

JOINT
Joints occur where bones meet. Major examples include the shoulders, elbows, wrists, hips, knees, ankles and jaw. Most joints are movable, but not all. Those between the separate bones that make up the skull are completely fixed. Joints between the two halves of the pelvis in the pubic area are fixed most of the time but move during childbirth. On the other hand, the

KNEE JOINT

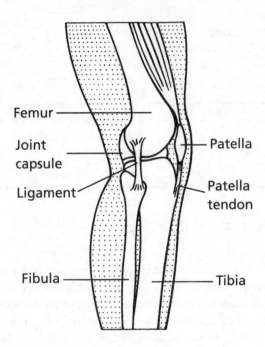

Femur

Joint capsule

Ligament

Patella

Patella tendon

Fibula

Tibia

shoulders are the most mobile joints in the body.

Ligaments are tough fibrous tissue that hold bones together at a joint. The ends of the bones are covered with a smooth layer of cartilage (gristle) providing a low-friction surface for easy movement. Joints such as the knees contain extra cartilage pads as shock absorbers. The bones in a joint never actually touch – they are always separated by a thin layer of synovial fluid contained in a capsule surrounding the joint.

The occasional cracking noise heard when a joint is flexed or bent may be caused by the tightly stretched ligaments moving from the surface of one bone to another. Alternatively, it might be the result of microscopic air bubbles bursting in the lubricating fluid.

A stretched or torn ligament around a joint is referred to as a sprain and can be as serious as a broken bone, needing proper rest and care until completely healed. Cartilage doesn't contain any blood vessels and so cannot heal itself if it is damaged. A torn cartilage isn't always troublesome, but if it does cause recurrent pain, it may be surgically removed.

Joints are divided into different types. Hinge joints such as those in the fingers, elbows and knees can move backwards and forwards. The hips and shoulders, on the other hand, are ball-and-socket joints which can move in almost any direction. The wrists and ankles have gliding joints.

People who have an unusually wide range of movement and who can bend their fingers and various other parts of their body into peculiar positions are sometimes said to be double-jointed – ie. they are alleged to have extra joints which enable their contortions. In reality there is no such thing. Such people actually have naturally slack ligaments and tendons which they have loosened still further by stretching and twisting until movement is no longer as restricted as it is in a normal person (hypermobility syndrome).

See also ARTHRITIS; BONES; BURSITIS; ELBOW; GOUT; HIP; JOINT RED; JOINT SWOLLEN; KNEE; LIGAMENT; OSTEOARTHRITIS; RHEUMATOID ARTHRITIS; SHOULDER; SLING; SPRAIN; STRAPPING; SYNOVIAL FLUID; SYNOVITIS; WRIST

JOINT INFECTION
See SEPTIC ARTHRITIS

JOINT MOBILITY INCREASED
See HYPERMOBILITY SYNDROME

JOINT PAIN
See ARTHRITIS

JOINT RED
There are three serious diseases that can make the skin over almost any joint red – cellulitis, septic arthritis and gout.

Cellulitis is an infection of the tissue immediately under the skin, and can occur anywhere on the body, but is more common at points where the skin is more easily injured, such as over joints. The skin is hot to touch as well as red, and often swollen and tender. The infection may spread to the adjacent joint or other tissues, or into the blood to cause septicaemia. The skin may also break down into an ulcer. Rapid treatment with an effective antibiotic is essential.

Septic arthritis is a bacterial infection of the fluid within a joint, which becomes red, swollen and painful. Urgent treatment with antibiotics is vital to prevent permanent joint damage.

Gout is caused by the build up of excess levels of uric acid in the blood. Uric acid itself is a break down product of proteins, particularly those found in red meat, offal and shellfish. The uric acid level in the fluid in all joints (synovial fluid) is the same as in the blood. If this reaches a critical level, particularly in joints that are put under considerable pressure (eg. ball of the foot), the uric acid may come out of solution and form crystals which under the microscope look like double ended needles. Indeed, in the affected joint they feel like double ended needles, and cause severe pain, tenderness, redness and swelling of the joint. The onset of a gout attack may be triggered by excess alcohol intake, although alcohol does not itself break down into uric acid.

Less common causes of a red joint include pseudogout (caused by a different crystal depositing in the joint), Reiter syndrome (which is associated with conjunctivitis, burning on passing urine and arthritis), severe osteoarthritis and rheumatoid arthritis, rheumatic fever and erythema nodosum (an autoimmune disease that also causes a rash). *See also* ARTHRITIS; CELLULITIS; GOUT; JOINT; SEPTIC ARTHRITIS and separate entries for diseases mentioned above.

JOINT SWOLLEN

Any injury to a joint from excessive twisting or turning, a blow or stretching, that causes even minor damage to the lining of the joint (synovial membrane), or the ligaments or cartilage in or around the joint, will cause the accumulation of inflammatory fluid and swelling. Rest, ice, compression and elevation (RICE) are the first aid measures for an injured joint, with heat, rest, strapping, pain relievers and anti-inflammatory medications following later.

There are a number of medical conditions that can cause a joint to become swollen.

Osteoarthritis is a wear and tear type injury to the lining of a joint that results in pain, reduced movement and swelling. This type of arthritis affects large joints more than small ones, but any joint may be affected.

Rheumatoid arthritis is the other major cause of joint swelling and deformity associated with both pain and loss of function. The body develops antibodies that inappropriately reject the lining membrane of the affected joint, in the same way that the body attempts to reject a donated transplanted kidney.

Septic arthritis is a bacterial infection of the fluid within a joint, which becomes red, swollen and painful. Urgent treatment with antibiotics is vital to prevent permanent joint damage.

Gout will cause severe pain, tenderness, redness and swelling of the affected joint. Bursitis is the inflammation of a sac beside a joint.

Inflammation of tissue outside a joint, including ligaments, tendons and fat (eg. deep bruising) may give the appearance that a joint is swollen.

A number of rare conditions may cause joints to swell including a Charcot joint (painless joint swelling after nerve supply to the joint has been destroyed), sarcoidosis (inflammation of tissue in many organs), synovitis (inflammation of joint lining membrane) and avascular necrosis (death of bone in a joint after its blood supply is cut off by blood clot or infection).

Tumours and cancers may rarely develop in a joint, and may first present as a painless swelling of the joint.
See also ARTHRITIS; JOINT; JOINT RED; SPRAIN and separate entries for diseases mentioned above.

JUGULAR VEIN
See VEIN

JUVENILE DIABETES
See DIABETES MELLITUS TYPE ONE

JUVENILE RHEUMATOID ARTHRITIS
See STILL'S DISEASE

K

K
See POTASSIUM

KA
See KERATOACANTHOMA

KALA-AZAR
Kala-Azar (visceral leischmaniasis) is a widespread internal infection by the protozoan (tiny single celled animal) *Leischmania donovani* that is transmitted from one person to another by sand-fly bites. It is found throughout the tropics in America, Asia and Africa.

The disease has a slow onset with fever, enlarged spleen and liver, anaemia, weight loss, pigmentation of skin on face (mainly forehead) and hands. Bleeding from the nose and mouth, and warty skin ulcers sometimes occur. It is diagnosed by blood tests and biopsy of the liver or spleen.

Quite toxic medications must be given regularly by injection for a long time to control the infection, which is fatal without treatment. Recurrences are common for years after apparently successful treatment, and a permanent cure is difficult.
See also CUTANEOUS
LEISCHMANIASIS

KAOLIN
See ANTIDIARRHOEALS

KAPOSI SARCOMA
A Kaposi sarcoma was initially a very rare form of cancer of muscle and fat tissue found only in central Africa, but it is now far more widespread because of the AIDS virus. Advanced stages of AIDS reduce the body's ability to defend itself from this rare type of cancer. Patients notice the growth of one or more tender, painful, firm tumours in muscle and other soft tissues, and the cancer then spreads to nearby lymph nodes and other tissues. It is diagnosed by a biopsy of the tumour.

Treatment involves surgical excision of the cancer, followed by irradiation and chemotherapy but, in advanced cases, only chemotherapy may be practical to slow the progress of the disease. No long term cure is possible, but progression of the condition may be slowed by treatment.
See also AIDS; SARCOMA

KARTAGENER SYNDROME
Kartagener syndrome is an inherited abnormality of organ position in which the heart is on the right side of the chest (dextrocardia) instead of the left, and recurrent sinus and lung infections (bronchiectasis) occur. In some patients, the organs in the abdomen (liver, spleen, gut etc.) are also reversed in position (situs inversus). An x-ray of the chest will show the abnormal heart position. Sometimes surgical correction of defects is required, but in most cases it is merely necessary to use antibiotic and symptomatic treatment of lung and sinus problems. There is no cure, but most problems can be corrected or controlled.
See also BRONCHIECTASIS; SINUSITIS;
SITUS INVERSUS

KATAYAMA FEVER
See SCHISTOSOMIASIS

KAYSER-FLEISCHER RING
See WILSON DISEASE

KELOID
Some people have an inherited tendency in which there is excessive healing of a scar that results in a keloid. It is more common in Negroes, and on the chest, back and neck. A red or brown, raised, thick scar that may become painful or itchy, forms at the site of skin injury. It may be improved by an injection or application, under a plastic dressing, of powerful steroids. Most keloids stop enlarging after a few months, and then persist for many years, before very slowly subsiding in some cases.
See also SKIN PIGMENTATION EXCESS

KENYA TICK TYPHUS
See TYPHUS

KERATIN
See SKIN

KERATIN CYSTS
See MILIA

KERATITIS
Keratitis is an inflammation of the cornea (the outer layer of the eye), caused by ultraviolet lights, exposure to reflected sun (snow blindness), cement dust, and irritating chemicals (eg. alkalis) that may splash into the eye. It may also be due to a bacterial or fungal infection in contact lens wearers.

Severe burning pain starts in the eye some hours after exposure to bright light, but immediately with direct irritants. The eyes water and are very sensitive to bright light and pain occurs whenever the pupil contracts or dilates due to changes in light intensity. Scarring of the cornea may occur with chemical burns. Examination of the eye under magnification shows damage to cornea.

Treatment involves irrigating the eye to remove any irritant chemicals or substances, instilling drops to paralyse any pupil movement, and an eye patch. Recovery usually occurs within one to two days.
See also EYE; FLASH BURN TO EYE

KERATOACANTHOMA
A keratoacanthoma (KA) is a rapidly enlarging skin growth that is often confused with a skin cancer. They are more common in the elderly and on the face, hands and other sun-exposed areas of the body, but rare in dark-skinned races.

They initially appear as a small, scale-covered lump, but over a couple of months they enlarge rapidly to become a red, shiny, firm blister topped with a plug of hard scaly material that may be 2cm or more in diameter. Over the next few months or years they slowly disappear, and eventually little or no trace of their presence remains, but they take about twice as long to resolve as they take to develop. No treatment is required, but as most KA are very disfiguring and unsightly they are usually removed surgically. If there is any doubt at all about the diagnosis a biopsy must be taken. Except for the disfigurement they cause, they are quite harmless.
See also SQUAMOUS CELL CARCINOMA OF THE SKIN

KERATOCONJUNCTIVITIS SICCA
Keratoconjunctivitis sicca is a severe form of the dry eye syndrome (xerophthalmia) that commonly occurs in elderly women whose lacrimal (tear producing) glands fail. It may also be a complication of autoimmune diseases such as systemic lupus erythematosus, rheumatoid arthritis and Sjögren syndrome. Patients have continued eye irritation and discomfort from a dry eye surface, and rarely it may be a threat to sight.

The diagnosis can be confirmed by a simple test; a thin strip of blotting paper, touched to the lower eye surface for a minute, remains abnormally dry with this condition.

Very regular and long term use of lubricating eye drops and ointment are the main treatments. Inserts that are placed under the lower lid and ooze a lubricant constantly for many hours can also be used. There is no cure, it is difficult to control, and usually continues lifelong.
See also DRY EYE SYNDROME; RHEUMATOID ARTHRITIS; SJÖGREN SYNDROME; SYSTEMIC LUPUS ERYTHEMATOSUS

KERATOCONUS
Keratoconus is a cone shaped protrusion and thinning of the cornea, which is the clear dome over the pupil and iris (coloured part of the eye). It is a condition that may be inherited or associated with Down syndrome, Turner syndrome, Marfan syndrome and numerous eye diseases, and causes distorted vision (astigmatism) in the affected eye that steadily worsens to the point where scarring or rupture of the clear corneal membrane may occur. It is diagnosed by examining the eye with a magnifying light (ophthalmoscope).

In early stages treatment merely requires spectacles or contact lenses to correct the vision, but in late stages, surgery to the surface of the cornea or replacement of the cornea with a transplant is necessary.

Patients get good results from treatment, but it is a progressive condition if left untreated.
See also DOWN SYNDROME; MARFAN SYNDROME; TURNER SYNDROME; VISION

KERATOLYTICS
Keratolytics are skin preparations that are designed to remove the outermost layer of the skin (the keratin layer) and therefore act as the

ultimate skin cleanser. Most are available without prescription and are used to treat diseases such as acne, psoriasis and some forms of dermatitis. Excessive or inappropriate use may cause reddening, burning and discolouration of the skin, particularly on the face. It is wise to make a test application on an area of skin that is not cosmetically important before applying a keratolytic to the face. Isotretinoin is a tablet and all others are creams, lotions, pastes, gels, ointments or soaps.

Examples include benzyl peroxide, isotretinoin (Roaccutane), salicylic acid, tretinoin and triclosan. Side effects may include stinging, redness, skin swelling and skin peeling. In addition, isotretinoin may cause sore mouth, dry eyes, dry skin, joint pain, thin hair and sun sensitivity. Patients should avoid eyes, mouth, nostrils and wounds. Care is necessary with sun exposure. Tretinoin must be used with caution in pregnancy. Isotretinoin is very dangerous in pregnancy, and must be used with caution in all patients.
See also ACNE; PSORIASIS; SKIN

KERATOSIS
See HYPERKERATOSIS; SEBORRHOEIC KERATOSES

KERATOTOMY
See REFRACTIVE SURGERY

KERION
A kerion is an abscess of the scalp caused by the fungi *Trichophyton*, *Microsporum* and other fungi that normally cause tinea (ringworm). A sore, boggy, raised abscess develops on the scalp and there may be spread of the fungal infection to other areas of the skin. A swab can be taken to identify the responsible fungus, then potent antifungal tablets and creams used to cure the infection.
See also TINEA CAPITIS

KETAMINE
Ketamine was initially used as an anaesthetic, but is now rarely used on humans except in areas where an anaesthetist is not available. It is now widely used as a veterinary anaesthetic, and used illegally as a mood enhancer. It may be referred to by drug addicts as 'Special K'.

Ketamine is colourless and odourless and may be used illegally as a tablet, liquid or injected. In low doses it acts as a stimulant,

causes loss of coordination (users may dance for hours in an uncoordinated manner), and induces artificial happiness and a floating sensation. Side effects may include nausea, vomiting, slurred speech, headache, muscle spasms and numbness. Some users may feel they are about to die, and become very stressed when the drug wears off. In other cases, the anaesthetic effect may cause users to unknowingly injure themselves (eg. not be aware that a cigarette has burnt down to their fingers). Psychological dependence may occur.

In overdose, breathing slows and heart rate increases, vision is impaired and convulsions may occur.
See also ANAESTHETICS; COCAINE; ECSTASY; GAMMA-HYDROXYBUTYRATE; HEROIN; LSD; MARIJUANA; STIMULANTS

KETOACIDOSIS
See DIABETIC KETOACIDOSIS

KETOCONAZOLE
See ANTIFUNGALS

KETOPROFEN
See NONSTEROIDAL ANTI-INFLAMMATORY DRUGS

KETOSIS
See APPETITE, LACK OF; DIABETES MELLITUS TYPE ONE

KEYHOLE SURGERY
See SURGERY

KIDNEY
The kidneys are a pair of reddish-brown organs lying on each side of the spine just above the waist. If you grip your waist with your hands, your thumbs will be over your kidneys. The kidneys are soft to the touch and are about ten cm. long and six cm. wide. One side is concave and the other is convex – the classic kidney shape. The right kidney is slightly lower than the left one because of the space taken up by the liver above it.

Each kidney is cushioned by a mass of fat and is also protected by the bottom ribs. The kidneys are, nevertheless, quite vulnerable and can be injured by a blow to the small of the back.

KIDNEY

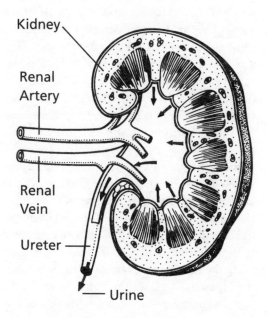

Kidney

Renal Artery

Renal Vein

Ureter

Urine

Their function is to filter the blood to remove impurities and waste products, and also ensure that various elements in our blood such as proteins, salts, vitamins and nutrients remain in perfect balance. They also monitor and regulate the balance of fluid in the body. Although the amount of water consumed in a day can vary enormously, the volume of body water at any given time remains remarkably stable. Water may be lost from the body in several ways – through the skin as perspiration, from the respiratory system when breathing out, in faeces and by passing urine. Normally the amount of water taken in is approximately equal to the amount lost. The kidneys are the main monitoring organs. If the body is short of fluid, the kidneys return more water to the bloodstream, and as a result the amount of urine is reduced and is more concentrated. Messages are also sent to the brain and to cause the person to feel thirsty. Correspondingly, if the intake of water is greater than needed, the kidneys return proportionally less fluid to the blood and the amount of urine passed increases. The amount of salts contained in the body is regulated in similar fashion.

To keep the kidneys functioning as effectively as possible it is important to drink sufficient water and not to overload them with products the body doesn't need, such as food additives, drugs and vitamins.

About a litre of blood is pumped into the kidneys every minute, and the entire bloodstream is purified every fifty minutes.

The kidneys have considerable reserve capacity. If one fails, the other can generally carry the load on its own and in fact even a third of one kidney may be enough to keep the body functioning. If the kidneys fail completely, however, the victim will die within a few days.

See also BLADDER; CREATININE; GLOMERULONEPHRITIS; INTRAVENOUS PYELOGRAM; KIDNEY FAILURE, ACUTE; KIDNEY FAILURE, CHRONIC; NEPHRON; POLYCYSTIC KIDNEY; PYELONEPHRITIS; UREA; URETER; WILMS' TUMOUR

KIDNEY CANCER
See WILMS' TUMOUR

KIDNEY FAILURE, ACUTE

Acute kidney (renal) failure is a sudden failure of the kidney to remove waste products from the body and to retain the correct amount of water in the body. It may be triggered by a severe injury (particularly crush injuries), major surgery, poisons (eg. mercury, dry cleaning fluid, mushrooms), heart attacks, severe burns, severe infections, and a number of rarer causes. It may also occur as a complication of pregnancy.

Patients experience a sudden severe reduction in the output of urine associated with a loss of appetite, tiredness, nausea, vomiting and raised blood pressure. The diagnosis is confirmed by blood and urine tests, which show waste products in the blood and very dilute urine.

Any specific cause must first be treated. In severe cases, an artificial kidney machine may be needed (dialysis). The amount of fluids the patient drinks must be carefully regulated, and a strict diet that limits the number of waste products in the body is given. Bacterial and viral infections are a common complication.

The prognosis depends on the cause. Some patients die within a couple of days, but most can be managed in a good hospital to a successful outcome. After a few days or weeks, the kidneys usually start to work again, and over a month or two the urine and kidney function return to normal, and there is usually no long-lasting kidney damage.

See also BURN; DIALYSIS; KIDNEY;
KIDNEY FAILURE, CHRONIC;
MERCURY POISONING

KIDNEY FAILURE, CHRONIC

Chronic kidney (renal) failure, or uraemia, is a slow, gradual failure of kidney function. Old age is the most common cause, but it may also be due to many other conditions including a damaged blood supply to the kidney from hardened arteries (arteriosclerosis), poisons, infections, the body trying to reject the kidney in autoimmune conditions such as systemic lupus erythematosus, and many rarer diseases.

Because of its slow onset, patients may not present to a doctor until the condition is well advanced, by which time they have weakness, tiredness, lack of appetite, weight loss, nausea, headaches, passing urine frequently (including overnight) and in advanced cases itchy skin, vomiting, high blood pressure and anaemia. Abnormal blood and urine tests are diagnostic, but further investigations are carried out to discover any specific cause.

It is necessary to treat any cause of the condition if possible, followed by a strict diet (low in protein), and control of all fluids that are drunk. Unless the cause can be corrected, long-term treatment with an artificial kidney machine (dialysis), or a kidney transplant operation is necessary. Patients must also be very careful with medications, as they are likely to be far more effective, last longer in the body than normal, have more side effects and may be toxic.

Kidney transplants have an 80% cure rate, while dialysis can be continued for many years if necessary.
See also ANALGESIC NEPHROPATHY;
AUTOIMMUNE DISEASES;
ARTERIOSCLEROSIS; DIALYSIS;
KIDNEY; KIDNEY FAILURE, ACUTE;
NEPHROTIC SYNDROME

KIDNEY INFECTION
See PYELONEPHRITIS, ACUTE;
PYELONEPHRITIS, CHRONIC

KIDNEY MEDICATIONS
See ALKALINISERS; DIURETICS

KIDNEY PAIN
See LOIN PAIN

KIDNEY STONE

The kidney acts to filter the blood, and removes excess water and wastes. If these wastes become too concentrated or altered in some way, they can precipitate out and form a crystal that slowly grows into a stone (renal calculus or nephrolithiasis). Most stones are flushed down the ureter (the tube that leads from the kidney to the bladder) and are passed out with the urine while still very small. A small proportion of stones slowly grow in size until they are the size of a grape or larger and completely fill the urine collection chamber of the kidney where they cause repeated kidney infections and pain. Medium sized stones, from one to five millimetres in length, enter the thin very sensitive ureter, and as the stone is pushed along the tube by the pressure of urine behind, it scrapes the tube wall to cause intense pain (renal or ureteric colic) that can thus come and go for several days every time the stone moves. Kidney stones are more common in men than women, and in hot climates more than cold due to the higher incidence of dehydration.

Patients experience excruciating, intermittent pain in the loin (side of the belly) that goes down to the groin. Patients may note blood in their urine because the stone is damaging the ureter to make it bleed. Severe intractable kidney infections may be due to an undiagnosed stone, and rarely a kidney may be so severely damaged by a stone that it fails. X-rays of the kidney after the injection of a dye (intravenous pyelogram – IVP) show the stone, its size and position, and the progress of the stone down the ureter can be seen on repeat x-rays. Ultrasound scans may also show the presence of a stone. Blood tests are done to check for the cause of the stone.

Most patients are given pain relief and lots of fluids to wash the stone down the ureter, and after a few hours or days, the stone enters the bladder and passes out without causing any further pain, but some stones get stuck in the ureter and must be removed. This can be done in a number of ways: –
• Lithotripsy uses intense sound shock waves that are passed through the body to shatter the stone. The remnants, which are the size of sand particles, can then be passed normally through the urine.
• Passing a tiny umbrella into the bladder and up the ureter to a point above the stone where the umbrella is then opened, and slowly

removed, dragging the stone along with it.

• Under the control of a radiologist (x-ray specialist), a tube can be placed through the skin into the kidney, and the stone removed.

• Rarely an open operation through the abdominal wall may be necessary.

Almost invariably kidney stones can be successfully treated, but up to 50% of patients will have a recurrence within five years if measures are not taken to prevent their formation.

See also COLIC;
HYPERPARATHYROIDISM;
INTRAVENOUS PYELOGRAM;
KIDNEY; LITHOTRIPSY; URETER

KILOJOULES AND CALORIES

Kilojoules (calories in the old British system of measurement) are a measure of energy, and can be applied to the energy content of foods. One calorie equals 4.2 kilojoules (kJ).

Different foods provide different amounts of energy and so have different kilojoule values. Fat generally supplies more than twice the number of kilojoules per gram than is provided by carbohydrates and proteins, while water and fibre have no kilojoules at all. Every kilogram your body weighs equals 35 000 kilojoules. If you eat 2500 kJ less than you expend every day for a week, you will lose about 500g.

See also FOOD; WEIGHT LOSS DIET

'KING'S EVIL'

See SCROFULA

KISSING DISEASE

See GLANDULAR FEVER

KISS OF LIFE

See RESUSCITATION

kJ

See KILOJOULES AND CALORIES

KLEINE-LEVIN SYNDROME

The Kleine-Levin syndrome is a sleep and mood disorder of no known cause in which patients experience recurrent periods of severe excessive sleepiness, increased appetite, mood disturbances, increased sexual activity, disorientation, hallucinations and memory loss. There may be no symptoms for months between attacks and it is more common in men, with onset from twelve to twenty years of age. It is treated with stimulants, and is self-limiting by about forty years of age.

See also SLEEP EXCESS

KLEPTOMANIA

Kleptomania is a form of mania (compulsion) in which there is an irresistible desire to steal, despite usually having adequate resources to pay for the stolen goods.

See also MANIA

KLINEFELTER SYNDROME

The Klinefelter syndrome (XXY syndrome) is a congenital sexual abnormality that affects one in every 500 males. The chromosomes from the mother and father of these men combine incorrectly with two X chromosomes and one Y being present (XXY) instead of one of each (XY). Patients have very small testes and penis, scanty body hair, small breasts develop and they are impotent and sterile. It is diagnosed by chromosomal analysis of blood sample.

Testosterone (male hormone) tablets or injections can be given to improve the body shape and impotence, and plastic surgery to remove the breasts is sometimes necessary, but the infertility cannot be corrected and no cure is possible.

See also CHROMOSOME; TURNER SYNDROME; XYY SYNDROME

KLUMPKE PALSY

Klumpke (Déjerine-Klumpke) palsy is a form of arm damage to an infant that occurs during birth due to stretching of the lower nerves in the armpit during a forceps or difficult delivery. The infant's hand is limp below the wrist. Nerve conduction studies are sometimes performed to confirm the diagnosis, and the wrist is then splinted in neutral position. Most babies fully recover.

See also ERB-DUCHENNE PALSY

KNEE

The joint formed by the femur above and the tibia below. The patella (kneecap) lies in front of the knee, and is an integral part of the joint. The fibula, the smaller bone in the lower leg, does not form part of the knee joint as its upper end attaches to the tibia. The knee can move in only one plane, forward and back, as it is a hinge joint.

See also ARTHROSCOPY; FEMUR;

JOINT; KNEE CAP ABNORMAL; KNEE LOCKED; KNEE MENISCUS TEAR; KNEE PAIN; KNEE SWOLLEN; KNEE UNSTABLE; KNOCK KNEES; PATELLA; TIBIA

KNEE CAP
See PATELLA

KNEE CAP ABNORMAL
The patella (kneecap) may be very loose and have abnormal amount of side to side movement when the leg is straight if the muscles of the leg are weakened for any reason, or as an inherited characteristic. With these conditions the patella is more likely to dislocate (slide sideways off the front of the knee) when the knee is twisted or knocked.

A dislocated kneecap only occurs when the knee is bent and is extremely painful, but the dislocation can be corrected, and the pain almost instantly relieved, if a bystander gently straightens the knee. Strapping, physiotherapy and surgery may be necessary to prevent subsequent dislocations.

Chondromalacia is damage to the cartilage on the underside of the patella. Cartilage usually enables the kneecap to slide smoothly across the end of the femur (thigh bone) when the knee is bent and straightened. Movement of a patella with chondromalacia will cause a grating sensation and pain. There may be associated swelling around the knee joint.

Other less common causes include the synovial plica syndrome (folding of the smooth membrane within the knee), and the nail-patella syndrome (patella is very small or absent, and the nails of fingers and toes are deformed).
See also KNEE PAIN; PATELLA and separate entries for diseases mentioned above.

KNEE LOCKED
The most common reason for the knee becoming difficult or impossible to move is a tear in the meniscal cartilage that surrounds the upper end of the tibia. The top of the tibia (the larger of the two bones in the lower leg) is shaped like a shallow double cup to fit the rounded lower end of the femur (thigh bone). This cupping is deepened by a cartilage (meniscus) that runs around the edge of the cup, to further stabilise the knee. A twist to the knee may result in tearing of this cartilage, and the torn section can move into the joint to cause pain, clicking and locking. Surgery is often necessary to repair these tears, but this can usually be done through an arthroscope (thin tube).

Other injuries to the knee may cause a fracture or dislocation of one of the bones forming the joint, or rupture of one or both of the strong cruciate ligaments in the centre of the joint. These injuries may cause locking of the joint, as well as swelling and pain.

Occasionally a piece of cartilage or other tissue may break off and float loosely in the knee joint. In certain positions this may cause the knee to lock.

Severe arthritis of the knee may so damage the joint that it may occasionally lock. Osteoarthritis and septic arthritis (infection in the joint) are most often responsible.
See also KNEE; KNEE MENISCUS TEAR; KNEE PAIN; KNEE UNSTABLE; PATELLA and separate entries for diseases mentioned above.

KNEE MENISCUS TEAR
The menisci are cartilages that run around the top end of the tibia (main lower leg bone) to deepen the socket of the joint and stabilise it. Abnormal twisting of the knee may result in tearing of a meniscus which causes pain, swelling, clicking and sometimes locking of the knee joint that is worse with movement. Patients often describe a feeling of instability in the joint. Doctors apply various stress tests to the knee in different positions to make the diagnosis.

Initially, resting the knee with strapping and using crutches may allow the knee to recover, and a locked knee can be released by manipulation. In persistent or severe cases, particularly if there is locking, an operation (meniscectomy) is necessary to remove the torn cartilage. This can usually be done through an arthroscope (small tube that is passed into the knee joint). Sometimes the knee may become unstable after a meniscectomy, and premature arthritis may develop, but generally there are good results from treatment.
See also ARTHROSCOPY; KNEE; KNEE PAIN; TIBIA

KNEE PAIN
The knee is designed in much the same way

as a finger joint. It can bend and straighten, but not twist, rotate or move from side to side. Any stress that tries to move the knee in one of these abnormal directions may result in damage to the bones (fracture, dislocation), ligaments (sprain), cartilages, tendons (tendinitis) and muscles around the knee to cause pain. In more severe injuries, bleeding into the joint may aggravate the pain and slow the healing. Time, rest, splinting and strapping are often the only effective treatments, although physiotherapy and anti-inflammatory medications may make the knee more comfortable.

The top of the tibia (the larger of the two bones in the lower leg) is shaped like a shallow double cup to fit the rounded lower end of the femur (thigh bone). This cupping is deepened by a cartilage (meniscus) that runs around the edge of the cup, to further stabilise the knee. A twist to the knee may result in a tear to this cartilage, which can cause pain, clicking, locking and instability in the joint. Tenderness along the joint line just beside the kneecap is characteristic of this type of injury.

Any form of arthritis may cause pain in the knee. Osteoarthritis is the most common type in the knee.

If the ligaments in and around the knee are slack or unstable after previous injury or surgery, there may be abnormal movement between the bone ends, leading to increased wear and tear on the lining of the joint and surrounding cartilages to cause inflammation and pain.

Osgood-Schlatter's disease is a relatively common condition, occurring in older children and teenagers, caused by inflammation of the point where the thick tendon (patella tendon) that runs from the bottom end of the knee cap attaches to the top front of the tibia. This is also the point at which the bone softens to grow in children and teenagers, so if there is a growth spurt associated with a period of vigourous exercise of the knee, the bone may become inflamed, tender and painful at this point. Unfortunately, the only treatment is prolonged rest.

Other causes of knee pain include bursitis (inflammation or infection of one of the many small sacs around the knee joint that produce the synovial fluid that normally fills the joint), osteochondritis dessicans (cartilage inflammation), chondromalacia (cartilage wear), sciatica (pain that runs down the leg from the buttock), a popliteal cyst (hard cyst that forms behind the knee), and unusually severe cases of knock knees and bandy knees in children which may put abnormal pressure on the joints to cause pain.

Rarer causes of knee pain include Paget's disease (a thickening but weakening of bones), septic arthritis (joint infection), patellofemoral pain syndrome (pain in, around and behind the knee cap a day or two after unaccustomed vigourous exercise), Still's disease (childhood rheumatoid arthritis), iliotibial band friction syndrome (inflammation of a band of ligaments that run up the outside of the knee), synovial plica syndrome (infolding of the synovial membrane lining the joint) and the Johansson-Sinding-Larsen syndrome (tearing of the thick tendon which runs from the lower end of the patella to the upper part of the tibia).
See also JOINT PAIN; KNEE; KNEE LOCKED; OSTEOARTHRITIS and separate entries for diseases mentioned above.

KNEE SWOLLEN
The knee may be swollen without any other symptoms, or the swelling may be associated with pain.

Swelling without pain in elderly people is most commonly caused by long-standing osteoarthritis, when the lining of a joint degenerates with time, and becomes swollen and inflamed.

In younger people, knee swelling is usually associated with an injury to one of the bones, cartilages, synovial membrane (lining membrane of the joint), ligaments or tendons in or around the knee. An injury can occur with a sudden painful movement, or it may develop gradually and painlessly with overuse.

Pigmented villonodular synovitis is an inflammation of the smooth membrane (synovial membrane) which lines the inside of the joint. The membrane develops multiple tiny projections that are damaged and bleed.

Tiny deposits of bone may also form in a persistently inflamed synovial membrane (synovial osteochondromatosis) to roughen it and cause inflammation and swelling.
See also KNEE; KNEE PAIN and separate entries for diseases mentioned above.

KNEE UNSTABLE

Individuals, particularly the elderly, may find that their knee suddenly gives way or is unstable, causing them to stumble or fall.

If the knee cap (patella) does not run smoothly and evenly across the end of the femur (thigh bone) as the knee bends and straightens, it may come partly out of the groove on the end of femur in which it normally runs (subluxation), resulting in a sudden loss of strength in the leg. This may occur with minimal discomfort if it is a recurrent problem, and correct itself almost immediately as the knee is straightened. Occasionally the patella may completely dislocate, but this is almost invariably associated with considerable pain, and requires someone else to straighten the leg in order to place the patella back in its correct position.

Significant arthritis in the knee may cause an abnormal side-to-side wobble in the joint and unsteadiness in walking.

Tears to the strong cruciate ligaments within the knee that join the femur (thigh bone) to the tibia (major bone in the calf) will result in an abnormal front to back movement in the knee, and instability.

A piece of cartilage or other tissue may break off and float loosely in the knee joint and in certain positions this may cause abnormal joint movement and the knee becomes unstable. Osteochondritis is a degeneration of the cartilage on the bone surfaces in the joint.

Any damage to the nerves supplying the knee caused by multiple sclerosis, nerve pinching in the back or direct injury to the nerve, may result in the brain being unable to automatically sense the position of the knee and leg, and an unsteady walk occurs.
See also KNEE; KNEE LOCKED; KNEE PAIN; KNEE SWOLLEN and separate entries for diseases mentioned above.

KNOCK KNEES

Knock knees (genu valgum) is a common condition of children, that is diagnosed when a child standing straight tries to bring the bony bumps (medial malleoli) on the inside of the ankles together. If they are unable to do this because the knees come together first, the diagnosis is confirmed. It is usually a developmental and growth problem, but in rare cases it may be due to rickets, poorly healed fractures of the leg bones or other very uncommon diseases.

These children have an awkward way of walking and possible knee and ankle discomfort.

In the majority of cases the problem corrects itself without any treatment, but in severe cases a wedge may be inserted into the inside edge of the shoes to turn the foot slightly outwards. Rarely, if the problem continues into the early teenage years and causes difficulty in walking or abnormal appearance and posture, an operation may be necessary.
See also BOW LEGS; KNEE

KOEBNER PHENOMENON

The Koebner phenomenon is the development of a rash at the site of a skin injury.

Injury to the skin (a cut, burn, graze or scar) can allow an autoimmune type skin reaction to develop and a rash on the area of damaged skin follows the outline of the damaged area exactly. Psoriasis and lichen planus are the most common conditions to develop. A biopsy is sometimes necessary to diagnose difficult cases. The identified skin disease is then treated.
See also AUTOIMMUNE DISEASES; LICHEN PLANUS; PSORIASIS

KORSAKOFF PSYCHOSIS
See WERNICKE-KORSAKOFF PSYCHOSIS

KUGELBERG-WELANDER SYNDROME

The Kugelberg-Welander syndrome is a familial (runs in families) nerve disease that affects muscle function. It is due to an abnormality of the point where a nerve joins to a muscle.

Patients develop muscular weakness of the shoulder girdle and pelvis and an abnormal gait. Some patients develop over large calf muscles and tongue weakness. It is diagnosed by abnormalities in blood tests, nerve conduction studies and muscle biopsy. Reflexes involving affected muscles are also abnormal. Physiotherapy may help, but there is no specific treatment available. Patients have a relatively normal life span, but the disease process is slowly progressive.
See also MOTOR NEURONE DISEASE; MUSCLE WEAKNESS

KURU

Kuru is a now extinct disease that occurred in the cannibalistic Fore tribe in the New Guinea highlands, and is closely related to Creutzfeldt-Jakob disease. A primitive virus-like particle known as a prion was probably responsible, and was transmitted from person to person by eating the infected brains of their victims. Symptoms included twitching, incoordination, tremor and mental deterioration. No treatment was available and death was inevitable.
See also CREUTZFELDT-JAKOB DISEASE; PRION

KWASHIORKOR

Kwashiorkor is a severe form of malnutrition caused by a lack of protein in the diet, although adequate amounts of carbohydrates and fatty foods may be eaten.

The symptoms may include a swollen belly, tiredness, thin limbs with swollen ankles, wasted muscles, a dry dermatitis, sparse hair, conjunctivitis and inflamed gums. Protein levels in the blood drop to a very low level, which allows water to escape from the blood into tissues to give the characteristic bloated belly appearance. Permanent organ damage may occur if malnutrition is prolonged.

Small amounts of nutritious food must be given frequently over several weeks before returning to a normal diet as an imbalance of chemicals in the blood may occur if too much protein is given quickly. Good recovery is possible with an appropriate diet, but it is fatal otherwise.
See also MARASMUS

KYPHOSCOLIOSIS

Kyphoscoliosis is a combination of both abnormal side to side (scoliosis) and front to back (kyphosis) curvature of the spine. Minor degrees are seen in many teenagers as they go through periods of rapid growth, particularly if they have poor posture, but in some the deformity becomes severe. Other causes include one leg being shorter than the other, a severe back injury, diseases of the muscles that support the vertebrae, cerebral palsy, osteoporosis, compressed and collapsed vertebrae, ankylosing spondylitis, tuberculous

damage to vertebrae, tumours, and a number of less common diseases.

There is an excessive outward curve of the spine at the back of the chest, and abnormal side to side curvature that may vary from a slightly increased prominence to a severe hunchback deformity. Nerves may be pinched as they leave the deformed back, causing severe pain, and permanent deformity is a rare possibility. The diagnosis is confirmed by x-rays of the spine, which may show the cause at the same time.

The cause should be treated if possible, otherwise muscle strengthening exercises, physiotherapy, braces and rarely surgery are used to correct the deformity. The prognosis depends upon severity, but most patients cope well with the deformity and have no outward signs of the condition.
See also BACK PAIN; KYPHOSIS; SCOLIOSIS; SPINE; VERTEBRA

KYPHOSIS

Kyphosis is an abnormal curvature of the back with an excessive outward curve of the spine at the back of the chest that may vary from a slightly increased prominence to a severe hunchback deformity. The pinching of nerves as they leave the deformed back may cause severe pain. The back normally curves gently from front to back in a double S-shape, curving in at the neck, out over the back of the chest, in at the small of the back, and out again between the buttocks.

Kyphosis may be caused by osteoporosis in older women, compressed and collapsed vertebrae, ankylosing spondylitis in the elderly, tuberculosis, tumours, constant muscle spasm in cerebral palsy, and a number of less common diseases.

The diagnosis is confirmed by x-rays of the spine, which may show the cause at the same time. If possible the cause should be treated; otherwise exercise, physiotherapy, braces and rarely surgery are used to correct the deformity. Many patients have remarkably pain-free backs despite quite horrendous deformities.
See also ANKYLOSING SPONDYLITIS; KYPHOSCOLIOSIS; OSTEOPOROSIS; SCOLIOSIS; SPINE; VERTEBRA

L

LABOUR

For weeks you have been waddling around uncomfortably. Every few hours you have Braxton-Hicks contractions that can be quite uncomfortable and sometimes wake you at night, but they always fade away. Your back aches, and you are going to the toilet every hour because your bladder has nowhere to expand. The long awaited date is due, and still nothing dramatic has occurred.

Suddenly you notice that you have lost some bloodstained fluid through the vagina, and the contractions are worse than usual. You have passed the mucus plug that seals the cervix during pregnancy, and if a lot of fluid is lost, you may have ruptured the membranes around the baby as well. Labour should start very soon after this 'show'.

Shortly afterwards you can feel the first contraction. It passes quickly, but every ten to fifteen minutes more contractions occur. Most are mild, but some make you stop in your tracks for a few seconds. When you find that two contractions have occurred only five to seven minutes apart, it is time to be taken to hospital or the birthing centre.

You are now in the first of the three stages of labour. This stage will last for about twelve hours with a first pregnancy, but will be much shorter (four to eight hours) with subsequent pregnancies. These times can vary significantly from one woman to another.

The hospital nurses fuss over you and answer questions. Soon afterwards, you may be given an enema. By the time the obstetrician calls in to see how you are progressing, the contractions are occurring every three or four minutes. The obstetrician examines you internally to check how far the cervix (the opening into the womb) has opened. This check may be performed several times during labour, and leads may be attached through the vagina to the baby's head to monitor its heart and general condition. The cervix steadily opens until it merges with the walls of the uterus. A fully dilated cervix is about 10cm. in diameter, and you may hear the doctors and nurses discussing the cervix dilation and measurement.

As the labour progresses, you are moved into the delivery room. In a typical hospital delivery room, white drapes hide bulky pieces of equipment, there are large lights on the ceiling, shiny sinks on one wall, and often a cheerful baby poster above them. The contractions become steadily more intense. If the pain in your abdomen doesn't attack you, the backache does, and your partner (who has hopefully attended one or two of your antenatal classes) massages your back between pains. You begin to wonder when it will all end. The breathing exercises you were taught at the antenatal classes should prove remarkably effective in helping you with the more severe contractions. Even so, the combined backache and sharp stabs of pain may need to be relieved by an injection offered by the nurse. Breathing nitrous oxide gas on a mask when the contractions start can also make them more bearable.

If you experience severe pain or require some intervention (eg. forceps), an epidural or spinal anaesthetic is given. This involves an injection into the spine, which numbs the body from the waist down. You feel nothing but remain quite conscious and alert, and you can assist in the birth process. Even a Caesarean section can be performed using this type of anaesthetic.

Eventually you develop an irresistible desire to start pushing with all your might. Your cervix will be fully dilated by this stage, and you are now entering the second stage of labour, which will last from only a few minutes to an hour or more.

Suddenly there is action around you. The obstetrician has returned and is dressed in gown, gloves and mask. You are being urged to push, and even though it hurts, it doesn't seem to matter any more, and you labour with all your might to force the head of the baby out of your body. The contractions are much more intense than before, but you should push only at the time of a contraction, as pushing at other times is wasted effort.

Another push, and another, and another, and then a sudden sweeping, elating relief, followed by a healthy cry from your new baby.

Immediately after the delivery, you are given an injection to help contract the uterus. A minute or so after the baby is born, the umbilical cord which has been the lifeline between you and the baby for the last nine months is clamped and cut. A small sample of cord blood is often taken from the cord to check for any problems in the baby.

About five minutes after the baby is born, the doctor will urge you to push again and help to expel the placenta (afterbirth). This is the third stage of labour.

If you have had an episiotomy (cut) to help open your passage for the baby's head, or if there has been a tear, the doctor will now repair this with a few sutures.

You should be allowed to nurse the baby for a while (on the breast if you wish) after the birth. Then both you and the baby will be washed and cleaned, and taken back to the ward for a good rest.
See also APGAR SCORE; BABIES; BREECH BIRTH; CAESAREAN SECTION; FACE PRESENTATION; FORCEPS DELIVERY; INDUCTION OF LABOUR; LABOUR PROLONGED; PLACENTA; PLACENTAL RETENTION; PREGNANCY; PREMATURE BABY; PREMATURE LABOUR; PROLAPSED CORD

LABOUR PREMATURE
See PREMATURE LABOUR

LABOUR PROLONGED
Labour of pregnancy may be prolonged for several reasons. The muscles of the uterus may not produce sufficiently strong contractions, or may not contract regularly. Some women have incoordinate contractions, which cause different parts of the uterine muscle to contract at different times. This can result in significant discomfort but minimal progress in labour. Injections may help the contractions, but sometimes a Caesarean section is necessary.

There may also be an obstruction to the passage of the baby through the birth canal. This can be caused by the baby having a large head, having the head twisted in an awkward position, or having an abnormal part of the baby presenting (eg. shoulder or face instead of head); or the mother may have a narrow pelvis that does not allow sufficient room for the baby to pass. Sometimes these situations can be assisted by forceps, but often a Caesarean section is necessary for the well-being of the baby.

In some women, the cervix fails to dilate and remains as a thick fibrous ring that resists any progress of the baby down the birth canal. In an emergency the cervix may be cut, but in most cases doctors would again prefer to perform a Caesarean section.
See also CAESAREAN SECTION; FACE PRESENTATION; FORCEPS DELIVERY; LABOUR; PREGNANCY

LABYRINTHITIS
Labyrinthitis is an inflammation, viral infection, or rarely bacterial infection, of the semicircular canals (labyrinth) in the inner ear that control balance. Sometimes toxins or ear damage may be responsible. Severe dizziness occurs along with abnormal eye movements, and non-existent noises may be heard. Rarely, permanent damage to the balance mechanism may occur. Caloric tests (alternating heat and cold in the outer ear canal) induce worse dizziness and confirm the diagnosis.

Medications can be used to reduce inflammation and dizziness, and antibiotics are sometimes necessary. Most cases settle in a few days but some persist for weeks.
See also BENIGN PAROXYSMAL POSITIONAL VERTIGO; DIZZINESS; EAR; VESTIBULITIS

LACERATION
A laceration is any cut or tear that penetrates through the skin.
See also CUT; SUTURING

LACRIMAL GLAND
See EYE, DRY; TEARS

LACRIMATION
See TEARS; TEARS EXCESS

LACTATION
See BREAST FEEDING

LACTEAL
See LYMPHATIC SYSTEM

LACTIC ACID
See MUSCLE

LACTULOSE
See OTHER

LAËNNEC, RENÉ
René Laënnec (born 1781) was a physician at the Salpétrière Hospital in Paris who in 1816 invented the stethoscope, which initially was a wooden tube with flared ends. This dramatically improved the examination of the heart and lungs, improved diagnoses and therefore treatments.
See also STETHOSCOPE

LAMIVUDINE
See ANTIVIRALS

LAMOTRIGINE
See ANTICONVULSANTS

LANDAU-KLEFFNER SYNDROME
The Landau-Kleffner syndrome is a rare form of epilepsy of no known cause. The patient has muscular seizures, followed by a slow failure of the ability to speak or understand language, and behavioural disorders. The syndrome usually starts between four and nine years of age and is treated with anticonvulsant medications and speech therapy. Fifty percent recover, but the prognosis is poor with early onset
See also CONVULSION; EPILEPSY

LANDRY-GUILLAIN-BARRÉ SYNDROME
See GUILLAIN-BARRÉ SYNDROME

LANGERHANS CELL
See DIABETES MELLITUS TYPE ONE; INSULIN; PANCREAS

LANGERHANS CELL GRANULOMATOSIS
See HISTIOCYTOSIS X

LANGE SYNDROME
See de LANGE SYNDROME

LANGUAGE
See SPEAKING DIFFICULT; STUTTER; SWEARING UNCONTROLLED

LANOXIN
See DIGOXIN

LANSOPRAZOLE
See PROTON PUMP INHIBITORS

LAPAROSCOPY
Laparoscopy is an endoscopic examination of the inside of the abdomen and pelvis, including a woman's internal reproductive organs. It allows a clear view of anything in the belly from the gall bladder to the appendix or the tubes of the womb and the ovaries. This has made it very useful in diagnosing various intestinal and gynaecological diseases, such as appendicitis, pelvic infection and ovarian cysts and tumours. It has also proved to be valuable as a means of checking that some gynaecological complaints, such as endometriosis (tissue resembling the lining of the womb, growing outside the womb) and cancer of the ovaries, are responding to treatment.

As a test for infertility that may be caused by blocked Fallopian tubes, it is possible to send dye into the uterus and see by laparoscopy if it spills out of the Fallopian tube into the abdomen. If it does, it means that the passages that allow the egg and the sperm to meet are open. At the same time, a piece of tissue from the lining of the womb can be removed for examination in the laboratory to see if the woman is ovulating.

An increasing use for laparoscopy is the removal of a woman's eggs by suction for fertilisation in a dish as part of IVF (in vitro fertilisation) procedures. Other uses for laparoscopy include removing an infected appendix, repairing a hernia or removing the gall bladder. Two or three 1cm. incisions are necessary for these procedures, as the doctor looks through a laparoscope in one incision, and operates using other instruments in the other incisions.

A laparoscopy involves a stay in hospital, usually with a general anaesthetic, although sometimes an epidural anaesthetic is performed in which the anaesthetic is injected into the spinal cord and the woman remains conscious. Under some circumstances only a local anaesthetic is required.

A small incision is made in the abdomen just below the navel so the scar is barely visible afterwards. A needle is inserted into the abdomen, and carbon dioxide gas is pumped into the abdominal cavity to inflate it so that the area can be seen more easily. The needle is withdrawn and the laparoscope inserted. The doctor (usually a specialist surgeon or gynaecologist) will then be able to see any abnormalities, and if necessary will take a small sample of tissue for further analysis through a second incision. Operations on some organs (eg. gall bladder removal) require a third incision so two operating instruments can be introduced.

The procedure usually takes about half an hour and will be concluded with one or two stitches in the cut. The patient may be allowed home within a few hours, provided they have someone to assist, or they may stay in hospital overnight. The cut and some remaining gas may produce a degree of discomfort for a day or so.

It is also possible for a tubal ligation (tying of the woman's tubes for the purposes of sterilisation) to be done by laparoscopy. For this operation there may be two or three incisions, the second of which is generally made just inside the line of the pubic hair (its tiny size and the fact that the hair grows back mean that the scar is invisible in even the briefest bikini).
See also ABDOMEN; APPENDECTOMY; ENDOSCOPE; INFERTILITY; TUBAL LIGATION

LARGACTIL
See ANTIPSYCHOTICS

LARGE BOWEL CANCER
See COLORECTAL CANCER

LARGE CELL CARCINOMA OF THE LUNG
See LUNG CANCER

LARGE HEAD
See ACROMEGALY; HEAD LARGE; HYDROCEPHALUS

LARGE INTESTINE
The large intestine consists of a large loop of bowel that circuits the belly. It is about 65 mm. in diameter and about 1.8 metres in length, compared with the seven to ten metres of the small intestine. Dividing the small intestine from the large intestine is a muscular valve that opens to let food into the large intestine but otherwise remains closed to prevent the food passing back into the small intestine.

The large intestine begins in the lower part of the abdomen on the right side. The first part, consisting of a small pouch into which the small intestine opens, is the caecum. The

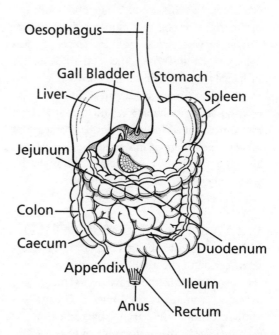

LARGE INTESTINE

second part is the colon, and the third part is the rectum, which passes straight down through the back part of the pelvis and opens to the exterior through the anus.
See also CAECUM; COLON; RECTUM.

LARVA MIGRANS
See CUTANEOUS LARVA MIGRANS; VISCERAL LARVA MIGRANS

LARYNGITIS
Laryngitis is an infection of the larynx (voice box or Adam's apple) at the front of the throat, which contains the vocal cords that are responsible for speech. Hoarseness or total loss of voice may occur, with associated pain, difficulty in swallowing, a dry cough and a fever. Almost invariably it is a viral infection and cannot be cured by antibiotics. Time, voice rest, aspirin and other anti-inflammatory medications are used to reduce inflammation and swelling of the vocal cords, and to ease the fever.

Recurrent attacks may cause small nodules to form on the vocal cords, and huskiness in later life.

Complete recovery after five to ten days is usual, but recovery will be delayed in smokers and those who persist in using their voice excessively.
See also HOARSE VOICE; LARYNX; PHARYNGITIS

LARYNGOMALACIA

Laryngomalacia is a rare congenital condition of the throat in children in which the cartilage of the larynx (voice box) is softened and collapses easily. When the patient breathes in heavily with exercise, a croupy cough and shortness of breath occur. It is diagnosed by laryngoscopy (looking down the throat with an instrument) and treated by surgical bracing of the larynx. There is no cure, but treatment allows a relatively normal life, although the voice may be permanently distorted.
See also HOARSE VOICE; LARYNX

LARYNGOTRACHEOBRONCHITIS

Laryngotracheobronchitis is a viral or bacterial infection of the airways from the voice box (larynx) through the trachea to the larger airways (bronchi) of the lungs. It is usually a viral infection, but various bacteria may be responsible. In the first couple of years of life, the infection is relatively common, and is better known as croup.

Patients experience hoarseness or total loss of voice, neck and chest pain, difficulty in swallowing, pain with breathing, shortness of breath, a productive cough and a fever.

Sputum may be cultured to identify the responsible organism and correct antibiotic to treat it, but if the infection is viral, time, rest, cough mixtures, aspirin and other anti-inflammatory medications are used to reduce inflammation and ease the fever. Bacterial infections settle rapidly with antibiotics, but untreated bacterial infections may progress to pneumonia. Viral infections recover after five to ten days, but recovery is delayed in smokers.
See also BRONCHITIS, ACUTE; CROUP; HOARSE VOICE; LARYNGITIS; PHARYNGITIS; TRACHEITIS

LARYNX

The larynx is the voice box where sound is produced by the vocal cords. It is also part of the mechanism used during a cough to remove excess mucus or foreign matter from the lungs. It lies below the pharynx and leads into the trachea and thence to the lungs. The pharynx transmits both food and air. The epiglottis at the top of the larynx separates food from air into its correct channels so that, when we breathe, air enters the lungs through the larynx and not the stomach and, when we swallow, food goes into the stomach and not the lungs.

The framework of the larynx protrudes slightly at the front to form the so-called Adam's apple. A man's Adam's apple is usually more obvious than a woman's because the male hormones act to enlarge the larynx

LARYNX

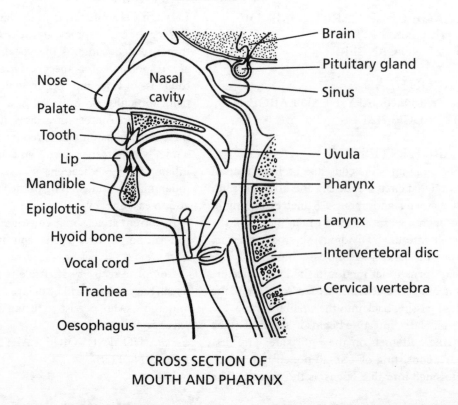

CROSS SECTION OF
MOUTH AND PHARYNX

and give the man a deeper voice.

The vocal cords are two folds of tissue protruding from the sides of the larynx so that the passage of air is narrowed into a small space called the glottis (situated beneath the epiglottis). As air is passed over the vocal cords, they vibrate to produce sound. By means of muscular control, this sound can be varied both in tone and pitch. The chambers of the throat and mouth then amplify the sound.

The type of sound depends on a number of extraordinarily complex factors, but generally speaking a large larynx with long vocal cords produces low notes. Hence men usually have deeper voices than women and, because the larynx of a child is smaller than that of an adult, children have shriller voices than adults. The breaking of the voice in boys in puberty is due to the rapid development of the larynx at this time, together with a degree of uncertain muscular control.

Voice is also affected by sex hormones and singers often notice a slight decrease in the quality of the higher notes during menstruation and in pregnancy. Similarly the voice may change at menopause and as old age advances.
See also EPIGLOTTIS; LUNG; PHARYNX; TRACHEA

LASER IN-SITU KERATOMILEUSIS
See REFRACTIVE SURGERY

LASER KERATECTOMY
See REFRACTIVE SURGERY

LASIK
See REFRACTIVE SURGERY

LASIX
See DIURETICS

LASSA FEVER
Lassa fever is an extremely contagious form of viral haemorrhagic fever (viral infection of the blood) that occurs in central and west Africa. The virus is spread by rats and from person to person in conditions of poor hygiene. Outbreaks have occurred in Sierra Leone, Nigeria and the Congo, and are more common in women.

Symptoms include muscle pains, headache, sore throat, joint pains, diarrhoea, vomiting, red eyes and abnormal bleeding, and blood tests show significant abnormalities.

There is no cure or preventive vaccine, but a number of drugs are being used experimentally to modify the disease. Patients must be nursed in strict isolation. Internal bleeding causes death in about 90% of patients.
See also EBOLA VIRUS; MARBURG VIRUS

LATENT HEPATIC PORPHYRIA
See PORPHYRIA CUTANEA TARDA

LATERAL
The term lateral refers to the side of the body, further away from the centre, or the outer side of an organ or structure. Something may be referred to as left or right lateral to indicate the relevant side.
See also DORSAL; MEDIAL; VENTRAL

LATERAL EPICONDYLITIS
See TENNIS ELBOW

LATERAL POSITION
See UNCONSCIOUS

LATEX ALLERGY
Latex is used to make nearly all rubber products (from gloves to condoms and tyres), and is also found in toys, adhesives and many medical devices. Allergies occur more in those who are constantly exposed to latex such as rubber workers, health care workers (who wear latex gloves) and patients who use latex products (eg. catheters), and it sometimes occurs after using latex products without problems for many years. There are unusual cross sensitivities with avocados, tomatoes, peaches and bananas.

Patients develop an itchy, red, raised rash on the skin that has been in contact with latex. The rash may start within minutes, or its onset may be delayed for a couple of days, and may persist for days or weeks. Some patients may develop severe asthma on exposure to latex. Skin and blood tests can be performed to confirm the diagnosis.

Treatment involves antihistamine tablets or injections, steroid creams and sometimes steroid tablets or injections. Rarely, the allergy may be so severe it requires an injection of adrenaline. Unfortunately, desensitisation is not normally possible, and the problem usually persists long term.
See also ALLERGY; HIVES

LAUGHING GAS

The common name for the general anaesthetic nitrous oxide is laughing gas. It is often used in maternity wards to ease pain during delivery, and less commonly as a general anaesthetic for other surgical procedures.

See also ANAESTHETICS

LAURENCE-MOON-BIEDL SYNDROME

The Laurence-Moon-Biedl syndrome is an inherited condition of the eye, brain and genitals that causes night blindness due to excessive amounts of pigment in the retina at the back of the eye, obesity, mental retardation, extra fingers and toes and underdeveloped genitals. Examination of the back of the eye through an ophthalmoscope (magnifying light) will show the excess pigment. There is no treatment available and no cure.

See also EYE

LAXATIVES

When you've just got to go, but you can't go, a laxative may be the answer to a large bowel's prayer. Constipation is a relative matter, as some people consider it normal to pass faeces three times a day, while others consider once a week to be normal. If retained faeces and the attempts to pass them cause pain or discomfort, then constipation needs treatment. Laxatives should be the last resort in the treatment of constipation, after increased fluid intake and alterations to increase the bulk residue of the food in your diet have been tried.

Laxatives vary from simple lubricants, such as paraffin, to bulking agents that contain senna and other fibres, different sugars that draw fluid into the gut (eg. lactulose, galactose), and gut stimulants (eg. bisacodyl) that actually increase the contractions of the gut. They are available as tablets, mixtures, granules, suppositories and enemas (the last two for anal use). All are available without prescription.

The main complication with laxatives is their overuse. Patients may use laxatives to pass faeces excessively, and become dependent upon them for the natural functioning of the bowel. Patients trying to lose weight by increasing the rate of faeces output may create this type of dependence, and it is a practice to be deplored. Laxatives should never be used if there is any suspicion of more sinister disease in the gut. Many patients have treated a pain in the abdomen with laxatives, only to find that they have worsened a case of appendicitis. Laxatives should be used with great caution in children and during pregnancy. Many other substances, foods and fibres are used as laxatives.

Side effects are usually minimal, but may include belly colic, diarrhoea and wind. Use lactulose with care in diabetes, elderly and pregnancy.

See also CONSTIPATION

LEAD POISONING

Lead (Pb) has been widely used in industry including batteries, paints (particularly dangerous in flaking old paint), crystal glass, ceramics, old plumbing fixtures, leaded petrol and some old-fashioned medications. Swallowing or inhaling lead compounds may lead to lead poisoning (plumbism) which causes belly pains, irritability, tiredness, loss of appetite, anaemia, poor coordination, slurred speech, convulsions, coma and death. Permanent damage to nerves (neuropathy) and kidneys is possible in survivors.

Lead can be detected in the body by specific blood tests.

If lead has been recently swallowed, induce vomiting and give activated charcoal. In chronic cases, medications can slowly remove the lead from the body. The prognosis depends on age, health and weight of the patient, and the dose of lead.

See also PEWTER

LEATHER-BOTTLE STOMACH

A leather-bottle stomach (linitis plastica) is a stomach that is firm and rigid (like a leather bottle) with a thickened wall, rather than being soft and flexible. The usual cause is a form of cancer of the stomach (10% of all stomach cancers) that spreads through one particular layer of the stomach, but uncommonly it may be due to persistent inflammation of the stomach.

Patients have nausea with eating, difficulty in swallowing, discomfort after eating, constant feeling of stomach fullness and weight loss. This form of cancer often spreads early to surrounding lymph nodes, liver, spleen and other organs. It is diagnosed by a gastroscopy, barium meal x-ray or CT scan of the stomach, although biopsies of the stomach wall are often normal.

Often no treatment is available, although

complete surgical removal of the stomach is sometimes performed.
See also STOMACH CANCER

LEDDERHOSE DISEASE
A fibrous sheet (the plantar fascia) stretches under the skin of the sole to give it a smooth appearance, strength and firmness, and to protect and control the movement of the muscle tendons that cross under it to the toes. If damaged, the plantar fascia may become scarred, contract and thicken into hard lumps that can be felt under the skin (Ledderhose disease). As the damage progresses, the contraction of the fibrous sheet pulls on the tendons that run underneath it to prevent their free movement. Men are affected more than women. It is a similar condition to Dupuytren's contracture of the hand.

The cause is unknown, but may be due to a poor blood supply to the foot (eg. diabetes), and injury to the foot from repeated blows (eg. running).

Patients develop one or more hard, fixed nodules under the skin of the sole that gradually extend lengthwise along the sole to cause discomfort, pain with walking and loss of toe mobility. Eventually the toes cannot fully extend, and contract into a claw-like appearance. The middle toes are usually more severely affected than the others.

Treatments include soft shoe insoles, injection of steroids around the nodule, and in severe cases only the nodule may be surgically excised, but recurrence after surgery is common.
See also DUPUYTREN CONTRACTURE OF HAND; FOOT

LEG
See FEMUR; FIBULA; FOOT; HAMSTRING MUSCLES; HIP; KNEE; LEG PAIN; LEG SWOLLEN; PATELLA; QUADRICEPS MUSCLES; TIBIA

LEG CRAMP
Nocturnal (night time) leg cramps are a very common, painful leg condition caused by a combination of minor muscle injury due to vigorous or unusual exercise, a buildup of waste products in the muscle and dehydration. They worsen with age and pregnancy.

Sudden, painful spasms occur in the muscles in the calf, or elsewhere in the body, usually following exercise. Minor muscle tears and persisting muscle aches may occur.

Stretching the affected muscles by standing on the balls of the feet can ease the spasm. Prevention is better than cure, and taking adequate amounts of fluid during and after exercise prevents dehydration. If this is insufficient, prescription medications (eg. quinine) can be taken after sport to prevent the cramps. Tonic water or bitter lemon drunk after exercise may also help as these drinks contain quinine. The cramps usually settle quickly, but recurrences are common.
See also MUSCLE CRAMP

LEGIONNAIRE'S DISEASE
Legionnaire's disease is a serious form of bacterial pneumonia caused by the bacterium *Legionella pneumophila*. It is usually spread by contamination of air-conditioning systems in large buildings with water cooling towers, and is named because of an epidemic that occurred at a Legionnaire's (ex-serviceman's) convention in the USA. Once an epidemic occurs, it is essential for the responsible building and air-conditioning system to be identified so that it can be thoroughly cleaned and disinfected. Victims inhale the Legionella bacteria into their lungs in microscopic droplets of water.

The symptoms are variable but may include a fever, productive cough and chest pains. Some patients may develop only a mild infection and recover without treatment, but others (particularly smokers) will rapidly deteriorate. Permanent lung damage such as chronic bronchitis and emphysema may also occur.

It is diagnosed by listening to the chest with a stethoscope, chest x-rays and tests on the sputum, to differentiate legionnaire's disease from other types of pneumonia. The antibiotic erythromycin will slowly cure most cases, but ancillary treatment, such as physiotherapy and expectorant medications, are also necessary.

Even with good hospital care up to 15% of patients will die, particularly if they are elderly, smokers or have other lung disease.
See also BRONCHITIS, CHRONIC; COUGH; EMPHYSEMA; PNEUMONIA

LEG PAIN
Pain may occur in part of or all of a leg, or in both legs. The location of the pain, its nature, what makes it better and worse, and any ten-

derness at the site of pain will help a doctor to diagnose the cause. X-rays show bones, but not any soft tissue, so many forms of leg pain cannot be diagnosed this way. Sometimes CT scans (computerised cross sectional x-rays that do show some soft tissue), doppler studies (measuring sound waves to determine the flow of blood in arteries and veins) and electromyography (EMG – measurement of electrical activity in muscles) may be useful. In most cases it is the clinical acumen of the examining doctor, who will check the movement of the leg and its joints, check pulses and reflexes, determine the position of tenderness, and check for swelling, redness and heat in tissue, that will determine the diagnosis.

Any injury to the leg that results in any degree of damage to a bone (fracture), ligament (sprain), muscle (bruise, tear), tendon (tendinitis, rupture), cartilage (tear), fat (bruise) or skin (cut, graze) will cause pain.

Muscle cramps often occur in the calf at night after exercise. They are caused by waste products building up in the muscle from the use of sugars, fats and proteins during the muscle activity. Sudden severe pain occurs, and may persist for some minutes.

Arthritis of any type may cause pain in the main joints of the leg – the hip, knee and ankle. Osteoarthritis is the most common form of arthritis in these joints.

The sciatic nerve is the main nerve running from the lower back, across the buttocks, and down the back of the thigh to the outside of the lower leg and foot. If this nerve is pinched or damaged at any point along its long course, abnormal sensations will be felt beyond that point, varying from a pins and needles sensation to numbness and quite severe pain. The most common point for pinching to occur is in the lower back, where arthritis, a slipped disc or other injury may be responsible. The resultant pain is known as sciatica.

Claudication is the term used to describe the pain experienced when the blood supply to tissue is reduced below its requirements. If the arteries to one or both legs are narrowed by cholesterol deposits (atherosclerosis) adequate amounts of blood may not get to the leg muscles. Any activity (eg. walking) will require extra supplies of oxygen and nutrition, which the narrowed arteries cannot supply, and a deep ache will occur.

Other common causes of leg pain include shin splints (tibia of very active young people becomes very tender and sore), fibromyositis (occurs in large muscles that have been overused and damaged repeatedly by heavy work or exercise), varicose veins, a blood clot (thrombophlebitis) in one of the deep veins in the calf or thigh, growing pains (limb pain syndrome), anterior compartment syndrome (lower leg pain in athletes) and the restless legs syndrome (constant desire to move the legs while trying to rest).

Uncommon causes of leg pain include osteoporosis, tumours or cancers in bone or the bone marrow, Paget's disease (thickening but weakening of bones), Buerger's disease (damage to the small arteries in the feet and hands caused by smoking), osteomyelitis (infection of bone), bursitis (inflammation or infection of the sacs around joints that produce synovial fluid), fasciitis (inflammation of the membrane surrounding a muscle), the patello-femoral pain syndrome (pain in, around and behind the knee cap) and polyneuritis (inflammation of nerves).

There are many rarer causes of leg pain, which include osteomalacia and rickets (due to a lack of vitamin D), scurvy (lack of vitamin C), beriberi (lack of vitamin B), Perthe's disease (damage to the artery supplying blood to the head of the femur in the hip joint), Leriche syndrome (large blood clot in the arteries of the pelvis) and impingement syndromes can occur around the ankle when the bones at the front or back of the joint become enlarged due to stress or injury, and pinch tendons, muscles, nerves and press on adjacent bones in the ankle.

See also ARTHRITIS; FOOT PAIN; KNEE PAIN; LEG SWOLLEN; MUSCLE CRAMP and separate entries for most diseases mentioned above.

LEG SWOLLEN

Swelling in the legs may be due to a simple problem such as prolonged standing (eg. shop assistant, hairdresser), sitting for a long period of time in one place (eg. on a long air flight), tight clothing (eg. garter at top of socks), or bandages around the leg. On the other hand, quite significant diseases may also be responsible for the problem.

Swelling of the ankles and feet of both legs can be an indication of serious heart problems, as the failing heart is unable to adequately pump blood through the legs. The swelling usually settles overnight when the legs are elevated, but recurs gradually through the next day.

The veins in the legs contain one-way valves that allow blood to only travel up towards the heart when they are squeezed by muscle action. If these valves are damaged by increased pressure (eg. during pregnancy, prolonged standing), obesity or direct injury, the blood is unable to move out of the leg as quickly, and the veins dilate with blood to form varicose veins. These may ache and cause the leg to swell, as well as being unsightly.

A blood clot (thrombophlebitis) in one of the deep veins in the calf or thigh will cause a deep ache and tenderness at that point, and sometimes swelling of the leg below the blockage.

Other causes include a blockage of the lymphatic drainage by infection or surgery (lymphoedema), malnutrition (a severely protein depleted diet may allow fluid to leak out of the tissue to cause swelling of the lower legs) and kidney failure.
See also KNEE SWOLLEN; LEG PAIN and separate entries for diseases mentioned above.

LEISCHMANIASIS
See CUTANEOUS LEISCHMANIASIS; KALA AZAR

LENNOX-GESTAUT SYNDROME
The Lennox-Gestaut syndrome is a very severe form of epilepsy of no known cause in which patients have multiple variable types of seizures, mental retardation, sudden drop attacks, and intractable epilepsy. Self-injury or death from persistent fitting is possible. An abnormal EEG (electroencephalogram – measures electrical activity in brain) confirms the diagnosis.

Combinations of potent anti-epilepsy drugs are used in treatment, but brain surgery may be required in resistant cases. There is no cure, and control of seizures is usually very difficult.
See also CONVULSION; EPILEPSY

LENTIGO
Lentigo is a skin pigmentation condition that starts in childhood and affects mainly Caucasians. There is an inherited tendency that is aggravated by sun exposure.

Small, permanent, pigmented spots appear on the skin. Plastic surgery can be performed to remove disfiguring spots.

See also HUTCHISON MELANOTIC FRECKLE; SKIN PIGMENTATION EXCESS

LENTIGO MALIGNA
See HUTCHISON MELANOTIC FRECKLE

LEPROSY
Leprosy (Hansen's disease) is a very slowly progressive infection caused by the bacterium Mycobacterium leprae that damages the skin and nerves (neuropathy). It is spread from one person to another by prolonged close contact, most commonly in childhood.

Pale, thick patches of skin on the hands and feet are the first sign, followed by slowly enlarging nodules, then nerves supplying the affected areas of skin become involved and sensation is lost. The cooler parts of the body, furthest from the heart, are affected first. As the disease progresses, pins and needles may be felt, ulcers form, and bones in the fingers and toes begin to disintegrate. There is rarely any pain. Damage and deformity is due to unintentional burns and injuries to totally numb tissue. In severe cases, fingers and toes do fall off, but this is very rare. The diagnosis can be confirmed by microscopic examination of a skin biopsy.

A number of antileprotic drugs are available that will slowly cure leprosy over several years. Any existing deformities must be treated with plastic surgery. With good management, cure is possible and patients can live normally in the community. Untreated, the disease progresses to death over ten to twenty years.
See also SKIN DRY AND SCALY; SKIN THICK; SWEATING LACK

LEPTOSPIROSIS
Leptospirosis is a bacterial infection of the liver and other organs caught from infected cattle and pigs by abattoir workers, veterinarians and farmers. In third-world countries, dogs and rats may also be carriers. The bacteria enter through minor abrasions or by being swallowed. The incubation period varies from three days to three weeks.

Patients develop a sudden high fever, headache, stomach pain, muscle aches and inflamed eyes. After a couple of days, these symptoms disappear, and the second stage of the infection commences which lasts for one to four weeks, and the patient complains of swollen lymph nodes, a generalised rash, eye pain, and in severe cases yellowing of the skin (jaundice). The second stage may cause permanent liver damage and Weil Syndrome. The diagnosis is confirmed by a specific blood test.

Antibiotics such as penicillin are prescribed as treatment, but sometimes they have remarkably little effect. Careful nursing is important. The disease can usually be prevented by taking an antibiotic tablet, doxycycline, once a week.

It is usually cured by correct treatment, but if jaundice develops, the death rate may be as high as 10%.
See also JAUNDICE; WEIL SYNDROME

LERICHE SYNDROME
Patients with high cholesterol levels may develop arteriosclerosis (hardening of the arteries) at the point where the aorta (main artery down back of body) divides at the back of the belly to supply the blood to each leg. This causes narrowing of the aorta and leg arteries, and symptoms due to an inadequate blood supply to the legs beyond this point (Leriche syndrome).

Symptoms include pain in the legs when walking, impotence and cold feet. Sometimes fragments of hard plaque can break off from the artery wall and travel down to small arteries in the feet, blocking them to cause gangrene of the toes.

A characteristic noise can be heard through a stethoscope as blood gurgles through the narrowed section of the aorta, while the diagnosis can be confirmed by doppler flow studies (a type of ultrasound) or x-rays of the aorta.

Treatment involves surgically cleaning out the artery (thromboendarterectomy), or bypassing the blockage with a synthetic graft (flexible plastic tube). The post-operative outcome is usually very good.
See also ARTERIOSCLEROSIS; CHOLESTEROL

LESBIAN
See HOMOSEXUALITY

LESCH-NYHAN SYNDROME
The Lesch-Nyhan syndrome is a rare X-linked inherited genetic error of metabolism involving uric acid, which is produced by the breakdown of protein in the diet. It passes through the female line but only affects males.

Symptoms include mental deficiency, severe gout, self-mutilation, and abnormal uncontrolled writhing movements of arms and legs. Severe arthritis may be a complication.

Blood and urine tests show very high levels of uric acid, and medications to remove uric acid are prescribed. There is no cure and control is often poor.
See also GOUT; URIC ACID; X-LINKED CONDITION

LET DOWN REFLEX
See BREAST FEEDING

LETHARGY
See FATIGUE

LETTERER-SIWE DISEASE
Letterer-Siwe disease is one of a number of rare diseases grouped together as histiocytosis X, which are lung diseases in which normal tissue is replaced by abnormal fibrous tissue. The cause is unknown, but it occurs in infants under two years of age who develop a fever, muscle wasting, a raised itchy rash, enlarged lymph nodes in the neck, armpit and groin, and enlargement of the liver and spleen. There are three stages of the disease, depending on its severity. The outcome is very good in stage one of the disease, but worsens in the other two stages, with a 70% mortality rate in stage three when it may spread to bone.

It is diagnosed by x-rays, CT scans and blood tests, and treatment involves potent chemotherapy drugs and radiotherapy.
See also HAND-SCHUELLER-CHRISTIAN DISEASE; HISTIOCYTOSIS X

LEUCO-
'Leuco-' is a prefix derived from the Greek word 'leukos' which means 'white', and used in medicine for reference to any cell, tissue or discharge etc. that is white in colour (eg. a leucocyte is a white blood cell).

LEUCOCYTES
See WHITE BLOOD CELLS

LEUCOCYTOSIS
Leucocytosis is a medical term indicating a high level of white blood cells (leucocytes). This may indicate a bacterial infection, pregnancy, leukaemia or liver damage. Children also have higher levels than adults.

See also FULL BLOOD COUNT; WHITE BLOOD CELLS

LEUCOPENIA
Leucopenia is a medical term indicating a low level of white blood cells (leucocytes). This may indicate a viral infection or leukaemia. In an adult the normal range is between 4000 and 10 000 leucocytes per cubic millimetre. The elderly have lower levels than younger adults.
See also AGRANULOCYTOSIS; FULL BLOOD COUNT; WHITE BLOOD CELLS

LEUCOPLAKIA
See MOUTH WHITE PATCHES

LEUCORRHOEA
See VAGINAL DISCHARGE

LEUKAEMIA
Leukaemia is cancer of the white blood cells. Primitive white blood cells are formed in the bone marrow then gradually change into many specialised different types of cell, and so there are many types of leukaemia. At the simplest level, white blood cells are divided into two groups called lymphocytes and myelocytes. Cancer in these can cause lymphocytic (or lymphatic) leukaemia and myeloid leukaemia. There are two other large divisions in leukaemia – the rapidly developing forms (acute leukaemias), and the slowly developing forms (chronic leukaemias). Combining these there are four possible combinations – acute lymphocytic, acute myeloid, chronic lymphocytic and chronic myeloid leukaemia. There are many rarer types of leukaemia known (eg. hairy cell leukaemia, T cell leukaemia).
See also BONE MARROW BIOPSY; LEUKAEMIA, ACUTE LYMPHOCYTIC; LEUKAEMIA, ACUTE MYELOID; LEUKAEMIA, CHRONIC LYMPHOCYTIC; LEUKAEMIA, CHRONIC MYELOID; LEUKAEMIA, HAIRY CELL; WHITE BLOOD CELLS

LEUKAEMIA, ACUTE LYMPHOCYTIC
Acute lymphocytic (lymphatic) leukaemia is the most common form of leukaemia (cancer of one type of white blood cell) in childhood and usually starts between three and seven years of age, but only thirty-three in every one million children will develop any form of leukaemia. 20% of this type occurs in adults.

Tiredness, recurrent infections, bruising, nose bleeds and bleeding from the gums are the main symptoms. Children develop progressively more severe infections, including skin infections, abscesses and pneumonia. Bleeding into joints may cause arthritic pains, and the liver, spleen and lymph nodes in the neck, armpit and groin may be enlarged. The child may become very ill with multiple serious infections.

The diagnosis is confirmed by blood tests and taking a biopsy of bone marrow.

Treatment will continue intermittently or continuously for some years, and a wide range of drugs are used, including cytotoxics and immunosupressants, all of which have significant side effects. Constant monitoring and testing of the patient is required. Other treatments include blood transfusions, radiotherapy, spinal injections and bone marrow transplants.

Acute lymphocytic leukaemia can be cured in 60% of children, and 95% achieve some remission. Adults have slightly poorer results.
See also LEUKAEMIA

LEUKAEMIA, ACUTE MYELOID
Acute myeloid leukaemia is cancer of one type of white blood cell, and is normally a disease of the elderly but may also occur in children and young adults. The symptoms include tiredness, recurrent infections, bruising, nose bleeds, bleeding from the gums and joints, and enlargement of the liver, spleen and lymph nodes. Serious bleeding into organs and rapidly progressive infection may occur.

The various types of leukaemia are differentiated by blood tests and a bone marrow biopsy. The marrow biopsy is usually taken from the breastbone or the pelvic bone under local anaesthetic.

Cytotoxic and immunosupressant drugs are used initially in treatment but later, blood transfusions and intensive radiotherapy are commonly required. Bone marrow transplants are possible in younger patients.

70% of adults can be given remission but fewer than 30% can be cured. If bone marrow transplantation is possible in younger patients, the cure rate rises to 50%.
See also LEUKAEMIA; SWEET SYNDROME

LEUKAEMIA, CHRONIC LYMPHOCYTIC

Chronic lymphocytic (lymphatic) leukaemia is a very slowly progressive form of white blood cell cancer found almost exclusively in the elderly. Most patients have only vague symptoms of tiredness or enlarged lymph nodes. The liver and spleen may enlarge, and in severe cases bleeding from nose and gums and into the skin may occur. The diagnosis is frequently made after a routine blood test for another reason.

Because of its slow progress many patients are given no treatment, but if it becomes more active, steroid and cytotoxic drugs are given. Severe anaemia or excessive bleeding may require an operation to remove the spleen. The disease is slowly but relentlessly progressive, with an average survival time of eight years, but because the patients are elderly, they frequently succumb to other diseases before the leukaemia.
See also LEUKAEMIA

LEUKAEMIA, CHRONIC MYELOID

Chronic myeloid leukaemia is a slowly progressive form of white blood cell cancer that occurs in middle-aged to elderly people. Patients complain of an intermittent fever, tiredness, excessive sweating and fullness in the abdomen. The spleen may also be enlarged. It is often discovered incidentally on a routine blood test, then the diagnosis is confirmed by further blood tests and a bone marrow biopsy.

There is no great urgency in treatment until blood test results reach certain levels, then cytotoxic or immunosuppressive drugs are given. Medication does not cure the disease, but slows its progress and makes the patient feel better. Another form of treatment is bone marrow transplantation but finding a compatible donor is difficult.

Once blood tests deteriorate to the point where treatment is necessary, on drug therapy alone the average survival time is four years. If a donor can be found and marrow can be transplanted, 60% of patients can be cured.
See also LEUKAEMIA

LEUKAEMIA, HAIRY CELL

Hairy cell leukaemia is a rare progressive chronic leukaemia that usually occurs in males over forty years of age. Tiredness, enlarged lymph nodes and spleen, and bleeding into the skin are the main symptoms, but serious infections due to destruction of white blood cells may also occur. It is diagnosed by blood tests and bone marrow biopsy.

The drug cladribine has been remarkably successful in inducing remissions, but splenectomy is the main form of treatment. 60% of patients survive for four years, but a permanent cure is uncommon.
See also LEUKAEMIA

LEVATOR LABII SUPERIORUS ALEQUAE NASI

The tiny muscle, levator labii superiorus alequae nasi, has the longest name of any human muscle, but is merely used to flare the nostrils and raise the lip in a sneer.
See also MUSCLE

LEVONORGESTREL

See CONTRACEPTIVE PILL

LFT

See LIVER FUNCTION TESTS

LIBIDO

Libido is the emotional desire for sexual intercourse and the natural instinct for sexual satisfaction.
See also LIBIDO LACKING; LOVE; SEXUAL INTERCOURSE

LIBIDO LACKING

Libido is controlled by the brain and not the testes or ovaries, although diseases of these glands can certainly have an adverse effect on libido as they do not respond to stimuli from the brain.

To enjoy, and be successful in achieving, sexual intercourse, both partners must be relaxed, secure and comfortable. Psychological stress of any sort will reduce sexual desire. Examples can be as wide ranging as worries about job, money, pregnancy, discovery (will the children come in?), the relationship itself or disease.

Many psychiatric conditions, but particularly depression, will remove any desire for sex. Difficulty in sleeping, loss of interest in other activities and poor self esteem are other signs of depression.

Failure of any major organ of the body

(eg. heart, liver, kidney) or any other serious disease will affect the normal hormonal and chemical balances, as well as causing stress and anxiety, and sex becomes something to be remembered rather than sought.

Disease, infection, tumour (eg. Fröhlich syndrome), injury or cancer of the pituitary gland under the centre of the brain will affect libido. This tiny gland is the conductor of the gland orchestra in the body, and is itself directly controlled by the brain. If for one of these reasons it does not produce the necessary hormones to stimulate the testes or ovaries, they will not release the appropriate sex hormones (testosterone and oestrogen) to allow appropriate sexual responses. Rarely the pituitary gland may become over active, and over stimulate the sex glands to drain them of their hormones.

The part of the brain controlling the pituitary gland can itself be affected by a stroke, bleeding, injury, tumour, cancer or abscess. Parkinson's disease and other degenerative conditions of the brain will both reduce desire and ability.

In men, any disease that reduces the production of testosterone (male hormone) in the testes will reduce libido. Examples include infections (orchitis), tumours (eg. cancer), cysts and torsion (twisting to cut off the blood supply). Other causes of low libido in men include enlargement of the prostate gland and poorly controlled diabetes mellitus.

Women find that their libido varies during the month, usually being highest at the time of ovulation (when they are most likely to get pregnant, half way between the start of one period and the next), and lowest during a menstrual period. Pregnancy also lowers libido for its duration, and breast feeding has a similar effect on the hormones. Other causes of low libido in women include tumours or cysts of the ovary, and during the menopause, when there is a lack of oestrogen, sex may be uncomfortable as well as undesirable.

Numerous drugs, legal, illegal and prescribed, can reduce libido. Examples include alcohol, heroin, marijuana, steroids, antihistamines (eg. cold preparations), benzodiazepines (eg. diazepam, oxazepam), fluid pills and some of those used to treat depression (tricyclics) and decrease high blood pressure (beta blockers).
See also FRIGIDITY; IMPOTENCE;

SEXUAL INTERCOURSE and separate entries for diseases mentioned above.

LICE
See also ANTIPARASITICS; CRABS; HEAD LICE

LICHEN PLANUS
Lichen planus is an uncommon skin condition which normally affects people in their twenties or thirties. It may start where the skin has been injured, may be a chronic viral infection of the skin, or may be triggered by drugs, but the actual cause is unknown.

Small, shiny, flat topped, itchy skin growths develop and may enlarge and join together to form a plaque. They are more common in skin creases such as the inside of the wrists and elbows, but can occur anywhere on the body, including the insides of the mouth, nose, ears, vagina and anus. It is diagnosed by a skin biopsy.

Mild cases are often not treated, but more serious cases are treated with steroid creams and occlusive plastic dressings. Further treatments include steroid tablets or injections under a plaque, ultraviolet light, and potent medications such as retinoic acid and dapsone.

The long term course is very variable. Some patients recover in a few months, while others may suffer for years, but eventually complete recovery does occur. Some pigmentation of the skin may remain after the rash has cleared.
See also LICHEN SCLEROSIS; LICHEN SIMPLEX; SKIN ITCH; SKIN LUMPS; SKIN RED

LICHEN SCLEROSIS
Lichen sclerosis et atrophicus (to give its full name) causes scarring of the tissue on the genitals and affects women more than men. The cause is unknown, but infection or injury to the genitals may be a factor.

In men a thickened area of skin develops on one side of the penis which causes a sideways curve to the penis that may be painful during an erection, and sexual intercourse may be difficult. In women, a shiny white itchy area with a red margin appears on the vulva. It may also occur in skin on other parts of the body. Biopsy of affected skin is sometimes necessary to make a diagnosis.

Minor surgery can be performed to stretch the scarred penis tissue, and steroid creams are prescribed for the itch.
See also LICHEN PLANUS; LICHEN SIMPLEX; SKIN THICK

LICHEN SIMPLEX
Lichen simplex chronicus (circumscribed dermatitis) is a type of persistent dermatitis that is thought to be a form of nerve rash, and patients who are anxious, tense, nervous or aggressive are more likely to develop it. In some cases, mild stimulants such as tea or coffee may aggravate the condition.

Intensely itchy, dry, scaling, thick plaques develop on the skin. They may appear anywhere, but usually occur in areas that are easy to scratch, such as the wrist, neck, thigh and groin. Permanent skin scarring may occur from scratching. A skin biopsy may help with the diagnosis.

Stopping tea and coffee may dramatically improve the itch, and it is important for patients to avoid any further damage to the skin from scratching, by using protective bandages or applying a plaster. Steroid creams and injections into the affected areas of skin may be beneficial. Avoiding stressful situations is helpful, but often not practical.

If the patient can stop scratching the skin, the disease will cure itself.
See also ECZEMA; LICHEN PLANUS; LICHEN SCLEROSIS; SKIN ITCH

LIGAMENT
The point where two bones meet is a joint. Joints enable the body to move. Consequently, bones meeting at a joint need to be held together firmly while still being sufficiently flexible to allow movement. The tough fibrous tissues that carry out this task are ligaments.

Ligaments are flexible and allow the joint to move while maintaining strength in the joint. Some ligaments are like a cord; others form flat bands. A major joint, such as the elbow, has several overlapping ligaments to support the three bones that meet there. Joints such as the knees and elbows, which need strength, are bound together by ligaments that prevent excessive movement.

Despite their flexibility, ligaments are not elastic, and if too much stress is placed on a ligament it will stretch or even tear, causing a sprain. Torn ligaments can be as serious as

a broken bone and need proper rest and care until completely healed.
See also JOINT; LIGAMENT OR TENDON RUPTURE; SPRAIN; TENDON

LIGAMENT OR TENDON RUPTURE
A ligament joins one bone to another, while a tendon joins a muscle to a bone. Complete or partial rupture of a ligament (eg. at sides of ankle) or tendon (eg. Achilles tendon at back of ankle) may occur due to excessive force being applied to the tendon or ligament. Severe pain and loss of function of the joint or muscle occurs, followed by swelling and bruising. X-rays may be taken to exclude fracture, while an ultrasound scan can show a rupture.

The treatment depends on the site and severity. A joint may be immobilised in a cast for weeks or months, or the rupture may be surgically repaired. A ligament may be slack after healing, allowing excessive movement in the joint, increased risk of further damage and premature arthritis, but usually there are very good results from treatment.
See also LIGAMENT; SPRAIN; TENDON

LIGHT ALLERGY
See ERYTHROPOIETIC PROTOPORPHYRIA; LIGHT SENSITIVE SKIN

LIGHTHEADED
The vague feeling of lightheadedness is commonly associated with an excessive intake of alcohol, illegal drugs (eg. marijuana, heroin) or adverse effects of some medications (eg. tranquillisers, narcotics, sedatives, antihistamines). Overdoses of other medications, particularly those that affect heart function and lower blood pressure, may also be responsible. Dizziness and disorientation after a rapid ride on a side show amusement, rough boat trip (sea sickness) or other causes of motion sickness, persistent stress and anxiety, and a prolonged lack of sleep are other causes.

Numerous medical conditions may also be responsible for this unpleasant sensation.

Any severe infection by a bacteria or virus, and its associated fever, may result in both lightheadedness and dizziness.

Poor circulation of blood to the brain due

to hardening of the arteries with cholesterol deposits (atherosclerosis) will make it difficult for the brain to receive an adequate blood supply, particularly when the patient changes from lying to sitting, or sitting to standing. Gravity drains blood from the head above to the feet below (postural hypotension). Elderly people are usually affected, and must ensure they move gradually from one position to another.

Other causes of lightheadedness include migraines (often associated with visual symptoms and headache), a lack of food and poor nutrition, disorientation and confusion (due to dementia, deafness or poor vision), hyperventilation (very rapid shallow breathing), transient ischaemic attacks (temporary blockage of a small artery in the brain), psychiatric conditions (particularly those that cause excitement or over activity), arthritis or spondylosis of the neck and disturbances of the balance mechanism in the inner ear (eg. infection, glue ear, Ménière's disease, tumour).
See also DIZZINESS; FAINT and separate entries for diseases mentioned above.

LIGHT SENSITIVE EYES
See PHOTOPHOBIA

LIGHT SENSITIVE SKIN
People with a pale complexion are obviously more sensitive to sunlight (photosensitive) than those with naturally darker skin tones, but there are a number of medical conditions which increase the sensitivity of any colour skin to sunlight.

Photodermatitis is a congenital (present since birth) allergy type reaction to sunlight that results in a red, raised itchy rash on sunlight exposed skin.

Systemic lupus erythematosus is an autoimmune disease (inappropriate rejection of the body's own tissue) that can affect tissues throughout the body causing arthritis, mouth ulcers and discolouration, abnormal muscle movements, high blood pressure and a characteristic red rash across the sun exposed areas of the cheeks and bridge of the nose in a butterfly pattern.

Other causes of photosensitivity include photosensitive eczema, porphyria, pellagra (lack of vitamin B3), phenylketonuria (inability of the body to process proteins containing phenylalanine), erythropoietic protoporphyria, Bloom syndrome and Hartnup disease.

A wide range of medications may cause the skin to become more sensitive to the sun. Examples include tetracyclines (antibiotic often used for acne), phenothiazines (used in psychiatry), sulphonamides (broad spectrum antibiotic), thiazide and frusemide diuretics (fluid removers), malaria medications (eg. quinine), griseofulvin (for fungal infections) and nalidixic acid (for urine infections).
See also ALBINISM; SKIN DEPIGMENTED and separate entries for diseases mentioned above.

LIGNOCAINE
See ANAESTHETICS

L'ILLUSION DE SOSIES
See CAPGRAS SYNDROME

LIMB-GIRDLE DYSTROPHY
See ERB MUSCULAR DYSTROPHY

LIMB-PAIN SYNDROME
See GROWING PAINS

LINEAR RASH
See LINES IN SKIN; STRETCH MARKS

LINES IN SKIN
A rash that develops in lines is called linear. The lines of the rash normally follow the 'fingerprint' pattern of the skin, but some conditions such as scabies can cause lines that run in any direction.

Scabies is an infestation (not an infection) that occurs when a tiny insect called *Sarcoptes scabiei* burrows under the skin to create tracks that can be one centimetre or more in length. These burrows and the tissue around them become red, itchy and inflamed. It is caught by close contact with someone who already has the disease.

Stretch marks (striae) are the curse of pregnant women, when they develop on their belly and breasts, and overweight people may develop stretch marks which persist after they have lost weight.

Lichen planus is an uncommon skin condition which causes small, shiny, flat topped growths that may grow and join together to form a linear plaque. It can occur anywhere on the body surface, including the insides of the mouth, nose, ears, vagina and anus.

The Koebner phenomenon is the tendency of some skin diseases such as psoriasis, flat warts (caused by a very slowly developing virus in the skin), and pigmented skin moles (naevi) to follow skin creases and form a line, particularly on the chest, back and abdomen.

Contact dermatitis from the application of perfumes or other substances will cause a rash that is the same shape as the area where the substance was applied.

Dermographia occurs in some people who have particularly sensitive skin. When a blunt object (eg. finger nail) is moved firmly over the skin, a raised red line will appear in the skin a few seconds after the pressure is removed. This effect is more common on the back, and lines or letters can be drawn on the patient's skin that will remain visible for some minutes or hours.

Jellyfish tentacles, stinging and irritating plants will cause a red, raised, itchy and/or painful linear rash where they have touched the skin.
See also STRETCH MARKS and separate entries for diseases mentioned above.

LINIMENT
Liniments or rubefacients, are creams or lotions that are rubbed into the skin to create local warmth and skin redness. There are scores of liniments available from chemists to treat bruises, sprains, fibrositis and arthritic conditions (eg. camphor, menthol, alcohol, salicylates). They should not be used on the face, near body openings (eg. anus, vagina), or on grazes or cuts. Many nonsteroidal anti-inflammatory drugs are also available as creams and gels. The more potent liniments include benzydamine (Difflam), butoxy ethyl nicotinate, nonivamide, capsaicin, heparinoid and salicylic acid.
See also NONSTEROIDAL ANTI-INFLAMMATORY DRUGS

LINITIS PLASTICA
See LEATHER-BOTTLE STOMACH

LIP CANCER
See MOUTH CANCER; SQUAMOUS CELL CARCINOMA OF THE SKIN

LIPIDS
If excess levels of the fats cholesterol and triglyceride (known collectively as lipids) are present in the blood, fatty plaques may develop in arteries restricting the blood supply to organs such as the heart and brain. The relevant blood test must be performed after a twelve hour overnight fast to ensure that base levels are obtained. Alcohol should be avoided for three days before a triglyceride test. A level below 5.5 mmol/L for cholesterol, and 2.5 mmol/L for triglyceride is normally considered satisfactory, but there are several different types of cholesterol (high density, low density and very low density), and the ratios between these types, as well as the patient's individual medical and family history, are also very important in determining the appropriate levels for both lipids.
See also BLOOD TESTS; CHOLESTEROL; FAT; TRIGLYCERIDE

LIPOMA
A lipoma (fat cyst) is a discrete collection of fat under the skin. It often appears for no apparent reason, but may be due to injury to the area months before the lump is noticed. It is felt as a soft, movable lump under the skin, and may be very small or several centimetres in diameter. Surgical excision can be performed if it is cosmetically unacceptable or worrying. Pressure on overlying skin rarely causes irritation and an ulcer.
See also FAT; SKIN LUMPS

LIP-PIT SYNDROME
The lip-pit syndrome is an inherited facial deformity that has dominant inheritance with 50% of siblings and offspring affected. Small pits develop on both sides of lower lip, sometimes with associated cleft palate and/or cleft lip. Plastic surgical correction of the deformity gives good results.
See also CLEFT LIP AND PALATE

LISINOPRIL
See ACE INHIBITORS

LISTERIOSIS
Listeriosis is a rare form of meningitis (infection of the membranes surrounding the brain) in newborn babies caused by the bacteria *Listeria monocytogenes* which can be caught from contaminated food, particularly soft cheeses (eg. brie) and salads.

In adults and children, the bacteria usually causes no symptoms and is harmless, but if a pregnant woman is infected, the bacteria may spread through her bloodstream to the placenta and foetus, where it may cause widespread infection, miscarriage, or death of the foetus and a stillbirth.

Antibiotics can be used in newborn infants, but they are often not successful. Treatment is more successful if started during pregnancy, but the infection is rarely detected before the infant is born. Infants that survive birth suffer from a form of septicaemia (blood infection) that soon progresses to meningitis, which is frequently fatal.
See also MENINGITIS; SEPTICAEMIA

LITHIUM
See ANTIPSYCHOTICS

LITHOTRIPSY
Stones are not normally part of the human anatomy, but those that form in the kidney, gall bladder and salivary glands may be just as solid and hard as those found in the average quarry. Stones are formed by a compound being present in an excessively high concentration in a bodily fluid, such as urine, bile or saliva. The substance then comes out of solution as a crystal, or precipitates out of suspension and starts to grow with the deposition of successive layers of the substance around the original seed. Stones in the kidney and salivary glands tend to be angular in shape and crystalline, while those in the gall bladder are smooth and rounded.

Until the 1980s, the only way to remove a stone was by an operation, but there is now a quick alternative for urinary stones and some gallstones – lithotripsy – which works by focusing high-intensity sound waves (shock waves) at the stone, and shattering it. Unfortunately this form of treatment cannot be used for salivary stones.

During lithotripsy, the patient is lightly sedated to make it easier to remain perfectly still, the smooth cone of the machine is then placed against the skin, and with the aid of ultrasound or x-rays, is accurately focused on the stone. Some older machines require the patient to be partly immersed in a bath of warm water. Care is taken in the positioning of the machine so that no bones or other vital structures are in the path of the shock wave.

Once positioned, very powerful but very brief shock waves are passed through the body and stone. During this time the patient is awake and feels minimal discomfort. Every fifteen to thirty minutes, further x-rays or ultrasound examinations will be performed to see if the stone has disintegrated.

The whole procedure takes anything from fifteen minutes to two hours, depending on the size and hardness of the stone. Once the stone has been shattered, the remnants, which are the size of sand particles, can be passed normally through the urine or bile. The patient can go home the same day, return to work the next day, and should have no further problems with the stone.
See also KIDNEY STONE

LIVER
The liver is the largest gland and internal organ in the body. Wedge-shaped, smooth and rubbery, it lies behind the lower few ribs on the right side, weighs about 1.5kg and has the same reddish brown colour as the animal livers we are familiar with in the butcher shop. The liver plays an integral part in the processing of food (metabolism).

The liver is the body's chemical processing plant. It regulates the amount of blood sugar, assists in producing the blood clotting mechanisms, helps to nourish new blood cells, destroys old blood cells, breaks down excess acids to be eliminated as urine, stores and modifies fats so they can be more efficiently utilised by cells all over the body, stores certain vitamins and minerals, and removes poisons from harmful substances such as alcohol and drugs. The liver is also an important source of heat, which is essential to maintain the body's temperature.

The liver aids the digestive process by manufacturing bile, which mixes with the digestive juices in the duodenum. Bile is a thick yellow-green liquid and contains salts that break down fat into small droplets so it can more easily be digested. Bile is manufactured constantly, but because it may be required only a few times a day, it is carried from the liver through ducts to the gall bladder, a small pear-shaped bag lying just under the liver, where it is stored until it is needed.

Once bile salts are manufactured, the body makes the most of them. Having fulfilled their digestive purpose in the small intestine, they are not simply discarded but are recycled through the blood and back to the liver to be used again. It is estimated that this recycling process takes place about eighteen times with only about 5% of salts being eliminated in the faeces each time.

One of the functions of the liver is to remove from the blood a yellow pigment called bilirubin, produced by the destruction of old red blood cells. If the liver becomes diseased and cannot function properly, this yellow pigment stays in the bloodstream and gives a yellowish tinge to the skin and whites of the eyes – the jaundice that is a striking symptom of liver diseases such as hepatitis.

THE LIVER AND GALL BLADDER

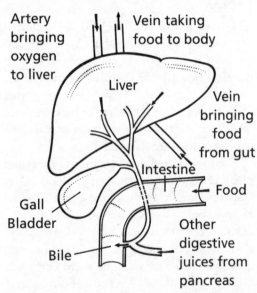

Artery bringing oxygen to liver

Vein taking food to body

Liver

Vein bringing food from gut

Intestine

Food

Gall Bladder

Bile

Other digestive juices from pancreas

The chemical processing capability of the liver is amazingly complex and wide-ranging. Substances which enter as one thing frequently leave as something else, depending on the body's needs. For example, most amino acids are converted into proteins, but if the body is short of glucose, the liver will combine some of the amino acids with fat to make extra sugar. Similarly if the level of blood sugar is too high, glucose is converted into a substance that can be stored.

The liver's storage capacity is equally attuned to the body's specific needs at any given time. If more vitamins are consumed than the body immediately needs, certain of them will be stored to be released if the supply falls off. A person could survive as long as twelve months without taking in any vitamin A, and for up to four months

without new supplies of vitamins B12 and D. *See also* ACUTE HEPATIC PORPHYRIA; BILE; BUDD-CHIARI SYNDROME; CIRRHOSIS; CRIGLER-NAJJAR SYNDROME; GALL BLADDER; GALLSTONES; GLYCOGEN STORAGE DISEASES; HEPATITIS A; HEPATITIS B; HEPATITIS C; LIVER ABSCESS; LIVER CANCER; LIVER ENLARGED; LIVER FUNCTION TESTS; WILSON DISEASE; YELLOW FEVER.

LIVER ABSCESS

A liver (hepatic) abscess is a collection of pus within the liver caused by a bacterial or rarely a fungal infection. It may be due to the spread of bacteria from other organs to the liver through the bloodstream or may spread through the abdomen to the liver from other infections within the belly such as appendicitis, salpingitis (infected Fallopian tubes) or cholecystitis (an infected gall bladder).

The symptoms may include a fever, pain and tenderness in the upper abdomen, loss of appetite, nausea, vomiting and weight loss. Multiple abscesses may develop, or abscesses may burst into the abdominal cavity to cause peritonitis. The abscess may be diagnosed by an ultrasound or CT scan.

Surgical drainage of the abscess is necessary and appropriate antibiotics are prescribed.

This is a serious condition, with up to 15% mortality, and those who survive may have long term problems with liver function. *See also* ABSCESS; APPENDICITIS; CHOLECYSTITIS; LIVER; PERITONITIS; SALPINGITIS

LIVER CANCER

Liver cancer (hepatic carcinoma or a hepatoma) is a form of cancer that starts in the liver itself, not having spread to the liver from some other organ. It occurs most commonly in patients who have long-standing alcoholic cirrhosis, hepatitis B or C, liver parasites and malnutrition, and is far more common in developing countries.

Often there are no symptoms until the cancer is well advanced, at which point the liver begins to fail and the patient becomes jaundiced (yellow), nauseated, very weak, loses weight and is unable to eat. At a late stage of the disease the abdomen may become swollen with fluid. The diagnosis is confirmed by blood tests, liver biopsy, ultrasound and CT scans.

No surgical or medical treatment available in most cases, as almost invariably the cancer has spread too far by the time it is diagnosed, and unfortunately death within a short time of diagnosis is the usual result.
See also CIRRHOSIS; HEPATITIS B; HEPATITIS C; JAUNDICE; LIVER

LIVER ENLARGED

The liver lies in the upper part of the belly on the right side, and is normally completely behind, and protected by, the lower ribs on that side. If the edge of the liver can be felt below the ribs, it is enlarged. This finding is usually made by a doctor examining a patient, but sometimes a thin individual will notice the firm smooth mass under the skin, or the edge of an enlarged liver.

An enormous range of medical conditions can cause an enlarged liver (hepatomegaly), which by itself merely indicates that there is a problem somewhere in the body, and not necessarily in the liver.

Hepatitis is a viral infection of the liver that may cause jaundice (yellow skin), fever, general tiredness and hepatomegaly. The type of hepatitis (A to E) will determine the exact symptoms, their duration and seriousness.

Many other infections may also cause liver enlargement. Glandular fever (infectious mononucleosis) is a common example, but others include AIDS, syphilis and even severe influenza.

Heart failure after a heart attack or other injury may result in back-pressure in the veins, causing swelling of the feet, congestion of the lungs (with a moist cough) and swelling of the liver. Inflammation or infection of the sac in which the heart lies (pericarditis) is an uncommon cause of heart failure as it may prevent the heart from contracting and functioning properly.

Blockages of the bile drainage ducts in or outside the liver (eg. by gallstones) will prevent bile from leaving the organ, and it will swell. Jaundice (yellow skin) is also usually present.

The liver tissue may be replaced by fibrous scar tissue due to repeated infection, or damage from poisons, toxins or alcohol. This is known as cirrhosis. A hard, large liver due to blockage of bile ducts will result in some cases, while in others it may still be hard, but will shrink as normal liver tissue is lost.

Tumours or cancers in the liver may arise in the liver tissue itself (hepatoma, lymphoma) or more commonly settle in the liver as secondary deposits from a cancer almost anywhere else in the body (eg. bowel, breast, lung). The liver tends to have hard lumps spread through it rather than be smoothly enlarged. Leukaemia is a cancer of the white blood cells that is almost invariably accompanied by liver enlargement.

Other causes of hepatomegaly include some types of anaemia (eg. haemolytic, sickle cell, aplastic), parasitic diseases (eg. malaria, hydatid cysts, amoebiasis), bacterial infections of the liver, poorly controlled diabetes, polyarteritis nodosa (inflammation of arteries) and liver cysts.

Rarer causes include Budd-Chiari syndrome (vein draining blood from the liver becomes blocked by a clot), tuberculosis, starvation (kwashiorkor), haemosiderosis (excess of iron in the body), thalassaemia major, Felty syndrome (complication of rheumatoid arthritis), amyloidosis, sarcoidosis, and glycogen storage diseases. Some children have genetic conditions that cause liver enlargement from birth, or shortly afterwards (eg. Gaucher disease, Letterer-Siwe syndrome, Pompe syndrome, Schiei syndrome, Sly syndrome and von Gierke syndrome).

Sometimes the liver may appear enlarged when it is not, because it has been pushed down into the belly by an enlarged right lung (eg. asthma, emphysema), paralysed right diaphragm (the muscle sheet between the chest and belly) or an abscess between the liver and diaphragm. The liver may sometimes be formed with an abnormal shape that makes it appear to be abnormally large.

Some medications may have hepatomegaly as an uncommon side effect.
See also JAUNDICE; LIVER and separate entries for diseases mentioned above.

LIVER FAILURE
See CIRRHOSIS; JAUNDICE

LIVER FUNCTION TESTS
Liver function tests measure the presence of certain enzymes in the blood that are produced by the liver. If the liver is under stress

or is damaged, some of these enzymes will be present in excessive quantities. Conditions such as hepatitis, liver abscess, gall bladder disease, cancer, drug reactions (eg. to epilepsy medications) and alcoholism may cause abnormal liver enzyme levels. One particular enzyme, gamma glutamyl transferase (GGT), is usually raised in association with alcohol abuse. Bilirubin is also measured to assess liver and blood health.

See also BILIRUBIN; BLOOD TESTS; GAMMA-GLUTAMYL TRANSFERASE; LIVER

LOCAL ANAESTHETIC

Local anaesthetics are used in three ways: –
• A local area may be injected with anaesthetic solution to numb that area, eg. while a mole is being cut out or a cut sutured. This method is commonly used by general practitioners, plastic surgeons, skin specialists and others, for small procedures. The injection stings for a few seconds, but this sensation subsides rapidly as the anaesthetic takes effect.
• A local anaesthetic can be injected around a nerve to stop that nerve from receiving pain impulses from beyond the point of injection. These nerve blocks are commonly used in fingers and toes and in dental procedures, but almost any nerve in the body may be injected.
• A tourniquet can be placed around the thigh or upper arm and a large amount of anaesthetic injected into the dilated veins below the tourniquet to give a regional block. This effectively numbs the entire area below the tourniquet, and this type of anaesthesia is commonly used to set minor fractures.

The most commonly used local anaesthetic is lignocaine (Xylocaine). This has an effect that lasts for one to two hours, depending upon the site of injection, the amount injected, and the concentration of anaesthetic used. Adrenaline may be added to the anaesthetic to reduce bleeding and prolong its effectiveness, but this cannot be used in toes, fingers, the penis and some other areas.

See also ANAESTHETICS; EPIDURAL ANAESTHETIC; EXCISION; GENERAL ANAESTHETIC; SPINAL ANAESTHETIC

LOCKED KNEE
See KNEE LOCKED

LOCKED-IN SYNDROME

The locked-in syndrome is a horrendous complication of certain types of brain damage caused by a stroke, tumour or injury to particular parts of the brain, or late stage multiple sclerosis. The patient has total paralysis of limbs and facial nerves, but normal consciousness, and is able to communicate only by eye movements. No treatment is available, and death from pneumonia due to lack of movement and poor function of muscles of breathing is usually a blessed release.

See also MULTIPLE SCLEROSIS; STROKE

LOCKJAW
See TETANUS

LOEFFLER SYNDROME

Loeffler syndrome (PIE syndrome) is a form of allergy reaction affecting the lungs. The underlying cause may be a reaction to drugs, an allergy reaction to a huge variety of substances, visceral larva migrans and other worm infestations. Asthmatics are more prone to this syndrome.

The main characteristic is technically called pulmonary infiltrates with eosinophilia, which gives the syndrome its alternative acronym name of PIE syndrome. In plain English this means that the lungs have too many allergy response cells, which results in a wheeze, cough and fever. Allergy reactions may also occur in other organs and areas of the body.

A lung biopsy is abnormal, and blood tests show very high levels of eosinophils (allergy response cells). Doctors treat the underlying cause if possible, but otherwise treatment is the same as asthma. The prognosis depends on the cause, but is usually good.

See also ASTHMA; ERYTHEMA NODOSUM; VISCERAL LARVA MIGRANS

LÖFGREN SYNDROME

Löfgren syndrome is a complication of sarcoidosis in its acute stage, which tends to occur in women of Scandinavian or Irish heritage. Erythema nodosum (a skin condition) occurs, and enlarged lymph nodes are seen on a chest x-ray. Anti-inflammatory medications control leg and skin symptoms, while the sarcoidosis is also treated. There is an 80% chance of spontaneous recovery

See also ERYTHEMA NODOSUM;
HEERFORDT SYNDROME;
SARCOIDOSIS

LOIN PAIN

The loin is that area at each side of the belly between the top of the pelvic bone and the bottom rib. The kidneys lie in the back of this area on each side, the liver and gall bladder on the top right, and the spleen on the top left. The pancreas intrudes slightly onto the right side, and the colon (part of the large intestine) runs up the right side and down the left. Any of these organs can cause pain in this region.

An infection of the kidney (pyelonephritis) will cause a constant dull ache in the affected side and loin, associated with frequent passing of urine and sometimes discomfort in the lower belly.

A stone in the kidney will cause a constant dull ache, but also an excruciatingly severe pain that runs down into the groin and testes every time the stone moves along with the pressure of urine behind it. Blood is usually present in the urine, but sometimes can only be detected by a specific test.

Inflammation or infection of the gall bladder (cholecystitis) and gallstones (cholelithiasis) will cause an intermittent pain that is made worse by eating, particularly fatty foods. Gall stones moving down the duct from the liver or gall bladder to the intestine will cause severe pain whenever they are pushed along by the pressure of bile behind them.

Other causes include diverticulitis (inflammation of outpocketings on the large intestine), ulcerative colitis (inflammation and ulceration of the large bowel), spleen enlargement or inflammation (eg. glandular fever, septicaemia, tuberculosis, malaria, leukaemia and severe anaemias), cancer in the spleen, pinched nerves between vertebrae in the back (pain felt along the course of the nerve as it runs around the body), shingles (infection of a spinal nerve caused by the chickenpox virus), and rarely a weakness in the muscle wall in the loin, which may allow a loop of gut to push out through a weak area to form a lump under the skin at the back of the loin (a lumbar hernia).

See also ABDOMINAL PAIN; COLON;
GROIN PAIN; KIDNEY; SPLEEN and
separate entries for diseases mentioned above.

LOMOTIL
See ANTIDIARRHOEALS

LONG QT SYNDROME

The long QT syndrome is an uncommon heart condition that may occur for no known reason, or may be due to body chemistry abnormalities, follow a heart attack or angina, or may be a side effect of some heart and psychiatric medications. The patient notices that one or more heart beats are missed, and it is diagnosed by an electrocardiogram (ECG). Each point on the graph produced by an ECG is labelled with a letter. In this condition there is a long gap between the Q and T points on the graph.

The treatment and prognosis depends on the cause. Treatments include adding or removing medications, or implanting an artificial pacemaker. Very rarely, sudden death may occur.

See also ARRHYTHMIA;
ELECTROCARDIOGRAM

NORMAL ECG TRACING

LONG SIGHTED

Long sightedness (hyperopia) is a defect in visual acuity that is usually present from birth. The eyeball is too short, and close objects cannot be focused precisely on the retina (light sensitive cells) at the back of the eye. Distant objects can be seen clearly, while close objects are blurred.

HYPEROPIA

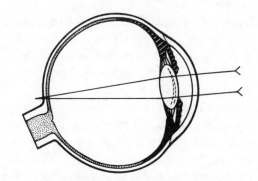

Light focuses beyond retina

It is diagnosed by refractive tests using a number of different lenses until near objects can be seen as clearly as possible. Appropriate spectacles are then prescribed, and must be worn when reading or looking at close objects. Children may grow out of the problem at puberty; otherwise it is a lifelong problem.
See also ASTIGMATISM; PRESBYOPIA; REFRACTIVE SURGERY; SHORT SIGHTED; VISION

LOOP DIURETICS
See DIURETICS

LOPERAMIDE
See ANTIDIARRHOEALS

LORATADINE
See ANTIHISTAMINES

LORDOSIS
Lordosis is an abnormally large inward curvature of the lumbar vertebrae in the small of the back. When looked at from the side, a normal back curves in at the neck, out over the back of the chest, in at the small of the back, and out again between the buttocks. Lordosis is often associated with poor posture, slack muscles and obesity, but it may be present to compensate for kyphosis (outward curvature) of the vertebrae at the back of the chest, or an abnormal hip. X-rays of the spine can demonstrate the abnormality more clearly. No treatment is required unless pain and discomfort are present, in which case weight loss, exercise and physiotherapy are appropriate.
See also KYPHOSIS; SCOLIOSIS; SPINE

LOU GEHRIG DISEASE
See AMYOTROPHIC LATERAL SCLEROSIS

LOVE
Look in the index of any anthology of poetry or dictionary of quotations, and there are more entries under love than any other. Men and women have tried to define love for millennia, mainly without success.

Medically, love is an emotion emanating from the frontal lobes of the brain that increases the desire of one person for another, and is associated with caring, pleasure, attachment and a feeling of well-being in the presence of the other person.

It is natural for one party to be emotionally upset if the other party does not return the love. In a medical sense, the stress associated with the break up of a relationship can be eased by counselling, and occasionally medications.
See also de CLERAMBAULT SYNDROME; LIBIDO

LOW BLOOD PRESSURE
See HYPOTENSION; POSTURAL HYPOTENSION

LOWE SYNDROME
The Lowe syndrome is a rare, inherited, body chemistry disorder passed to males only through the female side of the family. These boys have mental retardation, eye cataracts, clouding of the cornea (outer surface of eye), abnormal skin folds beside the eyes, and abnormal eye socket shape. Some patients have rickets and Fanconi syndrome. Abnormal levels of amino acids (protein breakdown products) are found in the urine. There is no cure, but they have a reasonable life span.
See also FANCONI SYNDROME; RICKETS

LOWN-GANONG-LEVINE SYNDROME
In Lown-Ganong-Levine syndrome, the ventricles (main chambers of heart) contract too early in a cycle of heart contraction because of an abnormal nerve pathway from the heart pacemaker to the ventricles. This results in an irregular heart rate and palpitations. An ECG (electrocardiogram) is diagnostically abnormal.

Attacks can be stopped by stimulation of nerves supplying the heart (vagus nerve) by swallowing, holding the breath or other manoeuvres. Numerous medications (eg. procainamide, quinidine, verapamil, beta-blockers) may be taken regularly to prevent attacks. In persistent cases, DC cardioversion (electric shock to the heart) can be given. The syndrome can usually be controlled, but recurs if treatment is ceased.
See also ARRHYTHMIA; ELECTROCARDIOGRAM; PAROXYSMAL ATRIAL TACHYCARDIA

LSD
LSD (lysergic acid diethylamide) is a synthetic

psychedelic drug first developed in 1947. Its use peaked in the late 1960s, and it is no longer in favour amongst the underground cult of drug abusers.

LSD is taken by mouth in pill form. It causes a rapid heart rate, high blood pressure, dilation of pupils, tremor, terror, panic and high fever within a few minutes of being swallowed. Addicts seek the hallucinations, illusions and happy mood that also occur. The actions last for twelve to eighteen hours after swallowing the tablet. Long-term effects include psychoses, personality changes, schizophrenia, deterioration in intelligence, poor memory and inability to think in abstract terms. Tolerance to LSD develops rapidly, and higher and higher doses must be taken to obtain the same effect. Death as a direct effect of LSD is rare, and there are no significant effects after withdrawal of the drug.
See also COCAINE; ECSTASY; GAMMA-HYDROXYBUTYRATE; KETAMINE; HEROIN; MARIJUANA; MESCALINE; STIMULANTS

LUMBAGO
Lumbago is an old-fashioned term that describes a collection of back and leg symptoms rather than a specific disease. Patients have sudden, severe pain in the lower back that spreads to the buttocks, leg or groin and is triggered by any movement in the back. It is caused by the pinching of a nerve as it leaves the spinal cord in the lower back due to a ligamentous strain, disc injury, arthritis or a misplaced vertebra. Lifting, coughing or straining often triggers attacks. Bed rest, a corset, physiotherapy, painkillers and nonsteroidal anti-inflammatory drugs are used in treatment.
See also NONSTEROIDAL ANTI-INFLAMMATORY DRUGS; SCIATICA

LUMBAR PUNCTURE
Cerebrospinal fluid (CSF) is the clear, watery fluid that surrounds the brain and spinal cord. The chemical composition of CSF changes in the presence of certain diseases of the nervous system, and in cases of suspected multiple sclerosis, stroke, poliomyelitis, meningitis, tumour and similar disorders, a sample of the spinal fluid may be analysed to help diagnose the disease.

The extraction of CSF is commonly called a spinal tap or lumbar puncture. The procedure is carried out in a hospital or clinic. The patient lies on the side, legs drawn up to the abdomen and chin bent down to the chest so that the spine is stretched and the spaces between the vertebrae are opened up. Local anaesthetic is injected just under the skin to numb the area. A hollow needle is then passed between the vertebrae in the lower part of the spine. A probe from the centre of the needle is removed and fluid flows up the hollow channel. A pressure-measuring manometer is connected so that the spinal fluid pressure can be measured and then, using a three-way tap, a sample of fluid is run off into a bottle. The procedure takes about fifteen minutes and some people find it uncomfortable, although not usually painful. The patient will normally be required to remain lying down for several hours to reduce the likelihood of headache, although they may still have a moderate to severe headache for up to twenty-four hours afterwards.
See also CEREBROSPINAL FLUID

LUMP
See ABDOMINAL LUMP; BONE LUMP; BREAST LUMP; GOITRE; LYMPH NODES ENLARGED AND/OR PAINFUL; MOUTH LUMP; NECK LUMP; SKIN NODULES; TESTICLE AND SCROTUM LUMP; THROAT LUMP

LUNATE BONE
See WRIST

LUNG
The lungs lie in the chest on either side of the heart. Each lung is shaped something like a pyramid, with the apex at the top extending into the neck and the broad base resting on the diaphragm – the dome-shaped wall of muscle dividing the chest from the abdomen. When breathing in, muscles cause the diaphragm and chest area to increase in volume so that the lungs can expand and suck in air. When breathing out, the lungs contract and force the air out. Breathing in involves muscular effort, but under normal circumstances breathing out does not – the muscles simply relax which allows the lungs to return to their normal size.

Each lung has an airtight cavity around it, lined with a double membrane called the pleura. The outer pleura is attached to the rib cage. Between the membranes is a lubricating fluid so that they can glide smoothly over one another as the lung expands and contracts with breathing. If this area becomes inflamed – called pleurisy – breathing becomes painful.

In the lungs, blood absorbs oxygen from air breathed in, and breathing out eliminates the waste product carbon dioxide. Air is brought into the body through the nose or mouth, and travels through the pharynx, larynx and trachea to the right and left bronchi, which lead to the lungs. Each main bronchus divides further after it has entered the lung into many small branches which then subdivide again and again into smaller branches in the bronchial tree. The smallest of the divisions are called the bronchioles – of which each person has about a million. At the end of the bronchial tree are clusters of air sacs, called alveoli, which look like minuscule bunches of grapes. It is in these tiny sacs that the new air and the old air are exchanged. There are about 300 million alveoli providing a surface area equivalent to that of a tennis court.

The structure of the lungs means that they are like a sponge; light, fluffy and full of air. If a lung becomes infected, the affected part becomes filled with pus so that air is excluded and pneumonia results.

The lungs are connected to the heart via the pulmonary artery and the pulmonary vein. Used blood, low in oxygen, is pumped through the right side of the heart, via the pulmonary artery, into the lungs to be re-oxygenated. Oxygen-enriched blood is then returned to the left side of the heart through the pulmonary vein to be pumped throughout the body.

The brain and nervous system constantly check the levels of both oxygen and carbon dioxide in the blood. If the carbon dioxide level becomes too high, or the oxygen level too low, our breathing process is speeded up. Yawning is not primarily due to boredom but is simply the body's way of getting more oxygen into the lungs. The faster breathing rate during exercise is also the means by which the body copes with the increased demand for oxygen by the muscles. If the demand is so high that the lungs cannot keep up with it, the person becomes 'out of breath' – gasping and panting for more air until the supply of oxygen catches up.

If breathing stops for longer than three or four minutes, cells will start to die, beginning with the brain cells. Breathing is normally involuntary. It continues while we are asleep or even if completely unconscious. However, up to a point, it can be switched to voluntarily control if the need arises, eg. taking a deep breath before diving under water. On the other hand, it is not possible to commit suicide by deliberately holding one's breath.

Before birth the lungs are yellowish brown and solid. When a baby takes its first breath after birth, the lungs expand like a rapidly opening flower and the colour changes to a pinkish red. The tissue of the lungs becomes spongy and would float in water, whereas prior

RESPIRATORY SYSTEM

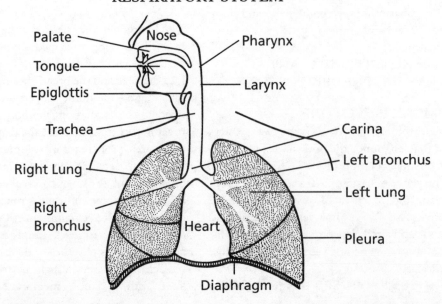

Palate, Nose, Pharynx, Tongue, Epiglottis, Larynx, Trachea, Carina, Right Lung, Left Bronchus, Right Bronchus, Left Lung, Heart, Pleura, Diaphragm

to birth it would sink. These changes will be evident even if the baby dies after only a few breaths. This can sometimes have medico-legal significance as it establishes whether the child was born alive or not.

See also ASBESTOSIS; ASTHMA; BREATHING DIFFICULT; BREATHING RAPID; BREATH, SHORT OF; BRONCHIOLITIS; BRONCHITIS, ACUTE; BRONCHITIS, CHRONIC; BRONCHOSCOPY; CHEST PAIN; COUGH; EMPHYSEMA; LUNG ABSCESS; LUNG CANCER; MELIOIDOSIS; MESOTHELIOMA; PLEURISY; PNEUMONIA; RESPIRATORY FUNCTION TESTS; TRACHEA; TUBERCULOSIS; WHEEZE and other diseases and symptoms associated with the lung.

LUNG ABSCESS

A lung (pulmonary) abscess is a localised collection of pus within the lung that may be a complication of pneumonia or a wound that penetrates into the lung. The symptoms may include chest pain, shortness of breath, fever, a cough and collapse. Permanent scarring of lungs, uncontrolled spread of infection and rarely death may also occur.

A chest x-ray or CT scan shows the presence and location of an abscess, then surgery is performed to drain the abscess and potent antibiotics are prescribed. Recovery is often stormy, but treatment is usually successful.

See also ABSCESS; LUNG; PNEUMONIA

LUNG CANCER

The terms lung cancer, bronchial carcinoma and bronchogenic carcinoma describe any of several different types of cancer affecting lung tissue. The incidence of this type of cancer is steadily increasing, particularly in women, and it is the most common form of internal cancer.

Smoking causes 90% of all lung cancers, but this effect of smoking is usually delayed until the patient is fifty-five or older. Other causes of lung cancer include asbestos dust, irradiation and chrome dust.

There are several different types of lung cancer, depending on the cells within the lung that are affected. The common types are: –
• Squamous cell carcinoma, a relatively common form in which symptoms usually occur early, but the cancer doubles in size every three months on average, and spreads early to lymph nodes.
• Oat cell (small cell) carcinomas, far more serious. They double in size every month on average, spread rapidly to other parts of the body, and are almost impossible to cure.
• Adenocarcinomas and large cell carcinomas, which develop at the edge of the lung, have few symptoms, are not easily detected, double in size every three to six months and spread early to distant parts of the body.
• Secondary cancers, which are the spread of cancer from other parts of the body to the lungs. These are common, but they are not caused by smoking, and their treatment involves the treatment of the original cancer as well as that in the lung.

Many other rarer types of lung cancer are known.

The early warning signs are weight loss, a persistent cough, a change in the normal type of cough, coughing blood and worsening breathlessness. Later symptoms include loss of appetite, chest pain, hoarseness and enlarged tender lymph nodes in the armpit. Spread of the cancer to other organs is the next stage, most commonly to bone and the brain, and the veins draining the head and arms may become blocked (superior vena cava syndrome). One quarter of patients have no symptoms when the diagnosis is made, often by a routine chest x-ray, so smokers should consider having a routine chest x-ray every few years.

The cancer is diagnosed by chest x-rays, CT scans, sputum examination, and a biopsy of the tumour using a bronchoscope if possible.

Prevention is always better than cure, and that means stop smoking. Even in heavy smokers, after five years of non-smoking, the risk of developing lung cancer will reduce to near normal. Treatment involves major surgery, irradiation and potent drugs, depending on the type of cancer present. Radiation may be used to shrink the original tumour, but is primarily used to treat cancers that have spread to other organs.

Fewer than 20% of all patients with lung cancer survive more than five years from diagnosis. Those with small cell (oat cell) carcinoma usually die within a year, while those with squamous cell carcinoma tend to live longer.

See also ASBESTOSIS;

BRONCHOSCOPY; CANCER; LUNG; MESOTHELIOMA; PANCOAST SYNDROME; PANCOAST TUMOUR; SMOKING

LUNG CLOT
See PULMONARY EMBOLISM

LUNG FUNCTION TESTS
See BLOOD GAS ANALYSIS; PEAK EXPIRATORY FLOW RATE; SLEEP STUDIES; TOTAL LUNG CAPACITY; VITAL CAPACITY

LUPUS
See DISCOID LUPUS ERYTHEMATOSUS; SYSTEMIC LUPUS ERYTHEMATOSUS

LUTEAL CYST
See OVARIAN CYST

LYELL SYNDROME
See SCALDED SKIN SYNDROME

LYME DISEASE
Lyme disease is a relatively common blood infection caused by the bacterium *Borrelia burgdorferi* that occurs in the northeast United States. It is spread by the bite of the tick *Ixodes* from infected mice or deer to humans. The tic may lie dormant for up to a year before passing on the infection with a bite.

The disease has three stages: –
• In stage one the patient has a flat or slightly raised red patchy rash, fever, muscle aches and headache.
• Stage two comes two to four weeks later with a stiff neck, severe headache, meningitis (inflammation of the membrane around the brain) and possibly Bell's palsy.
• In stage three, which may come three to twelve months later, the patient has muscle pains, and most seriously a long lasting severe form of arthritis that may move from joint to joint. Persistent crippling arthritis sometimes occurs.

The diagnosis is confirmed by specific blood tests, then a prolonged course of antibiotics is prescribed.

Long term, one third of patients may suffer from continuing muscle and joint pains, while a smaller percentage have after-effects of the meningitis.

See also BELL'S PALSY; MENINGITIS; TICK

LYMPH
See LYMPHATIC SYSTEM

LYMPHADENITIS
See ADENITIS

LYMPHADENOPATHY
See LYMPH NODES ENLARGED AND/OR PAINFUL

LYMPHANGITIS
Lymphangitis is a bacterial infection or inflammation of the lymph ducts under the skin that drain waste products from tissues back to the heart. It often starts from a skin wound, with *Streptococcus* and *Staphylococcus aureus* being the most common bacteria involved.

The usual symptom is a red, tender streak running under the skin, usually along an arm or leg, narrowing as it approaches the body. Other symptoms may include enlarged and tender lymph nodes and a fever. Ulceration may occur at the site of the skin injury, or over infected lymph nodes, if left untreated.

The white cell count is elevated on blood tests, but usually no specific tests are necessary, and appropriate antibiotics by mouth give a very good result.
See also LYMPHATIC SYSTEM

LYMPHATIC SYSTEM
The lymphatic system regulates tissue fluid throughout the body. For example if you injure your knee, the surrounding tissues will swell up with excess fluid. This fluid will be removed and returned to circulation by the lymphatic system.

All the cells in the body are surrounded by fluid. This fluid is constantly fed with oxygen and nutrients from the bloodstream. As well as being topped up, fluid must be constantly removed; otherwise it would accumulate in the tissues. Some of it is removed through the bloodstream and some through the lymphatic system. This consists of minute lymphatic capillaries (very narrow vessels with very thin walls) leading into progressively larger lymphatic vessels, or channels, which eventually unite to form two big ducts emptying into veins at the base of the neck – returning the fluid to the bloodstream. The lymphatic system thus complements the circulatory system.

The tissue fluid that is filtered into the lymphatic capillaries is called lymph. It is a colourless liquid not unlike blood plasma in its consistency and appearance, although it has a slightly different chemical composition. There are special lymph vessels in the small intestine to absorb fat after a fatty meal. These are called lacteals, because their fluid has a milky appearance.

All along the lymphatic vessels are tiny lymph nodes (often incorrectly called glands). These are tiny, bead-like structures that filter out bacteria, viruses and poisons from the lymph, rather like an oil filter in a car. The lymph glands also produce white blood cells and antibodies. There are especially high concentrations of lymph nodes in the armpits, groin and neck and these may become noticeably painful and swollen during an infection.

Unlike the circulatory system which includes the heart, there is no pump to keep lymph moving through the lymphatic system. Therefore, frequent valves exist to stop the fluid flowing backwards and the circulation of lymph is maintained by intermittent pressure on the lymph ducts from breathing, muscle contractions and body movement.

The lymphatic network also includes three large glands – the tonsils, the spleen and the thymus. Each of these consists of lymphatic tissue and produces antibodies and white blood cells to fight infection. In particular, the tonsils act as a barrier to infections entering through the mouth. The thymus is present in the lower neck of children but shrinks after puberty. The spleen is a gland in the abdomen.

See also ADENITIS; LYMPH NODE BIOPSY; LYMPHANGITIS; LYMPHOEDEMA; SPLEEN; THYMUS; TONSIL; WHIPPLE'S DISEASE

LYMPH NODE
See ADENITIS; LYMPHATIC SYSTEM; LYMPH NODE BIOPSY; LYMPH NODES ENLARGED AND/OR PAINFUL; TONSIL

LYMPH NODE BIOPSY
Lymph nodes are tiny collections of white cells in the lymphatic system that filter out infections and poisons that occur in the body. A lymph node biopsy is a procedure in which a lymph node is removed and analysed for abnormalities. It may give information about certain infections or about one of the cancers attacking the lymphatic system, including the spleen, such as Hodgkin's disease.

To remove a lymph node, the area of skin over the node is anaesthetised and then cut so that access can be gained to the node, which then is removed. The cut is then stitched with one or two stitches. The procedure takes about fifteen to thirty minutes and is not painful, although as with any cut the area will be sore for a day or so. A child may be given a general anaesthetic.

See also BIOPSY; LYMPHATIC SYSTEM; LYMPH NODES ENLARGED AND/OR PAINFUL

LYMPH NODES ENLARGED AND/OR PAINFUL
Lymph nodes are collections of infection fighting white cells that filter out bacteria, viruses and other organisms, and abnormal cells (eg. cancer cells), from the organs whose waste products they drain. These nodes (often incorrectly called glands) are concentrated around the neck, in the armpits, groin and in the membrane (mesentery) that loosely connects the intestine to the back wall of the abdomen.

The term lymphadenopathy refers to any disease affecting the lymph nodes, while adenitis is an infection or inflammation of the lymph nodes.

Any infection, bacterial or viral, may result in the draining nodes becoming enlarged and painful. For example, if a finger is infected, the lymph nodes in the armpit may become involved, while a throat infection will cause swelling and pain in neck nodes.

Some infections are more likely to cause swollen painful lymph nodes than others. These include glandular fever (infectious mononucleosis), measles, brucellosis (caught by meat workers), septicaemia (blood infection), tuberculosis (TB), toxoplasmosis (carried by cats), cat scratch disease, and the cytomegalovirus (with fever, joint pain and large liver). The sexually transmitted diseases syphilis, gonorrhoea and AIDS are other possible causes.

Parasites may enter the blood stream and infest lymph nodes. These are very uncommon in developed countries, but in poorer tropical countries diseases such as filariasis (elephantiasis) and trypanosomiasis may occur. The bacterial infections lymphogranuloma venereum (sexually transmitted disease with large lymph nodes in groin), tularaemia (infection of rats) and plague (Black Death with pus oozing nodes in armpits and groin) are also mainly limited to these countries.

Lyme disease is an infection passed from mice and deer to humans by tics. It is common in North America, but rare elsewhere. It causes a spreading rash, fever, chills, muscle pains, headache, arthritis and enlarged lymph nodes.

Other causes of lymph node pain or enlargement include cancer, which may spread (metastasise) from its original organ along the lymph ducts to the nearby lymph nodes, leukaemia, Hodgkin's lymphoma and other lymphomas (cancer starting in the lymph nodes). Immunisation (eg. for cholera and typhoid) may cause a temporary reaction in the nearby lymph nodes and some drugs (eg. phenytoin for epilepsy) may have enlarged lymph nodes as a side effect.

There are many rare causes of lymph node problems including systemic lupus erythematosus (an autoimmune disease in which the body inappropriately rejects some of its own tissue), serum sickness (a reaction to receiving a blood transfusion or other blood products), chronic fatigue syndrome, AIDS and Felty syndrome (a complication of rheumatoid arthritis).
See also ADENITIS; LYMPHATIC SYSTEM; LYMPH NODE BIOPSY and separate entries for diseases mentioned above.

LYMPHOEDEMA
Lymph is a waste products of all cells that returns to the circulation through a complex network of fine tubes that eventually drain into a major vein near the heart. The lymph ducts pass through the lymph nodes that are concentrated in the arm pit, groin and neck, and act to remove any bacteria or abnormal cells. Lymphoedema is a common complication of surgery when lymph channels are disrupted by the removal of lymph nodes in the armpit or groin because of breast or other cancers. The lymphatic fluid is unable to return to the circulation normally and accumulates in the limb. The limb becomes very swollen, tense and sore. In severe cases the arm is rock hard and three times its normal size, and ulceration and infection of the skin and deeper tissues in the affected limb may occur. The Stewart-Treves syndrome is another complication.

It is a very difficult problem to treat. Possible treatments include elevation, exercises, pressure bandages and a plastic sleeve that envelopes the arm and is rhythmically inflated by a machine. The severity varies dramatically from one patient to another, with only a partial relationship to the severity of the surgery. It often persists for many years before gradually subsiding as new lymph channels are formed.
See also BREAST CANCER; LYMPHATIC SYSTEM; STEWART-TREVES SYNDROME

LYMPHOGRANULOMA VENEREUM
Lymphogranuloma venereum is a sexually transmitted disease that is rare in developed countries but common in Africa and Asia. It is caused by the *Chlamydia* organism which is a bacteria-like germ that lives inside cells and destroys them. The incubation period after sexual contact is one to three weeks.

A sore develops on the penis or vulva, then the lymph nodes in the groin become infected, swollen, soften and suppurate (drain pus) onto the skin. The infection may spread to cause joint, skin, brain and eye infections. If anal intercourse has occurred, sores and pus discharging lymph nodes may form in and around the anus. The initial sore and pus-discharging lymph nodes are not painful, and only if the disease spreads does a fever develop. It is diagnosed by special skin and blood tests.

Antibiotics such as tetracyclines are prescribed and surgical procedures to drain pus from lymph nodes may be necessary. If left untreated, disfiguring scarring will occur in the groin at the site of the infected lymph nodes, and the genitals may become permanently swollen, and if the infection spreads to other organs, they may be seriously damaged. The majority of cases are cured by appropriate treatment.

See also CHLAMYDIAL INFECTION;
TETRACYCLINES; VENEREAL
DISEASES

LYMPHOMA

Lymphomas are any form of cancer involving
the lymphatic system, stem cells, white blood
cells and lymph nodes.
See also HODGKIN'S LYMPHOMA;
NON-HODGKIN'S LYMPHOMA;
LEUKAEMIA; WALDENSTRÖM'S
MACROGLOBULINAEMIA

LYMPHOPLASMACYTOID LYMPHOMA

See WALDENSTRÖM'S
MACROGLOBULINAEMIA

LYSOSOME

See CELL

LYSSAVIRUS

See RABIES

M

MACROGLOBULINAEMIA
See WALDENSTRÖM'S
MACROGLOBULINAEMIA

MACROLIDES
Macrolides are a class of antibiotics that act against bacteria by interfering with the way their internal chemical reactions occur. They are most commonly used in chest, sinus and ear infections. They can interact badly with theophylline, which is used by some asthmatics and is in some cough mixtures. Some people who are allergic to penicillin are also allergic to erythromycin. They are available as tablets, mixtures and injections.

Examples (with brand names in brackets) include azithromycin (Zithromax), clarithromycin (Klacid), erythromycin (Eryc, EES) and roxithromycin (Biaxsig, Rulide). Side effects may include nausea, diarrhoea and belly pain. Lower doses must be used in the elderly and debilitated. Use with care in pregnancy.
See also ANTIBIOTICS; *MYCOPLASMA* INFECTION

MACULAR DEGENERATION
Macular degeneration is a common form of vision deterioration in the elderly. The macula is the part of the retina at the back of the eye that is most sensitive to light. It degenerates because of a poor blood supply with advancing age and cholesterol build up in arteries and diabetes. Patients experience a gradual loss of central vision while peripheral vision may be normal. It is diagnosed by examining the eye through an ophthalmoscope (magnifying light), but there is no effective treatment, although progress is usually very slow.
See also BLINDNESS; DRUSEN; EYE; VISION

MAD COW DISEASE
See CREUTZFELDT-JAKOB DISEASE

MAGNESIUM
About half of the small amount of magnesium (Mg) in the body is found in bones. Excess is removed from the body through the kidneys. It is important in the functioning of over 300 enzymes, and acts in a similar way to calcium in the nervous system. Alterations in the level of magnesium in the blood also cause a change in the level of calcium.

Blood tests can be performed to determine the amount of magnesium present. The normal range is between 0.7 and 1.0 mmol/L (1.7-2.3 mg/100 mL). High levels occur in long term kidney failure. Low levels may be a sign of kidney abnormalities, chronic alcoholism, hyperaldosteronism, liver cirrhosis, malabsorption syndromes, diarrhoea, diabetic ketoacidosis, malnutrition, vomiting, and prolonged intravenous therapy. Medications such as diuretics, amphotericin, gentamicin, laxatives, cisplatin and cytotoxics may also be responsible. Low levels may cause an irregular heart beat.
See also BLOOD TESTS; CALCIUM; MINERALS

MAGNESIUM HYDROXIDE
See ANTACIDS

MAGNETIC RESONANCE IMAGING
See MRI SCAN

MAIDENHEAD
See HYMEN

MAIMONEDES
See PRAYER OF MAIMONEDES

MALABSORPTION
Patients with malabsorption receive adequate amounts of food, but are unable to take it into their bodies from the gut in sufficient quantities to maintain nutrition. Weight loss will occur in adults, or failure to grow and develop in children. The poorly absorbed food may result in diarrhoea.

The thyroid gland in the front of the neck produces the hormone thyroxine, which acts as an accelerator for every cell in the body. If there is an excess of thyroxine, all organs will function too rapidly, and symptoms will include sweating, weight loss, diarrhoea, malabsorption, nervousness, heat intolerance, rapid heart rate, warm skin, tremor and prominent eyes.

Tumours or cancers of the intestine may cause inflammation that results in diarrhoea and malabsorption of food.

Surgery to the intestine or abdomen may cause inflammation of the gut and a temporary malabsorption during recovery. If part of the intestine or stomach is surgically removed (eg. for cancer, Crohn's disease), it may be too small to allow adequate digestion or too short to adequately absorb all food.

Patients with coeliac disease (sprue) are unable to digest the protein gluten, which is found in cereal grains such as wheat, rye, barley and oats, but not in rice or corn. Eating any foods containing gluten will cause diarrhoea, belly discomfort, weight loss, excess wind and bloating. The disease may start at any age from childhood to mid-life, and the only treatment is to exclude all these cereals from the diet.

Other causes of malabsorption include diverticular disease (formation of numerous small outpocketings of the large gut), poorly controlled or undiagnosed diabetes, infections of the gut with parasites (eg. Giardia), Crohn's disease (thickening and inflammation of the small or large intestine), diseases of the liver (eg. cirrhosis) and gall bladder (eg. gall stones), which may prevent or reduce the production of bile which enables fat to be absorbed, and diseases of the pancreas (eg. cancer and infection) can result in malabsorption as well as abdominal pain.

Less common causes of poor food absorption include cystic fibrosis (genetic condition in which thick mucus lines the gut and lungs), irradiation to the abdomen during cancer treatment, a lack of digestive enzymes that specifically attack lipase (fat) or lactose (milk sugar), tropical sprue (long term intestinal infection contracted in equatorial countries), alcoholism, partial obstruction to the blood supply to the gut caused by plaques of cholesterol or blood clots (thromboses), Whipple's disease (serious long term infection of the gut), Bassen-Kornzweig syndrome (abetalipoproteinaemia) and amyloidosis.

Some medications (eg. neomycin, cholestyramine, metformin) may have malabsorption as a side effect.

See also DIARRHOEA; FAILURE TO THRIVE; WEIGHT LOSS and separate entries for diseases mentioned above.

MALAISE
Term used to describe a feeling of being generally unwell, but with no specific symptoms. *See also* FATIGUE

MALARIA
Malaria is a serious blood parasite infestation that damages liver and red blood cells and is widespread in the tropics. The single celled parasite *Plasmodium* is responsible. There are four different types (falciparum, malariae, vivax, ovale) that cause slightly different types of malaria.

It is passed from person to person through a bite from the *Anopheles* mosquito. During a bite, the mosquito draws a malaria patient's blood into its belly to be digested, and becomes a carrier to every subsequent person it bites. During a bite a small amount of parasite-infested saliva is injected before the blood is drawn up. The disease is found throughout the tropics, but in Indonesia, New Guinea, Thailand, and other south-east Asian and west Pacific nations, a more serious chloroquine resistant form of malaria has developed.

MALARIA AFFECTED AREAS
The symptoms of malaria include attacks of severe fevers, sweats and chills every three to four days, the patient becomes very ill, and red blood cells are destroyed to cause jaundice (yellow skin), headaches and muscle pain. Late symptoms include delirium, convulsions, coma and sometimes death. The pattern of fever attacks and temporary recovery varies from one type of malaria to another. In severe cases, brain infections, extremely high fevers that may cause brain and other organ damage, and gut infections may occur. Blackwater fever is a complication in which large amounts of blood are passed in the urine ('black water') due to the massive breakdown of red blood cells, and the patient becomes very anaemic, a deep yellow colour, feverish and desperately ill.

The first symptoms of malaria develop eight to thirty days after being bitten by a mosquito, but in some cases may not occur for six months or more.

The diagnosis and the type of malaria are

MALARIA AFFECTED AREAS

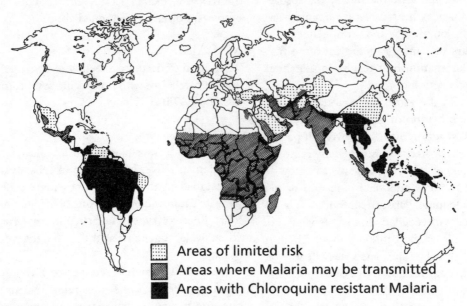

Areas of limited risk
Areas where Malaria may be transmitted
Areas with Chloroquine resistant Malaria

confirmed by examining the patient's blood under a microscope. Because the parasite goes through cycles of infecting the liver and then the blood, it is sometimes necessary to take several tests before it can be detected.

Appropriate drugs can slowly cure most cases, but relapses may occur for months or years. No vaccine is yet available, but most forms of malaria can be prevented by tablets that are taken either daily (eg. doxycycline) or weekly (eg. chloroquine). Some must be started as much as two weeks before entering a malarial area and continued for up to four weeks after leaving. As an added precaution, use an appropriate insect repellent, and wear long sleeved shirts and slacks or trousers.

With good treatment, 95% of patients recover, but it kills millions of people in poorer tropical countries every year. With blackwater fever the death rate exceeds 25%.
See also ANTIMALARIALS; SICKLE CELL ANAEMIA; TETRACYCLINES

MALARIA MEDICATIONS
See ANTIMALARIALS

MALDISON
See ANTIPARASITICS

MALE MENOPAUSE
See ANDROPAUSE

MALIGNANT
A malignant condition, growth or tumour is one that is cancerous or harmful.

See also BENIGN; CANCER

MALIGNANT LEUCOPENIA
See AGRANULOCYTOSIS

MALLET FINGER
A mallet finger is caused by a rupture of one of the tendons that straightens (extends) the finger tip. It commonly occurs through injury, or occasionally as a complication of rheumatoid arthritis. The patient is unable to straighten (extend) the tip of the affected finger, and it droops down. Splinting in the straight position for six weeks or more may correct the problem, but often surgery is necessary to repair the damaged tendon.
See also TRIGGER FINGER

MALLEUS
See EAR

MALLORY-WEIS SYNDROME
The Mallory-Weis syndrome is a serious inflammation of, and damage to, the lower end of the oesophagus (gullet) caused by a patient vomiting forcibly for a prolonged period of time, resulting in a tear at the lower end of the oesophagus where it joins the stomach. Massive bleeding occurs from the tear.

There is persistent vomiting of fresh blood, sometimes associated with pain behind and below the lower end of the breast bone. Massive blood loss may lead to other organ damage or death.

Gastroscopy is essential to confirm the diag-

nosis. Medications are given to stop the vomiting, and gastroscopy, surgery or a balloon device used to stop the tear from bleeding. Most patients recover with good treatment, but there is a significant mortality rate.
See also OESOPHAGUS; REFLUX OESOPHAGITIS; VOMITING BLOOD

MALNUTRITION
See FAILURE TO THRIVE; KWASHIORKOR; MALABSORPTION; MARASMUS

MAMM-
'Mamm-' is a prefix derived from the Latin word for breast, and used in medicine to indicate the breasts (mammary glands), or diseases or investigations relating to the breasts (eg. mammogram).

MAMMARY CARCINOMA
See BREAST CANCER

MAMMARY DYSPLASIA
Mammary dysplasia is also known as chronic cystic mastitis or fibrocystic disease of the breast. It is a common cause of breast lumps and cysts, and breast discomfort in middle aged women, and is caused by overactivity of the ovaries in producing too much oestrogen. It is often an inherited characteristic.

Affected women develop multiple, tender, painful, small lumps in the breasts that vary in size and severity with the monthly hormonal cycle. They are usually worse just before a menstrual period. Large cysts may form permanently in the breast, and persistent pain and discomfort may significantly affect the woman's lifestyle.

Mammography (breast x-ray) and ultrasound may be used initially, but in most cases needle or surgical biopsy is necessary to confirm the diagnosis.

Initially a firm bra should be worn day and night. Individual cysts may be drained through a needle when they become too large or uncomfortable. Medical treatment involves using drugs such as the contraceptive pill to regulate the menstrual cycle, nonsteroidal anti-inflammatories, danazol and progestogens. Avoiding caffeine helps some patients. The condition often persists until menopause, when it naturally subsides.
See also BEAST; BREAST CANCER; BREAST LUMP; FIBROADENOMA OF THE BREAST

MAMMOGRAM
A mammogram is an x-ray of the breast using a special technique to reveal the structure of the breast. It is one of the most significant diagnostic tools available for the detection of breast cancer.

A mammogram may be ordered to investigate a lump that has been found during a physical examination of the breasts, either by the patient herself, or by her doctor. However, women are being urged to have routine mammograms even before a lump can be felt, since it is the only reliable method of detecting cancer at the earliest possible stage. Unfortunately they are not 100% reliable, and a mammogram should always be preceded or followed by a breast examination by a doctor.

Cancer cells are denser than ordinary cells and are impenetrable to certain x-rays. A tumour will therefore appear as a white patch on the mammogram picture. Mammography can sometimes detect the difference between benign and malignant tumours.

The rate of breast cancer rises markedly in women aged over fifty, and regular mammograms are recommended for all women over this age, generally once every two years. Women younger than this should have regular mammograms if there is a high risk of developing breast cancer. Studies carried out in various parts of the world estimate that the death rate from breast cancer is reduced by up to 70% in screened women.

To have a mammogram, the woman will strip to the waist and sit or stand in front of a small table, leaning in such a way that her breast is resting on the table, where it will be placed in various positions and photographed by the x-ray machine above. The breasts will be compressed to reduce the distance the x-rays must pass through them, and to reduce distortion caused by the curvature of the breast surface. The technique is especially valuable in the examination of large breasts, because the contrast is greater. However, a trained radiologist will detect any abnormalities in even the smallest breasts.

Having a mammogram is painless, although some women find the compression of their breasts uncomfortable. For routine mammograms, it is better to make the appointment in the first two weeks of the menstrual cycle when the breasts are not swollen and painful because of normal hormonal changes.

Modern mammography equipment delivers very little radiation and so is considered safe. Nevertheless, even small amounts of radiation increase the likelihood of getting cancer to a degree, and this needs to be taken into account when deciding on the frequency of routine tests. The older a woman gets, the less she is at risk from radiation, so those for whom a mammogram is of most value are at least risk from exposure to radiation.

If an abnormality is detected, it may be further investigated by an ultrasound and biopsy.
See also BREAST; ULTRASOUND; X-RAY

MANDIBLE
The jaw bone is known as the mandible. It connects with the skull at the jaw (temporomandibular) joint, which lies just in front of the ear, and enables the mouth to open and close, and move slightly from side to side when chewing. The teeth of the lower jaw are imbedded in the mandible.

Viewed from the side, the mandible looks like the letter L, with a long lower arm. Powerful muscles run from the temples to the mandible and act to allow chewing. Other smaller muscles connect the mandible to the base of the skull to open the mouth, and to the tongue.
See also MOUTH; TEETH; TONGUE

MANE
The prescription notation 'mane' is derived from the Latin word for 'morning' which means 'take in the morning'.
See also PRESCRIPTION NOTATIONS

MANIA
Mania is the opposite of depression, but often associated with depression, as patients may swing from one mood extreme to the other (bipolar affective disorder or manic-depressive disorder). More serious forms of mania include pyromania (the inability to resist the temptation to light fires) and kleptomania (the inability to resist the temptation to steal). The cause is generally unknown, but attacks may be triggered by stress and anxiety, drug abuse or epilepsy, and it is more common in women than men.

Patients change their ideas rapidly, speak quickly on different topics that are not apparently connected, become over-involved in activities, move very quickly to the point where minor accidents are common, require little sleep, are very irritable and lose their temper easily. In severe cases, marked aggression may occur, there may be exceedingly grand ideas about their importance and ability, and rash decisions may be made such as resigning from a job or making inappropriate major purchases. Exhibitionism, excessive sexual desires (nymphomania), pointless travel and attempting to obtain media coverage are other symptoms. The patient may believe that others are persecuting him/her (paranoia), have hallucina-

FACIAL BONES

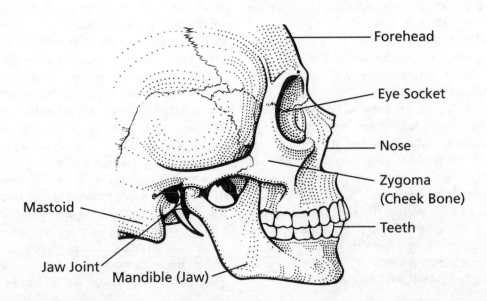

Forehead

Eye Socket

Nose

Zygoma
(Cheek Bone)

Teeth

Mastoid

Jaw Joint

Mandible (Jaw)

tions, hear imaginary voices, and feel rejected by society. Episodes usually commence suddenly, and may last from hours to months, and may be preceded or followed by a period of intense depression during which suicide is a risk. There is sometimes a risk that patients who are manic will injure themselves or others by their rash actions.

Antipsychotic medications such as lithium are used in treatment. If the patient is perceived by a doctor to be at risk of suicide or of injuring others and refuses to accept treatment, the doctor may, with the cooperation of relatives or another doctor, certify the patient so that the police are empowered to take the patient to a psychiatric hospital for compulsory treatment. If the patient can be convinced to remain on medication, good control can be obtained, but unfortunately, many patients cannot see why they should take drugs for many months or years, and stop them prematurely which leads to a relapse into the mania or depression.
See also ANTIPSYCHOTICS;
DEPRESSION; HALLUCINATION;
MANIC-DEPRESSIVE;
SCHIZOPHRENIA

MANIC-DEPRESSIVE

The manic-depressive disorder, which is also known as the bipolar affective disorder, results in severe swings in mood that start most commonly around thirty years of age and almost never after sixty.

The patient suffers dramatic changes in mood from very depressed to manic and vice versa. When depressed, the patient is sad, loses interest in pleasure, loses weight, wakes through night and cannot get back to sleep, becomes restless, fatigues easily, feels worthless, cannot concentrate and may think of death. In the manic stage which may follow days, or even hours after the depression, the patient has an inflated self esteem, decreased need for sleep, is very talkative, has sudden changes in thoughts, poor attention span, increased sexual activity including promiscuity, spends excessively and takes risks.

There are no specific diagnostic tests for manic-depression; a diagnosis can only be made after careful assessment by a doctor. Once diagnosed, specific medications to control mood swings (eg. lithium, valproic acid, carbamazepine) can be prescribed.

There is generally a good response to treatment, but there is a risk of suicide in the depressive phase, and of self-injury from dangerous activities in the manic phase.
See also DEPRESSION

MANIPULATION

Manipulative therapy by a physiotherapist can involve passive mobilisation and manipulation. Mobilisation is a rhythmical movement gently applied to joints and soft tissues by the physiotherapist's hands. A manipulation is a single joint movement performed quickly.

The techniques of manipulative therapy are used to treat joints and muscles which have become painful and lack their normal range of movement. This dysfunction can occur in the spine or limbs, or indeed in the joint of the jaw. The pain and loss of movement can result from injury, overuse or poor use of the joints, or from osteoarthritis. Dysfunction in the small joints, discs and muscles of the neck can give symptoms of headache, neck pain and stiffness. The pain may spread into the arm. In the low back, the pain may spread down the leg.

After a thorough history and examination, together with information from x-rays and other medical tests, the physiotherapist selects an appropriate manipulative therapy technique. Often this is a passive mobilisation technique, gently moving the joint to relieve its pain and help it regain movement. On occasion it is also necessary to manipulate the joint. Manipulation on the whole is a safe procedure, but as with any form of treatment, there are several conditions in which its use is unsafe (eg. in dizziness caused by vertebral artery problems, spinal cancer, fractures, rheumatoid arthritis, and osteoporosis).

In conjunction with the manipulative therapy treatment, the physiotherapist teaches the patient-specific, gentle exercises to help maintain and improve spinal movement. As the pain settles, therapeutic exercises are begun to ensure the patient has a good muscle system and good general fitness to help support and protect the spine from further injury.
See also CHIROPRACTIC;
OSTEOPATHY; PHYSIOTHERAPY

MANTOUX TEST

A Mantoux test establishes if someone has ever had tuberculosis. It is similar to an

allergy test in that a solution containing dead tuberculosis bacteria is injected into the skin. If the person has had the disease or has been immunised against it, their system will contain antibodies and these will rush to the site of the injection (normally the arm) leading to a raised red swelling. The reaction takes two to three days. The larger the patch, the more likely it is that the person has, or has had, tuberculosis, or has developed immunity to it following vaccination.
See also TUBERCULOSIS

MANUBRIUM
See STERNUM

MAOI
See ANTIDEPRESSANTS

MARASMUS
Marasmus is a severe form of malnutrition caused by starvation, with a lack of both protein and carbohydrates in the diet. Some elderly and intellectually handicapped people become malnourished because they are unable to care for themselves adequately. Victims have wasted muscles, retarded growth, no fat under the skin, dry skin, and look far older than their years. If weight loss exceeds one third of normal body weight, heart, liver, kidney and other organ damage becomes significant and sudden death may occur. Resistance to infection is reduced, and severe lung and skin infections may also cause death. Blood tests show widespread chemical abnormalities.

Before returning to a normal diet it is essential to give small amounts of nutritious food frequently over several weeks, to prevent an imbalance of chemicals in the blood.
See also FAILURE TO THRIVE; KWASHIORKOR

MARBURG VIRUS
The Marburg virus is an extremely contagious form of viral haemorrhagic fever (viral infection of the blood) that occurs in central Africa. The virus is spread by monkeys and from person to person in conditions of poor hygiene. Outbreaks have occurred throughout central Africa, and in zoo monkey handlers elsewhere in the world. Occasionally, those infected have minimal symptoms, but these patients may pass the infection on to others.

Patients develop muscle pains, headache, sore throat, joint pains, diarrhoea, vomiting, red eyes and abnormal bleeding. Internal bleeding causes death.

There is no cure or vaccine for prevention, and treatment is restricted to managing the symptoms and nursing care. Patients must be nursed in strict isolation, and it is fatal in about 80% of patients.
See also EBOLA VIRUS; LASSA FEVER

MARCAINE
See ANAESTHETICS

MARCH-A-PETIT-PAS
See WALK ABNORMAL

MARCH FRACTURE
A march fracture is a stress fracture of a forefoot (metatarsal) bone caused by prolonged running, jumping or walking, usually on hard surfaces (eg. soldiers on a route march). More significant metatarsal fractures may occur with direct injury.

Severe pain is felt in the ball of the foot and excruciating pain on attempting to walk. There may be minimal changes on x-ray and a bone scan may be necessary to detect the fracture. Six weeks rest in plaster and on crutches heals these fractures.
See also FRACTURE; STRESS FRACTURE

MARFAN SYNDROME
Marfan syndrome is an uncommon inherited condition that affects the skeleton, heart and eye, and occurs in all races but only in one out of every 20 000 people.

Its characteristics include very long thin bones in the arms, legs, fingers and toes, a tall skull, excessive joint movement and a humped back. Half the patients have an eye lens that is in the wrong position, and they may develop keratoconus (protruding eye surface) and a detached retina (the light-sensitive area at the back of the eyes), which results in partial or total blindness. An abnormality in the elastic tissue of the heart valves and major arteries causes these to fail and the pumping of the heart to be inefficient. The main artery of the body, the aorta, becomes overly dilated and distorted and may eventually rupture, and heart infections (endocarditis) are common. Most patients do not have all these symptoms, as there is great variation between them. Some may be totally unaware that they are affected and just appear to be very tall and thin.

It is diagnosed by the characteristic appearance of the long bones on x-ray, and by assessing the heart abnormalities with echocardiograms. The problems in the heart and aorta are controlled and corrected by both medication and surgery, but death in middle age is common unless corrective surgery is successful.
See also ENDOCARDITIS; HEART; HEIGHT EXCESSIVE; KERATOCONUS; RETINAL DETACHMENT

MARIJUANA
Marijuana (cannabis, hashish or 'pot') is an addictive drug that is taken into the body by smoking or eating. The concentrated resin from the plant (hashish) is stronger and more dangerous than marijuana, and produces a more noticeable effect. Marijuana is made from the hemp plant, *Cannabis sativa* which has as its active ingredient the chemical tetrahydrocannabinol (THC). THC occurs in all parts of the cannabis plant and is a depressant drug, not a stimulant.

Possibly one in every 100 people is dependent upon illicit drugs in Western society, and a far higher percentage have experimented with them at one time or another. Users tend to have a poor self-image and ego.

Initially the drug causes excessive happiness, followed by a long period of depression and drowsiness. If used daily for a few weeks it eventually ceases to have its original effect, and the user must increase the dose to reach the same level of intoxication, which is how addiction develops. Blood and urine tests can detect the presence of THC.

Most drugs dissolve in water, but THC dissolves in the body's fat, and so stores of the drug can be established in the system. This leads to a prolonged withdrawal stage, and the frightening flashbacks that regular users experience when a sudden release of the drug from the body's fat stores occurs. These flashbacks can occur without warning for weeks after the last use of marijuana, and may cause hallucinations while working or driving and can therefore place others at risk. Long-term use may cause an increased risk of bronchitis, lung cancer and other respiratory diseases associated with smoking; decreased concen-

tration, memory and learning abilities; interference with sex hormone production; and cannabis psychosis, which is similar to schizophrenia. Cannabis is often also used with other drugs to intensify its effects, often in unpredictable ways. Using cannabis and alcohol together can be much more dangerous than using either drug by itself.

The treatment options available are: –
• gradual withdrawal while receiving counselling and medical support
• immediate drug withdrawal ("cold turkey") while medically supervised
• halfway houses that remove the patient from the environment in which drug taking is encouraged
• individual or group psychotherapy

Marijuana is more addictive and damaging than alcohol, but there is a better long term prognosis than with other illicit drugs, unless the patient moves to using stronger and more addictive substances.
See also COCAINE; ECSTASY; GAMMA-HYDROXYBUTYRATE; HEROIN; KETAMINE; LSD; MESCALINE; STIMULANTS

MARROW
See BONE

MASS IN ABDOMEN
See ABDOMINAL LUMP

MAST CELL
See ALLERGY; ANTIHISTAMINES

MASTITIS
Mastitis is an infection of the breast tissue, almost invariably in a breast feeding woman. It usually occurs if one of the many lobes in the breast does not adequately empty its milk, and may spread from a sore, cracked nipple. Women nursing for the first time are more frequently affected.

The breast becomes painful, very tender, red and sore, and the woman may become feverish, and quite unwell. Antibiotic tablets such as penicillin or a cephalosporin usually cure the infection rapidly and the woman can continue breast feeding, but if an abscess forms, an operation to drain away the accumulated pus is necessary. In recurrent cases, bromocriptine may be used to stop or reduce breast milk production.

See also BREAST; MAMMARY DYSPLASIA

MASTOCYTOSIS
See URTICARIA PIGMENTOSA

MASTOIDITIS
Mastoiditis is a bacterial infection of the mastoid bone, which is a small bump of bone at the bottom of the skull immediately behind the ear that contains a microscopic honeycomb of air filled spaces. The infection almost invariably occurs as a result of infection spreading from the middle ear in patients who have recurrent or severe attacks of middle ear infection (otitis media).

Severe pain occurs behind the ear, as well as fever, and redness and tenderness over the mastoid bone. In some cases the infection will eat away the bone at the back of the ear canal and allow the pus to escape into the ear. The hole between the ear canal and the mastoid air cells, and the cavity in the mastoid bone that results from the infection, are permanent. If left untreated, the infection may spread into the brain.

An x-ray of the mastoid shows the destroyed air spaces within it, filled with pus (an abscess). Potent antibiotics are prescribed, sometimes given by injection. If these fail, an operation to drain the pus out of the mastoid bone will be necessary (a mastoidectomy). The prognosis is good with appropriate treatment.
See also ABSCESS; EARACHE; OTITIS MEDIA; TEMPORAL BONE

MASTOID PROCESS
See MASTOIDITIS; TEMPORAL BONE

MASTURBATION
Masturbation is sexual stimulation by oneself. Most people, both men and women, masturbate, especially during adolescence and at times of their lives when they do not have a sexual partner. Men masturbate by rubbing the penis or otherwise stimulating this organ. In women, a dildo (artificial penis) or finger is inserted in the vagina, or the clitoris is stimulated.

Some religions have frowned on the practice and insisted on their adherents regarding it as sinful. Dire threats have sometimes been made that unpleasant physical consequences such as blindness will result. This is nonsense.

Masturbation is harmless, and if it provides pleasure and sexual relief it is quite reasonable to engage in it.
See also EJACULATION; ORGASM

MATURE CAPILLARY NAEVUS
See PORTWINE NAEVUS

MATURITY ONSET DIABETES
See DIABETES MELLITUS TYPE TWO

MAXILLA
The maxilla is the upper jaw bone at the front of the skull.
See also MANDIBLE; SINUS; SKULL; ZYGOMA

MB
'MB' is an abbreviation used to indicate that the doctor has a Bachelor of Medicine qualification, which is part of basic medical degree.
See also MEDICAL TRAINING

MBA
A multiple biochemical analysis (MBA) is a catch-all collection of blood tests that screen for a wide range of diseases and abnormalities. It usually includes tests for liver function, kidney function, blood glucose (sugar), iron, cholesterol, triglycerides, electrolytes (eg. sodium, bicarbonate, potassium, chloride), proteins and calcium.
See also BLOOD TESTS; CREATININE; ELECTROLYTES; IRON; LIVER FUNCTION TESTS; UREA

McARDLE SYNDROME
See GLYCOGEN STORAGE DISEASES

MD
'MD' is an abbreviation used to indicate that the doctor is a Doctor of Medicine, which indicates a basic medical degree in North America and Europe, but a higher qualification in Australia and Britain.
See also MEDICAL TRAINING

ME
See CHRONIC FATIGUE SYNDROME

MEASLES
Measles (technically called morbilli or rubeola) is a *Morbilli* virus infection that is highly contagious from five days before the rash appears until it disappears. The incubation

period is ten to fourteen days. It was originally a disease of cattle that was only passed to humans after these animals were domesticated many thousands of years ago.

It starts with the cold-like symptoms of a snuffly nose, cough and red eyes. A rash develops about four days later, starting in the mouth where tiny white spots appear on the lining of the cheeks. Dark red blotches then develop on the face and gradually spread across the body, remaining for a week or more before gradually fading. Other symptoms include a high fever and eye discomfort with bright lights. The patient often starts to feel better once the rash has reached its maximum spread.

The diagnosis can be confirmed by blood tests if necessary, and previous exposure to the measles virus or vaccine can also be confirmed by blood tests.

There is no specific treatment. Rest, paracetamol and medication are used to relieve the cold symptoms, and vitamin A supplements appear to reduce the severity of an attack. It may be prevented by vaccination, usually given at one and four years of age in combination with the mumps and rubella (German measles) vaccine. With widespread vaccination, it is becoming a rare infection in developed countries and may be totally eradicated in the next decade.

Complications include encephalitis (a serious brain infection), pneumonia, ear infections and damage, and possibly the increased risk of developing multiple sclerosis later in life. Immediately after an attack patients are susceptible to other infections, and a significant number will develop tonsillitis, ear and lymph node infections.

The prognosis is usually very good, but significant complications occur in one in every 200 cases, and death occurs in one in every 5000 cases in developed countries, while in third-world countries one in ten children or adults who catch measles will die.
See also GERMAN MEASLES; ROSEOLA INFANTUM; SKIN RED SPOTS; VIRUS

MEBENDAZOLE
See ANTHELMINTICS

MEBEVERINE
See ANTISPASMODICS

MECKEL'S DIVERTICULITIS
Meckel's diverticulitis is a bacterial infection or inflammation of an outpocketing (Meckel's diverticulum) on the last part of the small intestine (ileum) that is left over from the individual's life as a foetus before birth when the diverticulum was attached to the umbilicus. In 2% of people it remains after birth, and may become blocked with food or other debris.

When infected the patient feels pain in the belly and develops a fever. Blood tests may show inflammation or infection but not its location. The diagnosis is often confused with appendicitis and it is usually not diagnosed until operation when a normal appendix is found, and further examination of the bowel reveals an infected Meckel's diverticulum. The problem is easily remedied by surgery, but if left untreated, may burst to cause life-threatening peritonitis, or an abscess that results in long term illness.
See also ABDOMINAL PAIN; APPENDICITIS

MEDIAL
The term medial refers to the middle of the body, closer to the centre or the inner side of an organ or structure.
See also DORSAL; LATERAL; VENTRAL

MEDIAL EPICONDYLITIS
See GOLFER'S ELBOW

MEDIASTINUM
Mediastinum is a medical term to describe the central part of the chest behind the sternum (breast bone) which contains the heart and its major vessels. The oesophagus runs through the back part of the mediastinum behind the heart.
See also CHEST PAIN; HEART; THORAX

MEDICAL ETHICS
The ethics of the medical profession have regulated doctor/patient relationships since the time of Hippocrates 2350 years ago. Most patients do not understand many of the intricacies of the medical code of ethics, and may become confused or annoyed at the way in which matters proceed as a result. The basis of the relationship between a doctor and his/her patients is that of absolute confidence and mutual respect. The patient expects the

doctor not only to exercise professional skill, but also to observe secrecy with respect to the information s/he acquires as a result of his/her examination and treatment of the patient. This means that a doctor has a strict obligation to refrain from disclosing to any person or organisation, without the consent of the patient (except where laws stipulate otherwise), any information which s/he has learnt in his/her consultation with the patient.

Ethics in the medical profession extend to the issuing of certificates, and under no circumstances may a doctor change the date, alter, or issue a certificate which is not true in every sense, as such certificates may be used to obtain unfair advantage for the patient, or disadvantage others.

Doctors must be in continual contact with their colleagues, and must exchange medical information freely in order to learn new techniques and better manage their patients. If a patient wishes to change doctors, they have a perfect right to do so. The correct procedure is for a patient to notify the present doctor (by mail if preferred) that s/he wishes to change to a new doctor. Relevant information can then be sent from the old doctor to the new one, so that there is no gap in care or confusion regarding the patient's case.

It is unethical for a doctor to hold himself/herself out to possess skills in a certain direction that s/he does not possess. For this reason, medical boards regulate who can and cannot call themselves a specialist in certain areas of medicine that require higher levels of skill (eg. surgery, obstetrics).

Doctors must not use the media or other methods to promote themselves as being better than other doctors in order to attract patients. As a result, many media doctors use a pseudonym to maintain their anonymity and therefore do not run foul of the ethical rules. If doctors were permitted to promote themselves in this way, the doctor most able to manipulate the media or to pay for the biggest advertisements would attract the most patients, rather than the doctor best able to care for the individual.

See also DICHOTOMY; HIPPOCRATES; HIPPOCRATIC OATH; PRAYER OF MAIMONEDES

MEDICAL TRAINING

The typical steps necessary for a school leaver to becoming a private medical practitioner are as follows: –

• Complete the final year at school with a high enough pass to enter University.

• Undertake and pass any undergraduate university course and achieve very high grades.

• At the end of the undergraduate course, a special medical aptitude test must be completed and passed.

• The candidate for medical school then goes for an interview before an expert panel of academics and doctors for final assessment.

• If accepted for medical school from a science course that has included all the prerequisite subjects (eg. biochemistry, physiology, physics) the student can enter directly into the medical course. If the prerequisite subjects have not been studied, a one-year bridging course must be completed.

• A four-year intensive clinical medical course at university must be completed and passed.

• Two years of supervised practice as an intern in a public hospital. Often several months will be spent in a country hospital.

• The young doctor's future career is chosen at this point. Primary exams for specialist colleges must be completed, or application must be made to enter the GP Training Program.

• Undertake a three to six year programme of training with the GP or specialist college training program.

• Pass the difficult exams to become a fellow of the appropriate GP or specialist college.

• Apply for registration.

• Go into private, unsupervised medical practice, a minimum of twelve years after leaving school.

There will be variations from this scenario in different countries, but most will take a similar time.

To remain registered, doctors must undertake compulsory continuing medical education which involves a variety of activities in the areas of courses, lectures, conferences, completing quizzes, reading journals, having their practice assessed, teaching other doctors and medical students, and acting as an examiner. A certain number of points must be obtained every year to remain on the register and in practice as a private medical specialist or GP.

See also GENERAL PRACTITIONER; MEDICAL ETHICS

MEDICATION

An illness may be treated by surgical procedures, psychological counselling, physical therapies, irradiation, or by the modification of the body's processes with medications (drugs). Medication can be given by mouth (tablet, capsule, mixture, pellets), through the skin (creams, ointments, patches), through the anus (suppository), the vagina (pessary), by injection or implantation, inhalation, nasal spray, ear drops, eye drops and by an infusion into a vein or other body cavity.

Almost every medication belongs to a particular class of drugs, all of which have similar properties, uses and actions. Some drugs may belong to two or more classes. Many drug classes and medications are listed in this text.

All medications have a generic (common) name which is the same world wide (with some exceptions in the USA and Canada). They also have one or many brand (or trade) names assigned by the manufacturer, which are usually much simpler and easier to remember than the generic name, and which may vary from country to country. For example, paracetamol is a generic name for the brand name products Dymadon, Panadol, Panamax, Tylenol etc. in Australia. The same medication has the generic name acetaminophen in the USA and Canada.

Some brand names are listed after generic names in this text, but only those that have become household names (eg. Viagra) have main headings.
See also BRAND NAMES; DRUGS; PESSARY; SUPPOSITORY and under individual medication generic names.

MEDITERRANEAN SPOTTED FEVER
See TYPHUS

MEDROXYPROGESTERONE INJECTIONS

Medroxyprogesterone (Depo-Provera or Depo-Ralovera) injections are a means of contraception in which a synthetic form of the female sex hormone progesterone is injected into a woman's muscle (usually the buttock or thigh) and slowly released into the body, causing the ovaries to stop producing eggs. It has been widely used since the late 1960s.

One injection lasts for three to six months depending on the dose given, but after the first injection, it is necessary to use another method of contraception for seven days. Follow-up injections are effective immediately, provided they are administered regularly. If an injection is more than a week late, you could become pregnant and should use another method of contraception until seven days after the next injection.

During the first few months, medroxyprogesterone injections sometimes cause a change in the menstrual pattern, such as missed periods, irregular spotting, continual light bleeding, or heavy bleeding. Occasionally it gives rise to nausea, headaches, mild depression, abdominal cramps, breast tenderness and weight gain. These are not a cause for concern, but if they are prolonged or a source of discomfort a different method of contraception may be more appropriate. Side effects cannot quickly be reversed because of the long-lasting nature of the injection.

In many women, the injections result in periods becoming lighter and less frequent, and eventually stopping. This is quite harmless and may even be welcome. It may take twelve months or longer after ceasing the injections for fertility to return to normal. However, there is no risk of permanent infertility.

The medroxyprogesterone injection has the advantage that it is highly effective, long-acting, cannot be forgotten, is convenient, and avoids the possible side effects of the pill with its oestrogen base.
See also CONTRACEPTION; SEX HORMONES

MEDRYSONE
See STEROIDS

MEFENAMIC ACID
See NONSTEROIDAL ANTI-INFLAMMATORY DRUGS

MEFLOQUINE
See ANTIMALARIALS

MEGACOLON

A megacolon is a massive distension of the descending and sigmoid colon, the last parts of the large intestine.

Causes include long term constipation and retention of faeces, which stretch the large bowel, or it may be a complication of ulcerative colitis, associated with some psychiatric and low intellect disorders, a symptom of an underactive thyroid gland (hypothyroidism), or due to excessive use of narcotics, or a birth defect (Hirschsprung disease).

The symptoms include severe constipation, sometimes associated with lower abdominal pain and watery diarrhoea as liquid faeces flows around the blockage. Rarely the bowel may rupture causing life threatening peritonitis.

It is diagnosed by colonoscopy (passing a flexible tube up the bowel through the anus) or x-rays. Doctors then treat any underlying disease, remove faeces build up, recommend a special high fibre diet, and advise the careful use of laxatives. Surgery in the form of a colostomy (opening bowel onto skin) is a last resort, but it is often a persistent condition that requires constant and repeated treatment.
See also COLON, CONSTIPATION; DIVERTICULITIS; HIRSCHSPRUNG DISEASE; ULCERATIVE COLITIS

MEGALOBLASTIC ANAEMIA
See PERNICIOUS ANAEMIA

MEIBOMIAN CYST
The upper and lower eyelids each contain about twenty Meibomian glands, which secrete an oily substance that lubricates the surface of the eye. If the tiny tube leading out of one a gland becomes blocked, it will swell up into a cyst that is felt and seen as a lump in the eyelid. It may become infected by bacteria to form a chalazion. The problem is more common in those over forty years of age, and may follow a period of eye irritation or conjunctivitis. A small cut into the cyst will drain out the contents.
See also CHALAZION; EYELID

MEIGS SYNDROME
Meigs syndrome (Demons-Meigs syndrome) is a fibrous growth in an ovary that causes abnormal levels of sex hormone production and swelling of the belly from fluid retention. Surgical removal of the ovarian tumour is necessary and infertility is a complication.
See also OVARY

MELAENA
See FAECES BLOOD

MELANCHOLIA
See DEPRESSION

MELANIN
See SKIN

MELANOMA
A melanoma is the most serious form of skin cancer, and it starts in the skin cells that create pigment. In Europeans (Caucasians), these cells are relatively inactive, giving a pale colour to the skin, but in Asians (Mongols) they are moderately active, and in Africans (Negroes) they are very active, giving a darker skin colour.

The actual cause is unknown, but exposure to sunlight, particularly in childhood and teen years, dramatically increases the risk. Ultraviolet radiation, most of which is filtered out of sunlight by the ozone layer in the upper atmosphere, is the part of the spectrum that causes the damage. Fair-skinned people have a higher incidence than those with dark complexions. It is rare in children, slightly more common in women than men, and most common between thirty and fifty years of age and on the legs and back. One in every 150 people in Australia will develop a melanoma at some time.

It appears as a skin spot that may be black, brown, pink or blue, and the colours may be found individually or mixed. They usually have an irregular edge, enlarge steadily, have an uneven and bumpy surface, and the pigment can be seen advancing into the surrounding skin and in advanced cases the spot will bleed, scab and ulcerate. They have a tendency to grow deep into the body and migrate to other organs, particularly the liver, lungs and lymph nodes in the armpit and groin. Melanomas can occur under the nail (where they may be mistaken for a bruise), in the mouth, under the eyelids, on the retina inside the eye, and in the anus, but the sun-exposed parts of the skin are the most commonly affected.

It is diagnosed by biopsy or excision of the suspected mole, then the melanoma and a large area of skin around and under it, must be cut out. The lymph nodes around the melanoma may also need to be removed. If there is evidence that it has spread to other areas, the patient will also be treated with irradiation and injected medications to control its further growth.

In the very early stages there is a 97% cure rate, but as the cancer enlarges, the cure rate drops dramatically. The cancer may appear to

be cured but can flare up decades later, but one third of all patients who develop a melanoma will eventually die from it.
See also CANCER; EXCISION; HUTCHISON MELANOTIC FRECKLE; SKIN PIGMENTATION EXCESS

MELASMA
See CHLOASMA

MELATONIN
See PINEAL GLAND

MELIOIDOSIS
Melioidosis is an uncommon infection of the lungs caused by the bacterium *Pseudomonas pseudomallei* which occurs throughout south and east Asia, and has been reported in Aboriginal communities in northern Australia. It is widespread in soil, and is caught by inhaling dust, with person to person spread being rare. Occasionally, dirt or food can infect wounds, the gut and other internal organs.

It is usually a low-grade persistent infection with minimal symptoms, but in a minority it develops rapidly with symptoms similar to pneumonia such as a cough, fever, muscle pains, loss of appetite and chest pain. It is diagnosed by examination of sputum and specific blood tests.

Treatment is only necessary if the patient has symptoms, and it involves long term use of antibiotics, with possible relapses after treatment has been completed. No form of prevention or vaccination is available. The prognosis is good with appropriate treatment, but without treatment, patients who develop pneumonia usually die.
See also PNEUMONIA

MELLERIL
See ANTIPSYCHOTICS

MEMORY
Memory is the most complex and least understood function of the brain. It requires several steps including acquisition of information, storage, and recall.

Memory is stored in the brain in three forms – immediate, short term and long term.

Immediate memory lasts about half a minute and can store between five and ten items. It is very susceptible to distraction and requires concentration. Doctors test this by asking a patient to remember and repeat four numbers backwards.

The short term memory lasts for a few minutes to hours, and has a much larger storage capacity than immediate memory. After this time it is sorted so that important memories are placed in the long term section of the brain, while other less important memories fade as they are gradually discarded. Doctors test this form of memory by asking the patient to repeat a list of three or four objects after several minutes.

Long term memory lasts weeks to a lifetime, and contains knowledge, personal experiences and social interactions. Long term memory requires the production of new proteins and new connections between nerve cells (neurones) in the brain.

Memory can be further subdivided into reference memory (previous experiences), episodic memory (information about a specific place and/or time), working memory (updates of old memory by current experiences), semantic memory (unchanging facts of everyday life), explicit memory (detailed facts about past experiences), and procedural memory (learned skills).

The exact nature of memory, and its location in the brain, is still a matter of debate amongst physiologists, but long term memory probably involves patterns of nerve connections throughout the brain rather than only one area.
See also BRAIN; INTELLIGENCE QUOTIENT; MEMORY DISTURBANCE; MEMORY LOSS

MEMORY DISTURBANCE
Memory disturbance is different to memory loss (amnesia). In this section causes of abnormal or inappropriate memories are discussed.

Dementia is caused by degeneration of the brain in old age, and is associated with abnormal thought processes, poor memory and hallucinations.

Alzheimer disease (senile dementia or second childhood), is one of the most common forms of dementia in the elderly, and is characterised by loss of recent memory, loss of initiative, reduced physical activity, confusion, loss of orientation (patients become confused about where they are and dates), and then it gradually progresses to loss of speech, difficulty in swallowing (drooling results), stiff muscles, incontinence of both faeces and urine, and a bedridden state in which the patients are totally unaware of themselves or anything that is happening around them. It is caused by a faster than normal loss of nerve cells in the brain.

The female sex hormone, oestrogen, has an effect upon every cell in the body, not just the breast, uterus and other reproductive organs. During and after the menopause, the levels of oestrogen fluctuate irregularly, and then it disappears altogether. A lack of oestrogen will have effects on the brain that include memory disturbances. Hormone replacement therapy can correct the problem.

The organic brain syndrome is a result of severe emotional disturbance (eg. horror, fear) and causes memory disturbances, disorientation, poor logic and behavioural changes. Drug use, epilepsy, cancer outside the head and severe infections may also trigger this syndrome.

Some illegal drugs (eg. heroin, marijuana) and prescribed narcotics and sedatives may affect memory. Long term alcoholism may cause memory disturbances.
See also MEMORY; MEMORY LOSS and separate entries for diseases mentioned above.

MEMORY LOSS

A loss of existing memories (amnesia) may be caused by any injury to the brain such as a blow, stroke (cerebrovascular accident), bleeding blood vessel, tumour, abscess, infection (encephalitis, meningitis), convulsion (eg. due to epilepsy) or cancer. The memory loss may be temporary or permanent.

Other causes include hysteria associated with severe shocks or stress, post-traumatic stress syndrome, a number of psychiatric conditions (eg. fugue states) and a high fever (may result in amnesia for the period of the fever). Exposure to extreme cold (hypothermia) may cause the body's functions to slow dramatically and there may be no memory of a prolonged period (eg. trapped in snow). Dramatic changes to the blood chemistry (eg. low blood sugar and salt levels) may result in the brain malfunctioning and the loss of short term memory.

If the brain is deprived of oxygen for a period (eg. near drowning), it will cease to function properly and all short term memory will be lost.

The brain is surrounded by a supportive fluid (cerebrospinal fluid – CSF), and there are interconnected cavities within the brain that also contain CSF. If there is too much CSF produced, or insufficient is absorbed, the pressure of this fluid in and around the brain will gradually increase (hydrocephalus). The resultant pressure on the brain will affect its function and result in headaches, personality changes, reduced intelligence, memory loss and convulsions.

Alcohol intoxication will result in loss of memory during the time of intoxication. Wernicke's encephalopathy (Korsakoff syndrome) is a permanent form of brain damage caused by a lack of thiamine (vitamin B1) and alcoholism.
See also ALZHEIMER DISEASE; DEMENTIA; MEMORY; MEMORY DISTURBANCE and separate entries for diseases mentioned above.

MENARCHE
See PUBERTY

MÉNIÈRE'S DISEASE

Ménière's disease is a syndrome causing dizziness, deafness and a constant noise in the ears.

The inner ear contains both the hearing and balance mechanisms. The latter consists of three tiny semicircular canals full of fluid. The exact cause of the disease is unknown, but there is a buildup of pressure inside the hearing and balance mechanisms, and it may occur after a head injury or ear infection. It is more common in men and with advancing age, but avoiding prolonged episodes of loud noise (eg. jet engines, rock bands) reduces the incidence.

The most distressing symptom is a constant high-pitched ringing noise (tinnitus) in the ear. Patients also have attacks of dizziness and nausea that come and go for no apparent reason, and a slowly progressive and permanent deafness. Other symptoms may include sweating, nausea and vomiting. There are no specific tests that can diagnose the disease.

Numerous medications may be tried including betahistine (increases the blood supply to the inner ear), antihistamines, diuretics, prochlorperazine, amitriptyline and chlorpromazine, but none have more than a

fifty-fifty chance of success. A tinnitus masker is a hearing-aid device that emits a constant tone that counteracts the noise already heard in the ear. Microsurgical techniques involve draining the high-pressure fluid from the affected parts of the inner ear, or as a last resort destroying the auditory nerve, leaving the patient deaf in that ear but without the distressing buzz saw noise. There is no cure and treatment is not very satisfactory, but some cases settle spontaneously.
See also BENIGN PAROXYSMAL POSITIONAL VERTIGO; DEAF; DIZZINESS; NAUSEA AND VOMITING; VASODILATORS

MENINGES
The brain and spinal cord are surrounded, supported and protected by three layers of fibrous connective tissue known as the meninges. These are called, from the outside to the inside, the dura mater, arachnoid mater and pia mater. The cerebrospinal fluid circulates in the space between the arachnoid and pia mater. An infection or inflammation of the meninges is known as meningitis.
See also BRAIN; MENINGITIS; MENINGOCOCCAL MENIGITIS

MENINGIOMA
A meningioma is a slowly progressive, mildly malignant cancer of the meninges, the membranes that surround and support the brain. The cause is unknown, but they are more common in women and older people and often grow to a large size before symptoms develop. The tumour compresses the brain, causing symptoms that relate to the part of the brain compressed. For example, if the area of the brain controlling the arm is compressed, the arm may become weak or paralysed. Seizures are common. The tumour can be visualised by CT and MRI scans, but a biopsy is required for definitive diagnosis. Surgical removal of the tumour is the only treatment, and most cases can be cured.
See also BRAIN; MENINGES; NEUROSURGERY

MENINGITIS
Meningitis is a viral (aseptic) or bacterial (septic) infection of the meninges, membranes which wrap all the way around the brain and spinal cord, and act to contain the cerebro-

spinal fluid in which the brain is supported.

The diagnosis of both types of meningitis is confirmed by taking a sample of cerebrospinal fluid from the lower end of the spine (which is an extension of the brain) and examining it under a microscope for the presence of certain cells. The fluid can be cultured to find the responsible bacteria. Blood tests also show abnormalities.

Viral (aseptic) meningitis is a relatively benign condition that may be caught by close contact with someone who has a viral infection, or it may be a complication of diseases such as mumps, glandular fever and Herpes. It causes a fever, headache, nausea and vomiting, tiredness and sometimes muscle weakness or paralysis, and neck stiffness may be present. No specific treatment or prevention available, but bed rest, good nursing, paracetamol, and sometimes medication for vomiting are prescribed. It is rare for there to be any after-effects and patients usually recover in one or two weeks.

Bacterial (septic) meningitis is caught from people who are carriers of the bacteria, but the victims are usually weak, ill, under stress or have their ability to resist infection reduced in some way. The most common form of bacterial meningitis is caused by *Haemophilus influenzae B* (HiB), while the most serious is meningococcal meningitis (caused by *Neisseria meningitidis*). It is a much more serious condition, with the severity and symptoms varying depending upon which type of bacteria is responsible. Common symptoms include severe headaches, vomiting, confusion and high fevers. Patients become delirious, unconscious and may convulse. Neck stiffness is quite obvious, and patients may lie with their neck constantly extended as though they are looking up. Meningococcal meningitis is accompanied by a bruise-like rash on the skin and inside the mouth. Complications include permanent deafness in one or both ears, damage to different parts of the brain, heart or kidney, arthritis and the excess production of cerebrospinal fluid which can put pressure on the brain (hydrocephalus). The worst complication is intravascular coagulation, which involves the blood clotting within the arteries and blocking them.

The treatment of septic meningitis involves antibiotics in high doses, usually by injection or a continuous drip into a vein, and patients always require hospitalisation. Patients can deteriorate very rapidly and most deaths occur within the first twenty four hours. The overall mortality rate is about 20%, although it is higher in children and with the Meningococcal form. Both common causes of bacterial meningitis can be prevented by a vaccine. The HiB vaccine is routine in childhood, but the meningococcal vaccine is an optional extra childhood vaccine or may be given during epidemics to close contacts of victims. Other forms of bacterial and viral meningitis cannot be prevented.

See also BRAIN; HAEMOPHILUS INFLUENZAE B INFECTION; LISTERIOSIS; LYME DISEASE; MENINGES; MENINGOCOCCAL MENIGITIS

MENINGOCELE
See SPINA BIFIDA

MENINGOCOCCAL MENIGITIS
Meningococcal meningitis is an uncommon, serious bacterial infection of the meninges (membranes around the brain) and blood stream (septicaemia). Sporadic outbreaks occur worldwide, usually in winter, but up to 40% of the population carry the responsible bacteria in their nose and throat without any symptoms. Infection is more common in closed communities such as military camps and boarding schools. It affects about one person in every 100 000 every year.

The infection is caused by the bacteria *Neisseria meningitidis*, which occurs in five common strains (forms), and several dozen uncommon strains. It is spread by sputum and phlegm in coughs and sneezes.

Symptoms include a high fever, severe headache, vomiting, neck and back stiffness, limb pains, confusion, convulsions and a rapidly spreading bruise-like rash that starts on the arms and legs. In terminal stages the patient becomes delirious, and goes into a coma. Rarely, abscesses may form in the brain, and pneumonia may develop.

Cultures of blood and/or spinal fluid from the lower back can confirm the presence of the responsible bacteria. Penicillin, or more potent antibiotics, is given by injection as soon as the diagnosis is suspected. The patient should be admitted to hospital for confirmation of the diagnosis, and continuation of antibiotics given through a drip into a vein. Life support in an intensive care unit may be necessary. The infection may be rapidly progressive causing death within hours, but overall 80% to 90% of all cases survive, with only 5% of survivors developing long term consequences such as epilepsy.

A vaccine is available against a couple of strains of the bacteria, and can be given to infants, but is not part of the routine vaccination schedule.

See also MENINGES; MENINGITIS; WATERHOUSE-FRIDERICHSEN SYNDROME

MENINGOMYELOCELE
See SPINA BIFIDA

MENISCUS TEAR
See KNEE MENISCUS TEAR

MENOPAUSE
Mothers teach their daughters all about periods and procreation, but nobody teaches them about what happens when it all stops. Menopause (called the climacteric in the old days) has only been a fact of life for most women in the last century or two. Prior to this the majority of women did not live long enough to reach menopause, many dying from the complications of childbirth. Once a woman passes her menopause, her ovaries will no longer produce eggs, her monthly periods will cease and no more female hormones will be manufactured. The process usually occurs gradually over several years, between the early forties and the mid-fifties, but it may occur as early as thirty-five or as late as fifty-eight. It is therefore not unusual for a woman to spend more of her life after the menopause (or change of life) than she spends being fertile, but this does not mean that she loses her femininity. Many women treat the end of their periods as a blessing and lead very active lives for many years afterwards (active sexually as well as physically and mentally).

The unpleasant part of the menopause is the change from one stage to another, when the hormones 'go crazy', the headaches and hot flushes take over, and depression occurs. The first sign is usually an irregularity in the frequency and nature of the periods, and their gradual disappearance may be the only symptom in 25% of women. About 50% have other symptoms that cause discomfort, and the remaining 25% go through severe and very distressing symptoms.

The menopause is a natural event, and psychologically most women take it in their stride, as simply another stage of life, but it is wrong to dismiss the unpleasant physical symptoms without seeking medical assistance. Doctors find the biggest problem to be the failure of their patients to tell them exactly what they are feeling and what effects the menopause is having on them. The first step in treating someone with menopausal symptoms is explanation. If they know why something is happening, it often makes the problem more bearable.

The sex hormones are controlled by the brain and released from the ovaries into the bloodstream on regular signals from the pituitary gland, which sits underneath the centre of the brain. Once in the blood, these hormones have an effect on every part of the body, but more particularly the uterus, vagina, breasts and pubic areas. It is these hormones that make the breasts grow in a teenage girl, give the woman regular periods as their levels change during the month, and cause hair to grow in the groin and armpits.

For an unknown reason, once a woman reaches an age somewhere between the early forties and early fifties, the brain breaks rhythm in sending the messages to the ovaries. The signals become irregular – sometimes too strong, at other times too weak. The ovaries respond by putting out the sex hormones in varying levels, and this causes side effects for the owner of those ovaries. The periods become irregular, vary in length and intensity, and may become painful. Other symptoms may include bloating and associated headaches and irritability, as excess fluid collects in the brain, breasts and pelvis; hot flushes when hormone surges rush through the bloodstream after excess amounts are released by the ovaries; abdominal cramps caused by spasms of the uterine muscles; and depression, which can be a reaction to the changes in the body, a fear of ageing or a direct effect of the hormones on the brain.

Menopause cannot be cured, because it is a natural occurrence, but doctors can relieve most of the symptoms. Sex hormone tablets are the mainstay of treatment. They can be taken constantly after the change has finished, but during the menopause they are usually taken cyclically. One hormone (oestrogen) is taken for three weeks per month, and a different one (progestogen) is added in for the last ten to fourteen days. This maintains a near normal hormonal balance, and the woman will keep having periods, while underneath the artificial hormones, her natural menopause is occurring, so that when the tablets are stopped after a year or two the menopausal symptoms will have gone. Hormones may also be given as skin patches, vaginal cream and by injection.

After the menopause, women should continue the hormones for many years to prevent osteoporosis, skin thinning, Alzheimer disease and to slow ageing. Taking combined oestrogen and progestogen hormone replacement for longer than five years slightly increases the risk of breast cancer, although it slightly decreases the risk of some other cancers.

Minor symptoms can be controlled individually. Fluid tablets can help bloating and headaches; other agents can help uterine cramps and heavy bleeding. Depression can be treated with specific medications.

An obvious problem faced by a woman passing through the menopause is when to stop using contraceptives. As a rule of thumb, doctors advise that contraception should be continued for six months after the last period, or for a year if the woman is under fifty. Taking the contraceptive pill may actually mask many of the menopausal symptoms and cause the periods to continue. It may be necessary to use another form of contraception to determine whether the woman has gone through the menopause.

Doctors can also perform blood tests to determine relative hormone levels and tell a woman if she is through the change of life or not. These tests are very difficult to interpret if the woman is taking the contraceptive pill.

Help is available, and there is no need for any woman to suffer as she changes from one stage of her life to another.

See also ANDROPAUSE; HORMONE REPLACEMENT THERAPY; SEX HORMONES

MENOPAUSE, MALE
See ANDROPAUSE

MENORRHAGIA
See MENSTRUAL PERIODS HEAVY

MENTHOL
See LINIMENT

MENSTRUAL PERIOD

Once a month, just after a woman releases the egg (at ovulation) from her ovary, the lining (endometrium) of the womb (uterus) is at its peak to allow the embedding of a fertilised egg.

If pregnancy does not occur, the endometrium starts to deteriorate as the hormones that sustain it in peak condition alter. After a few days, the lining breaks down completely, sloughs off the wall of the uterus, and is washed away by the blood released from the arteries that supplied it – a process known as menstruation. Contractions of the uterus help remove the debris.

After three to five days, the bleeding stops, and a new lining starts to develop ready for the next month's ovulation.

See also MENSTRUAL PERIOD, FAILURE TO START; MENSTRUAL PERIOD, LACK OF; MENSTRUAL PERIODS HEAVY; MENSTRUAL PERIODS PAINFUL; PUBERTY; UTERUS; VAGINAL BLEEDING ABNORMAL

MENSTRUAL PERIODS, FAILURE TO START

Normally, a young woman starts her menstrual periods between eleven and fourteen years of age, but some commence earlier or later, without any subsequent problems. If a girl fails to start her periods by the age of sixteen, investigation is appropriate. If the breasts have not developed, and there is no sign of pubic hair by the age of fourteen, investigation may be commenced earlier.

A number of uncommon medical conditions may be responsible for the problem, which is medically known as primary amenorrhoea.

In some girls, the hymen completely covers the vaginal opening and has no hole, so that menstrual blood accumulates in the vagina with no way to escape. The periods are occurring, but no blood appears.

The hypothalamus is the part of the brain that controls the pituitary gland at the base of the brain. The pituitary gland in turn controls all other glands in the body, including the ovaries. If there is damage to the hypothalamus or pituitary gland from a tumour, cancer, abscess, infection, poor blood supply or other disease, the appropriate signals may not be received by the ovary to activate its production of the sex hormone oestrogen, which is essential for the transformation of a girl into a woman at puberty.

The ovaries may not develop normally in some girls due to a birth defect, or chromosomal abnormalities such as Turner syndrome.

Congenital adrenal hyperplasia (adrenogenital syndrome) affects the adrenal glands

SCHEMATIC REPRESENTATION OF HORMONE CHANGES DURING MENSTRUAL CYCLE

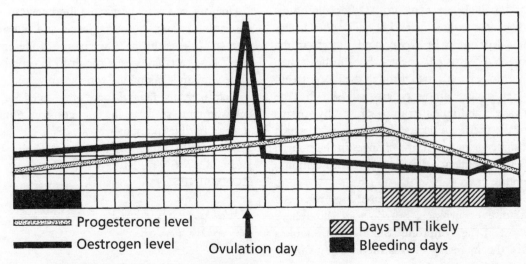

that sit on top of each kidney, and stimulates them to produce abnormal steroids, which affect sexual development.

The ovaries, or very rarely other tissue, may develop tumours that produce inappropriate levels of the male sex hormone testosterone, which blocks the effect of any oestrogen that may be produced.

See also HYMEN; MENSTRUAL PERIODS, LACK OF; PUBERTY DELAYED and separate entries for diseases mentioned above.

MENSTRUAL PERIODS HEAVY

Excessive blood loss during a menstrual period (menorrhagia) is uncomfortable, distressing and may lead to anaemia and other health problems. In most women it is a constitutional problem, meaning there is no specific disease or condition causing the problem, but instead it is merely the way that their body deals with the monthly hormonal changes. In a few cases though, there is an underlying medical problem. This is more likely if the periods have changed to become heavier over a few months.

The menopause occurs in the late forties and early fifties in most women. Instead of cycling smoothly and evenly through the monthly changes, sex hormone (oestrogen and progestogen) levels start to change suddenly, irregularly and inappropriately. This causes the symptoms of menopause, which include irregular menstrual periods that can vary from very light to very heavy, hot flushes, headaches, irritability, personality changes, breast tenderness, tiredness and pelvic discomfort.

Inappropriately high levels of oestrogen being prescribed for hormone replacement therapy may cause heavy periods.

Psychological disturbances (eg. severe stress, shock or anxiety) may affect oestrogen production and irregular heavy periods may follow.

Intrauterine contraceptive devices (IUDs) may irritate the lining of the uterus to cause heavier and more painful periods in some women.

Other causes of menorrhagia include fibroids (hard balls of fibrous tissue that form in the muscular wall of the uterus), cysts in an ovary, ulcers and erosions of the cervix (opening of the uterus into the vagina), endometriosis, a miscarriage (may cause abnormal bleeding before a woman is aware that she is pregnant), an ectopic pregnancy (development of a growing foetus in the fallopian tubes instead of the uterus), salpingitis (infection of the fallopian tubes) and hypothyroidism (an underactive thyroid gland). Tumours, polyps or cancers of the uterus or cervix may cause irregular heavy bleeding that may not be related to the menstrual cycle, but be caused by direct bleeding from the growth.

Uncommon causes include the Stein-Leventhal syndrome (multiple cysts in the ovaries affect their function) and thrombocytopenia.

See also CURETTE; MENSTRUAL PERIODS; MENSTRUAL PERIODS PAINFUL; VAGINAL BLEEDING ABNORMAL and separate entries for diseases mentioned above.

MENSTRUAL PERIOD, LACK OF

Women expect their menstrual periods to occur regularly every month, and become concerned when this does not happen. The obvious causes for periods stopping are pregnancy and menopause, and every woman between fifteen and fifty who misses a period should be considered pregnant until proved otherwise. Breast feeding will delay the return of regular menstrual periods. There are also a number of medical conditions which may be responsible for amenorrhoea (a lack of menstruation) or oligomenorrhoea (infrequent menstruation).

Any significant emotional trauma (eg. loss of job, death in family), physical stress (eg. vigourous athletic training), serious illness (eg. major infection) or poor nutrition (eg. lack of food, vomiting and diarrhoea) can affect the menstrual cycle. This is a very common phenomenon.

Significant weight loss as a result of deliberate dieting, disease (eg. cancer) or psychiatric disturbance (eg. anorexia nervosa) will also stop menstruation.

The oral contraceptive pill may cause menstrual periods to become lighter and lighter until they disappear completely. Some women take the pill constantly, without a monthly break off the pill or taking sugar tablets, and stop their periods for the sake of convenience. This practice is completely safe and causes no long term harm.

Uncommon causes include tumours, cysts or cancer in an ovary that affect the regular cyclical production of oestrogen, a lack of thyroxine (hypothyroidism), Asherman syndrome, Addison's disease and the Stein-Leventhal syndrome.
See also CONTRACEPTIVE PILL; MENSTRUAL PERIODS; MENSTRUAL PERIODS, FAILURE TO START; PREGNANCY and separate entries for diseases mentioned above.

MENSTRUAL PERIODS PAINFUL

In more than eight out of ten cases, there is no serious cause for painful periods (dysmenorrhoea). Although distressing, they are merely the way in which a woman, and her uterus, copes with menstruation.

The uterus mainly consists of powerful muscle fibres, which should only come into use during the delivery of a baby, and to a minor extent when blood and the unused lining of the uterus is expelled in the monthly menstrual period. Period pain is usually caused by excessive spasms of these muscles in the uterus, but sometimes may be due to other medical problems.

During the menopause, the natural sex hormones produced by the ovaries may be produced irregularly and in greater quantities, leading to an increased build up of the uterine lining during the month, or excessive stimulation of the uterine muscles during a period.

An intrauterine contraceptive device (IUD) may irritate the uterus to trigger more powerful contractions than usual.

Salpingitis (infection of the fallopian tubes), often by sexually transmitted diseases, may result in the tubes becoming blocked and painful. Pelvic inflammatory disease is a more widespread infection of the organs within the pelvis. During a period, contractions of the uterus may irritate these infected organs to cause pain.

Endometriosis is a disease in which the cells that normally line the inside of the uterus become displaced, and move through the fallopian tubes to settle around the ovary, in the tubes themselves, or on other organs in the belly. In these abnormal positions they proliferate, and when a menstrual period occurs, they bleed as though they were still in the uterus. This results in pain, adhesions,

damage to the organs they are attached to, and infertility.

Fibroids are hard balls of fibrous tissue that form in the muscular wall of the uterus, often after pregnancy. They can distort the shape of the uterus to cause pain when the uterus contracts during a period or orgasm.

The uterus is normally bent forwards at about 60° to the vagina. In some women, the uterus is straighter, or bent backwards (retroverted). These women seem to suffer from more painful periods.

Other causes of dysmenorrhoea include a prolapse of the uterus (uterus slips down into the vagina), pelvic congestion syndrome (veins in the pelvis become dilated), narrowing of the cervix after surgery, adhesions and tumours, or polyps or cancers of the uterus or surrounding organs.
See also CERVIX; INTRAUTERINE DEVICE; MENSTRUAL PERIODS; UTERUS and separate entries for diseases mentioned above.

MENSTRUATION
See MENSTRUAL PERIOD; PUBERTY

MENTAL RETARDATION

Mental retardation is an inability to function mentally at a level compatible with living independently in the community. It may be present from infancy, or may develop later in life, and may be genetic (present since conception), or due to brain injury or environmental, metabolic (body chemistry) or psychological causes.

Be warned that deafness and partial or complete blindness may mimic mental retardation.

Any injury to the brain, from a blow, tumour, abscess, cancer, stroke (cerebrovascular accident), bleeding blood vessel or repeated convulsions (status epilepticus) may result in mental retardation.

Mental retardation may also be caused by birth injury, when the head is compressed for a prolonged period in the birth canal (vagina), a sudden release of pressure at the moment of birth resulting in bleeding into the brain, premature separation of the placenta (which supplies all oxygen and nutrition to the baby) from the wall of the womb (uterus), or compression of the umbilical cord for a long time to reduce the flow of blood and oxygen to the baby.

Cerebral palsy (spasticity) is a form of brain damage that occurs during the pregnancy, usually for no obvious reason. A poorly functioning placenta, and a foetus that has its nutrition taken by its twin, are possibilities.

If too much cerebrospinal fluid (the fluid around the brain) is produced, or insufficient is absorbed, the pressure of this fluid in and around the brain will gradually increase (hydrocephalus). The resultant pressure on the brain will affect its function and result in headaches, reduced intelligence, personality changes, memory loss and convulsions. In babies, the head will enlarge dramatically unless the excess fluid is drained.

Hundreds of different rare syndromes are known to cause mental retardation. Some of these are inherited (passed from one generation to the next) while others are the result of the faulty joining of chromosomes at the moment of conception when an egg (ova) and sperm fuse. Some of the more common examples include: –

• Down syndrome (mongolism) which is due to the presence of three copies of chromosome 21 instead of two. Other features are flattened facial features, short stature, low set ears, thick tongue, broad hands with only a single transverse crease and slanted eyes. It occurs more commonly in children of older mothers.

• The fragile X syndrome is believed to cause a quarter of the mental retardation in males. All men have only one X chromosome paired with a Y chromosome. Females, who have two X chromosomes, may be carriers from one generation to the next. The X and Y chromosomes determine the sex of every individual. Other symptoms include overactivity, epilepsy, large build, large jaw and testes, and short sightedness.

• Klinefelter syndrome also only affects males. They have additional X chromosomes matched with a single Y chromosome. Their genetic make up is therefore XXY or XXXY instead of the normal XY. Other features are delayed puberty, tall slim build, emotional disturbances and underdeveloped genitalia.

• Savants (idiot savant syndrome) have extraordinary talents in one narrow area (eg. music, maths), but are otherwise subnormal. It may be due to overdevelopment of one area of the brain at the expense of others.

Rarer syndromes that may be responsible for mental retardation include Niemann-Pick disease (excess storage of certain fats), Gaucher disease (fat storage disorder), galactosaemia (a disturbance of the breakdown of the sugar galactose in milk), Rubenstein-Taybi syndrome, tuberous sclerosis (red nodules on the face, deformed nails and eye damage), Prader-Willi syndrome (small at birth, have poor muscle tone, eat compulsively to become obese and have small genitals), Angelman syndrome (abnormal walk, convulsions, inappropriate laughter and abnormal facial appearance), Coffin-Lowry syndrome (males with prominent lips, coarse facial features, slanted eyes and curved back), cri-du-chat (cat cry) syndrome, Dubowitz syndrome (droopy eyelids), de Lange syndrome (dwarfism) and Sturge-Weber syndrome (dark red birth mark on the face, convulsions, paralysis of one side of the body and eye abnormalities).

Various toxins and infections may adversely affect the brain and its mental capacity. Examples include foetal alcohol syndrome (caused by the mother drinking excessive amounts of alcohol during pregnancy), lead or copper poisoning, and overdoses of prescribed drugs or addiction to illegal drugs (eg. amphetamines, cocaine).

Infections of a pregnant woman may affect her unborn child. Examples include German measles (rubella), toxoplasmosis (caught from cats), cytomegalovirus (CMV, which is usually harmless to adults) and syphilis (a sexually transmitted bacteria).

Disturbances to the body's chemistry may also damage the brain and prevent it from functioning to its full potential. Examples of conditions that can cause this are phenylketonuria (PKU), malnutrition and untreated or poorly controlled diabetes mellitus.

Psychological conditions may also be responsible for mental retardation. Examples include autism, psychoses, and isolation and stimulus deprivation of a child.
See also BRAIN; INTELLIGENCE QUOTIENT and separate entries for diseases mentioned above.

MEPROBOMATE
See ANXIOLYTICS

MERCAPTOPURINE
See CYTOTOXICS AND ANTINEOPLASTICS

MERCURY POISONING

Mercury poisoning (Minamata or pink disease) can be caused by swallowing mercury or mercury-containing compounds or inhaling mercury vapour. Mercury is used in industry in thermometers, batteries, thermostats, dental fillings and chemical processing. Contamination of the food chain (particularly fish) from mercury-containing industrial wastes may lead to poisoning in humans, and a serious series of poisonings occurred in Minamata, Japan by this route. Mercury used to be present in medications such as teething powders until the 1950s.

If a large amount of mercury is swallowed at one time symptoms include a metallic taste, thirst, burning in the throat, excessive saliva formation, belly pain, vomiting, bloody diarrhoea, collapse and kidney failure. Inhaling mercury vapour can cause an intractable form of pneumonia. Chronic mercury poisoning, in which small amounts of mercury are swallowed over a long period of time, causes 'pink disease' with red and swollen hands and feet, irritability, fever, hair loss and damaged nails. Later problems include tremor, convulsions, brain damage and death. Mercury may cause birth defects in the children of mothers with chronic lead poisoning (Minamata disease).

The presence of mercury can be detected by specific blood tests.

If mercury is swallowed, induce vomiting, give egg whites and milk, then take the patient to hospital for stomach wash out. Mercury can also slowly be removed from the body by some medications in a process known as chelation.
See also CHELATION; KIDNEY FAILURE, ACUTE; LEAD POISONING

MESCALINE

Mescaline is a naturally occurring psychedelic drug found in several types of cactus species, but most commonly the Peyote and San Pedro cacti, which also contain a large variety of related psychoactive compounds. Mescaline belongs to a family of compounds known as phenethylamines, making it quite distinct from the other major psychedelics such as LSD, but the synthetic psychedelic ecstasy is also a phenethylamine.

In prehistoric times peyote was used throughout central and South America in various rituals.

Mescaline was first extracted from cacti in 1896. From 1919 it was used by psychiatrists, but in 1953 the popular novelist Aldous Huxley brought it to the attention of the public. Today, natives throughout America still perform sacred Peyote rituals that purportedly put one in touch with supernatural and divinatory powers.

In the most countries Peyote and mescaline are illegal, but in the USA members of the Native American Church are permitted to use it. It causes relaxation, an intensity of senses and hallucinations lasting six to eighteen hours, but stomach discomfort is a common side effect of mescaline use, and the cacti are difficult to eat without processing.
See also COCAINE; ECSTASY; GAMMA-HYDROXYBUTYRATE; HEROIN; KETAMINE; LSD; MARIJUANA; STIMULANTS

MESENTERIC ADENITIS

The mesentery is a thin membrane which connects the small intestine within the abdomen to the back wall of the abdomen and contains the arteries, veins and nerves that supply the intestine. Scattered through the mesentery are numerous lymph nodes that may become infected or inflamed to cause mesenteric adenitis.

It is almost invariably caused by a viral infection that is far more common in children than adults, and is often preceded by another infection such as a bad cold or bronchitis. The symptoms are identical to those of appendicitis, and many patients at operation for acute appendicitis are found to have mesenteric adenitis. Blood tests are unable to differentiate between the two diseases, as an infected appendix causes the same changes in the blood as infected lymph nodes. Both cause severe abdominal pain, nausea, diarrhoea and fever.

No specific treatment is available and symptoms usually settle without treatment after five to ten days.
See also ABDOMINAL PAIN; ADENITIS; LYMPHATIC SYSTEM

MESENTERIC ARTERY THROMBOSIS

A mesenteric artery thrombosis causes a reduction in the blood supply to the small intestine, which is loosely attached to the back wall of the belly by a fine membrane (the mesentery) which contains the two mesenteric arteries. If one of the mesenteric arteries is partially blocked by a plaque of cholesterol, a blood clot (thrombosis) or pressure from another organ or adhesion, the small intestine will not receive sufficient blood to function properly.

After a meal the patient experiences belly pain and aches that vary with the size of the meal, and so they eat very small infrequent meals, and lose weight. When an artery becomes completely blocked, severe belly pain and tenderness occurs, the patient will collapse and the intestine supplied by the thrombosed artery may become gangrenous. X-rays of the abdomen will show abnormal bowel patterns.

This is a surgical emergency, as the blocked artery must be cleared and the affected intestine removed as quickly as possible. The prognosis depends on the severity of bowel damage at time of surgery, but even in good hospitals there is significant mortality.
See also THROMBOSIS

MESOTHELIOMA
Mesothelioma is a serious form of lung cancer caused by inhalation of asbestos fibres, smoking, or the long term inhalation of other irritants (eg. talc dust, coal dust). Up to 7% of patients with asbestosis develop mesothelioma, but half the time it occurs in non-asbestosis sufferers. The average age of onset is sixty and the latent period between exposure to asbestos and development of mesothelioma can be up to forty years. It has a very insidious onset, with symptoms little different to asbestosis itself.

X-ray changes may not be apparent until the disease is quite advanced, and CT scans are more useful in making the diagnosis in suspicious cases. A biopsy of the cancerous area is the only way to make a definite diagnosis.

Treatment with surgery, drugs and radiation has been tried, but with virtually no success as the cancer is extremely virulent and spreads rapidly. Three quarters of victims die within a year of the diagnosis, and 98% within two years.
See also ASBESTOSIS; LUNG CANCER

MESTEROLONE
See SEX HORMONES

MESTRANOL
See CONTRACEPTIVE PILL

METABOLISM
Metabolism is a chemical process that breaks large molecules into smaller ones and in the process releases the energy necessary for all forms of life. The process occurs in every cell of the body, but primarily in the liver.

METASTATIC CANCER
Metastatic or secondary cancer occurs with the spread of cancer from one organ to another, often to lymph nodes, the liver (hepatic metastases), bone or lungs. Cancer can eat into a blood vessel or lymph channel and spread to distant parts of the body, but localised spread is also possible.

The symptoms depend upon the usual function of the affected organ. Nausea, weight loss, loss of appetite and general tiredness are symptoms of most forms of cancer that occur in addition to the symptoms caused by the failure of the affected organ.

Detecting a metastatic deposit of cancer may be difficult, and blood tests, x-rays, ultrasound, CT and MRI scans are used in the search. Treatment depends on the site of cancer deposits, and may involve surgery, anticancer drugs and irradiation. Metastases usually indicate a worsening of the primary cancer and a greater difficulty in treatment.
See also CANCER

METATARSAL FRACTURE
See MARCH FRACTURE

METATARSALGIA
Metatarsalgia is an inflammation of one or more of the long bones in the front half of the foot (metatarsals). It may be caused by a stress fracture (march fracture), by inflammation of one of the nerves that run beside the metatarsal bone (Morton's metatarsalgia), or by flattening and thinning of the forefoot fat pad and transverse arch that protects the foot bones when walking or running.

The cause is usually running or jogging on hard surfaces and in poor footwear, but an unusually long walk or climb may also trigger an attack, while Morton's metatarsalgia is more common in middle-aged women. Patients experience varying degrees of pain in the ball of the foot, or in the front half of the foot beside the ball. Every step may be painful, running excruciating, and patients often adopt an unusual way of walking by taking the weight on their heels or one side of the foot. Knee, hip and back pain may develop from the unusual walking pattern (gait).

Morton's metatarsalgia is treated by inserting a shock absorbing insole into the shoes, taking anti-inflammatory medications, steroid injections around the nerve, or in severe cases having an operation to remove the damaged section of nerve.

Damage to the forefoot arch and fat pad requires physiotherapy to strengthen the small muscles within the foot, sponge rubber insoles and anti-inflammatory medications to give relief from persistent pain.
See also FOOT; MARCH FRACTURE

METFORMIN
See HYPOGLYCAEMICS

METHICILLIN RESISTANT *STAPHYLOCOCCUS AUREUS*
See STAPHYLOCOCCUS AUREUS

METHOTREXATE
See CYTOTOXICS AND ANTINEOPLASTICS

METHOXYPHENAMINE
See EXPECTORANTS

METHYCLOTHIAZIDE
See DIURETICS

METHYLDOPA
Methyldopa (Aldomet) is an old fashioned medication used in the treatment of high blood pressure (hypertension). It may still be used today in patients in whom more sophisticated medications are inappropriate. It is inconvenient as it must be taken three or four times a day. It is safe in pregnancy and children, but side effects may include fever, sedation and headache.
See also HYPERTENSION; MEDICATION

METHYLPHENIDATE
See STIMULANTS

METOCLOPRAMIDE
See ANTIEMETICS

METRONIDAZOLE
See ANTIANAEROBES

MEXILETINE
See ANTIARRHYTHMICS

Mg
See MAGNESIUM

MI
See HEART ATTACK

MICONAZOLE
See ANTIFUNGALS

MICROCEPHALY
See HEAD SMALL

MICROSPORUM
See FUNGI; ONYCHOGRYPHOSIS; TINEA CAPITIS; TINEA CORPORIS; TINEA CRURIS

MICROWAVE ENDOMETRIAL ABLATION
An alternative to hysterectomy in some circumstances (eg. heavy bleeding) is microwave endometrial ablation. Investigations by ultrasound scans and/or hysteroscopy will be performed before the procedure is considered.

In this simple procedure, the patient is given a general anaesthetic, and the cervix is dilated to allow a small instrument to be introduced into the uterus. At the end of this probe is a rolling ball, through which an electrical current is passed. The ball is moved around the inside of the uterus and the electrical current permanently destroys the lining of the womb, which is normally responsible for nurturing a growing foetus in pregnancy, or a woman's monthly periods at other times. The woman can usually go home the same day, and can return to work in two or three days.

The procedure may not totally remove a woman's symptoms, and up to a quarter of patients need to go on to have a full hysterectomy at a later date.
See also HYSTERECTOMY; HYSTEROSCOPY; UTERUS

MICTURITION
Micturition is the medical term for the passing of urine through the urethra to the outside of the body.

See also BLADDER; URETHRA;
URINATION FREQUENT; URINE

MIDDLE EAR EFFUSION
See GLUE EAR

MIDDLE EAR INFECTION
See OTITIS MEDIA

MIGRAINE
Migraine is a form of headache that is usually associated with other significant symptoms. They may occur once in a person's life, or three times a week; may cause a relatively mild head pain, or may totally disable the patient.

They are caused by the contraction of an artery in the brain, which may give the patient an unusual sensation and warning of an attack (aura), followed within a few seconds or minutes by an over-dilation of the artery. Excess blood passes to the part of the brain that the artery supplies and it is unable to function properly. The patient feels intense pressure, pain and other symptoms. The artery dilation may occur for no apparent reason, or be triggered by certain foods, anxiety and stress, hormonal changes, allergies, loud noises or flashing lights. The frequency and severity of migraines tends to decrease with age and an initial attack over the age of forty is unusual. They may cease in old age.

The effects vary dramatically from one patient to another, depending on the part of the brain involved. As well as intense head pain, most patients suffer nausea and vomiting and loud noises or bright lights aggravate the pain. Other symptoms may include partial blindness, personality changes, loss of hearing, noises in the ears, paralysis, numbness, and violence. Migraines are rarely serious, but patients may be disabled for some hours or days.

There are no specific diagnostic tests, but doctors can sometimes diagnose a migraine by their description of a visual pattern. If the patient closes their eyes, s/he can see patterns on the back of the eyelids which are actually the random activity of the nerves in the light sensitive retina at the back of the eye and in the visual centre of the brain. In normal people, a swirling smooth pattern will be seen, but a patient with a migraine will see flashes of light, bright colours and jagged patterns.

Migraines may be prevented by regular medication, or treated each time they occur.

Many different drugs can be taken regularly to prevent migraines including propranolol, methysergide, clonidine, sodium valproate, ketoprofen and pizotifen. It is often a matter of trial and error to find the most effective one.

The longer a migraine has been present, the more difficult it is to treat. They can be rapidly cured in most patients by nose sprays, tablets or injections containing naratriptan, sumatriptan or zolmitriptan. The more often these medications are used, the more effective they become. Other treatments include tablets which may be placed under the tongue or swallowed (eg. ergotamine), or normal painkillers (eg. paracetamol, aspirin), antihistamines, mild sedatives and anti-vomiting medications (eg. promethazine). Strong narcotic painkillers should be avoided if possible. Resting in a cool, dark room is also helpful.

Most cases can be prevented or effectively treated, but a small number are resistant to all medications.
See also BETA-BLOCKERS; CLUSTER HEADACHE; ERGOTAMINES; 5HT RECEPTOR AGONISTS; HEADACHE; NONSTEROIDAL ANTI-INFLAMMATORIES

MILESTONES OF DEVELOPMENT
See BABIES; CHILDREN; TALKING; TOILET TRAINING

MILIA
Milia (keratin cysts) is a problem of excess keratin (scale) production by oil glands in the skin, commonly in areas of skin damage. Tiny, firm, creamy lumps (papules) appear on the skin, usually of the face. They can be removed for cosmetic reasons by piercing with a needle or cryosurgery (freezing). They persist long term unless removed.
See also SKIN LUMPS

MILK INADEQUATE
See BREAST FEEDING FAILURE

MINAMATA DISEASE
See MERCURY POISONING

MINERALS
Minerals are inorganic substances (i.e. not vegetable or animal in origin) that are necessary

for the normal functioning of the body. The common ones found in the body are calcium, sodium, fluoride, iodine, magnesium, phosphorus, potassium and zinc, but many others are also present in extraordinarily tiny quantities (eg. aluminium, copper). The medical uses of these minerals are detailed below.

Calcium is used to treat and prevent osteoporosis and rarely osteomalacia. Side effects include constipation, flushing and sweats. It should not be used in kidney disease.

Fluoride is used to prevent tooth decay, and treat osteoporosis, Paget's disease and multiple myeloma. Side effects are minimal, but it should not be used in kidney disease.

Iodine is used to treat goitre, and specific iodine deficiency. Side effects are minimal.

Iron treats some types of anaemia and any specific iron deficiency. Stomach upsets may be a side effect, and it should not be used in haemochromatosis.

Magnesium can be used to replace specific deficiencies. Side effects are minimal.

Phosphorus is used in hyperparathyroidism, bone cancer, rickets and multiple myeloma. Diarrhoea is the usual side effect.

Potassium is used to replace electrolyte deficiencies, particularly in patients using diuretics. It should be used with care in kidney and liver disease.

Zinc may help acne, and dries secretions. It should be used with care in pregnancy, and may cause constipation.
See also CALCIUM; FLUORIDATION; IODINE; MAGNESIUM; PHOSPHORUS; POTASSIUM; SODIUM; VITAMINS; ZINC

MINI CONTRACEPTIVE PILL
See CONTRACEPTIVE PILL

MINIPRESS
See ALPHA BLOCKERS

MINOCYCLINE
See TETRACYCLINES

MIOSIS
See PUPIL SMALL

MIOTICS
Miotics are medications used as eye drops, which cause contraction of the pupil in the centre of the eye. Examples include pilocarpine, carbachol and acetylcholine. They are not designed for long term use and may cause blurred vision.
See also MYDRIATICS; PUPIL SMALL

MISCARRIAGE
A miscarriage (spontaneous abortion) is always most upsetting to the parents, particularly if the woman has had difficulty in falling pregnant in the first place. A miscarriage usually starts with a slight vaginal bleed, then period-type cramps low in the abdomen. The bleeding becomes heavier and eventually, clots and tissue may pass.

A miscarriage occurs when a pregnancy fails to progress, due to the death of the foetus or a developmental abnormality in the foetus or placenta.

If the baby is lost before twenty weeks, it is considered to be a miscarriage. After twenty weeks, doctors consider it to be a premature birth, although the chances of the baby surviving if born before twenty eight weeks are slim. Most miscarriages occur in the first twelve weeks of pregnancy and many occur so early that the woman may not even know that she has been pregnant and may dismiss the problem as an abnormal period.

In more than half the cases, the miscarriage occurs because there is no baby developing. What develops in the womb can be considered to be just a placenta, without the presence of a foetus (a blighted ovum is the technical term). There is obviously no point in continuing with this type of pregnancy, and the body rejects the growth in a miscarriage.

Some women do not secrete sufficient hormones from their ovaries to sustain a pregnancy, and this can also result in a miscarriage. These women can be given additional hormones in subsequent pregnancies to prevent a recurrence of the problem.

Malformations of the womb are another, though rarer, cause. This problem may be surgically corrected to prevent the cervix from opening prematurely, or to remove fibrous growths that may be distorting the womb.

There are dozens of other reasons for a miscarriage, including stress (both mental and physical), other diseases of the mother (eg. diabetes, infections), injuries, and drugs taken in early pregnancy. Each case has to be considered individually.

Miscarriages are far more common than

most women realise. Up to 15% of diagnosed pregnancies, and possibly 50% percent of all pregnancies, fail to reach twenty weeks. There is virtually no treatment for a threatened miscarriage except strict rest, sedatives and pain relievers. If the body has decided to reject the foetus, medical science is normally helpless to prevent it.

Once a miscarriage is inevitable, doctors usually perform a simple operation to clean out the womb, and ready it as soon as possible for the next pregnancy.

The most common complications are infections in the uterus, heavy bleeding that may lead to anaemia, and the retention of some tissue in the uterus. Retained tissue may make it difficult for a further pregnancy to occur.

In most cases, there is no reason why a subsequent pregnancy should not be successful. It is only if a woman has two miscarriages in succession that doctors judge it is helpful to investigate the situation further.
See also CURETTE; PREGNANCY; VAGINAL BLEEDING ABNORMAL

MITOCHONDRIA
See CELL

MITRAL VALVE
The very strong valve between the left atrium and left ventricle in the heart. It is made of two cusps (halves) that resemble a mitre – the hat worn by a bishop. When the atrium, which receives oxygenated blood from the lungs, contracts, the valve opens to allow the blood into the largest and strongest chamber of the heart, the left ventricle.

When the left ventricle contracts to pump blood through the aortic valve and into the aorta, the mitral valve closes to prevent regurgitation of blood back into the left atrium.

If formed incorrectly at birth, or damaged later in life, it may be surgically repaired or replaced.
See also AORTIC VALVE; HEART; MITRAL VALVE INCOMPETENCE; MITRAL VALVE STENOSIS

MITRAL VALVE INCOMPETENCE
A leak of the mitral valve between the upper and lower chambers on the left side of the heart is called incompetence. The valve receives its name because its two halves resemble a bishop's mitre. The leak may be caused by rheumatic fever, endocarditis, heart tumours (eg. myxoma) or Marfan syndrome. When the large left ventricle (lower heart chamber) contracts, blood is forced not only into the aorta (where it should go) but back through the damaged valve and up into the smaller left atrium (upper heart chamber) from where it has just come. This puts pressure back into the lungs and patients develop shortness of breath and abnormal fatigue. An irregular heartbeat, lung failure and infections of the damaged valve are possible complications.

It is diagnosed by echocardiography (ultrasound scan) or passing a catheter through an artery into the heart.

Patients with only minimal symptoms require no treatment, but if complications or progressive symptoms develop, surgical repair or replacement of the valve is necessary, and has very good results.
See also ENDOCARDITIS; HEART; MARFAN SYNDROME; MITRAL VALVE; MITRAL VALVE STENOSIS; MYXOMA; RHEUMATIC FEVER;

MITRAL VALVE STENOSIS
A narrowing of the mitral valve between the upper and lower chambers on the left side of the heart is called a stenosis. Rheumatic fever is the cause in most patients, but this is becoming a rare disease in developed countries. The symptoms include shortness of breath, tiredness, an irregular heartbeat (caused by atrial fibrillation), coughing of blood, and cor pulmonale. The most significant complication is an embolism (blood clot) that may cause a stroke or death if it travels through arteries to the brain.

The stenosis is diagnosed by echocardiography (ultrasound scan) or passing a catheter through an artery into the heart. Patients with only minimal symptoms require no treatment, but if complications or progressive symptoms develop, medications to control heart rate and surgical repair or replacement of the valve are necessary. Anticoagulants (eg. warfarin) are given to prevent emboli. Very good results are obtained by surgery, but the irregular heart rate may be difficult to control.
See also ATRIAL FIBRILLATION; COR PULMONALE; ECHOCARDIOGRAPHY; HEART; MITRAL VALVE; MITRAL VALVE INCOMPETENCE

MITTE

The prescription notation 'mitte' is derived from the Latin word for 'send' which means 'dispense' and refers to the number of tablets, or amount of cream etc. to be dispensed.
See also PRESCRIPTION NOTATIONS

MITTELSHMERZ

Mittelschmerz ('middle pain' in German – i.e. pain in the middle of the menstrual cycle) is pain associated with ovulation (release of an egg from the ovary) that occurs in about 20% of women. Halfway between menstrual periods, the woman feels a sudden sharp pain occurring on one side or other of the lower belly that lasts from a few minutes to a couple of hours. Sometimes it is associated with a small vaginal bleed, which is light and brief. No treatment is normally necessary, but simple pain relievers may be used, and the contraceptive pill will prevent ovulation and thus the pain.
See also OVARIAN CYST; OVULATION

MIXED PAROTID TUMOUR

See PAROTID TUMOUR

MOBILISATION

See MANIPULATION

MO'CLOBEMIDE

See ANTIDEPRESSANTS

MOGADON

See SEDATIVES

MOLE

A mole (melanocytic naevus) is a very common skin mark that is completely harmless. Moles may be a family characteristic. They start in childhood and the numbers increase steadily with age and sun exposure. They often increase dramatically during puberty and pregnancy. They appear as brown, black or even pink, flat or slightly raised, evenly coloured spots on the skin that may have hair growing from them. Moles may sometimes fade and disappear with age.

A biopsy may be taken if there is any doubt about the diagnosis, but no treatment is normally necessary, although if they are unsightly or annoying they may be removed by shaving off or excision under local anaesthetic. Very rarely they may become a skin cancer, but a mole has no greater chance of becoming a skin cancer than any other area of skin.
See also BROWN PATCHES ON SKIN; SKIN LUMPS

MOLE, INVASIVE UTERINE

See UTERINE MOLE

MOLLUSCUM CONTAGIOSUM

Molluscum contagiosum is a mild contagious viral skin infection spread from one person to another by close contact. If the blisters occur on the genitals, it has probably been caught by sexual contact. Multiple small (2-4mm.), dome-shaped, white blisters with a central dimple appear on scattered parts of their body. The abdomen, chest and face are the most commonly affected areas.

No treatment is normally required, but unsightly or persistent blisters can be removed by a doctor scraping out their contents or heating them with an electrical cautery needle. Secondary bacterial infection of a scratched blister can occur. The rash disappears spontaneously after three to twelve months.
See also SKIN NODULES

MOMETASONE

See STEROIDS

MONGOLISM

See DOWN SYNDROME

MONGOLOIDS

See RACE

MONILIASIS

See THRUSH

MONOAMINE OXIDASE INHIBITORS

See ANTIDEPRESSANTS

MONONUCLEOSIS, INFECTIOUS

See GLANDULAR FEVER

MONTEGGIA FRACTURE

A Monteggia fracture is a particularly nasty fracture of the shaft or upper end of the ulna bone associated with a dislocation of the upper end of the radius bone at the elbow joint. The radius and ulna are the two bones in the forearm. The usual cause is a heavy fall onto the arm resulting in severe inwards twisting of the forearm.

Patients have significant pain in the elbow and forearm, inability to use the elbow and distortion of the forearm.

It requires accurate reduction of the dislocation and fracture into correct position under a general anaesthetic, followed by keeping the forearm and elbow in plaster for eight to twelve weeks. If the dislocation and fracture cannot be adequately corrected by manipulation, an open operation may be required. Inadequate treatment will result in some permanent loss of movement in the elbow.
See also ELBOW; FRACTURE

MOOD
See DEPRESSION; MANIA

MORBIDITY
Morbidity is a term used in statistical analyses to indicate sickness or poor health, the rate of sickness and ill health, or the prevalence of a disease in a particular area.
See also MORTALITY

MORBILLI
See MEASLES

MORNING-AFTER PILL
The morning-after pill is a short course of a high dose of sex hormones (often an oral contraceptive) which must be taken within seventy two hours of sexual intercourse. There are two main methods: –
• High dose of a progestogen only pill (levonorgestrel – Postinor).
• Yutzpe method, which involves taking a high dose combined oestrogen and progestogen contraceptive pill.

Two doses are taken twelve hours apart and the Yutzpe method is given with a second medication to prevent vomiting, which is the most common side effect. Some women also experience breast tenderness, dizziness and headaches, but these symptoms usually go away without any treatment.

The progestogen method is more effective than the Yutzpe method, with a 95% success rate for the former and 82% for the latter if the pills are started within twenty-four hours of sex. The success rate is only 58% for the progestogen method at seventy-two hours.

The morning-after pill prevents pregnancy in one of two ways – by preventing ovulation, or by preventing implantation of the fertilised egg in the womb, depending on when it is taken. It can be used after unprotected sex at the woman's fertile period, in cases of condom or diaphragm misuse or mishap, and is also used in cases of rape.

An abnormal, light period may come a couple of days after taking the morning-after pill, or it may be on time or delayed. The woman must use some other form of contraception until she has had her next normal period, as she is still at risk of pregnancy.

The morning-after pill should not be used as ongoing contraception and it should not be used more than once a month. Regular contraceptive methods should be discussed with a doctor or family planning clinic.
See also CONTRACEPTIVE PILL

MORNING SICKNESS
The nausea and vomiting that affects some pregnant women between the sixth and fourteenth weeks of pregnancy is called morning sickness, but it can occur at any time of the day. Its severity varies markedly, with about one third of pregnant women having no morning sickness, one half having it badly enough to vomit at least once, and in 5% the condition is serious enough result in prolonged bed rest or even hospitalisation, when it is called hyperemesis gravidarum.

Morning sickness is caused by the unusually high levels of oestrogen present in the mother's bloodstream during the first three months of pregnancy. Although it usually ceases after about three months, it may persist for far longer in some unlucky women. It is usually worse in the first pregnancy and with twins.

Because morning sickness is a self-limiting condition, treatment is usually given only when absolutely necessary. A light diet, with small, frequent meals of dry fat-free foods, is often helpful. A concentrated carbohydrate solution (Emetrol) may be taken to help relieve the nausea. Only in severe cases, and with some reluctance, will doctors prescribe more potent medications. In rare cases, fluids given by a drip into a vein are necessary for a woman hospitalised because of continued vomiting.

Morning sickness has no effect upon the development of the baby.
See also NAUSEA AND VOMITING; PREGNANCY

MORPHINE
See also NARCOTICS

MORTALITY
Derived from the Latin word for death, the term mortality is used in statistical analyses to indicate death, or a rate of death. For example, plague has a high mortality rate.
See also DEATH; MORBIDITY

MORTON'S METATARSALGIA
See METATARSALGIA

MOTION SICKNESS
Nausea and vomiting associated with any form of transport is caused by the same combination of factors. The main problem is that the two senses we use to balance – the eyes and the balance mechanism in the inner ears – do not synchronise. On a ship, the deck appears to be level, but we sense motion; in an aircraft, the interior of the plane appears to be horizontal, but the aircraft may be climbing steeply. Reconciling these conflicting sensations from our eyes and balance mechanism helps to overcome motion sickness. In a ship, sitting on deck (ideally amidships) and watching the horizon will help. In an aircraft, a window seat from which the earth below can be seen and a seat over the wings (where there is least motion) are helpful. In a car, sitting in the front seat or in the centre of the rear seat, from where the road can be easily seen, will assist.

Being overdressed, too warm, in a stuffy environment, eating too much, and drinking alcoholic drinks will aggravate motion sickness. A sufferer should be lightly dressed, slightly cold, have plenty of fresh air, eat small amounts of dry easily digestible food before and during the trip (no greasy chips or fatty sausages) and avoid alcohol. Fresh air is available by going on deck in a ship, opening a car window and opening the air ducts wider on an aircraft (don't hesitate to ask a flight attendant for assistance).

If the person still feels queasy, there are a number of medications (usually antihistamines) available in tablet, mixture and injection forms for the prevention or treatment of motion sickness. Milder ones are available without prescription, while stronger ones will require a prescription. Sedatives are used in some severely affected patients.

See also ANTIHISTAMINES, SEDATING; NAUSEA AND VOMITING; TRAVEL MEDICINE

MOTOR NEURONE DISEASE
Motor neurone disease is a horribly insidious disease of no known cause that affects the nerves that supply the muscles of the body.

Nerves are divided into two main groups – sensory nerves that feel heat, cold, touch and pain; and motor nerves that take the signals from the brain to the muscles and instruct the muscles to contract or relax. Motor neurone (neurone means nerve) disease is a steadily progressive degeneration of the motor nerves in the body, or the areas in the brain that control motor nerves. It normally affects adults between thirty-five and seventy years of age.

Muscles in various parts of the body become steadily weaker until complete paralysis results, but the muscles affected, and therefore the symptoms, vary between patients. Common symptoms include difficulty in swallowing and talking, drooling of saliva, inability to cough effectively, reduced tongue movement, and weakness of the arms and legs. As the disease progresses, weakness of the muscles required for breathing cause severe shortness of breath occur and lung infections such as pneumonia develop, and often lead to death. Some muscles may go into spasms that cause jerking movements and speech.

Electrical tests of the motor nerves to determine how well they are functioning, and a nerve biopsy, are used to confirm the diagnosis.

No cure is available, and treatment is aimed at relieving muscle spasm, assisting feeding, preventing infections, aiding breathing and making the patient as comfortable as possible. Physiotherapy on a very regular basis is essential. It is steadily progressive to death within three to five years.
See also AMYOTROPHIC LATERAL SCLEROSIS; MUSCLE WEAKNESS; NERVE; WERDIG-HOFFMAN SYNDROME

MOUNTAIN SICKNESS
See ALTITUDE SICKNESS

MOUTH
The mouth, or oral cavity, is the beginning of the digestive tract. Food and other nutrients

are taken in through the mouth and prepared for digestion. The mouth is also used in the production of speech and, together with the nose, is a channel for breath.

The cavity comprising the mouth is bounded above by the hard and soft palates, and below by a layer of muscles, salivary glands and other soft tissues. The sides are formed by the inside of the cheeks. The lips form the outer opening, while at the back the cavity narrows to the pharynx, which in turn divides into the oesophagus (the tube carrying food into the stomach) and the larynx (which takes air to the lungs). Protruding into the mouth are the teeth, which are used to chew food, and the tongue, used in both chewing and swallowing. In addition, there are three pairs of salivary glands, one pair situated under the tongue, another in the lower jaw, and the parotid glands in the cheeks just in front of the ear. The parotid glands swell up in an attack of mumps.

When food is taken into the mouth, it is torn apart by the front teeth and ground down and pulped by the back teeth. At the same time the glands produce saliva, which mixes with the food with the help of the tongue. The production of saliva is stimulated simply by the thought of food or even just its smell – we have all experienced mouth-watering aromas. When the food is actually in the mouth and can be tasted, the production of saliva increases.

The saliva not only moistens and lubricates food so that it will slide easily down the oesophagus; it actually starts the digestive process by inducing a chemical change by converting carbohydrates into sugars, which are easily absorbed. In the brief time the food is in the mouth before being swallowed, about 5% of starches will be converted to sugar.

Saliva also helps to keep the mouth healthy. It washes away leftover food particles and bacteria, and can even kill some of the bacteria causing tooth decay. Sometimes saliva is produced in response to indigestion, since swallowed saliva can help to dilute or neutralise acid.

See also GUM PAIN; MOUTH DRY; MOUTH LUMP; MOUTH OPENING DIFFICULT; MOUTH PAIN; MOUTH PIGMENTATION; MOUTH ULCER; MOUTH WHITE PATCHES; NOSE; PHARYNX; SALIVARY GLAND; TEETH; TONGUE

MOUTH CANCER

Mouth (oral) cancer is any cancer involving the lip, tongue, palate, gums or floor of the mouth. These cancers are rare under forty five years of age, and are associated with smoking in most cases. They may appear as an abnormally coloured or firm patch, tender lump, a persistent ulcer or painful swelling within the mouth. Spread to nearby lymph nodes and other organs is possible.

CROSS SECTION OF MOUTH AND NOSE

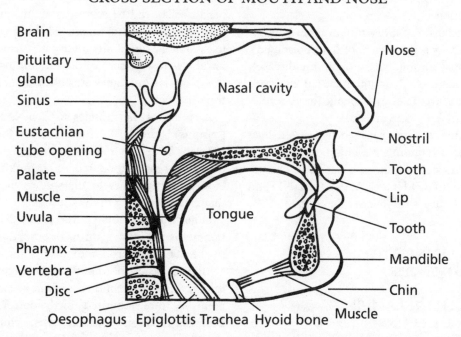

Brain · Pituitary gland · Sinus · Eustachian tube opening · Palate · Muscle · Uvula · Pharynx · Vertebra · Disc · Oesophagus · Epiglottis · Trachea · Hyoid bone · Muscle · Chin · Mandible · Tooth · Lip · Tooth · Nostril · Nose · Nasal cavity · Tongue

Scrapings taken from the surface of the suspected cancer can be examined under a microscope to confirm the diagnosis, followed by surgical removal and/or irradiation of the cancer. Overall one third of patients survive for five years, but there are better results with early detection.

See also CANCER; MOUTH

MOUTH DERMATITIS
See PERIORAL DERMATITIS

MOUTH DRY
Anxiety, fear, dehydration and a fever are the most common causes of a dry mouth (xerostomia). Doctors often judge the degree of dehydration in a baby by feeling the inside of the mouth and assessing the degree of moisture.

Medications are another common cause. A wide range of drugs may be responsible including those used to treat diarrhoea, depression, high blood pressure and a runny nose (antihistamines).

Many elderly people have salivary glands that do not function as effectively as in the past, and develop a dry mouth as a result.

People who habitually breathe through their mouth, or do so because of a blocked nose (eg. common cold, polyps), will dry out the inside of their mouth with the constant passage of air.

Infections, stones or tumours in any of the six salivary glands (three under each side of the jaw) will result in a reduction of saliva production.

Rare causes of a dry mouth include botulism (a very serious form of food poisoning), Sjögren syndrome (an autoimmune disease), poorly controlled or undiagnosed diabetes, cirrhosis (liver failure), systemic lupus erythematosus, AIDS and anaemia.

Alcoholism may cause dehydration, liver damage and mouth breathing, all of which result in a dry mouth.

See also MOUTH; SALIVARY GLAND and separate entries for diseases mentioned above.

MOUTH INFECTION
See STOMATITIS

MOUTH INFLAMED
See MOUTH PAIN

MOUTH LUMP
The most common cause of a swelling inside the mouth is a reaction to an injury of the moist mucous membrane that lines it. Causes include very hot foods or drinks, sharp object (eg. bone in food) inadvertently placed in the mouth, biting the inside of the cheek, and medical procedures such as irradiation for skin cancer on the face.

The gums may swell as a reaction to poorly fitting dentures, or as a side effect of medications such as phenytoin (for epilepsy) and cyclosporin A (for cancer).

Food sensitivities and allergies may cause a reaction in the mouth that results in swelling and ulceration.

Polyps may develop inside the mouth and cause discomfort, even when quite small.

A salivary gland may swell and bulge into the floor of the mouth if a stone blocks its duct or if it is infected or cancerous. All these conditions are very painful, and eating worsens the pain.

Cancer of the gums, bone of the upper or lower jaw or palate, mucous membrane and tongue may cause a hard painful swelling. Non-cancerous cysts may also develop in all these tissues, but these are soft and not usually painful. Cysts of a tooth root are hard, but not painful.

See also MOUTH; GUM PAIN and separate entries for diseases mentioned above.

MOUTH OPENING DIFFICULT
A difficulty in opening the mouth, fully or partly, will be due to a disorder of the muscles that control this movement, or the jaw joint itself. The jaw joint sits a long way from the lower jaw, just in front of the ear, and pain in this joint is sometimes mistaken as coming from the ear.

A spasm of the muscles used in chewing (trismus) is the most common reason for this problem. This may follow a prolonged period of chewing tough food, talking, shouting or a blow or other injury to the side of the face that causes bruising in the muscle.

Other causes include a fracture or dislocation of the jaw joint, arthritis or other damage to the jaw (temporomandibular) joint, scars on the inside of the mouth from surgery or injury, which may contract to limit jaw movement. A rare inherited birth defect, the Freeman-Sheldon syndrome, causes club feet

and distorted hands, pursed lips, a facial grimace and limited mouth opening.
See also MOUTH; MOUTH PAIN; MUSCLE SPASM and separate entries for diseases mentioned above.

MOUTH PAIN

Pain in the mouth may arise from the teeth, gums, tongue, salivary glands or the moist mucous membrane that lines the mouth. Any form of mouth infection or inflammation may be called stomatitis.

By far the most common cause is an ulcer of the mucous membrane. The saliva in the mouth contains a huge number of different viruses, bacteria and fungi that are constantly interacting with each other and the body's immune system. Every individual's proportions of these normally harmless germs is different, but those in the mouth of a husband and wife are almost identical. The balance is one that suits each person, but if that balance is disturbed by an additional infection, emotional or physical stress, or an injury, the brew of germs may start to attack the lining of the mouth to cause an ulcer.

Bacterial (eg. *Streptococcus*, tuberculosis), viral (eg. *Herpes*) or fungal (eg. thrush) infections of the mouth may also cause mouth pain and ulcers.

Dental disease is a very common cause. Damage to teeth or fillings, dental decay or infection, and an abscess of a tooth root may all cause significant pain. Tapping on the affected tooth with a metal object (eg. spoon handle) will often identify the affected tooth by causing a sudden worsening of the pain. In all cases, seeing a dentist as soon as possible will minimise both pain and permanent damage to the tooth.

Injury to the mucous membrane lining the mouth may be caused by very hot foods or drinks, sharp objects (eg. bone in food) inadvertently placed in the mouth, poorly fitting false teeth, and by medical procedures such as irradiation for skin cancer on the face.

Teething pains, as the first teeth cut through gums in children between six months and two years of age, may cause considerable distress. The pain may be felt in the ear, and the child may pull at the ear as though there is an infection there, but this is a referred pain.

Less common causes of stomatitis include infections or stones in the any of the six salivary glands (three on each side, under and behind the lower jaw), deficiencies of essential vitamins and minerals (such as vitamin B, vitamin C and iron), erythema multiforme (an acute inflammation), ulcerative colitis (lining of the large intestine becomes ulcerated and bleeds), lichen planus (uncommon skin condition), Reiter syndrome (conjunctivitis, inflammation of the urethra, arthritis and painful ulceration of the gums), cancer in the mouth, leukaemia and Behçet syndrome (mouth and gum ulcers, genital ulcers, eye inflammation, arthritis and brain damage).

Some medications, such as phenytoin (for epilepsy) and captopril (for blood pressure and heart disease), may cause mouth soreness.
See also GUM PAIN; MOUTH OPENING DIFFICULT; MOUTH ULCER; NECK PAIN; THROAT PAIN; TONGUE PAIN and separate entries for most diseases mentioned above.

MOUTH PIGMENTATION

The inside of the mouth may become darker in colour, or have patches of dark pigmentation, for a number of reasons. These include Addison's disease (the adrenal glands do not produce sufficient quantities of hormones and pigmentation occurs inside the mouth and on the lips and fingers), Peutz-Jegher syndrome (gut polyps) and Kaposi sarcoma (rare tumour that causes raised purple patches on the skin and in the mouth, usually as a complication of AIDS).

Negroes may naturally have some patchy pigmentation inside their mouths.
See also SKIN PIGMENTATION EXCESS and separate entries for diseases mentioned above.

MOUTH TO MOUTH RESUSCITATION
See RESUSCITATION

MOUTH ULCER

Mouth ulcers are common, painful and annoying. By far the most common cause is aphthous ulcers which everyone experiences every few months or so. They are caused by an imbalance between the bacteria, viruses and fungi which normally inhabit the mouth. Every individual's proportions of these normally harmless germs is different, but those in the mouth of a husband and wife are almost identical. The balance is one that suits each person, but if that balance is disturbed by an additional infection, emotional or physical stress, or an injury, the brew of germs may start to attack the lining of the mouth to cause an ulcer. These are easily treated by antiseptic and pain killing mouth washes, paints and gels. Vitamin B and folic acid supplements may also be beneficial, and in resistant cases pastes that contain steroids and antibiotics can be prescribed.

Other causes include an injury to the moist mucous membrane lining the mouth (eg. from very hot foods or drinks, sharp objects, biting the inside of the cheek, poorly fitting false teeth, medical procedures), infections of the skin (eg. chickenpox, glandular fever, shingles, hand foot mouth disease, tuberculosis), food sensitivities and allergies, cancer in the mouth, leukaemia and Behçet syndrome (recurrent mouth and gum ulcers, genital ulcers, eye inflammation, arthritis and brain damage).

Medications used to treat cancer (cytotoxics) are notorious for causing mouth ulcers. Antibiotics may also upset the normal balance of germs to create the problem.
See also GUM PAIN; MOUTH PAIN; ULCER and separate entries for diseases mentioned above.

MOUTH WHITE PATCHES
Medically, white patches within the mouth are called leucoplakia.

In babies, milk may be retained in the mouth for some time after feeding, and worried mothers have been known to bring them to a doctor for assessment, only to see the white patches of curdled milk disappear after a drink of water.

Thrush, a fungal infection of the mouth, is a very common cause of white patches that don't wash away, particularly in babies. Bacterial and viral (eg. herpes) infections in the mouth may also cause white patches.

Injury to the inside of the mouth, particularly burns from very hot food, may result in a dirty white scab forming during healing. Dentists may inadvertently lose some amalgam while filling a tooth and temporarily tattoo the inside of the mouth to give a patch that looks as though salt has been scattered on the red mouth lining.

Smokers may have damaged surface cells lining their mouth that gives a dirty white appearance, particularly on the tongue.

If an aspirin is held in one place in the mouth to dissolve, a white patch will remain at that point for some time afterwards.

Leucoderma is a permanent white discolouration of the mouth lining that occurs in some Negroes and other dark skinned races.

Uncommon causes for leucoplakia include systemic lupus erythematosus (an autoimmune disease), lichen planus (skin condition which causes small, shiny, flat topped growths), erythema multiforme (acute inflammation of the skin) and cancer of the mouth.

Medications that may cause mouth discolouration include ACE inhibitors (used for high blood pressure and heart disease), allopurinol (for gout), fluid tablets, anti-inflammatory drugs (for arthritis etc.) and methyldopa.
See also MOUTH; WHITE PATCHES ON SKIN and separate entries for diseases mentioned above.

MOVEMENT ABNORMAL
See JERKING; TREMOR; WALK ABNORMAL

MOXIBUSTION
See CHINESE MEDICINE

MRI SCAN
Magnetic resonance imaging (MRI), or nuclear magnetic resonance (NMR) as it used to be called, is a technique of scanning the body, especially the tissues that are hidden deep inside, and is a further advance on x-rays and CT scans. It is based on the fact that living tissues give off their own special electromagnetic signals, depending largely on their water content, and if the tissues are exposed to a magnetic field the signals can be picked up and read. Special magnets create an extremely strong magnetic field, and different areas of the body absorb different amounts of magnetism according to their water content. A magnetic absorption photograph is then built up, and can be seen and analysed, slice by slice, on a computer screen in much the same way as a CT scan. MRI is particularly useful as it ignores bones (which contain little water) and shows up soft tissue, which is the opposite of x-rays.

MRI is especially helpful in diagnosing diseases in the brain and spinal cord (eg. multiple sclerosis which involves abnormalities of the nerve fibres), and the ligaments and tendons around joints. The picture obtained by MRI of the brain clearly shows the difference between the white matter (nerve fibres) and the grey matter (nerve cells). MRI sometimes reveals tumours that are not apparent on a CT scan, not only in the brain but also in organs deep within the abdomen such as the liver.

MRI is completely safe. Its main disadvantage is that the equipment is enormously expensive (approximately twice as expensive as a CT scanner) and must be housed in a special magnetically sealed room.
See also CT SCAN; X-RAY

MRSA
See STAPHYLOCOCCUS AUREUS

MS
See MULTIPLE SCLEROSIS

MUCOLYTICS
Mucolytics liquefy mucus. Mucus produced during colds, flu, bronchitis and other infections of the airways, is often sticky and tenacious. Mucolytics make this phlegm watery and runny, so that coughing and sneezing can more easily clear it from the body. They are available as tablets and mixtures.

The most commonly used medication in this class is bromhexine (Bisolvon). Side effects are uncommon but may include nausea, indigestion, rash, diarrhoea and a feeling of belly fullness. It is safe in pregnancy, but should not be used in patients with peptic ulcers.
See also BRONCHITIS; MEDICATION

MUCOPOLYSACCHAROIDOSIS TYPE 1
See HURLER SYNDROME

MUCOPOLYSACCHAROIDOSIS TYPE 11
See HUNTER SYNDROME

MUCOUS CYST
See MYXOID CYST

MUCUS COLITIS
See IRRITABLE BOWEL SYNDROME

MULTIPLE BIOCHEMICAL ANALYSIS
See MBA

MULTIPLE MYELOMA
Multiple myeloma (myelomatosis) is a cancer of the cells in the bone marrow of the elderly that causes destruction of the marrow and damage to the surrounding bone. Patients develop bone pain (back, ribs and thighs are the most common sites), tiredness from anaemia, and recurrent infections because of reduced immunity. Further symptoms include fractures of weakened bones, and kidney and heart failure caused by the toxic by-products of the marrow and bone destruction. The blood becomes excessively thick and viscous, which leads to a wide range of other symptoms including dizziness, vomiting, bleeding gums, mental changes and partial blindness.

Because the marrow cancer destroys bone, calcium is released, and very high levels of calcium are found on blood tests. The diagnosis can be confirmed by specific tests on the blood, a biopsy of bone marrow, and x-rays show a 'moth-eaten' appearance of the bone in areas where it has been eaten away, particularly in the skull, ribs and long bones of the arms and legs.

There is no cure, but potent cytotoxic drugs and radiotherapy are used to reduce the symptoms and prolong life. Patients usually survive for one to four years after diagnosis, depending upon their age, the aggressiveness of the cancer, and their general health.
See also BONE

MULTIPLE PERSONALITY DISORDER
The multiple personality disorder is a very rare disorder in which multiple personalities alternate within the one body, but it attracts a lot of attention because of its bizarre symptoms. It may be started by stress in childhood or adolescence (eg. a sexual assault, emotional cruelty, repressed aggression), but in most cases no specific cause is found.

Two or more (sometimes more than twenty) different personalities occur within the same body, and they may switch from being dominant and obvious to being totally suppressed in a matter of seconds. One personality is usually present for most of the time, and others for far shorter periods, but in some patients it is difficult to determine which personality is the most common. Each personality is totally independent of the others, with its own likes and dislikes, friends and hobbies; but the different personalities may be aware of each other's presence in the one body, and there may be friends and enemies between the personalities. At other times, one personality may not be aware of the activities of the other. The change from one personality to another is often triggered by stress, but sometimes a particular action, activity, place or word may trigger the change. The personalities are often opposites – shy or extrovert, teetotaller or alcoholic, sportsman or studious. A normally faithful husband may suddenly become involved with prostitutes; a rabid antismoker may change into a chain-smoker. The possibilities are endless, but the risk of suicide while in one of the alternate personalities is high.

The aim of psychiatrists is to determine which personality is dominant and to promote that personality over the others in a lifelong course of psychotherapy. The prognosis varies significantly from one patient to another.
See also PERSONALITY CHANGE; PSYCHIATRY

MULTIPLE SCLEROSIS
Multiple sclerosis (MS) or disseminated sclerosis, is an uncommon disease of the brain and spinal cord that interferes with the brain's ability to control the body.

The cause is not known precisely, but there are several theories. It is possibly due to an unidentified virus, it may be that the body becomes allergic to itself, and starts attacking its own cells in an immune response, or it may start as a transverse myelitis. Scattered parts of the brain and spinal cord are damaged at random, the affected areas fail to function properly, and nerve messages from the brain to the muscles do not flow smoothly. Sometimes the message cannot get through at all, and paralysis results, while at other times the message may go to the wrong place, causing abnormal movement or a tremor. MS often attacks people in the prime of life rather than old age, it is more common in people with Western European ancestry, and is rare in the tropics between 30°S and 30°N. It is not contagious or preventable.

Symptoms vary greatly from one patient to another, but usually include vision problems, unusual forms of paralysis, tremor, loss of balance, poor coordination, general tiredness and numbness. Patients may experience difficulty in controlling an arm or leg, cannot talk, or may have periods of blindness. Symptoms also change in a patient because damaged tissue can repair itself and start functioning again, while other nerves becomes damaged, causing yet another set of symptoms. Pressure to skin areas and bacterial infections of various organs may occur due to lack of movement.

The diagnosis can be difficult to confirm. Electroencephalograms (EEG), electromyelograms (EMG), blood tests (no specific test is diagnostic) and magnetic resonance imaging (MRI) are all used.

There is no effective treatment available, but some medications (eg. beta interferon, steroids) can slow its progress, control acute attacks and bring about remissions. Physiotherapists, speech therapists and occupational therapists are also used.

The disease goes through a series of attacks and remissions, and periods of good health between attacks can last for months or years. Most patients can lead independent, active and satisfying lives and take care of their own needs for many years after the diagnosis is made. The life span of victims is not significantly altered.
See also TRANSVERSE MYELITIS

MUMPS
Mumps is a viral infection of the salivary glands in the neck that usually occurs in childhood. The responsible virus spreads in microscopic droplets of fluid that come from the nose and mouth with every breath. The incubation period is two to three weeks, and the patient is infectious from one or two days before the symptoms appear until all the swelling of the glands has disappeared. An attack usually gives lifelong immunity.

The symptoms may include a fever, swollen tender salivary glands just under and behind the jaw, headache, and a general feeling of being unwell. Sometimes only one side of the neck is involved, then the other side may swell up several days after the first side has subsided. Patients often experience additional pain in the gland if spicy or highly flavoured food is eaten, or even smelled. It may be a significant disease, particularly in adults, when inflammation of the brain, testicles and ovaries may occur. The kidneys, heart and thyroid gland may also be damaged and, very rarely, death may occur.

Treatment involves rest, with aspirin or paracetamol and/or codeine for the pain and fever, but if complications occur, further medical advice should be sought. Recovery is usually uneventful after an eight to twelve day course. Exclusion from school is mandatory for the course of the disease.

A vaccine is available that gives lifelong protection, and is usually given combined with those against measles and German measles (rubella) at twelve months and five years of age.
See also SALIVARY GLAND

MUNCHAUSEN SYNDROME
Named after Baron von Munchausen, a 16th century German fraudster, Munchausen syndrome is a serious psychiatric condition that involves lying and faking the symptoms of a serious illness. A disturbing form occurs when parents induce false illnesses in their children, and demand inappropriate investigations and surgery for them (Polle syndrome or Munchausen syndrome by proxy).

The cause is unknown, but patients have usually studied medical textbooks and are able to describe and mimic a wide range of medical symptoms and diseases. They travel from one hospital and doctor to another and tell extraordinary lies in order to obtain the most elaborate and extensive medical investigations and treatment possible. They may convulse, roll in agony, vomit, pretend to be unconscious and even mutilate themselves so that they bleed in front of examining doctors. By these means, they convince doctors to subject them to numerous operations for imaginary ills, and then they discharge themselves prematurely from hospital so that they can present to another doctor or hospital for further treatment of the 'complications' of the last operation or to complain about the 'incompetence' of the previous doctor. Patients may actually succeed in committing suicide or develop serious complications of surgery by the actions of unsuspecting, but caring, doctors.

Treatment is usually difficult, and involves a thorough assessment by a psychiatrist followed by prolonged counselling and psychotherapy, but even after apparent success the relapse rate is high.
See also HYPOCHONDRIA; POLLE SYNDROME; SHAFT SYNDROME

MUNCHAUSEN SYNDROME BY PROXY
See POLLE SYNDROME

MUPIROCIN
See ANTISEPTICS

MURMUR
See HEART MURMUR

MURRAY VALLEY ENCEPHALITIS
Murray Valley encephalitis is a viral infection of the brain spread from water birds to man by a mosquito bite. It is found in the Murray River valley of Victoria and NSW in Australia, and epidemics occur every few years after flooding when both bird life and mosquitoes multiply. The incubation period is three to six days.

Fever and a rash are often the only symptoms, but in severe cases it may cause eye pain, enlarged tender lymph nodes, dizziness, sore throat, joint pains, headache, neck stiffness, nausea, vomiting, tiredness, disturbed mental function and disorientation, although it rarely causes any long term problems. Death is rare.

No specific treatment or vaccine is available, and an acute attack lasts for one to three weeks.
See also ENCEPHALITIS

MUSCLE
Muscles hold various parts of the body in position, maintain posture and enable the body to move. Walking involves the coordinated contraction and relaxation of about 200 muscles from the neck to the toes.

Muscles may act because we instruct them to by a voluntary effort of will, or involuntarily, regardless of any conscious choice on our part.

The voluntary or consciously controlled muscles (skeletal muscles) attach to the bones of the skeleton to produce movement. If a person wants to lift an arm, the brain sends a message through nerves to the appropriate muscles, which contract to make the arm rise. Voluntary muscles are always kept in slight tension, commonly known as muscle tone, so that they are always ready to move.

Involuntary muscles, which carry out their task without any conscious instruction, are divided into cardiac muscle and smooth muscles. Cardiac muscle keeps the heart beating more than once every second from before birth to death, which may involve some two hundred and fifty billion contractions. Smooth muscles are found in the walls of all cavities of the body, such as the intestine and the stomach, blood vessels and gall bladder. They help to propel food along the digestive tract, expel waste from the bladder and control blood pressure in arteries and veins.

Viewed under a microscope, voluntary muscle fibres consist of alternately dark and light tissue and therefore are said to be striated or striped. Involuntary muscles are mostly unstriped or plain. However, there are some exceptions; the heart muscle is partly striped, and certain muscles in the throat and ear, which are not controlled voluntarily, are also striped.

A typical skeletal muscle is made up of bundles of fibre which look rather like a telephone cable. On the outside the fibres contain nerves, blood vessels and connective tissue. Within this there are smaller strands called myofibrils, comprised of overlapping filaments of protein that can expand and contract.

Muscles work by contracting and relaxing. Skeletal muscles usually work in pairs, one contracting to produce the desired movement, at the same time as its pair relaxes. This can be felt by bending the arm. As it bends, the biceps in the front of the upper arm contract and the triceps at the back relaxes. If the arm is then straightened, the opposite occurs. If muscles are not adequately warmed up before vigourous exercise, they may tear. This happens when a muscle is required to contract suddenly and its pair is unable to relax quickly enough.

As the body ages, in a process called fibrosis, the muscle tissue is gradually replaced by less resilient tissue, hence the reduced strength and slower muscular response of elderly people.

When a muscle contracts, its component parts slide over one another so that the muscle is shortened. Muscles require energy to move, which comes from a molecule called adenosine triphosphate, (ATP). During exercise, muscles break down ATP into ADP (adenosine diphosphate). When ATP is broken down, creatine phosphate comes in and releases phosphate to change ADP back to ATP. As creatine phosphate levels drop during exercise, performance

deteriorates. Skeletal muscle only stores enough creatine and ATP for about ten seconds of high intensity activity.

This is the end result of a complex chemical process begun when the brain first gives notice via the nerves that movement is required. A muscle can contract by approximately one third of its length.

To provide energy for the contraction a compound called glycogen, which is stored in the muscles, is converted into glucose. The conversion process involves the transfer of oxygen by the blood from the lungs to the muscle. During strenuous exercise, oxygen may not be breathed in quickly enough to keep the muscles adequately supplied, in which event a waste product called lactic acid accumulates. It is the build-up of lactic acid, and not the wearing out of the muscle's power, that causes cramps and muscle fatigue (and so prevents the muscle from being destroyed from overactivity). After the exercise has stopped, oxygen must be taken in at an increased rate (causing the person to puff and pant) to break down remaining lactic acid. A fatigued muscle will recover quite quickly after a rest, especially if accompanied by a massage to increase circulation.

There are about 650 muscles in the body and they make up about a third of the body weight in women and nearly half in men – hence the fact that, weight for weight, men are usually stronger than women. The longest muscle in the body is the sartorius, which runs from the pelvis across the front of the thigh to the knee. The biggest muscle is the gluteus maximus in the buttock, while the levator labii superiorus alequae nasi has the longest name of any muscle, but is merely used to flare the nostrils and raise the lip in a sneer.

By their movement muscles generate heat, helping to maintain the temperature of the body. It has been estimated that the heat in muscles could keep a litre of water boiling for an hour. Shivering is simply muscles moving involuntarily as an emergency measure to combat sudden or extreme cold.

Most muscles have the ability to regenerate after injury. However, the heart muscle is an exception. If a coronary artery is blocked in a heart attack so that the muscle is deprived of oxygen, the affected muscle will die. Surrounding muscle cells may increase in size to compensate for the dead section, but the overall number of the cells will always be fewer.

See also BICEPS BRACHII; CREATINE; ELECTROMYOGRAM; GLUTEUS MAXIMUS; HAMSTRING MUSCLES; MUSCLE CRAMPS; MUSCLE PAIN; MUSCLE RELAXANTS; MUSCLE TONE INCREASED; MUSCLE TONE REDUCED; MUSCLE WEAKNESS; MUSCLE STIFFNESS AND/OR RIGIDITY; PECTORALIS MAJOR; QUADRICEPS MUSCLE; RIGOR MORTIS; TENDON

MUSCLE CRAMP

Night-time cramps of the calf and foot muscles are very common and suffered by nearly everyone at some time. Patients experience a sudden, painful spasm of the muscles in the calf muscles, or of muscles elsewhere in the body. Although far more common at night and in the legs, they may occur at any time and in any muscle. Their cause is a build up of waste products in the muscles, usually after exercise, but sometimes after a prolonged period of inactivity (eg. a long air flight). Pregnant women are particularly prone to these cramps. Prevention involves having plenty of fluids, particularly tonic water which contains quinine, or taking quinine tablets.

Vigourous exercise may cause microscopic tears to muscles, particularly in the legs, and they may go into spasm during the exercise or soon afterwards. A similar effect may be responsible for the repetitive strain injury (RSI) of typists and pianists when overuse of muscles causes damage and spasm.

Compression of nerves as they leave the spinal cord through small holes between the vertebrae in the back may result in inappropriate stimulation of the nerves and contractions of the muscles they supply.

Rapid shallow breathing (hyperventilation) reduces the amount of carbon dioxide in the blood, which becomes more alkaline (raises the pH). Small muscles in the hand are sensitive to this change in the blood to the point that they go into spasm with the wrist bent and fingers and thumb bunched together and pointed towards the wrist. This is known as tetany (totally different to the disease tetanus) and can be cured by getting the patient to breathe into a paper bag for a few minutes while they slow down their breathing with repeated reassurance. Hyperventilation may start after a shock, surprise, injury or vigourous exercise. A low level of blood calcium due to diseases of the parathyroid glands in the neck may cause the same effect.

Severe diarrhoea (eg. cholera), kidney failure or an overdose of fluid tablets (diuretics) may cause very low levels of salt in the body. Salt is an essential substance for the effective function of nerves and muscles, and very low levels will result in inappropriate nerve stimulation and muscle spasm.

Tetanus and hypothyroidism (underactive thyroid gland) may also cause muscle cramps.

Many medications (eg. phenothiazines used for psychiatric conditions), particularly in overdose, may cause muscle spasms. The poison strychnine acts by causing painful muscle spasms that affect the heart.

Nighttime leg cramps may be treated by stretching the affected muscles, by standing on the balls of the feet to ease the spasm. Prevention is better than cure, and taking adequate amounts of fluid during and after exercise prevents dehydration. If this is insufficient, medications (eg. quinine) can be taken after sport to prevent the cramps. Tonic water or bitter lemon drunk after exercise may also help as these drinks contain quinine.

The treatment of other types of muscle cramps will depend on their cause.

See also JERKING; LEG CRAMP; MUSCLE; MUSCLE PAIN; MUSCLE SPASM; TIC and separate entries for diseases mentioned above.

MUSCLE MELTDOWN
See RHABDOMYOLYSIS

MUSCLE PAIN

Muscle pain (myalgia) may affect the large muscles of the legs and back, or tiny muscles in the hands or face. It is often mistaken for pain coming from deeper in the body, particularly if the muscles of the belly or chest are affected.

By far the most common and obvious cause of myalgia (muscular pain) is overuse of the muscle with excessive and unaccustomed exercise. This may cause microscopic tears in the muscle, resulting in both cramps and pain.

The next cause in order of importance is infection, viral or bacterial, that involve muscles. Dozens, if not hundreds, of different infections may be responsible. Examples include influenza (muscle pain is a feature that separates influenza from a common cold), hepatitis (most forms), glandular fever (infectious mononucleosis), measles, Ross River fever (joint pains), encephalitis (brain infection with neck stiffness), dengue fever, brucellosis (caught by meat workers from cattle), Lyme disease (spread by tics from mice and deer), toxoplasmosis (from cats), polio (prevented by vaccination, but if caught may cause permanent muscle damage) and leptospirosis (inflamed eyes and fever).

Fibrositis is the replacement of some muscle fibres with scar tissue after injury to the muscle from over use or repetitive use. The affected muscles may ache, become stiff and harder than usual. The discomfort is eased by heat and worsened by cold.

While passing through the menopause, women may suffer muscle pains as well as hot flushes, irregular menstrual periods, depression and headaches.

Less common causes of myalgia include low blood sugar (caused by overdoses of medication for the treatment of diabetes), polymyalgia rheumatica (inflammatory condition involving many muscles), motor neurone disease (progressive and permanent degeneration of the nerves that control muscle movement), chronic fatigue syndrome, severe deficiencies of vitamins B (beriberi) and C (scurvy) and rheumatic fever.

Rarer still are causes such as the Guillain-Barré syndrome (progressive symmetrical weakness of the limbs and face), eosinophilia-myalgia syndrome (eating excessive amounts of the protein L-tryptophan), some psychiatric conditions, hyperparathyroidism (overactive parathyroid glands), Bornholm disease (a viral infection that attacks the membrane surrounding the lungs) and Weil syndrome (complication of an infection by the bacteria Leptospirosis).

Some medications (eg. methyldopa for high blood pressure) may also cause muscle pains.
See also ARM PAIN; LEG PAIN; MUSCLE CRAMP; MUSCLE SPASM and separate entries for diseases mentioned above.

MUSCLE RELAXANTS
Muscle relaxants are used to relieve muscle cramps and the spasms associated with spasticity (cerebral palsy), paralysis (paraplegia and quadriplegia), multiple sclerosis and some rare brain diseases.

Quinine and orphenadrine are the most commonly used muscle relaxants to relieve night-time cramps. They prevent the development of these cramps but do not relieve them once they have occurred. Quinine is also used in the treatment of some types of malaria. It may have the side effects of ear noises, headache, nausea and blurred vision. It must never be used in pregnancy, and only cautiously in patients with an irregular heart beat.

Dantrolene (injection and tablets) and baclofen (tablets only) are potent muscle relaxants used in more severe and constant forms of muscle spasm.

Baclofen's side effects may include sedation and nausea, and it must be used with care in pregnancy, epilepsy, and patients with a head injury.

Dantrolene may cause liver problems, and regular blood tests to check the liver must be undertaken while on treatment. There are many side effects (eg. drowsiness, weakness, dizziness, diarrhoea) and drug interactions, and these must be balanced against the benefits received by the patient. It must be used with care in pregnancy and patients with liver disease.
See also BENZODIAZEPINES

MUSCLE SPASM
See HAND SPASM; JERKING; MOUTH OPENING DIFFICULT; MUSCLE CRAMP; MUSCLE STIFFNESS AND/OR RIGIDITY; MUSCLE TONE INCREASED; TIC; TREMOR

MUSCLE SPASM HEADACHE
See HEADACHE

MUSCLE STIFFNESS AND/OR RIGIDITY
The medical conditions that may cause muscle stiffness and rigidity tend to overlap.

Nerves run from the brain down the spinal cord to connect with a peripheral nerve at the point where the peripheral nerve leaves the spinal cord between each vertebra in the back. If the nerve from the brain is damaged by an injury, tumour, abscess or other disease (an upper motor neurone lesion) the brain will be unable to control the contraction and relaxation of the muscle, and it will go into a mild spasm to become stiffer and more rigid.

Damage by an injury, stroke, tumour, abscess or infection to the parts of the brain that control muscle movement will have the same effect as an upper motor neurone lesion.

Other causes include Parkinson's disease (degeneration of part of the brain that co-ordinates muscle movement), Steele-Richardson-Olszewski syndrome (muscle rigidity, severe hypothyroidism (underactive thyroid gland) and the Shy-Drager syndrome (progressive brain degeneration).
See also HAND SPASM; MUSCLE; MUSCLE CRAMP; MUSCLE TONE INCREASED; TREMOR and separate entries for diseases mentioned above.

MUSCLE TIC
See TIC

MUSCLE TONE INCREASED
An increase in muscle tone (hypertonicity) is indicated by an increase in the resistance to movement of a major joint (eg. elbow, knee) when moved by another person while the patient is at complete rest. The muscles will also feel firmer than normal to touch. It may involve only one group of muscles, or the problem may be widespread.

Nerves run from the brain down the spinal cord to connect with a peripheral nerve at the point where the nerve leaves the spinal cord between each vertebra in the back. If the nerve from the brain is damaged by an injury, tumour, abscess or other disease (an upper motor neurone lesion) the brain will be unable to control the contraction and relaxation of the muscle, and it will go into a mild spasm to increase tone. Stimulation of the muscle by a knock may cause a severe spasm and inappropriate movements.

A generalised increase in tone may be due to cerebral palsy (spasticity), a stroke (cerebrovascular accident), damage to the spinal cord (paraplegia or quadriplegia), Parkinson's disease (degeneration of part of the brain that co-ordinates muscle movement) and other injuries to the brain (eg. asphyxiation, very premature infants, swelling of the brain after severe concussion, encephalitis, meningitis and tumours or abscesses in the brain).
See also MUSCLE; MUSCLE CRAMP; MUSCLE STIFFNESS AND/OR RIGIDITY; MUSCLE TONE REDUCED and separate entries for diseases mentioned above.

MUSCLE TONE REDUCED
A reduction in muscle tone (hypotonia) is due to complete relaxation of a muscle, without any muscle fibres in contraction. The muscles feel soft and flabby, and adjacent joints can be moved without any resistance through their full range.

Nerves run from the brain down the spinal cord to connect with a peripheral nerve at the point where the nerve leaves the spinal cord between each vertebra in the back. If the peripheral nerve from the spinal cord to the muscle is damaged by an injury, tumour or other disease (a lower motor neurone lesion) the brain will be unable to contract the muscle, and it will completely relax.

If a patient is badly debilitated or semi-comatose because of a severe disease of any sort, all muscles may totally relax.

Other causes of hypotonia include tabes dorsalis (degeneration of the spinal cord caused by an advanced form of the sexually transmitted disease syphilis), damage to the cerebellum at the base of the brain (eg. from a stroke, tumour, injury or abscess), polio (a viral infection that affects the brain and spinal cord), myopathies, Sydenham's chorea (complication of rheumatic fever) and the Prader-Willi syndrome.

Very premature infants often have very low muscle tone for some weeks after birth.
See also MUSCLE; MUSCLE TONE INCREASED; MUSCLE WEAKNESS and separate entries for diseases mentioned above.

MUSCLE TWITCH
See JERKING; TIC; TREMOR

MUSCLE WEAKNESS
Weak muscles may occur in one small area (eg. the face) or the problem may be widespread. The cause may be in the brain, nerves or muscles, or may be due to body chemistry (metabolic) disorders.

Brain causes for muscle weakness include a stroke (cerebrovascular accident), transient ischaemic attack (a temporary spasm or blockage of an artery in the brain), an injury to the head that causes bleeding into or around the brain, Parkinson's disease (degeneration of part of the brain that co-ordinates muscle movement) and polio (viral infection that affects the brain and spinal cord) or its long term complication, the post-polio syndrome.

Nerves pass between the vertebrae in the back on their way from the spinal cord to the muscles they supply. If a nerve is pinched by a slipped or narrowed disc, arthritis in the back or a swollen strained ligament or muscle, its function may be affected, and the muscle it supplies may weaken. Pain and numbness are other common effects.

Other nerve causes of muscle weakness include Bell's palsy (nerve that controls the movement of muscles on one side of the face stops working), the carpal tunnel syndrome (inflammation in the narrow tunnel on the palm side of the wrist through which all the hand flexing tendons, nerves and blood vessels run), multiple sclerosis (a nerve disease that can affect any nerve in the body in a random and intermittent way), myasthenia gravis (varying weakness of the muscles that control the eyelids, eyes and swallowing), motor neurone disease (progressive and permanent degeneration of nerves), polyneuritis (painful inflammation of nerves), amyotrophic lateral sclerosis (Lou Gehrig disease), an extra rib in the neck above the normal first rib (Nafziger syndrome), the Guillain-Barré syndrome and Erb-Duchenne palsy.

If the blood supply to an arm or leg is reduced because of plaques of cholesterol building up in an artery, or a blood clot, the muscles supplied by the affected artery will not receive sufficient nutrition or oxygen, and will weaken.

There are numerous forms of inherited muscular dystrophy that usually affect children and sometimes adults. Duchenne muscular dystrophy is the most common type but other forms include Becker dystrophy and limb-girdle dystrophy.

Other muscle causes of muscle weakness include distal muscular dystrophy (starts in mid life and causes a slowly progressive muscle weakness that moves from the feet and hands towards the trunk), dermatomyositis (persistent dark red rash and gradually progressive weakness and pain of the muscles), severe rheumatoid arthritis and inclusion body myositis (progressive destruction of muscle cells in the hands, forearms, feet and lower legs).

The metabolic causes of muscle weakness include osteomalacia (lack of calcium in the body), an under or over active thyroid gland (hypothyroidism and hyperthyroidism), Cushing syndrome (from over production of steroids, or taking large doses of cortisone), botulism (very serious form of food poisoning) and ticks, which may inject a toxin with their bite that affects muscle strength in children and small adults.

Other possible causes of muscle weakness include severe psychological stress, syphilis, syringomyelia (cavity in spinal cord), Sturge-Weber syndrome (dark red birth mark on the face, convulsions, paralysis of one side of the body and eye abnormalities), Charcot-Marie-Tooth disease (nerve degeneration) and Bartter syndrome (short stature, thirst, frequent passing of urine, and muscle weakness and spasms).

There are numerous other rare birth defects and syndromes (eg. Kugelberg-Welander syndrome, Pompe syndrome, Roussy-Levy syndrome, Werdig-Hoffman syndrome) that may result in muscle weakness.
See also FACE, WEAK MUSCLES; FLOPPY BABY; HAND WEAK; MUSCLE; MUSCLE TONE REDUCED; PARAPLEGIA AND QUADRIPLEGIA; REFLEXES REDUCED and separate entries for diseases mentioned above.

MUSCULAR DYSTROPHY
See AMYOTROPHIC LATERAL SCLEROSIS; BECKER MUSCULAR DYSTROPHY; DUCHENNE MUSCULAR DYSTROPHY; ERB MUSCULAR DYSTROPHY; INCLUSION BODY MYOSITIS; MOTOR NEURONE DISEASE; MULTIPLE SCLEROSIS; MYASTHENIA GRAVIS

MUSCULOSKELETAL SYSTEM
See BONE; JOINT; LIGAMENT; MUSCLE; SPINE; VERTEBRA

MUTILATION
See CHILD ABUSE; SEXUAL SADISM; VIOLENCE

MYALGIA
See MUSCLE PAIN

MYALGIC ENCEPHALOMYELITIS
See CHRONIC FATIGUE SYNDROME

MYASTHENIA GRAVIS

Myasthenia gravis is an uncommon condition characterised by varying weakness of the muscles that control the eyelids, the movement of the eyes and swallowing. Signals from the nerves that supply affected muscles are blocked, for which there may be an immunological cause when antibodies that normally fight off infection actually attack nerve tissue (autoimmune response). It may occur at any age, but is most common in young women and may be associated with rheumatoid arthritis, systemic lupus erythematosus, thymus and thyroid disease.

Drooping eyelids (ptosis), double vision and difficulty in swallowing are the main symptoms. In severe cases the muscles used in breathing and walking are also affected. Muscle weakness varies in severity during the day and can disappear entirely for days or weeks before recurring, but over a period of months or years, the attacks become more severe. Unless adequate treatment is obtained, death eventually results from breathing difficulties.

The diagnosis is confirmed by the patient's reaction to an anticholinergic drug, which immediately reverses all the muscle weakness.

Treatment involves surgically removing the thymus gland, which is the source of most of the antibodies in the blood, and using anticholinergic drugs on a regular basis to control the muscle weakness. Steroids can be used in patients who respond poorly to other treatments. There is no cure and patients require treatment for the rest of their lives, but some have lengthy periods when the disease is inactive, during which they may be able to cease their medication.

See also AUTOIMMUNE DISEASES; MUSCLE WEAKNESS; RHEUMATOID ARTHRITIS; SYSTEMIC LUPUS ERYTHEMATOSUS

MYCOPLASMA INFECTION

The bacterium *Mycoplasma pneumoniae* may cause a particularly insidious form of pneumonia, which tends to attack teenagers and young adults, and often occurs in summer rather than winter.

The symptoms in lung infections are frequently mild at the beginning and slowly worsen over many weeks. A wheeze, persistent cough, tiredness, intermittent fever and loss of appetite are most common and it is often confused with asthma or viral infections.

A chest x-ray shows a typical pneumonia pattern, and a sputum sample can then be cultured to determine the bacteria present. Blood tests show the presence of infection, but not the type. Antibiotics such as erythromycin (a macrolide) and tetracycline are successfully used in treatment.

See also BACTERIA; MACROLIDES; PNEUMONIA; TETRACYCLINES

MYCOSIS FUNGOIDES

Mycosis fungoides is a rare form of cancer involving the lymphatic tissue in the skin. It may be caused by spread from other lymphatic cancers (eg. Hodgkin's disease) elsewhere in the body, or may arise in the skin.

Red circular patches appear on the skin, which initially may be confused with a fungal skin infection (thus the disease name), and gradually spread across the body, and may spread to other organs.

It is diagnosed by taking a biopsy (surgical sample) of the rash, then applications of anticancer medications are applied directly to the skin, and ultraviolet light therapy, irradiation of the affected areas of skin and, in more severe cases, anticancer tablets and injections are used. From when first diagnosed, average life expectancy is seven years.

See also CANCER; HODGKIN'S DISEASE; LYMPHATIC SYSTEM; PARAPSORIASIS EN PLAQUE; SÉZARY SYNDROME

MYDRIASIS

See PUPIL LARGE

MYDRIATICS

Mydriatics are drops that cause dilation (an increase in size) of the pupil in the eye. By contrast, miotics are used to decrease the size of the pupil. Atropine and cyclopentolate are the main mydriatics in use. They are used in examination of the eye to enable doctors to see into the eye, and during and after some types of eye surgery. They must not be used by patients with glaucoma. Side effects include blurred vision and sensitivity to bright light.

See also BELLADONNA; EYE; MIOTICS; PUPIL LARGE

MYELITIS
See MULTIPLE SCLEROSIS;
TRANSVERSE MYELITIS

MYELOFIBROSIS
Idiopathic myelofibrosis is an uncommon condition in which white blood cell producing bone marrow is replaced by fibrous scar-like tissue. The cause is unknown in most cases, but it may follow a severe infection of the bone marrow, cancer that spreads to the marrow, or be a complication of a lymphoma (cancer of lymph tissue) or leukaemia.

Often there are no symptoms until the disease is well advanced, when a large spleen and liver, and anaemia are noticed. Later, night sweats, weight loss and fevers occur. Complications may include fluid accumulation in the belly, bone overgrowth and nerve pinching, severe infections that do not respond to antibiotics, lymphatic cancers, leukaemia and destruction of the body's immune system.

Blood cell tests and bone marrow biopsy are abnormal, and bone x-rays may also show marrow damage.

Unfortunately no specific treatment is available, and the average survival time is five years from time of diagnosis.
See also BONE; LEUKAEMIA;
LYMPHOMA

MYELOGRAM
A myelogram is a special x-ray used to detect abnormalities in the spinal canal, such as tumours, fractures or damage to the vertebrae or discs, and other conditions that compress the spinal cord or the nerve roots. It is performed in a clinic or hospital under sedation. A radio-opaque (x-ray visible) dye is injected into the space surrounding the spinal cord by means of a lumbar puncture (needle into the lower spine). The patient is placed on a special table which can be tipped so that the dye can be distributed along the length of the spinal cord. The x-ray pictures are then taken. The main side effect is a headache that may persist for some days afterwards.

This test has largely been superseded by CT and MRI scans.
See also CT SCAN; LUMBAR
PUNCTURE; MRI SCAN; SPINE; X-RAY

MYELOMA
See MULTIPLE MYELOMA

MYELOMATOSIS
See MULTIPLE MYELOMA

MYOCARDIAL INFARCT
See HEART ATTACK

MYOCARDITIS
Myocarditis is an uncommon but serious bacterial, viral (most common), parasitic (rarest) or fungal (most serious) infection of the muscle in the heart wall. Patients usually remember another infection a week or two prior to the onset. Myocarditis may also be due to an inflammation of the heart muscle caused by poisons (eg. arsenic), toxins, irradiation and potent drugs (eg. cytotoxics used in cancer treatment).

Chest pain is a common symptom, and may be accompanied by a rapid pulse, tiredness, shortness of breath, swollen ankles and a cough. Heart failure may develop as damaged heart muscle cannot contract normally. An electrocardiogram (ECG), blood tests, and an echocardiogram confirm the diagnosis.

Treatment depends upon the cause. Bacterial infections can be cured by antibiotics, but there is no specific treatment for viral myocarditis, which tends to persist for many months and then slowly resolve. Permanent heart damage is a common result.
See also ARSENIC; CYTOTOXICS;
ENDOCARDITIS; HEART; HEART
FAILURE

MYOCARDIUM
See HEART

MYOMETRIUM
See UTERUS

MYOPIA
See SHORT-SIGHTED; VISION

MYOSITIS
See DERMATOMYOSITIS; INCLUSION
BODY MYOSITIS

MYRINGOTOMY
A myringotomy is an operation in which a small hole is surgically cut through the eardrum (tympanic membrane) to allow air

into, and secretions out of, the middle ear. It may be performed to ease a glue ear or persistent middle ear infection (otitis media) or abscess.
See also EAR; GROMMET; OTITIS MEDIA

MYXOEDEMA
See HYPOTHYROIDISM

MYXOID CYST
A myxoid or mucous cyst is a common, annoying but harmless cyst that forms on fingers due to degeneration of tissue under the skin on the back of the last segment of a finger. A small, smooth, shiny cyst forms under the skin on the back of a finger between the base of the nail and the last joint. The cyst contains a thick jelly-like substance and the nail may develop a lengthwise groove. Uncommonly, they may become infected.

They can be removed by freezing or injection if small, but larger cysts must be removed surgically under local anaesthetic. The surgical result is good, but recurrence is common.
See also NAIL

MYXOMA
A cardiac myxoma is the most common form of benign tumour occurring inside the heart. The cause is unknown in most cases, but it may be familial (run in families). The symptoms are very variable depending upon position of the myxoma within the heart, its size and the effect it has on heart function. Non-specific symptoms include a fever, weight loss, tiredness and loss of appetite, and it can be diagnosed by echocardiography (ultrasound scan). Sudden death due to blockage of a heart valve or irregular heart beat (ventricular fibrillation) is possible. Surgical removal of the tumour is necessary and gives good results if diagnosed early enough.
See also HEART

N

Na

See SODIUM

NAEVUS

A naevus is a small area of abnormal, but benign, rough raised pigmented skin that may be single or multiple. Many different forms exist including blue naevus (benign blue coloured and smooth), Becker naevus (hairy, in males, shoulders), sebaceous (yellow, bumpy, on scalp), epidermal (very common, may be extensive), halo, portwine, strawberry and spider naevi. If there is any suspicion that the spot may be malignant, it should be biopsied or cut out, otherwise they usually remain life long.

See also BLUE NAEVUS; BROWN PATCHES ON SKIN; HALO NAEVUS; MOLE; PORTWINE NAEVUS; SKIN PIGMENTATION EXCESS; SPIDER NAEVI; STRAWBERRY NAEVUS

NAFFZIGER SYNDROME

Naffziger syndrome is also known as the cervical rib syndrome, scalenus anticus syndrome and thoracic outlet obstruction syndrome. The cause is the congenital presence of an additional rib in the lower neck above the normal first rib. Nerves and arteries can be compressed between this extra cervical rib and the scalenus anticus muscle in the neck. The abnormal pressure on the ulnar nerve causes pain and a pins and needles sensation in the arm and hand, muscular weakness of small hand muscles, and altered sensation in forearm and hand. In severe cases patients have cold blue hands and reduced pulsation and blood flow in the radial and ulnar arteries in the arm.

An x-ray of the neck shows the extra cervical rib.

Rest, neck traction and surgical excision of extra rib are the possible treatments. The condition is usually slowly progressive, with an intermittent course, but good results are obtained from surgery.

See also ARM PAIN; RIB

NAIL

Nails consist of dead cells, and the visible hard part is composed of the same protein, keratin, that makes up hair.

Nails form a kind of armour plating for the sensitive and vulnerable ends of the fingers and toes. They lie over the nail bed. At the bottom of the nail bed is an overlapping fold of skin topped by the cuticle. The nail bed has a very good blood supply and it is this, together with the fact that the nail is thin (barely 0.5mm. thick) and transparent, which gives nails their pinkish colour. At its base the nail becomes denser and the blood supply less generous, giving rise to the white half-moon, technically called a lunula.

NAIL CROSS SECTION

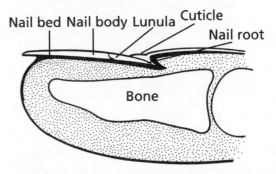

Hidden under the fold of skin at the base of the nail is the root from which the nail grows. The growth is continuous in finger nails and takes place at the rate of three to four cm. a year – considerably slower than hair which grows three or four times as rapidly. Nail growth is quickest in early adulthood and slowest in infancy and old age. The right thumbnail in right-handed people usually grows faster than the other nails and similarly the left thumbnail in left-handed people – possibly because usage leads to increased blood supply. Fingernails grow more quickly than toe nails – by about four times. Nails usually grow more quickly in summer than in winter.

Nail growth also depends on nutrition and general state of health. Poor health will lead to discoloured, dry and cracked nails. Transverse ridges in the nails will sometimes reflect a period of ill health, because the illness will have slowed nail growth for a time.

Nails are extremely porous and can absorb 100 times as much water as an equivalent amount of skin. This causes them to swell and, although they dry out fairly efficiently and resume their normal shape, if the process is repeated too often they may split and become painful.

See also FINGER TIPS SWOLLEN; FOOT; HAIR; HAND; NAIL DISCOLOURED; NAIL PAIN; NAIL PITTING; NAIL RIDGE; NAIL THICK; NAIL UNDERDEVELOPED; SUBUNGAL HAEMATOMA; ZADEK PROCEDURE

NAIL ABNORMAL
See FINGER TIPS SWOLLEN; FONG SYNDROME; NAIL DISCOLOURED; NAIL PITTING; NAIL RIDGE; NAIL THICK; NAIL UNDERDEVELOPED

NAIL BED INFECTION
See PARONYCHIA

NAIL BRUISE
See SUBUNGAL HAEMATOMA

NAIL DISCOLOURED
BLACK
A black nail may be due to injury to the nail and its bed that causes bleeding under the nail (subungual haematoma). The blood may initially appear red, but will slowly turn black in colour. A melanoma is the most serious form of skin cancer, and in rare cases it may develop under the nails to form a black patch. A benign (non-cancerous) black naevi may be confused with a melanoma in this position. Some bacterial and fungal infections under the nail may give a blackish appearance to the nail.
BROWN
Brown nails may be caused by nicotine staining of the nails of heavy smokers, chemicals that interact with the nails (eg. in laboratory and process workers), uraemia (advanced kidney failure), Addison's disease (failure of the adrenal glands), and poisoning by mercury or silver salts.
YELLOW
Yellow nails may be due to jaundice (liver failure from hepatitis, gall stones etc.), fungal

infections of the nails (onychomycosis) or lymphoedema (build up of waste products in an arm or leg due to a blockage of the lymph ducts). The antibiotic tetracycline, if taken for a long period, may cause yellow discolouration of the nails, teeth and bones of children.
BLUE
If insufficient oxygen enters the blood, usually because of lung or heart disease, the blood will become a bluer colour than normal, and a blue tinge will appear on the lips, under the nails, and in severe cases on other thin skinned areas of the body. Other causes of blue nails include Wilson's disease (excess deposition of copper in tissues) and the medications mepacrine, chloroquine and amodiaquine (all used for prevention and treatment of malaria).
WHITE
White patches under one or more nails may be due to lifting the nail from its bed, the skin disease psoriasis (the nails are also pitted), fungal infections under the nail, a lack of albumin in the blood (often associated with poor nutrition), severe heart or liver disease, low body temperature, kidney failure, arsenic poisoning, or a side effect of medications used to treat cancer (cytotoxics).
RED
Red nails may be due to blood collecting under the nail from an injury and exposure of a hand or foot to cold will increase the microcirculation and redden the nail bed. The white half moons at the base of the nails may become red with congestive heart failure.
GREEN
Infections under the nail caused by the bacteria Pseudomonas , or the fungi *Aspergillus* and *Candida* may give a dark green tinge to the affected nail.
See also NAIL and separate entries for diseases mentioned above.

NAIL INGROWN
See INGROWN TOE NAIL; ZADEK PROCEDURE

NAIL PAIN
The most obvious cause of nail pain is an injury to the nail, or more precisely, the sensitive nail bed over which the nail slides as it grows. The nail itself has no sensation. Lifting the nail from the nail bed, or injuring the nail

so that bleeding occurs under it (eg. accidentally hitting it with a hammer) are both very painful. If blood accumulates under the nail, it should be released as soon as possible to both relieve pain and give the nail a chance to reattach to the nail bed.

Other common causes of nail pain include an ingrown nail, when one leading corner of the nail grows into the adjacent flesh (often caused by tearing the nail rather than cutting, or tight shoes), and infections of the nail bed (paronychia), which require antibiotic and anti-inflammatory treatment, and sometimes minor surgery to lance an abscess.

Less common causes include a herpes virus infection around the edge of the nail (a whitlow), and tumours or cancers (eg. melanoma) under the nail.
See also NAIL; PARONYCHIA; SUBUNGAL HAEMATOMA

NAIL-PATELLA SYNDROME
See FONG SYNDROME

NAIL PITTING
Small, isolated or joined pits on the surface of one nail may be due to a persistent infection at the base of the nail (paronychia). If several nails are involved it may be due to eczema on the adjacent finger or toe skin.

If most nails are affected, the skin disease psoriasis may be a cause.

Strangely, patients with alopecia areata (patchy hair loss on the scalp) may also have pitted fingernails.

If every nail is affected, it may be an inherited trait.
See also NAIL and separate entries for diseases mentioned above.

NAIL RIDGE
The development of multiple ridges along the length of the nail is a common phenomenon in elderly people. This is due to reduced blood supply to the fingertips, and other generalised diseases such as rheumatoid arthritis, diabetes and other causes of damage to small arteries may also be responsible. The skin disease lichen planus is an unusual cause. A tiny cyst or tumour in the nail bed or base of the nail may cause a single ridge in a particular nail.

Multiple ridges across one or a small number of nails may be due to a persistent infection at the base of the nail (paronychia) or eczema on the adjacent skin. If most nails are affected by cross ridges, a generalised condition will be responsible. Examples include Raynaud's disease (excessive spasm of arteries due to cold), carpal tunnel syndrome (constriction of arteries and nerves in the wrist), a deficiency of protein in the diet and persistently wet nails (eg. from dish washing).

Women who have very painful and heavy periods may develop a small ridge across most nails every month.

Some people develop a habit of pulling back the quick at the base of the nail. This will damage the nail growth to cause cross ridging of the affected nails.

A single cross ridge (Beau's line) on most nails may occur after an episode of severe physical stress, major illness or significant emotional upset, during which time nail growth may slow temporarily.
See also NAIL and separate entries for diseases mentioned above.

NAIL ROUNDED
See FINGER TIPS SWOLLEN

NAIL THICK
If the nail is thicker than normal, a severe fungal infection of the nail bed is by far the most common cause. These infections have been notoriously difficult to treat, but in recent years a number of expensive lacquers and tablets have been developed that if used for a long period of time, will completely cure the problem, and remove the embarrassment of ugly nails.

Other causes of nail thickening include the skin diseases psoriasis and lichen planus.

Rarely, it may be a congenital defect of nail development.
See also NAIL and separate entries for diseases mentioned above.

NAIL UNDERDEVELOPED
A number of unusual conditions may cause most nails to be poorly developed or even absent. These include the Fong syndrome (poorly developed or defective nails and knee caps), Coffin-Siris syndrome (excess body hair, mental retardation and coarse facial features), foetal alcohol syndrome (caused by the mother drinking excessive amounts of alcohol during pregnancy) and Goltz

syndrome (scar-like areas of thin skin on the scalp, thighs and sides of the belly).
See also NAIL and separate entries for diseases mentioned above.

NALTREXONE

Naltrexone is a medication used to treat narcotic drug and alcohol dependence. It must be used with caution in pregnancy, breast feeding and children, and with caution in liver and kidney disease. Patients must have a negative urine test for narcotics before the first dose is given, and must never under any circumstances use narcotics.

Common side effects include severe withdrawal effects if not previously completely withdrawn from alcohol or narcotics, diarrhoea, nausea, dizziness and tiredness. Unusual side effects may include liver damage, nervousness, fatigue, anxiety, joint and muscle pains.

It interacts with all narcotic drugs (eg. codeine, pethidine, morphine, heroin, opium), and with thioridazine and alcohol, and this interaction may result in death.

A prescription is required, and its use must be combined with a drug or alcohol withdrawal program.
See also HEROIN

NANDROLONE
See ANABOLIC STEROIDS

NAPHAZOLINE
See VASOCONSTRICTORS

NAPPY ECZEMA
See NAPPY RASH; SEBORRHOEIC ECZEMA

NAPPY RASH

A nappy rash is not a reflection on the mother or a sign of neglect, but a very common problem. The baby develops an angry red area of skin under the nappy due to excess moisture on the skin from wet nappies, pilchers and plastic overpants that can cause skin damage, eczema and fungal infections (tinea cruris). Over bathing, soap and detergents left in nappies may also irritate the skin.

Red, peeling, irritated skin appears on the buttocks. If the skin folds are spared, it is probably a pure dermatitis, but if the rash extends to the skin folds and there are red satellite lesions beyond the edge of the rash, it probably has a fungal component. Uncommonly, bacterial infections may occur.

Zinc cream, lanolin or petroleum jelly applied to the bottom will protect it against moisture, and fungal infections will settle with antifungal creams, but eczema may require a mild steroid cream. The results of treatment are good, and even the most resistant cases settle once the child is toilet trained.
See also SEBORRHOEIC ECZEMA; TINEA CRURIS

NAPROXEN
See NONSTEROIDAL ANTI-INFLAMMATORY DRUGS

NARAMIG
See 5HT RECEPTOR AGONISTS

NARATRIPTAN
See 5HT RECEPTOR AGONISTS

NARCOLEPSY

Narcolepsy is an unusual disorder of the brain's electrical activity that is characterised by sudden uncontrolled episodes of sleep. The cause is unknown, but patients go from wakefulness almost immediately into the deepest type of sleep, known as REM (rapid eye movement) sleep, without passing through the normal intermediate stages. They have sudden periods of sleeping for five to thirty minutes several times a day, sudden muscle weakness, hallucinations before and during sleep periods, and paralysis immediately before and during sleep. Patients suddenly fall asleep, sometimes in the middle of a sentence, or when halfway across a pedestrian crossing. There is a wide range of severity from those who merely appear to sleep excessively, to those who are barely able to function or care for themselves.

The diagnosis is confirmed by an electroencephalogram (EEG) and by observing the patient in a sleep laboratory.

Stimulants such as amphetamine must be used on a regular basis, and patients must not be allowed to drive, swim or operate machinery until they have been well controlled for a long time, as there is the obvious danger that the patient may accidentally harm themselves or others. In many patients, good control of symptoms is quite difficult to achieve.

See also ELECTROENCEPHALOGRAM; SLEEP EXCESS

NARCOTICS

Narcotics are strong, addictive and effective painkillers that are derived from the opium poppy. They are available as injections, tablets, suppositories (for anal use), patches and mixtures. They are highly restricted in their use, and must be kept in safes by chemists and doctors. If used appropriately, they give relief from severe pain to patients with acute injuries, and pain from diseases such as cancer and kidney stones. They are often used before, during and after operations to ease the pain of the procedure. If used in this way, it is unlikely that addiction will occur. If used excessively, a psychological and physical addiction can rapidly develop. Heroin is an infamous illegal narcotic, which is broken down to morphine in the body.

Narcotics not only relieve severe pain, they also reduce anxiety, stop coughs, slow diarrhoea, sedate and cause euphoria (a 'high' – artificial happiness). They should be used with caution in asthma and other lung diseases, liver disease and after head injuries.

Examples include codeine, dextropropoxyphene, fentanyl, morphine and pethidine.

Side effects may include dizziness, drowsiness, nausea, fainting, insomnia, nausea, rash, sedation and constipation. They should be used only if essential in pregnancy and with care in liver disease and asthma.
See also ANALGESICS; HEROIN

NASAL

The medical term for any matters relating to the nose is 'nasal'.
See also NOSE

NATURAL FAMILY PLANNING

Natural family planning, or the rhythm method, is really a form of periodic abstinence from sex (not having sex at those times of the month when a woman is fertile). The trick is knowing just what are the safe and not so safe times. Obviously, it is essential for both sexual partners in this situation to co-operate fully in the contraceptive process. The man must be as aware of the woman's cycle as she is herself. For this reason alone, this method of contraception does not suit all couples.

A woman can only become pregnant for a short time each month, a few days either side of ovulation. There are many different ways of calculating the fertile time of the month. Because sperm can live for up to five days in the woman after ejaculation, and because the woman is fertile for two or three days after ovulation every month, sex must be avoided for seven to eight days during every cycle.

The most common is a simple mathematical calculation, as a woman usually ovulates fourteen days before her next period starts. If the woman has a regular twenty-eight day cycle, she should not have sex from days nine to sixteen of her cycle (where day one is the first day of the period) in order to avoid pregnancy. If her cycle varies significantly, other clues to ovulation must be observed.

Changes in body temperature can give a guide to ovulation, as the temperature first dips, then rises about half a degree centigrade at the time of ovulation. Changes in vaginal secretions also occur just before ovulation, and these can be noted on a glass slide. Breast tenderness and lower abdominal pain may be other relevant signs in some women. The Billing's method of contraception is a combination of the above factors.

Many people practise this form of contraception successfully for several years, but it is notoriously unreliable. The failure rate depends a great deal on the couple's commitment to follow the rules strictly, and the woman's own ability to note her own bodily changes. The percentage of women falling pregnant in one year while using natural family planning has varied from 5% to 25% in different clinical studies.

Natural family planning can be used in combination with other forms of contraception, such as condoms, spermicidal foam or diaphragms, which are used at the time of the month when pregnancy may occur. No couple should undertake this form of contraception without consulting a doctor who understands, and is prepared to teach, natural family planning.
See also CONTRACEPTION

NATUROPATHY

Naturopathy is a natural therapy discipline which encompasses various modes or subdisciplines, including nutrition, herbalism, homeopathy, and remedial therapies such as massage and exercise. By the use of these, the naturopath aims to create the conditions within the body that are most conducive to healing.

Nutrition therapy consists of an assessment of the nutritional needs of the individual patient and any special requirements arising from the complaint for which help is sought. Advice is given (as by dieticians) on how best to support the healing process by a sound diet, including adequate fluid intake, the avoidance of smoking and of using other toxic or potentially toxic substances, etc. The advice may extend to the selective use of vitamins, minerals and other supplements, and in some cases to the use of fasting and hydrotherapy.

Herbalism is the use of plants and plant extracts (other than those used in pharmaceutical drugs, such as quinine, opium, digitalis etc.) for the treatment of ailments. It is one of the forms of therapy used in naturopathy and also a sub-discipline within traditional Chinese medicine. In naturopathy it has developed mainly from a European tradition and is sometimes referred to as Western herbalism to distinguish it from Chinese herbalism.

Western remedial therapies used by naturopaths include different forms of massage, exercise, postural and relaxation therapies. Criticism of naturopaths is often aimed at their limited skills in diagnosing serious diseases and also at the orthomolecular treatment (i.e. the use of very large doses of vitamins and minerals) some of them recommend.
See also AYURVEDIC MEDICINE; CHINESE MEDICINE; CHIROPRACTIC; DIETICIANS; HOMEOPATHY; IRIDOLOGY; ORTHOMOLECULAR MEDICINE; OSTEOPATHY

NAUSEA AND VOMITING

Vomiting, and the nausea that usually precedes it, are some of the most common symptoms experienced by humans, and are almost unavoidable at some time in life. An enormous range of infections, gut diseases, liver disorders, brain conditions, glandular disorders, and even urinary tract abnormalities, as well as many other problems that cannot be easily categorised, can cause nausea and vomiting.

Gastroenteritis is the most common infective cause of vomiting, and it is usually associated with diarrhoea. A viral infection is the normal cause, but bacteria may sometimes be responsible. The infection is passed from one person to another by close contact or on the breath, and usually occurs in epidemics, often in springtime.

The nausea and vomiting associated with sea sickness, car sickness and other motion-induced forms of vomiting are due to an inability of the brain to co-ordinate what it is sensing from the balance mechanisms in the inner ears with what is being seen by the eyes. In a ship, the cabin appears to be perfectly still, while the balance senses movement. For this reason, sufferers should try watching the horizon while on the ship deck, which enables the brain to see the motion and reconcile the visual and balance senses.

Migraines are often associated with nausea and vomiting, as well as head pain and visual symptoms (eg. flashing lights, shimmering, seeing zigzag lines and loss of part of the area of vision). Pain usually occurs on only one side of the head, and is described as throbbing, and causes intolerance of exercise, light and noise.

Morning sickness usually occurs between the sixth and twelfth weeks of pregnancy, but in some women may persist for much longer. It is caused by a hormonal effect on the brain, probably arising from the developing placenta (afterbirth).

Bulimia is a psychiatric condition in which anxious patients consume excessive amounts of food (often sweets or fatty foods), and then vomit to get rid of the food and so stay slim. The patient (almost invariably high achieving, middle to upper class young females) may gorge and vomit or purge themselves for hours, days or weeks. The condition may be associated with anorexia nervosa. Complications can include menstrual period irregularities, sore throat, bowel problems, dehydration, lethargy, and dental problems due to the repeated exposure of the teeth to stomach acid.

Severe pain of any cause may result in nausea and vomiting as a reaction to the pain.

Other causes of nausea and vomiting include meningitis (infection of the supporting membranes around the brain), many different bacterial and viral infections (eg. cystitis, sinusitis), labyrinthitis (infection or inflammation of the balance mechanism in the inner ear), gastritis (inflammation of the stomach from acid irritation), appendicitis, mesenteric adenitis (infected lymph nodes in the abdomen), cholecystitis (inflammation or infection of the gall bladder), gall stones, hepatitis (several different types of liver infection), cirrhosis (damaged liver), a stroke (cerebrovascular accident), Ménière's disease (dizziness, deafness and ringing in the ears), and an increase in the pressure of the cerebrospinal fluid (CSF) which surrounds the brain and spinal cord due to ahead injury, tumour, cancer, abscess or infection in the brain or surrounding tissues.

Less common causes include kidney stones, uraemia (kidney failure), malaria, stomach cancer, Crohn's disease (inflamed and thickened intestine), intussusception (infolding of the gut on itself, usually in children), a blood clot in the main artery supplying the gut, epilepsy, a reduction in the blood supply to the brain (from suffocation, near drowning, inhalation of smoke or toxic gases, narrowing of the arteries to the brain, or any form of heart failure), abnormalities of most glands (may affect the body's chemical balances), the premenstrual tension syndrome (hormonal changes that precede a menstrual period), poorly controlled diabetes, hyperthyroidism (overactive thyroid gland), Addison's disease (adrenal gland failure), glaucoma (increased pressure in the eye), altitude sickness, severe high blood pressure, heart attack (myocardial infarct), congestive cardiac failure (damaged heart is unable to beat effectively), Chinese restaurant syndrome (reaction to preservatives and flavour enhancers in food), anaphylactic reaction (immediate, severe, life-threatening reactions to an allergy-causing substance), polyarteritis nodosa (inflammation of arteries) and AIDS.

In infants, particularly boys, severe projectile vomiting may be due to pyloric stenosis (narrowing of the drainage valve from the stomach).

Alcohol abuse, either a binge or long term overuse, will lead to vomiting. Binge drinking and intoxication causes vomiting, headaches and hangovers because of the effect of alcohol on the brain and stomach.

Many medications may have nausea and vomiting as a side effect. Common examples include most medications used for the treatment of cancer, narcotics (eg. morphine), digoxin (used in heart disease), theophylline (used in lung diseases) and overdoses of hormones (eg. contraceptive pill, hormone replacement therapy).

Radiotherapy (powerful x-rays) and nuclear irradiation used for the treatment of cancer often cause nausea and vomiting as a side effect.

Vomiting may sometimes by caused by psychological disturbances and used as an attention-seeking device.

There are many other rare conditions that may have nausea and vomiting as a symptom. *See also* ANTIEMETICS; MORNING SICKNESS; MOTION SICKNESS; STOMACH; VOMITING BLOOD and separate entries for diseases mentioned above.

NECK
See GOITRE; LARYNX; NECK LUMP; NECK PAIN; NECK STIFF; OESOPHAGUS; PHARYNX; SPINE; THROAT LUMP; THROAT PAIN; THYROID GLAND; TRACHEA; VERTEBRA

NECK LUMP
The neck contains the major arteries and veins supplying the head, the vertebrae and its enclosed spinal cord, the trachea (wind pipe) and larynx (voice box), oesophagus (gullet), thyroid gland, salivary glands under the angle of the jaw, muscles, nerves and numerous lymph nodes.

Lumps associated with skin and fat disorders may appear anywhere on the body, including the neck. Common examples are soft lipomas (fat collections), sebaceous cysts (blocked oil glands) and dermoid cysts in the skin itself.

Multiple lymph nodes surround the neck. They are collections of infection fighting white cells that filter out bacteria, viruses and abnormal cells (eg. cancer cells) from the structures in the neck whose waste products they drain. If these become infected, inflamed or cancerous, they may cause painful lumps in the neck.

Untreated infection in any of the neck tissues, but particularly the lymph nodes, may result in the formation of an abscess. These are usually tender, sore and may be accompanied by a fever and skin redness.

Goitre is an enlarged thyroid gland in the front of the neck. This can be due to an over- or under-active thyroid gland. Other causes include cysts, tumours or cancer in the thyroid gland.

A cancer, cyst or tumour of any of the structures in the neck may cause a lump, which is usually hard and tender.

Uncommon causes of a neck lump include a branchial cyst, pharyngeal pouch, a ranula (salivary gland cyst), a tumour or cancer in the carotid body, and a tumour or infection of the parotid salivary gland.

See also GOITRE; LYMPH NODES ENLARGED AND/OR PAINFUL; PHARYNX; SKIN NODULES; THROAT LUMP and separate entries for diseases mentioned above.

NECK PAIN

Pain in the neck may come from any of the structures in the neck (eg. vertebrae, trachea, oesophagus, lymph nodes, thyroid gland), or may be caused by damage to organs outside the neck (eg. heart, thymus) that inflame nerves running into the neck (referred pain).

Lymph nodes are collections of infection fighting white cells that filter out bacteria, viruses, other organisms and abnormal cells (eg. cancer cells) from the tissues whose waste products they drain. These nodes (often incorrectly called glands) are concentrated in the neck, armpits, groin and abdomen. If those in the neck become infected (adenitis) or cancerous, they can cause significant pain and discomfort. Mumps and glandular fever are examples of viral infections that may affect neck nodes.

A bacterial or viral infection of the pharynx (throat), trachea (windpipe) or larynx (voice box – laryngitis) will cause pain, fever, and possibly a cough, hoarseness and pain with swallowing.

Any injury to the vertebrae (eg. fracture, dislocation), ligaments (eg. strain, whiplash), discs (eg. slipped disc), joints (eg. arthritis) or muscles (eg. spasm, torticollis) in the neck may cause pain.

A fish or chicken bone, or other foreign body stuck in the throat or oesophagus (gullet) will cause neck pain.

The thyroid gland in the front of the neck produces the hormone thyroxine, which acts as an accelerator for every cell in the body. If the thyroid gland becomes inflamed, infected (thyroiditis) or cancerous, it may become extremely painful and tender.

Less common causes of neck pain include a cancer developing in any of the structures of the neck, an extra rib in the neck above the normal first rib (cervical rib), pressure on the nerves running from the neck to the arm (Nafziger syndrome), rheumatoid arthritis, osteomyelitis (infection of bone), a tumour or cancer in the carotid body (structure on the carotid artery that controls blood pressure), a tumour in the main muscle (sternomastoid) at the side of the neck and Pott's disease (tuberculosis of bones).

Pain may be referred to the neck from medical conditions outside the neck. The most significant cause of referred pain is that coming from the heart. This may be angina (a reduced blood supply to the heart muscle) or a heart attack (complete blockage of blood supply to one part of the heart muscle). The left side of the neck is affected far more often than the right in these cases.

Other causes of referred pain include lung infections (eg. pneumonia, bronchitis), lung cancer (eg. Pancoast tumour), a fracture of the collar bone (clavicle), an aneurysm of the aorta and an infected, inflamed or cancerous thymus gland.

See also ADENITIS; GOITRE; MOUTH PAIN; NECK STIFF; THROAT PAIN and separate entries for diseases mentioned above.

NECK STIFF

Stiffness when bending the neck forward (trying to put the chin on your chest) may be due to problems with the bones (vertebrae), nerves, spinal cord or muscles in the neck. Any cause of pain in the neck will limit neck movement, but will not necessarily cause neck stiffness.

Straining, tearing or stretching of the muscles and ligaments at the back of the neck in a whiplash injury is the most common cause of prolonged stiffness in the neck, which may persist for months after the pain from the injury has passed. Muscles may go into spasm when injured or overused, because microscopic tears occur in the tissue. The resulting scar tissue may cause prolonged stiffness.

Arthritis (usually osteoarthritis) of the joints between the vertebrae in the neck may limit neck movement, sometimes with minimal or no pain.

Infections of the numerous lymph nodes in the neck (adenitis) may cause scarring and contraction of the surrounding tissues and resultant neck stiffness, particularly if an abscess has developed in the infected node.

The most serious cause of neck stiffness, and the main reason that doctors check for this, is meningeal irritation. The three layers of membranes that surround the brain and the spinal cord, which runs down the back through the vertebrae, are called the meninges. If the meninges become inflamed, any stretching of them will activate a protective reflex which acts on the neck muscles to reduce movement and prevent pain. Bending the neck will irritate the inflamed meninges slightly because they surround the spinal cord as well as the brain. Therefore, neck stiffness may indicate inflammation or irritation of the meninges.

The possible causes of meningeal irritation or inflammation include a viral or bacterial infection of the meninges (meningitis) or brain itself (encephalitis), an abscess in or around the brain, bleeding between the meninges and the brain, or sometimes a severe migraine.
See also NECK PAIN; MUSCLE SPASM; THROAT PAIN and separate entries for diseases mentioned above.

NECK SWOLLEN
See GOITRE; LYMPH NODES ENLARGED AND/OR PAINFUL; NECK LUMP

NECROSIS
Necrosis is a medical term indicating the death of tissue or a part of an organ. Ischaemic necrosis is the death of tissue due to an inadequate blood supply.

NECROTISING FASCIITIS
Necrotising fasciitis is often portrayed as 'flesh eating disease' in the media. It is a very serious, but rare, bacterial infection and causes destruction of the fascia, the fibrous material around muscles and other internal organs that binds them together. Because the fascia is fibrous tissue, it has a very poor blood supply, and antibiotics have difficulty in reaching the infection. Bacteria in the *Streptococcus* group are usually responsible.

The bacteria spread extensively through the body and painfully destroy all the flesh surrounded by the infected fascia, converting it into pus or scar tissue. Swabs taken from infected tissue can identify the bacteria responsible, and then massive doses of potent antibiotics are given by a drip into a vein, and extensive and radical surgery is performed to cut away the infected flesh (eg. limb amputation). The infecting forms of *Streptococci* are sometimes resistant to many antibiotics. These infections are difficult to treat and may cause severe tissue damage or death.
See also STREPTOCOCCAL INFECTION

NEDOCROMIL SODIUM
See ASTHMA PREVENTION MEDICATION

NEGROIDS
See RACE

NEISSERIA GONORRHOEAE
See GONORRHOEA

NEISSERIA MININGITIDIS
See MENINGOCOCCAL MENINGITIS

NEMATODE
Nematodes are threadlike round worms that may be free living, or parasites within humans, other animals and plants.
See also ANGIOSTRONGYLIASIS; ASCARIASIS; CUTANEOUS LARVA MIGRANS; HOOKWORM; ONCHOCERCIASIS; ROUNDWORM; TRICHINOSIS; VISCERAL LARVA MIGRANS; WORMS

NEOMYCIN
See AMINOGLYCOSIDES

NEOPLASM
Neoplasm is a medical term indicating a tumour or cancer. It is derived from the Latin words for 'new growth' as cancer results in the growth of new abnormal tissue.
See also CANCER

NEPHRITIS
See GLOMERULONEPHRITIS; NEPHROTIC SYNDROME; PYELONEPHRITIS, ACUTE; PYELONEPHRITIS, CHRONIC

NEPHROBLASTOMA
See WILMS' TUMOUR

NEPHROLITHIASIS
See KIDNEY STONE

NEPHRON
A nephron is the microscopic blood-filtering unit within the kidney that removes waste products from blood and produces urine. There are over one million nephrons in each kidney.
See also KIDNEY

NEPHROPATHY
See ANALGESIC NEPHROPATHY

NEPHROTIC SYNDROME
The nephrotic syndrome is a form of kidney failure resulting in symptoms that are a result of the kidney's inability to remove fluid and waste products from the body. It is usually caused by glomerulonephritis, but may be a complication of diabetes, multiple myeloma, poisons or other diseases. It is far more common in places where there are poor standards of nutrition and hygiene.

Symptoms include a dramatic swelling (caused by fluid) of the body; the feet, abdomen and hands being the most commonly affected areas. If the chest is affected, the patient becomes very short of breath. Other symptoms include high blood pressure, stretch marks (striae) on the skin of the swollen belly, loss of appetite and a pale complexion. The patient is obviously very ill and may deteriorate rapidly.

Urine and blood tests confirm the diagnosis, and a biopsy of the kidney is often performed to determine the severity of the damage.

No specific treatment is available, but prolonged bed rest, usually in a hospital, is essential. Steroids are often prescribed to limit further damage and, if a specific cause for the disease is present (eg. diabetes), this can be treated. Total kidney failure may require kidney transplantation or dialysis.

The outcome in children is far better than in adults, and the majority recover after a few weeks, but in adults, long-term kidney problems are more likely.
See also GLOMERULONEPHRITIS; KIDNEY FAILURE, CHRONIC

NERVE
Nerves are the means by which all the parts of the body communicate with the brain, and in the entire body we have over seventy-five kilometres of nerves. Every structure in the body has its own set of nerves which, somewhat like a telephone system, come together in one central cable called the spinal cord. The spinal cord links with the brain, which has been likened to a central switchboard. The brain receives messages and transmits orders without ceasing throughout our lives. The entire communication system, or nervous system, including the brain, is made up of nerve tissue.

Each nerve consists of bundles of fibres called neurones. A typical neurone is made up of a central body, or nucleus, surrounded by threadlike projections, rather like a piece of coral. These are called dendrites and they carry messages to the cell body. There is also a longer cable-like projection called an axon which carries messages away from the cell body towards whatever tissue it serves (eg. a muscle). Axons can be quite long; those from the spinal cord to the toes measure up to a metre or more.

When a nerve ending, or receptor, is activated by a stimulus, such as heat or cold or light or sound, the message is first transmitted inwards to the brain, and the response is then transmitted outwards towards the appropriate muscle or gland. All of this occurs so quickly that we are virtually unconscious of it. For example, if your hand touches a hot stove it will take only a tiny fraction of a second for your arm muscles to receive the order to pull your hand away. Nerve impulses travel at about 400 km/hr.

All the neurones we will ever have (many millions) are formed before birth. If neurones are damaged, at best repair is slow and uncertain. The nerve body cannot regenerate; only the extensions can grow again. Neurones in the spinal cord and brain cannot be repaired at all; damage is permanent. However, the fact that there are so many neurones provides a safety net – even if some are destroyed the nervous system as a whole can still function.

The nerves send both chemical and electrical impulses. Like electrical wires, some nerves are insulated to prevent short-circuiting with a white coloured fatty tissue called myelin. Other nerves, including those in the outer layer of the brain, are a greyish colour – hence the popular description of the brain as grey matter.

See also AUTONOMIC NERVOUS
SYSTEM; BRAIN; CRANIAL NERVES;
GANGLION; NERVOUS SYSTEM;
SPINAL CORD

NERVE BLOCK
See LOCAL ANAESTHETIC

NERVE RASH
See NEURODERMATITIS

NERVE ROOT
See GANGLION; SPINAL CORD

NERVOUS BREAKDOWN
See ANXIETY NEUROSIS; DEPRESSION

NERVOUS DYSPEPSIA
See IRRITABLE BOWEL SYNDROME

NERVOUS SYSTEM
The nervous system is the complicated
network of nerve cells that enables all parts of
the body to communicate with the brain and
with each other to bring about bodily activity.
The brain is the centre of the nervous system,
and together with the spinal cord forms what
is called the central nervous system. The
remaining nerves are called the peripheral
nervous system.

There are two networks of nerves. One is
under conscious control and, for example,
enables us to move our legs when we want to
walk. The other network is unconscious and
operates irrespective of any control on our
part. This network is called the autonomic
nervous system and is responsible for such
bodily functions as breathing and digestion.

The nervous system receives messages
through receptors in the skin and throughout
the body which record sensations such as heat,
cold, balance, heartbeat and position. This is
called the sensory system. Responses to these
inward messages are then transmitted to the
muscles and glands by the motor system.

Damage to the central nervous system can
be very serious, possibly leading to paralysis
of some or all of the limbs. To provide as
much protection as possible, it is encased by
the extremely hard, rigid bones of the skull
and vertebrae of the spine.

Infections of the central nervous system
include encephalitis (inflammation of the
brain) and meningitis (inflammation of the
membrane covering the brain and spinal cord).
See also AUTONOMIC NERVOUS
SYSTEM; BRAIN; ENCEPHALITIS;
NERVE; REFLEX; SPINAL CORD

NEURALGIA
Neuralgia is a pain in any nerve. It may be due
to pinching of a nerve between other tissues
(eg. between ribs with prolonged coughing), a
reduced blood supply to a nerve (eg. migraine,
diabetes), an infection of the nerve (eg. shingles), an injury to the nerve, or joint arthritis
(eg. back arthritis causing sciatica).

Patients experience sudden, severe, shooting
and often brief stabs of pain that may occur
anywhere, but the chest, face and arms are
more frequently affected. Permanent damage
to the nerve may cause loss of sensation to
the affected area.

The cause must be investigated by x-rays
and sometimes blood tests, and treatment
depends on the cause. Anti-inflammatory
drugs can reduce inflammation associated
with muscle strain and arthritis, and steroids
can be given as injections into the damaged
area. Physiotherapy is often useful.
See also SHINGLES; TRIGEMINAL
NEURALGIA

NEURODERMATITIS
Neurodermatitis, a nerve rash, is a rapidly
developing form of dermatitis associated with
stress such as an exam, job interview, marriage or any other event. It does not mean that
the patient is neurotic or in need of psychiatric care; the rash is merely an outward
manifestation of a sometimes minor stress in
an otherwise normal person.

Multiple, very itchy, small red raised lumps
develop on the skin and they may fluctuate
quite rapidly in their intensity. The front of
the wrist, inside of the elbow and backs of the
knees are the most commonly affected areas,
but it may occur anywhere.

A mild steroid cream is used to reduce
inflammation in the skin, and if the cream is
applied as soon as the rash appears, it should
settle almost immediately.
See also DERMATITIS; LICHEN SIMPLEX

NEUROMA
See ACOUSTIC NEUROMA; von
RECKLINGHAUSEN'S DISEASE OF
MULTIPLE NEUROFIBROMATOSIS

NEURONE
See NERVE

NEUROPATHY
A neuropathy is any disease causing damage to, or loss of function of, nerves or the brain. *See also* AMYLOIDOSIS; ALCOHOLISM; BELL'S PALSY; BERIBERI; DIABETES MELLITUS TYPE ONE; DIABETES MELLITUS TYPE TWO; GUILLAIN-BARRÉ SYNDROME; LEAD POISONING; MULTIPLE SCLEROSIS; PERIPHERAL NEUROPATHY; TRIGEMINAL NEURALGIA

NEUROSES
Psychiatric conditions are divided into two broad classes, neuroses and psychoses. In neuroses, the patient has insight into the fact that they are mentally disturbed. The most common forms of neuroses are depression and anxiety neurosis.
See ANTIDEPRESSANTS; ANXIETY; ANXIETY NEUROSIS; DE CLERAMBAULT SYNDROME; DEPRESSION; OBSESSIVE COMPULSIVE NEUROSES; PHOBIA; POST-TRAUMATIC STRESS DISORDER; PSYCHOANALYSIS; PSYCHOSES; SOCIAL ANXIETY DISORDER

NEUROSIS
See ANXIETY NEUROSIS

NEUROSURGERY
Brain surgery (neurosurgery) may be performed in various situations, including to remove a tumour, to treat infection, to deal with abnormal, blocked or bleeding blood vessels, to relieve chronic pain, modify behaviour, manage Parkinson's disease or control epilepsy.

In operating on the brain for a tumour or cancer, the surgeon aims to reduce the amount (bulk) of tumour tissue present, and to reduce the excessive pressure in the patient's skull caused by the tumour. This initial operation is often followed by radiotherapy and sometimes further surgery. Some growths in the brain are benign and not cancerous, and brain surgery may be able to totally remove them.

The actual surgery for a tumour may be performed in one of three ways: –
• In a recently developed procedure known as stereo-tactic biopsy, a small hole is made through the scalp and skull and, using a CT scan to precisely locate the tumour, a small amount of tissue is taken from the tumour for later analysis and diagnosis by a pathologist.
• Burr hole biopsy is more traditional. In this procedure, a hole is drilled in the scalp in the vicinity of the tumour, and through this a larger sample of tumour tissue may be taken for analysis.
• A craniotomy is the third form of brain surgery. This involves the removal of a large flap of the scalp and a piece of the skull to reveal the brain. A large amount of tumour tissue can be removed, and pressure can usually be completely relieved by this technique. The removed piece of skull is replaced and held in position by sturdy stitches, and the flap of scalp is sewn down after the operation. Craniotomies are also used to gain access to the brain for some of the operations mentioned below.

An infection of the brain or surrounding tissues (eg. middle ear infection) may cause an abscess to form within or on the surface of the brain. Treatment involves drilling a small hole in the skull, and sucking out the pus from within the abscess, and giving antibiotics.

Bleeding within or around the brain can be due to the rupture of a berry aneurysm, or damage to an artery caused by high blood pressure or hardening of the artery (arteriosclerosis). Once special x-rays (angiograms) locate the site of bleeding, an operation can sometimes be performed to place a tiny silver clip on the bleeding artery or aneurysm and prevent further blood loss. The clip remains permanently on the artery and may be seen on later x-rays of the skull. This operation is considered to be major surgery, and there are some risks attached to it.

A partial or total blockage of an artery within the brain results in a stroke. In a small number of stroke victims, surgery may be possible to remove the blockage and restore function to the damaged area of brain.

Surgery on the brain may be performed to relieve some types of severe pain. Unfortunately only certain types of neuralgia (eg. trigeminal neuralgia) that cause excruciating facial pain respond to this type of surgery. The procedure involves the very careful separation of the accompanying artery from the affected nerve, when the artery has been pressing on the nerve to cause pain. This is a very difficult procedure and may have complications.

Surgery to modify behaviour is rarely performed today, but a prefrontal lobotomy (cutting away the front of the brain) was a common form of treatment for severe personality disorders in past decades.

An operation known as stereo-tactic ablation can be performed on those who have an extremely severe form of Parkinson's disease and who fail to respond to all medication. The malfunctioning control centres in the brain are destroyed in this operation, but locating the actual areas of the brain involved can be very complex and requires the assistance of a CT or MRI scan and a computer.

Some forms of epilepsy (eg. temporal lobe epilepsy) can also be controlled by surgery. Through a craniotomy the short-circuiting part of the brain that is responsible for the fits can be partially or completely removed.
See also CT SCAN; GENERAL ANAESTHETIC; RADIOTHERAPY and separate entries for diseases mentioned above.

NEUROTOMY
Neurotomy is a procedure in which a nerve is cut or destroyed to relieve pain or cause paralysis of muscles that are in spasm.
See also PERCUTANEOUS RADIOFREQUENCY NEUROTOMY

NICOTINE
Nicotine is a highly addictive toxic alkaloid (chemical) found in tobacco, and one of the main reasons that smokers find it so hard to stop their health damaging habit. Nicotine stimulates the pleasure centres in the brain, but tolerance develops so that a greater dosage (i.e. more smoking) is necessary to obtain the same effect. Withdrawal causes anxiety, cravings, anger, frustration, inability to concentrate, increased appetite and irritability.

Nicotine also affects the heart (increased blood pressure and pulse rate), increases blood sugar and has numerous other biological and physiological effects on almost every organ.

In medicine, nicotine gums and patches, or anti-craving tablets, are used to assist patients to stop smoking.
See also SMOKING

NICOTINIC ACID
See HYPOLIPIDAEMICS; VITAMIN B

NIDDM
See DIABETES MELLITUS TYPE TWO

NIFEDIPINE
See CALCIUM CHANNEL BLOCKERS

NIPPLE
The nipple is located at the apex of the breast and, in men, over the space between the fourth and fifth ribs.

In both sexes it is an erogenous area, meaning stimulation of the nipple is sexually stimulating, but in men it serves no other purpose. The nipple contains numerous small muscles that contract to make the nipple erect when stimulated by suckling, plucking, cold or anxiety. These muscles are more numerous in women, as the nipple is considerably larger.

In women fifteen to twenty ducts from the milk glands in the breast open through the nipple.

The nipple is surrounded by pigmented skin called the areola, which enlarges at puberty and may darken further (chloasma) after pregnancy or hormonal medication use (eg. contraceptive pill). The areola contains sebaceous (oil) glands that give it a bumpy appearance, particularly around its edge.

Cancer of the breast (Paget's disease of the nipple) can develop solely in the nipple.
See also BREAST; NIPPLE CRACKED; NIPPLE DISCHARGE; NIPPLE INVERTED; PAGET'S DISEASE OF THE NIPPLE

NIPPLE CANCER
See PAGET'S DISEASE OF THE NIPPLE

NIPPLE CRACKED
A common complaint, especially in breast feeding first-time mothers, is a cracked nipple. It usually starts a few days after the baby starts feeding and can be excruciatingly painful. Correction of breast feeding technique should lessen the likelihood of this problem. If a crack does appear, soothing creams (or anti-thrush creams, if relevant) are available from chemists or doctors to settle the problem. Often the baby will have to be fed from the other breast for a few days, with milk being expressed from the sore breast,

until the worst of the discomfort passes.
See also BREAST FEEDING; NIPPLE

NIPPLE DISCHARGE

The nipple of the breast will obviously discharge milk in a woman who is breast feeding, and will often leak milk between feeds, particularly when the breast is engorged with milk some hours after a feed. At other times a discharge will indicate some medical problem.

Sex hormone imbalances are the most common cause of abnormal nipple discharges. At almost any time during pregnancy, but particularly late in pregnancy, the higher levels of hormones in the body may stimulate premature breast milk production.

Hormones in the oral contraceptive pill, or hormone replacement therapy after the menopause, may over stimulate breast tissue to cause a discharge if the dose is too high.

The pituitary gland under the brain sends signals to the ovaries to increase or decrease sex hormone (oestrogen) production. A tumour or cancer of the pituitary gland or ovaries may result in excessive hormone levels and breast milk production.

Newborn infants of both sexes sometimes produce 'witch's milk', which is a discharge from the nipples in the first few days of life due to high levels of sex hormone passing over to the child from the mother through the placenta during birth. Despite the name, it is a harmless condition that settles quickly.

Other causes of an abnormal nipple discharge include breast cancer that involves the milk ducts (brown or blood stained discharge), kidney failure (may prevent the excretion of the normal amount of oestrogen and the levels of hormone increase), under or over active thyroid gland (hypothyroidism or hyperthyroidism), Cushing syndrome (over production of steroids, or taking large doses of cortisone) and excessive stimulation of a woman's nipples for a prolonged period of time may result in a reflex which increases oestrogen levels and results in milk production.

Some non-hormonal medications may increase sex hormone production as a side effect. Examples include methyldopa and reserpine (used for serious high blood pressure) and tricyclic antidepressants.
See also BREAST; BREAST FEEDING; NIPPLE and separate entries for diseases and medications mentioned above.

NIPPLE INVERTED

Some women have flat or inverted nipples. The nipple is also inverted if it retreats when the woman tries to express milk by hand. If a woman intends to breast feed, the doctor will examine the breasts during an antenatal visit, and if the nipples are flat or inverted, a nipple shield may be worn to correct the problem. The shield fits over the nipple, drawing it out gently, making it protrude enough for the baby to feed. Stimulating the nipple by rolling it between finger and thumb, and exposing the breasts to fresh air (but not direct sunlight) may also help.
See also BREAST FEEDING; NIPPLE

NIPPLE ITCH

Itchy nipples are a relatively common problem. Women with small breasts may go without a bra and clothing moving across them irritates their nipples, or a loose fitting bra may constantly move across the nipple. Other causes include synthetic materials in a bra, allergies to soaps, perfumes and washing powders, and fungal infections such as thrush (common in breast feeding mothers).

Treatments include lanolin and other skin moisturisers, anti-itch creams, antifungal creams if thrush is present, or prescribed mild steroid creams. Padding a bra may help small breasted women, and an adhesive dressing over the nipple can give quick relief.
See also NIPPLE

NITRAZEPAM
See SEDATIVES

NITROGEN

Nitrogen (N) is a colourless, odourless, relatively inert gas that makes up 80% of the air we breathe. It may cause problems if the body is subjected to rapid pressure changes (eg. a scuba diver surfacing quickly) when nitrogen dissolved in blood comes out of solution to form bubbles in the blood (the bends).

Nitrogen is used in a liquid form during cryotherapy to freeze skin spots.
See also BENDS; CRYOTHERAPY

NITROGLYCERINE
See ANTIANGINALS

NITROUS OXIDE
See ANAESTHETICS; LAUGHING GAS

NOCTE

The prescription notation 'nocte' is derived from the Latin word for 'night' and on a prescription means 'take at night'.
See also PRESCRIPTION NOTATIONS

NOCTURIA

See URINATION NIGHTLY

NOCTURNAL MUSCLE CRAMP

See LEG CRAMP; MUSCLE CRAMP

NODULES

See SKIN NODULES

NOISE IN EARS

See TINNITUS

NOISY BOWELS

See BOWEL NOISY

NON-GONOCOCCAL URETHRITIS

See NON-SPECIFIC URETHRITIS

NON-HODGKIN'S LYMPHOMA

A non-Hodgkin's lymphoma is a form of cancer of the lymph nodes. The cause is unknown, but this disease is closely related to some forms of leukaemia. This form of lymphoma is much more common than Hodgkin's disease.

A persistent, painless enlargement of the lymph nodes develops in the neck, armpit, groin or other areas including the belly. Patients may be tired and develop an itch, but rarely any fever. The cancer may spread to distant lymph nodes and other organs.

It is diagnosed by biopsy of an affected lymph node, and blood tests may also be abnormal. Treatment depends upon the stage at which the cancer is detected, and may involve surgery, irradiation and chemotherapy (anticancer drugs). Remission is common, but complete cure rare, although even in advanced stages, ten year survival is now common.
See also CANCER; HODGKIN'S LYMPHOMA; LYMPHOMA

NON-INSULIN DEPENDENT DIABETES MELLITUS

See DIABETES MELLITUS TYPE TWO

NONIVAMIDE

See LINIMENT

NON-SPECIFIC URETHRITIS

Non-specific urethritis (NSU) is also known as Chlamydial urethritis and non-Gonococcal urethritis, and is a sexually transmitted disease that is carried by women and infects men. Most (but not all) cases of NSU are caused by a Chlamydial infection, while unidentified bacteria are responsible for the other cases. *Chlamydiae* are a group of organisms that are not bacteria, but act as parasites inside human cells and eventually destroy the cell. They spread by passing from the man to female sexual partners where they remain in the vagina to infect the woman's next sex partner. In homosexuals, the infection may occur around the anus.

Men have a white discharge from the penis, painful passing of urine, but rarely other symptoms, although sometimes the infection may spread from the penis up into the testes or prostate gland. In women there are usually no symptoms, but sometimes the infection may spread to cause salpingitis (infection of the Fallopian tubes).

Chlamydiae may be identified by specific blood and swab tests, but these are not always reliable, and a negative test does not mean that the infection is not present.

Antibiotics such as tetracyclines and erythromycins are used very successfully in treatment, and all sexual contacts should be treated when the infection is discovered.
See also CHLAMYDIAL INFECTION; SALPINGITIS; VENEREAL DISEASES

NONSTEROIDAL ANTI-INFLAMMATORY DRUGS

Despite their long name and unpronounceable acronym, the nonsteroidal anti-inflammatory drugs (NSAIDs) are some of the most widely used drugs in modern medicine. They are drugs that reduce inflammation in tissue, without being steroids, which are the most potent anti-inflammatory drugs available.

Inflammation is the redness, swelling, pain and heat that occurs in tissue that is subjected to some form of irritation or injury. NSAIDs not only reduce inflammation but also ease pain and lower fevers. Their main uses are in the treatment of rheumatoid and osteoarthritis, sporting injuries to joints, muscles and tendons, and to reduce the inflammation in the pelvis associated with menstrual period pain. Some are used for reasons as diverse as migraines and inflamed throats. They are all available as tablets or capsules, but some are also available as injections, and even as creams, gels and a rub-on lotion.

Salicylates are a subgroup of the NSAIDs, derived from salicylic acid. The most commonly known member of this subgroup is aspirin, which acts as a painkiller (analgesic), fever-reducing agent (antipyretic) and anti-inflammatory medication. It has the same side effects as the other NSAIDs.

The greatest problem with the use of NSAIDs is the possibility of causing stomach irritation, and peptic ulcers in the stomach or small intestine. Unfortunately, a significant proportion of the patients using these medications will develop some intestinal problem. This can be prevented to some extent by always taking the drugs after food, or in conjunction with an antacid or other ulcer-preventing medication. Any patient who develops stomach pains, vomits blood or passes black stools while on NSAIDs must cease them and see a doctor immediately.

A new subclass of NSAIDs (the COX-2 inhibitors) has significantly reduced adverse effects on the stomach. These include rofe-coxib (Vioxx) and celecoxib (Celebrex).

Despite the problems associated with the use of NSAIDs, many patients with arthritis find that these drugs have improved their lives dramatically by controlling their previously painful and swollen joints. They can also enable sportsmen and women to overcome painful sprains and strains, allowing them to return to competition as quickly as possible.

Examples of NSAIDs include aspirin, diclofenac (Voltaren), diflunisal (Dolobid), ibuprofen (Brufen, Nurofen), indomethacin (Indocid), ketoprofen (Orudis), mefenamic acid (Ponstan), naproxen (Naprosyn), piroxicam (Feldene), sulindac (Clinoril), tenoxicam (Tilcotil) and tiaprofenic acid (Surgam).

Side effects may include stomach discomfort, diarrhoea, heartburn, constipation, nausea, ringing in ears and dizziness. They should not be used in pregnancy or breast feeding, or in those with peptic ulcers or indigestion. They must be used with care in the elderly, and patients with epilepsy, heart failure or kidney disease. They must be stopped before surgery, and not used with anticoagulants.

See also ANALGESICS; MEDICATION; OSTEOARTHRITIS; RHEUMATOID ARTHRITIS; STEROIDS

NON-TROPICAL SPRUE
See COELIAC DISEASE

NOONAN SYNDROME
Noonan syndrome is an uncommon congenital (present from birth) developmental abnormality with widespread effects that occurs in both sexes and without any chromosomal defects. These people are short in stature, and have a wide neck, broad chest, abnormal heart valves, slanted eyes, low set ears, depressed bridge of the nose, broad tip of the nose and some mental retardation. Surgical correction of the heart problems and plastic surgery to cosmetic deformities is possible, but although there is no cure, they have a relatively normal life expectancy.

NORETHISTERONE
See CONTRACEPTIVE PILL; SEX HORMONES

NORFLOXACIN
See QUINOLONES

NORMISON
See SEDATIVES

NORTRIPTYLINE
See ANTIDEPRESSANTS

NORWEGIAN SCABIES
See SCABIES

NOSE
Air is breathed in through the nostrils (the openings to the nose), then passes into the pharynx (throat) and down the larynx and trachea to the lungs. The nose warms the air to blood temperature and moistens it so that it will not harm the delicate tissues of the lungs.

The part of the nose we can see consists of cartilage and bone covered with skin. Behind it is the internal nose consisting of two nasal cavities divided by a septum, which is also made up of cartilage and bone. The septum has three curled bones called turbinates attached to it that swirl the air around as it moves through the nose to improve the efficiency of the warming and moisturising process.

CROSS SECTION OF MOUTH AND NOSE

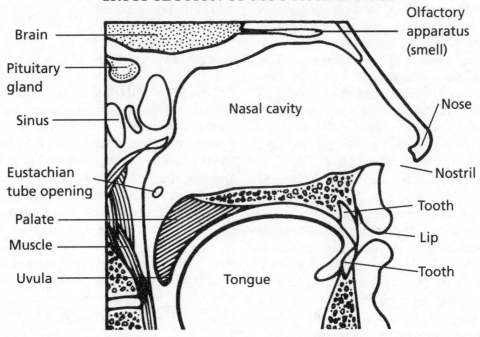

Brain — Olfactory apparatus (smell)

Pituitary gland

Sinus

Nasal cavity

Eustachian tube opening

Palate

Muscle

Uvula

Nose

Nostril

Tooth

Lip

Tooth

Tongue

As well as providing a passage for air, one of the main functions of the nose and pharynx is to filter air and trap infections before they reach the lungs – hence the frequency of coughs and colds and other minor upper respiratory ailments which, although tiresome, are preferable to serious lung diseases such as pneumonia.

The nose begins this filtering process very efficiently with its lining of tiny hairs, called cilia, which trap particles of foreign matter. The hairs at the front of the nose are bigger and coarser than those at the back, so large particles such as grit and dirt are caught before they get very far. Smaller particles which manage to find their way through the front hairs will usually come to grief in the finer hairs at the back. Once particles such as dust and bacteria are trapped, a sneeze will expel them, or they cling to the mucous membrane lining of the nose which itself has bacteria-destroying properties, and are moved by the waving of the hairs down to the throat and on to the stomach where they are processed by the digestive system. Alternatively they may be expelled in the mucus by coughing. Particularly harmful substances cause a sneeze and expel the irritant at the beginning. The reason it is better to breathe through the nose than the mouth is that the nose is much more effective at dealing with foreign matter and bacteria.

A healthy adult produces about a litre of mucus in a day. If an infection takes hold, this amount will increase substantially to cope with the extra load involved in ridding the infection from the body – hence the blocked or runny nose of a cold.

Surrounding the nasal cavities are air spaces opening into the bones of the skull through small gaps. These are the nasal sinuses. Matching pairs of sinuses exist in the forehead, the cheeks and the front and back of the nose itself. The sinuses do not seem to fulfil any specific respiratory function but rather exist to lighten the skull and add resonance to the voice. They enlarge significantly at puberty and so are a factor in the size and shape of the face. Despite their apparent lack of usefulness, the sinuses are very vulnerable to infection.

The nose is also the organ of smell. Odour receptors are situated in the roof of the nasal passages and these communicate with the brain.

See also MOUTH; NOSE BLEED; NOSE BLOCKED; NOSE DISCHARGE; PHARYNX; SMELL; SNEEZE; VASOMOTOR RHINITIS

NOSE BLEED

Everyone has a bloody nose (medically known as epistaxis) at some time. It can be one of the most annoying, embarrassing and distressing symptoms, but fortunately the vast majority of cases have no serious cause.

The lining of the nose is normally damp, and the side of the nostril against the nasal septum (central division of the nose) is covered with a network of tiny arteries that keep this area particularly warm and moist. Thus, air entering the nose on its way to the lungs is warmed and moistened as soon as possible to reduce the risk of the lungs drying out and becoming cold. There are also three curled bones called turbinates, which come off the septum further into the nostril. These are also covered by a warm moist membrane, and they are designed to swirl the air around to further add to its warmth and moisture.

If the moist nose-lining membrane dries out because of a hot dry climate, high altitude, or infections, it will crack and the tiny arteries under it will suddenly start bleeding quite profusely. If the drying occurs further back in the nose, the arteries on the turbinates may bleed, and most of the blood will go down the back of the throat rather than out the nose.

If the nostril lining is damaged by picking the nose or trauma, bleeding may also occur. A severe blow to the nose may fracture the bone, and this almost invariably causes bleeding.

High blood pressure may increase the risk of a nose bleed, but other causes are usually also present.

Polyps, tumours and very rarely cancer in the nostril may bleed unpredictably.

Children often place objects in the nose, and they may be difficult to see without proper instruments. A foreign body should always be suspected as a cause of a nose bleed in children and in adults with subnormal mentality.

All causes of generalised abnormal bleeding may be responsible for nose bleeds. Examples include a lack of cells (platelets) or substances necessary for normal clotting (eg. haemophilia), and medications that are used to reduce the risk of blood clots (eg. aspirin, warfarin).

Leukaemia is a rare cause of abnormal and excessive bleeding.

If recurrent nose bleeds occur, investigations must be undertaken to determine the cause.

In order to stop a nose bleed, the patient should sit (not lie) still and hold the nostrils firmly without letting go for ten minutes. Ice applied to the nose will also help. If bleeding continues after repeating the above three times, medical attention is necessary to find and treat the cause of the bleeding (eg. cauterising the bleeding point with heat, removing a nasal polyp). A Foley catheter (normally used to drain the bladder) can be inserted into the nose and then the balloon at the end of the tube can be inflated to stop an intractable nose bleed.

Very rarely, repeated severe nose bleeds may cause anaemia, but most cases of epistaxis settle quickly with appropriate treatment.
See also BLEEDING, EXCESSIVE; NOSE and separate entries for diseases mentioned above.

NOSE BLOCKED

Everyone will have experienced the sensations caused by a viral (eg. common cold) or bacterial (eg. sinusitis) infection in the nose, or rarely a fungal (eg. *Candida*) infection, that results in the excessive production of thick sticky phlegm and mucus.

Hay fever and vasomotor rhinitis may swell the lining of the nostrils and produce so much watery mucus that they become blocked.

Polyps are quite common in the nose, and may enlarge to completely block one nostril. Other growths, such as tumours and cancers, may also do this, but are quite rare.

The nasal septum (mid line divider of the nose) may be pushed to one side and block a nostril due to a birth defect or a fracture of the nose.

The incidence of diphtheria in children is now low due to vaccination. It causes a sore throat, thick grey sticky membrane across the throat, fever, nasal discharge, hoarse voice and obvious illness, with overwhelming tiredness and muscle aches.

Numerous medications, including methyldopa (for high blood pressure), may have a blocked stuffy nose as a side effect. Significantly, most decongestant sprays that are used to clear blocked noses will actually make the blockage worse if used too often or for too long.
See also NOSE DISCHARGE and separate entries for diseases mentioned above.

NOSE DISCHARGE

By far the most common cause for a runny nose is a viral infection such as common cold or influenza, or a bacterial infection such as sinusitis. Viral infections usually have a lightly coloured discharge, but in bacterial infections the patient is sicker with a fever, face ache and green or dark yellow discharge.

Hay fever (allergic rhinitis) is the next most common cause. The discharge is watery and profuse, and sneezing may be almost continuous, but the patient is otherwise well. Almost any substance (eg. pollens, dust, chemicals) may be inhaled and cause this reaction in a sensitive individual.

Vasomotor rhinitis is a reaction of the moist lining in the nose to a change in temperature (eg. walking into an air-conditioned room), position (eg. lying down), eating hot or cold food, or drinking (particularly alcohol) that results in the production of copious amounts of watery mucus. The problem usually settles after ten to thirty minutes, unless there is a further irritation of the nostril.

Children often place objects in the nose, and these may be difficult to see without proper instruments. A foreign body may be the cause of a nasal discharge, which is often infected, in children and in adults with subnormal mentality.

Other causes include hormonal changes (eg. at different times during the menstrual cycle, on the contraceptive pill, during pregnancy), tumours or polyps in a nostril, ozaena (lining of the nostril withers away almost completely), a fracture at the base of the skull (loss of the cerebrospinal fluid through the nose), sick building syndrome and France's triad (combination of asthma, aspirin sensitivity and hay fever).

The seldom used medications reserpine and guanethedine that treat uncontrolled high blood pressure may have a watery nose as a side effect.

See also NOSE BLEED; NOSE BLOCKED; SNEEZE and separate entries for most diseases mentioned above.

NSAID

See NONSTEROIDAL ANTI-INFLAMMATORY DRUGS

NSU

See NON-SPECIFIC URETHRITIS

NUCLEAR MAGNETIC RESONANCE IMAGING

See MRI SCAN

NUCLEAR SCAN

Nuclear scanning or imaging (also called isotope scanning) is used to measure the function of various organs, rather than examine their structure. It involves introducing into the body a radioactive chemical that is specifically tailored to go to the part of the body being investigated, and the nuclear energy it gives off will then be picked up by a gamma camera (working like a normal camera but picking up radiation instead of light) which is moved over the relevant area. This will provide a picture of how well the organ under investigation is functioning. An area of under or overactivity may indicate a cyst, abscess, tumour or other abnormality, depending on the organ and on the radioactive chemical being used.

Nuclear scanning can be used to look at many different organs in the body, including the heart, bones, lungs, thyroid gland, liver, spleen and kidneys. It is particularly useful in detecting abnormal heart function and cancer in bone, where normal x-rays are not able to give enough information.

A nuclear heart scan may be performed for angina or cardiomyopathy or after a heart attack to locate and measure damage to heart muscle caused by a clot or embolism. A radioactive substance that is specifically attracted to heart muscle is injected into a vein in the patient's arm. It travels through the circulation to the heart, where it is concentrated in the heart muscle, and will clearly show the site of any damage when photographed with a camera that can detect the rays released from the radioactive substance. The whole process takes less than an hour, and will be performed in a major hospital.

Bone cancer may just show as a nonspecific abnormality of bone on a normal x-ray. To differentiate normal bone from a bone cancer, a similar technique to the heart scan is undertaken, but with a different radioactive substance that concentrates in the abnormal bone.

Nuclear scanning is very safe because the amount of radiation given off by the radioactive chemical is very small – less than that from a detailed kidney X-ray (IVP). The residual chemical is eliminated from the body through the kidneys and bowels in a matter of days or hours, depending on where it has been concentrated. Nevertheless, the test is avoided in pregnant and breast feeding women, unless absolutely essential, to protect the unborn or newborn baby from any irradiation.

NUCLEUS

The nucleus is the control centre in the middle of every cell. It contains the chromosomes, which carry genetic material.
See also CELL

NUELIN

See THEOPHYLLINES

NUMB

See PAIN LOSS; PINS AND NEEDLES SENSATION IN SKIN

NUMMULAR ECZEMA

See DISCOID ECZEMA

NUTRITIONISTS

See DIETICIANS; FOOD

NYMPHOMANIA

Nymphomania is a psychiatric disturbance and a form of mania in women in which there are episodes when the woman has an insatiable desire for sexual activity and gratification, despite there being no emotional attachment to the person with whom she is interacting.
See also MANIA

NYSTAGMUS

Nystagmus is the technical term for an uncontrolled rhythmic or jerking side to side movement of the eye. Usually, only one eye is involved, and the vision is often remarkably normal as the brain compensates for the sudden changes in eye direction. It is a serious sign of disease, and if noticed, must always be checked by a doctor.

Most commonly, infections, inflammation or tumours of the balance mechanism in the inner ear may trigger nystagmus.

Tumours, cysts, abscesses or bleeding into the brain, particularly the base of the brain (brain stem) which is responsible for coordination of movements, is another common cause.

Less common causes include multiple sclerosis (nerve disease), Parinaud syndrome (tumour or inflammation of the pineal gland at the front of the brain), and Friedreich's ataxia (inherited condition caused by damage to chromosome nine).

In some rare cases, babies are born with nystagmus that does not affect them in any other way.

Nystagmus may be an unwanted side effect of medications such as barbiturates (used for sedation and epilepsy) or a result of over indulgence in alcohol.
See also EYE; EYE PARALYSED

NYSTATIN

See ANTIFUNGALS

OAT CELL CARCINOMA
See LUNG CANCER

OATH OF HIPPOCRATES
See HIPPOCRATIC OATH

OBESITY

In Roman times, a beautiful woman was considered to be well proportioned and rounded in the style of Venus de Milo (plus arms of course!). During the Renaissance, voluptuous females of Junoesque proportions were appreciated. Today the tall, skinny, anorexic fashion model is considered to be in vogue. It is possible that those overweight by today's standards were merely born in the wrong era!

Two centuries ago the average person walked twelve kilometres a day, getting adequate exercise and burning off excess weight. As a result, obesity was a sign of wealth as the person did not need to walk long distances for work, or had access to a carriage rather than a horse (horse riding also uses energy).

Up to 40% of people in developed countries are overweight, but only 5% are considered to be obese by medical standards. Obesity is medically defined as being more than 40% over the ideal weight for sex, height and age. Men tend to develop 'apple' obesity (fat around the middle of the body) while women are 'pears' (fat deposits around the buttocks). The 'apple' form has a far higher risk of heart complications.

Those whose weight is within 20% of their recommended weight have little to fear health-wise. Those who exceed this limit are more likely to develop strokes, heart disease, diabetes, arthritis and liver disease.

The causes of obesity can be simply listed (in order of importance) as: –
• inherited tendency
• too much food eaten
• too little exercise
• metabolic (body chemistry) disorders

The vast majority of cases of obesity are due to excessive food and physical inactivity, but if your parents were obese, your chances of also being obese are greatly increased. Some people have very efficient bodies (like a fuel efficient car), and require remarkably little energy in the form of food to remain healthy and active. If the amount of energy used (calories/kilojoules) in exercise and normal body function exceeds the amount of energy taken in as food and drink, the person will always lose weight. If the reverse is true, weight will increase. It should be remembered that calories and kilojoules are a measure of the energy content of food, and not the fat content.

Middle age spread occurs as the metabolic rate of the body (the rate at which all organs in the body function) slows with age, at the same time that exercise levels tend to reduce, and food intake increases with more leisure and security. Many women gain weight after the menopause due to a slowing of the body's metabolic rate when oestrogen levels drop. This effect may be slowed by hormone replacement therapy.

Other metabolic causes of obesity include disorders of the pituitary gland under the brain (caused by a tumour, cancer, stroke, infection, injury or other disease), an under active thyroid gland (hypothyroidism), Cushing syndrome (over production of steroids, or taking large doses of cortisone), poorly controlled insulin dependent diabetes, the chromosomal defect of Prader-Willi syndrome, syndrome X (also known as Reaven syndrome and insulin resistance syndrome), Stein-Leventhal syndrome (multiple cysts in the ovaries), Fröhlich syndrome (late onset of puberty, thin wrinkled skin, scanty body hair) and the Laurence-Moon-Biedl syndrome (night blindness, mental retardation, obesity, small genitals and sometimes extra fingers or toes).

The metabolic cases of obesity must have the underlying condition treated, and not the obesity itself.

Obese men and women tend to spend an incredible amount of money in their attempts to become thin by buying special foods and medicines. The cheapest and most effective way to lose weight is to spend less, by buying less food, particularly less of the expensive processed foods. If you find your willpower is lacking, or the craving for rich foods becomes unbearable, doctors can prescribe tablets that are designed to reduce your appetite (anorectics). These drugs are expensive, and should not be used for long periods, but they are effective.

Orlistat (Xenical) is a drug that reduces the body's ability to absorb fat, and is quite successful in assisting obese people to lose weight, but it must be used in conjunction with a diet program, and some degree of diarrhoea is an almost invariable side effect.

Sibutramine (Reductil) is a medication that was released in 2002, that acts on the brain to reduce appetite. A weight reduction of 5% can be expected in three months in most patients. Patients who are on certain antidepressants and patients with heart disease or high blood pressure cannot use it, blood pressure must be monitored regularly, and the medication is quite expensive. Many other groups should not use this medication, including those over sixty-five years. Its use should be carefully discussed with a doctor.

The long term success rate for those who are truly obese and try to lose weight is very discouraging. Most have yo-yo weights, which fluctuate up and down over the years by 20Kg. or more as they try different diets and exercise programs. This weight fluctuation can be more harmful than staying fat. Overall, less than one in twenty of obese people manage to return to within normal weight limits and stay there for more than five years.

If you do manage to stay on a diet for about five years, and maintain your weight constantly within the desired range, the body will adapt to its new shape, and the metabolic rate may also adjust, so that you may suddenly find after years of dieting that you can relax a little, and still maintain the new weight.
See also ANORECTICS; APPETITE, EXCESS; ORLISTAT; PICKWICKIAN SYNDROME; WEIGHT GAIN; WEIGHT LOSS DIET

OBSESSIVE COMPULSIVE NEUROSIS

The obsessive compulsive neurosis is a psychiatric condition in which the patient has a totally irrational desire to undertake a repetitive task. It is more common in women than in men and occasionally related to previous brain injury or infection (eg. encephalitis).

The desire to perform a task constantly intrudes into the patient's thoughts, and even after completing the task they feel that they must do it again and again. One of the most common desires is hand washing, when a patient cannot be convinced that his/her hands are clean, and must scrub them repeatedly, often to the point where serious dermatitis of the hands develops. Other repetitive desires include constantly checking that a tap is turned off, a door is closed, the fly is zipped up, a window is locked, or innumerable other similar routine tasks have been carried out. Compulsive exercise or running to the point of total exhaustion is another form of obsessive compulsive neurosis. The patient may feel that by performing the rituals, s/he will regain control of a personality and emotions that are felt to be out of control. The patient is well aware that the habit is abnormal, but is powerless to stop it. More frightening compulsions may occur such as the constant desire to hit or hurt someone else, to steal, to vandalise or to injure oneself in some way. In extreme cases, these desires may lead to criminal acts or suicide.

Another form is the body dysmorphic disorder, in which patients are obsessed with their appearance, and particularly their facial appearance, and constantly check in mirrors for any abnormality in the way they look.

Treatment involves psychotherapy, behavioural therapy and medication (eg. antidepressants such as paroxetine, sertraline). Long term treatment usually required, and the control of symptoms is only reasonable.
See also GAMBLING; NEUROSIS

OBSTETRICS

The science of dealing with pregnancy and birth is obstetrics. Doctors specialising in this field are known as obstetricians, and often also deal with gynaecology (the science of medical problems specific to women).
See also LABOUR; PREGNANCY

OCCIPITAL BONE

The occipital bone forms the back and lower back part of the skull.
See also SKULL

OCCUPATIONAL OVERUSE SYNDROME

See REPETITIVE STRAIN INJURY

OCCUPATIONAL THERAPY

Occupational therapists have completed a specific university degree in their area of skill and knowledge. The philosophy of occupational therapy rests with the assumption that the health level of individuals is affected by the activities and functions which are open to them or denied them. Occupational therapists therefore, through the use of therapeutic activities, specialised equipment and techniques, help individuals regain, maintain and develop functional competence which has been impaired or thwarted by disease, trauma, developmental abnormalities, psychological problems or social disadvantage. The activities include work, feeding, dressing and personal care, education, creative media, recreation, and social activities.

Occupational therapists may teach patients with heart disease or AIDS ways of getting tasks done with less effort, help stroke victims with their movement problems, assist intellectually disabled to manage a variety of jobs by breaking them down into simple and easily handled units, educate the institutionalised patient on the use of community facilities, or use relaxation and other psychosocial techniques, individually or in groups, to improve the coping strategies or self-image of both children and adults.

Equipment commonly used includes devices for measuring performance, splints, a variety of aids to facilitate performance in daily living tasks (from cooking to driving), wheelchairs, and computers which may be used for clinical assessment, vocational training, communication, or as devices to facilitate the interface between the disabled and their environment. *See also* PHYSIOTHERAPY

OCULAR LARVA MIGRANS
See VISCERAL LARVA MIGRANS

OCULOGYRIC CRISIS

An oculogyric crisis is a rare complication of encephalitis (brain inflammation), Parkinson's disease and some drugs (eg. the antiemetic prochlorperazine – Stemetil). Patients develop a constant upward movement of the eyes, and painful extension of the neck so the head is tilted backwards as far as possible, that last for minutes or hours. It is rapidly cured by injection of the drug benztropine into a vein. *See also* ANTIEMETICS

ODYNOPHAGIA
See SWALLOWING PAINFUL

OEDEMA

Oedema is the technical term for the swelling of tissues anywhere in the body due to accumulation of fluid. The fluid may be blood, serum (blood without cells) or lymph (waste fluid from cells).

The tissue around any part of the body that is injured by a blow, break or cut will swell up as a reaction (inflammation) to the injury.

Urticaria (hives) is an allergy reaction in skin that causes marked swelling in patches across the affected area, which becomes red and itchy. If the eyes are affected, quite dramatic swelling of the eyelids and the whites of the eyes may occur. Severe allergy reactions (anaphylaxis) may cause swelling in the throat, lungs and heart and may be life threatening. Any one of several billion substances from plants, animals or chemicals, may be responsible.

Infections of skin (erysipelas) or the underlying fat and other tissues (cellulitis) will cause redness, pain and swelling, sometimes associated with blistering.

Several types of severe dermatitis, due to contact with various irritating substances, overexposure to sunlight (photodermatitis) and allergies will cause swelling of the affected skin and an overlying rash.

Failure of the heart to contract effectively because of high blood pressure, narrowed arteries, heart attack or other disease will lead to a back up of blood in the distant parts of the body (eg. feet, hands) and swelling of these. This is congestive cardiac failure.

The veins in the legs contain one-way valves that allow blood to only travel up towards the heart when they are squeezed by muscle action. If these valves are damaged by increased pressure (eg. during pregnancy, prolonged standing), obesity or direct injury, the blood is unable to move out of the leg as quickly, and the veins dilate with blood to form varicose veins. These may ache and cause oedema of the legs as well as being unsightly.

Many women experience swelling of their hands and feet, and sometimes breasts and pelvis, in the few days before a menstrual period due to the generalised retention of fluid. Headache and irritability at this time may be caused by fluid retention in the brain.

Other causes of oedema include the

nephrotic syndrome (kidney failure), a blood clot in a vein (thrombophlebitis), lymphoedema (build up of waste products in an arm or leg due to a blockage of the lymph ducts), myxoedema (due to an underactive thyroid gland – hypothyroidism), Cushing syndrome (over production of steroids, or taking large doses of cortisone) and stasis dermatitis (due to prolonged sitting without moving).

Uncommon causes of fluid retention include glomerulonephritis (a form of kidney failure), liver failure (from hepatitis, cirrhosis etc.), liver cancer, carcinoid syndrome (due to a rare tumour – argentaffinoma – in the intestine or lungs), beriberi (severe lack of vitamin B), the eosinophilia-myalgia syndrome (eating excessive amounts of the protein L-tryptophan), a severe lack of protein in the diet (kwashiorkor) and the African diseases of sleeping sickness (trypanosomiasis) and elephantiasis (filariasis).

Some medications, including calcium channel blockers (used for high blood pressure), indomethacin (used for arthritis), clonidine and prednisone may cause oedema as a side effect.
See also ANGIONEUROTIC OEDEMA; FACE SWOLLEN and separate entries for diseases mentioned above.

OESOPHAGEAL ACHALASIA
See ACHALASIA

OESOPHAGEAL CANCER
Known risk factors for cancer of the gullet (oesophagus) include excess alcohol (particularly whisky) consumption, smoking, eating very large quantities of pickled vegetables, maize overcooked in iron pots and persistent reflux of stomach acid. It is uncommon in western society, but relatively common in central Asia and southern Africa.

Patients develop difficulty and pain with swallowing that steadily worsens, and associated weight loss. Food that the patient attempts to swallow may be vomited and inhaled, causing pneumonia.

It is diagnosed by oesophagoscopy (passing a flexible tube into the oesophagus) or a barium swallow x-ray, then radical surgery may be performed to remove the cancer. The prognosis is unfortunately very poor with only 5% surviving five years.
See also OESOPHAGUS;

PLUMMER-VINSON SYNDROME; REFLUX OESOPHAGITIS

OESOPHAGITIS
See BARRETT SYNDROME; PLUMMER-VINSON SYNDROME; REFLUX OESOPHAGITIS

OESOPHAGOSCOPY
See GASTROSCOPY

OESOPHAGUS
The oesophagus, or gullet, is the muscular tube connecting the pharynx at the back of the mouth with the stomach. When food has been chewed in the mouth and mixed with saliva, it forms into a soft mass called a bolus, ready for swallowing. The tongue pushes the bolus into the throat, or pharynx, and from there it moves to the oesophagus.

The two outer layers of the oesophagus consist of strong muscle to propel the food along, while the lining is a mucous membrane able to keep the food lubricated. Although the food under normal circumstances moves downward and so is assisted by gravity, gravity is not absolutely essential, and the oesophagus can do the job by itself if it has to.

Once the process of swallowing is under way, for the first few seconds you cannot breathe or talk, and several muscular movements automatically come into play. The soft palate in the roof of the mouth is raised so that the food won't go up the nose; the pharynx rises and widens to accommodate the food; the tongue is raised to seal the back of the mouth and prevent unchewed food or other substances from sliding down as well; and a flap of cartilage called the epiglottis covers the opening to the larynx and lungs. An attempt to laugh or talk during swallowing sometimes causes one of these movements to malfunction and so food goes down the wrong way or is forced up into the nasal cavity with all its attendant discomfort.

Once the food is in the oesophagus, a series of muscular contractions force it down the tube and into the stomach. A ring of muscle (the cardiac or lower oesophageal sphincter) at the top of the stomach opens to let the food through. It takes three to five seconds for food to travel this far.

On its way to the stomach, the oesophagus has to pass through a hole in the diaphragm.

If there is a weakness in the diaphragm at this point, part of the stomach may protrude through it and cause what is called a hiatus hernia, allowing acid to flow back up from the stomach into the oesophagus.
See also BOERHAAVE SYNDROME; DIAPHRAGM; HEARTBURN; HIATUS HERNIA; PHARYNX; REFLUX OESOPHAGITIS; STOMACH; SWALLOWING PAINFUL

OESTRADIOL
See SEX HORMONES

OESTRIOL
See SEX HORMONES

OESTROGEN
See OVARY; SEX HORMONES

OILY SKIN
See SEBACEOUS GLANDS; SEBORRHOEIC ECZEMA

OLANZAPINE
See ANTIPSYCHOTICS

OLEANDER POISONING
See POISONOUS PLANTS

OLECRANON
See ULNAR

OLFACTORY NERVES
See SMELL

OLIGOHYDRAMNIOS
In the womb, the baby is surrounded by, and floats in, a sac filled with amniotic fluid. This fluid acts to protect the foetus from bumps and jarring, recirculates waste, and acts as a fluid for the baby to drink. If insufficient fluid is present, the condition is called oligohydramnios.

Normally there is about a litre (1000mL) of amniotic fluid at birth. A volume less than 200mL is considered to be diagnostic of oligohydramnios. It may be caused by abnormal development of the foetus, or abnormal function of the placenta, but in most cases there is no reason for the problem.

The condition is diagnosed by an ultrasound scan, and if proved, further investigations to determine the cause of the condition follow. Treatment will depend upon the result of these tests, but often none is necessary.
See also POLYHYDRAMNIOS; PREGNANCY

OLIGOMENORRHOEA
Oligomenorrhoea is a medical term that means infrequent menstrual periods.
See MENSTRUAL PERIODS, LACK OF

OLIGURIA
See URINE REDUCED

-OLOGY
'-ology' is a suffix derived from the Greek word for study and used in science and medicine to indicate a particular branch of medicine or interest. For example, dermatology means 'skin study'.

-OMA
'-oma' is a suffix derived from the Greek and used in medicine to indicate an abnormal growth or tumour. For example, carcinoma means 'cancer growth'.

OMEPRAZOLE
See PROTON PUMP INHIBITORS

ONCHOCERCIASIS
Onchocerciasis (river blindness) is caused by the nematode worm *Onchocerciasis volvulus*. The nematode is carried from one person to another by the bite of a small black fly that only lives along rivers. Larvae are deposited in the skin by the bite, mature after six to thirty-six months into adult worms which are up to 60cm. long and live tightly coiled under the skin. The adult worm releases tiny microfilariae into the blood and these spread throughout the body, particularly to the skin, eyes and lymph nodes. A biting fly can pick up the microfilariae when it sucks up blood, and there they develop into larvae. Adult worms can live up to eighteen years. It only occurs in equatorial Africa, southern Arabia and central America.

The symptoms include extremely itchy skin, generalised rash, lumps under the skin usually over the lower back and thighs, premature ageing and wrinkling of the skin, changes in skin pigmentation and grossly enlarged lymph nodes in the groin. Blindness occurs in 5% of patients when the microfilariae spread to the eye and damage the cornea (clear surface layer of the eye). Rarely, muscles and the intestine may be affected to cause weakness and weight loss.

Surgical removal and examination of a skin lump reveals an adult worm, and medication can be given to kill the microfilariae. The medication often must be repeated every six months for some years to give a cure. The death rate in untreated patients is about one in a hundred.

See also NEMATODE

ONYCHOGRYPHOSIS

Onychogryphosis or tinea unguium, is a fungal infection that occurs under finger and toe nails and distorts the nails. Fungi such as *Trichophyton rubrum* and *Microsporum* may infect damaged or softened nails and surrounding tissue. If the nail is infected but not damaged the condition is called onychomycosis. The nails appear white or yellow and gradually thicken. It is more common in the middle-aged and elderly, and toe nails are usually more severely affected than the fingers, and sometimes the nail may be lost.

Scrapings from under nails are cultured and examined under a microscope to identify the fungus.

The infection is notoriously difficult to treat but amorolfine paint may be applied to the nail weekly for many months, or terbinafine tablets are taken daily for up to six months. In both cases, as the fungus is destroyed, new normal nail gradually grows out to replace the thick damaged nail, and these newer treatments are quite effective.

See also FUNGI; NAIL DISCOLOURED

ONYCHOMYCOSIS

See ONYCHOGRYPHOSIS

OPHTHALMOLOGY

The branch of medical science that deals with the eyes and related tissues is ophthalmology. Doctors specialising in this field are known as ophthalmologists.

See also EYE; OPTOMETRIST

OPHTHALMOSCOPY

Ophthalmoscopy is examination of the eye using an ophthalmoscope – a small device, held by hand, which shines a beam of light into the eye. The instrument has a series of lenses and by focusing these, the light beam can be directed through the pupil so that all the structures of the eye from the cornea in the front to the retina at the back are magnified and can easily be seen and investigated.

Ophthalmoscopy can help the ophthalmologist (eye specialist) diagnose cataracts (a clouding of the lens in the eye resulting in blurred vision, particularly common in elderly people), corneal ulcers, foreign bodies in the eye, and many other problems. Even the light-sensitive retina at the back of the eye can be inspected, together with the retinal blood vessels and the beginning of the optic nerve which links the eye with the brain, and detachment of the retina can be diagnosed. The blood vessels in the retina can also signal vascular abnormalities in other parts of the body and may give early warning of narrowing arteries to the heart, high blood pressure, anaemia, and diseases such as diabetes. The eye is the only place in the body where blood vessels can be seen directly.

An ophthalmoscope is also used to test how well the cornea and lens of the eye refract light, i.e. whether the patient's sight is as good as it should be or if they need glasses or contact lenses.

The patient is usually given eye drops before ophthalmoscopy so that the pupils dilate and allow the inside of the eye to be more easily examined. The drops make the vision blurry for an hour or so afterwards. If a more detailed examination of the retina is required, this may be carried out with a retinoscope, which is similar to an ophthalmoscope but provides higher magnification and is more sensitive, and takes a photo of the retina.

See also CATARACT; EYE; VISION

OPIUM

See HEROIN; NARCOTICS

OPTIC

The medical term for any matters relating to the eye is "optic".

See also EYE

OPTOMETRIST

An optometrist is a person who has undertaken university training to perform tests to determine visual acuity for the prescription of spectacles, and to detect (but not treat) eye diseases.

See also OPHTHALMOLOGY; VISION

ORAL
See MOUTH

ORAL CANCER
See MOUTH CANCER

ORAL CONTRACEPTIVE
See CONTRACEPTIVE PILL

ORCHITIS
See EPIDIDYMO-ORCHITIS

ORF
Orf is an unusual viral infection of sheep and goats that can infect the skin on the fingers and hands of people (eg. shearers, abattoir workers, veterinarians) who come into close contact with infected animals, when the *Parapoxvirus* can enter a minor injury to the skin. A sore develops at the site of infection about ten days later, and this enlarges to become a large, fluid-filled, ulcerating and scabbing lump that may be one to three centimetres across. The lymph nodes in the armpit or other areas may become tender and a secondary bacterial infection of the sore may occur. The lump becomes soft, breaks down, and heals completely after four to eight weeks, leaving no scar.

ORGAN INVERSION
See KARTAGENER SYNDROME; SITUS INVERSUS

ORGAN OF CORTI
See EAR

ORGANOPHOSPHATE POISONING
See INSECTICIDE POISONING

ORGASM
The female orgasm is a reflex, in the same way as a tap on the knee causes a reflex. Some people have a vigorous response to a knee tap, others have little. Thus it is difficult to determine what is a normal and abnormal reflex or orgasm.

An orgasm is the female equivalent of the male ejaculation.

The woman feels an intense sensation of pleasure sweeping over her associated with contractions of the muscles in the vagina and uterus and tingling of the nipples. This may last for a few seconds or half a minute.

Different women require different degrees and types of stimulation to have an orgasm. Some can only orgasm by stimulation of the clitoris, others require prolonged intercourse, while others may orgasm frequently and easily with merely breast stimulation or thinking about sex. A woman may find that one particular sex position causes orgasm more easily than other positions.
See also EJACULATION; MASTURBATION; ORGASM, LACK OF; SEXUAL INTERCOURSE

ORGASM, LACK OF
The muscles in the wall of the vagina contract in pleasurable spasms when a woman has an orgasm during intercourse. This rhythmic contraction aids the movement of the ejaculated sperm towards the cervix and uterus. Some women rarely, or never, experience orgasm. A woman may be sexually responsive, enjoy sex and have the physical signs of erotic arousal, but she may still fail to have an orgasm.

Different women require different degrees and types of stimulation to have an orgasm, which is a reflex, in the same way as a tap on the knee causes a reflex. Some women can only orgasm by stimulation of the clitoris, others require prolonged intercourse, while others may orgasm frequently and easily with merely breast stimulation or thinking about sex.

Common causes of occasional or regular lack of orgasm (anorgasmia) include psychological or physical stress, anxiety, fatigue, over indulgence in alcohol and poor sexual technique by her partner. Pain during sex is obviously not going to help the situation.

Infections (eg. thrush, *Trichomonas*) or ulceration (eg. *Herpes*) of the vagina or vulva will cause discomfort and reduce sensation.

Injuries to the spine (eg. paraplegia) or nerves (eg. pelvic fracture or surgery) that supply the vagina will affect the sensation of orgasm.

Underactivity of numerous hormone-producing glands in the body, including the ovaries (oestrogen), thyroid (thyroxine) and adrenal glands (adrenaline) because of infection, inflammation, tumours, cysts or cancer, will reduce all bodily responses and functions. The pituitary gland under the centre of the brain controls all other glands, and diseases affecting this gland can affect any other gland in the body.

If the woman is suffering some significant generalised disease (eg. infection, cancer), or is in any pain, her responses will be reduced.

Some medications, including antidepressants, narcotics, sedatives and blood pressure drugs may reduce the ability to experience an orgasm.

Treatment is difficult. Obviously, any underlying cause should be treated, but if all these are excluded the following procedure may be adopted.

The woman should be taught relaxation techniques, accompanied by masturbation by hand or mechanical devices, in order to bring herself to orgasm. Once she has experienced orgasm in this manner, she can move to the next stage of treatment with a male partner. This may involve the man using his hand to stimulate her to orgasm, or by using different sex positions (eg. man behind woman) during which the woman can stimulate her own clitoris. The supervision of a sex therapist (psychiatrist or psychologist) in this process is invaluable. Treatment is often successful if a woman and her partner are both well motivated.

See also ORGASM; SEXUAL INTERCOURSE PAIN and separate entries for diseases mentioned above.

ORIENTAL SORE
See CUTANEOUS LEISCHMANIASIS

ORIENTAL SPOTTED FEVER
See TYPHUS

ORLISTAT
Orlistat (Xenical) is a drug introduced in the year 2000 to treat significant obesity. It acts by preventing the absorption of fat from the intestine.

Common side effects include diarrhoea (worse if fat is eaten), flatulence, liquid faeces and headache.

It should be used with caution in pregnancy and children, and those with peptic ulcers, psychiatric disturbances, adhesions in belly, kidney stones, and serious heart, liver or kidney disease.

Patients should not take Orlistat if they are breast feeding, suffering from pancreatitis or some types of gall bladder disease, or are normal or under weight.

See also ANORECTICS; OBESITY

ORNITHOSIS
See PSITTACOSIS

ORPHENADRINE
See MUSCLE RELAXANTS

ORTHODONTICS
Orthodontics deals with the correction of teeth that are wrongly positioned. Ideally, teeth and jaws should match each other. As the face grows and the deciduous teeth are lost, the permanent teeth that replace them should slot neatly into place with no gaps and no crossing, forming a symmetrical elliptical arch like a string of pearls. The upper teeth should lock into the lower arch so that, when moved, the jaw joint moves smoothly in its socket.

Treatment is needed when the appearance or the function of teeth is less than satisfactory. Some faults are inherited; a small jaw may be characteristic of one side of the family, and large teeth a feature of the other side. Other faults are acquired; a disease suffered while the teeth are growing in the jaws can affect their formation. Teeth may be lost prematurely from decay or an accident and at times some teeth do not appear at all. Some undesirable habits, such as mouth-breathing due to a permanently blocked nose, thumb-sucking, tongue-thrusting or lip-sucking, can easily displace some of the teeth temporarily or permanently.

The orthodontist is trained to predict the growth pattern of the jaws and how to redirect it. Special x-rays of the head show how the teeth are lying in the skull and what influence they exert on the profile of the face. The jaw may be jutting aggressively forward, or lie too far back and give the appearance of a weak-looking chin. The orthodontist sets out to correct both the appearance and function of the misplaced teeth. If there is a shortage of room for all the teeth, either the arch is expanded to make more room, or some teeth are extracted. To expand the arch, small steel bands are cemented around the upper molar teeth. A detachable metal frame fits into the bands and, with the aid of an elastic strap passing behind the neck, the frame pulls those teeth backward and outwards to make a bigger arch and allow room for all the other teeth.

The optimum time for orthodontics is at

puberty. There is a sudden spurt of body growth at this age, when the last of the permanent teeth appear and the face and jaws expand to their final adult shape. The growing bone can be redirected to a desirable pattern. This is done by attaching wire springs to the teeth to guide them gently to their new positions. Under the small but constant pressure of the spring, the bone in front of the tooth is resorbed and the tooth moves into the space created. New bone is then formed behind the tooth to fill the space created by the movement. After several months when the teeth are in their new position, the bands are removed and often a temporary appliance is inserted to prevent the whole process from reversing to its original position.

Orthodontists sometimes move single teeth, particularly in adults, for reasons such as improving its position to take a crown or a bridge. At times an eye tooth may be held up in the palate, and in these cases a hook and spring are attached to its crown to pull it down into position.

Orthodontics may sometimes seem expensive in the short term, but when amortised over a lifetime of perceived benefit, it is very cost effective.
See also DENTISTRY; TEETH

ORTHOMOLECULAR MEDICINE
The treatment of disease by using vitamins and other chemicals normally present in the body, often in large doses, is known as orthomolecular medicine.
See also NATUROPATHY

ORTHOPAEDICS
The science of dealing with bones, joints, muscles, ligaments and related tissues is orthopaedics. Doctors specialising in this field are known as orthopaedic surgeons.
See also BONE; HIP REPLACEMENT; JOINT

OSELTAMIVIR
See ANTIVIRALS

OSGOOD-SCHLATTER'S DISEASE
Osgood-Schlatter's disease (apophysitis of the tibial tuberosity) is a relatively common but minor knee condition of children and teenagers.

At the top and front of the tibia (shin bone)

in the lower leg, there is a lump just below the knee (the tibial tuberosity). The large patellar tendon runs from the tibial tuberosity up to the knee cap (patella) and through this is connected to the large muscles on the front of the thigh (quadriceps). When the knee is straightened the thigh muscles contract, pull on the patella, which pulls on the patellar tendon, which is attached to the tibial tuberosity, which pulls the tibia into position and straightens the knee. Children who are growing rapidly tend to have slightly softened bones and, in a child who exercises a great deal, it is possible for the tibial tuberosity to be pulled slightly away from the softened growing area of the tibia behind it. This separation of the tibial tuberosity from the upper part of the tibia causes considerable pain.

The patient is usually a boy, a keen sportsman, and between nine and fifteen years of age, who develops pain, tenderness and sometimes an obvious swelling just below the knee. The pain is worse, or may only occur, whenever the knee is straightened, particularly when walking or running. The knee joint itself is pain-free. The diagnosis confirmed by x-rays that show the separation of the tibial tuberosity from the tibia.

The only treatment is time and rest. In severe cases, strapping or plaster and crutches may be necessary to rest the knee adequately. The prognosis is very good, but two to six months' rest may be required.
See also KNEE PAIN; TIBIA

OSLER, WILLIAM
Sir William Osler (1849-1919) was a Canadian physician who also practised in the USA and England. He was renowned as a teacher and clinician, and identified small red spots on the finger tips (Osler's nodes) as a sign of bacterial endocarditis. A number of more obscure medical signs and phenomena are also named after him.
See also ENDOCARDITIS

OSTEITIS DEFORMANS
See PAGET'S DISEASE OF BONE

OSTEO-
'Osteo-' is a prefix derived from the Greek word for bone (osteon) and used in medicine to indicate conditions, diseases, investigations etc. related to bone.

OSTEOARTHRITIS

Osteoarthritis is a degeneration of one or more joints that affects up to 15% of the population, most of them being elderly. The cartilage within joints breaks down, and inflammation of the bone exposed by the damaged cartilage occurs, which is then aggravated by injury and overuse of the joint. There is also a hereditary tendency to develop osteoarthritis.

Symptoms are usually mild at first, but slowly worsen with time and joint abuse. The knees, back, hips, feet and hands are most commonly affected. Stiffness and pain that are relieved by rest are the initial symptoms, but as the disease progresses, swelling, limitation of movement, deformity and partial dislocation (subluxation) of a joint may occur. A crackling noise may come from the joint when it is moved, and nodules may develop adjacent to joints on the fingers in severe cases. X-rays show characteristic changes from a relatively early stage, and repeated X-rays are used to follow the course of the disease. There are no diagnostic blood tests.

Patients should avoid any movement or action that causes pain in the affected joints, such as climbing stairs and carrying loads (obese patients should lose weight). Paracetamol, aspirin, heat and anti-inflammatory drugs may be used to reduce the pain in a damaged joint, and physiotherapy, acupuncture and massage have also been found to be useful. Surgery to replace affected joints is very successful, with the most common joints replaced being the hip, knee and fingers. Surgery to fuse together the joints in the back is sometimes necessary to prevent movement between them, as they cannot be replaced. Steroid injections into an acutely inflamed joint may give rapid relief, but they cannot be repeated frequently because of the risk of damage to the joint.

The prognosis depends on the joints involved and the disease severity. Cures can be achieved by joint replacement surgery, while other patients achieve reasonable control with medications. The inflammation in some severely affected joints can sometimes 'burn out' and disappear with time.
See also ARTHRITIS; JOINT;
RHEUMATOID ARTHRITIS

OSTEOCHONDRITIS DESSICANS

Osteochondritis dessicans is caused by an injury to the cartilage lining the knee joint. A fragment of cartilage separates from the joint surface and floats free in the joint (synovial) fluid, usually due to a sudden major injury, or repeated minor injuries, to the knee.

Patients experience dull aching pain in the knee joint that is worsened by exercise and may be accompanied by swelling, and locking of the knee in one position may be difficult to relieve. X-rays of the knee may be able to confirm the diagnosis, but otherwise it is diagnosed during arthroscopy (looking into the joint through a thin tube).

Initially, rest and strapping may be effective treatments, but persistent or severe cases require surgical treatment, usually by arthroscopy.
See also ARTHROSCOPY; CARTILAGE;
CHONDROMALACIA PATELLAE;
KNEE PAIN

OSTEOCLASTOMA
See BONE CANCER

OSTEOGENESIS IMPERFECTA

Osteogenesis imperfecta is a rare disease, commonly known as brittle bone disease, in which a child is born with fragile, brittle bones that break easily and heal poorly. The condition tends to run in families in an irregular pattern, and varying degrees of severity are possible, with some patients being far more severely affected than others.

These children suffer multiple painful fractures that take months to heal and often leave a permanent deformity. Other characteristics include deafness, a blue colour to the whites of the eyes, spinal deformities and teeth defects. It is diagnosed by x-rays, which show a typical appearance in the long bones of the legs and arms.

No treatment available and many patients die before puberty, but if they survive to adult life, the disease tends to become less severe, and a relatively normal life expectancy is possible.
See also BONE; FRACTURE

OSTEOGENIC SARCOMA
See BONE CANCER

OSTEOMA
See BONE CANCER

OSTEOMALACIA

Osteomalacia is the adult form of the bone disease rickets (which occurs only in growing children, and results in softening of the bones). The cause is a lack of calcium, usually due to overactivity of the parathyroid gland (which controls the calcium balance of the body) in the neck. Other causes include a deficiency in vitamin D or phosphate (both are essential to control calcium activity within the body), kidney failure, Fanconi syndrome, alcoholism and other poisons.

The symptoms of osteomalacia may be very mild, or the patient may have muscle weakness, tiredness and bone pain. Fractures are only slightly more common than would normally be expected. The condition is diagnosed by blood tests, x-ray and bone biopsy. Treatment involves improving the diet, prescribing vitamin D, giving calcium supplements and taking medications that force calcium into the bones. A further deterioration of bone strength is unlikely with correct treatment.
See also BONE; CALCIUM; FANCONI SYNDROME; RICKETS

OSTEOMYELITIS

Osteomyelitis is a serious but uncommon infection of a bone which is more common in children. The femur (thigh bone), tibia (shin bone) and humerus (upper arm bone) are most commonly affected, but any bone in the body may be involved. Often there is no obvious cause (presumably the infecting bacteria reaches the bone through the blood), but any cut or injury that penetrates through to the bone leaves it open to infection.

The infected bone becomes painful, tender and warm, the tissue over it is red and swollen, and the patient is feverish and feels ill. Complications may include septicaemia, permanent damage to the bone and nearby joints, bone death and collapse, persistent infection and damage to the growing area of a bone in a child.

X-rays show bone damage, but often not until several days after the infection has started. Blood tests for the presence of bacteria, plus the appearance of the patient, are usually sufficient to allow the commencement of treatment using potent antibiotics, which are often given by injection for several weeks. Once the infecting bacteria have been correctly identified, the antibiotic may be changed, if necessary. Strict bed rest is required and if pus is present in the bone, an operation to drain it is essential. The majority of osteomyelitis cases are controlled and cured by correct treatment.
See also BONE; SEPTICAEMIA

OSTEOPATHY

Osteopathy is a system of manipulating the spine and other joints and their surrounding soft tissues to enhance nerve and blood supply and thereby improve back problems, other joint disorders and all body tissues. Orthodox medicine looks upon manipulation as merely one therapeutic action among a range of treatments available to patients with disorders of joints and muscles. Manipulation is also carried out by doctors and physiotherapists.
See also CHIROPRACTIC; MANIPULATION; NATUROPATHY

OSTEOPOROSIS

Osteoporosis is a common bone condition affecting one quarter of women over the age of fifty, in which the basic constituent of bone, calcium, drops to a dangerously low level, and the bones soften and may bend, break or collapse. Calcium is found in all dairy food (particularly cheese), sardines, shellfish, beans, nuts and tripe. Adults require up to 800 mg. of calcium, and children and pregnant women up to 1400 mg. a day. The structure of bones is constantly renewed, and a lack of calcium over many years leads to a gradual deterioration in bone strength. Once women reach the menopause, the drop in hormone levels accelerates the loss of calcium from bones. It may be hereditary and is more common in petite, small-boned women.

Most patients do not know they have the disease until they fracture a bone (particularly the hip or a vertebra) with minimal injury, or on a routine x-ray their bones are seen to be more transparent than normal. Dual photon densitometry, a procedure similar to an x-ray, can diagnose osteoporosis at an early stage. Deformity of the back, severe arthritis, and neuralgia caused by the collapsing bones pinching nerves, can occur in due course.

Prevention involves adding calcium to the diet before menopause, and by taking calcium supplements and hormone replacement therapy after menopause. Regular exercise is important, as the minor stresses on the bones keep them stronger. In more serious cases,

sophisticated, very effective medications (eg. alendronate, calcitriol, disodium etidronate) that force calcium into bones to strengthen them, may be prescribed to be taken daily for several years. Other factors that can help are reducing the intake of coffee and alcohol, and stopping smoking. Control is good once the condition is diagnosed, but reversal of existing damage is difficult.
See also BONE; CALCIUM; FRACTURE; SEX HORMONES

OSTEOSARCOMA
See BONE CANCER

OTIC
The medical term for any matters relating to the ear is 'otic'.
See also EAR

OTIC FURUNCULOSIS
See FURUNCULOSIS, EAR

OTITIS EXTERNA
Otitis externa is commonly known as swimmer's ear, and is an infection of the ear canal. The most common cause is retained water in the ear canal, while other causes include irritating the ear canal with a cotton bud or similar object, badly fitting hearing aids, excess ear wax, sweating in dirty and dusty conditions, and dermatitis in the ear canal.

The outer ear normally contains harmless bacteria, but if the canal remains constantly wet, the bacteria can invade tissue to cause an infection. If a fungus is the cause it is called tropical ear. These infections are more common in children because their narrower ear canals retain water easily, but they can be prevented by using drying drops in the ear after each period of swimming, or inserting ear plugs before swimming. Sea water is less likely to be a problem than fresh water.

The outer ear canal and the outer surface of the eardrum become excruciatingly painful. The onset is often very rapid and, as the infection progresses, a discharge from the ear usually develops. The infection can injure the eardrum and repeated attacks may cause permanent damage. Untreated infections can spread through the eardrum and cause a more serious middle ear infection (otitis media).

In most cases, no investigations are necessary but, if the infection is persistent, swabs may be taken so that the responsible bacteria and fungi can be identified. Treatment involves cleaning the ear of any wax or debris that may be present in the canal, and inserting antibiotic drops or ointment. In difficult cases a wick (piece of light material) soaked in antibiotic ointment or drops may be put in the ear. Tropical ear, a severe form of otitis externa caught in hot, humid environments, is more difficult to cure and a prolonged course of antifungal drops or ointment and antifungal tablets is necessary.
See also EAR; EARACHE; OTITIS MEDIA

OTITIS MEDIA
Otitis media is a bacterial infection of the middle ear.

The middle ear is a cavity that contains three tiny bones, which transmit the vibrations of the eardrum to the hearing mechanism in the inner ear. There is a small tube (the Eustachian tube) connecting the middle ear to the back of the nose, and infection can enter the middle ear from there. Infection can also spread from the outer ear to the middle ear. Children are more commonly affected than adults.

Patients experience a sudden onset of severe pain, often at night, and a fever. Pressure on the outside of the ear causes additional pain and relative deafness. Antibiotics and medications are prescribed to dry up phlegm, but it is sometimes necessary to perform a small operation on the eardrum to relieve the pressure. The use of antibiotics in early otitis media is probably less effective than once thought, although most doctors still advocate their use. If there is rapid worsening of the infection, the bulging eardrum may burst, and blood and pus will ooze out of the ear canal. A rupture of the eardrum may relieve the pain, but treatment with antibiotics is essential to ensure that the eardrum repairs itself. If the hole in the eardrum fails to heal after several months, it may be necessary to have an operation to repair it. Rarer complications include a spread of the infection into the surrounding bone (mastoiditis), or into the bloodstream or brain.

Patients get very good results with appropriate treatment, and a ruptured eardrum usually heals in one or two weeks.
See also CHOLESTEATOMA; EAR;

EARACHE; EUSTACHIAN TUBE; GLUE EAR; OTITIS EXTERNA; TYMPANIC RUPTURE

OTORHINOLARYNGOLOGY

This is the science of dealing with the ear, nose and throat and related tissues. Doctors specialising in this field are often known as ENT (ear, nose and throat) surgeons rather than the more technical and unpronounceable otorhinolaryngologist. 'Oto' refers to the ear, 'rhino' to the nose and 'laryng' to the throat or larynx, while 'ology' is the term used to denote an area of study.

See also EAR; NOSE; LARYNX; PHARYNX; TONSILLECTOMY

OTOSCLEROSIS

Otosclerosis is a relatively common form of arthritis in the tiny bones (malleus, incus and stapes) in the middle ear, which vibrate to transmit sounds from the eardrum to the hearing mechanism in the inner ear. The middle ear bones become soft and enlarged, which reduces their ability to transmit vibration, and thus sound. It is more common in women, usually starts in the late teens or twenties, and its onset may be triggered by pregnancy. There is a significant tendency for it to pass from one generation to the next, and eventually it affects about one person in every 200 in old age.

There is a steadily worsening deafness and a constant ringing noise in the ears (tinnitus), and dizziness occurs in some patients. Special tests on ear function are used to make the diagnosis.

A hearing aid can be very effective, but the treatment of choice is a permanent operative cure in which the affected bones in the middle ear are replaced with Teflon substitutes. The disease progresses very slowly, and it never results in total deafness, but the earlier in life the condition starts, the worse the noises become, and the greater the final hearing loss.

See also DEAF; EAR

OTOSCOPE

See AURISCOPE

OVARIAN CANCER

The absolute cause of cancer of the ovary is unknown, but there is a family tendency. It is a relatively uncommon cancer, affecting about one in every 20 000 women in developed countries every year, and the majority of them will be over sixty years of age.

Most women present with a large, painless lump in the lower abdomen, or with pelvic discomfort. The cancer is diagnosed by a CT or ultrasound scan of the pelvis, and then surgery to remove the affected ovary and surrounding tissue is performed, followed by drug treatment (chemotherapy) with cytotoxics. The overall five-year survival rate for all ovarian cancer patients is only 35%, usually due to the early spread of the cancer to other parts of the body.

See also CANCER; MEIGS SYNDROME; OVARY; TERATOMA

OVARIAN CYST

An ovarian cyst (fluid-filled sac) is usually less than five centimetres across, but rarely they may form giant cysts the size of a football. Several types are known, including follicular cysts, luteal cysts, cysts caused by infections of the ovary and tubes, cysts associated with endometriosis, and rare cases associated with some types of ovarian cancers.

Every time a woman releases an egg from her ovary it is surrounded by a tiny sac of fluid, and some women experience a slight stab of pain (mittelschmerz) as the fluid around the egg is released with ovulation in the middle of each month. If these normal tiny cysts re-form and enlarge after releasing the egg, a follicular cyst of the ovary results. Luteal cysts tend to be larger and are due to persistence of the tissue that is designed to nurture any growing embryo in its first few weeks of life.

The woman is often not aware that a follicular cyst is present unless it is discovered at surgery, or it bursts. They cause some irregularity of the periods but if a cyst bursts, the woman experiences sudden, severe pain on one side, low down in her abdomen. The pain eases slowly over several hours or days, as the irritating fluid contained in the cyst disperses. They are quite common in teenage girls and young women.

Luteal ovarian cysts cause delayed or irregular periods and rarely any other trouble.

The cyst may be diagnosed by an ultrasound scan of the lower abdomen.

Women who develop follicular cysts frequently can be given the oral contraceptive pill, which will prevent ovulation, and therefore the formation of further cysts. The pill will also shrink existing cysts, but large cysts need to be removed surgically.

No treatment is necessary for a luteal cyst unless it is very large, when it must be surgically removed.

Infertility may occur until a large cyst is removed, and the fluid from a ruptured cyst may cause inflammation of the bowel and other abdominal organs, resulting in adhesion formation.
See also ENDOMETRIOSIS; MITTELSCHMERZ; OVARY; POLYCYSTIC OVARIAN SYNDROME

OVARIAN TORSION

Ovarian torsion is an uncommon cause of sudden severe ovarian pain and tenderness low down in the abdomen on one side, due to the twisting of an ovary on the stalk of tissue that supplies it with blood and nerves, cutting off the blood supply and inflaming the nerves. An ultrasound scan may show some abnormalities, but the condition is often diagnosed at surgery. The torsion usually results in the loss of the affected ovary, and the inflammation in the abdomen may cause adhesions. Although one ovary may be lost, the remaining ovary can maintain fertility and normal production of female hormones.
See also OVARY; TORSION OF THE TESTIS

OVARY

The two ovaries are the main female reproductive organs. Shaped like an almond, each ovary is about 3cm long, 1.5cm wide and 1cm thick. They lie in the pelvis, one on either side of the uterus. The ovaries have two functions – the development and release of eggs, and the production of hormones. All the eggs (ova) a woman will ever have – and considerably more than she will ever need – are contained in her ovaries when she is born. At birth, there are something like two million immature eggs in each ovary. By puberty these are reduced to about 40 000, and only about 400 will be released during the childbearing years. The ovum (egg) is the largest single cell in the body, but still needs a powerful microscope to be seen.

Each egg (ovum) is surrounded by a small sac called a follicle. When puberty is reached, a cycle is established in which a few of the egg cells develop each month, with one reaching full maturity. When this happens the follicle bursts and releases the egg in a process called ovulation. A woman is fertile and can become pregnant a day or two either side of ovulation – and not at other times.

When an egg is released, it is swept into the adjacent Fallopian tube, the other end of which connects with the uterus.

FEMALE REPRODUCTIVE SYSTEM

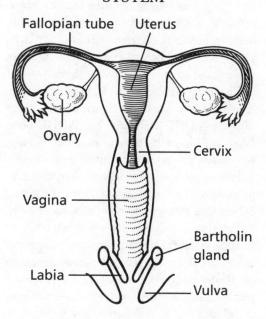

The ovaries also produce the hormones oestrogen and progesterone. Oestrogen predominates during the ripening of the egg, which takes about two weeks. It is this hormone that causes the lining of the uterus to thicken and the body to prepare for pregnancy. When the egg is released, the production of the second hormone, progesterone, increases, preparing the lining (endometrium) still further and bringing it to total readiness for a fertilised egg. If there is no conception, the oestrogen and progesterone levels fall suddenly and the uterine lining is shed during menstruation. The whole process then begins again. The monthly cycle continues throughout a woman's childbearing years from puberty to the menopause.

It is the female hormones that also give a woman her secondary sexual characteristics, for instance her broader hips than the male, her breasts, pubic and armpit hair, and her rounder, more feminine shape.

See also FALLOPIAN TUBE; OVARIAN
CANCER; OVARIAN CYST;
POLYCYSTIC OVARIAN SYNDROME;
SEX HORMONES; UTERUS

OVERACTIVE

Many children are overactive, particularly
boys between the ages of two and five, but very
few are truly hyperactive. Hyperactive children
are uncontrollable and destructive and do not
appear to respond to normal discipline. They
are also more often at the extremes of intelligence. Very intelligent children may be bored
by the activities available to them, and misbe-
have to obtain further stimulation. Children
with low intelligence may be confused and not
understand what is expected of them.

The most severe form of hyperactivity is
known as the attention deficit hyperactivity
disorder (ADHD). Children with ADHD often
fidget and are unable to remain seated for long,
are easily distracted and unable to sustain
attention, are always impatient, have difficulty
in following instructions, often move from one
incomplete task to the next, talk excessively,
are unable to play quietly, often interrupt or
intrude, do not seem to listen, have poor short
term memory, often lose items and engage in
physically dangerous activities. These symptoms create learning disabilities, emotional,
social and family difficulties, low self-esteem
and sometimes depression.

Behaviour problems other than ADHD
may also develop in children who receive no
or inappropriate discipline, poor parenting or
suffer from repeated significant illnesses.

Autism is thought to be an abnormality in
the development of the brain, and may be due
to brain damage during growth in the womb,
at birth, or in the first years of life. The child
fails to develop normal social, language and
communication skills. Repetitive habits are
common.

Minimal brain dysfunction is a term used
to describe those children who are not significantly below average intelligence, but may
lack normal social graces, have developmental
problems, poor coordination and may not
understand the consequences of their actions.
They may be seen to be overactive and dangerous to themselves and others (hyperkinetic
syndrome).

The fragile X syndrome is believed to cause
a quarter of the mental retardation in males.

All men have only one X chromosome paired
with a Y chromosome. A defect in the X chromosome has no spare 'backup copy' to protect
it. Females, who have two X chromosomes,
may be carriers from one generation to the
next. Other symptoms include over activity,
epilepsy, large build, large jaw and testes, and
short sightedness.
See also ATTENTION DEFICIT
HYPERACTIVITY DISORDER;
SWEARING UNCONTROLLED;
VIOLENCE and separate entries for diseases
mentioned above.

OVERDOSE

A person who has taken an overdose of drugs
may feel faint, slur their speech, have convulsions and gasp for breath. They will generally
have a rapid, weak pulse and they may be
unconscious. Excessive doses of medication
can be taken by accident (eg. children finding
a bottle of pills, confused elderly people) or
deliberately (eg. suicide attempt). Appropriate
first aid by the person discovering the overdose may be lifesaving. Some medications are
far more dangerous than others when taken in
excess.

Try to find out what drug has been taken
and whether it has been swallowed, inhaled or
injected. If you can find any containers,
syringes or ampoules, send them to the hospital with the victim. If the victim has vomited,
try to collect a sample.

For virtually all medication overdoses, the
first aid treatment is to administer charcoal to
neutralise the medication. Charcoal tablets and
solutions are readily available from chemists
without a prescription, and should be included
in any home medicine chest. If charcoal is
not available and there will be some delay in
obtaining medical attention, it is preferable to
induce vomiting rather than allow the medication to be absorbed. Do not induce vomiting
unless you are sure it is appropriate. Vomiting
should NOT be induced if the patient is
unconscious or otherwise liable to inhale any
vomitus.

Charcoal should be given at any time after
the overdose being taken. Induction of vomiting is most beneficial within thirty minutes of
the overdose being taken, but even up to two
hours later it may be beneficial. Many medications cause vomiting as part of their overdose
effects, but by this time the drug has already

been absorbed and the vomiting is unlikely to reduce the effects of the drug significantly.

Vomiting can be induced by giving ipecacuanha syrup and water, by giving soapy water to drink, by applying pressure to the upper belly or by putting a finger down the back of the persons throat (be careful not to be bitten, particularly if the patient is likely to convulse). The patient should be lying on their side with the neck extended, or sitting up and leaning over to avoid inhaling vomitus.

Carers should seek medical advice as soon as possible and sometimes urgent medical attention must be obtained. If the victim is unconscious, place them in the recovery position and continue to monitor breathing and pulse until help arrives. If breathing or the heart stops, carry out the ABC (airway, breathing circulation) of first aid and give mouth-to-mouth resuscitation and/or cardiopulmonary resuscitation as required.
See also CONVULSION; FIRST AID; POISONING; RESUSCITATION; UNCONSCIOUS

OVERWEIGHT
See OBESITY; WEIGHT GAIN

OVULATION
Ovulation is the release of an ovum (egg) from a woman's ovary. This occurs monthly, about fourteen days before the next menstrual period, and continues regularly from puberty to menopause. Ovulation may be missed due to emotional or physical stress or hormonal factors.
See also INFERTILITY; MITTELSCHMERZ; OVARIAN CYST; OVARY

OVULATION PAIN
See MITTELSCHMERZ

OXANDROLONE
See SEX HORMONES

OXPENTIFYLLINE
See VASODILATORS

OXYGEN
Oxygen (O) makes up 21% of the air we breathe and is essential for the metabolic processes of the body to proceed. If cells are deprived of oxygen for more than a few minutes, they die and degenerate.
See BLOOD GAS ANALYSIS

OXYMETAZOLINE
See DECONGESTANTS

P

P
See PHOSPHORUS

PACEMAKER

The heart has a collection of nerve cells near its top end that act as a natural pacemaker. This fires off signals about once a second to make the muscles of the heart contract and pump blood around the body. If this natural pacemaker is damaged, or the nerve fibres leading away from it are damaged, it will not function properly, and the heart will beat irregularly, at the wrong rate or not at all.

There are many reasons for the heart's pacemaker malfunctioning, the most common being a heart attack and a subsequent blockage of the nerve pathways within the heart, but many elderly people's pacemaker fail for no apparent reason.

To correct the failure of the natural pacemaker, a small but expensive electrical device is surgically implanted in the chest, usually under a local anaesthetic, with tiny wires leading to the appropriate parts of the heart. This device is an artificial pacemaker, and it sends electrical signals to the heart on a regular basis to make the heart contract correctly. The pacemaker contains a battery, a timing device and the electrical stimulation mechanism.

The latest, more sophisticated pacemakers contain a computer that actually monitors the heart and only sends off an artificial signal when the heart's natural rhythm is disrupted. Variable rate pacemakers, which increase the heart's rate with exercise, are also available.

The pacemaker's electronics have to be checked every six to twelve months, but they will last from ten to fifteen years or more. These marvels of electronic miniaturisation are keeping many people alive and giving many more a much better quality of life.
See also HEART; SICK SINUS SYNDROME

PAEDODONTICS

Paedodontics is the provision of dentistry for children. Children have special dental needs, as they produce two sets of teeth and hence have more teeth to care for than adults.

Teeth start forming below the gums at a very early stage before birth. As the teeth calcify and grow, they push their way into the mouth. As teeth are forming in the jaws, they should be exposed to an optimum amount of fluoride in the blood supply. Teeth that come through crookedly will generally straighten themselves out as they grow, if they have enough room to move. If not, they should be corrected by an orthodontist at about the age of twelve or when all the permanent teeth appear.

A child's diet should be sensible; foods rich in sugar are dangerous to teeth and poor nutritionally.

Children's teeth should be brushed from an early age and the habit firmly established. Self-brushing should be encouraged, but supervision is needed for many years.

Children should be introduced to the dentist at about the age of two and a half years, and then return every six months. Fear of dentistry is readily avoided and early detection of trouble makes correction easy.
See also DENTISTRY; ORTHODONTICS; TEETH

PAEDOPHILIA

Paedophilia is a psychiatric disturbance that results in the sexual abuse of a child by adult men (most commonly) or women. It may develop from childhood abuse of the pedophile by his or her parents, or other psychological traumas as a child. Paedophilia is NOT more common in homosexuals, but pederasty is by definition a homosexual act between a man and a boy.

The condition involves mentally disturbed adults who use children to become sexually aroused to the point of orgasm. Sexual contact varies from feeling, to oral sex, or sexual penetration that may progress to serious injury or rarely murder. Paedophiles have difficulty in establishing normal intimate relationships with adults of the opposite sex, have inadequate personalities, low self esteem, and male paedophiles are often impotent.

Treatment involves prolonged counselling by a psychiatrist and sometimes medications to reduce sexual desire and increase control. If discovered, paedophiles are invariably charged in the courts, but courts are more likely to treat leniently a person who comes forward voluntarily and seeks help. Unfortunately the long term success of treatment is poor.

See also CHILD ABUSE; SEXUAL SADISM

PAGET'S DISEASE OF BONE

Sir James Paget (1814–99) was a London surgeon after whom a number of diseases, tests, tissues and structures were named. In Paget's disease of bone (osteitis deformans), bone in scattered parts of the body becomes thickened and soft, causing compression of nerves and collapse of those bones that support weight. There is no known cause, but it is unusual under sixty years of age.

The disease has a very insidious onset, and may be quite advanced before diagnosis, and can vary from very mild to rapidly progressive. The skull, thighbone (femur) and shinbone (tibia) are often involved, giving a characteristic head appearance and bowing of the legs as they bend under the body's weight. Skull enlargement causes pressure on nerves and constant headaches, while fractures may occur in long bones with only slight injury, and the back becomes bent, painful and deformed.

The diagnosis made on the characteristic x-ray appearance, and blood tests show specific chemical imbalances, including excess calcium. The excess calcium may cause kidney damage, extra blood flow to the bones can cause circulatory and heart problems, and a small number of patients develop a form of bone cancer.

Medications such as disodium etidronate are taken regularly for the rest of the patient's life to control the disease. Drugs slow the disease progress, but there is no cure, and the earlier it occurs in life, the more likely it is to be severe.

See also BACK PAIN; BONE; PAGET'S DISEASE OF THE NIPPLE

PAGET'S DISEASE OF THE NIPPLE

Paget's disease of the nipple (nipple cancer) is an uncommon type of cancer that starts in the milk ducts of the nipple, and may spread rapidly along these ducts, deep into the breast. The cause is unknown, but it is uncommon, occurring in only one in every 100 breast cancers.

There are often very few symptoms until the cancer is well advanced, and no lump is felt. Symptoms include itching and irritation of the nipple, a thickening of the nipple and in advanced cases an ulcer may form. The cancer may spread to breast tissue and nearby lymph nodes. The diagnosis is confirmed by biopsy of the nipple.

Surgery to remove the nipple and the affected part of the breast is performed, followed by radiotherapy and chemotherapy when necessary. The more advanced the cancer when first treated, the poorer the survival rate.

See also BREAST CANCER; PAGET'S DISEASE OF BONE

PAIN

Cars have red lights that appear on the dashboard to indicate there is a fault somewhere in the vehicle. Sensible motorists take their vehicle to a garage for a check as soon as a red light appears, to have the problem corrected and prevent further damage to the car.

Humans do not have red lights or dashboards, but we do have pain fibres that run to almost every cell in the body (the brain being a notable, but unexpected, exception). These pain nerves serve the same purpose as red lights in cars – they indicate that there is something wrong with the cells in the area they supply. Sometimes the pain appears to come from an area that is perfectly normal (eg. pain in the leg caused by a pinched nerve in the back – sciatica). This is because the pain nerves supplying one area are damaged at a point closer to the brain (short circuits in a car's red light). This is known as referred pain, and can be quite a trap for both doctor and patient.

Unfortunately, patients are not always as sensible as motorists, and often ignore their red warning lights (pain) until it is too late to prevent serious damage or cure a problem. Any pain that has no obvious cause and persists should be checked by a doctor so that any serious problem can be remedied, or you can be reassured and relieved of discomfort at an early stage.

Pain is by far the most common symptom

experienced by humans, and it is explained in further detail under the anatomical locations of the pain.

See also ABDOMINAL PAIN; ANALGESICS; ANAL PAIN; ARM PAIN; ARTHRITIS; BACK PAIN; BREAST PAIN; BURN; CHEST PAIN; DYSPEPSIA; EARACHE; EYE PAIN; FACE PAIN; FOOT PAIN; FRACTURE; GROIN PAIN; GUM PAIN; HAND PAIN; HEADACHE; HEARTBURN; KNEE PAIN; LEG PAIN; LOIN PAIN; LYMPH NODES ENLARGED AND/OR PAINFUL; MENSTRUAL PERIODS PAINFUL; MOUTH PAIN; MUSCLE PAIN; NECK PAIN; PAIN LOSS; PALLIATIVE CARE; PELVIC PAIN; PHOTOPHOBIA; SALIVARY GLAND PAIN; SEXUAL INTERCOURSE PAIN; SHOULDER PAIN; SKIN PAIN; SWALLOWING PAINFUL; TESTICLE AND SCROTUM PAIN; THROAT PAIN; TONGUE PAIN; URINATION PAIN; WRIST PAIN etc.

PAINFUL ARC SYNDROME

The painful arc syndrome causes pain in part of the range of movement of the shoulder. It may be caused by an injury or fracture to the very top of the humerus (upper arm bone), stretching damage (tendinitis) to the tendon that pulls the arm through the painful arc, inflammation of the bursae (fluid-producing sacs for the shoulder joint) that surround the shoulder joint, or microscopic bone formation (calcification) in tendons that move the shoulder joint.

If the arm is held by the side, and then moved away from the body while being kept straight until it is above the head, it describes an arc of 180°. In this syndrome there is pain with movement through the mid part of the arc between about 45° and 135°. There is no pain in the lower or upper parts of the arc of movement.

X-rays may show microscopic calcification of a tendon, but in most cases are normal.

Treatment is a combination of physiotherapy, anti-inflammatory drugs and rarely surgery. Recovery is commonly slow, but long term good recovery is normal.

See also BURSITIS; ROTATOR CUFF SYNDROME; SHOULDER PAIN; SUPRASPINATUS TENDINITIS; TENDINITIS

PAIN-KILLERS

See ANALGESICS; NARCOTICS; NONSTEROIDAL ANTI-INFLAMMATORY DRUGS

PAIN LOSS

A loss of pain sensation (anaesthesia) in part or all of the body may initially be seen as a benefit, but in fact these patients inadvertently injure themselves and may cause significant damage to the affected part of the body.

In a stroke (cerebrovascular accident) various parts of the brain may be affected by having its blood supply cut off by a blockage in an artery, or a blood vessel in the brain may burst causing bleeding and damage to part of the brain. It may be associated with a wide variety of symptoms from paralysis and headache to weakness, loss of sensation, anaesthesia, confusion and coma.

Transient ischaemic attacks are a temporary blocking of a small artery in the brain by a blood clot, piece of plaque from a cholesterol deposit in an artery, or spasm of an artery, which results in that part of the brain failing to function for a short time.

Other causes of reduced pain sensation include poorly controlled diabetes, a blood clot in an artery anywhere in the body (may damage the sensory (pain) nerves beyond that point), and spinal cord disease (eg. tumour, infection, slipped disc) or damage (eg. fracture or partial dislocation of vertebrae) may reduce or remove all pain sensation below the point of injury.

Less common causes include polyneuritis (inflammation of nerves), leprosy, Refsum syndrome and some psychiatrically disturbed patients will describe a loss of all sensation in the areas normally covered by gloves and socks in the hands and feet.

If a sensory nerve is cut during surgery, the skin around the surgical incision may remain permanently anaesthetised. Local anaesthetics will obviously cause a loss of pain sensation in the areas injected.

See also PAIN and separate entries for diseases mentioned above.

PALATE

The roof of the mouth is called the palate. The two-thirds of the palate closest to the lips has a bony backing (the hard palate), but the back one-third (the soft palate) has no bony structure and is held in tension by elastic tissue. The soft palate ends in a soft loop of tissue known as the uvula, which can be seen dangling down the back of the throat when the mouth is wide open. The tongue compresses food against the hard palate to break and squash it, and mix in saliva to aid with digestion.

Above the palate are the nasal cavity and the sinuses.

See also CLEFT LIP AND PALATE

PALLIATIVE CARE

Palliative care is the care of those who are dying, in a way that ensures their comfort, dignity and freedom from pain. It is definitely not euthanasia (the deliberate ending of life in a terminally ill patient), but those giving palliative care will not unnecessarily prolong an individual's life.

Teams of doctors, nurses, physiotherapists, dieticians and other carers who specialise in palliative care will attend to the patient to help with food and drink, toileting, positioning, movement, relaxation, and medications to relieve anxiety, depression and (most importantly) pain, while attempting to make the last days or weeks of a patient's life as meaningful as possible by keeping him/her as aware and alert as possible.

Palliative care may be carried out in a hospital, nursing home, hospice or the patient's own home, depending on the resources available and the desires of the patient and his/her family.

Pain relieving medication may be given by tablets, mixtures, injection, an infusion into a vein, a very slow infusion into the fat tissue under the skin, or an infusion into the fluid (cerebrospinal fluid) that surrounds the spinal cord in the back. In some situations, some pain nerves may be surgically destroyed. Narcotics and anaesthetics are the most common medications used, but these may be augmented by muscle relaxants, medications for nausea and vomiting, laxatives or antidiarrhoeals, antidepressants and anxiolytics (anxiety relievers).

See also ANXIOLYTICS; DEATH; NARCOTICS; PAIN

PALMAR APONEUROSIS
See DUPUYTREN CONTRACTURE OF HAND; HAND

PALPEBRAE
See EYELID

PALPITATIONS

Palpitations are an excessively rapid and strong heartbeat, which may be irregular. They occur in everyone during exercise, anxiety, stress, pain or a fright, but usually settle quite quickly.

Heavy smoking, caffeine in cola drinks, tea or coffee, excess alcohol, food sensitivities and some food preservatives and colourings may trigger palpitations.

Pregnant women generally have a faster heart rate, and hormonal surges may trigger brief episodes of palpitations.

Bacterial and viral infections, or any other disease that causes a fever, will cause an increased heart rate while the fever is present.

Paroxysmal atrial tachycardia (PAT) is a very common condition, particularly in women. For no apparent reason, but sometimes because of hormonal changes during the menstrual cycle and menopause, the heart will start beating rapidly, usually at double its normal rate. This harmless but distressing condition may last for a few seconds or several hours before settling spontaneously.

Other causes include a heart attack (myocardial infarct), atrial fibrillation (due to heart damage) and ectopic beats.

Less common causes for palpitations include anaemia, infections (endocarditis, myocarditis) or inflammation of the heart muscle, an overactive thyroid gland (hyperthyroidism), reflux oesophagitis, phaeochromocytoma (black-celled tumour of the adrenal glands) and da Costa syndrome (a psychiatric disturbance).

Medications such as salbutamol (Ventolin – for asthma), glyceryl trinitrate (Anginine – for heart pain), terbutaline (Bricanyl – for asthma), aminophylline (for lung conditions) and imipramine (for depression) may have palpitations as a side effect.

See also da COSTA SYNDROME; FEVER; HEART and separate entries for diseases and medications mentioned above.

PAN
See POLYARTERITIS NODOSA

PANACEA
Panacea was the Greek god of healing. It is

also a term used to refer to a universal remedy for all illness.
See also AESCULAPIUS

PANCOAST SYNDROME

Pancoast syndrome is a complication of lung cancer that occurs in patients with cancer in the top part of the lung, and is a sign that the cancer is progressing very rapidly. The syndrome symptoms consist of shoulder, arm and chest pain with an associated Horner syndrome (a drooping eyelid, lack of sweating on one side of the face and a contracted pupil in the eye). Death usually follows soon after the syndrome is diagnosed.
See also HORNER SYNDROME; LUNG CANCER; PANCOAST TUMOUR

PANCOAST TUMOUR

Lung cancer occurring at the very top of the lung is known as a Pancoast tumour, after the Philadelphia radiologist Henry Pancoast (b.1875). As with other forms of lung cancer, smoking is by far the most common cause, but asbestos exposure and toxic fumes may also be responsible.

Pain in the shoulder may be the only symptom until the cancer is well advanced. Other possible symptoms include shortness of breath, weight loss and coughing blood. The cancer may spread to nearby bones early, and later to the liver and other organs. Chest x-rays may show the cancer, but it may be hidden by the shoulder bones, and a CT scan is often necessary to reveal the tumour.

Radiotherapy is the main form of treatment, but early cancers may be removed surgically. Unfortunately the prognosis is usually poor, as diagnosis is usually made late.
See also LUNG CANCER; PANCOAST SYNDROME

PANCREAS

The pancreas is a large gland situated almost exactly behind the navel in the belly. It is about 15cm. long and lies horizontally across the abdomen and is surrounded by the duodenum and stomach.

The pancreas has two quite distinct roles to play in the functioning of our body.

Insulin, the chemical vital for the control of the body's use of sugar and the prevention of diabetes, is produced by special cells (islets of Langerhan) scattered throughout the tissue of the pancreas. The insulin is produced and released according to how much we eat, not only of sugar but also carbohydrate. The cells that produce the insulin have no ducts to take the chemical away, but discharge it directly into the blood vessels surrounding each cell. Once in the bloodstream, insulin controls the level of sugar inside the cells and in the blood. In diabetics, insulin is either not produced, or is made ineffective by other problems in the body.

Another hormone, glucagon, is also pro-

BILE AND PANCREAS DRAINAGE

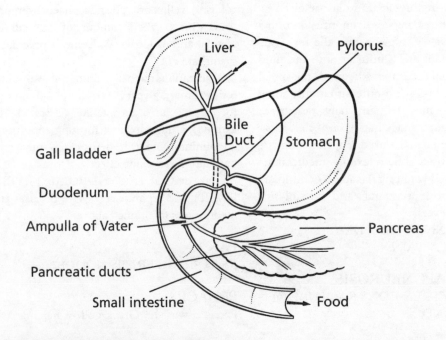

duced in the pancreas as a counter to insulin in controlling blood sugar levels.

The other function of the pancreas is to produce the main juices used in the digestion of food in our stomach. Millions of tiny glands produce powerful enzymes which are taken through a maze of ducts finally joining into one main duct that in turn joins with the bile duct to empty into the duodenum. As food passes through the duodenum, the digestive juices produced in the pancreas are squirted onto it. The churning action produced by contractions of the intestine mix these juices into the food, where they break it down into its basic components so that it can be absorbed into the body.

The duct coming from the pancreas joins with the bile duct then this common duct opens into the duodenum through a small hole in the side of the intestine called the ampulla of Vater. Thus stones coming down from the gall bladder can block off the pancreatic juices too. This can lead to a build-up of pressure in the pancreas, forcing the powerful pancreatic enzymes to leak into the abdominal cavity. When this happens the juices digest normal tissues instead of the food they are intended for. This causes the severe pain of acute pancreatitis, and serious illness and even death can result.
See also ENDOSCOPIC RETROGRADE CHOLECYSTOPANCREATOGRAPHY; GALL BLADDER; GLANDS; INSULIN; PANCREATIC CANCER; PANCREATITIS

PANCREATIC CANCER
The pancreas is an organ that sits in the centre of the belly behind the umbilicus and secretes digestive enzymes that are discharged through a duct, which it shares with the gall bladder, into the small intestine. Cancer usually occurs in the end nearest the discharging duct (the head of the pancreas), but its cause is unknown.

The enlarging cancer puts pressure on the adjacent duct from the gall bladder, preventing bile from escaping. The build up in bile results in liver damage and jaundice (yellow skin), which is often the first symptom. Other symptoms include vague belly and back pain, weight loss, poor food digestion, diarrhoea and blood clots in veins. Liver failure and spread of the cancer to adjacent lymph nodes and organs, may be complications.

The diagnosis is confirmed by blood tests and a CT or MRI scan, then treatment involves major surgery to remove the cancer and reroute the duct from the gall bladder to the gut. Follow-up radiotherapy and chemotherapy may be undertaken. The prognosis depends upon the type of cancer and how far it has spread, but is generally poor.
See also CANCER; PANCREAS

PANCREATITIS
Pancreatitis is a well recognised but uncommon complication of alcoholism causing inflammation or infection of the pancreas gland, which sits in the centre of the abdomen directly behind the navel. The main task of the pancreas is to produce the digestive enzymes that attack food. A tiny duct leads from the pancreas to the bile duct and then to the small intestine to transport enzymes to the food.

In pancreatitis the gland may become infected, damaged by excess alcohol intake, injured in an accident, or a gallstone may block the pancreatic duct. The digestive enzymes then leak out of the pancreas and start dissolving the gland itself, the intestines and other abdominal organs.

Patients develop excruciating pain in the centre of the abdomen that may also be felt in the back and sides, nausea, vomiting, weakness, fever and sweats. Recurrences of attacks, particularly in alcoholics, are common. The diagnosis can be confirmed by specific blood tests.

Treatment is difficult, and often involves long hospital stays for resuscitation, prolonged bed rest and pain relief. The cause of the pancreatitis must also be treated, with antibiotics and occasionally surgery. Despite the best treatment, there is a significant death rate, which rises with subsequent attacks.
See also ALCOHOLISM; PANCREAS

PANHYPOPITUITARISM
See HYPOPITUITARISM

PANIC ATTACK
See ANXIETY NEUROSIS

PANTOPRAZOLE
See PROTON PUMP INHIBITORS

PANTOTHENIC ACID
See VITAMIN B

PAPANICOLOU SMEAR
See PAP SMEAR

PAPILLOMA
See SEBORRHOEIC KERATOSES

PAP SMEAR
Pap is short for Papanicolou, the name of the Greek/American doctor who developed this cervical smear test in 1932. A Pap smear is used to detect any abnormality of the cervix, including infections and erosions.

Unquestionably, the main value of the Pap smear has been its ability to detect precancerous conditions of the cervix and cervical cancer at an early stage so that it can be treated. Also, chronic infections of the cervix of which the patient is not aware can cause infertility and other problems, and a Pap smear can enable the doctor to diagnose these and prescribe appropriate treatment. All women of any age who are sexually active should have regular Pap smear tests – generally every two years, although once every three years may be enough for women who are past menopause.

The test is quite simple. The doctor introduces a collapsible metal or plastic tube, called a speculum, into the woman's vagina. This is painless although it may feel a bit intrusive. The speculum is shaped like a duck's bill. When the upper and lower blades are separated, the doctor can see the cervix, and a soft plastic brush is gently inserted into the opening of the uterus in the middle of the cervix and rotated. This lifts off a superficial layer of cells. The brush is then wiped across a glass slide to form a smear and is sprayed with a solution to preserve the cells.

The slide is sent to a pathologist who examines the smeared cells under a microscope and sends a report to the doctor. Sophisticated computers, that are more accurate than human technicians, are now being used in most laboratories to scan Pap smears for abnormalities. The collecting of the cells takes only a minute or two, and the report is usually available within a week.

An abnormal result from a smear test does not mean that the woman necessarily has cancer, but it does mean that she should have a further test; this will usually be a colposcopy. If as a result of the colposcopy an early stage of cancer is detected, diathermy or laser may be used to burn the abnormal cells away, or a cone-shaped area of tissue may be excised. These forms of treatment will not interfere with a woman's normal sexual functioning or her ability to fall pregnant. Only if the cancer has already spread will she need to have the uterus removed in a hysterectomy, or undergo radiation therapy.

Cancer of the cervix is one of the more common forms of cancer in women, and yet if all women had a Pap smear regularly it could be largely prevented.

At the same time as a Pap smear is done, the doctor will usually insert two gloved fingers into the woman's vagina and feel for any abnormalities of the uterus or ovaries. The doctor may examine the rectum as well, and will often check the breasts and blood pressure at the same visit.
See also CERVICAL CANCER; CERVIX; COLPOSCOPY; GENITAL WART

PAPULES
See LUMPS IN SKIN

PARACETAMOL
See ANALGESICS

PARAESTHESIA
See PINS AND NEEDLES SENSATION IN SKIN

PARAFFIN
Paraffin is both a laxative and a lubricant that is used for constipation, preventing straining at stool, vaginal dryness, skin dryness and eye dryness. It is available as a liquid, cream and in eye drops. It should be used long term only under medical advice. Side effects are minimal, but excess may cause diarrhoea. It is a safe and widely used laxative that has been available for thousands of years. White soft paraffin and liquid paraffin are used in many creams as a vehicle for other medications.
See also LAXATIVES

PARALYSIS
See FACE, WEAK MUSCLES; HAND WEAK; KLUMPKE PALSY; MUSCLE WEAKNESS; PARAPLEGIA AND QUADRIPLEGIA

PARALYSIS AGITANS
See PARKINSON DISEASE

PARANOIA
See MANIA; PARANOID DISORDER; SCHIZOPHRENIA

PARANOID DISORDER
Paranoia is a delusion that makes a patient believe that s/he is being persecuted by individuals or organisations. The preoccupation with imagined persecutions may have a marked effect upon the patient's home life, and may cause disruption to a marriage or family. Examples include the belief that the secret service has bugged the home and is listening to all the conversations of the family, or that the next-door neighbour is deliberately undertaking activities that are constantly irritating. It may occur alone, or as a part of schizophrenia, and may progress to become seriously antisocial behaviour.

Antipsychotic medications and psychotherapy are used in treatment, and most patients can live relatively normally in society, but they may express their unreasoned fears of persecution at inappropriate times.
See also PSYCHOSES; SCHIZOPHRENIA

PARAPERTUSSIS
See WHOOPING COUGH

PARAPHIMOSIS
Paraphimosis is entrapment of the head of the penis in a tight band of foreskin, which usually occurs with a penile erection in a man suffering from phimosis (narrow opening in foreskin). The tight foreskin becomes painfully trapped behind head of penis after an erection has subsided.

The problem may be solved by manipulation of the foreskin back over the head of the penis by firm pressure, or surgically cutting the tight band of foreskin around the head. Circumcision may be necessary to prevent recurrences. If unrelieved, permanent damage to the head of the penis may occur.
See also CIRCUMCISION; PENIS; PHIMOSIS

PARAPLEGIA AND QUADRIPLEGIA
Paraplegia is paralysis and loss of sensation below the waist affecting both legs, while quadriplegia (tetraplegia) is paralysis and loss of sensation below the neck affecting all four limbs. Both conditions are serious and obviously extremely devastating to the patient.

All parts of the human body are capable of healing and repairing damage, except the central nervous system, which comprises the brain and spinal cord. The spinal cord runs from the base of the brain, down through the vertebrae that form the backbone, and ends just below the waist. Nerves run out from it to the muscles, skin and other tissues, with one bundle of nerves emerging from between each of the twenty four vertebrae. If the spinal cord is cut by a broken back or other injury, it is impossible for nerve signals to pass backwards and forwards from the brain to the body. Involuntary muscles, which control the internal organs such as the gut and heart movements, are supplied by a different set of nerves, and are not affected by spinal injury.

The most common cause of these conditions is a serious injury to the back or neck that results in a dislocation or fracture of the vertebrae, and significant damage to the spinal cord.

Between each vertebra is a disc of dense rubbery material that has a soft core. If this disc is damaged, it may push back onto the spinal cord (slipped disc) to cause pins and needles sensation, numbness, pain and eventually loss of sensation and paralysis. This condition can usually be corrected by surgery at an early stage.

Other causes include tumours or cancer of the spinal cord or the membranes covering it (meninges), bone cancer or tumours involving vertebrae, a dilated artery (aneurysm) in the spinal cord or surrounding tissues, infections of the spinal cord, osteomyelitis of the vertebrae, meningitis (infection of membrane around spinal cord), syringomyelia (cavity in the cord) and multiple sclerosis (a nerve disease that can affect any nerve in the body in a random and intermittent way).

The only treatment that can be offered is rehabilitation so patients can cope with their disability.
See also PINS AND NEEDLES SENSATION IN SKIN; QUADRIPLEGIA; SPINE; VERTEBRA and separate entries for diseases mentioned above.

PARAPOXVIRUS
See ORF

PARAPSORIASIS
See PARAPSORIASIS EN PLAQUE;
PITYRIASIS LICHENOIDES

PARAPSORIASIS EN PLAQUE
Parapsoriasis en plaque is an uncommon skin disease of no known cause, divided into two types, small and large plaque. The condition is characterised by the slow development over many months of multiple, oval to cigar shaped, red, slightly raised, scaly, non-itchy patches. They tend to avoid the forearms and lower legs and head, and to follow nerve pathways in skin. Large plaques (patches over ten cm. in diameter) may progress to mycosis fungoides. A skin biopsy can confirm the diagnosis.

Steroid creams and ultraviolet therapy control the condition, but there is no cure.
See also MYCOSIS FUNGOIDES;
PSORIASIS

PARASITES
Small or microscopic animals or plants that live on or in another animal, from which they receive nutrition, are parasites.
See ANTHELMINTICS;
ANTIPARASITICS; HOOKWORMS;
LICE; SCABIES; SYMBIOSIS;
TOXOPLASMOSIS; WORMS

PARASYMPATHETIC NERVOUS SYSTEM
See AUTONOMIC NERVOUS SYSTEM

PARATHORMONE
See PARATHYROID GLAND

PARATHYROID GLAND
Four tiny parathyroid glands can be found in the neck; two behind each lobe of the thyroid gland on either side of the trachea. They produce a hormone (parathormone) that circulates throughout the body in the blood to regulate the amount of calcium and phosphorus in cells, the blood and in bones. If the cells lack calcium, this hormone takes it from the bones, and releases it into the blood so that it can reach the cells that require it. Nerve cells are particularly dependent on having the correct amount of calcium for their function.

If excess calcium is present in the blood, the reverse process occurs, or an extreme excess of calcium is expelled in the urine.

Phosphorus and calcium are in balance in the blood. If calcium is high, phosphorus is low and vice versa. This balance is maintained by parathormone.
See also CALCIUM;
HYPERPARATHYROIDISM;
HYPOPARATHYROIDISM; THYROID GLAND

PARAUMBILICAL HERNIA
See UMBILICAL HERNIA

PARIETAL BONE
The two parietal bones form the sides of the cranial cavity at the top of the skull and protect the sides of the brain.
See also SKULL

PARKINSON DISEASE
Parkinson disease, which is also known as paralysis agitans, Parkinsonism and shaking palsy, is one of the more common causes of a tremor in elderly people. It is named after the English physician James Parkinson (1755–1824) who first described the condition in the medical literature.

There is no known cause, but what happens in the brain to cause the symptoms is understood. When a muscle contracts, the opposite muscle must relax. For example, when you bend your finger, the muscles on the palm side of the finger contract, while those on the back of the finger must relax. This coordination occurs in the brain. In Parkinsonism, the brain cells that control this coordination have degenerated so that smooth control of movement is lost.

Early signs of the disease are a failure to swing the arm when walking, a deterioration in handwriting, and poor balance. Later symptoms are a constant tremor, general body stiffness, loss of facial expression, a stiff way of walking and lack of coordination. The intelligence and mental powers of victims are not affected in the early stages of the disease, and this causes great frustration, particularly when speech may be impaired. Patients may become depressed, anxious and emotionally disturbed.

No blood or other test is diagnostic. CT scans (special x-rays) may reveal changes in certain parts of the brain, as may electroencephalograms (EEG) which measure the electrical brain waves. Magnetic resonance imaging (MRI) and positron emission tomography (PET) scans are now being used in some centres.

A number of drugs are available to control the symptoms and slow the progress of the disease, but it is a matter of trial and error to determine which medications will help any particular patient. Physiotherapy is also very important. In rare cases, brain surgery, in which part of the brain is destroyed in an attempt to block nerve pathways that cause the constant tremor, is performed.

There is no cure, but medications allow some patients to lead normal lives. The disease progresses steadily over many years, rarely causing death, but causing otherwise normal people to become invalids, totally dependent on others for everyday tasks.
See also ESSENTIAL TREMOR; STEELE-RICHARDSON-OLSZEWSKI SYNDROME; TREMOR

PARKINSONISM
See PARKINSON DISEASE

PARONYCHIA
A paronychia is an infection of the nail bed (pink tissue under a nail) and surrounding tissues caused by an ingrown nail, damage to the side and base of the nail from habitually picking at the area, working in water, working with chemicals (eg. detergents and soaps), dermatitis, or gardening (particles of dirt may be pushed between nail and skin).

A red, tender, painful swelling develops at the side and base of the nail.

Treatment involves applying antibiotic ointment to the infected skin around the nail, taking antibiotic tablets and, if an abscess is present, having it lanced to drain pus. If not treated, infected tissue can break down to form an abscess, which may damage the nail bed and cause the nail to come off. Most settle quickly with treatment.
See also INGROWN NAIL; NAIL; NAIL PAIN

PAROTID GLAND
See SALIVARY GLAND

PAROTID TUMOUR
The parotid glands sit under the angle of the jaw on each side to secrete saliva into the back of the mouth. Several different types of tumour can develop in this gland, and the other salivary glands (submandibular and submental glands) that sit under the chin. The most common form is called a mixed parotid tumour, which is not malignant (cancerous).

The tumour appears as a slowly enlarging painless lump at the angle of the jaw, but as it enlarges the tumour puts pressure on surrounding tissue and nerves to eventually cause discomfort and pain. The diagnosis is often difficult, but can be made by a CT or MRI scan and needle biopsy (sticking a needle into the gland to take a tissue sample).

Extremely intricate surgery is necessary to remove the enlarged gland and the tumour it contains. If the tumour is cancerous, irradiation of the area to prevent a recurrence is necessary. The nerve supplying the face runs through the parotid gland, and it is very easy to damage this during surgery, leaving the face numb and paralysed. The prognosis is generally very good, but if the tumour is cancerous it is far more serious.
See also FACE SWOLLEN; SALIVARY GLAND PAIN

PAROTITIS
See SIALITIS

PAROXETINE
See ANTIDEPRESSANTS

PAROXYSMAL ATRIAL TACHYCARDIA
Paroxysmal atrial tachycardia (a form of supraventricular tachycardia) is a sudden, irregular, rapid beating of the heart, that is relatively common in women, and may be triggered by hormonal, emotional or other factors. Most attacks last only a few minutes and cause minimal discomfort, but often significant anxiety.

The diagnosis is confirmed by an electrocardiogram (ECG) while an attack is present, but the ECG is normal at other times. Holter monitoring (long term ECG) may be necessary to confirm the diagnosis.

If the attacks last for long periods or occur frequently, medication (eg. beta-blockers such as propranolol and sotalol, or lanoxin) can be given to prevent them. Firm massage of the eyeballs, holding the breath and dunking the face in icy water may also stop an attack.

They are not harmful, and most attacks settle spontaneously within a couple of hours.

See also ARRHYTHMIA; BETA-
BLOCKERS; HOLTER MONITOR;
LOWN-GANONG-LEVINE
SYNDROME; SUPRAVENTRICULAR
TACHYCARDIA

PAROXYSMAL VENTRICULAR TACHYCARDIA

A paroxysmal ventricular tachycardia is a
sudden very rapid heart rate, often due to
a heart attack. It is accompanied by chest
tightness, palpitations, shortness of breath and
collapse. It may progress to ventricular fibrillation, which is usually fatal.

An ECG (electrocardiogram) will show the
abnormal rhythm. Medications (eg. lignocaine) are injected into a vein followed by
cardioversion (electric shock), stabilisation in
hospital, and then tablets to prevent a recurrence. The outcome depends on cause and
severity.
See also HEART ATTACK;
PALPITATION; TACHYCARDIA;
VENTRICULAR FIBRILLATION

PAROXYSMAL VERTIGO
See BENIGN PAROXYSMAL
POSITIONAL VERTIGO

PARTHENOGENESIS

Parthenogenesis is a term that describes a form
of reproduction which requires only a female,
without a sexual partner, and parthenogenesis
is thus a form of virgin birth (the meaning of
the term in Greek). It occurs naturally in many
lower orders of animals, particularly insects
(eg. aphids, bees, ants), but also in birds
(eg. turkey), amphibians (eg. frogs) and snakes.
Experimentally, parthenogenesis has been
achieved in mammals such as rabbits.

The ovum (egg) is released from the ovary,
implants into the uterus (or egg duct) and
develops into a new baby. The offspring is
always female, and identical in every way to
the mother, as the genetic make up is the
same as that of the mother, and the sex chromosomes available from the mother are only
the X ones. Males require a Y chromosome.

No successful experiments with human
parthenogenesis have been achieved.
See also GENE

PARTIAL SEIZURE
See EPILEPSY

PARVOVIRUS INFECTION
See FIFTH DISEASE

PASSIVE SMOKING
See SMOKING

PAT
See PAROXYSMAL ATRIAL
TACHYCARDIA

PATAU SYNDROME

Patau syndrome (trisomy 13-15) is a rare
congenital defect affecting numerous parts of
the body, caused by the presence of three
copies of chromosomes 13 and 15 instead of
two. The infant has extra fingers and toes,
abnormal heart structure, cleft lip and palate,
small eyes and brain malformations. Tests are
performed on heart and brain function
(eg. CT scan, echocardiogram) to confirm
the diagnosis. No treatment is available, and
the prognosis is poor.

PATCHES ON SKIN
See BROWN PATCHES ON SKIN; RED
PATCHES ON SKIN; WHITE PATCHES
ON SKIN

PATELLA

The medical term used for the knee cap. The
patella is not directly attached to any other
bone but slides up and down across the end of
the femur (thigh bone). Above it is attached to
the powerful quadriceps muscles at the front
of the thigh, and below to the patella tendon
which inserts into the top and front of
the tibia (shin bone). When the quadriceps
muscles contract, they pull on the patella,
which in turn pulls on the patellar tendon and
the tibia to straighten the knee.

The patella may slip out of position slightly
(subluxate), or completely (dislocate) with a
twisting of the knee, or may be fractured by
a severe blow. Arthritis may develop between
the patella and femur to cause a grating
sensation with knee movement.
See also CHONDROMALACIA
PATELLAE; DISLOCATION; KNEE;
KNEE CAP ABNORMAL; FEMUR;
PATELLO-FEMORAL PAIN
SYNDROME; SESAMOID BONE

PATELLA ABNORMAL
See KNEE CAP ABNORMAL

PATELLO-FEMORAL PAIN SYNDROME

The patello-femoral pain syndrome is due to overuse or straining of the knee. Pain occurs in the front of part of the knee behind or around patella (knee cap), a dull ache with sharp exacerbations aggravated by climbing or descending stairs or slopes.

There are no specific diagnostic tests, but on examination there is pain when pressing on the patella, which is eased by pushing the patella towards the other knee during knee movement. Pushing the patella away from the other knee worsens pain during knee movement. Physiotherapy, strapping, rest and anti-inflammatory medications are the treatments used.
See also CHONDROMALACIA PATELLAE; KNEE; PATELLA

PATENT DUCTUS ARTERIOSUS

Patent ductus arteriosus (PDA) is a failure of an artery near the heart that bypasses the lungs, to close immediately after birth.

A foetus inside the mother's womb (uterus) does not breathe, but obtains its oxygen directly from the mother's blood. The foetal blood is diverted away from the lungs through an artery (ductus arteriosus) which connects the pulmonary artery to the aorta. Immediately after birth, this special artery contracts and closes, diverting the full supply of blood into the lungs, which assists in their expansion, and enables the newborn baby to obtain its oxygen requirements by breathing. If the ductus arteriosus remains open after birth ('patent') it will divert unoxygenated blood away from the lungs and into the general circulation. This prevents sufficient oxygen from reaching the body, and eventually the baby may become blue.

There are no early symptoms, but as the heart has to work harder it will gradually enlarge, and over a period of several months or years, the heart will gradually fail because of the extra work it is required to undertake. There may also be other serious malformations of the heart present.

Babies have a characteristic heart murmur that can be heard through a stethoscope. The diagnosis is confirmed by sophisticated x-rays of the heart, electrocardiograms and other specialised tests.

The drug indomethacin, commonly used for treating arthritis, causes a patent ductus arteriosus to close in most cases, but sometimes surgery is necessary. In some patients, the ductus arteriosus may be partially closed, and the problem is not significant enough to warrant treatment. In others, the dilated patent ductus arteriosus may be life-threatening. Patients have a normal life expectancy once the ductus arteriosus has been closed.
See also DUCTUS ARTERIOSUS; EISENMENGER SYNDROME; FALLOT'S TETRALOGY

PATERSON-BROWN-KELLY SYNDROME
See PLUMMER-VINSON SYNDROME

PATHOLOGICAL FRACTURE

Any bone can obviously fracture if excessive force is applied to it, but sometimes a bone may break (the terms break and fracture are identical in meaning) with minimal force. This is considered to be an abnormal (or pathological) fracture.

The most common reason for such a fracture is osteoporosis, which is a thinning of the bone structure caused by a lack of calcium in the bone. This usually occurs in elderly women, and can be corrected by adequate calcium in the diet at younger ages, or special medications that place calcium in bones.

All other causes are rare, and include osteomalacia (softened bone due to lack of vitamin D), osteogenesis imperfecta (a genetic condition resulting in fragile bones) and Riley-Day

PATENT DUCTUS ARTERIOSUS

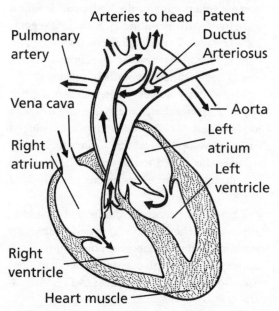

Arteries to head
Patent Ductus Arteriosus
Pulmonary artery
Vena cava
Aorta
Left atrium
Left ventricle
Right atrium
Right ventricle
Heart muscle

syndrome (occurs only in Jews, and is associated with a lack of tears, fever and sweating).
See also BONE; FRACTURE;
OSTEOPOROSIS and separate entries for diseases mentioned above.

PATHOLOGY

Pathology is the study of disease, and in particular the organisms that cause disease and the alterations to cells and tissue caused by disease. Pathologists are doctors who specialise in pathology. For a pathology test to be carried out, a sample of body tissue or fluid will be taken and sent to a laboratory for analysis. Blood, urine, faeces, sputum, pus, an excised lump, tissue removed at surgery, a discharge from the vagina or penis, cerebrospinal fluid, fluid from a joint or a cyst, a Pap or other form of smear, tissue obtained by scraping or biopsy and any other substance even remotely connected to a human may all be tested to determine a diagnosis or the cause of a problem.
See also BIOPSY; BLOOD TAKING;
BLOOD TESTING; BLOOD TESTS;
CHORIONIC VILLUS SAMPLING;
FAECES TESTS; PREGNANCY TESTS;
SCHILLING TEST; SKIN TESTS;
SPUTUM TESTS; URINE TESTS

Pb

Pb is the chemical symbol for lead, derived from the Latin word for lead, 'plumbum'.
See also LEAD POISONING

PC

The prescription notation 'pc' is derived from the Latin 'post cibum' which means 'after food'.
See also PRESCRIPTION NOTATIONS

PDA

See PATENT DUCTUS ARTERIOSUS

PEAK EXPIRATORY FLOW RATE

Peak expiratory flow rate (PEFR) is the maximum rate at which you can exhale (breath out). The patient is asked to blow as hard as possible into a small hand-held tube with a gauge and a mouthpiece attached (a peak flow meter). The rate at which you blow is measured in litres per minute, and the normal value will vary significantly depending on your sex, age and height. Doctors have tables which can compare the patient's performance to that of the average person. A poor result is characteristic of asthma, and some asthmatics have these simple measuring devices at home to determine the severity of their asthma attacks.
See also ASTHMA; LUNG;
RESPIRATORY FUNCTION TESTS

PECTORALIS MAJOR

The pectoralis major is a large, strong, fan shaped muscle found on the upper front wall of the chest. It acts to bring the arm closer to the chest in pulling actions. The fan end of the muscle attaches to the clavicle (collar bone), sternum (breast bone) and ribs, while the tendon at the outside end is inserted into the side of the top end of the humerus (upper arm bone).
See also CLAVICLE; HUMERUS;
MUSCLE; STERNUM

PEDERASTY
See PAEDOPHILIA

PEDICULOSIS
See CRABS; HEAD LICE

PEFR
See PEAK EXPIRATORY FLOW RATE

PEG
See GASTROSTOMY

PELLAGRA

Pellagra is caused by a lack of niacin (vitamin B3) in the diet. Niacin is essential for the normal functioning of the body, and is found in many foods including rice, meats, vegetables and dairy products. Pellagra occurs in countries where the diet is primarily corn, which has minimal amounts of niacin.

In the early stages patients have a poor appetite, general weakness, irritability, sore mouth and weight loss. More advanced cases develop dermatitis, diarrhoea, and become demented to the point where severe psychiatric disturbances occur in advanced cases.

The diagnosis can be confirmed by blood tests, then the disease is easily cured by vitamin B supplements given by mouth. If left untreated, death will eventually occur.
See also HARTNUP DISEASE; VITAMIN B

PELVIC CONGESTION SYNDROME

The pelvic congestion syndrome is a pelvic discomfort, ache and heaviness in women associated with fluid retention in the pelvis before a menstrual period. It can be relieved by fluid tablets or sexual orgasm.
See also PREMENSTRUAL TENSION SYNDROME

PELVIC INFLAMMATORY DISEASE

Pelvic inflammatory disease (PID) is an infection of the uterus (womb), Fallopian tubes, ovaries and the tissues immediately around these organs, usually associated with the sexual transmission of bacteria from one person to another, although less commonly it may occur as a result of non-sexually transmitted infections. It is most common in young, sexually promiscuous women. The use of intrauterine devices (IUD) doubles the risk of developing PID, while condoms provide significant protection. A wide range of different bacteria may be responsible, and frequently two, three or more different types are present.

Symptoms may include pain low in the abdomen, fevers, a vaginal discharge, abnormal menstrual periods, pain with intercourse, and infertility. The pain may become very severe, and the patient may appear extremely ill. One quarter of all women who develop PID will have long-term problems including repeat infections, infertility (10% after one attack of PID, 55% after three attacks of PID), persistent pain in the pelvis or with sex, and ectopic pregnancy (pregnancy that develops in the wrong position). There may be no symptoms in the male partner of the patient, although a discharge from the penis is sometimes present.

Swabs are usually taken from the vagina and cervix (opening into the womb) to determine the responsible bacteria and appropriate antibiotic. Treatment involves antibiotics by mouth or injected in severe cases. Sex should be avoided until complete recovery, which may take several weeks or months. If an abscess develops in the pelvis, an operation will be necessary to drain it. Fortunately, many women are completely cured by early treatment.
See also PELVIC PAIN; SALPINGITIS; VAGINITIS

PELVIC LUMP

A doctor may feel an abnormal lump or mass in the pelvis while feeling the lower abdomen or doing an internal examination through the vagina or anus. Occasionally patients discover such a lump themselves.

Lumps in the pelvis may come from the last part of the large bowel (rectum), bladder, vagina, uterus, ovaries, Fallopian tubes or lymph nodes.

Cancer of any of the organs in the pelvis listed above may be responsible for a lump. There is usually accompanying pain, tenderness and abnormal function of the organ (eg. bleeding and abnormal bowel function in bowel cancer).

Pregnancy is a certain cause of an enlarging mass in the pelvis, and some women have presented to doctors after finding it, without being aware that they are pregnant.

Other gynaecological causes include an ectopic pregnancy (development of a growing foetus in the Fallopian tubes instead of the uterus), fibroids (hard balls of fibrous tissue that form in the muscular wall of the uterus), endometriosis, pelvic inflammatory disease (generalised infection of the organs in the pelvis), ovarian cysts (sometimes of enormous size) and a severely inflamed Fallopian tube may swell dramatically with fluid (hydrosalpinx).

Other causes of a mass in the pelvis include severe constipation, an abscess in the pelvis, lymphoma (cancer of the lymph nodes) and very rarely an abnormally positioned kidney.
See also CANCER; PELVIC PAIN; PELVIS; UTERUS and separate entries for diseases mentioned above.

PELVIC PAIN

Pain in the pelvis or lower abdomen (hypogastrium) may come from any of the organs in the pelvis including the last part of the large bowel (rectum), bladder, vagina, uterus, ovaries, Fallopian tubes, prostate gland, testes or lymph nodes.

Painful periods, and the associated spasms and cramps of the uterus are a common cause of pelvic pain on a regular basis. The intra-uterine contraceptive device (IUD) may aggravate these period pains.

Similar cramping pains to those of a period may be felt before and during a miscarriage of pregnancy.

An ectopic pregnancy is the development of a growing foetus in the Fallopian tubes instead of the uterus. The tube becomes swollen and sensitive, and pain during deep sex may be noticed some days before other painful symptoms develop.

Fibroids are hard balls of fibrous tissue that form in the muscular wall of the uterus, often after pregnancy. They can distort the shape of the uterus to cause pain when the uterus contracts during a menstrual period or orgasm.

Cysts may form on a regular basis in an ovary because of errors in the release of ova (eggs) every month. When they leak or burst they release a fluid that is very irritating and causes inflammation and pain.

Other gynaecological causes of pelvic pain include salpingitis (infection of the Fallopian tubes), endometriosis, retrograde menstruation (menstrual blood goes up a Fallopian tube and out into the pelvic cavity), ovarian torsion (twisting of an ovary on the stalk of tissue that supplies it with blood and nerves), cancer of an ovary and pelvic congestion syndrome (associated with fluid retention in the pelvis).

Other causes of pelvic pain include severe constipation, a hernia (inguinal or femoral), cystitis (bladder infection), bladder stones, diverticular disease (formation of numerous small outpocketings of the large gut), irritable bowel syndrome, ulcerative colitis (lining of the large intestine becomes ulcerated and bleeds), adhesions, prostatitis (bacterial infection of the prostate), torsion of the testis (a medical emergency in which the testicle twists around and cuts off the blood vessels that supply it), appendicitis and peritonitis (infection of the lining the belly cavity).
See also ABDOMINAL PAIN; GROIN PAIN; PELVIS and separate entries for diseases mentioned above.

PELVIS

The pelvis is a basin-shaped group of bones which support the lower end of the abdominal cavity and contain the rectum, loops of small intestine, the bladder and, in women, the uterus and ovaries.

At the back of the basin is the sacrum, which is really five fused vertebrae. The top of the sacrum supports the spinal column and its vertebrae.

The sides of the pelvis are formed by the iliac bones, which can be felt as the arch of bone above the hip. We sit on a very thick arch of bone called the ischium. The front of the pelvis is formed by the pubic bone. These three bones fuse together as fixed joints where there is no movement. At the point where the three bones meet is the socket (acetabulum) for the hip joint.
See also ABDOMEN; BLADDER; FEMUR; PELVIC LUMP; PELVIC PAIN; SPINE; UTERUS; VERTEBRA

PEMPHIGOID

Bullous pemphigoid is an uncommon but serious autoimmune skin disease that usually affects elderly women. There is an inappropriate immune reaction within the body that causes the skin to be rejected in the same way as a transplanted kidney is rejected by the body. The actual cause of the autoimmune reaction is unknown.

Patients develop red, scaling, itchy patches, which after a few days break down into large, fluid-filled blisters on widespread areas of the body. These huge, soft bubbles develop on the arms and legs initially, but soon spread to the trunk. The face and head are rarely affected. Severe fluid loss from the body through the blisters may cause dehydration and heart rhythm irregularities.

The diagnosis is confirmed by a skin biopsy (taking a sample of the affected skin, and examining it under a microscope). Treatment involves high doses of prednisone, a steroid that reduces the immune response and allows the skin to repair itself. Once the disease is under control, the dosage is slowly reduced over a period of many months, but some patients need to remain on a low dose for years. Cytotoxic drugs may also be used. Without treatment, pemphigoid is fatal in one third of patients. With treatment, deaths are very rare, and one third of patients will require no treatment after two years.
See also AUTOIMMUNE DISEASES; BLISTERS; PEMPHIGUS; SKIN ITCH

PEMPHIGUS

Pemphigus is a rare but severe autoimmune skin disease that occurs in all age groups and both sexes, but is very uncommon in children. There is an inappropriate immune reaction within the body that causes the skin to be rejected in the same way as a transplanted kidney is rejected by the body. The actual cause of the autoimmune reaction is unknown.

The rash varies dramatically in its form from shallow ulcers, to multiple blisters, red scaling patches or massive peeling of skin. Any part of the body, including the face and the inside of the mouth, may be affected.

A biopsy (sample) of the affected skin is examined to confirm the diagnosis, then large doses of prednisone or other steroids, immunosuppressive and cytotoxic drugs, all of which may have significant side effects, must be used long-term. Without treatment, pemphigus is invariably fatal. With adequate treatment, the mortality rate is below 25%.
See also AUTOIMMUNE DISEASES; BLISTERS; PEMPHIGOID; SCALDED SKIN SYNDROME

PEMPHIGUS NEONATORUM
See SCALDED SKIN SYNDROME

PENICILLAMINE
See ANTIRHEUMATICS

PENICILLINS
Penicillins are the most widely used antibiotics in the world. There are many different types of penicillin now available. They are broad-spectrum antibiotics that kill a wide range of bacteria, and have been used for almost every conceivable type of infection at some time. Unfortunately many bacteria are now becoming resistant to penicillin. The penicillins are available as tablets, capsules, drops, syrup, injection and chewable tablets.

Allergies to penicillin are not more common than to other drugs, but appear to be so because it is so widely used. Patients who know they have a penicillin allergy should tell their doctors and wear a warning pendant or bracelet. Penicillin may cause a skin rash if given to a patient with glandular fever, and may start a vaginal thrush infection in some women.

Examples of medications in this class include amoxycillin (Amoxil), flucloxacillin (Flopen) and phenoxymethyl penicillin. Side effects may include diarrhoea, nausea and a rash. They are safe to use in pregnancy.
See also ANTIBIOTICS; FLEMING, ALEXANDER; FLOREY, HOWARD;

PENIS
The penis has the twin tasks of passing urine out of the body in a controlled manner, and being the organ used in male sexual intercourse. During sex, its length is designed to allow sperm to be deposited as close to the cervix as possible.

At rest, the penis is a soft sausage-like structure hanging limply down from the base of the

MALE GENITAL ANATOMY

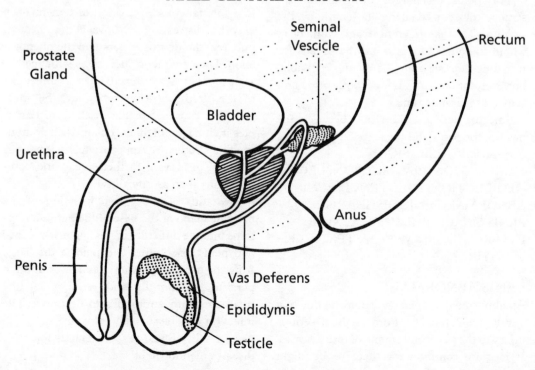

abdomen where it is attached to the bones of the pelvis. However, it is made up of several masses of spongy tissue and these fill with blood when the man is sexually aroused so that the penis becomes firm, erect and distended and is thus able to penetrate the vagina.

Sperm are manufactured in the testicles and travel through the male reproductive system, combining with a white sticky fluid to form semen. At the height of sexual excitation, or orgasm, the semen is ejaculated.

The head of the penis, or glans, is a highly sensitive zone which is easily sexually stimulated. Where the glans meets the shaft of the penis, the sensitive skin covering the penis folds back on itself to form the prepuce or foreskin. It is this part of the skin that is removed by circumcision. Circumcision has been commonly performed in much of the English-speaking world for several generations, but in more recent times it has been seen as unnecessary surgery performed for no medical reason. Indeed, because the foreskin is the most sexually sensitive part of the penis, it is now considered possible that a man's later sexual pleasure may be diminished by the operation. Sometimes the foreskin is so tight that the child cannot urinate properly (a condition called phimosis) and in this case circumcision may be essential. The condition will not usually become apparent until the age of about five.

The penis discharges both urine and semen, transported along its length by the urethra. This is different from women in whom the organs for sex and the organs for urinating are separate. It is not possible, however, for a man to release both urine and semen at the same time.

Smegma acts as a lubricant between the head of the penis and the foreskin.

See also CIRCUMCISION; EJACULATION; EJACULATION, LACK OF; ERECTION; IMPOTENCE; PENIS ABNORMAL; PENIS DISCHARGE; PENIS SMALL; PHIMOSIS; SEXUAL INTERCOURSE; SMEGMA; TESTICLE; URETHRA

PENIS ABNORMAL

An abnormally shaped penis may be due to a developmental defect from birth, a serious injury to the penis or a couple of rare diseases. It is quite common for there to be slight curvature to the left or right, and an upward curve in the erect penis is totally normal.

Hypospadias is a developmental abnormality in which some boys are born with the opening of the urethra (urine tube) on the underside or at the base of the penis instead of at the end. It can usually be surgically corrected.

Peyronie's disease is an abnormal curvature of the penis caused by scarring, poor blood supply, infection or other damage to the erection sustaining blood sacs on only one side of the organ.

Lichen sclerosis is a scarring and thickening of the skin on one side of the penis, caused by infection or injury to the penis. It causes a sideways curve to the penis that may be painful during an erection.

Smith-Lemli-Opitz syndrome is an inherited disorder that causes drooping of the eyelids, a narrow forehead, mental retardation, hypospadias (see above), prominent nostrils and webbed toes.

See also IMPOTENCE; PENIS SMALL and separate entries for diseases mentioned above.

PENIS CANCER
See SQUAMOUS CELL CARCINOMA OF THE SKIN

PENIS DISCHARGE
Wet dreams are a normal occasional event during deep sleep for all men, and are due to a spontaneous ejaculation of semen. They may be distressing to boys going through puberty who do not understand the phenomenon. Their frequency decreases with age.

Sexually transmitted bacterial infections of the urethra (urine tube) are the most common cause of penile discharges. Examples include gonorrhoea, chlamydia and non-specific urethritis. Appropriate treatment is essential to prevent further spread and complications such as infertility.

Prostatitis is a bacterial infection of the prostate gland at the base of the penis. Symptoms include difficulty in passing urine, pelvic and penis discomfort and pain, a discharge from the penis and sometimes a fever. It often persists for months and requires lengthy treatment with antibiotics to be cured. The infection may be sexually transmitted.

See also PENIS and separate entries for diseases mentioned above.

PENIS SHORT
See PENIS SMALL

PENIS SMALL
A lot of rubbish is spoken of about penis size in locker rooms and other areas where men congregate, but medical texts indicate that the average male erect penis measured along the top is 12.9 cm. in length, and 90% of men have an erect penis that is between 9cm. and 17 cm. in length. The other 10% are evenly divided between longer and shorter. The longest medically recorded erect penis was 32 cm. but this is as much of a freak as the man who is 270 cm. (nine feet) tall. There is no direct correlation between height, or any other obvious physical attribute, and penis size.

Usually no treatment is necessary as a small penis has no effect upon a man's fertility, and does not determine whether a man is a good lover. During intercourse, the most sensitive part of a woman's sexual organs are the clitoris, which is at the outside entrance to the vagina, and the 'G spot' which is just inside, and on the front wall of the vagina, at a point where even the shortest penis can give stimulation. If desired, there are plastic surgery procedures available that will both lengthen and thicken the penis, but these may have significant complications.

No man with a relatively small penis should underestimate his sexual prowess, as he will be able to satisfy the sexual appetite of any woman if he approaches her in the right way. It is not the size of the equipment that counts, but how it is used.
See also PENIS

PENIS ULCER
See GENITAL ULCER

PEPTIC ULCER
Ulcers of the duodenum (first part of the small intestine), stomach or pylorus (muscle ring separating the stomach and duodenum) are known as peptic ulcers. A gastric ulcer is an ulcer of the stomach.

Ulcers are caused by hydrochloric acid, which is a potent acid naturally produced in the stomach to aid food digestion. The stomach protects itself with a layer of thick mucus. If there is excess acid or insufficient mucus present, the acid may eat into the stomach wall. The most common causes for excess acid or reduced mucus are smoking, stress, anxiety, alcohol, aspirin and the nonsteroidal anti-inflammatory drugs used to treat arthritis. The bacterium *Helicobacter pylori* may damage the mucus lining of the stomach to allow an ulcer to form.

An ulcer may penetrate into a blood vessel to cause bleeding, anaemia and weakness before any pain is felt. Most ulcers cause pain high up in the belly which is often worst just before a meal and relieved by eating. Other symptoms include a feeling of fullness, excess burping and indigestion.

The diagnosis can be proved by a barium meal x-ray or gastroscopy. During gastroscopy a biopsy can be taken of an ulcer to exclude cancer, and a test can be performed to identify the presence *Helicobacter pylori*. The bacteria can also be detected by a test on a sample of breath that is collected in an airtight container, and there is a blood test, but this is less accurate.

A sensible diet, stopping smoking and relaxation can all help. If *Helicobacter pylori* is detected, a specific course of antibiotics and anti-ulcer medication (triple therapy) can be given to eradicate it, heal the ulcer, and prevent a recurrence. Numerous tablets are available to control and often cure peptic ulcers, and because of the effectiveness of these medications, surgery for peptic ulcers is now rarely required.

Excessive bleeding from an ulcer can cause serious anaemia, and a very small percentage of ulcers can be cancerous.
See also ANTACIDS; DUODENUM; GASTRITIS; H2 RECEPTOR ANTAGONISTS; HYDROCHLORIC ACID; PROTON PUMP INHIBITORS; STOMACH; ZOLLINGER-ELLISON SYNDROME

PERCUTANEOUS ENDOSCOPIC GASTROSTOMY
See GASTROSTOMY

PERCUTANEOUS RADIOFREQUENCY NEUROTOMY
Percutaneous radiofrequency neurotomy is a procedure undertaken under x-ray control in which nerves in the back that are causing severe chronic pain are destroyed. Under local

anaesthetic, a needle is introduced into the back to reach the point where the nerve leaves the spinal cord and passes between the vertebrae. When the needle is in the correct position, a high frequency radio wave is passed through the needle to destroy the segment of the nerve beside the needle tip, thus relieving the pain.

It is normally only performed after an injection of local anaesthetic into the nerve has proved that the pain can be relieved by its destruction. The procedure has effects that usually last for several months to a year, but it may need to be repeated as the nerve recovers after each neurotomy. Complications of the procedure are few, but may include temporary leg weakness from the local anaesthetic, and rarely damage to other nerves or tissue.
See also NEUROTOMY

PERHEXILENE
See ANTIANGINALS

PERIARTERITIS NODOSA
See POLYARTERITIS NODOSA

PERICARDITIS
Pericarditis is an uncommon inflammation or infection of the pericardium, the fibrous sac that surrounds the heart. It may be caused by a viral (common – often secondary to mumps, hepatitis or influenza) or bacterial (rare) infection, and may also occur if the pericardium is affected by the spread of cancer cells from the lung, lymph nodes or other organs. Other causes include heart attacks, tuberculosis, kidney failure and irradiation.

All forms cause chest pain, shortness of breath and a fever. The secretion of fluid by the damaged pericardium into the tiny space between the pericardium and heart (pericardial effusion) puts pressure on the heart, and scarring of the pericardium from infection may contract and constrict the heart. In both these cases, the heart may not be able to expand fully between each beat, and becomes steadily more constricted (constrictive pericarditis), causing the heart to fail as a pump.

It is diagnosed by a combination of x-ray, CT scan, electrocardiogram (ECG), blood tests and biopsy examinations.

There is no specific cure for a viral infection, and treatment involves aspirin, anti-inflammatory drugs and prednisone. Bacterial pericarditis can be treated with antibiotics. A pericardial effusion (collection of fluid within the pericardial sac) can be treated by inserting a long needle through the chest wall and draining the fluid. Patients with constrictive pericarditis (fibrous sac becomes scarred and contracts tightly around the heart) may require surgery on the heart to cut away the scarred part of the pericardium.

The prognosis depends upon the cause and severity of the infection, and the age and health of the patient. Death occurs in a significant number of cases, particularly if the patient is elderly or debilitated.
See also CHEST PAIN; DRESSLER SYNDROME; ENDOCARDITIS; HEART; HEART FAILURE; MYOCARDITIS

PERICARDIUM
See HEART

PERICYAZINE
See ANTIPSYCHOTICS

PERINDOPRIL
See ACE INHIBITORS

PERINEUM
The area between the base of the penis and anus in the man, and the vulva and anus in a woman, is called the perineum.
See also ANUS; RAPHE; VULVA

PERIODONTICS
Periodontics is the dental science that deals with the gum and bones that lie around the teeth. Periodontal disease may cause tooth loss, especially in later years, as it is an insidious disease, for the most part painless, and often not recognised until it is too late. Like dental decay, it is preventable in most people, and is caused in the first instance by the accumulation of dental plaque around the teeth.
See also DENTAL PLAQUE; DENTISTRY

PERIODS, MENSTRUAL
See MENSTRUAL PERIOD; MENSTRUAL PERIOD, FAILURE TO START; MENSTRUAL PERIOD, LACK OF; MENSTRUAL PERIODS HEAVY; MENSTRUAL PERIODS PAINFUL

PERIORAL DERMATITIS
Perioral dermatitis is a common facial skin

problem that tends to occur more in women who have oily skin, do not wash their face thoroughly, and use face creams, foundation and cosmetics that clog skin pores. The overuse of strong steroid creams on delicate facial skin may also be responsible.

Clumps of small, red, itchy, tender spots develop on the skin around the mouth, but not on the lips. The rash may also occur around the nose and eyes. Tetracycline antibiotics clear the rash, but patients should avoid all face creams, sunscreens, cosmetics and steroid creams, and wash their face regularly with warm water without soap. The rash settles well with treatment, but sometimes recurs.
See also DERMATITIS; FACE RED

PERIPHERAL NEUROPATHY

Peripheral neuropathy is abnormal nerve function in the arms and legs. There are many causes including toxins, poisons, alcoholism, poor blood supply, poorly controlled diabetes mellitus, kidney failure, vitamin deficiencies, liver failure (eg. cirrhosis) and an underactive thyroid gland.

Patients feel tingling and burning sensations in the hands and feet, other abnormal sensations, and have abnormal reflexes. Clumsiness and difficulty in walking, muscle wasting and weakness may occur.

Electromyography (EMG) measures the electrical activity and function of muscles and can be used to confirm the diagnosis. Numerous clinical tests can also be performed to check sensation, and blood tests and other tests are undertaken to find the cause. Appropriately treating the cause may slow the progress of the disease, or reverse its affects.

The prognosis depends on the cause, its severity and response to treatment.
See also ALCOHOLISM; CIRRHOSIS; PINS AND NEEDLES SENSATION IN SKIN; WERNICKE-KORSAKOFF PSYCHOSIS

PERISTALSIS

The wave-like contractions that move food slowly through the gut from the oesophagus to the anus are referred to as peristalsis. The walls of the intestine contract behind a bolus of food and relax in front of it to create movement.
See also LARGE INTESTINE; SMALL INTESTINE; STOMACH

PERITONEAL DIALYSIS
See DIALYSIS; PERITONEUM

PERITONEUM

The peritoneum is a tough membrane which forms a sac that lines the abdominal cavity and contains the small and large intestine, stomach, liver, spleen and pancreas. The kidneys lie behind the peritoneum, and the bladder is below it. In women, the uterus and vagina are also below the peritoneal sac, but the ovaries are within it.
See also ABDOMEN; PERITONITIS

PERITONITIS

Within the belly (abdomen) is a large membranous sac called the peritoneum, which contains the intestine and other organs. Peritonitis occurs if this sac becomes inflamed or infected.

A wide range of diseases of any organ within the abdomen may be responsible for peritonitis. Examples include gut infections such as appendicitis or diverticulitis, a hole in the gut from an ulcer that allows the gut contents to escape into the abdominal cavity, liver infections such as hepatitis and cirrhosis, pancreatitis, pelvic inflammatory disease, bleeding within the abdomen from injury, a ruptured ovarian cyst, cancer of any organ in the abdomen, mesenteric adenitis, or it may be a rare side effect of some drugs and poisons.

Patients have severe abdominal pain, nausea, fever and sometimes diarrhoea. As the infection progresses, they may become shocked and collapse, and further complications such as temporary paralysis of the gut, abscess formation in the abdomen, liver damage and adhesions may occur.

It is essential that the cause of the peritonitis be determined by further investigations before treatment is started. These investigations may include blood tests, x-rays, placing a needle into the abdomen to sample any fluid that may be present, vaginal and rectal examinations, or an operation to explore the abdomen. Treatment will include appropriate antibiotics by injection, as well as dealing with the cause.

With good treatment, recovery is normal, but without adequate medical care, death can occur.
See also ABDOMEN; INFECTION;

PERITONEUM and separate entries for diseases mentioned above.

PERITONSILLAR ABSCESS
See QUINSY

PERMETHRIN
See ANTIPARASITICS

PERNICIOUS ANAEMIA

Pernicious or megaloblastic anaemia is due to a lack of vitamin B12 (cyanocobalamin), which is essential for the formation of haemoglobin, the red oxygen-carrying substance in red blood cells. For vitamin B12 to be absorbed from the stomach and into the blood a substance called intrinsic factor is required. Patients with pernicious anaemia lack intrinsic factor and therefore develop a lack of vitamin B12, which in turn leads to an inability to produce haemoglobin. It is common in middle aged women and is given its name because of its very gradual and 'pernicious' onset over many years.

In addition to tiredness and pallor, patients have a smooth and sore tongue, indigestion, lack of appetite, and occasionally jaundice (yellow skin). It is diagnosed by blood tests, which show abnormal blood cells (megaloblasts).

Regular injections of vitamin B12 are necessary for the rest of the patient's life. The injections may be weekly at first, then reduced to one every two or three months. Although pernicious anaemia cannot be cured, it can be very effectively controlled. Untreated, the disease is fatal.
See also ANAEMIA; SCHILLING TEST; VITAMIN B

PERSONALITY CHANGE

Changes in personality are rarely noticed by patients, and often not by acquaintances; it is only close friends and family who will bring the affected person to a doctor with the complaint that "s/he is just not him/her self anymore". This very vague symptom may lead to the diagnosis of quite severe psychiatric or brain disorders, so if there is no obvious reason for a personality change in someone that you care about, ensure that s/he is adequately assessed by a doctor.

Tumours, cancer, injury, an abscess or bleeding into the frontal lobes of the brain, where the personality is formed, may cause a gradual and subtle change in personality that is detected only when quite advanced.

Alzheimer disease (senile dementia or second childhood) is one of the most common forms of dementia in the elderly. It is characterised by loss of recent memory, loss of initiative, reduced physical activity, confusion, loss of orientation, and then gradually progresses to loss of speech, difficulty in swallowing, stiff muscles, incontinence and a bedridden state. It is caused by a faster than normal loss of nerve cells in the brain.

A stroke (cerebrovascular accident) may have unusual or bizarre effects depending upon which area of the brain is damaged.

Numerous psychiatric disorders may be responsible for a progressive or intermittent alteration in the personality. These include paranoid delusions (eccentric ideas about persecution or obsession with a particular subject), schizophrenia (distorted view of the world because of delusions and hallucinations), obsessive compulsive disorder (patients repeat unnecessary actions or constantly check things), histrionic personality (subconsciously use personality changes as an attention seeking device), narcissistic personality (self centred and react badly to criticism), antisocial personality disorders (violent, disruptive and insensitive to others), phobias (abnormal fears) and manic depressive psychoses (wild mood swings from extremely happy and extroverted, to very depressed and suicidal).
See also MULTIPLE PERSONALITY DISORDER; PSYCHIATRY and separate entries for diseases mentioned above.

PERTHES' DISEASE

Perthes' disease is a hip joint disease that develops in children between five and eleven years of age. Softening of the growing area of the thigh bone (femur) occurs immediately below the hip joint due to an abnormal blood supply to the bone. The softened bone becomes distorted and damaged as the child continues to walk on it.

The first sign is a limp, as the affected leg does not grow as well as the other, and becomes slightly shorter. Pain is the next symptom, and eventually walking may become impossible. The diagnosis is confirmed by an x-ray of the hip.

Treatment involves resting the affected leg by keeping the child in bed, on crutches or in a caliper for many months. If there is significant deformity, or the bone at the top of the femur dies, an operation is necessary. Permanent deformity of the hip and the development of early arthritis may occur if treatment is inadequate or delayed. In most cases, the condition settles after two years.
See also ARTHRITIS; FEMUR; HIP

PERTUSSIS
See WHOOPING COUGH

PES CAVUS
Pes cavus is the opposite of flat feet, in that there is an increased height of the foot arch causing shortening of the foot. It may be a developmental abnormality, due to injury, or secondary to muscle spasm diseases such as cerebral palsy and polio.

The foot is painful, abnormally shaped and the toes are often clawed, and x-rays demonstrate the bone deformity. Premature osteoarthritis may develop in the foot as well as a limp.

Treatment depends on the severity and varies from supportive arches in shoes to strengthening exercises under the supervision of a physiotherapist and surgery to reduce the height of the arch. There are good results from treatment.
See also FLAT FEET; FOOT; FOOT PAIN

PES PLANUS
See FLAT FEET

PESSARY
A pessary is a tablet or other form of medication that is inserted into the vagina to act locally (eg. spermicide, moisturiser), or be absorbed into the bloodstream through the wall of the vagina (eg. hormone).
See also MEDICATION; VAGINA

PETECHIAE
See SKIN RED DOTS

PETHIDINE
See NARCOTICS

PETIT MAL
See EPILEPSY

PET SCAN
PET stands for positron emission tomography, and a PET scan is a way of measuring the chemical activity of the brain, which varies under different conditions. Unlike CT and MRI scanning, which show what the brain looks like, PET provides information about how the brain is working. It produces a three-dimensional map that differentiates those areas where a lot of chemical activity is taking place from those where there is little chemical activity. For example, some tumours produce more and some less chemical activity than the surrounding tissue, and a PET scan will identify them.

To carry out the scan, a radioactive chemical is injected. As it flows throughout the brain's blood vessels it is absorbed in the greatest amounts by the most chemically active areas. As the radioactive substance breaks down, minute particles called positrons are given off. These are picked up by the scan, analysed by computer as to what part of the brain they came from, and a picture is built up of how the radioactive chemical is distributed. The number of positrons emitted from a particular area reflects how much radioactive substance has been taken up, and therefore how chemically active that section of the brain is.

PET can help to diagnose tumours (where there is usually virtually no chemical activity) and epilepsy (where there is excessive activity), and also give information about the functioning of the brain in various mental illnesses such as schizophrenia. It is also used to assess Parkinson disease.
See also CT SCAN; MRI SCAN

PEUTZ-JEGHER SYNDROME
The Peutz-Jegher syndrome is a congenital (present from birth) abnormality. Patches of brown or black pigment can be seen in the mouth and on the lips and fingers, and multiple polyps occur throughout the intestine that can bleed and sometimes obstruct the gut. Anaemia may occur from loss of blood.

It is diagnosed and treated by gastroscopy and/or colonoscopy (passing a flexible tube into the gut through the mouth or anus), during which the largest and bleeding polyps are removed. Sometimes open surgery is necessary. There is no cure, and repeated operations to remove polyps are required.
See also COLONOSCOPY;

GASTROSCOPY; MOUTH
PIGMENTATION; POLYPOSIS COLI

PEWTER

Pewter is a bluish silver-grey coloured alloy of tin, antimony and copper, although lead was used originally. It was discovered that small amounts of lead were absorbed into the food and drink in or on pewter plates and jugs, which resulted in lead poisoning.

Pewter plates, jugs and mugs (without the lead) will kill *Staphylococci* and other bacteria. These were widely used in 18th century hospitals to reduce infection, although there was no contemporary knowledge of the method of disease transmission by micro-organisms.
See also LEAD POISONING

PEXID

See ANTIANGINALS

PEYOTE

See MESCALINE

PEYRONIE DISEASE

Peyronie disease is an uncommon problem that causes deformity of the erect penis. The cause may be injury to the penis, narrowing of the artery to one side of the penis (common with poorly controlled diabetes or high cholesterol), abnormal nerve supply to the penis or most frequently, for no known cause. The incidence increases with age.

These men have significant side to side (not vertical) curvature of the erect penis and a less firm than normal erection as the normal tissue of the penis is replaced by fibrous tissue on one side only. A hard piece of tissue can often be felt at the base of the penis on the affected side. Ultrasound scans can show the abnormal fibrous tissue in the penis. Note that a small degree of side to side curvature (up to 15°) is quite normal.

Most forms of treatment are not very successful. Surgery, steroid injections and radiotherapy may be tried, but the most radical, and most successful, treatment is surgical replacement of the contents of the penis with an inflatable bladder that can be pumped up when an erection is desired. This is up to 80% effective.
See also PENIS ABNORMAL

PHAEOCHROMOCYTOMA

A phaeochromocytoma is a rare black-celled tumour in the adrenal glands (which sit on top of each kidney) which releases a substance into the blood stream that causes very high blood pressure (hypertension). It is sometimes a hereditary tendency, but most arise for no apparent reason.

Patients have extremely high blood pressure, severe headaches, palpitations of the heart, abnormal sweating, nausea and vomiting, abdominal pains, blurred vision, and brain damage that may result in loss of speech, blindness or unconsciousness. Other symptoms may include increased appetite, nervousness and irritability, shortness of breath, weight loss, light-headedness and chest pain (angina). Some patients have multiple tumours in other parts of the body, and an unexplained sudden death may be due to a heart attack caused by an undiagnosed tumour. Some forms are associated with cancer, but a phaeochromocytoma is not a cancer itself.

The diagnosis is confirmed by special blood tests that measure excessive levels of catecholamines (the chemical released by the tumour). A CT scan or a magnetic resonance imaging scan (MRI) is performed to locate the tumour.

Controlling the high blood pressure with medication is the initial aim of treatment, and then surgically removing the tumour. Long-term management with medication, but without surgery, is not practical.

The prognosis depends on the damage caused by the high blood pressure before diagnosis and how many tumours are present. If the tumour is removed early, a complete recovery is expected. Without treatment, the disease is invariably fatal, and even in the best medical centres, a small percentage of patients will die from complications of the disease or the surgery.
See also ADRENAL GLAND;
HYPERTENSION

PHARYNGEAL CANCER

Cancer occurring in the throat (pharynx), almost invariably occurs after the age of fifty years, and smoking is by far the most common cause, but it is also more common in patients who are alcoholics, eat large quantities of salted fish and avoid fruit and vegetables.

Symptoms may include hoarseness, altered

ability to use the tongue, changes in speech patterns, throat and neck pain, difficulty in swallowing, cough, swelling of the neck and enlarged lymph nodes. The cancer may spread to surrounding bones and tissue. It is diagnosed by a biopsy of affected tissue in the throat.

Treatments include surgery and/or radiation, depending on location, type and severity of cancer. Chemotherapy (potent anticancer drugs) may be used in patients when other treatments are inappropriate or have failed. Treatment may result in removal of, or damage to the larynx, and the permanent loss of speech, difficulty in swallowing and a dry throat. The prognosis depends on the severity of cancer at time of diagnosis.
See also CANCER; PHARYNX; RADIOTHERAPY

PHARYNGITIS
Pharyngitis is a very common bacterial or viral infection of the throat (pharynx). Viruses cause the vast majority, while a minority is due to bacteria. The most serious bacterial pharyngitis is caused by *Staphylococcus aureus* (golden staph), but by far the most common is caused by *Streptococci*. The infection is passed from one person to another in tiny water droplets in the breath, and most cases occur in winter.

The symptoms may vary from one day of mild discomfort to a severe infection causing dramatic swelling of the throat for more than a week. The patient may have a fever, throat pain and soreness, pain on swallowing, dry cough, headache and enlarged lymph nodes in the neck. Severe bacterial infections may rarely cause a throat abscess.

Most cases require no investigation, but if the infection is serious, a throat swab may be taken to identify the responsible bacteria and appropriate antibiotic. Blood tests may be performed if diseases such as glandular fever, which also causes throat pain, are suspected.

The treatment of a viral pharyngitis is aspirin, paracetamol or ibuprofen, anaesthetic gargles, and soothing lozenges. Bacterial pharyngitis is treated with antibiotics such as penicillin as well as the medications for a viral infection.

Viral infections last for a week or ten days, while antibiotics will cure a bacterial infection in a day or two.

See also COLD, COMMON; GLANDULAR FEVER; LARYNGITIS; PHARYNGITIS; PHARYNX; STAPHYLOCOCCUS AUREUS; STREPTOCOCCAL INFECTION; TONSILLITIS; THROAT PAIN; UVULITIS

PHARYNX
The pharynx is a passageway for both food and air. It is commonly known as the throat although in fact the throat forms only part of it. The pharynx extends down from the back of the mouth where it joins the nasal cavity, past the opening to the larynx to the top of the oesophagus. Its overall length is about 11 cm. Once food reaches the pharynx, swallowing becomes an involuntary reflex action and cannot be stopped. The pharynx also functions as a resonating chamber for sounds produced in the larynx.

The back of the pharynx is a solid wall of muscle, lined with mucous membrane, while the front opens into the nose, mouth and larynx. The epiglottis protects the opening into the larynx. Tiny tubes called the Eustachian tubes open off the upper part of the pharynx and connect it with the ears.

If you open your mouth in front of a mirror you can see the back of the middle section of the pharynx. Hanging down in front of the opening is a soft, fleshy V-shaped mass known as the uvula. It is the vibration of the uvula that causes snoring.

At the top of the pharynx is a mass of lymphoid tissue called the adenoids. On each side of the uvula are two similar masses called the tonsils. Both tonsils and adenoids help to combat infection but are themselves prone to chronic infection, in which case they may be surgically removed.

The pharynx is prone to inflammation because of infection or overuse, which leads to the painful symptoms of pharyngitis.
See also EPIGLOTTIS; LARYNX; MOUTH; NOSE; OESOPHAGUS; PHARYNGITIS; THROAT LUMP; THROAT PAIN; TONSIL

PHENACETIN
See ANALGESIC NEPHROPATHY

PHENELZINE
See ANTIDEPRESSANTS

PHENERGAN
See ANTIHISTAMINES

PHENIRAMINE
See ANTIHISTAMINES

PHENOTHIAZINES
See ANTIPSYCHOTICS

PHENOXYMETHYL PENICILLIN
See PENICILLINS

PHENTERMINE
See ANORECTICS

PHENYLEPHRINE
See DECONGESTANTS

PHENYLKETONURIA
Phenylketonuria (PKU) is an uncommon congenital (present from birth) metabolic (body chemistry) disorder that may have serious consequences. The disease runs in families from one generation to the next, and is more common in people of Scottish or Irish descent (1 in 5000 children), but extremely rare in Negroes (1 in 300 000).

A baby with PKU cannot tolerate foodstuffs which contain the amino acid, phenylalanine, and a buildup of this in the blood causes brain damage, mental retardation, epilepsy, behaviour problems and eczema. As a result, every baby in Western countries is routinely tested a couple of days after birth using a single drop of blood taken from a heel prick. If the condition is diagnosed, further blood tests are performed regularly to ensure that the amount of phenylalanine does not rise above normal.

A protein free diet from before two months of age until the patient is at least eight years old is essential. Phenylalanine is found in most proteins, but other amino acids (the building blocks of protein) can be provided in a special milk formula. A correct diet started early will prevent the disease from damaging the brain, and the child will grow up to be a normal adult with normal intelligence.
See also MENTAL RETARDATION; PROTEIN

PHENYTOIN
See ANTICONVULSANTS

PHIMOSIS
Phimosis is a narrowed opening in the foreskin of the penis. This is normal up to six years of age, and the foreskin should never be forcibly retracted before this age. In older boys and men it may be due to infection in or under the foreskin, injury or a minor birth defect.

The man is unable to retract the foreskin over the head of the penis, and sometimes there is ballooning of the foreskin when passing urine. Balanitis (an infection of the head of the penis) due to an inability to clean under the foreskin, may be a problem.

Circumcision cures the condition.
See also BALANITIS; CIRCUMCISION; PARAPHIMOSIS; PENIS

PHLEBITIS
Phlebitis is inflammation of a vein, usually due to a blood clot (thrombosis) in the vein, but it may occur for no apparent reason. Pain, tenderness and redness are felt along the course of a vein. There may be swelling of the tissue drained by the affected vein due to reduced blood flow back to the heart. Anti-inflammatory gels, creams or tablets can be used to ease the discomfort and inflammation.
See also THROMBOPHLEBITIS; THROMBOSIS; VEIN

PHOLCODINE
See COUGH MEDICINES

PHOBIA
A phobia is an unreasonable fear of some thing, place or activity that should not normally provoke fear. There are people who fear enclosed spaces (claustrophobia), spiders (arachnophobia), open spaces (agoraphobia), heights (acrophobia), water (hydrophobia), sharp implements, specific animals, eating in public or almost any thing or activity imaginable.

Phobias most commonly develop in anxious people in the late teens and early adult years, and are more common in women than men. Some patients have a fear of a particular circumstance because of an unpleasant experience in the past (eg. claustrophobia after being trapped in a lift), but this is not a true phobia as it is a rational fear triggered by a previous unpleasant experience.

An anxious patient may rationalise their

anxiety and the palpitations, sweating, nausea and headaches caused by the anxiety, by considering it to be a reasonable fear of something. It may become a neurotic obsession that dominates the patient's life, particularly if the fear is of contamination, dirt or disease, which leads to repetitive actions such as constant, excessive hand-washing. In other situations, patients may go to extreme lengths to avoid the object of their fear (eg. stay in rooms on the ground floor of hotels), or undertake rituals that make a fearful activity safe (eg. always wear a certain piece of clothing when flying). The patient with one serious phobia usually develops more and more phobias of less and less fearful objects and situations, and as the neurotic disease or anxiety worsens they may become housebound or unable to function in society.

Obsessive compulsive disorder is a form of neurosis in which the patient (usually a woman) has a totally irrational desire to undertake a repetitive task (eg. hand washing). Even after completing the task, the patient feels that s/he must do it again and again, despite being well aware that the habit is abnormal, because s/he fears some disaster will befall them if s/he does not.

Schizophrenia is a mental illness which causes the sufferer to have a distorted view of the world because of delusions and hallucinations. Patients often change the topic of conversation for no apparent reason, do not look after themselves, become dishevelled in appearance, withdrawn, fail to communicate properly with others, hear unfriendly voices, have frightening visions, believe they are being persecuted and develop other mood and behaviour changes that seem bizarre. They may appear to have a phobia but it is really a psychotic delusion.

Psychiatrists can help patients deal with the underlying anxieties, give behavioural treatment that gradually exposes the patient to the fear, and prescribe medication that controls the problem. Schizophrenia requires intensive treatment with antipsychotic medications.

Most patients can cope with appropriate treatment, but the phobia often lasts lifelong.
See also ABREACTION; ANXIETY NEUROSIS; NEUROSES; PHOTOPHOBIA; PSYCHIATRY and separate entries for diseases mentioned above.

PHOSPHORUS

Virtually all the phosphorus (P) in the body is combined with calcium in the bones and teeth. About 20% is involved in organic and other compounds. It is vital for forming the structure of the bones, and plays a part in electrical conduction in nerves. Compounds containing phosphorus are involved in the transfer of energy when carbohydrates, protein and fat are broken down. The amount of phosphorus in the body is controlled by parathormone, a hormone produced by the parathyroid glands in the neck.

The amount of phosphorus in the blood can be measured and this will indicate the level of phosphorus in the entire body. The normal range is from 0.9 to 1.5 mmol/L (3-4.5 mg/100 mL). High levels may indicate poor kidney function, an underactive parathyroid gland or excess vitamin D in the body. Low levels may be due to an overactive parathyroid gland, lack of vitamin D, rickets, osteomalacia and other diseases of the kidney and bones. Phosphorus levels can drop temporarily after a large meal. The concentration of phosphate in the blood is influenced by parathyroid gland function, intestinal absorption of phosphorus from food, kidney function, bone metabolism and nutrition.
See also BLOOD TESTS; MINERALS; PARATHYROID GLAND

PHOTODERMATITIS

Photodermatitis is a congenital (present since birth) abnormal allergy type reaction of skin to sunlight. There are several different forms including Hutchison prurigo, polymorphic light eruption and solar urticaria. The sufferer develops a red, raised itchy rash on sun exposed skin that may result in permanent skin damage and scarring.

There is no cure, and the only treatment is to use clothing that covers all sun exposed skin and broad brimmed hats.
See also DERMATITIS; LIGHT SENSITIVE SKIN; PHOTOSENSITIVE ECZEMA; SKIN RED

PHOTOPHOBIA

Abnormal pain in the eye caused by a bright light is photophobia. Everyone has eye pain if a very bright spotlight is shone into the eyes, but patients with photophobia have excessive sensitivity to light, sometimes as dim as that from a bedside lamp.

A multiplicity of eye disorders may be responsible for photophobia including iritis (inflammation of the coloured part of the eye), conjunctivitis (bacterial infection of the eye), ulcers on the eye surface, viral infection of the eye, glaucoma (increased pressure inside the eye), a foreign body (eg. speck of dust) on the eye surface and episcleritis (infection of white of the eye).

Inflammation of the membranes around the brain (meninges) can cause photophobia. The most significant example of this is meningitis, and anyone with photophobia and a fever, or who is becoming increasingly unwell, should consult a doctor urgently.

Migraines are often associated with eye symptoms including flashing lights, photophobia, shimmering, seeing zigzag lines and loss of part of the area of vision. Pain usually occurs on only one side of the head, and causes intolerance of exercise, light and noise. Nausea and vomiting are common.

Numerous generalised viral infections, but most commonly measles and influenza, may have photophobia as a relatively minor symptom.

Rare causes include underactive parathyroid glands and the Richner-Hanhart syndrome. *See also* EYE PAIN; LIGHT SENSITIVE SKIN and separate entries for diseases mentioned above.

PHOTOREFRACTIVE LASER KERATECTOMY
See REFRACTIVE SURGERY

PHOTOSENSITIVE ECZEMA
Photosensitive eczema is an uncommon type of eczema that usually occurs in middle-aged and elderly men and affects areas of skin that are exposed to light. It is due to a reaction in the skin to the ultraviolet wavelengths in sunlight. Fluorescent lights also give off ultraviolet radiation and can cause this reaction.

An intensely itchy, red rash covered with scales develops on the face, forearms and hands, but other areas exposed to sunlight may also be affected. In rare cases, the reaction may be so severe that the patient cannot go outside during the day, and they must reverse their lifestyle – sleeping during the day and being active at night – in order to avoid the sun. A skin biopsy may assist in the diagnosis.

Wearing long-sleeved shirts and hats, and applying UV sunscreen creams and very strong steroid creams are the main treatment. Occasionally steroid tablets are also required. Once established, the condition persists for life.
See also ECZEMA; LIGHT SENSITIVE SKIN; PHOTODERMATITIS

PHOTOSENSITIVITY
See LIGHT SENSITIVE SKIN; PHOTODERMATITIS; PHOTOSENSITIVE ECZEMA; PHOTOPHOBIA

PHTHIRUS PUBIS
See CRABS

PHTHISIS
See TUBERCULOSIS

PHYLOQUINONE
See VITAMIN K

PHYSIOTHERAPY
Physiotherapists have completed a specific university degree in their area of skill and knowledge. They care for people with physical disabilities and for those with pain and loss of function caused by physical disorders. Such disabilities and disorders can arise from a variety of causes, including injury, disease, congenital abnormalities, the ageing and degenerative processes.

People at any stage of their life span may present with movement disorders and functional loss. For example, physiotherapists may need to promote motor development in some children or treat their problems of incoordination. In teenagers and adults, the problems may be related to sports injuries, pain and disability from neck and back injuries, arthritis, breathing problems associated with lung disorders, or movement disabilities arising from disorders of the nervous system, such as multiple sclerosis, stroke and spinal injury.

Physiotherapists use physical methods of treatment, which include therapeutic exercise and movement retraining, manipulative therapy and electrophysical agents. Patient education and self-help procedures are an integral part of all management programs. Physiotherapists are also involved in the

important areas of health promotion, injury prevention programs and clinical research.
See also MANIPULATION; OCCUPATIONAL THERAPY; SHORT-WAVE DIATHERMY; ULTRASOUND

PHYTOMENADIONE
See VITAMIN K

PICKWICKIAN SYNDROME
The Pickwickian syndrome is named after the extraordinarily obese Dickens character, and is a complication of being seriously obese that usually occurs in women. Patients have significant shortness of breath, gross obesity, tiredness, blue skin (cyanosis), shallow breathing, cor pulmonale, high blood pressure (hypertension) and heart failure. Pneumonia and other serious infections are common.

Blood tests show abnormal levels of acidity, oxygen, carbon dioxide and red blood cells, and respiratory function tests and a chest x-ray show abnormal results.

The only treatment is significant weight loss while medications are used to control heart failure and hypertension. The prognosis is poor unless the patient succeeds in losing a large amount of weight.
See also COR PULMONALE; CYANOSIS; HYPERTENSION; OBESITY

PID
See PELVIC INFLAMMATORY DISEASE

PIE SYNDROME
See LOEFFLER SYNDROME

PIGMENTED VILLONODULAR SYNOVITIS
Pigmented villonodular synovitis is a specific type of synovitis of the knee, in which the smooth synovial membrane that lines the inside of the joint becomes covered with dark-coloured (i.e. pigmented) microscopic protuberances and lumps. It may be caused by injury to the knee, or may be associated with rheumatoid arthritis.

The patient develops a painful, swollen, red knee that has limited movement. The condition is diagnosed at arthroscopy (looking into the knee joint through a small tube) by a biopsy of the synovial membrane.

Pain is controlled by anti-inflammatory drugs and the swelling is eased by removing excess fluid from the joint through a needle. These measures are only temporary, and most patients will needle to have the knee joint replaced. The knee joint may fuse solid and immovably if left untreated, but there are good results from knee replacement surgery.
See also ARTHROSCOPY; KNEE; KNEE SWOLLEN; RHEUMATOID ARTHRITIS; SYNOVITIS

PIGMENTATION OF MOUTH
See MOUTH PIGMENTATION

PIGMENTED SKIN
See SKIN PIGMENTATION EXCESS

PIGMENT MISSING
See ALBINISM; SKIN DEPIGMENTATION

PILES
Haemorrhoids (also known as piles) are caused by dilation, damage to, bleeding from and blood clot formation in veins around the anus. Internal and external versions exist, depending on whether veins inside or outside the anus are damaged.

A vein circles around the anus close to the skin surface. When a motion is passed, the anal canal dilates, but if this dilation is excessive, these fine veins can be stretched, then rupture and form piles. They may be intermittent, painless swellings, or they can be excruciatingly tender and painful, and bleed profusely. Excessive bleeding from the pile may cause anaemia. Once formed, a weak area will always be present, and even though one pile may settle, the same one may flare up again and again. There is an inherited predisposition to develop piles.

Constipation is by far the most common cause of a pile. Passing a large hard faecal motion overstretches the anal canal to cause bleeding from the surrounding vein.

Straining to lift a heavy weight while squatting is another common cause, as excessive pressure builds up inside the anal veins. Advanced pregnancy has a similar effect.

Obesity may also place excessive pressure on the veins around the anus.

Portal hypertension is an increase in the blood pressure in the veins of the abdomen that take nutrition from the intestine to the liver. Many different liver diseases may be

DIAGRAMATIC REPRESENTATION OF ANAL CANAL AND THE FORMATION OF A PILE

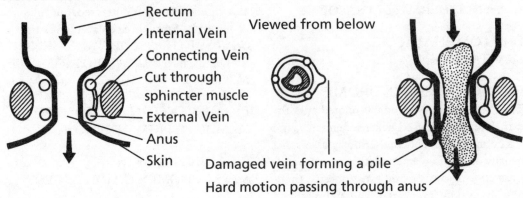

Viewed in vertical section
- Rectum
- Internal Vein
- Connecting Vein
- Cut through sphincter muscle
- External Vein
- Anus
- Skin

Viewed from below

Damaged vein forming a pile
Hard motion passing through anus

responsible, and piles are a common consequence.

Proctoscopy (passing an examination tube through the anus into the rectum) can be performed to examine the piles in greater detail, and to see internal piles.

Keeping the bowels regular and soft prevents piles. Initially, ice packs and simple soothing creams can be used in treatment, but if relief is not obtained, steroid and antiseptic creams or soothing suppositories are prescribed. If there is a clot of blood in the haemorrhoid, it is cut open to allow the clot to escape. If it persists, further treatment may involve clipping a rubber band around the base of the pile, injecting or electrically coagulating the pile, or an operation to cut away part of the anal canal. The operation is normally successful in permanently removing the problem.

See also ANAL BLEEDING; ANAL FISSURE; ANUS

PILL, CONTRACEPTIVE
See CONTRACEPTIVE PILL

PILOCARPINE
See MIOTICS; PUPIL SMALL

PILONIDAL SINUS

A pilonidal sinus is the infection of a hair follicle on or between the buttocks, and they are more common in hairy men who sit all day at work (eg. truck drivers).

Hair is found all over the body, except on the palms and soles, and every hair follicle is supplied with a gland that secretes thick,

viscous oil. If the hair follicle becomes clogged with oil, it may become infected. Waxing the hairs will aggravate the situation by damaging the hair follicles. A sinus can also be formed by a loose hair after a haircut falling down between the buttocks and slowly burrowing its way into the skin. It is a painful infection that rapidly develops into an abscess.

Antibiotic tablets and surgical drainage of the abscess are required. Long term antibiotics, may be necessary in some patients to prevent recurrences, and a severe abscesses may require significant surgery to remove a large area of surrounding tissue.

See also ABSCESS; HAIR

PIMPLES
See ACNE

PINEAL GLAND

The pineal gland is about the size of a grain of rice and sits at the front of the brain between the two hemispheres, immediately behind the point midway between the inside ends of your eyebrows. Its function was completely unknown until about 1970, and even today is not fully understood.

Sometimes known as the third eye, it is far more developed in primitive animals such as frogs and some lizards. In humans it is able to sense the difference between light and dark by nerve connections to the part of the brain (optic chiasma) where images from the eyes are first processed.

In simple terms the pineal gland is the clock of the body, and by releasing the hormone

melatonin it is able to regulate body functions that change with time. This includes the slowing of the body's metabolic (biochemistry) activity at night, the cyclical nature of a woman's menstrual periods, and the time at which puberty should commence, and possibly when menopause should occur.
See also CEREBRUM; PITUITARY GLAND

PINEALOMA

A pinealoma is a rare benign or cancerous tumour of the pineal gland. Patients develop a headache, difficulty in looking upward, personality changes, nausea and tiredness. An increase in the pressure of cerebrospinal fluid that surrounds the brain due to the tumour may cause epileptic fits. The growth is diagnosed by CT and MRI scans, and treatment involves surgical removal or irradiation of the tumour. The prognosis is good if the tumour is benign, but poor if cancerous.
See also PINEAL GLAND

PINEAL TUMOUR
See PINEALOMA

PINGUECULUM

A pingueculum is a growth on the eye surface that develops very slowly over many years, and is caused by recurrent mild sunburn to the cornea (eye surface) which irritates the tissue that overgrows.

It appears as a pale yellow fleshy overgrowth of the white part of the eye (cornea) that occurs on the side of the eye closest to the nose. It may become irritated, red and itchy and grow into a pterygium with further irritation.

Simple drops ease any redness and irritation, while a cure requires simple surgery. It can be prevented by wearing good quality (polarised) sunglasses.
See also EYE; EYE RED; PTERYGIUM

PINK DISEASE
See MERCURY POISONING

PINK EYES
See ALBINISM

PINNA

Pinna is the medical term used to describe the outer ear flap, including all parts of the ear that protrude from the head behind, above and below the ear canal. The tragus is the firm nub of skin-covered cartilage that protrudes in front of the ear canal.
See also EAR; TRAGUS

PINS AND NEEDLES SENSATION IN SKIN

A prickling pins and needles sensation (paraesthesia) is something experienced by everyone at some time, often after knocking the 'funny bone' (ulnar nerve) in the elbow.

Paraesthesia may be caused by pressure on a nerve anywhere in the body, from arthritis, a muscle or ligament strain, bruising, a tumour or cancer, abscess, polyp, swollen artery (aneurysm) or external pressure from tight clothing or prolonged sitting. It may progress to numbness and total loss of all sensation in the area supplied by the nerve.

Fear and other extreme emotions may cause generalised paraesthesia. Over-breathing (hyperventilation) often causes paraesthesia localised to the hands and around the mouth.

Transient ischaemic attacks are a temporary blocking of a small artery in the brain by a blood clot, piece of plaque from a cholesterol deposit in an artery, or spasm of an artery, which results in that part of the brain failing to function for a short time. A wide variety of symptoms may be experienced, depending upon which parts of the brain are affected.

Pernicious anaemia is caused by an inability of the stomach to absorb vitamin B12 (cyanocobalamin) from food. This vitamin is essential for the formation of haemoglobin, which transports oxygen in red blood cells. Symptoms include tiredness and pallor, a red smooth and sore tongue, indigestion, lack of appetite, paraesthesia and occasionally jaundice (yellow skin).

The carpal tunnel syndrome is caused by inflammation in the narrow tunnel on the palm side of the wrist through which many of the hand-flexing tendons, nerves and blood vessels that supply the hand must run. If any of these tissues are damaged or strained, they will swell to place pressure on the adjacent nerves, and therefore paraesthesia, numbness and pain. Common causes of the carpal tunnel syndrome are pregnancy, weight gain, an underactive thyroid gland, diabetes, rheumatoid arthritis and systemic lupus erythematosus.

Raynaud's phenomenon is a spasm of arteries when tissue is exposed to cold. It causes affected tissue to tingle, then go white, blue and red, before becoming swollen and painful. The hands and feet are usually affected, and it is far more common in women than men.

Other causes of paraesthesia include peripheral neuropathy, the restless legs syndrome (constant desire to move the legs while trying to rest), some psychiatric conditions (eg. psychoses) may cause paraesthesia in a glove and stocking distribution on the arms and legs, an extra rib in the neck can put pressure on the nerves running from the neck to the arm (Nafziger syndrome), poorly controlled diabetes, and a blood clot (thrombosis) in a major artery supplying a limb will markedly reduce the blood supply to that limb and cause symptoms that vary from pins and needles sensation, to numbness, severe pain and possibly gangrene.

Uncommon causes include uraemia (kidney failure), multiple sclerosis, Ciguatera poisoning (from eating large tropical reef fish that contain the ciguatera toxin), beriberi (severe lack of vitamin B1), Conn syndrome, acromegaly and leprosy.
See also NERVE; SKIN and separate entries for diseases mentioned above.

PINWORM
The gut may easily become infested by the 1cm. long pinworm (threadworm) *Enterobius vermicularis*. The pinworm lives in the large intestine, but migrates to around the anus to lay eggs, from where they may be transferred to the fingers during wiping or scratching, and then re-enter the original patient's mouth or pass to another person, where the cycle starts again. The worm dies after depositing the eggs and passes out with the faeces, where they may sometimes be seen. The eggs can survive for up to three weeks outside the body. Children are the most commonly affected group, and they spread the infestation to others by poor personal hygiene. It is very easy for all the members of one family to be affected. Most patients have no symptoms but some will experience anal itching at night, mild diarrhoea and minor abdominal pains. In rare cases the worms may migrate to the vagina and urethra of women and girls.

It is diagnosed by microscopically examining the faeces for the presence of worms or eggs.

Treatment should involve all members of the patient's immediate family. A number of anthelmintic medications can be used to kill the worms. Good hygiene involves careful hand-washing after going to the toilet and not scratching the anus. If patients do not re-infect themselves the worms will die out in six to seven weeks.
See also ANTHELMINTICS; WORMS

PIPERAZINE OESTRONE
See SEX HORMONES

PIROXICAM
See NONSTEROIDAL ANTI-INFLAMMATORY DRUGS

PISIFORM BONE
See WRIST

PITTED NAILS
See NAIL PITTING

PITUITARY FAILURE
See HYPOPITUITARISM

PITUITARY GLAND
The pituitary gland is situated at the base of the brain about eye level in the centre of the skull and is connected directly to a part of the brain known as the hypothalamus. The pituitary not only has its own activity but also regulates the activity of other glands, acting as the conductor of the endocrine (gland) orchestra. It is no bigger than the size of a walnut. In total the pituitary gland produces nine different hormones.

The human growth hormone is one of these hormones and possibly the most important. If too little of this hormone is produced during childhood, the child's growth will be stunted and it will be a dwarf. If too much is produced, the child will grow to an abnormal size.

Other hormones stimulate the thyroid gland and the adrenal glands.

Antidiuretic hormone acts on the kidneys and regulates the balance of water and salts in body fluids.

The follicle stimulating hormone tells the female ovaries and the male testicles when to produce oestrogen and testosterone, and the hormone prolactin stimulates the manufacture of milk in nursing mothers and controls the menstrual cycle.

At the end of pregnancy when the time comes for the child to be born, the pituitary stimulates the muscles in the uterus to contract and start labour.

Adrenocortico trophic hormone (ACTH) controls the activity of the outer part of the adrenal glands, which sit on top of each kidney.

The direct connection of the pituitary gland, and through it the other endocrine glands, to the brain and thus the nervous system is the reason why our mental and emotional states can influence our hormone levels and vice versa. If the pituitary gland malfunctions, the effects can obviously be wide-ranging because of the gland's importance in so many parts of the body.
See also ADRENAL GLAND; DIABETES INSIPIDUS; GLANDS; GROWTH REDUCED; HORMONES; HYPERPROLACTINAEMIA; HYPOPITUITARISM; SYNDROME OF INAPPROPRIATE ANTIDIURETIC HORMONE SECRETION; THYROID GLAND

PITYRIASIS

Pityriasis is a term used in skin diseases to indicate the presence of a fine scale resembling natural bran flakes.
See also PITYRIASIS ALBA; PITYRIASIS LICHENOIDES; PITYRIASIS ROSEA; PITYRIASIS VERSICOLOR

PITYRIASIS ALBA

Pityriasis alba is a common skin condition of children and teenagers. Several round or oval, scaly, pale pink patches occur on the skin, and there is usually no irritation or itchiness. The patches are more apparent on tanned skin, as the condition prevents tanning. It settles spontaneously without treatment after a few months, although moisturising creams may remove scale, and mild steroid creams reduce redness.
See also PITYRIASIS VERSICOLOR; SKIN DEPIGMENTED

PITYRIASIS LICHENOIDES

Pityriasis lichenoides, or guttae parapsoriasis, is an uncommon skin rash that is more common in males and usually affects teenagers and young adults. A mild form is known as pityriasis lichenoides chronica, while the more severe rapidly developing form is pityriasis lichenoides et varioliformis acuta (PLEVA). The cause is unknown, but it may be a reaction to a bacteria or virus in the skin, although it is not contagious.

Small, firm, raised, non-irritating, red to brown spots develop on sun protected areas such as the trunk, thighs and inside the upper arms. A fine scale covers the spots which are two to 15mm. across, and slowly flatten out over several weeks to leave a brown mark, which disappears after several months. PLEVA may be accompanied by a headache and fever. A biopsy of a spot confirms the diagnosis.

Treatment is not usually necessary, but in severe cases steroid creams, sun exposure and antibiotics (erythromycin or tetracycline) may help. Severe cases of PLEVA are treated with methotrexate or oral steroids. The condition always settles without treatment eventually, but this may take many months or years.
See also PARAPSORIASIS EN PLAQUE; PITYRIASIS; PSORIASIS

PITYRIASIS ROSEA

Pityriasis rosea is a skin disease of no known cause that occurs in older children and adults up to middle age. Dark red, scaling, slightly raised, oval-shaped patches appear on the chest, upper arms, thighs, neck, abdomen and back. Usually a large patch ('herald patch') precedes other smaller patches by a week or two. There is only very slight itching or irritation, and minimal discomfort, and the forearms, lower legs and face are not usually affected.

Antihistamine tablets may be taken at night for itching, and steroid creams can be applied, but the condition settles without treatment in six to eight weeks.
See also PITYRIASIS; SKIN ITCH

PITYRIASIS VERSICOLOR

Pityriasis versicolor (tinea versicolor) is a relatively common fungal skin disease that occurs in the tropics. It is more common in young adults than the elderly and children, and the chest, upper arms, neck, upper back and armpits are the most commonly affected areas.

Pink/brown patches develop on the skin, which may have a very faint scale upon them. After a few weeks, the skin underlying the rash has less pigment, so the rash appears as white patches which are due to sunlight being unable to tan the skin underlying the fungus. Areas not exposed to sunlight (eg. armpits, breasts) may retain the pink/brown patch appearance. This effect does not occur on Aborigines, Chinese, Negroes and other dark-skinned races. There are no other symptoms other than an occasional very mild itch.

The diagnosis can be proved by examining skin scrapings under a microscope, and then it is treated by regular use of antifungal lotions, rinses or creams. An antifungal tablet (ketaconazole) is used in persistent and wide-spread cases. The white patches will remain for some time after the fungus has been destroyed, until the sun tans the area again.

Episodes of infection are quite easy to clear, but they often recur in the next summer.
See also FUNGI; SKIN DEPIGMENTED

PKU
See PHENYLKETONURIA

PLACENTA
The placenta is a special outgrowth of the foetus that is firmly attached to the inside of the mother's uterus (womb). It has blood vessels that penetrate into the wall of the uterus and interact with the mother's arteries and veins to enable the foetus to draw oxygen and food from the mother's system and send waste products to the mother for removal. As the foetus grows, it floats in a fluid-filled sac like a water-filled balloon (the amniotic sac), and the foetus drinks the amniotic fluid and excretes into it through the kidneys. The amniotic sac and its fluid act as a very effective shock absorber so that the foetus can survive unharmed quite serious injuries to its mother (eg. a car crash). One side of the sac is especially modified into the placenta, while the rest is a fine but tough transparent membrane.

The foetus is connected to the placenta by the umbilical cord, which contains three inter-twined blood vessels (an artery and two veins) which convey nourishment from the mother to the foetus and waste products the other way. At birth, this is between 15 and 120cm. long and runs from the navel to the placenta, where the artery and veins it contains fan out to interact with the mother's circulatory system. The mother's and baby's blood streams remain separate and do not mingle. Doctors will check the cord after birth, and if only one vein is present instead of two, it is

probable that the baby will have some hidden birth defect.

The placenta is a flat, circular organ con-sisting of a spongy network of blood vessels. It acts as a combined lung, liver, kidney and digestive tract for the developing foetus. Oxygen, nutrients, waste products and other substances (eg. alcohol and some drugs) can pass freely through the placenta from the bloodstream of the mother to the blood-stream of the foetus. Infections (particularly viruses such as German measles) may also pass to the foetus through the placenta.

Several minutes after the birth, the placenta (the afterbirth) is expelled by further contrac-tions of the uterus, assisted by gentle traction on the cord by the doctor or midwife. Occa-sionally the placenta may not be expelled, which leads to intervention by a doctor.
See also CHORIONIC VILLUS SAMPLING; PLACENTA ACCRETA; PLACENTA PRAEVIA; PLACENTAL RETENTION; PREGNANCY; LABOUR; UTERINE MOLE

PLACENTA ACCRETA
Placenta accreta is a rare condition that occurs when the placenta attaches itself too firmly to the wall of the uterus and cannot be removed after birth. Heavy bleeding often occurs after the delivery of the baby, and the usual treatment is removal of the uterus (a hysterectomy) as an emergency procedure.
See also PLACENTA

PLACENTA CANCER
See CHORIOCARCINOMA OF THE UTERUS

PLACENTA PRAEVIA
Normally the placenta attaches to the front, back or side of the uterus, but if it attaches to the lower part, it may cover the opening of the uterus, through the cervix to the outside. This is placenta praevia. It is more common in women who have had several pregnancies, and it occurs in one in every 150 pregnancies.

In the later stages of pregnancy, the cervix starts to dilate to allow the head of the baby to drop, prior to labour starting. If the placenta is over the opening, it will be damaged by the dilation of the cervix and the pressure from the baby's head, and heavy bleeding may occur suddenly.

Placenta praevia may be suspected by the presence of a baby that is unusually high in the womb, and the position of the placenta can be seen accurately on an ultrasound scan. When diagnosed, the mother will be watched carefully, often in hospital, and about a month before the due date, a Caesarean section will be performed to remove both baby and placenta safely.

A bleeding placenta praevia can be a medical emergency, as quite torrential bleeding can occur which may threaten the lives of both mother and baby. The only treatment is an urgent Caesarean section.
See also PLACENTA

PLACENTAL RETENTION
After the delivery of the baby, the placenta normally separates away from the wall of the uterus and is expelled by the contractions of the uterus within a few minutes. The process may be assisted by a doctor using injections to improve the uterine contractions and manoeuvres to assist the separation of the placenta. If it fails to separate from the uterus and remains retained within the uterus, it is necessary to perform a simple procedure to remove the retained placenta. Without this procedure, the mother would continue to bleed, and this could threaten her life.

Under a general anaesthetic, the doctor slides his hand into the uterus, and uses his fingers to separate the placenta from the uterus and lift it away from the wall of the uterus, so that it can be drawn to the outside of the body through the vagina.
See also LABOUR; PLACENTA; PREGNANCY

PLAGUE
See BLACK DEATH; BUBONIC PLAGUE

PLANE WARTS
Plane or flat warts are mildly disfiguring growths on the face caused by a human papilloma virus (HPV) infection of the skin. Small (1 to 5mm.), round or oval, smooth, flat topped, slightly elevated, skin coloured or grey/cream raised areas of skin occur. They tend to follow the line of a scratch or graze and may become red, swollen and itchy. Tretinoin cream or other irritants can be applied to warts, but they disappear spontaneously in one to six months, although they do resolve faster with treatment.
See also PLANTAR WART; WART

PLANTAR FASCIA
See FOOT; PLANTAR FASCIITIS

PLANTAR FASCIITIS
Plantar fasciitis is an inflammation of the fibrous band of tissue that forms the support for the sole of the foot. It may start after excessive exercise (eg. an unusually long run or walk), after a sudden sharp injury (eg. landing heavily after jumping), or for no apparent reason.

The victim has a constantly aching sole, that becomes sharply painful with every step when walking.

The main treatment is complete rest, sometimes requiring several weeks on crutches. Other treatments include anti-inflammatory drugs, painkillers, physiotherapy and occasionally steroid injections into the foot. As a last resort, the foot may be put in plaster for a few weeks to ensure total rest.
See also FOOT; FOOT PAIN

PLANTAR WART
A plantar wart is known as a verruca in England. It is a type of wart that grows on the soles of the feet, and they tend to grow inwards rather than out. The cause is a very slow developing virus (human papillomavirus) that attacks softened skin. A hard, slightly raised, scar like growth forms on the sole of the foot, and becomes painful with walking. Verrucae are like icebergs, with only a small part showing on the surface and a much larger area affected deeper in the sole. They may become so large, widespread and painful that walking is very difficult.

There are numerous treatments available including diathermy (burning), acid ointments, freezing, cutting out, or injecting under the wart. After surgery, a far larger hole than expected is usually left in the sole that may take some weeks to heal. Unfortunately, recurrence is common despite the best treatment.
See also WART

PLANT POISONING
See POISONOUS PLANTS

PLAQUE
See DENTAL PLAQUE; PERIODONTICS

PLASMA
See BLOOD

PLASMODIUM
See MALARIA

PLASTER

The traditional plaster cast is made from plaster of paris, although lighter, stronger, more durable and expensive fibreglass casts are available.

If a plaster cast is applied, it is important to look after it properly while it does its job.

Under no circumstances should the patient: –
• get the plaster wet (it will become soft)
• walk on or put pressure on the plaster (it will crack or weaken)
• poke sticks under the plaster to ease any skin irritation (this will roll up the padding and cause pressure sores).

It is important to return to see the doctor the day after the plaster is applied to ensure that it is correctly fitted, and not too tight or loose.

If fingers or toes become swollen, bright red, blue, stiff or cannot be moved, contact a doctor immediately, as the plaster may have become too tight as the injured tissue swells. Do not wait until morning if this happens at night.

Elevate the affected limb. If the plaster is on a leg, keep it up on a pillow in bed, and on a footstool whenever sitting. If on an arm, keep the arm in a sling so that the hand is as high as possible. Elevation prevents swelling, stiffness and pain.

Some plasters are made of fibreglass. These have to be treated in the same way as normal plaster, although they are much lighter and are not badly affected by water.

Wiggle the fingers and toes regularly while the plaster is applied to maintain circulation and mobility.

If the plaster becomes soft, loose or cracked, return to the doctor as soon as possible to have the plaster reinforced or replaced.

A walking heel is sometimes attached to a plaster. These are designed to be used over short distances around the house only, and not on long expeditions to the shopping centre or into the garden. Crutches must still be used in these situations.
See also FRACTURE

PLASTIC SURGERY

Plastic surgeons are usually thought of as performing face lifts, tucking in sagging tummies, and cosmetically improving the appearance of vain movie stars. In fact, the major part of their work is the time-consuming surgery required to correct the gross disfigurement caused by serious burns and the intricate correction of the serious deformities that some children have at birth. They also play a major role in helping patients recover from disfiguring surgery that may be performed for cancer of the face, breast or other areas. Breast reconstruction after removal of a breast for cancer can help a woman recover both physically and psychologically. These surgeons join with dental and ENT surgeons to correct gross facial abnormalities (facio-maxillary surgery), correct harelips, cleft palates and abnormal noses and ears that may lead to social embarrassment. Birth marks and skin blemishes can also be reduced or removed.

Unfortunately, despite their skills and techniques of operating through very small holes and in areas where scars will not easily show, even plastic surgeons leave some scar behind when they operate. It is important for a patient to be aware of these limitations before undergoing any form of plastic surgery.
See also BAT EARS; BREAST AUGMENTATION; BREAST REDUCTION; FACE LIFT

PLATELETS

Blood clotting occurs when the blood turns from liquid to solid. A blood clot can be fatal if it forms in an artery and blocks it, but clotting is also an important part of human survival. If the blood did not clot, every time a person sustained even a minor cut they would bleed to death – and indeed someone suffering from the disease haemophilia has precisely that problem. The clotting in blood is primarily due to platelets. When an injury occurs and the blood comes into contact with something that is different from the lining of the blood vessels it is accustomed to, a chain of chemical reactions involving numerous different factors within the blood causes the platelets to stick together to form a clot and seal the wound.

Platelets are manufactured in the spleen and bone marrow, and live for a relatively short period compared with other blood cells – about ten days.

The term thrombocytopenia is used to indicate a lack of platelets.
See also BERNARD-SOULIER SYNDROME; BLEEDING, EXCESSIVE; BLOOD CLOTTING TEST; FULL BLOOD COUNT; STICKY PLATELET SYNDROME; THROMBOCYTOPENIA

PLEURA
See LUNG

PLEURAL EFFUSION
A pleural effusion is the accumulation of a large amount of serous fluid (the liquid part of blood without cells) between the pleura (a smooth, slippery, shiny membrane that lines the inside of the chest cavity) and the lung. The possible causes include heart failure, cirrhosis, nephrotic syndrome, lung embolus, cancer, tuberculosis and bacterial or viral infections of the lung. The fluid restricts lung movement and may cause significant shortness of breath and a dry cough. Pleurisy may be a complication.

The excess fluid can be seen on a chest x-ray, and then removed by passing a needle through the chest wall and into the fluid collection and drawing it off into a syringe. The fluid is then examined to determine which disease is responsible for the effusion, and further treatment will depend upon the cause of the effusion.
See also LUNG; PLEURISY and separate entries for diseases mentioned above.

PLEURISY
Pleurisy is an infection, while pleuritis is an inflammation, of the pleura, which is the smooth, slippery, shiny membrane that lines the inside of the chest cavity and allows the lung to move freely within the chest as it contracts and expands with every breath. The pleura is covered with a very thin layer of fluid that acts as a lubricant.

Pleurisy may be caused by a viral infection of the chest, a fractured rib that damages the pleura, or bacterial infections associated with acute bronchitis, pneumonia and tuberculosis.

Patients experience severe pain that can often be localised to one point on the chest or back and is worse with breathing, sneezing, coughing, laughing or any movement of the chest. A pleural effusion may be a complication. A chest x-ray may show an area of fluid accumulation or inflammation on the lung.

Viral and inflammatory pleurisy will settle with rest and minor pain killers or anti-inflammatory drugs (eg. indomethacin), while bacterial pleurisy associated with pneumonia requires antibiotics and stronger painkillers. The prognosis is generally good, but depends on the underlying cause.
See also BRONCHITIS, ACUTE; LUNG; PLEURAL EFFUSION; PNEUMONIA

PLEURITIS
See PLEURISY

PLEURODYNIA
See BORNHOLM DISEASE

PLEVA
See PITYRIASIS LICHENOIDES

PLUMBISM
See LEAD POISONING

PLUMMER-VINSON SYNDROME
The Plummer-Vinson syndrome is known as the Paterson-Brown-Kelly syndrome in the United States. It is an inflammatory condition of gullet (oesophagus) of no known cause, but it tends to occur in middle aged women. Patients develop difficulty and pain on swallowing, fibrous web formation across the oesophagus, an enlarged spleen, iron deficiency anaemia, inflamed mouth, their finger nails curve upwards, and in some patients the lips are thin and the mouth is beak shaped. It often leads to cancer of the oesophagus.

An x-ray barium swallow and oesophagoscopy (passing a flexible tube down the oesophagus) are both abnormal, and blood tests show anaemia.

Treatment involves swallowing oesophageal dilators under sedation, iron supplements, and a good diet, but the problem often recurs after treatment.
See also OESOPHAGEAL CANCER; OESOPHAGUS

PMR
See POLYMYALGIA RHEUMATICA

PMT
See PREMENSTRUAL TENSION

PNEUMATURIA
See URINE GASSY

PNEUMOCONIOSIS

Pneumoconiosis is the replacement of normal lung tissue by fibrous scar tissue and is a form of chronic obstructive airways disease caused by long-term inhalation of fine coal dust particles in underground coal miners. It is aggravated by cigarette smoking.

There are no symptoms until the condition is quite advanced, when patients become short of breath, and a chest x-ray shows numerous small pellets of coal dust concentrated in the lungs. The upper part of the lung is more affected than the lower. There is no treatment available, and lung infections such as pneumonia are common.

See also ASBESTOSIS; LUNG; PNEUMONIA; SILICOSIS

PNEUMONIA

Pneumonia is a bacterial, or rarely fungal, infection of the lung alveoli (tiny air bubbles that form the major part of the lung and enable the oxygen to cross into the bloodstream), which fill with pus. Usually only one part of the lungs, often at the bottom of the chest, is affected, but it may spread to other parts of the lung. If both lungs are affected, it is sometimes referred to as double pneumonia. Almost invariably the bronchi (main air tubes) are also infected, so the disease should correctly be called bronchopneumonia.

The infection starts when bacteria are inhaled into the lungs, and overcome the body's defence mechanisms, particularly if the patient is tired, run-down, overworked, elderly, bedridden or suffering from other illnesses.

The symptoms of pneumonia may be obvious with fever, productive cough and chest pains, but some infections are more insidious and cause minimal symptoms for some months while the patient feels tired, short of breath and has intermittent sweats.

Chest x-rays are diagnostic, and are repeated at regular intervals to ensure that the infection is resolving. A sample of sputum is taken before treatment is started, and is sent to a laboratory to identify the infecting bacteria.

One or more antibiotics are given by tablet, injection or drip into a vein to treat the infection. Expectorants to open up the airways and loosen the phlegm are also prescribed, along with cough mixtures and painkillers. Regular physiotherapy is very important to drain phlegm and pus out of the chest, while rest and the cessation of smoking are vital. Occasionally oxygen is required for seriously ill patients, and in rare cases, surgery to drain out collections of pus or remove areas of chronically infected lung is required. Some forms of pneumonia can be prevented by a vaccine (Pneumovax).

Inadequately treated pneumonia can cause chronic ill health, or an abscess may form in the lung and lead to permanent lung damage. Once the lung is damaged, the chance of developing a subsequent attack of pneumonia is increased, and smoking will accelerate this process. Pneumonia puts a great strain on the heart, and it may fail in older or debilitated patients.

With correct treatment the majority of patients recover in a couple of weeks, but some may take months, and there is a small mortality rate amongst the elderly and debilitated, even in the best hospitals. Up to half of all patients affected died before the advent of modern antibiotics in the 1940s.

See also BRONCHITIS, ACUTE; DOUBLE PNEUMONIA; EMPHYSEMA; LUNG; LUNG ABSCESS; MELIOIDOSIS; PSITTACOSIS; SPUTUM TESTS

PNEUMOTHORAX

A pneumothorax is the presence of air between the lung and its surrounding pleura. The lung lies in a smooth, slippery sac (the pleura). If the lung develops a puncture, air will leak into the pleural sac around the lung and is unable to escape. More and more air accumulates in the sac, causing pressure on the lung, which eventually collapses. It often occurs for no apparent reason (spontaneous pneumothorax), or may be due to a chest injury, and lung diseases such as asthma, tuberculosis, cancer or cystic fibrosis.

The patient develops worsening shortness of breath and chest pain, and a chest x-ray will show the partly collapsed lung.

A small pneumothorax may be observed and its progress checked by regular x-rays, but if the pneumothorax is large or growing larger, a tube is placed through the chest wall to remove the escaped air, which allows the lung to expand. The outside end of the tube is

LUNG WITH A PNEUMOTHORAX

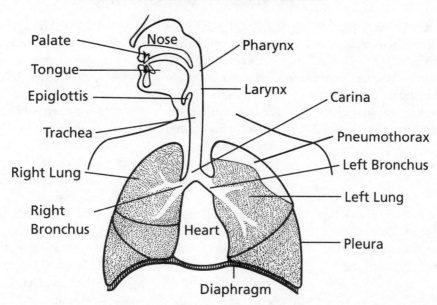

placed under water to stop air re-entering the lungs. Patients who have repeated attacks of spontaneous pneumothorax, may require surgery to repair the damaged area of lung. All patients must stop smoking.

A tension pneumothorax may be fatal in a few minutes, as every breath pumps large amounts of air out of the lungs and into the pleural cavity. The pressure in the pleural cavity builds up rapidly and causes the lungs to collapse. A large needle or tube must be immediately pushed through the chest wall into the pleural cavity to save the patient's life.

Complete recovery in a few hours or a day or two is normal with correct treatment.
See also BREATH, SHORT OF; LUNG; VALSALVA MANOEUVRE

PODIATRY

Podiatrists (previously called chiropodists) are responsible for the care of feet. They have been trained in their area of expertise by attending a course at a technical college or university, from where they receive the appropriate diploma or degree. Podiatrists can trim difficult nails, deal with some types of ingrown toenails, pare down corns and bunions, treat warts on the feet, and advise patients on footwear and general foot hygiene. A large part of their work involves the care of feet in the elderly.
See also FOOT

POISONING

A person can be poisoned by taking an overdose of drugs, either accidentally or deliberately, or by swallowing or inhaling some substance that upsets the functioning of their body. It is necessary to act quickly to minimise the effect of the poison. In children, a common cause of poisoning is raiding the family medicine chest, or the kitchen cabinet with its supply of cleaning fluids, solvents and so on.

If someone is poisoned, ring an ambulance, hospital or Poisons Information Service and ask them what to do in the case of the specific substance involved.

In general terms: –
• if the victim is unconscious, place them on their side in the coma position and check that the airway is clear
• monitor their breathing and pulse constantly. If breathing stops, give expired air respiration, and if the pulse becomes weak or stops, give cardiopulmonary resuscitation

Do not induce vomiting if: –
• the poisonous substance is unknown
• a corrosive substance such as battery acid, oven cleaner, toilet cleaner, a strong disinfectant or any acid or alkaline substance has been swallowed
• a petroleum-based product (eg. kerosene, petrol, diesel oil, turpentine) is swallowed. If these substances are vomited they will burn the throat a second time, or damage the lungs by inhalation
• the patient is drowsy and may become unconscious. Such patients risk choking if they vomit.

FIRST AID TREATMENT OF POISONING

CHEMICAL/DRUG	EFFECT OF POISON	FIRST AID TREATMENT
Alkalis (household bleaches)	Burning, vomiting, shock, difficult breathing.	Dilute with milk, allow vomiting, give vinegar.
Antidepressants (Tryptanol, Sinequan, Tofranil etc.)	Coma, muscle spasm, convulsions, death.	Give charcoal or induce vomiting, assist breathing.
Aspirin (Aspro, Disprin etc.)	Rapid breathing, brain disturbance, coma, kidney failure.	Give charcoal or induce vomiting.
Barbiturates	Drowsiness, confusion, coma, breathing difficulty.	Give charcoal or induce vomiting, black coffee, assist breathing.
Codeine (in pain killers, coughmixtures, antidiarrhoeals)	Constipation, reduced breathing, stupor, coma, heart attack.	Give charcoal or induce, assist breathing.
Digoxin (Lanoxin)	Vomiting, irregular pulse, heart failure.	Dilute with milk or water then give charcoal or induce vomiting.
Insecticides	Vomiting, diarrhoea, difficult breathing, convulsions.	Dilute with large amount of milk, give charcoal or induce vomiting, assist breathing.
Lysol and creosote	Burning of throat, vomiting, shock, breathing difficulty.	Dilute with large amount of milk. Do NOT induce vomiting.
Mushrooms	Varies depending on type.	Dilute with water, give charcoal or induce vomiting, assist breathing.
Narcotics (morphine, heroin)	Headache, nausea, excitement, weak pulse, shock, coma.	Give charcoal or induce vomiting if narcotic swallowed, assist breathing.
Paracetamol (Panadol, Dymadon, Panamax etc.)	Vomiting, low blood pressure, liver damage, death [>40 tabs]	Give charcoal or induce vomiting.
Petroleum products (petrol, kerosene, etc.)	Liver damage, lung damage.	Do NOT induce vomiting, dilute with milk.
Tranquillisers (phenothiazines)	Drowsiness, low blood pressure, rapid pulse, convulsions, coma.	Give charcoal or induce vomiting.

Someone who has swallowed a corrosive substance can be given small sips of water or milk, but otherwise simply wipe the substance away from the mouth and face, make the victim as comfortable as possible and get urgent medical advice.

If the substance is a medicine or similar substance, it may help to induce vomiting, depending on the age of the victim and how long ago the substance was ingested – if possible ask a doctor first.

To induce vomiting, give syrup of ipecacuanha according to instructions on the bottle, or stimulate the back of the victim's throat with a finger. Do NOT give salt or soapy water to drink. Keep a sample of the vomit in a clean jar to send to the hospital.

If the poison has been inhaled, move the victim away from the fumes or turn the fumes (eg. gas) off at the source. DO NOT BECOME A VICTIM YOURSELF. Once the victim is in the fresh air, loosen any tight clothing and check breathing and pulse constantly – if either ceases or becomes weak, administer artificial respiration.

Sometimes poisons are absorbed through

the skin (eg. pesticides, weed killer). In this case, remove the victim's clothes and get them to wash or shower thoroughly. If they become dizzy or sick, or complain of blurred vision or show any other sign of distress, get medical help immediately. Wash the contaminated clothes separately from other clothes.
See also ARSENIC; BOTULISM; CARBON MONOXIDE POISONING; CIGUATERA POISONING; CONVULSION; CYANIDE; FIRST AID; FOOD POISONING; INSECTICIDE POISONING; IRON POISONING; LEAD POISONING; MERCURY POISONING; OVERDOSE; POISONOUS PLANTS; RESUSCITATION; STRYCHNINE; UNCONSCIOUS

POISONOUS PLANTS
The plants found in many gardens are poisonous if they are eaten.

One of the prettiest and deadliest trees is the oleander. These are widely grown as an ornamental tree, but are extremely poisonous. A leaf, a flower or a fruit is sufficient to kill a child, and the sap can be equally dangerous. The early symptoms of poisoning are vomiting, diarrhoea, palpitations and dilated pupils, which can lead to coma and death.

The castor oil plant grows wild in many scrub areas along Australia's eastern seaboard. It has seeds the size of a golf ball, which children often play with, but which if eaten can cause severe diarrhoea, cramps, vomiting and sometimes even death. Most councils consider it a noxious weed.

Dieffenbachia (sometimes called dumb cane) is a decorative shrub often found in indoor pots. Chewing or biting the large fleshy leaves of this attractive plant produces copious salivation and severe burning and irritation of the mouth, which may last for many days.

Angel's trumpet is a small tree that may be three metres or more high and has white trumpet-shaped flowers. Eating any part of the plant, especially the flowers, can caused severe gastrointestinal symptoms, delirium and death.

Other common plants that may cause severe illness, if not death, include the broad-leafed rainforest plant cunjevoi, the stunted pineapple zamia palm; the blue-black plumb-like fruit of the African wintersweet, the prickly Duranta or golden dewdrop, the attractive fruit of the pot or rock plant called coral bush

or psychic nut, and the seeds of the Moreton Bay chestnut tree.

First aid in case of poisoning varies with the plant. Induction of vomiting is the normal immediate step if a child is found eating a potentially poisonous plant, but unless in a remote area, more details should be obtained from a doctor or hospital.
See also POISONING; RESUSCITATION; UNCONSCIOUS

POLIO
Polio (the full name is poliomyelitis) is a generalised viral infection which passes from one person to another through droplets in the breath or by touch, and attacks muscles. It has been eradicated in developed countries, but still occurs in some poorer countries.

The symptoms are severe muscle spasm followed by paralysis and muscle contractures. If the muscles of breathing or the heart are affected, the patient may die or remain on a respirator for life. It is diagnosed by specific blood tests.

No treatment is available other than general physical support and muscle relaxants, but an oral (Sabin) or injected vaccine is available that is extremely effective, safe, and has no side effects.

The overall prognosis is poor. Many patients recover, but most of them have significant disabilities.
See also POST-POLIO SYNDROME; VACCINATION OF CHILDREN; VIRUS

POLLE SYNDROME
Polle syndrome is more commonly known as Munchausen syndrome by proxy, and is an obscure form of child abuse due to a psychiatric disturbance in a parent.

The child has an apparently caring parent who consults excessively with doctors and hospitals about their child and demands extensive investigation of the child who is emotionally stressed. The parent deliberately falsifies symptoms and/or test results. As a result the child is usually over investigated by innumerable tests before diagnosis made, and may be injured by unnecessary procedures.

Psychotherapy and family counselling have poor results for the family and the child may need to be taken into protective custody.
See also CHILD ABUSE; MUNCHAUSEN SYNDROME

POLY-

'Poly-' is a prefix used in medicine to indicate many, too much or an excess amount. It is derived from the Greek words 'polus' mean-ing 'much' and 'polloi' meaning 'many'. For example, 'polyuria' means 'too much urine'.

POLYARTERITIS NODOSA

Polyarteritis nodosa (PAN or periarteritis nodosa) is an inflammation of small to medium-sized arteries. The damaged artery may become weakened and balloon out to several times its normal diameter, it may scar and shrink down, or the blood passing through the inflamed section of artery may clot and completely block the artery (a throm-bosis). The arteries affected may be anywhere in the body, but the gut, liver, heart, testes, kidney, and muscles are most commonly involved. The cause is unknown, but it is more common in drug abusers and in patients with hepatitis B. Rarely it may be a side effect of medication. Men are three times more likely to develop the disease than women, and it is most common in young adults.

The symptoms are very varied, depending on which arteries and organs are involved. The patient is usually feverish, and has pain in the area involved. Specific complaints may include muscle pain, palpitations, arthritis, skin ulcers, spots in the vision, abdominal pain, nausea, vomiting, diarrhoea and high blood pressure.

There are no diagnostic blood tests, and the diagnosis must be confirmed by a biopsy (sample) taken from an involved artery. Taking steroids (eg. prednisone) in high doses for a long period of time is the main treat-ment, and immunosuppressive drugs may also be used.

The prognosis varies markedly from one patient to another, depending upon the areas and arteries involved. Some patients do recover, but most slowly deteriorate to die within a few months or years.
See also ARTERY

POLYCYSTIC KIDNEY

A polycystic kidney has multiple fluid-filled cysts in it that are formed when tiny urine-collecting tubes within the kidney become blocked or do not connect up to the main urine-collecting system of the kidney.

It is a familial (inherited) condition that usually has no symptoms, and is found during investigations of a family that is known to have the disease, during an operation or other routine investigation. In other cases it may be a cause of high blood pressure, blood in the urine, or constant pain in one loin. The liver and pancreas may be involved and develop cysts in a small number of patients. It is diag-nosed by ultrasound scan, CT scan or special x-rays of the kidney.

Most patients require no treatment, but in serious cases where the kidneys do fail, dialy-sis (artificial kidney machine) or a kidney transplant is possible. The prognosis is gener-ally good. Although damaged, the kidney tissue remaining between the cysts is able to function adequately.
See also KIDNEY

POLYCYSTIC OVARIAN SYNDROME

In the polycystic ovarian, or Stein-Leventhal, syndrome, multiple small cysts form in one or both ovaries. The cause is unknown, but the cysts interfere with the production of hor-mones by the ovaries and the patient develops facial hairs, gains weight, stops her menstrual periods, is infertile and loses breast firmness.

Abnormal levels of hormones can be meas-ured in the bloodstream, but the syndrome is often discovered on an ultrasound scan while investigating infertility.

Treatment involves surgically cutting away part of the affected ovarian tissue, and using hormones to stimulate the ovary to restart its correct function. Specific medications (eg. spironolactone or progestogens) are used for excessive hair growth. Some women find the discomfort of the condition and the side effects of medication unacceptable and decide to have a total hysterectomy.
See also INFERTILITY; OVARIAN CYST; OVARY

POLYCYTHAEMIA RUBRA VERA

Polycythaemia rubra vera (the 'rubra' is sometimes omitted) is an excessive produc-tion of red blood cells that is most common in middle-aged to elderly, overweight men, but may occur in both sexes. It is rare under forty years of age.

Red blood cells are made in the spleen and bone marrow, primarily in the breastbone (sternum), pelvis and thighbone (femur). If

the marrow becomes overactive, excessive numbers of cells may be produced, and the patient develops a headache, dizziness, tiredness, blurred vision, generalised itching, noises in the ears, high blood pressure and an enlarged spleen. Blood clots may occur in vital organs (eg. brain to cause a stroke), and some patients develop a form of chronic leukaemia.

The diagnosis can be confirmed by finding excess red blood cells in a blood test, and further tests on bone marrow determine the severity of the disease.

The disease can be controlled, but not cured, by draining large quantities of blood out of a vein initially, and smaller amounts on a regular basis long term. Medications to reduce the activity of the bone marrow may also be used. The average survival time after diagnosis is twelve years.
See also BONE; LEUKAEMIA; RED BLOOD CELL; SPLEEN

POLYDIPSIA
See THIRST

POLYHYDRAMNIOS
In the womb, the baby is surrounded by and floats in a sac filled with amniotic fluid. This fluid acts to protect the foetus from bumps and jarring, recirculates waste, and acts as a fluid for the baby to drink. If an excessive amount of fluid is present, the condition is called polyhydramnios.

Normally there is about a litre (1000mL) of amniotic fluid at birth. A volume greater than 1500mL is considered to be diagnostic of polyhydramnios, but it may not become apparent until 2500mL or more is present.

Polyhydramnios occurs in about one in every 100 pregnancies, and it may be a sign that the foetus has a significant abnormality that prevents it from drinking or causes the excess production of urine. Other causes include a twin pregnancy, and diabetes or heart disease in the mother. In over half the cases no specific cause for the excess fluid can ever be found.

The condition is diagnosed by an ultrasound scan, and if proved, further investigations to determine the cause of the condition must follow. The treatment will depend upon the result of these tests, but often none is necessary.

There is an increased risk to the mother of amniotic fluid embolism, a potentially fatal complication that occurs when some of the fluid enters the mother's blood stream, but most pregnancies proceed relatively normally, although there is an increased risk of foetal abnormality.
See also OLIGOHYDRAMNIOS; PLACENTA; PREGNANCY

POLYMYALGIA RHEUMATICA
Polymyalgia rheumatica (PMR) is one of a number of post-viral syndromes that may trigger an autoimmune reaction in which the body rejects its own tissue inappropriately. In some people, for no known reason, a viral infection such as influenza is followed by a chronic random inflammation of many muscles anywhere in the body. Women are affected five times more often than men.

Patients experience severe aches and pains in a group of muscles for a few days before the pain subsides, then another muscle group is attacked. The muscles are also weak and the patient is irritable, tired, unable to concentrate, and depressed. Other symptoms may include nausea, headache, arthritis and loss of appetite. Temporal arteritis may be a very unwelcome complication.

No investigations can confirm the diagnosis but blood tests indicate a generalised inflammation of the body.

Heat, painkillers and anti-inflammatory medications are used in treatment, but if these are not successful, steroids can be prescribed.

The symptoms may last for weeks or months, then recur after a long absence, but eventually recovery occurs in most patients.
See also ARM PAIN; AUTOIMMUNE DISEASES; MUSCLE PAIN; TEMPORAL ARTERITIS

POLYMYOSITIS
See DERMATOMYOSITIS

POLYPOSIS COLI
Polyposis coli or familial polyposis is the presence of multiple polyps in the colon (large intestine). The condition is often familial (runs in families), but may arise for no apparent reason. Symptoms include vague abdominal pain, irregular bowel habits, bleeding from the bowel, anaemia and a significantly increased

risk of bowel cancer. It is diagnosed by colonoscopy or barium enema x-ray.

Treatment consists of removing as many polyps as possible through a colonoscope, and anti-inflammatory agents such as celecoxib may be used to prevent polyp formation. In severe cases, sections of, or the whole large intestine may need to be surgically removed.
See also COLON; COLONOSCOPY; PEUTZ-JEGHER SYNDROME

POLYURIA
See URINATION FREQUENT

POMPE SYNDROME
See GLYCOGEN STORAGE DISEASES

POMPHOLYX
Pompholyx (dyshidrosis or dyshidrotic dermatitis) is a skin condition that affects the sides of the palms of the hands and soles of the feet, and is more common in young adults. It may be triggered by excess sweating, emotional stress, fungal infections of the skin, and touching irritating substances or plants.

Small blisters that are deep in the skin and moderately itchy form at the edges of the palms and soles. With irritation, the blisters burst, the skin peels and leaves small brown scale-covered ulcers.

Avoiding all soaps, irritants, detergents and chemicals is the only treatment necessary for mild cases, while steroid or coal tar creams are used for moderate attacks, and severe attacks may require steroid tablets. With appropriate treatment the rash settles slowly but frequently recurs.
See also DERMATITIS

'POPPING' EARS
See EUSTACHIAN TUBE; VALSALVA MANOEUVRE

POROKERATOSIS
See DISSEMINATED SUPERFICIAL ACTINIC POROKERATOSIS

PORPHYRIA
See ACUTE HEPATIC PORPHYRIA; ERYTHROPOIETIC PROTOPORPHYRIA; PORPHYRIA CUTANEA TARDA

PORPHYRIA CUTANEA TARDA
Porphyria cutanea tarda (latent hepatic por-phyria) is the most common form of porphyria, which are a group of liver diseases. It is usually inherited, but may be triggered by some poisons, and occurs in all races but is more common amongst the Bantu tribes of Africa.

Patients have skin that is very sensitive to sunlight, with skin thickening and pigmentation occurring in sun exposed areas such as the face and forearms. The urine has a strange characteristic in that it turns a dark purple colour, then brown, if left standing. Liver damage may occur, and may progress to liver failure or liver cancer (hepatoma). It occurs in varying degrees of severity from so mild that it is undetected to a rapidly fatal form.

It is diagnosed by special blood tests, and treatment involves careful genetic counselling of families and the use of a complex drug regime. It may be controlled, but not cured, and is rarely fatal.
See also ACUTE HEPATIC PORPHYRIA; HEPATOMA; URINE COLOUR ABNORMAL

PORTAL SYSTEM
Totally separate to the main network of veins in the lower part of the trunk is the portal system. Unlike other veins, which drain blood to the heart, the veins in the portal system drain blood from the digestive tract (stomach and intestines) into the portal vein. This drains into the liver where it branches down into tiny capillaries, and nutrients taken from the gut are processed. After passing through the liver this blood then links up again with the main venous system and moves on to the heart.
See also PORTAL HYPERTENSION; VEIN

PORTAL HYPERTENSION
Portal hypertension is an increase in the blood pressure in the portal veins of the abdomen that take nutrition from the intestine to the liver. It may be caused by many different liver diseases including cirrhosis, a blood clot (thrombosis) in the portal vein or spleen, and schistosomiasis.

There are no symptoms, other than piles, until severe bleeding occurs from massively dilated veins around the lower oesophagus (gullet) and in the stomach. Torrential internal bleeding into the stomach may be fatal.

Angiography (x-rays of arteries) of portal

veins in the abdomen are diagnostic, and liver biopsy and blood tests may be abnormal if liver disease is responsible for the problem. Gastroscopy shows enlarged veins in the oesophagus and stomach.

Surgery is necessary to bypass any blockage in the veins or liver, and the spleen may be removed if veins in this organ are thrombosed. The prognosis depends on the cause, but is often poor.
See also CIRRHOSIS; GASTROSCOPY; PORTAL SYSTEM; SCHISTOSOMIASIS

PORTUGUESE MAN-OF-WAR JELLYFISH
See JELLYFISH STING

PORTWINE NAEVUS
A portwine or mature capillary naevus is a congenital, disfiguring skin condition due to overdilated blood vessels. Patients have a flat or slightly raised, pale pink to red or dark purple stain on the skin, usually on the face or upper chest, and on only one side of the body. Plastic surgery is sometimes possible to remove the naevus, depending on its site, otherwise these harmless marks persist life long.
See also NAEVUS

POSITRON EMISSION TOMOGRAPHY
See PET SCAN

POSTERIOR FACET SYNDROME
The posterior facet syndrome may be the cause of persistent lower back pain due to long standing inflammation of the synovial membrane which lines the small joints between the back outer edges on the arch of the vertebrae (posterior facet joints). It may also cause degeneration (osteoarthritis) and instability of these joints in the lower back (lumbar vertebrae).

Patients have pain in the lower back that runs down one or both legs, with the greatest pain occurring with bending back sideways and backwards. X-rays or CT scans of the lower back may show joint degeneration.

Treatments used may include physiotherapy, manipulation, injection of local anaesthetic and steroid into facet joints, and as a last resort surgical fusion of the adjacent joint surfaces. The problem is often persistent, and cure is difficult but control is reasonable.
See also BACK PAIN; VERTEBRA

POSTGASTRECTOMY SYNDROME
See DUMPING SYNDROME

POSTHERPETIC NEURALGIA
See SHINGLES

POSTMENOPAUSAL VAGINITIS
See ATROPHIC VAGINITIS

POST-NASAL DRIP
The inside of the nose and sinuses is lined with a moist (mucus) membrane. If inflamed, the glands in the mucus membrane swell up and secrete extra amounts of mucus that overflows the sinus cavities, and runs down the back of the throat as catarrh or a post-nasal drip.

The causes of mucus membrane inflammation include infections with bacteria (eg. sinusitis) or a virus (eg. the common cold or flu), allergies (eg. hay fever, cigarette smoke), temperature changes (vasomotor rhinitis), hormone changes (more mucus may be produced at certain times in a woman's monthly cycle), anxiety and stress (eg. an exam or interview), eating, drinking alcohol and changes in position (eg. getting out of bed may start a sneezing fit). Secondary bacterial infections may cause sinusitis or pharyngitis, and flying or changing altitude can force phlegm up the Eustachian tubes into the middle ears to cause pain and infection.

Patients have episodes of sneezing, irritated throat, recurrent cough, bad breath, blocked nose, snore more readily and develop nausea (from swallowed mucus). Examination of the nose with a special instrument, and x-rays or CT scans of the sinuses may be useful in showing the congested mucosa.

Antibiotics cure bacterial infection, if present. Antihistamines shrink down the swollen mucus membranes and reduce the production of mucus, mucolytics liquefy the phlegm, decongestants in tablets and nasal sprays clear the airways, and steroid or anti-allergy nasal sprays prevent the nose from reacting excessively. The minority who continue to have long term symptoms may be helped by surgery to reduce the amount of mucus membrane in the nose, and removing some curled up bones inside the nose (turbinates) that are covered with mucus membrane. The condition usually settles spontaneously, but sometimes becomes persistent.

See also CATARRH; HAY FEVER; NOSE; PHARYNGITIS; SINUSITIS; VASOMOTOR RHINITIS

POSTNATAL DEPRESSION

Postnatal or postpartum depression is a spontaneous form of depression that occurs in some women just before, or soon after childbirth, and is a response to the effect on the brain of sudden changes in hormone levels.

The woman experiences constant unhappiness for which there is no reason. They are unable to sleep, lose appetite and weight, and feel there is no purpose in living. They may feel unnecessarily guilty, have a very poor opinion of themselves, feel life is hopeless, find it difficult to think or concentrate, worry excessively about their infant or neglect the child. Rarely it may lead to attempted or actual suicide. It is diagnosed after careful psychiatric assessment.

Medications are prescribed to control the production of depressing chemicals in the brain (eg. fluvoxamine, moclobemide, nefazodone, paroxetine, venlafaxine) while hospitalised or given intensive home support. Shock therapy (electroconvulsive therapy – ECT) may be used as a last resort. Virtually all cases settle with support and medication in a few weeks.

See also DEPRESSION; PREGNANCY

POSTPARTUM DEPRESSION
See POSTNATAL DEPRESSION

POST-POLIO SYNDROME

The post-polio syndrome occurs in some survivors of polio, thirty to forty years after recovery from the infection, and may be due to the overuse of muscles previously damaged by polio. They develop unaccustomed tiredness, joint and muscle pain and muscle weakness. Because of muscle weakness, more stress is put on joints, and arthritis of major joints and in the back may also occur. In a small number of severely affected patients, difficulty in breathing may lead to sleep apnoea and the necessity for breathing aids. There is no cure, and the condition persists long term, but anti-inflammatory medications and steroids may help.

See also MUSCLE WEAKNESS; POLIO

POST-TRAUMATIC STRESS DISORDER

PTSD is not new, as a century ago the post-traumatic stress disorder was known as shell shock. It occurs after experiencing a situation that causes extreme stress and a feeling of horror and helplessness (eg. armed hold-up, serious accident, war violence, being assaulted or raped, observing atrocities etc.). Most symptoms start between two weeks and three months of the triggering catastrophe, but may start as late as six months.

There are no specific diagnostic tests, but patients must have at least one symptom from each of the following categories to be diagnosed: –

General: –
• Symptom duration more than one month, with significant distress or inability to function normally in society.
• Re-experiencing phenomena.
• Experience intrusive recollections, nightmares, flashbacks as if the event was recurring, psychological distress on exposure to cues that may trigger memories, or physiological effects (eg. rapid pulse, rapid breathing) on exposure to cues.

Avoidance behaviour: –
• Avoiding thoughts, feelings or conversations about the incident
• Avoiding places, people or activities connected with the incident
• Selective amnesia about the traumatic event
• Reduced interest in everyday activities or detachment from others
• Unable to look forward to future events with pleasure
• Abnormal personality compared to before the incident

Excessively aroused: –
• Insomnia, irritability, anger, poor concentration, increased vigilance or increased startle response to frights.

Treatment involves psychological counselling and debriefing immediately after the event, and a trained counsellor should follow up the victim for at least six months. Normal work and activities should be resumed as soon as possible. Referral to a psychiatrist is necessary if the patient does not appear to recover within six months, or deteriorates sooner, when medication may be necessary.

PTSD may become chronic and lead to recurrent minor illnesses, poor physical

health, and in extreme cases, suicide, but in most cases it usually settles within three to six months.
See also DEJA VU; NEUROSIS; STRESS

POSTURAL HYPOTENSION

Postural or positional hypotension is a brief drop in blood pressure (hypotension) caused by the altered relative positions of the brain and the heart when the patient moves from lying to sitting or standing. The heart must pump harder, and the arteries must contract more to maintain blood flow by means of the blood pressure to a brain that is now thirty centimetres above the heart, rather than one that is at the same level as the heart. It takes a few seconds for this adjustment to be made, particularly in patients who have hardening of the arteries (arteriosclerosis). Sometimes, medications to lower blood pressure and remove fluid may aggravate the condition.

The patient experiences light-headedness and dizziness, and sometimes blackouts or faints, when rising quickly from lying or sitting to a standing position. Fainting and falling may cause serious injuries.

The condition is diagnosed by measuring the blood pressure when the patient is lying, and again immediately after standing. The doctor should advise elderly patients to be slow in changing position, and review medications that may be responsible. The prognosis depends on the cause, but the problem may be difficult to control.
See also ARTERIOSCLEROSIS; FAINT; HYPOTENSION

POST-VIRAL SYNDROMES
See CHRONIC FATIGUE SYNDROME; POLYMYALGIA RHEUMATICA

'POT'
See MARIJUANA

POTASSIUM

Potassium is a mineral that is vital for muscle contraction and conduction of nerve impulses. It is also involved in cell wall function and the formation and function of enzymes. Potassium (the chemical symbol is K) is balanced against sodium in the body – as one rises the other falls. Changes in the level of potassium can affect heart muscle function and the rate at which impulses are conducted in nerves.

Potassium is lost from the body through the kidneys and colon; but it is readily absorbed from the gut. Bananas and apricots are both good dietary sources of potassium.

The amount of potassium in the blood can be easily measured. The normal range is between 3.5 and 5.2 mmol/L. High levels may be found in kidney failure, Addison's disease, after massive trauma, severe infections and with very vigorous exercise. Medications such as digoxin, ACE inhibitors, NSAIDs, triamterene, amiloride and spironolactone may also be responsible.

Low levels of potassium may be due to vomiting, diarrhoea, ulcerative colitis, malabsorption syndromes, excessive laxatives, diabetes mellitus, Conn syndrome, Cushing syndrome, dietary deficiency and as a side effect of medications such as diuretics, steroids, laxatives, insulin and sympathomimetics.
See also BLOOD TESTS; MINERALS and separate entries for diseases and medications mentioned above.

POTASSIUM IODIDE
See EXPECTORANTS

POTT'S FRACTURE

A Pott's fracture is a fracture above the ankle, when the bottom ends of the two bones in the lower leg (the tibia and fibula) are broken off by a twisting force to the lower leg, often after catching the foot in a hole while running.

POTT'S FRACTURE

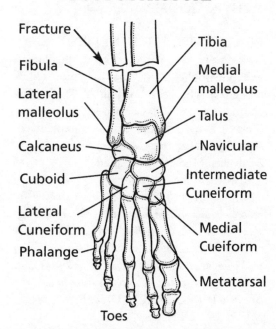

Fracture · Tibia · Fibula · Medial malleolus · Lateral malleolus · Talus · Calcaneus · Navicular · Cuboid · Intermediate Cuneiform · Lateral Cuneiform · Medial Cueiform · Phalange · Metatarsal · Toes

There is pain, swelling, tenderness and loss of function of the lower leg and ankle. The fracture is diagnosed by an x-ray.

Manipulation of bone ends under anaesthetic is undertaken to achieve good alignment, then the ankle is encased in plaster. Sometimes open operation and fixation of the bones by plates and screws is required. Possible complications include failure to heal, poorly aligned bone ends and infection after open operation.

These fractures require up to three months rest to heal adequately.
See also ANKLE; FRACTURE; TIBIA

POVIDONE-IODINE
See ANTISEPTICS

PRADER-WILLI SYNDROME
The Prader-Willi syndrome is a rare congenital (present since birth) brain condition caused by a chromosomal defect that affects only boys. The syndrome is characterised by a small infant who develops into an obese child due to compulsive overeating from an abnormality in the part of the brain that controls hunger. The child is usually short, has underdeveloped genitals, is mentally retarded, muscles are weak with very poor tone, and the belly is very flabby. There is no effective treatment, and they tend to develop diabetes later in life.
See also MENTAL RETARDATION; OBESITY

PRAVASTATIN
See HYPOLIPIDAEMICS

PRAYER OF MAIMONEDES
Written by the Jewish doctor, theologian and philosopher Moses ben Maimon (Maimonedes) who was born in 1135 in Fez, Morocco, and died in Cairo in 1204, his prayer (below) is used in the ethical statements of several medical organisations, including the Australian Medical Association.

"Inspire in me a love for my Art and for thy creatures. Let no thirst for profit or seeking for renown or admiration take away from my calling. Keep within me strength of body and soul, ever ready, with cheerfulness, to help and succour rich and poor, good and bad, enemy as well as friend. In the sufferer let me see only the human being".
See also HIPPOCRATIC OATH; MEDICAL ETHICS

PRAZOSIN
See ALPHA BLOCKERS

PRECOCIOUS PUBERTY
See PUBERTY EARLY

PREDNISOLONE
See STEROIDS

PREDNISONE
See STEROIDS

PRE-ECLAMPSIA AND ECLAMPSIA
Eclampsia is a rare but very serious disease that occurs only in pregnancy. In developed countries it is very uncommon, because most women undertake regular antenatal visits and checks. Pre-eclampsia is a condition that precedes eclampsia, and this is detected in about 10% of all pregnant women. The correct treatment of pre-eclampsia prevents eclampsia.

The exact cause of pre-eclampsia is unknown, but it is thought to be due to the production of abnormal quantities of hormones by the placenta. It is more common in first pregnancies, twins and diabetes. Pre-eclampsia normally develops in the last three months of pregnancy, but may not develop until labour commences, when it may progress rapidly to eclampsia if not detected.

The early detection of pre-eclampsia is essential for the good health of both mother and baby. Doctors diagnose the condition by noting high blood pressure, swollen ankles, urine abnormalities (excess protein) and excessive weight gain (fluid retention). Not until the condition is well established does the patient develop the symptoms of headache, nausea, vomiting, abdominal pain and disturbances of vision.

If no treatment is given, the mother may develop eclampsia. This causes convulsions, coma, strokes, heart attacks, death of the baby and possibly death of the mother.

Pre-eclampsia is treated by strict rest (which can be very effective), drugs to lower blood pressure and remove excess fluid, sedatives, and in severe cases, early delivery of the baby. The correct treatment of pre-eclampsia prevents eclampsia, and the prognosis is very good if detected early and treated correctly.
See also PREGNANCY

PREFRONTAL LOBOTOMY
See NEUROSURGERY

PREGNANCY

The first sign that a woman may be pregnant is that she fails to have a menstrual period when one is normally due. At about the same time as the period is missed, the woman may feel unwell, unduly tired, and her breasts may become swollen and uncomfortable.

A pregnant woman should not smoke because smoking adversely affects the baby's growth, and smaller babies have more problems in the early months of life. The chemicals inhaled from cigarette smoke are absorbed into the bloodstream and pass through the placenta into the baby's bloodstream, so that when the mother has a smoke, so does the baby.

Alcohol should be avoided especially during the first three months of pregnancy when the vital organs of the foetus are developing. Later in pregnancy it is advisable to have no more than one drink every few days with a meal.

Early in the pregnancy the breasts start to prepare for the task of feeding the baby and one of the first things the woman notices is enlarged tender breasts and a tingling in the nipples. With a first pregnancy, the skin around the nipple (the areola) will darken, and the small lubricating glands may become more prominent to create small bumps. This darkening may also occur with the oral contraceptive pill.

Hormonal changes cause the woman to urinate more frequently. This settles down after about three months, but later in pregnancy the size of the uterus puts pressure on the bladder, and frequent urination again occurs.

Some women develop dark patches on the forehead and cheeks called chloasma, which are caused by hormonal changes affecting the pigment cells in the skin. This can also be a side effect of the contraceptive pill. The navel and a line down the centre of the woman's belly may also darken. These pigment changes fade somewhat after the pregnancy but will always remain darker than before.

After the pregnancy has been diagnosed, the woman should see her doctor at about ten weeks of pregnancy for the first antenatal check-up and referral to an obstetrician. At this check-up she is given a thorough examination (including an internal one), and blood and urine tests will be ordered to exclude any medical problems and to give the doctor a baseline for later comparison.

Routine antenatal checks will then be performed by the general practitioner or obstetrician at monthly intervals until about thirty four weeks pregnant, when the frequency will increase to fortnightly or weekly. Blood

PREGNANCY AT FULL TERM

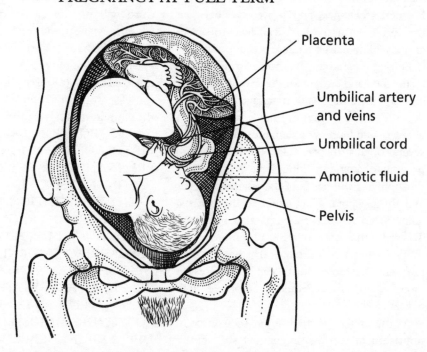

Placenta

Umbilical artery and veins

Umbilical cord

Amniotic fluid

Pelvis

pressure and weight measurement and a quick physical check are normally performed. A small ultrasound instrument may be used to listen for the baby's heart from quite an early stage. Further blood tests will be performed once or twice during this period, and a simple test will be carried out on a urine sample at every visit. An ultrasound scan is usually performed to check on the size and development of the foetus.

Most women are advised to take tablets containing iron and folic acid throughout pregnancy and breast feeding, in order to prevent both the mild anaemia that often accompanies pregnancy, and nerve developmental abnormalities in the foetus.

As the skin of the belly stretches to accommodate the growing baby, and in other areas where fat may be found in the skin (such as breasts and buttocks), stretch marks in the form of reddish/purple streaks may develop. These will fade to a white/silver colour after the baby is born, but unfortunately they will not normally disappear completely.

By about the fourth or fifth month, the thickening waistline will turn into a bulge, and by the sixth month, the swollen belly is unmistakable. The increased bulk will change the woman's sense of balance, and this can cause muscles to become fatigued unless she can make a conscious effort to maintain a good upright posture. Care of the back is vitally important in later pregnancy, as the ligaments become slightly softer and slacker with the hormonal changes, and movement between the vertebrae in the back can lead to severe and disabling pain if a nerve is pinched.

During pregnancy, the mother must supply all the food and oxygen for the developing baby and eliminate its waste materials. Because of these demands, the mother's metabolism changes, and increasing demands are made on several organs. In particular, the heart has to pump harder, and the lungs have more work to do supplying the needs of the enlarged uterus and the placenta. Circulation to the breasts, kidneys, skin and even gums also increases. Towards the end of the pregnancy, the mother's heart is working 40% harder than normal. The lungs must keep the increased blood circulation adequately supplied with oxygen.

As the mother is the baby's sole source of nourishment during pregnancy, she should pay attention to her diet. A balanced and varied diet containing plenty of fresh fruit and vegetables, as well as dairy products (calcium is required for the bones of both mother and baby), meat and cereal foods, is appropriate.

During the last three months of the pregnancy, antenatal classes are very beneficial. Women are taught exercises to strengthen the back and abdominal muscles, breathing exercises to help with the various stages of labour, and strategies to cope with them. Women who attend these classes generally do far better in labour than those who do not.

In the month or so before delivery, it will be difficult for the mother to get comfortable in any position, sleeplessness will be common, and the pressure of the baby's head will make passing urine a far too regular event. Aches and pains will develop in unusual areas as muscles that are not normally used are called into play to support the extra weight, normally between 7 and 12kg. (baby + fluid + placenta + enlarged uterus + enlarged breasts), that the mother is carrying around.

Attending lectures run by the Australian Breastfeeding Association (formerly the Nursing Mothers Association) to learn about breast feeding, how to prepare for it and how to avoid problems, is useful in the last few weeks of pregnancy and for a time after the baby is born.

Visiting the hospital or birthing centre that you have booked into for the confinement can be helpful, so that the facilities and the labour ward will not appear cold and impersonal when they are used.

After the baby is born, visits to a physiotherapist to get the tone back into your abdominal muscles and to strengthen the stretched muscles around the uterus and pelvis will help the woman regain her former figure.

See also ABORTION; BABIES; BREECH BIRTH; CONSTIPATION IN PREGNANCY; DIABETES IN PREGNANCY; ECTOPIC PREGNANCY; FACE PRESENTATION; FOETUS; HEARTBURN IN PREGNANCY; LABOUR; LABOUR, PROLONGED; MISCARRIAGE; MORNING SICKNESS; OLIGOHYDRAMNIOS; PLACENTA; PLACENTA ACCRETA; PLACENTA PRAEVIA; PLACENTAL RETENTION; POLYHYDRAMNIOS; POSTNATAL DEPRESSION; PRE-ECLAMPSIA AND

ECLAMPSIA; PREGNANCY
BACKACHE; PREGNANCY BLEEDING;
PREGNANCY DATES; PREGNANCY
TESTS; PREMATURE BABY;
PREMATURE LABOUR; PROLAPSED
CORD; SEX IN PREGNANCY;
STRETCH MARKS etc.

PREGNANCY BACKACHE

A pregnant woman's pelvis has to expand at the time of birth to allow the baby through. To facilitate this expansion, the ligaments that normally hold the joints of the pelvis (and other parts of the body) together become slightly softer and more elastic which makes them more susceptible to strain. The joints of the spine are particularly at risk because the expanding uterus shifts the centre of balance and changes posture. Standing for any length of time is likely to impose unusual stresses on the back, and this strains the supporting ligaments and results in backache.

Slight movements of the vertebrae, one on the other, can cause nerves to be pinched and result in pain such as sciatica. This nerve pinching is further aggravated by the retention of fluid in the whole body, which causes the nerves to be slightly swollen and therefore more easily pinched.

The best way to reduce the likelihood of backache is not to gain weight excessively and to avoid all heavy lifting. At antenatal classes, physiotherapists show the correct way to lift, and teach exercises to help relieve the backache.
See also PREGNANCY

PREGNANCY BLEEDING

Extensive studies have not shown any increase in infant abnormalities after bleeding in early pregnancy. The bleeding may be due to a slight separation of the placenta from the wall of the womb as it grows, and it almost certainly does not involve the baby directly. About 30% of all pregnant women suffer from some degree of bleeding during pregnancy, and some have quite severe bleeds without losing the baby.

Bleeding in early pregnancy may also be a sign of an impending miscarriage. Unfortunately nothing except rest can help the mother in this situation. Doctors cannot usually prevent miscarriages once bleeding has started.

Other causes of bleeding in pregnancy include an ectopic pregnancy, vaginal ulcers or erosions, or hormonal imbalances.
See also ECTOPIC PREGNANCY;
MISCARRIAGE; PREGNANCY

PREGNANCY COMPLICATIONS

See BREECH BIRTH; ECTOPIC
PREGNANCY; MISCARRIAGE;
OLIGOHYDRAMNIOS; PLACENTA
ACCRETA; PLACENTA PRAEVIA;
PLACENTAL RETENTION;
POLYHYDRAMNIOS; POSTNATAL
DEPRESSION; PRE-ECLAMPSIA AND
ECLAMPSIA; PROLAPSED CORD;
RUBELLA; SMOKING; SYPHILIS;
TOXOPLASMOSIS

PREGNANCY DATES

The date a pregnant woman is due to deliver can be calculated in the following way. Add seven days to the day the woman's last period started, and nine months to the month of her last period. For example, if the last period started on 5 January 2003, she will be due to deliver on 12 October 2003.

A pregnancy lasts forty weeks (280 days) from the beginning of the woman's last period, but only thirty-eight weeks from conception, because she ovulates two weeks after her period starts. It is not unusual for the pregnancy to be one or two weeks shorter or longer than this.
See also PREGNANCY

PREGNANCY TESTS

Pregnancy tests are based on the detection of a hormone called human chorionic gonadotrophin (HCG), which is produced in the first few months of pregnancy by the placenta and can be detected in blood or urine as early as twelve days after conception (i.e. before a period is even missed). At this early stage, a false negative result is possible, and the tests are more reliable if carried out a couple of days after the missed period. A negative test may mean that the pregnancy is not far enough advanced to be detected, rather than that the woman is not pregnant, while a positive test is almost invariably correct.

The pregnancy test consists of mixing a few drops of the woman's urine with specific chemicals. If HCG is present, a chemical reaction will take place. In a test carried out in a test tube, the mix of urine and chemicals will form a characteristic deposit; but more often the urine is added to one side of a small flat plastic container and as the urine moves across this it interacts with chemicals that will change colour if the test is positive. To ensure a reliable result, the test is generally carried out 2-7 days after the first missed period (ie. 16-21 days after conception).

A pregnancy test can be carried out at home with a kit purchased from the chemist, but more reliable tests are performed by doctors using a sample of blood.

Although pregnancy actually occurs about two weeks after a woman had her last period, for convenience doctors always date a pregnancy from the first day of that last menstrual period.

See also PREGNANCY; PREGNANCY DATES

PREMATURE BABY

The survival of a baby born before thirty-seven weeks of pregnancy depends more upon the weight of the baby than the actual number of weeks of pregnancy. Babies under 500g have only a 40% chance of survival, under 1000g a 65% chance, and over 1500g a nearly 100% chance of survival. These figures are for the best hospitals in developed countries, but babies born prematurely in remote areas will have a far lower survival rate.

The problems that very premature babies face include liver failure and jaundice, inability to maintain body temperature, immature lungs, inability to maintain the correct balance of chemicals in the blood, patent ductus arteriosus, increased risk of infection due to an immature defence system, bleeding excessively, and eye problems including blindness. The smaller the baby, the greater the problems, and the more intensive the care required from specialised units in major hospitals.

The activity and processes of immature babies must be monitored carefully. Tubes and leads to and from the infant may appear to overwhelm it but are necessary to monitor the heart and breathing, supply oxygen, assist breathing in some cases, feed the baby, drain away urine, keep the temperature at the correct level, and maintain the correct chemical balance in the blood.

Even some of the treatments to help these babies can have serious complications. Many require oxygen to allow them to breathe, but too much oxygen can cause a condition called retrolental fibroplasia that damages the retina (light sensitive area) at the back of the eye to cause permanent blindness. Premature babies also progress better if their intensive care nursery is darkened and quiet for the twelve night hours.

A baby born prematurely will be a little later in reaching the milestones of infancy and should have routine immunisations in the first six months slightly delayed. The delay is roughly the number of weeks of prematurity before 37 weeks (ie. a baby born at 31 weeks is 6 weeks before 37 weeks, and can expect its milestones and vaccinations to be delayed by 6 weeks). The delay is halved by the time the child reaches six months of age, and disappears completely by one year of age.

See also PREGNANCY; PREMATURE LABOUR; RESPIRATORY DISTRESS SYNDROME, INFANT and separate entries for diseases mentioned above.

PREMATURE EJACULATION

See EJACULATION, PREMATURE

PREMATURE LABOUR

A pregnancy normally lasts 40 weeks from the last menstrual period. A birth that occurs at less than 37 weeks is considered to be premature. Before 20 weeks, any birth that occurs is considered to be a miscarriage. It is rare for an infant born before 24 weeks to survive, and only after 30 weeks are the chances of survival considered to be good.

Premature labour occurs in about 7% of pregnancies. There is no apparent cause in over half the cases, but in others, high blood pressure, diabetes, two or more babies, more than six previous pregnancies, foetal abnormalities, polyhydramnios and abnormalities of the uterus may be responsible.

Premature labour may now be prevented or controlled in some cases by injections of drugs such as ritodrine (Yutopar) or salbutamol (Ventolin, which is also used to treat asthma). Strict bed rest is the only other form of treatment.

See also LABOUR; PREGNANCY and separate entries for diseases mentioned above.

PREMENSTRUAL DYSPHORIC DISORDER

See PREMENSTRUAL TENSION

PREMENSTRUAL TENSION

Premenstrual tension (PMT or premenstrual syndrome) may vary from a slight discomfort for a couple of hours before the onset of a woman's menstrual period to a severely distressing condition.

During the two weeks leading up to a menstrual period, the body retains fluid. If the balance between the sex hormones oestrogen and progestogen is not quite right, an excessive amount of fluid may be retained in the pelvis, brain, breasts, hands and feet to cause gradually increasing discomfort in the pelvis and breasts, with swelling of the hands and feet, pounding headaches and depression. The worst sufferers will experience abdominal pain, swollen tender breasts, anxiety, irritability and clumsiness, and may be unable to concentrate, work or exercise effectively. The most severe form is known as premenstrual dysphoric disorder when symptoms seriously interfere with a woman's lifestyle, mental and physical functioning, and relationships. Depression, very rarely severe enough to lead to suicide, and a psychosis that has been used in court as a defence for murder, can be extreme complications. The symptoms usually disappear within a few hours when the period starts.

The oral contraceptive pill or similar hormones can be used to regulate the hormonal balance and prevent excess fluid retention, and diuretics (tablets that remove fluid from the body) may be used alone or in combination with the contraceptive pill. Other medications that may be beneficial include antidepressants (eg: citalopram), vitamin B6, mefenamic acid, naproxen, indomethacin and evening primrose oil. Other approaches include a sensible balanced diet, and avoiding coffee, chocolate and rich foods in the two weeks before the period.

The majority of women can be helped adequately by good treatment.
See also CONTRACEPTIVE PILL; DEPRESSION; DIURETICS; PELVIC CONGESTION SYNDROME

PRE-PATELLAR BURSITIS
See HOUSEMAID'S KNEE

PREPUCE
See PENIS

PRESBYOPIA

Presbyopia is a deterioration of close vision that starts in middle age. The cause is stiffening of the lens with age which prevents it focussing light rays from close objects accurately on the retina (light sensitive layer of cells at the back of the eye). Patients experience steadily worsening difficulty in reading small print or seeing close objects in detail. Correct spectacles can be prescribed after suitable vision tests to assist with focusing.
See also LONG-SIGHTED; VISION

PRESCRIPTION NOTATIONS

When writing a prescription, doctors often use abbreviations of Latin or Greek terms for the instructions about what is to be dispensed and the instructions for the use of the medication. These are usually written in lower case (i.e. 'prn' not 'PRN'). Numerous notations are explained as listed below.
See also AC; BD; GUTTAE; MANE; MITTE; NOCTE; PC; PRN; QID; QH; TDS; TID

PRESSURE IMMOBILISATION

Pressure immobilisation is used in the first aid treatment of most venomous bites and stings. The steps involved are: –
• Apply pressure to the bite until a bandage is available.
• Bandage the limb firmly. The purpose of this is to restrict the venom as much as possible to the bitten area, so the bandage should be firm but not so tight that the blood supply is completely cut off. A crepe bandage is ideal, but otherwise improvise with torn strips of clothing, pantyhose or the like. Start at the bitten area and work to the fingers or toes. Then return and cover the limb to the armpit or groin.
• Immobilise the limb with a splint (eg. a small branch of a tree) or by bandaging it to the other limb.

DO use PRESSURE IMMOBILISATION for bites and stings of: –
• snakes
• funnel-web spider
• blue-ringed octopus
• cone shell
• insects (bees, wasps, ants, etc.) if the victim is allergic to them.

Do NOT use pressure immobilisation for bites and stings of: –

- red-back spider
- box jellyfish
- stonefish
- ticks

See also BEE STING: BLUE RINGED OCTOPUS STING; SNAKE BITE

PRESSURE ULCER
See BED SORE

PRIAPISM
Priapism is an abnormality in which the penis remains persistently, inappropriately and painfully erect for a long period of time. There are multiple possible causes including spinal cord injury, bladder stones, blood diseases (eg. leukaemia in children), stroke, uncontrolled diabetes, some forms of widespread cancer, injury to the penis, excess dose of alprostadil (Caverject, Muse), illegal drugs (eg. cocaine, marijuana) and prescription drugs (eg. prazosin, heparin). It rarely occurs a result of excessive sexual stimulation.

Treatment involves warm packs, pseudoephedrine (Sudafed) tablets, and syringes to draw excess blood from the penis. Any underlying cause needs to be excluded by appropriate tests. Permanent damage to the penis may occur due to the constant pressure on the tissue if it is not treated within four hours.
See ERECTION PROLONGED AND PAINFUL; PENIS

PRILOCAINE
See ANAESTHETICS

PRIMIDONE
See ANTICONVULSANTS

PRIMOBOLAN
See ANABOLIC STEROIDS

PRIMUM NON NOCERE
'Primum non nocere' means 'first do no harm' in Latin, one of the prime tenets of medical practice. This phrase may be used by doctors as a gentle warning to each other when considering a treatment, procedure or investigation that has significant risks or side-effects.

PRION
Prions are recently discovered infective agents that are smaller and more basic than viruses. Prions are complex protein particles that are able to replicate themselves, but are not destroyed by normal cooking, stomach acid or antiseptics. A small number of diseases are known to be caused by prions, including Creutzfeldt-Jakob disease (CJD), Kuru and Gerstmann-Straussler-Scheinker syndrome, but many more ailments whose cause is as yet unknown may eventually be found to be caused by prions.

Because they are so small, and very difficult to differentiate from normal protein particles that are meant to be in the tissue, prions are extremely difficult to isolate and identify.

There is no treatment available for any prion disease.
See also CREUTZFELDT-JAKOB DISEASE; KURU

PRK
See REFRACTIVE SURGERY

PRN
The prescription notation 'prn' is derived from the Latin 'pro re nata' which means 'when necessary'.
See also PRESCRIPTION NOTATIONS

PROBENECID
See HYPOURICAEMICS

PROBUCOL
See HYPOLIPIDAEMICS

PROCAINAMIDE
See ANTIARRHYTHMICS

PROCHLORPERAZINE
See ANTIEMETICS

PROCTALGIA FUGAX
Proctalgia fugax causes a severe, brief, very sharp pain that is felt in the anus for a few seconds or minutes several times a day. Patients describe the sensation as having a thin knife pushed into the anal canal and twisted. It is caused by spasm of the muscle that controls the opening and closing of the anus (the sphincter). Normally this is in constant contraction to prevent the passage of faeces and gas, but if it contracts excessively into a cramp, pain is felt.

Treatment is difficult, and involves using ice

packs, ice suppositories (large tablets of ice inserted into the anus) and anal injections. Strangely, inhaling salbutamol (Ventolin – normally used for asthma) will sometimes ease the pain. The condition may persist for months or years, but eventually settles.
See also ANAL PAIN; ANUS; PROCTITIS; PRURITUS ANI

PROCTITIS
Proctitis is inflammation or infection of the anal canal. It may be due to a bacterial, viral (eg. Herpes) or fungal infection. The main symptoms are pain and irritation in the anus that is worse with passing faeces, a constant feeling that there is a motion to be passed when there is none, and sometimes a discharge.

A swab may be taken from the anus to identify the infecting organism, and then the appropriate antibiotic/antifungal creams or antibiotic/antiviral tablets by mouth can be used to treat the condition. Soothing steroid creams and suppositories (anal tablets) may also be used.

Persistent infection may cause scar tissue formation and a narrowing of the anal canal, but the outcome is usually good with treatment.
See also ANAL ITCH; ANAL FISSURE; ANUS; PROCTALGIA FUGAX

PROCTOSCOPY
See COLONOSCOPY

PROGESTOGEN
See SEX HORMONES

PROGESTERONE
See OVARY

PROGNOSIS
Prognosis is a term used in medicine to indicate the probable outcome of a disease process. It is normally used in the future tense as a forecast. If a patient is likely to fully recover, the prognosis is good. If the patient is not likely to recover, the prognosis is poor.

PROGRESSIVE SUPRANUCLEAR PALSY
See STEELE-RICHARDSON-OLSZEWSKI SYNDROME

PROKINETIC AGENTS
These medications increase the rate at which the stomach empties its contents into the small bowel. The only widely used medication in this class is cisapride (Prepulsid). It is used for the treatment of reflux oesophagitis, heartburn and vomiting in babies. Side effects may include bowel cramps and noises and diarrhoea. It may rarely cause irregularities of the heart beat, and because of this it is not often prescribed. It is safe in pregnancy and children.
See also MEDICATION; REFLUX OESOPHAGITIS

PROLACTIN
See HYPERPROLACTINAEMIA; PITUITARY GLAND

PROLAPSE
A prolapse is the slippage or protrusion of an internal organ out through its natural opening (eg. part of the uterus may slip out through the vagina in a vaginal prolapse).
See also RECTAL PROLAPSE; VAGINAL PROLAPSE

PROLAPSED CORD
Very rarely, when the waters break during pregnancy at the start of labour, the umbilical cord slips down into the birth canal (a prolapsed cord). This is a medical emergency, as the start of labour usually follows soon after the waters break, and the cord will be compressed as the baby moves down into the birth canal, cutting off its oxygen supply. This problem is more common with breech births, as the smaller bottom is more likely than the larger head to allow the cord to slip past it into the birth canal.

The only treatment for a prolapsed cord is a Caesarean section as soon as possible. In the meantime, the mother may be placed in a kneeling position, with her head down on the bed and her bottom in the air. Drugs may be given to stop labour as well.
See also CAESAREAN SECTION; LABOUR; PREGNANCY

PROMAZINE
See ANTIPSYCHOTICS

PROMETHAZINE
See ANTIHISTAMINES

PROPANTHELINE
See ANTISPASMODICS

PROPTOSIS
See EYE PROTRUDING

PROPYLTHIOURACIL
See ANTITHYROID DRUGS

PROSTAGLANDIN E1
See ALPROSTADIL

PROSTATE CANCER
Prostate or prostatic cancer describes any one of several different types of cancer of the prostate gland, depending on which cells in the gland become cancerous. The cause is unknown, but those who have sex infrequently may be more susceptible. It is rare before fifty years of age, but up to 20% of all men over sixty may have an enlargement of the prostate. The percentage of these men whose enlargement is due to cancer steadily increases with age, with virtually every male over ninety years of age having some degree of prostate cancer.

This is a very slow-growing cancer that may give no symptoms until many years after it has developed. Symptoms usually start with difficulty in passing urine and difficulty in starting the urinary stream. In advanced stages there may be spread of cancer to the bones of the pelvis and back.

Specific blood tests can detect most cases, but it is often diagnosed by feeling the gland using a gloved finger in the back passage. Ultrasound scans and biopsy of the gland may also be performed.

It is treated with a combination of surgery, drugs and irradiation. Early stages may not be treated in the very elderly, because it is unlikely to cause trouble in their lifetime. Brachytherapy is a process in which tiny radioactive particles are injected into the prostate to create radiation which destroys the cancer. Orchidectomy (removal of the testes) is sometimes performed to remove all testosterone from the man's body, as this stimulates growth of the cancer.

If the cancer is localised to the gland itself, the five-year survival rate is over 90%. With local spread, the survival rate drops to about 70%, but with spread to the bone, only 30% of patients survive five years.
See also CANCER; PROSTATE GLAND; PROSTATE GLAND ENLARGED; PROSTATE SPECIFIC ANTIGEN; SEX HORMONES

PROSTATE GLAND
The prostate gland is situated behind the base of the penis. The bladder is above and behind the gland, and the tube which carries urine from the bladder to the outside (the urethra) passes through the centre of the prostate. It is found only in men and there is no female equivalent.

The prostate is about the size of a golf ball and consists of glands, fibrous tissue and muscle. Its primary purpose is to produce a substance that makes up part of the semen a man ejaculates during sexual intercourse. This substance is essential for the nutrition of the sperm as they try to fertilise an egg in the woman. Most men are totally unaware of the presence of the prostate unless it causes trouble.

In younger men, the most common cause of disease is infection, when the gland may swell up and become very tender. In older men the disease process is quite different. Up to 20% of all men over sixty may have an enlargement of the prostate which causes symptoms, and a small percentage of these may have cancer of the prostate.

Doctors can often diagnose diseases of the prostate by feeling the gland. This involves putting a gloved finger in the back passage so as to gauge its size and hardness.
See also BLADDER; PENIS; PROSTATITIS; PROSTATE CANCER; PROSTATE GLAND ENLARGED; PROSTATE SPECIFIC ANTIGEN; URETHRA

PROSTATE GLAND ENLARGED
Unless extraordinarily dexterous, no man can feel his own prostate, as this small organ which sits behind the base of the penis can only be felt by placing a finger through the anus, where the prostate can be felt as a firm lump on the front wall of the rectum (last part of the large bowel).

The prostate is about the size of a golf ball and consists of glands, fibrous tissue and muscle. Its produces a substance that makes up part of the semen a man ejaculates during intercourse that is essential for the nutrition of the sperm. If the prostate enlarges (prostatomegaly), the patient will have difficulty in starting the urinary stream, and when it does start, the urine will dribble out onto his shoes, rather than jet onto the porcelain. Up to 20%

of all men over sixty have benign enlargement of the prostate gland, which is usually associated with a drop in sexual activity. The absolute cause unknown, but as the gland enlarges, it squeezes the urethra (urine-carrying tube) which passes through it, making it steadily harder to urinate.

There are only three causes for prostate enlargement (prostatomegaly): –
• Prostatomegaly (prostate enlargement) is normal with age, and virtually all men over the age of seventy have some degree of this problem.
• Prostate cancer is a very slowly progressing cancer that increases in incidence with age. It spreads to bone early, and bone pain is the first symptom in some men.
• Prostatitis (infection of the gland), often from a sexually transmitted disease, may cause a temporary swelling and difficulty in passing urine at any age.

With prostate enlargement the man develops increasing difficulty in passing urine, and eventually the urethra becomes completely blocked, causing extreme distress as the pressure of urine in the bladder increases. If back pressure of urine in the bladder persists, kidney damage can occur.

In an acute situation, a flexible tube is passed up the urethra through the penis into the bladder to release urine, but if this is unsuccessful a large needle must be pushed through the lower wall of the abdomen into the bladder. In some cases drugs (eg. finasteride, prazosin, terazosin) can be used to shrink the enlarged prostate slightly. Most cases require surgery once symptoms develop. The operation can vary from simply dilating the urethra, to scraping away the part of the prostate constricting the urethra by passing a specially shaped knife up it (transurethral resection of prostate – TURP), or completely removing the gland.

Treatment almost invariably successful, with no subsequent effect on the general health of the patient, but there is sometimes subsequent sexual dysfunction.
See also FOLEY CATHETER; PROSTATE CANCER; PROSTATE GLAND; PROSTATE SPECIFIC ANTIGEN; URINATION DIFFICULT and separate entries for diseases mentioned above.

PROSTATE INFECTION
See PROSTATITIS

PROSTATE SPECIFIC ANTIGEN
A test for the prostate specific antigen (PSA) can be used to follow the success of treatment for prostate cancer and infection. If the levels drop, treatment is successful, if they rise it is not.

There has been a lot of controversy about the use of this test as a screening test for prostate cancer. A level of PSA below 4 micrograms per litre is usually normal, but unfortunately, many conditions other than cancer can cause the results to be high (eg. infection or enlargement of the gland), and so it is not an absolute test for prostate cancer. A combination of tests for different types of PSA (free and combined PSA) may be a better form of screening, but is still quite expensive.
See ANTIGEN; BLOOD TEST; CANCER ASSOCIATED ANTIGEN; PROSTATE GLAND; PROSTATE CANCER; PROSTATOMEGALY

PROSTATIC CANCER
See PROSTATE CANCER

PROSTATITIS
Prostatitis is an infection of the prostate gland, which sits behind the base of the penis, by bacteria that may enter the prostate by moving up the urethra (urine tube) from the outside, from a sexually transmitted infection (eg. gonorrhoea), or uncommonly from an infection spreading from other parts of the body.

Pain occurs behind the base of the penis, and there is a discharge from the penis, pain on passing urine, fever and patients pass urine frequently. The infection may spread to the man's sexual partner, in whom it can cause pelvic inflammatory disease.

The diagnosis is confirmed by taking a swab from the urethra, and identifying the bacteria and treatment requires taking a long course of antibiotics.

Acute cases usually settle with treatment, but recurrences are common and a low-grade persistent infection may develop, which is difficult to treat.
See also PELVIC INFLAMMATORY DISEASE; PROSTATE GLAND

PROSTATOMEGALY
See PROSTATE GLAND ENLARGED;

PROTEIN
A protein is a complex molecule that forms the basis of all life, and is composed of two or more amino acids. Protein is essential in the diet for growth, repair and replacement of tissue. Animal products (meat, fish, eggs, cheese) provide much protein in a form able to be used by the body. Vegetable proteins exist in peas, beans and other legumes, as well as in grains (and thus bread). If more protein is eaten than the body needs it will provide extra energy, but if not used it will be converted to fat and stored.
See also AMINO ACID; ANTIBODY; CARBOHYDRATE; CREATINE; FAT; FOOD; GAMMAGLOBULIN; GLUTEN; PHENYLKETONURIA

PROTEUS SYNDROME
Proteus syndrome is a rare congenital bone and tissue growth abnormality that is also known as the elephant man deformity, after Joseph Merrick, who suffered from this condition in the 19th century.

Excessive and unequal bone growth in face, arms, legs and hands results in severe facial and body disfigurement, bony growths on the skull that cause a great increase in skull circumference, and wrinkled bumps on feet, face and hands. X-rays show the abnormal bone growth.

Plastic surgery helps some deformities, and there is near normal life expectancy, but deformities persist.

PROTON PUMP INHIBITORS
This very effective class of medications was introduced in 1991, and has revolutionised the treatment of more resistant peptic ulcers and persistent reflux oesophagitis. They are usually prescribed when the presence of an ulcer or reflux is strongly suspected on clinical grounds, or after a gastroscopy proves the presence of an ulcer. They act by inhibiting the activity of the enzyme in the stomach lining that is responsible for acid production.

Examples include lansoprazole (Zoton), omeprazole (Losec) and pantoprazole sodium (Somac). Their side effects are minimal, but they must be used with care in pregnancy.
See also MEDICATION; PEPTIC ULCER

PROTOZOA
Protozoa are microscopic single-celled organisms like bacteria, but they are significantly larger and closer to what we normally think of as animal-like. Most protozoa are harmless but a few are parasites (i.e. live on a host body) and cause disease, usually of a singularly unpleasant kind. They are found all over the world in the soil and in almost any body of water from moist grass to mud puddles to the sea.

There are various kinds of protozoa, their classification depending on how they travel, either propelling themselves by one means or another, or in the case of the type that causes malaria, having no inbuilt means of propulsion but relying on a type of mosquito for transport. African sleeping sickness (affecting the nervous system) is caused by a species of protozoa and is transmitted by the tsetse fly, although the organism also has the ability to propel itself with a long whip-like tail.

Other diseases caused by protozoa are various gastrointestinal disorders and infections of the genitals such as vaginitis (inflammation and discharge from the vagina) or urethritis in men. A particularly unpleasant disease is called kala-azar, which is transmitted by the bite of a sandfly, and leads to anaemia and an enlarged liver and spleen. Another form of the disease attacks the mucous membrane and skin of the nose and spreads to the lips and mouth, causing ulcers, and as it progresses the cartilage of the nose may be destroyed, resulting in severe facial damage.

Toxoplasmosis, which can be transmitted by cats and raw meat, and which can cause fatal or severe damage to an unborn child if a pregnant woman becomes infected, is also caused by a protozoan organism.

Another type of protozoa is the amoeba. This is an irregularly shaped fluid blob enclosed in a membrane. There are several varieties of amoebae, one of which lives in the sockets of the teeth and gives rise to gum disease, while others are a cause of brain disease. One variety is the cause of amoebic dysentery, a disorder characterised by severe diarrhoea, common in the tropics, and is frequently spread by drinking contaminated water, especially where human excrement is used as fertiliser. It can be an insidious disease in that it sometimes lives harmlessly in the intestines for many years and then, for no apparent reason, invades the intestinal wall

and travels to the liver or other organs, where it forms an abscess.
See also AMOEBA; AMOEBIASIS; BACTERIA; BLASTOCYSTIS; CUTANEOUS LEISCHMANIASIS; FUNGI; GIARDIASIS; KALA-AZAR; TOXOPLASMOSIS

PROTRUDING EYE
See EYE PROTRUDING

PROZAC
See ANTIDEPRESSANTS

PRURITUS
See ANAL ITCH; SKIN ITCH; VULVA ITCH

PRURITUS ANI
See ANAL ITCH

PSA
See PROSTATE SPECIFIC ANTIGEN

PSEUDOCUSHING SYNDROME
Pseudocushing syndrome is caused by excessive levels of steroids in the blood, secondary to alcoholism and liver damage which prevents steroids that are normally produced in the body from being destroyed, allowing their blood levels to increase. Unlike Cushing syndrome, there is no excess steroid production. Patients have a combination of symptoms due to Cushing syndrome and alcoholism. Blood tests confirm the diagnosis.

Once the alcoholism has been controlled, symptoms may settle, provided organ damage is not severe, but sometimes liver damage may be so severe that the organ is unable to recover, and a liver transplant is required. The prognosis is reasonable if alcohol consumption is ceased, but it is fatal if alcohol consumption is continued.
See also ALCOHOLISM; CUSHING SYNDROME

PSEUDOEPHEDRINE
See DECONGESTANTS; VASOCONSTRICTORS

PSEUDOFOLLICULITIS BARBAE
See RAZOR RASH

PSEUDOGOUT
Pseudogout (calcium pyrophosphate deposi-

tion disease) is the deposition of calcium pyrophosphate crystals in joints due to a metabolic disorder.

Pseudogout has exactly the same symptoms as gout with acute pain in, and redness over, a joint but it affects the knees and other large joints. Patients are usually elderly, and complain of recurrent, severe attacks of pain. Permanent arthritis may develop in repeatedly affected joints. It is diagnosed by identifying the responsible crystals in the fluid that may be drawn out of the affected joint through a needle. X-rays show arthritis and calcification around the joint.

Treatment involves the use of nonsteroidal anti-inflammatory drugs (eg. indomethacin, naproxen), and injections of steroids into the joint. Unlike gout, there are no medications that can be used in the long term to prevent further attacks. Medication can control each attack, but repeated attacks may occur.
See also ARTHRITIS; CHONDROCALCINOSIS; GOUT

PSEUDOMEMBRANOUS COLITIS
Pseudomembranous colitis is a form of severe inflammation of the large intestine associated with a fine membrane over the gut wall caused by an overgrowth in the bowel of the bacteria *Clostridium difficile* due to an adverse reaction to antibiotics (eg. clindamycin, ampicillin, cephalosporins).

The symptoms include severe, intractable, watery diarrhoea, cramping belly pain and fever, and sometimes the motions become bloody. Dehydration, body chemistry abnormalities, perforation of the inflamed bowel, and rarely death may be complications.

Colonoscopy reveals the inflamed gut and false membrane. The antibiotic vancomycin is used in treatment, and fluid loss is replaced by a drip into a vein. Most patients recover with appropriate treatment.
See also COLON; COLONOSCOPY

PSEUDOMONAS AERUGINOSA INFECTION
Pseudomonas aeruginosa causes serious bacterial infections, usually of the lungs (eg. bronchitis, pneumonia), urine (eg. cystitis), ears and heart. Lung infections cause a persistent cough that produces yellow to green phlegm, chest pain, fever and tiredness. Antibiotics such as gentamicin give a slow but

successful response.
See also BACTERIA; BRONCHITIS,
ACUTE; PNEUMONIA

PSEUDOMONAS PSEDOMALLEI INFECTION
See MELIOIDOSIS

PSITTACOSIS

Psittacosis (bird fancier's lung or ornithosis) is a rare form of pneumonia caught from birds. It is caused by the bacteria-like organism *Chlamydia*, which is normally an infection of parrots, pigeons, chickens and ducks, but may very occasionally be transmitted to humans, although it rarely passes from one person to another.

There is a gradual onset of fever, headache, muscle pains, tiredness, dry cough and nose bleeds. Some patients develop skin spots, shortness of breath, and abdominal pains. Spread of the infection to the heart or brain is possible, and sometimes a second bacterium may cause double pneumonia. The incubation period is one to two weeks after exposure to an infected bird. The diagnosis may be suspected in bird fanciers, chicken farmers and veterinarians and is confirmed by sputum culture or a specific blood test. A chest x-ray can show the presence of pneumonia, but not that the pneumonia is necessarily caused by psittacosis.
See also CHLAMYDIAL INFECTION;
PNEUMONIA

PSORIASIS

Psoriasis vulgaris (to use the full name) is an annoying, distressing, persistent and difficult to treat skin disease that affects 2% of the population. It is an autoimmune disease in which the body's immune system is inappropriately triggered to reject tissue as though it was a foreign material. In psoriasis, varying parts of the skin are rejected. It is unusual in children but becomes more common as age increases.

The rash appears as a small patch of red skin covered with fine scales that gradually enlarges, roughens and thickens the skin, and other spots may start over a period of months. The elbows, knees and scalp are the most common sites, while on the scalp, it may appear to be a bad case of dandruff. The nails may also be affected, and become rough and pitted.

The Koebner phenomenon occurs when psoriasis develops on areas of skin that have been injured, and may appear as a line of inflamed skin along a healed cut or surgical incision, or a patch at the site of a previous graze.

In severe cases the joints may be attacked to cause a type of arthritis.

Psoriasis has many subtypes, and it is often necessary to perform a biopsy to confirm the exact diagnosis.

Treatment involves one or more of a number of keratolytic creams or ointments that are used regularly on the skin. Coal tar is the mainstay of treatment, but calcipotriol and steroid creams are also very effective. Other skin preparations include dithranol, salicylic acid and psoralen. Ultraviolet light may be used in conjunction with psoralen to promote healing. In very severe cases, steroid tablets or injections, or acitretin tablets, may be given. The rash may come and go without any treatment.

There is no cure for psoriasis, but it can usually be successfully controlled.
See also AUTOIMMUNE DISEASES;
DERMATITIS; GUTTAE PSORIASIS;
KERATOLYTICS; PARAPSORIASIS EN
PLAQUE; PITYRIASIS LICHENOIDES;
SKIN DRY AND SCALY

PSYCHIATRY

Psychiatry is the science of dealing with medical problems that are specific to disorders of brain function and perception. Doctors specialising in this field are known as psychiatrists. Psychiatrists treat mental diseases (eg. depression, phobias, schizophrenia) and teach patients how to maintain good mental health.
See also ABREACTION; ANOREXIA
NERVOSA; BULIMIA NERVOSA;
CATATONIC SYNDROME;
CLÉRAMBAULT SYNDROME;
DEPRESSION; ELECTROCONVULSIVE
THERAPY; HYPOCHONDRIA;
HYSTERIA; MANIA; MULTIPLE
PERSONALITY DISORDER;
MUNCHAUSEN SYNDROME;
NEUROSES; OBSESSIVE COMPULSIVE
NEUROSIS; PERSONALITY CHANGE;
PHOBIA; POSTNATAL DEPRESSION;
POST-TRAUMATIC STRESS
DISORDER; PSYCHOANALYSIS;

PSYCHOLOGIST; PSYCHOSES; SCHIZOPHRENIA; SUICIDE etc.

PSYCHIATRY MEDICATIONS
See ANTIDEPRESSANTS; ANTIPSYCHOTICS; ANXIOLYTICS; BENZODIAZEPINES

PSYCHOANALYSIS
In psychoanalysis, a patient sees a psychiatrist with further training in this area of psychiatry on a very regular basis (eg. three to five times a week) for an hour or more at a time over several weeks, months or years. It is essential for a close rapport to develop between the doctor and patient. Only a small number of patients with specific character disorders or neuroses are suitable for psychoanalysis.

The patient is placed in a comfortable position, sometimes lying down, sometimes in a comfortable chair, and the doctor usually sits out of the patient's sight. The patient is urged to express their thoughts, feelings, urges, desires, fantasies, memories and dreams. Using the free flow of thoughts between patient and doctor, the patient's personality and mind can be analysed (psychoanalysis).

The aim of the process is to give the patient insight into their lifestyle so that any problems and concerns can be worked through and controlled or rationalised. This process is called psychotherapy. The treatment is continued until the patient is content with their life and situation.
See also ABREACTION; NEUROSES; PSYCHIATRY

PSYCHOLOGIST
Psychologists are not medical doctors but have undertaken a course of training to obtain a Master of Arts degree in psychology from a university. Many further their studies to earn postgraduate degrees and doctorates (PhD). Psychologists deal with behavioural, social and emotional problems (eg. marriage counselling, dealing with badly behaved children, coping with stress).
See also PSYCHIATRY

PSYCHOSES
Psychiatric conditions are divided into two broad classes, neuroses and psychoses. In psychoses, the patient has no insight into the fact that they are mentally disturbed. The most

severe form of psychosis is schizophrenia.
See ANTIPSYCHOTICS; CAPGRAS SYNDROME; DIOGENES SYNDROME; HYPOCHONDRIA; MANIA; NEUROSES; SCHIZOPHRENIA

PSYCHOTHERAPY
See PSYCHOANALYSIS

PTERYGIUM
A pterygium (the P is silent, and this is pronounced as 'terrigium') is a form of damage to the eye surface. Glare and sun exposure cause recurrent mild sunburn to the cornea and the irritated tissue overgrows to form a pingueculum. This then spreads across the eye as a pterygium. The condition is more common in tropical climates.

A pale yellow fleshy overgrowth develops of the white part of the eye (cornea) and spreads across the coloured part of the eye (iris). If the growth spreads across the pupil it causes blindness. It may become irritated, red and itchy at times. Once present it will remain until removed by a simple surgical procedure, but they can be prevented by wearing good quality (polarised) sunglasses.
See also EYE; PINGUECULUM

EYE SHOWING PTERYGIUM

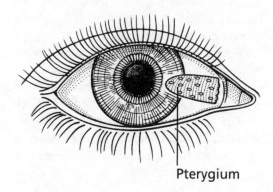

Pterygium

PTOSIS
See EYELID DROOP

PTSD
See POST-TRAUMATIC STRESS DISORDER

PTYALOCELE
See RANULA

PUBERTY
The trigger for puberty is the production of sex

hormone releasing factors from the pituitary gland at the base of the brain, which cause sex hormones to be manufactured in the gonads – oestrogen from the ovaries of females, and testosterone from the testes of males.

Both sexes show a marked increase in weight and height, while boys develop more muscle and girls acquire the fatty deposits, which give their rounded feminine shape. There are also gender-based differences in the way the skeleton grows – boys develop wider shoulders leading to greater physical strength, and girls develop wider hips to facilitate childbearing. As a general rule, the bones stop growing in girls by the age of about sixteen and in boys by the age of about eighteen, although sometimes growth continues until the early twenties.

Some parts of the body are affected by the adolescent growth spurt more than others. The hands and feet mature first, then the legs, then the trunk, so children stop growing out of their jeans a year or so before they stop growing out of their jumpers.

On average puberty starts in girls a year or two earlier than in boys – usually about ten or eleven years of age in girls, and twelve or thirteen in boys. Girls have been known to reach puberty as early as eight and as late as fifteen or sixteen. Boys vary similarly. Heredity is an important factor in the age of maturity. A girl whose mother started her periods late is likely also to be somewhat later than average in developing.

Puberty is also affected by general health. A child who has been undernourished or experienced a lot of illness may have the onset of maturity delayed. Children who are much smaller than the norm also may not mature as early as usual. Generally speaking there is no cause for concern unless a child shows no signs of development by the age of about fifteen or sixteen.

The physical changes of puberty are accompanied by psychological and emotional changes, also due to the production of sex hormones. In both boys and girls, there is an increased interest in sexuality as well as greater natural assertiveness, which helps to explain why teenagers are rebellious and often seen by their despairing parents as turning life into a never-ending argument. Rising levels of the male hormone testosterone are thought to be the reason adolescent boys are so often adventurous and aggressive.

In girls the physical changes include the development of the breasts, including an increase in the size of the nipples and possibly a darkening of the pigmentation. As well as the widening of the hips, the vagina and uterus develop further. Glands which will supply lubrication during sexual intercourse develop in and around the vagina. Hair grows in the armpits and the pubic region. In girls the pubic hair triangle has the base of the triangle closest to the navel and the apex points to the genitals. Fine hair may develop on the forearms, parts of the legs and the upper lip.

The major change in any girl's life is the start of menstruation (the onset of her periods – the menarche). From this time on, every month the uterus prepares itself for a possible pregnancy by increasing the thickness of its lining so as to nourish a fertilised egg. If a fertilised egg does not arrive, the thickened lining is not needed and breaks down to be discarded from the body. It is this lining, together with some blood, that flows out through the vagina as the monthly menstrual flow. The first time a girl has a period, it shows that her body has started releasing its eggs (all of which are present from birth) and is capable of becoming pregnant. An entire cycle normally takes twenty eight days, with menstruation lasting four or five days. A girl's periods are usually irregular for the first few months, since it takes a while for a pattern to be established. Some women continue to have irregular periods for their entire reproductive lives, other women are as regular as clockwork

In boys the main physical signs of maturity are an enlargement of the penis and testicles and the ability to produce sperm and so fertilise a female egg. Most boys will experience wet dreams or the involuntary emission of semen (the fluid in which sperm is contained) while they are asleep. These are completely normal, and no reason for concern.

The boy will also grow a triangular patch of body hair in the pubic region and under the arms. In boys, the pubic hair triangle is widest near the genitals and has its apex pointing towards the navel. Hair also appears on the face, and he will need to shave. Generally the hair is soft and downy to start with and becomes thicker and coarser as the maturing process progresses. Finally a boy's voice breaks and the pitch becomes lower due to the thickening of the vocal cords.

See also MENSTRUAL PERIODS;
MENSTRUAL PERIODS, FAILURE TO
START; OVARY; PUBERTY DELAYED;
PUBERTY EARLY; SEX HORMONES;
TESTES

PUBERTY DELAYED

Puberty is the transition from boy to man
or girl to woman, and is characterised by
the development of pubic hair in both sexes;
the enlargement of the penis, scrotum and
testes and the development of a beard in men;
or enlargement of the vulva (opening lips of
the vagina), fat deposition on the hips, development of breasts and the start of menstrual
periods in women. After puberty, a man and
woman can create new life with a child; before
they cannot.

Many of the causes of delayed puberty apply
to both sexes, while others are sex specific.

The onset of puberty is triggered by the
hypothalamus (part of the brain) sending
nerve signals to the pituitary gland which lies
in the centre of the head underneath the
brain. This gland controls every other gland in
the body, including the ovaries and testes, by
sending chemical messages (hormones) to
them through the blood stream. When the
testes and ovaries receive the appropriate hormonal signals from the pituitary gland, they in
turn start to produce the sex hormones
testosterone and oestrogen, which are responsible for the development of normal sexual
characteristics. A tumour, cyst, cancer,
abscess, infection or damage to the blood
supply of the hypothalamus or pituitary gland
may adversely affect these organs and therefore prevent the start of puberty. Irradiation
to the brain and cytotoxic drugs to treat
cancer will have a similar effect.

A significant long term illness, persistent
major infection, regular extremely vigourous
exercise, cancer, malnutrition or serious emotional stress will affect the body's functions
generally, including the production of sex
hormones.

Other causes of a delayed onset of puberty
that may occur in both sexes include hypothyroidism (an underactive thyroid gland), a
serious infection that involves both ovaries or
both testes, Addison's disease (under active
adrenal glands), Noonan syndrome and
Laurence-Moon-Biedl syndrome (inherited
condition that causes night blindness, mental

retardation, obesity, small genitals and sometimes extra fingers or toes).

Many different diseases may seriously affect
the liver, lungs, heart and other major organs
to place sufficient stress on a child's body to
delay the production of sex hormones.

In boys, late sexual development may be due
to undescended testes (testes remain in
abdomen), torsion of both testis (testicle twists
around and cuts off the blood vessels that
supply it), Klinefelter syndrome (additional X
chromosomes matched with a single Y chromosome) and the Prader-Willi syndrome
(obese and small genitals).

In girls the possible causes include anorexia
nervosa (psychiatric condition of under
eating), ovarian torsion (the twisting of both
ovaries on the stalk of tissue that supplies it
with blood and nerves), multiple ovarian cysts
and Turner syndrome (women with only one
X chromosome instead of two).
See also PUBERTY; MENSTRUAL
PERIODS, FAILURE TO START and
separate entries for diseases mentioned above.

PUBERTY EARLY

Some children may start the development
from girl to woman or boy to man (precocious puberty) earlier than normal. Only one
in ten girls passes through puberty before
eleven, and boys before twelve years of age.
Over the last two centuries, the average age of
puberty has dropped by more than eighteen
months due to better nutrition and health.

If both parents started puberty early, then
there is an inherited tendency for their children to do the same.

Most causes of precocious puberty are
common to both sexes.

If sex hormones are given to children deliberately or accidentally by tablet or injection,
adult sexual characteristics will develop,
although true puberty may not occur, and the
child will remain infertile. Tumours of the
ovary, testes, brain or pituitary gland under
the brain may also stimulate production of
sex hormones at an early age.

Other causes include hydrocephalus (too
much fluid around and in the brain), Cushing
syndrome (an over production of steroids, or
taking large doses of cortisone), encephalitis
(infection of the brain), congenital adrenal
hyperplasia (adrenogenital syndrome – overactivity of the adrenal glands) and tuberous

sclerosis (convulsions and mental retardation). *See also* PUBERTY and separate entries for diseases mentioned above.

PUBIC AREA
See VAGINA; VULVA

PUBIC BONE
See PELVIS

PUBIC PEDICULOSIS
See CRABS

PULMO-
'Pulmo-' is a prefix derived from the Latin word for the lung ('pulmonis') and used in medicine to indicate tests, conditions or diseases related to the lungs.

PULMONARY ABSCESS
See LUNG ABSCESS

PULMONARY ARTERY
See HEART; PULMONARY VALVE

PULMONARY EMBOLISM
A pulmonary embolism occurs when a blood clot or other substance (embolus – eg. fatty plaque from high cholesterol levels in the blood) travels through the bloodstream and the pulmonary artery to a small artery in the lung which it then blocks.

Blood clots may occur in the veins of leg muscles (deep venous thrombosis, DVT), but may also arise in other parts of the body. They travel through veins to the right side of the heart, and then into the lungs where they cut off the blood supply to a segment of lung which will collapse and die. Emboli are more common after major surgery, in patients who are bedridden for long periods, and in the elderly.

The symptoms may include chest pain, shortness of breath, coughing of blood, fainting, increased heart rate, and a fever. After a pulmonary embolism, increased back pressure of blood on the heart may lead to right heart failure (cor pulmonale), and an extending clot can cut off more arteries in the lung, and destroy a larger area of lung tissue.

The condition is diagnosed by chest x-ray or CT scans. Blood tests can show signs of clotting within the body, and an electrocardiogram (ECG) shows strain on the heart.

Specialised tests of lung function are sometimes necessary, and an x-ray in which dye is injected into the veins and can be seen moving through the arteries in the lung may be performed in cases of doubt.

Treatment must start as soon as possible to prevent extension of the clot and further damage to the lung. Anticoagulant drugs that prevent blood clotting (eg. heparin) are initially given as an injection, and later as tablets (eg. warfarin, aspirin). Regular blood tests are performed throughout anticoagulant treatment, to check the dosage required. Anticoagulant therapy is continued for some months after the attack, but in high-risk patients it may be continued for life. In severe cases thrombolytics (clot dissolving drugs) are injected directly into the involved veins. In rare circumstances, surgery to remove the clot from the lungs or leg is undertaken, or a filter is inserted surgically into the main vein of the body leading from the legs to the heart, to filter out any blood clots that may form in the future. Blood clots in the legs can be prevented by using pressure stockings during long operations, early mobilisation after surgery, physiotherapy to keep leg muscles active, and elevation of the legs in bed-bound patients.

Rapid death occurs in 10% of patients who have a large area of lung involved, but the majority of patients recover provided appropriate treatment is given quickly.
See also ANTICOAGULANTS; BREATH, SHORT OF; COR PULMONALE; DEEP VENOUS THROMBOSIS; LUNG; THROMBOSIS

PULMONARY FUNCTION TESTS
See BLOOD GAS ANALYSIS; PEAK EXPIRATORY FLOW RATE; SLEEP STUDIES; TOTAL LUNG CAPACITY; VITAL CAPACITY

PULMONARY HYPERTENSION
See COR PULMONALE

PULMONARY VALVE
The pulmonary valve sits between the right ventricle of the heart and the pulmonary artery, which takes blood lacking in oxygen from the heart to the lungs. When the heart contracts, blood is forced out of the right ventricle into the pulmonary artery through the pulmonary valve. The valve then closes to

prevent the back flow of blood when the heart relaxes.

See also HEART; PULMONARY VALVE INCOMPETENCE; PULMONARY VALVE STENOSIS; TRICUSPID VALVE

PULMONARY VALVE INCOMPETENCE

Leakage of the pulmonary heart valve, which controls the flow of blood from the right ventricle (right lower chamber) of the heart to the pulmonary artery, which goes to the lungs, is called incompetence or regurgitation. It is an uncommon form of heart valve disease that is often a result of endocarditis or cor pulmonale. No significant symptoms are usually present, and the problem is usually found by accident when listening to the heart for other reasons. No treatment is normally necessary for the valve, but the cause must be treated.

See also COR PULMONALE; ENDOCARDITIIS; HEART; PULMONARY VALVE

PULMONARY VALVE STENOSIS

Narrowing of the pulmonary heart valve which controls the flow of blood from the right ventricle (right lower chamber) of the heart to the pulmonary artery, which goes to the lungs is called stenosis. It is usually a birth defect, and a mild stenosis causes no symptoms. Severe stenosis may cause chest pain, fainting on exertion and shortness of breath and must be corrected surgically. It is diagnosed by echocardiography (ultrasound scan). If left untreated, sudden death or heart failure may occur.

See also ECHOCARDIOGRAPHY; HEART; PULMONARY VALVE

PULMONARY VEIN

See HEART; LUNG; VEIN

PULMONIC REGURGITATION

See PULMONARY VALVE INCOMPETENCE

PULSE

The rate at which the heart beats, measured in beats per minute, as felt in an artery in the arm, leg or neck, is referred to as the pulse rate. The most common place to feel a pulse is the radial artery, just above the wrist on the thumb side. Other common pulse points are the carotid artery in the neck, the posterior tibial artery on the inside of the ankle, the dorsalis pedis artery on top of the foot, and the femoral artery behind the knee.

The regularity and strength of the heart beat may also be determined by feeling a pulse.

A normal pulse rate is about seventy beats a minute.

See also HEART; PALPITATIONS; PULSE SLOW

PULSE IRREGULAR

See PALPITATIONS

PULSE RAPID

See PALPITATIONS; TACHYCARDIA

PULSE SLOW

A slow heart rate (below sixty beats a minute at rest) is usually felt by patients as a slow pulse in their wrist or neck. It is common in very fit athletes, the very old, patients who are recovering from a serious illness, after a bad fright, and in some others who have an inborn tendency to this condition. Provided there is no serious underlying disease, a slow pulse (bradycardia) is not dangerous.

In a faint, the blood pressure drops to a low level (resulting in the faint) and the heart rate also slows significantly.

Other causes may include a heart attack (myocardial infarct), congestive cardiac failure (damaged heart is unable to beat effectively) sick sinus syndrome and damage to the heart pacemaker.

Numerous other diseases that affect the heart and its function, may also cause bradycardia, including an under active thyroid gland (hypothyroidism), Stokes-Adams attacks (sudden change in the heart rate), and tumours, cancer or infection of the brain or its surrounding tissues, or an increase in the pressure of the fluid surrounding the brain (cerebrospinal fluid).

Many medications are available to slow the heart rate, and others have this as a side effect. Examples include digoxin (Lanoxin), beta-blockers (eg. propranolol), sedatives and narcotics (eg. morphine, codeine).

See also FAINT; PULSE and separate entries for diseases and medications mentioned above.

PUPIL LARGE

Mydriasis is the technical name for a large dilated pupil (the black part in the centre of the eye). It may be due to a natural phenomenon at night or in a dark room, or may be a sign of anxiety, fright or sexual attraction. The size of the pupil is controlled by contraction or relaxation of the tiny muscle that forms the iris (coloured part of the eye) in response to messages from the brain or reflexes in the eye (eg. to light changes).

An abnormally dilated pupil may be caused by a head injury that is affecting brain function and is a serious sign that urgent medical attention is necessary. Less common causes include an overactive thyroid gland (hyperthyroidism), injuries to the eye, poisoning (eg. botulism), syphilis, syringomyelia, Tolosa-Hunt syndrome and Holmes-Adie syndrome. Legal medications (eg. atropine) and illegal drugs such as marijuana and amphetamines may also be responsible.

See also BELLADONNA; EYE; MYDRIATICS; PUPIL SMALL and separate entries for diseases mentioned above.

PUPIL SMALL

Miosis is the technical name for a small contracted pupil (the black part in the centre of the eye) which may be a natural phenomenon due to bright light, or looking at something that is very close to the eyes.

An abnormally contracted pupil may be caused by a brain tumour or injury to the brain, an injury to the eye, Horner syndrome, tabes dorsalis (a complication of syphilis), hysteria or may be defect present from birth. Legal medications (eg. narcotics, pilocarpine) and illegal drugs such as heroin or cocaine may also be responsible.

See also EYE; MIOTICS; PUPIL LARGE and separate entries for diseases mentioned above.

PURPURA

See SKIN RED DOTS; THROMBOCYTOPENIA

PUS

Pus is formed by the destruction of normal tissue by a bacterial, or rarely fungal, infection. The breakdown and waste products of the destroyed cells accumulate as pus.

See also ABSCESS; PUSTULES

PUSTULES

Pustules are small, elevated skin blisters filled with pus. They are only caused by a bacterial or viral infection, but a number of diseases may be responsible.

Pimples (acne) are due to a blockage in the outflow of oil from the oil glands in the skin due to dirt, flakes of dead skin, or most commonly a thickening and excess production of the oil. The gland becomes dilated with oil, then inflamed and eventually infected to cause acne spots. Stress, an infection or hormonal changes may see the number of spots increase dramatically.

School sores (impetigo) are a very common bacterial skin infection that virtually every child will catch at some stage. It is most commonly caused by the bacteria *Staphylococcus aureus*. The infection spreads easily to cause one or more itchy, tender, red, raised, weeping or crusting sores on the skin.

A virus called *Herpes zoster* causes chickenpox. It can be found in the fluid-containing blisters, breath and saliva of patients. The rash usually starts on the head or chest as red pimples, then spreads onto the legs and arms, and develops into blisters before drying up and scabbing over.

Shingles is an infection of a spinal nerve also caused by the *Herpes zoster* virus (the same virus that causes chickenpox). At times of stress or reduced immunity, the virus may start to multiply again in one particular nerve, to cause sharp pain that gradually moves along the nerve on one side only from the back to the front of the abdomen. Shortly after the pain starts, a patchy blistering rash will appear in a line along the course of the nerve.

Genital herpes causes a pus filled blister that bursts to form a very painful, tender, shallow ulcer that persists for ten to twenty days. The virus that causes the infection (*Herpes simplex*) is highly contagious.

Other causes include folliculitis (bacterial infection of a hair follicle), rosacea (skin disease of the face), melioidosis and chancroid (bacterial sexually transmitted infection).

See also BLISTERS; PUS; SKIN and separate entries for diseases mentioned above.

PUTTI-PLATT PROCEDURE

See SHOULDER DISLOCATION

PYELOGRAM
See INTRAVENOUS PYELOGRAM

PYELONEPHRITIS, ACUTE
Acute pyelonephritis is a bacterial infection of the kidneys. The infection may reach the kidney through the blood stream, or up the ureter from the bladder. They are more common in women, after operations to the urinary tract, during pregnancy, and in those who are very sexually active.

Symptoms start suddenly with pain in the loin, fever, nausea, headaches and sometimes nausea and vomiting. There may be associated cystitis (bladder infection) which causes pain on passing urine, and urinary frequency. The diagnosis is confirmed by examining a sample of urine to identify the responsible bacteria and the correct antibiotic. Further tests may be indicated if infections are repeated, including x-rays and/or ultrasound scans of the kidney, and cystoscopy (a fine flexible tube is passed into the bladder).

Antibiotics are the primary treatment, usually as a tablet or capsule by mouth for five to ten days, but occasionally by injection, and patients should take as much fluid as possible to flush out the infection. Some patients will require long courses of antibiotics to prevent further attacks. Passing urine after sexual intercourse will reduce the incidence of recurrences in women. With correct treatment, most infections settle quickly.
See also CYSTITIS; CYSTOSCOPY; INTRAVENOUS PYELOGRAM; KIDNEY; PYELONEPHRITIS, CHRONIC

PYELONEPHRITIS, CHRONIC
Chronic pyelonephritis is a persistent bacterial infection of the kidneys. It may occur in both sexes and at any age, but those most commonly affected are elderly, incontinent (unable to control their bladder) and may have a catheter into the bladder.

Often there are no or minimal symptoms, but the infection is detected on a routine urine test. Some patients have vague loin pain, feel tired and pass urine frequently. Scarring of the kidney, high blood pressure, anaemia and functional failure of the kidney are possible complications.

X-rays, CT and ultrasound scans of the kidneys, blood tests, urine culture tests, and cystoscopy (passing a flexible tube into the bladder) are used to investigate the condition.

Treatment involves a very long course of the appropriate antibiotic, urinary antiseptics and alkalising agents (eg. Ural, Citravescent), and patients are encouraged to drink large quantities of fluids. If a kidney abnormality is found, this may be surgically corrected. One third of patients are cured by a six-week course of antibiotics, another third cured after six months of antibiotics and antiseptics, 10% progress to severe kidney damage and failure, and the remainder continue to have a chronic infection without symptoms or kidney damage.
See also CYSTOSCOPY; KIDNEY; PYELONEPHRITIS, ACUTE

PYLORIC STENOSIS
A congenital (present from birth) narrowing of the pylorus (the drainage valve at the lower end of the stomach) that prevents or slows food from leaving the stomach. Affected infants develop projectile vomiting soon after birth, and fail to gain weight. Boys are affected far more often than girls. On examination, a thickened ball of muscle at the site of the pylorus can often be felt in the abdomen. The problem can be corrected by a relatively simple operation, and there are no long term adverse effects.
See also FAILURE TO THRIVE; NAUSEA AND VOMITING; STOMACH

PYLORIC ULCER
See PEPTIC ULCER

PYLORUS
See STOMACH

PYRANTEL
See ANTHELMINTICS

PYRAZINAMIDE
See TUBERCULOSIS MEDICATIONS

PYREXIA
See FEVER; TEMPERATURE MEASUREMENT

PYRIDOXINE
See VITAMIN B

PYRIMETHAMINE
See ANTIMALARIALS

PYROMANIA

A form of mania in which there is an irresistible desire to light fires, despite usually having the knowledge that considerable damage may be done to property. The perpetrator is often found helping to fight the fire s/he has started, and sometimes achieves inappropriate personal satisfaction and sexual gratification from seeing the flames.

See also MANIA

Q

Q FEVER

Q fever is a lung infection by primitive bacteria of the genus *Rickettsia*, which was unidentified for many years. The disease may derive its name from the fact that doctors were constantly questioning (Q) the cause of the fever, or Q may stand for Queensland, where the disease was very common and first researched.

Coxiella burnetti is the responsible Rickettsia. It is a parasite of sheep, cattle and goats, and passes from these animals in the milk and faeces, then may be inhaled by humans in the form of droplets and dust containing the bacteria, but it does not spread from one human to another. Farmers, shearers and abattoir workers are at a high risk. The incubation period is one to three weeks.

It often causes very mild, barely noticeable symptoms, but in more severe cases the patient will develop a fever, weakness, headache, muscle pains and a dry cough. In advanced cases, jaundice (yellow skin) and stomach pains occur and rarely heart and brain involvement is possible. A specific blood test can diagnose the disease, and a chest x-ray may show lung abnormalities in severe cases.

Tetracyclines (antibiotic) are used to suppress the infection, but it does not always eliminate the disease completely. It may be prevented by a vaccination given to those who are at high risk.

Treatment is not completely satisfactory, and relapses are common, but death is rare unless the heart becomes involved.
See also BRUCELLOSIS; RICKETTSIAL INFECTIONS; TETRACYCLINES

QH

The prescription notation 'qh' is derived from the Latin 'quaque hors' which means 'every hour'.
See also PRESCRIPTION NOTATIONS

QID

The prescription notation 'qid' is derived from the Latin 'quater in die' which means 'four times a day'.
See also PRESCRIPTION NOTATIONS

QUADRICEPS MUSCLE

The bulk of muscles on the front of the thigh are collectively called the quadriceps. Four muscles, the rectus femoris, vastus lateralis, vastus intermedius and vastus medialis act together when they contract to extend the knee. At the top end they are attached to the front of the pelvis (rectus femoris) or front of the femur (vastus muscles). Their lower ends insert together as a common tendon into the patella (knee cap).
See also FEMUR; HAMSTRING MUSCLES; MUSCLE; PATELLA

QUADRIPLEGIA

Quadriplegia (tetraplegia) is a complication of a neck injury or disease that severs the spinal cord.

All parts of the human body are capable of healing and repairing damage, except the central nervous system, which comprises the brain and spinal cord. The spinal cord runs from the base of the brain, down through the vertebrae that form the backbone, and ends just below the waist. Nerves run out from it to the muscles, skin and other tissues, with one bundle of nerves emerging from between each of the twenty four vertebrae. If the spinal cord is cut by a broken neck or other injury or disease, it is impossible for nerve signals to pass backwards and forwards from the brain to the body and paralysis occurs below the level of the injury. Involuntary muscles which control the internal organs such as the gut and heart movements, are supplied by a different set of nerves, and are not affected by spinal injury.

Patients cannot feel heat or cold, hard or soft, sharp or dull, or any other sensation below the level of the injury. There is no control of muscles, so patients cannot walk, move their arms or control their bowels or bladder. Pressure sores may develop on the skin, and lung and urinary infections occur from immobility.

The cause is diagnosed by x-rays, CT and MRI scans, and electrical tests on nerves and muscles.

The only help that can be offered is

rehabilitation so patients can cope with their disability, as there is no cure. Life span is often slightly shortened by lung complications.
See also PARAPLEGIA AND QUADRIPLEGIA; SPINAL CORD

QUEENSLAND TICK TYPHUS
See TYPHUS

QUETIAPINE
See ANTIPSYCHOTICS

QUINAPRIL
See ACE INHIBITORS

QUINIDINE
See ANTIARRHYTHMICS

QUININE
See ANTIMALARIALS; MUSCLE RELAXANTS

QUINOLONES
Quinolones are a class of potent antibiotics that are used to treat serious bacterial infections, particularly in the urinary tract. Examples include ciprofloxacin (Ciproxin), enoxacin (Enoxin) and norfloxacin (Noroxin). Side effects may include nausea, headache and dizziness. They must be used with care in pregnancy.
See also ANTIBIOTICS

QUINSY
Quinsy is a peritonsillar (around the tonsil) abscess involving the tonsil at one side of the back of the throat. It is more common in adults and males.

If tonsillitis is severe enough to cause destruction of the tonsil tissue, pus will form and collect between the tonsil and the wall of the throat to form an abscess. An attack of tonsillitis may initially appear to settle, but then the patient develops a high fever, severe pain on one side of the throat, a swollen throat, and difficulty in swallowing and opening the mouth. Swabs are taken from the tonsil to identify the bacteria responsible and the appropriate antibiotic to treat it.

Large doses of antibiotics (often penicillin) must be given by injection or tablet, and an operation to either drain the abscess or remove the tonsil and abscess together. If the pus alone is drained at operation, the tonsils are often removed a few weeks later to prevent a recurrence. Rarely, the infection can spread to the bloodstream to cause septicaemia, but most patients settle well with appropriate treatment.
See also ABSCESS; SEPTICAEMIA; TONSILLITIS

R

RABIES

Rabies is an invariably fatal viral infection spread by animal bites (eg. dog, cat, bat, monkey, rat), that is found throughout Asia, Europe (except Spain, Italy, Scandinavia and Britain), Africa and the Americas, but is not present in Australia and the Pacific. Other forms of the rabies virus have been implicated in rare infections, including a fatal encephalitis that can be caught from infected bats in north-eastern Australia.

The virus responsible is the *Lyssavirus*, which infects the salivary glands of animals, so that any bite causes the injection of the virus into the victim's wound. The incubation period after a bite is three to seven weeks. If possible, the animal causing the bite should be isolated and observed to see if it is affected. The diagnosis can be confirmed by a specific blood test.

The classic symptom is fear of water (hydrophobia) which is due to the severe pain that swallowing any food or liquid causes as a result of muscle spasm in the throat. Further symptoms include skin pain and tingling, generalised muscle spasms, convulsions, the production of copious amounts of thick saliva and eventually muscle paralysis.

First aid after a bite from a possibly infected animal is thorough washing of the wound with soap and water, then drenching the bite in antiseptic (eg. Betadine). If rabies is suspected it is essential for the patient to receive a rabies vaccine because no treatment is available once symptoms appear, and death occurs within two or three days of symptoms appearing.
See also VIRUS

RACE

All humans belong to the one species – Homo sapiens sapiens – and as such can produce offspring that are fertile, no matter which race they come from. Race is a more subtle variation than breed (as in dogs), so a Finn is more closely related to a Pygmy than an Alsatian is to a Dachshund.

It is impossible to tell one race from another by examining the internal organs, or by any blood test or other biological feature. Genetic studies can give some indication of race, but it is really a very subjective determination made on skin colour, facial features and body shape.

Virtually all humans belong to one of three races, with the remainder (less than one in a thousand) being the remnants of ancient aboriginal peoples. An increasing number of people are blends between races, and many people carry genes of a race of which they have no knowledge.

Caucasians make up approximately 60% of the world population, and are native to Europe, North Africa and the Middle East (Arabs), Southern Asia (India, Iran) and western Siberia. By migration, Caucasians have populated most of North and South America, and Australasia. They vary from the fair haired, blue eyed and freckled Scandinavians and Scots to the mid-brown skinned, black haired and brown eyed Ceylonese. They tend to have a moderate beard.

Mongoloids make up approximately 30% of the world population, and are native to Eastern Asia, Japan and Southeast Asia. Pacific islanders and Native Americans are also of Mongoloid origin. Their skin colour is a fairly uniform light brown, and hair is black and straight. Their features vary from the heavy rounded face of the Western Chinese to the more sharply and lightly structured faces of the Indonesians. Beards tend to be scanty.

Negroids make up approximately 10% of the world population, and are native to Africa below the Sahara. Negroids are found in the Americas due to involuntary migration as slaves. Their skin colour varies from the mid brown of the South African Bantu to the jet black of the Sudanese, while their hair is curly and black, and eyes are brown. They often have a strong but curly beard.

Aboriginals make up less than 0.1% of the world population, and the few surviving groups are totally unrelated to each other. Most Aboriginal tribes have been assimilated into other races or annihilated. Examples include the Pygmies of central Africa, the Bushmen of Southern Africa, the natives of New Guinea and the Aborigines of Australia. *See also* GENE

RADIAL KERATOTOMY
See REFRACTIVE SURGERY

RADIATION SICKNESS
A high dose of irradiation from a nuclear reactor accident, the mishandling of radioactive material used in medicine or industry, or an atomic bomb, will damage all body tissues. However, bone marrow, which is responsible for producing cells that maintain the immune system, is particularly susceptible and will cease to function, allowing the body to be overwhelmed by what would otherwise be minor infections. Other vulnerable organs include the liver, lungs, thyroid, testes, ovaries and breasts.

Symptoms may include nausea, vomiting, weakness, delirium, blindness (the cornea of the eye being damaged to cause a cataract), mouth ulcers, bleeding gums, bleeding into the skin (bruises), and convulsions. The testes and ovaries may be affected to cause deformities or infertility. Unborn babies are at particular risk of irradiation, and miscarriages are common. Some body damage may be permanent (eg. skin scarring, thyroid destruction), and there are long-term risks of increased cancer rates. Tests can be performed to assess the function of specific organs and the types of cells present in the blood.

First aid involves removing the patient from the contaminated area, thorough washing, providing fresh uncontaminated clothing, and purging the gut. If evacuation is not immediately practical, place as many walls and objects (eg. upturned table) as possible between the source of radiation and any people. Further treatment involves blood transfusions, marrow transplants and drugs that will remove any inhaled or swallowed radioactive dust from the body. The thyroid gland can be protected by taking high doses of normal iodine in pill form to prevent the thyroid from absorbing any radioactive iodine from the environment.

With time, natural repair of radiation damage is possible, but the risk of death will depend upon the dosage of radiation received.

RADIOGRAPHER
A radiographer is not a doctor but a person who has undertaken tertiary training to perform, but not report on, x-ray examinations. *See also* RADIOLOGY; SONOGRAPHER

RADIOGRAPHY
See RADIOLOGY; X-RAYS

RADIOLOGY
The science of dealing with x-rays, ultrasound, CT and MRI scans is radiology. Doctors specialising in this field are known as radiologists.
See also RADIOGRAPHER; SONOGRAPHER

RADIONUCLIDE SCAN
See NUCLEAR SCAN

RADIOTHERAPY
Radiotherapy had its beginnings when Madame Curie, the discoverer of nuclear radiation, noted the effect that radiation had upon her hands, and theorised on the possibility of these invisible rays being used to destroy unwanted tissue. Radiotherapy is the treatment of disease (usually cancer) with various forms of ionising radiation. Different types of radiation may be used for different degrees of penetration into the tissue. The time of exposure also varies, depending upon the depth and sensitivity of the cancer. Some cancers are known to be very susceptible to irradiation, while others are quite resistant.

Once a patient is diagnosed as having a tumour that is sensitive to radiotherapy, they will be referred to one of the special clinics attached to major hospitals that have the facilities to apply radiotherapy. There the patient is assessed, the location of the cancer is determined, and special marks will be applied to the patient's skin to allow the beam of radiation to be accurately directed at the cancer. The patient is firmly secured to a stretcher so that no movement of the area affected by cancer is possible. Then following the plotted guide lines on the skin, the radiation machine is rotated around the patient to give the maximum possible dose of irradiation to the cancer, while avoiding damage to the skin and other vital internal organs. Depending on the site of the cancer, it may be attacked from only a few directions, or every imaginable direction that is safe. The aim is to destroy the cancer cells and allow the body's natural defence mechanisms and waste clearance cells do the rest of the work.

In other situations, a small amount of radioactive material may be briefly implanted into the cancer within the body, to destroy the surrounding malignant cells.
See also CANCER; X-RAYS

RADIUS

The radius is one of the two bones in the forearm (the ulna is the other one), and runs from the elbow to the wrist. If the arm is held out with the palm facing up, the radius is on the thumb side of the forearm. The radius and ulna can twist around each other to enable the hand to be turned over.
See also BONE; COLLES FRACTURE; WRIST

RAMIPRIL

See ACE INHIBITORS

RAMSAY-HUNT SYNDROME

The Ramsay-Hunt syndrome is the infection of a facial nerve with the virus *Herpes zoster*, which also causes chickenpox and shingles.

Shingles may affect any nerve leading out from the brain or spinal cord, but if the nerve affected (the geniculate ganglion) is the one supplying the ear and face, the patient will develop this syndrome.

It causes severe earache, dizziness, and a painful blistering rash across the upper face and ear. No investigations are normally necessary, but if required the diagnosis can be confirmed by taking special swabs from a sore.

Antiviral medication (eg. aciclovir, valaciclovir) must be taken as soon as the shingles starts, to prevent its spread. Steroids may also be used to reduce complications, but permanent deafness and dizziness can result if treatment starts too late.
See also CHICKENPOX; SHINGLES; VIRUS

RANITIDINE

See H2 RECEPTOR ANTAGONISTS

RANULA

A ranula also has many other names including the almost unpronounceable one of ptyalocele, as well as sialocele and sublingual cyst. It is a cyst forming in the submental salivary gland that lies under the front of the tongue.

There are two forms of ranula – simple or plunging. Simple ranulas are located in the floor of the mouth, while plunging ranulas track down the front of the neck. Simple ranulas are caused by obstruction to the outlet duct from the salivary gland, or sometimes due to an injury to the mouth, while plunging ranulas are usually a developmental abnormality in children.

A lump may be felt in the floor of the mouth at the point where it meets the tongue, and may also be apparent under the chin. The lump may be painful or painless. A plunging ranula also causes a swelling on the front of the neck that may vary in size. Both types may become infected and painful and very rarely, a plunging ranula may become cancerous. Thick saliva can be obtained if a needle is put into the cyst, and an ultrasound of the neck may be used to diagnose a plunging ranula.

Surgical excision of the cyst is the only treatment, and this may involve quite intricate surgery in the case of a plunging ranula.
See also NECK LUMP; SALIVARY GLAND; SALIVARY GLAND PAIN; SIALITIS

RAPE

Rape is the sexual penetration of the vagina, anus or mouth of a woman by a man without her consent. Rarely, a woman may rape a man. The penetration may be by a man's penis or hand, or with an object, and is always a terrifying experience for the victim, despite sometimes appearing to co-operate in order to save themselves from further injury or even death.

Most rape victims know their assailant, while rape by a total stranger is relatively uncommon. Rape may occur within a marriage. Fewer than 10% of rape victims receive physical injuries that require medical treatment, and fewer than 20% of victims report their rape to police, because of the further mental trauma that questioning, medical examination and court appearances would involve.

Rapists have a desire to wield power over their victim by demonstrating their strength and sexual potency. A man may feel downtrodden by women in general, or by a particular woman, and use a hostile act to show in his mind that he is actually dominant over a woman who may be more attractive, intelligent or capable. His main aim may be to humiliate the woman. The bravado of groups of young men who may be intoxicated and determined to show off their supposed domination over women may also lead to rape.

There is a fallacious belief amongst a minority of men that women secretly want to be raped and enjoy it. This is most definitely not the case.

All rape victims suffer from some form of psychological stress after the event, and even if they do not see the police, should seek professional counselling from a doctor or psychologist, who will treat them in the strictest confidence. Sexually transmitted diseases and pregnancy should also be excluded.

Psychological support from professionals and family will be necessary for many months after the rape in order to enable the woman to continue in society without fear and establish normal intimate relationships in the future.
See also INCEST; POST TRAUMATIC STRESS DISORDER; VIOLENCE

RAPHE
The raphe is the ridge of skin separating the two halves of the body, that runs in men from the base of the penis to the anus and separates the scrotum into its two halves, and in women runs from the back of the vulva to the anus.
See also PERINEUM; SCROTUM

RAPID BREATHING
See BREATHING, RAPID

RASH
See BLISTERS; BROWN PATCHES ON SKIN; DERMATITIS; ECZEMA; FACE RED; JAUNDICE; LIGHT SENSITIVE SKIN; LINES IN SKIN; PERIORAL DERMATITIS; PSORIASIS; PUSTULES; RED PATCHES ON SKIN; SKIN DEPIGMENTED; SKIN DRY AND SCALY; SKIN ITCH; SKIN LUMPS; SKIN NODULES; SKIN PIGMENTATION EXCESS; SKIN RED; SKIN RED SPOTS; SKIN THICK; SKIN THIN; SKIN ULCER; STRETCH MARKS; WHITE PATCHES ON SKIN
and separate entries for skin diseases.

RAYNAUD'S DISEASE
Raynaud's disease is a widespread constriction of small arteries of unknown cause, but aggravated by cold conditions. The hands go white then blue, swell and become very painful and there is constriction of blood vessels in the feet, face, chest, abdomen and sometimes internal organs. Patients have intense feelings of cold in these areas. Poor blood supply to the fingers and toes may lead to ulceration and eventually gangrene.

A wide range of medications may be used regularly to dilate the constricted arteries.
See also RAYNAUD'S PHENOMENON

RAYNAUD'S PHENOMENON
Raynaud's phenomenon is a distressing spasm of small arteries, almost invariably affecting women. Attacks are usually triggered by cold conditions, such as entering an air-conditioned building or a cold climate. Other triggers may be hormonal changes, stress and anxiety, exercise and some foods. Raynaud's disease is the most common cause, but in most cases no specific cause can be found, although it may be associated with rheumatoid arthritis, CREST syndrome and scleroderma.

The hands go white then blue, swell and become very painful episodically. It usually starts in the teenage years or early twenties, may remain lifelong, and affects one in every five women, but often eases after the menopause.

Patients should keep their hands warm, and alcohol in low doses may be useful. A wide range of tablets and ointments can be used to dilate the tiny arteries in the fingers. As a last resort, operations to cut the nerves that cause the artery spasm can be performed.
See also CREST SYNDROME; RAYNAUD'S DISEASE; SCLERODERMA

RAZOR RASH
Doctors seem to insist that even the simplest medical conditions have technical names, and in the case of razor rash it is pseudofolliculitis barbae. This is a skin irritation of face and neck caused by minor damage to facial hair follicles from the scraping of a razor, and the ingrowing of hairs. It occurs more commonly in people who have curly hair.

An ugly, raised, red, itchy rash develops on the neck and face. Initially, affected men should let the beard grow for a month to eliminate ingrown hairs, then use a polyester skin-cleansing pad twice a day or a moisturising shaving foam, a single blade razor, or shave frequently and as lightly as possible with an

electric razor. They should not stretch the skin when shaving. Astringents and alcohol rubs may harden the skin to prevent the problem, and a mild steroid cream will settle the rash when it flares. As a last resort, they can grow a beard!
See also SKIN

REACTIVE ARTHRITIS
See REITER SYNDROME

REACTIVE DEPRESSION
See DEPRESSION

READING DIFFICULTY
See DYSLEXIA

REAVEN SYNDROME
See SYNDROME X

RECREATIONAL DRUGS
See CANNABIS; COCAINE; ECSTASY; GAMMA-HYDROXYBUTYRATE; HEROIN; KETAMINE; LSD; MARIJUANA; MESCALINE

RECTAL BLEEDING
See COLORECTAL CANCER; FAECES BLOOD; RECTUM

RECTAL CANCER
See COLORECTAL CANCER

RECTAL PROLAPSE
A rectal or anal prolapse is a slippage of part of the lining of the lower gut out through the anus. It tends to occur in babies and the frail elderly who strain at stool with constipation, and severe diarrhoea. Patients develop anal pain, discomfort and constant moistness, and a lump protrudes through the anus. Ulceration and bleeding may occur from the prolapsed bowel, and in severe cases the prolapsed bowel may become gangrenous. Proctoscopy (passing a viewing tube into the anus) may be performed to inspect the rectum (last part of the large intestine).

Surgery is the only way to correct the prolapse, and gives good results.
See also ANUS; PROLAPSE; RECTUM; VAGINAL PROLAPSE

RECTOCOELE
See VAGINAL PROLAPSE

RECTUM
At the bottom of the descending colon is an S-bend called the sigmoid colon, which empties into the last part of the large intestine, the rectum.

Food that cannot be digested or absorbed (faeces), is passed into the rectum for temporary storage. For the first time since the food left the mouth and was passed into the oesophagus, the person has some voluntary control over it. When the rectum is full, it sends messages to the brain, and at a convenient time a conscious decision can be made to expel the waste material through the back passage or anus in a process called defecation. However, if defecation does not take place within a reasonable time and the rectum becomes over full, the involuntary muscles will take over so that the muscle keeping the rectum closed will open and the faeces will be expelled regardless of any effort or will (faecal incontinence).

The conscious control of defecation does not occur in babies but is a response acquired in childhood. For the first couple of years of life, the anal sphincter (ring muscle) opens unconsciously in an involuntary nervous reflex. It is from about the age of two years that the brain is able to exercise conscious control.
See also ANUS; COLON; COLORECTAL CANCER; FAECES; INCONTINENCE OF FAECES; SUPPOSITORY

RECTUS FEMORIS
See QUADRICEPS MUSCLE

RED-BACK SPIDER BITE
See SPIDER BITE

RED BLOOD CELLS
Not surprisingly, the red colour of blood comes from its red blood cells (erythrocytes). The colour is produced by an iron-containing pigment called haemoglobin. Haemoglobin acts as a carrier for oxygen. Red blood cells are shaped like a disc, hollowed out on both sides so that they have as large a surface area as possible. They are the only cells without a nucleus.

As it passes through the lungs, one cell can attract as many as four oxygen molecules from the air that has been breathed in. Haemoglobin also attracts carbon dioxide so that, as blood travels through the body, the red blood cells operate a sort of exchange system, dropping off life-giving oxygen and picking up used and toxic carbon dioxide to be discharged in the lungs on the return journey.

The more oxygen the blood is carrying, the redder it is. Blood in the arteries flowing from the lungs, full of oxygen, is bright red, whereas blood in the veins, which has been depleted of oxygen on its journey throughout the body, is more bluish in colour. Interestingly, the red colour can only be seen if there is a lot of blood. If looked at as a smear under a microscope, it appears to be pale yellow.

Every cubic millimetre of blood contains about five million red blood cells. Women have slightly fewer than men. One red blood cell lives for about four months, during which time it will circuit the system about 300 000 times. At the end of this period it will die and eventually be discarded through the bile. New red blood cells are made in the spleen and bone marrow.

See also ANAEMIA; BLOOD; BONE; ESR; POLYCYTHAEMIA RUBRA VERA; SICKLE CELL ANAEMIA; SPLEEN

RED DOTS
See RED PATCHES ON SKIN; SKIN RED DOTS

RED EYE
See EYE RED

RED FACE
See FACE RED

RED NAIL
See NAIL DISCOLOURED; SUBUNGAL HAEMATOMA

RED PATCHES ON SKIN
Tinea is a fungal infection of the skin that may occur almost anywhere on the body, but most commonly on the scalp and in the groin. It starts as a red spot that slowly expands in size to form a red ring (ringworm) with a paler centre that may return to skin colour if the ring becomes very large.

Mycosis fungoides is a severe form of tinea that causes disfiguring raised plaques of red scaling skin.

Psoriasis is a skin disease characterised by plaques of red, scaly skin, most commonly on the elbows, knees and scalp. Guttae psoriasis is a very active form that tends to occur in young people.

Discoid lupus erythematosus is an auto-immune disease (inappropriate rejection of normal body tissue) that varies from the more common systemic lupus erythematosus (SLE) in that there are multiple red patches on the skin, that occur most commonly on the face. The rash is not itchy or sore, but may have a fine scale and there may be permanent scar damage to the affected skin.

Many forms of dermatitis can cause red skin, but the redness is usually diffuse rather than occurring in distinct patches.

See also FACE RED; FLUSH; SKIN RED; SKIN RED SPOTS and separate entries for diseases mentioned above.

RED PATCHES ON TONGUE
See TONGUE DISCOLOURED

RED SKIN
See FACE RED; FLUSH, ABNORMAL; RED PATCHES ON SKIN; SKIN RED

REDUCTIL
See OBESITY

RED URINE
See URINE BLOOD; URINE COLOUR ABNORMAL

REFLEX
Some nervous activity takes place in the spinal cord without involving the brain. These are the spinal reflexes. The best known is the knee-jerk. If your legs are crossed and the upper leg is tapped just below the knee, a sensory impulse will travel along the nerves to the spinal cord and make a connection with a motor nerve which will cause your leg to jerk forward. The brain is aware of what is happening but is not involved in the response.

Other reflexes occur at the elbow, wrist, on the sole of the foot, and even at the point of the chin if they are tapped. More complex reflexes involve sneezing, urinating, and digestion.

See also GASTRO-COLIC REFLEX; NERVOUS SYSTEM; REFLEXES EXCESSIVE; REFLEXES REDUCED; SPINAL CORD

REFLEXES EXCESSIVE

Most people know of the classic reflex which makes a bent knee straighten when the tendon below the knee cap is tapped gently. Doctors perform this test to see if the reflex is normal (slight, smooth straightening of the knee occurs), reduced (no or minimal knee straightening occurs) or excessive (sudden or violent straightening of the knee occurs). A reflex occurs because the sudden tension on the tendon caused by the tapping triggers a sensory nerve that runs to the spinal cord, which in turn triggers a motor nerve to contract a muscle.

Reflexes can be tested at many joints other than the knee, including the ankle, elbow, jaw, wrist, and under the sole.

An excessive reflex may be caused by damage to the spinal cord that runs from the brain down through the vertebrae of the back. If the control of sensory and motor nerves is restricted by damage to the spinal cord from an injury (eg. fractured or dislocated vertebra), tumour, cyst or infection, the nerves performing the reflex action will be able to act without hindrance and control, causing an exaggerated response.

Other causes include an overactive thyroid gland (hyperthyroidism), encephalitis (infection of the brain), and significant anxiety, which may cause generalised muscle tenseness. *See also* REFLEX; SPINAL CORD and separate entries for diseases mentioned above.

REFLEXES REDUCED

Reduced reflexes may be caused by damage to a nerve (neuropathy) that runs between the joint being tested and the spinal cord. The nerve may be pinched as it passes a joint, or affected by pressure from a growth, tumour, scar or even tight clothing. Infections of nerves may also occur.

Tumours or other damage to the nerves that connect the spinal cord to the nerves running to and from the tested joint will affect their function and prevent a reflex from occurring.

Other less common causes include polio (viral infection that causes muscle spasm then paralysis), syphilis in advanced stages, hypothyroidism (underactive thyroid gland) and beriberi (severe lack of vitamin B).

If a muscle is weak for any reason, although the nerves may be normal, the reflex will not occur.
See also MUSCLE WEAKNESS; REFLEX; SPINAL CORD and separate entries for diseases mentioned above.

REFLEX SYMPATHETIC DYSTROPHY SYNDROME

Reflex sympathetic dystrophy syndrome (also known as complex regional pain syndrome type one and Sudeck atrophy) is an over stimulation of the sympathetic nervous system, which controls subconscious bodily functions (eg. sweating), resulting in a self-perpetuating closed cycle of sensory nerves stimulating sympathetic nerves and vice versa. The syndrome is often triggered initially by major injury or surgery to a limb.

Patients experience prolonged exaggerated burning pain associated with very minor injury to affected area, and a hot dry limb initially, that becomes a cold clammy blue limb later. The limb may also be swollen. When the foot is involved, it is known as Sudeck atrophy.

Strong pain-killers, physiotherapy, injections into sympathetic nerves, and medications to reduce the perception of pain (psychotropics) are used in treatment. Unfortunately treatment is often unsatisfactory, but the condition may settle spontaneously after a prolonged period.
See also CAUSALGIA

REFLUX OESOPHAGITIS

Reflux oesophagitis (gastro-oesophageal reflux) is the back flow of acid from the stomach up through a normally closed muscle ring into the lower end of the oesophagus (gullet). It most commonly occurs in babies and overweight elderly men. Some infants have a defect or temporary weakness in the muscle ring at the bottom of the oesophagus. In adults, factors such as obesity, smoking, overeating, a hiatus hernia, rapid eating, alcohol, stress, anxiety, and poor posture may cause the excessive production of acid in the stomach and/or slackness in the muscle ring.

Infants with reflux are in pain, with crying and irritability the main symptoms. Adults experience a burning sensation behind the breast bone (heartburn), a bitter taste on the back of the tongue and burping as gas escapes easily from the stomach. It is often worse at night after a large meal when the patient is lying down. If attacks are regular, ulcers may develop. Complications include scarring and narrowing of the lower end of the oesophagus to the point where it may be difficult to swallow food (Barrett syndrome), severe bleeding from ulcers in the oesophagus, and cancer of the oesophagus.

The reflux can be proved by gastroscopy or a barium meal x-ray.

Most children will grow out of the problem, but to ease the symptoms position the child with head elevated while feeding, give small frequent thickened feeds, burp the baby regularly, loosen the nappy before feeds and do not allow the child to lie flat after a feed. If not adequately helped, preventive medication is given as a mixture.

Treatment in adults involves weight loss, raising the head of the bed, having the main meal in the middle of the day, avoiding bending and heavy lifting, stopping smoking and reducing alcohol. Antacids to reduce the acid concentration in the stomach, and medication to empty the stomach faster (eg. prokinetic agents such as cisapride) and reduce acid production (eg. H2 receptor antagonists and proton pump inhibitors). In resistant cases is it necessary to resort to quite major surgery.

See also BARRETT SYNDROME; CHEST PAIN; H2 RECEPTOR ANTAGONISTS; HEARTBURN; HIATUS HERNIA; MALLORY-WEIS SYNDROME; OESOPHAGUS; PROKINETIC AGENTS; PROTON PUMP INHIBITORS

REFRACTIVE SURGERY

Refractive surgery involves one of a number of procedures on the cornea (transparent front surface of the eye over the pupil) to alter its curvature and correct short or long sightedness. These procedures can revolutionise the vision of a person who is short sighted, but the patient must be at least eighteen years of age, and normally under seventy.

All procedures are expensive and only undertaken after very careful discussion, then mapping and measuring of the eye surface and the degree of vision correction required. The patient usually returns at a later time for the procedure. Both eyes may be done at once, but the eyes must remain bandaged for twelve to twenty-four hours after the procedure. There is often some pain for the first day

after the operation, and the eyes must not be rubbed or knocked for a couple of weeks, but much clearer vision is usually obtained as soon as the eye patches are removed.

Originally radial keratotomy was performed using tiny radial knife cuts, in Russia, but now lasers are used to reshape the cornea.

Laser photorefractive laser keratectomy (PRK) was the next procedure developed. The patient is placed on a table under a computer driven laser machine, and is given a light anaesthetic in order to keep the head and eye totally still. The ophthalmic surgeon then removes the outer surface of the cornea with a fine scalpel, and the laser is applied for thirty to sixty seconds to reshape the deeper layers of the cornea. The cornea usually heals within seventy-two hours, but a haze may develop and persist for a few months. This does not affect vision but sometimes causes glare with lights at night. It may take six months for the eye surface shape to stabilise.

Laser in-situ keratomileusis (LASIK) is the latest and now most common procedure. Up to -16 myopia can be corrected by this technique, and it has less post operative pain and more rapid stabilisation of vision than PRK. Under the same circumstances as PRK, the surgeon lifts a small flap on the surface of the cornea in front of the pupil. The tissue under this is then given a carefully programmed momentary burn with the laser to reshape it to focus the light appropriately. The flap is then replaced and the eye bandaged.

See also EYE; SHORT-SIGHTED; VISION

REGIONAL BLOCK
See LOCAL ANAESTHETIC

REITER SYNDROME

Reiter syndrome (reactive arthritis) is an inflammatory condition involving the eyes, urethra and joints. The cause is unknown, but it is more common in young men, and often follows a bacterial infection.

It has the unusual and apparently unconnected symptoms of conjunctivitis (eye inflammation), urethritis (inflammation of the urine tube – the urethra) and arthritis (joint inflammation). Other symptoms that may occur include mouth ulcers, skin sores, inflammation of the foreskin of the penis and a fever. Rarely, the heart becomes inflamed.

Blood tests are not diagnostic, but indicate

presence of inflammation, and x-rays show arthritis in the joints of the back only after several attacks.

It heals without treatment after a few days or weeks, but the arthritis tends to last longer and recurrences are common. The disease course can be shortened by anti-inflammatory drugs such as indomethacin.
See also ARTHRITIS; CONJUNCTIVITIS; URETHRITIS

REGIONAL ENTERITIS
See CROHN'S DISEASE

RELAPSING FEVER
Relapsing fever is a generalised bacterial infection found worldwide in areas of poor hygiene. It is particularly common in the western United States, but rare in western Europe and Australasia. Several bacteria of the species *Borrelia* are responsible. They spread from rats to man by the bite of a tick, or may spread from man to man by the bite of human body lice.

Some days after being bitten by an infected insect, the patient suddenly develops a fever, chills, nausea, vomiting, rapid heart rate, joint pains, rash and headache. Sometimes they become delirious and hallucinate. The attack stops as suddenly as it started after three to ten days, but relapses occur after one or two weeks. Uncommonly, in the elderly and debilitated, it may be fatal.

It is diagnosed by specific blood tests. Up to a dozen relapses may occur before final recovery, but five is the average, and each subsequent attack is milder than the preceding one. Treatment with appropriate antibiotics cures the infection and stops the relapses.
See also BACTERIA; FEVER

RELAXANTS, MUSCLE
See MUSCLE RELAXANTS

RENAL
Renal is a medical term used when referring to the kidney and its diseases.
See KIDNEY FAILURE, ACUTE;
KIDNEY FAILURE, CHRONIC; KIDNEY STONE

RENAL CALCULUS
See KIDNEY STONE

RENAL COLIC
See KIDNEY STONE

RENAL FAILURE
See KIDNEY FAILURE, ACUTE;
KIDNEY FAILURE, CHRONIC

REPETITIVE STRAIN INJURY
A repetitive strain injury (RSI) or occupational overuse syndrome, is a controversial diagnosis as the symptoms are almost invariably due to a condition such as tenosynovitis, tendinitis, carpal tunnel syndrome, osteoarthritis, rheumatoid arthritis, synovitis or a combination of these. It tends to occur in those undertaking repetitive tasks such as typing, playing the piano, or working on a production line.

Pain, swelling and stiffness of the wrist, elbow or the small joints in the hand occurs. The pain may actually be worse while the patient is at rest and immediately upon returning to work after a break, and may result in long-term stiffness, pain and limited joint movement.

There are no specific tests, and the diagnosis is only made after all other possible conditions have been excluded by x-ray and other investigations.

Treatment involves resting the affected joint in a splint for a short time, altering the type of work undertaken, physiotherapy, alternating heat and cold to the area, and anti-inflammatory medications. A prolonged rest such as a holiday often settles the disorder. Some cases become chronic while others resolve completely after treatment.
See also CARPAL TUNNEL SYNDROME; OSTEOARTHRITIS; RHEUMATOID ARTHRITIS; SYNOVITIS; TENDINITIS; TENOSYNOVITIS

REPLACEMENTS
See HIP REPLACEMENT;
TRANSPLANTS AND IMPLANTS

REPRODUCTIVE SYSTEM
The reproductive systems of the male and female combined are responsible for the perpetuation of the human race, by producing both sperm and eggs (ova), anatomically arranging for a sperm to meet an ova, fertilise it and allow it to grow into an embryo, foetus and finally be born as a new infant.

The male reproductive system consists of

the penis, urethra, prostate gland, vas deferens, seminal vesicles and testicles.

The female reproductive system consists of the vulva, Bartholin's glands, vagina, cervix, uterus, Fallopian tubes and ovaries.
See BARTHOLIN CYST; FALLOPIAN TUBE; OVARY; PENIS; PREGNANCY; PROSTATE GLAND; SEMINAL VESICLE; TESTICLE; URETHRA; UTERUS; VAGINA; VAS DEFERENS; VULVA

RESPIRATORY DISTRESS SYNDROME, ADULT

The adult respiratory distress syndrome is difficulty in breathing in association with severe shock, very low blood pressure, significant blood loss or serious injury. Symptoms include anxiety, shortness of breath, rapid breathing, excess fluid in the lungs and a blue tinge may develop in the skin (cyanosis). Specific blood tests are performed to measure oxygen levels in the blood.

It is managed in a hospital intensive care unit. Doctors must control any bleeding and replace lost blood, give oxygen, ventilate mechanically if necessary, manage body fluids by a drip into a vein and fluid removing medications (diuretics), and prescribe antibiotics to prevent infection.

The prognosis depends on the cause, but recovery is normally expected, although permanent organ damage may occur.
See also LUNG; RESPIRATORY DISTRESS SYNDROME, INFANT; SHOCK

RESPIRATORY DISTRESS SYNDROME, INFANT

Hyaline membrane disease, or infantile respiratory distress syndrome, is a lung disease that occurs only in very premature babies. The more premature the infant, the greater the risk of developing the condition. Of babies born eight weeks premature, 75% will be affected.

Surfactant is a fluid essential within the lungs to enable them to open and fill with air after birth. It is not produced in adequate quantity in some premature babies, so their lungs do not open and they cannot obtain sufficient air and oxygen. The hyaline membrane that lines the tiny airways within the lungs, is responsible for producing surfactant. Hyaline membranes are not anatomical structures but restrictive membranes, formed by proteins exuded from the tiny blood vessels in the immature lungs of premature babies, which decrease the elasticity of the lungs and make breathing more difficult.

The condition develops some hours after birth, when the baby starts to breath rapidly, grunt with each breath, and has very marked movements of the chest and abdomen as it tries to breath. The baby will become blue in colour, and lapse into a coma.

The diagnosis is confirmed by a chest x-ray while a special test performed on a sample of the amniotic fluid in which the baby floats in the womb can assess the risk of developing the disease before birth. It can be prevented if the mother is given an injection of a steroid at least forty-eight hours before the birth. Every effort is made to delay a birth until the forty-eight hours has elapsed.

Once the disease is present, oxygen is given in a humidicrib. Death is common without treatment, but if the baby survives for forty-eight hours, it is almost certain to recover. A small number of children have permanent lung damage.
See also LUNG; PREMATURE BABY; RESPIRATORY DISTRESS SYNDROME, ADULT

RESPIRATORY FUNCTION TESTS

Pulmonary (respiratory) function tests are used to measure how effectively the lungs are working. These tests are useful in determining the severity of diseases such as asthma, chronic bronchitis, emphysema and cystic fibrosis. A wide range of tests are available, ranging from simple ones performed by a general practitioner to very complex ones undertaken in special units or hospitals.
See BLOOD GAS ANALYSIS; PEAK EXPIRATORY FLOW RATE; SLEEP STUDIES; TOTAL LUNG CAPACITY; VITAL CAPACITY

RESPIRATORY SYSTEM

The respiratory system refers to those organs of the body used for breathing. Air enters the upper respiratory system through the nose or mouth and is conveyed by way of the pharynx (throat), larynx (voice box) and trachea (windpipe), through the two bronchial tubes to the lungs. It is in the lungs or lower part of the respiratory system that the oxygen is extracted

RESPIRATORY SYSTEM

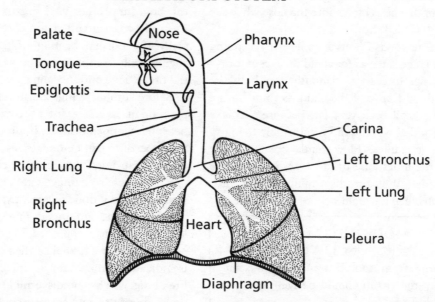

Palate — Nose — Pharynx

Tongue

Epiglottis — Larynx

Trachea — Carina

Right Lung — Left Bronchus

Right Bronchus — Left Lung

Heart — Pleura

Diaphragm

and absorbed into the blood, which in turn is sent to the heart to be pumped throughout the body's cells. At the same time, the waste product, carbon dioxide, is extracted by the lungs from the blood and sent back up through the respiratory system to be exhaled from the body.

The upper respiratory system not only provides a passage for air but also filters it so that impurities and infections are removed before it reaches the lungs where an impurity can have much more serious consequences. The most common problems occur in the upper respiratory system as a result of inhaling infections or allergy-causing substances from the air. Coughs, colds, hay fever and various inflammatory diseases such as sinusitis, pharyngitis and laryngitis keep doctors busy.

Diseases of the lower respiratory tract are more serious and may include asthma, bronchitis, emphysema, pneumonia and rarely tuberculosis.
See also NOSE; PHARYNX; LARYNX; RESPIRATORY FUNCTION TESTS; TRACHEA; LUNG

RESTLESS LEGS SYNDROME

Patients with the restless legs or Wittmaack-Ekbom syndrome have legs that feel as though they want to exercise when the body is trying to rest. The cause is unknown, but it is more common in women, made worse by pregnancy and heat, and is sometimes aggravated by antihistamine medications. It is not related to previous exercise.

When the patient goes to bed, or is resting, they can't get to sleep because they feel that they have to keep moving their legs. It can be helped by keeping the legs cooler than the body, and using paracetamol or a small dose of a mild muscle relaxant such as diazepam (Valium). Unfortunately, getting out of bed and going for a run doesn't help. It is a distressing but not serious problem that often occurs episodically for years, but is usually well controlled by treatment.
See also LEG PAIN

RESUSCITATION

If someone has stopped breathing, it is necessary for someone else to breathe for them. When breathing stops there will be no rise and fall movement of the chest, the face may be a bluish grey colour, and it will not be possible to feel any exhaled breath.

MOUTH TO MOUTH RESUSCITATION

The simplest and most effective form of expired air resuscitation is to exhale breath directly into the victim's lungs, usually by placing the first-aider's mouth over the mouth of the victim and performing mouth-to-mouth resuscitation. For obvious reasons this is also called the kiss of life.

Mouth-to-mouth resuscitation may be inappropriate if the person has facial injuries or their face is covered with poison, or if you are trying to operate in deep water. In this case mouth-to-nose resuscitation can be carried out following the same technique except that air is blown into the nose while the mouth is held shut.

The method of resuscitating a baby or young child is the same as for an adult, except it may be easier to seal your mouth over both the mouth and nose of the child. Do not tip the child's head back very far, because a child's neck and airway are more vulnerable to injury than an adult's. Blow gentle breaths of air into the lungs, one breath every two or three seconds (20-30 breaths a minute). Stop each breath when the child's chest starts to rise.

MOUTH TO MOUTH RESUSCITATION

To perform mouth-to-mouth resuscitation, the victim should be lying on their back. Then: –

- tilt the head backwards by placing one hand beneath the base of the head and lifting upwards
- put your face at right angles to the victim's face so that you have easy access to the mouth and take a deep breath
- pinch the victim's nose shut so that it does not provide an escape route for the air
- seal your lips around the lips of the victim and blow firmly so that your exhaled breath is pushed into the victim's lungs
- look to see if the chest rises. If it does not, check the airway again for any obstructions
- if the chest rises, remove your lips and look to see if the chest falls. At the same time, place your ear close to the mouth and listen for air leaving the lungs
- repeat the procedure again for four or five quick breaths
- feel the victim's neck pulse. If it is present, continue at the rate of one breath approximately every four seconds. If you cannot feel the neck pulse, start external cardiac compression (see below).

EXTERNAL CARDIAC COMPRESSION

External cardiac (heart) compression is a technique used to restart a heart that has stopped beating, and to maintain circulation so that damage caused by lack of oxygen to the brain and other vital organs is avoided. Basically it is intended to reproduce artificially the normal beating of the heart by rhythmically compressing the heart between the breastbone and the spine.

Before administering external cardiac compression it is important to ensure that the heart has stopped beating. If it is still beating, the procedure can be dangerous, even to the point of causing death. External cardiac compression can also damage vital organs as well as the ribcage if done incorrectly, so it should usually not be attempted unless you have learned how at an approved first aid course.

The need for external cardiac compression is indicated if the victim is unconscious, not breathing, and has no discernible pulse. Generally mouth-to-mouth resuscitation will be tried first. If the victim still shows no sign of life when the neck pulse is checked after the first five breaths, you should apply external cardiac compression together with the resuscitation. External cardiac compression must always be combined with mouth-to-mouth resuscitation.

CARDIOPULMONARY RESUSCITATION

Cardiopulmonary resuscitation (CPR) is a combination of expired air resuscitation and external cardiac compression. Essentially, it takes over both breathing and circulation in a person whose body has stopped carrying out these functions itself. It keeps vital organs supplied with oxygen and thus prevents death or brain damage. Although brain damage and death usually occur within three to six minutes there are cases where breathing and circulation have stopped for longer than this and the person has survived (usually young people and in very low temperatures), so CPR should always be administered.

It is possible for CPR to be undertaken by one person alone who alternates the two forms of resuscitation, carrying out expired air respiration for a period and then external cardiac compression before returning again to expired air respiration, and so on. However, it is difficult and tiring, and it is far better if two people can work together, one on the airway and one on the heart.

Anyone proposing to give CPR should first check the victim's neck pulse. This is located

CARDIOPULMONARY RESUSCITATION

To perform cardiopulmonary resuscitation, the victim should be lying on their back. Then: –

- check that the airway is clear, and tilt the head back so that the passage to the lungs is unrestricted
- place the heel of one hand on the middle of the lower half of the breastbone, keeping the palm and fingers raised clear of the chest. Place the heel of the second hand on top. With the arms straight, press down firmly so that the breastbone is depressed 4-5cm. Keeping the hands in position, release the pressure
- repeat fifteen times, faster than one compression per second (about five compressions in three seconds)
- give two mouth-to-mouth breaths (see above)
- give another fifteen chest compressions;
- continue with a pattern of fifteen compressions to two mouth-to-mouth breaths;
- after one minute, check the neck pulse. If it has returned, stop the compression immediately
- if the neck pulse cannot be felt, continue with the compression and check the pulse every two or three minutes. Stop as soon as the heart starts beating again.
- continue mouth-to-mouth resuscitation until the victim can breathe alone

between the Adam's apple and the large muscle running up the side of the neck. If there is no sign of a heartbeat, CPR is indicated.

The same techniques of CPR can be used on babies and young children, but the breastbone should be depressed only 1cm. in the case of a baby and 2cm. in the case of a child. It is only necessary to use one hand to press down on the chest of a child, and two fingers are sufficient for a baby.
See also ARTERIAL PRESSURE POINTS; BLEEDING; FIRST AID; NOSEBLEED; VOMITING BLOOD.

RETARDED
See MENTAL RETARDATION

RETINA
See EYE

RETINAL DETACHMENT
The light-sensitive retina at the back of the eye is loosely attached to the eyeball, but if it detaches from the back of the eye, full or partial blindness results. It may occur very slowly over a period of years, or be complete in a few minutes. The retina may detach if a blood vessel ruptures and bleeds behind the retina, if the fluid in the eye leaks behind the retina, if the eye is injured, or if there is high blood pressure or a tumour in the eye. Marfan syndrome is a rare cause, but frequently there is no obvious cause.

The patient describes a black curtain slowly moving across the field of vision, as the retina progressively lifts away from the eyeball and causes at first partial, and later complete blindness. The detachment can be seen by examining the eye with an ophthalmoscope (small magnifying glass attached to a light).

Rapid treatment is essential to save the sight. A surgical procedure, or a laser that is shone in short, sharp, accurately aimed bursts into the eye, are used to seal the retina back onto the eyeball. Ninety-five percent of retinal detachments can now be cured or controlled if treated immediately they occur.
See also BLINDNESS; EYE

RETINAL DETACHMENT DUE TO BLEED BEHIND RETINA

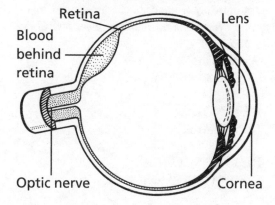

Retina · Lens · Blood behind retina · Optic nerve · Cornea

RETINITIS PIGMENTOSA
Retinitis pigmentosa is an inherited disease of the light-sensitive cells in the retina at the back of the eye that passes from one generation to

the next. It starts with night blindness in childhood, and slowly progresses to cause near total blindness in old age. The retinal cells steadily deteriorate, and pigmented cells replace them. The degeneration starts at the edge of the retina and progressively moves towards the centre. The field of vision slowly decreases until the patient can only see straight ahead as though through a tunnel, and has no peripheral vision.

The retina has a characteristic pigmented appearance when viewed by a magnifying light (ophthalmoscope).

No treatment is available, and the condition is slowly progressive over many years.
See also BLINDNESS; EYE

RETINOBLASTOMA
A retinoblastoma is cancer of the retina (light sensitive cells at the back of the eye) that usually occurs in children under three years of age. There is a familial (inherited tendency) in 40% of cases, but cause in others is unknown.

The pupil becomes white, a squint develops, the affected eye bulges forward, becomes reddened and the vision is affected. The cancer may spread (metastasise) from the eye along the optic (vision) nerve to the brain.

It is diagnosed by examining the eye with a magnifying light (ophthalmoscope) and a CT scan.

Small tumours may be treated by laser or chemotherapy (medication), but most are not diagnosed until large, and the eye must be removed. The prognosis depends on the size of the tumour at time of diagnosis. Survival rate with no spread is 85%, but this drops dramatically if cancer cells are found in the optic nerve. The overall five-year survival rate is about 70%.
See also CANCER; EYE;
NEUROSURGERY

RETINOL
See VITAMIN A

RETINOSCOPE
See OPHTHALMOSCOPY

RETROGRADE EJACULATION
See EJACULATION RETROGRADE

RETROGRADE PYELOGRAM
See INTRAVENOUS PYELOGRAM

REVERSIBLE INHIBITORS OF MONOAMINE OXIDASE
See ANTIDEPRESSANTS

REYE SYNDROME
Reye syndrome is a rare brain and liver inflammation that is more common in children under six years of age, and is named after the Australian pathologist who first described it. The cause is unknown, but it sometimes follows the use of aspirin in children. It also invariably follows two to three weeks after a viral infection such as influenza, chickenpox or a cold.

Liver failure and brain inflammation (encephalitis) occur, that cause vomiting, mental confusion and convulsions.

No specific treatment is available, but attempts are made to control the brain swelling and assist breathing. There is a death rate in excess of 30% and it is often rapidly fatal. Permanent liver or brain damage may occur in survivors.
See also ASPIRIN; ENCEPHALITIS

RHABDOMYOLYSIS
Rhabdomyolysis is commonly known as the muscle meltdown disease, and is a form of muscle destruction caused by massive overuse. In conditions of extreme exertion, when a muscle is forced to work despite an inadequate blood supply of oxygen and energy, the muscle will briefly use its own material as an energy source and destroy itself.

The athlete suddenly collapses during extreme exertion and is unable to use affected muscles, which become excruciatingly painful. The muscle is permanently damaged and is replaced by scar tissue or fat. No treatment is available.
See also MUSCLE

RHEUMATIC FEVER
Rheumatic fever is a damaging inflammation of the heart valves that follows some types of bacterial infections and was common before antibiotics were readily available, but is now rare in developed countries.

Patients have two or more of a number of widely different symptoms, so every case is completely different. Symptoms include inflammation of the heart and its valves, a rapid pulse, irregular heart beat, irregular shaped red patches and rings on the skin, chorea (uncontrolled twitching of the arms, legs and face), fever, and arthritis that moves from one large joint to another. In 70% of patients it causes permanent damage to heart valves which leak and fail in later life, and are susceptible to infection (endocarditis). All patients who have had rheumatic fever must take antibiotics whenever they have any dental treatment or operation.

The diagnosis is confirmed by blood tests, and an electrocardiogram (ECG), then antibiotics (commonly penicillin) are given to remove any remaining bacterial infection, aspirin to reduce fever and joint pains, and strict bed rest is ordered for several weeks or months.

The condition may last a few weeks to months, with children taking far longer to recover than adults. A significant number of patients have recurrences for years afterwards. 98% of patients recover from the first attack, but multiple repeat attacks may lead to death from heart damage.

See also ENDOCARDITIS; HEART; SYDENHAM'S CHOREA

RHEUMATISM

Rheumatism is not a disease, but an obsolete term used by patients to indicate generalised muscle and joint pains. It may be confused with rheumatic fever, rheumatoid arthritis and polymyalgia rheumatica.

See also ARTHRITIS; BACK PAIN; KNEE PAIN; RHEUMATIC FEVER; RHEUMATOID ARTHRITIS; POLYMYALGIA RHEUMATICA

RHEUMATOID ARTHRITIS

Rheumatoid arthritis is an inflammatory autoimmune disease that affects the entire body, and is not limited to the joints. The immune system is triggered off inappropriately, and the body starts to reject its own tissue. The main effect is inflammation (swelling and redness) of the smooth moist synovial membrane that lines the inside of joints. Those most affected are the hands and feet.

It tends to run in families from one generation to the next, and a viral infection or stress may trigger the onset. It occurs in one in every 100 people, females are three times more frequently affected than males, and it usually starts between twenty and forty years of age. A juvenile form is known as Still's disease.

Initial symptoms are very mild, with early morning stiffness in the small joints of the hands and feet, loss of weight, a feeling of tiredness and being unwell, pins and needles sensations, sometimes a slight intermittent fever, and gradual deterioration over many years. Occasionally the disease has a sudden onset with severe symptoms flaring in a few days, often after emotional stress or a serious illness. As the disease worsens, it causes increasing pain and stiffness in the small joints, progressing steadily to larger joints, the back being only rarely affected. The pain becomes more severe and constant, and the joints become swollen, tender and deformed. Additional effects can include wasting of muscle, lumps under the skin, inflamed blood vessels, heart and lung inflammation, an enlarged spleen (Felty syndrome) and lymph nodes, dry eyes and mouth, and changes to cells in the blood.

It is diagnosed by specific blood tests, x-rays, examination of joint fluid and the clinical findings. The level of indicators in the blood stream can give doctors a gauge to measure the severity of the disease and the response to treatment.

The condition requires constant care by doctors, physiotherapists and occupational therapists. The severity of cases varies greatly, so not all treatments are used in all patients, and the majority will only require minimal care.

In acute stages, general physical and emotional rest and splinting of the affected joints are important. Physiotherapists undertake regular passive movement of the joints to prevent permanent stiffness developing, and apply heat or cold as appropriate to reduce the inflammation.

In chronic stages, carefully graded exercise under the care of a physiotherapist is used. Medications for the inflammation include aspirin and other anti-inflammatory drugs. Steroids such as prednisone give dramatic, rapid relief from all the symptoms, but they may have long-term side effects (eg. bone and skin thinning, fluid retention, weight gain, peptic ulcers, lowered resistance to infection, etc.), and their use must balance the benefits against the risks. In some cases, steroids may be injected into a particularly troublesome joint. A number of unusual drugs are also used, including gold by injection or tablet, antimalarial drugs (eg. chloroquine) penicillamine (not the antibiotic), and cell-destroying drugs (cytotoxics). Surgery to specific painful joints can be useful in a limited number of patients.

There is no cure, but effective control is available for most patients, and the disease tends to burn out and become less debilitating in old age. Some patients have irregular acute attacks throughout their lives, while others may have only one or two acute episodes at times of physical or emotional stress. Yet others steadily progress until they become totally crippled by the disease.
See also ANTIRHEUMATICS; ARTHRITIS; AUTOIMMUNE DISEASES; FELTY SYNDROME; NONSTEROIDAL ANTI-INFLAMMATORY DRUGS; STEROIDS; STILL'S DISEASE

RHIN-
'Rhin-' is a prefix used in medical terms to indicate a reference to the nose.

RHINITIS
Rhinitis is a term used to indicate any form of inflammation of the moist membrane (nasal mucosa) lining the inside of the nose.
See also HAY FEVER; NOSE DISCHARGE; VASOMOTOR RHINITIS

RHINOPHYMA
Rhinophyma is a severe form of rosacea affecting the nose that usually occurs in men. There is an increase in size of the nose due to a dramatic enlargement of the oil glands in the skin and excessive deposition of fat and other tissue under the skin. In advanced cases it becomes very disfiguring and gives the appearance of a large growth on the nose.

A skin biopsy is sometimes necessary to confirm diagnosis, then plastic surgery can be performed to remove the excess tissue. Patients obtain reasonable results from surgery.
See also NOSE; ROSACEA

RHINOVIRUS
See COLD, COMMON

RHYTHM METHOD
See NATURAL FAMILY PLANNING

RIB
Each rib is a long, thin curved strip of bone. There are twelve ribs on each side of the chest in both sexes, despite Old Testament stories to

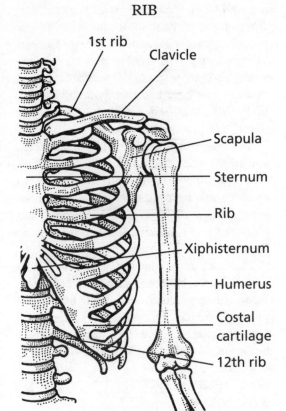

RIB

1st rib
Clavicle
Scapula
Sternum
Rib
Xiphisternum
Humerus
Costal cartilage
12th rib

the contrary. The top ten ribs are attached by strips of cartilage (costal cartilages) to the side of the sternum (breast bone). The eleventh and twelfth ribs are unattached at their front ends and are referred to as floating ribs.

The back end of each rib joins to one of the twelve thoracic vertebrae in the spine.

The ribs protect the heart and lungs, and enable expansion of the chest when breathing.

When broken, a rib may pierce into the lungs to cause serious damage or, lower down, the liver or spleen may be torn. In the vast majority of cases, broken ribs do not damage deeper structures, but remain painful for six to eight weeks until healed by time and rest.
See also SPINE; STERNUM

RIBOSOME
See CELL

RIBOFLAVINE
See VITAMIN B

RIB PAIN
See CHEST PAIN

RICKETS

Rickets is a rare disease in developed countries, but growing children in poorer countries may develop rickets if they have an inadequate intake of vitamin D. This vitamin is essential for the body to absorb calcium, which is the main constituent of bone. Vitamin D is obtained from dairy products (milk, cheese, yoghurt, etc.), eggs and fish, and can also be formed in the body by the action of sunlight on certain substances in the skin. In adults the same condition is known as osteomalacia.

Children with rickets have soft bones and grow slowly. The legs tend to bow outwards because of walking on the soft long bones of the legs, and there are abnormalities in the growth of the ribs, and excessive enlargement of the forehead may occur. Patients may also be 'double-jointed', with slack ligaments around the joints, and may have weak muscles. Any bone deformity that occurs may become permanent, resulting in premature arthritis.

Measurement of calcium and vitamin D levels in the blood and x-rays of long bones can be used to confirm the diagnosis. It is easily treated by supplying adequate amounts of vitamin D in the diet. No further damage is likely once a good diet is started.
See also BONE; OSTEOMALACIA; VITAMIN D

RICKETTSIAL INFECTIONS

Rickettsiae are a class of bacteria that are commonly found in the gut of lice, mites, ticks and fleas. They can spread to humans who are bitten by these insects, and cause diseases such as Q fever, rickettsialpox, Rocky Mountain spotted fever and typhus. Most forms respond to antibiotics such as tetracyclines.
See also BACTERIA; Q FEVER; RICKETSIALPOX; TETRACYCLINES; TYPHUS

RICKETSIALPOX

Rickettsialpox is an uncommon mild infection caused by the primitive bacteria *Rickettsia akar,* which has widespread effects. It passes from mice to humans through a mite bite in overcrowded unhygienic conditions. The incubation period is seven to twelve days.

The symptoms are a sudden onset of fever, chills, a single red lump on the skin at site of mite bite, headache and widespread muscular and joint pains. Two to four days later swelling of skin occurs with chickenpox-like blisters on the affected skin. It can be diagnosed by specific blood tests, and treated by tetracycline antibiotic tablets. Complete recovery is normal.
See also RICKETTSIAL INFECTIONS

RIDGED NAILS
See NAIL RIDGE

RIEDEL THYROIDITIS

Riedel thyroiditis is a rare form of inflammation involving the thyroid gland at the front of the neck. The normal structure of the thyroid is replaced by hard fibrous scar tissue for no known reason.

The gland becomes irregularly enlarged, inadequate thyroid hormone is produced and the patient develops a slow heart beat, dry skin, cold intolerance and other symptoms of hypothyroidism (thyroid failure). Other effects are caused by the enlargement of the gland and include difficulty in swallowing, shortness of breath and hoarseness, and it is often associated with other widespread organ damage. It is diagnosed by blood tests and thyroid gland biopsy.

Treatment is satisfactory and involves partial removal of the gland by surgery and taking thyroid hormone tablets long term.
See also de QUERVAIN THYROIDITIS; HASHIMOTO THYROIDITIS; HYPOTHYROIDISM; THYROID GLAND; THYROIDITIS

RIFAMPICIN
See TUBERCULOSIS MEDICATIONS

RIGHT HEART FAILURE
See COR PULMONALE

RIGIDITY
See MUSCLE STIFFNESS AND/OR RIGIDITY

RIGOR
See CONVULSION; SHIVER

RIGOR MORTIS

When someone dies, the muscles will start to contract and stiffen one to seven hours later depending on the temperature. The first muscles to be affected are the ones in the neck and lower jaw. This phenomenon is known

rigor mortis. The effect disappears after one to seven days as decomposition begins.
See also MUSCLE

RILEY-DAY SYNDROME

Riley-Day syndrome is an uncommon familial (runs in families from one generation to the next) syndrome that occurs in Jews of Middle Eastern extraction. Its symptoms include a lack of tears in the eyes, excessive sweating, intermittent fevers and episodes of low body temperature, blood pressure swings between being too high and too low, the surface of the eye may feel no pain, and generally patients feel only the most severe pains. As a result they may have fractures and other injuries of which they have no knowledge. Less commonly, they may have poor coordination, difficulty in swallowing, difficulty in talking, and extreme mood swings. They may suffer serious personal injury, particularly to the eye resulting in blindness. No treatment is available.
See also BLOOM SYNDROME

RIMA

See ANTIDEPRESSANTS

RINGWORM

Ringworm is not a worm infestation, but the term is used to describe any fungal infection of the skin, as they often create a ring shaped rash. The term 'tinea' may be used for fungal infection involving skin, hair or nails.
See also FUNGI; TINEA CORPORIS; TINEA CRURIS; TINEA MANUM

RITTER DISEASE

See SCALDED SKIN SYNDROME

RIVER BLINDNESS

See ONCHOCERCIASIS

RIZATADINE

See H2 RECEPTOR ANTAGONISTS

RODENT ULCER

See BASAL CELL CARCINOMA

ROENTGEN, WILHELM

Wilhelm Roentgen was born in 1845 in Würzburg, Germany, and was the discoverer of x-rays. The unit of dose for x-rays is named after him.
See also X-RAYS

ROFECOXIB

See NONSTEROIDAL ANTI-INFLAMMATORY DRUGS

ROHYPNOL

See SEDATIVES

ROSACEA

Acne rosacea is a skin disease of the face, of no known cause, found most commonly in middle-aged women. Patients develop intermittent flushing of the face that becomes a permanent redness of the facial skin. After a few days or weeks, sores similar to a severe case of acne develop. In advanced cases, the surface of the eyes may be involved in a form of conjunctivitis. Treatment involves antibiotic tablets (eg. tetracycline, erythromycin) and/or metronidazole gel applied to the affected skin. Both must be continued for two or three months. Relapses are common for years afterwards, but if medication is used immediately, it suppresses each attack effectively and, with good treatment, eventually a cure can be expected.
See also ANTIANAEROBES; MACROLIDES; RHINOPHYMA; TETRACYCLINES

ROSEA

See PITYRIASIS ROSEA

ROSEOLA INFANTUM

Roseola infantum (baby measles or exanthem subitum) is a contagious viral infection that is caught by virtually every child in the first two or three years of life. It has an incubation period from seven to seventeen days, and most children will have such a mild attack that it will be passed off as a slight cold. Those with a severe attack will develop a fever and a measles-like rash on the trunk and neck, which usually appears after the fever has gone. No treatment is necessary other than paracetamol for the fever, and the child recovers completely within two or three days.
See also GERMAN MEASLES; MEASLES; VIRUS

ROSS RIVER FEVER

The Ross River fever, or epidemic polyarthritis, is a generalised viral infection found throughout northern Australia, in the NSW Riverina irrigation area, New Guinea, Solomon Islands,

Samoa and Fiji. The responsible virus is transmitted by mosquitoes between animals (possibly bats) and humans. It is named after the river running through Townsville in north Queensland.

Symptoms may include fevers, muscle aches, arthritis (particularly of the hands and feet), swollen joints, headaches, swollen tender lymph nodes, poor appetite, nausea, flu-like symptoms, tiredness and a rash occurs in some patients. Symptoms worsen with age and children may be infected without having symptoms, but still act as reservoirs for further spread of the disease. It can be diagnosed by a specific blood test.

Aspirin and anti-inflammatory medications to ease pain and remove the fever are the only treatments, but it can be prevented by control of mosquitoes, insect repellents, window screens and protective clothing. There is no cure, and it may be debilitating for months and recur repeatedly when the patient becomes run-down.
See also ARTHRITIS; BARMAH FOREST VIRUS

ROTATOR CUFF SYNDROME
The shoulder can move through a greater range than any other joint in the body because the socket of this ball-and-socket joint is very shallow, but as a result, the joint is very unstable and dislocates easily. To stabilise the joint, a number of muscles and tendons crowd around the joint as a 'cuff' of firm tissue, inside which the shoulder can still freely rotate. The rotator cuff syndrome may occur as a result of any tear, stretching or rupture of the muscles, ligaments or tendons forming the rotator cuff around the shoulder joint, due to an obvious injury, overuse or ageing.

Pain and tenderness around the shoulder joint are the main symptoms. Depending upon the muscles injured, some movements of the joint may be very painful, while others cause no discomfort.

Treatment is a combination of rest, physiotherapy, anti-inflammatory medications, and in severe cases injections of steroids and anaesthetics into the affected muscles. If a muscle or tendon is torn badly or completely ruptured, surgery to repair the damage will be necessary. Recovery is normally slow but complete.
See also PAINFUL ARC SYNDROME; SHOULDER

ROTAVIRUS
See GASTROENTERITIS

ROTOR SYNDROME
The Rotor syndrome is a hereditary cause of yellow skin (jaundice) in a newborn infant. All liver function tests and liver biopsy are normal except for high levels of bilirubin. No treatment is necessary, and complete recovery is normal within a week or so.
See also DUBIN-JOHNSON SYNDROME

ROUNDED NAIL
See FINGER TIPS SWOLLEN

ROUND LIGAMENT
See UTERUS

ROUNDWORM
Most roundworms (nematodes) are free living worms, but some may infect the human gut and may spread to other tissues. Infections with roundworms are widespread in Asia, Africa and other less developed areas.
See also ASCARIASIS; CUTANEOUS LARVA MIGRANS; HOOKWORM; TRICHINOSIS; VISCERAL LARVA MIGRANS

ROXITHROMYCIN
See MACROLIDES

ROYAL FREE DISEASE
See CHRONIC FATIGUE SYNDROME

RSI
See REPETITIVE STRAIN INJURY

RUBEFACIENTS
See LINIMENT

RUBELLA
See GERMAN MEASLES

RUBENSTEIN-TAYBI SYNDROME
The Rubenstein-Taybi syndrome is a developmental abnormality of numerous structures that may be hereditary or occur spontaneously as a congenital malformation. Patients have under-developed cheek bones, broad thumbs and toes, slanted eyes, patent ductus arteriosus, heart malformations, and mild to moderate subnormal mentality.

There is no cure, but surgery is performed for heart and cosmetic deformities. Patients

have a reasonable life span provided the heart abnormalities are not severe.
See also MENTAL RETARDATION; PATENT DUCTUS ARTERIOSUS

RUBEOLA
See MEASLES

RUPTURED EAR DRUM
See TYMPANIC RUPTURE

RUSSELL-SILVER SYNDROME
The Russell-Silver syndrome is a form of dwarfism due to retarded development of growth plates at bone ends in the arms and legs. It is sporadically inherited within families. Babies are small at birth, have reduced growth, significant variation in size between left and right sides of body which tends to correct itself with growth, early onset of puberty and brown spots on the skin. Some patients may have an incurved and short little finger, down turning at the corner of the mouth, triangular shaped face, webbed toes, mental retardation, and kidney and penis abnormalities. X-rays show bone growth plate abnormalities. There is no cure, but growth and appearance improve in adolescence. Unfortunately, 10% develop Wilms' tumour.
See also GROWTH REDUCED; WILMS' TUMOUR

Rx
See EYE OF HORUS

S

SABIN VACCINE
See POLIO; VACCINATION OF CHILDREN

SACRUM
See PELVIS; SPINE

SAD
See DEPRESSION; SOCIAL ANXIETY DISORDER

SADISM
Sadism is a psychiatric disturbance in which a patient gains pleasure and enjoyment from inflicting pain or humiliation on others.
See also SEXUAL SADISM; VIOLENCE

St. VITUS DANCE
See SYDENHAM'S CHOREA

SALICYLATES
See ANALGESICS; LINIMENT; NONSTEROIDAL ANTI-INFLAMMATORY DRUGS

SALICYLIC ACID
See ACIDS; KERATOLYTICS

SALIVARY GLAND
The saliva that comes into the mouth when smelling or eating food is produced by six glands, three on each side of the mouth. The two parotid glands sit under the angle of the jaw, while the two submandibular and two submental glands are in the soft tissue under the chin.

The parotid glands have a duct each that opens into the back of the mouth near the base of the tongue. The four other glands have ducts that join up on each side of the mouth to open under the tongue.

When food is expected by the brain, it stimulates these glands to produce saliva, so that the mouth becomes moist in preparation. In animals, this may result in drooling. The saliva contains enzymes that commence the digestion of the food, as well as lubricating the mouth and easing the passage of the food down the throat.
See also MOUTH; MOUTH, DRY; MUMPS; PAROTID TUMOUR; RANULA; SALIVARY GLAND PAIN

SALIVARY GLAND PAIN
There are six salivary glands, three on each side on the inside the jaw bone. From back to front they are called the parotid, submandibular and submental glands.

In years past, mumps was by far the most common cause of painful, enlarged salivary glands (particularly the parotid glands), but with widespread vaccination of children against the disease since the early 1980s it is now an uncommon disease.

Parotitis is a viral or bacterial infection of the parotid glands, while sialitis is an infection of any of the salivary glands. Other symptoms include fever and redness over the affected gland.

If a salivary gland is damaged or infected or the saliva becomes too concentrated because of dehydration, or often for no apparent reason, a stone may form in the gland and block the narrow duct that leads from the gland into the mouth. Only one gland is involved, and this becomes excruciatingly painful and very swollen. The pain worsens with any salivation on eating or even smelling food.

Other possible causes of salivary gland pain include mixed parotid tumours, cancer of the salivary glands, Sjögren syndrome (an autoimmune disease), sarcoidosis, a ranula (salivary cyst) and tuberculosis.
See also LYMPH NODES ENLARGED AND/OR PAINFUL; SALIVARY GLAND and separate entries for diseases mentioned above.

SALIVARY STONE
The formation of a stone in a saliva-producing gland in the mouth is uncommon.

Under the tongue and in the side of the jaw there are six salivary glands, three on each side (the parotid glands at the angle of the jaw, submandibular glands under the side of the jaw, and submental glands under the chin). A small tube leads from each gland to open into the mouth under the tongue or at the back corner of the mouth. They produce saliva to keep the mouth moist and to start the digestion of food. If a salivary gland becomes infected or injured, or the saliva becomes too concentrated, a stone may form in the gland.

If a stone is present, salivation at the sight, smell or taste of food causes excruciating pain as the pressure of saliva behind the stone moves it in the delicate duct. Sialitis (salivary gland infection) and abscess formation in the gland may be complications.

The diagnosis can be confirmed by a special x-ray of the salivary gland after a passing a fine tube into its duct through the opening into the mouth.

Medication is given to temporarily dry up the saliva and ease the pain, followed by surgery to remove the stone.
See also PAROTID TUMOUR; SALIVARY GLAND; SALIVARY GLAND PAIN; SIALITIS

SALMONELLOSIS
See TYPHOID FEVER

SALPINGITIS
Salpingitis is a bacterial infection of the Fallopian tubes that lead from the ovaries to the uterus. Numerous sexually transmitted bacteria may be responsible, including *Chlamydia trachomatis* and *Neisseria gonorrhoea*.

Affected women develop a pain low in the abdomen, fevers, a vaginal discharge, abnormal menstrual periods and pain with intercourse. With repeated or prolonged infection, the Fallopian tubes may be damaged so eggs have difficulty in passing down to the uterus, resulting in infertility, or fertilised eggs may implant in the tube as an ectopic pregnancy (pregnancy that develops outside the uterus).

Blood tests and vaginal examination are performed, and vaginal swabs are taken, to determine which bacteria are present and the appropriate antibiotics that should be taken by tablet or injection to clear the infection. Sex should be avoided until the infection is cured.

Up to one quarter of affected women will have continuing problems including repeat infections, infertility, ectopic pregnancies, persistent pelvic pain and painful sex.
See also ECTOPIC PREGNANCY; FALLOPIAN TUBE; GONORRHOEA; PELVIC INFLAMMATORY DISEASE; VENEREAL DISEASES

SARCOIDOSIS
Sarcoidosis is an uncommon disease which causes damage and inflammation to a wide range of organs within the body, but most commonly to the lungs. The cause is unknown, but women are more commonly affected than men, and the usual age of onset is forty to sixty years.

The symptoms can be very varied and sometimes bizarre because almost any part of the body may be involved as affected tissues fail to function correctly. Patients may have a fever, tiredness, shortness of breath, rashes, enlarged glands, liver or spleen enlargement, pain, arthritis, pins and needles sensation and heart failure. Gradual destruction of the lungs and other organs may occur.

Blood tests and lung x-rays show abnormalities, but cannot specifically diagnose sarcoidosis. A definitive diagnosis requires the microscopic examination of a biopsy.

Steroids are used to reduce the inflammation, but the disease is slowly progressive and cannot be cured, although control is usually sufficient to give the victim a relatively long life.
See also HYPERCALCAEMIA; LÖFGREN SYNDROME

SARCOMA
A sarcoma is a malignant tumour originating in connective tissue (bone, cartilage, muscle and fibre).
See also ANGIOSARCOMA; CANCER; KAPOSI SARCOMA; OSTEOSARCOMA

SARCOPTES SCABIEI
See SCABIES

SARS
See SEVERE ACUTE RESPIRATORY SYNDROME

SARTORIUS
The longest muscle in the body, which runs from the pelvis across the front of the thigh to the knee, is the sartorius.
See also MUSCLE

SAVANT SYNDROME
See IDIOT SAVANT SYNDROME

SCABIES

Scabies is an infestation (not an infection) by a tiny insect that burrows for one cm. or more through the outer layers of the skin. Most common areas affected are the fingers, palms, heels, groin and wrists, but it can spread across the entire body, although it is unusual for the head and neck to be involved. The scabies mite, *Sarcoptes scabiei,* is just visible to the naked eye, appearing like a spot of dust on a piece of black paper, but it cannot be seen on the skin. It spreads by close contact (eg. shaking hands) with someone who already has the disease, and can occur despite scrupulous personal cleanliness. In many third-world countries, the disease is in epidemic proportions, but it is relatively uncommon in developed countries.

The main symptom is incessant itching caused by the burrowing mite, as the tissue around them becomes red, itchy and inflamed. Scratching often damages the skin, making diagnose difficult, and allowing a secondary bacterial infection to enter the skin. Norwegian scabies is a very severe form of infestation that causes thickening and scaling of the skin (particularly the palms and soles) from huge numbers of mites.

The diagnosis can be confirmed when a skin scraping is examined under a microscope and the mites and their eggs can be seen.

Treatment involves covering the entire body with a lotion or cream (eg. benzyl benzoate, permethrin, crotamiton) that kills the mites. All other members of the family, and anyone else closely connected with the patient, should be treated at the same time. It is advisable to change all the bed linen, and to repeat the treatment after a week, so that any mites that hatch from the remaining eggs after the initial treatment will be killed. The itch may continue for ten to twenty days after treatment due to an allergy to the scabies bodies or their products (eggs, droppings, etc.).

There is a good response to treatment, but recurrences are common.
See also ANTIPARASITICS; INFESTATION

SCALD
See BURN

SCALDED SKIN SYNDROME

The scalded skin syndrome is a severe superficial bacterial skin infection known as Ritter disease in newborn infants, and toxic epidermal necrolysis in older children. Milder forms are known as pemphigus neonatorum or bullous impetigo. Scalded skin syndrome and Lyell syndrome are terms that cover all forms.

It is caused by the bacterium *Staphylococcus aureus* (golden Staph) that spreads from nose, eyes, mouth or umbilicus to areas of skin damaged by eczema or injury. It may be a complication of the Stevens-Johnson syndrome.

The infant or child has severe peeling of skin that commences on the face and genitals and spreads across body. The skin appears similar to very severe sunburn. Death from fluid loss through damaged skin or internal spread of infection is possible.

A culture of swabs from the nose, eyes, throat and umbilicus will confirm responsible bacteria and the appropriate antibiotic (eg. penicillin or erythromycin). The infection responds slowly to antibiotics, but most children recover.
See also IMPETIGO; STEVENS-JOHNSON SYNDROME

SCALENUS ANTICUS SYNDROME
See NAFFZIGER SYNDROME

SCALP

The scalp is the tissue covering the top of the skull from which hair grows. There are five layers. From the outside they are: –
• a thick layer of skin
• a small amount of fatty tissue
• the aponeurosis (sheet of fibrous tissue)
• loose layer of tissue containing veins (the subaponeurotic tissue)
• the periosteum that covers the bone of the skull

The outer three layers slide as a unit across the subaponeurotic tissue. Hair grows from the outermost layer.

There are fewer nerves in the scalp than most areas of skin, and it is therefore not as painful when injured. On the other hand the scalp bleeds profusely when cut as the blood vessels tend to be held open in the fibrous tissue rather than go into spasm and clamp shut when cut.
See also DANDRUFF; SKIN; SKULL; TINEA CAPITIS

SCALP SCALY
See DANDRUFF; TINEA CAPITIS

SCALY SKIN
See SKIN DRY AND SCALY

SCAN
See CT SCAN; DOPPLER STUDIES;
DUAL PHOTON DENSITOMETRY; MRI
SCAN; NUCLEAR SCAN; PET SCAN;
ULTRASOUND

SCAPHOID BONE
See WRIST

SCAPHOID FRACTURE
The scaphoid bone is one of the eight small
wrist bones, and it lies on the thumb side of
the wrist. A scaphoid fracture is usually
caused by falling on the outstretched hand.

Although there may be pain and tenderness
on the thumb side of the wrist, these fractures
are often hard to detect, and x-rays ten days
apart may be necessary.

Immobilisation of the wrist in plaster for
four to six weeks is the usual treatment, but in
a small number of cases, part of this small
bone may die after a fracture and result in a
constantly painful wrist joint. An artificial
scaphoid bone can be inserted if complications occur.
See also COLLES' FRACTURE;
FRACTURE; SMITH FRACTURE;
WRIST

SCAPULA
The shoulder blade (scapula) forms the inner
side of the shoulder joint with a socket that
meets the ball at the top end of the humerus.
On the inside of the socket (glenoid) it fans
out as a thin triangular bone across the upper
and outer part of the back. A side arm of the
bone (the acromion) curves out across the top
of the shoulder joint to stabilise it, and join
with the clavicle (collar bone). Strong muscles
are attached to all its surfaces to move the
shoulder and brace the upper back.
See also CLAVICLE; HUMERUS; JOINT

SC AR
See KELOID

SCARLET FEVER
Scarlet fever is a bacterial infection of children

caused by bacteria from the Streptococcal
family. These infections are now very uncommon because of the widespread use of antibiotics for minor infections.

The patient is unwell with a fever and sore
throat for a few hours to two days before the
typical 'scarlet red' rash develops, which
consists of bright red, pinhead size dots on
the face, neck, armpits, groin and other areas.
The skin immediately around the mouth
often remains a normal colour. The tonsils are
usually enlarged, red and painful, and the
tongue may be red and swollen. The skin of
the palms and soles may flake away in severe
cases.

The diagnosis is confirmed by taking a
swab from the throat, and by specific blood
tests. It can be very effectively treated and
prevented by antibiotics such as penicillin
and erythromycin.
See also BACTERIA; SKIN RED

SCC
See SQUAMOUS CELL CARCINOMA
OF THE SKIN

SCHEURMANN DISEASE
Scheurmann disease is a relatively uncommon bone condition that affects the shape of
the vertebrae in rapidly growing teenagers,
but it may not be diagnosed until later in life
when back pain occurs. The vertebrae in the
middle part of the back, behind the chest,
do not grow properly, and instead of being
roughly square in cross section, become
slightly wedge-shaped. As a result the back
curves forward excessively giving a slightly
humped appearance, back movement is
reduced and pain may occur due to compression of nerves. Osteoarthritis often develops
prematurely. The diagnosis is made by seeing
abnormal vertebrae on a back x-ray.

Physiotherapy is given to correct posture,
anti-inflammatory medications to ease pain
and exercise to mobilise the back. In rare
cases surgery is required.

Although there is no cure, reasonable
control of symptoms is usually possible.
See also OSTEOARTHRITIS; VERTEBRA

SCHICK TEST
A Schick test establishes a person's immunity
to diphtheria. In this test a weak solution of
the toxins produced by the bacteria which

causes diphtheria is injected into the skin on the forearm. In this case, there will be no reaction if the antibodies are present, since the toxin will be neutralised. Instead the reaction occurs within three or four days if the person has not had the disease and so needs immunising against it.

Diphtheria vaccination is routine in childhood and this test is now rarely performed.
See also ANTIBODIES; DIPHTHERIA

SCHILLING TEST

A patient suspected of being anaemic may be given a Schilling test to find out how well the body is absorbing vitamin B12. The patient is given two doses of vitamin B12, one as an injection and one in tablet form, and then urine is collected over a twenty-four hour period and analysed to establish how much of the vitamin has been absorbed. If a deficiency is established, another test may be taken.

The level of vitamin B12 in the body can now be directly measured so this test is rarely performed.

Certain neurological disorders can be caused by vitamin B12 deficiency.
See also PERNICIOUS ANAEMIA

SCHISTOSOMIASIS

Schistosomiasis (bilharzia) is a fluke infestation transmitted by a species of snail found in fresh water streams, rivers and lakes in Egypt, tropical Africa as far south as Zimbabwe, the Caribbean and eastern South America. It is often caught by bathing or washing in fresh water.

The cause is a microscopic animal (trematode fluke) that enters the body by burrowing through the skin, often of the foot. Three different flukes – *Schistosoma mansoni, Schistosoma japonicum,* and *Schistosoma mekongi* – may be responsible. Once in the blood it travels to the veins around the large intestine, where eggs are laid. These pass out with the faeces or urine to infect water supplies. Once in fresh water, the eggs hatch, and the larvae seek out and burrow into the flesh of specific species of fresh water snail. They mature in the snail, and emerge from it ready to enter and infect another human. Patients do not pass out all the eggs that are laid by the fluke, and they may spread to the liver, lungs or spinal cord to cause further symptoms. Damage caused to organs by the fluke may be permanent.

The first symptom is an itchy patch at the site of skin penetration. Varying symptoms then follow, depending on the areas affected by the fluke as it moves through the body, and the individual's reaction to those changes. Long-term symptoms include diarrhoea, abdominal pain and bloody urine. A particularly severe and rapidly progressive form of the disease is known as Katayama Fever.

The diagnosis involves blood, urine and skin tests, and liver and gut biopsies.

Treatment is difficult, particularly late in the disease, although a number of drugs can be used to kill the fluke inside the body. Untreated it may cause a low-grade chronic illness, or may progress to death in a matter of months. The results of treatment are good if commenced early in the course of the disease, but advanced disease may be incurable.

SCHIZOPHRENIA

Schizophrenia is a psychotic mental illness which causes abnormal behaviour and perceptions. The idea that schizophrenics suffer from a 'split personality' is not true though. That idea comes from the origin of the word schizophrenia, which comes from the Greek word meaning 'to split', but rather than meaning 'split personality' it actually means a 'split from reality'.

The exact cause unknown, but there is a family tendency and the environment in which the patient is raised, and emotional stress, may trigger a person to escape into schizophrenia. If a person has two parents with schizophrenia there is about a 40% chance of developing the disease. Marijuana abuse is often a trigger in young people.

Patients have a distorted view of the world because of delusions and hallucinations. They often change the topic of conversation for no apparent reason, may not look after themselves, become dishevelled in appearance, withdrawn, and fail to communicate properly with others. Their mood and behaviour changes seem bizarre and they often believe that others are persecuting them. They may hear unfriendly voices, or have frightening hallucinations.

A lot of people think that schizophrenics are much more violent and dangerous than people who don't have schizophrenia, but in fact crime and violent behaviour is no more common amongst schizophrenics than it is other people. They can become violent, but generally speaking, people with schizophrenia are more of a danger to themselves than to others as suicide is possible. Many patients refuse medication and treatment because they lack insight into their condition.

There are no diagnostic blood or other tests, and the diagnosis rests on the ability of the doctor to recognise a characteristic form of behaviour.

There are a wide range of effective medications (antipsychotics) available to treat schizophrenia, including clozapine, fluphenazine, olanzapine, promazine, risperidone, thioridazine, thiothixene and trifluoperazine. They can be given as tablets or injections to control the disease. Just as important are a supportive environment and psychological counselling for the patient and their family.

A permanent cure is not usually possible, but the condition can be well controlled if the patient remains on long term medication.
See also ANTIPSYCHOTICS; CAPGRAS SYNDROME; CATATONIC SYNDROME; DIOGENES SYNDROME; HALLUCINATION; PARANOID DISORDER; PSYCHOSES

SCHOOL SORES
See IMPETIGO

SCIATICA
Sciatica is caused by the pinching of a nerve as it emerges from the spinal cord and passes between two vertebrae in the lower back. It is often due to arthritis, ligament strains or disc damage. More sinister diseases (eg. bone cancer) may also be responsible. The sciatic nerve is made from several spinal nerves that join together in the middle of the buttock, at a point where the pain of sciatica is often first felt, then it runs down the back of the thigh and calf to the foot.

Patients experience severe pain that spreads from the lower back to the buttock and then down one or both legs. The pain is felt where the nerve runs, not usually at the point in the back where the nerve is pinched, and shooting pains may be experienced all the way from the back to the foot. Severe nerve damage can cause temporary or eventually permanent paralysis of muscles or a leg.

X-rays and CT scans of the lower back can usually determine where the nerve is damaged.

In difficult cases, an MRI scan or myelogram (x-ray of dye injected into the back) may be performed

Treatment involves pain killers, anti-inflammatory medications, physiotherapy, rest, heat, back braces, steroid or other injections into the back and occasionally surgery. Most patients can be helped by adequate treatment.
See also BACK PAIN; LEG PAIN; LUMBAGO; SPINE

SCISSOR GAIT
See WALK ABNORMAL

SCLERITIS
Scleritis is an uncommon inflammation of the whites (sclera) of an eye. Numerous different types are recognised (eg. anterior scleritis, posterior scleritis, diffuse scleritis, nodular scleritis).

The cause is often unknown, but it may be associated with rheumatoid arthritis, polyarteritis nodosa, systemic lupus erythematosus and other autoimmune diseases.

Redness, discomfort, and sometimes painful ulceration, of the sclera occurs. The sclera may become thickened and affect vision, while cataracts and glaucoma may occur in severe forms.

Anti-inflammatory or steroid eye drops and tablets give a good response.
See also AUTOIMMUNE DISEASES; EPISCLERITIS; EYE; EYE DISCHARGE; EYE PAIN

SCLERODACTYLY
Sclerodactyly is a medical term for thickening and hardening of the skin on the fingers and toes.
See also CREST SYNDROME

SCLERODERMA
Scleroderma (progressive systemic sclerosis) is an inflammatory condition most commonly affecting the skin and gut, then the oesophagus (gullet), lungs, heart and other internal organs. It is an autoimmune disease, in which the body inappropriately rejects its own tissue, and usually starts between thirty and fifty years of age, with women being more commonly affected.

Symptoms vary widely but include thickening of the skin, arthritis that moves between joints, patchy changes in skin colouration, poor circulation to the hands, difficulty in swallowing, lung infections, fevers and diarrhoea. Damage to vital organs such as the heart may occur.

Blood tests show abnormalities but are not diagnostic, and a biopsy (sample) of skin or other affected tissue must be taken to confirm the diagnosis.

Medications can relieve the symptoms, but there is no cure, and the disease is slowly progressive over many years. Men and the elderly deteriorate more rapidly.
See also AUTOIMMUNE DISEASES; CREST SYNDROME; SKIN THICK

SCOLIOSIS

Scoliosis is abnormal lateral (side to side) curvature of the spine. Kyphosis is excessive antero-posterior (front to back) curvature of the spine. The two conditions can be combined in kyphoscoliosis. Spinal curves are usually double. If there is a curve in one direction, there must also be a curve in the opposite direction further up or down the spine. If this were not so, the shoulders would tilt to one side.

The easiest way to detect curvature is to have the child touch their toes. When looking along their back, one side will be seen to rise higher than the other, even though the spine may appear relatively straight when erect. If scoliosis is detected, the cause must be determined.

Minor degrees of both kyphosis and scoliosis are seen in many teenagers at puberty and in children as they go through rapid growth spurts, particularly if they have poor posture, which accentuates the deformity. Only significant curvature warrants medical attention. This is the type that must be watched most carefully to prevent permanent deformity. The younger the onset of the problem, the greater the need for concern, but babies nearly always recover spontaneously.

If one leg is shorter than the other due to injury or other causes, the pelvis will be tilted, and the spine will curve to compensate.

Abnormal vertebrae in the back that may have been present since birth or damaged by a severe injury, or a collapse of one or more of the discs between vertebrae (slipped disc), may also lead to scoliosis.

Diseases of the muscles that support the vertebral bones are another cause. This occurs in patients with polio, muscular dystrophy or quadriplegia. Spasm of the same muscles in spastics can pull the backbone out of shape.

Rare causes of scoliosis include Marfan syndrome (long limbs and fingers, thin body, heart defects), Coffin-Lowry syndrome and Roussy-Levy syndrome.

Once diagnosed, careful measurements are taken, and the patient is then checked at regular intervals to assess the progress of the scoliosis. If there is deterioration or the curvature exceeds 15-20 degrees, treatment is necessary, by means of physiotherapy, structured exercises, braces, or in severe cases surgery. Surgical techniques include the insertion of steel rods into the back to keep it straight, or fusing several vertebrae together in a straight line to prevent them from moving. The younger the onset of the problem, the greater the need for concern, but babies nearly always recover spontaneously. With proper medical care severe deformity is almost unknown.
See also BACK PAIN; KYPHOSCOLIOSIS; KYPHOSIS; SPINE; VERTEBRA and separate entries for diseases mentioned above.

SCORPION STING

Stings from scorpions can be very painful but, except in the case of allergy, the reaction is normally confined to the area of the sting. Apply ice to the affected area, and if symptoms persist see a doctor.
See also BEE AND WASP STING

SCRAPIE
See CREUTZFELDT-JAKOB DISEASE

SCROFULA

Scrofula ('king's evil') is an uncommon form of tuberculosis that occurs in the lymph nodes of the neck in areas with very poor hygiene. In the Middle Ages it was thought that it could be cured by the touch of a king, thus giving the disease its nickname.

Large, hard masses develop in the lymph nodes of the neck and they may drain pus out onto the skin. In severe cases the infection may spread from the lymph nodes to other organs including the lungs, brain and heart. The bacterium *Mycobacterium tuberculosis* is responsible.

Swabs taken from discharging lymph nodes are examined to confirm the diagnosis.

Treatment involves cutting out the affected lymph nodes and giving antituberculotic medications. Results are good with appropriate treatment, but permanent scarring usually occurs.
See also TUBERCULOSIS

SCROTUM

The pouch of thin skin behind and below the base of the penis that contains and supports the testicles. It is divided into two compartments, one for each testicle, separated by a ridge of skin (raphe), and the left side usually hangs lower than the right in right handed men. The skin is usually a darker colour than the skin of the adjacent thigh in most races, and contains more oil glands and fewer hairs than other skin.
See also RAPHE; TESTICLE; TESTICLE AND SCROTUM LUMP; TESTICLE AND SCROTUM PAIN

SCURVY

Scurvy was the scourge of sailors on long voyages over two centuries ago, particularly voyages of exploration to places where fresh food supplies could not be relied upon, but it is a very uncommon condition today. The cause is a lack of ascorbic acid (vitamin C) in the diet, and it may occur in people on unusual fad diets or in malnourished alcoholics. Captain James Cook made a name for himself early in his career by insisting that all his crew had rations of lime juice (which contains high levels of vitamin C) every day.

In early stages patients develop vague tiredness and weakness. As the vitamin deficiency becomes more severe, bleeding into the skin, rashes, bleeding gums, joint pain and bleeding into joints, slow wound healing and tender bones are experienced. The patient becomes severely anaemic, and bleeds readily. In advanced cases the kidneys fail, the body swells, bleeding occurs in the brain and death follows.

The diagnosis is confirmed by measuring ascorbic acid level in blood, and noting the marked anaemia. Between 100 and 300 mg. of vitamin C a day is required for treatment, while 50 mg. a day is sufficient for prevention.
See also VITAMIN C

SEA SICKNESS
See MOTION SICKNESS

SEASONAL AFFECTIVE DISORDER

Seasonal affective disorder is a common condition in far northern climates where there may be daylight for only two or three hours a day during winter. The cause is an inappropriate regulation of time by the body's internal clock, which is controlled by the hormone melatonin produced in the pineal gland at the front of the brain.

Patients become irritable and depressed, and suicide may occur in severe cases.

It is difficult to manage, but living in very bright light for part of the day, antidepressant medications, or taking melatonin may help.
See also DEPRESSION

SEA WASP
See BOX JELLYFISH

SEBACEOUS CYST

A sebaceous cyst (epidermal cyst or wen) is full of sebum (the oil that keeps the skin moist and supple) which is produced in sebaceous glands beneath the skin all over the body, and is discharged through small ducts. In areas that become sweaty, dirty or injured it is possible to block the duct draining the sebaceous gland. The sebum continues to be produced, and a cyst slowly forms under the skin.

Cysts usually appear on the back, chest and neck. They are slightly soft and often have a tiny dimple at the point where the original duct opened onto the skin. Sometimes pressure in the cyst is sufficient for its contents to be discharged through the previously blocked duct, but the cyst usually reforms. Cysts may become infected, and if antibiotics are not given soon enough, an abscess may form.

Any cyst that is unsightly may be cut out, while infected cysts are treated with antibiotic tablets.
See also CYST

SEBACEOUS GLANDS

The millions of sebaceous glands in the skin produce an oil called sebum, which lubricates the skin and hair and prevents drying. The ducts of these glands open into the side of every hair follicle. It is when the opening of a sebaceous gland becomes blocked with a mixture of dirt and sebum that a blackhead develops. A gland may become infected to form a pimple. A gland that becomes blocked

by accumulated sebum so that a sebum-filled sac forms is called a sebaceous cyst and may have to be removed by minor surgery.
See also ACNE; HAIR; SEBACEOUS CYST; SKIN; SKIN, DRY AND SCALY; SWEAT GLANDS

SEBORRHOEIC ECZEMA
This is a widespread, common form of eczema that can occur at any age.

It is caused by inflammation of the oil-producing sebaceous glands in the skin, but the cause of the inflammation is unknown.

In infants, seborrhoeic eczema frequently affects the scalp to cause cradle cap or the buttocks to cause nappy eczema. Other frequently affected areas are the cheeks, neck, armpits, groin and folds behind the knees and elbows and under the breasts. In adults, it is responsible for some forms of dandruff. On the scalp, it appears as a red, scaly, greasy rash. In skin folds, the skin is red, moist and breaks down into tiny ulcers. On exposed areas such as the face, the rash is red, scaling and may contain tiny blisters.

The scalp is treated with a lotion or cream to remove the oil and scale, and regular shampooing. Tar solutions are applied in resistant cases. In other areas, mild steroid lotions or creams are used. Soap should be avoided and substitutes used.

A complication may be the development of a secondary fungal infection.

Seborrhoeic eczema tends to be chronic and recurrent. Children often grow out of it in the early teens, but in adults it may persist intermittently for years.
See also DANDRUFF; ECZEMA; SKIN

SEBORRHOEIC KERATOSES
Seborrhoeic keratoses (basal cell papillomas or senile warts) are very common harmless skin growths that increase in number with age and may occur anywhere on the body, but particularly on the trunk. There is an inherited tendency to develop them, and they are more common in patients who have had any form of dermatitis.

These keratoses appear as raised, light brown, greasy surfaced spots that slowly enlarge and thicken to the point where they appear to be stuck onto the skin. The surface eventually becomes rough and cracked, and the colour darkens. If damaged, they bleed easily, and they persist long term.

They may be removed by diathermy, laser or shaving off the skin under a local anaesthetic. Smaller ones may be removed by freezing with liquid nitrogen, but they are harmless and only removed if unsightly or irritating as a significant scar may be left after removal.
See also HYPERKERATOSIS; SKIN NODULES

SEBUM
See SEBACEOUS GLANDS

SECONDARY CANCER
See METASTATIC CANCER

SECOND CHILDHOOD
See ALZHEIMER DISEASE; DEMENTIA

SEDATIVES
Sedatives and hypnotics are overlapping groups of drugs that induce sleep (hypnotics), or reduce bodily awareness and activity (sedative). Most sleeping pills are very safe provided they are taken in the recommended manner, but if used constantly for many weeks or months, patients may become dependent upon them. The greatest problem with the use of sleeping pills is that too often they are taken unnecessarily, particularly by elderly people who do not need large amounts of sleep. The pills are better taken intermittently when really needed, when they will work far more effectively. Care must be exercised when taking hypnotics in the evening so that the patient is not still affected by the sedation the following morning.

Examples of sedatives include flunitrazepam (Hypnodorm, Rohypnol), nitrazepam (Mogadon), temazepam (Normison), triazolam (Halcion) and zopiclone (Imovane).

Side effects may include confusion and reduced alertness, and they may cause dependence or addiction if taken regularly. They must be used with caution in pregnancy and glaucoma, and should not be given to infants. Lower doses are required in the elderly.
See also BENZODIAZEPINES

SEIZURE
See CONVULSION; EPILEPSY

SELECTIVE SEROTONIN REUPTAKE INHIBITORS
See ANTIDEPRESSANTS

SEMEN TEST

The purpose of a semen test is to determine the health of a man's sperm if he and his partner are having difficulty in conceiving a child. The man will ejaculate a sperm sample into a sterile container, which will be sent to a laboratory and examined to establish the number of sperm, whether they are normal and if they are able to swim sufficiently strongly to make their way to the woman's Fallopian tubes to fertilise an egg. The semen sample must reach the laboratory as soon as possible after ejaculation.

Semen tests are also performed about six weeks after a vasectomy to ensure that the operation has been a success and the man is infertile.

They may also be useful to diagnose the bacteria causing an infection of the prostate gland or epididymis (sperm draining tubules at the back of the testicle).
See also INFERTILITY; TESTICLE; VASECTOMY

SEMINAL VESICLE

The male reproductive cells, the sperm, are manufactured in the testicles. Once mature, the sperm swim along a small tube called the vas deferens for storage in two small pouches called the seminal vesicles, situated just below the prostate gland. Both the vas deferens and the seminal vesicles produce a white sticky fluid in which the sperm are suspended.

When a man has an orgasm at the climax of sexual arousal, vigourous contractions are triggered in the muscular walls of the vas deferens, seminal vesicles and prostate, as well as rhythmic contractions of the muscles at the base of the penis. The sperm-filled fluid, called semen, is pushed into the urethra, passing through the prostate, where it collects more fluid, down the length of the penis to the tip from which it is ejaculated. There may be as many as 500 million sperm in one ejaculation.
See also PENIS; PROSTATE; TESTICLE; VAS DEFERENS

SEMINOMA
See TESTICULAR CANCER

SENEGA
See COUGH MEDICINES; EXPECTORANTS

SENILE

Senility is the loss of mental and physical abilities in old age.
See also ALZHEIMER DISEASE; DEMENTIA

SENILE HAEMANGIOMAS
See CAMPBELL de MORGAN SPOTS

SENILE WARTS
See SEBORRHOEIC KERATOSES

SENILE VAGINITIS
See ATROPHIC VAGINITIS

SENNA
See LAXATIVES

SENSATION LOSS
See PAIN, LACK OF

SENSES

The senses are our contact points with the world that enable us to experience what goes on around us in the world. There are five main senses – vision, hearing, smell, taste and touch.

Our eyes enable us to see, our ears to hear, our nose to smell, and taste buds in our mouth to taste.

The sense of touch is actually quite complex. Tiny receptors all over our body, just under the skin enable us to have a sense of touch, with its associated sensations of pressure (sharp, blunt, vibration), heat, cold and pain. As well, receptors in our muscles and joints, together with those in our ears, allow us to experience position and balance.

Regardless of the type of receptor or the type of stimulus, they all communicate with the brain. A stimulus only becomes a sensation when the nerve impulse it triggers is interpreted by the brain.
See also EARS; EYES; NERVOUS SYSTEM; SMELL; TASTE; TOUCH

SEPTAL DEFECT
See ATRIAL SEPTAL DEFECT; VENTRICULAR SEPTAL DEFECT

SEPTIC

An instrument, material, wound, organ, tissue etc. that is infected, normally with bacteria, but sometimes by a fungus or virus, is referred

to as being septic. In living tissue, pus is an indication that sepsis is present. A septic tank is a receptacle for holding faeces and urine, that is then broken down by the bacteria that infect these waste products.
See also ANTISEPTIC

SEPTICAEMIA
Septicaemia, or blood poisoning, is a bacterial infection of the blood. The infection usually starts in another part of the body, such as the lungs, tonsils (quinsy) or after childbirth (now very rare), but in some cases the origin of the infection may never be found. Many different bacterial infections have septicaemia as a complication.

Patients are usually very ill, with a high fever, prostration and generalised aches and pains. A small number will have an overwhelming infection with resistant bacteria, which leads to death.

Many different bacteria may be responsible for the infection, and it is important to identify them by blood tests before antibiotic treatment commences. Potent antibiotics are given by mouth, injection or drip infusion in hospital to cure the infection. The original site of infection must also be treated if possible.

Provided an appropriate antibiotic can be found, most patients can be cured.
See also BACTERAEMIA; INFECTION; QUINSY; SEPTIC SHOCK

SEPTIC ARTHRITIS
Septic arthritis is an uncommon but serious bacterial infection of a joint that requires urgent and effective treatment. The responsible bacteria usually enter the joint through the bloodstream, but sometimes injury to the joint or adjacent bone can allow bacteria to enter. It may also follow an injection into, or the draining of fluid from a joint. Premature babies are at particularly high risk.

The infection starts with a fever and the rapid onset of severe pain in a joint that is tender to touch, swollen, hot, red, and painful to move. The knees, hips and wrists are most commonly involved. Joint destruction, severe chronic arthritis, or complete fusion and stiffness of a joint can occur if the disease is not treated correctly.

Blood tests show infection is present in the body, but not the location or type. Fluid drawn from the joint through a needle is cultured to identify the responsible bacteria. X-rays only show changes late in the disease.

A culture of joint fluid should be started before treatment is commenced, so that the bacteria can be correctly identified. While awaiting results, antibiotics are started and are initially given by intramuscular injection. Regular removal of the infected fluid from the joint by needle aspiration or open operation, is also necessary. Further treatment involves hot compresses, elevation and immobilisation of the joint, and pain relieving medication. Gentle movement of the joint should commence under the supervision of a physiotherapist as recovery occurs.

Recovery within a week to ten days is normal with good treatment.
See also ARTHRITIS; JOINT

SEPTIC SHOCK
Septic shock is a serious widespread reaction to a severe bacterial infection of the blood (septicaemia). Patients have a high fever, very low blood pressure, rapid breathing and heart rate, confusion, poor output of urine and eventually coma. Permanent damage to organs from poor blood supply or blood clots (thrombosis) may occur.

The responsible bacteria is identified by a blood culture.

Treatment consists of fluids by drip into a vein to increase blood pressure, and potent antibiotics into the drip. Management in a hospital intensive care unit is normal, and if necessary kidney dialysis and artificial respiration are performed. Despite the best treatment, there is a mortality rate of 50% within a month in good hospitals, and further deaths later from organ damage. Survival rates are better in the young, but worse in the elderly or debilitated.
See also SEPTICAEMIA; SHOCK; THROMBOSIS

SEROCONVERSION
See VACCINATION

SEROTONIN AND NORADRENALINE REUPTAKE INHIBITORS
See ANTIDEPRESSANTS

SERTRALINE
See ANTIDEPRESSANTS

SERUM
See BLOOD

SERUM HEPATITIS
See HEPATITIS B

SERUM SICKNESS
Serum sickness is an uncommon reaction to a blood or serum (liquid part of blood without the cells) transfusion, or use of a blood product (eg. globulin or proteins). Uncommonly it may be caused by the use of a drug. The reaction may be immediate, or delayed for up to two weeks after a transfusion.

The patient feels unwell, tired, nauseated and feverish; lymph nodes in the neck, armpit and groin become enlarged, an itchy rash develops, cramps occur in the belly, and joints may become painful.

No tests are diagnostic, but blood tests show generalised abnormalities characteristic of an allergy.

Antihistamines are given to counteract the allergy reaction, and steroids or adrenaline are prescribed to treat the results of the reaction. The reaction can vary widely in severity from being so mild that it passes almost unnoticed, to a very severe condition that can lead to death in a few hours.
See also ALLERGY; BLOOD GROUPS; TRANSFUSION REACTION

SESAMOID BONE
A sesamoid bone is found entirely within a tendon, usually at a point where the tendon rubs against another bone, and moves freely and independently of any other bone. The patella (knee cap) is effectively the largest sesamoid bone in the body, and sesamoid bones are often found in the ball of the foot, but others may be found in varying numbers in other parts of the foot, hand and rest of the body.
See also BONE; FOOT; PATELLA

SEVERE ACUTE RESPIRATORY SYNDROME
Severe acute respiratory syndrome (SARS) appears to be a totally new viral infection that attacks the lungs of humans. It is probably a mutated coronavirus, a form of virus that causes the common cold in humans, and is well known to cause infections in many animals. It is probable that it has been transferred from animals to humans by close contact between them, and the virus has mutated during the transfer.

First identified in southern China, Hong Kong and northern Vietnam in early 2003, it has spread rapidly with infected air travellers to many parts of the world.

The infection is spread from person to person on microscopic droplets of liquid exhaled through the mouth and nose. There is a three to five day incubation period.

The initial symptoms of the infection are the sudden onset of a high fever, muscle pains, chills, headache and loss of appetite. Three to seven days later a dry cough develops along with shortness of breath and difficulty in breathing, and chest x-rays show the presence of a widespread pneumonia. Most patients recover completely, but about 4% die from failure of the lungs.

Patients must be barrier nursed to prevent infection of nursing and medical staff, and the further spread of the infection. Extreme care must be used to wear a mask (both patient and contacts), gloves and gowns when in contact with the patient, and all surfaces and objects with which the patient has contact must be cleaned with an antiseptic. The information above is correct at the time of writing (April 2003) but may change as more information becomes available.
See also PNEUMONIA; VIRUS

SEX
See SEXUAL INTERCOURSE

SEX CHOICE
There is no way in which the sex of a child can be guaranteed, but the following system (known as Shettles' system) may increase the odds in your favour. At best, this system increases the chances of a child of a particular sex from 50% to 75%. It is definitely NOT a guarantee of success, and it may make it more difficult to fall pregnant at all!

Ovulation (release of the egg from the ovary) occurs 14 days before a period starts. If you usually have 28 days from the beginning of one period to the beginning of the next, you will ovulate 14 days after the first day of your last period. If your cycle is usually 30 days, you will ovulate 16 days after the first day of your last period. For the following system to work, you must know when you usually ovulate.

To increase the chance of having a GIRL: –

1 Ten minutes before sex, use a vaginal douche consisting of 20mls. of white vinegar in 500mls. of cooled boiled water.

2 Have sex frequently in the seven to ten days before you ovulate.

3 No sex from one day before ovulation until ten days after ovulation.

4 Your partner should ejaculate just inside the vagina, and not deeply inside as usual.

5 Your partner should withdraw immediately after ejaculation.

6 It is better for the woman not to have an orgasm.

To increase the chance of having a BOY: –

1 Ten minutes before sex, use a vaginal douche consisting of 5g. of baking powder in 500mls. of cooled boiled water.

2 No sex from the end of your period until the day ovulation occurs.

3 Twice daily sex from the day of ovulation for four days.

4 Your partner should ejaculate deep inside the vagina.

5 Your partner should withdraw immediately after ejaculation.

6 It is better for the woman to have an orgasm, ideally just before ejaculation.

Couples who are having treatment for infertility and are using artificial methods of conception may be able to choose the sex of their child, as they can decide if a male or female embryo is implanted. There are significant ethical dilemmas associated with this decision and the use of this technique when sex choice rather than infertility is the main reason.

SEX HORMONES

Sex hormones are produced by the ovaries in the woman and the testes in the man to give each sex its characteristic appearance. In men, they are responsible for the enlargement of the penis and scrotum at puberty, the development of facial hair and the ability to produce sperm and ejaculate. In women, the sex hormones produced for the first time at puberty cause breast enlargement, hair growth in the armpit and groin, ovulation, the start of menstrual periods, and later act to maintain a pregnancy.

If the sex hormones are reduced or lacking, these characteristics disappear. This happens naturally during the female menopause and the male andropause. During the transition from normal sex hormone production to no production in the menopause, there may be some irregular or inappropriate release of these hormones, causing the symptoms commonly associated with menopause such as irregular periods, irritability and hot flushes. After the menopause, the breasts sag, pubic and armpit hair becomes scanty, and the periods cease due to the lack of sex hormones. Men also go through a form of menopause, the andropause, but more gradually and at a later age, so the effects are far less obvious than in the female.

Sex hormones, and many synthesised drugs that act artificially as sex hormones, are used in medicine for two main reasons. They correct natural deficiencies in sex hormone production; and they alter the balance between the two female hormones (oestrogen and progestogen), which causes ovulation, thereby preventing ovulation and acting as a contraceptive.

It is now well recognised that hormone replacement therapy (HRT) in middle-aged women who have entered the menopause significantly improves their quality of life by not only controlling the symptoms of the menopause itself, but by preventing osteoporosis (bone weakening), reducing the apparent rate of ageing and reducing the risk of dementia after the menopause. Women who have both their ovaries removed surgically at a time before their natural menopause will also require sex hormones to be given regularly by mouth, patch or implant.

Female sex hormones can also be used to control some forms of recurrent miscarriage and prolong a pregnancy until a baby is mature enough to deliver, to control a disease called endometriosis, and to treat certain types of cancer.

The female sex hormone oestrogen can be given as a tablet, patch, vaginal or skin cream, implanted capsule that is placed under the skin or as an injection.

If the woman has not had a hysterectomy, she will need to take progestogen as a pill or patch in a cyclical manner every month or two. This may result in a bleed similar to that of a natural menstrual period (although usually much lighter), but it protects the woman against uterine cancer.

The common sex hormones fall into the categories of oestrogens, progestogens and androgens (male sex hormones).

OESTROGENS

Oestrogens include dienoestrol, ethinyloestradiol (Estigyn), oestradiol, oestriol (Ovestin), conjugated oestrogen (Premarin) and piperazine oestrone (Ogen). They are used in contraceptive pills, for hormone replacement therapy during and after the menopause, and are usually combined with a progestogen unless the woman has had a hysterectomy. Side effects may include abnormal menstrual bleeding, vaginal thrush, nausea, fluid retention, breast tenderness, bloating and skin pigmentation. These side effects can usually be overcome by adjusting the dosage. They should not be used in pregnancy, breast feeding, children, and patients with liver disease or a bad history of blood clots. Care must be used in patients with breast cancer, epilepsy and hypertension.

PROGESTOGENS

Progestogens include dydrogesterone (Duphaston), medroxyprogesterone (Provera) and norethisterone (Primolut-N, Micronor, Noriday). They are used to control abnormal menstrual bleeds, endometriosis, for preventive contraception, 'morning-after' contraception, hormone replacement therapy and premenstrual tension. Medroxyprogesterone is an injectable progesterone that may be used for contraception or to treat certain types of cancer and endometriosis. As a contraceptive it is given every three months. Side effects include the cessation of menstrual periods, breakthrough vaginal bleeding, headaches, and possibly a prolonged contraceptive action (up to fifteen months). The other progestogens usually have minimal side effects, but they may include headache, abnormal vaginal bleeding, insomnia, breast tenderness, nausea and sweats. They should not be used in pregnancy, liver disease, or in patients with blood clots or breast lumps. Care must be used in patients with hypertension and diabetes.

Danazol (Danocrine) is a special type of sex hormone that acts against oestrogen and is used to treat endometriosis, severe menstrual period pain and severe breast pain. Side effects are common and may include acne, weight gain, excess body hair, retained fluid, dry vagina, sweats and the development of a deep voice. It must never be used in pregnancy or in patients with pelvic infection, liver disease, blood clots or heart failure.

ANDROGENS

The androgen (male sex hormone) testosterone, is available in synthetic form as a tablets, as an injection (Sustanon), and as implants. It is used to treat conditions such as failure of puberty to occur, pituitary gland dysfunction, impotence, decreased libido (in both sexes), and male osteoporosis. Side effects are unusual, but the prostate gland must be checked regularly for enlargement. It is used in women to treat breast cancer and in both sexes for severe anaemia. Natural lack of the male sex hormone testosterone will cause the man to be impotent and sterile. Synthetic testosterones include fluoxymestrone (Halotestin), mesterolone (Proviron), and oxandrolone (Lonavar). Fluoxymestrone is used to treat breast cancer, osteoporosis and aplastic anaemia. Mesterolone and testosterone are used for male infertility and impotence. Oxandrolone aids short stature, male puberty failure and aplastic anaemia. Side effects may include penis enlargement, infertility, fluid retention, increased body hair and nausea in men, and if used in women irregular periods, deep voice and an enlarged clitoris may develop. They must not be used in pregnancy, heart, liver or prostate disease.

Antiandrogens counteract the action of testosterone. The only common hormone in this group is androcur. It is used to treat excess body hair, severe acne and loss of scalp hair in women, and prostate cancer in men. Side effects may include reduced libido, tiredness, nausea, weight increase and irregular menstrual periods. They must not be used in pregnancy and in patients with blood clots or liver disease.

See also ANDROPAUSE;
CONTRACEPTIVE PILL; HORMONES;
HORMONE REPLACEMENT THERAPY;
MEDROXYPROGESTERONE
INJECTIONS; MENOPAUSE; OVARY;
PUBERTY; TESTICLE

SEX IN PREGNANCY

Unless a doctor has recommended otherwise (eg. for a threatened miscarriage), it is perfectly safe to engage in sex during pregnancy if both partners desire it. Some women find that their sex drive decreases at certain stages of pregnancy, while other women are the opposite. A man may also be affected, being more attracted to his pregnant wife, or deterred by the new life within her. As a general rule, the foetus will not be affected by

intercourse. In the last couple of months, only certain positions will be comfortable for the woman (eg. woman sits atop lying man).
See also PREGNANCY

SEX PROBLEMS
See EJACULATION, LACK OF; EJACULATION FAILURE; EJACULATION, PREMATURE; FRIGIDITY; HOMOSEXUALITY; IMPOTENCE; INFERTILITY; LIBIDO REDUCED; ORGASM, LACK OF; PAEDOPHILIA; PENIS SMALL; PEYRONIE DISEASE; PRIAPISM; SEXUAL SADISM; SEXUAL INTERCOURSE PAIN; VAGINISMUS; VULVODYNIA

SEXUAL INTERCOURSE
The purpose of sexual intercourse is to produce a baby and perpetuate one's genes. However, humans also have sex because it feels good. In the Western world, people reproduce on average no more than two or three times in their lives, but they will probably engage in sexual intercourse thousands of times.

Intercourse consists of the man inserting his penis into the woman's vagina. Before he does this, ideally, each partner will become sexually aroused. In the man this means that the penis will become engorged with blood so that it becomes larger, stiff and erect. In the woman, the vagina lengthens, and glands in the vagina produce a lubricating fluid which enables the man's penis to slide in easily. Thrusting movements by both partners stimulate the penis and vagina and produce pleasurable sensations that increase in intensity until a climax or orgasm is reached. In a woman an orgasm consists of contractions of the vagina, and the man will have an ejaculation of semen, which is a mix of seminal fluid and sperm.

Positions for intercourse vary. The commonest is the so-called missionary position in which the woman lies on her back with her legs bent up and the man lies on top of her. Penetration is generally deepest in this position.

In a man, orgasm and ejaculation go together. One usually does not occur without the other. Consequently a man has to have an orgasm before he can father a child. The situation is different in women. A woman does not need to have an orgasm to conceive and some women who have active sex lives rarely or never achieve orgasm.

Statistically, 85% of menstruating women will fall pregnant within one year if undertaking sexual intercourse at least once a week.

The frequency of sexual intercourse varies significantly between couples and with age. The frequency of sex in no way determines the affection a couple have for each other. In Australia, the average married couple of thirty to thirty five years of age will have sex 106 times a year, while the average for couples

SEXUAL INTERCOURSE

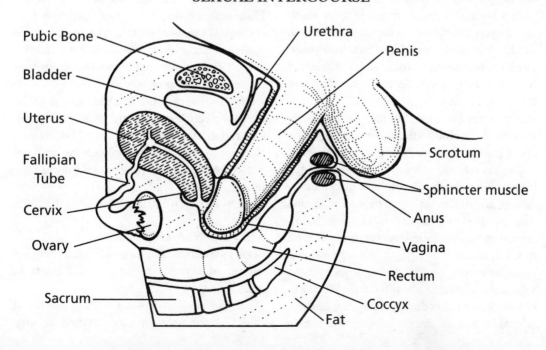

between fifty and fifty five years drops to forty-one times a year. Social circumstances, pregnancy, children and individual preferences will result in couples varying significantly from these averages.
See also HOMOSEXUALITY; IMPOTENCE; INCEST; LIBIDO; ORGASM; SEXUAL INTERCOURSE PAIN; RAPE; SEXUAL POSITIONS

SEXUAL INTERCOURSE PAIN

Pain experienced by a woman during sexual intercourse is called dyspareunia by doctors. It may occur superficially near the outside as the penis initially enters the vagina, during deep penetration of the penis, or may be a mixture of both.

Infections of the vagina caused by a fungus (eg. thrush) or bacteria may inflame both the vagina and the vulval tissue around the outside. These infections are usually accompanied by a discharge. Irritation of the inflamed tissue during sex will cause pain.

Deeper infections in the lower part of the belly involving the bladder (cystitis), urethra (tube that drains urine from the bladder), bowel (eg. diverticulitis), lining of the belly (peritonitis) or an abscess in the pelvis will be aggravated by intercourse.

A lack of the female hormone oestrogen after menopause may lead to a dryness of the vagina which makes sex difficult and painful. The natural lubrication of the vagina is maintained by glands that are stimulated by oestrogen. Some women may notice that their vagina is drier at some stages of their menstrual cycle than at others due to variations in the level of oestrogen. Underactive thyroid, pituitary or adrenal glands, which affect the functioning of all cells in the body, may also cause vaginal dryness.

A prolapse (dropping) of the uterus, usually as a result of childbirth, age or obesity, may cause back ache, which is aggravated by sex.

Causes of superficial pain during sex include vulvodynia, Bartholin's gland infection (glands near the opening of the vagina that produce its natural lubricating fluid), genital herpes infection (painful ulcers around the vulva and the lips of the vagina), an episiotomy scar (cut in the back wall of the vagina performed to allow the baby's head to emerge more easily during birth), vaginismus (strong spasm of the muscles in the vagina

that prevents the penis from entering), a allergy to soaps, perfumes, detergents in underwear or other substances, which may cause a swelling and inflammation of the delicate tissues of the vulva.

Causes of deep pain during sex include salpingitis and pelvic inflammatory disease (infections of the fallopian tubes and other organs in the pelvis), endometriosis, fibroids (hard balls of fibrous tissue that form in the muscular wall of the uterus), an ectopic pregnancy (a foetus in the Fallopian tubes instead of the uterus) and tumours or cancer of the cervix, uterus or ovaries.
See also ORGASM, LACK OF; SEXUAL INTERCOURSE; VAGINA and separate entries for diseases mentioned above.

SEXUALLY TRANSMITTED DISEASES
See VENEREAL DISEASES

SEXUAL SADISM

Sexual sadism is a psychiatric aberration that usually starts in males in their late teens and twenties, and sometimes persists long term. The cause is unknown, but sometimes it is blamed on sexual assaults in childhood. Rarely, a brain tumour or disease may be found to be responsible for a personality change, and is detected by a CT scan.

The man has prolonged, recurrent and intense sexual urges and fantasies involving real or imagined acts in which physical or psychological suffering occurs in a victim. Humiliation is one of the more common psychological fantasies or acts. Most patients are unable to achieve sexual satisfaction in other ways. The victim may be consenting or nonconsenting, and may be raped.

Psychotherapy and medications may be tried as treatments, but are often ineffective. Castration has been used as a last resort. Because of their interaction with the criminal justice system, many patients end up as long term prisoners.
See also PAEDOPHILIA; RAPE; VIOLENCE

SÉZARY SYNDROME

Sézary syndrome is a form of cancer that is a variant of mycosis fungoides and starts in middle age.

Patients develop persistently itchy patches of thick red skin, overlying hair loss on affected skin, and enlarged lymph nodes in neck, groin, armpits and elsewhere. It may spread to other areas of the body, and the nails may be damaged. Eventually the syndrome progresses to leukaemia or a type of sarcoma.

Skin and lymph node biopsy are diagnostic, and a blood test reveals abnormal white blood cells.

Low-grade irradiation of skin and cytotoxic drugs (chemotherapy) are the main treatments, but despite these the condition is usually very slowly progressive.
See also MYCOSIS FUNGOIDES; SARCOMA

SHAFT SYNDROME
SHAFT syndrome is a neurotic personality disorder that is a variation of Munchausen syndrome.

The disease name is an acronym for its major symptom characteristics – patients are Sad, Hostile, Anxious, Frustrated and Tenacious, and praise a doctor excessively to obtain unnecessary surgery, then have worsening of imagined symptoms after surgery, for which the doctor is blamed. Extensive investigations are invariably carried out, but all are normal.

Psychotherapy can be tried, but the prognosis is poor, and patients often persist with symptoms long term.
See also MUNCHAUSEN SYNDROME

SHAKING PALSY
See PARKINSON DISEASE

SHELL SHOCK
See POST-TRAUMATIC STRESS DISORDER

SHETTLES' SYSTEM
See SEX CHOICE

SHIATSU
Shiatsu is a form of treatment similar to acupuncture that was developed over 1000 years ago in Japan. Practitioners put pressure on specific points on the body known as 'tsubos', which purportedly connect through invisible meridians to all the organs of the body. By applying pressure to a point distant from the organ, but on the meridian of that organ, the shiatsu practitioner corrects abnormalities in body energy that are responsible for illness. The body energy known as 'ki' is primarily divided into water ki and fire ki, and believers in shiatsu claim that imbalances in these two forms of ki are responsible for illness and disease. Water ki is stored in the kidney, and when this runs out death occurs. Fire ki is produced by good food and can reduce the drain on water ki energy.

Undergoing a shiatsu treatment involves the practitioner applying varying degrees of pressure to the tsubo points that s/he believes are responsible for the symptoms, and the transfer of ki energy both ways between patient and practitioner.
See also ACUPUNCTURE; AYURVEDIC MEDICINE; CHINESE MEDICINE

SHIGELLOSIS
Shigellosis, or bacillary dysentery, is a common intestinal disease in third-world countries and the poorer areas of some developed countries. A number of different bacteria from the *Shigella* family can infect the gut under poor sanitary conditions. The infection spreads when bacteria in the faeces of a patient contaminate the food of another person.

Patients develop severe intermittent abdominal pain, copious diarrhoea, blood and mucus mixed in with the faeces, and a high fever. Severe dehydration may lead to blood clots (thrombosis) that damage the organ supplied by the affected artery. It is diagnosed by examining a sample of faeces for the presence of the infecting bacteria.

Treatment involves appropriate antibiotics, adequate fluid intake by an intravenous drip in severe cases, medications to relieve abdominal cramps, and a strict diet to avoid foods that may irritate the gut (eg. milk products, eggs and fatty foods). Carers should be very careful in the disposal of the faeces and soiled linen to prevent spread of the infection.

In children under three years of age and the elderly the infection may be life-threatening. In older children and adults it can be readily treated, or may persist for several weeks without adequate treatment.
See also CAMPYLOBACTER JEJUNI; CRYPTOSPORIDIOSIS; DIARRHOEA; GASTROENTERITIS; TYPHOID FEVER

SHINGLES
Shingles (varicella) is an infection of nerves and skin by the *Herpes zoster* virus, which is the same virus that causes chickenpox, and is

usually caught as a child. The virus is never completely eradicated by the body, but migrates to the roots of nerves along the spinal cord, where it remains inactive lifelong. At times of stress, the virus may reactivate and move along the nerve to cause the skin and other tissues to become very painful. Shingles is far more common in older people, and uncommon in children. You cannot catch shingles from another person, but a child who has not had chickenpox may catch this from a person who has active shingles.

An acutely tender, blistering rash develops, often in a belt-like line on one side of the body, and even the slightest touch causes severe shooting pain. Any nerve may be affected, and it can occur on the abdomen or chest (most common sites), or on the face or legs. Occasionally the rash leaves permanent scars, particularly on the face. A small number of elderly people develop chronic inflammation in the nerve, and pain that persists for years (post-herpetic neuralgia). The worst complication occurs if nerves around the eye and ear are involved, when dizziness, ear noises and rarely blindness may occur (Ramsay-Hunt syndrome).

No investigations are normally necessary but if required, the diagnosis can be confirmed by taking special swabs from a sore.

Shingles can be cured by specific antiviral tablets, but only if treatment is started within seventy two hours of the rash first appearing. If treatment is neglected until after three days from the onset of the rash, the only treatment is painkillers, drying antiseptic lotions and mild sedatives. Steroids may be used in severe cases.

The rash dries out slowly and disappears over several weeks, usually healing completely. The pain is slower to disappear, and may last a month longer than the rash, but the vast majority of patients make an excellent recovery.
See also ANTIVIRALS; CHICKENPOX; RAMSAY-HUNT SYNDROME; VIRUS

SHIN SPLINTS
Shin splints, or the tibial stress syndrome, is an inflammation of the periosteum (thin membrane) that covers the tibia (larger of the lower leg bones). It is caused by excessive stress on the periosteum at the point where major muscles attach to the back and outside surfaces of the tibia, particularly in novice athletes who exercise excessively. Running on a hard surface is notorious for triggering the condition because of the jarring at every step.

Patients experience pain and tenderness of the tibia that is worsened by running, jumping or sometimes just walking.

Prolonged rest and anti-inflammatory medications result in a slow recovery.
See also BONE; TIBIA

SHIVER
The medical term rigor is used to describe a shiver.

Shivering is an involuntary trembling, often associated with the goose bumps on the skin. It has the beneficial effect of increasing muscle activity, and therefore body temperature, when a person becomes very cold. This is the most common reason for shivering, but if the body temperature drops too far (hypothermia), shivering will actually cease, in order to preserve energy.

A fever from any cause, but most commonly an infection, will cause shivering, even though the person is quite warm. One of the most violent forms of shivering can occur with malaria.

Fear or a fright is another reason for shivering, due in this case to the release of excessive amounts of the stimulant adrenaline from the adrenal glands on top of each kidney. The adrenaline has a beneficial action of allowing flight when frightened by briefly increasing the strength and responsiveness of muscles.

The withdrawal from addictive drugs, including alcohol, heroin and even marijuana and nicotine (smoking) can result in uncontrollable shivering.
See also CONVULSION; FEVER; MUSCLE SPASM and separate entries for diseases mentioned above.

SHOCK
In a medical context, shock has a different meaning to that of fright or startle. Medically, any condition in which there is inadequate circulation of blood around the body can be described as shock (or shock syndrome). There are many serious causes including loss of blood from a major injury, severe burns, several fractures, extensive bleeding into the gut from an ulcer or other disease, massive diarrhoea, various forms of heart damage and failure, lung disease (eg. thrombosis or

embolism), heart valve disease or septicaemia.

The patient collapses, is obviously very ill, pale, sweaty, has a weak thready pulse, the blood pressure is very low, and the patient may become unconscious. Further symptoms depend on the cause, and may vary from pain to shortness of breath and fever. Extensive blood, urine, x-ray and other tests may need to be performed in order to determine the cause.

First aid involves lying the patient flat with legs raised if conscious to improve blood flow to the brain, or lying down flat and on the side if unconscious, controlling any bleeding, maintaining body temperature by the use of warm blankets, splinting fractures, protecting burnt areas, and if the patient deteriorates, mouth-to-mouth resuscitation and external cardiac massage may be necessary. In a hospital intensive care unit fluids or blood are given through a drip into a vein, and oxygen and painkilling injections are given when appropriate. Further treatment depends on the cause and may include a wide range of drugs and possibly surgery.

Permanent damage to almost any organ (including the brain and heart) may occur due to poor blood supply or blood clots (thrombosis).

The prognosis depends upon a multitude of factors including the cause of the shock, the patient's age and general health, and the speed with which medical assistance can be obtained.
See also ANAPHYLAXIS; ELECTROCUTION; FIRST AID; HYPOTENSION; RESPIRATORY DISTRESS SYNDROME, ADULT; SEPTIC SHOCK and separate entries for diseases mentioned above.

SHOCK TREATMENT
See ELECTROCONVULSIVE THERAPY

SHORT
See GROWTH REDUCED

SHORT OF BREATH
See BREATH, SHORT OF

SHORT-SIGHTED
Short-sightedness (myopia) is a developmental vision defect in which the eye ball is too long, and light rays from distant objects are focussed in front of the retina (layer of light

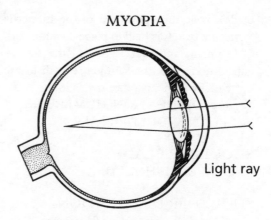

MYOPIA

Light ray

Light focuses in front of retina

sensitive cells at back of the eye). Distant objects appear blurred while close objects are clearly seen. Reading is easy but moving around difficult.

The problem can be corrected by spectacles with accurately prescribed corrective lenses. In some people, laser keratotomy, in which the shape of the cornea (outer layer of the eye) is permanently reshaped, may cure the problem. This procedure is not carried out before the late teen years as vision can change with growth.
See also LONG-SIGHTED; PRESBYOPIA; REFRACTIVE SURGERY; VISION

SHORT-WAVE DIATHERMY
Physiotherapists may apply heat to damaged tissue by the use of hot packs (a superficial moist heat) or, if deep warming of the tissues is required, by the administration of short-wave diathermy. The latter is particularly useful for chronically sprained and arthritic joints, and deep muscle problems. In this modality, high-frequency electrical energy is converted to heat within the tissues. However, in some instances short-wave diathermy should not be used. These include where metal is present in joint replacements and some intrauterine devices, because it concentrates the electrical field and may cause local burning; where the electrical field may interfere with cardiac pacemakers; in pregnancy; and in patients who suffer severe circulatory disorders.
See also PHYSIOTHERAPY

SHOULDER
The ball and socket shoulder joint can move more freely than any other joint. The socket (glenoid) is part of the scapula (shoulder

blade) while the upper end of the humerus forms the ball. It is held in place by a network of ligaments and muscles called the rotator cuff, but even so, the shoulder can dislocate more easily than any other major joint.
See also DISLOCATION; HUMERUS; SCAPULA; SHOULDER PAIN

SHOULDER BLADE
See SCAPULA; SHOULDER

SHOULDER DISLOCATION
Shoulder dislocation is a disruption of the joint between the scapula (shoulder blade) and humerus (upper arm bone). The shoulder is a ball and socket joint, but the socket is very shallow to allow maximum movement. A cuff of muscles and ligaments surrounds the joint to keep it in position. This joint can move through a greater range than any other, but as a result is relatively unstable, and it is the most commonly dislocated major joint.

If excessive force is applied to the shoulder joint, it may dislocate forwards, or less commonly, backwards. Patients experience severe pain, do not like the shoulder joint to be moved, and often hold the elbow of the affected arm at right angles and against their side with the other hand. Any shoulder dislocation is associated with tearing and damage to the surrounding muscles and ligaments of the rotator cuff and joint capsule, and a dislocation may also be associated with a fracture.

The dislocated shoulder can be put back into place by one of a number of different techniques, often with little or no anaesthetic if treated immediately, or after giving painkilling injections or a brief general anaesthetic if there is any delay. After treatment the arm is kept in a sling for a month. Recurrent shoulder dislocations may occur by merely picking up a heavy object or raising the arm and these patients require an operation (the Putti-Platt procedure) to repair the damaged tissues and prevent further dislocations. It can be diagnosed by x-rays.

Results of treatment are good after one dislocation, but after further dislocations surgery is advisable, and is usually very successful.
See also DISLOCATION; SHOULDER; SHOULDER PAIN

SHOULDER IMPINGEMENT SYNDROME
The shoulder impingement syndrome is caused by overuse or inappropriate use of the shoulder joint and the pinching of tissue between bones in the shoulder joint.

There is pain at the top of the shoulder in arc of movement between 60 and 120° when moving arm away from body. The diagnosis can be confirmed if local anaesthetic injected into top of shoulder joint temporarily relieves the pain. Treatment involves rest, anti-inflammatory drugs, cortisone injections into the shoulder, physiotherapy, and some-

SHOULDER

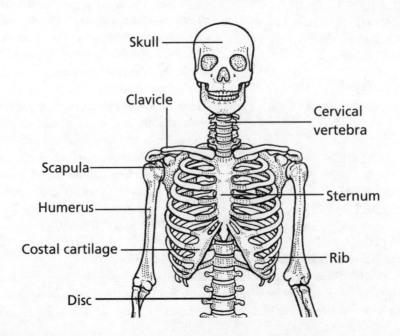

Skull — Clavicle — Cervical vertebra — Scapula — Humerus — Sternum — Costal cartilage — Rib — Disc

times surgery to release trapped tissue.
See also SHOULDER PAIN

SHOULDER PAIN

The shoulder joint is able to move through a greater range of movements than any other joint in the body, and so is more susceptible to injury than most joints.

Obviously, any injury to the joint resulting in a fracture to one of the bones making up the joint will cause pain.

The shoulder has a complex network of muscles, ligaments, bones and tendons to support it. These supporting structures are known as the rotator cuff. If there is a tear or rupture to any of the tissues that move and support the shoulder, due to injury, strain or ageing, pain will be felt with certain movements, depending upon which tissues are affected.

The tendons around the shoulder joint, particularly those above the joint (supraspinatus tendon), may become inflamed (tendinitis), torn, displaced, damaged, and even develop tiny flakes of bone in areas that are persistently inflamed. When this happens, any movement that involves the affected tendon will be painful.

Because of its ability to move very freely, the shoulder joint can also dislocate very easily. If excessive stress is put on the shoulder, the head of the humerus (upper arm bone) may slide partially (subluxate) or completely (dislocate) out of the socket on the outside end of the shoulder blade (scapula), tearing and stretching the surrounding ligaments, tendons and muscles and causing severe pain. Normally the shoulder dislocates forwards, but other directions are possible. After one dislocation, it is easier for the joint to dislocate again, and the problem can steadily worsen until surgery is necessary to prevent further dislocations.

Another common cause of shoulder pain is osteoarthritis. The lining of a joint degenerates with time, and becomes inflamed, resulting in pain with any movement or pressure on the joint. Arthritis may also affect the small joint (acromioclavicular joint) between the collar bone (clavicle) and the upward protrusion on the shoulder blade (acromion) to cause pain that is felt on top of the shoulder.

The painful arc syndrome causes pain during the mid-range movement of the shoulder joint as the arm is moved away from the body. There is no pain at the lower or upper end of the range of shoulder movement. It is caused by nipping of tissue between the top of the humerus (upper arm bone) and the shoulder blade.

If a pain nerve that runs from the shoulder to the neck to connect with nerves running to the brain in the spinal cord, becomes pinched in the neck due to disc damage, arthritis or other conditions or diseases in the neck, the patient will feel that the pain is coming from the shoulder, even though the problem is in the neck.

Other causes of shoulder pain include an inflamed or infected bursa (bursitis), synovitis (inflammation of the synovial membrane that lines the joint), the capsule around the joint becomes inflamed or infected (capsulitis), septic arthritis (bacterial infection of the fluid within the joint), the shoulder impingement syndrome and referred pain which occurs when an injury or disease in one place causes pain in another (eg. a heart attack or angina may cause pain in a shoulder or arm).

Rarer causes include neuropathy (infection, tumour or inflammation of a nerve), the scapulo-costal syndrome (due to faulty posture stressing the muscles, ligaments and nerves in the neck and upper back), tumours or cancer of the bones forming the joint, polymyalgia rheumatica (generalised inflammation of muscles), rheumatoid arthritis and Pancoast syndrome (due to cancer at the top of one lung).
See also ARTHRITIS; SCAPULA;
SHOULDER and separate entries for diseases mentioned above.

SHUNT

A shunt is a diversion tube that is placed in the body for the drainage of fluid (eg. blood, cerebrospinal fluid) from a cavity, to bypass a blockage or to allow connection from an artery to a vein through a machine (eg. dialysis).
See also DIALYSIS; HYDROCEPHALUS

SHY-DRAGER SYNDROME

The Shy-Drager syndrome is a severe form of multiple system failure of no known cause.

Patients have low blood pressure, reduced sweating, slight tremor, difficulty in speaking, rigidity, poor coordination, impotence, dizziness, varying muscle paralysis and incontinence.

Fainting may occur with changes in position. An MRI scan of the brain may be abnormal.

Treatment is unsatisfactory. Patients must take care with postural changes, wear elastic stockings and a support girdle, and take medication (eg. fludrocortisone, ephedrine sulphate). Unfortunately, it usually progresses to death within five to seven years.
See also FAINT

SIADH
See SYNDROME OF INAPPROPRIATE ANTIDIURETIC HORMONE SECRETION

SIALADENITIS
See SIALITIS

SIALITIS
Sialitis (sialadenitis) is an infection or inflammation of one or more of the three salivary glands on each side of the mouth (the parotid, submandibular and submental glands) that supply the saliva to the mouth. If the parotid gland (which is situated at the angle of the jaw and is the largest of the glands) alone is infected the condition is called parotitis.

It may be caused by a stone in the duct of the salivary gland, may be associated with Sjögren syndrome, a tumour, or may start for no apparent reason.

An acutely painful swelling of the gland develops, which may exude pus into the mouth, and if the infection is not adequately treated an abscess may form.

Potent antibiotics (often given by an intravenous drip), and massage of the gland to expel any pus, are successful treatments.
See also RANULA; SALIVARY GLAND; SALIVARY GLAND PAIN; SALIVARY STONE; SJÖGREN SYNDROME

SIALOCELE
See RANULA

SIBERIAN TICK TYPHUS
See TYPHUS

SIBUTRAMINE
See OBESITY

SICK
See NAUSEA AND VOMITING

SICK BUILDING SYNDROME
The sick building syndrome is a condition affecting workers in air-conditioned buildings.

In order to conserve cold air and therefore energy, some large air-conditioned buildings allow minimal amounts of fresh air into circulation with each cycle. This allows organic solvents (eg. from photocopiers, glues, paints), fungal spores, pollens, dusts and other contaminants to recirculate in increasing concentrations, particularly if the air conditioning filters are poorly maintained.

Residents and workers in the building develop snuffly noses, eye irritation, dry skin, headaches and tiredness. The longer they spend in the building, the worse the symptoms become. Increasing the amount of fresh air entering building and carefully maintaining filters solves the problem.
See also NOSE DISCHARGE

SICKLE CELL ANAEMIA
Sickle cell anaemia, or haemoglobin S disease, is a form of abnormal red cell development that occurs only in Negroes. This inherited condition causes red blood cells to become sickle shaped (like a crescent moon) rather than round, because of an abnormal form of haemoglobin called haemoglobin S. The responsible abnormal gene is found only in Negroes.

Victims are tired and weak, have large spleens, may become jaundiced (yellow), heal poorly, develop gallstones easily and cope poorly with infections. Sometimes clumping of the abnormal red cells may block small arteries, causing severe pain in wide areas of the body and permanently damaging the heart, liver or other organs.

Adults carrying the abnormal gene can be identified by blood tests, and if two carriers marry, one in four of their children will suffer from sickle cell anaemia. It can be diagnosed before birth by amniocentesis or other tests on the unborn child. After birth, examining blood under a microscope reveals the abnormal cells.

Treatment with folic acid supplements and occasional transfusions controls most cases. Maintaining adequate water intake and treating infections early are important. There is no cure but its effects can usually be controlled.

Interestingly, the disease gives protection against malaria, which may explain its selective benefit in tropical areas.

See also ANAEMIA; MALARIA; RED
BLOOD CELLS

SICK SINUS SYNDROME
The sick sinus syndrome is an abnormality
of heart rhythm, due to failure of the heart
pacemaker (sinus node) or nerve conduction
within the heart. Patients have a variable heart
rate from brief standstill or very slow (sinus
bradycardia) to markedly rapid beat or atrial
fibrillation and resultant fainting or collapse.
Heart attack and death may rarely occur. A
continuous ECG reading (Holter monitor) for
twenty four hours will be abnormal and can be
used to make the diagnosis.

Treatment involves an artificial pacemaker
and drugs to stabilise heart rhythm, which
give good control once diagnosed.
See also ATRIAL FIBRILLATION;
HEART; PACEMAKER; PULSE SLOW

SIDE PAIN
See LOIN PAIN

SIDS
See COT DEATH

SIGHT
See EYE; LONG-SIGHTED; SHORT-
SIGHTED; SQUINT; VISION

SIGMOIDOSCOPY
See COLONOSCOPY

SILDENAFIL
Better known by its brand name of Viagra,
sildenafil is a medication used for the treatment of impotence (inability to obtain erection
of the penis). After the medication is taken, it
may take one to four hours to be effective, and
its effect may last up to twelve hours. An erection does not occur just because the tablet is
taken; sexual stimulation is also necessary.

It must never be taken by patients with
heart disease or angina, while taking nitrate
drugs (eg. glyceryl trinitrate) used for angina,
or in patients with liver disease, high or low
blood pressure or with a history of a recent
stroke. Side effects may include headache,
flushing, blue haze in vision and indigestion.
See also ALPROSTADIL; IMPOTENCE;
MEDICATION

SILICOSIS
Silicosis is a form of permanent lung damage
caused by the long-term inhalation of tiny
silica dust particles by workers involved in rock
quarrying, stone cutting, tunnelling, pottery
and in those who use diatomaceous earth.
Multiple small hard round nodules develop in
the lung.

There are no symptoms in early stages of the
disease, but in advanced cases patients develop
shortness of breath, and a poor tolerance to
exercise. Lung infections such as pneumonia
may be a complication.

Chest x-ray shows characteristic abnormalities, but there is no treatment, no cure, and
the condition is slowly progressive over many
years.
See also ASBESTOSIS; LUNG;
PNEUMOCONIOSIS;

SIMETHICONE
See ANTACIDS

SIMMONDS DISEASE
See HYPOPITUITARISM

SIMVASTATIN
See HYPOLIPIDAEMICS

SINUS
Technically, a sinus is a cavity, and the term is
used in medicine to describe an abnormal
cavity or hollow in many parts of the body,
and in particular a cavity caused by an abscess
that opens onto the skin or into an internal
organ (eg. the intestine).

More commonly, a sinus refers to the
sinuses in the front of the skull.

Below, above, between and even behind the
eyes, the skull bone is riddled with spaces
called sinuses. All these sinuses are connected
together by small holes and tubes, making a
complex interconnecting system rather like a
cave explorer's nightmare in miniature. The
exact purpose of the sinuses is obscure, but
they certainly lighten the skull, and may act as
resonance chambers for speech.

Lining this network is a damp membrane
similar to that inside the nostrils. The whole
system is thus kept constantly moist, and this
moisture slowly flows out of the drain holes in
the sinuses, into the back of the nose and
down the throat. This system is designed to
keep the sinuses clean, as any dust or other

FACIAL SINUSES

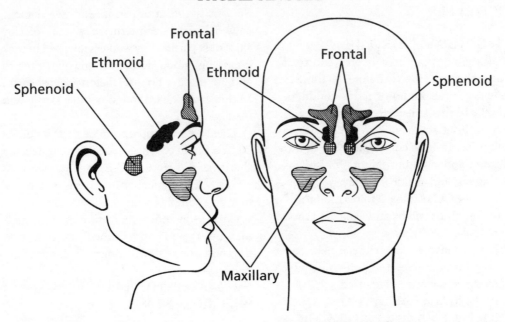

small particles that enter are washed out.

Unfortunately the system does not always work perfectly. Some people secrete excess fluid into the sinuses, while others may have drainage holes and tubes that are too small to cope with the secretions produced. If the sinuses become blocked, infection usually follows and sinusitis occurs.

See also FACE PAIN; SKULL; SINUSITIS

SINUSITIS

Sinusitis is a bacterial or viral infection of the moist membrane that lines the air-filled sinuses in the face. They lie in the skull bone below, above, between and behind the eyes and are connected together and to the nose by small holes and drainage tubes.

Some people secrete excess amounts of fluid in the sinuses because of hay fever, smoking or irritating fumes, while others may have drainage holes and tubes that are too small to cope with the secretions produced. If bacteria or viruses infect the sinus lining or secretions, sinusitis results.

Sinusitis causes thick and pus-like phlegm to drain from the nose and down the throat, the face is very painful and tender and there is fever, headache and tiredness. The infection may spread to the middle ear, and in severe cases, it may be necessary to insert needles through the nose into the sinuses to wash out the pus. X-rays of the sinuses show the abnormal presence of fluid, and swabs may be taken from the back of the nose so that the type of

bacteria causing the infection can be determined and the correct treatment selected.

Appropriate antibiotics are prescribed when the cause is bacterial, and other medications are used to dry phlegm and clear the sinuses. Inhalations of steam and nasal decongestant drops are beneficial. In patients who suffer from repeated attacks, surgical procedures to more effectively drain the sinuses can be performed. Untreated, the infection can spread to the teeth, eyes or brain, and abscesses may form. Most patients settle quickly with appropriate treatment, but recurrences are common.

See also COLD, COMMON; FACE PAIN; SINUS

SINUS PAIN

See FACE PAIN; SINUSITIS

SITUS INVERSUS

In the condition known as situs inversus, the organs within the chest and abdomen are reversed in position, so that the heart is on the right instead of left, and the liver on the left instead of right, and all other organs are similarly reversed in position.

See also KARTAGENER SYNDROME

SIX-WEEK COLIC

See INFANTILE COLIC

SJÖGREN SYNDROME

Sjögren syndrome is a chronic widespread autoimmune inflammatory condition in which the body inappropriately rejects its own tissue. It is closely related to rheumatoid arthritis, but affects more organs.

Common symptoms include widespread arthritis, dry eyes, dry mouth, dry skin and dry throat. Other symptoms may include difficulty in swallowing, decaying teeth, loss of taste and smell, and a hoarse voice. Nearly all patients are women, and it usually commences in the fifth decade. Complications may involve inflammation of the pancreas, thyroid and other organs. It is diagnosed by specific blood tests.

Patients are prescribed anti-inflammatory drugs, steroids (eg. prednisone), and a number of unusual drugs such as gold by injection or tablet, antimalarial drugs (eg. chloroquine) penicillamine (not the antibiotic), and cell-destroying drugs (cytotoxics). Artificial tears and skin moisturisers, and good dental hygiene are also necessary.

There is no cure, but reasonable long-term control is usually possible.
See also AUTOIMMUNE DISEASES; RHEUMATOID ARTHRITIS

SKELETAL HYPEROSTOSIS
See DIFFUSE IDIOPATHIC SPINAL HYPEROSTOSIS

SKELETON
The bones of the skeleton protect the internal organs and support the body. The rib cage shields the heart and lungs and the skull protects the brain. In an adult body, bone makes up about 16% of the total weight.

Adults have fewer bones than children. A baby is born with 350 bones. Many of these then fuse as the child grows, and by the time a person has reached twenty to twenty-five years of age, they will typically have 206 permanent bones.

Some cartilage remains as part of the skeletal structure into adult life, particularly as the costal cartilages which join the ribs to the breast bone, in the discs between the vertebrae in the back, and at major fixed joints (eg. at the front of the pelvis where the two halves join at the pubic symphysis).
See also BONE; FEMUR; FIBULA; HUMERUS; PELVIS; RADIUS; RIB;

SKELETON

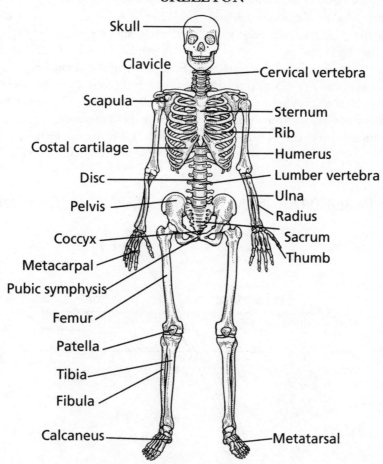

Skull — Clavicle — Cervical vertebra — Scapula — Sternum — Rib — Costal cartilage — Humerus — Disc — Lumber vertebra — Pelvis — Ulna — Coccyx — Radius — Metacarpal — Sacrum — Pubic symphysis — Thumb — Femur — Patella — Tibia — Fibula — Calcaneus — Metatarsal

SKULL; STERNUM; TIBIA; ULNAR;
VERTEBRA

SKIN

Skin is the outer covering of the body. It is much more complex than one might think as it protects the body against infection and parasites and provides a tough resilient cushion to safeguard the tissues underneath from injury. It also helps to maintain body temperature and prevent the body from becoming dehydrated. The skin is also the main organ of the sensation of touch and it can perceive heat, cold, sharp, blunt, vibration and pain.

The skin consists of two main layers which are quite different from each other in the way they are made up and the way they function. The top layer, the one we see, is the epidermis. This contains no blood vessels, nerves or connective tissue fibres and, in turn, is subdivided into two layers. The outer layer consists mainly of dead cells that are constantly being shed. The inner layer consists of cells with the capacity to multiply at a rapid rate, which they do continually, pushing up and replacing the discarded dead cells. The dying cells produce a protein called keratin which thickens and protects the skin. Keratin developed in a particular way together with dead cells also forms the hair and nails.

Under normal circumstances, the time it takes between a skin cell's production to the time it dies and flakes off, is about a month. However, if injury occurs, even just a minor scratch, the multiplication of cells speeds up to repair the damage. If the damage is repeated, deeper tissues may thicken to compensate and form a callus.

The inner layer of the epidermis also produces the pigment melanin, which gives the skin its colour. Freckles are simply irregular patches of melanin. We all have the same number of melanin-producing cells, irrespective of our racial origin, but dark-skinned races produce more melanin than light-skinned races. Exposure to the sun encourages the production of melanin as a protection against the sun's rays, giving a suntan. Complete absence of the pigment melanin leads to the abnormally white skin and general appearance of people classified as albino.

Beneath the epidermis is the dermis, which is the so-called true skin. The dermis is well supplied with blood vessels and nerves and has a framework of elastic connective tissue as well as the proteins collagen and elastin. The blood vessels provide the nourishment for the epidermis. The thickness of both the dermis and the epidermis varies so that some areas (eg. the soles of the feet and the palms of the hands) are covered with thick layers, whereas other areas (eg. the eyelids) are covered with thin and delicate layers.

The dermis rests on a layer of fatty tissue called the subcutaneous layer. The fat serves as both insulation and a reserve store of energy. Embedded in the dermis and extending into the subcutaneous layer are sweat and sebaceous glands which are essential for the proper functioning of the body.

Most skin is covered by hair, with the exception of that on the soles of the feet and the

ENLARGED DIAGRAMATIC CROSS SECTION OF SKIN

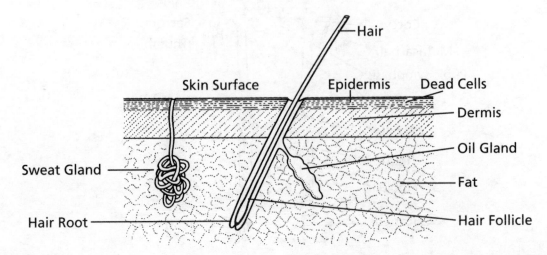

palms of the hands. These areas are covered with alternately ridged and grooved patterns that increase the body's ability to grip at these points. These patterns are different in every single individual and remain the same throughout life; hence the use of fingerprints as a means of identification.

Disorders of the skin are not usually life-threatening but can be unsightly and psychologically damaging.

See also BLISTERS; BLUE SKIN; BROWN PATCHES ON SKIN; CRAWLING SENSATION ON SKIN; DERMATITIS; ECZEMA; FACE RED; HAIR; JAUNDICE; LIGHT SENSITIVE SKIN; LINES IN SKIN; NAIL; PINS AND NEEDLES SENSATION IN SKIN; PSORIASIS; PUSTULES; RED PATCHES ON SKIN; SCALP; SEBACEOUS GLANDS; SKIN COLOUR; SKIN DEPIGMENTED; SKIN DRY AND SCALY; SKIN ITCH; SKIN LUMPS; SKIN NODULES; SKIN PAIN; SKIN PIGMENTATION EXCESS; SKIN RED; SKIN RED SPOTS; SKIN THICK; SKIN THIN; SKIN ULCER; STRETCH MARKS; SWEAT GLANDS; TOUCH; WHITE PATCHES ON SKIN

SKIN BLISTERS
See BLISTERS

SKIN BLUE
A blue tinge to the skin (cyanosis) is a serious symptom that can indicate significant disease, usually of the heart or lungs. Cyanosis is caused by the blood carrying too much waste carbon dioxide and not sufficient oxygen, and so remaining a dark blue colour rather than the bright red of well-oxygenated blood.

Cyanosis in an infant usually indicates a serious structural defect of the heart (eg. ventricular septal defect) and/or lungs. These are usually congenital (present as a developmental defect since the embryo stage).

In adults cyanosis may be due to extensive involvement of both lungs with pneumonia, emphysema, bronchiectasis, heart failure, pulmonary thrombosis (blood clot in lungs), severe anaemia and abnormal connections between major arteries and veins, or defects in the muscular wall between the right and left sides of the heart.

Blue fingers and toes are a common symptom of extreme cold in everyone. Initially they will go white, then if neglected will become blue and painful before the permanent damage of frostbite occurs. A specific form of this problem is Raynaud's phenomenon, which is a spasm of arteries when tissue is exposed to only mild cold. It causes affected tissue to go white, then blue and red, before becoming swollen and painful. The hands and feet are usually affected, and it is far more common in women than men.

Buerger's disease is damage to the small arteries in the feet and hands caused by smoking. Polycythaemia rubra vera is an uncommon condition in which there are an excessive number of red blood cells which can clog up the fine capillaries that supply blood to individual cells leading to painful finger tips, itchy blue skin and a general tiredness. In Pickwickian syndrome, grossly obese patients are unable to circulate sufficient blood due to heart failure.

See also SKIN; SKIN RED and separate entries for diseases mentioned above.

SKIN CANCER
Forms of skin cancer vary from the relatively innocuous to those which can spread rapidly enough to eventually kill. Most are caused by sun exposure, primarily in childhood, but some chemicals may also be responsible and there is sometimes a familial tendency. Tropical countries with a predominantly white-skinned population have a far higher incidence.

Skin cancers fall into several different categories – squamous cell carcinomas (SCC), intraepithelial carcinoma (IEC), basal cell carcinomas (BCC), Bowen's disease and melanomas are the most common and are dealt with separately. Signs to watch for in a spot or sore, which may indicate that it is a skin cancer, are any irregularity in colour, shape or outline; soreness or itchiness; bleeding or weeping. A biopsy can give a definitive diagnosis, but it may be more practical to excise whole growth.

Prevention involves protecting the skin from the sun.

They may be treated by freezing with liquid nitrogen, diathermy (burning), cutting out the growth, injecting anticancer drugs in and under it, or applying acid or anticancer ointments.

See also BASAL CELL CARCINOMA; BOWEN'S DISEASE; INTRAEPITHELIAL CARCINOMA;

MELANOMA; MERKEL CARCINOMA;
SQUAMOUS CELL CARCINOMA OF
THE SKIN

SKIN COLOUR

Skin pigmentation is an inherited characteristic
that can vary from the pale white of the Scandinavians to the pitch black of the Sudanese,
and every shade in between. Every human has
the same concentration of pigment-producing
melanin cells in their skin, but skin colour is
determined by the activity of these cells and
how much black melanin they produce.

It is impossible to determine the skin
colour of a person by examining their internal
organs.
See also FACE PIGMENTED; SKIN; SKIN
PIGMENTATION EXCESS

SKIN DEPIGMENTED

A lack of skin pigment, even in northern
Europeans, can be seen as a total lack of
pigment everywhere on the skin, or patchy
loss of pigment. The darker the natural skin
colour, the more obvious the problem.

Severe burns and other skin injuries may
heal with a scar that is dead white or significantly paler than the surrounding skin.

Pityriasis versicolor is a relatively common
fungal infection of the outermost layers of the
skin that occurs in warm climates. The fungus
prevents the skin under it from tanning on
exposure to the sun, so the patient appears to
have white blotches of varying sizes scattered
across their body. Pityriasis alba causes a
similar effect.

Albinism is an inherited disorder in which
the skin lacks pigment cells, and explains the
occasional appearance of completely white
Negroes, or normally dark skinned animals.
The iris (coloured part of the eye) also lacks
pigment and appears pink because of the
blood vessels in it.

Chediak-Higashi syndrome is an inherited condition that can pass to subsequent
generations. It causes recurrent skin and lung
infections, partial albinism (skin depigmentation) and sometimes liver, spleen and lung
damage.
See also ALBINISM; SKIN; WHITE
PATCHES ON SKIN and separate entries
for diseases mentioned above.

SKIN DRY AND SCALY

The skin is normally kept moist and supple by
the production of oil from millions of tiny
sebaceous glands that are distributed everywhere on the body surface. Dry skin (xeroderma) is often susceptible to infection, itchy,
irritated and uncomfortable. There are many
different causes for dry and scaly skin.

Seborrhoeic dermatitis is an inflammation
of the skin oil glands in the affected area,
which reduced oil production and causes a
red, itchy, scaly rash.

High fevers from any cause can increase
evaporation from the skin and make it feel
both hot and dry.

The thyroid gland in the front of the neck
produces the hormone thyroxine, which acts
as an accelerator for every cell in the body. If
there is a lack of thyroxine (hypothyroidism),
all organs will function slowly, and symptoms
will include intolerance of cold, constipation,
weakness, hoarse voice, heavy periods, dry
skin, hair loss, slow heart rate and anaemia.

Psoriasis is a skin disease characterised by
plaques of red, dry, scaly skin, most commonly on the elbows, knees and scalp. Guttae
psoriasis is a very active variant.

Some patients have an inherited tendency
towards dry skin that can pass from one generation to the next. The extreme cases of this
are known as ichthyosis.

Some drugs, such as cimetidine (Tagamet –
for stomach ulcers), nicotinic acid (for high
cholesterol) and retinoids (for acne) have dry
skin as a side effect.

Uncommon causes of dry skin include a
severe deficiency of vitamin A, sarcoidosis,
ichthyosis, leprosy and Refsum syndrome.
See also SEBACEOUS GLANDS; SKIN
and separate entries for diseases mentioned
above.

SKIN ITCH

Everyone experiences itchy skin (pruritus) at
some time or another, but in most cases it
settles rapidly and easily. There are scores of
different conditions which may be responsible
for an itch that may arise in the skin itself, due
to infections or infestations, result from liver
diseases, or may arise from other organs in
the body.

Over-cleaning the skin with soap removes
the oil that is necessary for the health of the
body's surface, and causes the skin to dry out

and become itchy. Soaps and skin cleansers may also cause a mild allergy reaction in the skin that is itchy.

Urticaria (hives) is an allergy reaction in skin that causes marked swelling in patches across the affected area, which is also red and itchy. Any one of several trillion substances, from plants, animals or chemicals, may be responsible.

Bites from insects (eg. mosquitoes, sand flies, fleas) or spiders may cause a red itchy spot or patch on the skin.

Fibreglass (eg. in ceiling insulation) and other irritants can act on the skin to cause microscopic damage, redness and itching.

Heat rash (miliaria) is a skin reaction of the arms, trunk and groin that occurs in hot, humid climates, and more commonly in overweight people due to the blocking of overactive sweat ducts. It causes a burning, itching, red, slightly bumpy rash that is eased by cool lotions.

Atopic eczema occurs almost exclusively in children and young adults. It is a skin reaction that may be triggered by changes in climate or diet, stress or fibres in clothing, and there is a genetic predisposition. The rash occurs in areas where the skin folds in upon itself (eg. groin, arm pits, inside elbows and eyelids), and is more common in winter and urban areas. The rash is extremely itchy, and any blisters that form are rapidly destroyed by scratching which changes the appearance of the eczema, so that it appears as red, scaly, grazed skin.

Contact dermatitis is very common. The skin is red, itchy, swollen, burning and may be blistered in an area that has come into contact with a substance to which the patient has reacted. After a few days, the area may become crusted, weeping and infected with bacteria. Substances that a person has used or touched regularly for many years without any adverse effect may suddenly sensitise them, and cause a reaction. This is particularly common in the workplace (eg. solvents, dyes, rubber, inks) and with cosmetics.

Scabies is an infestation (not an infection) that occurs when a tiny insect called *Sarcoptes scabiei* burrows under the skin to create tracks that can be one centimetre or more in length. These burrows and the tissue around them become red, itchy and inflamed. It is caught by close contact with someone who already has the disease. The most common areas for it to settle are the fingers, palms, heels, groin and wrists; but it can spread across the entire body.

Both bacterial (impetigo) and fungal (tinea) infections of the skin may cause an itch.

Severe lice infestations may cause a mild itching from the bites on the skin or scalp.

Other skin causes for an itch include seborrhoeic dermatitis (excess oil on the skin), psoriasis (plaques of red, itchy, scaly skin), intertrigo (due to heat, sweat and friction), Grover disease (triggered by heat and sweat), pressure areas on the skin, pityriasis rosea, lichen simplex, ichthyosis (inherited condition in which the skin lacks oil glands), dermatitis herpetiformis, lichen planus, stasis dermatitis (develops in areas of the body that are not drained of blood, particularly the feet of disabled and elderly people), and pemphigoid.

Less common causes for an itch include bilharzia (caused by a microscopic animal that enters into the body by burrowing through the skin), other infestations of the body by microscopic animals (eg. hookworm, hydatid, echinococcus), a viral infection of the liver (hepatitis A and B), cholecystitis (inflammation or infection of the gall bladder), cirrhosis (damaged liver), jaundice, underactive thyroid gland (hypothyroidism), poorly controlled diabetes, severe emotional upsets (eg. divorce) or stress (eg. exam nerves) may cause a nerve rash (neurodermatitis), a fixed drug eruption (adverse reaction to a drug), itchy upper arm syndrome, uraemia (kidney failure), polyarteritis nodosa (an inflammation of arteries), haemochromatosis (excess iron in the body), Sjögren syndrome (an autoimmune disease), AIDS, many different cancers and leukaemia.

Some medications may cause an allergy reaction, resulting in red, itchy skin, or may cause an itch without any associated rash.

There are many other possible causes of itchy skin.
See also ANAL ITCH; ECZEMA; GENITAL ITCH; SKIN and separate entries for diseases mentioned above.

SKIN LIGHT SENSITIVE
See LIGHT SENSITIVE SKIN

SKIN LUMPS

Papules are small, discrete, firm, solid, raised lumps on or in the skin. They may be skin colour, red, brown or black. The lump created by acne, before it becomes filled with pus and blisters (becomes a pustule), is a typical papule.

Naevi are dark brown or black, raised moles. More develop on the skin with age, and most are benign (not cancer) but there is always a chance that they may be nasty.

Melanomas are the most serious form of skin cancer, and may be black, brown, pink or blue. The surface of a melanoma is often uneven and bumpy.

Cancers of the deeper layers of the skin (basal cell carcinomas) are not nearly as serious as melanomas. They appear as shiny, pink, rounded lumps that often change in size and colour.

Neurodermatitis (nerve rash) causes multiple small red itchy lumps to develop in response to stress or anxiety. The wrists, ankles, inside the elbows and behind the knees are the most commonly affected areas.

Other causes of a papular rash include dermatofibromas (yellow-brown nodules), folliculitis (infection of the oil gland at the base of a hair), molluscum contagiosum (viral infection of the skin in children), xanthoma (creamy yellow, soft, smooth, fatty lumps that often appear around the eyes), granulomas (single, soft lumps that develop in response to skin damage), granuloma annulare (ring shaped lumps), lichen planus, milia (keratin cysts), heat rash (miliaria) and tularaemia (bacterial infection of rats and rabbits that can spread to humans via a tick bite).

Various types of dermatitis can appear in many forms, including solitary or multiple small lumps. Contact dermatitis, where the skin is reacting excessively to a substance, is particularly likely to form papules.

Large lumps under the skin may be due to enlarged lymph nodes, fatty cysts (lipomas) or Von Recklinghausen's disease of multiple neurofibromatosis.

See also ACNE; SKIN NODULES and separate entries for diseases mentioned above.

SKIN NODULES

Nodules are discreet, separate, lumps in or on the skin. There may be one solitary nodule (eg. a wart) or hundreds (eg. molluscum contagiosum) present, and they can vary in size from a couple of millimetres to over a centimetre.

Warts cause a persistent, rough elevation of an area of skin, usually less than 5mm. in diameter. They are caused by a very slow-growing virus, and are most common in children from eight to sixteen years of age.

Genital warts are caused by the human papilloma virus, which is passed from one partner to another during sex. These warts are usually external on the male, but internal in the woman. They can become itchy, but more seriously, the virus can cause cancer of the cervix in women.

Blood vessels in the skin may sometimes dilate and overdevelop dramatically to form a small red lump that blanches on pressure, and bleeds dramatically if injured. These haemangiomas are harmless, but annoying and sometimes cosmetically unacceptable.

Cancers of the deeper layers of the skin are called basal cell carcinomas (BCC). They may appear as shiny, pink, rounded lumps that often change in size and colour, or they may present as an ulcer that fails to heal.

Molluscum contagiosum is a viral infection of the skin in children that causes dozens or hundreds of tiny pus filled blisters with dimpled tops to appear on the body over a few weeks. They remain for several weeks or months before disappearing spontaneously.

Lipomas are soft, poorly defined, round lumps under the skin that consist of fat. They may develop due to an injury to the fat layer under the skin.

Other causes of skin lumps include seborrhoeic keratoses, xanthomata (creamy yellow, smooth, fatty lumps that commonly occur around the eyes), Heberden's nodes (bony lumps that develop beside finger joints in patients with severe osteoarthritis), gouty tophi (white, hard lumps that develop beside joints affected by gout), chilblains (develop as a result of exposure to extreme cold), melanomas (serious form of skin cancer), rheumatoid nodules (around joints affected by rheumatoid arthritis), erythema nodosum (very tender, painful red lumps that develop on the front of the leg), Von Recklinghausen's disease of multiple neurofibromatosis, and granuloma inguinale (a sexually transmitted disease).

See also BLISTERS; PUSTULES; SKIN;

SKIN LUMPS and separate entries for diseases mentioned above.

SKIN PAIN

The most common and obvious cause of skin pain is an injury such as a bruise, graze, scald or sunburn, but the most important causes are infections.

Shingles is an infection of a spinal nerve caused by the virus *Herpes zoster*. This is the same virus that causes chickenpox. At times of stress or reduced immunity, the virus may start to multiply in one particular nerve, to cause sharp pain that gradually moves along the nerve on one side only from the back to the front of the abdomen. A day or so after the pain starts, a patchy blistering rash will appear in a line along the course of the nerve.

Cellulitis is an infection of the tissue immediately under the skin, and can occur anywhere on the body, but is more common at points where the skin is more easily injured, such as over joints. The skin is hot to touch as well as red and painful, and often swollen and tender.

See also SKIN and separate entries for diseases mentioned above.

SKIN PIGMENTATION EXCESS

Skin pigmentation can be patchy, but still normal as in freckles, but there are a multiplicity of medical conditions that can cause excessive pigmentation that is obviously more noticeable in those whose natural colouring is fair.

The most common cause of excessive skin pigmentation in Caucasians is tanning from excessive exposure to the sun.

Bruising is an obvious but temporary cause of skin pigmentation. The initially black bruise will fade to dark blue, brown and finally yellow before disappearing.

Many people have naevi (pigmented spots) of varying shades on their skin that increase in number with age and skin exposure. These are completely harmless, but may be mistaken for a melanoma.

Lentigo is the technical name for the flat brown 'age spots' that increase in size and number on the skin of many elderly people. They also are harmless, but may be cosmetically undesirable. Sebaceous moles are fatty, soft, irregular, raised lumps that also occur with age.

Some people heal poorly and any wound leaves a dark coloured, and often raised scar, known as a keloid.

The mongoloid spot is an area of mid brown pigmentation seen at the base of the spine of many people of Chinese and other Asian ancestry. It is an inherited characteristic that can be found in some families as far west as eastern Europe, as it was introduced by ancient Mongol invasions.

Chloasma is a mark of motherhood, as pregnancy results in pigment being deposited in the skin of the forehead, cheeks and nipples. Unfortunately, it is also an uncommon side effect of using the contraceptive pill.

Long standing varicose veins often cause pigmentation of the overlying skin due to tiny amounts of blood leaking out of the veins and staining the skin.

Other causes of excessive skin pigmentation include melanomas (serious form of skin cancer), Hutchison melanotic freckle, haemochromatosis (excess iron in the body), carotenaemia (excessive eating of yellow fruit and vegetables), xeroderma pigmentosa (disfiguring fatty brown lumps that occur in the skin folds of people with high cholesterol levels), Cushing syndrome (over production of steroids such in the body, or taking large doses of cortisone), Addison disease (underactive adrenal glands), Von Recklinghausen's disease of multiple neurofibromatosis, scleroderma and the Peutz-Jegher syndrome.

See also BROWN PATCHES ON SKIN; FACE PIGMENTED; SKIN COLOUR and separate entries for diseases mentioned above.

SKIN PINS AND NEEDLES SENSATION

See PINS AND NEEDLES SENSATION IN SKIN

SKIN PUSTULES

See PUSTULES

SKIN RED

Any infection (eg. cellulitis, joint infection, mastitis – breast infection), inflammation (eg. eczema, gout, arthritis), injury (eg. sunburn, scald, bruise), or dilation of arteries (eg. flush, allergy, alcohol) can cause the skin to become redder than normal (erythema). There are therefore literally hundreds of different causes of red skin. A number of typical examples will be explained below.

There are many different types of dermatitis which can cause red skin. Some examples include those caused by contact of the skin with substances to which it is sensitive (contact dermatitis), sitting or lying for prolonged periods (stasis dermatitis), inflammation of the outer layers of the skin that cause excessive peeling (exfoliative dermatitis), excessive sensitivity to sunlight (photodermatitis) and inflammation of the oil glands in the skin (seborrhoeic dermatitis).

The term eczema describes a large range of skin diseases that cause itching and burning of the skin. It typically appears as red, swollen skin that is initially covered with small fluid-filled blisters that later break down to a scale or crust. The many different forms of eczema also have innumerable causes, both from within the body (eg. stress) and outside (eg. allergies, chemicals). The appearance of eczema depends more on its position on the body, duration, severity and degree of scratching than the actual cause. The specific diagnosis of the type of eczema is therefore quite difficult.

Viral infections such as measles, rubella (german measles) and infectious mononucleosis (glandular fever), as well as many other unnamed viruses, may cause a widespread slightly itchy, red rash (viral exanthema).

Urticaria (hives) is an allergy reaction in skin that causes marked swelling in patches across the affected area, and is also red and itchy. Any one of several trillion substances, from plants, animals or chemicals, may be responsible.

Cellulitis is a bacterial infection of the skin that may cause very thin-walled, soft blisters over the site of an intense infection. These blisters burst very easily, while the skin underneath is hot, red, tender, swollen and painful. The patient may have a fever, and nearby lymph nodes are often tender and enlarged.

Other causes of erythema include acne, tinea (a fungal infection of the skin), psoriasis, intertrigo (caused by heat sweat and friction in skin folds), erysipelas (bacterial infection of the layer of fat just under the skin), rosacea (skin disease of the face found most commonly in middle aged women), scarlet fever (Streptococcal bacterial infection), systemic lupus erythematosus, lichen planus, erythema multiforme and erythema nodosum.

Uncommon causes of red skin may include pellagra (a lack of vitamin B3), Lyme disease (an infection passed from mice and deer to man by tics), Sézary syndrome and Stevens-Johnson syndrome.

See also ECZEMA; FACE RED; FLUSH; RED PATCHES ON SKIN; SKIN; SKIN RED SPOTS and separate entries for most diseases mentioned above.

SKIN RED PATCHES
See RED PATCHES ON SKIN

SKIN RED SPOTS
Petechiae and purpura are tiny and small red dots respectively (there is no defined cut off size when one becomes the other) that appear in the skin when the smallest blood vessels (capillaries and arterioles) leak or burst. Leakage may be associated with a lack of platelets (blood cells that are required for the formation of clots), or one of the other factors that are essential for the formation of a blood clot.

Senile purpura occur in the elderly as their blood vessels weaken and break easily with advancing age.

An injury to the skin may cause a bruise that is surrounded by purpura.

Several severe viral infections may cause bleeding into the skin, including measles, cytomegalovirus (CMV), aseptic meningitis (infection of the membranes around the brain) and yellow fever.

Bacterial infections may also be responsible for purpura, the most serious being *Meningococcal* meningitis which may cause death within hours. Other examples include endocarditis (heart infection), tuberculosis and septicaemia (blood infection).

Thrombocytopenia is a lack of platelets in the blood, and without adequate numbers, abnormal bleeding and bruising occurs. Thrombocytopenia often occurs for no apparent reason, or it may be triggered by diseases of the bone marrow or liver, autoimmune diseases (inappropriate rejection of the body's own tissue), severe infections, alcoholism, many types of cancer, or a reaction to some medications (eg. those used to treat cancer).

Many different medications may have bleeding into the skin as an unwanted or overdose effect. Examples include aspirin, warfarin and heparin (used to prevent blood clots), quinine (for malaria and rheumatoid arthritis), thiazide diuretics (remove excess fluid), and sulpha antibiotics.

Other cases of petechiae and purpura include Cushing syndrome (over production of steroids such as cortisone in the body, or taking large doses of cortisone), polyarteritis nodosa (inflammation of arteries), vasculitis (inflammation of blood vessels that occurs because of an allergy or an autoimmune reaction), uraemia (kidney failure), Henoch-Schoenlein purpura (self-limiting disorder of the immune system that causes bleeding into the skin), severe lack of vitamin K (which is normally produced by bacteria in the gut) and scurvy (lack of vitamin C).

There are many rare causes of this problem including aplastic anaemia, disseminated intravascular coagulation, inborn defects in the chemical pathways necessary to form a blood clot (eg. haemophilia, Christmas disease) and Waterhouse-Friderichsen syndrome.
See also BLEEDING, EXCESSIVE; SKIN RED; SPIDER NAEVI and separate entries for diseases mentioned above.

SKIN SCALY
See SKIN DRY AND SCALY

SKIN STREAKS
See STRETCH MARKS

SKIN SUN SENSITIVE
See LIGHT SENSITIVE SKIN

SKIN TESTS
See ALLERGY TESTS; MANTOUX TEST; SCHICK TEST

SKIN THICK
Prolonged exposure to the sun over many years will lead to thickening of the skin, particularly on the forearms, back of the neck and face.

Skin that is constantly subjected to hard work, scratched or irritated for any reason will slowly thicken and harden.

Other causes include scleroderma (an autoimmune disease in which the skin and gut are most commonly affected), porphyria, leprosy, ichthyosis (congenital condition which causes widespread scaling and thickening of the skin), lichen sclerosis (scarring of the skin

on one side of the penis), the eosinophilia-myalgia syndrome and the Neu-Lexova syndrome.
See also SKIN; SKIN ITCH and separate entries for diseases mentioned above.

SKIN THIN
The most common cause of skin thinning is without doubt ageing. Old people have far thinner and more fragile skin than the young due to the loss of connective tissue from the skin structure. The skin replaces itself every three weeks, but this process slowly falters with age. The average eighty-year-old has skin only half as thick as when they were twenty.

Cushing syndrome is caused by an over production of steroids such as cortisone in the body, or taking large doses of cortisone to control a wide range of diseases, and causes headache, obesity, thirst, easy bruising, thin skin, impotence, menstrual period irregularities, red face, acne, high blood pressure, bone pain and muscle weakness.

In the same way, the excessive use of steroid creams on the skin for the treatment of eczema and dermatitis may cause thinning of the skin, particularly on the face.

Other causes include Ehlers-Danlos syndrome (joints that are excessively loose), Fröhlich syndrome (late onset of puberty) and the very rare Goltz syndrome (causes abnormally formed nails and scar-like areas of thin skin on the scalp, thighs and sides of the belly).
See also SKIN and separate entries for most diseases mentioned above.

SKIN ULCER
A skin ulcer is a break in the skin that penetrates to the tissue layers beneath the skin and fails to heal in a reasonable time. There are a huge number of conditions that may be responsible.

Any cut, deep graze or other skin injury that becomes infected may become an ulcer, and a persisting infection usually prevents the ulcer from healing.

Constant pressure on an area of skin, from lying or sitting in the one position without moving for many hours, will prevent the normal circulation of blood to and from that area of skin, which will die and break down into an ulcer that may be very difficult to heal (also called a bed sore). This is a common problem in the elderly and those with some form of paralysis.

Sitting still for long periods may cause a stasis ulcer because blood pools in the feet and ankles to put pressure on the skin, which again may break down into an ulcer. Elevation of the feet, pressure stockings and regular movement of the legs of people who are unable to move their own legs will prevent this problem.

The veins in the legs contain one-way valves that allow blood to only travel up towards the heart when they are squeezed by muscle action. If these valves are damaged by increased pressure (eg. during pregnancy, prolonged standing), obesity or direct injury, the blood is unable to move out of the leg as quickly, and the veins dilate with blood to form varicose veins. These may ache and put pressure on skin, which may discolour and break down into an ulcer, as they are unsightly.

Diabetes results in a higher than normal amount of sugar (glucose) circulating in the blood. The symptoms of untreated diabetes are unusual tiredness, increased thirst and hunger, excess passing of urine, weight loss despite a large food intake, itchy rashes, recurrent vaginal thrush infections, pins and needles, nerve damage, foot ulcers, dizziness, light headedness and blurred vision. Effective treatment is essential to prevent serious complications.

Other causes of ulceration include skin cancers (advanced basal cell carcinomas, squamous cell carcinomas and melanomas), chilblains (a result of exposure to extreme cold), a blood clot in a vein or artery near the skin, and damage to the sensory nerves, which will reduce pain sensation and allow patients to injure themselves without being aware of the injury. Sometimes a biopsy of the edge of an ulcer is necessary to exclude skin cancer as a cause.

Rarer causes include any cancer of an internal organ or tissue that is close to the skin surface (eg. breast cancer), Behçet syndrome, syphilis, Buerger's disease (caused by smoking), polyarteritis nodosa (inflammation of arteries), chancroid (bacterial sexually transmitted infection), granuloma inguinale, lymphogranuloma venereum and leprosy.

The treatment of an ulcer will depend on its cause, and may include covering the ulcer with a dressing that prevents irritation, removing excessive pressure on the area by regularly changing position or special mattresses or cushions, and special healing gels, plasters and dressings. Surgically excising a persistent ulcer and closing the defect by suturing or with a skin graft can be used in some cases.
See also BED SORE; GENITAL ULCER; SKIN; VENOUS ULCER

SKIN WHITE
See ALBINISM; SKIN DEPIGMENTED

SKIN YELLOW
See JAUNDICE

SKULL
The skull (cranium) acts to protect the brain, eyes, hearing mechanism of the middle and inner ears, and other organs within it, and to support the muscles, teeth, jaw (mandible) and other tissues of the head. It has openings that allow food, fluids and air to enter the body, and allow sight, hearing and communication by speech.

The skull consists of fifteen major bones, many of which fuse together at sutures. Major sutures run along the top of the skull, down behind each temple, and form a triangle at the back of the head.

The single occipital bone forms the back of the skull, while there is one parietal bone on each side, and the two frontal bones fuse soon after birth to form the forehead. The maxilla forms the upper jaw, while the zygoma arches out from the skull to support the cheek. Separate nasal bones form the base of the nose. The sphenoid bone has a very complex shape and supports the structures in the centre of the skull behind the eye. The eye socket is made of from parts of the sphenoid, frontal, zygoma and maxilla. The mastoid is a protrusion of the temporal bones, which form the lower sides of the skull and contain the ear canal. The sinuses are hollows in the front of the skull and around the eye sockets and nose.

There are about eighty five openings in the skull that vary from the large ones for the eyes and spine, to smaller ones for arteries and major nerves, and tiny ones for individual nerves and small veins.
See also BONE; CRANIAL NERVES; CRANIOSTENOSIS; HEAD LARGE; HEAD SMALL; SCALP; SINUS; SPINE

SKULL

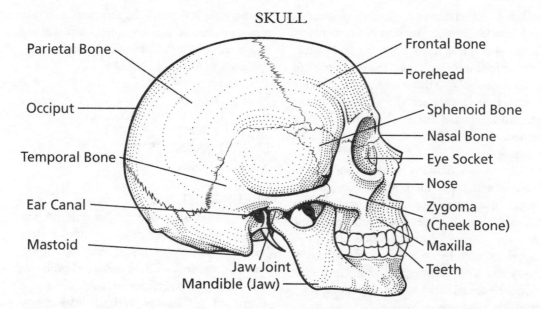

Parietal Bone

Occiput

Temporal Bone

Ear Canal

Mastoid

Jaw Joint

Mandible (Jaw)

Frontal Bone

Forehead

Sphenoid Bone

Nasal Bone

Eye Socket

Nose

Zygoma (Cheek Bone)

Maxilla

Teeth

SLAPPED CHEEK DISEASE
See FIFTH DISEASE

SLE
See SYSTEMIC LUPUS
ERYTHEMATOSUS

SLEEP APNOEA
A cessation of breathing (apnoea) during sleep most commonly occurs in overweight middle-aged men due to a complete relaxation of the small muscles at the back of the throat. The throat tissue becomes very soft, flabby and collapses as the patient breathes in, closing off the throat and preventing breathing. Snoring is caused in the same way. In elderly men with high blood pressure there may be a suppression of the urge to breathe by the brain during very deep sleep.

In sufferers, breathing stops for periods from ten to sixty seconds on many occasions during the night while asleep, resulting in tiredness during the day, morning headaches, personality changes, poor concentration, bed-wetting and impotence. The sleeping partner complains about the patient's loud snoring and thrashing, restless sleep. Minor brain damage may occur with every episode of apnoea, and this eventually leads to a noticeable deficit in brain function.

The diagnosis is best made in a sleep laboratory, where the patient's sleep and breathing pattern can be monitored through an entire night.

Treatment involves weight loss, and avoiding alcohol, sedatives and smoking. In persistent cases a small mask is fitted to the patient's nose, and air is blown up the nose at a slightly increased pressure with a small electrically driven blower (continuous positive airway pressure – CPAP). In severe cases surgery to the back of the throat and nose to remove the uvula and part of the soft palate opens the airway. A significant deterioration in the quality of life may occur unless successfully treated.
See also CONTINUOUS POSITIVE
AIRWAY PRESSURE MACHINE;
SNORING

SLEEP EXCESS
Excessive sleeping is usually due to exhaustion from extra physical exercise, mental activity, stress or anxiety, but may be due to some unusual medical conditions.

Excessive sleeping from concussion after a head injury is relatively common, but if this becomes prolonged, or is associated with vomiting, confusion, changes in the size of the pupils in the eyes, bleeding from the nose or an ear, fits, spasms, severe headache or double vision, further medical assistance is essential.

A number of psychiatric conditions may have excess sleeping as an effect as the patient attempts to escape reality.

Epilepsy is a condition that causes recurrent seizures (fits). Fits can vary from very mild 'absences' to the grand mal convulsion. After a major fit, it is very common for a patient to sleep, sometimes for some hours.

Narcolepsy is an unusual disorder of the brain's electrical activity that is characterised by sudden periods of sleeping for five to thirty minutes several times a day, hallucinations and sudden muscle weakness immediately before and during sleep. There is a wide range of severity from those who merely appear to sleep excessively, to those who are barely able to function or care for themselves. Patients may suddenly fall asleep in the middle of a sentence, or when halfway across a pedestrian crossing.

Other causes include a tumour, cancer, cyst, bleed or abscess in the brain or surrounding tissues that puts pressure on vital centres in the brain to affect sleeping patterns, and the Kleine-Levin syndrome (episodes every few months of severe excessive sleepiness, increased appetite, mood disturbances, increased sexual activity, disorientation, hallucinations and memory loss).

Excess sleeping may be the result of excess alcohol, or the effect of medications such as sedatives, antihistamines (used for allergy and colds) and tricyclic antidepressants.
See also FATIGUE and separate entries for diseases and medications mentioned above.

SLEEP JERKS
See HYPNIC JERKS

SLEEPING SICKNESS
Sleeping sickness (African trypanosomiasis) is a parasitic disease of lymph nodes and the brain that only occurs in tropical Africa. It is caused by the tiny parasite *Trypanosoma brucei* (of which there are three further subtypes), which is transmitted from game animals, cattle and sheep to humans by the bite of the tsetse fly.

A sore develops at the site of the tsetse fly bite, followed a few days later by tender and enlarged lymph nodes in the groin armpit and neck, fever, headache, rashes and joint pain. Often there are week-long periods of perfect health, followed by a recurrence of the symptoms. As the disease progresses, the patient loses weight, becomes very tired and, as the brain becomes involved, wants to sleep constantly. It can be diagnosed by specific blood tests.

Travellers to tropical Africa should avoid tsetse bites by wearing trousers and long-sleeved shirts, using insect nets at night and an insect repellent by day. Drugs are available to treat the disease, but early treatment is essential as permanent brain damage may

remain after recovery. The infection may take many months to run its course but without treatment, it is almost invariably fatal.
See also CHAGAS' DISEASE

SLEEP LACK
See CHILDHOOD; INSOMNIA

SLEEPLESSNESS
See INSOMNIA

SLEEP STUDIES
Sleep studies are performed mainly on patients with respiratory problems during sleep (eg. sleep apnoea, snoring), but also sometimes on patients with neurological problems and insomnia. Obstructive sleep apnoea is diagnosed by having various instruments attached and a series of measurements made throughout the night while the patient is sleeping – electrodes on the head to establish sleep states, special bands around the chest and abdomen to detect movement, a sensor to detect air flow at the nose and mouth, and an oximeter on the finger or ear to detect oxygen levels in the blood.
See also INSOMNIA; RESPIRATORY FUNCTION TESTS; SLEEP APNOEA; SNORING

SLING
Slings are used to rest, support or immobilise injuries to an upper limb or shoulder. They are triangular in shape and can be adapted from any suitably shaped piece of material.

An arm sling is used to support an injured forearm in a position roughly parallel to the ground. The victim should support the injured arm, with the wrist and hand raised higher than the elbow. Place the open sling between the chest and forearm, with the apex of the triangle stretching well beyond the elbow, the top point hanging over the shoulder on the uninjured side. The bottom point is towards the ground so that the long side of the triangle hangs down, parallel to the body. Bring the apex round the elbow so that it lies flat along the arm. Bring the base point up over the forearm and the top point around the neck so that the two points meet in the hollow just above the collar bone on the injured side. Tie the two ends in a reef knot.

An elevation sling is used if the hand or forearm is injured, or to provide support for an injured shoulder without causing pressure on the shoulder or upper chest. The victim should rest the hand of the injured side on the opposite shoulder, with the elbow and upper arm held close against the chest. Cover the forearm and hand with a sling, with the apex of the triangle pointing towards the bent elbow, and the top point over the victim's shoulder on the uninjured side. The base point should be hanging down, so that the long side of the triangle extends down the length of the body. Gently push the base of the sling under the hand, forearm and elbow of the injured limb. Then bring the lower end of the base up and around the victim's back on the injured side. Bring the two ends of the sling together around the back of the victim and secure with a reef knot on the uninjured side. Fold the top of the sling at the elbow, and fasten it with a pin or tape, or tuck it in.

Check the victim's fingernails to make sure they have not turned blue. If they have, loosen the sling or bandage.
See also FIRST AID; FRACTURE; SPRAIN

SLIPPED DISC
See INTERVERTEBRAL DISC PROLAPSE

SMALL CELL CARCINOMA
See LUNG CANCER

SMALL HEAD
See HEAD SMALL

SMALL INTESTINE
The small intestine is the part of the gut where the main and final process of digestion takes place. By the time the ingested food reaches the small intestine, it will have passed from the mouth to the oesophagus (gullet) and down through the stomach. It is here that food is converted into tiny chemical units, small enough to pass through the wall of the intestine into blood vessels and lymphatic vessels which carry the nutrients from the food to provide fuel for the body's cells.

The small intestine is a narrow tube, seven to ten metres long, consisting of a series of loosely packed loops. It is actually considerably longer than the large intestine but is referred to as small because it is much narrower. Its structure is much the same as the stomach – a muscular wall that propels food along in waves and an inner mucous lining that contains glands which produce digestive juices.

The rate of absorption of digested food depends on the extent of the surface area over which it must pass. The larger the area, the more rapidly matter can pass over it. To increase the surface area of the small intestine, the inner lining is covered with millions of tiny finger-like projections called villi. The villi give the surface a velvety texture and facilitate the absorption of digested food into the body.

The small intestine is divided into three parts – the top part attached to the stomach is called the duodenum, the middle section is called the jejunum, and the remaining portion is called the ileum.
See also DUODENUM; ILEUM; JEJUNUM; LARGE INTESTINE; LYMPHATIC SYSTEM; PORTAL SYSTEM

SMALL PENIS
See PENIS SMALL

SMALLPOX
Smallpox (variola major) was a highly contagious virus infection, and the first disease in history to be totally eradicated by vaccination, the last case occurring in Somalia in 1978. Vaccination is no longer necessary anywhere in the world.

Symptoms included blistering sores on the skin, severe headache and high fever. No treatment was available, and more than half of all patients died.
See also CHICKENPOX; JENNER, EDWARD; VIRUS

SMEAR TEST
See PAP SMEAR

SMEGMA
Smegma is the natural lubricant found under the foreskin of males that enables the foreskin to slide back and forward across the head of the penis. It may appear as a white discharge similar to milk curds if present in excess, particularly in uncircumcised boys and men who have a narrow opening to the foreskin.

It is not necessary to clean smegma away, and excessive cleaning under the foreskin may cause soreness and dryness due to a lack of smegma.
See also PENIS

612   THE COMPLETE FAMILY MEDICAL GUIDE

SMELL

Our sense of smell is closely linked with the sense of taste. When eating, aromas from the food pass from the mouth through the throat to the nose, where they stimulate the smell receptors. This is why there is such a strong connection between the smell of food and appetite.

The sense of smell is extremely acute – about 10 000 times more sensitive than the sense of taste, but in modern humans it is not as important to our effective functioning as other senses such as sight and hearing. Smell can detect a far greater variety of substances than taste (there are thousands of smells and only four tastes).

Smell operates by means of hair-like organs called the olfactory nerves which are located high in the nose. Substances that have a smell give out gases or vapours into the air. The olfactory nerves detect these gases and pass the information to the nerve centre of the brain. Substances that are converted easily to gas or vapour, such as petrol or ammonia, have a strong smell. Sometimes strong smells trigger the sense of touch in the nose (eg. the smell of ammonia may cause the nose to sting, and the smell of camphor may cause a feeling of cold). The fact that the olfactory nerves are so far back and high up in the nose is the reason it is necessary to sniff to smell something carefully. The olfactory organ of smell is actually level with the eyebrows.

The sense of smell adapts quickly. A smell that at first might be extremely unpleasant becomes tolerable after a relatively short period as the person gets used to it.

Smell seems to be supported by an extremely good memory. Once something has been smelt it is usually readily recalled and identified.

Smell deteriorates with age and the sense of smell becomes less acute. It is therefore important to provide attractive-looking meals for elderly people so that their appetite will be stimulated. Smell is also affected by respiratory illness. If the nose becomes congested because of a cold, air is stopped from reaching the smell receptors, and the ability to smell temporarily disappears.

Because smell is so closely linked with taste, if the sense of smell is not working, patients may think they have lost their sense of taste as well. But this is not the case – what the patient has is actually pure taste. The close connection between smell and taste can be experienced in another way too. If someone closes their eyes and blocks their nose, onions and apples will taste almost the same!
See also NOSE; SMELL LOSS; TASTE

SMELL LOSS

Smell is perceived by a network of sensitive hairs at the top of the nose cavity. A permanent loss of the sense of smell (anosmia) is uncommon, but a temporary loss may be due to a common cold or other infection in the nose.

The sense of smell becomes less sensitive in the elderly, and some medications (eg. phenol) and metal poisoning (eg. chrome) may affect the sense of smell. After exposure to a very strong smell (eg. ammonia), it may take some hours for the sense of smell to return to normal.

Fractures of the front of the skull may damage the olfactory (smell) nerve and affect the sense of smell, as may tumours, cancer, abscesses or cysts in the part of the brain that is responsible for processing the signals from this nerve.

An underactive thyroid gland (hypothyroidism) may also be responsible.
See also SMELL; TASTE ABNORMAL and separate entries for diseases mentioned above.

SMELLY EAR
See EAR SMELL

SMITH'S FRACTURE

A Smith's fracture occurs if the wrist is bent forward excessively to cause a fracture of the forearm bones (ulna and radius) just above the wrist. Falling onto the back of the outstretched hand is a common cause.

There is pain, tenderness, swelling, deformity and loss of function of the forearm and wrist.

The fracture is diagnosed by an x-ray, and then the bones must be put back into place under an anaesthetic and held in position by plaster. A persistent deformity may occur if incorrectly aligned.

This fracture normally heals well after six weeks in plaster in an adult, and three to four weeks in a child.
See also COLLES' FRACTURE;
FRACTURE; RADIUS; SCAPHOID
FRACTURE; ULNAR; WRIST

SMOKING

If beetroot and rhubarb, just for instance, were found not only to cause cancer in 10% of their heavy consumers, but eventually to bring 25% to an early death, no-one would consume them, and the government would long ago have legislated against growing them. Sadly, this is just what cigarette smoking does, but the sale of cigarettes is permitted, cigarettes have been heavily promoted by advertising, and large profits are made from their sale.

Over the centuries, since the introduction of tobacco to Europe in the 1590s, more and more people have become addicted to nicotine. Women started smoking in public only during the First World War, and the habit reached a peak during the Second World War when 75% of the adult population of most western countries were smokers. When today's grandparents were children, they were warned against smoking because 'it stunts the growth' (something it only does to the babies of smoking mothers), but generally it was not regarded as harmful, at least for adults. Cigarettes, cigars, lighters, pipes, ashtrays, etc., were standard gifts at Christmas and birthday for a generation. Vast factories poured out billions of cigarettes that were made, packed, wrapped and boxed untouched by human hands. Multinational tobacco corporations gained enormous profits, and became powerful friends of government as taxpayers and revenue earners. Governments even subsidised the growth of tobacco in some areas. Then came the crunch. It was found that smoking tobacco killed people. There is a long delay, and more than half the smokers escape, but there was little doubt about it – for many people smoking was lethal.

Nicotine is a very powerful and toxic substance that acts initially as a stimulant on the central nervous system, but this effect is followed by a reduction of brain and nervous system activity. Nicotine causes narrowing of blood vessels, which then affects the circulation and causes blood pressure to rise. This is why regular absorption of nicotine through smoking can cause chronic heart problems and increases the possibility of heart attacks. In addition to nicotine, tobacco smoke contains many other chemicals which are harmful, including tar and carbon monoxide. Tar released in the form of particles in the smoke is the main cause of lung and throat cancer in smokers and also aggravates bronchial and respiratory disease.

We now know that 11% of smokers will get lung cancer, and 90% of these patients will die. Coronary heart disease will kill many prematurely. Chronic lung disease will cripple a large proportion of the remainder. Women smokers have an increased risk of cancer of the cervix. The medical facts are conclusive – smoking is the biggest preventable health problem in the Western world. It contributes to more deaths than alcohol and illicit drugs together, and costs the economies of these countries millions of dollars a year. If nobody smoked, there would be 30% less cancer.

Smokers just can't win in any way. In a Boston study smokers were found to have 50% more traffic accidents and 46% more traffic violation convictions than non-smokers.

SMOKING IN PREGNANCY

There is no doubt that the babies of mothers who smoke are smaller (by 200g on average) than those of non-smoking mothers. There is also an increased rate of premature labour (delivering the baby too early), miscarriage and stillbirth in these women. After birth, babies of smoking mothers continue to suffer both directly and indirectly from their mother's smoking. The smoking by the mother appears to reduce their resistance to disease, in particular to infection, so that babies born to smoking mothers die in infancy more often than average. By inhaling the smoke from either of their parents, these infants have more colds, bronchitis and other respiratory problems than babies in non-smoking homes.

Any woman who smokes should ideally cease before she falls pregnant, but certainly should do so when the pregnancy is diagnosed. This is far easier said than done, but if her partner stops at the same time, support and encouragement is given by family and friends, and assistance is obtained from the family doctor, women who are motivated to give their baby the best possible chance in life will succeed in kicking this very addictive habit.

SMOKING CESSATION

Before anyone can stop smoking, they must really want to stop. No one who is half-hearted about wanting to stop will ever succeed. Once you have decided to stop, set a time and date for the event. Tell everyone you know of your intentions, and take side-bets if you can, to reinforce your incentive. Make lists of reasons why you must stop, and leave them everywhere at home and at work. Make sure that from the moment you stop, you have no cigarettes available to you, and resist the temptation to buy or beg for more. Start a savings account with the money you save by not smoking, and if you don't succeed, pay the balance to the Cancer Fund! Nicotine-containing gum or patches can be used to ease the craving for cigarettes.

If these incentives are not sufficient, see a doctor. They can prescribe a medication (bupropion) that can reduce the craving for nicotine, or teach you how to best use nicotine patches or gum. Group therapy sessions, hypnotherapy, psychological counselling, support groups, rewards at the end of each successful week and reinforcement visits to your doctor can all help win the fight.

At present, 26% of the adult population in western Europe smokes, but this figure is decreasing every year. The lowest rate of smoking in the world is in Australia where only 19% of adults indulge. It will soon become so antisocial that it will only be permitted by consenting adults in private!

PASSIVE SMOKING

Almost everyone is forced to inhale fumes containing toxins such as formaldehyde, acetone, arsenic, carbon monoxide, hydrogen cyanide and nicotine at some time. You have no choice in the matter and have to suffer the consequences, because these chemicals are just a few of the scores of irritants found in cigarette smoke. Fortunately for most of us, the result of passive involuntary smoking is only a minor itch of the nose, a cough or a sneeze, but some people can develop life-threatening asthma attacks or have their heart condition aggravated by inhaling tobacco smoke. Being trapped in a vehicle or other enclosed space with a smoker can be a nightmare experience for such people. In some situations the non-smoker may be more affected than the smoker, because the smoke coming directly from a cigarette contains more toxins, nicotine and carbon monoxide than that inhaled by the smoker, which has been more completely burnt and passed through a filter.

The most unfortunate victims of passive smoking are the children of smokers. The incidence of pneumonia and bronchitis and the severity of asthma in children whose parents smoke are far higher than in the children of non-smokers. In babies of women who smoke, health problems caused by passive smoking begin before birth (see above).

In the workplace, more and more offices are becoming smoke-free zones. Unfortunately some people still smoke at work, and if their subordinates have adverse reactions to passive smoking, they may have to put up with it or change jobs. This situation may change in the future, as more and more workers are successfully claiming workers compensation payments for complications of passive smoking at work.

The non-smoking spouse or partner of a smoker is also at great risk. They have a significantly increased risk of lung cancer, reduced lung capacity, a higher incidence of asthma, and more respiratory infections than those whose spouses or partners do not smoke.

Smokers should now be aware of the health risks that they are taking every day, and they can no longer claim personal freedom to smoke where and when they like, as their habit is adversely affecting the health of those around them. All smokers should have the courtesy to only light up when there is no possibility of others inhaling the resultant toxic fumes. Legal suits by passive smokers against smokers for causing bodily harm have been successful in the United States.

DISEASES CAUSED BY SMOKING

As well as slowing wound healing after injury or surgery, there are many diseases that may be caused or aggravated by smoking including asbestosis, amblyopia, aneurysm, angina, asthma, bronchiectasis, bronchitis, Buerger's disease, catarrh, cervical cancer, common cold, cor pulmonale, emphysema, histiocytosis X, hypercholesterolaemia, hypertension, laryngitis, laryngotracheobronchitis, Legionnaire's disease, lung cancer, mesothelioma, mouth cancer, oesophageal cancer, osteoporosis, peptic ulcer, pneumoconiosis, pneumonia, reflux oesophagitis, sleep apnoea, snoring, tachycardia, talcosis, thrombosis and many others.

See also BREATH BAD; BUPROPION; LUNG CANCER; NICOTINE and separate entries for diseases listed above.

SNAKE BITE

Snakes usually retreat from a human intruding into their habitat unless surprised or cornered,

---

FIRST AID FOR SNAKE BITE

- keep the victim calm and move them as little as possible to prevent spread of poison.
- apply pressure directly to the bite.
- if the bite is on a limb, apply pressure immobilisation by bandaging the limb firmly, starting at the bitten area and working to the fingers or toes, then back up the limb to the armpit or groin.
- immobilise the limb with a splint (eg. a small branch) or by bandaging it to the other limb.
- check the victim's breathing and pulse regularly, and give mouth-to-mouth resuscitation if breathing stops, and cardiopulmonary resuscitation if the pulse stops.
- get medical assistance as soon as possible.

---

and most non-venomous snakes do not bite (the carpet python is an exception). A bite from a snake is more serious in a child than an adult because the proportion of venom relative to body size is greater.

Signs of envenomation may include nausea, vomiting, headache, giddiness, double vision, drowsiness, tightening in the chest, diarrhoea, sweating, difficulty in breathing, and there may be reddening, swelling, bruising or persistent bleeding at the site of the bite. Symptoms may occur from fifteen minutes to two hours after the bite. Ulceration and permanent damage to tissue around the site of the bite may be complications.

NEVER cauterise the bite or try to suck the venom out – this will cause the victim's blood to flow more swiftly as it hurries to plug the wound, and will only spread the poison.

The responsible snake can be identified by taking swabs from around the bite site, then an antivenene is given (these are available for all poisonous snake bites), and specific blood and other tests are used to monitor a patient's progress in hospital. In developed countries with good health care, only 2% of bites from potentially deadly snakes are now fatal.
See also ANTIVENENE; RESUSCITATION

SNEEZE
The usual cause of sneezing is an increase in the secretions in the nose, but sudden changes in temperature (eg. walking in or out of an air-conditioned building), drinking alcohol, eating spicy food and emotional upsets may also be responsible (vasomotor rhinitis).

Nasal secretions may be increased by a viral (eg. common cold) or bacterial (eg. sinusitis) infection, allergies (eg. hay fever), enlarged adenoid lymph nodes at the back of the nose, a foreign body in the nose (eg. a child putting a peanut in their nose), polyps in the nose or an injury (eg. blow) to the nose.

Women may find that the sensitivity of their nose to many irritants (eg. hay fever, temperature changes) will vary at different times of the month due to differences in the levels of their sex hormones (eg. oestrogen). Pregnancy and the oral contraceptive pill will also alter hormone levels.

Some uncommon medications may have increased nasal secretions as a side effect (eg. reserpine and guanethidine used for high blood pressure), while other medications (eg. aspirin) may cause an allergy reaction that include sneezing as one of its features.
See also NOSE DISCHARGE and separate entries for diseases mentioned above.

SNORING
The noises, sounds, eruptions, gargles and other auditory traumas associated with snoring are impossible to express adequately in print. The effects upon a spouse or entire family may be sufficient to lead to arguments, fights or even divorce and mental illness. The greatest problem with snoring is that the

VIEW INTO MOUTH

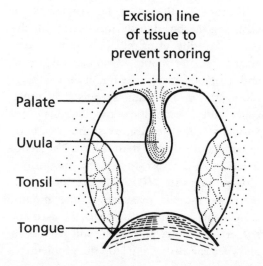

Excision line
of tissue to
prevent snoring

Palate

Uvula

Tonsil

Tongue

snorer is often unaffected, but those around him (and most snorers are male) are the victims.

Snoring is the production of a harsh, rough sound caused by the passage of air through the mouth, throat and nose during sleep. It can occur intermittently during colds, flu or throat infections and with hay fever because of the excess production of phlegm and the swelling of tissues at these times, or it may occur almost every night.

In persistent cases, snoring is due to the vibration of the uvula or soft palate with the movement of air in and out of the mouth. The uvula is the piece of tissue that can be seen hanging down the back of the throat when the mouth is wide open, and the soft palate is the back part of the roof of the mouth, to which the uvula is attached. In some cases snoring is associated with periods when the breathing stops completely for up to a minute (sleep apnoea), which is due to collapse of the soft tissues of the throat during sleep. It may cause significant health problems to the sufferer.

Other causes include enlargement of the tonsils or adenoids at the back of the throat, a broken nose that has an abnormal shape, polyps in the nose, or other distortions of the shape of the nose or throat.

The excessive use of alcohol, sleeping pills or sedatives will relax the tissues and muscles in the throat to make snoring more likely.

Smoking can increase the secretion of phlegm in the nose and sinuses, and cause persistent inflammation of the throat, which also increases the risk of snoring.

If severe, snoring may need to be investigated in a sleep laboratory, where the patient can be monitored through an entire night.

Treatments that may be tried include changing the position during sleep from the back to the side, using pillows or straps if necessary. Patients should lose weight if obese, and stop sedatives, alcohol and smoking. Nose clips and dilating springs may prove successful. Sometimes medications (eg. antidepressants, respiratory stimulants, anti-inflammatory drugs, steroids) may be beneficial. In severe cases a continuous positive airway pressure (CPAP) machine that increases the air pressure in the mouth, throat and major airways can be used, or surgery to remove part of the soft palate can allow a clear airway and stop the problem.

See also CONTINUOUS POSITIVE AIRWAY PRESSURE MACHINE; SLEEP APNOEA and separate entries for diseases mentioned above.

SNOW BLIND
See KERATITIS

SNRI
See ANTIDEPRESSANTS

SOCIAL ANXIETY DISORDER
The social anxiety disorder (SAD) is a common form of neurosis in which the patient realises that they have an irrational level of anxiety or fear. It may be due to an unfortunate experience earlier in life, depression, trauma or stress, but often no cause can be identified.

Patients have a prolonged (greater than six months), marked and persistent abnormal fear about one or more social activities such that fear of embarrassment causes avoidance of others, avoidance of activities that draw attention, and a fear of looking stupid in the eyes of others. The patient does everything possible to avoid these situations, or they are endured with intense anxiety. If exposed to a feared situation, patients may develop a tremor, stuttering, sweating, rapid heart rate and collapse. Severely affected patients may become totally housebound and unable to function in society. Other psychiatric conditions (eg. schizophrenia, anorexia nervosa), physiological and metabolic disorders may need to be excluded.

Counselling, abreaction (gradual exposure under supervision to situations that provoke fear), and some types of antidepressant medications are used in treatment. There is usually a good response to appropriate treatment.
See also ANXIETY; NEUROSIS; POST-TRAUMATIC STRESS DISORDER

SODIUM
Sodium (Na) is a vital element in the body as a part of common salt (sodium chloride – NaCl), and as such is found in every bodily fluid and tissue. It plays a vital part in electrical conduction in nerves, plays a role in muscle contraction and regulates the amount of fluid in the body. The more sodium in the body, the more fluid is retained by the kidneys, and vice

versa. Dehydration may be due to lack of water or lack of salt (sodium).

The amount of sodium in the body is regulated by the hormone aldosterone, which is produced in the adrenal glands that sit on top of each kidney. Salt is obtained from a very wide range of foods. Excess intake in the diet may increase blood pressure.

Blood tests can be performed to determine the level of sodium present. The normal range is from 135 to 145 mmol/L.

The amount of sodium in the body can be measured by blood tests. Low levels of sodium (hyponatraemia) may be due to excess water intake, severe diarrhoea, kidney disease, an underactive thyroid gland, diabetes mellitus, Addison's disease, and numerous other medical conditions. Medications such as diuretics, tricyclic antidepressants, carbamazepine, phenothiazines and clofibrate may also be responsible.

High levels of sodium (hypernatraemia) may be caused by dehydration, salt water drowning, uraemia, diabetes insipidus, an over active adrenal gland, excess salt intake and mechanical ventilation.
See also ALDOSTERONE; BLOOD TESTS; MINERALS

SODIUM CITROTARTRATE
See ALKALINISERS

SODIUM CROMOGLYCATE
See ASTHMA PREVENTION MEDICATION

SODIUM VALPROATE
See ANTICONVULSANTS

SOILING
See INCONTINENCE OF FAECES

SOLAR KERATOSIS
See HYPERKERATOSIS

SOLAR PLEXUS
See GANGLION

SONOGRAPHER
A sonographer is a person who has undertaken tertiary training to perform, but not report on, ultrasound examinations.
See also RADIOGRAPHER

SORE THROAT
See THROAT PAIN

SOTALOL
See ANTIARRHYTHMICS

SPASM
See HAND SPASM; MUSCLE CRAMP; MUSCLE TONE EXCESSIVE; TIC; TREMOR

SPASTIC COLON
See IRRITABLE BOWEL SYNDROME

SPASTICITY
See CEREBRAL PALSY

SPEAKING
See HOARSE VOICE; SPEECH DIFFICULT

SPECIAL K
See KETAMINE

SPEECH DIFFICULT
Difficulty in speaking (dysarthria) may be caused by an intellectual handicap, damage to the brain, or damage to nerves supplying the muscles responsible for speech. The specific speech disability of a stammer (stutter) is dealt with separately.

Damage to or scarring of the vocal cords or throat from shouting or speaking for a long time (hoarse voice), inhaling hot or toxic gases, surgery or injury to the throat will affect the ability to speak.

In a stroke (cerebrovascular accident) part of the brain is affected by having its blood supply cut off by a blockage in an artery, or a blood vessel in the brain may burst causing bleeding and damage to part of the brain. It may be associated with paralysis in various parts of the body, headache, shortness of breath and other abnormalities that can vary from minor discomfort and confusion to widespread paralysis and coma, depending upon which parts of the brain are affected.

Transient ischaemic attacks are a temporary blocking of a small artery in the brain by a blood clot, piece of plaque from a cholesterol deposit in an artery, or spasm of an artery, which results in that part of the brain failing to function for a short time.

A tumour, cancer, abscess, or cyst in the

brain or surrounding tissues, or a bleed (eg. from a head injury) anywhere in the skull, may put pressure on the brain that affects its function.

Other causes of difficulty in speech include multiple sclerosis (a degenerative nerve disease), motor neurone disease, the Guillain-Barré syndrome (progressive symmetrical weakness of the limbs and face), hypothyroidism (underactive thyroid gland), Shy-Drager syndrome (progressive brain degeneration), Sydenham's chorea (complication of rheumatic fever) and Moebius syndrome (failure of nerves from the brain to develop properly before birth).

Alcohol, heroin, marijuana and some medications (eg. sedatives) may affect brain function and cause slurring or difficulty in speech.

See also HOARSE VOICE; SPEECH PATHOLOGY; STUTTER and separate entries for diseases mentioned above.

SPEECH PATHOLOGY

Speech pathologists (also known as speech therapists) have completed a degree at a university in their particular area of knowledge and skill, which involves the diagnosis and treatment of speech, language, stuttering and voice problems. The aim of speech pathology is to help a person to communicate as effectively as possible. Speech pathology does NOT involve the art of fine speech (elocution), diction or teaching English as a foreign language.

Children are often referred for speech pathology because they may jumble their sounds, which causes them frustration or embarrassment if they are unable to make themselves understood. A speech pathologist can recognise the difference between an immature sound pattern that will improve spontaneously and a confused pattern where therapy will be needed to teach the child to hear and correct wrong sounds.

Children may also need speech pathology to help in the development of language skills. They may be slow in acquiring words or in using sentences compared with their peers. Parents should also seek therapy if their child appears confused or is having difficulty understanding what others say.

Adults with speech difficulties can be limited in their choice of employment, as clear speech is essential in many careers. They may seek the assistance of a speech pathologist.

Sometimes accident, illness or injury interferes with speech and language which has been developing normally. A person who has had a stroke may have good hearing but because of brain damage may not understand what is heard. Also he or she may be confused in the use of words to express his/her thoughts and intentions and have a marked loss in speech. A speech pathologist will organise exercises to help the person relearn to communicate to the best of his/her ability.

In some cases, therapy may not be able to help in the development of oral communication. For example, in severe cerebral palsy, the speech therapist may teach the use of alternative means of communication, such as word boards or electronic aids.

Speech pathology can also help overcome the problem of stuttering. It can offer a person a new way of talking smoothly, but it does not provide a cure.

See also SPEECH DIFFICULT; STUTTER

SPEED
See AMPHETAMINE ABUSE

SPERM

Microscopically small sperm cells are made in the testicles and are shaped like microscopic tadpoles with a long thin tail that propels them along at 18cm. an hour. Millions are released by each ejaculation. Only one sperm cell out of these millions is able to fertilise an egg. The sperm need to be produced at a slightly lower temperature than that which is normal in the body, so the testicles hang down away from the body in the scrotum, and are about 4°C cooler than the body.

The sperm is divided into a head and a tail. The head contains the nucleus and its genetic material (chromosomes) and the acrosome, which is used to penetrate into an ovum

HUMAN SPERM

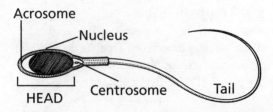

Acrosome
Nucleus
HEAD
Centrosome
Tail

(egg). The tail allows propulsion while the centrosome at the base of the tail plays a part in the preparation of the genetic material.
See also SPERMICIDES; TESTICLE

SPERMATOCELE

A spermatocele is a sperm filled cyst in the epididymis at the top end of the testicle. The epididymis consists of hundreds of tiny tubules that collect sperm from the testes, and join up to lead into the vas deferens which takes the sperm to the seminal vesicle (sperm storage sac) and penis. Cyst formation may follow an injury to the testicle or a vasectomy, but often appears for no apparent reason.

A lump is felt at the top of the testicle, but separate from the testicle. It is usually painless, but may become painful if injured or infected. Bleeding into the cyst after an injury may cause a sudden increase in size and pain.

It is usually a clinical diagnosis, but an ultrasound scan can confirm the diagnosis if there is any concern.

No treatment is necessary unless the patient finds the cyst painful, uncomfortable or worrying, when it can be drained or removed.
See also HYDROCELE; TESTICLE

SPERMICIDES

There are creams, foams, gels and pessaries (tablets) which act to kill sperm on contact. A pessary can be inserted high into the vagina at the opening to the womb by hand, but creams, gels and foams are usually inserted with an applicator. A spermicide should be inserted no more than twenty minutes before intercourse and a new application must be inserted before each ejaculation. Even used strictly as directed, the failure rate of such contraceptives is high, and they are more suitable for use in conjunction with other methods (eg. diaphragm, condom) rather than on their own.
See also CONTRACEPTIVES

SPHENOID BONE
See SKULL

SPHEROCYTIC ANAEMIA
See SPHEROCYTOSIS

SPHEROCYTOSIS

Spherocytosis is an uncommon inherited form of anaemia caused by red blood cells that swell and become more rounded (spherical) than they should be. These large cells cannot fit through the smallest capillaries, block them, and damage organs such as the spleen.

The severity can vary markedly from one patient to another, but most patients are ill from soon after birth with weakness, jaundice (yellow skin) from excess red cell destruction and an enlarged spleen. It is diagnosed by the abnormal appearance of red blood cells seen through a microscope on a blood film.

Treatment involves folic acid supplements and surgery to remove the spleen, which is responsible for the anaemia by destroying too many red cells. There is no cure, but reasonable control is usually possible.
See also ANAEMIA; RED BLOOD CELLS

SPHYGMOMANOMETER

The heart contracts regularly to pump blood through the arteries under high (systolic) pressure. When the heart relaxes between beats, the blood continues to flow due to the lower (diastolic) pressure exerted by the elasticity of the artery walls. Blood pressure readings are written as systolic pressure/diastolic pressure (eg. 125/70) and are measured with a sphygmomanometer.

A sphygmomanometer works by compressing the artery in the upper arm. The cuff is inflated to a high pressure so that the artery is completely compressed and no blood can pass. The pressure is then slowly lowered until the blood can squirt past the constriction when the variable pressure is at its maximum. This squirting can be heard by a doctor through a stethoscope which is placed over the artery, just below the cuff on the inside of the elbow. As the pressure drops further, the lower pressure is eventually sufficient to keep the artery open at all times, so that the squirting through the narrowed segment that occurs at a higher pressure can no longer be heard. The doctor notes on the gauge of the sphygmomanometer the pressures at which the noise can first be heard, and when it disappears. The blood pressure can also be measured in the thigh in the same way.

Electronic sphygmomanometers that work almost automatically are available, and are reasonably accurate. They are most useful for people who are being investigated for hypertension to use for a week or two at home with readings being taken several times a day, with the results being assessed by a doctor at the

end of that time. The devices that measure blood pressure in the finger or wrist are less accurate.
See also HEART; HYPERTENSION; STETHOSCOPE

SPIDER BITE

There are very few spiders in the world that can inflict serious injury to humans. There are none in Europe or North America, but Australia has two potentially fatal spiders.

The eastern Australian funnel-web spider is a large black, furry spider about 2-3cm. across. It lives in rock crevices, burrows, post holes, under houses or around dead tree roots. The bite is intensely painful, and the victim will usually be frightened and distressed. Further symptoms include tingling around the mouth, muscular spasm or weakness, excessive sweating, profuse salivation, nausea, abdominal pain, numbness, coughing up of secretions from the lungs, weeping eyes, cold shivers and breathing difficulty. Long term, ulcer formation and scarring may occur at the bite site.

Keep the victim calm and move them as little as possible, apply pressure immobilisation to the limb and get medical help as soon as possible. Check the victim's breathing and pulse regularly, and give mouth-to-mouth resuscitation if breathing stops, and cardiopulmonary resuscitation if the pulse stops. An effective antivenene injection is available. Death may occur with funnel web spider bites, but is uncommon.

The Australian red-back spider is found in dark and protected areas, often hiding under cast-off tins and other rubbish. Only the female bites, and her body is the size of a pea, dark brown to black in colour, with the distinctive red or orange stripe running down the back. Symptoms include intense pain at the site of the bite, tingling around the mouth, generalised pain, nausea and vomiting, profuse sweating, weakness and faintness, swelling around the bite and a rapid pulse. An ulcer may form at the bite site.

Reassure the victim, relieve the pain by applying an ice cube wrapped in damp material to the bite (but do not freeze or damage the skin) and get medical help. Do NOT apply pressure immobilisation. An antivenene injection is available. Red-back spider venom is relatively slow-acting, and provided there is no undue delay in obtaining treatment the victim should recover. Deaths have occurred in infants, but not older children.

No investigations are normally necessary with either type of bite, but swabs may be taken from the bite site for venom identification.
See also ANTIVENENE; RESUSCITATION; SNAKE BITE

SPIDER NAEVI

Spider naevi (telangiectasia) are an over dilation of a capillary that becomes visible on the skin. They are commonly caused by sun damage to the skin, but pregnancy and a number of diseases may also be responsible, including liver failure, an overactive thyroid gland, alcoholism and rheumatoid arthritis.

The dilated blood vessels usually appear on the nose and cheeks and look like tiny red spiders. The small blood vessels can be seen diverging from a central point.

Each individual naevus can be treated by cryotherapy (freezing), laser or diathermy (electrical heat) to the central blood vessel which destroys it. A small white spot will remain at the site.

These naevi may bleed excessively if damaged.
See also SKIN RED SPOTS

SPIGELIAN HERNIA

This is a rare hernia occurring between muscle bundles in the lower belly wall, due to weakness in the muscle wall from obesity, or wasting of muscles in chronic disease. A soft lump appears just above the pubic bone to the left or right of centre in the lower belly, and if the intestine or other tissue becomes trapped in the hernia, it may be painful and tender. Usually the lump can be pushed back into the belly when the patient lies down.

Surgery can be performed to repair the defect in the muscle wall, but obesity may make it complicated.
See also ABDOMINAL LUMP; HERNIA

SPINA BIFIDA

The spinal cord runs from the base of the brain, through the vertebrae of the back, and carries nerve messages from the brain to the body. Spina bifida is a failure of the vertebra to close over the spinal cord during development as a foetus. There are several degrees of severity: –
• Spina bifida occulta is the mildest form in

which only the vertebral arch is affected, and the spinal cord works normally.

• Meningocele is more serious as there is a protuberant sac at the level of the failed fusion, which contains cerebrospinal fluid only, but the spinal cord has some damage.

• Meningomyelocele is the most serious form in which a raw, uncovered sac containing nerve tissue and cerebrospinal fluid protrudes onto the surface of the back. There is a significant risk of infection in the spine and brain and it may be associated with other birth deformities such as hydrocephalus and anencephaly (failure of the brain to develop).

The cause is unknown, but the incidence of spina bifida is higher in subsequent pregnancies after one child has been born with the condition, and in those of Irish and Welsh ancestry. The foetus develops its spinal cord and vertebrae in the first three months of pregnancy from a flat strip of nerve tissue that folds in upon itself lengthwise and fuses into a rod. It is then surrounded by the bony arch of the vertebrae. Spina bifida is the failure of the vertebral arch to form, usually in the lower back, allowing the spinal cord to be easily damaged. The unfused vertebral arch has a double pointed (bifid) appearance on x-ray examination.

Spina bifida occulta has no symptoms, but with a meningocele only some of the necessary nerve messages are transmitted to the legs and bladder causing some muscle weakness, abnormal sensations and poor bladder control. Patients with a meningomyelocele have paralysis and loss of all sensation below the level of damage and no control of the bladder or legs (paraplegia).

Mothers who are at high risk can have a test performed on the amniotic fluid that surrounds the baby in the womb between the fourteenth and sixteenth week of pregnancy to detect the defect. It may also be detected by an ultrasound scan during pregnancy. After birth, x-rays, and MRI and CT scans of the back show every detail of the defect. Folic acid supplements taken during pregnancy appear to prevent the condition.

Spina bifida occulta requires no treatment, but with a meningocele an operation to close the defect in the back is performed in childhood, while with a meningomyelocele a major operation to close the defect in the back is performed early in life, but this does not cure the paraplegia.

See also HYDROCEPHALUS; PARAPLEGIA AND QUADRIPLEGIA; SPINAL CORD

SPINAL ANAESTHETIC

A spinal anaesthetic can be administered when operations below the waist are being performed. The patient remains awake, but is often sedated, while an anaesthetist or surgeon places a needle into the lower back. The needle is inserted between the vertebrae so that the tip enters the spinal canal, which contains cerebrospinal fluid and surrounds the spinal cord. The spinal cord carries all the nerve messages to and from the brain, and runs through the centre of the twenty-four vertebrae that form the backbone. A small amount of anaesthetic is injected into the spinal canal, so that the nerves below the level of injection no longer work and pain from the operation cannot be felt. The patient is often tilted slightly to prevent the anaesthetic from flowing further up the spine and affecting nerves above the level required for adequate anaesthesia.

The side effects of a spinal anaesthetic include low blood pressure, a headache for several days, and a slow heart rate. Nausea and vomiting are less common complications.

This type of anaesthetic is usually given when the patient is not well enough to stand a general anaesthetic, for Caesarean sections, and in other circumstances when it is desirable for the patient to be awake.

See also ANAESTHETICS; EPIDURAL ANAESTHETIC; GENERAL ANAESTHETIC; LOCAL ANAESTHETIC; SPINE

SPINAL CORD

Together with the brain, the spinal cord is part of the central nervous system. The spinal cord is where all the nerves of the body join together in one large cable and travel up to the brain. The cord extends from the brain about two thirds of the way down the backbone (spine). It is encased within the vertebrae that make up the spine so that it is well protected from harm. All nervous impulses, with the exception of those in the head, travel up and down the spinal cord.

Thirty-one pairs of nerves radiate out from the spinal cord to form (together with twelve pairs radiating from the brain) the peripheral nervous system.

Nerves that record information from the senses join at the back of the cord, and those that relay instructions for movement to various parts of the body leave from the front. The nerve root, where the nerve joins the spinal cord, runs between the spinal vertebrae, and it is this that causes such severe pain if it is squeezed because one of the discs moves out of place (popularly called a 'slipped disc').

Reflexes take place in the spinal cord without involving the brain, which is aware of what is happening but is not involved in the response.

Like the brain, the spinal cord is cushioned by a layer of fluid – the cerebrospinal fluid. Some of this fluid is sometimes withdrawn by a needle inserted in the lower part of the spine in a process called a lumbar puncture or cerebrospinal fluid test and used to provide information on the nervous system.
See also BRAIN; BROWN-SÉQUARD SYNDROME; CEREBELLUM; CEREBROSPINAL FLUID; GANGLION; PARAPLEGIA AND QUADRIPLEGIA; REFLEX; SPINA BIFIDA; SPINE; SYRINGOMYELIA; TABES DORSALIS

SPINAL STENOSIS

Narrowing (stenosis) of the canal in the vertebrae through which the spinal cord runs, results in pressure on the cord that affects its function. It may be caused by an injury to the back, collapse of vertebrae with osteoporosis (bone thinning), Paget's disease of bone, a tumour of bone or the membranes (meninges) that surround the spinal cord, or it may be a birth defect.

Patients develop back and leg pain that are worsened by walking or prolonged standing, and relieved by sitting or lying. As the stenosis worsens, there may be abnormal sensations (eg. pins and needles), then loss of sensation and muscle weakness. Finally paralysis (paraplegia) occurs below the level in the back where the narrowing occurs, with associated loss of control of bladder and bowels.

The narrowing can be demonstrated by CT or MRI scans, or special x-rays in which a dye is injected into the spinal canal (myelogram).

Anti-inflammatory medications, exercise and physiotherapy, and pain relievers may be used initially, but as the condition progresses surgery is essential to ease the pressure on the spinal cord. The prognosis depends on the cause, but overall one quarter of patients have progressive disease that eventually results in paraplegia.
See also OSTEOPOROSIS; PAGET'S DISEASE OF BONE; PARAPLEGIA AND QUADRIPLEGIA

SPINAL TAP
See LUMBAR PUNCTURE

SPINE

The spine (backbone) supports the rest of the skeleton, and therefore the entire body. It consists of twenty four bones (vertebrae) arranged in a column, surrounding and protecting the spinal cord. It extends from the base of the skull to the tail bone, and attaches directly to the skull at the top, to each of the twelve ribs on each side, and forms the back of the pelvis.

It is the spinal cord and the surrounding vertebrae that distinguish the higher animals from the lower and that give rise to the name vertebrates. Of the vertebrates, human beings are the only ones that stand absolutely erect.

Everyone's spine is much the same length once they reach adulthood – about seventy centimetres in men and sixty centimetres in women. Individual differences in height depend mainly on the length of the legs.

There are seven cervical vertebrae in the neck, twelve thoracic at the back of the chest, and five lumbar vertebrae in the lower back. Five vertebrae fuse together to form the sacrum at the back of the pelvis, and four are fused in the coccyx or tail bone. Nearly all

SPINE

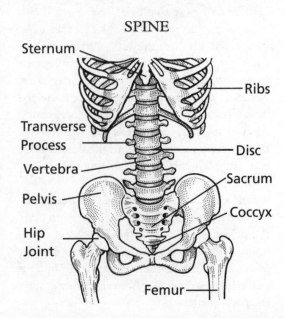

Sternum — Ribs — Transverse Process — Disc — Vertebra — Sacrum — Pelvis — Coccyx — Hip Joint — Femur

mammals have seven vertebrae in the neck, regardless of their overall shape – even the giraffe.

Each vertebra is separated from the next one by a disc made of cartilage. The discs act as shock absorbers and give the spine its pliability. It is when an injury causes one of these discs to be squeezed by the vertebrae so that a part of it protrudes to the side and presses on a nerve branching out from the spinal cord, that the acute pain of a so-called slipped disc is experienced.

Each ring has three sharp bony protrusions, two pointing sideways and one pointing backwards, to which muscles and ligaments are attached. The protrusions can be seen or felt under the skin of the back as small spines – hence the name spinal column.

The cervical vertebrae do not have much weight to support, and they are smaller than the others. The vertebrae get progressively larger down the spine to support the greater weight they are required to bear.

The top two cervical vertebrae have special features so that the head can move. The very top vertebra has no body but a very large and strong ring, enabling nodding movements. The second vertebra fits into the first vertebra on a pivot so that the head can rotate from side to side.

Each of the twelve thoracic vertebrae join a pair of ribs which arch forward to the breast bone at the front of the chest, thus enclosing and protecting the heart and lungs in the ribcage. The sacrum and coccyx form part of the pelvis.

Viewed from the side, the spinal column has four curves, alternately forward and back, corresponding to the various groups of vertebrae. The two backward curves (i.e. the ones with the hollow facing towards the front), one in the thoracic region and one in the pelvis, can be seen at birth, so that the spine of a newborn baby is entirely concave from the front. As the baby begins to hold its head up at three or four months and then to sit up at about nine months, the cervical curve appears, bending the other way. When the child begins to walk, the compensating lumbar curve appears, so that the spine acquires its classic double S-shape. The curves make the spine a kind of spring, able to absorb jolting and jarring that would otherwise damage internal organs, especially the brain.

Unduly pronounced curves of the spine can cause problems. Abnormal curves can be congenital, caused by disease, fracture or bad posture.

See also ANKYLOSING SPONDYLITIS; BACK; BACK PAIN; INTERVERTEBRAL DISC PROLAPSE; KYPHOSIS; LUMBAR PUNCTURE; MYELOGRAM; SCOLIOSIS; SKULL; SPINAL CORD; VERTEBRA

SPINE CURVED
See BACK PAIN; KYPHOSCOLIOSIS; KYPHOSIS; SCOLIOSIS

SPINOCEREBELLAR DEGENERATION
See FRIEDREICH'S ATAXIA

SPIROMETER
See VITAL CAPACITY

SPIRONOLACTONE
See DIURETICS

REGIONS OF SPINE

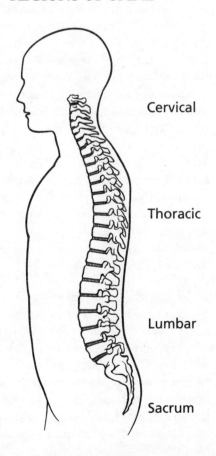

Cervical

Thoracic

Lumbar

Sacrum

SPLEEN

The spleen is the largest and most sophisticated gland in the human body. It is a soft dark red organ that weighs about 100g and is roughly the same size as a clenched fist. Shaped rather like an inverted pudding bowl, it is in the abdominal cavity tucked under the lower ribs on the left side.

The spleen has three main functions: –

• It filters blood, removing damaged cells and extracting and storing reusable elements such as iron from these cells.

• It stores antibodies developed by the body during an infection, so that when a similar infection occurs in the future the antibodies can be called into play quickly.

• It helps to produce from stem cells, along with bone marrow, new red and white blood cells. White cells fight infection and red cells transport oxygen.

The most frequent reason for medical attention is that the spleen is damaged in an accident. If the chest is squashed, for example in a car accident, the spleen may be pierced by a rib or ruptured by the pressure. Because it consists of a very large number of blood vessels, it bleeds freely, and the blood loss into the abdomen may be life-threatening. It is difficult to repair surgically because it is a bit like trying to sew up sponge rubber – the stitches tear out very easily and every stitch hole bleeds. It is therefore sometimes necessary to remove it to save the victim's life. The removal of the spleen has remarkably little effect on an adult, because the bone marrow can take over most of its functions. In babies, the situation is rather different, as the spleen is essential for the early formation of blood cells, and it is removed from children only if there is no alternative.

If the spleen becomes overactive, it may destroy blood cells too rapidly so that the person becomes severely anaemic, susceptible to infection, and bleeds and bruises excessively.
See also ANTIBODIES; BLOOD; RED BLOOD CELLS; SPLEEN ENLARGED; SPLEEN RUPTURED; STEM CELLS; WHITE BLOOD CELLS

SPLEEN ENLARGED

The spleen cannot normally be felt, but if enlarged (splenomegaly), may be found as a firm area below the bottom edge of the left side ribs.

The most common causes for enlargement of the spleen are viral infections such as glandular fever (infectious mononucleosis) and brucellosis (from cattle), bacterial infections of the blood (eg. septicaemia) and serious generalised infections (eg. tuberculosis).

The spleen can be injured and bleed in severe accidents that involve a blow to the lower ribs on the left side. If the bleeding is inside the fibrous capsule that surrounds the organ, it will enlarge and become painful.

Malaria kills millions of people in developing countries every year. The malarial parasite is injected into a patient by a mosquito, and then invades red blood cells, destroying them and releasing their haemoglobin, which then degenerates to bilirubin to give the characteristic jaundice (yellow skin). The spleen will enlarge as it tries to produce new red blood cells and remove the damaged ones.

Other causes of splenomegaly include haemolytic anaemia (the body rapidly destroys its own blood cells), cancer in the spleen (either as the primary site, or more commonly because the cancer has spread from another area), Hodgkin's disease (cancer of the lymph nodes), leukaemia (cancer of the white blood cells), portal hypertension (increase in the blood pressure in the veins of the abdomen), sarcoidosis (inflammation of a wide range of organs), thalassaemia major (inherited condition of fragile red blood cells), AIDS and sickle cell anaemia (found only in Negroes).

Rarer causes include Gaucher disease (inherited condition that causes fat to accumulate in cells throughout the body), Wilson disease (excess copper in the body), Felty syndrome (complication of rheumatoid arthritis), Scheie syndrome, Letterer-Siwe syndrome and Niemann-Pick (excess storage of certain fats).

There are many other very rare conditions that may be responsible.
See also SPLEEN and separate entries for diseases mentioned above.

SPLEEN RUPTURED

In a car or other accident, the chest may be squashed, and the spleen may be pierced by a rib or ruptured by the pressure. Pain is felt in the lower left chest and upper left abdomen, and the patient becomes weak, short of breath and collapses. An ultrasound scan of the spleen may show the damage, and free blood may be found in the abdominal cavity when a needle is pushed through the muscle wall. Blood loss into the abdomen can be life-threatening.

Repairing the spleen surgically is difficult as it is too friable, and as a result it is often necessary to remove it in order to stop bleeding. This lifesaving operation has remarkably little effect on an adult, as bone marrow can take over most of its functions. In babies the spleen is essential for the early formation of blood cells, and it is removed from children only in extreme circumstances.
See also SPLEEN

SPLENOMEGALY
See SPLEEN ENLARGED

SPLINTER
Small pieces of wood, glass, thorn, prickles and the like may penetrate the skin and can cause infection if they are not removed. Most splinters can be removed at home, but if the splinter is very large or does not protrude from the skin, a doctor may need to be consulted.

To remove a splinter: –
• sterilise a pair of tweezers by passing the ends through a flame or by boiling them in water for ten minutes
• wash the area around the splinter thoroughly with antiseptic lotion and wash away from the wound so that dirt is not carried into it, then dry gently
• pull the splinter out with the tweezers
• wash the wound with a mild antiseptic again and cover with a dressing

If it is not possible to dislodge a splinter, or if the wound swells or becomes painful after the splinter has been removed, consult a doctor.
See also CUT; FIRST AID

SPONDYLITIS
Spondylitis is an inflammation of the spine. There are several different types, the most common being rheumatoid spondylitis, ankylosing spondylitis and arthritic spondylitis. The rheumatoid form is caused by a rejection reaction of the body to the tissue lining the small joints of the back (autoimmune condition) and usually affects the small joints of the hands and feet as well. The arthritic form is usually a wear and tear injury to a part of the spine in heavy manual workers or those who have participated in rugged sports. Ankylosing spondylitis is discussed separately.

Patients develop significant pain in localised areas of the back bone. The damage may be seen on an x-ray or CT scan, and blood tests show inflammatory changes.

Anti-inflammatory medications, painkillers, physiotherapy (most important), surgery and some exotic drugs for the rheumatic form (eg. chloroquine, gold) are used in treatment. There is no permanent cure for most forms, and continuing care is normally required.
See also ANKYLOSING SPONDYLITIS; RHEUMATOID ARTHRITIS; SPINE; SPONDYLOSIS

SPONDYLOLISTHESIS
Spondylolisthesis is an abnormality of the vertebrae in the lower back in which one vertebra moves forward in the back in relation to the adjacent vertebrae causing nerves to be pinched. It may be present from birth, or caused by injury or degeneration (arthritis).

Sufferers develop significant back pain that spreads to the buttocks and down the legs (sciatica). Severe nerve pinching may cause muscle spasm or weakness.

It is diagnosed by x-ray and CT scan, and treated by physiotherapy, anti-inflammatory drugs, and in intractable cases, surgery. The management often difficult, but in most cases surgery is eventually successful.
See also OSTEOARTHRITIS; VERTEBRA

SPONDYLOSIS
Spondylosis is an abnormality in the mechanical structure of the spine due to incorrect alignment of the joints between the vertebral arches (the arch of bone protecting the spinal cord) in the back. It usually occurs in the elderly, obese or after a back injury. If the joints become inflamed, the condition is spondylitis.

Dull aching pain in the neck or back that is relieved by a change in position is the main symptom. This may be associated with a protective spasm of the back muscles.

X-rays and CT scans of the back may show arthritic changes in the involved joints.

Exercises and spine movements under the supervision of a physiotherapist, anti-inflammatory medications, support corset or neck brace, pain killers, and in severe cases surgery, are the treatments used. It is often persistent and recurrent, but with good temporary response to treatment. Surgery may be curative.
See also SPINE; SPONDYLITIS

SPONTANEOUS ABORTION
See MISCARRIAGE

SPOTS IN VISION
See VISUAL BLACK SPOTS

SPRAIN
A sprain is tearing of ligaments that support a joint, due to excessive force being applied to the joint. Pain, swelling and bruising occur in and around the joint. X-rays may be performed to exclude any possible fracture, but will not demonstrate a sprain.

The first aid of a sprain involves the RICE principles: –
• Rest; place the victim in a comfortable position (if possible with the injured limb supported with pillows) and advise them to stay quietly
• Ice; apply cold packs (with the ice in damp material so that it does not come in direct contact with the skin)
• Compression; apply a firm bandage to the injured part
• Elevation; if possible, elevate the injured limb to reduce pressure and swelling using pillows or a sling

Medical treatment involves immobilisation of the joint to allow ligaments to heal by use of bandages or plaster, and a sling or crutches. If healing is poor, there may be permanent slackness in the ligaments, allowing excessive movement in the joint and increased risk of further injury and premature arthritis.
See also JOINT; LIGAMENT OR
TENDON RUPTURE; SLING; STRAIN;
STRAPPING; WHIPLASH

SPRUE
See COELIAC DISEASE; TROPICAL
SPRUE

SPUTUM TESTS
Sputum consists of mucus and fluids produced by the lungs, trachea and pharynx, and if there is an infection in any of these areas, the organisms will usually be found in the sputum. Generally a sputum sample will be obtained quite easily by the patient coughing it up. If they have trouble producing it, they may be given a container to take home overnight or be sent to a physiotherapist to be given chest drainage treatment.

The sample is sent to a laboratory and initially examined under a microscope. If there is a bacterial infection, it may be diagnosed at this stage and treatment can begin. If the result is uncertain, the specimen may be cultured in a special liquid or jelly to see what disease-causing organisms grow, and what antibiotics will destroy it.

A problem which sometimes arises with sputum tests is that the sample may be contaminated with organisms from the mouth. In this case, the test becomes largely useless.
See also BRONCHITIS; LUNG;
PNEUMONIA

SQUAMOUS CELL CARCINOMA OF THE LUNG
See LUNG CANCER

SQUAMOUS CELL CARCINOMA OF THE SKIN
A squamous cell carcinoma (SCC) is a cancer of the outermost layer of skin that occurs on sun-exposed parts of the body, usually in patients who are over fifty years of age. They are caused by prolonged exposure to sunlight or irritant chemicals. The rims of the ears, the face, scalp, arms and hands are commonly affected, but the cancer may also occur on the penis.

SCCs look like a red spot covered in fine white scales. They may be itchy or sore but often attract attention because they are unsightly. In severe cases they can spread by blood or lymphatics to distant parts of the body.

If suspected, excision or biopsy is necessary to make the diagnosis. Small SCCs are easily removed by burning with a diathermy machine or freezing with liquid nitrogen. If it is larger, or if the diagnosis is not certain, it is necessary to excise the spot and surrounding tissue. Any SCC that recurs after freezing or burning must be surgically excised.

Treatment is very effective in early stages of the disease.
See also BOWEN'S DISEASE;
HYPERKERATOSIS;
INTRAEPITHELIAL CARCINOMA;
KERATOACANTHOMA; SKIN

SQUINT
A squint (strabismus) occurs when the eyes appear to look in slightly different directions away from each other. When the eyes are

both turned inwards the condition is called esotropia. It is critical that this is detected and treated when it occurs in childhood, because if allowed to persist, the brain will permanently suppress the vision in one eye in order to overcome the double image it receives. Even if the good eye becomes blind later in life, the eye in which vision has been suppressed will not be able to see.

In children a squint is usually due to an inherited tendency with weakness or abnormal development of the tiny muscles within the eye socket which move and align the eyes, or abnormal vision in one eye due to a cataract (cloudy lens).

In older patients a squint may be caused by damage to the muscles that control eye movement from a direct blow to the eye or surrounding skull, a poor blood supply to the muscles of one eye, a stroke that affects the nervous control of the eye muscles, a tumour or cancer in the eye socket, an over active thyroid gland (causes eyes to protrude slightly) or multiple sclerosis (affects nerves to eye muscles).

Special spectacles may be used long term to correct the problem by reducing the angle of the squint. In more severe cases an eye patch may cover the good eye to strengthen the poorer one and eye exercises may be added. In marked degrees of squint, it is necessary to operate to change the tightness of the tiny muscles that control eye movement, which is a technically difficult operation for the surgeon, but relatively minor surgery for the patient. Provided medical advice is followed, the long-term cosmetic and vision results are excellent.
See also DOUBLE VISION; DUANE SYNDROME; VISION

SSRI
See ANTIDEPRESSANTS

STAFF OF AESCULAPIUS
See CADUCEUS

STAMMER
See STUTTER

STAPES
See EAR

STAPHYLOCOCCUS AUREUS
Commonly known as the 'golden Staph', the bacteria *Staphylococcus aureus* is responsible for a wide range of infections in organs and tissues such as the lungs, throat, sinuses, ears, skin, eyes, gut, meninges, heart, bone and joints. Most infections respond rapidly to appropriate antibiotics such as penicillin and cephalosporin, but resistant forms have developed, particularly in hospitals, and may be very difficult to eradicate.

Methicillin is one of the most potent forms of penicillin, and methicillin-resistant *Staphylococcus aureus* (MRSA) is becoming a serious problem, because it is difficult to treat and tends to occur in hospitals where large quantities of antibiotics are used. A fortunately rare development is that of vancomycin and methicillin-resistant *Staphylococcus aureus* (VMRSA) infections, which usually cause pneumonia in debilitated patients admitted to large hospitals.

The treatment of infections with these resistant forms of the bacteria is more difficult: –
• MRSA; patients will need to be given high doses of special antibiotics (eg. vancomycin) by injection or drip, and isolated and nursed in such a way that the hospital staff cannot transmit the infection to other patients (barrier nursing).
• VMRSA; at present there are no antibiotics available to treat this infection.
See also BACTERIA; IMPETIGO; PHARYNGITIS; SCALDED SKIN SYNDROME; TOXIC SHOCK SYNDROME

STARVATION
See FAILURE TO THRIVE; GROWTH REDUCED; KWASHIORKOR; MARASMUS; WEIGHT LOSS

STATINS
See HYPOLIPIDAEMICS

STATUS EPILEPTICUS
See EPILEPSY

STEATORRHOEA
Steatorrhoea is the presence of excess fat in the faeces, which becomes a pale yellow colour. The stools tend to float in the toilet, and may be difficult to flush away. The excess fat may be due to a fatty diet, or more commonly because a lack of digestive enzymes from the pancreas

or gall bladder is preventing the fat from being digested. Diseases that cause steatorrhoea may be serious, and investigation at an early stage is important.
See also FAECAL COLOUR ABNORMAL; FAT

STEELE-RICHARDSON-OLSZEWSKI SYNDROME
The Steele-Richardson-Olszewski syndrome (progressive supranuclear palsy) is a deterioration of the part of the brain responsible for muscle control. Its cause is unknown, but it occurs twice as often in males as females, and is often confused with Parkinson disease.

The typical patient is an elderly person whose back is rigidly extended, falls backwards easily, is demented, eyes are unable to look down, reflexes are increased and has difficulty swallowing.

Physiotherapy, occupational and speech therapy, and medications to ease muscle rigidity and spasm are used in treatment, but the condition is slowly progressive.
See also PARKINSON DISEASE

STEIN-LEVENTHAL SYNDROME
See POLYCYSTIC OVARIAN SYNDROME

STEM CELL
A stem cell is the most basic type of cell, and as well as reproducing itself, it may develop into any of the more than 200 different types of cell found in the human body. If correctly stimulated or placed amongst other cells, a stem cell may develop into a bone cell, gut cell or nerve cell. The primitive ball of cells that forms immediately after conception (a blastocyst) is made up of a few dozen stem cells, but these soon start developing into different types of cells as the embryo forms.

Stem cells are found in the human embryo, in the umbilical cord and in the spleen and bone marrow of both children and adults. The more primitive the stem cell, the more potential diversity it possesses, so embryonic stem cells are far more useful than those from the umbilical cord and bone marrow.
See also BLASTOCYST; BONE; CELL; SPLEEN

STEMETIL
See ANTIEMETICS

STENOSIS
Stenosis is a term used in medicine to indicate the narrowing of a tube, or opening, in the body.
See also AORTIC VALVE STENOSIS; COARCTATION OF THE AORTA; PYLORIC STENOSIS

STENT
A stent is a synthetic tube, either solid or made of a mesh, placed in an artery, vein or duct (eg. bile duct) to keep it open after surgery or injury.
See also ARTERIOSCLEROSIS; BALLOON ANGIOPLASTY

STEREO-TACTIC BIOPSY
See NEUROSURGERY

STERNOCLEIDOMASTOID TORTICOLLIS
See TORTICOLLIS

STERNUM
The sternum is the breast bone that protects the front of the chest and the heart behind it.

It is divided into three section – an upper bony part called the manubrium, the main body, and a lower cartilaginous lump called the xiphisternum which can sometimes be felt just below the skin between the ribs at the front.

Ribs one to ten on each side are indirectly attached to the sternum by the costal cartilages. At the top corners of the sternum there is a joint with the clavicle (collar bone).
See also RIB; CLAVICLE

STEROIDS
Cholesterol is the base substance from which the body produces natural steroids. There are many different types of steroids, including sex hormones, anabolic steroids (that are often abused by athletes) and trophic hormones. The type being described here is more correctly called corticosteroid hormones. They act as powerful reducers of inflammation in damaged tissue. Artificial steroids have been synthesised to control a wide range of diseases, including asthma, arthritis, dermatitis, eczema, and severe allergy reactions.

Steroids are available as tablets (prednisone, prednisolone etc.), mixtures, injections, creams (hydrocortisone, betamethasone, mometasone, triamcinolone etc.), nasal sprays (eg. budesonide), inhaled sprays (eg. beclomethasone, fluticasone etc.), eye drops (eg. medrysone), ear drops and suppositories. They are therefore an extremely useful group of drugs in a wide variety of conditions.

The actions of steroids include shrinking down inflamed tissue (eg. in allergies, injuries, piles) to normal, reducing itching (eg. in eczema and bites), and opening up airways by reducing mucus secretion and shrinking swollen tissue (eg. hay fever, asthma).

When used on the skin or on the surface of the airways (lungs, nose), side effects are uncommon. Overuse of sprays used for asthma is relatively safe, but overuse in the nose can cause tissue damage. Creams and ointments that contain strong steroids should not be overused, particularly in children and on the face, as they can cause skin thinning and damage. Taken as injection into joints, steroids are very successful at controlling arthritis, but again, overuse may cause weakness and damage to the joint tissue instead of controlling the disease.

The greatest dangers occur when steroids are taken as tablets. Short courses, in which a high dose is given at the start and then reduced rapidly to zero over a couple of weeks, are quite safe. Low doses given for quite long periods of time are also relatively safe, but when high doses are given for months on end, damage can occur in the body.

Side effects of prolonged steroid tablet use include tissue swelling, an imbalance in blood chemicals, high blood pressure, weight gain, peptic ulcers, brittle bones (fracturing easily), heart failure, muscle weakness, delayed wound healing, headache, abnormal menstrual periods, fatty deposits under the skin, blood clots, cataracts, glaucoma and a host of rarer conditions. It is therefore obvious why doctors use these remarkably effective drugs with great caution. In some situations, the seriousness of the disease warrants taking the risk of using steroids to give a patient relief, or even saving a life.

If used judiciously, steroids can dramatically improve a patient's quality of life, but doctors must always be aware of the pros and cons of their use in every individual.

See also ADRENAL GLAND; ANABOLIC STEROIDS; ASTHMA PREVENTION MEDICATION; ECZEMA; MEDICATION; SEX HORMONES; TROPHIC HORMONES.

STETHOSCOPE

The stethoscope is an instrument used to listen to sounds within the body using a bell or diaphragm covered cup connected to a flexible plastic or rubber tube. The tube splits in two with one arm going to each ear of the doctor. It effectively magnifies and clarifies sounds by its shape, enabling doctors to diagnose conditions within the chest and abdomen, but also hear blood flow in arteries and therefore take a blood pressure reading. It was initially invented by the French physician René Laënnec in 1816, and modified into its present form in 1852 by the American Dr. George Cammann.

See also LAËNNEC, RENÉ; SPHYGMOMANOMETER

STEVENS-JOHNSON SYNDROME

The Stevens-Johnson syndrome is a severe complication of erythema multiforme that may be triggered by drugs or infection.

The characteristics of the syndrome include erythema multiforme; severe purulent ulcerating conjunctivitis; high fever; inflamed mouth (stomatitis); blisters or ulcers in nose, vagina, urethra, and anal canal; and ulceration, pain and swelling extending down the throat and into the lungs to give a form of bronchitis. The heart and lungs may become involved, and the scalded skin syndrome may develop. There is no specific diagnostic test.

Treatment involves intensive steroid therapy and removal of the cause of erythema multiforme if possible. Most patients recover slowly, but death is possible in the elderly and debilitated.

See also ERYTHEMA MULTIFORME; SCALDED SKIN SYNDROME

STEWART-TREVES SYNDROME

The Stewart-Treves syndrome is a sarcoma (form of cancer) of an arm affected by lymphoedema (hard swelling) in the elderly, that often follows mastectomy (breast removal) for cancer. A purplish red growth (angiosarcoma) develops on the lymphoedematous limb. The diagnosis is confirmed after surgical removal of the tumour and examination under a microscope. These are relentlessly aggressive tumours with a poor prognosis.

See also ANGIOSARCOMA; BREAST CANCER; LYMPHOEDEMA; SARCOMA

STICKY PLATELET SYNDROME

The sticky platelet syndrome is an uncommon cause of abnormal blood clots (thromboses) in young patients. Platelets are the cells in blood that stick together to form a clot. The excess stickiness of the platelets causes migraines and thromboses, but the symptoms vary markedly depending on the organs affected. Stroke may occur in the brain in severe cases. The cause is unknown.

Medications that reduce platelet stickiness such as aspirin and dipyridamole are taken long term, and good control is possible, but serious permanent organ damage may occur before the condition is diagnosed.

See also PLATELETS; THROMBOSIS

STIFF MUSCLES

See MUSCLE STIFFNESS AND/OR RIGIDITY

STILL'S DISEASE

Still's disease is a rare juvenile form of rheumatoid arthritis-type disease that occurs in children and teenagers for no known reason. There are several forms of the disease that vary in their symptoms, severity and outcome.

The symptoms include a widespread measles-type rash; a fever that rises and falls rapidly; enlarged lymph nodes, spleen and liver; and one or more hot, red, painful, swollen joints. Nodules may develop under the skin near affected joints, and the heart, lungs and muscles may also become inflamed. The knees, hips, elbows and ankles are the joints most commonly affected. Some patients develop long term joint damage and deformity. It is rare under one year of age and over fourteen, and girls are twice as likely as boys to develop the condition.

Blood tests show signs of inflammation, but the tests that diagnose adult rheumatoid arthritis are usually normal.

Prolonged rest, with passive movement of affected joints by physiotherapists on a regular basis, is the main treatment. Heat often relieves the pain and swelling, while drug treatments include aspirin, anti-inflammatory drugs, and steroids.

Although the course is often prolonged, most children eventually recover.

See also RHEUMATOID ARTHRITIS

STIMULANTS

The most common stimulants are amphetamines, and tablets are used in medicine to treat mild depression, disorders of excessive sleep, some types of senility and (rather strangely) overactivity in children. They are sometimes abused by long-distance truck drivers and others who wish to stay awake for long periods of time. Dependence upon these drugs can develop rapidly.

Examples include dexamphetamine and methylphenidate (Ritalin). Side effects may include insomnia, restless, nausea, dry mouth, difficult urination and tremor. They must not be used in pregnancy, depression, hypertension and thyroid disease.

See also ADRENERGIC STIMULANTS; CAFFEINE; MEDICATION; MESCALINE

STINGS

See BEE AND WASP STING; BLUE RINGED OCTOPUS; BOX JELLYFISH; IRUKANDJI SYNDROME; JELLYFISH STING; SCORPION STING

STITCHING

See CUT; SUTURING

STOCKHOLM SYNDROME

In 1973, four hostages were taken in a bank robbery in Stockholm, Sweden. Six days later, when they were released from captivity, they resisted rescue. Later they refused to testify against their captors and raised money for their defence.

This strange behaviour has been seen in other similar circumstances, and has been named Stockholm syndrome after this first reported case.

A similar well-publicised case occurred in the United States. Patty Hearst was kidnapped and tortured by the Symbionese Liberation Army. She later took up arms and joined their cause, helping them rob banks.

The Stockholm syndrome occurs when a captive cannot escape, is isolated and threatened with death, but is shown token acts of kindness by the captor. It typically takes four or five days for the psychological shift to take hold. Captives develop a strategy of trying to keep their captor happy in order to stay alive. This becomes an obsession as the captive identifies with the likes and dislikes of the captor.

This affects their psyche in a way that they come to sympathise with their tormenter.

The syndrome can also be used to understand the behaviour of battered wives, members of religious cults, and victims of other forms of torture and abuse.
See also VIOLENCE

STOKES-ADAMS ATTACK
A Stokes-Adams attack (or Adams-Stokes syndrome) is a sudden slowing of the heart rate due to an electrical problem within the heart, resulting in inadequate blood supply to the brain. It often occurs after a heart attack, may have no apparent cause, or may be a side effect of medication.

The patient faints suddenly, convulses, and has a slow heart rate or multiple missed heart beats. Facial flushing occurs for a minute or so on recovery. Rarely an attack may cause permanent damage to heart leading to further heart complications.

The diagnosis of a series of unexplained faints can be made by monitoring the heart electrical activity for a prolonged period (Holter monitor) while maintaining normal lifestyle until an attack occurs and the heart electrical problem can be identified. Once diagnosed, appropriate medications can be prescribed to regulate the heart rhythm or surgical implantation of an electrical pacemaker can be performed.

Recovery from a sudden attack is usually rapid, but recurrences may be frequent. Attacks are usually well controlled by appropriate treatment once cause identified, and patients get good result from a pacemaker.
See also FAINT; HEART ATTACK;
HOLTER MONITOR

STOMA
Any opening in the human body is a stoma, but the ones doctors are concerned about are the artificial stomas (or stomata) that an increasing number of people must deal with, often for the rest of their lives. An artificial stoma occurs when surgeons bring part of the gut through the front wall of the abdomen so that the patient will pass faeces through this opening and not through the anus. It looks rather like a small pink doughnut sitting on the skin and is usually covered by a specially designed plastic bag that collects the waste products and gut secretions. If the colon is used to form the stoma it is called a colostomy, but if the ileum of the small intestine is used, an ileostomy is formed. In a gastrostomy the stoma is used to feed the patient, with food introduced directly into the stomach.

Many varied diseases make a stoma necessary. Some babies are born without part of the gut and are unable to pass waste products. For their survival, the large intestine is opened to form a stoma on the abdomen. When they are older, it is sometimes possible to reconnect the gut or fashion a new anus for these children to enable them to lead a normal life. Cancer is a very common reason for a stoma.

There are two main problems affecting people with stomas – embarrassment if others find out about the problem (the person sitting next to you in the bus may have one without you knowing), and difficulties with the skin around the stoma caused by excoriation from the gut contents and the adhesives used to hold the collecting bag in place. A wide range of different bags, adhesives and deodorants are available to help with these problems. It is often a matter of trial and error to find the combination best suited to a particular patient.
See also COLOSTOMY;
GASTROSTOMY; ILEAL CONDUIT;
ILEOSTOMY

STOMACH
The process of digestion, which begins in the mouth, continues in the stomach. Chewed food is passed from the mouth down the oesophagus (gullet) to the stomach. The stomach is a J shaped bag that expands with the intake of food, and after a large meal may be thirty cm. long and twelve cm. in diameter. It can hold up to three litres in a large person when full. It is soft and pliable when empty but becomes firm when filled with food. It is on the left side of the body, behind the lower ribs, high in the abdomen not far below the heart, and not down behind the navel as people often assume.

The stomach digests food and also stores food, which usually has been taken in quite quickly as a meal, but is released slowly to be processed by the small intestine.

The outside layers of the stomach consist of muscle, while the inside lining is a mucous membrane, much the same as that lining the oesophagus. The membrane in the stomach, however, forms many folds which allow it to expand as food is taken in. The muscles in the stomach wall grind and churn food so that it is pulverised and mixed with gastric juices. The semi-liquid, fairly acidic product is called chyme (pronounced 'kime').

The gastric juices contain digestive enzymes and concentrated hydrochloric acid but the stomach wall is protected from this by a thick layer of alkaline mucus. If acid does manage to eat into the stomach walls, an ulcer develops.

At each end of the stomach is a muscular ring, a sphincter. These rings are normally closed, opening only to allow food in from the oesophagus and out to the small intestine. The ring at the top is called the lower oesophageal or cardiac sphincter because it is close to the heart. Sometimes this sphincter does not open properly, which leads to a feeling of being unable to swallow past this point. If the sphincter opens too easily, reflux oesophagitis and heartburn occur as stomach acid comes up into the oesophagus.

The sphincter at the bottom of the stomach that leads into the duodenum of the small intestine is the pylorus (pyloric sphincter). This sphincter occasionally malfunctions in newborn babies, leading to projectile vomiting in which food is brought up in a forceful spurt. Males are more often affected than females. It can be successfully corrected by surgery. Ulcers (pyloric ulcer) can also develop at this point.

The action of the stomach consists of a series of waves propelling the contents along it towards the pylorus, which relaxes as each wave reaches it to allow some of the softened mass to pass through into the duodenum. The waves also separate out any remaining lumps and ensure that these remain in the upper part of the stomach for further digestion. Each wave takes about half a minute. Usually a person is quite unaware of these wavelike movements, but if the stomach is irritated so that the digestive process is upset, it may give rise to irregular spasms causing indigestion. If the stomach is empty, it is these waves that give a rumbling noise (borborygmi). Under some circumstances, (eg. if the stomach is irritated by consumption of too much alcohol), the waves will work in reverse and the cardiac sphincter will open to allow the contents of the stomach to be ejected back up the oesophagus, causing vomiting. Milder reverse action causes belching.

The first amounts of semi-liquid food will begin to leave the stomach about half an hour after a meal, with the whole process usually taking about two to six hours, depending on what has been eaten. Different types of food stay in the stomach for different periods of time. For example, fatty foods stay longer than carbohydrates – hence the ability of a meal rich in carbohydrates to provide a quick source of energy. Obviously a heavy meal will take longer to digest than a light meal.

Alcohol and some drugs are absorbed directly into the bloodstream from the stomach.

The passage of food through the stomach is also affected by temperature, so cold foods such as ice cream slow it down. The natural inclination to relax after a meal and perhaps go to sleep is to enable the body to concentrate its resources on digesting food as quickly as possible, whereas strenuous exercise diverts the blood to the heart and muscles and therefore slows down the digestive process.

Diseases involving the stomach tend to start with the prefix gastric (eg. gastric ulcer, gastritis, gastroenteritis).
See also DIGESTIVE ENZYMES; DUODENUM; DYSPEPSIA; GASTRO-COLIC REFLEX; GASTROSCOPY; GASTROSTOMY; OESOPHAGUS; PEPTIC ULCER; PYLORIC STENOSIS

STOMACH CANCER

Stomach cancer (gastric carcinoma) is one of the less common cancers in Europeans (4% of all cancers), but very common amongst Japanese. It is more than twice as common in men than women, and usually occurs over the age of sixty years. The consumption of green and yellow vegetables decreases the risk, but it rises in lower socio-economic groups and in those who have pernicious anaemia.

Often it has mild symptoms such as indigestion and heartburn, so patients frequently do not attend a doctor until the cancer is quite advanced. Other symptoms include burping, feeling very full in the upper belly, nausea, weight loss and a loss in appetite. Vomiting blood and passing black faeces are late complications. The liver is a common site for the spread of the cancer, but once this is involved, a cure is most unlikely.

The diagnosis is confirmed by gastroscopy

and biopsy of any suspicious areas, but the investigator must be very careful as stomach cancer often looks like, and may be confused with, a peptic ulcer.

Surgical removal of the stomach, and surrounding lymph nodes, to which the cancer may have spread, is the primary treatment. Irradiation may be used as additional treatment. The five-year survival rate is about 20%.
See also CANCER; LEATHER-BOTTLE STOMACH; PEPTIC ULCER; STOMACH

STOMACH ULCER
See PEPTIC ULCER

STOMATITIS
Stomatitis is an infection of the mouth, and may be the result of one or more mouth ulcers, or a fungal, viral or bacterial infection.

Fungal infection (thrush) is common in babies and in those who are on antibiotics or taking anticancer drugs (cytotoxics). The inside of the mouth and tongue have patches of off-white slough sticking to them, and if this is scratched away, a red sore area is exposed. The infection is often painful and aggravated by sweet or spicy foods. Antifungal drops, ointments or lozenges are effective treatments.

Viral infections that may cause stomatitis include chickenpox, hand foot and mouth disease, and most seriously, Herpes simplex – cold sores. The main symptom is painful ulcers that are worse with eating or drinking. Herpangina is a special type of stomatitis that occurs in children under six years of age and is caused by the coxsackievirus. It causes sudden pain in the mouth, fever, difficulty in swallowing, mouth ulcers and grey coloured blisters.

Bacterial stomatitis may arise from poor dental hygiene and causes a generalised soreness of the mouth and bad breath. Hydrogen peroxide mouth washes and antibiotics give rapid relief.
See also COLD SORES; COXSACKIE VIRUS INFECTION; GINGIVOSTOMATITIS; MOUTH PAIN; MOUTH ULCER; THRUSH

STONE
See GALLSTONE; KIDNEY STONE; SALIVARY STONE

STONEFISH
Stonefish are found around coral reefs in the waters of the tropics. They look astonishingly like a stone, and generally lie immobile in the sand under water, moving only if disturbed. Thongs or sandshoes should be worn if walking in tropical waters. Prodding or kicking with bare feet a 'funny-looking stone' is a dangerous pastime.

A sting from a stonefish will cause intense pain spreading along the limb, blue or grey discolouration, swelling, sweating and signs of shock. The victim may become quite irrational as a result of the intense pain.

Anyone bitten by a stonefish needs urgent medical attention. While help is being obtained, you should relieve the pain by soaking the affected area in hot water, and remove any foreign body. Reassure the victim and keep them calm so that anxiety does not encourage the spread of the poison. Do NOT apply pressure immobilisation, as this increases the pain and may cause damage to the tissues.
See also FIRST AID; RESUSCITATION

STRABISMUS
See SQUINT

STRAIN
A strain is an over stretching of a muscle or tendon by excessive stress being placed on the muscle or tendon, often during sport. The symptoms include pain, swelling and inability to use the muscle without discomfort. Weakness in an affected muscle may make future injury easier.

X-rays and ultrasound scans are sometimes necessary to exclude a sprain or fracture.

Rest, ice, compression and elevation are the initial treatments. Strapping, pain killers and anti-inflammatory medications may be necessary later. Full recovery in a few days is usual.
See also ILEOLUMBAR SYNDROME; MUSCLE; SPRAIN; STRAPPING; TENDON

STRANGUARY
See URINATION DIFFICULT

STRAPPING
The best bandage to strap an injured joint is an elasticised rolled bandage. Ideally, the size of the bandage should be related to the size of

the injured limb, eg. finger bandages should be small and body bandages should be wide.

To strap an injured joint: –
• place the joint in the position in which it is to remain
• stand or sit opposite the victim, supporting the injury while bandaging
• hold the roll in one hand and apply the outer surface on the bandage to the injured area, unrolling a few centimetres at a time
• start about two or three bandage turns above the injury and bandage outwards from the victim's body, maintaining an even pressure. Finish two or three turns below the injury, overlapping each turn for maximum support. The bandage should be firm but not so tight that it will impede circulation.
• cut the end, tuck it in and pin, or cut the end in two strips and tie a reef knot
See also JOINT; SPRAIN; STRAIN

STRAWBERRY NAEVUS
A strawberry naevus (immature haemangioma) is a temporarily disfiguring skin blemish of children caused by the overgrowth of small blood vessels. A bright red, raised, irregular, rapidly enlarging spot appears shortly after birth, but growth ceases by nine months of age. Virtually all disappear spontaneously, completely and without a scar by the age of five years. Surgery to remove the naevus leaves a permanent scar, and is never considered until at least the age of six years.
See also HAEMANGIOMA; NAEVUS

STREPTOCOCCAL INFECTION
Beta-haemolytic streptococci, which are divided into two major groups – A and B – are a common cause of bacterial infections. Group A is responsible for infections in the throat and on the skin, and less commonly rheumatic fever and glomerulonephritis, while group B causes some types of genital infections, meningitis and pneumonia.

A specific blood test is available to detect the A group anywhere in the body, but the B group can only be detected by a culture of the blood, sputum or other infected tissue.

Antibiotics such as penicillin, erythromycin and cephalosporins result in rapid recovery in most cases.
See also BACTERIA; ERYSIPELAS; GLOMERULONEPHRITIS; MENINGITIS; NECROTISING FASCIITIS; PHARYNGITIS; PNEUMONIA; RHEUMATIC FEVER

STRESS
Stress is excessive anxiety about problems of daily living. Mortgage repayments, marriage strife, young children, job security, family finances, separation and divorce, leaving home, poor health, work responsibilities, or a death in the family. All of these, and hundreds of other situations, are causes of stress.

Stress may cause a very wide range of symptoms including a persistent headache, peptic ulcers, heart disease, migraines, diarrhoea, shortness of breath, sweating, passing excess urine, rashes and vomiting. Stress may worsen or trigger other physical illnesses, or progress to a neurosis, depression, or in severe cases, suicide is possible.

There are three possible treatment strategies: –
• Remove the cause of the stress, which is much easier said than done in most cases.
• Rationalise stress by talking over the problem with a spouse, relatives, friends, doctor or priest. Writing down details of the problem makes it appear more manageable, particularly when all possible options are diagrammatically attached to it to give a rational view of the situation. Professional assistance may be given by a general practitioner, psychiatrist, psychologist, marriage guidance counsellor, child guidance officer or social worker.
• Medications that alter mood, sedate or relieve anxiety are used in a crisis, intermittently or for short periods of time. Some antidepressant drugs and treatments for psychiatric conditions are designed for long-term use, but most of the anxiety-relieving drugs can cause dependency if used regularly.

The prognosis depends on the cause, but most people eventually cope with their problems.
See also CONVERSION DISORDER; NEUROSIS; POST-TRAUMATIC STRESS DISORDER; SUICIDE

STRESS FRACTURE
A stress or fatigue fracture is an abnormal break of a bone, often in the foot (march fracture), or lower leg (fibula or tibia) due to repeated excessive stress on a bone. Pain and tenderness develops in the affected bone that is worsened by use.

The fracture is diagnosed by x-ray, CT or radionucleotide scan, and treated by rest in a plaster cast.
See also FRACTURE; MARCH FRACTURE

STRESS INCONTINENCE
See INCONTINENCE OF URINE

STRESS TEST
A cardiac stress test explores the activity of the heart – not the amount of mental tension to which you are being subjected. It is generally carried out if heart disease is suspected.

Just like an ordinary pump, the heart is more likely to break down when it is called on to work hard. Consequently, if you are suffering from chest pain and an electrocardiogram (ECG) recorded in the doctor's surgery is normal, you may be asked to undergo an exercise ECG or stress test. It involves having an ECG done while you are exercising in a carefully controlled manner, and also having your blood pressure measured.

First, a calculation is made of your maximum safe heart rate, based on variables such as your age and weight. You are then connected to the ECG machine and start off walking slowly on a treadmill machine, or riding an exercise bicycle. The pace is gradually increased by speeding up the machine until your heart is beating steadily at the calculated rate. An ECG is taken before, during and after the exercise, so that adverse results of the increased activity on the heart quickly become apparent.

People whose arteries have narrowed so that the heart is not getting enough blood often have a characteristic ECG pattern. A stress test is also used for someone who is recovering from a heart attack to determine how much blood is getting through to the heart.

The test is painless, but it is possible that the patient may feel dizzy or weak, or become conscious of their heartbeat becoming irregular, or even experience some chest pain. However, it is obviously vital for the doctor supervising the test to ensure that the exercise does not bring on a heart attack, and the ECG readings will constantly be monitored so that the test can be stopped if there is any hint of heart distress.

As with an ordinary ECG, an exercise ECG can only show what is happening at the time it is taken. It is not unknown for a person to have a stress test which appears normal and then have a heart attack shortly afterwards.
See also ANGIOGRAM; ELECTROCARDIOGRAPH; HEART

STRETCH MARKS
Stretch marks (striae) are the curse of pregnant women, when they develop on their belly and breasts, and overweight people whose stretch marks persist after they have lost weight. The tendency to develop striae is one that may be inherited.

They are caused by a breakdown and stretching of the elastic fibres in the skin by changes in the body's hormone levels as well as direct stretching of the skin. Once they form they usually remain permanently unless removed by plastic surgery or reduced by creams containing retinoic acids.

Cushing syndrome is caused by an over production of steroids such as cortisone in the body, or taking large doses of cortisone. Headache, obesity, thirst, easy bruising, impotence, menstrual period irregularities, stretch marks, acne, high blood pressure, bone pain and muscle weakness are common symptoms of this syndrome.
See also CUSHING SYNDROME; LINES IN SKIN; PREGNANCY; SKIN

STRIAE
See STRETCH MARKS

STRIDOR
See BREATHING, DIFFICULT; CROUP; WHEEZE

STROKE
A stroke is an accident involving the blood vessels in the brain, and is technically known as a cerebral infarct or cerebrovascular accident (CVA). If a clot, or piece of material from elsewhere in the body, blocks an artery in the brain (cerebral thrombosis), or if an artery bursts in the brain, a stroke may occur. The risk of stroke is higher in those who smoke, have high blood pressure, high cholesterol levels, are diabetic or drink alcohol to excess.

Any blood vessel in the brain may be involved, so any part of the brain may be damaged, and the area damaged determines the effects on that person's body. The symptoms are therefore very varied. If a motor area of the brain which controls movement is affected, the patient becomes paralysed down the opposite side of the body because the nerves supplying the body cross over to the opposite side at the base of the brain (the right side of the brain controls the left arm and leg). Other patients may lose their memory, power of speech, become uncoordinated, unbalanced, start fitting, have strange smells, hear abnormal noises or any of dozens of other possibilities. The area of the brain affected may increase as a blood clot extends along an artery, or bleeding into the brain continues.

The cause of the stroke can be determined by using special x-rays, CT scans, MRI (magnetic resonance imaging), blood tests, tests on the fluid around the brain, and measuring the brain waves electrically (EEG).

A wait-and-watch attitude is adopted in most cases, with medication given to prevent the stroke from worsening and to protect other organs. Surgery to a bleeding or blocked artery in the brain may occasionally be appropriate. Physiotherapists, speech pathologists and occupational therapists will assist in recovery. Further strokes can often be prevented by the long term use of low dose aspirin or warfarin, which prevent blood clots. Patients who are at a high risk can also use these medications.

It will be several days or even weeks before doctors can give an accurate prognosis. The brain does not repair itself, but it can often find different ways of doing a task and bypassing damaged areas. Most improvement occurs in the first week, but full recovery may take months. Patients who become unconscious during a stroke generally have a poorer outcome than those who do not. Strokes are the third major cause of death in developed countries after heart disease and cancer.
See also BRAIN; CHOLESTEROL; HYPERTENSION; LOCKED-IN SYNDROME; NEUROSURGERY; TRANSIENT ISCHAEMIC ATTACK

STRONGYLOIDIASIS

Strongyloidiasis is an infestation of the human by the tiny two millimetre long worm *Strongyloides stercoralis*. This worm can live freely in moist soil or its larvae may penetrate the skin of a human, enter the bloodstream, pass through the heart into the lungs, and pass from the blood into the air passages of the lung. From there it moves up into the throat, is swallowed and develops into an adult worm, which then produces eggs which pass out with the faeces and contaminate the soil. The eggs may also hatch into larvae in the intestine and these larvae can penetrate the bowel wall to enter the blood and reinfect the host human. There are no male and female worms, only a single asexual form, found throughout the tropics.

Many patients have no or minimal symptoms, but in long standing or severe cases symptoms may include itchy buttocks and wrists, raised rashes, belly pains, nausea, diarrhoea and weight loss. Rarely in severe chronic cases the larvae may invade the liver, kidney and brain.

It is diagnosed by finding the eggs or worms in the faeces or by a specific blood test, and then appropriate medication can be prescribed to eradicate the infestation.
See also WORMS

STRYCHNINE

Strychnine is a poison obtained from the seeds of the plant species *Strychnos*. It is a bitter tasting white powder in pure form, and acts as a powerful stimulant of the nervous system. If swallowed, the victim will experience muscle spasms, convulsions and vomiting before brain death occurs. Symptoms start within fifteen to thirty minutes of swallowing the poison.

In hospital intensive care unit, medications are given to paralyse the patient, preventing convulsions, while life is sustained by artificial ventilation. The prognosis depends on the dose. If a patient survives for twelve hours, recovery is likely, but permanent heart, nerve or muscle damage is possible.
See also ARSENIC; CYANIDE

STURGE-WEBER SYNDROME

The Sturge-Weber syndrome is a congenital developmental disorder of the brain and skin that causes mental retardation, a red stain across part of the face, convulsions, paralysis down one side of the body and eye abnormalities.

Medication can control the convulsions, surgery can correct the cosmetic deformities, and a combination of drugs and surgery are used for the eye abnormalities. Although there is no cure, reasonable control of symptoms is possible.
See also MENTAL RETARDATION; MUSCLE WEAKNESS

STUTTER

Stuttering (stammering) is the involuntary repetition of a sound while trying to talk. The speaker is unable to proceed past a certain point for some seconds but eventually overcomes the barrier, and the remaining part of the phrase comes out in a rush.

The cause is unknown, but it tends to start between two and four years of age. It is more common in boys than girls, and more likely if one parent is or was a stutterer. Some experts believe that emotional insecurity, anxiety and disturbances in childhood can be a trigger, but it may be that the insecurity and anxiety is caused by the stammer, rather than the opposite. An association between left-right confusion and stuttering has also been noted.

If the person is tense, hurried or confused, the stammer will be worse. Helping a stammerer to finish a sentence only agitates him /her more and worsens the problem with the next sentence. The consonants are the usual blocks for stammerers, and the letters 'p' and 'b' are the most commonly involved.

Interestingly, stammerers can usually sing without stammering, even if it is a sentence they had been totally unable to complete previously, and some patients use a singsong cadence to their speech pattern to overcome their problem.

Long-term treatment by a speech pathologist is necessary, and psychologists and/or psychiatrists may also be involved. Other than brief use of minor anti-anxiety drugs, no medication can help. With persistence over many months or years, most patients can learn to cope with their disorder.
See also SPEECH DIFFICULT; SPEECH PATHOLOGY and separate entries for diseases mentioned above.

STYE

A stye or external hordeolum, is a miniature abscess in an eyelid, due to a bacterial infection in one of the tiny sweat or oil glands (glands of Zeiss) on the margin of the eyelid that keep the eyelashes moist and lubricated. Often there is no apparent reason for the infection, but it may follow excessively rubbing the eye or an injury to the eyelid.

The infected gland becomes painful, red, swollen, and fills with pus.

It is treated with frequent warm compresses to the eye, and antibiotic ointment under the upper eyelid. A persistent stye can be incised to drain away pus.
See also MEIBOMIAN CYST

SUB-

'Sub-' is a prefix used in medical terms to indicate under or below, as in subnormal (below normal) and subcutaneous (under the skin).

SUBARACHNOID HAEMORRHAGE

A subarachnoid or intracerebral haemorrhage is a bleed into the substance of the brain. The arachnoid mater is the middle of the three meninges (membranes) that surround and support the brain, so by definition a subarachnoid haemorrhage is a bleed within the arachnoid membrane. The innermost membrane is the pia mater.

Rupture of a blood vessel in the brain may be due to high blood pressure (stroke), the rupture of an aneurysm (ballooning on the side of an artery), a bleeding disorder (eg. thrombocytopenia, leukaemia), brain tumour, head injury or as a side effect of medication (eg. warfarin).

Patients experience a sudden loss of consciousness or confusion, vomiting, dizziness, headache and abnormal brain function (eg. partial paralysis, strange sensations), depending on the position of the bleed within the brain. A CT scan or angiogram (x-ray of arteries after injecting a dye) is used to locate the bleed.

Treatment will depend on the cause of the bleed, and can vary from time and rest, to surgery to stop continued bleeding. The prognosis is very variable depending on the position and severity of the bleed. Some patients recover rapidly, while other may lapse into a long term coma or die, or develop permanent brain damage and epilepsy.
See also ANEURYSM; BRAIN; LEUKAEMIA; MENINGES; STROKE; SUBDURAL HAEMATOMA; THROMBOCYTOPENIA

SUBCUTANEOUS EMPHYSEMA

Subcutaneous emphysema is the presence of gas (air) in tissues under the skin due to a lung injury, major surgery, fractured rib, gas gangrene, serious gas-producing skin infections (cellulitis), severe tissue injuries, or damage to the throat (larynx). There is a spongy crackling sensation and/or sound when skin is indented.

The gas may show on ultrasound scan, and the cause must be investigated by x-rays or blood tests.

Treatment depends on the cause, but the problem usually settles without treatment if the cause is not serious.
See also CELLULITIS; GAS GANGRENE

SUBDURAL HAEMATOMA
A subdural haematoma is a collection of blood between the brain and the skull that puts pressure on the brain and affects its function. The dura mater is the outermost of the three meninges (membranes) that surround and support the brain, so by definition this is a bleed between the dura mater and the arachnoid mater, which is the middle membrane. The innermost membrane is the pia mater.

The bleeding is usually due to a significant head injury, but sometimes may be due to the rupture of a blood vessel affected by arteriosclerosis (hardening of the artery), high blood pressure or for no obvious reason. The onset may be sudden, or may be delayed for some weeks after a head injury if the bleed and build up of pressure is very gradual.

Symptoms may include confusion, vomiting, dizziness, headache and abnormal brain function (eg. partial paralysis, strange sensations) depending on the position of the blood collection and the pressure it applies to the brain.

A CT or MRI scan is used to find blood collection, and this is followed by urgent surgical removal of the blood collection.

It may be fatal or cause permanent disability if left untreated, but there are good results from surgical treatment.
See also ARTERIOSCLEROSIS; CONCUSSION; HEAD INJURY; SUBARACHNOID HAEMORRHAGE

SUBLINGUAL CYST
See RANULA

SUBNORMAL
See MENTAL RETARDATION

SUBUNGAL HAEMATOMA
A subungal haematoma (nail bruise) is a collection of blood under a finger or toe nail. They are caused by an injury to the nail, and

result in a very painful nail that is black in colour and loose on its bed.

Blood can be released from under a nail using the following simple trick. Partially unbend a metal paper clip so that one end is at right angles to the folded part. Heat the end in a flame (eg. candle) until it is red hot. Apply the end to the nail over the blood collection. The paper clip will burn through the nail to form a hole through which the blood can escape. The patient will feel no pain until the hot tip penetrates the nail, at which point a small burn will be felt, and the paper clip can be immediately removed.

This results in immediate relief of pain, but the nail is usually lost as a new nail grows out underneath old one.
See also NAIL; NAIL PAIN

SUDDEN INFANT DEATH SYNDROME
See COT DEATH

SUDEK ATROPHY
See REFLEX SYMPATHETIC DYSTROPHY SYNDROME

SUFFOCATION
If the supply of oxygen to the blood is cut off, the person will suffocate. The most common cause of suffocation is a blockage to the victim's nose and mouth, such as by a plastic bag. Other causes are smoke inhalation and fumes from toxic substances, such as gas and petrol-based products.

A person who is suffocating will have laboured, noisy breathing, a swollen neck and head veins. Their face, fingernails and toenails will turn blue, and their pulse will be rapid, then weak before stopping altogether. Their breathing will change to shuddering spasms, and then cease and they will be unconscious.

If you witness this, the first step in management is to deal with the cause (i.e. tear off plastic bag, remove patient from toxic fumes). If the cause is smoke, you must ensure that you do not become a casualty as well. Tie a piece of cloth (preferably wet) over your nose and mouth before entering the room, and remove the victim as quickly as possible. In the case of fire, do NOT open windows and doors as this will increase the risk of the fire spreading. Keep low to avoid smoke, but if the atmosphere is too contaminated, wait for the fire brigade.

Once the victim is in a safe place, perform mouth to mouth or cardiopulmonary resuscitation if necessary, or if the victim is breathing but still unconscious, place them in the coma position and send for medical help.
See also CARBON MONOXIDE POISONING; FIRST AID; RESUSCITATION; UNCONSCIOUS

SUGAR, BLOOD
See GLUCOSE, BLOOD

SUGAR DIABETES
See DIABETES MELLITUS TYPE ONE; DIABETES MELLITUS TYPE TWO

SUICIDE
Suicide is eighth in importance as a cause of all deaths in Western countries, but in young adults it is far higher in the rankings. Twice as many women as men attempt suicide, but men are three times more successful and are more likely to use violent means (eg. gun, jumping). Those who live alone and who have poor general health are also at a higher risk.

It may be triggered by an emotional crisis such as divorce, death of a close family member, loss of a job, financial crisis or as a result of some other form of rejection, but often there is no apparent reason. Alcoholism makes suicide attempts more likely, and the sudden excessive use of alcohol in an already stressed or depressed person is cause for considerable concern.

Those who contemplate suicide often provide clues of their intentions, but unfortunately these clues are sometimes not obvious or are ignored. A person who jokes about 'ending it all', or that the family is 'better off without me', may well be trying to judge the reaction of others to this idea. Other similar conversational clues may be introduced in the third person by expressing ideas such as 'my friend often talks of suicide' or 'did you read about that suicide in the paper?' Further clues may include changes in behaviour such as giving away prized possessions, enquiring about cremations, or sudden changes in religious attitudes and investigating alternate religions. A decision to attempt suicide may be a long slow process over many weeks or months, in which cases clues may be identified and a doctor alerted, or a sudden bout of deep depression may result in the decision being made in a matter of minutes.

Once there is reasonable suspicion that an individual may attempt suicide, a medical practitioner (usually the person's general practitioner) should be made aware of the clues that have been noticed. The doctor will then take all possible measures to ensure that the person is treated and counselled appropriately. No-one can be forced to undergo medical treatment, but if the doctor's efforts to persuade the patient to accept treatment are unsuccessful, and if the doctor is convinced that a suicide attempt is imminent, documents may be signed to allow the person to be taken into a hospital for further assessment and treatment. This measure is only taken as a last resort. If the patient accepts treatment, it will involve counselling and medication to correct the biochemical imbalance in the brain that may be causing depression.

Suicide attempts are at least ten times more common than successful suicides. Many can be prevented, and the patient can be successfully treated so that they can lead a happy and productive life, but the early involvement of doctors is essential.
See also DEPRESSION; POST TRAUMATIC STRESS DISORDER; STRESS

SULFA ANTIBIOTICS
See SULPHA ANTIBIOTICS

SULFASALAZINE
See ANTIRHEUMATICS

SULINDAC
See NONSTEROIDAL ANTI-INFLAMMATORY DRUGS

SULPHA ANTIBIOTICS
Sulphas were the very first antibiotics developed, but the ones available in the late 1930s had severe side effects and were not very effective. Sulphas today are not as widely used as penicillins but still play a part in the treatment of some types of infections. The most commonly prescribed sulpha preparation is co-trimoxazole (Bactrim, Septrin), which has a sulpha antibiotic (sulphamethoxazole) combined with a second type of antibiotic (trimethoprim). Sulphas should be avoided in patients with liver disease and used with caution in the elderly. They are available in

tablet, mixture and injection forms. They are used for infections of skin, sinuses, urine and the lungs.

Side effects may include nausea, poor appetite, a rash and rarely the skin condition erythema multiforme. They must be used with care in pregnancy, but are safe in children.
See also ANTIBIOTICS; ERYTHEMA MULTIFORME

SULPHAMETHOXAZOLE
See SULPHA ANTIBIOTICS

SULPHONYLUREAS
See HYPOGLYCAEMICS

SULTHIAME
See ANTICONVULSANTS

SUMATRIPTAN
See 5HT RECEPTOR AGONISTS

SUNBURN
The sun is extremely hot and will burn in the same way as fire, except that the sun is so far away we are not aware of the burning sensation that makes us draw back from fire. Obviously, people with fair complexions are most susceptible to sunburn and should take extra precautions, especially in the middle of the day when the sun is at its height.

When the skin is burnt by the sun, it becomes red, painful and hot to the touch. If the burning is severe, the skin will blister. After a few days the skin dries and a layer peels off. Long-term effects of overexposure to the sun are permanent freckling, blotching and premature ageing of the skin.

Most cases of sunburn can be dealt with by taking a cool bath or shower, and applying cool compresses (although not iced since these may chill the victim) to the most affected parts. Calamine lotion or one of the commercial anti-sunburn moisturising creams will usually help. Paracetamol may reduce the pain, but if the sunburn is severe, the victim may develop cold shivers and a temperature, and if a child is the sufferer, medical advice may be necessary.

Do not allow the victim of sunburn back in the sun without light-protective clothing until the burns have healed.
See also BURN

SUNCT SYNDROME
The SUNCT syndrome is a variant form of cluster headache whose name is an acronym of its major symptoms (short lasting, unilateral, neuralgiform, conjunctival injection, tears). It may be triggered by alcohol, stress, exercise, certain foods and glare.

The symptoms are severe headaches that are short lasting (seconds to minutes), one sided (unilateral) and piercing (neuralgiform) with associated red eyes (conjunctival injection) and excess tear production. They may occur regularly or spasmodically.

Medication such as sumatriptan and ergotamine, nasal capsaicin spray, and inhaling pure oxygen are used as treatments. The headaches are very annoying but not serious.
See also CLUSTER HEADACHE; HEADACHE

SUN SENSITIVE SKIN
See ERYTHROPOIETIC PROTOPORPHYRIA; LIGHT SENSITIVE SKIN

SUPERFICIAL VENOUS THROMBOSIS
A superficial venous thrombosis (SVT) is a blood clot (thrombus) in the superficial veins just under the skin in the legs or arms. It may follow injury to the area, an intravenous drip insertion, or other localised disease, and the affected vein becomes red, hard and tender. Rarely there may be secondary infection or skin ulceration over the thrombosis.

Heat, rest of the limb, and aspirin or other anti-inflammatory medication are the main treatments, and recovery without complications in a week or two is normal.
See also DEEP VENOUS THROMBOSIS; THROMBOSIS; VARICOSE VEINS

SUPERIOR VENA CAVA SYNDROME
See LUNG CANCER

SUPPOSITORY
A suppository is a bullet shaped medication that is inserted into the rectum through the anus to act locally (eg. on piles), or be absorbed into the bloodstream through the wall of the rectum (eg. naproxen to treat arthritis).
See also MEDICATION; RECTUM

SUPRA-

'Supra-' is a prefix used in medical terms to indicate above or over as in supraventricular (above the ventricle).

SUPRASPINATUS TENDINITIS

Supraspinatus tendinitis is an inflammation of the supraspinatus tendon, which runs across the top of the shoulder and acts to move the whole arm away from the body. The tendon may be damaged by repeatedly using the tendon excessively, or by one specific severe wrench to the shoulder. Long term damage to the tendon may result in hard lumps of calcium depositing in the damaged section of tendon, which in turn cause more problems when the tendon is used.

Patients experience pain on top of the shoulder when moving the arm away from the body. An ultrasound of the tendon can show swelling and damage to the tendon, while an x-ray of the shoulder may show calcium deposits in a more severely damaged tendon.

Anti-inflammatory medications, physiotherapy, steroid injections and rarely surgery, may be used in treatment, which gives good but slow results.
See also PAINFUL ARC SYNDROME; ROTATOR CUFF SYNDROME; TENDINITIS

SUPRAVENTRICULAR TACHYCARDIA

A supraventricular tachycardia (SVT) is an abnormally rapid heart rate (tachycardia) caused by an abnormal nerve signal coming from the pacemaker or atria of the heart. It may be due to disease in the atria (upper chambers of the heart) or abnormal nerve pathways between the atria and ventricles (lower chambers of the heart), but often no specific cause can be found.

Patients experience prolonged rapid beating of the heart above 100 beats a minute which may be irregular. Sudden death from heart failure is rarely possible.

The diagnosis confirmed by an electrocardiogram (ECG), then beta-blocker (eg. propranolol, sotalol) or lanoxin medication can be given to control the tachycardia. Destruction of the abnormal nerve pathways by high frequency radio waves, administered through a catheter inserted into the heart through an artery or vein, can cure the condition.

Preventive medication and surgical treatment are both very successful.
See also PAROXYSMAL ATRIAL TACHYCARDIA; WOLFF-PARKINSON-WHITE SYNDROME

SURFACTANT
See RESPIRATORY DISTRESS SYNDROME, INFANT

SURGERY

Surgery is performed to remove or repair tissues within or upon the body, to drain away pus or other unwanted substances, to remove foreign bodies or to insert artificial body parts. Any operation usually involves penetrating through tissue that contains nerves, so an anaesthetic of one type or another is necessary. The penetration may be very minor (eg. a needle to drain an abscess or suck out a cyst), or a major part of the body may need to be widely exposed.

An operation may proceed by using a scalpel (a sharp, specially shaped knife), scissors, diathermy (electric needle) or laser (hot concentrated light beam) to cut through the tissues. Diathermy and lasers have the advantage of sealing most blood vessels as they cut, therefore preventing bleeding. Any bleeding must be controlled or prevented as the operation proceeds by clipping and tying bleeding vessels, or by destroying them with diathermy or laser.

Keyhole surgery is a term that is used when an operation is performed through the smallest possible incision in order to minimise tissue damage and scarring. It has now been superseded in many cases by laparoscopic surgery.

Once the operation has been performed, the wound is normally closed. This can be done by the traditional needle and thread, by staples, by special glues or by adhesive tape. The thread used can be absorbable or non-absorbable. Absorbable threads, such as catgut and more modern dissolving synthetics, are normally used internally; the non-absorbable threads such as silk, nylon and other synthetics are commonly used on the surface, from where they must be later removed. Some non-absorbable sutures are used internally, and remain permanently, in areas where their continued support of a structure (eg. hernia repair) is necessary.

Staples are applied by a special gun or forceps. Some sophisticated staple guns can now join together pieces of gut with one action. Internal staples are designed to remain forever, but external ones are normally removed. Glues are used in eye surgery and skin repair, which can enable a cut to be sealed without requiring local anaesthetic injections. Tape is often used to close minor cuts or small wounds, particularly on fingers, and where only slight pressure is likely to be applied to the wound.

Drains are often inserted during or after an operation to remove any blood, secretions or pus that may slow the healing process. These drains empty into a sealed container or a clean dressing, and are usually removed after a few days.

See also GENERAL ANAESTHETIC; LAPAROSCOPIC SURGERY; SUTURING and separate entries for specific operations.

SURGERY EXCESS

Munchausen syndrome is one of the more famous extremes of hypochondria, and is named after an 18th century German baron who suffered from the condition. Patients falsify symptoms by elaborate means in order to obtain medical attention, medications, investigations and surgery.

Patients with SHAFT syndrome have a personality disorder that causes them to be Sad, Hostile, Anxious, Frustrated and Tenacious (the name is an acronym of these symptoms). They praise doctors excessively to obtain unnecessary surgery, then claim worsening of symptoms after surgery for which the doctor is blamed. It is a psychiatric neurosis that requires long term psychotherapy.

See also MUNCHAUSEN SYNDROME; SHAFT SYNDROME

SUTURING

Sutures are threads used to close a wound anywhere in the body, be it caused by an injury or operation, in the skin or an internal organ. The thread of the suture can be made from silk, linen, gut, nylon, or any one of innumerable other synthetics. Some are designed to remain permanently, while others must be removed after healing has occurred, or will dissolve and disappear after a predetermined time. Almost invariably the thread is bonded almost seamlessly with a steel needle which will vary in shape and size depending on its intended use. Needles used in the skin are usually diamond shaped in cross section, while those used on internal tissues are usually round in cross section.

If a cut (laceration) is being sutured, a local anaesthetic will usually be given into the tissue around the wound by injection. After this there should be no pain felt, although there may be sensations of pulling or pressure.

The doctor inserts the needle through the skin to one side of the cut, curls it around under the skin, and brings it out through the skin on the other side, then pulls on the two ends of the thread to bring the wound edges together, and ties the ends firmly so that it is kept closed.

Sutures usually must be removed from the skin, and the timing will depend on the site and size of the wound. A small cut on the face may have sutures removed in three or four days, while a large deep cut on the thigh may need the support of the sutures for two weeks or more.

The removal of sutures is a painless procedure, with only a pulling sensation, but if their removal is delayed beyond the ideal time, the healing process may bury the sutures making removal more difficult. Sutures must be removed in a way that prevents any infection entering the healing wound as the thread is pulled through.

See also CUT; LACERATION; SURGERY

SVT

See SUPERFICIAL VENOUS THROMBOSIS; SUPRAVENTRICULAR TACHYCARDIA

SWALLOWING

Swallowing is achieved by the rhythmic relaxation and contraction of the muscles along the

SUTURING A CUT
Cross Section

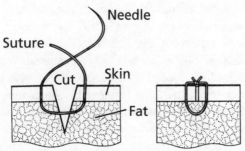

Insertion of suture   After tying suture

length of the oesophagus (gullet). The oesophagus is a muscular tube that runs from the back of the throat, down the chest, through a hole in the diaphragm (sheet of muscle that separates the chest cavity from the abdomen) to join the stomach.

See also DYSPEPSIA; OESOPHAGUS; PHARYNX; SWALLOWING PAINFUL

SWALLOWING PAINFUL

Difficult swallowing (dysphagia) or pain on swallowing (odynophagia) are often related, and most causes come from conditions in the oesophagus. However, problems with the nerve supply to the oesophagus and other diseases in the throat and elsewhere in the chest and abdomen may also be responsible.

The stomach contains concentrated hydrochloric acid, and is protected from this by a thick lining of mucus. A muscle ring (sphincter) normally prevents acid from coming up into the oesophagus, but if the sphincter weakens and acid comes back up into the unprotected oesophagus (reflux oesophagitis), intense burning may be felt behind the breast bone, as well as a bitter taste, shortness of breath, pain on swallowing and burping.

A hiatus hernia occurs when part of the stomach pushes up through the diaphragm (the sheet of muscle that separates the chest and abdominal cavities) into the chest. The muscle ring that prevents stomach acid from coming back up into the oesophagus then fails to work effectively, and both acid and gas can then enter the lower oesophagus to cause burning pain behind the breast bone, burping and an acid taste at the back of the tongue.

If reflux oesophagitis, due to a hiatus hernia or merely a weak sphincter, occurs for a prolonged time, the oesophagus may become scarred, and a stricture can develop which makes swallowing difficult.

Any infection of the throat, tonsils, larynx (vocal cords) or lymph nodes in the neck may cause pain when swallowing due to the inflammation of these tissues.

Globus is a relatively common phenomenon, but often goes unrecognised. The patient complains of a distressing intermittent lump in the throat, but on examination by a doctor, nothing can be found. It is caused by subconscious tension and anxiety which causes a spasm and uncomfortable tightness of the throat muscles. It may also extend down into the gullet (oesophagus) to cause swallowing difficulties.

Less common causes of difficulty and pain with swallowing include thrush (fungal infection of the mouth and throat), a swallowed foreign body (eg. fish or chicken bone, needle), epiglottitis (bacterial infection at the back of the throat), cancer of the oesophagus or throat, a goitre (enlarged thyroid gland), Parkinson disease, abscess in the throat or tonsil (quinsy), a stroke (cerebrovascular accident), severe arthritis in the neck, myasthenia gravis, Sjögren syndrome and irradiation of the chest to treat cancer of the lung or other chest organs.

There are many other rare causes of swallowing problems.

See also CHEST PAIN; DYSPEPSIA; HEARTBURN; OESOPHAGUS and separate entries for diseases mentioned above.

SWEARING UNCONTROLLED

Occasionally children or adults who swear uncontrollably are encountered.

In adults this is normally due to a head injury that has affected the control centres of the brain, or psychiatric conditions that reduce inhibitions.

In children, attention deficit hyperactivity disorder is the most common cause. The classic symptoms include fidgeting, inability to remain seated for long, being easily distracted and unable to sustain attention, always impatient, difficulty in following instructions, often moving from one incomplete task to the next, inability to play quietly, violence towards others and objects, talking excessively, often interrupting or intruding, not seeming to listen, poor short term memory, often losing items, and engaging in physically dangerous activities.

Rarely, Giles de la Tourette syndrome may be responsible. Children with this very uncommon disorder have convulsions and twitching as well as uncontrolled swearing.

See also ATTENTION DEFICIT HYPERACTIVITY DISORDER; GILES de la TOURETTE SYNDROME; VIOLENCE

SWEAT GLANDS

The sweat glands are an important factor in regulating body temperature. They are coiled tubes, and when it is hot they produce a mixture of salty water and some waste products which are evaporated through pores (tiny openings) in the surface of the skin, cooling the body's temperature in the process. Different sweat glands (apocrine glands) are located in the armpits and the groin. These react to emotional stress and sexual stimulation and secrete a fluid which, combined with bacteria, produces body odour. When the environment is too cold, the sweat glands cease to operate and surrounding tiny blood vessels contract. Cold causes the hairs on the surface to become erect, raising the skin into 'goose pimples' and trapping a layer of insulating air over the epidermis. To some extent the sweat glands also regulate the amount and composition of fluid in the body.

See also SEBACEOUS GLANDS; SKIN; SWEATING EXCESS; SWEATING LACK

SWEATING EXCESS

Increased sweating (hyperhidrosis or diaphoresis) is obviously associated with hot conditions, but may also occur with anxiety and fear, eating hot (spicy hot or temperature hot) foods, significant pain from any cause, and drinking excess alcohol. There are a number of medical conditions which may also be responsible.

Any bacterial or viral infection that causes a fever will have excessive sweating associated with it. Some infections, such as malaria, AIDS and tuberculosis, may result in sweating out of proportion to the level of fever.

The menopause occurs in the late forties and early fifties in most women. The symptoms of menopause include irregular menstrual periods, hot flushes, sweats, headaches, irritability, personality changes, breast tenderness, tiredness and pelvic discomfort.

The thyroid gland in the front of the neck produces the hormone thyroxine, which acts as an accelerator for every cell in the body. Excess thyroxine will cause sweating, weight loss, diarrhoea, poor absorption of food, nervousness, heat intolerance, rapid heart rate, warm skin, tremor and prominent eyes.

A heart attack (myocardial infarct) may cause chest pain and pressure, shortness of breath and the patient often sweats profusely. The seriousness and effects of a heart attack vary depending on which part, and how much of the heart, is affected.

Other causes of excess sweating include many different types of cancer (particularly in advanced stages), a blood clot in one of the major arteries within the lungs (pulmonary thrombosis), poorly controlled diabetes, overactive pituitary gland (eg. from a tumour or infection) and hyperthyroidism (overactive thyroid gland). Some psychoses may cause patients to have abnormal fears which cause the normal responses to fear, such as rapid heart rate, sweating and pins and needles sensation.

Rarer causes of excessive sweating include the Irukandji syndrome (excessive and abnormal response to some jellyfish stings), porphyria, Frey syndrome, phaeochromocytoma (tumour of the adrenal glands) and the Riley-Day syndrome (occurs only in Jewish people).

See also FEVER; SWEAT GLANDS and separate entries for diseases mentioned above.

SWEATING LACK

A total inability to sweat (anhidrosis) is extremely rare, and usually leads to death, but it is relatively common for there to be a generalised reduction in sweating, or absence of sweating in just one area of skin.

Severe dehydration from lack of fluid, inability to avoid hot environment, extreme exercise (heat stroke) or excessive passing of urine, may cause all sweating to cease, despite a hot climate, in a desperate attempt by the body to retain water. This phenomenon is critically serious as it only occurs close to death.

The thyroid gland in the front of the neck produces the hormone thyroxine, which acts as an accelerator for every cell in the body. If there is a lack of thyroxine, all organs will function slowly, and symptoms will include intolerance of cold, constipation, weakness, hoarse voice, heavy periods, dry skin, reduced sweating, hair loss, slow heart rate and anaemia.

Diabetes results in a higher than normal amount of sugar (glucose) circulating in the blood. The symptoms of untreated diabetes are unusual tiredness, increased thirst and hunger, excess passing of urine, weight loss despite a large food intake, itchy rashes, reduced sweating, recurrent vaginal thrush infections, pins and needles, dizziness, belly pains, light headedness and blurred vision.

Other causes of a generalised reduction in sweating include some types of lung cancer, quadriplegia (paralysis of all four limbs),

Hodgkin's disease (cancer of lymph nodes) and multiple myeloma (cancer of the cells in the bone marrow). Very premature babies will not sweat normally as their sweat glands are immature, but this problem settles as they develop, and should have disappeared by the time they reach their expected date of delivery.

Some drugs (eg. mepacrine) and poisons (eg. arsenic) can damage sweat glands.

Most causes of localised loss of sweating are caused by damage to the nerves or arteries supplying the affected area of skin. Damage to a nerve in an arm or leg, from an injury or being pinched near an arthritic joint, may cause sweating to stop beyond the point at which the nerve is damaged.

Sweat glands may be destroyed or damaged over a small area that is deliberately irradiated for the treatment of cancer.

Other causes of a localised reduction in sweating include rheumatoid arthritis, multiple sclerosis (nerve disease), polyarteritis nodosa (inflammation of arteries), Horner syndrome, leprosy and miliaria (development of multiple hard, cream coloured cysts on the skin, often of the face, that can block surrounding sweat glands).
See also SWEAT GLANDS and separate entries for diseases mentioned above.

SWEET SYNDROME
Sweet syndrome (acute febrile neutrophilic dermatosis) is a generalised skin disease of no known cause that is more common in women. Multiple tender, red or purple skin plaques develop on the neck and limbs, and are associated with muscle pains, fever, and joint pains and swelling. Acute myeloid leukaemia develops in 20% of patients, and rarely ulcerative colitis occurs.

Blood tests show excess white cells (neutrophils) and skin plaque biopsy is diagnostic. Prednisone is used in treatment. The plaques heal spontaneously over two or more months, but recurrences are common.
See also LEUKAEMIA, ACUTE MYELOID

SWIMMER'S EAR
See OTITIS EXTERNA

SWOLLEN
See ASCITES; OEDEMA

SWOLLEN JOINT
See KNEE SWOLLEN; JOINT SWOLLEN

SYDENHAM'S CHOREA
Sydenham's chorea used to be called St. Vitus dance. It is a complication of rheumatic fever or other bacterial infections, and now a rare condition, but was more common before the development of antibiotics.

Patients have irregular jerky movements of a limb or the body, with a complete loss of muscle tone between each movement. The underlying infection must be treated with antibiotics (eg. penicillin).
See also JERKING; RHEUMATIC FEVER

SYMBIOSIS
Symbiosis is two or more animals and/or plants and/or bacteria living together for their mutual benefit (eg. bacteria living within the human gut that aid digestion, fungi and algae living together to form lichen). In many cases the relationship is essential for the survival of both organisms.
See also PARASITES

SYMPATHETIC NERVOUS SYSTEM
See AUTONOMIC NERVOUS SYSTEM

SYMPATHOMIMETICS
See BETA-2 AGONISTS

SYNCOPE
See FAINT

SYNDROME
A syndrome is a collection of several symptoms that occur consistently in patients with a particular medical condition. Several hundred syndromes are recognised.
See also under individual syndrome names.

SYNDROME OF INAPPROPRIATE ANTIDIURETIC HORMONE SECRETION
The syndrome of inappropriate antidiuretic hormone secretion, despite its long name, is an important medical condition that is usually abbreviated to SIADH, although it has an alternative name of the syndrome of inappropriate vasopressin secretion.

It is a complex condition in which excess ADH (antidiuretic hormone or vasopressin) is released by the pituitary gland in the centre of the head. ADH controls the rate at which the kidneys produce urine and excrete salt and if excess is produced, the kidneys do not release sufficient water in the urine, and it builds up in the body.

The syndrome may occur as a result of a pituitary gland tumour, strokes in the part of the brain (hypothalamus) which controls the pituitary gland, or bleeding into the brain from a head injury. Some types of cancer, particularly of the lungs and pancreas, can start producing ADH independent from the pituitary gland. A number of other diseases (eg. tuberculosis, thyroid gland underactivity) may rarely also inappropriately produce ADH. Uncommon side effects from drugs and prolonged resuscitation may also trigger the syndrome.

The symptoms include weight gain, reduced urine output, generalised weakness, mental confusion, and eventually convulsions due to retention of excessive amounts of water and very low levels of salt in the blood. Heart, brain and other organ damage may occur if it is not controlled

Both blood and urine tests are abnormal, and the syndrome is controlled by medications (diuretics) to make the kidneys produce more urine, taking salt and restricting fluid intake.

Good control is possible with treatment, but a cure may be difficult as the exact cause must be found and corrected. It is fatal if not controlled.
See also DIURETICS; PITUITARY GLAND;

SYNDROME OF INAPPROPRIATE VASOPRESSIN SECRETION
See SYNDROME OF INAPPROPRIATE ANTIDIURETIC HORMONE SECRETION

SYNDROME X
Syndrome X (insulin resistance syndrome or Reaven syndrome) is a newly recognised autoimmune condition that may be a cause of high blood pressure. The body inappropriately rejects its own tissue, in this case the cells that respond to insulin.

The symptoms may include high blood pressure, a tendency to develop diabetes, obesity and cholesterol imbalances. There is a significantly increased risk of stroke and heart attack. It is diagnosed by sophisticated blood

tests, then medication is prescribed to control blood pressure, diabetes and cholesterol levels. No cure is possible, but good control normally achieved.
See also HYPERTENSION

SYNOVIAL FLUID
Synovial fluid is the clear, thick, slightly amber coloured lubricating fluid found between the bone ends in all mobile joints. It is produced by the synovial membrane lining joints and in small sacs (bursae) that lie near the joint and connect to it by a tiny duct. These bursae are themselves very small in smaller joints, while larger joints may have several.

The fluid moves from the bursa to the joint cavity and is then slowly absorbed through the joint cartilage into the bone ends, before entering veins to return to the bloodstream, thus giving a steady circulation to refresh joint and nurture the bone ends.

If a joint is infected the synovial fluid may become thicker and cloudy. Some joint diseases are diagnosed by inserting a needle into the joint and drawing out a sample of the fluid.
See also BURSITIS; HOUSEMAID'S KNEE; JOINT; SEPTIC ARTHRITIS; SYNOVITIS

SYNOVITIS
Synovitis is an inflammation or infection of the synovial membrane that lines all joint cavities, covering all surfaces within the joint except those where weight-bearing cartilage is present. The membrane secretes synovial fluid, which acts as a lubricant within joints and allows them to move smoothly and freely.

The cause of synovitis may be a bacterial infection, injury to the joint, rheumatoid arthritis, tuberculosis (now rare), gonorrhoea or other infecting organisms. It is usually associated with the excessive secretion of synovial fluid into the joint. It is sometimes necessary to drain some fluid from the joint through a needle and examine it to diagnose the cause.

There is swelling, restricted movement, pain and sometimes redness and heat in the affected joint. Any joint may be involved, but the hip, knee and ankle are the most commonly affected ones. The cause must be treated (eg. antibiotics for a bacterial infection) and the joint must be rested until pain and swelling subside. If left untreated, permanent damage to the joint may occur, or arthritis may develop prematurely.

See also GONORRHOEA; JOINT SWOLLEN; PIGMENTED VILLONODULAR SYNOVITIS; REPETITIVE STRAIN INJURY; RHEUMATOID ARTHRITIS; SEPTIC ARTHRITIS; SYNOVIAL FLUID

SYPHILIS

Syphilis is an infection that is usually sexually transmitted, and which passes through three main stages over many months or years. It is relatively uncommon in developed countries, but still widespread in poorer societies. The cause is the spirochete bacterium *Treponema pallidum,* which is transmitted by heterosexual or homosexual contact, sharing injecting needles, blood transfusions, or from a mother to her child during pregnancy (congenital syphilis). The same bacterium also causes yaws, which is transmitted by close body contact, but not necessarily sexual contact.

The symptoms are totally different in each of the three stages: –

• First stage syphilis causes a painless sore (chancre) on the penis, the female genitals, or around the anus of homosexuals, which heals after three to six weeks. There may be painless, enlarged lymph nodes in the armpit and groin that also disappear.

• Second stage syphilis starts a few weeks or months later with a widespread rash, mouth and vaginal ulcers, and a slight fever. The patient is highly infectious but will usually recover and enter a latent period that may last many years.

• Third (tertiary) stage syphilis develops years later with tumours (gumma) in the liver, major arteries, bones, brain, spinal cord (tabes dorsalis), skin and other organs. Symptoms vary depending on organs involved but may include arthritis, bone weakness, severe bone pain, paralysis, strokes, heart attacks, internal bleeding from aneurysms, blindness, headaches, jaundice (liver failure), muscle spasms, skin ulcers, scars, nodules in the larynx and lungs, vomiting, confusion, insanity and death.

Congenital syphilis occurs in newborn infants who have teeth abnormalities, deafness, misshapen bones, deformed nose, pneumonia, and mental retardation.

It can be diagnosed at all stages by specific blood tests, or by finding the responsible bacteria on a swab taken from a genital sore in the first stage of the disease. All pregnant women should be routinely tested.

First and second stages are treated by antibiotics such as penicillin (often as an injection), tetracycline or erythromycin. In the third (tertiary) stage, antibiotics are also used, but can merely prevent further deterioration as organ damage is irreversible. A child suffering from congenital syphilis is infectious when born and is treated with antibiotics.

There are many complications associated with syphilis infection. In the first stage there are usually none, but in second stage syphilis there may be spread of the infection to involve the joints, brain, liver and kidney which may be severely damaged. In the third (tertiary) stage almost any organ can be seriously damaged. Infants with congenital syphilis may develop more serious problems if the condition is not treated aggressively.

A course of antibiotics for a few weeks almost invariably cures the disease in its first two stages, but there is no cure for tertiary or congenital syphilis. Plastic surgery may correct the more obvious congenital deformities.

See also TABES DORSALIS; VENEREAL DISEASES; YAWS

SYRINGOMYELIA

Syringomyelia is an expansion of a cavity within the spinal cord that places pressure on the nerves passing this point, and affects nerve function and circulation of the surrounding cerebrospinal fluid below it. It most commonly occurs in the neck, and may be a developmental disorder (congenital), or due to tumours, injury or inflammation. Sometimes it is associated with the Arnold-Chiari malformation, in which the lowest part of the brain (cerebellum) slips down into the spinal canal.

Patients experience a gradually worsening reduction in sensation and muscle weakness below the affected point of the spine. It is diagnosed by CT and MRI scans, and then surgical drainage of the cavity in the spinal cord and removal of any tumour is performed. Untreated, quadriplegia or paraplegia may occur, but good results are obtained from treatment.

See also MUSCLE WEAKNESS; PARAPLEGIA AND QUADRIPLEGIA; SPINAL CORD

SYSTEMIC LUPUS ERYTHEMATOSUS

Systemic (or disseminated) lupus erythematosus (SLE) is a relatively common inflammatory condition affecting joints, skin, liver, and kidney most commonly, but almost any tissue in the body may be involved. 85% of cases occur in women (usually young), and it is more common in Negroes than Caucasians.

Lupus is an autoimmune disorder in which the body inappropriately rejects normal tissue for no known reason. Attacks may be precipitated by stress, some medications or chemicals. There is also a familial tendency.

Common symptoms include arthritis of several joints, a red rash across both cheeks and the bridge of the nose ('butterfly rash'), rashes on other areas that are exposed to sunlight, mouth ulcers, poorly functioning kidneys and anaemia. Additional symptoms may include a fever, loss of appetite, tiredness, weight loss, damaged nails, loss of hair and painfully cold fingers. Less common complaints include conjunctivitis, blurred vision, chest pain, pneumonia, heart failure, belly pain, constipation, depression and convulsions. The symptoms vary significantly from one patient to another, and none will have them all. Many patients are free of symptoms for months before a recurrence. After each attack, there is slightly more permanent liver, kidney or heart damage, and eventually these problems accumulate to the point where the disease becomes life-threatening. In rare cases it proceeds relentlessly to death within a relatively short time. Specific blood tests can diagnose the condition.

Treatment depends upon the severity of the disease, and with mild symptoms no treatment is required. Sun exposure should be avoided and all non-essential medications ceased. In severe cases, a wide range of drugs, including steroids, cytotoxics, immunosuppressives and antimalarials may all be used. Regular blood tests follow the course of the condition, which is very variable, from a mild arthritic complaint to a rapidly progressive disease. There is no cure, but with careful management, compliance with treatment, and regular check-ups, 90% of patients are alive more than ten years after the diagnosis is made.

See also AUTOIMMUNE DISEASES; DISCOID LUPUS ERYTHEMATOSUS

SYSTEMIC MASTOCYTOSIS
See URTICARIA PIGMENTOSA

SYSTEMIC SCLEROSIS
See SCLERODERMA

SYSTOLIC PRESSURE

The heart contracts regularly to pump blood through the arteries under high (systolic) pressure. When the heart relaxes between beats, the blood continues to flow due to the lower (diastolic) pressure exerted by the elasticity of the artery walls. Hypertension occurs when one, or both, of these pressures exceeds a safe level. Blood pressure readings are written as systolic pressure/diastolic pressure (eg. 125/70) and are measured with a sphygmomanometer.

See also HEART; HYPERTENSION; SPHYGMOMANOMETER

T

TABES DORSALIS

Tabes dorsalis is a rare complication of third stage syphilis due to the development of a syphilitic deposit in the spinal cord. Patients experience repetitive, brief, severe pain in the legs, back, chest, and sometimes arms and face. Some patients develop poor coordination of the legs and difficulty in walking, loss of bladder control, vomiting, abdominal pain, and abnormal sensations.

Antibiotics can treat the syphilis and prevent progression of the disease, but there is no cure for existing symptoms.
See also SPINAL CORD; SYPHILIS

TACHYCARDIA

Tachycardia is a medical term that indicates a rapid heart rate above the normal resting rate of about seventy beats a minute in an adult. Normally the heart beats without any conscious awareness, but if a patient becomes aware of the heartbeat, it is usually because it is beating faster than normal. Patients may become excessively tired and feel the cold more than normal.

Causes include exertion, fear or emotion, eating or drinking too much caffeine (eg. colas, coffee), smoking, diseases (eg. anaemia, overactive thyroid gland, cancer, chronic kidney or liver disease), numerous heart diseases (eg. paroxysmal atrial or ventricular tachycardia), and drugs (eg. thyroxine, appetite suppressants).

An ECG (electrocardiogram) will show tachycardia and sometimes its cause. Blood and other tests will be necessary to find the cause, and this will determine the treatment.
See also ELECTROCARDIOGRAPH; PALPITATIONS; PAROXYSMAL ATRIAL TACHYCARDIA; PAROXYSMAL VENTRICULAR TACHYCARDIA

TAENIASIS
See TAPEWORMS

TAGAMET
See H2 RECEPTOR ANTAGONISTS

TALIPES EQUINOVARUS
See CLUB FOOT

TALKING

Babies often make repetitive sounds from six months of age. By eight to nine months the child will recognise its own name, and at about the same age s/he will say 'mama' and know what it means. By twelve months the child will be able to name a few objects and people, although they may not necessarily use the correct name. By eighteen months of age a child will have a vocabulary of about twenty words, but some children with normal intelligence do not speak coherently until much older. By the time they are two years old, most children can make a short sentence of three or four words.
See also BABIES; CHILDHOOD

TALL
See HEIGHT EXCESSIVE

TALUS
See ANKLE

TAMOXIFEN
See CYTOTOXICS AND ANTINEOPLASTICS

TAPANUI FLU
See CHRONIC FATIGUE SYNDROME

TAPEWORMS

Mature tapeworms live in the gut of humans or other animals. Six different types of tapeworm (Taeniasis) can infect humans. They vary in length from half a centimetre (dwarf tapeworm) to more than twenty five metres (beef tapeworm) and are members of a class of worms known as Cestodes. Tapeworms were named because they are divided into segments in much the same way as a tape measure. At one end there is a head (scolex) that has a large sucker on it, and this is used to attach the worm to the inside of the gut.

Segments that are full of eggs constantly drop off from the end of the worm and pass out with the faeces and remain in the soil until eaten by another animal. When the egg is swallowed, it hatches an embryo that burrows into the muscle of the animal and remains there for the rest of that animal's life. If the animal's flesh is eaten, the embryo enters the gut of the new host, attaches to it and grows into a mature tapeworm. Tiny tapeworm embryos may be found in the flesh of cattle, pigs, and fish but are destroyed by cooking. Less common tapeworms can be transmitted by fleas and other insects from rats and dogs to man, and another uncommon form passes directly from the gut of one human to another through faeces and contaminated food. Tapeworms may be caught in many parts of the world but are rare in developed countries.

There may be no symptoms until the numbers of worms present is quite high when nausea, diarrhoea, abdominal discomfort, hunger, weight loss and tiredness may occur. Sometimes patients find segments of the worm in their underclothes or bedding. Except for the rare cases where the embryo stage spreads to the brain, there are no long-term complications.

The presence of tapeworms can be confirmed by examining faeces under a microscope for the presence of segments or eggs. It is then cured by the use of appropriate medication.
See also HYDATID DISEASE; WORMS

TARSAL PLATE
See EYELID

TARSAL TUNNEL SYNDROME
Tarsal tunnel syndrome is due to compression of the posterior tibial nerve as it passes around the ankle joint, and usually follows an injury to the ankle from repetitive use or a sudden strain.

A pins and needles sensation is felt in the toes and sole of the foot, and there may be weakness of muscles in the foot. Permanent damage to the nerve may result in loss of sensation and function in the foot. Electromyography (EMG) shows abnormal nerve and muscle function.

Treatment involves corticosteroid injection around the nerve at the point where it is being pinched, or surgery to release the trapped nerve.
See also ANKLE; CARPAL TUNNEL SYNDROME; ELECTROMYOGRAM

TARTAR
See DENTAL PLAQUE

TASTE
The organ that allows us to experience different tastes is the tongue. On the upper surface of the tongue are millions of tiny projections called papillae. It is these papillae that give the tongue its rough feel. Housed within them are microscopic nerve endings known as taste buds. There are about 1000 taste buds on an adult tongue, but far more in a baby.

When food is taken into the mouth and liquefied by the chewing and the saliva, the taste buds react to the various chemicals that are released, sending messages to the taste centres of the brain. The taste buds will only be activated if there is moisture. Dry food taken into a dry mouth would have no taste at all.

There are only four primary tastes – sweet, sour, bitter and salty. The variety of flavours we experience are different combinations of these four, combined with smell. The different tastes are detected on different areas of the tongue. Bitterness is experienced at the rear, sourness at the sides, and saltiness and sweetness at the front. The tongue's centre has almost no sense of taste.

The strongest taste sensation is that of bitterness, and this has a protective aspect to it. Poisons and other toxic substances are usually bitter and, because of the extreme unpleasantness of their taste on the tongue, we are prompted to spit them out before they are swallowed and cause damage to internal organs.

It is possible for taste buds to be educated to a high degree of sensitivity, eg. to wine. The sense of taste is closely linked with the sense of smell, which is some ten thousand times stronger.
See also ACID TASTE; MOUTH; SMELL; TASTE ABNORMAL

TASTE ABNORMAL
Taste is determined by taste buds that are found on the tongue, with sweet receptors at the tip of the tongue, salt and sour along the sides from front to back, and bitter at the back centre of the tongue. This can explain the bitter aftertaste to some foods and drinks.

The elderly gradually lose their sense of both taste and smell, and for this reason many older people complain that all their food is bland and uninteresting.

Smoking coats the tongue and damages the taste buds. When smokers give up their habit, taste returns after a few weeks, food is better appreciated, more is eaten, and weight increases if the diet is not carefully watched.

Dentures can trap food particles, and if not properly cleaned, these particles can rot or ferment to cause unpleasant tastes.

Any bacterial, viral or fungal infection in the mouth, teeth, salivary glands, throat, sinuses or other surrounding tissues can create a bad taste from the pus and other waste products it produces.

A dry tongue, caused by mouth breathing, dehydration, mouth infections or failure of the salivary glands with age or other disease, will reduce the tongue's ability to detect taste.

Other causes of abnormal taste include migraines (varied symptoms may affect sight, taste and/or smell with or without a headache), hypothyroidism (an underactive thyroid gland in the neck), tumours or cancers of the mouth and nose can discharge foul tasting waste products, an injury to the nerves of taste or smell (from infection, tumours, cancer or fractured skull), poisoning with heavy metals (eg. lead, mercury) and irradiation of the head for various types of cancer.

Many medications may cause a bad taste, particularly metronidazole (antibiotic), ACE inhibitors (for high blood pressure), cancer treating drugs and antithyroid drugs.
See also ACID TASTE; SMELL LOSS; TASTE and separate entries for diseases mentioned above.

TASTE ACID
See ACID TASTE

TASTE LOSS
See TASTE ABNORMAL

TB
See TUBERCULOSIS

TDS
The prescription notation 'tds' is derived from the Latin 'ter die sumendum' which means 'three times a day'.
See also PRESCRIPTION NOTATIONS

TEAR DUCT BLOCKED
See CONJUNCTIVITIS

TEARS
Tears are produced in the small lacrimal glands situated above the outside corner of each eye. Numerous small ducts lead into the eyes. Tears are salty and contain antibacterial substances to protect against infection. Tears lubricate the eyes with a blink, and may be produced in greater quantities when the eyes are irritated or the person is experiencing intense emotion. Tears are an important part of the functioning of the eye, and an inability to produce them can lead to serious problems caused by dryness of the eye surface.

To keep the eyes moist, most people blink ten to twenty times a minute.

At the inner corner of the eyes the tear duct (lacrimal duct) drains tears from the eye through a small storage area (the lacrimal sac)

EYE FROM FRONT

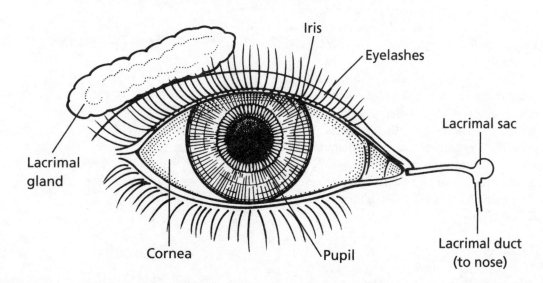

into the top of the nose. When we cry, excess tears are produced, and will overflow the eyes, or run through the tear ducts into the nose and thence down the throat, and the salt they contain can be tasted.

See also EYE; EYE, DRY; EYELID; TEARS EXCESS

TEARS EXCESS

Tears are produced by the lacrimal gland at the outside corner of the eye, move across the eye surface to keep it moist, and then flow through a tiny duct at the inside corner of the eye into the back of the nose. It is normal to cry when upset, distressed or in pain, but there are a number of conditions which may cause excessive tear production at other times.

Ectropion is an outwards tilting of the lower lid that occurs in elderly people due to the poor tissue strength around the eye. This allows tears to escape and give the appearance of crying

If the facial nerve, which supplies the muscles and tissue around the eye, is damaged by an injury, infection or tumour, the lower eyelid will also become slack, and tilt outwards to allow tears to escape.

Bell's palsy is a peculiar condition in which the facial nerve, which controls the movement of muscles in the face, stops working. The cause is unknown. The onset is quite sudden, and a patient may find that one side of their face becomes totally paralysed in a matter of hours. Completely recovery without treatment or discomfort is usual in two to ten weeks. The patient has no expression on the affected side of the face, and the mouth appears to be crooked. The eye on the affected side may need to be protected with lubricants, as it cannot be closed properly, and leaks tears constantly.

Mikulicz syndrome is a rare condition, more common in Scandinavia, which causes enlargement of the salivary and lacrimal glands to create excess saliva and tears.

SUNCT syndrome is a nerve inflammation that causes intermittent spasms of severe headache, stabs of face pain and watery eyes.
See also EYE DISCHARGE; EYE DRY; EYE WATERY

TEETH

Two sets of teeth grow in a lifetime. The baby,

or primary, teeth start to appear a few months after birth (although they have begun forming while the baby is still in the womb) and will usually have reached their full complement of twenty by about two and a half years of age with ten on the top and ten on the bottom jaw. The front cutting teeth are the incisors, and the back grinding teeth are the molars. Dividing these are sharp pointed eye teeth, or canines.

At the age of about six, a child develops the permanent six-year-old molars. Some time after this, the roots of the baby teeth begin gradually to dissolve and the teeth fall out, in order to be replaced by the permanent teeth. This process will usually be completed during the teens, with individual children varying a great deal. The permanent teeth have started forming in the gum from the age of about two. Care and hygiene of baby teeth are no less important because the teeth will eventually be lost. Decay and infection can spread to the developing teeth and the baby teeth are important in guiding the permanent teeth as they grow out through the jaw.

Permanent teeth are larger than baby teeth and total thirty two. They are accommodated by the increased size of the older child's jawbone. Starting from the front there are two incisors, one canine tooth, two premolars and three molars (the one furthest back is the wisdom tooth). This pattern is repeated on both sides, and in the top and bottom jaws.

Sometimes the jaw isn't large enough for the wisdom teeth, which may not appear until the late teens or early twenties. In this case,

INCISOR TOOTH

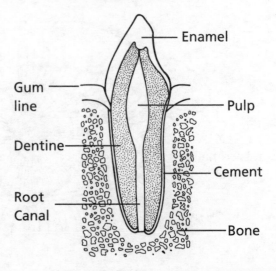

they may remain embedded in the jaw, and if this causes problems they may have to be removed by dental surgery. However, some people never grow their wisdom teeth and never develop any problems.

The visible part of the tooth is the crown and is covered with shiny white enamel – the hardest substance in the human body. The lower part of the tooth that fits into a socket in the jaw is the root, and this is covered by a bony material called cementum. The area where the root and crown meet is called the neck. The root is attached to the jaw by a membrane. The bulk of the tooth consists of a bone-like substance called dentine. In the centre of each tooth is the pulp, which contains the living matter such as nerves, blood vessels and connective tissue. This is the part that hurts if the tooth becomes infected or damaged. A fine canal (the root canal) runs from the pulp down either side of the root, and joins up with the body's main nerve and circulation systems.

The jawbone in which the teeth sit is covered by the gum, technically known as the gingiva, which is attached to the tooth enamel around the neck of the tooth. The sockets in the jaw in which the teeth sit correspond in shape to the teeth although they are slightly larger. The upper and lower teeth themselves are designed to fit perfectly one into the other when the jaw is closed, a feature that gives maximum chewing efficiency.

The lower jaw (mandible) is joined to the base of the skull by the temporomandibular or jaw joints.

MOLAR TOOTH

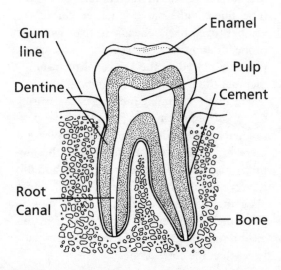

The saying 'long in the tooth' comes from the retraction of the gingiva (gums) from the teeth that is common in old age.
See also DENTAL PLAQUE; DENTISTRY; FLUORIDATION; MOUTH; ORTHODONTICS; PAEDODONTICS; PERIODONTICS; SALIVARY GLAND; TONGUE; TOOTH DISCOLOURED; TOOTH LOOSE

TEETH GRINDING
See BRUXISM

TEETHING
Most babies have some discomfort while they are teething. They may dribble and become fretful and irritable. Sometimes bowel movements become slightly loose, but it is a mistake to blame diarrhoea, vomiting, fever or any other sign of illness on teething, although teething may lower resistance so that the child is more susceptible to viral infections.

The reason a child cries when teething is that its gums are hurting. Chewing on a rattle or teething ring may help, as may rubbing the gums with a finger. If necessary, gels that contain a mild pain reliever and gum soother can be rubbed on the gums. These are available without a prescription from chemists.

Teeth normally start to appear around five or six months, although babies vary widely, with some cutting a tooth as early as three months (some children have even been born with teeth eg. Napoleon Bonaparte) and some not until seven or eight months. A baby who cuts teeth earlier than average is not brighter or more advanced than one who cuts them later.

Teeth usually appear quite rapidly in the child's second six months, and by the time they are nine or ten months, most babies have both the top and bottom four front teeth. The molars then start to appear around the age of one. These are likely to cause some discomfort even in a baby who has had none before, since the larger, broader shape makes it difficult for them to push through the gum. Most of the first or 'milk' teeth will have arrived by the age of two and a half. Chewing on a teething ring, rubbing the gums with gels that contain a mild pain reliever, and paracetamol drops or elixir, will ease any discomfort. Infants are more susceptible to infections while stressed by teething.

The baby teeth will start to loosen and fall

out when the child is about five, and the permanent teeth will then begin to erupt. It is a complete mistake to assume that because a child will lose the first teeth therefore dental care is of reduced importance. The second teeth are already in the gums and a child whose first teeth are allowed to decay faces a lifetime of dental problems.
See also BABIES; CHILDHOOD; TEETH

TELANGIECTASIA
Telangiectasia is a medical term for multiple dilated blood vessels in the skin.
See also CREST SYNDROME; SPIDER NAEVI

TELMISARTAN
See ANGIOTENSIN II RECEPTOR ANTAGONISTS

TELOGEN EFFLUVIUM
Telogen effluvium is a form of diffuse hair loss. Both men and women have fewer hairs as they grow older, but excessive generalised hair loss from the scalp, and sometimes other hairy areas of the body (eg. eyebrows, pubic area, chest) may be a symptom of disease such as sex hormone disturbances (eg. pregnancy, menopause), an over or underactive thyroid gland, pituitary gland diseases, many other serious illness, drugs used to treat cancer, radiation therapy, too much vitamin A, and sudden and excessive loss of weight (eg. anorexia nervosa). Extreme mental or physical stress may also be responsible. Blood and other tests may be done to exclude specific causes but are often normal.

If a cause can be found this should be treated. When the cause is medication, the hair usually grows back when it is ceased.
See also ALOPECIA AREATA; BALD; HAIR LOSS

TEMAZEPAM
See SEDATIVES

TEMPERATURE
The normal active human has a temperature of about 37°C. The word 'about' is used advisedly, because the temperature is not an absolute value. A woman's temperature rises by up to half a degree after she ovulates in the middle of her cycle. Many people have temperatures up to a degree below the average

with no adverse effects. The body temperature will also vary slightly depending on the time of day, food intake and the climate. All these factors must be taken into account when the notion of a normal temperature is considered.

The body's temperature is controlled by balancing the heat produced by the body with the heat lost. Heat is produced by the exertion of muscles, the breakdown of food and the basic functioning of the body's organs (the metabolic rate, particularly the liver). Heat is lost by the evaporation of sweat, radiation from the skin (a person feels hot or cold to the touch), loss of heat in breathing out warm air, and in the warmth of the urine and faeces.

The balance of these inputs and losses is maintained by an area in the base of brain known as the hypothalamus. If the hypothalamus perceives that a body is too hot, it will increase heat loss by sweating. If it perceives that the body is too cold, muscle activity will be increased by shivering. In between these ranges, the individual will also sense heat or cold, and adjust their clothing or environment accordingly.

An individual who feels the cold (or heat) more than another is reflecting that person's variation in basic metabolic rate (the rate at which the bowel, kidneys, heart, liver and all the other organs work), or their learned experience of temperature change (eg. a Tasmanian can swim in winter in Queensland, while a local finds it far too cold to do so).
See also FEVER; TEMPERATURE MEASUREMENT

TEMPERATURE MEASUREMENT
A person's temperature is measured using a thermometer. Thermometers may be a glass tube filled with mercury (silver colour) or alcohol (dyed red), a heat sensitive electronic probe, or an infrared measuring device which is gently placed in the ear canal to instantly measure the body's temperature.

The most common method of measuring the body temperature is to place the thermometer bulb under the tongue, and leave it there for at least two minutes. The thermometer may also be placed in the anus, and this is very useful in children who might bite a glass thermometer. The third method is to place the instrument in the arm pit, but this gives a reading about half a degree centigrade lower than the correct one.

The heat sensitive strips that can be placed on the forehead, give only a very rough guide to the patient's true internal temperature.
See also FEVER; TEMPERATURE

TEMPERATURE RAISED
See FEVER

TEMPER TANTRUMS
Most children will scream and cry with rage if they are frustrated. Nearly all children have the occasional tantrum, and some children have them frequently.

Tantrums seem to reach their peak around the age of two when the child is beginning to assert its own independence – hence the 'terrible twos'. Toddlers who have a lot of tantrums are usually lively children, and may be very intelligent and have a strong desire to extend their horizons to things that are still beyond them. It is important to be aware that a child who has a tantrum is a child whose frustration has gone beyond the limits of their tolerance and the child can no longer help their behaviour.

A tantrum is as frightening for a child as it is unpleasant for you. The best way to deal with tantrums is to prevent them by organising the child's life so that frustration is at a minimum. If a child is having a tantrum, it is pointless to try to remonstrate or argue – the child is not capable of any rational response. Try to prevent the child from getting hurt or causing damage by holding them gently but firmly on the floor. As the child calms down, they will usually find comfort in your being there. A child should neither be rewarded nor punished for a tantrum. If the tantrum was because you wouldn't let them go out to play, don't change your mind once the tantrum has taken place. On the other hand, if you were about to go for a drive in the car, continue with your plans once the tantrum has ended. As the child gets bigger, stronger and feels more confident in its ability to cope with life, the tantrums will usually come to an end.

One of the most frightening forms of tantrum (for parents) is the young baby who holds its breath, possibly until it turns blue and even loses consciousness for a brief period. Older children sometimes bang their heads on the ground or the sides of their cot. Despite their obvious unpleasantness for parents, these forms of behaviour do not seem to cause any harm, although a parent worried about some serious abnormality shouldn't hesitate to consult a doctor.
See also BABIES; CHILDHOOD

TEMPORAL ARTERITIS
Temporal or giant cell arteritis, is an inflammation of medium to large arteries throughout the body, but most commonly the arteries in the temples at the side of the head. The cause is unknown but it may an autoimmune disease and often follows a significant viral infection.

Involved arteries become extremely tender and swollen. Symptoms depend on which arteries are inflamed, but may include headache, scalp tenderness, pain in the jaw with chewing, throat pain and vision disturbances. Less commonly a cough, shoulder pain, weakness and a fever occur. Blindness due to involvement of the arteries in the eye, and aneurysms (dilations) of arteries are complications. About half of all patients also have polymyalgia rheumatica

Blood tests are usually performed to detect the inflammation, and a biopsy of an artery will reveal the presence of characteristic giant cells. Treatment involves taking steroid tablets (eg: prednisone) for several months. It is usually well controlled and eventually cured, but recurrences when medication is ceased are common.
See also AUTOIMMUNE DISEASES;
POLYMYALGIA RHEUMATICA

TEMPORAL BONE
The temporal bone forms the lower part of the side of the skull, and contains the ear canal. It joins to the occipital bone at the back, the parietal bone above, and the sphenoid bone at the front. The mastoid process is a protrusion of the temporal bone behind each ear. The mastoid is filled with less dense bone that may become infected by a severe or untreated ear infection.
See also MASTOIDITIS; SKULL

TEMPORAL LOBE EPILEPSY
See EPILEPSY

TEMPOROMANDIBULAR JOINT
See MANDIBLE

TEMPOROMANDIBULAR JOINT DYSFUNCTION
The temporomandibular joint is the jaw joint,

and malfunctioning of this joint is a common cause of face pain. The joint lies just in front of the ear, and problems may be due to poor alignment of teeth, muscle imbalances in the face associated with emotional stress, grinding of the teeth (bruxism) or an injury to the joint. Problems are more common in women

Patients develop a tight aching pain which spreads to the ear and across the face, is worse with chewing and may be associated with a click in the joint. With prolonged symptoms, arthritis may develop in the joint. X-rays and other tests are usually normal.

Treatment involves muscle relaxants (eg. diazepam), mobilisation of the joint under the supervision of a physiotherapist, anti-inflammatory medications and pain relievers, and as a last resort surgery may be performed. There is a good response to treatment.
See also MANDIBLE

TENDINITIS
Tendinitis is inflammation of a tendon due to overuse or injury. Tendons connect a muscle to a bone so that when a muscle contracts, the tendon pulls the bone. If a tendon becomes strained, stretched, overused or damaged it will become inflamed. The tendon swells, becomes acutely painful and does not work effectively. Sometimes tiny flecks of bone form in the tendon if it has been inflamed for a long time, and these can be seen on x-ray. Supraspinatus tendinitis is one of the most common types of tendinitis, and is caused by inflammation of the tendon that runs across the top of the shoulder to move the arm away from the body.

Treatment involves rest of the affected part, which may be strapped, bandaged, splinted or plastered to ensure there is no movement. Anti-inflammatory medicines and steroid injections may also be used along with physiotherapy, which is particularly valuable on return to work to prevent a recurrence of the problem.
See also REPETITIVE STRAIN INJURY; SUPRASPINATUS TENDINITIS; TENDON; TENOSYNOVITIS

TENDON
In the same way as ligaments are the means by which bones are attached to other bones, tendons are the strong fibrous cords attaching muscles to bones and controlling muscular movement. Tendons are similar to ligaments but are not as elastic.

Some tendons are round and some are flat bands. Some tendons are so short that the muscle fibres are attached almost directly to the bone. Most tendons are surrounded by a sheath lined with a membrane and containing fluid so that the tendon can glide smoothly over surrounding parts. On contact with the bone, tendon fibres gradually pass into the substance of the bone and blend with it. One of the largest tendons in the body is the Achilles tendon which attaches the calf muscle to the heel bone.

The sudden imposition of an unbalanced load can result in a ruptured tendon which is extremely painful and, if the rupture is total, usually requires surgical repair and immobilisation for six weeks. The rupture of the Achilles tendon is a well-known sports injury.

Tendinitis, or inflammation of a tendon, can also result from misuse or overuse.
See also BONE; LIGAMENT; LIGAMENT OR TENDON RUPTURE; MUSCLE; STRAIN; TENDINITIS; TENOSYNOVITIS; TRIGGER FINGER

TENESMUS
See FAECES, ABNORMAL DESIRE TO PASS

TENNIS ELBOW
Tennis elbow (lateral epicondylitis) is an inflammation of the tendon on the outside of the bony lump at the side of the elbow (epicondyle). The cause is overstraining of the extensor tendon at the outer back of the elbow due to excessive bending and twisting movements of the arm. In tennis, the injury is more likely if the backhand action is faulty, with excessive wrist action and insufficient follow-through. Being unfit, having a tautly strung racquet, a heavy racquet and wet balls all add to the elbow strain. This leads to tears of the minute fibres in the tendon; scar tissue forms, which is then broken down again by further strains. It may also occur in tradesmen who undertake repetitive tasks, housewives, musicians and many others who may put excessive strain on their elbows.

Painful inflammation occurs, which can be constant or may only occur when the elbow is moved or stressed. The whole forearm can ache in some patients, especially when trying to grip or twist with the hand.

Prolonged rest is the most important treatment. Exercises to strengthen the elbow and anti-inflammatory drugs may also be used, and cortisone injections may be given in resistant cases. The strengthening exercises are done under the supervision of a physiotherapist and involve using the wrist to raise and lower a weight with the palm facing down. Some patients find pressure pads over the tendon, or elbow guards (elastic tubes around the elbow) help relieve the symptoms and prevent recurrences by adding extra support. The condition is not easy to treat and can easily become chronic.

No matter what form of treatment is used, most cases seem to last for about eighteen months and then settle spontaneously.
See also GOLFER'S ELBOW

TENOSYNOVITIS
Tenosynovitis is inflammation of the fibrous sheath that surrounds a tendon, particularly in the hands and feet. Overuse or repetitive use may reduce the volume of the very thin film of lubricating synovial fluid that allows a tendon to slide smoothly through its sheath, triggering inflammation.

Pain occurs with any movement involving use of the inflamed tendon sheath, and there is tenderness if pressure is applied to the tendon. Rarely permanent contractures of the tendon and limited movement of the joint may occur.

Treatment involves resting the affected part by strapping, bandages, splints or even plaster to prevent any movement of the tendon. Anti-inflammatory medicines may also be used along with physiotherapy. In severe cases injections of steroids may be given around the tendon sheath, but these cannot be repeated too frequently. The last resort is an operation to remove the tendon sheath.
See also de QUERVAIN
TENOSYNOVITIS; REPETITIVE
STRAIN INJURY; TENDON;
TENDINITIS

TENOVAGINITIS
See de QUERVAIN TENOSYNOVITIS

TENOXICAM
See NONSTEROIDAL ANTI-INFLAMMATORY DRUGS

TENSION HEADACHE
See HEADACHE

TERATOMA
A teratoma is an uncommon and unusual form of cancer that occurs in the ovaries or testes. As the ovaries are the source of eggs, and the testes of sperm, that are used for fertilisation and growth into new humans, the cells (stem cells) in the ovary and testes, when cancerous may develop into many different types of tissue. All types of strange tissue may develop in the tumour, including gland tissue, muscle tissue, skin and even teeth.

In women, symptoms are often minimal until the cancer is quite large, or bleeding occurs into it to cause an abdominal lump or pain. Men feel a hard, tender lump in a testicle.

The tumour is diagnosed by x-ray, CT scan and biopsy of the tumour. Surgical removal of the cancer and surrounding tissue is usually all that is necessary, but rarely, an aggressive cancer may be present, that spreads to other parts of the body. The overall cure rate is close to 90%.
See also OVARIAN CANCER; OVARY;
TESTICLE; TESTICULAR CANCER

TERBINAFINE
See ANTIFUNGALS

TESTES
See TESTICLE

TESTICLE
The testicles, or testes, are the male sex glands and correspond to the ovaries in the female. Like small chicken eggs in size and shape, they develop up near the kidneys while the child is still in the womb. Just before birth they descend through openings in the lower part of the front of the abdomen to their permanent position suspended between the thighs behind the penis in a pouch of skin called the scrotum. Like the ovaries, the testicles have two functions – to produce male sex cells, or sperm, and to manufacture male hormones.

The reason why the testicles are located outside the body is that sperm production requires a slightly lower temperature (by about 3-5 degrees) than that maintained by the rest of the body. The correct temperature is so important that if it is varied even slightly (eg. by the wearing of tight pants), the production

MALE GENITALS

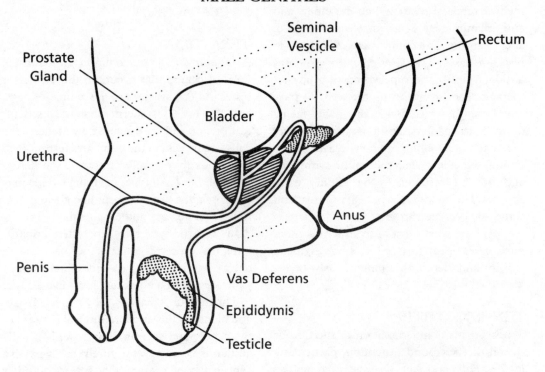

of sperm may temporarily cease. The scrotum provides its own temperature control, contracting to keep the testicles warm in cold weather and relaxing when the temperature rises.

Each testicle is made up of millions of tiny coiled tubes in which sperm (spermatozoa) are continuously manufactured. About 300 million sperm are produced every day. Once manufactured, the sperm mature in a network of tubes called the epididymis, situated at the back of the testicle. After about two to four weeks when they acquire the ability to propel themselves, they are transferred through a duct called the vas deferens, extending upwards into the body from the epididymis, looping beside the bladder until they reach the seminal vesicles, which are two small pouches just behind the prostate gland. Here the sperm are stored until they are either ejaculated or eventually die and are reabsorbed into the body.

The testicles also produce the male hormone, testosterone, which at puberty gives rise to the development of the recognisable male characteristics, such as a deep voice, the growth of facial and bodily hair, and the development of the male genitals.

Unlike women, men's ability to reproduce does not come to a definite end in mid-life. The production of sperm and testosterone starts to decrease as early as twenty years of age, but it merely continues to decline rather than ceasing completely. Even men in their seventies can produce sperm, and a few (about 10%) continue into their eighties.

Occasionally one or both testicles fail to descend fully as they should in a young child, in which case they will not function properly.

It is normal for the testicles to hang unevenly. In most men the left testicle hangs lower than the right, but in some dominantly left handed men the reverse arrangement applies.

See also ANDROPAUSE; CASTRATION; EJACULATION; INGUINAL HERNIA; OVARY; SCROTUM; SEMEN TEST; SEX HORMONES; SPERM; TERATOMA; TESTICLE AND SCROTUM LUMP; TESTICLE AND SCROTUM PAIN; TESTICLE SMALL; TESTICLE UNDESCENDED; TESTICULAR CANCER; TORSION OF THE TESTICLE; VAS DEFERENS

TESTICLE AND SCROTUM LUMP

Men seldom examine their own scrotum for lumps, but when they do, they may become concerned about structures that are quite normal (eg. the epididymis which drains sperm from the testes), but at other times a lump can be due to a serious disease. For this reason, any unexplained scrotal lump must be checked by a doctor.

A bruise in the scrotum after an injury or operation will settle very slowly, and if blood has pooled in the area, it may form a solid clot that persists for months.

A hydrocele is a collection of fluid around the testicle. It is painless, but the testicle may slowly enlarge to two or three times its normal size.

A spermatocele is a cyst full of sperm that develops in the epididymis (sperm collecting ducts on top of and behind the testes) or the vas deferens (tube leading from the testes to the penis), often after a vasectomy. The cyst is usually small, painless, soft and separate from the testicle.

A lump caused by a hernia in the groin (inguinal hernia) may contain gut and extend down into the scrotum to make one side appear far larger than the other.

A varicocele is a knot of varicose veins in the scrotum that can cause a soft, slightly tender blue swelling.

Cancer of the testicle is rare, and usually detected early because of a hard lump, pain or discomfort.
See also TESTICLE; TESTICLE AND SCROTUM PAIN and separate entries for diseases mentioned above.

TESTICLE AND SCROTUM PAIN
Testicular pain can develop suddenly or gradually, but in all cases must be checked by a doctor, particularly in children or young men.

Torsion of the testis is a medical emergency in which the testicle twists around and blocks the blood vessels that supply it. Pain occurs in both the testicle and the groin. Surgery must be performed within twelve hours or the testicle will die.

Epididymo-orchitis is a bacterial or viral infection of the epididymis (sperm collecting ducts on the back and top of the testicle) and the testicle itself. The symptoms include pain, tenderness and fever.

Orchitis is a viral infection of the testicle, usually as a complication of a generalised glandular infection such as mumps, brucellosis (caught from cattle) or glandular fever (infectious mononucleosis). The testicle becomes acutely tender, painful and swollen, and in rare cases may be permanently damaged.

Other causes of testicular pain include a torted hydatid of Morgagni (twisting of a tiny dead end sac on the epididymis), gonorrhoea (a common sexually transmitted disease caused by the bacterium *Neisseria gonorrhoeae*), referred pain from the lower back and cancer of the testicle.
See also TESTICLE; TESTICLE AND SCROTUM LUMP and separate entries for diseases mentioned above.

TESTICLE LARGE
See TESTICLE AND SCROTUM LUMP

TESTICLE SMALL
It is not unusual for there to be a difference in size between the testicles, but this is usually no more than 25%. If one testicle is markedly larger than the other it is possible that one is too small or the other too large. A man can function sexually, and father children, quite successfully with only one testicle.

A small testicle can be a developmental abnormality caused by a poor blood supply to one testicle, or it can be caused by an injury or irradiation (eg. for cancer) to the testicle at a later time.

Serious infections of a testicle (orchitis) may damage the gland and cause it to scar and shrink.

Torsion of the testis is a medical emergency in which the testicle twists around and cuts off the blood vessels that supply it. Pain occurs in both the testicle and the groin. If surgery is not performed within twelve hours, the testicle will die and shrink in size.

Other less common causes of a small testicle include an underactive pituitary gland (controls every other gland in the body),

TESTICLE AND EPIDIDYMIS

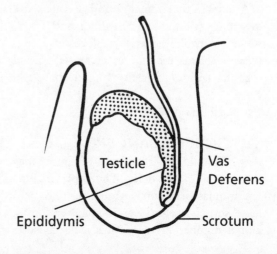

Testicle

Vas Deferens

Epididymis

Scrotum

poorly controlled diabetes (damages small blood vessels that supply the testes), cirrhosis (damage to the liver that causes abnormal levels of hormones), excess thyroxine from the thyroid gland in the neck (hyperthyroidism), Klinefelter syndrome (additional X chromosomes matched with a single Y chromosome) and tuberculosis (TB) infection of a testicle.

As a side effect, some drugs may cause the testicles to become smaller and function poorly. Examples include cell destroying drugs (cytotoxics) used to treat cancer, spironolactone (fluid remover), digoxin (for heart disease), narcotics (for pain), ketaconazole (for fungal infections), alcohol and marijuana. *See also* TESTICLE; TESTICLE AND SCROTUM LUMP and separate entries for diseases mentioned above.

TESTICLE UNDESCENDED

The migration of the testes from where they develop inside the abdomen to the scrotum occurs in 97% of boys by the time they are born, but the process may be delayed in premature babies.

If the testes remain inside the abdomen and do not descend into the scrotum, the scrotum is empty and no testicles can be felt, but in some boys the testes can be found in the groin and manipulated into the scrotum by gentle finger movements. An ultrasound scan is sometimes performed to find the missing testes.

If the testes can be manipulated out of the groin into the scrotum no treatment is usually required, but they must be checked regularly to ensure that they do eventually enter and stay in the scrotum. If the testes do not descend in the first year of life, an operation to place them in the correct position is necessary.

A testicle that remains undescended will eventually fail due to overheating, and if both testes are involved, sterility will result. Long-term problems include an increased risk of inguinal hernias, torsion of the testicle and cancer.
See also TESTICLE

TESTICULAR CANCER

Any of several different types of cancer may develop in the testicles. The types include embryomas, seminomas (most common and least serious), choriocarcinoma, teratomas, and a number of rarer ones. The cause is unknown, but it is a rare form of cancer that develops in one in every 50 000 adult men every year. It is most common in early adult and middle age.

The man finds a firm lump, hardening, unusual tenderness or gradual enlargement of the testicle. There is often no pain, but unusually some patients develop small breasts due to excess production of female oestrogen by the tumour. The cancer may spread to the lymph nodes in the groin, the lungs and liver.

Some types of cancer can be detected by blood tests, but any hard lump in the scrotum must be investigated by ultrasound, and if necessary surgically biopsied, to determine the exact cause. Treatment involves removing the affected testicle and nearby lymph nodes, followed by irradiation or cytotoxic drugs, depending upon the type of cancer present. Overall the cure rate is over 90%.
See also TERATOMA; TESTICLE

TESTICULAR INFECTION
See EPIDIDYMO-ORCHITIS

TESTICULAR TORSION
See TORSION OF THE TESTIS

TESTOSTERONE
See ANDROPAUSE; SEX HORMONES; TESTICLE

TETANUS

Tetanus (lockjaw) is a very serious worldwide disease that attacks muscles. The bacterium *Clostridium tetani*, which lives harmlessly in the gut of many animals, particularly horses, is responsible. When it passes out in faeces it forms a hard microscopic cyst which contaminates soil. It can remain inactive for many years until it enters a cut or wound where it starts multiplying and produces a chemical (toxin) which spreads throughout the body in the blood. Deep wounds, such as treading on a nail, are particularly susceptible to a tetanus infection.

The toxin attacks the small muscles used for chewing making it difficult to open the mouth (thus the common name of lockjaw). Larger and larger muscles are then attacked, irritating them and causing severe spasm. Excruciating pain from widespread muscle spasms may be triggered by the slightest noise. The patient remains conscious, but eventually the muscles which control breathing and the heart are affected.

There is no effective treatment other than muscle relaxants and mechanical ventilation. Although the bacteria may be killed by antibiotics, the toxin remains in the body. A vaccine is available, but it does not give lifelong protection, and revaccination is necessary every ten years, or after five years with a deep wound.

Death occurs in about 50% of patients, even in good hospitals.
See also VACCINES

TETANY

Tetany is a form of muscle spasm that is totally different to a tetanus infection. The small muscles in the hand go into spasm with the wrist bent and fingers and thumb bunched together and pointed towards the wrist. Sometimes muscles in the forearms and feet also go into a firm spasm.

Tetany may be due to low levels of calcium, potassium or magnesium in the blood, but is most commonly caused by rapid over breathing (hyperventilation) after a shock, surprise, injury or vigourous exercise.

Rapid shallow breathing causes the amount of carbon dioxide in the blood to decrease. This makes the blood more alkaline (high pH) than normal, and small muscles in the hand and elsewhere are sensitive to this change in blood chemistry.

Breathing into a paper bag for a few minutes slows the breathing, lowers the level of carbon dioxide in the lungs, and eases the spasm. It is also assisted by giving repeated reassurance to the patient.

Tetany is not serious, and settles spontaneously eventually, but sometimes not until after the patient has collapsed. There is quick recovery with treatment.
See also TETANUS

TETRACYCLINES

Tetracyclines are antibiotics that act by preventing the multiplication of bacteria. Other antibiotics, such as penicillins or sulphas, act by directly killing the bacteria. As a result, tetracyclines are sometimes slower to act than other antibiotics. Prolonged use in children can cause yellow discolouration of teeth and nails, and they can retard the development of the skeleton in a foetus if taken during pregnancy.

They are very effective in the treatment of many infections, particularly in the chest and sinuses, and are frequently used in the long term for the treatment of pimples in teenagers. Interestingly they also inhibit the development of the malaria parasite and so are used as a form of protection against this tropical disease. The most common side effect is vaginal thrush in women. Other side effects may include poor appetite, nausea, sore mouth, diarrhoea and sun sensitivity.

The more recently developed synthetic tetracyclines need be given only once or twice a day, and are far more effective than their antecedents. They are most commonly used as capsules or tablets, but injections are available.

Examples include (with brand names in brackets) doxycycline (Doryx, Vibramycin), minocycline (Minomycin) and tetracycline (Mysteclin).
See also ACNE; ANTIBIOTICS; MALARIA

TETRAHYDRAZOLIN
See VASOCONSTRICTORS

TETRAHYDROCANNABINOL
See MARIJUANA

TETRALOGY OF FALLOT
See FALLOT'S TETRALOGY

TETRAPLEGIA
See QUADRIPLEGIA

TETROCOSACTRIN
See TROPHIC HORMONES

TFT
See THYROID FUNCTION TESTS

THALASSAEMIA BETA MAJOR

Thalassaemia beta major is a familial blood disease (passes from one generation to the next) found in people who live in an area that stretches across Europe and Asia from southern Italy to Malaya, and in some Negro tribes. It occurs in two main forms, minor and major. There are a number of further subdivisions. The major form only occurs if both parents have the minor form.

Patients develop severe anaemia, generalised weakness, increased susceptibility to other diseases, and children grow slowly, develop large livers and spleens, and may become jaundiced (yellow). The heart is put under great strain trying to cope with severe anaemia, and becomes very enlarged. It can be diagnosed by specific blood tests.

Regular blood transfusions for severe anaemia are the only treatment. Death from heart failure, infection or other complications is common in early adult life, but the outcome will depend on the severity of the disease. *See also* ANAEMIA; THALASSAEMIA BETA MINOR

THALASSAEMIA BETA MINOR

Thalassaemia is a familial blood disease that may cause mild anaemia, and occurs in two main forms, minor and major. The minor form is far more common than the major. If someone with thalassaemia beta minor marries a normal person, half their children have the chance of having the minor form of the disease. If two people with thalassaemia beta minor marry, statistically one quarter of their children will have the far more serious and disabling major form of the disease, one half will have the minor form, and the other quarter will have neither.

It is diagnosed by specific blood tests. Those with a family history should have tests to see if they have the minor form. If a person is positive any marriage partner should also have the test.

No treatment is normally necessary. The prognosis is very good and the condition is only an inconvenience. *See also* THALASSAEMIA BETA MAJOR

THC
See MARIJUANA

THEOPHYLLINES

Xanthinates or theophyllines are a rather old fashioned class of drugs available as tablets, mixtures and injections. One form (Nuelin) is available as a sprinkle for adding to food. They are used for patients with asthma and chronic lung diseases, and are often used as additives to beta-2 agonists. Their use is slowly declining as more effective inhaled medications are becoming available. Patients who smoke require higher dosages.

Examples include aminophylline (Brondecon) and theophylline (Austyn, Nuelin, Theo-Dur).

Side effects include nausea, vomiting, rapid heart rate, tremor, belly discomfort, palpitations and a headache. *See also* BETA-2 AGONISTS; BRONCHODILATORS

THIAMINE
See VITAMIN B

THIAZIDE DIURETICS
See DIURETICS

THICK NAIL
See NAIL THICK

THICK SKIN
See SKIN THICK

DIAGRAM SHOWING INHERITANCE OF THALASSAEMIA FROM EITHER ONE OR TWO PARENTS WITH THALASSAEMIA MINOR

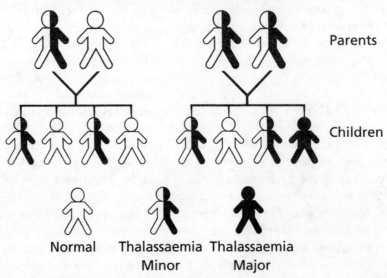

Parents

Children

Normal   Thalassaemia   Thalassaemia
           Minor   Major

THIGH BONE
See FEMUR

THIN SKIN
See SKIN THIN

THIOPENTONE
See ANAESTHETICS

THIORIDAZINE
See ANTIPSYCHOTICS

THIRST
Thirst is controlled by sensors in the brain which detect the fluid balance of the body. Excessive thirst (polydipsia) will obviously be associated with hot weather, exercise and dehydration, but there are also a number of medical conditions that may be responsible for an abnormal thirst.

Diabetes mellitus is caused by a lack of insulin production in the pancreas (type 1 or juvenile diabetes), or is due to the cells of the body becoming resistant to insulin and preventing it from transporting sugar from the blood into the cells (type 2 or maturity onset diabetes). The early symptoms are unusual tiredness, increased thirst and hunger, excess passing of urine, weight loss despite a large food intake, belly pains, itchy rashes, recurrent vaginal thrush infections, pins and needles and blurred vision.

Uraemia occurs when the kidneys fail to function adequately due to a persistent disease, infection, tumour or cyst in the organs. The result is a steady increase in waste products in the blood and body until these cause symptoms due to their adverse effects on other tissues. Symptoms may include tiredness, weakness, itchy skin, excessive thirst, easy bruising, abnormal bleeding, shortness of breath, loss of appetite, vomiting, diarrhoea, impotence, poor libido, irritability, inability to concentrate, leg cramps and restlessness.

Less common causes of excessive thirst include diabetes insipidus (caused by damage to the pituitary gland), acromegaly (excessive growth of the hands, feet, jaw, face, tongue and internal organs), Cushing syndrome (over production of steroids, or taking large doses of cortisone), over active parathyroid glands (hyperparathyroidism), Conn syndrome (tumour of adrenal gland) and some psychiatric conditions (eg. psychoses may cause excessive thirst because patient subconsciously restricts their fluid intake).

See also HUNGER and separate entries for diseases mentioned above.

THORACIC OUTLET OBSTRUCTION SYNDROME
See NAFFZIGER SYNDROME

THORAX
The medical term for the chest is the thorax. This pyramid shaped hollow cavity is protected in front by the sternum (breast bone), at the sides by the ribs and at the back by the thoracic vertebrae. It is separated from the abdomen by the diaphragm (a sheet of muscle). At the top, the apex of the chest is crowded by the pharynx, oesophagus, major blood vessels and the clavicles (collar bones). It contains the heart, two lungs, trachea, oesophagus and the aorta, as well as numerous smaller blood vessels and nerves. The central part of the thorax is known as the mediastinum.

See also ABDOMEN; CHEST PAIN; HEART; LUNGS; MEDIASTINUM

THREADWORM
See PINWORM

THROAT
See GOITRE; LARYNX; NECK PAIN; PHARYNX; THROAT LUMP; THROAT PAIN; VOICE

THROAT INFECTION
See LARYNGITIS; PHARYNGITIS; THROAT PAIN; TONSILLITIS; UVULITIS

THROAT LUMP
People may comment that they have a lump in their throat (pharynx) when they become upset or emotional, and this is caused by a spasm of muscles surrounding the pharynx, but there are numerous medical conditions that may also be responsible.

A bacterial, viral or fungal infection of the pharynx (pharyngitis), vocal cords (laryngitis), epiglottis (cartilage that stops food going into the lungs – epiglottitis) or surrounding lymph nodes (eg. tonsillitis) will cause both throat pain and the sensation that a lump is present. An untreated infection may progress to an abscess of the tonsils (quinsy) or of the throat itself.

Irritation of the pharynx from a swallowed foreign body (eg. bone in food), inhaled gases (eg. smoking) or chemical irritation (eg. inhaling ammonia while cleaning) will cause swelling of the tissues in the throat.

Globus is a relatively common phenomenon, but often goes unrecognised. The patient complains of a distressing intermittent lump in the throat, but on examination by a doctor, nothing can be found. It is caused by subconscious tension and anxiety which causes a spasm and uncomfortable tightness of the throat muscles. It may also extend down into the gullet (oesophagus) to cause swallowing difficulties.

Other causes include glandular fever (infectious mononucleosis), cancer and other tumours of the throat (occur almost exclusively in smokers and workers who have been exposed to toxic gases), angina (restriction of blood supply to the heart), a hiatus hernia (part of the stomach pushes up through the diaphragm into the chest), poorly controlled diabetes, Sjögren syndrome (an autoimmune disease) and severe arthritis of the joints between the vertebrae in the neck may allow one vertebra to shift forward on another (spondylolisthesis).

As an embryo in the early stages of pregnancy, humans have structures on the side of their throat that resemble primitive fish gills. These tiny pockets normally disappear, but in some people remain as pharyngeal pouches or cysts around the thyroid gland (thyroglossal cysts). They may slowly enlarge and be felt as a lump in the throat.
See also PHARYNX; THROAT PAIN; TONSIL and separate entries for diseases mentioned above.

THROAT PAIN
A bacterial, viral or fungal infection of the pharynx (pharyngitis), tonsils, vocal cords (laryngitis), epiglottis (cartilage that stops food going into the lungs – epiglottitis) or surrounding lymph nodes (eg. mumps) will cause throat pain and sometimes the sensation that a lump is present. An untreated bacterial infection may progress to an abscess of the tonsils (quinsy) or the throat itself.

Glandular fever (infectious mononucleosis) is very common in teenagers and in the early twenties. Patients usually have a sore throat, raised temperature, croupy cough, large glands in the neck and other parts of the body, extreme lethargy, and generally feel absolutely lousy for about four weeks.

Irritation of the pharynx from a swallowed foreign body (eg. bone in food), inhaled gases (eg. smoking) or chemical irritation (eg. inhaling ammonia while cleaning) may cause throat pain.

Less common causes include reflux oesophagitis (bringing up stomach acid into the throat), cancer and other tumours of the throat (occur almost exclusively in smokers, and workers who have been exposed to toxic gases), angina (pain referred from the heart) and severe arthritis of the joints between the vertebrae in the neck may pinch the nerves supplying the throat to cause both neck pain and referred pain to the throat.
See also MOUTH PAIN; NECK PAIN; PHARYNX; THROAT LUMP and separate entries for diseases mentioned above.

THROMBOANGIITIS OBLITERANS
See BUERGER'S DISEASE

THROMBOCYTOPENIA
Thrombocytopenia (idiopathic thrombocytopenic purpura) is a complex, uncommon condition due to a lack of platelets (also known as thrombocytes), the blood cells that are responsible for controlling the rate at which blood clots. In children the condition often follows a viral illness and settles quickly, but in adults it is usually an autoimmune condition (body rejects its own cells) in which platelets are inappropriately destroyed by the spleen for no apparent reason. It can also occur as a result of adverse drug reactions, infections and other rare disorders.

Patients are unable to clot their blood as quickly as normal, so they bleed excessively. They develop purpura (red dots under the skin caused by microscopic bleeding) across a wide area, bleed internally to cause black motions, have nosebleeds that are difficult to stop, may vomit and cough blood, bruise very easily, bleed around their teeth after eating and may bleed very heavily during a menstrual period. Bleeding into the brain may cause a stroke, or very rarely, death. The diagnosis is confirmed by a simple blood test.

In some children, rest and time are the only necessary treatments. In all adults and most children, high doses of prednisone (a steroid) are given to settle the condition and allow more platelets to be made in the bone marrow. Immunoglobulin injections may also be used. As the spleen is the organ destroying the platelets, surgical removal of this can cure the disease in resistant cases. Other exotic medications may be used in severe cases.

The disease may last for a long time in adults, but the vast majority of patients respond well to treatment, although there are significant dangers before the patient presents to a doctor and in the first few days of treatment. It may occasionally recur in adults, but rarely in children.
See also AUTOIMMUNE DISEASES; BLEEDING, EXCESSIVE; FULL BLOOD COUNT; PLATELETS; SKIN RED DOTS

THROMBOPHLEBITIS

Thrombophlebitis is a combination of thrombosis and phlebitis in a vein. Thrombosis is a clot in a vein and phlebitis is inflammation of the involved blood vessel, and the condition often occurs in a vein which has had a drip inserted into it. A long, rope-like, painful, hard, red lump can be felt under the skin along the course of an artery or vein. Rarely, a clot may spread and damage blood supply to or from major organs.

Anti-inflammatory medication is given for the phlebitis and sometimes anticoagulant treatment for the thrombosis. It settles with treatment, but the rope-like lump may remain long term.
See also PHLEBITIS; THROMBOSIS

THROMBOSIS

Thrombosis is the process that allows a thrombus (blood clot) to develop inside a vein or artery, partially or completely blocking it. Blood vessels in any part of the body may be involved. The cause may be an injury, prolonged immobility, hardening of the arteries from cholesterol deposits (atherosclerosis), smoking, cancer, major surgery and a number of rarer conditions.

Patients develop pain at the site of the thrombus, and other symptoms depending on blood vessel affected. If a thrombus occurs in an artery supplying the heart muscle a heart attack occurs, in the brain a stroke, and in the lung a pulmonary embolism. Blood tests can demonstrate the presence of a thrombus somewhere in the body, but not its location. Sophisticated x-rays, ultrasound and CT scans are used to find the blood clot.

Treatment depends on the site and severity of the blood clot, but generally anticoagulant medication (eg. warfarin, heparin) is given to prevent both the spread of the thrombus and the formation of new clots.
See also ATHEROSCLEROSIS; BLOOD CLOTTING TEST; COAGULATION; DEEP VENOUS THROMBOSIS; MESENTERIC ARTERY THROMBOSIS; PULMONARY EMBOLISM; SEPTIC SHOCK; STROKE; SUPERFICIAL VENOUS THROMBOSIS; THROMBOPHLEBITIS

THRUSH

Thrush (candidiasis or moniliasis) is a fungal infection that occurs most commonly in the mouth and the vagina, caused by the fungus *Candida albicans*.

The oral form is quite common in infancy, particularly in bottle-fed babies, and may be triggered by a course of antibiotics that destroy the bacteria in the mouth that normally control the growth of excess fungi. Babies develop grey/white patches on the tongue, gums and inside of the cheeks that cannot be rubbed away with a finger tip or cotton bud. The infection may spread through the intestine and emerge to infect the skin around the anus, where it causes a bright red rash that is slightly paler towards the centre. Antifungal drops or gels in the mouth, and antifungal creams around the anus rapidly settle the problem.

The vaginal form is very common in sexually active women. *Candida albicans* lives in the gut where it causes little or no trouble. When it comes out on to the skin around the anus, it usually dies off; but if that skin is warm, moist and irritated, it can grow and spread forward to the lips of the vagina (the vulva). A warm climate and the aggravating factors of tight jeans, pantyhose, the contraceptive pill, nylon bathers, antibiotics and sex give the area between a woman's legs the right degree of warmth, moisture and irritation to make the spread of the fungus relatively easy. Antibiotics aggravate the problem as they can kill off the bacteria that normally keep fungi under control. Entry of the fungus into the vagina is aided by the mechanical action of sex and the alteration in the acidity of the vagina caused by the contraceptive pill.

An unpleasant white vaginal discharge develops, along with intense itching of the vulva and surrounding skin, and often inflammation of the urine opening so that passing urine causes discomfort. Swabs may be taken from the vagina to confirm the identity of the responsible fungus.

Antifungal vaginal pessaries (tablets), vaginal creams or antifungal tablets taken by mouth are the available treatments. The sex partner must also be treated as he can give the infection back to the woman after she has been successfully treated. It is prevented by wearing loose cotton panties, drying the genital area carefully after swimming or showering, avoiding tight clothing, wiping from front to back after going to the toilet and not using tampons when an infection is likely. Many women have repeated attacks, which may be due to inadequate treatment, contamination from the gut, or reinfection from their sex partner.
See also FUNGI; STOMATITIS; VAGINAL DISCHARGE

THUMB SUCKING

In a young baby, sucking is a very strong reflex, and most babies suck their thumbs or fingers at some stage. Most will stop on their own after a few months, or perhaps after they begin toddling around and have more interesting activities to occupy them. Some parents feel they should stop a baby sucking, but this is likely to do more harm than good as the baby's sucking reflex remains unsatisfied. If necessary, a dummy may be substituted for the thumb.

If a toddler of two or three is still sucking its thumb, a parent may wish to remove the thumb gently and distract the child with another activity, but to get cross or force the issue will frustrate and upset the child and usually be unsuccessful.
See also DUMMIES

THYMIC HYPOPLASIA
See di GEORGE SYNDROME

THYMOL
See COUGH MEDICINES

THYMUS

The thymus in the adult is a small irregular strip of glandular tissue that lies behind the upper part of the breast bone (sternum) and extends up into the front of the neck. In a child it is proportionally much larger and more important. It reaches its maximum size of about thirty grams at puberty.

The thymus plays a major role in the development and maintenance of the immune system. It produces specific types of white cells (B and T cells) that are vital in allowing the body to become immune to infection. It also secretes a hormone that maintains the competence of the cells it produces.

If the thymus fails to develop or is removed, the patient will be unable to fight off infection or cancer effectively. Excess activity of the gland can cause the disease myasthenia gravis. *See also* di GEORGE SYNDROME; LYMPHATIC SYSTEM; MYASTHENIA GRAVIS

THYROID CANCER

There are several different types of cancer of the thyroid gland, which sits in the front of the neck between the Adam's apple (larynx) and the top of the breast bone, and produces hormones that control the metabolic rate of the body. Cancers are more common in elderly women, although the cause in unknown. Cancer may also spread from other organs to the thyroid.

The cancer is usually felt as a painless lump in the gland that steadily enlarges. It does not normally interfere with the workings of the gland until it is very advanced, and there are no other symptoms in the early stages. An advanced cancer may spread to surrounding lymph nodes, bone, liver and other organs. Any hard lump in the thyroid gland is considered to be a cancer until proved otherwise.

The proof usually involves scanning the thyroid gland with radioactive iodine, an ultrasound scan, taking a biopsy of the lump, or removing the lump surgically. It cannot be detected by a blood test.

Surgery to remove the gland is the main treatment. Irradiation and cytotoxic drugs may be added in some cases.

Several different types of cancer occur in the thyroid, and outcome will depend upon the type present. Anaplastic carcinoma of the thyroid has the worst prognosis and usually proceeds rapidly to death, while papillary tumours are rarely fatal.

See also THYROID GLAND

THYROID FUNCTION TESTS

The thyroid gland in the front of the neck controls the rate at which every cell in the body functions by secreting a hormone (thyroxine) which circulates in the blood stream. The pituitary gland in the centre of the head secretes a hormone (thyroid stimulating hormone – TSH) which in turn controls the rate at which the thyroid gland produces thyroxine. The levels of thyroxine and TSH in the blood can be measured to check the function of both the thyroid and pituitary glands. If the level of TSH is high, the thyroid gland is underactive and not producing sufficient thyroxine, a common problem, particularly in middle-aged women.

See also BLOOD TESTS; THYROID GLAND

THYROID GLAND

The thyroid gland controls the rate with which the whole body functions, the rate at which it converts food into energy (metabolism), and the rate of development in adolescence. It is situated at the front of the throat just below the Adam's apple. The gland consists of two wings, rather like a butterfly, one on each side of the windpipe.

To carry out its functions, the thyroid produces the hormone thyroxine. Thyroxine contains iodine, so a certain amount of iodine must be included in the diet to ensure the proper functioning of the thyroid. The amount of iodine required is only small and most normal diets contain enough, especially if iodised salt is used.

If the production of hormones is too much or too little, the metabolic rate will be either too fast or too slow. If it is too slow the person will feel tired, and if it is too fast they may feel nervous and jumpy. If the variation is too far removed from normal, serious disorders may result.

If too much hormone is produced, the patient will become hyperactive and be unable to sleep, have palpitations and hand tremors, sweating and sometimes severe emotional disturbance. Various drug treatments are available, or more usually the gland is destroyed altogether, and substitute hormones are provided in the form of medication. This is a common condition in young and middle-aged women. The reverse occurs if too little thyroxine is produced. Everything will slow down and the patient will become tired, cold and constipated.

Goitre is an enlarged thyroid gland. It may be due to an overactive gland, or to a lack of iodine in the diet.

Some children are born without an adequate thyroid gland, in which case they will be subnormal physically and mentally in the condition known as cretinism. This is routinely tested for, shortly after birth, usually before the newborn leaves the hospital. The condition may then be treated, and the children grow up

LOCATION OF THYROID GLAND AT FRONT OF NECK

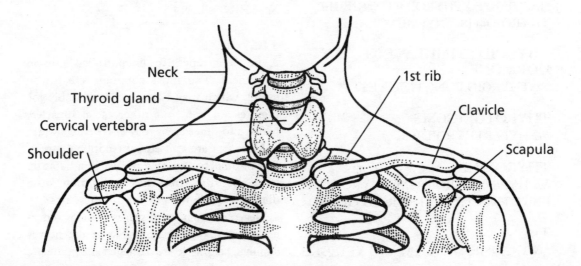

Neck — Thyroid gland — Cervical vertebra — Shoulder — 1st rib — Clavicle — Scapula

normally and unaffected by cretinism. It is one of the most important screening tests of the newborn, as the consequences of not detecting and treating this condition are very serious.

The most common disease of the thyroid gland is underactivity due to loss of thyroid tissue with ageing. Many elderly people suffer from this condition and take tablets to keep them functioning normally.

Cancer may also occur in the gland and is usually characterised by a painless swelling in one part of the gland. Treatment is usually very effective and may involve a combination of surgery, radiotherapy and drugs.

Embedded within the thyroid gland are the parathyroid glands, which help regulate the level of calcium in the blood. The activity of the thyroid gland itself is regulated by the pituitary gland at the base of the brain.
See also ANTITHYROID DRUGS; CRETINISM; GOITRE; HYPERTHYROIDISM; HYPOTHYROIDISM; PARATHYROID GLAND; PITUITARY GLAND; THYROID CANCER; THYROID FUNCTION TESTS; THYROIDITIS

THYROID GLAND ENLARGED
See GOITRE

THYROIDITIS
Thyroiditis is an inflammation or infection of the thyroid gland, which lies in the front of the neck. The most common type is Hashimoto thyroiditis, while others include de Quervain thyroiditis and Riedel thyroiditis. Suppurative thyroiditis is a rare disorder caused by a bacterial infection of the gland.
See also de QUERVAIN THYROIDITIS; HASHIMOTO THYROIDITIS; RIEDEL THYROIDITIS; THYROID GLAND

THYROID STIMULATING HORMONE
See THYROID FUNCTION TESTS

THYROTOXICOSIS
See HYPERTHYROIDISM

THYROXINE
See HYPERTHYROIDISM; THYROID FUNCTION TESTS; THYROID GLAND

TIA
See TRANSIENT ISCHAEMIC ATTACK

TIAPROFENIC ACID
See NONSTEROIDAL ANTI-INFLAMMATORY DRUGS

TIBIA
The tibia is the larger of the two bones in the lower leg (the fibula is the other one). The top end is shaped like a plateau to bear the weight of the femur (thigh bone) and forms the lower part of the knee joint. At its lower end it forms part of the ankle joint. The lump of bone on the inside of the ankle is the lower end of the tibia. It acts as the main weight-bearing part of the lower leg.
See also JOINT; FIBULA; KNEE; PATELLA; SHIN SPLINTS

LOWER LEG

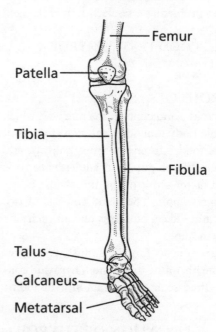

TIBIAL STRESS SYNDROME
See SHIN SPLINTS

TIC
A tic is a repetitive uncontrolled muscle movement. The most common site is the eyelid, which may twitch uncontrollably for minutes on end, but other facial muscles, hands and other areas may also be involved.

Most tics are caused by emotional stress, fear or anxiety, but may persist as a habit tic long after the stress has gone. Low dose diazepam (Valium) will control these tics.

Degenerative nerve diseases of many different types may be responsible as the nerves supplying a muscle are damaged and stimulate the muscle inappropriately. The nerve bundles around the spine are particularly liable to damage, resulting in a tic.

Some psychiatric conditions may cause repetitive muscle movements that may be thought of as a tic, while others may have a habit tic from performing an unnecessary task many times over.

Huntington's chorea is a devastating inherited condition that does not make its presence felt until the patient is forty or fifty years old. These patients suffer progressive loss of limb control, muscle spasms and mental deterioration.
See also CONVULSION; JERKING; MUSCLE; MUSCLE CRAMP and separate entries for diseases mentioned above.

TIC DOLOUREUX
See TRIGEMINAL NEURALGIA

TICKS
Ticks are from the same family as spiders (arachnids) but are modified so much that they look nothing like their distant cousins. They have a large black body from which mouthparts protrude and grasp the skin. The tick does not have a head as such. A tube-like mouthpart pierces the victim's skin to suck up blood. When the tick is full of blood, it drops off and waits for its next victim, which may be almost any warm-blooded animal, although some species preferentially attack certain animals. A full feed of blood may last the tick for a year or more.

Ticks are most active in the spring and summer. Bush ticks, which are the only dangerous form of tick, live on the eastern coastal strip of Australia. The most common victims of ticks are children playing in the bush, and golfers, since ticks shelter in foliage and drop on a victim and burrow in as they engorge themselves on blood. Ticks are usually found on the head, burrowing in amongst the hair, or in body crevices.

Ticks generally cause painful irritation and a raised lump on the skin. Uncommonly they may lead to paralysis if left untreated, especially in children.

Symptoms of tick bite are irritation and pins and needles at the site of the bite, nausea, double vision, unsteadiness, and eventually weakness and difficulty in moving first the lower limbs, then the upper limbs, and finally the face and breathing apparatus.

Do NOT attempt to pull the tick off or cut it out or squeeze it – this forces more venom into the system.

To remove a tick, wash it and the surrounding skin with an alcohol solution, such as methylated spirits. Place a pair of tweezers flat on the skin so that the jaws are on either side of the tick. Grasp the tick firmly, as close to the skin as possible, twist through ninety degrees, and then lift off. The tick will come away easily with minimal pain. Some tiny black marks, the mouthparts, may be left behind, but these rarely cause any trouble. Place some antiseptic cream or lotion on the bite and leave it alone to heal over the next couple of days. If the area becomes red and angry, it may have become infected, and a doctor should be consulted.
See also LYME DISEASE

TID
The prescription notation 'tid' is derived from the Latin 'ter in die' which means "three times a day".
See also PRESCRIPTION NOTATIONS

TIETZE SYNDROME
Tietze syndrome (anterior chest wall syndrome; costochondral syndrome; costochondritis) is a harmless, relatively common chest wall condition which tends to mimic the pain of a heart attack. Patients are usually middle aged, and there is normally only one attack, and the cause is unknown.

RIB CAGE AND COSTAL CARTILAGES

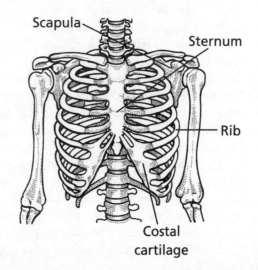

Scapula

Sternum

Rib

Costal cartilage

The ribs sweep around the chest from the vertebrae in the back towards the breast bone (sternum) but stop a few centimetres short. The ribs are joined to the sternum by a strip of cartilage (costal cartilage). Inflammation occurs at the point where the cartilage joins onto the rib (costochondral junction). The second rib is most commonly involved, but any rib, and any number of ribs may be affected.

Patients develop painful, tender swellings of one or more costal cartilages, just under the skin on the front of the chest at the side of the sternum. Anti-inflammatory drugs, steroid injections and painkillers may be used in treatment.

The syndrome settles spontaneously in two weeks to six months.
See also RIB; STERNUM; XIPHOIDALGIA

TIGABINE
See ANTICONVULSANTS

TINEA
Tinea is a term used to describe any fungal infection of the skin, hair or nails. Ringworm is a lay term that may be used for a fungal infection involving skin only.
See also ATHLETE'S FOOT; FUNGI; ONYCHOGRYPHOSIS; PITYRIASIS VERSICOLOR; TINEA CAPITIS; TINEA CORPORIS; TINEA CRURIS; TINEA MANUM

TINEA CAPITIS
Tinea capitis is a fungal infection of the skin on the scalp that usually occurs in children. The fungi usually come from the *Trichophyton*, *Microsporum* and *Epidermophyton* families. It is caught by close contact with another infected human or animal (eg. cat, dog).

The child develops an irregular, relatively bald patch on the scalp covered in a fine scale and broken hair stubble (the fungus invades the hairs and causes them to become fragile and break). A severely affected patch may develop a thick build-up of scale and form a fungal abscess (kerion).

The diagnosis can be proved by taking a skin scraping or hair sample and examining it under a microscope for fungal spores. Ultraviolet light (Wood's light) in an otherwise dark room, will cause a bright green fluorescence of hair and skin affected by a fungus.

Antifungal ointments, lotions, tinctures and shampoos are all very effective treatments.
See also DANDRUFF; FUNGI; KERION; TINEA

TINEA CORPORIS
Tinea corporis (ringworm) is an infection of the skin that is caused by a fungus, not a worm. The fungi usually come from the *Trichophyton*, *Microsporum* and *Epidermophyton* families, and are caught by close contact with another infected human or animal (eg. cat, dog). The fungi prefer areas of the body where there is heat (under clothing, in shoes), friction (from tight clothes or skin folds rubbing together) and moisture (from sweat), and infection is more common in the tropics. It affects both sexes and all ages equally.

The fungus settles in one spot on the skin, where a red dot may be seen. This slowly enlarges as the fungus spreads, and after a few days the centre of the red patch becomes pale again and similar to normal skin, because the infection is no longer active at this point. The infection continues to spread and forms an enlarging red ring on the skin. Multiple ring-shaped spots with a pale centre are seen on the chest, abdomen and back. It usually does not cause an itch or discomfort. The diagnosis is proved by taking a skin scraping and examining it under a microscope for fungal spores.

Antifungal creams, ointments, lotions and tinctures are usually effective. Antifungal tablets are available for more serious infections, but sometimes they are very slow to work, and may need to be taken for up to six months. Without treatment, the ringworm may persist for many months.

The prognosis is very good with proper treatment, but the infection tends to recur if treatment is ceased prematurely.
See also FUNGI; TINEA; TINEA MANUM

TINEA CRURIS
Tinea cruris ('crotch rot') is a fungal infection of the skin in the groin. The fungi usually come from the *Trichophyton*, *Microsporum* and *Epidermophyton* families and are caught by close contact (eg. sexual) with an infected person, or in babies may be due to wet nappies or sweaty skin. Infection is more common in men than women, has a peak incidence in the twenties and thirties and tends to occur more in summer and with exercise.

A red, scaly rash spreads out from the skin folds in the groin to cover the inside of the thighs, the lower abdomen and the buttocks. It is often itchy and feels constantly uncomfortable. A secondary bacterial infection of damaged skin is possible. The diagnosis is proved by taking a skin scraping and examining it under a microscope for fungal spores.

Antifungal creams, ointments, lotions and tinctures are usually effective. Antifungal tablets are available for more serious infections, but sometimes they are very slow to work, and may need to be taken for up to six months.

The prognosis is good with proper treatment, but recurrences are common.
See also FUNGI; TINEA; TINEA CORPORIS

TINEA MANUM
Tinea manum is a fungal infection of the palm of the hand. The fungi usually come from the *Trichophyton*, *Microsporum* and *Epidermophyton* families, and are caught by close contact with another infected human or animal (eg. cat, dog). This form of tinea is uncommon in children.

Patients develop a fine scale with a faint red edge that affects the palms and palm side of the fingers. The diagnosis proved by taking a skin scraping and examining it under a microscope for fungal spores.

Treatment involves antifungal tablets taken for a month or more, rather than cream, because the thick skin of the palm makes it difficult for creams to penetrate. Results are good with proper treatment.
See also ATHLETE'S FOOT; FUNGI; TINEA; TINEA CRURIS

TINEA UNGUIUM
See ONYCHOGRYPHOSIS

TINEA PEDIS
See ATHLETE'S FOOT

TINEA VERSICOLOR
See PITYRIASIS VERSICOLOR

TINIDAZOLE
See ANTIANAEROBES

TINNITUS
A persistent, high pitched ringing noise in an ear, when there is no sound actually present, is called tinnitus. It is a very annoying symptom, as the noise may continue day and night without relief, and drown out quieter noises that the person is trying to hear.

Ménière's disease may occur after a head injury or ear infection, but in most patients it has no apparent cause. It is more common in men, and with advancing age. The cause is a build-up in the pressure of the fluid inside the hearing and balance mechanisms of the inner ear. The increase in pressure causes tinnitus as well as dizziness, nausea and slowly progressive permanent deafness. Avoiding prolonged episodes of loud noise (eg, jet engines, rock bands) helps to reduce the incidence of the condition.

Damage to the blood supply of the inner ear from a head injury, aneurysm (swelling of an artery) or hardening of the arteries (arteriosclerosis) will affect the sensitive hair cells in the inner ear that detect sound, and cause them to trigger off inappropriate nerve signals that are interpreted by the brain as a high pitched noise.

The tiny semicircular canals of the inner ear that control balance are known as the labyrinth. If this structure becomes inflamed or infected (labyrinthitis) the patient will become dizzy, abnormal eye movements will occur and noises may be heard in the ear.

Other causes include degeneration of the hearing mechanism (cochlear in the inner ear) with advancing age, middle ear infections (otitis media), a direct injury to the ear, a sudden change in pressure on the ear (with decompression of an aircraft or surfacing too quickly from a scuba dive), acoustic neuroma (tumour of hearing nerve), endolymphatic hydrops (increased pressure in the inner ear) and otosclerosis (a form of arthritis in the bones of the middle ear).

Rare causes include persistent high blood pressure, some neuroses (eg. schizophrenia), altitude sickness (ascending rapidly to heights over 3000m), Costen syndrome (abnormal stresses are placed on the jaw joint and muscles of chewing) and Cogan syndrome.

Excess caffeine from coffee, cola drinks or medications (eg. stimulants) can cause tinnitus as a side effect, as may excess aspirin and some malaria medications (eg. quinine).
See also DEAF; EAR and separate entries for diseases mentioned above.

TIRED
See FATIGUE; SLEEP EXCESS

TOCOPHEROLS
See VITAMIN E

TOENAIL
See NAIL; NAIL ABNORMAL; NAIL PAIN

TOGAVIRUS
See GERMAN MEASLES

TOILET TRAINING
Babies have no control over their bladder or bowels. They simply eliminate their waste material as the organs become full. Around the age of two, the ability to exercise control develops, and gradually, in a combination of both physical development and learning, a child acquires the ability to urinate and defecate only when appropriate. Obviously there is no point in trying to toilet-train a child who is not physically ready to control its bladder or bowels. To try is the equivalent of trying to teach a six-month-old baby to talk and will simply lead to frustration on both sides.

Parents often feel a child should be clean by the age of two, and dry at night by the age of two and a half. In fact, only about half of all children achieve these goals and many are at least a year later. Complete control is rarely reached before three in any child.

Toilet training usually starts around fifteen to eighteen months by placing the child on a potty after meals. This is the time they are most likely to want to void, and gradually, with much praise if the potty is used, the child will learn that this is what is required. A young child, of course, has no way of knowing what is expected and patience is needed. A child with an older brother or sister who sits on a potty will usually latch on more quickly than a child without such a model to imitate.

Most toddlers react vigorously against being forced into things, and a parent who is aggressively insistent about toilet training is likely to find the attitude counterproductive. Toilet training can only succeed with the voluntary cooperation of the child, and if you make the process a battleground, you are the one likely to lose out.

It is much easier for a child to learn to be clean than dry. Most children only move their bowels once or twice a day, usually at regular intervals. You are likely to be able to recognise the signs of an approaching motion and provide a potty or take them to the toilet to collect it. Generally, after a few weeks, especially if you make it clear you regard it as desirable and grown-up behaviour, your child is likely to have become proud of its new skill and will seek out the potty or toilet when it is needed.

Urinating is more haphazard. Children urinate many times in a day and, since it is a less major event, they may not even notice it if they are absorbed in play. The urge to urinate is also not enough to wake them in the early days of developing control, so they remain urinating in their nappy while they are asleep. If a child wakes dry, make the potty available or take them to the toilet and be liberal with praise if it is used.

Gradually the child will learn that when the urge to urinate is felt they should head for the potty or toilet. It is worth remembering that children want to learn and want to acquire new skills – also that all children do eventually stop wetting themselves, even those who seem impossibly slow. As a rule, the only children who are referred to a doctor because of failure to learn bladder control are those who have been subjected to excessive training. Bed-wetting that persists in an older child is a rather different problem, for which various types of treatment are available.
See also BABIES; BED WETTING; CHILDHOOD

TOLBUTAMIDE
See HYPOGLYCAEMICS

TONE INCREASED
See MUSCLE TONE INCREASED

TONGUE
The tongue is effectively a powerful network of muscles covered with a tough, rough, moist membrane that contains taste buds at its back and sides.

It is used to move food under the teeth where it can be broken up, and then roll the food into a ball (bolus) before propelling it down the pharynx (throat) and into the oesophagus (gullet).
See also MOUTH; PHARYNX; TASTE;

TEETH; TONGUE ABNORMAL;
TONGUE DISCOLOURED; TONGUE
PAIN

TONGUE ABNORMAL
A small number of rare syndromes may cause tongue abnormalities.

Down syndrome (mongolism) is one of the commonest causes of mental retardation, and is due to the presence of three copies of chromosome 21 instead of two. Other features are flattened facial features, short stature, low set ears, thick protruding tongue, broad hands with only a single transverse crease and slanted eyes. It occurs more commonly in the children of older mothers.

Beckwith syndrome is often inherited and causes prominent eyes, a large tongue, enlarged organs in the abdomen and low blood sugar levels.

A tumour, cancer, stroke or abscess affecting the lower part of the brain may affect the nerves supplying the tongue, throat and neck so that these muscles function abnormally (Sicard syndrome).
See also TONGUE; TONGUE DISCOLOURED; TONGUE PAIN and separate entries for diseases mentioned above.

TONGUE DISCOLOURED
A healthy tongue is a dark pink colour, but discolourations may indicate significant disease.

Strongly coloured foods and drinks can temporarily give the same colour to the tongue.

Patchy discolouration of the tongue is known as geographic tongue. The most common pattern is smooth red patches with a greyish margin. It is a relatively common, harmless condition for which there is no specific cause, but rarely may be due to tuberculosis or allergy reactions on the tongue.
BROWN TONGUE
A brown tongue may be caused by smoking, and poor dental hygiene (allows persistent low-grade infections in the mouth).
WHITE TONGUE
A white discolouration may be due to milk curds (may persist in the mouth of a baby for some time after a feed), thrush (infection of the mouth caused by the fungus *Candida albicans*), leucoplakia (inflammation after a tongue injury), lichen planus (white patches), and scars on the tongue after a serious burn, which may remain white for some weeks or months.
BLACK TONGUE
The tongue may become black or dark grey due to overgrowth of normal bacteria in the mouth (particularly after using antibiotics such as penicillin), some drugs used for the treatment of severe arthritis (eg. gold), mercury dental amalgam may harmlessly tattoo the tongue with black spots if carelessly used by a dentist and rarely, a black melanoma cancer may grow on the tongue to give a very obvious black patch.
RED TONGUE
A red tongue may be due to pernicious anaemia (an inability of the stomach to absorb vitamin B12 from food), scarlet fever (streptococcal bacterial infection that attacks the throat, tonsils and tongue to give a scarlet red appearance), and pellagra (lack of niacin – vitamin B3 – in the diet).
BLUE TONGUE
Cyanosis is caused by inadequate oxygen being taken up from the lungs by the blood and it results in blue lips and tongue. There are many serious lung, blood and heart diseases that can cause this, and patients with a blue tongue or lips should always be checked by a doctor.
See also TONGUE; TONGUE ABNORMAL and separate entries for diseases mentioned above.

TONGUE PAIN
Painful ulcers may form on the tongue because of bacterial or viral infections, or injury to the tongue (eg. from broken tooth, biting tongue).

Thrush is an infection of the mouth caused by the fungus *Candida albicans*, and virtually every baby will have several episodes. The fungus lives normally in the gut, but may spread from the skin around the anus to the mouth when the baby scratches and plays. The result is white patches that irritate the surface of the tongue and lining of the mouth.

Other causes include pernicious anaemia (an inability of the stomach to absorb vitamin B12 from food), iron and folic acid deficiencies and very rarely cancer of the tongue.
See also MOUTH PAIN; TONGUE; TONGUE DISCOLOURED and separate entries for diseases mentioned above.

TONOMETRY

Glaucoma is a serious eye disease that can lead to blindness. There are various types, but the most common one, chronic glaucoma, typically develops in older people and is basically a buildup of pressure in the eyeball, which arises if a blockage prevents normal drainage of fluid from the eye. If the pressure gets too high for too long, the sight may be permanently damaged. Because chronic glaucoma develops very gradually and in its initial stages causes no pain, it is possible to have it and not know until it is too late. Everyone over forty should have their eyes regularly checked, especially if they have a family history of the disease. Glaucoma can be controlled successfully if it is discovered early enough.

Whether a person visits an ophthalmologist (an eye specialist) or an optometrist (a person trained to test for glasses), they will usually be tested for glaucoma as a matter of routine with an instrument called a tonometer. This is a relatively simple instrument consisting of a gauge with a pointer. A few drops of anaesthetic will be put into the eye and the lid held open while the doctor places the tonometer on the eyeball. The handle of the tonometer will be lowered until it hovers at a point on the dial, indicating the tension of your eyeball. If the reading is greater than a certain amount, disease may be indicated. Most ophthalmologists and optometrists now use more accurate and sensitive computerised machines that do not require an anaesthetic drop and measure the pressure in the eye by blowing a very brief puff of air onto the eye.

See also EYE; GLAUCOMA

TONSIL

The tonsils are located at either side of the pharynx at the back of the mouth. They are made of a large number of infection-fighting white cells, and are the main protector from infection of the throat and airways. In children they are almost invariably enlarged as children are building up their immunity to many bacteria and viruses while they develop one respiratory or throat and nose infection after another.

Infections of the tonsils themselves are relatively common, but most viral infections settle with time, and bacterial infections (tonsillitis) can be settled by appropriate antibiotics. If the tonsils become repeatedly infected they may be surgically removed.

See also MOUTH; PHARYNX; QUINSY; TONSILLECTOMY; TONSILLITIS

TONSILLECTOMY

The tonsils are lymph nodes, similar to those in the neck, armpit or groin, which lie in the throat on either side of the back of the tongue. They are made of lymphoid tissue which is responsible for producing antibodies to fight off infection. The tonsils are only 1% of the total body lymphoid tissue, so they are not essential from this point of view.

Tonsillectomy (often accompanied by the removal of other lymphoid tissue at the back of the nose – the adenoids) is a very old operation, the first ones being performed in Egypt around 3000 BC. It was a much more common operation in the pre-antibiotic era before the second world war, as tonsillitis without antibiotics was a severe disabling disease that could be life-threatening. Today the operation is still necessary under certain circumstances. These include: –
• five attacks of tonsillitis in a year in a child, or three a year in an adult
• an attack of quinsy (the formation of an abscess under the tonsil)
• obstruction of the airway or food passage by grossly enlarged tonsils
• tonsillitis complicated by middle ear infections on two occasions
• other rarer complications of tonsillitis

Age is no barrier to tonsillectomy, provided the reasons for the operation are present, but it is unusual to perform it on babies under twelve months of age and on the elderly.

Tonsillectomy is normally done under a general anaesthetic by an ENT (ear, nose and throat) surgeon. Adults stay in hospital for two to four days, children just overnight. Adults can return to work after two weeks, children can return to school after ten days. The degree of discomfort is about the same as an attack of tonsillitis, but without the accompanying fever and muscular aches. The operation is normally postponed until antibiotics control any acute infection.

Complications are uncommon, the most common being bleeding from the operation site in the throat. This may be treated by local measures, or occasionally by a minor repeat operation. Bleeding may occur immediately after the procedure or a week to ten days later, and medical advice should be sought if it occurs.

Tonsillectomy is only performed to improve the quality of life in patients who suffer from repeated attacks of infection or constant discomfort from a blocked throat or ears. The Eustachian tube that drains fluid from, and allows air to enter into the middle ear, opens into the back of the throat between the tonsils and adenoid glands. By removing the large amount of obstructing tissue, tonsillectomy and adenoidectomy can also help chronic ear diseases.
See also EUSTACHIAN TUBE; LYMPHATIC SYSTEM; PHARYNX; TONSIL; TONSILLITIS

TONSILLITIS

Tonsillitis is infection of the tonsils, which are modified lymph nodes that sit on either side of the throat at the back of the mouth. They intercept and destroy bacteria and viruses that enter the body, but if a tonsil is overwhelmed by these organisms, tonsillitis occurs. Infection may occur at any age, but is far more common amongst children. The cause may be bacteria (eg. *Streptococci, Staphylococci, Haemophilus*) or viruses (eg. glandular fever) that enter through the mouth or nose.

The tonsil(s) becomes enlarged, red and covered in pus, and the patient develops a sudden high fever, headache, throat pain, has offensive breath and finds it difficult to swallow or speak. It can easily spread to the other tonsil and to lymph nodes below the jaw and around the ear. The Eustachian tube that drains fluid from, and allows air to enter into the middle ear, opens into the back of the throat between the tonsils and adenoids. As a result infection may spread from the tonsils to the ear. Uncontrolled bacterial infection may cause an abscess (quinsy) or septicaemia.

Tonsillitis is infectious, and may be passed to another person who is in close contact with the patient.

The types of bacteria can be differentiated by a throat swab, and blood tests can detect glandular fever and the likelihood of other viral infections.

Bacterial infections are readily treated by bed rest, fluid diet, aspirin or paracetamol, antiseptic mouthwashes and antibiotics (eg. penicillin, erythromycin, tetracycline). No cure is available for viral infections, and painkilling tablets and gargles are used to give relief, while prolonged rest allows recovery. Recurrent attacks may lead to surgical removal of the tonsils (tonsillectomy).
See also QUINSY; SEPTICAEMIA; TONSIL; TONSILLECTOMY

TOOTH
See TEETH; TOOTH DISCOLOURED; TOOTH LOOSE

TOOTH DISCOLOURED

According to television advertisements, everyone should have the whitest of white teeth, but there are many reasons for this not being so.

Smoking can cause staining of teeth that may last for months, while strongly coloured foods can temporarily stain teeth, sometimes for many hours.

Poor dental hygiene can result in persistent low grade infections of the teeth and gums which can give them a dull grey colour.

Mercury dental amalgam can cause staining of the tooth adjacent to a filling.

An injured tooth may die, and although it will remain in its socket for many months or years, will be a duller white colour than a healthy tooth.

Other causes include fungal infections (eg. oral thrush) which can create a scum that coats teeth, internal absorption of the tooth surface in a damaged or infected tooth (multiple pink spots on tooth surface), fluorosis (brown stain caused by excessive fluoride in the water supply or taking too many fluoride tablets), kernicterus (form of jaundice that occurs in newborn babies because of an immature liver), and a number of uncommon diseases of tooth structure and development may also be responsible for long term discolouration.

Numerous medications, including tetracyclines (antibiotic) and iron may cause tooth discolouration as a side effect, if given to children before tooth development is complete.
See also TEETH and separate entries for diseases mentioned above.

TOOTH LOOSE

An injury (eg. blow, fall) to a tooth may dislodge it from its socket. If any dirt is rinsed off with milk, and the tooth is replaced in the socket and temporarily held in place with aluminium foil wrapped around it and surrounding teeth, there is a good chance it will heal back into place. Dental treatment should be sought as soon as possible.

A fracture of the upper or lower jaw may dislodge teeth adjacent to the fracture.

Periodontitis is an infection or inflammation of the gum around the base of the teeth. As this recedes, teeth may become loose and eventually fall out.

Other causes include Down syndrome (mongolism), poorly controlled diabetes, scurvy (lack of vitamin C in the diet), Ehlers-Danlos syndrome (excessively loose joints), Chediak-Higashi syndrome (inherited condition) and very rarely cancer of the gums.
See also TEETH and separate entries for diseases mentioned above.

TOPIRAMATE
See ANTICONVULSANTS

TORSION OF THE TESTIS
Torsion of the testis occurs if a testicle, hanging in the scrotum from its network of veins, arteries and nerves, twists horizontally, and its blood supply is cut off.

Severe testicular pain, tenderness, redness and swelling occur. It usually occurs in teenage boys, and is almost unknown over thirty years of age.

Testicular torsion is a medical emergency, and the testis will die unless it is surgically untwisted within about twelve hours. Gangrene and death of the testicle will occur if surgery is delayed, necessitating its removal. Infection of the testes (epididymo-orchitis) can also occur, and may be confused with torsion, but the pain is usually less severe, the patient is feverish and both testes may be involved.

The prognosis depends on how quickly surgery is undertaken, but few reach surgery in time for the testicle to be saved. A man is still able to function normally sexually, and is still fertile, despite having only one testicle.
See also EPIDIDYMO-ORCHITIS;
HYDATID OF MORGAGNI; TESTICLE

TORTICOLLIS
Torticollis is a severe spasm of a muscle in the neck. Most commonly involved is the sternocleidomastoid muscle that runs diagonally from the mastoid process at the base of the skull behind the ear, across the neck to the top of the breast bone (sternum).

It is usually caused by repeated turning of the head (eg. watching a tennis match) or sleeping heavily (eg. after excess alcohol) and awkwardly (eg. in a chair), but rarely may be due to a tumour of the brain affecting the nerves to the involved muscles.

The patient has a very painful spasm of muscles, usually on only one side of the neck, which limits neck movement and causes the head to be held at an abnormal angle. No investigations are normally necessary unless a brain cause is suspected. Treatment involves muscle relaxants (eg. diazepam – Valium) and powerful painkillers (eg. pethidine), often by injection, with pain relieving tablets to follow. Heat and physiotherapy are also useful.

Symptoms usually settle in a day or two with treatment.
See also NECK PAIN

TOTAL LUNG CAPACITY
Total lung capacity is sometimes measured in special laboratories. This involves breathing a mixture of helium and oxygen into a complex machine that can use the information obtained to measure quite accurately the total amount of gas in the lungs. It can also be measured with the patient seated inside a body plethysmograph (body box) while performing various breathing manoeuvres.
See also RESPIRATORY
FUNCTION TESTS

TOUCH
Touch is the sense that enables us to experience not only contact, but also heat and cold, pressure, position, vibration and, most importantly of all, pain. The capacity to feel pain is one of our most fundamental protective mechanisms – without it we would lose much of our ability to recognise potential harm (eg. burning heat) and thus to take steps to avoid it, and damage to our body would result.

Touch is also essential in the maintenance of intimacy and affection.

Unlike the other senses, such as taste, sight and hearing, which we experience in specific parts of the body, touch sensors, or receptors, are located over the entire surface of the body. They are tiny bulb-like organs (called endorgans) situated just under the skin. Touch sensors are also incorporated in the muscles where they are known as muscle spindles, and it is these that enable our bodies to remain steady and upright. Touch receptors vary in structure according to their specific purpose (ie. to feel pain, heat, cold, or pressure).

Touch is one of the first senses we develop and is more important in the maintenance of human life than perhaps was recognised until recently. It is now generally acknowledged that newborn babies who are given all the medical care they need but are never stroked or held or touched in a normal way, will not do as well as babies who are treated normally.

The extent to which things are felt varies greatly from one part of the body to another, depending on the number of touch receptors. The fingertips and the lips have a large number of receptors and are especially sensitive, whereas the skin on the back has relatively few receptors. The greater the concentration of receptors, the easier it is to discriminate between separate points of contact. If a compass with its two points pricks a lip, it is possible to distinguish the two pricks if the points are separated by only 1mm. If the finger is pricked, it is necessary to widen the points to 2mm before two separate pricks are felt. If an arm or leg is pricked, the points need to be separated to 25mm, and separate pricks of pain are only felt on the back if the points are 50mm apart.

Different sensations are also felt more acutely in different parts of the body. For example, while the tongue and fingertips are the most sensitive to touch, they are comparatively insensitive to heat and can bear temperatures that would be intolerable to the cheek or elbow. This is why mothers are often advised to test the temperature of the water for the baby's bath with an elbow rather than a hand.

The most sensitive areas of the skin are hairless (eg. tongue, lips, fingertips, sexual organs). These have their own special methods of recording sensation. Elsewhere the skin surface is covered with hair, varying from the long and thick hair on our head, to the less dense hair on our legs, to the fine almost invisible hairs on our trunk. These hairs act as antennae, detecting sensations and transmitting them to the touch receptors below the hair follicle. From here they are carried by the nerves to the spinal cord and finally to the brain, where they are registered so that we feel whatever the original stimulus was. The hairs are amazingly sensitive. If someone touches the end of the hair on your head, even long hair, the touch receptors in your head will detect it.

Pain receptors are more common than other types of receptors, and these record different qualities of sensation depending on where they are situated in the skin. The receptors in the surface layer, the epidermis, produce an itch when stimulated; the receptors a little lower down in the upper dermis produce a sharp pain; and the receptors in the lower dermis give rise to an ache. The touch receptors for pressure are located relatively deep in the body's tissues, and pressure can sometimes be felt even under anaesthetic.

Hot and cold receptors can adapt. Anyone who has ever plunged an arm into steaming hot or icy cold water will know that, while it can seem unbearable at first, the body adjusts quite quickly and before too long the discomfort disappears. Pain receptors do not adapt nearly so readily – perhaps because nature wants to be sure that the warnings are heeded.

It is not always easy to distinguish between one sensation and another. This is because the same thing may stimulate two or more types of receptors simultaneously, and the brain experiences them in the same way. For example, extremes of temperature, hot or cold, stimulate both the temperature receptors and the pain receptors and we then feel both sensations as pain.

Excessive skin sensitivity (hyperaesthesia) and significantly decreased skin sensitivity causing a feeling of numbness (anaesthesia) can be symptoms of diseases of the spinal cord. Similarly, some diseases are manifested by abnormal sensations such as burning, pricking or tingling.
See also SKIN

TOURETTE SYNDROME

Gilles de la Tourette syndrome (to give the condition its full title) is a severe behaviour disorder of children. The cause is unknown, but it is possibly associated with the Crigler-Najjar syndrome.

Patients suffer seizures, other forms of uncontrollable body movements, and often swear and shout excessively. No investigations can specifically diagnose the condition.

Medications are available to control the more serious symptoms. The syndrome usually persists long term but often fades in adult life.
See also ATTENTION DEFICIT HYPERACTIVITY DISORDER; CRIGLER-NAJJAR SYNDROME; VIOLENCE

TOXIC EPIDERMAL NECROLYSIS
See SCALDED SKIN SYNDROME

TOXIC SHOCK SYNDROME
Toxic shock syndrome is a rare syndrome that usually affects women in which a toxin (poison) released by the bacterium *Staphylococcus aureus* (golden staph) damages tissue. It may occur after childbirth, using contraceptive diaphragms, after gynaecological surgery, with an abscess, or as a complication of influenza, but more than 90% of cases are associated with the use of menstrual tampons. The blood-soaked material in a tampon may become invaded by the bacteria, which release the toxin into the bloodstream through the vaginal wall, although the woman herself is not infected by the bacteria.

Symptoms include fever, widespread red rash, headache, muscle aches, vomiting, diarrhoea and a dangerously low blood pressure. The low blood pressure may threaten the blood supply to the brain, liver, kidney and other vital organs, and eventually causes them to fail. Numerous blood tests may be performed in an attempt to identify the cause and monitor progress, but no specific diagnostic test is available.

Treatments that may be used include injected steroids, kidney dialysis (artificial kidney machine), blood transfusions and antibiotics in a hospital intensive care unit. Overall the mortality rate is 15%.
See also BACTERIA; TOXIN

TOXIN
A toxin is a substance poisonous to humans that may be released by a bacteria, plant or animal.
See also BOTULISM; DIPHTHERIA; TETANUS; TOXIC SHOCK SYNDROME

TRACHEA
The trachea (windpipe) forms the air passage between the larynx (voice box) and the lungs. It passes from just below the Adam's apple to the top of the chest behind the breastbone.

The trachea is about 12cm. long and 2cm. in diameter. So that it won't collapse, it is supported by regularly spaced rings of cartilage. These rings are shaped like a horseshoe or a reversed letter C, open at the back so that the oesophagus can expand into this area when swallowing. The rings mean that whatever position the body is in, the trachea will remain open and allow air through.

Once it enters the chest, the trachea divides into two main bronchi, one leading to each lung.

Infection of the trachea causing inflammation is a fairly common upper respiratory ailment called tracheitis. This is generally associated with infection in the nose or throat and may cause a sore chest and painful cough.

Sometimes the trachea becomes obstructed because of a disease such as diphtheria, or because a foreign body becomes lodged there. This is life-threatening. In an operation called a tracheotomy it is possible for a tube to be inserted to bypass the obstruction and allow air to enter directly.
See also LARYNX; LUNG; RESPIRATORY SYSTEM; TRACHEITIS; TRACHEOTOMY

TRACHEITIS
Tracheitis is infection of the trachea (windpipe), usually by viruses, but sometimes by bacteria. The infecting viruses or bacteria are inhaled from the breath of someone who has some form of respiratory tract infection (eg. common cold, bronchitis, sinusitis).

Symptoms may include painful breathing, persistent dry cough, pain in the chest behind the upper end of the breast bone, fever and tiredness. The infection may spread up to the throat to cause laryngitis, or down into the lungs to cause bronchitis.

Antibiotics can cure the condition if it is caused by bacteria, but viral infections can only be treated with aspirin and other antiinflammatory medications, cough suppressants, and paracetamol for pain. In severe cases, inhaled steroids may be used to settle the inflammation, which may persist for two or more weeks before settling.
See also BACTERIA; BRONCHITIS, ACUTE; LARYNGITIS; PHARYNGITIS; TRACHEA; VIRUS

TRACHEOTOMY

A tracheotomy is performed in order to enable a patient to breathe more easily, or sometimes as an emergency procedure to allow breathing at all. Most patients are those who are on a ventilator to assist breathing for a prolonged period.

Usually under a general anaesthetic, but sometimes using several local injections of anaesthetic, an incision is made in the front of the neck about half way between the Adam's apple (larynx) and the top of the breast bone. Through this an opening is made into the trachea (windpipe), and a plastic tube is inserted to allow air direct access to the lungs, bypassing the nose mouth and throat. Unless a special valve is installed, the patient will be unable to speak, because air cannot pass above the tracheotomy and through the vocal cords.

When the tube is removed, the tracheotomy hole will heal up completely, and a small scar on the neck will be the only long term result.
See also TRACHEA

TRACHOMA

Trachoma is a type of conjunctivitis (superficial eye infection) caused by the bacteria-like *Chlamydia* organism, which is very common in areas of low hygiene where flies can transmit the infection from one person to another. It is particularly common among Australian Aborigines.

Mild infections may not be very noticeable, and in children may cause no symptoms. In more severe cases, eye pain, intolerance to bright lights, and a weeping swollen eye develop. Small bubbles on the underside of the eyelids are the earliest sign of the disease. Chronic trachoma causes scarring of the cornea (the outer surface of the eye) and subsequent blindness. Blood vessels grow into the scar tissue, and the coloured part of the eye and the pupil may be covered with a thick scar and obvious small arteries and veins. The gland that produces tears (the lacrimal gland) can also be damaged so that tears no longer form, the eye dries out, and is further damaged and scarred.

It is diagnosed by culture and examination of swabs from the eye.

A one to three month course of antibiotics and antibiotic eye ointment are required for treatment. Once blindness has occurred from corneal scarring, the only treatment is surgical replacement of the damaged cornea by one donated by a deceased person.

It is usually cured if treated within the first year, and the outcome is excellent, but if left longer some scarring of the eye surface may occur.
See also CHLAMYDIAL INFECTION; CONJUNCTIVITIS; EYE; EYE DISCHARGE

TRADE NAMES
See BRAND NAMES; MEDICATION

TRAGUS

The tragus is the medical name for the firm nub of skin covered cartilage that protrudes out from the head in front of the ear canal.
See also EAR; PINNA

TRANDOLAPRIL
See ACE INHIBITORS

TRANSFUSION REACTION

A transfusion reaction is an abnormal reaction to a blood transfusion.

It is necessary to cross-match blood before it is given to a patient, so that the blood of the patient and the donor are compatible. There are four main blood groups (A, B, O, AB) that are further subdivided into those that are Rhesus negative and Rhesus positive. A person can therefore be one of eight different combinations (ie. A+ or A-, O+ or O-, B+ or B-, AB+ or AB-). There are several dozen subgroups beyond this classification and usually these make no significant difference to the patient receiving the blood, but in some cases a transfusion reaction can occur if there is a very slight mismatch of the blood between one of these minor subgroups.

Most commonly a minor reaction causes only a raised temperature. Other possible symptoms if the reaction is more severe include muscle pains, headaches, and shortness of breath. Very rarely do symptoms become worse than this, but a severe reaction may permanently damage organs or be life threatening.

Often no treatment is required, but in more severe cases aspirin, antihistamines or steroids may be necessary. Recovery within a few hours or days is usual.

See also BLOOD GROUPS; SERUM SICKNESS

TRANSIENT ACANTHOLYTIC DERMATOSIS
See GROVER DISEASE

TRANSIENT ISCHAEMIC ATTACK

A transient ischaemic attack (TIA) may be the cause for a type of funny turn in elderly people due to a temporary (less than twenty-four hours) miniature stroke. The usual cause is hardening and narrowing of arteries (arteriosclerosis) in the neck and brain by excessive deposition of cholesterol that causes small blood clots to form. A clot may break off from the artery wall and travel through the arteries into the brain, where it may briefly obstruct an artery, causing temporary damage to the brain tissue beyond the blockage. Spasms of arteries caused by stress, toxins or allergies, and Fabry disease may also be responsible.

The patient feels strange and acts peculiarly. There may be weakness in one arm or leg, abnormal sensations (eg. pins and needles, numbness), disturbances in vision, abnormally slurred speech, dizziness, confusion, tremor and blackouts. The symptoms may last for a few seconds or several hours. A TIA may be an early warning of narrowed arteries in the brain, and can forewarn of strokes.

All patients experiencing a TIA needs to be fully investigated by blood tests, ultrasound examination of arteries in the neck, special x-rays of arteries in the brain, and CT scans of the brain to determine the cause.

There is no specific treatment, but aspirin or warfarin taken long term in low doses prevent most TIAs, and often prevent strokes too, by preventing blood clots. The patient usually returns to normal within twenty-four hours.
See also ARTERIOSCLEROSIS; FABRY DISEASE; STROKE

TRANSPLANTS AND IMPLANTS

Many parts of the human can be replaced, but it will be centuries, if ever, before it will be possible to produce anything approaching an artificial person. Replacements can be of two types: –
• Transplants, where human tissue is transferred from one person to another (eg. kidney and heart transplants).
• Implants, where totally synthetic material replaces a body part (eg. artificial hip or heart valve).

Many different medical specialties are involved in these fields, but the unsung heroes, particularly of the transplants, are the immunologists who have now developed means of combating the body's normal rejection processes.

Heart transplants were grabbing headlines a few years ago, but they have now moved out of the experimental area into accepted medical practice. Unfortunately the demand for this procedure outstrips supply, as the supply of hearts from fatally injured people is limited.

The problem of supply has been overcome to some extent in liver transplants, where an operation in which a part of a living adult's liver can be successfully transplanted into a child has been developed. Liver transplants are now routine, and since the late 1960s kidney transplants have been performed at major hospitals. Lungs can be transplanted along with the heart they belong to, as a heart-lung transplant, and sometimes the recipient's own heart can be transplanted to someone else, if it was only the patient's lungs that were damaged.

Orthopaedic surgeons perform more replacement operations than any other group of doctors. Almost every joint has been replaced experimentally, but the ones most commonly implanted are the hip and knee. The hip replacement operation is very common, and has made the lives of people with serious arthritis far more enjoyable. Patients who can barely crawl into their hospital bed find themselves walking normally only a couple of weeks after the operation.

Knee joints are also replaced when necessary, as are the small joints of the fingers in victims of severe rheumatoid arthritis. There is even a small bone in the wrist (the scaphoid) that can be completely replaced if it is damaged by a fracture. Major whole bones of the arm and leg have been replaced experimentally.

Vascular surgeons bypass blocked arteries with pieces of vein taken from other parts of the body, or with specially prepared nylon tubing. This can enable those who have poor blood supply anywhere from the legs to the heart to recover normal use of those parts.

Ophthalmologists (eye doctors) have transplanted the cornea (the clear outer part of the eye that may become cloudy from age or disease) from the dead to the living for decades. The lens of the eye can also be replaced with an artificial one to cure cataracts. Ear nose and throat surgeons can replace the tiny bones in the middle ear with a teflon piston to restore hearing to some deaf patients.

Cardiac surgeons can replace faulty heart valves in newborn infants or elderly adults with those taken from animals, or with totally artificial valves.

Plastic surgeons can repair damaged noses and ears with artificial cartilage, or replace breasts lost by cancer. Operations to use part of your own body to replace those lost by disease or accident are legion (eg. skin grafts, bone grafts).
See also GRAFT VERSUS HOST DISEASE; HIP REPLACEMENT; IMMUNOSUPRESSANTS

TRANSVERSE MYELITIS
Transverse myelitis is an inflammatory autoimmune disorder of the spinal cord, often associated with a recent viral (eg. influenza, measles, mumps) or bacterial (eg. Mycoplasma) infection, or very rarely a vaccination.

Patients develop neck or back pain, followed by altered sensations (eg. pins and needles, loss of sense of touch) and muscle weakness in the body below the area of pain, and reflexes are abnormal. It may progress to complete paraplegia or quadriplegia.

It is diagnosed by an MRI scan. Steroid injections into the spinal cord may be tried as a treatment, but they are often ineffective. There may be some spontaneous recovery, but effects are usually permanent.
See also AUTOIMMUNE DISEASES; BROWN-SÉQUARD SYNDROME; MULTIPLE SCLEROSIS; PARAPLEGIA; QUADRIPLEGIA; SPINAL CORD

TRANYLCYPROMINE
See ANTIDEPRESSANTS

TRAPEZIUM BONE
See WRIST

TRAPEZOID BONE
See WRIST

TRAUMATIC CERVICAL SYNDROME
See WHIPLASH

TRAVEL IMMUNISATION
The following countries require no immunisations or health protection for the benefit of the traveller, but may require proof of appropriate immunisation if coming from a country with serious health problems (eg. yellow fever).

No immunisations are normally required for: –

Australia, Austria, Bahamas, Belgium, Bermuda, Canada, Croatia, Czech Republic, Denmark, Estonia, Finland, France, Germany, Greece, Greenland, Grenada, Hong Kong, Hungary, Iceland, Ireland, Italy, Japan, Latvia, Lithuania, Luxembourg, Malta, Moldova, Nauru, Netherlands, New Zealand, Norway, Poland, Portugal, Slovakia, Spain, St.Vincent, Singapore, Slovenia, Swaziland, Sweden, Switzerland, Trinidad, United Kingdom, United States.

If you are visiting other countries, discuss your immunisation requirements with your doctor at least six weeks before departure.

Travel vaccinations that may be required for other countries include: –
• Cholera. This is now an oral vaccine that gives good protection. Injections are not normally given now. It is a very severe disease that causes incredibly profuse diarrhoea, and death can occur very rapidly from gross dehydration.
• Typhoid vaccine can be given as an injection which lasts for three years, or by three capsules taken by mouth over five days, which gives twelve months protection. Both typhoid and cholera are caught by eating contaminated food.
• Yellow fever is found in central America, central Africa and around the Red Sea. The vaccine for this lasts for ten years. Yellow fever vaccinations are a condition of entry to some countries.
• Malaria occurs in practically every tropical country. Particularly vicious forms that are resistant to many medications are occurring in south-east Asia and some Pacific islands. To prevent malaria, it is necessary to take tablets regularly for up to a fortnight before departure and sometimes for a month after return. The malaria-carrying mosquito bites only between dusk and dawn, so travellers should take precautions against being bitten after dark – wear clothes that cover as much skin as possible, avoid perfumes, and use repellents and insecticides.

• Hepatitis A occurs world-wide, but is more prevalent in countries with poor hygiene, particularly those in South America, central Asia and Africa. One vaccination will give six to twelve months protection. A booster at this time will give long term protection.

• Hepatitis B. Two vaccinations four to six weeks apart will give six months protection. A booster at six months will usually give long term protection. Southeast Asia is one of the areas with the highest incidence of hepatitis B, but it is not a routine travel vaccination, as it can only be caught by sex or contact with the blood of an infected person. A combined hepatitis A and B vaccination is available.

• Immunoglobulin. In situations where there has been exposure to hepatitis A or other serious illnesses, or there is insufficient time for a normal course of vaccinations, one immunoglobulin injection gives protection for six to twelve weeks against numerous viral infections, depending on dose.

• Japanese encephalitis. Two vaccinations, two weeks apart. It is required only for residence in rural areas of India, Nepal, China and south-east Asia.

• Meningococcal meningitis. One injection, five weeks before departure to live in areas of poor hygiene.

See also CHOLERA; HEPATITIS A; HEPATITIS B; MALARIA; TRAVEL MEDICINE; TRAVELLER'S DIARRHOEA; TYPHOID; VACCINATION; YELLOW FEVER

TRAVELLER'S DIARRHOEA

The most common ailment affecting overseas travellers is diarrhoea. Most diarrhoea is caused by contaminated water resulting from inadequate water and sewerage systems. If you are travelling in any third-world or tropical country, you should avoid drinking the water unless it has been filtered and boiled. Bottled water is best (preferably fizzy water, so that you can ensure that it has not been replaced by tap water), and most reasonable hotels will provide bottled water in your room, but that still leaves the water you use to clean your teeth and ice blocks in all the cool drinks you will undoubtedly consume. Don't have ice in your drinks; if necessary add mineral water from a bottle or can, and use bottled water to clean your teeth. If this is not possible, there are tiny purifying tablets you can pop into a glass, but these will give the water a taste (which you may be able to overcome with a small sachet of fruit-flavoured powder).

Food too can be a source of diarrhoea and food poisoning. Tempting as it is to try all those exotic dishes, steer clear of raw or underdone meat, uncooked seafood, unprocessed dairy products and uncooked fruits (unless you peel them yourself), vegetables and salad ingredients.

An attack of diarrhoea usually lasts only from one to three days but, especially if you are travelling around, it can be very uncomfortable and embarrassing. Ask your doctor to prescribe antidiarrhoea tablets before you go, and keep them with you in your personal baggage. If you are struck down with an attack, go on a 'fluid only' diet for twenty-four hours and eat lightly for several days. You may have stomach pains, nausea and possibly vomiting as well.

See also DIARRHOEA; TRAVEL IMMUNISATION; TRAVEL MEDICINE

TRAVEL MEDICINE

Getting sick on a holiday is always a major disappointment and in a strange environment can be very difficult to cope with. A few simple preparations can reduce the likelihood of disaster. If you are going overseas, find out what the conditions are like in the country or countries you will be visiting. You should ask about the climate, the food, any local diseases against which you should be immunised, and the availability and cost of medical treatment.

Remember, the only ways you can catch an exotic disease are to: –

• eat it

• drink it

• be bitten by it

• have sex with it!

Never travel overseas without health insurance. In developed countries you may be unlikely to be stricken with one of the more exotic third-world diseases, but medical treatment of any kind can be prohibitively expensive (eg. in the United States) and you may find yourself unable to afford the care you need unless you are insured for the cost.

If you get ill in one of the less developed countries, you might need a hasty return home – even flying first class with special nursing care. Don't risk not being able to afford it.

For vaccination schedules to be completed visit your doctor six weeks before departure. *See also* CHOLERA; DIARRHOEA; JET LAG; HEPATITIS A; HEPATITIS B; MALARIA; MOTION SICKNESS; TRAVEL IMMUNISATION; TRAVELLER'S DIARRHOEA; TYPHOID; YELLOW FEVER

TRAVEL SICKNESS
See MOTION SICKNESS

TREMOR
A tremor is an uncontrollable, rhythmic, purposeless, repetitive muscular movement, often of the hands, feet and/or mouth.

Anxiety, fright and emotional stress are the most common causes of a tremor. Anyone who is upset, nervous or excited will find that they have a fine tremor due to the extra adrenaline released into their body.

Anyone who uses a group of muscles excessively for a prolonged period of time will find that eventually those muscles will suffer fatigue, fail to function properly, and start twitching if forced to function.

An essential (familial) tremor is an inherited condition that commences in the twenties. It usually slowly worsens with age and with emotional upsets.

Parkinson disease is caused by degeneration of part of the brain that co-ordinates muscle movement. The usual symptoms are tremor, shuffling walk and increased muscle tone, but in advanced cases, muscle weakness of the face may occur. Repeated head injuries (eg. in boxers) may result in a variation of Parkinson disease known as the 'punch drunk' syndrome.

A senile tremor occurs with advancing age, and is worse when the patient tries to use the arm or leg. It is due to a gradual deterioration of the nerve pathways in the brain that co-ordinate movement.

Other causes of a tremor include a stroke (cerebrovascular accident), hyperthyroidism (overactive thyroid gland), damage to or pressure on nerves (can cause a tremor in the muscles supplied by those nerves), hypoglycaemia (low blood sugar), delirium tremens (occurs when an alcoholic is deprived of alcohol), multiple sclerosis (degenerative nerve disease), Huntington's chorea (inherited condition with progressive loss of limb control and mental deterioration), advanced syphilis and Wilson disease (excess deposition of copper in the liver, brain, eye, kidney and other tissues).

The neuroleptic-malignant syndrome is a side effect of the over use of tranquillising medication in psychiatric conditions. Symptoms include fever, muscle rigidity, tremor, loss of control of bodily functions and impaired consciousness.

Poisoning with mercury or arsenic may result in brain damage and a tremor.

Excess alcohol and caffeine (in coffee, cola drinks, and stimulants) may cause a tremor, and some medications may have a tremor as a side effect. Examples include salbutamol (Ventolin) and terbutaline (Bricanyl) for asthma, lithium (used in psychiatry) and phenytoin (for epilepsy).

There are many other rare causes of a tremor.
See also JERKING; TIC and separate entries for diseases mentioned above.

TREPONEMA PALLIDUM
See SYPHILIS; YAWS

TRETINOIN
See KERATOLYTICS

TRIAMCINOLONE
See STEROIDS

TRIAZOLAM
See SEDATIVES

TRIAMTERENE
See DIURETICS

TRICHINOSIS
Trichinosis is a roundworm infestation found world-wide (not Australia) with a maximum incidence in North America and Europe. It is caused by an infestation of the intestine and muscle tissue of humans, pigs and a wide range of other animals by a tiny nematode (round worm). Wild pigs are the most common source, but it has been caught from eating walrus in Alaska and bear in Canada. The nematode forms a cyst in the animal meat, and if not adequately cooked, may survive and enter the human intestine where larvae are released from the cyst, mature and reproduce. The larvae pass through the lining

of the gut into veins and are distributed by the blood throughout the body to form cysts in the tissue, where they may remain for up to ten years waiting to be eaten by another mammal. In more serious cases the heart, lungs and brain may be invaded.

Symptoms may include diarrhoea, muscle pain, fevers, tiredness and sometimes facial swelling. The infestation can be detected by specific blood and skin tests, and the larvae can be killed by appropriate medication. The cysts remain in the tissue after the larvae they contain have been destroyed, so symptoms may continue long term.
See also ROUNDWORM

TRICHOBEZOAR

A bezoar is a solid mass in the stomach formed from swallowed foreign bodies. A trichobezoar is the most common form and is composed of hair that may completely fill the stomach. It may occur as a side effect of stomach surgery (eg. vagotomy, partial gastrectomy) if the emptying ability of the stomach is affected and fibrous vegetable matter accumulates, but more commonly occurs in psychiatric patients who eat inappropriate objects that can vary from asphalt and cloth to leaves and plastic bags. Women with very long hair who chew their hair as a habit, and psychiatric patients who pull out their hair and eat it, may form a trichobezoar.

Symptoms may include stomach pain, nausea, vomiting, loss of appetite and weight loss. Stomach ulcers or rarely bowel obstruction, may also occur. The diagnosis is confirmed by a barium meal x-ray or gastroscopy.

Treatment is difficult. Removal through a gastroscope is usually attempted, but if the bezoar cannot be broken and allowed to pass on naturally, or withdrawn with or through the gastroscope, open surgery may be necessary. There are good results from treatment once the condition is diagnosed.
See also GASTROSCOPY; STOMACH

TRICHOMONIASIS

Trichomoniasis is an infection of a woman's vagina, and the urethra (urine tube) of both men and women, caused by the single-celled animal, Trichomonas vaginalis. It is transmitted from one victim to another by heterosexual or homosexual intercourse.

In women, vaginal infection causes a foul-smelling, yellow/green, frothy discharge, and there may be mild itching or soreness around the outside of the vagina. In men, there are often minimal symptoms, but it may cause discomfort on passing urine, often first thing in the morning. The diagnosis can be confirmed by examining a swab taken from the vagina or urethra.

Antibiotic tablets (eg. azithromycin) and/or vaginal cream are usually very effective, but all sexual contacts need to be treated at the same time.
See also VENEREAL DISEASES

TRICHOPHYTON
See FAVUS; FUNGI; ONYCHOGRYPHOSIS; TINEA CAPITIS; TINEA CORPORIS; TINEA CRURIS

TRICHOTILLOMANIA

Trichotillomania is a self-induced cause of hair loss that often starts in childhood or the teen years. Females are far more commonly affected than males, and any body hair, including pubic and eyebrows, may be involved.

Patients pull and twist the hair until it breaks, usually as a subconscious habit, but sometimes in association with a psychiatric disturbance, resulting in patchy hair loss, with hair of varying lengths in the affected area.

Strangely, shaving the head or pubic area (but not the eyebrows) may break the habit, but sometimes psychiatric medications required, although most patients grow out of the habit.
See also HAIR LOSS

TRICHURIASIS

Trichuriasis is an infestation of the large intestine with the three to five cm. long whipworm Trichuris. Adult whipworms live in the colon and produce eggs that pass out with the faeces to contaminate the soil. If contaminated food or water is consumed the eggs will hatch in the small intestine to form larvae that then migrate to the large intestine and mature into adult worms. The cycle takes a minimum of three months and adult worms may live for three years, and they are found throughout the tropics.

Most patients have no symptoms but, with severe infestations, abdominal pain, loss of appetite and diarrhoea may occur. Badly infested children may have bloody diarrhoea and become malnourished.

The condition is diagnosed by finding the eggs on microscopic examination of the faeces, then is very effectively treated by the drug mebendazole.

See also WORMS

TRICLOSAN
See ANTISEPTICS; KERATOLYTICS

TRICUSPID REGURGITATION
See TRICUSPID VALVE INCOMPETENCE

TRICUSPID VALVE
The valve between the right atrium and right ventricle in the heart. The right ventricle collects oxygen-depleted blood returning from the body through the veins, and contracts to pump it through the tricuspid valve into the right ventricle. When the right ventricle contracts to pump blood into the lungs, the tricuspid valve remains closed to prevent blood regurgitating back into the right atrium.

The valve is made from three leaves (cusps) of tough cartilage, and this is how its name is derived.

See also HEART; PULMONARY VALVE; TRICUSPID VALVE INCOMPETENCE; TRICUSPID VALVE STENOSIS

TRICUSPID VALVE INCOMPETENCE
Tricuspid incompetence or regurgitation, is leaking of the three-leafed tricuspid valve which controls the flow of blood between the upper chamber (the atrium) and lower chamber (the ventricle) on the right side of the heart. Causes include cor pulmonale, heart attack, heart tumours (eg. myxoma), or endocarditis.

Patients develop distended neck veins, an enlarged liver, fluid accumulates in the belly and around the lungs, and the ankles and feet become swollen. In severe cases, the reduced outflow of blood from the heart to the lungs may lead to heart failure or attack

It is diagnosed by hearing a characteristic heart murmur through a stethoscope, abnormal electrocardiogram (ECG), echocardiography (ultrasound scan) or passing a catheter through a vein and into the heart.

Symptoms are often controlled by medication rather than surgery, which is performed only in severe cases.

See also COR PULMONALE; EBSTEIN ANOMALY; ECHOCARDIOGRAM; ENDOCARDITIS; HEART; HEART ATTACK; MYXOMA; TRICUSPID VALVE

TRICUSPID VALVE STENOSIS
Tricuspid stenosis is a narrowing of the three-leafed tricuspid valve which controls the flow of blood between the upper chamber (the atrium) and lower chamber (the ventricle) on the right side of the heart. It is uncommon in developed countries and usually occurs as a result of rheumatic fever.

Symptoms include fluid accumulation in the belly, a large liver, shortness of breath, fatigue, dilation of the veins in the neck and a redness in the neck and face as blood finds it difficult to progress from the body and into the heart. Heart failure may occur in severe cases.

It is diagnosed by hearing a characteristic heart murmur through a stethoscope, and an abnormal electrocardiogram (ECG) and echocardiography (ultrasound scan).

Surgical correction is necessary for the narrowed heart valve, which has a very good prognosis.

See also ECHOCARDIOGRAM; HEART; RHEUMATIC FEVER; TRICUSPID VALVE

TRICYCLIC ANTIDEPRESSANTS
See ANTIDEPRESSANTS

TRIFLUOPERAZINE
See ANTIPSYCHOTICS

TRIGEMINAL NEURALGIA
Trigeminal neuralgia (tic doloureux) is an inflammation of the trigeminal nerve which leaves the brain and passes through a hole in the skull just beside the ear. It fans out across the face, to receive sensations from the skin of the face, and to give movement instructions to the muscles in the face. Occasionally it may be caused by a brain or nerve disease such as multiple sclerosis, or a tumour that presses on the nerve, but usually there is no specific cause

Patients develop a sudden severe pain in the face which often arises beside the mouth and spreads almost instantly up to the eye, down to the jaw, and across to the ear. The pain may last a few seconds or several minutes and only one side of the face is affected. Attacks may be started by cold winds, eating, yawning, or touching the face, and they tend to come in episodes, with attacks coming every few minutes for a few days or weeks, and then disappearing for a time. Unfortunately, each successive attack tends to last longer than the preceding one, and the pain-free periods become shorter. No specific tests are available to prove the diagnosis.

Painkillers are not particularly effective, but anti-epileptic drugs such as carbamazepine and phenytoin are quite successful treatments. If these medications prove unsuccessful, surgical exploration of the nerve may find an area of compression or abnormality as a cause of the pain. As a last resort, the nerve may be destroyed to give relief from intractable pain, but this leaves the face permanently numb.

Control is usually reasonable, but cure difficult, although spontaneous, permanent cures do occur.
See also MULTIPLE SCLEROSIS; NEURALGIA

TRIGGER FINGER
A trigger finger may occur as a consequence of an injury or inflammation to the tendon to the affected finger, resulting in the formation of a nodule (lump) in the tendon, restricting its ability to flex the finger. The finger (or thumb) becomes difficult to straighten (extend) and may do so with a sudden painful jerk, or may need to be moved back by pushing on an object. Sometimes the finger may become fixed in the bent position.

Injecting steroids around the swollen nodule on the tendon, or surgical removal of the nodule gives good results.
See also MALLET FINGER; TENDON

TRIGLYCERIDE
Triglycerides are formed when one of a group of fatty acids (oleic acid, stearic acid and palmitic acid) combines with glycerol. Triglycerides are found in most animal and vegetable fats and form an essential part of the human diet. Only when eaten in excess, or excessively concentrated in the bloodstream, do they become a problem. Oral contraceptives may also be responsible for raising the blood triglyceride level.

A high level of triglycerides in the blood (hypertriglyceridaemia) predisposes towards an increased risk of strokes and heart attacks, as the excess triglyceride is deposited along with cholesterol on the inside wall of arteries to cause hardening of the arteries (arteriosclerosis). The cholesterol levels are more important than those of triglyceride in this process.

The amount of triglyceride present in the blood can be readily measured in a pathology laboratory. For an accurate result, it is necessary for the patient to fast for twelve hours and avoid alcohol for three days before the test. A level below 2.3 mmol/L is considered normal.

Patients can usually control levels by a diet that excludes most animal and vegetable fat. A low triglyceride diet would exclude all fried food, most dairy products and fatty meats (eg. sausages, lamb chops). With hereditary disease or severe cases, medication must be taken long term as well as the diet.

Patients with obesity, diabetes, alcoholism, an underactive thyroid gland, and a number of rarer diseases have an increased risk of developing high blood levels of triglycerides.
See also ARTERIOSCLEROSIS; CHOLESTEROL; FAT; HYPOLIPIDAEMICS; LIPIDS

TRIMEPRAZINE
See ANTIHISTAMINES

TRIMETHOPRIM
See SULPHA ANTIBIOTICS

TRIMIPRAMINE
See ANTIDEPRESSANTS

TRISMUS
See MOUTH OPENING DIFFICULT

TRISOMY 13-15
See PATAU SYNDROME

TRISOMY 21
See DOWN SYNDROME

TROPHIC HORMONES
Trophic hormones are given as injections to aid infertility, prevent miscarriages, stimulate sperm production in men, control breast pain due to hormone imbalances, to start puberty in cases where it has been delayed, and to control some patients with asthma and arthritis. There

are a number of rarer diseases in which they are also useful.

Commonly used trophic hormones include gonadotrophins (Humegon) and tetrocosactrin (Synacthen). Adverse reactions are uncommon but severe when they do occur. They include nausea, headaches, peptic ulcers, fluid retention, high blood pressure, inappropriate sexual development and skin markings.
See also HORMONES; MEDICATION

TROPICAL EAR
See OTITIS EXTERNA

TROPICAL SPRUE
Tropical sprue is a failure to absorb fat from the gut caused by an inflammation of the small intestine that develops in people used to a European diet who live for prolonged periods in tropical countries.

Symptoms may include explosive diarrhoea with watery stools, rapid weight loss, indigestion, burping, abdominal cramps, muscle cramps, and as a result of the failed fat absorption, a failure to absorb vitamins A, D, E and K, which are all soluble in fat.

The diagnosis is made by examination of the faeces, which is found to contain high levels of fat, and by x-rays of the small intestine. Blood tests may show a particular type of anaemia.

Tetracycline (an antibiotic) for a week, and folic acid for several months, usually cures the condition. Further treatment may be required if severe anaemia has developed.
See also COELIAC DISEASE; VITAMIN A

TRYPANOSOMIASIS
See CHAGAS' DISEASE; SLEEPING SICKNESS

TRYPTOPHAN
See EOSINOPHILIA-MYALGIA SYNDROME

TSH
See THYROID FUNCTION TESTS

TUBAL LIGATION
A tubal ligation (having the tubes tied or clipped) renders a woman permanently unable to have children. As a contraceptive it is almost 100% effective, but as with all surgical procedures, failures may occur, and women should be aware of this when they have the procedure. On the other hand, as it is a procedure which must be regarded as irreversible at the time it is performed, it is only suitable for women who have completed their family or are sure they want no children. There is a very minimal, but theoretically possible, risk to the woman herself from the surgery.

A woman's Fallopian tubes are about seven cm long and lead from each of the two ovaries to the womb. The egg released every month travels down the tube where it may be fertilised by a male sperm, in which case it will become implanted in the wall of the womb and develop into a foetus. The purpose of tying or closing the tubes is to stop the egg and the sperm meeting.

Tubal ligation is a relatively simple operation, normally performed by laparoscopy. Two small 1cm. long cuts are made in the abdomen, one in the belly button and one low down on one side. Through these small cuts, long stainless-steel tubes are placed. The surgeon looks through one, and operates with very long, fine instruments through the other. The Fallopian tubes are closed with metal clips and electrically burnt in this procedure, which takes only fifteen minutes under a general or local anaesthetic in a hospital or clinic. It may be followed by an overnight stay in hospital. Laparoscopy can also be done through a cut in the top of the vagina, which

TUBAL LIGATION OPERATION

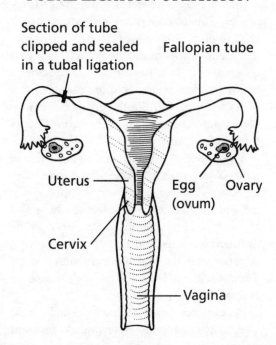

Section of tube clipped and sealed in a tubal ligation

Fallopian tube

Uterus

Egg (ovum)

Ovary

Cervix

Vagina

avoids any scars, but is technically more difficult and sex must be avoided for several weeks. With both methods, the woman can expect to be off work for about a week, with minor discomfort for a few days.

Developments in microsurgery sometimes make it possible to 'untie' the tubes but the success rate is not high (about 65%) and should not be taken into account when deciding on the operation.

A newer method involves inserting a spring-like device into the Fallopian tubes using an instrument that is placed though the vagina and cervix into the uterus. These take about three months to become effective, and the procedure is not reversible.

Because of its permanence, a woman and her partner need to consider all the aspects carefully and take into account all possible eventualities, for example a marriage break-up or the death of a child.
See also CONTRACEPTIVES;
LAPAROSCOPY; VASECTOMY

TUBAL PREGNANCY
See ECTOPIC PREGNANCY

TUBERCULOSIS
Tuberculosis (TB or phthisis) was originally a disease of cattle that only passed to humans after these animals were domesticated many thousands of years ago. It is now a bacterial infection that affects one third of the people on the planet.

Infection usually occurs in the lungs (pulmonary tuberculosis), but may attack bone, skin, joints, lymph nodes, kidney, gut, heart and membranes around the brain (meningeal tuberculosis). It is uncommon in developed countries, but widespread in poorer parts of Asia, Africa and South America. Because cattle and other animals may carry TB, its total eradication is difficult.

The responsible bacterium, *Mycobacterium tuberculosis*, passes from one person to another in moist droplets with every breath. When inhaled the bacteria may infect the lung and the surrounding lymph nodes, or may lie dormant for years, and then start multiplying to cause an initial or subsequent attack of the disease at a time when the patient's resistance is down.

Patients develop a productive cough, night sweats, loss of appetite, fever, weight loss and generalised tiredness. The infection may gradually spread to almost every other organ in untreated patients, when symptoms depend upon which areas are affected.

Chest x-rays show a characteristic pattern, and the infection may be confirmed by collecting sputum samples and identifying the bacteria through a microscope. Skin tests can determine whether the person has ever been exposed to tuberculosis.

Treatment involves a combination of different antibiotic and antituberculotic medications for a year or more. Patients should be hospitalised and isolated until they are no longer infectious, although this is not usually practical in poorer countries. All the other members of the patient's family must be investigated for early signs of the disease, and may be given treatment as a routine preventative measure. The BCG vaccine gives lifelong protection, and is given routinely at birth to babies in many poorer countries.

With effective treatment regimes, a complete cure can be expected, and most recurrences are due to patients failing to complete the full course of treatment. Without treatment, death occurs in a significant proportion of victims.
See also MANTOUX TEST; SCROFULA;
TUBERCULOSIS MEDICATIONS

TUBERCULOSIS MEDICATIONS
Sixty years ago in Western countries, tuberculosis (TB) killed thousands every year. Special hospitals were built in every city just to cope with the huge number of patients suffering from this lung disease. Today those hospitals have been converted to other uses, and thanks to x-ray screening, inoculations, pasteurisation of milk, better hygiene and effective antituberculotic drugs, tuberculosis has almost been eradicated in developed countries. Tuberculosis does still occur though, usually in migrants from poorer countries and in the homeless.

A number of drugs can be used for the treatment of TB. Normally two or three are given simultaneously, and in the early stages of treatment they may be given by injection. Treatment is very slow, and the medication must be taken for many months or years. Regular blood tests and x-rays are necessary while on treatment, and sometimes side effects may necessitate alterations in dosage or choice of medication. Common medications in this group include ethambutol, isoniazid,

pyrazinamide and rifampicin. Because the side effects and precautions are so variable from drug to drug and patient to patient, it is not possible to list them in any meaningful way.
See also MEDICATION; TUBERCULOSIS

TUBEROUS SCLEROSIS

Tuberous sclerosis (epiloia) is an uncommon nodule formation in organs of young children. It is a congenital condition (present since birth) that may occur in successive generations in the one family or develop randomly.

Repeated convulsions occur in infancy due to the presence of brain nodules. Later in childhood, mental retardation is noted and a rash consisting of red nodules (small lumps) appears on the face and neck. Other unusual rashes may develop elsewhere on the body, and lumps may form under the nails. Eye damage, cysts in the heart, bone and lungs, and nodules in the bowel, may also develop.

No curative treatment is available, but medication is given to control convulsions, and surgery is performed to remove some of the more serious nodules. Mental retardation usually steadily worsens with age.
See also CONVULSION; MENTAL RETARDATION

TULARAEMIA

Tularaemia is a bacterial infection of rats and rabbits that can spread to humans through a tick bite or direct contact with an infected animal. Symptoms include a fever, headache, enlarged lymph nodes, tender spleen and vomiting. A sore can usually be found at the site where the bacteria entered the body. Diarrhoea and pneumonia may occur in severe cases, and meningitis, bone and heart infections are rare serious complications.

The diagnosis can be confirmed by a blood culture, then antibiotics are given in high doses by injection or intravenous drip. Most patients recover.

TUMOUR

See CANCER; BONE LUMP; BREAST LUMP; GOITRE; TESTICLE AND SCROTUM LUMP

TUNICA VAGINALIS

See HYDROCELE

TURNER SYNDROME

The Turner syndrome (XO syndrome) is a rare defect in sex chromosomes. The person is born with only one X chromosome (XO), and no matching X or Y sex chromosome. The sex chromosomes are named X and Y. Normally two X chromosomes (XX) occur in a female, and one of each (XY) in a male.

Patients look female, but are really asexual, as they do not develop testes or ovaries and are infertile. At puberty, the breasts and pubic hair fail to develop, the genitals remain childlike in appearance, and menstrual periods do not start. Other signs are short stature and a web of skin that runs from the base of the skull down the neck and onto the top of the shoulder. Complications may include eye disorders (eg. keratoconus), heart valve defects, narrowing of the aorta (main body artery), a stocky chest, the early development of diabetes and thin frail bones (osteoporosis).

The diagnosis can be confirmed by blood and cell tests that show the abnormal chromosome structure.

Female hormones (oestrogens) are given in a cyclical manner from the time of expected puberty to encourage the development of female characteristics, growth hormone can be used to improve height, and surgery can correct the heart defects and neck webbing.

Patients can function as females in every way except fertility, and can lead a normal life.
See also CHROMOSOME; KERATOCONUS; NOONAN SYNDROME

TWINS

If, perchance, two eggs are released and fertilised, there will be two babies or twins. Twins produced from two separate eggs each have their own separate set of inherited characteristics and are not identical. Occasionally a fertilised egg or a blastocyst (ball of cells) divides into two to produce two separate embryos. The result is identical twins, each with the same genetic make-up, ie. they will be the same sex, have the same colour eyes and hair, and have similar features. It is not known why this occurs.

Triplets, quads and quins usually result from both the production of more than one egg and the division of a single fertilised egg, so some of the babies will look alike and some will be different. Nowadays multiple pregnancies not infrequently result from treatment for infertility with hormones which stimulate the production of several eggs.

Twins occur naturally once in every eighty births, and triplets once in every 640 births. *See also* BLASTOCYST

TWITCH
See JERKING; TIC; TREMOR

TYMPANIC RUPTURE
The rupture of the ear drum (tympanic membrane) leaves it with a slit or round hole. The cause may be increased pressure in the middle ear (eg. Eustachian tube blockage), infection (eg. otitis media), glue ear or direct injury to the ear (eg. extremely loud sudden noise, poking stick into ear).

Pain and deafness occur, and if infection is present there may be a discharge. Infection in the ear may lead to permanent deafness.

It is diagnosed by examining the ear with an otoscope (magnifying light). Antibiotics are then prescribed to prevent or treat infection and in persistent cases, surgery is performed to place a tiny skin graft is put over the defect.

Most ruptured ear drums heal in a few days to weeks, depending on size of hole and cause. *See also* DEAF; EAR; EAR DISCHARGE; EUSTACHIAN TUBE BLOCKAGE; GLUE EAR; OTITIS MEDIA

TYPHOID FEVER
Typhoid fever (enteric fever or intestinal Salmonellosis) is a widespread bacterial infection of the gut and surrounding lymph nodes, including the spleen, which occurs throughout Asia, Africa and South America.

The infection is caught by eating food contaminated with the bacterium *Salmonella typhi*, which passes out in the faeces and urine of those who have the infection, or are symptom-free carriers of the bacteria. The incubation period is five to fourteen days.

Symptoms include fever, headache, tiredness, cough, sore throat, abdominal pain and constipation. After a day or two, the constipation suddenly gives way to copious diarrhoea. Complications may include massive bleeding into the gut and perforation of the gut, which usually cause the death of the patient. In severe cases, it is possible for the infection to spread to the lungs, brain, kidneys and gall bladder.

The diagnosis confirmed by specific blood, urine and faeces tests.

Antibiotics are prescribed to destroy invading bacteria, steroids are given to reduce inflammation, and a low-residue diet and intravenous fluids prevent gut irritation and dehydration. The bacteria may be almost impossible to eradicate from people who become symptom-free carriers of the disease. Preventive vaccines are available as three tablets taken over five days that give at least six months protection, or injections that give three years protection.

Death occurs in up to 30% of untreated cases, but only in 2% of those who are treated in good facilities. With no treatment, survivors slowly improve after about ten days, but

AREAS OF THE WORLD AFFECTED BY TYPHOID FEVER

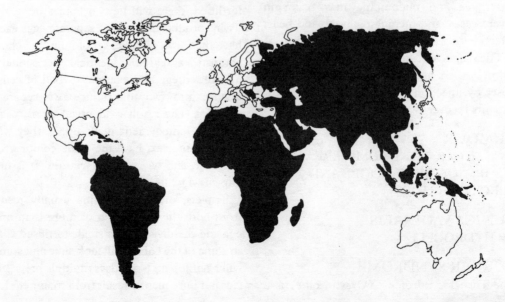

relapses may occur for the next two or three weeks.

See also DIARRHOEA; SHIGELLOSIS

TYPHUS

Typhus is a world-wide infection caused by various types of the primitive bacteria *Rickettsia*, that causes a significant generalised illness. The bacteria pass to humans through a tick bite, and the incubation period is three days to two weeks.

It is more common around the Mediterranean Sea, in the Middle East and in East Africa, and different names are given to the infection in different parts of the world, and to infections caused by different species of Rickettsia. These include: –

• *Rickettsia conorrii* – Mediterranean Sea and East Africa – Mediterranean Spotted Fever, Fievre Boutonneuse, Astrakhan Spotted Fever, Indian Tick Typhus, Kenya Tick Typhus, Israeli Spotted Fever.

• *Rickettsia sibirica* – North Asia – Siberian Tick Typhus.

• *Rickettsia africae* – East and Southern Africa – African Tick Bite Fever.

• *Rickettsia australis* – Tropical Australia – Queensland Tick Typhus.

• *Rickettsia japonica* – Japan – Oriental Spotted Fever.

• *Rickettsia honei* – Flinders Island, Tasmania – Flinders Island Spotted Fever.

All forms have similar symptoms and treatment.

Symptoms include a black spot on the skin at the site of the tick bite, swelling of skin, a widespread red large spot rash, fever, generalised aches and pains, tiredness, headache, joint pains, loss of appetite and enlarged lymph nodes. Liver damage and skin ulceration are possible complications.

It is diagnosed by specific blood tests and/or a skin biopsy.

Treatment involves antibiotics such as tetracycline and ciprofloxacin, which settle the infection in a few days. Without treatment, and with no complications, symptoms settle in three or four weeks.

The prognosis is usually good in Western countries with appropriate treatment, but up to 10% of patients die from liver damage without medical attention.

See also RICKETTSIAL INFECTIONS

U

ULCER
See BED SORE; GENITAL ULCER;
MOUTH ULCER; PEPTIC ULCER;
SKIN ULCER

ULCER MEDICATIONS
See ANTACIDS; H2
RECEPTOR ANTAGONISTS; PROTON
PUMP INHIBITORS

ULCERATIVE COLITIS
Ulcerative colitis is a severe and potentially life-threatening inflammation and subsequent ulceration of the large intestine (colon). Repeated attacks cause thickening and scarring of the colon to the point where it cannot adequately undertake its task of absorbing excess fluid from the faeces. The cause is unknown, but it is more common in whites than in blacks and orientals, and six times more common in Jews than other Caucasians. The overall incidence in developed countries is about one in every thousand people.

The symptoms are often quite mild at first, but subsequent attacks steadily worsen to cause bloody diarrhoea with severe abdominal cramps and pain. Large amounts of mucus may be present in the diarrhoea, and in severe cases the diarrhoea may occur twenty times a day, consist entirely of blood and mucus, and be severe enough to cause the patient to collapse. Occasionally, periods of apparent constipation can occur between attacks of diarrhoea. Further symptoms include fever, loss of appetite, weight loss and overwhelming tiredness.

Numerous serious complications include abscesses around the anus, a rupture of the colon (urgent surgery necessary), colon cancer, massive over dilation of the large intestine (megacolon), and false connections (fistula) from the gut to the bladder or vagina caused by ulcers breaking through to these adjacent organs. Inflammation in the colon may be associated with inflammation in other parts of the body, including the skin, joints, eye, mouth and liver.

The diagnosis is confirmed by a barium meal x-ray or colonoscopy (a tube is passed through the anus into the colon to allow it to be examined).

The disease passes through phases of active disease and remission, and treatment is aimed at treating the active disease when it occurs and preventing an attack from developing. Severe attacks require admission to hospital for drips into a vein, antibiotics, and steroids. Milder attacks may be treated by steroid tablets or suppositories (given through the anus). Prevention and the treatment of mild attacks require a specific diet that is high in protein but excludes dairy products, and the regular use of sulfasalazine, which reduces gut inflammation. Uncontrolled disease may require the surgical removal of the entire colon and an ileostomy (the small intestine is opened out onto the skin of the abdomen and wastes are collected in a bag).

Although there is no permanent cure, most cases can be adequately controlled by medication. Because of the long-term complications and related conditions in other organs, the average life expectancy of these patients is slightly less than normal.
See also COLON; COLONOSCOPY;
COLORECTAL CANCER; FISTULA;
MEGACOLON

ULCER
An ulcer is any persistent break in a body surface that exposes underlying tissue, be it the skin or lining of a hollow organ (eg. mouth, intestine).
See also BED SORE; GENITAL ULCER;
MOUTH ULCER; ORF; PEPTIC ULCER;
SKIN ULCER; VENOUS ULCER

ULNA
The ulna is one of the two bones in the forearm (the radius is the other one), and runs from the elbow to the wrist. At the elbow end it curls around the bottom of the humerus (upper arm bone) to form the lump of bone on the point of the elbow (the olecranon process). If the arm is held out with the palm facing up, the ulna is on the little finger side of

the forearm.
See also RADIUS; WRIST

FOREARM BONES

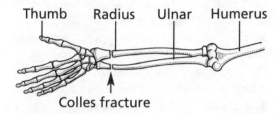

Thumb   Radius   Ulnar   Humerus

Colles fracture

ULTRASOUND

Ultrasound is based on the fact that high-frequency sound waves bounce off tissues of different density at different rates. For example, bone reflects back nearly all sound waves that hit it, whereas fluids allow the waves to pass through. Sound waves are bounced off the organ being investigated, and the reflected waves are translated into a picture so the doctor can see what they mean.

Ultrasound machines produce a moving image from which selected still photographs are taken. Part of the patient's body is coated with oil or gel, and a small pen-like probe that contains the sound recorder and microphone is placed on the skin. Once the area has been scanned, the instrument is moved a few centimetres and another scan is taken, and so on, until the entire area under investigation has been covered.

Almost any part of the body can be examined by ultrasound, with the exception of the head because the sound waves cannot penetrate bone. Because of the ribs, it is also difficult to see into the chest.

The most useful aspect of ultrasound is its ability to examine the foetus of a pregnant woman without the risks associated with x-rays. The size, position and sometimes sex of the baby can all be seen, and some of the internal organs of the baby, particularly the heart, can be checked. Abnormalities such as spina bifida, hydrocephalus and certain other congenital disorders can be identified. A routine scan may be performed between the sixteenth and eighteenth week of pregnancy when the foetus can easily be seen and transformed into an image. Another scan is sometimes performed later in the pregnancy, after about thirty-two weeks.

The breasts can be carefully checked for cysts, fibrous lumps or cancer by ultrasound, as the cancer cells reflect sound in a different way from normal cells. The gall bladder and liver can be checked for damage and stones, the kidneys and pancreas for cysts and stones, and the thyroid gland and spleen for enlargement, tumours and cysts, among many other uses.

Ultrasound can also be used to study the flow of the blood. Among other interesting pieces of information to emerge is that the blood flow in the carotid artery (the main artery carrying blood to the brain) is strongly influenced by external stimuli, such as the phone ringing or someone coming into the room.

Ultrasound is frequently used to guide a needle towards its destination in a biopsy.

Unlike x-rays, sound waves have no effect on the tissues exposed to them, so ultrasound is completely safe. It can be repeated as often as required without concern.

Ultrasound is also used by physiotherapists and doctors as a form of treatment. These high-frequency sound waves impart a mechanical energy into the tissues, and are used to disperse swelling and enhance healing of injured tissue, so are commonly used in the treatment of sporting and other soft-tissue injuries.

See also DOPPLER STUDIES; ECHOCARDIOGRAM; SONOGRAPHER

UMBILICAL HERNIA

An umbilical hernia is a protrusion of the gut under the skin of the navel. There are two very different forms in children and adults.

In children, there is a hole between the muscle layers of the abdomen where the arteries and veins that passed down the umbilical cord from the mother entered the baby. This hole normally closes quickly after birth, but in some children the hole is very large, or is slow to close. In these cases, bulging of the intestine into the area just below the skin of the umbilicus can occur. This is more common in premature babies, as the processes involved in closing the hole behind the umbilicus are slower. The hernia bulges out while the infant is crying or active, but usually disappears when the child is lying quietly, and almost never gives pain or discomfort to the child. The vast majority close spontaneously within twelve months but may take until three years of age. If the hernia persists, surgery may be necessary.

In adults, the hernia is not strictly speaking an umbilical hernia, but a paraumbilical hernia, as the rupture occurs not immediately underneath the umbilicus but in the slightly weakened fibrous tissue just above (more common) or below the navel. These steadily increase in size with time and are common in women who have had multiple pregnancies, in the very obese and those who have other causes for excess pressure in the abdomen. Large hernias can contain a significant amount of intestine and may cause discomfort and constipation. Small paraumbilical hernias are repaired surgically when discovered, as delay may lead to a larger hernia and more difficult repair later. In older patients with particularly large hernias, surgical repair may not be practical. Rarely the intestine may become trapped in the hernia, very painful and gangrenous. If this occurs, emergency surgery is essential. The recurrence rate after surgery depends upon the original size of the hernia, but is generally low.

See also ABDOMINAL LUMP; HERNIA

UNCONSCIOUS

If a person is unconscious, they cannot respond to their surroundings in a normal way and their usual reflexes may not operate. They cannot swallow or cough and so clear the throat of any mucus or foreign objects. An unconscious person's muscles relax and may be so floppy that if they are lying on their back their tongue may fall backwards and block their airway.

There are three levels of unconsciousness: –
• The victim can be easily aroused but slips back into a sleepy state.
• The victim can only be aroused with difficulty.
• The victim cannot be aroused at all.

Any level of unconsciousness can lead to a difficulty in breathing, so it is essential to attend to the victim quickly and to get medical help. If a person does not respond to shaking or shouting they are unconscious.

Leaving aside a temporary faint from which the person usually recovers quite quickly, reasons for becoming unconscious include a stroke or heart attack, a blow to the head, an overdose of alcohol or drugs, and diseases such as epilepsy or diabetes.

Do not move an unconscious person unless they are in immediate danger, and do not leave them alone (send someone else for help). Carry out the ABC (airways, breathing, circulation) of first aid as soon as possible. If necessary, administer mouth-to-mouth resuscitation or cardiopulmonary resuscitation. If the victim is breathing and has a pulse, put them in one of the positions described below and keep them there to ensure that the airway is kept clear. Monitor the airway and pulse continually until help arrives. Do NOT give anything to eat or drink – do not for example try to revive them with sips of water; they will be unable to swallow and may choke.

COMA POSITION
To put an unconscious person in the coma position: –
• lie the victim on their back and kneel on one side
• place the near arm straight down beside the body, tucking the hand, palm up, under the buttocks
• cross the far arm over the chest
• cross the far leg over the near one
• protect and support the head with one hand, and with the other hand grasp the clothing at the hip furthest from you and pull the victim towards you so they roll onto the side
• readjust the head to make sure the airway is still open
• bend the upper arm into a convenient position to support the upper body. Bend the upper leg at the knee to bring the thigh well forward so that it supports the lower body
• carefully pull the other arm out from under the body on the far side and leave it lying parallel so the victim cannot roll back

Do NOT use the coma position if you suspect the victim has an injured back or neck, unless breathing becomes noisy, laboured or irregular.

LATERAL POSITION
Provided there is adequate support for the head, an unconscious person may also be placed in the lateral position: –
• place the victim on their back and kneel beside them
• extend the far arm out at right angles to the body
• place the near arm across the chest
• bend the near knee so the leg is at right angles to the body, keeping the far leg straight
• grasp the victim's near shoulder and hip and

roll them on to their side so that they are facing away from you. Keep the back straight • place the top arm so that it rests comfortably across the lower arm

• tilt the head backwards with the face slightly downwards to maintain a clear airway
See also COMA; FAINT; FIRST AID; GLASGOW COMA SCALE

UNCOORDINATED
See COORDINATION POOR

UNDERWEIGHT
See APPETITE, LACK OF; FAILURE TO THRIVE; GROWTH REDUCED; MALABSORPTION; WEIGHT LOSS

UNDESCENDED TESTICLE
See TESTICLE UNDESCENDED

UNDULANT FEVER
See BRUCELLOSIS

UNFOLDING OF AORTA
See AORTIC UNFOLDING

UNIPOLAR ELECTROCAUTERY
See DIATHERMY

UNSTABLE ANGINA
See INTERMEDIATE CORONARY SYNDROME

UNSTABLE KNEE
See KNEE UNSTABLE

UPPER RESPIRATORY TRACT INFECTION
See COLD, COMMON; INFLUENZA; LARYNGITIS; PHARYNGITIS; SINUSITIS; TONSILLITIS; UVULITIS

URAEMIA
See KIDNEY FAILURE, CHRONIC

URAEMIC SYNDROME
See HAEMOLYTIC-URAEMIC SYNDROME

URATE
See URIC ACID

UREA
Urea is a chemical produced by the liver in the process of the body's use of proteins. It is normally excreted by the kidneys, and if the kidneys are not functioning properly it will accumulate in the blood. Hence a high level of urea in the blood indicates possible kidney disease. A urea level under 8 mmol/L is considered normal.
See also BLOOD TESTS; KIDNEY

URETER
The two ureters are slender tubes down which urine passes from the kidneys to the bladder where it is stored. Each ureter is about 30cm long, and in parts less than 1mm. in diameter. The ureters travel from the kidneys in the small of the back through the loins and the pelvis, and enter the bladder at an angle. This enables urine to run freely into the bladder but prevents it from flowing back upwards as the bladder fills up prior to being emptied. The walls of the ureters consist of thick layers of smooth muscle which contract to force urine down into the bladder.

The main problem that occurs in the ureter is when a stone is formed in the kidney and is then passed into one of the ureters. This can be extremely painful.
See also BLADDER; KIDNEY; KIDNEY STONE; URETHRA

URETERIC COLIC
See KIDNEY STONE

RENAL TRACT

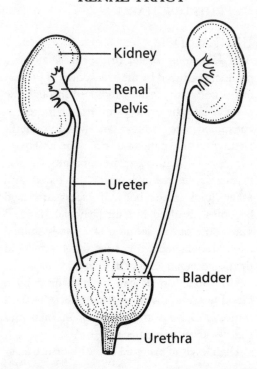

Kidney

Renal Pelvis

Ureter

Bladder

Urethra

URETHRA

The urethra is the tube leading from the bladder, along which urine passes to be emptied outside the body.

In women, the urethra is comparatively short (about two centimetres) and has only the one purpose of conveying urine. It is set within the muscle of the front wall of the vagina and has its external opening just in front of the vaginal opening.

In men, the urethra is considerably longer (about twenty centimetres) and runs from the bladder through the prostate down through the penis so that its external opening is at the tip of the penis. It serves as a passageway not only for urine but also for the ejaculation of semen, and so is also part of the male reproductive system. It is not possible for both semen and urine to be expelled at the same time, however, because when a man urinates, the process automatically seals the opening through which seminal fluid enters the urethra.

Inflammation of the urethra (urethritis) is caused when normally harmless bacteria in surrounding areas such as the rectum, or in the vagina in women, invade the urethra and give rise to infection.
See also BLADDER; KIDNEY; PENIS DISCHARGE; PROSTATE GLAND; URETER; URETHRITIS

URETHRAL DISCHARGE
See PENIS DISCHARGE

URIC ACID

Also known as urate, uric acid is a waste product produced by the breakdown of protein in the body. It is usually removed through the kidneys into the urine, but if excess protein is consumed, the kidneys are working inefficiently, or the patient has a poor ability to process uric acid, excessive amounts (hyperuricaemia) may build up in the blood and other fluids in the body. If excess uric acid becomes dissolved in joint (synovial) fluid, it may come out of solution as crystals shaped like a double pointed needle, which results in the excruciating joint pain of gout.

Uric acid (urate) can be measured by a blood test, and the normal range is 0.24-0.42 mmol/L (3.2-8.1 mg/100 mL) in men and slightly lower in women.

High levels of uric acid in the blood are diagnostic of gout if joint pain is present, but may also be caused by toxaemia of pregnancy, leukaemia, polycythaemia, kidney failure, myeloma, lymphoma, other cancers, prolonged high fever, hypothyroidism, high cholesterol, starvation, psoriasis, severe viral infections, alcoholism, haemolytic anaemia, rhabdomyolysis, acidosis, lead poisoning and the Lesch-Nyhan syndrome. Medications such as diuretics, salicylates and cytotoxics may also cause high levels. In some people levels may be high without any definable cause.
See also BLOOD TESTS; GOUT; HYPOURICAEMICS; LESCH-NYHAN SYNDROME; URINE; URINE TESTS

URINALYSIS
See URINE TESTS

URINARY INCONTINENCE
See INCONTINENCE OF URINE

URINATION DIFFICULT

Despite having a full bladder, it is sometimes difficult to pass urine (stranguary) because of anxiety, stress or the location in which it is being attempted. A number of diseases, almost invariably affecting men, may also be responsible.

The prostate gland at the base of the penis, is responsible for producing some of the fluid (semen) which is ejaculated during sex. With increasing age this tends to enlarge, putting pressure on the urethra (urine tube from bladder to the outside) which passes through the middle of the gland, and making it more difficult to pass urine. In extreme cases, it may become impossible to pass any urine, and the bladder will increase to an enormous size causing considerable pain.

Cancer of the prostate is a common condition of elderly men, but it progresses very slowly in most cases, and its presence may not be noticed until the enlarging cancer puts pressure on the urethra to make passing urine difficult. An aching pain at the front of the pelvis is the other possible symptom.

Other causes include prostatitis (a bacterial infection of the prostate gland), urethritis (infection of the urethra), an injury to the urethra, an inserted foreign body, and a stone, polyp, tumour, cancer or blood clot in the bladder that may block the opening of the bladder into the urethra.

Rarely, the nerve supply to the bladder may be damaged by an injury to the lower back or pelvis, making bladder emptying difficult or impossible.

See also PROSTATE GLAND ENLARGED and separate entries for diseases mentioned above.

URINATION FREQUENT

Passing more urine than normal (polyuria) may be due to drinking more fluid (particularly coffee, tea, cola or alcohol which stimulate urine production), cold weather, pregnancy (when pressure is put on the bladder by the growing baby), anxiety, fright or fear, but there are many different kidney, bladder and other organ diseases that may also be responsible.

If the bladder becomes infected by bacteria (cystitis) the patient will have a fever, feel pain low down in the front of the belly, will pass urine more frequently, and pain will be felt when passing urine. In severe cases the urine will be cloudy and sometimes blood will be seen in the urine.

Diabetes mellitus results in a higher than normal amount of sugar (glucose) circulating in the blood. The symptoms of untreated diabetes are unusual tiredness, increased thirst and hunger, belly pains, excess passing of urine, weight loss despite a large food intake, itchy rashes, recurrent vaginal thrush infections, pins and needles, dizziness, light headedness and blurred vision.

A prolapse (bulging) of the bladder into the front wall of the vagina in a woman will make passing urine difficult and uncomfortable, and increases the risk of infection. The bladder cannot be completely emptied, so the woman will find that she has to pass small amounts of urine very frequently. Damage to the vagina during childbirth is the most common cause of a prolapse.

Other causes of polyuria include prostatitis (bacterial infection of the prostate gland), kidney failure (from persistent infection or inflammation of the kidney, a poor blood supply to the kidneys, severe high blood pressure, or a number of rarer diseases), systemic lupus erythematosus (autoimmune condition), and a number of psychiatric conditions, particularly those associated with anxiety and depression, may increase bladder irritability.

Diuretics are medications designed to increase urine production in conditions such as high blood pressure, heart failure and kidney failure. Other medications may have increased urination as a side effect.

Rare causes of frequently passing urine include diabetes insipidus (failure of the pituitary gland in the centre of the head), Hand-Schueller-Christian syndrome, Cushing syndrome (over production of steroids in the body, or taking large doses of cortisone), Addison disease (adrenal gland failure), hyperparathyroidism (over activity of the parathyroid glands in the neck), acromegaly and Bartter syndrome.

See also BLADDER; CYSTITIS; PROLAPSE; URINATION NIGHTLY; URINE; URINE BLOOD and separate entries for diseases mentioned above.

URINATION NIGHTLY

Getting up during the night in order to pass urine (nocturia) is a real nuisance, but one that is endured by a very large percentage of the adult population. Women are five times as likely to need to do this than men, and the problem steadily worsens with age.

Women who have had children are more affected, as the structures in the pelvis that control the bladder are stretched during childbirth and never quite return to their former strength. Women also often find that the problem is worse at different times of the month, usually just before a menstrual period, and worse again after menopause as the lack of hormones also reduces tissue strength in the pelvis.

The kidney does not produce urine at a constant rate; it reduces its urine output at night, while increasing it during the day. This cycle becomes less pronounced with age as the controlling hormone from the pituitary gland under the brain fails to be produced in sufficient quantities.

There are a number of medical conditions (eg. cystitis, pyelonephritis, diabetes) which can increase urine production, or irritate the bladder to cause nocturia.

See also CYSTITIS; PYELONEPHRITIS; URINATION FREQUENT; URINE

URINATION PAIN

Distressing pain experienced when passing urine (dysuria) is due to inflammation of the bladder, surrounding tissues, or the urethra (tube from the bladder to the outside).

If the bladder becomes infected by bacteria (cystitis) the patient will have a fever, feel pain low down in the front of the belly, will pass urine more frequently, and pain will be felt when passing urine. In severe cases the urine will be cloudy and sometimes blood will be seen in the urine.

Pyelonephritis is an infection of a kidney that causes aching pain in a loin, fever, a general feeling of being unwell, and sometimes frequent uncomfortable passing of urine.

Prostatitis is a bacterial infection of the prostate gland at the base of the penis. Symptoms include difficulty in passing urine, dysuria, pelvic and penis discomfort and pain, and sometimes a fever.

Pelvic inflammatory disease is a widespread infection of the organs and tissues within a woman's pelvis, often caused by a sexually transmitted disease. Pain occurs with passing urine because the infected tissue moves as the bladder size suddenly shrinks.

Urethritis is an infection of the urethra by a bacteria or virus. It is usually a sexually transmitted disease, and there is often a discharge from the urethra, that is more easily seen in men.

Reiter syndrome causes conjunctivitis, inflammation of the urethra, arthritis and painful ulceration of the gums. Its cause is unknown, but settles slowly without treatment, although recurrences are possible.

A prolapse (bulging) of the bladder into the front wall of the vagina in a woman will make passing urine difficult and uncomfortable, and increases the risk of infection.
See also BLADDER; CYSTITIS; KIDNEY; URINATION DIFFICULT; URINE and separate entries for diseases mentioned above.

URINE
The body produces three waste products – urine from the kidneys, faeces from the bowels, and bile, which passes from the liver via the gall bladder to the small intestine and mixes with the faeces.

After being produced by the nephrons in the kidney by filtration of blood, urine moves down the ureters to the bladder where it stored before being expelled when convenient through the urethra to the outside of the body.

Urine consists mainly of water, with a very large number of dissolved waste products (eg. urea), salts (eg. urate), ammonia, enzymes, vitamins (eg. vitamins B and C), minerals, proteins (eg. creatinine), fats and carbohydrates. Many toxic substances and medications are removed from the body in the urine. The concentration of urine will depend on the amount of water in the body (hydration). If the person is well hydrated, dilute urine will be passed. If the person is dehydrated, the urine will be far more concentrated. The colour of the urine varies depending on its concentration from almost completely clear (dilute) to a dark yellow. The yellow colour comes from the pigment that gives blood its red colour, and is removed from the body as red blood cells are broken down and recycled.
See also BLADDER; CYSTITIS; INCONTINENCE OF URINE; KIDNEY; URIC ACID; URINATION DIFFICULT; URINATION FREQUENT; URINATION NIGHTLY; URINATION PAIN; URINE BLOOD; URINE COLOUR ABNORMAL; URINE TESTS

URINE BLOOD
Blood may be seen in the urine as a red tinge, dark red colour or even blood clots, but often the amount present is so small that no difference in colour can be detected by the patient. Doctors can test for extremely small amounts of blood in urine (haematuria) very simply by using a plastic strip with a spot of chemical on it which changes colour if blood is present. The greater the colour change, the greater the amount of blood present in the sample of urine. Examining the urine under a microscope will reveal red blood cells if blood is present.

Diseases of the kidney, ureter (tube from kidney to bladder), bladder, urethra (tube from bladder to outside) and prostate may cause bleeding into the urine. Blood may also find its way into the urine by contamination of a sample during a woman's menstrual period, bleeding piles or from a bleeding sore on the genitals. Red coloured foods (eg. beetroot, some medications) may give a false impression of blood.

By far the most common cause of blood in a urine sample is a bacterial bladder infection (cystitis). The patient will experience a fever, feel pain low down in the front of the belly, will pass urine more frequently, and pain will be felt when passing urine. Virtually every woman will have cystitis at some time, but it is far less common (and usually indicates more serious disease) in men.

Pyelonephritis is a bacterial infection of a kidney. The symptoms include a fever, loin pain (usually only on one side), frequent passing of urine, general tiredness and sometimes blood in the urine.

Glomerulonephritis is a degeneration of the filtering mechanism (glomeruli) of the kidney that occurs in two forms – acute and chronic. Acute glomerulonephritis is often triggered by a bacterial infection (eg. tonsillitis) but may start as a result of other diseases in the body. The patient feels tired, has no appetite, develops headaches and has a low-grade fever. Some patients do not recover from acute glomerulonephritis, and are considered to have chronic glomerulonephritis. There are usually no symptoms until the kidneys start to fail and excessive levels of waste products build up in the bloodstream.

Other causes of blood in the urine include prostatitis (bacterial infection of the prostate gland), a stone in the kidney, extremely vigorous exercise (eg. running a marathon) and a tumour or cancer that develops anywhere in the urinary system.

An injury to the kidneys, bladder or genitals (eg. car accident, fall, sport) may cause damage to these organs and bleeding. If the bleeding persists for more than a couple of days, investigations are necessary to find the exact site of bleeding so that it can be corrected.

Patients who are taking warfarin to thin their blood because of a risk of blood clots, and patients who have poor blood clotting due to other diseases (eg: haemophilia) often have small amounts of blood found in their urine.

Some people with haematuria can have no cause found for the condition, and it is thought that they may have been born with kidneys that leak blood into the urine without any disease being present. This diagnosis is only made after all other possibilities are excluded.

Rare causes of haematuria include haemolytic anaemia, tuberculosis involving the kidneys, septicaemia, autoimmune diseases (eg. systemic lupus erythematosus, polyarteritis nodosa, rheumatoid arthritis, scleroderma), leukaemia and bilharzia (transmitted by a species of snail that is found in freshwater streams, rivers and lakes in Egypt, tropical Africa, the Caribbean and South America). *See also* URINE; URINE COLOUR ABNORMAL and separate entries for diseases mentioned above.

URINE COLOUR ABNORMAL

The urine normally varies in colour from a very pale clear straw colour, to dark brownish yellow, depending on whether the body is trying to get rid of excess fluid, or preserve fluid when dehydrated. Any other colour may indicate a significant disease.

Whitish urine may be due to the presence of white cells (pus), or excess protein or fat.

Urine containing blood may appear brown or red. Red urine may also be due to eating lots of red food (eg. beetroot) and some medications (eg. phenytoin, phenothiazines, phenindione, rifampicin).

In the disease porphyria, brown urine is passed which turns purple on exposure to sunlight.

Excess bilirubin from liver failure will make urine brown, as will eating lots of deeply coloured foods (eg. rhubarb, fava beans, liquorice) or medications such as nitrofurantoin (for urine infections).

Blackish or very dark urine may be caused by the medication methyldopa, cascara and old blood.

With dehydration and diseases of the liver that cause jaundice, the urine may become a dark orange colour. The medications primaquine, riboflavin and sulfasalazine may also give urine an orange colour.

A few medications and naturopathic remedies may cause the urine to take on a blue/green tinge. Examples include amitriptyline (used in psychiatry), triamterene (used to increase urine production), phenol and indigo.
See also URINE BLOOD and separate entries for diseases mentioned above.

URINE GASSY

Very rarely a patient will notice that they are passing gassy urine (pneumaturia). This is a serious symptom that may be caused by a bladder or kidney infection with a gas producing bacteria, or a connection between the bladder and a hollow organ such as the gut or vagina allows air into the bladder.

A number of serious bowel diseases, including Crohn's disease (an inflammation and thickening of the bowel wall), bowel or bladder cancer, diverticulitis (out pocketing of the colon) and an abscess on the bowel may weaken tissue so that the walls of the bowel and bladder breaks down to form a connection (fistula) between them.

In a complicated child birth, the front wall of the vagina may be damaged and an opening into the bladder may be formed that will allow urine to leak constantly into the vagina and air into the bladder.
See also separate entries for diseases mentioned above.

URINE REDUCED

A markedly reduced production of urine (oliguria) is a serious symptom, while a total absence of urine (anuria) is a medical emergency. Kidney diseases and severe dehydration are the usual causes.

Glomerulonephritis is a degeneration of the filtering mechanism (glomeruli) of the kidney that occurs in two forms – acute and chronic. Acute glomerulonephritis is often triggered by a bacterial infection (eg. tonsillitis) but may start as a result of other diseases in the body. The patient feels tired, has no appetite, develops headaches and has a low-grade fever. Other symptoms can include a low urine output, loin (kidney) pain, swelling of the ankles and around the eyes, and cloudy urine. Some patients do not recover from acute glomerulonephritis, and are considered to have chronic glomerulonephritis. There are usually no symptoms until the kidneys start to fail and excessive levels of waste products build up in the bloodstream.

Other causes of kidney failure include infection of both kidneys, severe generalised infections (eg. septicaemia, yellow fever), long standing high blood pressure, blockages to the arteries supplying the kidneys or cysts replacing the kidney tissue. The main symptoms of kidney failure are slowly decreasing urine production, swelling of feet and hands (oedema), headaches, high blood pressure, and eventually lung and heart damage.

Severe dehydration will result in reduced urine production, particularly when associated with massive diarrhoea in diseases such as cholera.

Massive bleeding from an injury, or internally from disease, may result in a dramatically reduced blood volume in the body (shock), and a shutdown of kidney function that can lead rapidly to death if not treated as an emergency.

Some poisons and toxins can cause serious kidney damage that results in reduced urine production. Compounds that contain mercury are particularly insidious in their action as poisons, while carbon tetrachloride (used in dry cleaning) may cause quite a rapid deterioration in kidney function.
See also KIDNEY; URINE and separate entries for diseases mentioned above.

URINE TESTS

After blood tests, urine tests (urinalysis) are the most frequently ordered diagnostic tests. During the course of the day, all the blood is filtered through the kidneys, which means that not only are diseases of the urinary system and kidneys detectable in urine, but also a number of diseases which occur elsewhere in the body, the most common of which is diabetes. However, for something to show up in the urine, it must be a substance that is isolated by the kidneys or picked up as the urine flows from the kidneys to the bladder and out of the body. This does not include disease-fighting antibodies, some hormones, proteins and fats, and many other substances which are symptoms of disease – blood tests are necessary for these. Substances that are found in the urine include sugar, blood, pus, crystals, bile and some proteins.

Urine can be analysed by its appearance, by mixing it with various chemicals and noting the reaction, and by placing a specimen under a microscope to see if organisms are present.

A midstream urine sample is usually collected, so that the patient must pass a small amount of urine into the toilet, then about 10 mLs into a sterile container, then the rest may be passed into the toilet. This reduces the risk of contamination from the skin around the urine opening. On occasions a urine sample is collected straight from the bladder by means of a catheter.

A routine urinalysis begins with an evaluation of the colour, clarity and odour of the sample. Normal urine is clear, pale yellow to dark amber, and has an easily recognisable odour. If the urine is cloudy or has a foul odour, it may indicate the presence of infection. If it has a pinkish tinge, blood may be present, and if it is brownish, there is too much bilirubin – a pigment produced by the liver which is present in excess if the person is suffering from liver disease such as hepatitis. Certain foods, food colourings and drugs turn urine orange.

Urine that smells of ammonia may be a sign of cystitis, whereas the urine of someone suffering from diabetes smells like new-mown hay. What is eaten may be reflected in the smell urine gives off – the pungent smell of garlic is evident in the urine as well as in the breath, spinach produces an acrid smell, mushrooms produce a fetid odour, and truffles a stagnant smell. Even certain deodorants and talcum powders can be detected in the urine.

The most common form of analysis is a dipstick – a plastic strip impregnated with bands of chemicals that change colour when exposed to certain substances. Diabetes, kidney disease, urine infection, liver disease and dehydration can all be diagnosed in this way.

Urine can also be examined under a microscope for the presence of bacteria and cells. Although blood may be visible to the naked eye, the presence of blood cells will normally be confirmed by a microscope analysis. Blood indicates kidney disease or a stone, an infection, ulcer or tumour in the urinary system. If pus is present it generally shows that there is infection or ulceration somewhere in the urinary passages.

If bacteria are present, they can be cultured to confirm the type, and then tested against various antibiotics to see which one will work most effectively.
See also CYSTITIS; KIDNEY; PREGNANCY TESTING; URIC ACID; URINE

URTI

URTI is an acronym for upper respiratory tract infection.
See also COLD, COMMON; INFLUENZA; LARYNGITIS; PHARYNGITIS; SINUSITIS; TONSILLITIS; UVULITIS

URTICARIA

Hives or urticaria (angioedema) is an allergic reaction in the skin. Angioedema is a term used more commonly when the lips or eyelid is involved and becomes severely swollen, with only slight itchiness and redness. Common causes include brushing against plants that may have stinging nettles on their surface, insect bites and chemicals (in creams, cosmetics, soaps) that are applied to the skin. Urticaria may also occur in a non-allergic form, which may be a response to stress. Some patients with long-term and recurrent forms of urticaria may be reacting to salicylates and tartrazine, chemicals that occur naturally in a wide range of foods.

Patients develop red, raised, itchy wheals that may be limited to a small area, or spread widely over the skin. The rash develops rapidly over a few minutes or a couple of hours, and may persist for up to two weeks, although two or three days is average. Some rarer forms may become chronic and last for months or years.

Skin and blood tests can be undertaken in an attempt to identify the substance responsible for the reaction, but these are usually unsuccessful.

Antihistamines or steroids by mouth or injection are the main treatments. Tricyclic antidepressants also seem to benefit some patients with persistent hives. Soothing creams, lotions and baths can give relief to patients during the worst stages of an attack, and a diet which is free of salicylates and tartrazine may be of benefit.
See also ALLERGY; DERMOGRAPHISM; SKIN ITCH

URTICARIA PIGMENTOSA

Urticaria pigmentosa (mastocytosis) is an allergy-like patch reaction in skin that most often affects infants. The patches are made of abnormal collections of mast cells, which contain histamine, and when the cell is disturbed, the histamine is released into the skin. Histamine makes blood vessels leak, resulting in localised itching, swelling and redness.

Brown patches develop on the skin of young children that steadily increase in number over several months or years and blister when rubbed. If many patches are activated at the same time the skin becomes itchy and the infant may become irritable, but it is uncommon for severe symptoms to arise. A severe attack can result in flushing and faintness. Rarely it occurs in adults, when the condition is usually worse, spots are itchier, and may spread to involve internal organs (systemic mastocytosis).

Rubbing a patch causes redness, swelling and itching within a few minutes (Darier's sign). Occasionally a skin biopsy is needed to confirm the diagnosis.

No treatment is normally necessary. Exercise, heat, alcohol and some medications (eg. aspirin, narcotics – codeine and morphine) can aggravate the condition. If symptoms are significant, antihistamine mixture or tablets and steroid creams can be used. Over a few years the skin becomes less irritable and eventually the patches fade away. By the teenage years, most patches will have gone.
See also ALLERGY

UTA
See CUTANEOUS LEISCHMANIASIS

UTERINE CANCER
See CHORIOCARCINOMA OF THE UTERUS; ENDOMETRIAL CARCINOMA

UTERINE FIBROIDS
See FIBROIDS OF THE UTERUS

UTERINE MOLE
A uterine or hydatidiform mole is a dramatic abnormal overdevelopment of the placenta that occurs in one out of every 750 pregnancies. Any foetus that is present dies at a very early stage.

Multiple cysts develop in the placenta so that it appears like a large bunch of grapes. The woman may not be aware of the problem until it is well advanced, at fourteen to twenty weeks of pregnancy, when abnormal vaginal bleeding or discharge may occur, and the womb feels much larger than expected. Occasionally, some of the grape-like cysts may be passed. One complication is an invasive mole, in which the abnormal placenta penetrates through the wall of the uterus and damages it to the point where a hysterectomy is necessary. More seriously, 4% of women develop cancer in the abnormal tissue (choriocarcinoma).

An ultrasound scan and blood tests confirm the diagnosis, at which point immediate surgical removal of the abnormal placenta from the uterus through the cervix is essential.

The prognosis is usually very good, but careful follow-up with blood tests and gynaecological examinations is essential.
See also CHORIOCARCINOMA OF THE UTERUS; PLACENTA; UTERUS

UTERINE PROLAPSE
See VAGINAL PROLAPSE

UTERUS
The uterus or womb is the hollow muscular organ in women in which a baby grows. It is located in the pelvis and is loosely tethered to the pelvic walls by two ligaments on each side, the round and broad ligaments, giving it a high degree of mobility. It leans forwards when the rectum is full and backwards when the bladder is full. During pregnancy it expands upwards as far as the ribs. In a non-pregnant woman the uterus looks something like an upside-down pear. It is about 7.5cm. long and 5cm. wide. The cavity of a non-pregnant uterus is small and narrow, virtually a slit.

The upper part of the uterus is called the body, and is attached to the two egg-conducting Fallopian tubes. It narrows at the lower end to form the cervix, or neck, which protrudes into the vagina and provides a passage for sperm to enter and menstrual blood to flow out.

The wall of the uterus is made up of three separate layers. The outer layer is a tough protective covering called the perimetrium. In the middle is a thick layer of muscle called the myometrium, while the inner lining consists of a blood-enriched mucous membrane called the endometrium.

Each month the endometrium thickens to prepare for the implantation of a fertilised egg. If this does not eventuate, all but the deepest

FEMALE REPRODUCTIVE SYSTEM

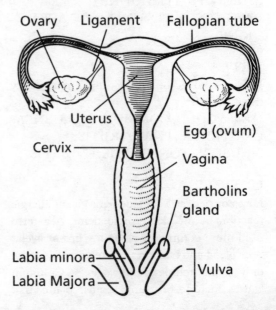

part of the endometrium is discarded, leading to the monthly menstrual period. This takes place about fourteen days after an egg has been released. The menstrual flow consists of the liquefied dead endometrium together with some blood lost in the process. If fertilisation, or pregnancy, does occur, the embryo is implanted in the endometrium and nourished by the mother's blood supply. The mother's and the embryo's blood circulations interact through the placenta.

The muscles in the myometrium are among the strongest in the human body. They expand to accommodate the growing foetus, and when the time comes for the baby to be born they engage in a series of contractions, helping the hitherto tightly closed cervix to open and propelling the baby into the vagina during labour. About six weeks after pregnancy, the muscles have shrunk again and the uterus has returned to its normal size.
See also CERVIX; ENDOMETRIAL CARCINOMA; FALLOPIAN TUBES; HYSTERECTOMY; HYSTEROSCOPY; LABOUR; MENSTRUAL PERIOD; MICROWAVE ENDOMETRIAL ABLATION; PREGNANCY; VAGINA.

UTERUS BLEEDING
See MENSTRUAL PERIOD; VAGINAL BLEEDING ABNORMAL

UVEITIS
Inflammation of the iris, the coloured part of the eye, is iritis. When the surrounding tissues are also involved (more common), it is called uveitis. Both conditions may be due to an infection such as toxoplasmosis, tuberculosis or syphilis (exogenous iritis), or may be associated with inflammatory diseases in other parts of the body, including psoriasis, ankylosing spondylitis, and some bowel conditions (endogenous iritis).

Usually it involves only one eye, which will suddenly become red and painful with blurred vision. Bright lights will aggravate the eye pain and the pupil is small. In the exogenous form, there is less pain and the onset is slower, but this form often results in some permanent deterioration in vision.

Any underlying infection or disease must be treated if possible, and the eye is made more comfortable with warm compresses. Steroid eye drops are used to reduce inflammation.

Usually recovery is satisfactorily, but recurrences are common.
See also ANKYLOSING SPONDYLITIS; EYE; EYE RED; PSORIASIS

UVULA
The soft palate that forms the back one-third of the roof of the mouth ends in a soft loop of tissue known as the uvula, which can be seen dangling down the back of the throat when the mouth is wide open. It acts to prevent food going into the back of the nose when swallowing.
See PALATE; PHARYNX

VIEW INTO MOUTH

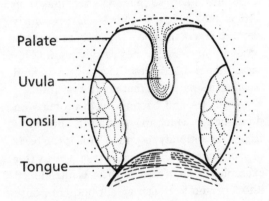

Palate — Uvula — Tonsil — Tongue

UVULITIS
A bacterial, viral or fungal infection of the uvula, which is the soft tag of flesh that hangs down the back of the throat from the soft palate, is called uvulitis. The symptoms include a painful throat, pain with swallowing, excess saliva production, enlarged lymph nodes in the neck and a fever. Sometimes the uvula may ulcerate, and the infection may spread to the tonsils or other nearby tissues.

Treatments include antibiotics for bacterial infections, and antifungal lozenges or gels for fungal infections. Sometimes a swab is taken to identify the responsible organism. All types of infection, including viral, are eased by anaesthetic and antiseptic gargles or lozenges, and paracetamol or aspirin. Bacterial and fungal infections settle rapidly with treatment, while viral infections settle after a few days.
See also BACTERIA; FUNGI; PHARYNGITIS; TONSILLITIS; VIRUS

V

VACCINATION

Vaccination is the process in which a substance (antigen) is injected, swallowed or otherwise taken into the body in order to trigger a reaction in the immune system, which causes the production of proteins (immunoglobulins) known as antibodies. A very small number of the antibodies against a particular antigen remain in the body for many years, or for the rest of the patient's life. While these antibodies remain, the body retains the memory of how to produce them, so that at a later time, if an antigen to which it has been previously exposed enters the body, the body can rapidly produce more antibodies to destroy it. This rapid response enables the body to defend itself against antigens that may be harmful.

All viruses and bacteria have proteins on their surface which may act as an antigen to trigger an antibody response. This is the basis of vaccination. A harmless part of a virus (for example), or all of a killed virus, is introduced into a person to trigger an antibody response without causing the disease for which the virus is normally responsible. This then gives long term immunity against the virus. The immune system sometimes needs several prompts by repeated doses of the antigen in order to obtain long term immunity. A patient whose immune system has responded appropriately to the vaccination so that they have immunity is said to have seroconverted (become seropositive). This means that the antibodies against the virus can be detected by the appropriate blood test. A small number of patients may not form adequate levels of antibodies in response to an antigen and are described as failing to seroconvert (they are seronegative).

Viruses are far simpler structures than bacteria, and as a result vaccines against viruses are far easier to produce than those against bacteria, or even more complex parasites. The majority of vaccines available act against viruses, there are a few against bacteria, and none as yet against parasites, although research is continuing on a vaccine that will act against the malaria parasite.

Once a person has caught a viral infection (eg. chickenpox), they normally have lifelong immunity to that disease due to the antibody response that the first infection triggered in the patient.

Many other substances can act as antigens, including all types of cells, many chemicals, foods, dusts, pollens etc. In most vases the body recognises that these antigens are not harmful and has no, or a minimal reaction to these antigens, but in some people the antibody response to a particular antigen may become excessive to create an allergy reaction due to an over reaction by the immune system. *See also* ANTIBODY; ANTIGEN; ALLERGY; BACTERIA; IMMUNE TESTS; JENNER, EDWARD; TRAVEL IMMUNISATION; VACCINATION OF CHILDREN; VACCINES; VIRUS

VACCINATION OF CHILDREN

Unless there are very good medical grounds not to vaccinate, all children should receive the full course of injections to protect them against tetanus, whooping cough and diphtheria; the HiB vaccine against Haemophilus influenzae B infections; the measles, mumps and rubella vaccine; hepatitis B vaccine; and the Sabin vaccine by mouth for polio. A chickenpox vaccine has been available since 2000 and is being steadily more widely used and a Meningococcal meningitis vaccine was introduced in 2002. The risk of vaccination is infinitesimal, and when compared with the potential side effects of any one of these diseases, it is a far preferable course of action. Another person (adult or child) only has to breathe the infecting germs in the direction of a child and he or she may catch one of these dread diseases.

Tetanus is around us constantly in the soil. The bacteria causing this disease are carried by animals and are therefore not likely to be eradicated in the near future. The series of tetanus injections received as a child do not give lifelong immunity, and boosters are required every ten years, or more frequently if injury occurs.

Most young doctors have never seen a case of diphtheria. The incidence of this disease is now low, but older citizens may recall losing childhood friends to it. Diphtheria is still around though, and many children still catch the disease each year, and suffer the difficulty in breathing, and possible heart complications that can accompany it.

Whooping cough is becoming a very worrying problem, as it is increasing in the community due to under-vaccination of many children. This is a potentially fatal disease, and even if the child survives the distress of weeks or months of severe coughing, they may be left with permanent brain or lung damage.

Haemophilus influenzae B causes a severe form of meningitis, and rarely a throat infection (epiglottitis) that can cause part of the throat to swell so much that the child suffocates. This infection can be prevented by three or four HiB vaccines starting at two months of age.

Hepatitis B is a viral infection of the liver, which may cause life long complications. It is spread by blood, bodily fluids and sex. It requires three vaccinations in childhood.

Measles is often considered to be a mild disease, but a small percentage of children even in developed countries develop debilitating ear, chest and brain complications that may affect them for the rest of their lives. The measles vaccine is combined with the mumps and rubella vaccination and is given at twelve months and again at four years of age, but it can be given at any age if vaccination has been neglected at the correct age.

Mumps is a relatively benign disease of childhood, but it too may have serious consequences, particularly if it is caught in adult life when it may spread to the testes and cause sterility, or infect the brain and cause permanent damage.

Polio was probably the most feared of childhood diseases. If it didn't kill a child, it probably left them crippled for life. 1956 was the last year before the original Salk injectable vaccine became available, and it was the year of the last polio epidemic in Australia. Parents were so scared for their children that when the vaccine became available, there were queues down the street from the clinic front doors that rivalled the scene before a modern pop concert. They wanted their children protected, and as soon as possible. The Sabin vaccine is now given by mouth to prevent this disease, but boosters are required into adult life every ten years.

German measles (rubella) vaccination is more important for girls as it can cause severe deformities to the foetus if contracted in pregnancy. To reduce the risk of spreading this disease, the vaccination is given in combination with measles and mumps at twelve months of age, and an additional booster is given at four years of age.

All routine childhood immunisations, except for polio, are now given by injection. The polio vaccine (Sabin) is given as a few drops that are swallowed. If the child has a high fever or other significant illness, the vaccination may be delayed for a few days until it has recovered.

Significant complications after all childhood vaccinations are rare. A sore arm or leg at the site of the injection is relatively common, and likely to be worse with bruising caused by movement of the child during the injection. Firm restraint by the parent for the fifteen seconds that the injection takes can prevent this.

Fever and irritability may occur after a triple antigen, and giving paracetamol before the injection is sensible.

Measles vaccines may cause a very mild case of measles (usually the rash only) in about 2% of children.

Any other risks are minimal, and certainly far rarer than the serious complications of any of these diseases.
See also BABIES; CHILDHOOD; VACCINATION; VACCINES and under individual diseases.

VACCINES

Vaccines are substances that are introduced into the body (by injection, tablet or mixture) to induce immunity to a particular disease. Vaccines commonly available include those that protect against the following diseases.

Side effects vary between different vaccines but are usually confined to local inflammation at the site of the injection, fevers, irritability, and in rare cases, a very mild dose of the disease (eg. measles).
See also VACCINATION; VACCINATION OF CHILDREN and under individual diseases.

COMMON VACCINES AVAILABLE

DISEASE	AGE GIVEN	BOOSTER	EFFECTIVE	COMMENTS
Chickenpox	9mo. to 12 years 13+ years	Nil 6 weeks	Not known	Introduced in 2000
Cholera	2 years+	6mo.	6mo.	Some travellers only Oral vaccine
Diphtheria	2mo.+	3 by 18mo.	10 years	Combined with tetanus and pertussis.
Haemophilus	2mo.+	2 by 18mo.	5 years	HiB meningitis and infantile throat infection.
Hepatitis A	16 years.+	6-12 mo.	20 years+	May be combined with hepatitis B.
Hepatitis B	Birth+	2 by 4 mo.	5 years+	May be combined with hepatitis A.
Influenza	6 years+	Annually	One year.	Form changes every year.
Measles	1 year	5 years	Long term	Combined with rubella & mumps
Meningococcus	2 years+	3 years	Long term	Form of meningitis. Now routine
Mumps	1 year	5 years	Long term	Combined with measles & rubella
Pertussis	2mo.+	3 by 18mo.	10 years	Whooping cough. Combined with tetanus
Plague	As required	As required	Short term	Given in epidemics only.
Pneumonia	60 years+	5 years	5 years	Lower age for those at high risk
Polio	2mo.+	4 by 5 years	10 years	Sabin oral vaccine
Q fever	Adults	No	Long term	After skin tests in high risk people.
Rabies	As required	No	Short term	Given immediately after suspect bite.
Rubella	1 year	5 years	Long term	May be combined with mumps & measles.
Tetanus	2mo.+	3 by 18mo.	5 to 10 years	Combined with diphtheria.
Tuberculosis	birth	Nil	Long term	BCG vaccine. Routine in some countries.
Typhoid	2 years+ 12 years+	3 years 6mo.	3 years 6mo.	Injection. Oral capsules
Yellow fever	6 years+	10 years	10 years	African & South American travellers only

VACUUM EXTRACTION
See FORCEPS DELIVERY

VAGINA
The vagina is the passage connecting the uterus (womb) to the outside of the body. Usually about eight cm. long, it is joined to the uterus at the cervix, and passes through the lower part of the woman's body behind the urethra and bladder and in front of the rectum. It is the passage into which the male penis is inserted during sexual intercourse. Vaginal secretions are released during sexual arousal and it can expand to facilitate intercourse. Sperm ejaculated during intercourse travel through the cervix and into the uterus and Fallopian tubes to fertilise an egg if one has been released.

The lining of the vaginal wall is made up of a moist mucous membrane arranged in folds, which enable its muscular tissue to expand for the purposes of sexual intercourse and childbirth. The muscles in the wall of the vagina will also contract in spasms when a woman has an orgasm during intercourse. This rhythmic contraction aids the movement of the ejaculated sperm towards the cervix and uterus.

In children the external opening to the vagina is partly covered by a thin mucous membrane called the hymen. This will be broken at the time of first sexual intercourse, or it may break spontaneously earlier than this.

FEMALE REPRODUCTIVE SYSTEM

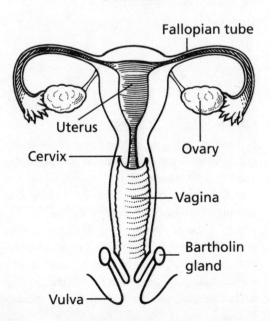

See also CERVIX; HYMEN; PESSARY; UTERUS; VAGINAL PROLAPSE; VAGINISMUS; VAGINITIS; VULVA

VAGINAL BLEEDING ABNORMAL
Abnormal vaginal bleeding that occurs away from the normal menstrual period, may be caused by conditions in the vagina, uterus and ovaries, or may be hormonal.

A woman may not realise that she is pregnant, and an abnormal bleed may be caused by a very early miscarriage. Up to 15% of all pregnancies end as a miscarriage, usually because of some abnormality in the developing foetus or placenta.

During the menopause, instead of cycling smoothly and evenly through the monthly changes, sex hormone levels start to change suddenly and inappropriately. This causes irregular menstrual periods, hot flushes, headaches, irritability, personality changes, breast tenderness, tiredness and pelvic discomfort.

Taking the oral contraceptive pill will normally regulate the menstrual cycle very effectively, but if a pill is missed, or fails to work because of vomiting, diarrhoea or interaction with other medications (eg. antibiotics), the sudden change in hormone levels may cause an irregular bleed. A similar effect can occur when taking hormone replacement therapy after the menopause.

Endometriosis is a sinister disease which is due to cells that normally line the inside of the uterus becoming displaced, and moving through the Fallopian tubes to settle around the ovary, in the tubes themselves, or on other organs in the belly. In these abnormal positions they proliferate, and when a menstrual period occurs, they bleed as though they were still in the uterus. This results in pain, adhesions, damage to the organs they are attached to, and infertility.

A psychological stress (eg. death in family, losing job) may affect a woman's pituitary gland under the brain and thus her sex hormone levels so that her menstrual periods stop or become frequent and irregular.

An intrauterine contraceptive device (IUD) may irritate the uterus to cause a vaginal discharge and irregular bleeding.

Other uterine causes of abnormal vaginal bleeding include fibroids (balls of scar tissue in the muscular wall of the uterus), pelvic inflammatory disease, ectopic pregnancy (pregnancy outside the uterus), a prolapsed uterus (uterus slips down into vagina), irritation of the uterus after an abortion, a hydatidiform mole (an overdeveloped cystic placenta) polyps, and tumours or cancer of the uterus (endometrial carcinoma).

Vaginal causes include an infection of the vagina (vaginitis), ulceration and bleeding from the wall of the vagina, ulcerated or cancerous cervix, an injury to the vagina from over enthusiastic sex, using mechanical sex aids or a fall astride a bar.

Ovarian causes include mittelschmerz (slight blood loss and pain at the time of ovulation), and tumours, cysts or cancer of the ovary.

Any disease that slows the rate at which blood clots, and any drugs used to slow blood clotting (eg. warfarin) may cause abnormal vaginal bleeding if the dose is too high.
See also MENSTRUAL PERIOD;
MENSTRUAL PERIODS HEAVY;
MENSTRUAL PERIODS, LACK OF;
VAGINAL DISCHARGE and separate entries for diseases mentioned above.

VAGINAL DISCHARGE
A vaginal discharge can vary from a minimal clear discharge due to excess production of the normal moisture in the vagina, to copious quantities of pus, and blood.

The most common cause is leucorrhoea, which is not a disease. The vagina is a moist cavity, and like the mouth, there are glands that produce the mucus that lubricates the vagina. If these glands become over active because of sexual stimulation, or taking oestrogen as a medication (eg. in the contraceptive pill or for symptoms of menopause), too much mucus will be produced, and overflow as a discharge. Some women produce more mucus than others, and may have long term trouble with this type of loss.

The hormonal stimulation of the uterus and vagina that occurs with pregnancy will often cause a clear discharge, particularly in the last couple of months.

Thrush is a fungal infection of the vagina caused by *Candida albicans*, and virtually every woman will have several episodes of this infection during her life. The fungus lives normally in the gut, but when there is moisture on the skin around the vagina and anus from sweating or sexual stimulation, the fungus can migrate into the vagina. Sexual intercourse helps the fungus into the vagina where it finds a warm, moist environment in which to live and prosper. The result is a white vaginal discharge that irritates the skin of the vulva, and creates an intense itch that is socially unacceptable to scratch in public.

A single-celled animal, *Trichomonas vaginalis*, may cause infections in a woman's vagina, and the urethra (urine tube) of both men and women. The infection is transmitted by sexual intercourse. In women, the vaginal infection causes a foul-smelling, yellow/green, frothy discharge. There may be mild itching or soreness around the outside of the vagina.

Other possible causes include oozing from a damaged or ulcerated cervix (particularly after childbirth), a forgotten tampon or other foreign body (particularly in little girls), an intrauterine contraceptive device (IUD), bacterial infections of the vagina (vaginitis), tumours or cancers of the cervix or uterus, pelvic inflammatory disease (widespread infection of the uterus and other organs within the pelvis), intestinal worms that migrate into the vagina, and after an abortion a coloured or smelly discharge is a serious sign that there may be an infection in the uterus.

A vaginal discharge in a young girl must be considered to be due to sexual abuse until proved otherwise. Infections and injury to the vagina are responsible.
See also VAGINA; VAGINAL BLEEDING ABNORMAL and separate entries for diseases mentioned above.

VAGINAL INFECTION
See VAGINITIS

VAGINAL ITCH
See GENITAL ITCH

VAGINAL PROLAPSE
A vaginal prolapse is the protrusion of an organ into the vagina, caused primarily by gravity. A uterine prolapse occurs when the uterus (womb) moves down the vagina and completely fills it. Occasionally the cervix, which is the lowest part of the uterus, may protrude through the vulva to the outside. Part of the bladder which is in front of the vagina, may push back into the vagina causing a bladder prolapse (cystocoele). The rectum

(last part of the large intestine) may push forward into the vagina as a rectal prolapse (rectocoele). Occasionally there is a combination of all three types of prolapse.

During childbirth, the vagina becomes very stretched, and does not always return to its original size. The muscles around the vagina weaken and the ligaments supporting the uterus may stretch and sag. All these factors may lead to vaginal prolapse years later.

A cystocoele may cause difficulty in passing urine, urinary infections and incontinence. A rectocoele causes difficulty in passing faeces and other bowel problems. A uterine prolapse causes discomfort and pain, and ulceration of the cervix may result in infections and bleeding.

The prolapse may be repaired by an operation that uses strong natural material in the pelvis and artificial slings to support the prolapsed organ. In elderly women, a ring inserted into the vagina may be used to hold prolapse in the correct place. Younger women can prevent the problem by pelvic floor exercises under the guidance of a physiotherapist both before and after the delivery of their babies. The results of surgery are reasonable, but recurrences are possible.
See also RECTAL PROLAPSE; UTERUS; VAGINA

VAGINAL THRUSH
See THRUSH

VAGINAL ULCER
See GENITAL ULCER

VAGINISMUS
Vaginismus is a strong spasm of the muscles around the vagina. It is an unconscious reaction, normally triggered by anxiety related to sex. The initial trigger may be fear (of pregnancy, pain, etc.), guilt, lack of privacy, anxiety about expectations, lack of self confidence, previous rape or sexual assault, and other psychological factors. Sexual intercourse is impossible, as the man is unable to penetrate the woman.

Treatment consists of psychological counselling, medication to reduce anxiety and vaginal dilators (dildo – artificial penises) of gradually increasing width. Confidence must be gained in using one size of dildo before the next size is attempted. Treatment gives reasonable results if the woman is well motivated and has an understanding partner.
See also SEXUAL INTERCOURSE PAIN; VAGINA; VULVODYNIA

VAGINITIS
Vaginitis is any form of inflammation of the vagina, or a vaginal infection by any of a

LONGITUDINAL SECTION OF FEMALE PELVIS

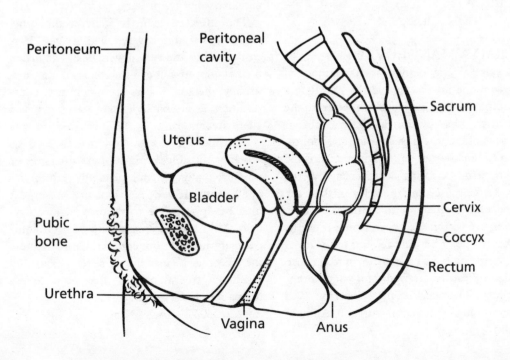

number of different bacteria. Many bacteria may be responsible, including *Gardnerella vaginalis*, which is slightly unusual in that it requires an oxygen-free and alkaline environment. The upper end of the vagina can be oxygen-free, but is normally slightly acid. It may become alkaline with semen after sex, changing sexual partners, hormonal changes at different times of the month, and using antibiotics. Most other infections (eg. gonorrhoea) are sexually transmitted venereal diseases. The infection may spread into the uterus and cause pelvic inflammatory disease, or to adjacent glands to cause a Bartholin cyst infection.

The woman develops a greyish fish-smelling vaginal discharge, with soreness and redness of the vagina. The diagnosis and type of bacteria present determined by taking a swab from the vagina and having it examined and cultured.

Treatments include appropriate antibiotic tablets by mouth, antiseptic douches (eg. iodine solution), and acidic gels or creams in the vagina. In recurrent cases the male sexual partner may need to be treated.
See also ATROPHIC VAGINITIS; BARTHOLIN'S CYST; PELVIC INFLAMMATORY DISEASE; VAGINA; VAGINAL DISCHARGE; VENEREAL DISEASES

VALACICLOVIR
See ANTIVIRALS

VALPROATE
See ANTICONVULSANTS

VALSALVA MANOEUVRE
The valsalva manoeuvre is a method of increasing the air pressure in the middle ear ('popping' the ear), which is connected to the back of the nose by the Eustachian tube. It involves holding the nose, closing the mouth, trying to breathe out and forcing air into the ears, hopefully clearing any blockage of the tube. At the same time the veins in the neck will become swollen due to an increase of the air pressure within the chest, which prevents the return of blood from the veins to the heart for a moment, and so the manoeuvre can also be used to test the strength of a pneumothorax repair. The name comes from the 17th century Italian (Bologna) surgeon Antonio Valsalva.

See also EUSTACHIAN TUBE BLOCKAGE; PNEUMOTHORAX

VANCOMYCIN
See ANTIANAEROBES

VANCOMYCIN AND METHICILLIN RESISTANT *STAPHYLOCOCCUS AUREUS*
See STAPHYLOCOCCUS AUREUS

VARICELLA
See CHICKENPOX; SHINGLES

VARICOCOELE
A varicocoele is a knot of soft, slightly tender, blue varicose veins surrounding the testes in the scrotum. The cause is unknown, but it is probably an inherited tendency. The extra heat produced by these veins can sometimes affect sperm production and fertility. Surgical removal can be performed if the varicocoele is uncomfortable or if infertility is a potential problem.
See also TESTICLE; VARICOSE VEINS

VARICOSE ECZEMA
Varicose or hypostatic eczema is a chronic skin deterioration that affects women more than men, and is far more common in the elderly. The cause is a poor return of blood through the veins from the feet to the heart, and as a result blood pools in the feet, causing pressure on the skin. It is more common if varicose veins are present.

The affected skin is itchy, red, shiny, swollen, dry and covered with scales. It is easily injured and very slow to heal. The inside of the shin, just above the ankle, is the area usually affected. Ulcers are a common complication, as are bacterial skin infections, and allergy reactions.

Treatment involves elevating the leg as much as possible, using support stockings or pressure bandages, and raising the foot of the bed slightly. If varicose veins are present, it may be appropriate to remove them surgically. Mild steroid creams and coal tar solutions are used on the eczema. Unfortunately the eczema is usually persistent, and the results of treatment are often poor unless the patient is very compliant.
See also ECZEMA; VENOUS ULCER

VARICOSE ULCER
See VENOUS ULCER

VARICOSE VEINS

Varicose veins are the over-dilation of the superficial veins in the legs. Two networks of veins in the legs move the blood from the feet back to the heart. One is superficial, lying just under the skin, while the other system of veins is deep in the muscles. The superficial venous system may dilate to form varicose veins.

Muscle contractions in the leg squeeze the veins, and with the aid of one-way valves scattered through the venous network, the blood is steadily pushed back towards the heart. Pregnancy (because the growing baby puts pressure on veins in the pelvis) and prolonged standing (eg. hairdressing, shop assistant) make it difficult for the blood to move up from the legs into the body and the pooled blood stretches the veins, which then damages the one-way valves. The damaged valves allow more blood to remain in the veins, stretching them further. Reducing the amount of standing, wearing elastic support stockings and regularly exercising the muscles in the legs while standing may prevent varicose veins.

Sufferers develop tired, aching, swollen legs, with large, ugly, blue, knotted veins under blotchy, red and sometimes ulcerated skin. Rupture of a vein may cause severe bruising, or a cut will bleed profusely (treated by elevating the leg and applying compression).

Tablets (eg. hydroxyethyl rutosides) can reduce the leg ache, but only surgical procedures can permanently remove the veins. Injections of a type of glue, diathermy (hot electric needle) or lasers may be used to destroy small, fine, spider-like networks of veins. Larger isolated veins can be removed one at a time by a 'nick and pick' procedure, with a small cut being made over each vein to allow its removal. Vein stripping involves removing most of the superficial veins on one side of the leg from the groin to the ankle.

Although there is no absolute cure, the symptoms can usually be reduced. Surgery is successful in most patients, but does not prevent the development of new veins, and skin staining caused by the varicosities is usually permanent.

See also VARICOCOELE; VEIN; VENOUS ULCER

VARIOLA MAJOR
See SMALLPOX

VAS DEFERENS

The tube that connects the epididymis at the back of the testicle to the urethra is the vas deferens. Sperm are manufactured in the testicles and stored in the epididymis. Once mature, the sperm swim along the vas deferens for storage in the seminal vesicles, situated just below the prostate gland. When a man ejaculates during sexual intercourse, vigourous contractions in the muscular walls of the vas deferens, seminal vesicles and prostate push semen into the urethra, passing through the prostate, where it collects more fluid, down the length of the penis to the tip from which it is ejaculated.

See also PENIS; PROSTATE; SEMINAL VESICLE; TESTICLE; VASECTOMY

VASECTOMY

A vasectomy is the procedure in which the vas deferens (sperm tubes) of a man are cut and tied or clipped in order to prevent him from fathering children. It is a simpler operation than the sterilisation (tubal ligation) of a woman and is growing in popularity as men increasingly accept responsibility for family planning. Many men are very anxious about a vasectomy, but there is no effect on their libido or masculinity.

Sperm are produced by the testes throughout adult life at a relatively constant rate. The sperm enter a complex network of small tubules in the epididymis which unite to form the vas deferens. The sperm pass along this tube to a storage sac (the seminal vesicle) in the groin where they await the next ejaculation.

The walls of the sperm storage sac secrete a fluid which nourishes the sperm and which, along with an exudate from the prostate gland, forms 95% of the semen passed by the man during intercourse. When he ejaculates, the sperm and supporting fluid (called semen when combined) pass down the sperm tube to its junction with the urethra, and then along this tube to the outside of the penis.

In a vasectomy operation, a local anaesthetic numbs the side of the scrotum, and through a small incision, the doctor cuts, burns and ties or clips the sperm tube (vas deferens) which lies just under the surface, so no further sperm can pass along it from the testes. Usually a small section of the vas is

MALE ANATOMY

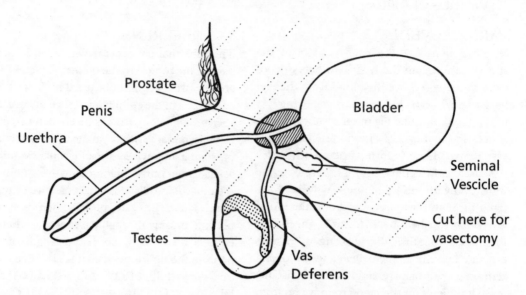

removed to prevent the ends from rejoining. The procedure may be done in the doctor's rooms, or as a day patient in a private hospital. The procedure is very simple and brief, and no pain is felt. There is usually some bruising and discomfort of the scrotum for a few days after the operation, but other complications are rare. There is always a small risk that the cut sperm tubes may spontaneously reconnect at a later time making the man fertile again.

The man is not immediately sterile after the operation. Because sperm are stored in the sac above where the tube is tied, this must be emptied by about a dozen ejaculations over the next few weeks. It is essential to have a test done about six weeks after the operation to check that no sperm are getting through or remaining in storage. The couple can stop their other contraceptive measures only after this test is confirmed.

The male hormones which establish and maintain masculinity are also produced in the testes. These are not affected in any way by the operation as they enter the blood stream directly from the testes and continue to function normally. The man's ejaculation is not affected either, as the fluid from the sperm storage sac is passed as normal.

Although reversal procedures are sometimes possible, it should be considered to be a permanent procedure at the time it is performed. The success rate of vasectomy reversal is higher than with a tubal ligation but by no means high enough for a couple to be able to

regard it as anything but a possibility. A decision about a vasectomy needs to be taken on the basis that it is permanent and that, even if his marriage breaks down or his child dies the man will be unable to have further children. *See also* CONTRACEPTIVES; SEMEN TEST; SEMINAL VESICLE; TUBAL LIGATION; VAS DEFERENS

VASOCONSTRICTORS

Vasoconstrictors are drugs that constrict (reduce in size) blood vessels (arteries in particular) and raise blood pressure. When a patient collapses with a heart attack, severe allergy or shock, it is often due to the sudden over dilation of all the arteries in the body, which causes a very low blood pressure. A doctor giving an injection of a vasoconstrictor such as adrenaline (an adrenergic stimulant) can correct this.

Otherwise, vasoconstrictors are used mainly as drops in the eye and nose, and as additives (eg. pseudoephedrine – a decongestant) to some cold and hay fever remedies.

Vasoconstrictor eye drops constrict any dilated arteries criss-crossing the white of the eye to leave it looking and feeling much better. Examples include antazoline, naphazoline and tetrahydrazolin. They may cause eye stinging for a few seconds after use and must not be used in patients with glaucoma.

Nose drops and sprays containing phenylephrine shrink down the dilated arteries in the nose that develop with hay fever. They can therefore ease the congestion and stuffiness in the nose and allow victims to breathe more easily. Overuse can cause a rebound effect, and the nose becomes inflamed because the drops cause it to swell again. Always follow the directions on these drops and sprays carefully.

All swallowed or injected vasoconstrictors should be used with caution in patients with high blood pressure, diabetes, thyroid disease or heart disease.
See also ADRENERGIC STIMULANTS; DECONGESTANTS; MEDICATION

VASODILATORS

Arteries, and to a lesser extent veins, are surrounded by tiny muscles that control the diameter of the blood vessel tube by contracting and relaxing it. If arteries in the arms and legs are excessively contracted or blocked by plaques of cholesterol (atherosclerosis), the amount of blood reaching the distant parts of the body may be insufficient for them to work properly. The earliest sign of a poor blood supply is pallor of the skin. This is followed by muscle weakness and pain. Vasodilators will relax the tiny muscles around the artery, enabling it to dilate to its maximum extent and allowing the greatest possible amount of blood to reach the affected areas. Vasodilators can also be used in the emergency treatment of very high blood pressure.

Vasodilator tablets and injections include many other drugs that have been classified elsewhere. For example, nifedipine (a calcium channel blocker) may be used for high blood pressure and also used to dilate arteries and veins.

Dizziness and noises in the ears (tinnitus) associated with Ménière's disease can be caused by a poor blood supply to the ears, and using vasodilators such as betahistine (Serc) can sometimes help this problem. Betahistine must not be used in pregnancy, children, asthmatics or patients with a peptic ulcer, but side effects are minimal.

Oxpentifylline (Trental) is used to help poor circulation to the arms and legs. Side effects may include nausea, heartburn, dizziness and a hot flush. It should not be used in patients with a peptic ulcer or heart disease.
See also ARTERY; CALCIUM CHANNEL BLOCKERS; MEDICATION

VASOMOTOR RHINITIS

The inside of the nose and sinuses is lined with a moist (mucus) membrane. If inflamed, the glands in the mucus membrane swell up and secrete extra amounts of mucus that overflows the sinus cavities. There are many causes of inflammation (eg. infection, allergy), but in vasomotor rhinitis the irritation of the nasal mucosa is caused by non-specific irritants such as temperature changes (eg. walking into an air-conditioned building), hormonal changes (more mucus may be produced at certain times in a woman's monthly cycle), anxiety and stress (eg. an exam or interview), eating, drinking alcohol and changes in position (eg. getting out of bed may start a sneezing fit).

Patients experience episodes of constant sneezing, and a constant drip of clear watery mucus from the nose. Secondary bacterial infections may occur and cause sinusitis or pharyngitis. Patients also need to be careful about flying or changing altitude, as this can force phlegm up the Eustachian tubes into the middle ears to cause pain and infection.

Cetrizine and other sedating antihistamines (non-sedating ones are not useful as they only act against allergies) shrink down the swollen mucus membranes and reduce the production of mucus, and steroid or ipratropium nasal sprays may prevent the nose from reacting excessively. The minority who continue to have long term symptoms may be helped by surgery to reduce the amount of mucus membrane in the nose, and removing some curled up bones inside the nose (turbinates) that are covered with mucus membrane.
See also HAY FEVER; NOSE; POST-NASAL DRIP; SINUSITIS; SNEEZE

VASOVAGAL SYNDROME

The vasovagal syndrome may be the cause of repeated fainting attacks. Triggers may include stress, anxiety, or significant emotional or physical upset. Past stresses may cause an attack by the recall of a memory at times when there is another minor stress or possibility of fainting.

Patients experience recurrent episodes of fainting, low blood pressure, a pale complexion and slow heart rate. There is always the possibility of injury from falling during an attack.

Doctors may detect low blood pressure, a slow pulse and abnormal ECG (electrocardiogram) during an attack.

Patients should avoid precipitating causes (eg. prolonged standing), and should lie down or bend forward with the start of symptoms, and use aromatic inhalations.
See also FAINT; POST-TRAUMATIC STRESS DISORDER

VASTUS MUSCLES
See QUADRICEPS MUSCLE

VATER, AMPULLA OF
See PANCREAS

VC
See VITAL CAPACITY

VD
See VENEREAL DISEASES

VEGAN
See VEGETARIAN DIET

VEGETARIAN DIET
There are far more vegetarians in the world than meat eaters, simply because vegetables, grains and the like are easier to keep without refrigeration and are usually more readily available. However, most people in the developed world, for many generations, have been enthusiastic consumers of meat. To a degree this is changing, for reasons including health, religion, environmental concerns and simple fashion.

There are three main types of vegetarian diet. The most common form is lacto-ovo-vegetarianism in which meat is excluded but fish is allowed, while a vegan diet excludes all animal products, ie. not only meat and fish but also dairy produce and eggs.

There is no reason why a vegetarian diet cannot be as healthy as a diet containing meat, provided that protein is obtained from nuts, cereals or pulses (eg. beans). Vegetarians also need to ensure they get adequate supplies of iron, zinc and calcium, which are found in good supply in meat and milk. Women in particular have double the iron needs of men and should take care to avoid iron deficiency. Women also seem to suffer more from loss of calcium. Generally an adequate supply of these minerals can be obtained from dairy products, but if these are not included in the diet, substitutes must be found. A vegan diet is likely to be deficient in vitamin B12, and supplements may need to be taken to avoid this.
See also CARBOHYDRATE; FAT; FOOD; PROTEIN; VITAMINS

VEIN
Veins are the blood vessels that carry the blood back to the heart after it has been circulated via the arteries through the tissues of the body.

As a general rule, veins lie alongside the corresponding arteries, although there are almost twice as many veins and they have a much bigger capacity. There are also extra veins near the outside of the body that can easily be seen just below the skin.

The pressure of blood in the veins is much lower than that in the arteries so the vein walls are not as thick. The pressure also varies only slightly, since blood in veins flows steadily rather than being forced along in spurts by the pumping of the heart. For this reason, if a vein is cut, the flow of blood is easier to stop than blood spouting from a cut artery.

Because the pressure in veins is so much lower than in the heart, there is a risk that blood could flow backwards, especially since much of it is flowing upwards against the force of gravity. To counteract this and to push the blood towards the heart, veins contain valves, which close off as the blood moves along in them, thus preventing any backward flow. If the muscles are contracting frequently such as during exercise, the blood in the veins will be pushed more quickly towards the heart so that it can be re-oxygenated and brought back as soon as possible to keep the cells nourished and able to perform the extra work.

The tiniest veins, scattered throughout the body, where the blood begins its return journey from the cells are called venules. These flow into progressively larger veins until they reach the heart. There are two main veins flowing into the heart – one bringing the blood from the head, neck and upper limbs (the superior vena cava), and the other bringing blood from the abdomen and lower limbs (the inferior vena cava). The large veins leading from the head are the jugular veins, which can usually be seen in the neck. The main veins carrying blood from the lungs to the heart are called the pulmonary veins. There are four of these, two from each lung.

In all the veins except the pulmonary veins, blood is low in oxygen and high in the waste

product, carbon dioxide. Blood in the pulmonary veins, having been through the lungs, is rich in oxygen.
See also ANGIOGRAM; ARTERY; HEART; PHLEBITIS; PORTAL SYSTEM

VEIN THROMBOSIS
See DEEP VEIN THROMBOSIS; PHLEBITIS; SUPERFICIAL VENOUS THROMBOSIS; THROMBOSIS

VENA CAVA
See VEIN

VENEREAL DISEASES
Venereal diseases are passed from one person to another by sexual contact. This includes homosexual, lesbian, oral and anal sex, as well as normal heterosexual intercourse.
See also AIDS; CHANCROID; CRABS; CYTOMEGALOVIRUS; DONOVANOSIS; GENITAL HERPES; GENITAL WARTS; GONORRHOEA; GRANULOMA INGUINALE; HEPATITIS B; HEPATITIS C; LICE; LYMPHOGRANULOMA VENEREUM; NON-SPECIFIC URETHRITIS; PELVIC INFLAMMATORY DISEASE; SYPHILIS; TRICHOMONIASIS; VAGINITIS

VENEREAL WARTS
See GENITAL WARTS

VENLAFAXINE
See ANTIDEPRESSANTS

VENOGRAM
See ANGIOGRAM

VENOUS LAKE
A venous lake is a common disfiguring problem affecting older people, that usually develops on the face and ears. It is caused by sun exposure that damages veins under the skin, or a direct injury to the skin. The damaged vein dilates to form a dark blue to black, painless, raised, smooth, soft, blood filled blister under the skin. It bleeds profusely if injured.

Electric cautery, laser or excision can be used to remove the spot if it is cosmetically unacceptable.
See also CAMPBELL de MORGAN SPOTS; HAEMANGIOMA

VENOUS ULCER
A venous or varicose ulcer may occur on the shin and ankle in middle-aged and elderly people due to a poor return of blood from the ankles and feet to the heart. The ankles may be swollen, and the skin may be thin and discoloured by eczema. A slight injury to a leg affected by varicose veins may cause an ulcer, and because of the high pressure from the swollen veins in the area and the poor quality of the skin, healing may be very slow. Women are affected far more often than men, and ulcers are more common in diabetics. Secondary bacterial infection of the ulcer is the only significant complication.

Treatment involves prolonged elevation of the leg to reduce the pressure in the veins, wearing compression bandages or stockings when walking, avoiding standing still for prolonged periods, and careful dressing of the ulcer with antiseptics and specialised pads or powders. In persistent cases, surgery to the swollen veins to relieve the pressure may be necessary before healing can occur. Recovery is often very slow, but most heal with persistence.
See also SKIN ULCER; VARICOSE ECZEMA

VENTOUSE
See FORCEPS DELIVERY

VENTRAL
Ventral is a term used by doctors to describe the front of the body. The ventral part of the trunk is the abdomen, and the palm side of the hand is also the ventral side.
See also DORSAL; LATERAL

VENTRICLE
See HEART

VENTRICULAR EXTRASYSTOLES
If an abnormal nerve impulse from part of the left ventricle (larger chamber on the left side of the heart) fires off before the normal heart pacemaker, it will cause a premature or extra heart beat (ventricular extrasystole). This is felt as a momentary irregularity in the heart beat, and may occur very infrequently, or every three or four beats. Occasionally it may progress to ventricular flutter or rarely ventricular fibrillation. It can be diagnosed by an electrocardiogram (ECG).

Often no treatment is necessary, but if

frequent, medications can be given to regulate the heart rhythm.

See also ARRHYTHMIA; ATRIAL EXTRASYSTOLES; HEART, EXTRA BEATS; VENTRICULAR FIBRILLATION

VENTRICULAR FAILURE
See CONGESTIVE CARDIAC FAILURE

VENTRICULAR FIBRILLATION
Ventricular fibrillation (VF) is an extremely rapid vibration of the heart muscle in the ventricles (larger heart chambers) that prevents any blood from being pumped out of the heart. A slower, but still very rapid, heart contraction rate that allows a small amount of blood flow, is called ventricular flutter. The most common causes are a heart attack and electrocution.

The patient suddenly collapses into a coma, and death occurs within minutes if not adequately treated. VF can be differentiated from other heart problems by an ECG (electrocardiogram).

Cardiopulmonary resuscitation (CPR – heart massage and mouth to mouth breathing) may save some patients long enough for specific treatment to be given. The only effective treatment is an electrical shock to the heart (cardioversion) applied as soon as possible after the patient collapses, and repeated until normal rhythm occurs, followed by injections into a vein of medications to prevent further heart beat irregularities.

If VF occurs in a hospital intensive care ward, a significant percentage of patients can be saved. In the community, death usually occurs before effective treatment can be given.

See also ARRHYTHMIA; HEART ATTACK; RESUSCITATION

VENTRICULAR FLUTTER
See VENTRICULAR FIBRILLATION

VENTRICULAR SEPTAL DEFECT
A ventricular septal defect is a congenital abnormal opening between the two main chambers (ventricles) in the heart, the most common form of 'hole in the heart' and the usual cause of a 'blue baby'. This defect is often combined with other heart and other organ developmental defects. Heart defects can be diagnosed by ultrasound examination (echocardiography).

The symptoms depend on the size of the abnormal opening. The infant may have no symptoms or in severe cases may develop congestive cardiac failure, cor pulmonale (lung failure), shortness of breath, blue tinged skin (cyanosis), chest pain, fainting attacks, coughing up blood and numerous other symptoms related to the heart and lungs.

HEART

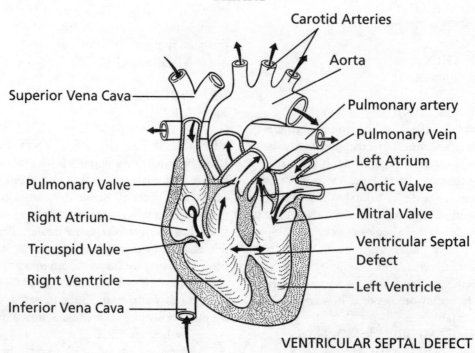

VENTRICULAR SEPTAL DEFECT

Small holes may close spontaneously, but open heart surgery is used to close larger holes that cause any symptoms. Usually there are good results from treatment, but if the defect is very severe, death in infancy is possible, before surgery can be performed.
See also ATRIAL SEPTAL DEFECT; CONGESTIVE CARDIAC FAILURE; COR PULMONALE; FALLOT'S TETRALOGY; HEART; SKIN BLUE

VENULE
See VEIN

VERAPAMIL
See CALCIUM CHANNEL BLOCKERS

VERBAL GARBAGE
See GARBLED VERBIAGE

VERTEBRA
Twenty-four vertebrae make up the spine from the skull to the pelvis. A single vertebra is hollow, with a thick cylindrically shaped bone in front, called the body, and a thin ring of bone (the lamina) curving around the back enclosing the spinal cord which runs up through the hollow centre. Each vertebra is separated from the next one by a disc made of cartilage.

Each ring has three sharp bony protrusion, two pointing sideways (transverse processes) and one pointing backwards (spine), to which muscles and ligaments are attached. The protrusions can be seen or felt under the skin of the back as small spines – hence the name spinal column.

VERTEBRA FROM ABOVE

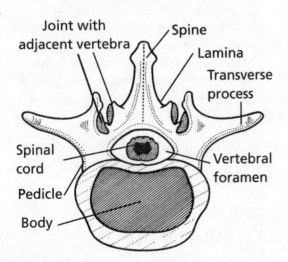

Joint with adjacent vertebra
Spine
Lamina
Transverse process
Spinal cord
Vertebral foramen
Pedicle
Body

See also BACK; INTERVERTEBRAL DISC PROLAPSE; LAMINECTOMY; SCHEURMANN DISEASE; SPINE; SPONDYLOLISTHESIS

VERTEBRAL PAIN
See BACK PAIN

VERTIGO
See BENIGN PAROXYSMAL POSITIONAL VERTIGO; DIZZINESS

VESICLE
In medical terms, a vesicle is a small fluid or air filled sac in or on the body. Vesicles commonly form on the skin as a blistering rash, or in the lungs with emphysema.
See also EMPHYSEMA; RASH BLISTERING

VESTIBULAR NEURONITIS
See VESTIBULITIS

VESTIBULITIS
Vestibulitis (vestibular neuronitis) is a disturbance to the function of the three semicircular canals that form the balance mechanism in the inner ear. It may be due to inflammation or viral infection of the nerve endings supplying the balance mechanism (vestibular apparatus), and may be associated with almost any viral infection, including influenza. Excess fluid accumulates in the balance mechanism to make it malfunction.

The patient suffers constant dizziness and unsteadiness, often at rest, but certainly with any movement. It may be associated with nausea, vomiting and a ringing noise in the ears, and abnormal side to side eye movements (nystagmus) may be present.

There is no cure but the disturbance settles slowly with time, and medications such as prochlorperazine and diuretics) ease the symptoms.
See also LABYRINTHITIS

VF
See VENTRICULAR FIBRILLATION

VIAGRA
See SILDENAFIL

VIBRIO CHOLERAE
See CHOLERA

VIGABATRIN
See ANTICONVULSANTS

VINCENT'S ANGINA
See GINGIVOSTOMATITIS

VIOLENCE
Abnormal levels of violence perpetrated by an individual may be due to a number of medical conditions, as well as a reaction to excess alcohol, abuse of illegal drugs (eg. stimulants, LSD), and a side effect of barbiturates (used in epilepsy and psychiatry).

Attention deficit hyperactivity disorder (ADHD) is a very complex problem of children. The classic symptoms include fidgeting, inability to remain seated for long, being easily distracted and unable to sustain attention, being always impatient, having difficulty in following instructions, often moving from one incomplete task to the next, being unable to play quietly, violence towards others and objects, talking excessively, often interrupting or intruding, not seeming to listen, poor short term memory, often losing items, and engaging in physically dangerous activities. These symptoms create learning disabilities, emotional, social and family difficulties, low self-esteem and sometimes depression.

Schizophrenia is a mental illness that causes the sufferer to have a distorted view of the world because of delusions and hallucinations. Patients often change the topic of conversation for no apparent reason, do not look after themselves, become dishevelled in appearance, withdrawn, fail to communicate properly with others, hear unfriendly voices, have frightening visions, believe they are being persecuted, become violent towards loved ones and develop other mood and behaviour changes that seem bizarre.

A grand mal fit during epilepsy may give the appearance of violence, but it is really uncontrolled muscle spasms.

Other possible causes of abnormal violence include a head injury that has effects on the brain, numerous psychiatric conditions (eg. episodic dyscontrol syndrome, psychopathy, hypomania), low blood sugar (hypoglycaemia), Klinefelter syndrome, XYY syndrome (chromosome abnormality), Lesch-Nyhan syndrome, Tourette syndrome and Asperger syndrome (inability to feel emotion, inappropriate social interactions, poor communication skills, poor coordination and violence).
See also CHILD ABUSE; OVERACTIVE; RAPE; SEXUAL SADISM; STOCKHOLM SYNDROME; SWEARING UNCONTROLLED and separate entries for diseases mentioned above.

VIRAEMIA
A viraemia is a generalised viral infection of the blood. Almost any virus that enters the body (often through the nose or mouth) and circulates in the blood, may be responsible. The infection lies in the blood rather than in any specific organ or tissue.

There is a general feeling of being unwell, variable fever, tiredness and generalised aches and pains. At a later stage the infection may attack a specific organ (eg. nose) to cause localised symptoms.

Aspirin or other anti-inflammatory medications, and pain killers such as paracetamol are the only treatments. Time and rest are the only cures.
See also VIRUS

VIRAL EXANTHEMA
A viral exanthema is any rash caused by a viral infection. These are much more common in children than adults and common examples include measles, roseola infantum (baby measles), chickenpox and German measles (rubella), but a wide range of other viral infections may be responsible.

The rashes are extremely variable in their appearance. Usually there is a red or maroon, flat, widely scattered, slightly itchy rash in a child with a mild fever who is vaguely unwell, but the rash may also be a raised, crusting and highly itchy, as in chickenpox.

No tests are normally necessary, but blood tests and swabs of sores can sometimes make a definite diagnosis.

The rash settles spontaneously within hours or days without treatment. Paracetamol and medication for the itch may be necessary.
See also VIRUS

VIRAL HAEMORRHAGIC FEVER
See EBOLA VIRUS; LASSA FEVER; MARBURG VIRUS

VIRGIN BIRTH
See PARTHENOGENESIS

VIRUS

Viruses are unimaginably small, and millions could exist on this full stop. They can be found anywhere in the environment – in the body, or in a drop of sweat, in saliva, or the skin of the family dog.

If the viruses are in the body, they will be under constant attack by the body's defence system. Every minute, millions more viruses enter the body through the mouth or nose. As they enter, the defence system uses its special cells and protein particles (antibodies) to repel the attack. Sometimes the defences are overwhelmed for a short time by the rapidly multiplying viruses. When this happens, the patient may feel off-colour for a day or two. If the virus numbers manage to totally defeat the defenders, a full-blown viral infection will develop. Viruses can cause diseases as diverse as measles, hepatitis, cold sores, chickenpox, glandular fever, AIDS and the common cold.

Virus particles are so small that they cannot be seen by even the most powerful light microscope, and special electron microscopes have to be used. They are neither animal nor plant, but particles that are so basic that they are classified into a group of their own. They are not alive in any sense that we understand, but are overgrown molecules that are intent on reproducing themselves at the expense of any host that happens along. Because they are not truly alive, they cannot be killed, and so antibiotics that are effective against the much larger living cells known as bacteria have no effect on viruses. Other than for a limited number of viruses that cause genital herpes, shingles and cold sores, doctors have no cure for virus infections.

The common cold can be caused by any one of several hundred different viruses. They cause the lining of the nose, sinuses and throat to become red, sore and swollen; and phlegm and mucus are produced in great quantities to give a stuffy head, sore throat and runny nose to their victim. The poisons created after the body destroys the viruses circulate around in the blood stream to cause the fever and muscular aches that are also associate with a cold. While the patient is suffering, the body is busy producing the appropriate antibodies to fight the infection. Once the number of antibodies produced is adequate to destroy most of the viruses, the symptoms of the disease disappear.

Doctors can vaccinate against some viral diseases, such as measles and influenza, to prevent them; but others such as the common cold cannot be prevented. Viral infections can best be avoided by a good, well-balanced diet, reasonable exercise, avoiding stress, avoiding extremes of temperature, and avoiding those who already have the infection.

See also ANTIBODY; ANTIVIRALS; BACTERIA; COLD, COMMON; CYTOMEGALOVIRUS INFECTION; INFECTION; INFLUENZA; PRION; VACCINATION; VIRAEMIA and specific entries for other viral infections

VISCERAL LARVA MIGRANS

Visceral (and ocular) larva migrans are internal infestations by the larvae of a roundworm (nematode). Dogs infected by the roundworm (*Toxocara canis*) pass worm eggs out with their faeces to contaminate the soil. Eggs swallowed by humans (often children) hatch into larvae which penetrate through the gut wall into the bloodstream, by which they are carried to a variety of organs, particularly the lungs, liver, brain and eye (ocular larva migrans).

The symptoms are very variable, depending on which organ the larvae are carried to, and the number of larvae present. They usually include fever, tiredness, loss of appetite and weight loss. Organ-specific symptoms include cough, wheeze, rash, large liver and spleen, visual disturbances, seizures and behavioural disorders. Heart infestation and pneumonia may lead to death.

There is a specific blood test to detect the presence of the larvae, and other blood tests show significant reactive changes. Chest x-rays may show lung inflammation. Masses of larvae in the eye can be seen by looking through the pupil with an ophthalmoscope (magnifying light). Medication is available to destroy the larvae, and steroids are used to reduce inflammation.

The larvae cannot develop into worms in humans, and die off naturally after several months, but permanent organ damage may occur. The treatment of eye disease is unsatisfactory.

See also CUTANEOUS LARVA MIGRANS; LOEFFLER SYNDROME; NEMATODE

VISCERAL LEISCHMANIASIS
See KALA AZAR

VISION

Because of their complexity, the eyes sometimes function less than perfectly. There are four main types of vision problems:

• People who are short-sighted (myopia) have eyeballs that are too long. This means that the light cannot accurately be focused by the lens and a blurred image results.

• The reverse problem occurs in long-sighted people (hypermetropia) where the eyeball is too short. These people can see objects at a distance but when close objects are seen, the muscles that change the shape of the lens to focus the light rays cannot cope with the shortened eyeball.

• Older people whose sight slowly deteriorates suffer from presbyopia, or the inability of the lens to change shape sufficiently to see objects that are close to them. This is caused by a weakening of the tiny muscles that pull on the lens to change its shape.

• The last group is those with astigmatism. These people have an uneven curve of the refractive surfaces at the front of the eye (ie. the lens and cornea), so that some parts of the vision are clear while other parts are blurred at the same time.

All these problems can be corrected by placing a lens (spectacles or contact lenses) in front of the eye to help the natural lens of the eye focus the image. Reshaping the cornea with laser surgery can also be used to help people with myopia.

See also DOUBLE VISION; EYE; HALLUCINATION; KERATOCONUS; OPTOMETRIST; REFRACTIVE SURGERY; SHORT-SIGHTED; VISION BLURRED; VISION HALF LOST; VISUAL ACUITY; VISUAL BLACK SPOTS; VISUAL HALO

VISION BLURRED

Seeing things that can't be focused and that remain blurred, is very frustrating, and the most obvious causes are long sightedness (inability to see close objects and read, usually associated with advancing age), short sightedness (inability to see distant objects and often a problem from childhood), or astigmatism (uneven focus). These problems can be corrected by spectacles or contact lenses, but there are some eye and other diseases which may cause blurred vision.

A cataract is clouding of the lens in the eye that will cause gradual blurring and loss of sight over many years in the elderly. Rarely, babies are born with a cataract.

Glaucoma is due to an increase in the pressure of the jelly like fluid inside the eye. This may come on gradually, or may be quite sudden. If inadequately treated, total blindness may result. Early symptoms include an eye ache or pain, blurred vision, seeing halos around objects, red eye, and a gradual loss of peripheral vision. There is a hereditary tendency.

The retina is the layer of light sensitive cells at the back of the eye. If this is damaged by a poor blood supply from narrowed hardened arteries, a blood clot in a tiny artery, or separation of the retina from the back of the eyeball, the vision will be blurred or totally absent in the affected area.

Other causes of blurred vision include iritis (inflammation of the coloured part of the eye), conjunctivitis (bacterial or viral infection on

HYPERMETROPIA

Light focuses beyond retina

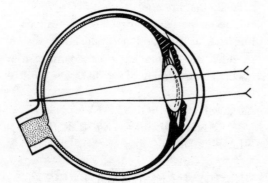

MYOPIA

Light focuses in front of retina

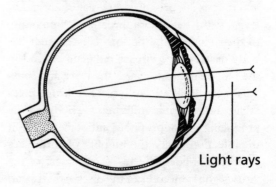

Light rays

the surface of the eye), an ulcer on the surface of the eye, a severe allergy reaction affecting the surface of the eye, exposure of the eye to the brilliant white light of an arc welding torch or prolonged exposure to ultraviolet light (eg. in a disco), migraines, amblyopia, poorly controlled diabetes, a stroke (cerebrovascular accident) and uraemia (kidney failure).

Medications such as atropine (used in eye surgery), nicotine in tobacco (smoking over forty cigarettes a day), and illegal drugs (eg. cocaine) may cause blurred vision as a side effect.
See also BLINDNESS; EYE; VISION and separate entries for diseases mentioned above.

VISION DOUBLE
See DOUBLE VISION

VISION HALF LOST
If you cover one eye, and while looking with the other eye find that you cannot see half of the objects in front of you, you are said to have hemianopia.

The most serious cause of this problem is damage to the optic nerve which carries the sight nerve messages from the eye to the brain. This damage may be caused by a poor blood supply to the nerve, or a tumour, cancer (eg. craniopharyngioma), abscess or infection in the nerve, brain or other surrounding tissues.

Far more commonly, a migraine may be responsible, and this may not always be accompanied by a headache. Migraines are often associated with visual symptoms including flashing lights, shimmering, seeing zigzag lines and loss of part of the area of vision. Any headache usually occurs on only one side of the head, is described as throbbing, and causes intolerance of exercise, light and noise. Nausea and vomiting are common.

In a stroke (cerebrovascular accident) part of the brain is affected by having its blood supply cut off by a blockage in an artery, or a blood vessel in the brain may burst, causing bleeding and damage to part of the brain. The onset is almost instantaneous, may be associated with paralysis in various parts of the body, headache, shortness of breath and other abnormalities that can vary from minor discomfort, confusion and visual disturbances to widespread paralysis and coma.

Temporal arteritis is an inflammation of the artery in the temple. There is severe tenderness over the artery, searing pain into the jaw and temples, and the eye may be affected in various ways.
See also BLINDNESS; EYE; VISION and separate entries for diseases mentioned above.

VISION LOSS
See BLINDNESS; VISION HALF LOST

VISUAL ACUITY
Visual acuity tests are a tests administered to determine if there are any defects in vision, what they are, and how severe they are.

The patient looks at a chart with letters on it on a wall six metres away and is asked to read it line by line. The letters vary in size from row to row. The top row has one large letter, the next row smaller letters, the next, smaller letters still, and so on. A person with normal vision should be able to read letters six millimetres high at a distance of six metres.

The doctor will generally guess which line the patient will be able to see, and asks them to start there and read the letters out. If they cannot see them, the doctor will move up a line until the patient reaches a line they can read without difficulty.

The result is given as two figures (eg. 6/12). The first figure refers to the distance at which the letters (six metres) are read. The second figure describes the distance at which a person with normal vision can read the smallest letters that the patient was able to read correctly. For example, if the smallest letters read from a distance of six metres would be seen from twelve metres by a person with normal sight the result is 6/12. The results may be different for each eye. 6/12 is the minimum visual acuity permissible for a normal driver's license.

Poor reading of the chart usually means that the eyes have an impaired ability to refract light – the basis of sight – either nearsighted (myopic) or far-sighted (hypermetropic). Occasionally it indicates a serious eye disease, such as glaucoma.

If the vision is faulty, the doctor or optometrist will ask the patient to look through a selection of lenses of different magnifications and to read the chart again, covering up one eye at a time. The combination of lenses which enable the person to see best are then prescribed as glasses or contact lenses.

Even people with previously good sight

usually find that they are having difficulty reading and seeing things up close as they get older, and most people need a visual acuity test by the time they are in their mid-forties.
See also EYE; VISION; VISION HALF LOST

VISUAL BLACK SPOTS

Seeing black spots floating across the vision, or fixed in one spot in the visual field (everything that can be seen), can be a frightening experience. Most causes are associated with diseases of the layer of light sensitive cells at the back of the eyeball (the retina).

The most common cause is suddenly noticing the blind spot in the visual field of one eye. It is a phenomenon that only occurs when one eye is covered and you are looking with the other. When both eyes are used, the brain compensates for this defect in the visual field by using information from the other eye.

Migraines are often associated with visual symptoms including flashing lights, black spots, shimmering, seeing zigzag lines and loss of part of the area of vision. They usually occur on only one side of the head, are described as throbbing, and cause intolerance of exercise, light and noise. Nausea and vomiting are common.

Floaters appear as a spot in the vision that won't go away, and may continue to move across the vision after the moving eye comes to rest. A floater is a collection of cells in the half-set jelly-like substance that fills the eyeball. The cells cast a shadow on the light-sensitive retina at the back of the eye, which the brain perceives as an object in front of the eye. They may be due to bleeding into the eye, a detached retina (which itself may cause a black spot or patch in the visual field), infection, or no apparent cause may be found.

Other possible causes include some forms of epilepsy, a cataract (clouding of the lens in the eye), tumours of the optic nerve which takes nerve signals from the eye to the brain, and a poor blood supply to the eye because of hardening of the arteries (arteriosclerosis) or a blood clot (thrombosis).
See also BLIND SPOT; EYE; VISION; VISION BLURRED; VISION HALF LOST; VISUAL FLASHES and separate entries for diseases mentioned above.

VISUAL FLASHES

Seeing flashing lights, often at the edge of vision, when there are none actually present, can be both an annoying and a serious symptom. There are only two possible causes.

By far the most common cause is a migraine. These are often associated with varied visual symptoms including flashing lights, shimmering, seeing zigzag lines and loss of part of the area of vision. Pain usually occurs on only one side of the head, and is described as throbbing, and causes intolerance of exercise, light and noise. Nausea and vomiting are common.

Damage to the retina (the layer of light sensitive cells at the back of the eye) is the other, and much more serious, cause. If the retina starts to lift off the back of the eye (retinal detachment), or if there is bleeding into or under the retina, the light sensitive cells will send inappropriate signals to the brain which are interpreted as flashing lights. If treated early, this problem can often be cured, but if left for too long, permanent damage to the sight may occur.
See also EYE; VISION; VISUAL BLACK SPOTS and separate entries for diseases mentioned above.

VISUAL HALO

When looking at a street light on a misty night, everyone sees a faint halo of light around it, but if this phenomenon occurs all the time and in all degrees of light and dark, a person is considered to have abnormal visual halos.

The most serious cause of this effect is glaucoma. This is caused by an increase in the pressure of the jelly-like fluid inside the eye. Other causes include cataracts (clouding of the lens in the eye), allergic conjunctivitis (reaction to a pollen, dust, chemical or other substances that enter the eye) and any injury, ulceration or infection which causes swelling of the surface of the eye to cause distortion and blurring of vision.

Contact lenses may be responsible if they are poorly fitting, the wrong strength, contaminated, or left in place for too long.
See also VISION and separate entries for diseases mentioned above.

VITAL CAPACITY

The vital capacity (VC) of the lungs is the difference in lung volume between the deepest breath you can take in and the maximum lung emptying possible by breathing out. This is

measured by a machine called a spirometer, into which you will be asked to blow as long and hard as you can after first having taken a deep breath in. These machines may produce a line on a piece of graph paper, or may have an electronic printout. The recordings of PEFR and VC and other measurements that can be made from the results enable doctors to obtain a very accurate picture of lung function in disease.
See also ASTHMA; LUNG; RESPIRATORY FUNCTION TESTS

VITAMINS

Vitamins are a group of totally unrelated chemicals that have only one thing in common – they are essential (usually in tiny amounts) for the normal functioning of the body. All vitamins have been given letter codes, sometimes with an additional number to differentiate vitamins within a group. The missing letters and numbers in the series are due to substances initially having been identified as vitamins but later being found to lack the essentials for the classification.

There is no evidence that vitamin supplements benefit anyone on a normal diet and in good health. The cheapest and most effective way to obtain adequate vitamins is to eat a well-balanced diet. Most vitamin supplements are expensive, pass rapidly through the body, and merely enrich the sewers.
See also FOLIC ACID and specific vitamins (eg. VITAMIN A; VITAMIN C)

VITAMIN A

A fat-soluble vitamin, retinol (vitamin A) is found in milk, butter, eggs, liver and most fruit and vegetables. Very high levels are found in orange-coloured foods (eg. pumpkin, carrots, pawpaw, etc.). It is essential for the normal function of the skin and eyes, but there is no evidence that extra amounts can improve vision in people with sight problems or can cure skin problems.

A vitamin A deficiency (hypovitaminosis A) may occur with starvation, tropical sprue, a poor or fad diet that lacks vitamin A, and alcoholism or narcotic addiction which may lead to the other causes. Symptoms include reduced night vision, dry eye surface, eye ulceration and dry skin. Permanent damage to the retina (light sensitive area at the back of the eye) is possible. Blood test measurements of low vitamin A levels are inaccurate, and the diagnosis must be made by history and clinical signs.

An excess of vitamin A (hypervitaminosis A) causes carotenaemia which is characterised by yellow skin, palms and soles, and may be cause foetal abnormalities in pregnant women.
See also CAROTENAEMIA; COELIAC DISEASE; EYE DRY; EYE ULCER; TROPICAL SPRUE; VITAMINS

VITAMIN B

This vitamin is divided into several subgroups numbered 1, 2, 3, 5, 6 and 12. All are water-soluble and occur in dairy products, meats and leafy vegetables. Vitamin B1 has the chemical name of thiamine, B2 is riboflavin and B5 is pantothenic acid. Vitamin B6 (pyridoxine) may be useful in mouth inflammation, morning sickness and nervous tension. Vitamin B12 (cyanocobalamin) is used as an injection to treat pernicious anaemia. Nicotinic acid (vitamin B3) is specifically found in peanuts, meat, grain and liver. It is used in the treatment of certain types of headache, nervous disorders, poor circulation and blood diseases.

It is almost impossible to have a lack of only one in the group. If one is missing, several will usually be missing. A deficiency may cause anaemia and other blood diseases. Beriberi is caused by a lack of vitamin B1, pellagra by a lack of vitamin B3, while pernicious anaemia is due to a lack of vitamin B12. A lack of vitamin B6 (pyridoxine), may be an uncommon side effect of some medications (eg. isoniazid, penicillamine), genetic disorders and in poor nutrition. It causes epileptic-like seizures, dermatitis, mouth sores and dryness, vomiting, weakness and dizziness. The blood levels of pyridoxine can be measured to confirm the diagnosis, which is easily corrected by vitamin B6 supplements.

Excessive blood levels of any of the B group vitamins may be due to taking too many vitamin B supplements. Usually there are no serious effects as excess passes out in the urine. Very high doses of pyridoxine (vitamin B6) may cause nerve damage and poor coordination, numbness around the mouth, clumsiness, muscle weakness and loss of position sense. Very high doses of niacin (vitamin B3) may cause severe flushing, itchy skin, diarrhoea and liver damage. Long term complications are uncommon.

See also AMBLYOPIA; BERIBERI; PERNICIOUS ANAEMIA; PELLAGRA; REFLEXES REDUCED; VITAMINS; WERNICKE-KORSAKOFF PSYCHOSIS

VITAMIN C

Ascorbic acid (vitamin C) is water-soluble and found in citrus fruits, tomatoes and greens, but its level in food is reduced by cooking, mincing and contact with copper utensils. Vitamin C can also be synthesised from non-food sources, and the synthetic form cannot be differentiated from the natural in any way. It is essential for the formation and maintenance of cartilage, bone and teeth, and is used in moderate amounts to promote the healing of wounds and during convalescence from prolonged illnesses. Unfortunately there is no evidence to support its use in preventing or treating the common cold. In one trial, 3000 Californian users of Vitamin C supplements were followed for ten years and had the same rate of illness and death as a control group of nonusers.

A lack of vitamin C in the diet will result in the disease scurvy.

Excess vitamin C in the body from taking too many vitamin C (ascorbic acid) supplements may have several unusual effects including increased blood levels of oestrogens which causes breast tenderness and menstrual period irregularities, increased risk of kidney stones, reduced absorption of vitamin B12 and the development of pernicious anaemia, and rebound scurvy in babies born to mothers who take too much vitamin C during pregnancy. The level of vitamin C can be measured in the blood. If the patient stops vitamin C supplements long term complications are uncommon.
See also FOLIC ACID; SCURVY; VITAMINS

VITAMIN D

This is a fat-soluble chemical found in egg yolks and butter, and it may be formed by a reaction of sunlight on skin. It is essential for the balance of calcium and phosphorus in the bones and bloodstream, but it is not used routinely in the treatment of disease. Vitamin D is actually composed of a number of chemicals including calcitriol and ergocalciferol.

A lack of vitamin D causes rickets and osteomalacia, while an excess causes hypercalcaemia (high blood calcium levels).

See also BABY FLOPPY; CALCIUM; COELIAC DISEASE; HYPERCALCAEMIA; OSTEOMALACIA; RICKETS; VITAMINS

VITAMIN E

Readily available in most foods, vitamin E (tocopherols) is a fat-soluble vitamin which acts as an antioxidant.

High doses may cause serious diseases and abnormalities including blood clots, high blood pressure, breast tumours, headaches, tiredness and diarrhoea. It may be harmful to the foetus in pregnancy, and prevent blood clotting in those who are taking warfarin. Vitamin E is a quite dangerous substance, and is only rarely used in medicine.

A lack of vitamin E from starvation, poor diet or malabsorption of fats may result in nerve damage. The patient has reduced reflexes, abnormal gait (way of walking), decreased senses of position and vibration, and eye movement abnormalities. Permanent degeneration of the spinal cord is a rare complication. The diagnosis is confirmed by measuring vitamin E levels in the blood. There is a good response to vitamin E supplements provided there has not been permanent nerve damage.
See also COELIAC DISEASE; VITAMINS

VITAMIN H

Biotin (vitamin H) has no specific medical use. A lack occurs only in severe starvation.
See also VITAMINS

VITAMIN K

Essential for the clotting of blood, vitamin K (phytomenadione or phylloquinone) is fat-soluble and is found in most vegetables, particularly those with green leaves. It is also manufactured by bacteria living in the gut. It is not commonly used clinically.

A lack of vitamin K is relatively common in newborn infants, or may rarely be due to diseases which prevent fat absorption from the gut and long term potent antibiotic use. Excessive bleeding and bruising are the symptoms, but it is easily and well treated by vitamin K injections, which rarely may be given to infants. The excessive bleeding may lead to anaemia if left untreated.

Excess vitamin K may occur with taking too many vitamin K supplements. This stops

anticoagulants (eg. warfarin) from working and may lead to strokes or heart attacks. In pregnancy, the baby may be born jaundiced (yellow skin due to liver damage) due to anaemia in infants from the breakdown of red blood cells.
See also BLEEDING, EXCESSIVE; COELIAC DISEASE; VITAMINS

VITAMIN M
See FOLIC ACID

VITILIGO
Vitiligo is a skin pigmentation disorder that can occur in all races, in both sexes, and at all ages, but onset is uncommon over fifty years of age. The cause is unknown, but it is probably an autoimmune disease, in which the body's defence mechanisms inappropriately attack normal cells and tissue, in this case destroying pigment-producing melanin cells (melanocytes) in the skin.

The loss of skin pigmentation in multiple patches that are sharply defined, may appear anywhere on the body, in any size and number, and overlying hair is usually white or grey. The affected skin is very sensitive to sunlight, and burns easily. In pale-skinned northern Europeans the patches may be barely noticed, but in southern Europeans, Arabs, Negroes and Chinese the resultant large white patches are quite disfiguring. There are no other side effects or complications of the disease

Cosmetic stains or dyes are used to disguise the affected areas of skin, and may be quite effective. A number of other treatments are available, but require long-term use of tablets and/or ultraviolet light exposure, and have only moderate success. The affected area of skin usually slowly extends to involve larger areas but eventually stabilises after several years. Spontaneous recovery is uncommon.
See also SKIN DEPIGMENTED

VMRSA
See STAPHYLOCOCCUS AUREUS

VOCAL CORDS
See LARYNX

VOGT-KOYANAGI-HARADA SYNDROME
The Vogt-Koyanagi-Harada syndrome is a form of inflammation of the brain, eyes and ears, of unknown cause.

Patients develop recurrent attacks of encephalitis and meningitis, with uveitis (eye inflammation), detachment of the light sensitive retina from the back of the eye (causes patches of blindness), fever, headache and dizziness. It may be associated with a white patch of hair and skin, hair loss (alopecia), cataracts and glaucoma in the eyes, and deafness and ringing in the ears (tinnitus). One or both eyes may be affected.

There is no specific diagnostic test and no treatment is available. Most cases settle spontaneously with time, but permanent eye damage often occurs.
See also BLINDNESS; ENCEPHALITIS; MENINGITIS; RETINAL DETACHMENT; UVEITIS

VOICE
See HOARSE VOICE; LARYNX; SPEECH DIFFICULT; STUTTER

VOLKMANN CONTRACTURE
Damage to the artery (brachial artery) supplying the muscles in the forearm from an elbow injury results in them being replaced by scar tissue, which causes pain in the forearm and an inability to straighten the wrist and fingers, which become fixed in a claw position. This forearm deformity is a Volkmann contracture.

On examination, the radial pulse is missing in the wrist. Surgical repair of artery in early stages sometimes possible, but the prognosis is poor once contractures are present.
See also PULSE

VOMITING
See NAUSEA AND VOMITING; VOMITING BLOOD

VOMITING BLOOD
Vomiting blood (haematemesis) can vary from a few specks of red in copious vomitus, to vomiting large amounts of blood with no other substance being present. Vomiting a small amount of blood on one occasion is not normally a reason for any concern, but if even small amounts are vomited repeatedly, or a large amount only once, medical attention must be obtained.

Prolonged vomiting from any cause may result in vomiting of blood as the junction between the oesophagus (gullet) and stomach becomes torn. This is known as the Mallory-Weis syndrome.

A peptic ulcer in the stomach is caused by the concentrated hydrochloric acid in the stomach penetrating the protective mucus that normally lines the organ, and eating into the stomach wall to cause significant pain. If the ulcer penetrates a vein or artery, severe bleeding into the stomach may occur.

Varicose veins can occur not only in the legs, but also in the lower oesophagus (gullet), when liver disease (eg. cirrhosis from alcohol, liver tumours or hepatitis) increases the pressure in the veins that drain from the gut into the liver. The dilated veins in the oesophagus (oesophageal varices) can be damaged and bleed torrentially because of vomiting, reflux of acid into the oesophagus (eg. with a hiatus hernia), straining with heavy lifting, or swallowing hard or sharp objects.

Uncommon causes of haematemesis include swallowing a sharp foreign body (eg. a pin, sharp bone), cancer of the stomach or oesophagus, abnormal arteries and veins that may be present in the stomach or oesophagus from birth, and yellow fever (a severe infection of the liver transmitted by mosquitoes).

Some medications, such as aspirin, anti-inflammatory medications (used for arthritis) and, more seriously, warfarin (used to thin blood), may cause bleeding into the stomach and vomiting blood.
See also NAUSEA AND VOMITING; OESOPHAGUS; STOMACH and separate entries for diseases mentioned above.

VOMITING MEDICATIONS
See ANTIEMETICS

von GIERKE SYNDROME
See GLYCOGEN STORAGE DISEASES

von WILLEBRAND DISEASE
Von Willebrand disease (vascular haemophilia) is a rare inherited cause of prolonged bleeding. Patients lack one of the essential factors involved in the complex process of blood clotting.

Most cases are mild, and patients experience nose bleeds, heavy periods, bleeding gums and bleeding into the gut. Excessive bleeding also occurs with any cut or surgery, bleeding into joints may cause premature arthritis, and the condition is dramatically worsened by aspirin.

The diagnosis is confirmed by appropriate blood tests.

No treatment is required in the majority of patients, but aspirin must be avoided. An injection of a blood extract that contains the missing factors is given before surgery and to those who experience excessive bleeding from a severe case of the disease. The long term prognosis is excellent.
See also BLEEDING, EXCESSIVE; BLOOD CLOTTING TEST; CHRISTMAS DISEASE; HAEMOPHILIA A

VULVA
The external female genitals are the site of sexual arousal. The vulva consists of two pairs of fleshy folds or lips, and a small highly sensitive organ, called the clitoris. The outer of the two pairs of lips is called the labia majora (Latin for larger lips) and the inner pair the labia minora (Latin for smaller lips). The labia minora are sometimes hidden by the labia majora and sometimes protrude beyond them. The space surrounded by the lips is called the vestibule and contains the entrance to the vagina and the opening of the urethra – the tube through which urine is passed from the bladder.

The clitoris is located at the front junction of the labia minora and is the main centre of female sexual sensation. It contains erectile tissue and when stimulated enlarges in much the same way as the male penis.

Situated on each side of the vaginal opening are small Bartholin glands, which are stimulated by sexual arousal and release a mucous-like secretion to provide lubrication for intercourse.

The pad of fat covered by pubic hair at the front of the vulva is called the mons veneris (mound of Venus), or sometimes the mons pubis (pubic mound). The area extending from the back of the vulva to the anus is the perineum. The perineum is sometimes cut by the doctor during childbirth (an episiotomy) to avoid tissues being torn, and then repaired immediately afterwards.
See also BARTHOLIN CYST; VAGINA; VULVODYNIA

VULVA ITCH
See GENITAL ITCH

VULVAR VESTIBULITIS
See VULVODYNIA

VULVODYNIA

Vulvodynia (burning vulva syndrome or vulvar vestibulitis) is a painful condition affecting the external genitals (vulva) of sexually active women, due to inflammation of the tiny lubricating glands in the skin of the vulva. The cause is unknown, but attacks sometimes follow a vaginal thrush infection.

The vulva appears normal, but there is intermittent tenderness and pain of the vulva and opening into the vagina which is worse with pressure or friction (eg. during sex, inserting a tampon, bike riding or wearing tight clothing) and persists for an hour or more once triggered. Muscle spasms in the vagina triggered by fear of pain occurring may cause vaginismus and make sexual intercourse impossible.

Patients should apply heat to the area (hot bath, warm water bottle) when pain occurs. Steroid creams may reduce inflammation and amitriptyline tablets my relax the woman and help her cope and patients should avoid using soap in the area. Sex can be assisted by an understanding partner, applying local anaesthetic ointment, adequate foreplay and the use of lubricants. The condition often persists for months or years before settling spontaneously. *See also* SEXUAL INTERCOURSE PAIN; VAGINISMUS; VULVA

W

WADDLE
See WALK ABNORMAL

WALDENSTRÖM'S MACROGLOBULINAEMIA
Waldenström's macroglobulinaemia (or lymphoplasmacytoid lymphoma) is a very complex condition that is a malignancy of an abnormal type of white cell in the blood. These B type white cells produce a protein that causes further symptoms in the patient. The cause is unknown, but it is more common in people over sixty years of age.

Fatigue is the only constant feature. Other symptoms may include abnormal bleeding from gums, blood (often dark or black) in faeces, nausea, dizziness, abnormal sensations and disturbances of vision. In severe cases the patient may become semiconscious or comatose. Various lymph nodes, the spleen and liver are often enlarged and other symptoms may be due to the development of abnormal lymphatic tissue growths in scattered parts of the body.

It is diagnosed after a series of blood tests gradually determine the cause and identify the presence of an abnormal protein.

Treatment involves plasmapheresis (taking blood from the body, removing the abnormal B cells and protein, and then returning the blood to the patient) and/or cancer-treating medications, but despite intensive treatment, the condition is often slowly progressive.
See also LYMPHOMA; WHITE BLOOD CELLS

WALK ABNORMAL
There are many abnormal ways of walking (gait), and each has its own medical description, and specific causes. Because of this, doctors can sometimes diagnose a problem as the patient walks into their consulting room. Each different gait will be described technically with an explanation, and its causes listed.

ATAXIC GAIT
An ataxic gait (unsteady, unbalanced and a lack of confidence in walking) is often caused by drugs such as alcohol, narcotics (including heroin) and sedatives. Other causes include hypothyroidism (underactive thyroid gland in the neck), degeneration of the balance mechanism in the back of the brain (cerebellum) with age or disease (eg. tumour, infection) or alcoholism, and transient ischaemic attacks (mini-strokes).

EXTRAPYRAMIDAL GAIT
An extrapyramidal gait is a shuffling, slow, stiff walk with no arm swinging. Parkinson disease is the most common cause, but some medications (eg. chlorpromazine, thioridazine, metoclopramide) may cause this gait as an unwanted side effect.

FESTINATION
Festination is a quick shuffle with a slightly bent back. This gait may also be caused by Parkinson disease, as well as damage to different parts of the brain by a stroke, tumour, cancer or abscess.

MARCHE-A-PETIT-PAS
Patients with the 'marche-a-petit-pas' (gait of little steps) have a jerky unbalanced walk in which the feet appear to stick to the floor. Multiple small strokes that interrupt multiple nerve pathways may cause this type of gait.

SCISSORS GAIT
The scissors gait occurs when the legs cross over with walking. Causes include a stroke that affects the motor control centre in the brain of one or both legs, diseases of the hip joint that make the use of the joint painful (eg. arthritis, partially dislocated hip), and severe injury to the lower back that partially severs or damages the spinal cord. Models tend to use this gait on the catwalk to emphasise their body movements.

SPASTIC GAIT
A spastic gait is one that is jerky, unsteady and unbalanced due to muscle spasms. Cerebral palsy (spasticity) is the most common cause, but a stroke (cerebrovascular accident), and severe untreated pernicious anaemia (inability of the stomach to absorb vitamin B12 from food) may also be responsible.

WADDLING GAIT
A waddling gait is the exaggerated dropping of the hip on the stepping side when the leg

is lifted off the ground, with marked side to side movement of the trunk. Weakness of the muscles in the buttocks causes this abnormal gait. A number of rare diseases that cause wasting of muscles around the pelvis may be responsible, as well as congenital (from birth) dislocation of the hips and Huntington's chorea (inherited condition that does not make its presence felt until middle age).
See also HIP and separate entries for diseases mentioned above.

WARFARIN
See ANTICOAGULANTS

WART
A wart is an unsightly, hard, rough, raised growth on the skin caused by a very slow-growing virus (papillomavirus), which takes months or years to cause a wart. Only about a quarter of the population is susceptible to the wart virus; the rest have natural immunity. They are most common in children from eight to sixteen years of age, but people with warts should not be isolated for fear of spreading the disease, as the virus is widespread in the community. The most common sites affected are the knees, elbows, hands and feet.

Possible treatments include acid paints applied regularly to eat away the wart tissue, freezing (cryotherapy) with liquid nitrogen which causes the wart to fall off after a few days, burning the wart tissue away with a high voltage electric current (diathermy) or laser, injecting a cell-destroying substance (bleomycin) under the wart, immunotherapy (inducing a skin reaction under and around the wart), or rarely cutting the wart out surgically. Warts may recur after all forms of treatment, and only warts that are causing disfigurement or discomfort should be treated, as a scar may remain after any form of surgery, diathermy or cryotherapy.

Warts usually go away by themselves without any treatment, but this may take many months or years. The average life span of a wart is about eighteen months, but some may last several years.
See also GENITAL WARTS; PLANTAR WART; SEBORRHOEIC KERATOSES

WASP STING
See BEE STING

WASTING
In medicine, wasting is used to describe an organ or tissue that is shrinking in size. This may be due to an inadequate blood supply, poor nutrition, or nerve damage to the affected part of the body. In some cases a lack of hormones may lead to a shrinkage of the organ (eg. breast shrinkage after menopause).

A reduced blood supply can starve the tissue of essential nutrients and oxygen. If nerves are damaged, there are no signals from the brain or spinal cord to activate the tissue (eg. muscles) so that they gradually shrink. In paraplegics there is no nerve stimulation to muscles below the level of the spinal damage, and the muscles shrink and waste away.
See also MUSCLE WEAKNESS

WATERBRASH
See ACID TASTE

WATER FEAR
See HYDROPHOBIA; RABIES

WATERHOUSE-FRIDERICHSEN SYNDROME
Waterhouse-Friderichsen syndrome (fulminant meningococcaemia) is a catastrophic infection of the adrenal glands, which sit on top of each kidney and secrete steroids to sustain the body. It is caused by a severe *Meningococcal* bacterial infection which causes bleeding into both adrenal glands, destroying them and causing an acute Addisonian crisis.

The patient collapses, and develops bleeding into and under the skin, a blue tinge to skin around the mouth, and a pale complexion. This is followed by coma, heart failure and death. A blood culture can identify the bacteria responsible and blood tests show numerous body chemistry abnormalities.

Immediate treatment is critically urgent. Large doses of antibiotics are given by a drip into a vein, followed by hydrocortisone injections and fluids into the drip.

The prognosis is poor. Death may occur within a few hours, and even in patients who survive, permanent Addison disease, brain or heart damage may occur.
See also ADDISON DISEASE; MENINGITIS; MENINGOCOCCAL MENINGITIS

WATER ON THE KNEE
See HOUSEMAID'S KNEE

WATER LACK
See DEHYDRATION

WATERY EYE
See EYE DISCHARGE; TEARS EXCESS

WAX
See EAR WAX

WEAK
See FACE, WEAK MUSCLES; HAND
WEAK; MUSCLE WEAKNESS;
PARAPLEGIA AND QUADRIPLEGIA

WEAL
See ALLERGY; DERMOGRAPHISM;
URTICARIA

WEANING
When weaning is desired, it is best done gradually over several weeks, with one breast feed at a time being stopped in favour of solids, formula or cow's milk. The milk supply will gradually reduce, and the breasts will return to their original size.

If a mother desires not to feed her baby at all, cannot feed because of disease or drug treatment, or the baby cannot be breastfed because of prematurity or other disease, it may be necessary to suppress milk production.

A firm bra should be worn and nipple stimulation should be avoided. Fluid tablets can assist in reducing engorgement, and occasionally oestrogens (as in the contraceptive pill) may be prescribed. The best medication to stop the production of breast milk is bromocriptine (Parlodel) which will dry up most women's milk in three or four days, but it must be taken for at least ten days to stop it from recurring. It may cause some nausea in the first few days, but this settles with time.

The traditional method of using cabbage leaves inside the bra probably works because the leaves are cold and reduce the blood supply to the breast, and the cabbage taste on the nipples will discourage the baby from suckling.
See also BREAST FEEDING

WEDGE RESECTION OF NAIL
See ZADEK PROCEDURE

WEIGHT GAIN
Weight gain (or loss) is really a function of energy (calories or kilojoules) in and energy out. If the energy in exceeds energy out, weight will increase, as food is merely a form of energy for our bodies, in the same way that petrol is the energy source for a car. The fact that eating is pleasurable and can therefore lead to excess, is a problem that humankind has yet to solve, leading to the present epidemic of obesity. If a person wishes to lose weight, they have to alter the equation by decreasing energy in (food), and/or increasing energy out (exercise).

There are a number of diseases which can affect this balance, but still do not alter the basic equation. Part of the energy output goes to maintaining the basic operations of the body, such as breathing, heart beat, digestion etc. This is the metabolic rate, and this rate varies from one person to the next. If the metabolic rate is high, the person needs more energy (food) to maintain it, and is unlikely to gain weight. If the metabolic rate is low, the reverse is true. Diseases which slow the metabolic rate can therefore affect weight by reducing the energy (food) needs of the body.

Diseases which may cause weight gain include hypothyroidism (an under active thyroid gland in the neck), congestive cardiac failure (a damaged heart that slows down and is unable to beat effectively), Cushing syndrome (over production of steroids in the body, or taking large doses of cortisone) and the Prader-Willi syndrome (chromosomal defect).

Some medications may have weight gain and increased appetite as an unwanted side effect. Examples include steroids, tricyclic antidepressants (for depression) and thioridazine (used in psychiatry).
See also APPETITE, EXCESS; DIET;
OBESITY

WEIGHT LOSS
Weight loss can be caused by diseases that increase metabolic rate (the rate at which the body's basic functions work), a lack of nutrition, an increase in exercise, excessive sweating, an inability to absorb food (malabsorption), diarrhoea, or any disease or inflammation that puts stress on the body. Weight loss that is not easily explained is a significant symptom that needs to be investigated by a doctor.

Any condition that causes persistent diarrhoea, nausea or vomiting will lead to weight loss. Sometimes, the diarrhoea and vomiting may be self-induced in order to lose weight, or may be part of a number of different psychiatric conditions, including depression.

Anorexia nervosa is a psychiatric condition that normally occurs in young women who have a distorted image of their own body. They believe that they are fat when they are not, and so starve themselves in order to lose excessive amounts of weight. The patient can become seriously undernourished and emaciated, to the point of death, if adequate treatment is not available. Other symptoms include a cessation of menstrual periods, diffuse hair loss, an intolerance of cold, a slow pulse, irregular heart beat and other complex hormonal disorders. Patients practice deceit to fool their family and doctors by appearing to eat normal meals but later vomit the food, use purgatives to clean out their bowel, or hide food during the meal.

Other common causes include any persistent infection (eg. tuberculosis, hepatitis, AIDS, brucellosis), autoimmune disorders (eg. rheumatoid arthritis, dermatomyositis, systemic lupus erythematosus), cancer of almost any organ, cirrhosis (damage to the liver), cholecystitis (inflammation or infection of the gall bladder), a peptic ulcer in the stomach and ulcerative colitis (lining of the large intestine ulcerates and bleeds).

Less common causes of weight loss include an overactive thyroid gland (hyperthyroidism), severe asthma, uncontrolled diabetes, parasites of the intestine, kidney failure, congestive cardiac failure, emphysema (incurable lung disease caused by smoking), and alcoholism and addictive drug abuse.

There are many rare conditions which may cause loss of weight including Crohn's disease (inflammation of the small or large intestine), pancreatitis, tropical sprue (long term intestinal infection), Addison disease (underactive adrenal glands), diabetes insipidus and Letterer-Siwe syndrome.
See also APPETITE, LACK OF; FAILURE TO THRIVE; GROWTH REDUCED; MALABSORPTION and separate entries for most diseases mentioned above.

WEIGHT LOSS DIET
Those who are serious about losing weight should follow the diet plan below. It is effective, and not expensive. It is inappropriate to spend more money to lose weight, as a correct diet is actually cheaper as less food is required, and the food purchased should be fresh rather than processed.

WEIGHT LOSS DIET
EAT ONLY THREE TIMES A DAY.
Never eat between, before or after your normal meals. Drink only water, black tea/coffee or diet drinks if thirsty.
EAT THE RIGHT FOODS.
Eat a balanced selection of the correct foods. This means that those foods with low kilojoule values, selected from all food groups (fruit, vegetables, meats, cereals) are the only ones to eat. Do not stick to one food group for long periods of time, as this can seriously upset the body's metabolism. Tables of relative food values are readily obtainable from doctors. For example, avocado is very rich in kilojoules, cucumber is low.
EXERCISE DAILY.
Exercise to the point where you are hot, sweaty and breathless. If you are over forty, you should check with your doctor to determine what level of exercise is appropriate. Walking briskly for twenty minutes, swimming for ten minutes, or running flat out for seven minutes will use 400 kilojoules (100 calories).
IF NECESSARY, EAT LESS.
If you are not losing weight at the rate of one kilogram per week, averaged over a month, you need to eat less!
KEEP GOING.
Continue until you reach your target weight, and continue dieting to maintain that weight.

See also FOOD; KILOJOULES AND CALORIES; OBESITY; WEIGHT GAIN

WEIGHT LOW
APPETITE, LACK OF; FAILURE TO THRIVE; GROWTH REDUCED; MALABSORPTION; WEIGHT LOSS

WEIL SYNDROME
Weil syndrome is a severe form of leptospirosis that causes pharyngitis (inflamed throat), muscle pains, diarrhoea with blood in faeces,

excessive bleeding internally and externally (eg. blood nose, unusual bruising), kidney and liver failure, a large spleen and severe jaundice (yellow skin). Lung involvement causes cough, bloodstained sputum, shortness of breath and the adult respiratory distress syndrome. Heart involvement (myocarditis) is also possible.

Antibiotics (eg. penicillin, tetracycline) and kidney dialysis (artificial kidney machine) are used in treatment, but there is significant morbidity (permanent organ damage), and it is occasionally fatal.

See also JAUNDICE; LEPTOSPIROSIS

WERDIG-HOFFMAN SYNDROME

Werdig-Hoffman syndrome is an inherited, progressive, permanent weakening and wasting of muscles.

Patients develop muscle weakness, which attacks the muscles of the trunk more than the limbs and makes breathing increasingly difficult to the point where pneumonia may occur. It is diagnosed by electrical studies of muscle action and by muscle biopsy.

No effective treatment is available, and there is no cure, but physiotherapy may be beneficial. Most patients die before the age of five years.

See also MOTOR NEURONE DISEASE; MUSCLE WEAKNESS

WERNICKE-KORSAKOFF PSYCHOSIS

Wernicke-Korsakoff psychosis, or encephalopathy, is damage to the brain caused by a deficiency in vitamin B, particularly thiamine (vitamin B1). It occurs most commonly in alcoholics who neglect their diet and elderly people who are malnourished. Blood tests can confirm the low level of thiamine in the blood.

Symptoms may include a tremor, poor coordination, confusion, sudden eye movements, double vision, and pins and needles in the hands and feet. If alcoholics are not treated early, permanent brain damage may result.

For treatment, thiamine is initially given by injection, and later by tablet, to replace that which is missing. Those affected should eat a good well-balanced diet and abstain from alcohol. Good treatment and patient cooperation brings most back to a reasonable lifestyle.

See also ALCOHOLISM; PERIPHERAL NEUROPATHY

WET DREAMS
See PENIS DISCHARGE; PUBERTY

WHEEZE

A wheeze occurs when a person has difficulty breathing out. They can usually get some air into the lungs, but then have to force the air out, creating a harsh rasping wheeze. The cause of a wheeze is usually a disease of the lungs or airways.

Asthma is a temporary narrowing of the tubes (bronchi) through which air flows into and out of the lungs. This narrowing is caused by a spasm in the tiny muscles which surround the bronchi. The problem is further aggravated by the excess production of phlegm in the lungs and swelling of the lung tissue through inflammation. The narrowing of the airways causes shortness of breath and wheezing. Asthmatics usually find they cannot breathe out easily, because as they try to exhale the lung collapses further, and the small amount of space left in the airways is obliterated. Asthmatic symptoms also include coughing, particularly in children, and tightness and discomfort in the chest.

An inhaled foreign body (eg. peanut, small Lego brick, poorly chewed food) is a serious and potentially life threatening cause of a wheeze. The Heimlich manoeuvre (standing behind an adult patient and suddenly squeezing their chest to expel the foreign body) may need to be applied by a person who has studied first aid in order to clear the airway before an ambulance or doctor can reach the victim. If the object cannot be expelled and the patient loses consciousness and stops trying to breathe, apply mouth to mouth resuscitation to force air past the obstruction.

Other causes of a wheeze include anaphylaxis (severe, life-threatening reaction to an allergy-causing substance), congestive cardiac failure (damaged heart is unable to beat effectively enough to clear blood out of the lungs), emphysema, bronchitis (infection of the bronchi that carry air within the lungs), and bronchiolitis (lung infection of children under two years of age).

Less common causes include bronchiectasis (bronchi are damaged, scarred and permanently overdilated), reflux oesophagitis (stomach acid is inhaled), lung cancer, cystic fibrosis (genetic defect of mucus glands), underactive parathyroid glands (hypoparathyroidism),

carcinoid syndrome (rare tumour in the intestine) and Loeffler syndrome.
See also ASTHMA; BREATHING, DIFFICULT; COUGH; CROUP; HEIMLICH MANOEUVRE and separate entries for diseases mentioned above.

WHEEZY BRONCHITIS
See ASTHMA

WHIPLASH
Whiplash (traumatic cervical syndrome) is a neck sprain injury that damages the ligaments and muscles that support the neck and head. If a person is suddenly accelerated forwards (eg. in a rear-end automobile accident), the head has a tendency to remain behind and the neck is bent backwards suddenly and excessively. The ligaments and muscles on the front of the vertebral column and neck are stretched and torn (sprained). In severe cases, nerve fibres may also be overstretched and damaged.

Symptoms vary dramatically from one patient to another. Pain, limited neck movement and stiffness may commence shortly after the injury or be delayed by twenty four hours or more. The pain may then spread to the shoulders, chest and back. Other possible symptoms include numbness in the fingers and forearm, difficulty in swallowing, blurred vision, dizziness, noises in the ears (tinnitus) and nausea. Sometimes there may be damage to the bony vertebrae in the neck, or very rarely the spinal cord. Neck x-rays are often performed, but are usually normal.

Treatment involves rest, immobilisation (neck brace), anti-inflammatory medications, pain relievers, heat and physiotherapy. Most patients recover within a couple of weeks, but a very small number continue with long-term discomfort, pain and movement limitation.
See also NECK PAIN; SPRAIN

WHIPPLE'S DISEASE
Whipple's disease is a rare disorder of the lymphatic system, which drains waste products back from cells to the heart, caused by obstruction of the lymphatic ducts draining the small intestine and a persistent bacterial infection of the gut.

Patients develop joint and belly pain, diarrhoea, weight loss and a slight fever. They may also have increased pigmentation of the skin and enlarged lymph nodes. Rarely, heart failure, uveitis (eye inflammation), confusion, memory loss and abnormal eye movements occur.

A faeces examination shows the presence of excess fat, and small bowel x-rays are abnormal. The diagnosis is confirmed by a biopsy of the small intestine.

There is no cure, but most cases are controlled by long term antibiotics (eg. sulphas).
See also LYMPHATIC SYSTEM

WHIPWORM
See TRICHURIASIS

WHITE BLOOD CELLS
The main task of white blood cells (leucocytes) is to fight infection. There are about 700 times more red blood cells than white ones, and on blood tests the normal adult range is between 4000 and 10 000 cells in every cubic millimetre of blood. Scientifically, white cells are known as leucocytes (hence leukaemia is the name for a disease in which they multiply out of control).

Despite their name, white blood cells are in fact colourless. There are different types of white cells, but the main task of all of them is to attack harmful substances that invade the body. They may do this directly, literally by engulfing up bacteria, or by producing antibodies that work through the body's immune system. When an invader enters the body's tissues, the white cells rush to the affected area and act to destroy the intruder. At the same time, extra supplies are produced so that an abnormally large number of white cells in the blood (leucocytosis) is frequently an indication of bacterial infection. On the other hand, a drop in the number of white blood cells (leucopenia) may be due to a viral infection. Pus is the combination of old white cells, dead bacteria, destroyed tissue and other waste matter.

White cells eventually die. Their life span depends on what they are called on to do in the body and varies from a few hours to days, months or even years.

White blood cells are manufactured in bone marrow, lymph nodes and the spleen.
See also AGRANULOCYTOSIS; BLOOD; BONE; FULL BLOOD COUNT; LEUCOCYTOSIS; LEUCOPENIA; LEUKAEMIA; SPLEEN

WHITE NAIL
See NAIL DISCOLOURED

WHITE PATCHES IN MOUTH
See MOUTH WHITE PATCHES

WHITE PATCHES ON SKIN
Pityriasis versicolor is a fungal skin disease of the tropics that initially causes pink/brown patches on the body, which may have a very faint scale upon them. After the disease has been present for a few weeks, the skin underlying the infection has the pigment reduced, so that the rash appears as white patches because sunlight is unable to tan the skin under the fungus. Areas not exposed to sunlight (eg. armpits, breasts) may retain the pink/brown patch appearance, while in sun-exposed areas (eg. back, arms) the same infection can cause white patches to appear on the sun-tanned skin. This effect does not occur in dark-skinned races.

Vitiligo is a patchy loss of skin pigmentation that in pale-skinned northern Europeans may be barely noticed, but in southern Europeans, Arabs, Negroes and Chinese the resultant large white patches can be quite disfiguring.

An area of skin that has been severely inflamed for any reason may remain white after the inflammation has settled for some period of time, or occasionally permanently.

A scar may appear as a white patch on the skin, particularly after the application of liquid nitrogen to remove a skin cancer.
See also ALBINISM; MOUTH WHITE PATCHES; SKIN DEPIGMENTED and separate entries for diseases mentioned above.

WHITE SKIN
See ALBINISM; SKIN DEPIGMENTED; WHITE PATCHES ON SKIN

WHITLOW
A whitlow (*Herpes simplex* type 1 infection) is a skin infection beside a finger nail, caused by the virus *Herpes simplex* type 1. Initially, the infection is caught as a child, when it is a simple mouth infection. The virus then migrates to the nerve endings around the finger or toe nail, and remains inactive there for many years. It may later reactivate at times of stress or illness. Recurrences tend to develop at the same spot.

Redness and soreness of the skin occurs, usually beside a nail, followed a day or two later by an eruption of small blisters, which rapidly burst to leave a shallow, weeping, painful ulcer. In rare cases, the infection can spread into the throat and lungs, and these patients become extremely ill.

If treated by appropriate creams and lotions immediately the redness and discomfort is felt and before the blisters form, it may be possible to stop further progress. Once established, a cure is not normally possible, but drying, antiseptic and anaesthetic creams or lotions may be used. The sore heals and the pain eases in about ten days.
See also COLD SORE; GENITAL HERPES

WHOOPING COUGH
Whooping cough (pertussis) was originally an infection of ducks that only passed to humans after these birds were domesticated many thousands of years ago. It is now a preventable bacterial infection of the respiratory tract that may be very serious in children. A much milder form of the disease (parapertussis) is also known, against which the pertussis vaccine gives no protection.

The cause is the bacterium *Bordetella pertussis*, which is widespread in the community. In adults an infection may merely cause the symptoms of a cold, but in young children the disease is more severe, and spreads from person to person in the microscopic droplets exhaled or coughed out in the breath of a patient, so an adult with minimal symptoms may carry the disease from one infant to another. The incubation period is one to two weeks.

It starts in a child as a cold that lasts a week or two, but then the cough becomes steadily more severe and occurs in increasingly distressing spasms, characterised by a sudden intake of breath before each cough. Coughing spasms may last up to thirty minutes, and leave the child exhausted, then another spasm starts after only a few minutes. As the infection worsens, the child may become blue, lose consciousness, and thick stringy mucus is coughed up and vomited. The patient has no appetite and rapidly loses weight. Severe coughing may cause bleeding in the lungs, throat and nose, that may be severe enough to cause suffocation. If the child survives, the spasms start to ease after a few weeks, but mild recurrences may occur for months.

Permanent lung damage is also possible.

The diagnosis can be confirmed by analysis of a sputum sample.

No cure is available, but the disease may be completely prevented by a vaccination that is usually combined with those for tetanus and diphtheria, and is given three times before six months of age, and again at eighteen months, and five years of age. Treatment involves oxygen, sedatives and careful nursing isolated within a hospital for several weeks. Antibiotics can be used to prevent the spread of the disease to others.

Even in good hospitals about 2% of patients die, and up to 10% have long term complications. In poorer countries, the mortality rate is much higher.

See also DIPHTHERIA; VACCINATION OF CHILDREN

WILMS' TUMOUR

A Wilms' tumour (nephroblastoma) is a form of cancer that arises in the supportive tissue immediately surrounding the kidneys of children. The cause is unknown, but more than 80% of patients are under four years of age when diagnosed, and it accounts for nearly 10% of all childhood cancers.

Affected children develop a swollen abdomen, but only one in five has pain, and even fewer develop the other possible symptoms of fever, bloody urine, weight loss and loss of appetite. It is usually detected by a parent feeling the large hard mass in the abdomen, and the diagnosis is confirmed by an x-ray or CT scan of the kidney, followed by a biopsy of the kidney

The affected kidney must be removed surgically, followed by irradiation of the abdomen to destroy any remaining cancer cells. Chemotherapy with cytotoxic drugs may also be given, but spread of the cancer to other tissues and organs, particularly the liver and lungs, and in rare cases to the bone and brain, may occur.

With localised disease 90% of patients now survive more than five years, and even if the cancer has spread to other organs, more than 50% survive for five years.

See also CANCER; KIDNEY

WILSON DISEASE

Wilson disease (hepatolenticular degeneration) is a rare inherited disorder of copper metabolism with symptoms relating to the brain, the liver or both, that occurs in both sexes and is usually diagnosed between ten and thirty years of age. It results in the excessive deposition of copper in the liver and brain.

Excess copper in the brain may cause psychiatric disorders, rigid muscles and a tremor. Liver disease symptoms include jaundice (yellow skin), an enlarged liver and/or spleen, anaemia and hepatitis. A brown/green ring (Kayser-Fleischer ring) around the iris (coloured part) in the eye is easily visible. The diagnosis is confirmed by blood tests that detect the excessive copper.

Copper can be removed by a number of drugs (eg. penicillamine), and a diet low in copper (eg. avoiding shellfish, beans and offal) must be followed. Lifelong treatment is necessary to keep copper levels low. Any damage to the brain or liver caused before the treatment is started cannot usually be reversed, but the long-term outlook is normally good.

See also COPPER; FANCONI SYNDROME; LIVER

WIND EXCESS
See FLATULENCE

WINDPIPE
See TRACHEA

WISKOTT-ALDRICH SYNDROME

Wiskott-Aldrich syndrome is an inherited X-linked (passes from mothers to sons) abnormal destruction of the cells which are responsible for blood clotting (platelets), and a lack of the cells necessary to protect the body from infection.

Patients have widespread eczema, recurrent severe infections, and excessive bleeding and bruising because of a lack of platelets in the blood. Severe life threatening infections may occur. It can be diagnosed by blood tests and bone marrow biopsy.

Vigorous treatment of infections is necessary, as are blood transfusions, bone marrow transplants and sometimes removal of the spleen (which is responsible for destroying the platelets), but despite the best treatment, few of these children survive into their teen years.

See also IMMUNODEFICIENCY; X-LINKED CONDITION

WITHDRAWAL CONTRACEPTION
See COITUS INTERRUPTUS

WITKOP
See FAVUS

WITTMAACK-EKBOM SYNDROME
See RESTLESS LEGS SYNDROME

WOLFF-PARKINSON-WHITE SYNDROME
The Wolff-Parkinson-White (WPW) or accelerated conduction syndrome, may be congenital or develop later in life. It is due to an abnormal nerve pathway in the heart that allows a short circuit between the upper (atria) and lower (ventricles) chambers of the heart.

Patients have a very abnormal heart rhythm and distressing palpitations, and an electrocardiogram (ECG) shows a typical abnormal pattern. Rarely, sudden death may occur.

Acute attacks are treated by medications (eg. verapamil, propranolol, procainamide) injected into a vein and cardioversion (electric shock to heart). Long term prevention of further attacks involves the regular use of medication and, sometimes, surgery on the heart to cut abnormal nerve pathways.
See also ARRHYTHMIA; HEART; ELECTROCARDIOGRAM; SUPRAVENTRICULAR TACHYCARDIA

WOMB
See UTERUS

WOMB PROLAPSE
See VAGINAL PROLAPSE

WOOD'S LIGHT
See TINEA CAPITIS

WORMS
The common worms (helminths) in developed countries are pinworms (threadworms), which appear as short pieces (about 3mm. long) of white cotton thread on the motions. They may also be seen around the anus, particularly at night. They cause itching around the anus and slight abdominal discomfort, but rarely anything more severe. The worms lay eggs in the faeces, and if a person is not careful with their personal hygiene, the eggs may contaminate the fingers, then food, and be swallowed by another person where the eggs hatch, grow into adult worms, and start the cycle again. Very effective treatments are available without a prescription from chemists, but if the problem recurs, a doctor's advice should be obtained.

There are many other worms which may infest humans.
See also ANGIOSTRONGYLIASIS; ASCARIASIS; CUTANEOUS LARVA MIGRANS; GUINEA WORM; HOOKWORM; HYDATID DISEASE; NEMATODE; PINWORM; STRONGYLOIDIASIS; TAPEWORM; TRICHURIASIS

WPW SYNDROME
See WOLFF-PARKINSON-WHITE SYNDROME

WRIST
The wrist is made of eight small bones arranged in two rows of four. The four bones nearest the arm (in order from the thumb side they are the scaphoid, lunate, cuneiform and pisiform bones) move against the lower end of the radius and ulnar bones. The outer row of bones (again in the same order they are the trapezium, trapezoid, capitate and hamate) forms joints with the metacarpal bones that make up the skeleton of the hand.

This arrangement enables the wrist to move up and down as well as from side to side, but rotation of the wrist is due to the radius twisting around the ulnar, not the wrist joint.

When falling on the outstretched hand, it is possible to fracture the scaphoid bone, but this fracture may not show up on x-rays for ten days after the injury, and may be very slow to heal. It is unusual to fracture the other wrist bones.
See also JOINT; HAND; RADIUS; SCAPHOID FRACTURE; ULNAR

WRIST PAIN
The wrist is a relatively small and delicate joint, with a complex network of tendons, nerves, arteries, veins, muscles, bones and ligaments running through it or forming its structure. Despite this, enormous forces are placed on the wrist with lifting, twisting and turning, it may be subjected to extraordinary degrees of repetitive movement for many hours on end with work on machines, typing or playing a musical instrument.

BONES OF THE HAND

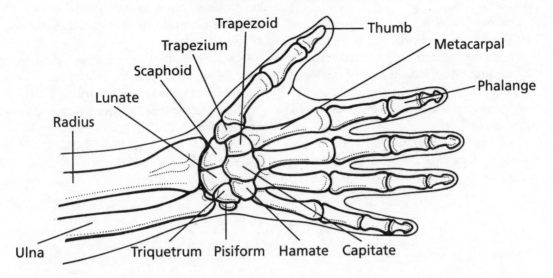

A sprain (tear) or strain (stretch) to any of the ligaments or tendons that form the wrist will cause pain, as will a fracture to the ends of the forearm bones (radius and ulna – Colles or Smith fracture) or any of the eight small bones that form the wrist joint. The most commonly fractured bone is the scaphoid, which is injured by a fall onto the outstretched hand.

The carpal tunnel syndrome is caused by inflammation in the narrow tunnel on the palm side of the wrist through which all the hand flexing tendons, nerves and blood vessels that supply the hand must run. If any of these tissues are damaged or strained, they will swell to place pressure on the adjacent nerves, and therefore cause pain. Common causes of the carpal tunnel syndrome are pregnancy, weight gain, an underactive thyroid gland, diabetes, rheumatoid arthritis and systemic lupus erythematosus (SLE).

Other causes of wrist pain include osteoarthritis, a ganglion cyst (caused by a small puncture in a tendon sheath), tendinitis (inflammation of a tendon due to overuse), de Quervain tenovaginitis, synovitis (inflammation of the synovial membrane that lines every joint), and tears or strains to the muscles in the hand or forearm.

Rarely, a severe injury to the wrist may result in a dislocation of the wrist, or one of the small bones within the joint, causing severe pain.
See also ARM PAIN; COLLES
FRACTURE; HAND PAIN and separate entries for diseases mentioned above.

WRITHING
Uncontrolled, slow, writhing (snake-like) movements of an arm or leg are described as athetosis by doctors. It is caused by various brain disorders.

In a stroke (cerebrovascular accident) various parts of the brain may be affected by having its blood supply cut off by a blockage in an artery, or a blood vessel in the brain may burst causing bleeding and damage to part of the brain. The onset is almost instantaneous, may be associated with a wide variety of symptoms from paralysis and headache to weakness, loss of sensation, anaesthesia, confusion, athetosis and coma.

Cerebral palsy (spasticity) is a form of brain damage that occurs during pregnancy, usually for no obvious reason. A poorly functioning placenta, or a foetus who takes nutrition from its twin, are possibilities. Muscle spasms and increased muscle tone are inevitable, and convulsions, athetosis and mental retardation may occur.

Other causes include Huntington's chorea (inherited condition), Wilson disease (excess deposition of copper in liver and kidneys), Lesch-Nyhan syndrome (genetic condition that affects only males) and Louis-Bar syndrome (spontaneous degeneration of the spinal cord and part of the brain).
See also JERKING and separate entries for diseases mentioned above.

WRITING DIFFICULT
Difficulty in writing (agraphia) may be caused by problems of learning, brain disorders, sight

disorders, or any cause of tremor or muscular weakness.

Dyslexia is a difficulty in learning to read and/or write due to varying degrees of minimal brain damage that usually occurs before or during birth. Most patients have normal intelligence, and are able to perform all other physical (eg. playing music) and mental (eg. maths) tasks normally.

In a stroke (cerebrovascular accident) the function of part of the brain is affected by having its blood supply cut off by a blockage in an artery, or a blood vessel in the brain may burst causing bleeding and damage to part of the brain. Writing is one function that may be affected by a stroke.

Other brain diseases, such as a tumour, cyst, infection or cancer, may affect brain function in ways that prevent writing.

Numerous psychiatric disorders may affect a patient's ability to concentrate and write. *See also* DYSLEXIA; TREMOR; MUSCLE WEAKNESS and separate entries for diseases mentioned above.

X

XANTHINATES
See THEOPHYLLINES

XANTHOMATOSIS
Xanthomatosis is a complication of excess cholesterol in the blood that settles in the skin. Small, fatty, yellow lumps appear that are almost on top of the skin. They most commonly develop around the eyes, on the knees, elbows and buttocks. Diet and medication can lower blood cholesterol levels, but skin lumps must be destroyed by cautery (burning) or removed surgically as they persist after cholesterol levels are controlled.
See also CHOLESTEROL

XENICAL
See ORLISTAT

XERODERMA
See SKIN, DRY AND SCALY

XEROPHTHALMIA
See DRY EYE SYNDROME; EYE DRY

XEROSTOMIA
See MOUTH DRY

XIPHISTERNUM
See ABDOMINAL LUMP; STERNUM

XIPHOIDALGIA
The xiphoid or xiphisternum is a piece of cartilage at the bottom end of the breast bone (sternum) that sticks down into the gap between the ribs on either side. Xiphoidalgia is inflammation of the xiphoid, which occurs for no known reason.

Significant pain and tenderness of the xiphoid cartilage occurs, worse with chest movement (eg. deep breath, cough). Irritation of underlying stomach may cause nausea and vomiting. Anti-inflammatory medications, anti-inflammatory and anaesthetic injections, or steroids can be used for treatment. The pain settles with time and treatment.
See also TIETZE SYNDROME

X-LINKED CONDITION
Women have two X chromosomes, while men have one X chromosome and a much smaller Y chromosome. If one X chromosome is defective, in women the other X chromosome can compensate. In males this compensation

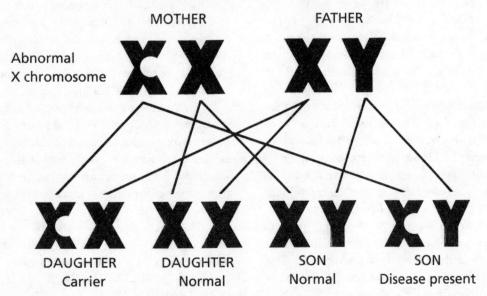

TRANSMISSION OF X-LINKED DISEASES

Females have two X chromosomes, and males one X and one Y. Individuals obtain one sex chromosome from each parent giving four possible combinations.

cannot occur, so there are a number of X-linked inherited conditions that only affect males. Statistically, one half of sons will have the disease and one half of daughters will be carriers.
See also AGAMMAGLOBULINAEMIA; CHROMOSOME; HAEMOPHILIA A; LESCH-NYHAN SYNDROME; WISKOTT-ALDRICH SYNDROME

XO SYNDROME
See TURNER SYNDROME

X-RAYS
X-rays were discovered in 1895 in Würzburg, Germany by Wilhelm Röntgen and virtually revolutionised medicine. It meant that for the first time it was possible to see inside the human body without cutting it open. They were called x-rays because in the beginning no-one knew exactly what they were. The study of x-rays and other types of radiation for use in diagnosis, treatment and medical research generally is called radiology. X-ray pictures of internal organs can be used to diagnose many conditions, including broken or diseased bones, pneumonia, tuberculosis, peptic ulcers, and obstructions in the intestines.

X-rays are a form of energy similar to light rays and radio waves but with their much higher frequency they have the power to penetrate soft tissue. If you turn on a bright torch in a darkened room and then place a leaf over the torch lens, a shadow of the leaf showing its internal structure will be projected onto the wall. X-rays work in the same way as the torch, but because they have to penetrate the human body, the intensity of the light required is far greater. The frequency of these waves is so great that they are invisible to the eye. Although the eye cannot see x-rays, they will register on photographic film and, in essence, the taking of x-rays is a form of photography. However, no lens is used for an x-ray photograph, which is different from an ordinary photograph in that it reproduces shadows rather than a pictorial image.

To take an x-ray, a photographic plate is placed in a black envelope to shield it from the light in the same way as photographic film is shielded by the camera body. The plate is then placed in close proximity to the limb or whatever part of the body is to be x-rayed. The x-ray tube is placed opposite the plate and on the other side of the limb. The tube must be some distance away from the limb to avoid distortion. When the x-ray tube is activated, the x-rays pass in parallel lines through the body opposite to the plate behind. Dense tissue such as bone prevents some of the rays from passing and thus projects a paler image than soft tissue, so that the image as a whole appears as dark and light shadows. The recorded image is developed in the same way as in ordinary photography. The taking of x-ray photographs is called radiography.

Because an x-ray picture is a shadow, it does not matter if the x-ray beam goes from front to back, or from back to front – the same picture will be produced. X-rays cannot show depth for this same reason, and side and oblique views are usually taken so the exact position of a bone or other structure in the body can be determined.

It is now possible, using the x-ray technique, to photograph hollow interior organs to study their position and shape, and whether there is any obstruction either in the organ itself or in the ducts leading from it. To do this, harmless substances which do not transmit x-rays are either given to the patient to swallow or are injected into the organs being investigated. These throw a dense shadow on the photographic plate, corresponding to the interior of the organ being examined. For example, a patient with a suspected gastric ulcer or other digestive tract disorder will usually be asked to swallow a glass of barium sulphate which will pass down into the stomach and duodenum, showing up the existence of any abnormality in the smooth wall of the organs. Similarly, organs that are not part of the digestive tract, such as the lungs, gall bladder and kidneys, can be highlighted by the injection of radio-opaque dyes which make it possible to see if there are stones or other obstructions. X-rays obtained in this way are called contrast x-rays.

Large doses of x-rays can destroy tissues. This means that they are sometimes used in a therapeutic way to destroy abnormal tissue, but it also means that x-rays should not be given unnecessarily, and these days their use as a diagnostic tool is kept to a minimum.
See also ANGIOGRAM; BARIUM ENEMA; BARIUM MEAL; CT SCAN; INTRAVENOUS PYELOGRAM; MAMMOGRAM; MYELOGRAM;

RADIOGRAPHER; RADIOLOGY;
ROENTGEN, WILHELM

XXX SYNDROME

XXX syndrome is a congenital chromosomal abnormality affecting one in 800 women, in which three X chromosomes are present instead of the normal two in a woman. These women appear totally normal, have normal fertility, their children are genetically normal, and their life span is normal, but they may suffer minor mental retardation. There is no cure.
See also CHROMOSOME; TURNER SYNDROME

XXY SYNDROME
See KLINEFELTER SYNDROME

XYLOCAINE
See ANAESTHETICS

XYY SYNDROME

XYY syndrome is a congenital sex chromosome abnormality of males. Usually males have an X and Y chromosome (XY) and females two X chromosomes (XX). In one in 500 males, an extra Y chromosome is found to cause the XYY syndrome. Rarely even more Y chromosomes may be added to create XYYY and XYYYY. It is diagnosed by examining the chromosomes in almost any bodily cell, and may be made before birth by amniocentesis or chorionic villus sampling.

These males are tall, heavily built, aggressive and violent. Behavioural therapy is the only treatment as there is no cure. The population in jails has a far higher proportion of men with this syndrome than is found in the general population.
See also AMNIOCENTESIS;
CHROMOSOME; KLINEFELTER
SYNDROME; VIOLENCE

Y

YAWS

Yaws is a bacterial infection that occurs in some third-world countries with very poor hygiene. *Treponema pallidum* is the responsible bacterium, and this is the same bacterium that causes syphilis. It is transmitted from one person to another by close contact and poor personal cleanliness.

Sores develop on the skin and in the nose and mouth, and inflamed lymph nodes appear in the armpits and groin. The sores may become large, ulcerate, penetrate to the bone and cause permanent disfigurement. The diagnosis can be confirmed by taking swabs from the sores.

Treatment involves antibiotics (eg. penicillin) and improved personal hygiene, which cure the infection.
See also SYPHILIS

YELLOW FEVER

Yellow fever is a serious tropical liver infection caused by a virus that is transmitted from one person to another by the *Aedes* mosquito. It occurs only in central Africa, and tropical Central and South America. The incubation period is three to six days.

Symptoms vary from vomiting, headache, tiredness, and eye pain in mild cases, to severe generalised body pains, high fevers, bleeding from the gums and intestine, bruising, copious vomiting, delirium, kidney failure and liver failure (which causes yellow skin – jaundice). Severe constipation may be a complication.

Specific blood tests are used to confirm the diagnosis, but they may not turn positive until a week or two after the symptoms develop, which makes early diagnosis difficult.

There is no effective treatment or cure, but a single vaccination gives protection for at least ten years. The patient must be carefully nursed, given fluids through a drip into a vein, and sedated. Unfortunately, death through massive internal bleeding and liver failure is common, even in good hospitals.
See also LIVER; VIRUS

YELLOW NAIL
See NAIL DISCOLOURED

YELLOW SKIN
See JAUNDICE

YUTZPE METHOD
See MORNING-AFTER PILL

COUNTRIES AFFECTED BY YELLOW FEVER

Z

ZADEK PROCEDURE

The Zadek procedure is one of the more radical methods of curing an ingrown toe nail, but will result in a permanent cure of the problem in most cases, although there may be a recurrence in about 10% of patients. It is only performed if the nail is significantly ingrown, or previous procedures have been unsuccessful. The aim of the operation is to permanently narrow the nail by one quarter to one third of its width.

After cleaning the toe with an antiseptic solution, the patient will be given an anaesthetic injection into either side of the base of the toe. There is then a five to ten minute wait for the anaesthetic to be effective. Sometimes a third injection is given into the end of the toe after this time.

A tourniquet (often a broad rubber band) is then placed around the base of the toe, it is again cleaned with antiseptic, and draped with a sterile dressing. The operation is then performed. The patient may feel pulling and tugging, but no pain should be felt. If pain is experienced, tell the doctor, and more anaesthetic will be given.

During the procedure a cut is made from the flesh behind the base of the nail, through the entire length of the nail. A second cut is made around the outside edge of the nail to curve around and meet the first cut at both ends. These cuts are deepened to meet in the flesh beneath the nail, and a wedge of nail and flesh is removed. Part of the nail bed behind the base of the nail is also removed in the wedge.

In most cases, the defect in the nail is then sewn up with stitches through both the flesh

and the nail, the tourniquet is removed, and a firm dressing is applied. It is necessary to return to have a lighter dressing applied after one day, and to have the stitches removed after ten days.

When the anaesthetic wears off after about ninety minutes there will be considerable discomfort in the toe due to the depth of the incision and the pressure from the bandage. The doctor will give the patient painkilling tablets to take as necessary for the next twenty-four hours. After the dressing is changed the next day, much of the pain will ease, and paracetamol is all that is normally needed for the next couple of days.

Bleeding from the wound into the dressing is common in the first few hours. Additional bandaging may be added to the original dressing if necessary. Keeping the foot elevated will prevent both bleeding and pain. The patient should not walk any more than is absolutely necessary for the first day, and shoes should not be worn until after the stitches are removed. Sandals, thongs and open toed shoes that do not put pressure on the wound are appropriate.

The wound should be kept clean, dry, covered and elevated as much as possible until the sutures are removed. The patient may shower briefly, remove the dressing after showering, pat the toe completely dry, then apply a clean dry dressing. The patient must not swim or take a bath unless the toe is kept out of the water. A soggy wound is more likely to get infected and heal poorly.

An immediate complication may be excessive bleeding from the wound, and this may require further suturing or dressing. Infection is an uncommon possibility that may occur one or more days after the procedure. If there is a foul ooze, smell, increasing pain or redness in the toe, the patient should return to the doctor for antibiotic treatment.

A long term complication may be the growth of a spicule of nail from the damaged nail bed. This can grow out parallel to the existing nail, or may grow into the flesh at an angle to cause pain and infection. If this

ZADEK PROCEDURE

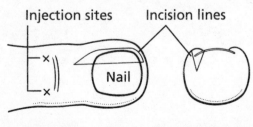

TOE FROM TOP   **TOE FROM END**

occurs, a further operation may be necessary.

In some cases the remaining nail may be distorted without growing into the flesh again, and may not be as cosmetically attractive as the patient may desire, although still pain free.
See also NAIL

ZANAMIVIR
See ANTIVIRALS

ZIDOVUDINE
See ANTIVIRALS

ZINC
Zinc (Zn) is essential in the body for the functioning of many enzymes. It is obtained from a wide range of foods in the diet, and the recommended daily intake is 15mg a day in adults. The amount present in the body can be measured by a blood test and the normal range is 12 to 20 µmol/L (80-140 µg/100 mL).

Low levels may be found in cirrhosis, diarrhoea, malabsorption syndromes, alcoholism, and after the use of drugs such as steroids and diuretics.
See also BLOOD TESTS; MINERALS

Zn
See ZINC

ZOLLINGER-ELLISON SYNDROME
Zollinger-Ellison syndrome (or gastrinoma) is a rare form of severe peptic ulceration in the stomach or small intestine caused by a tumour of the pancreas that produces high levels of a hormone which promotes excessive acid production in the stomach.

Patients have exaggerated symptoms of a peptic ulcer with severe pain in the upper abdomen, bloating, nausea and diarrhoea.

Symptoms usually start at a younger age than normal for a peptic ulcer, and severe bleeding from ulcers may lead to anaemia.

A specific blood test can measure the hormone gastrin, which is responsible for stimulating the stomach to produce hydrochloric acid. Other tests include gastroscopy and measuring the amount of acid in the stomach.

Treatment involves medications as for normal peptic ulcers, but in higher doses. Surgery is often required to control recurrent ulceration. Treatment must be continued life-long, but is usually successful in controlling the disease.
See also PROTON PUMP INHIBITORS; PEPTIC ULCER

ZOLMITRIPTAN
See 5HT RECEPTOR AGONISTS

ZOMIG
See 5HT RECEPTOR AGONISTS

ZOPICLONE
See SEDATIVES

ZYGOMA
The zygoma is the arch shaped cheek bone that may be referred to as the zygomatic arch as it curves away from the skull. Because of its shape, it can be easily fractured by a blow to the cheek.
See also SKULL

ZYGOTE
A woman's fertilised egg (ova) is called a zygote. The zygote divides quickly into two cells and then into four, eight, sixteen, thirty-two and so on to form a blastocyst.
See also BLASTOCYST; GAMETE